Computational Theories of Interaction and Agency

Computational Theories of Interaction and Agency

edited by
Philip E. Agre and Stanley J. Rosenschein

The MIT Press
Cambridge, Massachusetts
London, England

First MIT Press edition, 1996

© 1995 Elsevier Science Publishers B.V., Amsterdam, the Netherlands

Reprinted from *Artificial Intelligence*, Volume 72, Numbers 1–2 (January 1995) and Volume 73, Numbers 1–2 (February 1995). The MIT Press has exclusive license to sell this English-language book edition throughout the world.

Printed and bound in the United States of America.

Library of Congress Cataloging-in-Publication Data

Computational theories of interaction and agency / edited by Philip E. Agre and Stanley J. Rosenschein.
    p.   cm.—(Artificial intelligence)
  Includes bibliographical references.
  ISBN 0-262-5190-1 (pbk.: alk. paper)
   1. Artificial intelligence—Data processing. 2. Computational complexity. I. Agre, Philip. II. Rosenschein, Stanley J. III. Series: Artificial intelligence (Cambridge, Mass.)
Q336.C653   1996
006.3—dc20   96-6163
                                                   CIP

Contents

Series foreword   vii

Preface   ix

Computational research on interaction and agency   1
P. E. Agre

Sensorimotor transformations in the worlds of frogs and robots   53
M. A. Arbib and J.-S. Liaw

Learning to act using real-time dynamic programming   81
A. G. Barto, S. J. Bradtke, and S. P. Singh

Learning dynamics: systems identification for perceptually challenged agents   139
K. Basye, T. Dean, and L. P. Kaelbling

A dynamical systems perspective on agent-environment interaction   173
R. D. Beer

On information invariants in robotics   217
B. R. Donald

The stabilization of environments   305
K. J. Hammond, T. M. Converse, and J. W. Grass

An architecture for adaptive intelligent systems   329
B. Hayes-Roth

Analysis of adaptation and environment   367
I. Horswill

The intelligent use of space   397
D. Kirsh

Indexical knowledge and robot action—a logical account   435
Y. Lespérance and H. J. Levesque

Exploiting patterns of interaction to achieve reactive behavior   483
D. M. Lyons and A. J. Hendriks

A situated view of representation and control   515
S. J. Rosenschein and L P. Kaelbling

The use of dynamics in an intelligent controller for a space faring rescue robot   541
M. Schoppers

On social laws for artificial agent societies: off-line design   597
Y. Shoham and M. Tennenholtz

Instructions, intentions, and expectations   619
B. Webber, N. Badler, B. Di Eugenio, C. Geib, L. Levison, and M. Moore

Reinforcement learning of non-Markov decision processes   637
S. D. Whitehead and L.-J. Lin

Book review of *From Animals to Animats: Proceedings of the First International
Conference on Simulation of Adaptive Behavior* (Jean-Arcady Meyer and
Stewart W. Wilson, eds.)   673
M. Brand, P. Prokopowicz, and C. Elliott

Book review of *Reasoning Agents in a Dynamic World: The Frame Problem*
(Kenneth Ford and Patrick J. Hayes, eds.)   689
J. A. Toth

Book review of *Artificial Life* (Christopher G. Langton, ed.), *Artificial Life II*
(Christopher G. Langton, Charles Taylor, J. Doyne Farmer, Steen Rasmussen, eds.),
and *Artificial Life II: Video Proceedings* (Christopher G. Langton, ed.)   737
S. W. Smoliar

Book review of *Planning and Control* (Thomas Dean and Michael Wellman)   745
J. Hendler

Book review of *Vision, Instruction, and Action* (David Chapman)   753
D. M. Lyons

Series foreword

Artificial intelligence is the study of intelligence using the ideas and methods of computation. Unfortunately, a definition of intelligence seems impossible at the moment because intelligence appears to be an amalgam of so many information-processing and information-representation abilities.

Of course psychology, philosophy, linguistics, and related disciplines offer various perspectives and methodologies for studying intelligence. For the most part, however, the theories proposed in these fields are too incomplete and too vaguely stated to be realized in computational terms. Something more is needed, even though valuable ideas, relationships, and constraints can be gleaned from traditional studies of what are, after all, impressive existence proofs that intelligence is in fact possible.

Artificial intelligence offers a new perspective and a new methodology. Its central goal is to make computers intelligent, both to make them more useful and to understand the principles that make intelligence possible. That intelligent computers will be extremely useful is obvious. The more profound point is that artificial intelligence aims to understand intelligence using the ideas and methods of computation, thus offering a radically new and different basis for theory formation. Most of the people doing work in artificial intelligence believe that these theories will apply to any intelligent information processor, whether biological or solid state.

There are side effects that deserve attention, too. Any program that will successfully model even a small part of intelligence will be inherently massive and complex. Consequently, artificial intelligence continually confronts the limits of computer-science technology. The problems encountered have been hard enough and interesting enough to seduce artificial intelligence people into working on them with enthusiasm. It is natural, then, that there has been a steady flow of ideas from artificial intelligence to computer science, and the flow shows no sign of abating.

The purpose of this series in artificial intelligence is to provide people in many areas, both professionals and students, with timely, detailed information about what is happening on the frontiers in research centers all over the world.

J. Michael Brady
Daniel G. Bobrow
Randall Davis

Preface

Early artificial intelligence research focused on thinking. This was understandable, given the poor state of robotics and the Cartesian intellectual inheritance of that day, as well as the promise of symbolic programming as a tool for simulating cognition. Over time, though, the field has returned to the "agent perspective" that first emerged with early robotic projects such as Shakey, expanding its focus from thought to action, from search spaces to physical environments, and from problem-solving to long-term activity. It has sought computational ways of understanding an agent's embodiment, as well as its embedding in its familiar world.

Above all, the concept of an "agent" points to the need for a developed conception of "agency." The first steps in this direction have been difficult, as researchers have learned to untangle the web of assumptions that drove the field in its early days. Enough has been done, though, to identify some recurring themes and to paint a methodological picture that encourages cooperation among diverse disciplinary frameworks without imposing a premature unity upon them. Central to this picture is the principled characterization of agents' interactions with their environments. Building artificial agents that *do* interact with environments is a good first step. Past a certain point, though, it becomes important to conceptualize the structures and attributes of the interactions themselves. Although several existing fields offer useful concepts for this purpose, the computational research tradition provides the raw materials for powerful new frameworks for characterizing interactions.

This book gathers fundamental papers presenting several such frameworks. Originally published as a special double volume of *Artificial Intelligence*, this collection grew out of an intense three-year discussion among numerous distinct voices. This discussion reached a peak during the Workshop on Computational Theories of Interaction and Agency at the University of Chicago in February 1993. At this workshop, the contributors read and intensively discussed drafts of the papers, leading in many cases to extensive revisions. The point of this workshop, as of this book, is not to found a new field distinct from other fields. Instead, we hope that the themes of interaction and agency will continue to provide points of contact for researchers in several different fields, technical and nontechnical alike, whether they aim at explanatory theories or new designs.

Computational Theories of Interaction and Agency

Artificial Intelligence 72 (1995) 1–52

Computational research on interaction and agency

Philip E. Agre *

Department of Communication, University of California, San Diego, La Jolla, CA 92093-0503, USA

Abstract

Recent research in artificial intelligence has developed computational theories of agents' involvements in their environments. Although inspired by a great diversity of formalisms and architectures, these research projects are unified by a common concern: using principled characterizations of agents' interactions with their environments to guide analysis of living agents and design of artificial ones. This article offers a conceptual framework for such theories, surveys several other fields of research that hold the potential for dialogue with these new computational projects, and summarizes the principal contributions of the articles in this special double volume. It also briefly describes a case study in these ideas—a computer program called Toast that acts as a short-order breakfast cook. Because its designers have discovered useful structures in the world it inhabits, Toast can employ an extremely simple mechanism to decide what to do next.

1. Introduction

The papers in this special double volume illustrate an emerging way of doing research in artificial intelligence, which might be stated compactly as follows:

> Using principled characterizations of interactions between agents and their environments to guide explanation and design.

The purpose of this introduction is to explain this emerging style of research and to explore its relationship to other research in AI and elsewhere.

Let us begin with a familiar example. Consider a device (a "controller") that must direct the operations of an oil refinery. So far as control theory is concerned, an oil refinery is an enormous machine (the "plant") with a number of "control variables" that can be adjusted from the outside (the settings of various valves and burners) and a number of "output variables" whose values at any given moment can be determined from

---

* E-mail: pagre@ucsd.edu. Telephone: (619) 534-6328. Fax: (619) 534-7315.

SSDI 0004-3702(94)00054-9

the outside (the readings on various sensors and gauges). The task of the "controller", let us say, is to stabilize some of the output variables around certain values while maintaining other variables within certain fixed ranges. In concrete terms, the controller must adjust the valves and burners to sustain a fixed flow of oil without the plant blowing up.

Given a proposed design for this controller, how do we know whether it will work? It is impossible to answer this question simply by analyzing the controller itself. Nor, obviously, does it suffice to analyze the plant in isolation. Instead, it is crucial to analyze how the controller will interact with the plant. Given any particular set of initial values, and supposing for simplicity that the interaction is not stochastic, the combined system of plant plus controller will follow a determinate trajectory. The designer's goal is to ensure that the entire family of these interaction trajectories has certain properties. One way to characterize this family of trajectories is in terms of a differential equation that relates changes in the control variables to the current values (and perhaps the ongoing rates of change, or past values, or both) of the output variables.

The controller in this example might be regarded as an agent interacting with its environment, namely the plant, and differential equations provide one way of characterizing such interactions. Control theory, of course, provides only one way of thinking about interactions. It is tied to a particular model of interaction (through output and control variables), its historical development has been profoundly influenced by the need for safety and conservatism in relatively well-behaved systems, and it is thoroughly mathematical. A principled characterization of interaction, though, need not have any of these qualities to provide a useful guide to the design of artificial agents and the explanation of natural ones. Indeed, we have deliberately chosen the vague word "principled" (as opposed to, say, "formal") in order to include an unforeseeable range of possible types of theories of interaction. The important thing is that our characterization of interaction should allow us to address questions like these:

- What will our agent do in a given environment?
- Under what conditions will it achieve its goals or maintain desired relationships with other things?
- In what kinds of environments will it work?
- How do particular aspects of an environment, such as topography or mutability or the workings of artifacts, affect particular types of agents' abilities to engage in interactions that have particular properties?
- What forms of interaction require an agent to employ particular elements of internal architecture, such as memory?
- What forms of interaction permit an agent to learn particular knowledge or skills?

To ask these questions, we do not need to make any *a priori* assumptions about the architecture of our agents. To the contrary, the point is to understand, in as general a way as possible, the relationships among the properties of agents, environments, and forms of interaction between them. Of course, it is doubtful that any single theory can give a complete account of this vast topic. The papers in this special double volume, though, each provide detailed examples of the analysis of interactions within some particular domain of architectures and environments. This special double volume is thus explicitly ecumenical in approach, advocating no single architecture and no single formalism. Through the shared themes that arise within the principled characterization of interactions, we hope that each project can benefit from the others, and that readers can benefit from the three-dimensional picture of research in this area that this approach can offer.

This introduction cannot attempt a complete synthesis of research in this area, nor is it a manifesto representing a definite group or movement. Instead, it offers one perspective on how the research reported in this special double volume is situated in the larger intellectual and technical world. It is organized as follows. Section 2 outlines a series of themes that arise when doing computational research on interaction between agents and their environments, together with examples and conceptual discussion. In so doing, it also specifies more precisely the territory of research covered by this special double volume. Section 3 describes the conceptual connections between the research reported here and research in other fields. These connections may provide inspiration for further computational research on interaction. Section 4 summarizes the individual papers in this special double volume, offering comments on their distinctive contributions and their relationships to one another. Section 5 presents a case study in the ideas of the special double volume. Section 6 concludes with a prophesy and plea for interdisciplinary research.

2. Studying interaction

It is far too early to assemble a rulebook for research into computational theories of interaction and agency. It is possible, though, to convey some of the intuitions that have been developing through the progress of research in this area, both through the computational research reported here and through the existing traditions of research upon which it builds. Putting words to these intuitions is a hazardous matter, and the words offered here should be understood as heuristic devices, as first passes, and as invitations to formulate things in different ways, through different metaphors.

2.1. Mapping the territory

First it is necessary to define carefully the scope of research reported here. Let us imagine research on agents interacting with the world to be arrayed in a two-dimensional field, with one axis corresponding to the number of agents involved in the interaction and the other axis corresponding to the degree of realism with which the world is modeled. (See Fig. 1.) A single agent interacting with a very simple world would lie toward the origin of this diagram. Any project to model human life, or the lives of most animals, in a realistic way would lie in the upper-right corner of the diagram, and that is surely the future ideal of much of the field. As it is, most current research clusters in three areas:

(1) Research that explores single agents interacting with relatively simple environments, where particular aspects of the environment are analyzed in enough detail to bring out larger points.

(2) Research on relatively complex forms of interaction among several agents in extremely simple environments, where the interaction is largely symbolic and

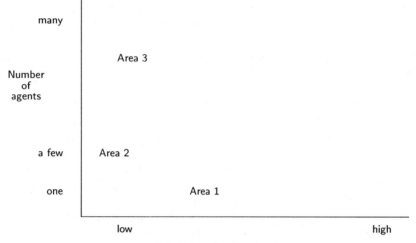

Fig. 1. Current AI research falls mostly into three clusters, which can be contrasted according to the degree of complexity of the environments they deal with and the number of interacting agents they employ.

    depends little on the agents' bodies. The emphasis is on the logical structure of the interaction.

(3) Research on relatively simple interaction among numerous agents in slightly more complex environments, where the interaction does depend in some way on the agents being embodied. The agents may be physical robots or simulations, and the emphasis is on the emergence of order from simple forms of interaction.

The papers in this special double volume lie exclusively in the first of these three clusters, with the exception of the paper by Shoham and Tennenholtz, which lies in the third. As a result, numerous important issues go unaddressed here, including symbolic forms of interaction among agents. Integration of the three approaches, leading to an exploration of the middle regions of the diagram, is obviously an important goal for the future, and we hope that the analyses developed here will contribute their part to that project.

2.2. Planning and reaction

    Computational research on interaction between agents and their environments has historically been structured by two sets of ideas: a dominant tradition focused on "planning" and a subordinate tradition focused on "reaction". Careful consideration of these ideas will make the distinctive position of the research reported here much clearer.

    Although the term "planning" is not always used with great precision, let it refer here to the notion of organizing action through the construction and execution of computer-program-like symbolic structures called plans (cf. [7]). This idea can be traced backwards through the history of AI to a number of sources. Perhaps the most important of these is Karl Lashley's 1951 lecture "The problem of serial order in behavior" [49]. As a neurophysiologist vitally concerned with the workings of human brains, Lashley urged an understanding of cognitive processes whose prototype was the phonetic structure of language. Utterances of language have a formal structure of great intricacy whose basic elements, the phonemes, follow upon one another so rapidly that the structure simply could not emerge through the chaining together of behavioristic stimuli and responses. It follows, Lashley argued, that the brain must be capable of generating these structures on its own internal resources.

Moreover, Lashley proposed understanding all human action on the model of language. The job of the brain was to string together the "expressive elements" (by analogy to words or lexical units) by means of "the syntax of the act" (the grammar of action) in accord with the "determining tendency" that the action is intended to express. Although the theoretical vocabulary has changed, the general shape of this proposal was enormously influential [3]. In a more familiar AI vocabulary, Lashley is suggesting that the brain generates sequences of primitive actions by applying stored habitual schemata. The vague idea of "determining tendency", which Lashley abstracted by analogy to the semantic content being expressed by a linguistic utterance, has been replaced by the simpler notion of the goal to be achieved at the end of an action sequence.

Another influential early proposal, better known in the AI world because it was accompanied by computer models, was Allen Newell and Herbert Simon's computational model of problem solving based on search [59]. Although linguistic metaphors were not central to their exposition, their proposal was similar to Lashley's. Thought was held to consist in a process of search through a space of possible sequences of "operators", some of which correspond to desirable situations which might be understood as problem solutions or goals. The term "planning" entered the AI lexicon as one of the heuristic devices that could abbreviate these searches. According to Newell and Simon's conception, planning takes place when a coarser search space is used to guide the exploration of a finer (and thus combinatorially much larger) search space. This notion of nested search spaces aligned neatly with the formal concept of the hierarchical decomposition of action that was already found in research on linguistics. Each utterance has a grammatical structure that can be drawn as a hierarchical parse tree, with each lexical item itself having a hierarchical structure of syllables and phonemes. To researchers such as Newell and Simon, hierarchical decomposition held the promise of a universal structuring principle for human cognition.

The ideas proposed by Lashley and by Newell and Simon were combined in the first synthesis of the computational theory of planning, *Plans and the Structure of Behavior* by George Miller, Eugene Galanter, and Karl Pribram [57]. There one encounters the first recognizable definition of "Plans":

> A Plan is any hierarchical process in the organism that can control the order in which a sequence of operations is to be performed. [57, p. 16]

Note that a Plan here is not necessarily a symbolic mental structure. It is less specific than that: a "hierarchical process" specified in terms of its ability to structure (in Lashley's terms) the serial order of the organism's behavior. Miller, Galanter, and Pribram's conception of a Plan shaped later AI research in numerous ways. But the most important of these for present purposes is a persistent ambiguity throughout the whole of their book between two conceptions of Plans and their use:

(1) A notion of "Plans", a relatively fixed repertoire of commonly employed structures of action. In more recent AI work, this would be called a "plan library". Miller, Galanter, and Pribram give no account, however, of where these Plans come from. The Plans are hierarchical in their structure, and they can be assembled into larger structures by treating them as elements in a larger hierarchy.

(2) A notion of "the Plan", a hierarchical structure or process which provides a sort of running transcription (in linguistic terms, a parse tree) of the organism's behavior. No commitment is made here to the mechanisms by which this Plan arises, and it could perfectly well be improvised from moment to moment, with the sole constraint that it be possible to the process in retrospect as having been hierarchical in nature.

These two concepts correspond conceptually to two strands of research in AI, which are commonly known as "planning" and "reaction". In Miller, Galanter, and Pribram's book, though, they are conflated in a wide variety of ways. Brief reflection on them makes it clear why. A computational theory of action has at least two central goals:

- to explain how action has the structure it does, and
- to explain how actions are chosen that are appropriate to the circumstances in which they are taken.

The notion of "Plans" addresses the question of structure: action has the structure it does, says this theory, because it arises through the execution of things called Plans which have that same structure. Yet this theory does not provide a convincing account of how these actions are adapted to their circumstances. Of course, if the organism is wholly in control of the circumstances then rational decisions about action can be made *a priori*, before the execution of one of these Plans. And this may indeed be true for short stretches, as when uttering a single word or phrase. But Miller, Galanter, and Pribram wished to explain the whole structure of everyday life, in which a wide variety of contingencies arise.

The notion of "the Plan" addresses this need. It allows for a greater degree of improvisation, since elements can be added to the hierarchical structure of the Plan at any time, including at the very moment when those Plan elements are about to be executed. But it offers no account of the reason why action has the structure it does. Action is still hierarchical in nature, but the particular shape of the hierarchy is wholly unspecified. Miller, Galanter, and Pribram do not seem aware of the problem, most likely because they do not clearly distinguish between their two proposals, shifting frequently back and forth between them as the details of their argument demand.

This ambiguity in Miller, Galanter, and Pribram's book foreshadowed the outlines of three subsequent decades of research. Starting with Fikes and Nilsson's STRIPS program [22], a long tradition of research focused its attention on the first of Miller, Galanter, and Pribram's concepts, that of Plans which are constructed and executed as packages, and which might be stored in Plan libraries to provide an organism or robot with a repertoire of habitual patterns of action for future occasions. STRIPS did address the question of improvisation in a simple way through certain flexibilities in the execution process [23,24]. But for the next decade or so, research generally focused upon the plan-construction process, assuming plan execution to be a relatively simple matter. This line of research into plan-construction shifted to a new phase in the late 1980s as researchers began to cast the classical problems of plan-construction in much more formal terms, and to explore the mathematical questions to which these formalized problems gave rise [14,31,42,55]. Yet all along, half of Miller, Galanter, and Pribram's original story was missing.

This situation was remedied in the mid 1980s with the rise of what has come to be called "situated action" or (somewhat unfortunately, in my own view) "reactive planning" [4,26,28,68,70]. These "reactive" systems should be understood not as a radical departure, but as filling in a hole in the existing system of ideas around planning—as reinventing the other half of Miller, Galanter, and Pribram's theory. Here the emphasis was on interaction with the environment and on the role of tightly coupled perception-action loops in organizing activity. Just as planning offered no robust account of moment-to-moment interaction with the world, reaction offered no robust account of how the organism or robot's actions could be guaranteed to "work", understood as rational, and so on. Conflict between the two schools of research has often been heated, as each school has been able to point at substantial weaknesses of the other's mechanisms without always possessing the necessary concepts to appreciate the weaknesses of its own.

Observing this impasse, a substantial literature immediately grew up attempting to synthesize the planning and reaction theories through "hybrid architectures" (e.g., [25,62]. Just as Miller, Galanter, and Pribram attempted (probably without realizing it) to reconcile planning and reaction through rhetorical ambiguity and logical improvisation, the designers of hybrid architectures recapitulate in computational terms (again, probably without realizing it) this same attempt at reconciliation. In each case, the implicit project is to fashion a whole theory out of two half-theories that presuppose incompatible views of action. Although it is conceivable that the resulting theory might work out, and probable that the resulting architectures may have some practical applications, such research will most likely be frustrated in its forward progress by its lack of a consistent conceptual framework. These things are easy to see with the benefit of hindsight, of course, but it is important to recognize them nonetheless because of their substantial implications for computational theories of action.

It is the central purpose of this special double volume to overcome the conceptual impasse between planning and reaction. The point is not necessarily to offer a better and newer architecture, though research informed by new ideas will presumably lead in that direction, but to identify some concepts and methods of research that will reconcile the unhappy split between planning and reaction by providing interesting accounts of both the structure of behavior and the dynamics of an agent's interactions with its environment. Symbolic plans might play a role in this story or they might not, but they are not ruled out *a priori*.

To reconcile planning and reaction, the important thing is to focus upon the structures of interaction between agents and their environments. Every agent that undertakes actions in some world has a structure of interaction with its environment, whether it is symbolic or connectionist, whether it has internal state or not, and so forth. To focus on interactions is not to legislate these things ahead of time. Nonetheless, a focus on interactions does impose a stiff constraint on the research process. Given an agent interacting with an environment, one must ask this question: "why do we think it should work?". Of course, the notion of "working" has no single definition, and different research programs can pursue a wide range of notions of "working" with equal legitimacy. The proposal of this special double volume is that approaches to this question will require researchers to formulate principled characterizations of the agent's interactions with its environment. As noted at the outset, the phrase "principled characterizations" is designed to cast a wide net, including both formal and informal theories, symbolic and quantitative theories, explanatory and prescriptive theories, biological and social theories, and so forth.

Whatever its faults, research on planning does at least offer a clear account of why the agent's actions ought to work. The environment is usually assumed to be basically stable, in the sense that the agent is the only significant source of disruption within it, and interaction proceeds in ways that can be anticipated in advance through some kind of search process. The agent itself formulates all of the characterizations of its interaction with its environment that it needs, and if its search for an adequate plan halts then the designer can be assured that that plan will actually work—the search process is effectively proving the theorem that some such plan will work. (In the case of probabilistic planning [45], the proposition being "proved" will be probabilistic in nature.) The problem, of course, is that the design of such provably correct plan-construction systems requires that highly restrictive conditions be imposed upon the world—roughly, that the world be representable using a formalism within which a proof of correctness can be performed as a practical matter. Of course, historically most such "proofs" have been informal. The point, though, has been to construct systems that produce correct plans if they halt with any plan at all.

The accomplishments of this research should certainly not be underestimated. It is not a simple matter to obtain any kind of correctness proof in domains as formally complex as those that AI research has investigated. Research on principled characterization of agent–environment interaction will surely build upon this existing work in a wide variety of ways. At the same time, it will also incorporate a wide variety of other influences. The remainder of this section sketches the outlines of the approach to AI research that results from this still emerging synthesis.

2.3. Correspondence and convergence

How does one argue that a particular agent–environment interaction will work? By far the most common approach in AI research has been to formulate arguments in terms of correspondence between internal representations and the outside world. In a simple form, such arguments work by induction: if it is assumed that the agent has correct knowledge of the world at some initial time, and if we can demonstrate that correctness of knowledge is preserved from one unitary action to the next, then it follows that the agent's knowledge of the world will remain correct for as long as it takes actions. If the correctness of an agent's actions is guaranteed by the correctness of its reasoning, the agent can then be shown to "work". This section contrasts this *correspondence method* of argument with a broader *convergence method* that is employed by many of the papers in this special double volume.

The correspondence method may seem unfamiliar when stated in the abstract form provided in the previous paragraph. Nonetheless, it is precisely what is at stake in attempts to solve the frame problem. Understood in its broadest terms, the frame problem is a lemma that must be proven in the midst of any attempt to design a plan-construction program. It asks, given that the agent correctly anticipates what the world will be like up to a certain point, how can it infer what the world will be like after a particular action is taken? In particular, which of the agent's beliefs can be assumed to stay in correspondence with the world after the action is taken? Answering these questions is a difficult matter, since it can take real work to infer all of the consequences of a given action. These consequences might be hard to catalog, yet we would not wish an agent to become disabled worrying that opening a door might have consequences far beyond its reasonable surmises, for example causing the sun to fall from the sky. Technical and philosophical research into the frame problem has determined that it can be usefully decomposed into a variety of separate problems [65], but this decomposition does not matter for the purposes of the present argument. The point is simply that the frame problem arises as part of any attempt to argue for an agent's correctness in a given environment by means of the correspondence method.

Some authors have made strong claims about the theoretical implications of the frame problem. Toth [73], for example, argues that the frame problem is fatal for a certain conception of AI research, whose unit of analysis is the individual's cognitive process. Likewise, the difficulty of bounding the necessary inferences from a given action is reminiscent of Dreyfus' [20] argument that real-life reasoning takes place against a large enough unarticulated background that attempts at logical formalization necessarily encounter an infinite regress of rules-about-how-to-apply-rules. These arguments should not be interpreted as grounds for the categorical rejection of a tradition of research, but rather as roughly indicating the contours of a complex phenomenon. Indeed, the paradoxes of the frame problem may simply be, at least in part, an inherent condition of life that is "solved" piecemeal by real agents through learning in particular cases. Although it is not possible to resolve the question here, we can explore how the question arises through the concepts that have historically guided AI research.

The correspondence method makes fairly specific assumptions about the process through which agents choose actions. These assumptions are not necessarily architectural in nature: the reasoning processes that encounter a version of the frame problem might operate on symbolic structures in an agent's memory, but they might also potentially be encoded in hardwired circuitry, simulated through neural networks, or subserved implicitly in the operation of other types of machinery. The point, though, is that the designer is approaching the design process in a certain way, maintaining a sense of the representational content of various machine states and making sure at all points that the correspondence method of argument constrains the design process.

This procedure might be contrasted with the *convergence method*. Here the design process is also constrained by an argument about correctness, whether formal or informal. The difference is that the method of argument focuses upon the agent's behavior and not on its internal states. Put another way, the method focuses upon particular relationships between the agent and its environment, characterizing these relationships in principled ways and making arguments about their invariants and their evolution. This approach is not wholly distinct from the correspondence method; it is a larger category that includes the correspondence method as a particular case—the relationship in that case being one of semantic correspondence. The term "convergence" is a little misleading in suggesting that the agent is necessarily evaluated by its eventual arrival at some kind of goal, but many other kinds of evaluation are possible as well.

The point is that principled arguments about correctness can be formulated in a variety of ways other than in terms of correspondence. Some of the most important invariants identified by these arguments might be located in the physical world, without any regard for the agent's internal states. To take a trivial example, an agent that performs an exhaustive search of a finite physical territory, placing breadcrumbs on each spot already searched and continually homing in on spots without breadcrumbs, can be easily demonstrated to find what it is looking for within a certain amount of time. Early AI theorists referred to this sort of thing as "external memory" and did not regard it as significantly different in its implications for cognitive architecture than internal memory [1,2]. Although this view is surely too simple once we take account of the geography of the physical world and the capacities of our organisms' physical bodies, note that the proof of correctness for this simple agent is entirely familiar from proofs of program correctness in computer science. The proof involves an invariant (the total of spots searched and unsearched), a progress function (the number of spots still unsearched), and a convergence condition (no more spots unsearched). Other arguments for correctness might employ considerably different methods. In each case, though, the argument will depend on some kind of principled characterization of the interaction— not necessarily of every detail of the interaction, just enough of its properties to allow an adequate argument to be formulated.

Another example may help to illustrate one of the correspondence method's inherent limitations for research on agents in environments with much qualitative structure. Consider an agent with a traditional set of symbolic "beliefs" that employs logical reasoning, based on these beliefs, to decide what actions seem indicated in particular situations. Since the agent is a finite being in a complicated world, it will probably have mistaken beliefs occasionally. Yet it may still be possible to demonstrate that the agent will necessarily achieve its goals anyway. Such a demonstration might proceed in several different ways, but in each case it will take into account specific properties of the relationship between the agent and its environment. For example, different paths may be easily distinguishable so long as the agent is registering certain properties of its environment, thus guarding against ending up on unintended routes. Likewise, the environment may be provided with signs that disambiguate all of the ambiguous situations that the agent might encounter. As with any other theory of erroneous beliefs (for example in computer perception research), demonstrating such things in a principled way requires an error model—a theory of the circumstances through which errors in belief might take place (cf. [77]). One might be able to demonstrate that mistaken beliefs will necessarily get corrected, that mistaken actions will necessarily provoke safe indications of the difficulty, or that uncorrected mistaken beliefs will lead at worst to alternative solution paths that are quantifiably less desirable than the optimum. In each case, the argument proceeds on the convergence model, even though symbolic beliefs are present and other, interrelated arguments might rest on the correspondence model.

A simple example might be provided by the control-theoretic notion of robust control: uncertainty about the plant is characterized by assuming that plant parameters are within certain known bounds. A controller that is robust under these conditions produces the desired behavior for all the possible plants consistent with these constraints.

These examples are obviously simple and abstract, meant for illustration. The rest of this introductory article will explain some of the concepts that have led the authors in this special double volume to develop more sophisticated forms of argument about interactions between agents and their environments.

2.4. Aerial and ground views

Another helpful distinction in research on interaction and agency is that between aerial and ground views of an agent's activities. When designing agents that operate in abstract territories such as search spaces, and that do not have bodies (simulated or not) in any real sense, it can be easy to lose the distinction between what the agent knows about a situation and what the designer knows about that situation. This distinction is not crucial when the design process is being constrained by the correspondence method, since in that case it is important for the agent to maintain enough knowledge about its environment to permit a proof to be constructed that the agent will do the things it is supposed to do. The agent need not be capable of actually performing that proof, since it suffices for the designer to have conducted the proof in a generalized way off-line, but the whole point of the correspondence method is that the agent knows those facts which permit it to get along successfully.

This is not true with the convergence method. An agent designed using the convergence method might be spoken of as having knowledge (or it might not), but this knowledge need not necessarily support a proof of convergence. The designer might be able to demonstrate that a large number of conditions about the agent's environment, together with the agent's internal states, afford a proof that the agent will be able to achieve its goals. For example, an agent that relies upon posted signs to find its way around will have great trouble in a world where such signs are sparse, but if the designer knows one particular world to have been adequately posted then it will be possible to prove that the agent will get where it is going, regardless of whether the agent itself can be sure of this.

This too is obviously a trivial example, and it is also a conceptually straightforward example in the sense that the agent is spoken of as having knowledge—the only question concerns the relationship between the agent's knowledge-set and the designer's. Things become more interesting when the agent is understood to have different kinds of knowledge from the designer—for example, indexical knowledge of its relationship to its surroundings—or when the agent is spoken of in wholly different terms, without reference to notions of knowledge. In such cases, it becomes particularly important to maintain a rigorous conceptual separation between the agent and the designer, so that the particularities of the agent's relationship to its environment can come out in full relief—and so that new theories about knowledge can arise that are rooted in the agent's having a body, being located in a physical environment, interacting with artifacts, and so forth.

The general point is that agents who are interacting with physical worlds have bodies, and embodiment has pervasive consequences for computational theories of action, knowledge, perception, and learning. In large part this is due to locality: agents with bodies, embedded in physical environments, only have direct access to limited regions of the world. These limited regions are not accidental or arbitrary in their shape, but have a structure that is made from the geometry of the space, the shapes of physical objects like hills and roads and walls and tools, and the causal interconnection of things. The simple partialness of the agent's access to these things already has significant consequences for theories of action that require agents to have substantially complete world models.

But more subtly, the local structure of an agent's involvements with the world brings to those involvements a pervasive indexicality: the agent is involved with *this* place, faces in *this* direction, interacts *now* with *these* artifacts. The agent does not necessarily know where it is, nor what time it is, nor what its heading is, nor which particular stone or can-opener or McDonald's it might be dealing with at any given time. Given this fact, the correspondence method, at least in its traditional forms, would suggest ensuring that the agent always know the answers to all these questions. The agent might possess a compass and a clock and a map, objects might be labeled with their identities, and so on. Another approach, compatible with the looser demands of the convergence method, is to explore the relationships between indexical knowledge ("this bike here now") and the more objective kinds of knowledge ("Karen's bike in Miami on Christmas"). Perception and action, after all, are inherently indexical in character: your retinas do not register "red" at a specific latitude and longitude, but rather "red here". Likewise, your hand does not close the door to room 317, but rather "this door". To interact with the world is to do things with your body, and your body is a physical thing that participates in the same locality and the same concrete particularity as any other.

It is this materiality of embodied action that makes the distinction between the aerial view and the ground view so compelling. The designer, taking a metaphorical position above the territory, can know a wide variety of things that an agent resting in a particular spot on the ground, with a particular heading, may not know. The agent's knowledge and ignorance are structured phenomena, and it is the designer's job to understand those structures. An agent might be going around in circles without ever knowing it, but the designer might be in a position to characterize the conditions under which the agent can and cannot avoid such a fate. An agent might be at risk of running out of stove burners without realizing it until it is too late, but the designer might be able to demonstrate that stove burners will necessarily be plentiful unless certain supplies run low. An agent may continually lose track of its tools, but the designer might be able to demonstrate that the tools will remain accessible so long as the agent makes a habit of putting them back where they belong.

2.5. Structure in the agent and the world

Having established the outlines of this emerging style of research, what kinds of things can be learned from it? Perhaps the most important lessons concern the ways in which agents are adapted to their environments. Although notions of adaptation are perhaps most familiar from biology, the most important ideas about adaptation in the history of AI are actually sociological. In his pre-AI book *Administrative Behavior* [71], Simon outlined many ways in which social organizations compensate for the "limited rationality" of their members. The orchestration of numerous workers within a larger organization, Simon argued, compensates for the individual's limited capacity for work. Likewise, the division of labor and the assignment of specialized tasks to individuals compensates for their limited abilities to learn new tasks. The flow of structured information through the organization compensates for their limited knowledge, and the precise formats of that organization, together with the precise definition of individual tasks, compensate for individuals' limited abilities to absorb information and apply it usefully in making decisions. Finally, Simon believed that the hierarchical structure of bureaucracies compensates for individuals' limited abilities to adopt their own values and goals.

Whatever the value system implicit in this analysis, the general form of argument has had an important influence on AI. This influence, though, has been indirect. When Simon moved from studies of organizations to studies of individual cognition in the 1950's, most of these ideas about the individual's cognitive environment did not survive the transition. The individual imagined in AI research has generally been isolated and self-reliant, except in the matter of goals, which in practice have almost invariably been assigned from the outside by the system's designer. Yet almost through the inherent logic of the enterprise, AI researchers have rediscovered the general form of argument outlined in *Administrative Behavior*: structure in the world compensates for the weaknesses of cognitive architectures. Some of these weaknesses might be imposed by the designers, for example when the goal is to explain human processing limitations, or they might derive from the weaknesses of all known architectures, or they might be inherent computational limitations deriving from undecidable problems and the like.

Despite this insight, perhaps the most significant shortcoming of research on "reactive" systems and "hybrid" planning–reaction architectures is a relative lack of concepts for discussing the useful structures of the world. When breaking free from the safe and constrained microworlds of classical planning research, these new schools emphasized environments which are "uncertain", "unpredictable", "complex", "changing", and the like (e.g., [33,40]). Unfortunately, it is next to impossible to say anything very general about environments that are characterized in these negative terms, as not-this and not-that. It is quite plausible that, by some measure, most environments are in fact wholly untenable, in the sense that they are so uncertain, unpredictable, and so forth that no organism above a certain primitive level could possibly survive in them. (Of course, these negative characteristics may be viewed as constitutive of warfare and other profoundly adversarial activities, and they are certainly part of American military discourse.) But given that the classical problems of plan-construction rapidly become intractable or undecidable as the qualitative complexity of the agent's environment increases (or, more precisely, as the planning formalism registers more and more of that complexity), it becomes imperative to discover the features of a given world—and of the agent's interaction with the world—that make life in that world tenable.

To be sure, AI research has employed a variety of concepts of "structure". Marr [52], for example, outlined a method of vision research that posits a set of modules, each computing a mapping from an input representation of the visual world to an output representation. Since this mapping is generally underconstrained (for example, when moving from a two-dimensional to a three-dimensional representation), it is necessary to make a series of "assumptions" about the objects being viewed [52, p.267]. These might include the rigidity of objects, the uniformity of light sources, the continuity of various physical curves, and the smoothness of occluding contours. The point is not that these assumptions always hold, but that they usually hold closely enough, and that visual illusions can result when they fail. For Marr, the relevant structures of the world are physical properties of objects, and more generally of the physical processes through which images arise (e.g., the reflection of light from textured surfaces). They do not pertain in any way to the agent's tasks or activities or interactions with the world.

Another concept of structure is found in AI research that frames problems in terms of heuristic search. Search spaces frequently have combinatorial properties that frustrate even relatively sophisticated heuristic search techniques. Discovering useful structures in these spaces, though, can lead to specially adapted search techniques with dramatically better properties. For example, one line of research in the plan-construction literature has explored the type of structure that Newell and Simon originally called "planning" but that has more commonly been known as "abstraction". In a typical plan-construction search problem, the nodes in the search space correspond to partially specified states of the world. When these states are represented in terms of conjunctions of ground terms, one promising strategy is to make a plan that only takes particular predicates into account (presumably the ones that correspond to the most difficult-to-achieve states of affairs in the world), and then determine whether that plan can be fleshed out to take the others into account. This was the idea behind the ABSTRIPS program [69]. Much later, Knoblock [44] derived conditions under which such schemes could be guaranteed to work.

While certainly useful, it is important to note that this latter conception of "structure" is not defined in terms of a physical or social world, but simply in terms of a search space. A further question is where the structure of a search space comes from. Is it simply a property of a representation scheme that can be arbitrarily chosen from among many possibilities? Yes and no: designers can often choose among different representation schemes, some of which might have significantly different computational properties than others for particular purposes. At the same time, of course, the choice of possible representation schemes is intimately tied to the world with which the agent in question must interact. If that world is inherently messy and complicated then no representation scheme can possibly smooth over the difficulties that will confront any agent living in it.

The general point here is independent of particular architectures: whatever architecture you employ, try to find structure in the world that fits the strengths and weaknesses of that architecture. Put another way, when a particular agent architecture runs into trouble, see if the world contains structures that compensate for its weaknesses. Of course, it is possible that a given architecture simply has inherent weaknesses. But the search for structure in the world will almost certainly be illuminating.

Where can structure in the world be found? And what does "the world" mean? Does it include what AI has historically called "the domain"? The various papers in this special double volume, which are summarized in a later section of this introduction, make numerous suggestions. By way of general orientation, though, here are some general categories that might aid the search for structure:

- *Artifacts.* How do the properties of tools simplify the reasoning that decisions that agents must undertake in choosing actions? How about buildings and streets? How about clothing and furniture?

- *Signs.* Where are signs placed in the particular world being studied? What do they say, and what assumptions about knowledge do they make? What other sorts of symbolic labels are placed on things? What kinds of instructions are provided? Does the language in those instructions have any reliable properties?

- *Physical dynamics.* What rhythms are established in a particular category of physical interactions with an environment? What properties of those interactions are conserved or remain invariant? Under what conditions do they converge to attractors or remain bounded by certain envelopes? Why?

- *Customs.* What conventions do the agents in this world maintain? If the agents can rely upon one another to maintain these customs, how can this simplify their reasoning? What invariants do these customs maintain in the physical world?

- *Practical constraints.* What orderings upon actions are dictated by plain physical practicality? A cupboard must normally be open before objects can be retrieved from it. Although often possible, it is usually impractical to put on your pants after putting on your shoes. You cannot normally pick something up without being near it. You cannot bake bread every day without periodically obtaining fresh supplies of flour. The sheer mass of such constraints will tend to channel activity in particular ways.

- *Learning situations.* In what situations are agents called upon to do something new? Do those situations have any reliable properties? Does anyone or anything ensure that agents need only perform reasoning that is incrementally more complex than they have performed in the past? When and how can the agent get help?

- *Mutual adaptation.* Does some pressure operate to incrementally adapt various entities to one another? Examples might include biological coevolution, accumulation of shared knowledge in joint activity, and moving parts wearing together. Each of these cases obviously has its own particular logic and its own way of conceiving adaptation.

- *Inertia.* Are there limits to the possible rates of change of important things in the world? Does this inertia provide agents in that world with a margin of safety in uncertain situations? Does it guarantee that dangerous situations will be detectable before they cause permanent damage?

- *Locality.* Are the effects of actions confined to relatively limited parts of the world? Such locality effects can arise either through physical distance or more subtle routes of causal connection. Do these effects simplify reasoning or perception? In particular, do they guarantee that particular important circumstances will be perceptible when the agent needs them to be? Do they provide provable bounds on the possible harm that mistakes can cause?

- *Stabilization.* (The term derives from the article by Hammond, Converse, and

Grass.) What actions do agents in this world take to ensure that the world maintains its computationally useful properties?

- *Geometry*. What properties of the physical environment bound the complexity of the reasoning required to act or learn in it? Are there useful notions of "diameter", "bottleneck", "critical path", "hillclimbing", and so forth?

These are elementary examples of the kinds of structure that one might seek in the environment. In hinting at their computational ramifications here, it has been necessary to employ terms such as "reasoning" and "perception" that might tend to presuppose particular architectures or philosophies of activity. But such commitments are not necessary *a priori*. As the articles in this special double volume will illustrate, analysis of the relationship between agent architectures and structures of the world can be conducted on a wide range of agents in a wide range of worlds. In each case, since the point of structure is to simplify computations, the questions one might address to the world will be shaped by the needs of the architecture. What is the architecture good and bad at? When has it been fragile or incapable of scaling up? When have the necessary computations been impossible or intractable? And so forth.

In particular, one should distinguish between two uses that a designer might make of these structures in the world, corresponding to the aerial view or the ground view. As part of the aerial view of the agent's activities, knowledge about structures of the world might enable the designer to prove that the agent's activities will necessarily have certain properties. For example, these structures might inspire the development of formalisms and methods of argument that enable the designer to demonstrate convergence to set goals. As a separate matter, knowledge about structures in the world might also be part of the *agent's* ground view of its situation. The agent might engage in explicit symbolic reasoning about these structures, it might communicate about these structures with other agents, or it might even use its ideas about the structures to set about creating, maintaining, or restoring them as the need arises. The agent's understandings of its environment need not correspond to the designer's understandings. The agent might have a subset of the designer's understanding of the world, or it might have a simplified or comparatively shallow version of the designer's understanding, or it might slowly discover that understanding for itself by increments and approximations. Clearly distinguishing between the aerial and ground views of the world will help designers keep track of the wide range of design options that are compatible with any particular designer's understanding of the agent's world.

A focus on structures in the world and upon principled characterizations of interactions has a further benefit. When research is focused upon architectures and mechanisms, little intellectual room exists for interchange between researchers pursuing different lines of research. Discoveries about structures in the world and properties of interactions, on the other hand, might be useful to researchers employing radically different architectures. Different research projects may employ incommensurable vocabularies, but each project can learn valuable lessons from the ways that the others have moved back and forth between the design of agent architectures and the exploration of structures of the world and properties of interactions.

2.6. Units of analysis

All of this attention to activities in the world can be misleading when it is viewed from within the context of the history of AI. Founders of AI such as Newell and Simon were engaged in a fight against behaviorism, as were other authors such as Lashley whose ideas were influential in the development of AI. As such, embedded in the concepts and values of AI is a powerful allergy to behaviorism born of the field's founding battles. One factor contributing to this allergy is a powerful distinction made within AI between "cognition" occurring inside agents and "the world" located outside of them. The earliest texts of AI were mostly framed with terms like "thinking" that pointed to internal cognition, perhaps with occasional perceptions and actions but with no strong sense of an embodied agent's continual and structured involvement in an outside world.

Perhaps as a result, research on agents' interactions with their environments can sound like covert advocacy of behaviorism. Indeed, it is easy enough for research that would rebel against AI's conventional ideas to slip into a reliance on behaviorist-type ideas such as the stimulus–response chains that Lashley argued against in his article on the structure of serially ordered behavior. The central conceptual challenge for computational research on interaction and agency is to formulate AI problems and methods in a way which does not fall into either extreme.

Borrowing a term from sociology, the conceptual issue here concerns the "units of analysis" within which research is conducted. There can be little doubt that human beings and other creatures have skins and skulls which provide a certain degree of causal isolation between the things that occur within them and the things that occur outside of them. To the extent that interactions between agents and their environments provide a useful focus of research, though, it will be necessary to define concepts that cross the boundaries between inside and outside. In other words, AI research will have to develop units of analysis that refer to interactions and not simply to an agent plus a world considered as two separate entities. This proposition can sound forbidding to people trained in computer science, inasmuch as an interaction is not a "thing" that can be spoken of as causing effects to happen, or else as being the object of effects caused elsewhere. Yet to speak of interactions as units of analysis is stronger than simply studying interactions: it requires that at least some of one's fundamental concepts be defined in terms of interactions and their properties. What does this mean?

To reconstruct in computational terms the idea of the interaction as a unit of analysis, let us return to the control-theory example with which this introduction began. A controller attached to a refinery (or, for that matter, to a walking robot) will receive a long series of inputs through its sensors, and it will produce a long series of outputs as well. Long-term observation of these numbers may reveal that they converge to certain values, or that they enter into an oscillation with a certain amplitude and frequency. Does the controller cause this behavior? Does the plant cause it? Of course, the behavior results from the interaction of the two, and responsibility for it cannot be pinned down any more precisely. That does not make the behavior mysterious; it only means that the structure of the behavior is (to employ one more term from sociology) "located" in the interaction between the controller and plant, and not in either of them separately.

The notion of units of analysis becomes more important when the agent and its environment are continually influencing each other, so that each one changes through the course of the interaction. If we watch the interaction proceed for a moderately long period of time, so that both organism and environment have had a chance to change in large and complex ways from their original states, then it can be a challenge to specify what the agent and its surroundings even *are*. Of course, one might make a list of every molecule or variable setting or memory address or synaptic weight, but such an enumeration would probably not be a useful or parsimonious description. In such a case, the very identity of the agent, as well as the identities of the various things in its environment, can only be conceptualized in terms of the interaction through which they arrived at their current states. Again, nothing is mysterious about this. The challenge for research is to develop principled ways of talking about it that allow useful arguments to be made about the properties of the interaction, and thence about the rationale behind the agent's architecture and design.

These ideas allow us to reformulate in a more sophisticated way the insights about "structure in the world" described in the previous subsection. The point is not exactly that the world has structure all by itself, but rather that the world has the kind of structure that makes a difference to the workings of that particular agent. This is a property of the relationship between the agent and the world, not of the world alone. For example, we might discover that certain tools have come to be designed in such a way that human hands are minimally likely to slip when using them as they are customarily used. Such tools are well adapted to their customary use, but they might be poorly adapted to use by other species or for other purposes. It is only in a very narrow sense, then, that the tool's adaptation is a property simply of the tool. It is better to conceptualize it as a property of the relationship among a number of entities (tool, hand, materials being worked on, etc.), and specifically as something that only makes sense in the context of a particular form of interaction among those entities. The unit of analysis in this case, then, is not the tool but rather the customary way of using the tool to interact with the world.

This is progress, but much remains to be done. The account of "interaction" in this special double volume is almost wholly individualistic in nature. Its units of analysis, likewise, frame research issues in terms of a single agent's interactions with a structured environment. To make full sense of these interactions from the designer's aerial view, though, it will be important for research on embodied interaction to merge with computational research on social interactions. Tools and the customary ways of using them, for example, are generally not properties of an individual's activities but of a culture's. Cultures provide forms of embodied interaction that offer us considerable guidance in adapting ourselves to a complex world, and computational research holds as much promise for analysis of these settings as it does for the more particular types of interaction treated here.

2.7. Representation

The revised theoretical orientation suggested here clears some new space for computational research on representation. So long as research is guided by the correspondence method and the maintenance of objective world models, representations have very specific jobs to do and in consequence are highly constrained in their forms and uses. Within the broader perspective suggested here, though, new possibilities open up. Some of these have already been sketched. Perhaps most fundamentally, designers need to understand the respective roles of indexical and objective forms of representations ("a couple of feet straight ahead" versus "latitude 41, longitude 13"). Indexical representations are more closely tied, in causal and epistemological terms, to the agent's immediate circumstances, but they are not as well suited for other purposes, such as distributing knowledge about spaces and times to agents at distant or unknown locations.

Reacting against conventional theories that have seemed to import an encumbering system of philosophical and architectural assumptions, computational research on situated action has been deeply ambivalent about the concept of representation. Authors such as Brooks [10] and Beer [9] have been willing to say that their agents employ no representations at all. Since representations obviously exist (inner monologues, visual imagery, tactile maps, etc.), this raises the question of what purposes representations actually serve. Brooks and Beer concentrate their attention on insects, and it is common to suppose that representations are late evolutionary developments [43]. Agre and Chapman [4] take another approach, describing a notion of "indexical-functional representation" in which the representational elements are not internal symbolic structures but stable interactional relationships between agents and the objects that serve particular functional roles in the agents' activities. Whether these things really deserve to be called "representations" is a valid question. The important thing, though, is not to provoke a binary argument framed in terms of "representations versus no representations", but to explore interactional concepts which might do similar theoretical work while providing alternatives to the correspondence model.

As the papers in this special double volume demonstrate, it is possible to take a variety of approaches to representation. The perspective advocated here does not dictate any single approach to the question, and the reality of the matter might be complex and heterogeneous. For present purposes, it will be valuable to review some of the history of the AI notion of representation. Most of the earliest explicit theorizing about representation in AI was tied to architectural assumptions and processing mechanisms. Quillian [66], for example, explored mechanisms for automated reasoning in network-like structures that resembled the structure of the brain, at least in the sense of consisting of a small set of basic units joined by connections that can transmit simple signals. Faced with the difficulty of building representations of complex things within these semantic network structures, AI researchers invested great effort into making their semantics clear (e.g., Woods [79]), with the result that the structures were eventually understood by most of the AI community as merely notational schemes for modified first-order logic [38]. Subsequent AI research on representation has primarily been concerned with logical semantics, which has widely been viewed as providing foundations for the whole of AI work [27]. Concern with the physical realization of logical reasoning has lately taken the form of complexity-theoretic analyses of the problems of making crucial types of inferences within logics with particular sets of expressive features [12]. Complexity analysis, though, does not yield detailed information about the consequences of particular architecture choices. Connectionist research, due to its strong focus on the possibilities of a particular class of architectures, has resumed the type of close analysis of distributed inference mechanisms that Quillian began [41].

The story of representational research in AI, then, has had two interacting aspects, semantics and physical realization, whose constraints upon one another have been explored in fits and starts. Computational research on agency and interaction will surely have these two aspects as well, but now each aspect will be placed in the context of agents' involvements in their environments. A basic observation in this regard, already remarked upon, is the inherent efficiency virtues of indexical representations that are tied to direct sensorimotor interaction with an environment. The research in this special double volume is deeply concerned with the physical realization of agents' reasoning (if, indeed, the vocabulary of "reasoning" is employed), but it has no fully developed interactional account of the meaning of representations, and in particular the relationship between what AI has historically understood as "internal" and "external" representations.

As already remarked, external representational materials are likely to provide a substantial amount of useful structure in the everyday world, including things like signs and instructions. What do people do with representational materials, how do these activities complement internal uses of representations, what role do representation-mediated interactions play in the rise of internal representations, and what properties do internal representational reasoning have as a result? These topics have been thoroughly investigated in a variety of other fields [16,17,29,37,50,80], so rather than speculating on the directions that future computational research in this area could take, let us simply survey some possible connections to these other fields that future research could develop more concretely.

3. Connecting to other fields

As the articles in this special double volume demonstrate, computational research on interaction and agency can benefit from contact with a wide variety of other fields of research. The common denominator of these contacts is the abstract notion of interaction, although an extraordinary number of other strands run through the various fields as well. This section offers a very brief outline of some of these fields and their potential connections to AI research. Control theory has been discussed briefly above, and several other fields might be mentioned as well, including philosophical logic, sociolinguistics, decision theory, and several varieties of psychology.

3.1. Dynamical systems theory

In recent years, researchers in numerous fields have developed mathematical models of dynamical systems, which are defined generally as any systems that can be described in terms of the changes over time of a set of interacting variables. Many such "systems", of course, have no very useful properties. And others are simple linear systems whose properties can be analyzed with traditional mathematical tools. Yet others fall within categories of differential equations for which robust solution or analysis methods are known. Dynamical systems theory extends the categories of systems for which useful analyses can be made. The most important cases are those in which the development over time of a system is driven by the repeated application of the same principle, for example the laws of mechanics or natural selection or economic choice. Since AI pursues computational understandings of organisms at all levels, from the neurological and mechanical to the social, the full range of these cases should ultimately be relevant to AI research.

A challenge for the relationship between AI and dynamical systems theory is to reconcile the quantitative and qualitative aspects of the various systems that AI research seeks to understand. Differential equations describe systems that can be characterized in terms of numerical variables, but symbolic systems require other types of analysis. In its broadest definition, systems theory is general enough to provide definitions of even very complex symbolic systems. But it does not follow that general results exist that cast useful light upon those systems. As the various fields develop, they will most likely begin to overlap in their approaches, particularly as the conceptions of structure in the world that inform the research in this special double volume also continue to influence research in other fields.

3.2. Robotics and vision

Inasmuch as roboticists construct actual embodied agents, research on robotics has led to several forms of principled analysis of interactions between agents and environments. The most innovative of these have been on the lower levels where the main analytical tools are built upon the theories of kinematics and dynamics in physics. Raibert [67], for example, analyzes the various types of symmetry found in animals' gaits and demonstrates how these might be represented mathematically and used to simplify analysis and synthesis of walking and running machines. The designer of a running machine cannot impose any arbitrary pattern of leg movements and foot landings that might come to mind. Only certain cycles of movement are physically possible, and principled analysis allows this space of possibilities to be characterized.

Or consider the theory of force control [78]. Whereas a position control system directs the movements of a robot effector by specifying a sequence of physical locations that it should occupy, force control is defined in terms of dynamic relationships between the robot and its physical environment, such as a specific force vector that should describe the robot's pressure upon a picked-up part regardless of any changes or variations in the parts' shapes. Because force relationships are indexical or relational in nature, it can be easier to build a sensor for them than for objective quantities like absolute position (unless, of course, the robot and the workpiece are made of rigid elements and fixed to the floor). The point is not that position control is useless, but that the space of possible designs is structured in large part by the kinds of epistemological considerations discussed in this special double volume.

Robot design must also be informed by dynamical analysis of the interactions among objects in the world that the robot's actions will set in motion. Mason [53], for example, presents a mathematical analysis of the interactions that arise when a robot must push an object across a surface. A part might move in a variety of ways due to the vagaries of friction, and anticipation of the space of possible trajectories allows motor plans to be fashioned that move the part into a desired configuration without wasted motion and even without sensors. In situations with greater uncertainty, such a system might visually observe the part's progress and update the dynamic analysis and motor strategy as new information becomes available.

Because computer vision programs can be presented with digital snapshots taken at distant places and times, research in vision has not always been forced to confront the embodied nature of visual activity. The theories of Marr, for example, do not envision an agent that is interacting in any complex way with its environment, assuming instead that the purpose of vision is to construct a three-dimensional model of the world with little reference to its purpose. But recent research on visual systems for robots has begun to demonstrate the depth of rethinking that the construction of embodied agents demands. Ballard [8], for example, presents a series of experiments in "animate vision", in which the architecture of visual processing is interconnected in tight and principled ways with the architecture of motor control. A paradigm of this kind of interconnection might be vergence control, in which the physical configuration of the visual system (eye orientation, for example) is dynamically adjusted to permit stereo focus upon a particular object at some determinate distance. And the architectural boundaries among reasoning, learning, and perception start to disappear altogether once one starts modeling the active choices agents make about what to perceive based on what information they need (cf. [15]).

3.3. Biology

Ecology and evolutionary biology offer several powerful concepts for thinking about the relationship between organisms and their environments. Perhaps the central such concept is adaptation. For an organism to be adapted to an environment is not a simple thing, since neither the organism nor the environment are likely to be simple themselves. Some aspects of adaptation, of course, can be explained in relative isolation from this full complexity, for example in terms of the mechanics of flying or swimming. The challenge for a full explanation of adaptation is that every organism's life has many aspects—locomotion, respiration, avoiding predation, finding and eating food and water, regulating body temperature, social interaction, and so forth—each of which brings its own adaptational demands.

Biologists sum up these demands by speaking of a particular species as filling a "niche" in its local ecosystem. Each component of the ecosystem provides part of the adaptational context for the others, and the result is a tendency for all of the elements to coevolve and to become adapted to one another in intricate ways. As the ecosystem changes through exogenous influences and the internal interactions of its various components, the adaptational demands of the niche will change as well. This dynamic notion of an agent's environment is much more complex and subtle than the conceptions historically employed by computational research.

At the same time, biology has historically had fairly simple concepts to describe organisms' activities in their environments and their interactions with one another, and it is here that computational ideas may make significant contributions. Research on "artificial life" [46,74] has commenced precisely this project. Building and analyzing artificial and simulated creatures may help clarify many biological concepts by forcing unarticulated assumptions and unasked questions to the surface.

3.4. Activity theory

Activity theory is a school of sociologically oriented psychology and education research that developed from the writings of the Russian psychologist Lev Vygotsky [76]. Vygotsky believed that human cognition is profoundly shaped by culture, and in particular that cognitive processes arise through the internalization of patterns of social interaction among people. Vygotsky believed that the process of learning has a great deal of structure. Specifically, he believed that most learning takes place in what he calls the "zone of proximal development". Watching caretakers and children interact in the context of shared activities like games and chores, he observed that the caretakers endeavored to dynamically shift the division of labor between the two, with the aim of ensuring that the child's portion of the activity lay near the outer edge of the child's current capabilities. Thus spared from overly simple and overly difficult tasks, the child could focus on incremental learning. Vygotsky argued that these complex structures of learning are reflected in the child's developing cognition, so that the child's processes of thinking could be viewed as internalizing the patterns of social interaction that gave rise to them.

A strong believer in the cultural dimensions of cognition, Vygotsky also emphasized the role of cultural artifacts such as tools in shaping cognition. The invention or refinement of a tool is an important event, inasmuch as it effectively encodes in a physical material the result of a beneficial process of thinking and experimenting. In learning to use the tool according to its affordances and the customs surrounding its use, future generations will be spared the tedious and haphazard burden of reinventing it. Moreover, in order to use a tool it is usually not necessary to fully understand the reasoning behind it, much less the alternative designs for the tool that had been tried out and discarded. The environment of daily life includes a rich collection of cultural artifacts—the tools and other artifacts to which Vygotsky's arguments apply—that provide a tremendous amount of support to individuals and groups who are organizing their activities. These artifacts include kitchen utensils, buildings and streets, machines like cars and computers, clothing, and much else.

Subsequent research has developed Vygotsky's ideas in numerous directions. The term "activity theory" was coined by Vygotsky's follower Leontiev, who proposed a conceptual framework for analyzing larger "activity systems" beyond the simple parent-child dyad. Leontiev shares with much AI research an interest in the process through which activities become habitual or automatic, no longer requiring conscious structuring and guidance. Activity theory has been brought to the English-speaking world by a number of psychologists and educationalists who are looking for ways to place children's cognition and learning in larger social contexts [60]. Engeström [21] has considerably broadened the activity theory framework to provide a principled means of intervening in complex organizational settings to bring about changes in the local activity system through the development among its members of an "expanded" awareness of its actual dynamics.

3.5. Genetic epistemology

Another relevant school of developmental psychology is that founded by Jean Piaget [63], whose work on "genetic epistemology" traces the ways in which the child grasps the nature of reality through its interactions with its environment. In contrast to Vygotsky, Piaget focuses upon the child as an individual figuring things out through a process that has been likened to scientific experimentation. He argued that the child's relationship to its environment proceeds through a series of discrete and identifiable "stages", each of which is defined by a different form of epistemology. A child in a very early sensorimotor stage, for example, might have difficulty connecting the object that it encounters on one occasion to the same object a few moments later, after it has been momentarily obscured. Later, though, the child will come to understand the "permanence" of objects across time, and this is the beginning of the child's understanding of a world that exists independently of thought.

Drescher [19] has conducted an extensive program of computational research based on Piaget's theories. Building on some suggestions of Piaget's, he has implemented a computer system that employs "sensorimotor schemata" to learn and represent knowledge. A schema, in Drescher's usage, does not represent the world through correspondence or mirroring. Instead, it states (roughly) "when the perceivable world is like *this*, and you take *this* action, then the world is likely to turn out like *this*". Such schemata can be learned through a relatively simple process of induction by simply trying numerous simple actions in numerous situations. More complex cognitive structures can then be built up by "chaining" these schemata, a process similar in form to the assembly of new plans through the stringing together of existing plans and primitive actions in traditional AI planning research. Another, more advanced mechanism is the creation of "synthetic items", which function similarly to "items" of sensory input except that they represent the much more abstract proposition that a certain schema is likely to be applicable in the ongoing situation. Drescher presents some extremely detailed scenarios that describe how the creation of these complex cognitive structures through the simpler sensorimotor schemata explains various features of the developmental process that Piaget traced in his work, including the detailed sequence of substages through which the child passes during the period leading up to the full establishment of object permanence. These scenarios allow Drescher to construct a theory of cognitive architecture that is consistent with Piaget's theories, as well as with recent empirical claims that Piaget underestimated the amount of innate cognitive structure in the infant. Specifically, he argues that the infant, in constructing its own cognitive apparatus in the process of development, effectively *re*constructs the functionality of many innate peripheral faculties, thereby allowing them to be integrated with one another more effectively than is possible on a simple modular design.

For present purposes, the great strength of Drescher's work is that its scenarios include numerous arguments that depend upon on the structure of the environment in which the human infant lives. Within Piagetian theory, the most fundamental fact about this environment is precisely the existence of permanent objects. When you rest something on a table and cover it with a cloth, it stays there until you take the cloth back off. When you put something in the refrigerator, it stays there until someone takes it back out again. As you move around a stationary object, the views of that object that become available to your eyes possess some stable, reliable, and predictable relationships to one another. And so forth. This observation about the environment of human activity gives substance to the scenarios, which follow the child through the discovery of a wide variety of simple but fundamental interactional regularities.

3.6. European phenomenology

Phenomenology is a branch of philosophy whose goal is to develop good vocabularies for describing the experience of ordinary activities. Put in plain language, phenomenology provides words for answering the question, "what is it like?". Although Merleau-Ponty's [56] phenomenological analysis of human embodiment has a straightforward relevance to the analyses in this special double volume, phenomenology is chiefly known in AI through the influence of Martin Heidegger, whose book *Being and Time* [39] provides a phenomenology of ordinary routine activities such as carpentry. Heidegger's work is notorious for its obscurity, and those who have been inspired by his writing to criticize various central tenets of AI routinely find themselves in the impossible situation of translating between intellectual languages and communities that could hardly be more different. In particular, attempts to read Heidegger as directly specifying alternative algorithms or architectures of cognition are doomed to especially intractable confusion, inasmuch as it was very much Heidegger's goal to avoid expressing himself in such terms.

Nonetheless, Heidegger's writing can, if handled with care, provide useful guidance for the development of computational theories of interaction. Heidegger places great emphasis on the customary forms of activity that structure much of everyday life, and in particular upon the customary uses of tools that give a conventional structure to actions, space, and materials. This "structure", for Heidegger, is not a cognitive symbolic structure, but a structure of experience within which things take on particular interrelated meanings. He emphasizes, for example, that we do not normally relate to a pencil as *this* particular pencil, but rather as *a* pencil that is used in a certain habitual way. We can choose to withdraw the pencil from this ordinary, routine kind of relationship to our activities, staring at it as an object of curiosity or levity or scientific inquiry, but that is a very different experience from simply using it to write. This idea suggests, in a loose sort of way, investigating how a computational theory of interaction might give a different status to routine interactions with generic things (writing with a pencil) than to exceptional interactions with specific things (examining or measuring this particular pencil).

But research like Heidegger's can have its most productive influence upon AI when AI itself recovers a sense of its own historical development. Despite the efforts of Dreyfus, Heidegger's work is not directly addressed to AI as it exists today, but rather to a larger tradition of which AI is one part. If Heidegger's analysis of the history of philosophical ideas can be viewed as indicating paths not taken—and, therefore, alternative ways in which AI research might be conceptualized—then it need not be taken as posing an all-or-nothing challenge to AI's foundations, but rather one critical perspective to assist in the field's self-examination and evolution.

3.7. Buddhist phenomenology

Whereas the European phenomenological literature is relatively recent (while, of course, building upon much older philosophical tradition), Buddhism has an ancient and continuously developed phenomenological system. The whole point of Buddhism is to seek enlightenment by using systematic meditation to pursue mindful awareness of one's own cognition, and Buddhist scholars have developed extensive descriptive accounts of cognitive processes that provide guidance for this process. These systems of description have evolved historically as communities of meditators have found previous formulations inadequate to describe their own experiences. Central to this evolving intellectual system is the idea of illusion, which holds that any particular conceptualization of reality must be understood as an imposition, perhaps possessing heuristic value but not providing any definitive or exhaustive representation. Prior to the cultivation of mindful awareness, cognition proceeds in a ceaseless cycle of imposing specific, prestructured interpretations upon the world and contracting desires and drives based on the unrecognized illusions that result. Mindfulness does not eliminate thought or paralyze action, but it does liberate the individual from the illusion that thought transparently grasps reality or inevitably compels action.

These ideas may seem distant from the concerns of computational research. Yet Varela, Thompson, and Rosch [75] have argued that the connections are actually numerous and deep. Both traditions of inquiry, after all, are concerned with the mind and its relationships with reality. The pivot through which these authors develop the connections between the two traditions is Maturana and Varela's notion of "structural coupling" [54]. Structural coupling is a biological notion rooted in the theory of evolution. Evolved species are adapted to their environments, and this adaptation ought to be conceptualized in interactional terms:

- the organism interacts in complex ways with its environment;
- this interaction both sustains the organism's internal functioning and has some range of effects upon the environment as well;
- the organism's internal structures and the structures of its external environment have both changed over historical time through mutual adaptation of species and ecosystem; and
- the changes in these structures have accumulated to such a degree that it is difficult if not impossible to understand them except in the context of their interaction.

The structures of the organism and its environment are, in this sense, "coupled" to one another. Varela, Thompson, and Rosch point out that this coupling is analogous in certain ways to the Buddhist notion of "codependent arising", which describes the experience of cognition: one does not experience cognition as rising up, searching for something in reality, and then settling upon it; nor does one experience reality as invading oneself and bringing a previously dormant cognition back to life. Instead, the processes of cognition and the structures of reality arise together, each proposing the other as its own illusory validation. Although further research will need to flesh out this analogy in more detail, it is certainly stimulating, and leads to innovative investigations of the processes through which perception and action guide one another in embodied activity.

This type of research has many skeptics among technical people. And indeed, phenomenology and computational research are not straightforwardly commensurable. Allowing each to influence the other requires drawing out the most promising analogies between them and pursuing the suggestions for research that these analogies might generate. Unfortunately, the phenomenological method strikes many people in the cognitive science tradition as akin to introspection, which was once pursued systematically by Russian and German psychologists but ultimately ran afoul of its lack of conceptual precision and empirical reproducibility. Phenomenology, though, makes no claim to identify internal mental mechanisms but only to provide compelling and detailed descriptions of experience. More importantly, phenomenological methodology, particularly in the Buddhist version, is simply far more rigorous than introspectionism, having developed over a long period in extensive communities of investigators.

3.8. Sociology

Sociology has numerous schools and subdisciplines, many of which have potential connections to research on interaction in AI. Perhaps the central question of all sociological research, though, is the question of social order: in virtue of what does society seem to have a relatively stable structure? It is impossible to survey the many formulations of this question in a short space, much less the available answers to it. Nonetheless, research within sociological schools such as ethnomethodology and symbolic interactionism has been distinguished by a commitment to detailed empirical investigation of how, in fact, people actually enact the structures of society in their dealings with one another.

The sociological research program that has had the greatest influence upon thinking in AI is arguably that of Lucy Suchman in her critique of AI planning research in *Plans and the Structure of Behavior* [72]. Suchman observed some people attempting to use a photocopier that had been equipped with a device that, based on AI planning theories, attempted to guide its users through complex copying operations by constructing a plan and then presenting the successive steps of the plan to the users. The users experienced a wide range of difficulties using these instructions, and they interpreted them in complex ways based on the situation as it presented itself in the moment. In particular, far from executing the instructions in the manner of a computer program, the people employed the instructions as resources—and as one set of resources among many—in figuring out what actions to take next. Both through Suchman's influence and other developments, a number of AI research projects have investigated the complex and varied uses that might actually be made of plans [5,30,64]. The deeper point, though, concerns the many subtle and improvised ways in which people structure their actions in accord with the demands of moment-to-moment meaningful interaction. These phenomena may lead future computational research to rethink its basic concepts in ways that can do justice to the improvisatory nature of human action.

3.9. Anthropology

Historically, anthropology differs from sociology in that it studies "them" rather than "us". Remarkably, even as this distinction has become untenable, anthropology has retained its distinctive character through its focus upon culture—and specifically upon the notion that cultures differ from one another in profound ways. Exploring the question of social order in a large variety of settings has led anthropologists to investigate numerous features of life that are normally too familiar to attract much attention. Among these is the role of habitual activities and customary artifacts in defining and maintaining a social order. Pierre Bourdieu [11], for example, disagreeing with a long tradition that locates social order in loud and visible things such as laws and ceremonies and conflicts, suggested to the contrary that the social order can best be found in the most ordinary details of everyday activities, and particularly in the habitual structuring of everyday uses of artifacts like houses, hearths, tools, clothing, pathways, and so forth. Anthropologists refer to this kind of theory as "practice anthropology" [61] because of its emphasis on the hidden order to be found in everyday cultural practices. While perhaps exaggerated in its emphasis on structured habit as opposed to conscious choice, this style of research has had a massive and generally salutary influence as anthropologists have chosen to view ever more ordinary and quotidian aspects of life as important and meaningful, and as legitimate topics of research.

In connecting anthropology with computational research on interaction and agency, a significant obstacle is the differing scales of research. Computational researchers must get things working, and that requires analyzing very small and specific actions. Whereas several schools of sociology, including those previously mentioned, have engaged in microscopic studies of human interaction, anthropology has mostly been concerned with larger things. Even when an author such as Bourdieu speaks of the fine details of habitual activities, it is rare for anything like a worked-out grammar of those activities to be provided. The focus, instead, is on articulating a set of analytical categories that allow apt descriptions to be given—descriptions that allow things on very different scales to be fitted together, so that economic structures, for example, can be related to the ways in which people teach and learn skills.

In this regard, a particularly promising analytical framework can be found in the work of Jean Lave. In her book *Cognition in Practice* [51], she provides a set of categories for analyzing people's interactions with their worlds on several different scales (more accurately, "levels"), from the moment-to-moment interleaving of different tasks to the historical structuring of an arena of activity such as a kitchen or supermarket. In contrast to much research in cognitive science and AI, she rejects the notion that people decide what to do by solving "problems" that can be abstracted from the complex and interconnected details of moment-to-moment activity. The people she observes do not so much solve problems as work through complicated dilemmas, resolving things just enough to keep moving. Her resolute focus upon units of analysis defined in terms of interactions leads her to theories that are hard to reconcile with computational research as it has historically been practiced. And indeed, numerous details will have to be worked out and rethought in order to strike up a productive relationship between conceptual systems such as Lave's and the concepts that guide computational research on interaction. An emphasis upon formulating computational ideas in terms of interactions, though, will ensure that the units of analysis in the two research projects are at least commensurable.

4. Papers in this double volume

The papers collected here are a diverse group, deriving from a remarkable variety of disciplinary backgrounds and technical literatures. Although they are described here within the agenda and vocabulary of this introductory article, it bears repeating that they each represent a distinctive approach to the issues. They should be understood as voices in a conversation, with numerous and subtle points of interconnection among them. Despite the temptation to impose an artificial structure upon them by sorting them into topical groups, they are arranged in alphabetical order by the first author.

4.1. Arbib and Liaw

Arbib and Liaw present an evolutionary scenario for explaining the complex functionality of the nervous system. Taking as their model the visual system of the frog, they summarize the evidence that motivates their model. Rather than directly specifying the operation of neurons, they frame their theory at an abstract level, in terms of the interacting "schemata" that give rise to the observed patterns of behavior. Schemata are abstract units of computational functionality that can be implemented on a variety of hardware substrates. In particular, schemata provide a level of abstraction that allows brains and computer hardware to be discussed in a common vocabulary. Arbib and Liaw and their colleagues have developed general formal models of schemata that allow precise accounts of particular systems to be formulated and reasoned about in principled ways.

Beginning with the life and ways of the frog, Arbib and Liaw develop an approach to the study of the visual system that places it squarely within the context of an embodied agent's interactions with its environment. Having done so, they discuss the issues that arise in making the difficult transition from sensorimotor behavior to symbolic reasoning. In particular, they sketch some processes through which novel schemata might arise in response to the demands of novel situations. They emphasize, however, that cognition within the schema model is not controlled by a centralized device but is a matter of cooperation and competition among a distributed set of schemata. Furthermore, these schemata do not employ any single representation scheme, but rather a patchwork of partial representations, each of which captures a particular aspect of the agent's interactions within a particular mode of processing.

Arbib and Liaw's argument illustrates an inversion of priorities that is common in computational research on interaction and agency. AI has traditionally been concerned with "higher" cognitive functions such as the construction of innovative plans to solve arbitrary goals, with less attention to evolutionarily prior phenomena. This is natural enough if one believes that, in fact, "thought" is a phenomenon that can be defined and studied by itself, without reference to the whole background of "low-level" processing and routine activity against which thought takes place. Rejecting this point of view leads to a considerably different approach: an emphasis on routine activities, on sensorimotor interactions with the world, and upon the ways in which "low-level" functions provide the functional, developmental, and evolutionary basis for the higher functions. In practice this means that the higher functions generally suffer the same methodological postponement that older AI research had visited upon the lower ones. The ultimate challenge, of course, is not to declare one set of functions to be more important than the other, but rather to provide substantive accounts of their interrelationship. Arbib and Liaw suggest some ways of seeing the higher functions as continuous with the lower ones. Although the higher and lower functions are made of the same stuff, so to speak, they do differ in the sense that the higher functions require schemata to be replicated and synthesized in a way that the lower functions do not. As Arbib and Liaw point out, this evolutionary shift is congruent with the theoretical movement that Newell referred to as the "Great Move" [58]—from a focus upon hardware, with its static interconnections, to a focus upon the interconnectable symbolic structures of higher thought.

4.2. Barto, Bradtke, and Singh

Barto, Bradtke, and Singh review and synthesize a great deal of research on the use of dynamic programming, applying their unified understanding of this class of algorithms to real-time control. Each of these algorithms enables an agent to learn how to improve its efficiency in achieving goals when interacting with dynamic, and possibly stochastic, systems. Through repeated trials of actual or simulated control of a given system, the agent draws on its accumulating experiences to produce improved control strategies. These methods differ from AI's heuristic state-space search techniques in that they must repetitively visit a large number of states, as opposed to threading their way through an explosive number of states. By improving their heuristic evaluation function using principles from dynamic programming, they improve their search strategy. Unlike classical dynamic programming systems, the algorithms described by Barto, Bradtke, and Singh do not need to visit all of the possible states. As the algorithm converges, effort is focused increasingly upon those states which must actually be visited by an optimal controller. It is possible to prove fairly strong results about the conditions under which these learning methods will converge to optimal controllers.

This research unifies results from a number of fields. In particular, by pointing out the relevance of asynchronous dynamic programming methods to research on learning in stochastic environments, it greatly strengthens the connections between AI research on search and learning and control theory research on adaptive control methods. The result is a nearly exhaustive investigation of a set of weak methods that can be applied to a wide range of problems. On the other hand, as with any weak method of any generality, the results guarantee convergence without making any strong promises about how long convergence will take. A project for future research will be to understand how the learning methods might be specialized to take advantage of particular kinds of structure in the environment.

4.3. Basye, Dean, and Kaelbling

Basye, Dean, and Kaelbling develop a series of algorithms for probabilistically solving the problem of "system identification". On an abstract level, system identification is the problem of reconstructing the structure of a state-transition graph by sampling its input–output behavior. That is, the algorithm is presented with a series of discrete options (such as turning left or right) and, upon choosing one of those options, is told what information can now be "seen" (red or green; hot, warm, or cold; etc.). Although system identification problems have been investigated in a wide variety of settings, their relevance here is to the problem of discovering the structure of an environment by traveling around in it according to some strategy. And since Basye, Dean, and Kaelbling have real robotic applications in mind, they have extended the problem to assume that the information about the environment that the agent receives is only probabilistically correct, perhaps because of noise in the operation of its sensors. As a result, their algorithms do not guarantee perfect correctness but a certain specifiable likelihood of correctness.

The problem cannot be solved in its most general form, since insufficient information may be available to sort through the fog and actually pin down which states are which. Intuitively, the difficulty is that the agent never knows where it is, has no guarantees that it can return to where it came from, and has no perfectly reliable way of knowing if its present location is the same as its location at any previous time. Its exploration, moreover, must begin wherever it happens to be located; it cannot, in other words, jump to an arbitrary location. Therefore, the authors explore the structures in the environment which can be exploited by particular search strategies to provably reduce uncertainty. It transpires that the problem can be solved in probabilistic polynomial time, provided that the world has certain properties such as reliable landmarks or tightly constrained structures which can be mapped with greater certainty than wide-open fields of densely interconnected vertices.

Although clearly simplified in relation to many real environments, Basye, Dean, and Kaelbling's paper is a sophisticated study in the interaction between learning, partial knowledge, action strategies, and environment structures. Their agent is not omniscient, does not reliably know where it is, may have wildly mistaken ideas about the structure of the environment, and follows trajectories that the designer can only characterize in abstract terms. Despite this, it is possible to characterize the agent's interactions with the environment in sufficient detail to demonstrate that the resulting models of the environment will converge to accuracy. Although it is convenient to explain the algorithm using the spatial metaphors of travel through a graph-structured space, the results will apply to environments in which the state-transitions represent other kinds of changes, such as the workings of artifacts. An important project for future research will be to understand what structures of particular categories of environments, especially these not-literally-spatial ones, correspond to the formal properties of graphs that permit Basye, Dean, and Kaelbling to prove their results.

4.4. Beer

Beer applies the mathematical machinery of dynamical systems theory to the formalization of agent–environment interactions. Specifically, he proposes viewing agent and environment as two coupled dynamical systems, so that the interaction between them can be viewed as the trajectory of one large system whose variables are simply the variables of both agent and environment together. This proposal provides a straightforward reading of the general notion of making interaction, not the internal cognitive processing, the unit of analysis for AI research. Having defined things in this way, dynamical systems theory provides an extensive vocabulary for discussing the space of possibilities through which a given agent–environment system travels. A given region of the space, for example, might form a basin within which all possible initial configurations eventually settle into a stable, periodic "limit set". The interaction might be defined as adaptive in relation to an arbitrary condition upon its trajectory.

One benefit of this general approach is in analysis. Research on interaction and agency will only progress if it becomes possible to inspect particular performances, and to characterize general categories of them, so as to understand what the agent is really doing and why. Since any given interaction can be understood as a trajectory through a space, this trajectory can be submitted to analysis using a variety of tools. Particular trajectories can be visualized by being plotted, though presumably in a reduced subset of the dimensions of the full coupled dynamical system. Beer provides several examples of this kind of analysis, and of the conclusions that can be drawn from it.

Beer's particular domain is a walking robotic insect whose leg parameters are driven by a simple neural network. The weights of this network, in turn, are set by a genetic algorithm that simulates many different settings of the weights and homes in through incremental, evolutionary refinements on a set of weights that maximizes certain measurements of the simulated insect's performances. Analysis of these performances demonstrates that the neural network has settled upon patterns of interaction with the environment (the insect walks on a horizontal floor) that correspond to the gaits used by insects. Moreover, when the sensors measuring the positions of the insect's legs are unreliable, the genetic algorithm settles upon a set of weights that permit the insect to switch among different dynamics for generating gaits as the situation demands.

Beer emphasizes, though, that his principal commitment is not to this particular architecture but to the dynamical-systems framework. He presents these discoveries as prototypes of an emerging style of AI research in which an agent's embodiment is accorded a central role. Once this is done, he argues, all of the traditional categories of AI research must be rethought. His robotic insects, for example, have internal states but do not have anything resembling traditional symbolic notions of representations. Of course, one might vindicate the notion of representation by defining it widely enough to include all possible uses of internal state. But so long as the notion retains any real content, Beer argues, his insects fall outside of it. Instead, the internal states in the robotic insects are grounded in, and take their functional "meanings" in relation to, the agent's interactions with its environment.

Dynamical systems theory provides a highly general framework for formalizing agent–environment interactions. Perhaps the principal challenge for research within this framework will be to formulate systems-theoretic definitions that capture the particular kinds of structure encountered in more general categories of agent–environment interaction. The structures of tool use, for example, presumably correspond to particular properties of enormous dynamical systems. But can these constraints be captured by relatively compact and comprehensible formulas for characterizing those properties? This question will presumably not have a single, simple answer. As Beer's analysis shows, development of this theory will require the elucidation of new, more appropriate conceptions of categories as basic as "representation". AI having been decades in the making, its reconstruction in terms of interactions will take unpredictable forms as well.

4.5. Donald

Donald presents a formalism for reasoning about the computational properties of distributed sensor systems. Given two sensor systems arranged in the world, one would like to ask a series of questions modeled on the theory of computational complexity: Can one sensor system detect every condition in the world that the other can? Are the two sensor systems equal in their sensory powers? If not, can we define precisely what would need to be added to the "weaker" sensor system to make it equivalent in power to the "stronger" one? And most generally, does there exist a formal sense in which information is "conserved" in the movement from one design to the other (for example, a design that involves two relatively simple mobile agents communicating via flashing lights versus a single relatively complex agent performing all of the necessary computations on its own)?

Formalizing these questions brings forth a large number of points that usually remain in the background of a design process. For example, a great deal of information is encoded into the calibration of sensors, and the formalism makes it possible to explain precisely what this information amounts to, and how it compares to the addition of another sensor or the addition of extra capabilities to an existing one. To take another example, it may turn out that one sensor system cannot be transformed into another, seemingly similar one, without the expenditure of considerable computational effort because that transformation would require a particular computation to be inverted; inverse problems, of course, are frequently much harder to solve than the problems they invert.

The form of analysis made concrete in Donald's paper would be extremely useful if extended to other aspects of the design of autonomous agents. An informal model in this regard might be found in Braitenberg's [13] speculations about the capacities of various kinds of agent machinery. Intuitively speaking, as an agent's machinery grows more sophisticated, it ought to be able to participate in a growing range of interactions with a given environment. Different forms of interaction would thus fall into a hierarchy, according to which categories of agent machinery are capable of participating in them. Of course, this hierarchy depends on the particular environment being considered, and the rearrangements of the hierarchy in different environments would provide a valuable indication of the degrees and kinds of adaptation that different varieties of agent machinery possess to environments with particular properties. These kinds of understandings would qualitatively improve our abilities to design novel situated agents and to understand and explain the ones that already exist.

4.6. Hammond, Converse, and Grass

Hammond, Converse, and Grass wish to develop computational models of what they call "long-term activity". Whereas classical planning was defined in terms of an agent pursuing a goal (and then, presumably, going to sleep or asking for a new goal), Hammond et al. wish to understand the strategies by which an agent can engage in productive activity in a given environment over long periods. In their contribution to this special double volume, they explore a category of action policies that contribute to orderly action over long periods. They refer to these policies as "stabilization"—actively changing the environment so as to maintain in effect the properties that the agent's actions rely upon. A simple example would be putting away your tools when you are finished with them. Hammond et al. provide a helpful taxonomy of the types of stabilization, with many examples, and they embody some of these examples in a simple demonstration program.

The underlying argument in Hammond et al. is important for the general project of making computational theories of interaction and agency. An omnipotent and omniscient agent would not need to put its tools away, since it would have no trouble finding them the next time it needs them. Agents with more realistic capacities, by contrast, need the world to have relatively stable properties. This observation takes on a specific form in the context of the case-based architectures that Hammond et al. employ. Their emphasis is not upon unique, complex, creative forms of reasoning but upon the stockpiling of "cases" that permit newly arising situations to be usefully assimilated by precedents from situations that have gone before. An agent with a large collection of cases will be able to act in a sophisticated fashion without necessarily engaging in sophisticated computation. But a collection of cases is only useful if those cases actually arise in the future. If the tools are always left in different places then new cases might be required much more frequently than if they are always left in the same place. It therefore makes sense, other things being equal, to actively manipulate the world so that the same cases tend to arise over and over.

Note the form of this argument: faced with a seeming lack of generality in their architecture, Hammond et al. did not immediately decide to make the architecture more general. Instead, they sought structures in the world—and, more specifically, in agents' interactions with the world—that, once properly articulated, actually revealed an adaptive "fit" between the architecture and its environment. This is similar to Simon's approach in *Administrative Behavior* [71], where he explained the functioning of organizations largely in terms of compensating for the limited rationality of individual employees. Hammond et al. are, of course, dealing with individual agents in a wider variety of environments, but the similarities remain. It could have transpired that no viable compensatory structures were found, in which case suspicion might have been transferred back to the architecture. But generalization of the architecture should be the second line of defense, not the first.

The approach of Hammond et al. ought to find application in a wider variety of settings. Social and organizational activities have their own forms of stabilization, and techniques of stabilization are supported by cultures in many ways, from artifacts such as toolboxes to teaching methods to linguistic phrases such as "this goes here". Analysis of the limits of stabilization, moreover, might lead to the discovery of new (seeming, apparent) weaknesses in the case-based architecture, which might in turn provoke a search for further types of structure in agents' interactions with the world.

4.7. Hayes-Roth

Hayes-Roth introduces the concept of the "niches" that can be occupied by particular categories of agent architectures. While inspired by the biological concept of a niche, Hayes-Roth defines a niche according to several dimensions, each calling for a particular architectural approach: perceptual strategies, control mode, reasoning choices, reasoning methods, and meta-control strategies. For example, some environments, perhaps due to their high reliability and their high demands for efficiency, call for control modes based on strict linear sequencing of actions; other environments, by contrast, may call for actions to be improvised based on relatively complex moment-to-moment adaptation to evolving circumstances.

Rather than looking for a single super-architecture that is equally responsive to the entire territory of niches, Hayes-Roth has developed an architecture that is capable of dynamically adapting itself to changing conditions, synthesizing control policies that select and combine certain elements of the system's architectural repertoire according to its analysis of the demands of the situation. This kind of dynamic adaptation is necessary in Hayes-Roth's target domain of intensive-care monitoring, an extraordinarily complex environment whose demands can qualitatively shift among extreme positions. When a patient has a sudden medical crisis, for example, long-term tracking and reasoning must give way to a much more urgent form of processing that is capable of rapid responses to shifting states. Likewise, the patient's response to treatment may drift into an unfamiliar pattern, requiring the agent to change its processing mode into a much more active policy of probing and diagnosing to determine what might be going on. This reasoning, in turn, might shift between more qualitative forms based on past precedents and more quantitative forms based on simulation, depending on what kinds of information and symbolic knowledge might be available.

Hayes-Roth's system is still evolving. In evaluating it, Hayes-Roth insists upon the accumulation of empirical experience in complex real-life domains such as intensive care monitoring. As a strategic matter, the architecture can be deemed promising if it is able to shift gracefully among the various modes of operation that changing conditions require of it. Detailed analysis of whether the system behaves optimally within each of its many modes will be required later on, of course, once each facet of the system is equipped with the mass of detailed knowledge that it will require. But qualitatively accurate responsiveness within a relatively parsimonious architectural framework will provide promising signs for future development.

4.8. Horswill

Horswill presents a methodology for the construction of specialized agent architectures. Observing that AI has long pursued the goal of wholly general architectures that can be adapted to arbitrary circumstances, Horswill considers the contrary project, a search for architectures that are maximally adapted to particular environments. He suggests a process of incremental refinement in which structures of the environment are, so to speak, "folded in" to the agent's computations as assumptions, yielding simpler versions of the architecture that require simpler forms of computation and perhaps, in extreme cases, no computation at all. Experience with this method ought to lead designers to fill out a space of possible designs, a kind of lattice structure within which a designer can move downward as new environmental regularities are discovered and upward as those regularities prove false or unstable.

His examples are chosen from the construction of an autonomous robot designed to provide tours of an office space. Suitable constraints are discovered in the level floor, reliable visual properties, and independence of variables in search spaces afforded by this environment, leading to a particularly simple agent design. The same design process in a different environment, of course, might lead to the discovery of different regularities and the making of different simplifications to the agent architecture. Horswill emphasizes that his analysis of his robot's architecture is largely retrospective. The point of the design methodology is not to provide a simple algorithm from which optimal designs can be cranked out, but to provide a framework for thinking within which the generalization and specialization of designs can be undertaken in a conscious and deliberate way.

Horswill's paper expresses in a particularly clear way a theme that runs throughout these papers: the desirability of parsimony in architectures. When the units of analysis for design and analysis are defined in terms of interactions, the mutual fit between an agent and its environment becomes the most important source of guidance for the design process. A highly general architecture may be able to function well in a wide variety of circumstances, assuming that its computations are not impossibly cumbersome, but this very generality will produce a great deal of "slack" in the architecture's relationship to the environment. By aiming for simple machinery, and by shifting the primary explanatory burden to interactions and not to the architecture, designers such as Horswill are forced to pay ever more detailed attention to the environment and the agent's place within it.

4.9. Kirsh

Kirsh explores the wide variety of ways in which people employ the space around them to complement their cognition. If we watch people as they work we note that they constantly manage the resources around them, not just to get things done, but for cognitive ends—to highlight opportunities, to encode useful information, and to keep the task-relevant complexity of the world to a manageable level. These cognitively oriented manipulations of the environment happen on all scales, from a slight repositioning of a single workpiece to a long-term structuring of a whole workplace. Considering a striking range of cases, he distinguishes among three phenomena: spatial arrangements of tools and materials that simplify an agent's choices among alternatives, spatial arrangements that simplify the gathering of information through perception, and spatial arrangements that permit calculations to be formulated in a way that fits better with the capacities of internal cognition. As we observe an individual interacting with a complicated array of physical things in an environment—particularly when participating in a familiar activity in a familiar setting—it can become difficult to draw lines between the "internal" and "external" aspects of cognition. Of course, it is simple enough to make one list of the causal events going on with hands and artifacts and a second list of the causal events going on within brains, but the fact is that these two categories of events are continually triggering one another, so that it is difficult to make sense of them except as a members of a closely coupled system.

It is here that the case for an interactional unit of analysis in computational research on situated agency starts to become compelling. This is not to say that analyses based upon traditional theories of cognition must be abandoned. To the contrary, Kirsh uses theories of cognition-as-search to provide an intuitive explanation of why certain spatial arrangements of things lessen the burden upon internal cognition. The resulting picture of interaction, though, takes those traditional concepts in new directions, placing them in the larger context of an agent's involvement in a highly structured environment.

Kirsh's analysis brings out some of the enormous complexity of the phenomenon of "adaptation". The metaphors used to explain adaptation are frequently structural: the agent is spoken of as "well-fitted" to its surroundings. Yet if we ask whether a particular cognitive architecture is well-adapted to a given environment, the question only makes sense in the context of a potentially elaborate set of practices by which the agent actively manipulates its surroundings from moment to moment to achieve that "fit". Many of these practices are cultural in nature, must be learned by the agent, are supported by artifacts, and so forth. Furthermore, the means by which agents actively manage their workplaces are inseparable from the means by which they actually get useful work done in those settings. With this realization, the boundary between "perception" and "action" becomes complicated, and it becomes necessary to take care about what these terms—so sharply distinguished by many conventional AI architectures—are to mean.

4.10. Lespérance and Levesque

Lespérance and Levesque adapt methods from philosophical logic to give an account of the distinction between objective knowledge and indexical knowledge. Their point of departure is the observation that agents routinely know things in indexical terms that they do not know in objective terms. For example, it is common to know things like "something red just went by here" without having any objective name for "here" (such as a conventional place name or a latitude and longitude) or any objective knowledge of the current or recent time (such as a clock reading). Of course, the designer or another outside observer might have this knowledge from an aerial point of view. But down on the ground, the world is immediately tangible in indexical forms. Requiring an agent to represent the world in objective terms, then, would impose a wholly unnecessary epistemological burden, as well as requiring that knowledge that is actually independent of objective information (like the right way to core an apple, which operates regardless of what county one inhabits or what month it is) must be formulated in unnecessarily cumbersome ways, quantifying over the possible places and times rather than in indexical terms.

Formalizing indexical knowledge accurately, though, presents significant challenges. Many of these pertain to time. Events can have a range of complex relationships to "now" and to various "thens", and Lespérance and Levesque develop a fairly sophisticated logic of time that permits a wide variety of types of partial knowledge to be expressed accurately. They are also able to express a wide variety of "knowledge preconditions" for action. A simple example is that you cannot call me on the phone without knowing my number. A more complex example is that you cannot reliably place a letter in my mailbox if you are only aware of being "here", as opposed to being on my front step.

The logical formalism that Lespérance and Levesque have developed is meant, as they explain, solely as an account of the "knowledge level" of indexical and objective reasoning. That is, they do not provide any account of how these forms of reasoning might be realized in hardware. It would be a mistake to assume that an agent would have to manipulate a mass of symbolic formulae corresponding to those in Lespérance and Levesque's paper. Instead, it is possible that their formalism is best employed by the designer as a tool for analyzing (and, of course, designing) an agent's patterns of reasoning. Before this possibility can be realized, though, it will be necessary to explore the computational properties of the formalism and the ways that it can be fitted to particular classes of machinery. Simple and straightforward realizations of their theory will of course be possible through the use of general-purpose logical theorem-proving programs. This approach is most likely impractical, though, and more sophisticated kinds of physical realization will probably require the logic to be adjusted in various ways. Research in this area is bound to produce an expanded understanding of the computational properties of various forms of situated reasoning.

4.11. Lyons and Hendriks

Lyons and Hendriks present an architecture for the automatic incremental synthesis of agents that participate in complex, structured interactions with their environments. Their research is founded upon a formal framework for the characterization and analysis of agent–environment interactions. The basic idea is to model the agent and environment as interacting mathematical automata. Each automaton is assembled from a vocabulary of basic computing elements, and the behavior and interaction of agent and environment can be modeled in terms of the trajectories followed by these automata as they evolve according to a fixed set of formal rules. This approach allows one to make precise a long list of important questions about interaction, most particularly whether the interaction will eventually converge to a specific desired state. Although the method is only as powerful as the proof techniques for demonstrating such conclusions within it, it stands as one of the most thoroughly worked out frameworks for analyzing qualitatively complex interactions.

In their paper, Lyons and Hendriks employ their automata-theoretic formalism to motivate the design of a system for controlling industrial robots as they engage in complex assembly tasks. Their architecture has two components, a "reactor" that employs a fixed circuit-structure to control the robot's moment-to-moment interaction with its environment, and a "planner" that is capable of incrementally adding to the reactor's structure so as to extend its behavioral repertoire. The automata-theoretic formalism provides Lyons and Hendriks with a principled basis for designing a language that a programmer can use to represent "dynamics" of interaction. A robot can "participate" in one of these dynamics just in case it can sense particular kinds of situations, and take particular actions in them, that will guarantee that the joint agent–environment system will evolve in a particular way.

This is a different and more complex concept than the traditional notion of "executing a plan to achieve a goal". First of all, Lyons and Hendriks take for granted that only a certain proportion of the action in the world will be controllable by the agent (for example, through the movement of its limbs). Secondly, the "planner" does not envision a definite sequence of actions and world-states through which the "execution" will travel. Instead, it specifies a potentially large and complex space of possible trajectories whose destinations can be sufficiently influenced through the adoption of particular action policies that can be physically realized by the reactor, through the particular kind of machinery of which the reactor is made.

4.12. Rosenschein and Kaelbling

Rosenschein and Kaelbling present a view of representation and control based on the theory of situated automata. They observe that AI ideas about representation have frequently been based on mathematical logic, or upon notations that can be formalized in logical terms. Unfortunately, these ideas have traditionally been accompanied by specific architectural commitments, according to which knowledge is formulated through structures modeled on the techniques of symbolic programming. Thought, in this view, is a matter of the explicit computational manipulation of these symbolic structures by mechanisms such as theorem-proving programs. The extreme inefficiency of most such schemes has cast shadows on formal logic as a research tool in AI. Rosenschein and Kaelbling point out, however, that the basic point of logic is not architectural but semantic: it is a formal means of sorting out the meanings of representational elements, with no inherent commitments about the manner in which these elements are physically realized.

Pursuing this observation, Rosenschein and Kaelbling present an agent synthesis methodology in which the machinery being generated is unusually simple and straight-forward. They present a logical formalism that allows them to represent the workings of a specific, wholly traditional class of digital machinery. The representational elements here are not symbolic structures but values in registers and on wires. Logical formalization permits the designer to give a precise account of the meanings of individual elements in terms of their correspondence to the world, and logical notation provides the basis for a set of languages for specifying the machinery for newly designed agents. The resulting circuitry need not be specified in complete detail. To the contrary, the compilers for these languages can perform a wide variety of manipulations on the logical forms and circuitry representation, and these manipulations can be proven to preserve the intended meanings of the computations because of the clear formal semantics of the underlying logical formalism.

The devices that are synthesized through Rosenschein and Kaelbling's methods are embodied agents whose activities take place across time. The authors point out that this is quite a different picture from the traditional notion of "solving a problem" by mapping a single, isolated input onto a single, isolated output. Instead, the picture is more like that of control theory, with a continual stream of inputs and a continual stream of outputs—in this case, tied to a discrete digital clock. The logic includes operators that can represent the relationships between values on adjacent ticks of this clock, thereby making it possible to reason in a principled way about the meanings of computational processes that unfold over a series of time units. A further valuable step would be to employ these methods to formalize the time-structures of activity in particular kinds of environments, in which strong guarantees might become possible regarding the correspondences between time-extended computations inside the agent and time-extended processes occurring in its surroundings.

4.13. Schoppers

Schoppers presents an architecture that combines a modal logic of time and belief with a control-theoretic philosophy of an agent's relationship to its environment. Rather than engaging in complex symbolic reasoning on-line, Schoppers' program compiles a sensorimotor decision tree that interacts with a variety of asynchronously operating subsystem controllers within a robot. One of these subsystems monitors the information available from the various sensors and maintains a consistent set of beliefs. This approach permits the agent to take advantage of complex dynamics within its relationship to its environment, intervening with specific corrective actions only when these dynamics are not headed for desired states. It also affords a high degree of parallelism in the agent's execution, as well as considerable resilience in the face of unexpected perturbations.

A reformulation of traditional AI ideas within a control-theoretic vocabulary leads Schoppers to fresh perspectives on a variety of AI issues. His point of departure is the observation that it is impossible to guarantee any sort of iron-clad coupling between the agent's internal states and the world outside. Instead, the agent can rely upon a variety of factors to ensure that it remains adequately coupled to the world. These include physical inertia, which ensures that incorrect actions undertaken based on transiently mistaken perceptions or deductions about the world cannot do too much harm before they are corrected. They also include the structure of the space around the agent, with its strong locality effects, so that the agent will necessarily get a better look at any object that it is in a position to affect. The result is a distinctive system modularity that focuses on managing the agent's relationship to its environment rather than upon dictating a predetermined sequence of actions.

Schoppers applies his architecture to the control of a rescue robot operating in space. It would be valuable to apply Schoppers' framework to environments with more and different types of interactional regularities, such as those involving interaction with artifacts and real-time cooperative interaction with other agents. Future research could characterize in more detail the loose coupling between robot and environment that is recognized by Schoppers' approach.

4.14. Shoham and Tennenholtz

Shoham and Tennenholtz explore in mathematical terms the conditions under which large numbers of simple agents can be programmed to avoid colliding with one another. They observe that strategies for programming such agents can be arrayed along a continuum, from one extreme at which the programmers specify detailed paths for each individual agent, to another extreme at which the agents engage in negotiations of unbounded complexity. In the middle region between these extremes are a wide variety of possible "social laws" that might guide agents' actions. While the agents themselves might develop these social laws through systematic reasoning or incremental evolution, Shoham and Tennenholtz focus on the problem of off-line methods for designing these laws.

Their paper develops in two stages. In the first stage, they consider at length a particular case study, in which the agents attempt to avoid colliding while traveling in a grid. The challenge is to define a social law that permits the designers to prove mathematically that the agents will reach their goals without colliding. This is difficult when the designers have limited knowledge of the precise arrangement of the agents upon the grid. In the second part of their paper, Shoham and Tennenholtz sketch a general formalism for proving things about social laws. In particular, they explore the computational complexity of the automatic synthesis of provably correct social laws for large numbers of agents. Although this problem is unsurprisingly intractable in the general case, they specific various conditions under which it can be made tractable.

Shoham and Tennenholtz's paper occupies a distinctive place among the papers in this special double volume. It is the only paper to deal with large numbers of agents, and with the use of customs to provide reliable structure in agents' interactions with the world. Nonetheless, their paper fits comfortably with the others in the sense that their agents are embodied. Their bodies are surely primitive, but it does matter to the definition of the problem, and to the proofs of correctness, that the agents have locations, occupy space, and have limited perceptual and motor capabilities. The social laws that Shoham and Tennenholtz specify for the agents traveling on the grid require the agents to use the space in specific ways by moving about in relatively conventional patterns. In particular, their proofs require them to characterize these emergent patterns of movement in enough detail to demonstrate that they converge. Their paper is thus a simple example of the ways in which interactional customs can provide reliable structure. The agents need not be able to prove that their social laws are adequate; they need only follow those laws.

Future research along these lines might explore the ways in which agents can improvise their interactions with one another. It would probably be impractical to posit agents which invent completely innovative ways of interacting every time they encounter one another; customs, after all, have the important computational benefit of making these kinds of impossibly open-ended reasoning processes unnecessary. Yet customs do evolve with time, and agents do improvise their interactions in a variety of ways, from incremental optimizations to private deals (both formal and informal) among small numbers of agents who deal with one another regularly. Although human beings clearly engage in a great deal of this sort of thing, computational research should probably begin with simple cases and work upward.

4.15. Webber et al.

Webber and her colleagues describe a project to build an system that can animate the movements of a human figure as it follows instructions written in English. Instructions, Webber et al. point out, differ in numerous ways from computer programs, as well as from the symbolic structures that AI has long referred to as "plans". The interpretation of instructions appears to be conditioned by the situation in which the instructions are given. This context dependence of instructions is reflected as well in the linguistic forms commonly found in instructions, for instance in users' manuals for machines, and Webber et al. adduce numerous examples from the naturally occurring instructions that they have studied.

These insights have numerous implications for research on computational theories of interaction and agency. They illustrate one sense in which the "higher-level" functions of language use and symbolic reasoning must interact with the "lower-level" functions of sensorimotor interaction. In particular, they suggest that the conventional modularity that separates the interpretation of linguistic meaning from motor skills might have to be rethought. They also suggest the significant role of pragmatics—features of language that relate to the situation of language-use—in the situated interpretation of instructions. Finally, they force clear thinking about notions such as intentions and expectations that are central to cognitive theories of action.

As this ambitious project develops, it will no doubt encounter other features of language and thought that relate to agents' interactions with their environments. The expectations upon which people rely in interpreting instructions are cultural, in the sense that different cultures organize their concepts about action and interaction in different ways. Interactions between people can presuppose a wide and very subtle range of shared background understandings, for example when the participants in an interaction are members of the same profession, and thus possess a shared vocabulary and a shared experience of training, or members of the same family or circle of friends, and thus possess a shared background of references to things that have happened in the past. A difficult challenge is to understand the senses in which these phenomena are grounded in embodied activities.

4.16. Whitehead and Lin

Whitehead and Lin explore a number of algorithms for learning to engage in serially ordered behavior within the technical framework of reinforcement learning. Historically, of course, reinforcement learning has a close association with the behaviorist school of psychology that the founders of artificial intelligence sought to overcome. Whitehead and Lin are not nearly behaviorists, but their work is clearly part of an alternative tradition within AI. Whereas the main stream of AI research focused on complex cognitive processes internal to agents, other work retained a focus upon agents' interactions with their environments. Behaviorists took this focus to extremes, arguing that it was pointless or meaningless to posit internal cognitive processing. But their search for means of explaining behavior based on sequences of stimuli and responses, guided through the learning process by positive and negative reinforcement, counterbalances explanatory principles based wholly on internal processing.

The architectures that Whitehead and Lin explore do not maintain complete world models. To the contrary, they maintain very simple representations of the world that are grounded in sensorimotor experience. As a result, it becomes necessary for their architectures to actively interpret their available sensory input in functional terms. The agent must actively decide which available stimuli to pay attention to, and it must learn which of these stimuli is likely to permit the agent to accurately predict the degree of "payoff" which its actions will receive. A stimulus that has low predictive value in a particular situation is most likely capable of being generated by things in the world with differing functional significances, with the result that it does not provide information that allows the agent to choose correctly among possible actions. A stimulus that has high predictive value, on the other hand, is probably generated by those things in the world whose states are relevant to the agent's decisions. This deep idea connects the indexicality and active nature of perception with the practicalities of learning from limited information.

The most immediate difficulty with this proposal is that it requires the agent's actions to be functions of its immediately available inputs. Whitehead and Lin therefore extend their analysis to architectures that can maintain limited types of internal state. In contrast once again to architectures that assume that a complex internal model is kept up to date, the authors explore much simpler schemes in which the architecture itself synthesizes state elements which assist it in predicting payoffs. The result is a notion of internal representation tied to the meaningful aspects of the agent's interactions with the world.

This model obviously requires much further development before it can undertake more complex tasks. One aspect of this development might be a more extensive analysis of the structures in the world that permit the algorithms to work well or poorly. The synthesis of internal states tied to functionally significant properties of the agent's sensorimotor interactions is a powerful idea, and it might work best when dealing with artifacts whose functional states are meant to be readily distinguishable, or in environments which have been heavily marked with indications of their normal roles in customary forms of activity. In such settings, the synthesis of internal states might be channeled in comprehensible ways, corresponding not simply to the objective structure of the environment but to the structure of the agent's involvements in it.

5. Case study

An informal review of research that I conducted with Ian Horswill [6] will provide an instructive case study in the themes of this special double volume. This research explores one of the ways in which cultural artifacts support activity by simplifying computational tasks that would otherwise be extremely complex. Its ideas are embodied in a computer program called Toast that acts as a short-order cook, cooking a continual stream of breakfast dishes by interleaving the various actions. It does so without having to construct any symbolic plans, perform any search, or engage in any explicit reasoning about the future. It can do so because certain properties of the artifacts of cooking tend to reduce the computational complexity of decisions about what to do next—or at least to permit simple strategies such as "find something that needs doing and do it" to provably converge to certain kinds of goals. The point is not that all activity is like this, either inside or outside the kitchen, but to indicate some of the ways in which structures in the world can simplify computational problems.

5.1. Model of action

One place to begin the story is with the assumptions of the classical planning literature. This literature takes a definite stand on the nature of action. Although some authors have explored the consequences of relaxing or complicating one or more of these assumptions by certain increments (for example, by introducing probabilities or concurrency), this underlying model of action continues to anchor the literature by providing a set of default assumptions for new projects. The model begins with the idea of "actions" and "situations" as discrete entities, so that the effects of an action can be represented in terms of the transition from one clearly defined situation to another. The result, of course, is that the agent's actual and potential activities can be represented in terms of the possible routes through a directed graph whose vertices correspond to situations and whose arcs are labeled with the actions which can lead from one situation to the next.

A great deal of planning research is concerned, implicitly or explicitly, with the structure of this graph. This structure is affected by many things, most prominently the agent's repertoire of actions, the representation scheme employed to identify the possible actions and dissect the possible situations in the world, and the structure of the world itself. If an agent is going to take actions in the world by executing a plan, that plan must be guaranteed (at least probabilistically) to trace a path through the graph that arrives at a desired end-point from a given beginning-point—or, more precisely, from any beginning-point that is consistent with whatever knowledge the agent has about the beginning-point. Whether, and how efficiently, it should be possible to discover such a plan will depend on the structure of the state graph (large or small, high or low branching factor, clear landmarks, etc.) and on the ways in which the structure of the graph can be exploited in designing algorithms to search it.

Investigation of the computational properties of the state-space graph structure, though, is conceptually independent of the idea of a plan or the idea of activity as plan-execution. The upshot of our research is that the world includes structures that permit a great deal of action to be conducted through simple forms of improvisation without the necessity of explicit plan-construction. It is sometimes necessary to engage in symbolic reasoning about the future, of course, and to make representations of action to help guide future activities. But we would like to suggest that these more complex forms of reasoning about action are delimited and controlled to a substantial extent by the structures in the world that support simpler forms of moment-to-moment action choice.

Our domain, once again, is that of cooking breakfast in a short-order restaurant, and I wish to make clear our intentions in choosing this domain. Cooking is an attractive domain (cf. [32,47]) because it is fairly complicated but still routine, has fairly well-defined properties but regularly admits of uncertainty and surprise, and has plainly been organized in customary ways to allow action to be driven in large part by vision (cf. [4,8,48]). We do not claim to analyze all of the complexities of actual breakfast-cooking, of course (cf. [34]). Rather, we formalize the activities of cooking breakfast for purposes of our analysis using the formal methods of the classical planning literature. In employing these methods our purpose is not to endorse the assumptions that underlie them, but rather to demonstrate how the research process points beyond them. Finally, our goal is not to invent a sophisticated new architecture for making breakfast, but rather to discover structures within the domain that make the invention of sophisticated architectures unnecessary. The real work, in other words, is taking place at the designer's level, in the "aerial view", discovering regularities that can permit an agent operating at the "ground level" to get along with relatively simple policies.

To explore the structure of cooking world, we elaborate the traditional formal framework by using an object-centered representation of action. The objects in question are those found in cooking tasks, such as pots and pans, tools and utensils, and materials such as food ingredients. The agent's actions all pertain in some way to these objects: moving them, transforming them, mixing them, cleaning them, and so forth. The state of the world can be decomposed into the states of these objects and a small number of possible relationships among them. The states of an egg, for example, can include being intact, being broken, being beaten, and being cooked. A bowl can be filled, empty-and-dirty, and empty-and-clean.

These descriptions of states obviously fail to capture all of the properties that the objects could possibly have. The formalization of these actions is analogous to the model of actions employed by a classical planning program: each possible action has a set of preconditions and a set of effects. The difference is that these preconditions and effects must be expressed in terms of the properties and relationships of objects. The action of cleaning a given spoon, for example, has no preconditions at all, since it makes sense to clean a spoon regardless of what state it is in; the effect of this action is to move the spoon into the "clean" state. The action of beating an egg with a fork in a bowl has the preconditions that the fork be clean (if the set of states is more elaborate, of course, the fork can be in the state of being dirty-with-beaten-egg, so that the egg-stirring fork need not be cleaned after each episode of stirring), that the egg be broken, and that the broken egg be located in the bowl; its effects are that the egg moves into the "beaten" state, the fork moves into the "dirty" state, and the beaten egg remains in the bowl.

Much of the formalism, then, concerns the states of objects. In particular, the state of the world at any given moment will consist in large part of the states of all objects. As with any conventional formalism, it would be possible to generate a graph structure that contains all of the possible world-states and the actions that can be taken to move from one world-state to the next. If the kitchen contains a large number of objects, of course, this graph will be enormous because of the large number of actions that can be taken at any moment and the huge number of possible combinations of individual object-states.

The enormity of this graph obviously conceals a great deal of structure within it. This becomes evident if we represent the state-space graph in another, object-centered way. If we neglect for the moment the relationships among objects, we can view each object as having its own state graph. The structure of this graph will depend on what type of object it is, so that the graph for eggs has one structure, which might include states corresponding to "intact", "broken", "beaten", and "cooked"; and the graph for forks will have another structure, which might have the states "clean" and "dirty". Given such graphs for each type of object, the state space of the whole world can be understood as the cross-product of the state-space graphs for each individual object. In fact, the whole world's state-space graph is a subset of this much larger cross-product graph, since it only includes actions that can actually be taken with the objects that are present. A world without forks, for example, will include no state-transitions in which eggs are beaten.

This idea of decomposing state graphs by interpreting them as the products of graphs for individual objects has already been introduced by Harel [34,35], who refers to his notation for these graphs as statecharts. Simply representing planning problems within such a notation, of course, does not change their inherent complexity. If the problem of identifying a correct plan within a given graph is unsolvable or intractable in the search space corresponding to the product graph then it is equally unsolvable or intractable when the graph is drawn in a different way. The purpose of the object-centered state-graph formalism, then, is not simply to reveal the implicit structure of domains like making breakfast as they are already defined, but also to provide a language within which to express additional structures that might be discovered within them. Such additional structure might transform cooking breakfast from a computationally difficult domain into a much more straightforward one.

Additional structure can indeed be found in the domain by categorizing the state-graphs for the types of objects actually found in kitchens. Let us consider two major categories, which might be called tools and materials. Informally speaking, materials include items of food like eggs, cups of water, and pats of butter. Tools include things like forks and spatulas which are primarily used to do things to materials. Every tool has a distinguished state in which it is clean, dry, and ready to use. Materials tend to have original, raw states, and they tend to pass through a series of further states as things are done to them with tools. Tools, furthermore, can be cleaned at any time, regardless of what state they are in, without the necessity of invoking other objects that might be in inconvenient states themselves. If a sponge or brush is used to clean a tool, then it will always be available and in a suitable state. These two categories, tools and materials, cover a large proportion of the objects found in kitchens, and their properties are much more specific than the worst, most complex state graphs and actions that might be imagined in the abstract.

5.2. Formalism

Given these intuitions, let us outline a simple formalism for domains that involve objects and actions. Such a domain will have a set of *object types*. (The term "object" can be used instead when the context makes clear that one is speaking of an object type and not a particular concrete object.) Each object type has an associated state graph, which is a finite directed graph whose vertices are called *states* and whose arcs are called *operations*. Note that the "operation" is the arc itself, not a label on the arc. Each operation is thus unique and is not shared by different object types. The domain will also have a set of *action types*, each of which has an associated set of operations drawn from the graphs associated with the domain's object types. For example, the action type of beating an egg might have two operations, corresponding to the egg's transition from "broken" to "beaten" and the fork's transition from "clean" to "dirty".

Let us say that an action is *focused* if it consists of a single operation (that is, if it involves a single object). A state in a given object type's state graph is *free* if it can be reached from any other state in that graph using only focused operations. A *tool*, then, is an object with at least one free state in its state graph. Each tool will have a distinguished free state, its *normal* state. An example of a normal state is "clean".

Given a set of tool types, it becomes possible to define a *material*. The basic idea is that one uses clean tools to do things to materials. A *tool action* is an action involving some finite number of tools (most commonly one tool), and possibly also one object class which is not a tool. A *normal tool action* is a tool action in which the actions involving tools require that those tools originate in their normal states. A *material* is an object with an acyclic state graph which includes a particular, distinguished state, the *raw* state, from which any other state in the graph can be reached purely by means of normal tool actions. The material might have other operations in its state graph besides the ones included in normal tool actions.

A *cooking task* is a task which has these four properties:
- all of the objects are tools and materials,
- enough tools exist to perform each of the actions required by each type of material,
- every instance of material starts out in its raw state, and
- the goal is to move some of the materials, all of which are instances of different material types, into other particular states.

Informally, it is possible to solve a cooking problem by repeatedly applying a simple policy:
- Choose a material that has a goal state but is not yet in it.
- Determine its current state, look up in a table which state it must pass through next in order to reach its goal state, and then look up in another table a normal tool action that is capable of affecting this necessary state change.
- Inspect the list of tool types required by this action. If the world contains a tool in its normal state for every one of these tool types then employ these tools to execute the action, thus causing the material and all of the tools to potentially change their states.
- If there exists a tool type in the required action that does not correspond to any tool in the world which is currently in its normal state, then choose one of these problematic tool types.
- Choose a tool of this type. Determine its current state, look up in a table which state it must pass through next in order to reach its goal state, and then look up in another table a focused action that can effect this necessary state change. Then take that action.

It is easy to see why this simple policy works. Each action either moves a material toward its goal state or moves a tool toward its normal state. When every tool is in its normal state (if not before), it becomes possible to move a material toward its goal state. Since every material type's state graph is finite, it is possible to calculate the total number of state transitions that the materials mentioned in the goal must go through. Likewise, since every tool type's state graph is finite as well, it is possible to place an upper bound on the number of state transitions that the tools in the world must go through in order for an action upon a material to become possible. Since every action reduces one of these quantities, since the total distance of the materials from their goals necessarily decreases whenever all of the tools are in their normal states, and since no action ever increases the total distance of the materials from their goals, it follows that the materials with goal states will eventually reach them.

This argument obviously relies on a large number of simplifying assumptions. For example, relations among objects have not been taken into account and objects cannot be mixed together or split into pieces. As well, it has been assumed that no object can be committed to a purpose over a long period, thus temporarily making it incapable of being used for any other purpose. The major category of objects for which this latter condition holds are "containers" such as cups, plates, bowls, frying pans, and stove burners. This category also includes clamps and vises, though very few other kitchen implements. The major pitfall associated with containers is running out of them, and the key to avoiding this pitfall is simply to have enough of them at hand. If enough of them are not available then it will become necessary to engage in some type of scheduling. Potentially complex plan-construction thus has its place, but analysis of the world's structure can isolate this place to a relatively small corner of the total activity. (The intuition here is similar to that of the algorithms for efficient constraint satisfaction presented by Dechter and Pearl [18].) Other simplifications can likewise be remedied by a judicious combination of appeals to structure in the world and limited extentions to the architecture. My purpose here, though, is not to develop the formalism in enough detail to accommodate these possibilities—or even to thoroughly vindicate its usefulness. Instead, I wish to present them as an instance of the ideas in this special double volume. Referring back to the discussions in Section 2, let us consider these in turn.

- *Aerial and ground views*. The whole formalism of states, actions, tools, materials, and so forth is part of the designer's aerial view, not the agent's ground view. The agent can employ a simple policy that involves looking up certain information in tables, and the designer can prove that this policy will always lead to a correct outcome, if not necessarily an optimal one.

- *Structure in the world*. The domain of cooking breakfast was discovered to have some useful kinds of structure that could assist an agent in choosing actions in a simple way. This structure can be viewed as an abstraction hierarchy, with the actions on tools forming one layer of abstraction and the actions on materials forming another layer. The model can obviously be generalized to several layers of abstraction [44].

- *Located in the practices*. The "structure in the world" was not located in the objects (the tools and materials) all by themselves. Instead, it was located in the objects together with a customary set of practices for using them. It is conceivable that another culture might employ eggs and forks and spatulas in wholly different activities with different computational properties. The proofs here depended on these objects being used in the ways that are familiar from the simplest recipes in American kitchens.

- *Looking for structure*. The search for this structure was motivated by the great computational complexity of unconstrained plan-construction problems, and in particular by the enormous search spaces that planning methods face in most realistic domains. This structure compensates for the difficulty of searching huge spaces by ensuring that the necessary spaces are small, and indeed that subgoal interactions are so constrained that search becomes unnecessary.

- *Convergence*. The proof of correctness is precisely, in computer science terms, a proof of convergence. It proceeds along the lines of classical program correctness proofs using progress functions that can be demonstrated to move continually toward the goal state of zero.

- *Cultural support*. The structure in the world is not a simple matter of physics but is located largely in artifacts such as tools. As Vygotsky suggested (see the account of Vygotsky's ideas above), the people who invented the artifacts of cooking effectively rendered concrete a type of knowledge for simplifying tasks without requiring everyone in future to understand this knowledge in any explicit way.

6. Conclusion

This introduction has sketched an emerging method of computational research on interaction and agency. It has placed this method in the context of a variety of other fields and it has illustrated them through summaries of the articles and a case study. The shape of future research in this area cannot be predicted in detail, this being the nature of research. The precedents offered by the papers in this double volume, though, do make clear that research on computational theories of interaction and agency provides a fertile territory for the cross-pollination of a wide variety of different fields, each with its own conception of interaction and its own models of agency. Changing the metaphor, perhaps the continuation of the trend will help to transform artificial intelligence from a self-contained discipline to a kind of interdisciplinary switchboard for the construction of principled characterizations of interaction between agents and their environments.

Acknowledgements

The electronic mail archive for this project contains over 4000 messages totaling nearly five megabytes (not including manuscripts). Clearly the editors ought to acknowledge the contributions of numerous individuals and organizations, and they are happy to do so. Danny Bobrow and Mike Brady supported the project over a long period. Approximately sixty referees wrote well over 300 pages of exceptionally useful comments on the manuscripts. The American Association for Artificial Intelligence and Philips Research Laboratories New York provided grants to support the Workshop on Computational Theories of Interaction and Agency at the University of Chicago in February 1993, in which the authors assembled to discuss early drafts of their papers. We wish to thank the University of Chicago Computer Science Department's AI Group for acting as our hosts for this workshop, and Tim Converse for coordinating the local arrangements. Finally, the authors themselves gracefully acceded to numerous requests for revisions and considerable delays in the mechanics of the editorial process. We hope that they and the reader will benefit from the result.

References

[1] P.E. Agre, The symbolic worldview: Reply to Vera and Simon, *Cogn. Sci.* **17** (1) (1993) 61–69.

[2] P.E. Agre, Interview with Allen Newell, *Artif. Intell.* **59** (1–2) (1993) 415–449.

[3] P.E. Agre, The soul gained and lost: Artificial intelligence as a philosophical project, *Stanford Humanities Review*, to appear.

[4] P.E. Agre and D. Chapman, Pengi: An implementation of a theory of activity, in: *Proceedings AAAI-87*, Seattle, WA (1987) 196–201.

[5] P.E. Agre and D. Chapman, What are plans for?, in: P. Maes, ed., *Designing Autonomous Agents: Theory and Practice from Biology to Engineering and Back* (MIT Press, Cambridge, MA, 1991).

[6] P.E. Agre and I. Horswill, Cultural support for improvisation, in: *Proceedings AAAI-92*, San Jose, CA (1992).

[7] J. Allen, J. Hendler and A. Tate, eds., *Readings in Planning* (Morgan Kaufmann, San Mateo, CA, 1990).

[8] D.H. Ballard, Animate vision, *Artif. Intell.* **48** (1) (1991) 57–86.

[9] R.D. Beer, *Intelligence as Adaptive Behavior: An Experiment in Computational Neuroethology* (Academic Press, Boston, MA, 1990).

[10] R.A. Brooks, Intelligence without representation, *Artif. Intell.* **47** (1–3) (1991) 139–160.

[11] P. Bourdieu, *Outline of a Theory of Practice*, translated by Richard Nice (Cambridge University Press, Cambridge, England, 1977). Originally published in French in 1972.

[12] R.J. Brachman and H.J. Levesque, The tractability of subsumption in frame-based description languages, in: *Proceedings AAAI-84*, Austin, TX (1984) 34–37.

[13] V. Braitenberg, *Vehicles: Experiments in Synthetic Psychology* (MIT Press, Cambridge, MA, 1984).

[14] D. Chapman, Planning for conjunctive goals, *Artif. Intell.* **32** (3) (1987) 333–377.

[15] D. Chapman, *Vision, Instruction, and Action* (MIT Press, Cambridge, MA, 1991).

[16] H.H. Clark and D. Wilkes-Gibbs, Referring as a collaborative process, *Cognition* **22** (1) (1986) 1–39.

[17] J.L. Comaroff and S. Roberts, *Rules and Processes: The Cultural Logic of Dispute in an African Context* (University of Chicago Press, Chicago, 1981).

[18] R. Dechter and J. Pearl, The anatomy of easy problems: a constraint-satisfaction formulation, in: *Proceedings IJCAI-85*, Los Angeles, CA (1985) 1066–1072.

[19] G.L. Drescher, *Made-Up Minds: A Constructivist Approach to Artificial Intelligence* (MIT Press, Cambridge, MA, 1991).

[20] H.L. Dreyfus, *What Computers Can't Do: A Critique of Artificial Reason* (Harper and Row, New York, 1972).

[21] Y. Engeström, *Learning by Expanding* (Orienta-Konsultit Oy, Helsinki, 1987).

[22] R.E. Fikes and N.J. Nilsson, STRIPS: a new approach to the application of theorem proving to problem solving, *Artif. Intell.* **2** (3) (1971) 189–208.

[23] R.E. Fikes, P.E. Hart and N.J. Nilsson, Learning and executing generalized robot plans, *Artif. Intell.* **3** (4) (1972) 251–288.

[24] R.E. Fikes, P.E. Hart and N.J. Nilsson, Some new directions in robot problem solving, in: B. Meltzer and D. Michie, eds., *Machine Intelligence* 7 (Wiley, New York, 1972).

[25] R.J. Firby, An investigation into reactive planning in complex domains, in: *Proceedings AAAI-87*, Seattle, WA (1987) 202–206.

[26] M.S. Fox and S. Smith, ISIS: A knowledge-based system for factory scheduling, *Expert Syst.* **1** (1) (1984) 25–49.

[27] M.R. Genesereth and N.J. Nilsson, *Logical Foundations of Artificial Intelligence* (Morgan Kaufmann, Los Altos, CA, 1987).

[28] M.P. Georgeff and A.L. Lansky, Reactive reasoning and planning, in: *Proceedings AAAI-87*, Seattle, WA (1987) 677–682.

[29] J. Goody, *The Logic of Writing and the Organization of Society* (Cambridge University Press, Cambridge, England, 1986).

[30] B.J. Grosz and C.L. Sidner, Plans for discourse, in: P.R. Cohen, J. Morgan and M.E. Pollack, *Intentions in Communication* (MIT Press, Cambridge, MA, 1988).

[31] N. Gupta and D. Nau, On the complexity of blocks-world planning, *Artif. Intell.* **56** (2) (1992) 223–254.

[32] K.J. Hammond, T. Converse and C. Martin, Integrating planning and acting in a case-based framework, in: *Proceedings AAAI-90*, Boston, MA (1990.

[33] S. Hanks and D. McDermott, Modeling a dynamic and uncertain world I: Symbolic and probabilistic reasoning about change, *Artif. Intell.* **66** (1) (1994) 1–55.

[34] C. Hardyment, *From Mangle to Microwave: The Mechanization of Household Work* (Polity Press, Oxford, England, 1988).

[35] D. Harel, Statecharts: A visual formalism for complex systems, *Sci. Comput. Program.* **8** (3) (1987) 231–274.

[36] D. Harel, On visual formalisms, *Commun. ACM* **31** (5) (1988) 514–530.

[37] H. Haste, Growing into rules, in: J. Bruner and H. Haste, eds., *Making Sense: The Child's Construction of the World* (Methuen, London, 1987).

[38] P.J. Hayes, In defense of logic, in: *Proceedings IJCAI-77*, Cambridge, MA (1977) 559–565.

[39] M. Heidegger, *Being and Time*, translated by J. Macquarrie and E. Robinson (Harper and Row, New York, 1961). Originally published in German in 1927.

[40] J. Hendler, ed., Planning in uncertain, unpredictable, or changing environments, proceedings of the AAAI symposium at Stanford, University of Maryland Systems Research Center Report SRC TR 90-45 (1990).

[41] G.E. Hinton and D.S. Touretzky, Symbols among the neurons: details of a connectionist inference architecture, in: *Proceedings IJCAI-85*, Los Angeles, CA (1985) 238–243.

[42] H.A. Kautz and E.P.D. Pednault, Planning and plan recognition, *AT & T Tech. J.* **67** (1) (1988) 25–41.

[43] D. Kirsh, Today the earwig, tomorrow man?, *Artif. Intell.* **47** (1–3) (1991) 161–184.

[44] C.A. Knoblock, Automatically generating abstractions for planning, *Artif. Intell.* **68** (2) (1994) 243–302.

[45] N. Kushmerick, S. Hanks and D.S. Weld, An algorithm for probabilistic least-commitment planning, in: *Proceedings AAAI-94*, Seattle, WA (1994).

[46] C.G. Langton, ed., *Artificial Life II: Proceedings of the Workshop on the Artificial Life*, Santa Fe, NM (1990).

[47] A.L. Lansky and D.S. Fogelsong, Localized representations and planning methods for parallel domains, in: *Proceedings AAAI-87*, Seattle, WA (1987) 240–245.

[48] J.H. Larkin, Display-based problem solving, in: D. Klahr and K. Kotovsky, eds., *Complex Information Processing: The Impact of Herbert A. Simon* (Erlbaum, Hillsdale, NJ, 1989).

[49] K.S. Lashley, The problem of serial order in behavior, in: L.A. Jeffress, ed., *Cerebral Mechanisms in Behavior: The Hixon Symposium* (Wiley, New York, 1951).

[50] B. Latour, Visualization and cognition: Thinking with eyes and hands, *Knowledge and Society: Studies in the Sociology of Culture Past and Present* **6** (1986) 1–40.

[51] J. Lave, *Cognition in Practice: Mind, Mathematics, and Culture in Everyday Life* (Cambridge University Press, Cambridge, England, 1988).

[52] D. Marr, *Vision* (Freeman, San Francisco, CA, 1982).

[53] M.T. Mason, Mechanics and planning of manipulator pushing operations, *Int. J. Rob. Res.* **5** (3) (1986) 53–71.

[54] H.R. Maturana and F.J. Varela, *The Tree of Knowledge: The Biological Roots of Human Understanding* (New Science Library, Boston, MA, 1987).

[55] D. McAllester and D. Rosenblitt, Systematic nonlinear planning, in: *Proceedings AAAI-91*, Anaheim, CA (1991) 634–639.

[56] M. Merleau-Ponty, *Phenomenology of Perception*, translated from the French by Colin Smith (Humanities Press, New York, 1962).

[57] G.A. Miller, E. Galanter and K.H. Pribram, *Plans and the Structure of Behavior* (Holt, New York, 1960).

[58] A. Newell, *Unified Theories of Cognition* (Harvard University Press, Cambridge, MA, 1990).

[59] A. Newell and H.A. Simon, GPS: A program that simulates human thought, in: E.A. Feigenbaum and J. Feldman, eds., *Computers and Thought* (McGraw-Hill, New York, 1963) 279–296.

[60] D. Newman, P. Griffin and M. Cole, *The Construction Zone: Working for Cognitive Change in School* (Cambridge University Press, Cambridge, England, 1989).

[61] S.B. Ortner, Theory in anthropology since the sixties, *Comparative Studies in Society and History* **26** (1) (1984) 126–166.

[62] D.W. Payton, J.K. Rosenblatt and D.M. Keirsey, Plan guided reaction, *IEEE Trans. Syst. Man Cybern.* **20** (6) (1990) 1370–1382.

[63] J. Piaget, *The Construction of Reality in the Child*, translated by Margaret Cook (Basic Books, New York, 1954).

[64] M.E. Pollack, The uses of plans, *Artif. Intell.* **57** (1) (1992) 43–68.

[65] Z.W. Pylyshyn, ed., *The Robot's Dilemma*: *The Frame Problem in Artificial Intelligence* (Ablex, Norwood, NJ, 1987).

[66] M.R. Quillian, Semantic memory, in: M. Minsky, ed., *Semantic Information Processing* (MIT Press, Cambridge, MA, 1968).

[67] M.H. Raibert, Running with symmetry, *Int. J. Rob. Res.* **5** (4) (1986) 3–19.

[68] S.J. Rosenschein and Leslie Pack Kaelbling, The synthesis of digital machines with provable epistemic properties, in: J. Halpern, ed., *Proceedings Conference on Theoretical Aspects of Reasoning About Knowledge*, Monterey, CA (1986).

[69] E.D. Sacerdoti, Planning in a hierarchy of abstraction spaces, *Artif. Intell.* **5** (2) (1974) 115–135.

[70] M. Schoppers, Universal plans for reactive robots in unpredictable environments, in: *Proceedings IJCAI-87*, Milan, Italy (1987) 1039–1046.

[71] H.A. Simon, *Administrative Behavior*: *A Study of Decision-Making Processes in Administrative Organization* (Macmillan, New York, 2nd ed., 1957).

[72] L.A. Suchman, *Plans and Situated Actions*: *The Problem of Human-Machine Communication* (Cambridge University Press, Cambridge, England, 1987).

[73] J.A. Toth, Review of Kenneth Ford and Patrick Hayes, eds., *Reasoning Agents in a Dynamic World*: *The Frame Problem Artif. Intell.* **73** (1995), to appear.

[74] F.J. Varela and P. Bourgine, eds., *Toward a Practice of Autonomous Systems*: *Proceedings of the First European Conference on Artificial Life* (MIT Press, Cambridge, MA, 1992).

[75] F.J. Varela, E. Thompson and E. Rosch, *The Embodied Mind*: *Cognitive Science and Human Experience* (MIT Press, Cambridge, MA, 1991).

[76] L.S. Vygotsky, *Mind in Society*: *The Development of Higher Psychological Processes*, M. Cole, V. John-Steiner, S. Scribner and E. Souberman, eds. (Harvard University Press, Cambridge, MA, 1978). Originally published in Russian in 1934.

[77] D.S. Weld, Reasoning about model accuracy, *Artif. Intell.* **56** (2) (1992) 255–300.

[78] D.E. Whitney, Historical perspective and state of the art in robot force control, *Int. J. Rob. Res.* **6** (1) (1987) 3–14.

[79] W.A. Woods, What's in a link?, in: D.G. Bobrow and A. Collins, eds., *Representation and Understanding*: *Studies in Cognitive Science* (New York, Academic Press, 1975).

[80] J. Yates, *Control through Communication*: *The Rise of System in American Management* (Johns Hopkins University Press, Baltimore, MD, 1989).

Artificial Intelligence 72 (1995) 53–79

Sensorimotor transformations in the worlds of frogs and robots[*]

Michael A. Arbib, Jim-Shih Liaw*

Center for Neural Engineering, University of Southern California, Los Angeles, CA 90089-2520, USA

Received September 1992; revised July 1993

Abstract

The paper develops a multilevel approach to the design and analysis of systems with "action-oriented perception", situating various robot and animal "designs" in an evolutionary perspective. We present a set of biological design principles within a broader perspective that shows their relevance for robot design. We introduce schemas to provide a coarse-grain analysis of "cooperative computation" in the brains of animals and the "brains" of robots, starting with an analysis of approach, avoidance, detour behavior, and path planning in frogs. An explicit account of neural mechanism of avoidance behavior in the frog illustrates how schemas may be implemented in neural networks. The focus of the rest of the article is on the relation of instinctive to reflective behavior. We generalize an analysis of the interaction of perceptual schemas in the VISIONS system for computer vision to a view of the interaction of perceptual and motor schemas in distributed planning which, we argue, has great promise for integrating mechanisms for action and perception in both animal and robot. We conclude with general observations on the lessons on relating structure and function which can be carried from biology to technology.

1. An evolutionary background

Agents do not have an unlimited repertoire of behavior. An animal evolves within a certain ecological niche, and even that "general-purpose" animal, the human, builds on its evolutionary heritage to acquire specialized skills that fit the person for a relatively limited set of roles in society. Similarly, when we write a

---

[*] The research described in this paper was supported in part by grant no. 1RO1 NS 24926 from the National Institutes of Health and Grant NOOO14-92-J-4026 from ONR (M.A. Arbib principal investigator).
* Corresponding author. E-mail: liaw@rana.usc.edu.

computer program or build a robot, we design it to carry out a certain repertoire of tasks. The animal or the robot comes with specialized receptors which allow it to sense only a subset of the energies available in the environment, and has specialized effectors, including those which can mediate active sensing. (For a formal characterization of evolutionary specialization based on environmental constraints see Horswill [20].)

We will focus upon a particular animal, the frog (and its close cousin, the toad) to construct a biological "robot" which will allow us to see more carefully the way in which a specific biological system has evolved—but our task will be to understand the integrated style of action and perception that such evolution yields, rather than to chart the evolutionary process itself. We start with an analysis of aspects of the basic survival behaviors of feeding and fleeing— approach and avoidance—and then model the control structures of the animal either as a network of interacting automata-like systems, which we call *schemas* (or in some cases, schema instances) [4], or as neural networks which implement the functionality of these schemas.

The work in the next three sections is part of a general research program called *Rana computatrix* (the frog that computes), an evolving testbed for multilevel modeling (in terms of both schemas and neural networks) of the mechanisms of visuomotor coordination [2]. Frog and toad are sufficiently similar that our generic model applies to both of them. Thus, except when referring to specific experiments carried out with one or the other animal, we will use the term "frog" throughout when the generic frog/toad is meant. While the core constraint of the *Rana computatrix* study is to understand the biological data, the work is at the same time designed to yield case studies which can point us to a more general understanding of principles of action-oriented perception of the animal/robot acting in the world.

2. Schemas for approach and avoidance

To simplify rather drastically, we may say that the frog's ability to find food and escape enemies can be reduced to the ability to tell small moving objects from large ones. A frog surrounded by dead flies will starve to death, but the frog will snap with equal "enthusiasm" at a moving fly or a pencil tip wiggled in a fly-like way. On the other hand, a larger moving object can trigger an escape reaction. Thus, at a very simple level, we might imagine that the brain of the toad has two basic pattern-recognition routines (what we shall call *perceptual schemas*), one for recognizing small moving objects (food-like stimuli) and one for recognizing large moving objects (enemy-like stimuli). We could then come up with the very simple model shown in Fig. 1(a) in which we have the signals from the eye routed to these two perceptual schemas. If the small-moving-object schema is activated, it will in turn trigger the *motor schema* (our term for an automaton or control system for controlling action) to get the animal to approach what is apparently its prey; while if the perceptual schema for large moving objects is activated, it will

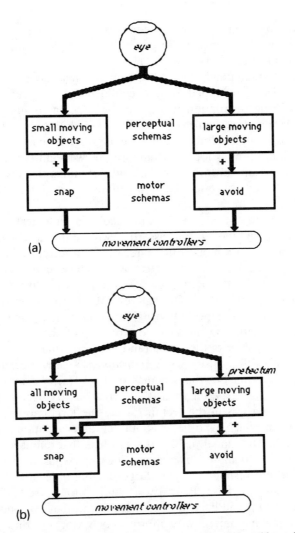

Fig. 1. (a) The "naive" schema program for the toad's snapping and avoidance behavior. (b) The schema program revised in light of data on the effect of lesioning the pretectum.

trigger the motor schema for avoidance, causing the animal to escape an apparent enemy.

Before going further, we may note that the system in Fig. 1(a) involves four simple automata, and Lyons and Arbib [34] have modeled schema instances as port automata in applying them to perceptual robotics. However, rather than simply process input symbols to yield output symbols, the individual automata have *activation levels* which measure some degree of confidence, and it is the more active of the two perceptual schemas that will trigger the appropriate motor schema to yield the appropriate response. We may say that the perceptual schemas *compete* to control the behaviour of the animal. This is a very simple example of the type of mechanisms of competition and cooperation that can be exhibited by a network of schemas. In particular, multiple motor schemas may be coactivated to control subtle behaviors [11].

Notice the important point that perceptual schemas do not serve simply as YES–NO recognizers, equipped with a confidence level, but rather serve to provide a parametric description which can be used in tuning motor behavior appropriately. When it recognizes prey, the animal does not respond with a launch in a standard or random direction, but rather it snaps at the position in 3-D space where the prey is located. Similarly, as we shall see in more detail in Section 4, when the animal sees a predator-like stimulus, it must find an escape direction that will have a good likelihood of taking it out of the path of the predator.

We now consider how such a model can become a biological model as distinct from a purely functional model. Our assertion will be that a schema-based model (we turn to neural network models in a later section) becomes a biological model when explicit hypotheses are offered as to how the constituent schemas are played over particular regions of the brain. For the examples to be offered in this paper, some simple anatomy will suffice: The right eye of the frog projects to the left half of the brain, with the most important visual midbrain target being the *tectum*. The projection from the retina to the layered structure of the tectum preserves the neighborhood relationships of the retina (and thus the visual field), and is called a *retinotopic* map. We will also study the *pretectum* (so called because it is in front of the tectum). Returning to the schemas of Fig. 1(a), we may note (without giving the details) that experimentalists had reason to suggest that the small-moving-object schema was in the tectum, while the large-moving-object schema was in the pretectum. Such hypotheses about neural localization may be tested by lesion experiments. The model of Fig. 1(a) predicts that animals with a pretectal lesion would continue to approach small moving objects just as the normal animal would, but would not respond at all to large moving objects.

However, the model is false! Peter Ewert studied toads (see [15] for a review) in which the pretectum had been lesioned. He found that not only did the toads respond to small moving objects with approach behavior, but they also responded to large moving objects with approach behavior! This observation leads to the new schema-level model shown in Fig. 1(b). The new data tell us that in the absence of the pretectum, the animal must be able to respond to all moving objects with approach. Thus, we replace the left-hand perceptual schema for *small* moving objects by a perceptual schema for *all* moving objects. On the other hand, in the normal animal, we have that recognition of large moving objects triggers avoidance and so we leave the right-hand column the way it was. However, although we have now explained the response of the lesioned animal to all moving objects, and the response of the normal animal to large moving objects, it remains to tune the model so that the normal animal will respond to small moving objects with approach but not avoidance. This we can achieve by having an inhibitory pathway running from the perceptual schema for large moving objects (in the pretectum) to the approach schema—or, equivalently, to the schema for all moving objects. With this model we can now explain our small database on the behavior of both normal animals and those with a lesion of the pretectum. We have thus established that hypotheses about neural localization of subschemas may be tested by lesion experiments. As we shall see below, we may then proceed further to model a brain region to see if its neural circuitry will indeed implement the posited schemas. The important point is that biological models can be expressed at the level of a network of interacting "automata", and that these can really be biological models that can be tested at the level of such a coarse-grained network, whether or not data or hypotheses are available about the fine-grain implementation of those automata in neural networks.

With this background, we are well on our way to understanding our first principle:

Principle 1 (*Cooperative computation of schemas*). The functions of perceptual-motor behavior and intelligent action of animals and robots situated in the world can be expressed as a network of interacting schemas/schema instances. The method of interaction of schemas/schema instances is "cooperative computation" (Competition/Cooperation) so that "computations" which are often seen as the province of traditional symbol-based processing are carried out by distributed "neuron-like" methods which do not involve explicit symbolic control. This not only serves as a basis for coordinated motor actions, but for reactive planning, and intelligent behavior, including the use of language.

In biology, we must discover how the schemas are distributed across biologically distinct brain regions. In robotics, the schema analysis and the allocation of processors may occur in tandem as part of an explicit design process (see Section 8).

3. Detours and path planning

In the present section, we show how a study of frog behavior led to a model of path planning that was then applied to the design of the control of mobile robots, and which anticipated an important area of robot control. The motivation for this work is provided by Ingle's study [22] of a frog observing a worm through a semi-transparent grating or barrier. Instead of launching directly at its prey as would occur if no barrier is present, the frog reacts appropriately, detouring around the barrier to get its prey. We note here how this behavior leads us to extend the schema picture of Fig. 1(b). Now, the perceptual schema for recognizing prey must be augmented by the perceptual schema for recognizing a barrier, and there can no longer be a simple direct path from prey recognition to the triggering of approach behavior. Rather, there must be some way for this path to be modulated by the recognition of the barrier to yield an indirect detour, rather than the direct response.

In the particular situation under consideration here, the animal must not only recognize prey and barrier, but must locate them in space. If it can recognize that the prey is in front of the barrier or at most a tongue's length behind, then the animal will indeed snap directly. But if the prey is further behind the barrier, then the animal must use its recognition of where the prey is and where the barrier is to come up with a path which will carry it around the barrier towards the prey.

Arbib and House [6] offered a model of this in which perceptual schemas for prey and barrier can drive motor schemas which compete and cooperate to yield the overall behavior (Fig. 2). We postulate that the ground plane in front of the animal is represented in the brain, with the worm being represented as a global attractor: each point in the "arena" has a vector pointing towards the worm, with the vectors decreasing in length with distance from the prey, but not vanishing (Fig. 2(a)). On the other hand, each fence post is represented as a local repellor, such that animal will be repelled either to left or right if it comes close to the fence post, but will not be affected if it is further away (Fig. 2(B)). When we combine the action of the individual fence posts, we get a strong vector field to the left of the post and a strong vector field to the right. If we combine all this activity we get the field shown in Fig. 2(c) which can be integrated to yield trajectories which either pass to the left or to the right of the fence and then continue en route to the prey.

It is not our claim here that that the brainstem of the frog implements the above potential field algorithm in its neural circuitry. Rather, the crucial point is that we have an evolutionary account of how such a system might arise (Fig. 3): The elements of the prey-recognition system—perceptual schema, motor schema, and motor pattern generator (MPG)—co-evolve so that activity in the prey-schema can represent a goal in such a way that the approach-schema provides the right control signals for the MPG to determine a path to the prey; while the detour system evolves (or co-evolves) by combining a perceptual schema for stationary objects with a motor schema that *modulates* the effect that the approach-schema has on the motor pattern generator.

In building upon this approach, Arkin [7] developed a hybrid architecture for the control of a mobile robot. The robot was equipped with a map of its "world" and, given a knowledge of its current position and of where it was to go, it could plan a path.[1] What Arkin did was to translate such a path into a vector field which consists of vectors pointing along the path plus "diagonal" vectors in the neighborhood of the path pointing the robot back onto the central path in a direction tending towards that of the path. He then added to the system a "frog brain" to navigate around obstacles—not actually grafting a biological brain onto the control computer of the robot, but augmenting the AI planner with a

---

[1] In fact, this planner was more "symbolic" than "neural". The study of animals rests on the expectation that all schemas will be implemented in neural networks, or will be expressed in the functional interactions of the neural networks and the biomechanical systems they control—i.e., they will represent the function of a dynamic system not all of which need be neural. However, in an artificial system, different implementations may be optimal for different schemas, and for many tasks symbolic processing will marry well with available VLSI technology.

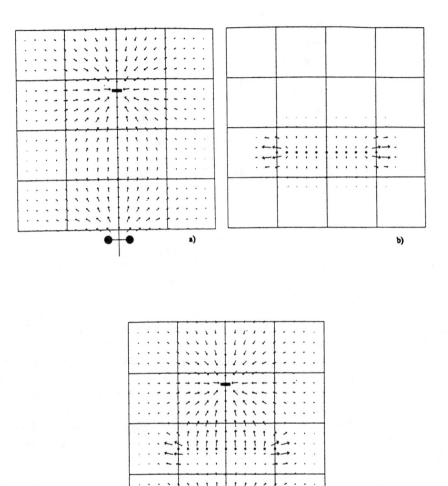

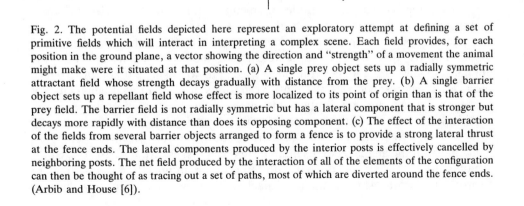

Fig. 2. The potential fields depicted here represent an exploratory attempt at defining a set of primitive fields which will interact in interpreting a complex scene. Each field provides, for each position in the ground plane, a vector showing the direction and "strength" of a movement the animal might make were it situated at that position. (a) A single prey object sets up a radially symmetric attractant field whose strength decays gradually with distance from the prey. (b) A single barrier object sets up a repellant field whose effect is more localized to its point of origin than is that of the prey field. The barrier field is not radially symmetric but has a lateral component that is stronger but decays more rapidly with distance than does its opposing component. (c) The effect of the interaction of the fields from several barrier objects arranged to form a fence is to provide a strong lateral thrust at the fence ends. The lateral components produced by the interior posts is effectively cancelled by neighboring posts. The net field produced by the interaction of all of the elements of the configuration can then be thought of as tracing out a set of paths, most of which are diverted around the fence ends. (Arbib and House [6]).

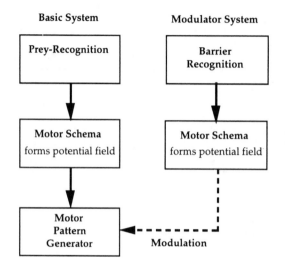

Fig. 3. The evolutionary refinement of adding detour behaviour to prey-approach by modulating the basic system for approaching prey.

potential field system similar to that in the Arbib–House study of the toad. When an obstacle was detected along the path, it set up a local repulsive field. The robot's path was then determined by the local field established by the path vectors and the obstacles. In general, the robot would follow the path, detouring to one side on detecting an obstacle. After being displaced toward the side and leaving the field of the obstacle, it would move back towards the center of the path and then continue following the path specified by the AI planner. Such a method has now been discussed many times as the "potential field" method for path planning in robotics (see, e.g., [25, 26]). See [38] for an alternative approach to path planning.

To close this section, we emphasize not so much the particular implementation of the schemas, but rather the evolving subtlety of the schema interactions. We start with two basic systems (Fig. 1(a)) for response to small and large moving objects, respectively, and then find that if we are to match the biological strategy we must come to the more subtle interactions shown in Fig. 1(b), in which recognition of small moving objects is not in fact localized in any one region, but is rather a system property involving the *modulation* of the tectum by the pretectum. We then extend the complexity of the environment to which the animal responds—it no longer contains a single prey or a single predator to which the animal may respond with the most basic forms of the "survival behaviors" of feeding or fleeing, but now contains the more subtle structure of obstacles which can block the animal's path and around which the animal must now be equipped to detour. In evolutionary terms, this corresponds to expansion of the ecological niche in which the animal is well suited to survive—just as Arkin's basic design for a mobile robot was extended from path-following in an uncluttered environment to work in a world which contains obstacles. We now have a sense of the new perceptual schemas that must be added (for barrier detection) as well as the type of modulation that must be involved. This leads us to our next principle:

Principle 2 (*Evolution and modulation*). New schemas often arise as "modulators" of existing schemas, rather than as new systems with independent functional roles.

Further examples of Principle 2 may be seen in the lesion-based analysis of schemas for approach and avoidance behavior [11]. Here it simply suffices to note that this strategy for the analysis for biological systems may be traced back to the work of Braitenberg [8] and Walter [47], and has a number of points in common with the approach to the design of robot controllers offered by Brooks [9].

4. Neural mechanism of avoidance behavior

We now complete our introduction to biological analysis of "robots" by briefly outlining a specific example of how the schemas which serve animal behavior can be traced down to the neural networks that implement them.[2] Fig. 4 shows a number of escape behaviors exhibited by the frog. In Figs. 4(a)–(c) [22], we see the direction of approach of a large moving object, and we see bars radiating from the head of the frog providing a histogram of the relative frequency with which the animal chooses a particular escape direction over a number of trials. The escape direction may be briefly characterized as a compromise between the forward direction of the animal and the direction immediately away from the looming stimulus. Barriers can modify avoidance behavior, just as they modify approach behavior. If we use the data from Fig. 4(b) to determine the preferred direction of the animal for a looming stimulus coming directly from the left of the frog and interpose a barrier to block that preferred direction, then, as we see in Fig. 4(d), the behavior of the animal changes and it no longer tends to jump in the previously preferred direction, but just to the left or just to the right of the barrier. In the rest of the section, we will not return to the study of barriers, but will instead look in more detail at how the looming stimulus is recognized, and how this recognition is transformed into action.

Before doing so, we look at more recent experimental data [23] which show that the behavior is actually more subtle (Fig. 4(e)). In Fig. 4(a)–(c), we saw that if a stimulus is looming directly at the frog, its escape direction will be a compromise between the direction away from the stimulus and the forward direction of the frog. However, Fig. 4(e) shows that if, instead of moving directly towards the animal, the stimulus is on a trajectory which will carry it in front of

---

[2] Among the many biologically based neural network models have been developed as part of *Rana computatrix* are models of retina (Teeters and Arbib [44]), tectal–pretectal interactions in prey recognition (Cervantes-Pérez, Lara and Arbib [10]), and the role of anterior thalamus and medial pallium in habituation (Wang and Arbib [48]), as well as the model presented here.

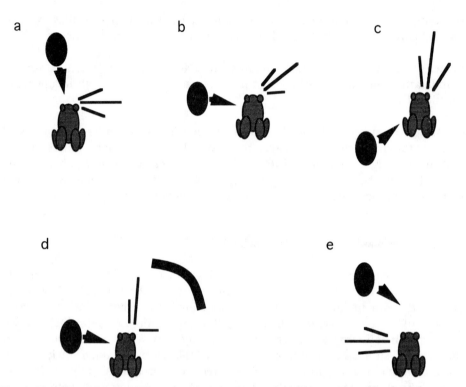

Fig. 4. The escape direction. When a looming stimulus is on a collision course with a frog, the escape direction of the frog is a compromise between the forward direction and that away from the looming object (a)–(c). However, if a barrier is interposed in the preferred direction, the animal will tend to jump to either side (d). If the stimulus is not on a colliding trajectory, the frog will jump in such a direction as to "cut back" behind the looming object (e). ((a)–(d) are adapted from Ingle [22] and (e) from Ingle and von Hoff [23]).

the animal, the frog will not respond based solely on the position of the looming stimulus, for in this case the animal would follow one of the trajectories shown in Fig. 4(a) which would carry it on a collision path with the predator, thus making it highly likely to be captured. Instead, the animal exhibits the highly adaptive "cutback" behavior shown in Fig. 4(e) which carries it on a path that is well away from that being pursued by the looming object. Here again we note an evolutionary refinement going from simple recognition of a predator to recognition of the trajectory that the predator is following to find an escape direction based on this extra information. Clearly, it is an interesting question to understand how evolutionary pressure could yield an animal able to exhibit this more subtle repertoire. However, in this section our concern is with the neural mechanisms which provide the frog with this functional repertoire. Unlike the previous sections in which we have simply sought a specification of schemas (whether or not analyzed in terms of specific brain regions) to provide a functional analysis of the behavior, we now look at the availability of neurophysiological data.

To start the discussion going, we recall why the frog was initially seen as an interesting candidate for a "biological robot". In one of the classic papers on neural networks, Pitts and McCulloch [40] offered a hypothetical network for the recognition of "universals"—in other words, for recognizing an object despite great variations in the size, position or orientation with which it was projected on the retina. They postulated ways in which arrays of feature detectors could be gathered together in such a way that invariants with respect to a variety of group operations could be found which would then yield a pattern of neural activity which corresponded to the "universals" of a pattern, rather than its particular presentation. On this basis, some ten years later Oliver Selfridge (well known for his 1959 paper on Pandemonium [43]) persuaded Lettvin to look for such a structure in the frog's brain. The calculation of group invariants was not found to be exemplified, but arrays of feature detectors were indeed found. The ganglion cells of the retina, those which send their axons back to the brain, were classified in four different classes, and these four classes of cells were found to project to different depths in the tectum, forming four specific retinotopic maps. Even more excitingly, these maps appeared to be tied to the behavioral repertoire of the animal. If we call the four classes R1, R2, R3 and R4 (remember each one is a spatially arrayed population of cells in the "output layer" of the retina) we find that the R3 cells seem to respond best to small moving objects—as if they were bug detectors—whereas the R4 cells seemed to respond best to the large moving objects—as if they were enemy detectors [29]. The slightly later work of Hubel and Wiesel (e.g., [21]) on cat and then monkey found cells in visual cortex which reported on the orientation of edges, and thus provided very low-level features for shape description. By contrast, it appeared that Lettvin et al. had hit the jackpot in linking vision to action by showing that the frog retina computed features specifically linked to the behavioral repertoire of approach and avoidance, feeding and fleeing. For this reason, as well as the linkage to the pioneering modeling of Pitts and McCulloch, the frog was seen in the 1960s to be an excellent candidate for a neural network analysis of a visual system which was not simply engaged in some sort of abstract pattern processing but was directly geared to the determination of appropriate actions.

Fortunately or unfortunately, research over the subsequent years—both by neurophysiologists and by modelers—has shown that the story is not so simple, and that the frog really does need a brain (!) and not just a retina to determine whether to feed or flee. For example, it has been shown that the activity of the R3 cells is quite complicated. To a first approximation it can be viewed as response to the *leading edge* of a moving object entering its receptive field (the region of the visual field in which patterns of illumination can affect the activity of the cell), rather than the presence of a prey-like object within the receptive field. Again (and this was already recognized by Lettvin et al.) the activity of the R4 cell can be better interpreted as just a measure of *dimming*—but clearly a predator by casting a larger shadow will dim the receptive field more than prey, and thus excite the R4 cell more strongly.

Many studies of visual processing or visually guided behavior ignore the particular transformations conducted by the retina, or simply reduce them to a contrast enhancement difference-of-Gaussians lateral inhibition mask. However, we [31] have taken as our starting point the properties of the R3 and R4 neurons. Recall that the R3 and R4 neurons (which have been modeled by Teeters and Arbib [44]) form an array which stretches across the output layer of the retina. If we consider the effect of a dark looming stimulus, we will then see greatest activity amongst those R3 cells whose receptive fields include the leading edge or expanding boundary of that looming stimulus, whereas the R4 cells which will respond most strongly are those contained within the interior of that expanding pattern. We can then combine these cells to provide a model of the T3 cells (so called because they are type 3 among cells of the Tectum as characterized by their physiological response). The T3 cell will respond more and more strongly as a stimulus looms to a position at the center of its receptor field if the connections from R3 cells to the T3 cell are radially symmetric but with a sort of inverted Gaussian form in which activity towards the periphery is more effective than activity at the center. The larger the looming stimulus, the further out the pattern of R3 activity and thus the stronger the input to the T3 cell. Since the T3 cells also form a retinotopic array, many cells will be activated by this looming stimulus but the T3 whose receptive field is centered on the center of the looming stimulus will have the strongest response. To complete the design of the T3 cell, and to make it responsive to a large looming stimulus, but not to several small objects flying apart from each other or to an expanding ring, we give the R4 cells a standard Gaussian projection to the T3 cells so that darkness at the center of the receptive field of the T3 cell will increase its response.

With this we have given analysis that does not simply explain how the presence of a looming stimulus can be represented by a peak of activity in an array of neurons, but also uses circuitry with cells whose firing rates provide a good model of firing rates actually observed neurophysiologically (see [31] for the details and simulations). We now have the neural network implementation of the perceptual schema required to explain the behavior shown in Figs. 4(a)–(c), where the current *position* of the looming stimulus on the retina implies the preferred direction of escape. However, to provide the necessary perceptual schema for the situation shown in Fig. 4(e), we must come up with cells that recognize the *temporal to nasal motion* across the retina. It turns out that the T2 neurons, also in tectum, do have this sensitivity. However, we have no neurophysiological data as to how these cells are actually wired up and so we use a standard model of directional selectivity to link an array of T3 neurons whose activity signals the current center of the looming stimulus feed to an array of T2 neurons in such a way that the passage of the stimulus from left to right will increase the likelihood of a T2 neuron firing. By contrast, if the pattern is moving in the opposite direction, then the direct activation of a T2 neuron by the corresponding T3 neuron will be diminished by the inhibition received via delay neurons to the right. The resultant neural network will respond more vigorously to a pattern moving from left to right than to a pattern moving from right to left, within a given velocity range.[3]

With this we have all the perceptual information we need to complete our model. In Fig. 5(a) we see the retinotopic map of T3 neurons (simplified from a two-dimensional to a one-dimensional retina for ease of comprehension here) with an appropriate projection pathway from neurons in the T3 array to neurons in what we call the motor heading map which will cause the animal to turn towards the retinotopically corresponding location. Unlike the projection from prey-recognition neurons to the motor heading map, in which retinotopically corresponding points are linked by the projection, we now set up the connections to replicate the data of Figs. 4(a)–4(c) so that each peak of activity on the T3 layer will yield a peak of activity in the motor heading map centered at the point

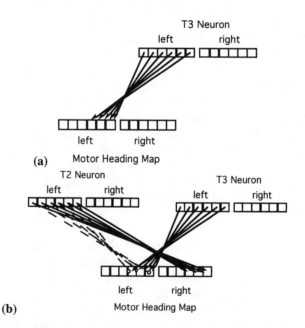

Fig. 5. Gating of the tectal projection onto motor heading map. Only half of the projections are shown here for simplicity. The T3 neurons project to the heading map to indicate the escape trajectory for looming object on a colliding trajectory. When the stimulus is crossing the visual field, the T2 signal blocks the T3 signals while exciting the contralateral heading map, thus resulting in a "cutback" jump.

---

[3] Direction-selective neurons in *mammalian* visual systems each have a preferred (small) range of velocity so that together they provide a sort of population coding of stimulus velocity. Motion-related neurons in the anuran (R2, R3, T2, T3, etc.), on the other hand, respond to the entire range of velocity. The stimulus velocity is coded in their firing rate—the greater the speed, the higher the firing rate. In terms of stimulus direction, most T2 cells prefer movement in the behaviorally significant temporal to nasal direction.

which is a compromise between the forward direction and the direction away from the looming stimulus. This will control the motor pattern generators to yield the Figs. 4(a)–(c) responses.

The situation must now be made more subtle to address the data of Fig. 4(e), and we show how this is done in Fig. 5(b). First, we add the T2 array which again is retinotopic but is now signaling not simply that there is a looming stimulus at that point of the retina but that this stimulus is moving from left to right. (We will not look at the corresponding connections for a stimulus on the right half of the visual field moving to the left—this will simply be the mirror image). This activity must block the normal escape response and so we see a projection from cells of the T2 array to the motor heading map which is a replica of the projection from the T3 array to the motor heading map—but this new projection is *inhibitory*. Thus, if there is no T2 activity the system will respond as in Fig. 5(a). To complete this extended model, we must now add a new excitatory pathway from the T2 neurons which project to the cutback direction, and thus can trigger the appropriate motor behavior in this case, while avoiding the normal escape behavior. What is perhaps worth stressing here is that the T3 neurons serve as the basis for the "evolution" of a more "sophisticated" set of neurons, the T2 neurons which not only signal the presence of a looming stimulus but the presence of a looming stimulus moving on a particular type of trajectory. This new system then *modulates* T3 activity by projecting to the same motor heading map and competing there with the T3 input, rather than acting upon the T3 array itself. This is another instance of Principle 2 on Evolution and Modulation.

We refer the reader to [31] for further details of the neurophysiological data which grounds the model, for further details of the circuitry involved in the model, and for a number of analyses of the simulations that we have conducted. Reflecting on the control schemes shown in Figs. 1, 3 and 5 we come to the third principle:

Principle 3 (*Interaction of partial representations*). A multiplicity of different representations—whether they be partial representations on a retinotopic basis, abstract representations of knowledge about types of object in the world, or more abstract "planning spaces"—must be linked into an integrated whole. Such linkage, however, may be mediated by distributed processes of competition and cooperation. There is no one place in the brain where an integrated representation of space plays the sole executive role in linking perception of the current environment to action.

We close the presentation by noting that simulation shows that as the stimulus speed increases, the time until the network yields a motor command decreases. This is a direct relation that follows from the network properties that we have sampled to explain the avoidance behavior. The velocity-dependent response time is due to the property of the T3 and other neurons whose firing rates increase as the speed of a looming stimulus increases. This result may be contrasted with the great body of work in the motion vision literature which interposes the computation of the optic flow field between the retinal input and the motor output. Where Gibson [17] noted that the optic flow could provide useful input for navigation, Lee and Lishman [26] explicitly showed how the time until contact of an approaching object could be inferred from the optic flow field, and suggested ways in which this explicit time parameter could be used to gate action. Here, we have offered an alternative model in which the action is controlled adaptively without the explicit extraction of time until contact from the optic flow.

5. Application of the looming avoidance model to robot control

The model for frog looming perception is directly applicable to obstacle avoidance in autonomous navigation, since, from a relative motion point of view, the situation where an object moves towards a robot is similar to one in which the robot moves towards the object. Moreover, the two situations become identical when a mobile robot has to negotiate moving obstacles. An experiment has been conducted to test the capability of the looming avoidance model in detecting obstacles and providing a detour path [30, 32]. The robotic experiment was carried out in an integrated testbed consisting of Neural Simulation Language (NSL) [49] for implementing the neural network model, and the Rapid Robotics Application Development environment (R^2AD) [16] for dynamic control of a robot arm. A camera mounted on the moving robot arm provides the visual inputs to the neural network, which computes the 3-D motion of the obstacles and determines an appropriate "escape" direction to guide the robot arm to go around the obstacles (Fig. 6).

Though the detection of obstacles and the computation of trajectory relative to the moving camera is performed in the same way as described above, there is one major difference between the looming avoidance behavior and obstacle avoidance. In the simulation of looming avoidance, only one approaching stimulus is presented at a time, whereas multiple obstacles are present in the robot experiment. This raises several interesting issues that the model must deal with, including occlusion, detection of gaps between obstacles, sizes constancy for obstacles of different sizes at different distances, and the interaction and integration of multiple obstacle signals.

Unlike avoiding a single looming object where the data of escape direction is obtained experimentally and the projection from the looming detectors is fixed, the heading for avoiding multiple obstacles has to be determined dynamically based on their spatial arrangement. Here we adopt the motor heading map [11] to provide a substrate on which signals of multiple obstacles interact and compete with each other and a heading of the next step for the robot to take emerges from such interaction. For this scheme to work, the signal should indicate not the location and extent of the obstacle, but rather, it should specify the opening beyond the edges of an obstacle. This is achieved by projecting looming detectors to the motor map via a connectivity patten that resembles an inverted DOG (Difference of Gaussians). Through such a convolution, neurons activated by an

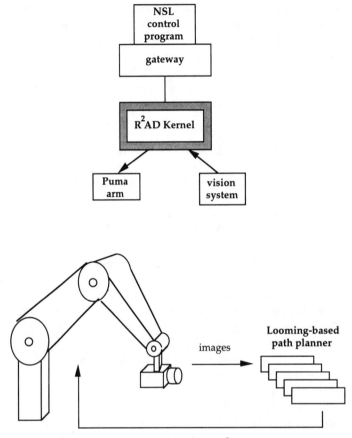

Fig. 6. Experimental setup for robot navigation. The illustration at the top shows the architecture of the integrated system. The high-level control is performed by neural network models written in NSL, whereas the low-level robot manipulation is computed by R^2AD. An interface (gateway) provides the protocol for communication between these two components. In addition to controlling the robot arm, R^2AD also provides frame grabbing routines for visual inputs from a camera. One image frame is taken after every move made by the robot and is fed into the looming perception neural network. The neural network locates the position of the obstacles based on the looming patterns and selects an optimal path based on some criteria (locally shortest path in this case) by specifying the direction of the next movement.

obstacle inhibit cells on the map that correspond to the same spatial location and excite those that are some distance away. As a result, only cells whose location corresponds to an opening (or gap between two obstacle) can be activated.

The presence of multiple obstacles (and hence multiple gaps) raises the question of which route to choose. A winner-takes-all mechanism proposed by Didday [13] is built into the motor map. A simple mechanism which gives higher preference to more centrally located gaps is employed to obtain a locally optimal path (shortest path length). This is implemented as a differential tonic firing rate for cells in the motor map such that more centrally located ones have higher background activity. Therefore, a more centrally located gap has a greater probability to emerge as the winner on the map. Here we see that the motor map offers a medium to which various sources can send biasing signals (e.g., the desirability of a path or deviation from the intended route, etc.) to modulate the competition (cf. Principles 1, 2 and 3).

Since the only available information is the expansion of the image of obstacles, the model is confronted by a problem, namely, without depth information, how can the model respond to a small obstacle at a closer distance instead of a larger one at a greater distance when the latter subtends a bigger visual angle (i.e., it casts a bigger image on the camera)? Although only expanding patterns in the image are available, it provides a crucial clue about the distance of an object, namely, motion parallax. Motion parallax refers to the fact that for two objects moving at the same speed at different distances, the closer one generates a greater retinal shift, i.e., its image moves at a higher speed than the more distant one. Therefore, once the camera starts moving, the looming detector will respond more strongly to the smaller and closer obstacle since it elicits more retinal ganglion cells. In several experiments with obstacles of different sizes, the model demonstrated the capability of correctly avoiding them based on motion parallax (Fig. 7; for details of the robotic application see [32]).

6. From instinctive to reflective behavior

So far we have focused on instinctive behavior with sensorimotor transformation at its core. The sensorimotor system is composed of schema assemblages that are "evolutionarily hardwired" into patterns of competition and cooperation between specific brain regions. The animal performs in a "reactive" mode to interact with a dynamic environment, with little or no lookahead planning. Although great efficiency can be achieved via such hardwired schema assemblages, they are unable to compose a truly flexible set of representations of the world or to provide a large functional repertoire to cope with the diversity of a natural environment beyond the niche to which they have evolved. Furthermore, the notion of goal is not explicitly represented. The evolutionary pressure of flexibility leads to the development of other systems (not necessarily one fully general such system) where explicit representation is employed to support goal-oriented reflective behavior which compensates for the shortcomings of the sensorimotor system. Furthermore, it is the mechanism that facilitates the intimate interaction between these two sets of systems that allows humans to achieve a high degree of flexibility and efficiency at the same time.

The same problem also arises in AI, though along quite a different (almost reversed) evolutionary course. In "classical" AI, explicit planning precedes execution, taking the form of a centralized sequential deliberation based on goals

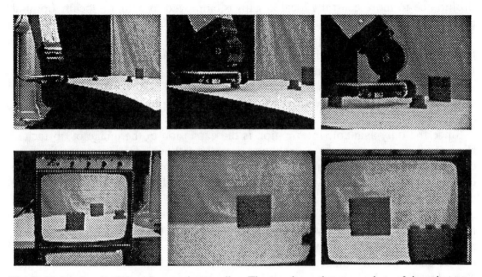

Fig. 7. Estimating depth based on motion parallax. The top shows three snap shots of the robot arm moving around three obstacles (from left to right). The frames in the bottom row show images seen through the robot's eye (the video camera). In this experiment, a large object is placed behind two small objects. The looming neural network is able to detect the small ones first based on motion parallax and guides the robot arm through them first.

and a world model to yield a sequence of actions. Such an approach may impose unrealistic requirements for modeling and perception since all relevant information must be available before planning begins. This makes it hard to adapt the plan to events not predicted by the model. In reaction to this, some critics have advocated *reactive systems* in which selection and execution of actions are inextricably intertwined (e.g., the subsumption architecture of Brooks [9], Kaelbling [24], Agre and Chapman [1]). Such reactive systems are parallel and distributed, with a hardwired priority scheme which is fixed at "compile time". There is no deliberation, and no model. Inhibition/suppression rules determine which models will control action, on the basis of current input. However, such reactive systems are hardwired, difficult to design, and completely data-oriented, and the goals are implicit and thus cannot be referred to in decision making. This leads to the development of hybrid systems to achieve a dynamic intertwining of planning and execution [35–37, 42] (see also [46] on dynamic planning). Here, though along an almost reversed evolutionary course, we see the need for reactive (instinctive) behavior and reflective behavior and, moreover, their integration into a coherent whole.

In the next section, we will outline a computer vision system constructed within the framework of schema theory to demonstrate how the integration of planning and reaction can be achieved in a manner consistent with the principles of cooperative computation and evolution by modulation. Before we do that, however, an important contrast between biological evolution and that of AI is worth noting. With its roots in symbolic representation, the AI tradition is carried over from planning to reactive systems and into the latest development of the hybrid approach of dynamic planning. In biological evolution, on the other hand, we see two distinct representational schemes subserving instinctive and reflective behaviors, namely, implicit (subsymbolic) and explicit (both symbolic and subsymbolic) representations. Using implicit representations, the animal achieves efficiency in "routine" performance of instinctive behaviors like feeding or fleeing, whereas explicit representation lends itself to contemplation and, through dynamic composition, provides a rich set of representations of the world as the basis for flexible reasoning and planning. The process of learning to drive a car with the help of verbal instruction shows that explicit representations may orchestrate a variety of implicit representations (such as visual recognition of an impending collision) and that constant rehearsal of explicit representations may yield to their automatization in which they come to form schemas that are normally under implicit control, while still possessing paths for explicit access in exceptional circumstances.

The distinction between the reflective and instinctive behaviors can be illustrated in the cortical visual systems of primates, i.e., the "what" pathway which performs object recognition and the "how" pathway which mediates interaction with objects [18, 45]. The "what" pathway runs along the ventral part of the brain whereas the "how" system involves the dorsal part (with massive interconnection between them along the way). Lesion to the "what" pathway in monkey impairs the performance of visual pattern discrimination and recognition but not object location tasks. Quite the opposite results were observed in monkeys with lesions to the "how" pathway. Further observations have been reported in human patients. Goodale and Milner [18] have noted the ability of a patient with a ventral lesion to carry out a variety of object manipulations even though unable to demonstrate explicit knowledge of the object parameters used to guide these actions. For example, when asked to pick up objects with various sizes or orientations, the patient is able to preshape the hand according to the size and orientation of the object to pick it up. Yet, when asked to indicate the size or the orientation of the objects either by means of her hand or verbally, the patient failed to do so. The opposite deficit was observed in another patient with lesion to the "how" pathway. While this patient had no difficulty in recognizing objects, her ability to pick up such objects is severely impaired. Further review of such data, and a fuller expansion of the argument in Section 7, may be found in [5].

The advantage of using the subsymbolic representation is efficiency. We have seen examples of such representation in previous sections, e.g., the retinotopic maps in the frog's for coding the location and direction of a looming stimulus or the potential field in detour behavior. The utilization of subsymbolic representations is not exclusive to instinctive behavior; indeed, as we saw in our discussion of learning to drive, instances of such representation can be found even in behaviors that are considered highly cognitive. Consider the process of acquiring a second language. One first learns a set of grammatical rules and uses the language poorly by applying those rules. Speaking a new language (or even one's native language, of that matter) in such a way is inefficient. However, as learning progresses and one's mastery of the language improves, more and more of the rules "disappear" from consciousness and one starts to use the language without explicitly thinking about it. Only after such transferring of the rules (or knowledge in more general situations) from explicit to implicit representation, so that the agent becomes capable of behaving without explicitly reasoning on the rules (or symbolic knowledge), can efficiency be achieved.

We have charted the nearly opposite evolutionary courses in biology and AI and shown that, in the end, the agents (both biological and artificial) come to be confronted with the same set of problems due to the demands of efficiency and flexibility in interaction with the environment which lead to the development of reflective and instinctive behaviors and the corresponding underlying representational schemes. We stress that it is the integration of these two behaviors that brings out the essence of intelligence.

7. From vision to distributed planning

Our study of animal-based robot design introduces an evolutionary basis for the design of intelligent systems. It is our task now to chart the "evolutionary breakthrough" which adds "reflective" capabilities to this basis in a fashion consistent with the principles of cooperative computation and evolution by modulation that we have enunciated above—but, to conserve space, we will do this very briefly, referring the reader to Arbib and Goodale [5] for details. We do this by addressing the integrative question of how complex visual scenes affect human behavior. The approach to schema-based interpretation in the VISIONS computer vision system [14] employs active, independent, schema instances, and the schemas encode mechanisms for using features in multiple representations, conducting information fusion and sensor fusion in a knowledge-directed manner. The knowledge required for interpretation is stored in LTM (long-term memory) as a network of perceptual schemas, while the state of interpretation of the particular scene unfolds in STM (working memory) in the form of a network of schema instances. Each schema instance has an associated activity level (or confidence level) which changes on the basis of interactions with other units in the (dynamically reconfigurable) STM network. The STM network makes context explicit: each object represents a context for further processing, using to advantage the relations among objects. When a schema instance is activated, it is with an associated area of the image and an associated set of local variables. Different instances of a given schema may be associated with separate portions of the image if they correspond to different instances of the "object" the schema represents. The structure of STM is further constrained in part by relationships encoded within LTM, both those between schemas for inter-object relations and those within a schema for geometric relations of parts.

In the VISIONS system, it is the user who starts the interpretation process by invoking general goals such as "interpret this image as a road scene" or such specific goals as "find the sidewalk in this image". The point we stress here is that the above considerations still have much to offer when applied to analyzing the vision of a robot or an animal. However, in such systems, it is the current goals of the autonomous system, not the demands of some user, that guide the process of *action-oriented* perception. Changing goals change the perceptual demands as action proceeds.

The VISIONS system exemplifies a distributed form of planning—as the result of activity emerging in a flexible network—involving generativity to form novel patterns of schema activation that may involve creation of novel "networks". However, if we extend the analysis so that motor schemas are activated as well as the perceptual schemas of STM, we see that planning will be intertwined with execution, with patterns of schema activation modified and thus the "plan" updated as action proceeds and new sensory stimulation is obtained (similar principles are adapted in the IPUS architecture for acoustic signal interpretation [28], see also [41] for active vision). We thus see planning as a process emerging from the cooperative computation of multiple agents rather than being imposed by a separate executive planning system, thus providing an approach to the reactive (we prefer the term "dynamic") planning reviewed by Lyons and Hendriks [35].

Schema theory provides a distributed model of computation, supporting many concurrent activities for recognition of objects, and the planning and control of different activities. Each instance of a schema has an associated *activity level*. That of a perceptual schema represents a "confidence level" that the object represented by the schema is indeed present; while that of a motor schema may signal its "degree of readiness" to control some course of action. The use, representation, and recall of knowledge is mediated through the activity of a network of interacting computing agents, the schema instances, which between them provide processes for going from a particular situation and a particular structure of goals and tasks to a suitable course of action (which may be overt or covert, as when learning occurs without action or the animal changes its state of readiness). This activity may involve passing of messages, changes of state (including activity level), instantiation to add new schema instances to the network, and deinstantiation to remove instances. Moreover, such activity may involve self-modification and self-organization, but the topic of learning (save by implication in our analysis of evolutionary design) is beyond the scope of this article (readers are referred to the extension by Earl and Firby to construct new schemas for reactive planning). A schema network does not, in general, need a top-level executor since schema instances can combine their effects by distributed processes of competition and cooperation (i.e., interactions which, respectively, decrease and increase the activity levels of these instances), rather than the operation of an inference engine on a passive store of knowledge. This may lead to apparently emergent behavior, due to the absence of global control.

The transition we have seen from frog visuometer coordination to human visual perception[4] is reminiscent of the "Great Move" charted by Newell [39] from using specialized materials to support different schemas to using a medium in which it is possible to compose copies of whatever schemas are needed to form novel representations. Contrasting the study of ethologists of the adaptive character of lower organisms with the rich repertoire of human cognitive abilities, Newell observes that:

> Finding feasible representations gets increasingly difficult with a richer and richer variety of things to be represented and richer and richer kinds of operational transformations that they undergo. More and more interlocking representation laws need to be satisfied. . . . Instead of moving towards more and more specialized materials with specialized dynamics to support an increasingly great variety and intricacy of representational demands, an entirely different turn is possible. This is the move [the Great Move] to using a neutral, stable medium that is capable of registering variety and then *composing* whatever transformations are needed to satisfy the requisite representation law. Far from representational constriction, this path opens up the whole world of indefinitely rich representations. (Newell [39, p. 61]).

We may note here that Brooks [9] sets an ethologically inspired hierarchy of levels of control (mentioned earlier as being in the spirit of our schema-based design principles), each biasing rather than replacing the one below it, in opposition to the "classical" view of abstract operators applied to uniform representations. In his general cognitive architecture for problem solving, SOAR, Newell offers a somewhat broader version of classical AI, since he allows a variety of problem spaces—but nonetheless sees these each as being implemented in some uniform medium. However, it is mistaken to see this as a sharp dichotomy in which one school or the other must prove triumphant. The schema theoriest (as in our discussion of the "what" and "how" visual systems) explains a complex cognitive function through the interaction of "instinctive" schemas, implemented in specifically evolved circuitry, and "abstract" schemas that are developed through learning and experience in relatively "general purpose" (highly adaptive, post-Great-Move) circuitry. An intelligent system needs to combine the ability to react rapidly (jumping out of the way of an unexpected vehicle when crossing the street) with the ability to abstractly weigh alternatives (deciding on the best way to get to the next appointment).

---

[4] The VISIONS model is not a biological model and, indeed, the *generic* architecture sketched above allows an unlimited number of schema instances to process simultaneously—ignoring crucial issues of focus of attention. However, Arbib and Goodale [5] review evidence on primate cerebral cortex to suggest how processing algorithms and memory strategies inspired by the distributed planning model outlined so briefly above may indeed be encoded in the brain. The result is not a brain model *per se*, but rather a sketch of a dramatically new approach to modeling the interaction of cortical mechanisms for vision and action.

In summary, a satisfactory account of Newell's "Great Move" should not seek a complete break from using specialized materials to support different schemas to using a medium in which it is possible to compose copies of whatever schemas are needed to form novel representations. Rather, we should provide—in the manner of schema theory—insight into how instinctive behavior provides a basis for, and is intertwined with, rational behavior. When we study frogs, we see the animal's behavior mediated by the dynamic interaction of multiple special-purpose schemas implemented in dedicated neural circuitry. But when we seek to understand human vision, we combine a model of low-level vision implemented across a set of dedicated brain regions [12] with a variety of "general-purpose" media in which copies of schemas (schema instances) can be assembled, parameterized, and bound to regions of the image as they compete and cooperate in a process of distributed planning which creates an interpretation of a visual scene (cf. [3], especially Sections 5.1, 5.2, 7.3, and 7.4). The contrast between frog visuomotor coordination and the flexibility of human visual perception makes explicit the contrast between those schema assemblages that are "evolutionarily hardwired" into patterns of competition and cooperation between specific brain regions, and those which can, through multiple instantiations (both data- and hypothesis-driven), yield totally novel forms to develop new skills and represent novel situations.

Principle 4 (*Interpretation as planning*). The mechanisms of distributed interaction seen in visual interpretation extend to distributed goal-directed planning.

Principle 5 (*Distributed goal-directed planning*). Moreover, the "Great Move" takes us from dedicated circuitry for every schema to the creation of novel schemas distributed across relatively general-purpose machinery. Distributed goal-directed planning combines reactive aspects (dynamic updating) with working memory and focus of attention mechanisms.

The hedge "relatively" in the expression "relatively general-purpose machinery" is important. Recent advances in neuroanatomy have increasingly demonstrated that what were once thought to be large undifferentiated brain regions can in fact be discriminated into far smaller regions with distinctive patterns of input and output connections [19]. Presumably, each of these regions can access a distinct set of other regions, and as these sets of subsets can be developed hierarchically, the result can be a "general-purpose" representation—but one which is distributed across more or less specialized partial representations (in the spirit of Principle 3) each in a specified brain region, rather than being a set of states of neutrally-addressed registers in the totally uniform computational medium of the serial general-purpose computers used in Newell's many contributions to "classical" AI.

8. Relating structure and function: from biology to technology

Many authors have emphasized that the brain can be analyzed at many different levels of detail going all the way from the overall brain through the various anatomically separable brain regions to layers or modules of cells down to the individual neurons, and from there down even further to various cellular components and even to the very molecules themselves. This corresponds to the right-hand path shown in Fig. 8(a). However, what this figure emphasizes is that in computational neuroscience we will as often start from a behavior of the organism as from a concern with particular brain regions of the organism. We must stress that a functional unit (a schema) must not be equated with a structural unit (a component or processor)—in general, a schema may be implemented across several components, and a component may contribute to several functions (Fig. 1(b)). When we start from the behavior we are committed to a functional analysis; when we start from one or more brain regions, we are committed to a structural analysis. In this paper we have given some sense of how schemas may be defined without any commitment as to their implementation within specific neural circuits, but we have then suggested how this functional analysis may be considered by the data of neurobiology. We can directly confront the functional decomposition of schemas with the structural decomposition of brain regions, etc., by using lesion analysis to see whether our account of interacting schemas when coupled with hypotheses about which particular brain regions are involved (recall Fig. 1) bear up when we look at the behavior of animals with brain lesions. However, structure and function may be brought even more directly together, as we saw in Section 4, when we analyze the neural circuitry in a brain region to see

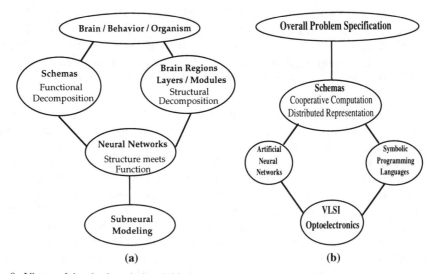

(a)   **(b)**

Fig. 8. Views of level of analysis of (a) brain and behavior and (b) a distributed AI system, highlighting the role of schemas as an intermediate level of functional analysis in each case.

whether it can provide the functionality demanded by the schemas mapped on to this region. Our examples from frog visuomotor coordination have shown both that a schema inferred on the basis of a functional analysis may indeed correspond to the interaction of many brain regions, and that a specific brain region may be implicated in a number of different schemas. Finally, although we have not discussed this above, Fig. 8(a) emphasizes that neuroscience often proceeds to the subneural level to explain how, for example, the properties of synapses can mediate the computations and learning properties of individual cells (see, e.g., Section 8.1 of [3]).

When we turn from the brain to artificial systems—whether under the rubric of distributed artificial intelligence, neural engineering, or perceptual robotics—we find a somewhat different situation, as shown in Fig. 8(b). In the study of the brain we are committed to the fact that any functionality must—at least in principle (though we may choose to stop our modeling of at least some functions at the schema level)—be played over neural networks. In contrast, in an artificial system there is no such commitment. We pick the optimal implementation for a particular functionality and this may indeed differ from function to function. Thus, rather than seeing schemas as providing a path alternate to that of the structural path, as we did for computational neuroscience in Fig. 8(a), we here see schemas as providing the language of cooperative computation and distributed representation in which we provide the coarse-grain analysis of the interacting functionalities required to meet the overall problem specification. Branching occurs from the schema level to the level of fine-grain implementations—Fig. 8(b) shows just two examples, namely artificial neural networks and symbolic programming. The unification may then occur at the lowest level where, irrespective of the intermediate level of implementation, we come to a computational medium such as VLSI or optoelectronics which may either be used uniformly as a substrate for many different intermediate forms, or may be chosen varyingly in the design of dedicated processors for different families of schemas. In the spirit of Principle 5, it will be a major design issue to determine which schemas are most efficiently implemented in special-purpose hardware, and which—and in which various subsets—are programmed to share general-purpose hardware with a variety of other schemas.

References

[1] P.E. Agre and D. Chapman, Pengi: an implementation of a theory of action, in: *Proceedings AAAI-87*, Seattle, WA (1987) 268–272.
[2] M.A. Arbib, Levels of Modeling of Visually Guided Behavior (with peer commentary and author's response), *Behav. Brain Sci.* **10** (1987) 407–465.
[3] M.A. Arbib, *The Metaphorical Brain 2: Neural Networks and Beyond* (Wiley-Interscience, New York, 1989).
[4] M.A. Arbib, Schema theory, in: S. Shapiro, ed., *The Encyclopedia of Artificial Intelligence* (Wiley-Interscience, New York, 2nd ed., 1992) 1427–1443.
[5] M.A. Arbib and M.A. Goodale, Visual routes to action and knowledge: a new perspective on the cognitive architecture of vision (to appear).

[6] M.A. Arbib and D.H. House, Depth and detours: an essay on visually-guided behavior, in: M.A. Arbib and A.R. Hanson, eds., *Vision, Brain, and Cooperative Computation* (Bradford Books/ MIT Press, Cambridge, MA, 1987) 129–163.

[7] R.C. Arkin, Neuroscience in motion: the application of schema theory to mobile robotics, in: J.-P. Ewert and M.A. Arbib, eds., *Visuomotor Coordination: Amphibians, Comparisons, Models, and Robots* (Plenum, New York, 1989) 649–671.

[8] V. Braitenberg, *Vehicles: Experiments in Synthetic Psychology* (Bradford Books/MIT Press, Cambridge, MA, 1984).

[9] R.A. Brooks, A robust layered control system for a mobile robot, *IEEE Trans. Rob. Automation* **2** (1986) 14–23.

[10] F. Cervantes-Pérez, R. Lara, and M.A. Arbib, A neural model of interactions subserving prey-predator discrimination and size preference in anuran amphibia, *J. Theor. Biology* **113** (1985) 117–152.

[11] A. Cobas and M.A. Arbib, Prey-catching and predator-avoidance in frog and toad: defining the schemas, *J. Theor. Biol.* **157** (1992) 271–304.

[12] E.A. DeYoe and D.C. Van Essen, Concurrent processing streams in monkey visual cortex, *Trends Neurosci.* **11** (5) (1988) 219–226.

[13] R.L. Didday, A model of visuomotor mechanisms in the frog optic tectum, *Math. Biosci.* **30** (1976) 169–180.

[14] B.A. Draper, R.T. Collins, J. Brolio, A.R. Hanson, and E.M. Riseman, The schema system, *Int. J. Comput. Vision* **2** (1989) 209–250.

[15] J.-P. Ewert, Neuroethology of releasing mechanisms: prey-catching in toads, *Behav. Brain Sci.* **10** (1987) 337–405.

[16] A.H. Fagg, M.A. Lewis, T. Iberall, and G. Bekey, R^2AD: Rapid Robotics Application Development environment, in: *Proceedings IEEE Conference of Robotics and Automation* (1991) 1420–1426.

[17] J.J. Gibson, The optical expansion-pattern in aerial location, *Am. J. Psychol.* **68** (1955) 480–484.

[18] M.A. Goodale and A.D. Milner, Separate visual pathways for perception and action, *Trends Neurosci.* **15** (1992) 20–25.

[19] P. Goldman-Rakic, Parallel systems in the cerebral cortex: the topography of cognition, in: M.A. Arbib and J.A. Robinson, eds., *Natural and Artificial Computation* (MIT Press, Cambridge, MA, 1991) 155–176.

[20] I. Horswill, Analysis of adaptation and environment, *Artif. Intell.* **73** (1995).

[21] D.H. Hubel and T.N. Wiesel, Receptive fields, binocular and functional architecture in the cat's visual cortex, *J. Physiol.* (*London*) **160** (1962) 106–154.

[22] D. Ingle, Spatial vision in anurans, in: K.V. Fite, ed., *The Amphibian Visual System* (Academic Press, New York, 1976) 119–140.

[23] D. Ingle and K. van Hoff, Visually elicited evasive behavior in frogs: giving memory research an ethological context, *BioSci.* **40** (4) (1990) 284–291.

[24] L.P. Kaelbling, An architecture for intelligent reactive systems, in: *Proceedings Workshop on Planning and Reasoning about Action*, Timberline, OR (1986) 235–250.

[25] O. Khatib, Real-time obstacle avoidance for manipulators and mobile robots, *Int. J. Rob. Res.* **5** (1986) 90–98.

[26] J.-C. Latombe, *Robot Motion Planning* (Kluwer Academic Publishers, Dordrecht, Netherlands, 1991).

[27] D.N. Lee and J.R. Lishman, Visual control of locomotion, *Scand. J. Psychol.* **18** (1977) 224–230.

[28] V.R. Lesser, S.H. Nawab and F.I. Klassner, IPUS: an architecture for the integrated processing and understanding of signals, *Artif. Intell.* **76** (1995).

[29] J.Y. Lettvin, H. Maturana, W.S. McCulloch, and W.H. Pitts, What the frog's eye tells the frog brain, *Proc. IRE* **47** (1959) 1940–1951.

[30] J.-S. Liaw, Visuomotor coordination in anurans, mammals, and robots, Ph.D. Thesis, Department of Computer Science, University of Southern California, Los Angeles, CA (1993).

[31] J.-S. Liaw and M.A. Arbib, Neural mechanisms underlying direction-selective avoidance behavior, *Adaptive Behav.* **1** (1993) 227–261.

[32] J.-S. Liaw, A.H. Fagg, and M.A. Arbib, Robot obstacle avoidance using a biologically-based looming perception neural network (to appear).

[33] J.-S. Liaw, I.K. King, and M.A. Arbib, Visual perception of translational and rotational motion in neural networks, in: M. Omidvar and R. Mohan, eds., *Vision, Progress in Neural Networks* (Ablex, Norwood NJ, to appear).

[34] D.M. Lyons and M.A. Arbib, A formal model of computation for sensory-based robotics, *IEEE Trans. Rob. Automation* **5** (1989) 280–293.

[35] D.M. Lyons and A.J. Hendriks, Planning, reactive, in: S. Shapiro, ed., *The Encyclopedia of Artificial Intelligence* (Wiley-Interscience, New York, 1992) 1171–1181.

[36] D.M. Lyons and A.J. Hendriks, Exploiting patterns of interaction to achieve reactive behavior, *Artif. Intell.* **73** (1995).

[37] P. Maes, A bottom-up mechanism for behavior selection in an artificial creature, in: S. Wilson and J.-A. Meyer, eds., *Simulation of Animal Behavior: From Animals to Animats* (MIT Press, Cambridge, MA, 1991) 238–246.

[38] B.W. Mel, *Connectionist Robot Motion Planning: A Neurally-Inspired Approach to Visually-Guided Reaching* (Academic Press, Boston, MA, 1990).

[39] A. Newell, *Unified Theories of Cognition* (Harvard University Press, Cambridge, MA, 1990).

[40] W.H. Pitts and W.S. McCulloch, How we know universals, the perception of auditory and visual forms, *Bull. Math. Biophys.* **9** (1947) 127–147.

[41] Y. Roth and R. Jain, Knowledge caching for sensor-based systems, *Artif. Intell.* **71** (1994) 257–280.

[42] M. Schoppers, The use of dynamics in an intelligent controller for a space faring rescue robot, *Artif. Intell.* **73** (1995).

[43] O.G. Selfridge, Pandemonium: a paradigm for learning, in: *Mechanisation of Thought Processes* (Her Majesty's Stationery Office, London, 1959) 511–531.

[44] J.L. Teeters and M.A. Arbib, A model of anuran retina relating interneurons to ganglion cell responses, *Biol. Cybern.* **64** (1991) 197–201.

[45] L.G. Ungerleider and M. Mishkin, Two cortical visual systems, in: D.J. Ingle, M.A. Goodale and J.W. Mansfield, eds., *Analysis of Visual Behavior* (MIT Press, Cambridge, MA, 1982).

[46] R. Vijaykumar, Y. Liu, and M.A. Arbib, Dynamic planning for sensor-based robots, in: *Proceedings, SYROCO (Symposium on Robot Control)* Barcelona, Spain (1985) 401–406.

[47] W.G. Walter, *The Living Brain* (Duckworth, London, 1953).

[48] D.L. Wang and M.A. Arbib, Modeling the dishabituation hierarchy: the role of the primordial hippocampus, *Biol. Cybern.* **67** (1992) 535–544.

[49] A. Weitzenfeld, NSL, Neural Simulation Language, Technical Report 91-05, Center for Neural Engineering, University of Southern California, Los Angeles, CA (1991).

Artificial Intelligence 72 (1995) 81–138

Learning to act using real-time dynamic programming

Andrew G. Barto [*], Steven J. Bradtke [1], Satinder P. Singh [2]

Department of Computer Science, University of Massachusetts, Amherst, MA 01003, USA

Received September 1991; revised February 1993

Abstract

Learning methods based on dynamic programming (DP) are receiving increasing attention in artificial intelligence. Researchers have argued that DP provides the appropriate basis for compiling planning results into reactive strategies for real-time control, as well as for learning such strategies when the system being controlled is incompletely known. We introduce an algorithm based on DP, which we call Real-Time DP (RTDP), by which an embedded system can improve its performance with experience. RTDP generalizes Korf's Learning-Real-Time-A* algorithm to problems involving uncertainty. We invoke results from the theory of asynchronous DP to prove that RTDP achieves optimal behavior in several different classes of problems. We also use the theory of asynchronous DP to illuminate aspects of other DP-based reinforcement learning methods such as Watkins' Q-Learning algorithm. A secondary aim of this article is to provide a bridge between AI research on real-time planning and learning and relevant concepts and algorithms from control theory.

1. Introduction

The increasing interest of artificial intelligence (AI) researchers in systems embedded in environments demanding real-time performance is narrowing the gulf between problem solving and control engineering. Similarly, machine learning techniques suited to embedded systems are becoming more comparable to methods for the adaptive control of dynamic systems. A growing number of researchers are investigating learning systems

---

[*] Corresponding author. E-mail: barto@cs.umass.edu.

[1] Present address: GTE Data Services, One E. Telcom Parkway, Temple Terrace, FL 33637, USA.

[2] Present address: Department of Brain and Cognitive Sciences, Massachusetts Institute of Technology, Cambridge, MA 02139, USA.

based on dynamic programming (DP) algorithms for solving stochastic optimal control problems, arguing that DP provides the appropriate basis for compiling planning results into reactive strategies for real-time control, as well as for learning such strategies when the system being controlled is incompletely known. Learning algorithms based on DP employ novel means for improving the computational efficiency of conventional DP algorithms. Werbos [83, 87] and Watkins [81] proposed incremental versions of DP as learning algorithms, and Sutton's *Dyna* architecture for learning, planning, and reacting [69, 70] is based on these principles. The key issue addressed by DP-based learning is the tradeoff between short- and long-term performance: how can an agent learn to improve long-term performance when this may require sacrificing short-term performance? DP-based learning algorithms are examples of *reinforcement learning* methods by which autonomous agents can improve skills in environments that do not contain explicit teachers [71].

In this article we introduce a learning algorithm based on DP, which we call Real-Time Dynamic Programming (RTDP), by which an embedded problem solving system can improve its long-term performance with experience, and we prove results about its behavior in several different types of problems. RTDP is the result of recognizing that Korf's [38] Learning-Real-Time A* (LRTA*) algorithm[3] is closely related to a form of DP known as asynchronous DP [10]. This novel observation permits us to generalize the ideas behind LRTA* so that they apply to real-time problem solving tasks involving uncertainty. In particular, we apply the theory of asynchronous DP developed by Bertsekas [10] and Bertsekas and Tsitsiklis [12] to show that RTDP converges to optimal solutions when applied to several types of real-time problem solving tasks involving uncertainty. Whereas the theory of asynchronous DP was motivated by the suitability of asynchronous DP for parallel processing, we adapt this theory to the case of performing DP concurrently with problem solving or control. We also present an extension of RTDP, called *Adaptive* RTDP, applicable when information is lacking about a problem's structure in addition to its solution.

Recognizing that the theory of asynchronous DP is relevant to learning also permits us to provide new insight into Watkins' Q-Learning [81, 82] algorithm, another DP-based learning algorithm which is being explored by AI researchers. We present simulation results comparing the performance of RTDP, Adaptive RTDP, Q-Learning, and a conventional DP algorithm on several simulated real-time problem solving tasks involving uncertainty.

Another aim of this article is to discuss some of the important issues that arise in using DP-based learning algorithms, with particular attention being devoted to indicating which aspects of their use have formal justification and which do not. In doing this, we attempt to clarify links between AI research on real-time planning and learning and relevant concepts from control theory. We discuss selected concepts from control theory that we believe are most relevant to the efforts in AI to develop autonomous systems capable of performing in real time and under uncertainty.

---

[3] We use the term real-time following this usage by Korf in which it refers to problems in which actions have to be performed under hard time constraints. We do not address details of the scheduling issues that arise in using these algorithms as components of complex real-time systems.

But there remain many issues relevant to using DP-based learning in AI that we do not discuss. For example, we adopt a rather abstract formalism and do not say much about how it might best apply to problems of interest in AI. A formalism this abstract is potentially applicable to a wide variety of specific problems, but it is not easy to specify exactly what subproblems within complex systems can best take advantage of these methods. In accord with Dean and Wellman [23], we regard DP-based reinforcement learning as a *component technology* that addresses some of the issues important for developing sophisticated embedded agents but that by itself does not address all of them.

Because the reader is unlikely to be familiar with all of the contributing lines of research, we provide the necessary background in Section 2, followed in Section 3 by a discussion of the proper relationship between some concepts from AI and control theory. Development of the theoretical material occupies Sections 4 through 9, with an introduction to a class of stochastic optimal control problems occupying Section 4 and an introduction to conventional DP occupying Section 5. There are two major parts to this theoretical development. The first part (Sections 5 and 6) concerns problems for which accurate models are available. Here, we describe RTDP, its convergence properties, and its relationship to LRTA*. The second part (Section 7) concerns the additional complexity present in the case of incomplete information, i.e., when an accurate model of the problem is lacking. Section 8 is a brief discussion of DP-based learning algorithms that are outside the theoretical scope of this article. In Section 9 we discuss some of the issues that practical implementations of DP-based learning algorithms must address. In Section 10 we use an example problem to illustrate RTDP and other algorithms. We conclude in Section 11 with an appraisal of the significance of our approach and discuss some of the open problems.

2. Background

A major influence on research leading to current DP-based algorithms has been the method Samuel [61, 62] used to modify a heuristic evaluation function for the game of checkers. His method updated board evaluations by comparing an evaluation of the current board position with an evaluation of a board position likely to arise later in the game:

> ... we are attempting to make the score, calculated for the current board position, look like that calculated for the terminal board position of the chain of moves which most probably occur during actual play. (Samuel [61])

As a result of this process of "backing up" board evaluations, the evaluation function should improve in its ability to evaluate the long-term consequences of moves. In one version of this algorithm, Samuel represented the evaluation function as a weighted sum of numerical features and adjusted the weights based on an error derived from comparing evaluations of current and predicted board positions.

Because of its compatibility with connectionist learning algorithms, this approach was refined and extended by Sutton [67, 68] and used heuristically in a number of single-agent problem solving tasks (e.g., Barto, Sutton, and Anderson [4], Anderson [1], and Sutton [67]). The algorithm was implemented as a neuron-like connectionist element called the Adaptive Critic Element [4]. Sutton [68] later called these algorithms Temporal Difference (TD) methods and obtained some theoretical results about their convergence. Following the proposals of Klopf [36,37], Sutton and Barto [72–74] developed these methods as models of animal learning. Minsky [53,54] discussed similar ideas in the context of the credit assignment problem for reinforcement learning systems; Hampson [28] independently developed some of these ideas and related them to animal behavior; Christensen and Korf [16] experimented with a Samuel-like method for updating evaluation function coefficients using linear regression; and Holland's [30] bucket-brigade algorithm for assigning credit in his classifier systems is closely related to Samuel's method. Tesauro's recent TD-Gammon [77], a program using a TD method together with a connectionist network to improve performance in playing backgammon, has achieved remarkable success.

Independently of the approaches inspired by Samuel's checkers player, other researchers suggested similar algorithms based on the theory of optimal control, where DP provides important solution methods. As applied to control problems, DP (a term introduced by Bellman [9]) consists of methods for successively approximating optimal evaluation functions and decision rules for both deterministic and stochastic problems. In its most general form, DP applies to optimization problems in which the costs of objects in the search space have a compositional structure that can be exploited to find an object of globally minimum cost without performing exhaustive search. Kumar and Kanal [40] discuss DP at this level of generality. However, we restrict attention to DP as it applies to problems in which the objects are state sequences that can be generated in problem solving or control tasks. DP solves these optimization problems by solving recurrence relations instead of explicitly searching in the space of state sequences. Backing up state evaluations is the basic step of DP procedures for solving these recurrence relations. We discuss several DP algorithms in detail in Section 5.

Although DP algorithms avoid exhaustive search in the state-sequence space, they are still exhaustive by AI standards because they require repeated generation and expansion of all possible states. For this reason, DP has not played a significant role in AI. Heuristic search algorithms, in contrast, are explicitly designed to avoid being exhaustive in this way. But DP algorithms are relevant to learning in a way that heuristic search algorithms are not because they systematically update the evaluations of the states; in effect, they adjust a problem's heuristic evaluation function by incorporating the results of repeated shallow searches. Although some heuristic search algorithms, such as A* [29], update estimates of the costs to reach states from an initial state (A*'s g function), they typically do not update the heuristic evaluation function estimating the cost to reach a goal from each state (the h function).[4]

Despite the fact that DP algorithms are exhaustive in the sense described above, it is possible to arrange their computational steps for use *during* control or real-time

---

[4] We have found only a few exceptions to this in the heuristic search literature in algorithms proposed by Mérő [51] and Gelperin [26]. Although these algorithms use DP-like backups to update heuristic evaluation functions, they were developed independently of DP.

problem solving. This is the basis of RTDP and the other algorithms we describe in this article. In most cases, convergence to an optimal evaluation function still requires repeated generation and expansion of all states, but performance improves incrementally (although not necessarily monotonically) while this is being accomplished. It is this improvement rather than ultimate convergence to optimality that becomes central. This perspective was taken by Werbos [85], who proposed a method similar to that used by the Adaptive Critic Element within the framework of DP. He called this approach *Heuristic Dynamic Programming* and has written extensively about it (e.g., [83, 86–88]). Related algorithms have been discussed by Witten [92, 93], and more recently, Watkins [81] extended Sutton's TD algorithms and developed others by explicitly utilizing the theory of DP. He used the term *Incremental Dynamic Programming* to refer to this class of algorithms and discussed many examples. Williams and Baird [91] theoretically analysed additional DP-based algorithms suitable for on-time application. We have also come across the work Jalali and Ferguson [32], who independently proposed a method similar to Adaptive RTDP. Sutton, Barto, and Williams [75] discussed reinforcement learning from the perspective of DP and adaptive control, and White and Jordan [89] and Barto [2] provide additional background and extensive references to current research.

Although aspects of this approach also apply to problems involving continuous time and/or state and action spaces, here we restrict attention to discrete-time problems with finite sets of states and actions because of their relative simplicity and their closer relationship to the non-numeric problems usually studied in AI. This excludes various "differential" approaches, which make use of optimization algorithms related to the connectionist error-backpropagation algorithm (e.g., Jacobson and Mayne [31], Jordan and Jacobs [33], Werbos [83, 84], White and Jordan [89]).

The relevance of DP for planning and learning in AI was articulated in Sutton's [69] *Dyna* architecture. The key idea in *Dyna* is that one can perform the computational steps of a DP algorithm sometimes using information obtained from state transitions actually taken by the system being controlled, and sometimes from hypothetical state transitions simulated using a model of this system. To satisfy time constraints, this approach interleaves phases of acting with planning performed using hypothetical state transitions. The underlying DP algorithm compiles the resulting information into an efficient form for directing the future course of action. Another aspect of *Dyna* is that the system model can be refined through a learning process deriving training information from the state transitions observed during control. Even without this on-line model refinement, however, executing a DP algorithm concurrently with the generation of actions has implications for planning in AI, as discussed by Sutton in [70].

In this article, we introduce the fact that the theory of asynchronous DP is applicable to the analysis of DP-based reinforcement learning algorithms. Asynchronous DP algorithms differ from conventional DP algorithms in that they do not have to proceed in systematic exhaustive sweeps of the problem's state set. Bertsekas [10] and Bertsekas and Tsitsiklis [12] proved general theorems about the convergence of asynchronous DP applied to discrete-time stochastic optimal control problems. However, because they were motivated by the suitability of asynchronous DP for parallel processing, they did not relate these results to real-time variants of DP as we do in this article. To the best of our knowledge, the only other work in which explicit use is made of the theory of asynchronous DP for real-time control is that of Jalali and Ferguson [32].

Korf's [38] LRTA* algorithm is a heuristic search algorithm that caches state evaluations so that search performance improves with repeated trials. Evaluations of the states visited by the problem solver are maintained in a hash table. Each cycle of the algorithm proceeds by expanding the current state by generating all of its immediate successor states and evaluating them using previously stored evaluations if they exist in the hash table, and otherwise using an initially given heuristic evaluation function. Assuming the objective is to find a minimum-cost path to a goal state, a score is computed for each neighboring state by adding to its evaluation the cost of the edge to it from the current state. The minimum of the resulting scores becomes the new evaluation for the current state, which is stored in the hash table.[5] Finally, a move is made to this lowest-scoring neighboring state. LRTA* therefore backs up state evaluations in much the same way as do Samuel's algorithm and DP. In fact, as we shall see in what follows, with a slight caveat, *LRTA* is the deterministic specialization of asynchronous DP applied on-line.*

3. Heuristic search and the control of dynamic systems

Whereas AI has focused on problems having relatively little mathematical structure, control theorists have studied more restrictive classes of problems but have developed correspondingly more detailed theories. Some concepts and methods from control theory are nevertheless relevant to problems of interest in AI as discussed, for example, by Dean and Wellman [23]. In this section, as a prelude to introducing the stochastic optimal control framework in which our results are cast, we discuss the relationship between heuristic search, real-time heuristic search, and selected concepts from control theory

3.1. Heuristic search and system control

Heuristic search algorithms apply to state-space search problems defined by a set of states, a set of operators that map states to states, an initial state, and a set of goal states. The objective is to find a sequence of operators that maps the initial state to one of the goal states and (possibly) optimizes some measure of cost, or merit, of the solution path. These components constitute a model of some real problem, such as solving a puzzle, proving a theorem, or planning a robot path. The term control as used in the literature on heuristic search and problem solving means the process of deciding what to do next in manipulating a model of the problem in question. Despite some similarities, this is not the meaning of the term control in control theory, where it refers to the process of manipulating the behavior of a physical system in real time by supplying it with appropriate input signals. In AI, control specifies the formal search process, whereas in control theory, it steers the behavior of a physical system over time. Unlike models manipulated by search algorithms, physical systems cannot be set

---

[5] In Korf's [38] related Real-Time A* (RTA*) algorithm, the *second* smallest score is stored. Because LRTA* is more closely related to control and DP than is RTA*, we do not discuss RTA*.

immediately into arbitrary states and do not suspend activity to await the controller's decisions. Models used to formalize system control problems, called *dynamic systems*, are explicit in taking into account the passage of time. In what follows, by control we mean the control of dynamic systems, not the control of search.

In many applications, a symbolic representation of a sequence of operators is not the final objective of a heuristic search algorithm. The intent may be to execute the operator sequence to generate a time sequence of actual inputs to a physical system. Here the result is the control engineer's form of control, but this control method differs substantially from the methods addressed by most of control theory. A sequence of inputs, or actions, produced in this way through heuristic search is an *open-loop control policy*, meaning that it is applied to the system without using information about the system's actual behavior while control is underway, i.e., without execution monitoring, or feedback. In terms of control theory, heuristic search is a *control design procedure* for producing an open-loop control policy from a system model; the policy is appropriate for the given initial state. Further, under normal circumstances, it is an *off-line* design procedure because it is completed before being used to control the system, i.e., under normal circumstances, the planning phase of the problem solving process strictly precedes the execution phase.

Open-loop control works fine when all of the following are true: (1) the model used to determine the control policy is a completely accurate model of the physical system, (2) the physical system's initial state can be exactly determined, (3) the physical system is deterministic, and (4) there are no unmodeled disturbances. These conditions hold for some of the problems studied in AI, but they are not true for most realistic control problems. Any uncertainty, either in the behavior of the physical system itself or in the process of modeling the system, implies that *closed-loop control* can produce better performance. Control is closed-loop when each action depends on current observations of the real system, perhaps together with past observations and other information internal to the controller.

A *closed-loop control policy* (also called a closed-loop control rule, law, or strategy) is a rule specifying each action as a function of current, and possibly past, information about the behavior of the controlled system. It closely corresponds to a "universal plan" [64] as discussed, for example, by Chapman [14], Ginsberg [27], and Schoppers [65]. In control theory, a closed-loop control policy usually specifies each action as a function of the controlled system's current state, not just the current values of observable variables (a distinction whose significance for universal planning is discussed by Chapman [14]). Although closed-loop control is closely associated with negative feedback, which counteracts deviations from desired system behavior, negative feedback control is merely a special case of closed-loop control.

When there is no uncertainty, closed-loop control is not in principle more competent than open-loop control. For a deterministic system with no disturbances, given any closed-loop policy and an initial state, there exists an open-loop policy that produces exactly the same system behavior, namely, the open-loop policy generated by running the system, or simulating it with a perfect model, under control of the given closed-loop policy. But this is not true in the stochastic case, or when there are unmodeled disturbances, because the outcome of random and unmodeled events cannot be anticipated in designing an open-loop policy. Note that game-playing systems always use closed-loop control for this reason: the opponent is a kind of disturbance. A game player always uses the opponent's actual previous moves in determining its next move For exactly the same reasons, closed-loop control can be better than open-loop control for single-agent problems involving uncertainty. A corollary of this explains the almost universal use of closed-loop control by control engineers: the system model used for designing an acceptable control policy can be significantly less faithful to the actual system when it is used for designing closed-loop instead of open-loop policies. Open-loop control only becomes a practical alternative when it is expensive or impossible to monitor the controlled system's behavior with detail sufficient for closed-loop control.

Most control theory addresses the problem of designing adequate closed-loop policies off-line under the assumption that an accurate model of the system to be controlled is available. The off-line design procedure typically yields a computationally efficient method for determining each action as a function of the observed system state. If it is possible to design a complete closed-loop policy off-line, as it is in many of the control problems studied by engineers, then it is not necessary to perform any additional re-design, i.e., re-planning, for problem instances differing only in initial state. Changing control objectives, on the other hand, often does require policy re-design.

One can also design closed-loop policies on-line through *repeated* on-line design of open-loop policies. This approach has been called *receding horizon control* [42, 50]. For each current state, an open-loop policy is designed with the current state playing the role of the initial state. The design procedure must terminate within the time constraints imposed by on-line operation. This can be done by designing a finite-horizon open-loop policy, for example, by using a model for searching to a fixed depth from the current state. After applying the first action specified by the resulting policy, the remainder of the policy is discarded, and the design process is repeated for the next observed state. Despite requiring on-line design, which in AI corresponds to on-line planning through projection, or prediction, using a system model, receding horizon control produces a control policy that is reactive to each current system state, i.e., a closed-loop policy. According to this view, then, a closed-loop policy can involve explicit planning through projection, but each planning phase has to complete in a fixed amount of time to retain the system's reactivity to the observed system states. In contrast to methods that design closed-loop policies off-line, receding horizon control can react on-line to changes in control objectives.

3.2. Optimal control

The most familiar control objective is to control a system so that its output matches a reference output or tracks a reference trajectory as closely as possible in the face of disturbances. These are called regulation and tracking problems respectively. In an optimal control problem, on the other hand, the control objective is to extremize some function of the controlled system's behavior, where this function need not be defined in terms of a reference output or trajectory. One typical optimal control problem requires controlling a system to go from an initial state to a goal state via a minimum-cost trajectory. In contrast to tracking problems—where the desired trajectory is part of the problem specification—the trajectory is part of the solution of this optimal control problem. Therefore, optimal control problems such as this are closely related to the problems to which heuristic search algorithms apply.

Specialized solution methods exist for optimal control problems involving linear systems and quadratic cost functions, and methods based on the calculus of variations can yield closed-form solutions for restricted classes of problems. Numerical methods applicable to problems involving nonlinear systems and/or nonquadratic costs include gradient methods as well as DP. Whereas gradient methods for optimal control are closely related to some of the gradient descent methods being studied by connectionists (such as the error-backpropagation algorithm [43, 86, 89]), DP methods are more closely related to heuristic search. Like a heuristic search algorithm, DP is an off-line procedure for designing an optimal control policy. However, unlike a heuristic search algorithm, DP produces an optimal closed-loop policy instead of an open-loop policy for a given initial state.

3.3. Real-time heuristic search

Algorithms for real-time heuristic search as defined by Korf [38] apply to state-space search problems in which the underlying model is extended to account for the passage of time. The model thus becomes a dynamic system. Real-time heuristic search algorithms apply to state-space search problems with the additional properties that (1) at each time there is a unique current state of the system being controlled, which is known by the searcher/controller, (2) during each of a sequence of time intervals of constant bounded duration, the searcher/controller must commit to a unique action, i.e., choice of operator, and (3) the system changes state at the end of each time interval in a manner depending on its current state and the searcher/controller's most recent action. These factors imply that there is a fixed upper bound on the amount of time the searcher/controller can take in deciding what action to make if that action is to be based on the most up-to-date state information. Thus, whereas a traditional heuristic search algorithm is a *design* procedure for an open-loop policy, a real-time heuristic search algorithm is a *control* procedure, and it can accommodate the possibility of closed-loop control.

Korf's [38] LRTA* algorithm is a kind of receding horizon control because it is an on-line method for designing a closed-loop policy. However, unlike receding horizon control as studied by control engineers, LRTA* *accumulates* the results of each local design procedure so that the effectiveness of the resulting closed-loop policy tends to improve over time. It stores information from the shallow searches forward from each current state by updating the evaluation function by which control decisions are made. Because these updates are the basic steps of DP, we view LRTA* as the result of interleaving the steps of DP with the actual process of control so that control policy design occurs concurrently with control.

This approach is advantageous when the control problem is so large and unstructured mathematically that complete control design is not even feasible off-line. This case requires a *partial* closed-loop policy, that is, a policy useful for a subregion of the problem's state space. Designing a partial policy on-line allows actual experience to influence the subregion of the state space where design effort is concentrated. Design effort is not expended for parts of the state space that are not likely to be visited during actual control. Although *in general* it is not possible to design a policy that is optimal for a subset of the states unless the design procedure considers the entire state set, this is possible under certain conditions such as those required by Korf's convergence theorem for LRTA*.

3.4. Adaptive control

Control theorists use the term adaptive control for cases in which an accurate model of the system to be controlled is not available for designing a policy off-line. These are sometimes called control problems with incomplete information. Adaptive control algorithms design policies on-line based on information about the control problem that accumulates over time as the controller and system interact. A distinction is sometimes made between adaptive control and learning control, where only the latter takes advantage of *repetitive* control experiences from which information is acquired that is useful over the long term. Although this distinction may be useful for some types of control problems, we think its utility is limited when applied to the kinds of problems and algorithms we consider in this article. According to what we mean by adaptive control in this article, even though algorithms like LRTA* and Samuel's algorithm [61] are learning algorithms, they are *not* adaptive control algorithms because they assume the existence of an accurate model of the problem being solved. Although it certainly seems odd to us that a control algorithm that learns is not ipso facto adaptive, this is forced upon us when we adopt the control engineer's restrictive definition of adaptive control. In Section 7 we describe several algorithms that have properties of both learning and adaptive control algorithms.

4. Markovian decision problems

The basis for our theoretical framework is a class of stochastic optimal control problems called *Markovian decision problems*. This is the simplest class of problems that is general enough to include stochastic versions of the problems to which heuristic search algorithms apply, while at the same time allowing us to borrow from a well-developed control and operations research literature. Frameworks that include stochastic problems are important due to the uncertainty present in applications and the fact that it is the presence of uncertainty that gives closed-loop, or reactive, control advantages over open-loop control. In a Markovian decision problem, operators take the form of actions, i.e., inputs to a dynamic system, that probabilistically determine successor states. Although an action is a "primitive" in the theory, it is important to understand that in applications an action can be a high-level command that executes one of a repertoire of complex behaviors. Many problems of practical importance have been formulated as Markovian decision problems, and extensive treatment of the theory and application of this framework can be found in many books, such as those by Bertsekas [11] and Ross [60].

A Markovian decision problem is defined in terms of a discrete-time stochastic dynamic system with finite state set $S = \{1, \ldots, n\}$. Time is represented by a sequence of time steps $t = 0, 1, \ldots$. In Section 6 introducing RTDP, we treat this as a sequence of specific instants of real time, but until then it is best to treat it merely as an abstract sequence. At each time step, a controller observes the system's current state and selects a control action, or simply an *action*,[6] which is executed by being applied as input to the system. If i is the observed state, then the action is selected from a finite set $U(i)$ of admissible actions. When the controller executes action $u \in U(i)$, the system's state at the next time step will be j with state-transition probability $p_{ij}(u)$. We further assume that the application of action u in state i incurs an *immediate cost* $c_i(u)$.[7] When necessary, we refer to states, actions, and immediate costs by the time steps at which they occur by using s_t, u_t, and c_t to denote, respectively, the state, action, and immediate cost at time step t, where $u_t \in U(s_t)$ and $c_t = c_{s_t}(u_t)$. We do not discuss a significant extension of this formalism in which the controller cannot observe the current state with complete certainty. Although this possibility has been studied extensively and is important in practice, the complexities it introduces are beyond the scope of this article.

A closed-loop policy specifies each action as a function of the observed state. Such a policy is denoted $\mu = [\mu(1), \ldots, \mu(n)]$, where the controller executes action $\mu(i) \in U(i)$ whenever it observes state i. This is a *stationary* policy because it does not change over time. Throughout this article, when we use the term policy, we always mean a stationary policy. For any policy μ, there is a function, f^μ, called the *evaluation function*, or the *cost function*, corresponding to policy μ. It assigns to each state the total cost expected to accumulate over time when the controller uses the policy μ starting from the given state. Here, for any policy μ and state i, we define $f^\mu(i)$ to be the expected value of the *infinite-horizon discounted cost* that will accrue over time given that the controller uses policy μ and i is the initial state:

$$f^\mu(i) = E_\mu \left[\sum_{t=0}^{\infty} \gamma^t c_t \middle| s_0 = i \right], \tag{1}$$

where γ, $0 \leqslant \gamma \leqslant 1$, is a factor used to discount future immediate costs, and E_μ is the expectation assuming the controller always uses policy μ. We refer to $f^\mu(i)$ simply as the *cost* of state i under policy μ. Thus, whereas the *immediate cost* of state i under policy μ is $c_i(\mu(i))$, the *cost* of state i under policy μ is the expected discounted sum of all the immediate costs that will be incurred over the future starting from state i. Theorists study Markovian decision problems with other types of evaluation functions, such as the function giving average cost per time step, but we do not consider those formulations here.

---

[6] In control theory, this is simply called a *control*. We use the term action because it is the term commonly used in AI.

[7] To be more general, we can alternatively regard the immediate costs as (bounded) random numbers depending on states and actions. In this case, if $c_i(u)$ denotes the *expected* immediate cost of the application of action u in state i, the theory discussed below remains unchanged.

The objective of the type of Markovian decision problem we consider is to find a policy that minimizes the cost of each state i as defined by Eq. (1). A policy that achieves this objective is an *optimal policy* which, although it depends on γ and is not always unique, we denote $\mu^* = [\mu^*(1), \ldots, \mu^*(n)]$. To each optimal policy corresponds the same evaluation function, which is the *optimal evaluation function*, or *optimal cost function*, denoted f^*; that is, if μ^* is any optimal policy, then $f^{\mu^*} = f^*$. For each state i, $f^*(i)$, the *optimal cost* of state i, is the least possible cost for state i for any policy.

This infinite-horizon discounted version of a Markovian decision problem is the simplest mathematically because discounting ensures that the costs of all states are finite for any policy and, further, that there is always an optimal policy that is stationary.[8] The discount factor, γ, determines how strongly expected future costs should influence current control decisions. When $\gamma = 0$, the cost of any state is just the immediate cost of the transition from that state. This is because $0^0 = 1$ in Eq. (1) so that $f^{\mu}(i) = E_{\mu}[c_0|s_0 = i] = c_i(\mu(i))$. In this case, an optimal policy simply selects actions to minimize the immediate cost for each state, and the optimal evaluation function just gives these minimum immediate costs. As γ increases toward one, future costs become more significant in determining optimal actions, and solution methods generally require more computation.

When $\gamma = 1$, the undiscounted case, the cost of a state given by Eq. (1) need not be finite, and additional assumptions are required to produce well-defined decision problems. We consider one set of assumptions for the undiscounted case because the resulting decision problems are closely related to problems to which heuristic search is applied. In these problems, which Bertsekas and Tsitsiklis [12] call *stochastic shortest path problems* (thinking of immediate costs as arc lengths in a graph whose nodes correspond to states), there is an absorbing set of states, i.e., a set of states that once entered is never left, and the immediate cost associated with applying an action to any of the states in the absorbing set is zero. These assumptions imply that the infinite-horizon evaluation function for any policy taking the system into the absorbing set assigns finite costs to every state even when $\gamma = 1$. This is true because all but a finite number of the immediate costs incurred by such a policy over time must be zero. Additionally, as in the discounted case, there is always at least one optimal policy that is stationary. The absorbing set of states corresponds to the set of goal states in a deterministic shortest path problem, and we call it the *goal set*. However, unlike tasks typically solved via heuristic search, here the objective is to find an optimal closed-loop policy, not just an optimal path from a given initial state.

AI researchers studying reinforcement learning often focus on shortest path problems in which all the immediate costs are zero until a goal state is reached, when a "reward" is delivered to the controller and a new trial begins. These are special kinds of the stochastic shortest path problems that address the issue of *delayed reinforcement* [67] in a particularly stark form. Rewards correspond to negative costs in the formalism we are using. In the discounted case when all the rewards are of the same

---

[8] In finite-horizon problems, optimal policies are generally nonstationary because different actions can be optimal for a given state depending on how many actions remain until the horizon is reached.

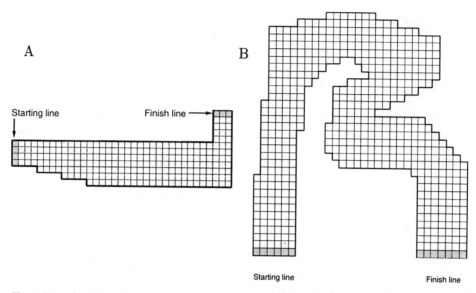

Fig. 1. Example race tracks. Panel A: small race track. Panel B: larger race track. See Table 1 (Section 10) for details.

magnitude, an optimal policy produces a shortest path to a rewarding state. Another example of a stochastic shortest path problem receiving attention is identical to this one except that all the non-rewarding immediate costs have the same positive value instead of zero. In this case, an optimal policy produces a shortest path to a goal state in the undiscounted case. Such problems are examples of minimum-time optimal control problems.

4.1. An example: the race track problem

To illustrate the Markovian decision framework, we formalize a game called Race Track described by Martin Gardner [25] that simulates automobile racing. We modify the game, which we use in Section 10 to compare the performance of various DP-based learning algorithms, by considering only a single car and by making it probabilistic.

A race track of any shape is drawn on graph paper, with a starting line at one end and a finish line at the other consisting of designated squares. Each square within the boundary of the track is a possible location of the car. Fig. 1 shows two example tracks. At the start of each of a sequence of trials, the car is placed on the starting line at a random position, and moves are made in which the car attempts to move down the track toward the finish line. Acceleration and deceleration are simulated as follows. If in the previous move the car moved h squares horizontally and v squares vertically, then the present move can be h' squares vertically and v' squares horizontally, where the difference between h' and h is -1, 0, or 1, and the difference between v' and v is -1, 0, or 1. This means that the car can maintain its speed in either dimension, or it can slow down or speed up in either dimension by one square per move. If the car hits the track boundary,[9] we move it back to a random position on the starting line, reduce its velocity to zero (i.e., $h' - h$ and $v' - v$ are considered to be zero), and continue the trial. The objective is to learn to control the car so that it crosses the finish line in as few moves as possible. Figs. 2 and 4 show examples of optimal and near-optimal paths for the race tracks shown in Fig. 1.

In addition to the difficulty of discovering faster ways to reach the finish line, it is very easy for the car to gather too much speed to negotiate the track's curves. To make matters worse, we introduce a random factor into the problem. With a probability p, the actual accelerations or decelerations at a move are zero independently of the intended accelerations or decelerations. Thus, $1 - p$ is the probability that the controller's intended actions are executed. One might think of this as simulating driving on a track that is unpredictably slippery so that sometimes braking and throttling up have no effect on the car's velocity.

Although the Race Track problem is suggestive of robot motion and navigation problems, it is not our intention to formulate it in a way best suited to the design of an autonomous vehicle with realistic sensory and motor capabilities. Instead, we regard it as a representative example of problems requiring learning difficult skills, and we formulate the entire task as an abstract stochastic shortest path problem. The first step in this formulation is to define the dynamic system being controlled. The state of the system at each time step $t = 0, 1, \ldots$ can be represented as a quadruple of integers $s_t = (x_t, y_t, \dot{x}_t, \dot{y}_t)$. The first two integers are the horizontal and vertical coordinates of the car's location, and the second two integers are its speeds in the horizontal and vertical directions. That is, $\dot{x}_t = x_t - x_{t-1}$ is the horizontal speed of the car at time step t; similarly $\dot{y}_t = y_t - y_{t-1}$ (we assume $x_{-1} = y_{-1} = 0$). The set of admissible actions for each state is the set of pairs (u^x, u^y), where u^x and u^y are both in the set $\{-1, 0, 1\}$. We let $u_t = (u_t^x, u_t^y)$ denote the action at time t. A closed-loop policy μ assigns an admissible action to each state: the action at time step t is

$$\mu(s_t) \in \{(-1,-1), (-1,0), (-1,1), (0,-1), (0,0), (0,1), (1,-1), \\ (1,0), (1,1)\}.$$

The following equations define the state transitions of this system. With probability $1 - p$, the controller's action is reliably executed so that the state at time step $t + 1$ is

$$\begin{aligned}
x_{t+1} &= x_t + \dot{x}_t + u_t^x, \\
y_{t+1} &= y_t + \dot{y}_t + u_t^y, \\
\dot{x}_{t+1} &= \dot{x}_t + u_t^x, \\
\dot{y}_{t+1} &= \dot{y}_t + u_t^y,
\end{aligned} \tag{2}$$

and with probability p, the system ignores the controller's action, so that the state at time step $t + 1$ is

---

[9] For the computational experiments described in Section 10, this means that the projected path of the car for a move intersects the track boundary at any place not on the finish line.

$$
\begin{aligned}
x_{t+1} &= x_t + \dot{x}_t, \\
y_{t+1} &= y_t + \dot{y}_t, \\
\dot{x}_{t+1} &= \dot{x}_t, \\
\dot{y}_{t+1} &= \dot{y}_t.
\end{aligned}
\tag{3}
$$

This assumes that the straight line joining the point (x_t, y_t) to the point (x_{t+1}, y_{t+1}) lies entirely within the track, or intersects only the finish line. If this is not the case, then the car has collided with the track's boundary, and the state at $t+1$ is $(x, y, 0, 0)$, where (x, y) is a randomly chosen position on the starting line. A move that takes the car across the finish line is treated as a valid move, but we assume that the car subsequently stays in the resulting state until a new trial begins. This method for keeping the car on the track, together with Eqs. (3) and (2), define the state-transition probabilities for all states and admissible actions.

To complete the formulation of the stochastic shortest path problem, we need to define the set of start states, the set of goal states, and the immediate costs associated with each action in each state. The set of start states consists of all the zero-velocity states on the starting line, i.e., all the states $(x, y, 0, 0)$ where (x, y) are coordinates of the squares making up the starting line. The set of goal states consists of all states that can be reached in one time step by crossing the finish line from inside the track. According to the state-transition function defined above, this set is absorbing. The immediate cost for all non-goal states is one independently of the action taken, i.e., $c_i(u) = 1$ for all non-goal states i and all admissible actions u. The immediate cost associated with a transition from any goal state is zero. If we restrict attention to policies that are guaranteed to take the car across the finish line, we do not need to use discounting. For such a policy μ, the undiscounted infinite-horizon cost, $f^\mu(i)$, of a state i under μ is the expected number of moves for the car to cross the finish line from state i when it is being controlled by a policy μ. An optimal policy, which minimizes this cost of each state, is therefore a policy by which the car is expected to cross the finish line as quickly as possible starting from any state. The optimal cost of a state i, $f^*(i)$, is the smallest expected number of moves to the finish line.

The total number of states depends on the configuration of the race track, but because we have not imposed a limit on the car's speed, it is potentially infinite. However, the set of states that can be reached from the set of start states via any policy is finite and can be considered to be the state set of the stochastic shortest path problem.

4.2. The optimality equation

To set the stage for discussing DP, we provide more detail about the relationship between policies and evaluation functions. Although the evaluation function f^μ gives the cost of each state under policy μ, μ does not necessarily select actions that lead to the best successor states as evaluated by f^μ. In other words, μ is not necessarily a greedy policy with respect to its own evaluation function.

To define a greedy policy in this stochastic case we use Watkins' [81] "Q" notation, which plays a role in the Q-Learning method described in Section 7.3. Let f be a real-valued function of the states; it may be the evaluation function for some policy, a guess for a good evaluation function (such as a heuristic evaluation function in heuristic search), or an arbitrary function. For each state i and action $u \in U(i)$, let

$$Q^f(i, u) = c_i(u) + \gamma \sum_{j \in S} p_{ij}(u) f(j). \tag{4}$$

$Q^f(i, u)$ is the cost of action u in state i as evaluated by f. It is the sum of the immediate cost and the discounted expected value of the costs of the possible successor states under action u. If the system's state transitions are deterministic, then Eq. (4) simplifies to

$$Q^f(i, u) = c_i(u) + \gamma f(j),$$

where j is the successor of state i under action u (i.e., node j is the child of node i along the edge corresponding to operator u). In the deterministic case, one can therefore think of $Q^f(i, u)$ as a summary of the result of a one-ply lookahead from node i along the edge corresponding to operator u as evaluated by f. The stochastic case requires a generalization of this view because many edges correspond to each operator, each having a different probability of being followed. If f is the evaluation function for some policy, $Q^f(i, u)$ gives the cost of generating action u in state i and thereafter following this policy.

Using these "Q-values", a policy μ is greedy with respect to f if for all states i, $\mu(i)$ is an action satisfying

$$Q^f(i, \mu(i)) = \min_{u \in U(i)} Q^f(i, u).$$

Although there can be more than one greedy policy with respect to f if more than one action minimizes the set of Q-values for some state, we let μ^f denote any policy that is greedy with respect to f. Also note that any policy is greedy with respect to many different evaluation functions.

A key fact underlying all DP methods is that *the only policies that are greedy with respect to their own evaluation functions are optimal policies*. That is, if μ^* is any optimal policy, then its evaluation function is the optimal evaluation function f^*, and $\mu^* = \mu^{f^*}$. This means that for any state i, $\mu^*(i)$ satisfies

$$Q^{f^*}(i, \mu^*(i)) = \min_{u \in U(i)} Q^{f^*}(i, u). \tag{5}$$

Furthermore, any policy that is greedy with respect to f^* is an optimal policy. Thus, if f^* is known, it is possible to define an optimal policy simply by defining it satisfy Eq. (5), i.e., defining it to be greedy with respect to f^*. Due to the definition of Q-values (Eq. (4)), this generalizes to the stochastic case the fact that an optimal policy is any policy that is best-first with respect to f^* as determined by a one-ply search from each current state. Deeper search is never necessary because f^* already summarizes all the information that such a search would obtain.

Letting $Q^*(i, u) = Q^{f^*}(i, u)$ to simplify notation, a related key fact is that a necessary and sufficient condition for f^* to be the optimal evaluation function is that for each state i it must be true that

$$f^*(i) = \min_{u \in U(i)} Q^*(i, u)$$

$$= \min_{u \in U(i)} \left[c_i(u) + \gamma \sum_{j \in S} p_{ij}(u) f^*(j) \right] \tag{6}$$

This is one form of the *Bellman Optimality Equation* which can be solved for each $f^*(i)$, $i \in S$, by a DP algorithm. It is a set of n (the number of states) simultaneous nonlinear equations. The form of the equations depends on the dynamic system and the immediate costs underlying the decision problem.

Once f^* has been found, an optimal action for state i can be determined as follows. The Q-values $Q^*(i, u)$ for all admissible actions $u \in U(i)$ are determined via Eq. (4). In general, this takes $O(mn)$ computational steps, where n is the number of states and m is the number of admissible actions for state i. However, if one knows which of the state-transition probabilities from state i are zero (as one usually does in the deterministic case), then the amount of computation can be much less ($O(m)$ in the deterministic case). Computing these Q-values amounts to a one-ply lookahead search from state i, which requires knowledge of the system's state-transition probabilities. Using these Q-values, an optimal action can be determined via Eq. (5), which takes $m-1$ comparisons. The computational complexity of finding an optimal action using this method is therefore dominated by the complexity of finding f^*, i.e., by the complexity of the DP algorithm.

5. Dynamic programming

Given a complete and accurate model of a Markovian decision problem in the form of knowledge of the state-transition probabilities, $p_{ij}(u)$, and the immediate costs, $c_i(u)$, for all states i and actions $u \in U(i)$, it is possible—at least in principle—to solve the decision problem off-line by applying one of various well-known DP algorithms. We describe several versions of a basic DP algorithm called *value iteration*. There are other DP algorithms, including one called *policy iteration*, but learning algorithms based on them are beyond the scope of this article, although we briefly discuss policy iteration in Section 8. We treat DP as referring only to value iteration unless otherwise noted. As used for solving Markovian decision problems, value iteration is a successive approximation procedure that converges to the optimal evaluation function, f^*. It is a successive approximation method for solving the Bellman Optimality Equation whose basic operation is "backing up" estimates of the optimal state costs. There are several variations of value interaction depending on how the computations are organized. We first describe the version that applies the backup operations synchronously.

5.1. Synchronous dynamic programming

Let f_k denote the estimate of f^* available at stage k of the DP computation, where $k = 0, 1, \ldots$. At stage k, $f_k(i)$ is the estimated optimal cost of state i, which we refer to simply as the *stage-k cost* of state i; similarly, we refer to f_k as the *stage-k evaluation function*, even though it may not actually be the evaluation function for any policy. (We use the index k for the stages of a DP computation, whereas we use t to denote the time step of the control problem being solved.) In synchronous DP, for $k = 0, 1, \ldots, f_{k+1}$ is defined in terms of f_k as follows: for each state i,

$$
\begin{aligned}
f_{k+1}(i) &= \min_{u \in U(i)} \left[c_i(u) + \gamma \sum_{j \in S} p_{ij}(u) f_k(j) \right] \\
&= \min_{u \in U(i)} Q^{f_k}(i, u),
\end{aligned}
\tag{7}
$$

where f_0 is some given initial estimate of f^*. We refer to the application of this update equation for state i as *backing up i's cost*. Although backing up costs is a common operation in a variety of search algorithms in AI, there it does not always mean that the backed-up cost is *saved* for future use. Here, however, the backed-up cost is always saved by updating the evaluation function.

The iteration defined by Eq. (7) is synchronous because no values of f_{k+1} appear on the right-hand side of the equation. If one imagines having a separate processor associated with each state, applying Eq. (7) for all states i means that each processor backs up the cost of its state at the same time, using the old costs of the other states supplied by the other processors. This process updates all values of f_k simultaneously. Alternatively, a sequential implementation of this iteration requires temporary storage locations so that all the stage-$(k + 1)$ costs are computed based on the stage-k costs. The sequential ordering of the backups is irrelevant to the result.

If there are n states and m is the largest number of admissible actions for any state, then each iteration, which consists of backing up the cost of each state exactly once, requires at most $O(mn^2)$ operations in the stochastic case and $O(mn)$ operations in the deterministic case. For the large state sets typical in AI and in many control problems, it is not desirable to try to complete even one iteration, let alone repeat the process until it converges to f^*. For example, because backgammon has about 10^{20} states, a single iteration of value iteration in this case would take more than 1,000 years using a 1,000 MIPS processor.

If $\gamma < 1$, repeated synchronous iterations produce a sequence of functions that converges to the optimal evaluation function, f^*, for any initial estimate, f_0. Although the cost of a state need not get closer to its optimal cost on each iteration, the *maximum* error between $f_k(i)$ and $f^*(i)$ over all states i must decrease (e.g., [11]).

Synchronous DP, as well as the other off-line versions of value iteration we discuss below, generates a sequence of functions that converges to f^* if $\gamma < 1$, *but it does not explicitly generate a sequence of policies*. To each stage-k evaluation function there corresponds at least one greedy policy, but these policies are never explicitly formed. Ideally, one would wait until the sequence converges to f^* and then form a greedy policy corresponding to f^*, which would be an optimal policy. But this is not possible in practice because value iteration converges asymptotically. Instead, one executes value iteration until it meets a test for approximate convergence and then forms a policy from the resulting evaluation function.[10]

It is important to note that a function in the sequence of evaluation functions generated by value iteration does not have to closely approximate f^* in order for a corresponding greedy policy to be an optimal policy. Indeed, a policy corresponding to the stage-k evaluation function for some k may be optimal long before the algorithm converges to f^*. *But unaided by other computations, value iteration does not detect when this first happens.* This fact is an important reason that the on-line variants of value iteration we discuss in this article can have advantages over the off-line variants. Because the controller always uses a policy defined by the current evaluation function, it can perform optimally before the evaluation function converges to the optimal evaluation function.

Bertsekas [11] and Bertsekas and Tsitsiklis [12] give conditions ensuring convergence of synchronous DP for stochastic shortest path problems in the undiscounted case ($\gamma = 1$). Using their terminology, a policy is *proper* if its use implies a nonzero probability of eventually reaching the goal set starting from any state. Using a proper policy also implies that the goal set will be reached eventually from any state with probability one. The existence of a proper policy is the generalization to the stochastic case of the existence of a path from any initial state to the goal set.

Synchronous DP converges to f^* in undiscounted stochastic shortest path problems under the following conditions:

(1) the initial cost of every goal state is zero,

(2) there is at least one proper policy, and

(3) all policies that are not proper incur infinite cost for at least one state.

The third condition ensures that every optimal policy is proper, i.e., it rules out the possibility that a least-cost path exists that never reaches the goal set. One condition under which this is true is when all immediate costs for transitions from non-goal states are positive, i.e., $c_i(u) > 0$ for all non-goal states i and actions $u \in U(i)$.[11] In the deterministic case, conditions (2) and (3) are satisfied if there is at least one solution path from every state and the sum of the immediate costs in every loop is positive.

5.2. Gauss–Seidel dynamic programming

Gauss–Seidel DP differs from the synchronous version in that the costs are backed up one state at a time in a sequential "sweep" of all the states, with the computation for each state using the most recent costs of the other states. If we assume that the states are numbered in order, as we have here, and that each sweep proceeds in this order, then the result of each iteration of Gauss–Seidel DP can be written as follows: for each state i and each $k = 0, 1, \ldots,$

---

[10] Policy iteration, in contrast, explicitly generates a sequence of policies that converges to an optimal policy after a finite number of iterations (when there are a finite number of states and admissible actions, as we are assuming here). However, policy iteration has other shortcomings which we discuss in Section 8.

[11] The assumption of positive immediate costs can be weakened to nonnegativity, i.e., $c_i(u) \geq 0$ for all $i \in S$ and $u \in U(i)$, if there exists at least one *optimal* proper policy [12].

$$f_{k+1}(i) = \min_{u \in U(i)} \left[c_i(u) + \gamma \sum_{j \in S} p_{ij}(u) f(j) \right]$$

$$= \min_{u \in U(i)} Q^f(i, u), \tag{8}$$

where

$$f(j) = \begin{cases} f_{k+1}(j), & \text{if } j < i, \\ f_k(j), & \text{otherwise.} \end{cases}$$

Unlike synchronous DP, the order in which the states' costs are backed up influences the computation. Nevertheless, Gauss–Seidel DP converges to f^* under the same conditions under which synchronous DP converges. When $\gamma < 1$, repeated Gauss–Seidel sweeps produce a sequence of functions that converges to f^*. For undiscounted stochastic shortest path problems, the conditions described above that ensure convergence of synchronous DP also ensure convergence of Gauss–Seidel DP [12]. Because each cost backup uses the latest costs of the other states, Gauss–Seidel DP generally converges faster than synchronous DP. Furthermore, it should be clear that some state orderings produce faster convergence than others, depending on the problem. For example, in shortest path problems, sweeping from goal states backwards along likely shortest paths usually leads to faster convergence than sweeping in the forward direction.

Although Gauss–Seidel DP is not one of the algorithms of direct interest in this article, we used it to solve the example problem described in Section 4.1 and it serves as a bridge between synchronous DP and the asynchronous form discussed next.

5.3. Asynchronous dynamic programming

Asynchronous DP is similar to Gauss–Seidel DP in that it does not back up state costs simultaneously. However, it is not organized in terms of systematic successive sweeps of the state set. As proposed by Bertsekas [10] and further developed by Bertsekas and Tsitsiklis [12], asynchronous DP is suitable for multi-processor systems with communication time delays and without a common clock. For each state $i \in S$ there is a separate processor dedicated to backing up the cost of state i (more generally, each processor may be responsible for a number of states). The times at which each processor backs up the cost of its state can be different for each processor. To back up the cost of its state, each processor uses the costs for other states that are available to it when it "awakens" to perform a backup. Multi-processor implementations have obvious utility in speeding up DP and thus have practical significance for all the algorithms we discuss below (see, e.g., Lemmon [44]). However, our interest in asynchronous DP lies in the fact that it does not require state costs to be backed up in any systematically organized fashion.

Although in the full asynchronous model, the notion of discrete computational stages does not apply because a processor can awaken at any of a continuum of times, we use a notion of an iteration stage because it facilitates our discussion of RTDP in the next section. As in the other forms of DP, let f_k denote the estimate of f^* available at stage

k of the computation. At each stage k, the costs of a *subset* of the states are backed up synchronously, and the costs remain unchanged for the other states. The subset of states whose costs are backed up changes from stage to stage, and the choice of these subsets determines the precise nature of the algorithm. For each $k = 0, 1, \ldots$, if $S_k \subseteq S$ is the set of states whose costs are backed up at stage k, then f_{k+1} is computed as follows:

$$f_{k+1}(i) = \begin{cases} \min_{u \in U(i)} Q^{f_k}(i, u), & \text{if } i \in S_k, \\ f_k(i), & \text{otherwise.} \end{cases} \tag{9}$$

According to this algorithm, then, f_{k+1} may differ from f_k on one state, on many states, or possibly none, depending on S_k. Further, unlike Gauss–Seidel DP, the costs of some states may be backed up several times before the costs of others are backed up once. Asynchronous DP includes the synchronous and Gauss–Seidel algorithms as special cases: synchronous DP results if $S_k = S$ for each k; Gauss–Seidel DP results when each S_k consists of a single state and the collection of S_k's is defined to implement successive sweeps of the entire state set (e.g., $S_0 = \{1\}$, $S_1 = \{2\}$, $\ldots$, $S_{n-1} = \{n\}$, $S_n = \{1\}$, $S_{n+1} = \{2\}$, $\ldots$).

Discounted asynchronous DP converges to f^* provided that the cost of each state is backed up infinitely often, i.e., provided that each state is contained in an infinite number of the subsets S_k, $k = 0, 1, \ldots$. In practice, this means that the strategy for selecting states for cost backups should never eliminate any state from possible selection in the future. In the undiscounted case ($\gamma = 1$), additional assumptions are necessary to ensure convergence. It follows from a result by Bertsekas and Tsitsiklis [12, p. 446] that asynchronous DP converges in undiscounted stochastic shortest path problems if the cost of each state is backed up infinitely often and the conditions given in Section 5.1 for convergence of synchronous DP are met: (1) the initial cost of every goal state is zero, (2) there is at least one proper policy, and (3) all policies that are not proper incur infinite cost for at least one state.

It is important to realize that a single backup of a state's cost in asynchronous DP *does not necessarily improve it as an estimate of the state's optimal cost*; it may in fact make it worse. However, under the appropriate conditions, the cost of each state converges to its optimal cost with repeated backups. Further, as in Gauss–Seidel DP, the order in which states' costs are backed up can influence the rate of convergence in a problem-dependent way. This fact underlies the utility of various strategies for "teaching" DP-based learning algorithms by supplying experience dictating selected orderings of the backups (e.g., Lin [48], Utgoff and Clouse [80], and Whitehead [90]).

6. Dynamic Programming in real time

The DP algorithms described above are off-line algorithms for solving Markovian decision problems. Although they successively approximate the optimal evaluation function through a sequence of stages, these stages are not related to the time steps of the decision problem being solved. Here we consider algorithms in which the controller performs asynchronous DP *concurrently* with the actual process of control, i.e., concurrently with the process of executing actions. The concurrent DP and control processes interact as follows: (1) control decisions are based on the most up-to-date information from the DP computation, and (2) the state sequences generated during control influence the selection of states to which the DP backup operation is applied and whose estimated costs have to be stored. The asynchronous version of DP is appropriate for this role due to the flexibility with which its stages can be defined. As a consequence of this interaction, the controller automatically uses intermediate results of the DP computation to guide its behavior, and the DP computation can *focus* on regions of the state set that are most relevant for control as revealed in the system's behavior. The algorithm we call Real-Time DP (RTDP) results when this interaction has specific characteristics that we present below.

Throughout this section we assume that there is a complete and accurate model of the decision problem, the case Sutton [70] discusses in relation to planning in AI. In Section 7, we discuss the adaptive case, in which a complete and accurate model of the decision problem is not available. When there is a model of the decision problem, then the concurrent execution of DP and control can also be carried out in *simulation mode*, where the model is used as a surrogate for the actual system underlying the decision problem. The result is a novel off-line DP computation that can have computational advantages over conventional off-line DP due to its ability to focus on relevant parts of the state set. Despite its not being a real-time computation, we regard the concurrent execution of DP and control in simulation mode to be a form of learning. This is in fact how learning was accomplished in the game-playing programs of Samuel [61,62] and Tesauro [77]. Learning occurred during many simulated games in which these learning systems competed against themselves. Although we emphasize the real-time use of DP-based learning algorithms, the reader should be aware that our discussion also applies to the use of these algorithms in simulation mode.

To describe the concurrent execution of DP and control, we think of the time steps $t = 0, 1, \ldots$ of the abstract discrete-time formulation of a Markovian decision problem as the indices of a sequence of instants of real time at which the controller must execute control actions. Let s_t be the last state observed before time t, and let k_t be the total number of asynchronous DP stages completed up to time t. Then f_{k_t} is the latest estimate of the optimal evaluation function available when the controller must select action $u_t \in U(s_t)$. When the controller executes u_t, it incurs the immediate cost $c_{s_t}(u_t)$, and the system's state changes to s_{t+1}. By the time the next action, u_{t+1}, has to be selected, some additional stages of asynchronous DP stages are completed to yield $f_{k_{t+1}}$. We let B_t denote the set of states whose costs are backed up in these stages. Note that some states in B_t might have their costs backed up more than once in these stages.

6.1. Real-time DP

RTDP refers to cases in which the concurrently executing DP and control processes influence one another as follows. First, the controller always follows a policy that is greedy with respect to the most recent estimate of f^*. This means that u_t is always the greedy action with respect to f_{k_t}. Moreover, any ties in selecting these actions must be resolved randomly, or in some other way that ensures the continuing selection of all the greedy actions. Second, between the execution of u_t and u_{t+1}, the cost of s_t is always backed up, i.e., $s_t \in B_t$ for all t. In the simplest case, $B_t = \{s_t\}$ for all t, i.e., the cost of *only* s_t is backed up at each time step t, but more generally, B_t can contain *any* states (in addition to s_t) such as those generated by any type of lookahead search. For example, B_t might consist of the states generated by an exhaustive search from s_t forward to some fixed search depth, or it might consist of the states generated by a search that is best-first according to f_{k_t}.

We say that RTDP converges when the associated asynchronous DP computation converges to f^*. Because the controller always takes actions that are greedy with respect to the current estimate of f^*, when RTDP converges, optimal control performance is attained.[12] The conditions described in Section 5.3 ensuring that asynchronous DP converges to f^* still apply when it is executed concurrently with control. Consequently, in the discounted case, the only condition required for convergence of RTDP is that no state is ever completely ruled out for having its cost backed up. Because RTDP always backs up the cost of the current state, one way to achieve this is to make sure that the controller always continues to visit each state. There are several approaches to ensuring this. One approach is to assume, as is often done in the engineering literature, that the Markov process resulting from the use of any policy is ergodic. This means that there is a nonzero probability of visiting any state no matter what actions are executed. Discounted RTDP converges under this assumption. However, this assumption is unsatisfactory for stochastic shortest path problems because it does not allow proper subsets of states to be absorbing; it is satisfied only in the trivial stochastic shortest path problem in which every state is a goal state.

A second way to ensure that each state is visited infinitely often is to use multiple *trials*. A trial consists of a time interval of nonzero bounded duration during which RTDP is performed. After this interval, the system is set to a new starting state, and a new trial begins.[13] Obviously, this method cannot be used when it is impossible to set the system state to selected start states, but for many problems this approach is possible, and it is always possible when RTDP is used in simulation mode.

6.2. Trial-based RTDP

If the initial states of trials are selected so that every state will be selected infinitely often in an infinite series of trials, then obviously every state will be visited infinitely often—if only at the start of an infinite number of trials. A simple way to accomplish this is to start each trial with a randomly selected state, where each state has a nonzero probability of being selected. By *Trial-Based* RTDP we mean RTDP used with trials initiated so that every state will, with probability one, be a start state infinitely often in an infinite series of trials. Then the following theorem is an immediate result of noting

---

[12] When there is more than one optimal policy, the controller will continue to switch between optimal policies because RTDP continues to select among all the greedy actions. This results in a *nonstationary* optimal policy because different optimal actions can be taken from the same state on different occasions.

[13] RTDP must be interrupted at the end of a trial so that the cost of the last state in a trial is not influenced by the cost of the starting state of the next trial. This prevents the state transitions caused by the "trainer" from influencing the evaluation function.

that, in the discounted case, Trial-Based RTDP gives rise to a convergent asynchronous DP computation with probability one for any method of terminating trials:

Theorem 1. *For any discounted Markov decision problem (as defined in Section 4) and any initial evaluation function, Trial-Based RTDP converges (with probability one).*

It is natural to use Trial-Based RTDP in undiscounted stochastic shortest path problems, where trials terminate when a goal state is first reached, or after a predetermined number of time steps. Because Trial-Based RTDP gives rise to a convergent asynchronous DP computation with probability one in an undiscounted stochastic shortest path problems under the conditions enumerated in Section 5.3, we have the following result:

Theorem 2. *In undiscounted stochastic shortest path problems, Trial-Based RTDP converges (with probability one) under the following conditions:*
  (1) *the initial cost of every goal state is zero,*
  (2) *there is at least one proper policy, and*
  (3) *all policies that are not proper incur infinite cost for at least one state.*

Trial-Based RTDP is more interesting if we relax the requirement that it should yield a *complete* optimal evaluation function and a *complete* optimal policy. Consider a trial-based approach to solving undiscounted stochastic shortest path problems in which there is a designated subset of *start states* from which trials always start. We say that a state i is *relevant* if a start state s and an optimal policy exist such that i can be reached from state s when the controller uses that policy. It suffices to find a policy that is optimal when restricted to relevant states because the other states (*irrelevant states*) will never occur during the use of that (or any other) optimal policy. If one somehow knew which states were relevant, then one could apply DP to just these states and possibly save a considerable amount of time and space. But clearly this is not possible because knowing which states are relevant requires knowledge of optimal policies, which is what one is seeking.

However, under certain conditions, without continuing to back up the costs of irrelevant states, Trial-Based RTDP converges to a function that equals f^* on all relevant states, and the controller's policy converges to a policy that is optimal on all relevant states. The costs of some irrelevant states may not have to be backed up at all. Moreover, if memory for the estimated state costs is allocated incrementally during trials, the exhaustive memory requirement of conventional DP can be avoided because Trial-Based RTDP tends to focus computation onto the set of relevant states, and eventually restricts computation to this set. Conditions under which this is possible are stated precisely in the following theorem, whose proof is given in Appendix A:

Theorem 3. *In undiscounted stochastic shortest path problems, Trial-Based RTDP, with the initial state of each trial restricted to a set of start states, converges (with probability one) to f^* on the set of relevant states, and the controller's policy converges to an* *optimal policy (possibly nonstationary) on the set of relevant states, under the following conditions*:

(1) *the initial cost of every goal state is zero,*

(2) *there is at least one proper policy,* [14]

(3) *all immediate costs incurred by transitions from non-goal states are positive, i.e., $c_i(u) > 0$ for all non-goal states i and actions $u \in U(i)$, and*

(4) *the initial costs of all states are non-overestimating, i.e., $f_0(i) \leqslant f^*(i)$ for all states $i \in S$.*

Condition (4) can be satisfied by simply setting $f_0(i) = 0$ for all i. The significance of Theorem 3 is that it gives conditions under which a policy that is optimal on the relevant states can be achieved without continuing to devote computational effort to backing up the costs of irrelevant states. Under these conditions, RTDP can yield an optimal policy when state and action sets are too large to feasibly apply conventional DP algorithms, although the amount of computation saved will clearly depend on characteristics of the problem being solved such as its branching structure. Moreover, if RTDP is applied on-line instead of in simulation mode, whenever the evaluation function changes so that its greedy policy shows improvement, the controller automatically takes advantage of this improvement. This can occur before the evaluation function is close to f^*.

Although in both discounted and undiscounted problems, the eventual convergence of RTDP does not depend critically on the choice of states whose costs are backed between the execution of actions (except that the cost of the current state must be backed up), judicious selection of these states can accelerate convergence. Sophisticated exploration strategies can be implemented by selecting these states based on prior knowledge and on the information contained in the current evaluation function. For example, in a trial-based approach to a stochastic shortest path problem, guided exploration can reduce the expected trial duration by helping the controller find goal states. It also makes sense for RTDP to back up the costs of states whose current costs are not yet accurate estimates of their optimal costs but whose successor states do have accurate current costs. Techniques for "teaching" DP-based learning systems by suggesting certain back ups over others [46, 80, 90] rely on the fact that the order in which the costs of states are backed up can influence the rate of convergence of asynchronous DP, whether applied off- or on-line. A promising approach recently developed by Peng and Williams [58] and Moore and Atkeson [57], which the latter authors call "prioritized sweeping", directs the application of DP backups to the most likely predecessors of states whose costs change significantly. Exploration such as this—whose objective is to facilitate finding an optimal policy when there is a complete model of the decision problem—must be distinguished from exploration designed to facilitate learning a model of the decision problem when one is not available. We discuss this latter objective for exploration in Section 7.

---

[14] If trials are allowed to time out before a goal state is reached, it is possible to eliminate the requirement that at least one proper policy exists. Timing out prevents getting stuck in fruitless cycles, and the time-out period can be extended systematically to ensure that it becomes long enough to let all the optimal paths be followed without interruption.

6.3. RTDP and LRTA*

Theorem 3 is a generalization of Korf's [38] convergence theorem for LRTA*. RTDP extends LRTA* in two ways: it generalizes LRTA* to stochastic problems, and it includes the option of backing up the costs of many states in the time intervals between the execution of actions. Using our notation, the simplest form of LRTA* operates as follows: to determine action $u_t \in U(s_t)$, the controller first backs up the cost of s_t by setting $f_t(s_t)$ to the minimum of the values $c_{s_t}(u) + \gamma f_{t-1}(j)$ for all actions $u \in U(s_t)$, where j is s_t's successor under action u and $f_{t-1}(j)$ is j's current cost. [15] The costs of all the other states remain the same. The controller then inputs this minimizing action to the system, observes s_{t+1}, and repeats the process.

This form of LRTA* is almost the special case of RTDP as applied to a deterministic problem in which $B_t = \{s_t\}$ for all $t = 0, 1, \ldots$. It differs from this special case in the following way. Whereas RTDP executes an action that is greedy with respect to f_t, LRTA* executes an action that is greedy with respect to f_{t-1}. This is usually an inconsequential difference because in LRTA* $f_t(j)$ can differ from $f_{t-1}(j)$ only when $j = s_t$, i.e., when s_t is its own successor. LRTA* saves computation by requiring only one minimization at each time step: the minimization required to perform the backup also gives the greedy action. However, in the general case, when RTDP backs up more than one state's cost during each time interval, it makes sense to use the latest estimate of f^* to select an action.

An extended form of LRTA* can also be related to RTDP. In his discussion, Korf [38] assumes that the evaluation of a state may be *augmented by lookahead search*. This means that instead of using the costs $f_{t-1}(j)$ of s_t's successor states, LRTA* can perform an off-line forward search from s_t to a depth determined by the amount of time and computational resources available. It applies the evaluation function f_{t-1} to the frontier nodes and then backs up these costs to s_t's immediate successors. This is done (roughly) by setting the backed-up cost of each state generated in the forward search to the minimum of the costs of its successors (Korf's "minimin" procedure). These backed-up costs of the successor states are then used to update $f_{t-1}(s_t)$, as described above, but neither these costs nor the backed-up costs of the states generated in the forward search are saved. Despite the fact that backed-up costs for many states have been computed, the new evaluation function, f_t, differs from the old only for s_t. However, within the limits of space constraints, it makes sense to store the backed-up costs for as many states as possible, especially when the controller will experience multiple trials with different starting states. In contrast to LRTA*, RTDP can save all of these backed-up costs in f_{k_t} by executing appropriately defined stages of asynchronous DP.

Specifically, saving the backed-up costs produced by Korf's minimin procedure corresponds to executing a number of stages of asynchronous DP equal to one less than the depth of the forward search tree. The first stage synchronously backs up the costs of all the immediate predecessors of the frontier states (using the current costs of the frontier states), the second stage backs up the costs of the states that are the immediate

---

[15] Note that because $B_t = \{s_t\}$ for all t in LRTA*, k_t always equals t.

predecessors of these states, etc. Then one additional stage of asynchronous DP to back up the cost of s_t completes the computation of f_{k_t}. Not only does this procedure also apply in the stochastic case, it suggests that other stages of asynchronous DP might be useful as well. These stages might back up the costs of states not in the forward search tree, or they might back up the costs of states in this tree more than once. For example, noting that in general the forward search might generate a graph with cycles, multiple backups of the costs of these states can further improve the information contained in f_{k_t}. All of these possibilities are basically different instances of RTDP and thus converge under the conditions described in the theorems above.

With repeated trials, the information accumulating in the developing estimate of the optimal evaluation function improves control performance. Consequently, LRTA* and RTDP are indeed learning algorithms, as suggested by the name chosen by Korf. However, they do not directly apply to *adaptive* control problems as this term is used in control theory, where it applies to problems in which a complete and accurate model of the system to be controlled is lacking. In the next section we discuss how RTDP can be used in adaptive control problems.

7. Adaptive control

The versions of value iteration described above—synchronous, Gauss–Seidel, asynchronous, and real-time—require prior knowledge of the system underlying the Markovian decision problem. That is, they require knowledge of the state-transition probabilities, $p_{ij}(u)$, for all states i, j, and all actions $u \in U(i)$, and they require knowledge of the immediate costs $c_i(u)$ for all states i and actions $u \in U(i)$. If the system is deterministic, this means that one must know the successor states and the immediate costs for all the admissible actions for every state. Finding, or approximating, an optimal policy when this knowledge is not available is known as a *Markovian decision problem with incomplete information*, and solution methods for these problems are examples of *adaptive control* methods.[16]

There are two major classes of adaptive methods for Markovian decision problems with incomplete information. Bayesian methods rest on the assumption of a known a priori probability distribution over the class of possible stochastic dynamic systems. As observations accumulate, this distribution is revised via Bayes' rule. Actions are selected by using DP to find a policy that minimizes the expected cost over the set of possible systems as well as over time. Non-Bayesian approaches, in contrast, attempt to arrive at an optimal policy *asymptotically* for *any* system within some pre-specified class of systems. Actions may not be optimal on the basis of prior assumptions and accumulated observations, but the policy should approach an optimal policy in the limit as experience accumulates. Kumar [39] surveys the large literature on both classes of

---

[16] Markovian decision problems with incomplete information are not the same as problems with incomplete *state* information in which the controller does not have complete knowledge of the system state at each time step of control. These are sometimes called *partially observable Markovian decision problems*, which despite their relevance for many applications, are beyond the scope of this article.

methods and conveys the subtlety of the issues as well as the sophistication of the existing theoretical results. Here we restrict attention to non-Bayesian methods because they are more practical for large problems.

Two types of non-Bayesian methods are distinguished. *Indirect* methods explicitly model the dynamic system being controlled. They use *system identification* algorithms to update parameters whose values determine the current system model at any time during control. They typically make control decisions under the assumption that the current model is the true model of the system (what control theorists call the *certainty equivalence principle* [11]). *Direct* methods, on the other hand, form policies without using explicit system models. They directly estimate a policy or information other than a system model, such as an evaluation function, from which a policy can be determined.

For both indirect and direct methods, a central issue is the conflict between controlling the system and exploring its behavior in order to discover how to control it better. This is often called the *conflict between identification and control* because it appears in indirect methods as the conflict between conducting enough exploration to achieve model convergence and the objective of eventually following an optimal policy. Direct methods also require exploration and involve these same issues. Adaptive optimal control algorithms require mechanisms for resolving these problems, but no mechanism is universally favored. Some of the approaches for which rigorous theoretical results are available are reviewed by Kumar [39], and a variety of more heuristic approaches have been studied by Barto and Singh [3], Kaelbling [34], Moore [55], Schmidhuber [63], Sutton [69], Watkins [81], Thrun [78], and Thrun and Möller [79].

In the following subsections, we describe several non-Bayesian methods for solving Markovian decision problems with incomplete information. Although these methods can form the basis of algorithms that can be proved to converge to optimal policies, we do not describe exploration mechanisms with enough rigor for developing the theory in this direction. We call the first method the *generic indirect method*. A system identification algorithm updates a system model at each time step of control, and a conventional DP algorithm is executed *at each time step* based on the current system model. Although this method's computational complexity severely limits its utility, it is representative of most of the approaches described in the engineering literature, and it serves as a reference point for comparative purposes. Next, we describe another indirect method that is the simplest modification of the generic indirect method that takes advantage of RTDP. We call this method *Adaptive* RTDP. The third method we describe is the direct Q-Learning method of Watkins [81]. We then briefly describe hybrid direct/indirect methods.

7.1. The generic indirect method

Indirect adaptive methods for Markovian decision problems with incomplete information estimate the unknown state-transition probabilities and immediate costs based on the history of state transitions and immediate costs observed while the controller and system interact. The usual approach is to define the state-transition probabilities in terms of a parameter, θ, contained in some parameter space, Θ. Thus, for each pair of states $i, j \in S$ and each action $u \in U(i)$, $p(i, j, u, \theta)$ is the state-transition probability corresponding to parameter $\theta \in \Theta$, where the functional dependence on θ has a known form. Further, one usually assumes that there is some $\theta^* \in \Theta$ that is the true parameter, so that $p_{ij}(u) = p(i, j, u, \theta^*)$. The identification task is to estimate θ^* from experience. A common approach takes as the estimate of θ^* at each time step the parameter having the highest probability of generating the observed history, i.e., the maximum-likelihood estimate of θ^*.

The simplest form of this approach to identification is to assume that the unknown parameter is a list of the actual transition probabilities. Then at each time step t the system model consists of the maximum-likelihood estimates, denoted $p_{ij}^t(u)$, of the unknown state-transition probabilities for all pairs of states i, j and actions $u \in U(i)$. Let $n_{ij}^u(t)$ be the observed number of times before time step t that action u was executed when the system was in state i and made a transition to state j. Then $n_i^u(t) = \sum_{j \in S} n_{ij}^u(t)$ is the number of times action u was executed in state i. The maximum-likelihood state-transition probabilities at time t are

$$p_{ij}^t(u) = \frac{n_{ij}^u(t)}{n_i^u(t)}. \tag{10}$$

If the immediate costs, $c_i(u)$, are also unknown, they can be determined simply by memorizing them as they are observed.[17] If in an infinite number of time steps each action would be taken infinitely often in each state, then this system model converges to the true system. As mentioned above, it is nontrivial to ensure that this occurs while the system is being controlled.

At each time step t, the generic indirect method uses some (non real-time) DP algorithm to determine the optimal evaluation function for the latest system model. Let f_t^* denote this optimal evaluation function. Of course, if the model were correct, then f_t^* would equal f^*, but this is generally not the case. A *certainty equivalence optimal policy* for time step t is any policy that is greedy with respect to f_t^*. Let $\mu_t^* = [\mu_t^*(1), \ldots, \mu_t^*(n)]$ denote any such policy. Then at time step t, $\mu_t^*(s_t)$ is the *certainty equivalence optimal action*. Any of the off-line DP algorithms described above can be used to determine f_t^*, including asynchronous DP. Here it makes sense at each time step to initialize the DP algorithm with final estimate of f^* produced by the DP algorithm completed at the previous time step. The small change in the system model from time step t to $t+1$ means that f_t^* and f_{t+1}^* probably do not differ significantly. As pointed out above, however, the computation required to perform even one DP iteration can be prohibitive in problems with large numbers of states.

What action should the controller execute at time t? The certainty equivalence optimal action, $\mu_t^*(s_t)$, *appears* to be the best based on observations up to time t. Consequently, in pursuing its objective of control, the controller should always execute this action. However, because the current model is not necessarily correct, the controller must also pursue the identification objective, which dictates that it must sometimes select actions other than certainty equivalence optimal actions. It is easy to generate examples in which

---

[17] In problems in which the immediate cost is a random function of the current state and action, the maximum-likelihood estimate of an immediate cost is the observed average of the immediate cost for that state and action.

always following the current certainty equivalence optimal policy prevents convergence to a true optimal policy due to lack of exploration (see, for example, Kumar [39]).

One of the simplest ways to induce exploratory behavior is to make the controller use randomized policies in which actions are chosen according to probabilities that depend on the current evaluation function. Each action always has a nonzero probability of being executed, with the current certainty equivalence optimal action having the highest probability. To facilitate comparison of algorithms in the simulations described in Section 4.1, we adopt the action-selection method based on the Boltzmann distribution that was used by Watkins [81], Lin [47], and Sutton [69].

This method assigns an execution probability to each admissible action for the current state, where this probability is determined by a rating of each action's utility. We compute a rating, $r(u)$, of each action $u \in U(s_t)$ as follows:

$$r(u) = Q^{f_t^*}(s_t, u).$$

We then transform these ratings (which can be negative and do not sum to one) into a probability mass function over the admissible actions using the Boltzmann distribution: at time step t, the probability that the controller executes action $u \in U(s_t)$ is

$$\text{Prob}(u) = \frac{e^{-r(u)/T}}{\sum_{v \in U(s_t)} e^{-r(v)/T}}, \tag{11}$$

where T is a positive parameter controlling how sharply these probabilities peak at the certainty equivalence optimal action, $\mu_t^*(s_t)$. As T increases, these probabilities become more uniform, and as T decreases, the probability of executing $\mu_t^*(s_t)$ approaches one, while the probabilities of the other actions approach zero. T acts as a kind of "computational temperature" as used in simulated annealing [35] in which T decreases over time. Here it controls the necessary tradeoff between identification and control. At "zero temperature" there is no exploration, and the randomized policy equals the certainty equivalence optimal policy, whereas at "infinite temperature" there is no attempt at control.

In the simulations described in Section 4.1, we introduced exploratory behavior by using the method just described for generating randomized policies, and we let T decrease over time to a pre-selected minimum value as learning progressed. Our choice of this method was dictated by simplicity and our desire to illustrate algorithms that are as "generic" as possible. Without doubt, more sophisticated exploratory behavior would have beneficial effects on the behavior of these algorithms.

7.2. Adaptive real-time dynamic programming

The generic indirect method just presented relies on executing a non real-time DP algorithm until convergence at each time step. It is straightforward to substitute RTDP, resulting in the indirect method we call *Adaptive* RTDP. This method is exactly the same as RTDP as described in Section 6.1 except that (1) a system model is updated using some on-line system identification method, such as the maximum-likelihood method given by Eq. (10); (2) the current system model is used in performing the stages of RTDP instead of the true system model; and (3) the action at each time step is determined by the randomized policy given by Eq. (11), or by some other method that balances the identification and control objectives.

Adaptive RTDP is related to a number of algorithms that have been investigated by others. Although Sutton's *Dyna* architecture [69] focuses on Q-Learning and methods based on policy iteration (Section 8), it also encompasses algorithms such as Adaptive RTDP, as he discusses in [70]. Lin [46,47] also discusses methods closely related to Adaptive RTDP. In the engineering literature, Jalali and Ferguson [32] describe an algorithm that is similar to Adaptive RTDP, although they focus on Markovian decision problems in which performance is measured by the average cost per time step instead of the discounted cost we have discussed.

Performing RTDP concurrently with system identification, as in Adaptive RTDP, provides an opportunity to let progress in identification influence the selection of states to which the backup operation is applied. Sutton [69] suggested that it can be advantageous to back up the costs of states for which there is good confidence in the accuracy of the estimated state-transition probabilities. One can devise various measures of confidence in these estimates and direct the algorithm to the states whose cost backups use the most reliable state-transition information according to this confidence measure. At the same time, it is possible to use a confidence measure to direct the selection of actions so that the controller tends to visit regions of the state space where the confidence is *low* so as to improve the model for these regions. This strategy produces exploration that aids identification but can conflict with control. Kaelbling [34], Lin [47], Moore [55], Schmidhuber [63], Sutton [69], Thrun [78], and Thrun and Möller [79] discuss these and other possibilities.

7.3. Q-learning

Q-Learning is a method proposed by Watkins [81] for solving Markovian decision problems with incomplete information.[18] Unlike the indirect adaptive methods discussed above, it is a direct method because it does not use an explicit model of the dynamic system underlying the decision problem. It directly estimates the optimal Q-values for pairs of states and admissible actions (which we call admissible state–action pairs). Recall from Eq. (6) that $Q^*(i, u)$, the optimal Q-value for state i and action $u \in U(i)$, is the cost of generating action u in state i and thereafter following an optimal policy. Any policy selecting actions that are greedy with respect to the optimal Q-values is an optimal policy. Thus, if the optimal Q-values are available, an optimal policy can be determined with relatively little computation.

---

[18] Watkins [81] actually proposed a family of Q-Learning methods, and what we call Q-Learning in this article is the simplest case, which he called "one-step Q-Learning". He observed that although Q-Learning methods are based on a simple idea, they had not been suggested previously as far as he knew. He further observed, however, that because these problems had been so intensively studied for over thirty years, it would be surprising if no one had studied them earlier. Although the idea of assigning values to state-action pairs formed the basis of Denardo's [24] approach to DP, we have not seen algorithms like Q-Learning for estimating these values that predate Watkins' 1989 dissertation.

We depart somewhat in our presentation from the view taken by Watkins [81] and others (e.g., Sutton [69], Barto and Singh [3]) of Q-Learning as a method for adaptive on-line control. To emphasize Q-Learning's relationship with asynchronous DP, we first present the basic Q-Learning algorithm as an *off-line* asynchronous DP method that is unique in not requiring direct access to the state-transition probabilities of the decision problem. We then describe the more usual on-line view of Q-Learning.

7.3.1. Off-Line Q-Learning

Instead of maintaining an explicit estimate of the optimal evaluation function, as is done by all the methods described above, Q-Learning maintains estimates of the optimal Q-values for each admissible state–action pair. For any state i and action $u \in U(i)$, let $Q_k(i,u)$ be the estimate of $Q^*(i,u)$ available at stage k of the computation. Recalling that f^* is the minimum of the optimal Q-values for each state (Eq. (6)), we can think of the Q-values at stage k as implicitly defining f_k, a stage-k estimate of f^*, which is given for each state i by

$$f_k(i) = \min_{u \in U(i)} Q_k(i,u). \tag{12}$$

Although Q-values define an evaluation function in this way, they contain more information than the evaluation function. For example, actions can be ranked on the basis of Q-values alone, whereas ranking actions using an evaluation function also requires knowledge of the state-transition probabilities and immediate costs.

Instead of having direct access to the state-transition probabilities, Off-Line Q-Learning only has access to a random function that can generate samples according to these probabilities. Thus, if a state i and an action $u \in U(i)$ are input to this function, it returns a state j with probability $p_{ij}(u)$. Let us call this function `successor` so that $j = \texttt{successor}(i,u)$. The `successor` function amounts to an accurate model of the system in the form of its state-transition probabilities, but Q-Learning does not have access to the probabilities themselves. As we shall see below, in on-line Q-Learning, the role of the `successor` function is played by the system itself.

At each stage k, Off-Line Q-Learning synchronously updates the Q-values of a subset of the admissible state–action pairs and leaves unchanged the Q-values for the other admissible pairs. The subset of admissible state–action pairs whose Q-values are updated changes from stage to stage, and the choice of these subsets determines the precise nature of the algorithm. For each $k = 0, 1, \ldots$, let $S_k^Q \subseteq \{(i,u) \mid i \in S, \; u \in U(i)\}$ denote the set of admissible state–action pairs whose Q-values are updated at stage k. For each state–action pair in S_k^Q, it is necessary to define a learning rate parameter that determines how much of the new Q-value is determined by its old value and how much by a backed-up value. Let $\alpha_k(i,u), 0 < \alpha_k(i,u) < 1$, denote the learning rate parameter for updating the Q-value of (i,u) at stage k. Then Q_{k+1} is computed as follows: if $(i,u) \in S_k^Q$ then

$$\begin{aligned}
Q_{k+1}(i,u) &= (1 - \alpha_k(i,u))Q_k(i,u) \\
&\quad + \alpha_k(i,u)[c_i(u) + \gamma f_k(\texttt{successor}(i,u))],
\end{aligned} \tag{13}$$

where f_k is given by Eq. (12). The Q-values for the other admissible state–action pairs remain the same, i.e.,

$$Q_{k+1}(i,u) = Q_k(i,u),$$

for all admissible $(i,u) \notin S_k^Q$. By a Q-Learning backup we mean the application of Eq. (13) for a single admissible state–action pair (i,u).

If the Q-value for each admissible state–action pair (i,u) is backed up infinitely often in an infinite number of stages, and if the learning rate parameters $\alpha_k(i,u)$ decrease over the stages k in an appropriate way, then the sequence $\{Q_k(i,u)\}$ generated by Off-Line Q-Learning converges with probability one to $Q^*(i,u)$ as $k \to \infty$ for all admissible pairs (i,u). This is essentially proved by Watkins [81], and Watkins and Dayan present a revised proof in [82]. Appendix B describes a method for meeting the required learning rate conditions that was developed by Darken and Moody [19]. We used this method in obtaining the results for Real-Time Q-Learning on our example problems presented in Section 4.1.

One can gain insight into Off-Line Q-Learning by relating it to asynchronous DP. The stage-k Q-values for all admissible state–action pairs define the evaluation function f_k given by Eq. (12). Thus, one can view a stage of Off-Line Q-Learning defined by Eq. (13) as updating f_k to f_{k+1}, where for each state i,

$$f_{k+1}(i) = \min_{u \in U(i)} Q_{k+1}(i,u).$$

This evaluation function update does not correspond to a stage of any of the usual DP algorithms because it is based only on samples from successor for selected actions determined by the state–action pairs in S_k^Q. A conventional DP backup, in contrast, uses the true expected successor costs over all the admissible actions for a given state. [19]

It is accurate to think of Off-Line Q-Learning as a *more asynchronous version of asynchronous DP*. Asynchronous DP is asynchronous at the level of states, and the backup operation for each state requires minimizing expected costs over all admissible actions for that state. The amount of computation required to determine the expected cost for each admissible action depends on the number of *possible* successor states for that action, which can be as large as the total number of states in stochastic problems. Off-Line Q-Learning, on the other hand, is asynchronous at the level of admissible state–action pairs. Although each Q-Learning backup requires minimizing over all the admissible actions for a give state in order to calculate (via Eq. (12)) $f_k(\texttt{successor}(i,u))$ used in Eq. (13), [20] it does not require computation proportional to the number of possible successor states. Thus, in the stochastic case, an asynchronous DP backup can require $O(mn)$ computational steps, whereas a Q-Learning backup

---

[19] However, stage k of Off-Line Q-Learning has the same effect as the stage of asynchronous DP using S_k in the special case in which (1) the problem is deterministic, (2) S_k^Q is the set of all admissible state–action pairs for states in S_k, and (3) $\alpha_k(i,u) = 1$ for all admissible state–action pairs (i,u).

[20] This complete minimization can sometimes be avoided as follows. Whenever a $Q_k(i,u)$ is backed up, if its new value, $Q_{k+1}(i,u)$, is smaller than $f_k(i)$, then $f_{k+1}(i)$ is set to this smaller value. If its new value is larger than $f_k(i)$, then if $f_k(i) = Q_k(i,u)$ and $f_k(i) \neq Q_k(i,u')$ for any $u' \neq u$, then $f_{k+1}(i)$ is found by explicitly minimizing the current Q-values for state i over the admissible actions. This is the case in which u is the sole greedy action with respect to $f_k(i)$. Otherwise, nothing is done, i.e., $f_{k+1}(i) = f_k(i)$. This procedure therefore computes the minimization in Eq. (12) explicitly only when updating the Q-values for state–action pairs (i,u) in which u is the sole greedy action for i and the Q-value increases.

requires only $O(m)$. This advantage is offset by the increased space complexity of Q-Learning and the fact that a Q-Learning backup takes less information into account than does a backup of asynchronous DP: an asynchronous DP backup is comparable to many Q-Learning backups. Nevertheless, because the computation required by a Q-Learning backup can be much less than that required by an asynchronous DP backup, Q-Learning can be advantageous when stages have to be computed quickly despite a large number of possible successor states, as in real-time applications which we discuss next.

7.3.2. Real-Time Q-Learning

Off-Line Q-Learning can be turned into an on-line algorithm by executing it concurrently with control. If a current system model provides an approximate successor function, the result is an indirect adaptive method identical to Adaptive RTDP (Section 7.2) except that stages of Off-Line Q-Learning substitute for stages of asynchronous DP. This can have advantages over Adaptive RTDP when the number of admissible actions is large. However, we use the term *Real-Time Q-Learning* for the case originally discussed by Watkins [81] in which there is no model of the system underlying the decision problem and the real system acts as the successor function. This direct adaptive algorithm backs up the Q-value for only a single state–action pair at each time step of control, where this state–action pair consists of the observed current state and the action actually executed. Using Real-Time Q-Learning, therefore, one can compute an optimal policy without forming an explicit model of the system underlying the decision problem.

Specifically, assume that at each time step t the controller observes state s_t and has available the estimated optimal Q-values produced by all the preceding stages of Real-Time Q-Learning. We denote these estimates $Q_t(i, u)$ for all admissible state–action pairs (i, u). The controller selects an action $u_t \in U(s_t)$ using this information in some manner that allows for exploration. After executing u_t, the controller receives the immediate cost $c_{s_t}(u_t)$ while the system state changes to s_{t+1}. Then Q_{t+1} is computed as follows:

$$Q_{t+1}(s_t, u_t) = (1 - \alpha_t(s_t, u_t))Q_t(s_t, u_t) + \alpha_t(s_t, u_t)[c_{s_t}(u_t) + \gamma f_t(s_{t+1})], \quad (14)$$

where $f_t(s_{t+1}) = \min_{u \in U(s_{t+1})} Q_t(s_{t+1}, u)$ and $\alpha_t(s_t, u_t)$ is the learning rate parameter at time step t for the current state–action pair. The Q-values for all the other admissible state–action pairs remain the same, i.e.,

$$Q_{t+1}(i, u) = Q_t(i, u),$$

for all admissible $(i, u) \neq (s_t, u_t)$. This process repeats for each time step.

As far as convergence is concerned, Real-Time Q-Learning is the special case of Off-Line Q-Learning in which S_t^Q, the set of state–action pairs whose Q-values are backed up at each step (or stage) t, is $\{(s_t, u_t)\}$. Thus, the sequence of Q-values generated by Real-Time Q-Learning converges to the true values given by Q^* under the conditions required by for convergence of Off-Line Q-Learning. This means that each admissible action must be performed in each state infinitely often in an infinite number of control steps. It is also noteworthy, as pointed out by Dayan [22], that when there is only one admissible action for each state, Real-Time Q-Learning reduces to the TD(0) algorithm investigated by Sutton [68].

To define a complete adaptive control algorithm making use of Real-Time Q-Learning it is necessary to specify how each action is selected based on the current Q-values. Convergence to an optimal policy requires the same kind of exploration required by indirect methods to facilitate system identification as discussed above. Therefore, given a method for selecting an action from a current evaluation function, such as the randomized method described above (Eq. (11)), if this method leads to convergence of an indirect method, it also leads to convergence of the corresponding direct method based on Real-Time Q-Learning.

7.3.3. Other Q-Learning methods

In Real-Time Q-Learning, the real system underlying the decision problem plays the role of the successor function. However, it is also possible to define the successor function sometimes by the real system and sometimes by a system model. For state–action pairs actually experienced during control, the real system provides the successor function; for other state–action pairs, a system model provides an approximate successor function. Sutton [69] has studied this approach in an algorithm called *Dyna-Q*, which performs the basic Q-Learning backup using both actual state transitions as well as hypothetical state transitions simulated by a system model. Performing the Q-Learning backup on hypothetical state transitions amounts to running multiple stages of Off-Line Q-Learning in the intervals between times at which the controller executes actions. A step of Real-Time Q-Learning is performed based on each actual state transition. This is obviously only one of many possible ways to combine direct and indirect adaptive methods as emphasized in Sutton's discussion of the general *Dyna* learning architecture [69].

It is also possible to modify the basic Q-Learning method in a variety of ways in order to enhance its efficiency. For example, Lin [47] has studied a method in which Real-Time Q-Learning is augmented with model-based Off-Line Q-Learning only if one action does not clearly stand out as preferable according to the current Q-values. In this case, Off-Line Q-Learning is carried out to backup the Q-values for all of the admissible actions that are "promising" according to the latest Q-values for the current state. Watkins [81] describes a family of Q-Learning methods in which Q-values are backed up based on information gained over sequences of state transitions. One way to implement this kind of extension is to use the "eligibility trace" idea [4, 37, 67, 68, 72] to back up the Q-values of all the state–action pairs experienced in the past, with the magnitudes of the backups decreasing to zero with increasing time in the past. Sutton's [68] TD(λ) algorithms illustrate this idea. Attempting to present all of the combinations and variations of Q-Learning methods that have been, or could be, described is well beyond the scope of the present article. Barto and Singh [3], Dayan [20,21], Lin [46,47], Moore [57], and Sutton [69] present comparative empirical studies of some of the adaptive algorithms based on Q-Learning.

8. Methods based on explicit policy representations

All of the DP-based learning algorithms described above, both non-adaptive and adaptive cases, use an explicit representation of either an evaluation function or a function giving the Q-values of admissible state–action pairs. These functions are used in computing the action at each time step, but the policy so defined is not explicitly stored. There are a number of other real-time learning and control methods based on DP in which policies as well as evaluation functions are stored and updated at each time step of control. Unlike the methods addressed in this article, these methods are more closely related to the *policy iteration* DP algorithm than the value iteration algorithms discussed in Section 5.

Policy iteration (see, e.g., Bertsekas [11]) alternates two phases: (1) a *policy eval-uation* phase, in which the evaluation function for the current policy is determined, and (2) a *policy improvement* phase, in which the current policy is updated to be greedy with respect to the current evaluation function. One way to evaluate a policy is by exe-cuting one of the value iteration algorithms discussed in Section 5 under the assumption that there is only one admissible action for each state, namely, the action specified by the policy being evaluated. Alternatively, explicit matrix inversion methods can be used. Although policy evaluation does not require repeated minimizing over all admissible actions, it can still require too much computation to be practical for large state sets. More feasible is *modified policy iteration* [59], which is policy iteration except that the policy evaluation phase is not executed to completion before each policy improvement phase. Real-time algorithms based on policy iteration effectively work by executing an asynchronous form of modified policy iteration concurrently with control.

Examples of such methods appear in the pole-balancing system of Barto, Sutton, and Anderson [4,67] (also [1,67]) and the *Dyna-PI* method of Sutton [69] (where PI means Policy Iteration). Barto, Sutton, and Watkins [5,6] discuss the connection between these methods and policy iteration in some detail. In this article we do not discuss learning algorithms based on policy iteration because their theory is not yet as well understood as is the theory of learning algorithms based on asynchronous value iteration. However, Williams and Baird [91] have made a valuable contribution to this theory by addressing DP algorithms that are asynchronous at a grain finer than that of either asynchronous DP or Q-Learning. These algorithms include value iteration, policy iteration, and modified policy iteration as special cases. Integrating their theory with that presented here is beyond the scope of this article.

9. Storing evaluation functions

An issue of great practical importance in implementing any of the algorithms de-scribed in this article is how evaluation functions are represented and stored.[21] The theoretical results we have described assume a lookup-table representation of evaluation functions, which—at least in principle—is always possible when the number of states

---

[21] All of our comments here also apply to storing the Q-values of admissible state–action pairs.

and admissible actions is finite, as assumed throughout this article. In applying conventional DP to problems involving continuous states and/or actions, the usual practice is to discretize the ranges of the continuous state variables and then use the lookup-table representation (cf. the "boxes" representation used by Michie and Chambers [52] and Barto, Sutton, and Anderson [4]). This leads to space complexity exponential in the number of state variables, the situation prompting Bellman [9] to coin the phrase "curse of dimensionality". The methods described in this article based on asynchronous DP and Q-Learning do not circumvent the curse of dimensionality, although the focusing behavior of Trial-Based RTDP in stochastic shortest path problems with designated start states can reduce the storage requirement if memory is allocated incrementally during trials.

A number of methods exist for making the lookup-table representation more efficient when it is not necessary to store the costs of all possible states. Hash table methods, as assumed by Korf [38] for LRTA*, permit efficient storage and retrieval when the costs of a small enough subset of the possible states need to be stored. Similarly, using the *kd-tree* data structure to access state costs, as explored by Moore [55, 56], can provide efficient storage and retrieval of the costs of a finite set of states from a k-dimensional state space. The theoretical results described in this article extend to these methods because they preserve the integrity of the stored costs (assuming hash collisions are resolved).

Other approaches to storing evaluation functions use function approximation methods based on parameterized models. For example, in Samuel's [61] checkers player, the evaluation function was approximated as a weighted sum of the values of a set of features describing checkerboard configurations. The basic backup operation was performed on the weights, not on the state costs themselves. The weights were adjusted to reduce to the discrepancy between the current cost of a state and its backed-up cost. This approach inspired a variety of more recent studies using parameterized function approximations. The discrepancy supplies the error for any error-correction procedure that approximates functions based on a training set of function samples. This is a form of supervised learning, or learning from examples, and provides the natural way to make use of connectionist networks as shown, for example, by Anderson [1] and Tesauro [77]. Parametric approximations of evaluation functions are useful because they can generalize beyond the training data to supply cost estimates for states that have not yet been visited, an important factor for large state sets.

In fact, almost any supervised learning method, and its associated manner of representing hypotheses, can be adapted for approximating evaluation functions. This includes symbolic methods for learning from examples. These methods also generalize beyond the training information, which is derived from the backup operations of various DP-based algorithms. For example, Chapman and Kaelbling [15] and Tan [76] adapt decision-tree methods, and Mahadevan and Connell [49] use a statistical clustering method. Yee [94] discusses function approximation from the perspective of its use with DP-based learning algorithms.

Despite the large number of studies in which the principles of DP have been combined with generalizing methods for approximating evaluation functions, *the theoretical results presented in this article do not automatically extend to these approaches*. Although generalization can be helpful in approximating an optimal evaluation function, it is often detrimental to the convergence of the underlying asynchronous DP algorithm, as pointed out by Watkins [81] and illustrated with a simple example by Bradtke [13]. Even if a function approximation scheme can adequately represent the optimal evaluation function when trained on samples from this function, it does not follow that an adequate representation will result from an iterative DP algorithm that uses such an approximation scheme at each stage. The issues are much the same as those that arise in numerically solving differential equations. The objective of these problems is to approximate the function that is the solution of a differential equation (for given boundary conditions) in the absence of training examples drawn from the true solution. In other words, the objective is to *solve approximately* the differential equation, not just to approximate its solution. Here, we are interested in approximately solving the Bellman Optimality Equation and not the easier problem of approximating a solution that is already available.

There is an extensive literature on function approximation methods and DP, such as multigrid methods and methods using splines and orthogonal polynomials (e.g., Bellman and Dreyfus [7], Bellman, Kalaba, and Kotkin [8], Daniel [18], Kushner and Dupuis [41]). However, most of this literature is devoted to off-line algorithms for cases in which there is a complete model of the decision problem. Adapting techniques from this literature to produce approximation methods for RTDP and other DP-based learning algorithms is a challenge for future research.

To the best of our knowledge, there are only a few theoretical results that directly address the use of generalizing methods with DP-based learning algorithms. The results of Sutton [68] and Dayan [22] concern using TD methods to evaluate a given policy as a linear combination of a complete set of linearly independent basis vectors. Unfortunately these results do not address the problem of representing an evaluation function more compactly than it would be represented in a lookup table. Bradtke [13] addresses the problem of learning Q-values that are quadratic functions of a continuous state, but these results are restricted to linear quadratic regulation problems. However, Singh and Yee [66] point out that in the discounted case, small errors in approximating an evaluation function (or a function giving Q-values) lead at worst to small decrements in the performance of a controller using the approximate evaluation function as the basis of control. Without such a result, it might seem plausible that small evaluation errors can drastically undermine control performance—a condition which, if true, would raise concerns about combining DP-based learning with function approximation. Much more research is needed to provide a better understanding of how function approximation methods can be used effectively with the algorithms described in this article.

10. Illustrations of DP-based learning

We used the race track problem described in Section 4.1 to illustrate and compare conventional DP, RTDP, Adaptive RTDP, and Real-Time Q-Learning using the two race tracks shown in Fig. 1. The small race track shown in Panel A has 4 start states, 87 goal states, and 9,115 states reachable from the start states by any policy. We have not shown the squares on which the car might land after crossing the finish line. The

Table 1

Example race track problems. The results were obtained by executing Gauss–Seidel DP (GSDP)

	Small Track	Larger Track
Number of reachable states	9,115	22,576
Number of goal states	87	590
Estimated number of relevant states	599	2,618
Optimum expected path length	14.67	24.10
Number of GSDP sweeps to convergence	28	38
Number of GSDP backups to convergence	252,784	835,468
Number of GSDP sweeps to optimal policy	15	24
Number of GSDP backups to optimal policy	136,725	541,824

larger race track shown in Panel B has 6 start states, 590 goal states, and 22,576 states reachable from the start states. We set $p = 0.1$ so that the controller's intended actions were executed with probability 0.9.

We applied conventional Gauss–Seidel DP to each race track problem, by which we mean Gauss–Seidel value iteration as defined in Section 5.2, with $\gamma = 1$ and with the initial evaluation function assigning zero cost to each state. Gauss–Seidel DP converges under these conditions because it is a special case of asynchronous DP, which converges here because the conditions given in Section 5.3 are satisfied. Specifically, it is clear that there is at least one proper policy for either track (it is possible for the car to reach the finish line from any reachable state, although it may have to hit the wall and restart to do so) and every improper policy incurs infinite cost for at least one state because the immediate costs of all non-goal states are positive. We selected a state ordering for applying Gauss–Seidel DP without concern for any influence it might have on convergence rate (although we found that with the selected ordering, Gauss–Seidel DP converged in approximately half the number of sweeps as did synchronous DP).

Table 1 summarizes the small and larger race track problems and the computational effort required to solve them using Gauss–Seidel DP. Gauss–Seidel DP was considered to have converged to the optimal evaluation function when the maximum cost change over all states between two successive sweeps was less than 10^{-4}. We estimated the number of relevant states for each race track, i.e., the number of states reachable from the start states under any optimal policy, by counting the states visited while executing optimal actions for 10^7 trials.

We also estimated the earliest point in the DP computation at which the optimal evaluation function approximation was good enough so that the corresponding greedy policy was an optimal policy. (Recall that an optimal policy can be a greedy policy with respect to many evaluation functions.) We did this by running 10^7 test trials after each sweep using a policy that was greedy with respect to the evaluation function produced by that sweep. For each sweep, we recorded the average path length produced over these test trials. After convergence of Gauss–Seidel DP, we compared these averages with the optimal expected path length obtained by the DP algorithm, noting the sweep after which the average path length was first within 10^{-2} of the optimal. The resulting numbers of sweeps and backups are listed in Table 1 in the rows labeled "Number of GSDP sweeps to optimal policy" and "Number of GSDP backups to optimal policy".

Although optimal policies emerged considerably earlier in these computations than did the optimal evaluation functions, it is important to note that this estimation process is not a part of conventional off-line value iteration algorithms and requires a considerable amount of additional computation.[22] Nevertheless, the resulting numbers of backups are useful in assessing the computational requirements of the real-time algorithms, which should allow controllers to follow optimal policies after comparable numbers of backups.

We applied RTDP, Adaptive RTDP, and Real-Time Q-Learning to both race track problems. Because all the immediate costs are positive, we know that $f^*(i)$ must be nonnegative for all states i. Thus, setting the initial costs of all the states to zero produces a non-overestimating initial evaluation function as required by Theorem 3. We applied the real-time algorithms in a trial-based manner, starting each trial with the car placed on the starting line with zero velocity, where each square on the starting line was selected with equal probability. A trial ended when the car reached a goal state. Thus, according to Theorem 3, with $\gamma = 1$, RTDP will converge to the optimal evaluation function with repeated trials. Although RTDP and Adaptive RTDP can back up the costs of many states at each control step, we restricted attention to the simplest case in which they only back up the cost of the current state at each time step. This is the case in which $B_t = \{s_t\}$ for all t. Obviously, all of these algorithms were applied in simulation mode.

We executed 25 runs of each algorithm using different random number seeds, where a run is a sequence of trials beginning with the evaluation function initialized to zero. To monitor the performance of each algorithm, we kept track of path lengths, that is, how many moves the car took in going from the starting line to the finish line, in each trial of each run. To record these data, we divided each run into a sequence of disjoint *epochs*, where an epoch is a sequence of 20 consecutive trials. By an *epoch path length* we mean the average of the path lengths generated during an epoch using a given algorithm. Adaptive RTDP and Real-Time Q-Learning were applied under conditions of incomplete information, and for these algorithms we induced exploratory behavior by using randomized policies based on the Boltzmann distribution as described in Section 7.1. To control the tradeoff between identification and control, we decreased the parameter T in Eq. (11) after each move until it reached a pre-selected minimum value; T was initialized at the beginning of each run. Parameter values and additional simulation details are provided in Appendix B.

Fig. 2 shows results for RTDP (Panel A), Adaptive RTDP (Panel B), and Real-Time Q-Learning (Panel C). The central line in each graph shows the epoch path length averaged over the 25 runs of the corresponding algorithm. The upper and lower lines show ± 1 standard deviation about this average for the sample of 25 runs. Although the average epoch path lengths for the initial several epochs of each algorithm are too large to show on the graphs, it is useful to note that the average epoch path lengths for the first epoch of RTDP, Adaptive RTDP, and Real-Time Q-Learning are respectively 455, 866, and 13,403 moves. That these initial average path lengths are so large, especially for Real-Time Q-Learning, reflects the primitive nature of our exploration strategy.

---

[22] Policy iteration algorithms address this problem by explicitly generating a sequence of improving policies, but updating a policy requires computing its corresponding evaluation function, which is generally a time-consuming computation.

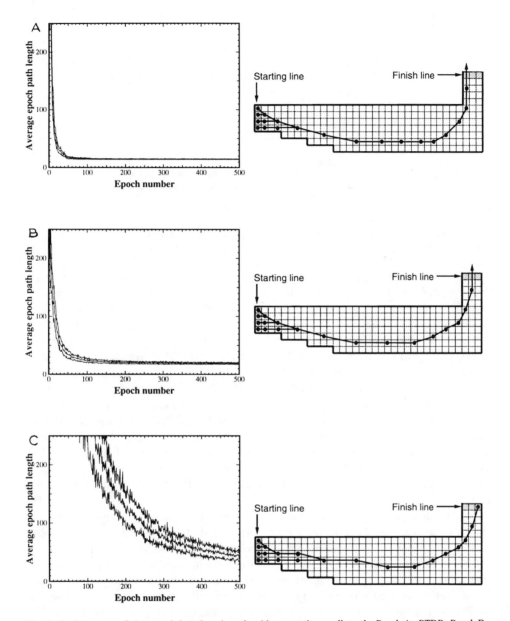

Fig. 2. Performance of three real-time learning algorithms on the small track. Panel A: RTDP. Panel B: Adaptive RTDP. Panel C: Real-Time Q-Learning. The central line in each graph shows the epoch path length averaged over the 25 runs of the corresponding algorithm. The upper and lower lines show ±1 standard deviation of the epoch path length for the sample of 25 runs. Exploration was controlled for Adaptive RTDP and Real-Time Q-Learning by decreasing T after each move until it reached a pre-selected minimum value. The right side of each panel shows the paths the car would follow in noiseless conditions from each start state after effective convergence of the corresponding algorithm.

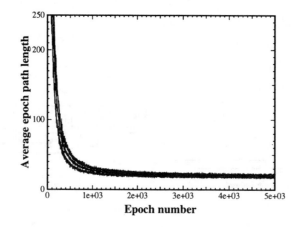

Fig. 3. Performance of Real-Time Q-Learning on the small track for 5,000 epochs. The initial part of the graph shows the data plotted in Panel C of Fig. 2 but at a different horizontal scale.

It is clear from the graphs that in this problem RTDP learned faster (and with less variance) than Adaptive RTDP and Real-Time Q-Learning, when learning rate is measured in terms of the number of epochs (numbers of moves are given in Table 2 discussed below). This is not surprising given the differences between the versions of the problem with complete information (Panel A) and with incomplete information (Panels B and C). That the performances of RTDP and Adaptive RTDP were so similar despite these differences reflects the fact that the maximum-likelihood system identification procedure used by the latter algorithm converged rapidly on relevant states due to the low level of stochasticity in the problem ($p = 0.1$). These graphs also show that Real-Time Q-Learning takes very many more epochs than do RTDP and Adaptive RTDP to reach a similar level of performance. This reflects the fact that each backup in Real-Time Q-Learning takes into account less information than do the backups in RTDP or Adaptive RTDP, a disadvantage somewhat offset by the relative computational simplicity of each Q-Learning backup. Fig. 3 shows the Real-Time Q-Learning results out to 5,000 epochs.

A convenient way to show the policies that result from these algorithms is to show the paths the car would follow from each start state if all sources of randomness were turned off; that is, if both random exploration and the randomness in the problem's state-transition function were turned off. At the right in each panel of Fig. 2 are paths generated in this way by the policies produced after each algorithm was judged to have "effectively converged". We inspected the graphs to find the smallest epoch numbers at which the average epoch path lengths essentially reached their asymptotic levels: 200 epochs for RTDP (Panel A), 300 epochs for Adaptive RTDP (Panel B), and 2,000 epochs for Real-Time Q-Learning (Panel C). Treated with appropriate caution, these effective convergence times are useful in comparing algorithms.

The path shown in Panel A of Fig. 2 is optimal in the sense that it was produced in noiseless conditions by a policy that is optimal for the stochastic problem. The paths in Panels B and C, on the other hand, were not generated by an optimal policy despite the fact that each is a move shorter than the path of Panel A. The control decisions made

Table 2
Summary of learning performance on the small track for Real-Time DP (RTDP), Adaptive Real-Time DP (ARTDP), and Real-Time Q-Learning (RTQ). The amount of computation required by Gauss–Seidel DP (GSDP) is included for comparative purposes

	GSDP	RTDP	ARTDP	RTQ
Average time to effective convergence	28 sweeps	200 epochs	300 epochs	2,000 epochs
Estimated path length at effective convergence	14.56	14.83	15.10	15.44
Average number of backups	252,784	127,538	218,554	2,961,790
Average number of backups per epoch	—	638	728	1,481
% of states backed up $\leqslant$ 100 times	—	98.45	96.47	53.34
% of states backed up $\leqslant$ 10 times	—	80.51	65.41	6.68
% of states backed up 0 times	—	3.18	1.74	1.56

toward the end of the track by these suboptimal policies produce higher probability that the car will collide with the track boundary under stochastic conditions. Although we do not illustrate it here, as the amount of uncertainty in the problem increases (increasing p), optimal policies generate paths that are more "conservative" in the sense of keeping safer distances from the track boundary and maintaining lower velocities.

Table 2 provides additional information about the performance of the real-time algorithms on the small track. For comparative purposes, the table includes a column for Gauss–Seidel DP. We estimated the path length after the effective convergence of RTDP, Adaptive RTDP, and Real-Time Q-Learning by executing 500 test trials with learning turned off using the policy produced at effective convergence of each algorithm. We also turned off the random exploration used by the latter two algorithms. The row of Table 2 labeled "Estimated path length at effective convergence" gives the average path length over these test trials.[23] RTDP is most directly comparable to Gauss–Seidel DP. After about 200 epochs, or 4,000 trials, RTDP improved control performance to the point where a trial took an average of 14.83 moves. RTDP performed an average of 127,538 backups in reaching this level of performance, about half the number required by Gauss–Seidel DP to converge to the optimal evaluation function. This number of backups is comparable to the 136,725 backups in the 15 sweeps of Gauss–Seidel DP after which the resulting evaluation function defines an optimal policy (Table 1).

Another way to compare Gauss–Seidel DP and RTDP is to examine how the backups they perform are distributed over the states. Whereas the cost of every state was backed up in each sweep of Gauss–Seidel DP, RTDP focused backups on fewer states. For example, in the first 200 epochs of an average run, RTDP backed up the costs of 98.45% of the states no more than 100 times and 80.51% of the states no more than 10 times; the costs of about 290 states were not backed up at all in an average run. Although we did not collect these statistics for RTDP after 200 epochs, it became even more focused on the states on optimal paths.

---

[23] These path length estimates are somewhat smaller than the average epoch path lengths shown at effective convergence in the graphs of Fig. 2 because they were produced with exploration turned off, whereas the graphs show path lengths produced with random exploration turned on. For Gauss–Seidel DP, we averaged over the costs of the start states given by the computed optimal evaluation function to obtain the estimated path length listed in Table 2.

Not surprisingly, solving the problem under conditions of incomplete information requires more backups. Adaptive RTDP took 300 epochs, or an average of 218,554 backups, to achieve trials averaging 15.1 moves at effective convergence. Real-time Q-Learning took 2,000 epochs, or an average of 2,961,790 backups, to achieve a somewhat less skillful level of performance (see Fig. 3). Examining how these backups were distributed over states shows that Adaptive RTDP was considerably more focused than was Real-Time Q-Learning. In the first 300 epochs Adaptive RTDP backed up 96.47% of the states no more than 100 times and 65.41% of the states no more than 10 times. On the other hand, in 2,000 epochs Real-Time Q-Learning backed up Q-values for 53.34% of the states no more than 100 times and only 6.68% of the states no more than 10 times. [24] Again, these results for Real-Time Q-Learning reflect the inadequacy of our primitive exploration strategy for this algorithm.

Fig. 4 shows results for RTDP, Adaptive RTDP, and Real-Time Q-Learning on the larger race track, and Table 3 provides additional information. These results were obtained under the same conditions described above for the small track. Fig. 5 shows the Real-Time Q-Learning results for the larger track out to 7,500 epochs. We judged that RTDP, Adaptive RTDP, and Real-Time Q-Learning effectively converged at 500, 400, and 3,000 epochs respectively. That Adaptive RTDP effectively converged faster than RTDP in terms of the number of epochs is partially due to the fact that its epochs tended to have more moves, and hence more backups, than the epochs of RTDP. We can see that to achieve slightly suboptimal performance, RTDP required about 62% of the computation of conventional Gauss–Seidel DP. The average epoch path lengths for the initial epoch of each algorithm, which are too large to show on the graphs, are 7,198, 8,749, and 180,358 moves, respectively, for RTDP, Adaptive RTDP, and Real-Time Q-Learning. Again, these large numbers of moves, especially for Real-Time Q-Learning, reflect the primitive nature of our exploration strategy. The paths shown at the right in each panel of Fig. 4 were generated in noiseless conditions by the policies produced at effective convergence of the corresponding algorithms. The path shown in Panel A of Fig. 4 is optimal in the sense that it was produced in noiseless conditions by a policy that is optimal for the stochastic problem. The paths in Panels B and C, on the other hand, were generated by slightly suboptimal policies.

Although these simulations are not definitive comparisons of the real-time algorithms with conventional DP, they illustrate some of their features. Whereas Gauss–Seidel DP continued to back up the costs of all the states, the real-time algorithms strongly focused on subsets of the states that were relevant to the control objectives. This focus became increasingly narrow as learning continued. Because the convergence theorem for Trial-Based RTDP applies to the simulations of RTDP, we know that this algorithm eventually would have focused only on relevant states, i.e., on states making up optimal paths. RTDP achieved nearly optimal control performance with about 50% of the computation of Gauss–Seidel DP on the small track and about 62% of the computation of Gauss–Seidel DP on the larger track. Adaptive RTDP and Real-Time Q-Learning also focused on progressively fewer states, but we did not run the generic indirect method for comparison because it is too inefficient to apply to problems with as many states as our race track

---

[24] We considered a Q-value for a state i to be backed up whenever $Q(i, u)$ was updated for some $u \in U(i)$.

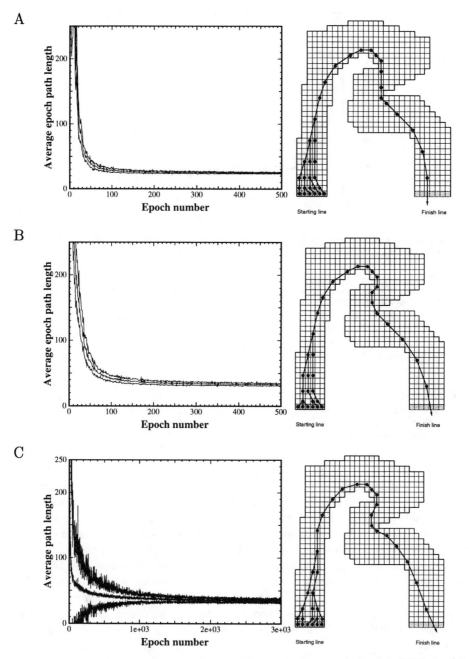

Fig. 4. Performance of three real-time learning algorithms on the larger track. Panel A: RTDP. Panel B: Adaptive RTDP. Panel C: Real-Time Q-Learning. The central line in each graph shows the epoch path length averaged over the 25 runs of the corresponding algorithm. The upper and lower lines show ±1 standard deviation of the epoch path length for the sample of 25 runs. Exploration was controlled for Adaptive RTDP and Real-Time Q-Learning by decreasing T after each move until it reached a pre-selected minimum value. The right side of each panel shows the paths the car would follow in noiseless conditions from each start state after effective convergence of the corresponding algorithm.

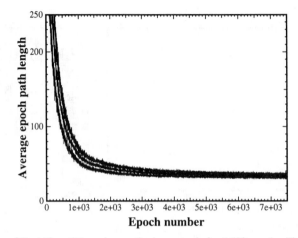

Epoch number

Fig. 5. Performance of Real-Time Q-Learning on the larger track for 7,500 epochs. The initial part of the graph shows the same data as plotted in Panel C of Fig. 4 but at a different horizontal scale.

Table 3
Summary of learning performance on the larger track for Real-Time DP (RTDP), Adaptive Real-Time DP (ARTDP), and Real-Time Q-Learning (RTQ). The amount of computation required by Gauss–Seidel DP (GSDP) is included for comparative purposes

	GSDP	RTDP	ARTDP	RTQ
Average time to effective convergence	38 sweeps	500 epochs	400 epochs	3,000 epochs
Estimated path length at effective convergence	24.10	24.62	24.72	25.04
Average number of backups	835,468	517,356	653,774	10,330,994
Average number of backups per epoch	—	1,035	1,634	3,444
% of states backed up $\leqslant$ 100 times	—	97.77	90.03	52.43
% of states backed up $\leqslant$ 10 times	—	70.46	59.90	8.28
% of states backed up 0 times	—	8.17	3.53	2.70

problems: It would have to perform at least one complete sweep for each move. In sharp contrast, the amount of computation required by each of the real-time algorithms for each move was small enough not to have been a limiting factor in the simulations.[25]

The results described here for Adaptive RTDP and Real-Time Q-Learning were produced by using an exploration strategy that decreased the randomness in selecting actions by decreasing T after each move until it reached a pre-selected minimum value. Although not described here, we also conducted experiments with different minimum values and with decreasing T after trials instead of after moves. Performance of the algorithms was much altered (for the worse) by these changes. Although we made no systematic attempt to investigate the effects of various exploration strategies, it is clear that the performance of these algorithms is highly sensitive to how exploration is introduced and controlled.

---

[25] However, in implementing Adaptive RTDP on the race track problems, we took advantage of our knowledge that for any action there are only two possible successors to any state. This allowed us to avoid performing at each move the n divisions required in a straightforward implementation of Eq. (10). This is not possible under the general conditions of incomplete information.

How the algorithms scale up to larger problems is also not adequately addressed by our simulations. Although the results with the small and the larger race track give some indication as to how the algorithms might scale, this collection of problems is not adequate for studying this issue. The variability of an algorithm's performance as a function of problem details other than the size of its state and action sets make it difficult to extrapolate from its performance on just two problems. Proceeding to larger problems is hampered by the large space requirements of these algorithms if they continue to use lookup tables for storing evaluation functions. Tesauro's TD-Gammon system [77] is an encouraging data point for using DP-based learning in conjunction with function approximation methods in problems much larger than those described here, but continued theoretical research is necessary to address the computational complexity of real-time DP algorithms. What is clear from our simulations, however, is that real-time DP algorithms can confer significant computational advantages over conventional off-line DP algorithms.

In concluding our discussion of the race track problem, we again point out that it is misleading to think of our application DP-based learning algorithms to this problem as the most productive way to apply them to realistic robot navigation tasks. For example, DP-based learning applied to this formulation of a race track problem refines skill in racing on a specific track. This skill does not transfer to other tracks due to the specificity with which a track is represented. More realistic applications of DP-based learning to robot navigation requires more abstract states and actions, as in the work of Lin [45] and Mahadevan and Connell [49].

11. Discussion

Conventional DP algorithms are of limited utility for problems with large state spaces, such as the combinatorial state spaces of many problems of interest in AI, because they require fully expanding all possible states and storing a cost for each state. Heuristic search, in contrast, selectively explores a problem's state space. However, because DP algorithms successively approximate optimal evaluation functions, they are relevant to learning in a way that heuristic search is not. They effectively cache in a permanent data structure the results of repeated searches forward from each state. This information improves as the algorithm proceeds, ultimately converging to the optimal evaluation function, from which one can determine optimal policies with relative ease. Although some heuristic search algorithms (such as A*) update an estimate of the cost to reach states from an initial state, they typically do not update the heuristic evaluation function estimating the cost to reach a goal state from each state.

Although the principles of DP are relevant to learning, conventional DP algorithms are not really learning algorithms because they operate off-line. They are not designed to be applied *during* problem solving or control, whereas learning occurs as experience accumulates during actual (or simulated) attempts at problem solving or control. However, it is possible to execute an otherwise off-line DP algorithm concurrently with actual or simulated control, where the DP algorithm can influence, and can be influenced by, the ongoing control process. Doing this so as to satisfy certain requirements results in the algorithm we call RTDP, a special case of which essentially coincides with Korf's LRTA* [38] algorithm. This general approach follows previous research by others in which DP principles have been used for problem solving and learning (e.g., [61, 69, 70, 81, 87, 88]).

Our contribution in this article has been to bring to bear on DP-based learning the theory of asynchronous DP as presented by Bertsekas and Tsitsiklis [12]. Although the suitability of asynchronous DP for implementation on multi-processor systems motivated this theory, we have made novel use of these results. Applying these results, especially the results on stochastic shortest path problems, to RTDP provides a new theoretical basis for DP-based learning algorithms. Convergence theorems for asynchronous DP imply that RTDP retains the competence of conventional synchronous and Gauss–Seidel DP algorithms, and the extension of Korf's LRTA* convergence theorem to this framework provides conditions under which RTDP avoids the exhaustive nature of off-line DP algorithms while still ultimately yielding optimal behavior.

We used the term *simulation mode* to refer to the execution of RTDP and related algorithms during simulated control instead of actual control. DP-based learning in simulation mode is illustrated by Samuel's checkers playing system [61, 62], Tesauro's backgammon playing system [77], and our illustrations of RTDP using the race track problem. Despite the fact that DP-based learning algorithms executed in simulation mode are actually off-line algorithms, we still treat them as learning algorithms because they incrementally improve control performance through simulated experience instead of solely through the application of more abstract computational methods. For algorithms, like RTDP, that require an accurate model of the decision problem, simulation mode is always an option and has obvious advantages due to the large number of trials often required. Applying RTDP during actual control makes sense when there is not enough time to compute a satisfactory policy by any off-line method before actual control must begin.

Whether applied during actual control or in simulation mode, RTDP can have significant advantages over conventional DP algorithms. Because RTDP is responsive to the demands of control in selecting states to which the backup operation is applied, it can focus computation onto parts of the state set for which control information is likely to be most important for improving control performance. The convergence theorem for Trial-Based RTDP applied to stochastic shortest path problems specifies conditions under which RTDP focuses on states that are on optimal paths—eventually abandoning all the other states—to produce a policy that is optimal on these relevant states without continuing to back up the costs of all the states, and possibly without backing up the costs of some states even once. Our illustrations using the race track problem show that RTDP can obtain near optimal policies in some problems with significantly less computation than is required by conventional DP. However, more compelling is the fact that the approach illustrated by RTDP can form useful approximations to optimal evaluation functions in problems to which conventional DP cannot be feasibly applied at all. We mentioned, for example, that in backgammon, a single sweep of conventional DP would take more than 1,000 years using a 1,000 MIPS processor. This is true despite the fact that a large fraction of the states of backgammon are irrelevant in normal play.

RTDP is closely related to Monte Carlo algorithms that achieve computational efficiency by automatically allocating computation so that, for example, unimportant terms in a sum correspond to very rare events in the computational process [17]. For this reason, the computational efficiency of Monte Carlo methods can exceed that of other methods for some classes of problems. However, Monte Carlo methods are generally not competitive with deterministic methods for small problems or when high-precision answers are required. More research is needed to fully elucidate these correspondences and to exploit them in refining DP-based learning methods and understanding their computational complexity.

For problems that have very large states sets (such as backgammon), the lookup-table method for storing evaluation functions to which we have restricted attention is not practical. Much of the research on DP-based learning methods has made use of other storage schemes. For problems in which DP-based learning algorithms focus on increasingly small subsets of states, as illustrated in our simulations of the race track problem, data structures such as hash tables and *kd*-trees can allow the algorithms to perform well despite dramatically reduced space requirements. One can also adapt supervised learning procedures to use each backup operation of a DP-based learning method to provide training information. If these methods can generalize adequately from the training data, they can provide efficient means for storing evaluation functions. Although some success has been achieved with methods that can generalize, such as connectionist networks, the theory we have presented in this article does not automatically extend to these cases. Generalization can disrupt the convergence of asynchronous DP. Additional research is needed to understand how one can effectively combine function approximation methods with asynchronous DP.

In addition to the case in which an accurate model of the decision problem is available, we also devoted considerable attention to Markovian decision problems with incomplete information, i.e., problems for which an accurate model is not available. Adopting the terminology of the engineering literature, these problems require adaptive control methods. We described indirect and direct approaches to these problems. The method we called the *generic indirect method* is representative of the majority of algorithms described in the engineering literature applicable to Markovian decision problems with incomplete information. A system identification algorithm adjusts a system model on-line during control, and the controller selects actions based on a current estimate of the optimal evaluation function computed by a conventional DP algorithm under the assumption that the current model accurately models the system. The DP algorithm is re-executed whenever the system model is updated. Although this approach is theoretically convenient, it is much too costly to apply to large problems.

Adaptive RTDP results from substituting RTDP for conventional DP in the generic indirect method. This means that RTDP is executed using the most recent system model generated by the system identification algorithm. Adaptive RTDP can be tailored for the available computational resources by adjusting the number of DP stages it executes at each time step of control. Due to the additional uncertainty in this case, learning is necessarily slower than in the non-adaptive case when measured by the number of backups required. However, the amount of computation required to select each control action is roughly the same. This means that it is practical to apply Adaptive RTDP to problems that are much larger than those for which it is practical to apply methods, such as the generic indirect method, that re-execute a conventional DP algorithm whenever the system model is updated.

In addition to indirect adaptive methods, we discussed direct adaptive methods. Direct methods do not form explicit models of the system underlying the decision problem. We described Watkin's [81] Q-Learning algorithm, which approximates the optimal evaluation function without forming estimates of state-transition probabilities. Q-Learning instead uses sample state transitions, either generated by a system model or observed during actual control. Q-Learning is an asynchronous DP algorithm that operates at a finer grain than the asynchronous DP algorithm described in Section 5.3. Whereas the basic operation of asynchronous DP is backing up the cost of a state, requiring computation proportional to the number of possible successor states, the basic operation of Q-Learning is backing up the Q-value of a state–action pair, a computation that does not depend on the number of possible successor states. The fine grain of the basic Q-Learning backup allows Real-Time Q-Learning to focus on selected actions in addition to selected states in a way that is responsive to the behavior of the controlled system. The cost of this flexibility is the increased space required to store the Q-values of state–action pairs and the fact that a Q-Learning backup does not gather as much information as does a complete DP backup operation.

Sophisticated exploration strategies are important in solving Markovian decision problems under conditions of both complete and incomplete information. With complete information, a sophisticated exploration strategy can improve control performance by decreasing the time required to reach goal states or, in the case of RTDP, by focusing DP stages on states from which information most useful for improving the evaluation function is likely to be gained. Knowledgeable ordering of backups can accelerate convergence of asynchronous DP, whether applied off- or on-line. When information is incomplete, sophisticated exploration is useful for other reasons as well. In this case, exploration strategies must also address the necessity to gather information about the unknown structure of the system being controlled. Unlike exploration in the case of complete information, which can be conducted in simulation mode, this kind of exploration must be conducted on-line. We discussed how exploration performed for this reason conflicts with the performance objective of control, at least on a short-term basis, and that a controller should not always execute actions that appear to be the best based on its current evaluation function.

Although we did not use sophisticated exploration strategies in our simulations of the race track problem, and we made no attempt in this article to analyse issues pertinent to exploration, sophisticated exploration strategies will play an essential role in making DP-based learning methods practical for larger problems. From what we did mention, however, it should be clear that it is not easy to devise a consistent set of desiderata for exploration strategies. For example, researchers have argued that an exploration strategy should (1) visit states in regions of the state space where information about the system is of low quality (to learn more about these regions), (2) visit states in regions of the state space where information about the system is of high quality (so that the backup operation uses accurate estimates of the state-transition probabilities), or (3) visit states having successors whose costs are close to their optimal costs (so that the backup operation efficiently propagates cost information). Each of these suggestions makes sense in the proper context, but it is not clear how to design a strategy that best incorporates all of them. It is encouraging, however, that the convergence results we have presented in this article are compatible with a wide range of exploration strategies.

Throughout this article we have assumed that the states of the system being controlled are completely and unambiguously observable by the controller. Although this assumption is critical to the theory and operation of all the algorithms we discussed, it can be very difficult to satisfy in practice. For example, the current state of a robot's world is vastly different from a list of the robot's current "sensations". On the positive side, effective closed-loop control policies do not have to distinguish between all possible sensations. However, exploiting this fact requires the ability to recognize states in the complex flow of sensations. Although the problem of state identification has been the subject of research in a variety of disciplines, and many approaches have been studied under many guises, it remains a critical factor in extending the applicability of DP-based learning methods. Any widely applicable approach to this problem must take the perspective that what constitutes a system's state for purposes of control—indeed what constitutes the system itself—is not independent of the control objectives. The framework adopted in this article in which "a dynamic system underlies the decision problem" is misleading in suggesting the existence of a single definitive grain with which to delineate events and to mark their passage. In actuality, control objectives dictate what is important in the flow of the controller's sensations, and multiple objective-dependent models at different levels of abstraction are needed to achieve them. If this caution is recognized, however, the algorithms described in this article should find wide application as components of sophisticated embedded systems.

Acknowledgment

The authors thank Rich Yee, Vijay Gullapalli, Brian Pinette, and Jonathan Bachrach for helping to clarify the relationships between heuristic search and control. We thank Rich Sutton, Chris Watkins, Paul Werbos, and Ron Williams for sharing their fundamental insights into this subject through numerous discussions, and we further thank Rich Sutton for first making us aware of Korf's research and for his very thoughtful comments on the manuscript. We are very grateful to Dimitri Bertsekas and Steven Sullivan for independently pointing out an error in an earlier version of this article. Finally, we thank Harry Klopf, whose insight and persistence encouraged our interest in this class of learning problems. This research was supported by grants to A.G. Barto from the National Science Foundation (ECS-8912623 and ECS-9214866) and the Air Force Office of Scientific Research, Bolling AFB (AFOSR-89-0526).

Appendix A. Proof of the trial-based RTDP theorem

Here we prove Theorem 3, which extends Korf's [38] convergence theorem for LRTA* to Trial-Based RTDP applied to undiscounted stochastic shortest path problems.

Proof of Theorem 3. We first prove the theorem for the special case in which only the cost of the current state is backed up at each time interval, i.e., $B_t = \{s_t\}$ and $k_t = t$, for $t = 0, 1, \ldots$ (see Section 6). We then observe that the proof does not change when each B_t is allowed to be an arbitrary set containing s_t. Let G denote the goal set and let s_t, u_t, and f_t respectively denote the state, action, and evaluation function at time step t in an arbitrary infinite sequence of states, actions, and evaluation functions generated by Trial-Based RTDP starting from an arbitrary start state.

First observe that the evaluation functions remain non-overestimating, i.e., at any time t, $f_t(i) \leqslant f^*(i)$ for all states i. This is true by induction because $f_{t+1}(i) = f_t(i)$ for all $i \neq s_t$ and if $f_t(j) \leqslant f^*(j)$ for all $j \in S$, then for all t

$$
f_{t+1}(s_t) = \min_{u \in U(i)} \left[c_{s_t}(u) + \sum_{j \in S} p_{s_t j}(u) f_t(j) \right]
$$

$$
\leqslant \min_{u \in U(i)} \left[c_{s_t}(u) + \sum_{j \in S} p_{s_t j}(u) f^*(j) \right] = f^*(s_t),
$$

where the last equality restates the Bellman Optimality Equation (Eq. 6).

Let $I \subseteq S$ be the set of all states that appear infinitely often in this arbitrary sequence; I must be nonempty because the state set is finite. Let $A(i) \subset U(i)$ be the set of admissible actions for state i that have zero probability of causing a transition to a state not in I, i.e., $A(i)$ is the set of all actions $u \in U(i)$ such that $p_{ij}(u) = 0$ for all $j \in (S - I)$. Because states in $S - I$ appear a finite number of times, there is a finite time T_0 after which all states visited are in I. Then with probability one any action chosen an infinite number of times for any state i that occurs after T_0 must be in $A(i)$ (or else with probability one a transition out of I would occur), and so with probability one there must exist a time $T_1 \geqslant T_0$ such that for all $t > T_1$, we not only have that $s_t \in I$ but also that $u_t \in A(s_t)$.

We know that at each time step t, RTDP backs up the cost of s_t because $s_t \in B_t$. We can write the backup operation as follows:

$$
f_{t+1}(s_t) = \min_{u \in U(i)} \left[c_{s_t}(u_t) + \sum_{j \in I} p_{s_t j}(u_t) f_t(j) + \sum_{j \in (S-I)} p_{s_t j}(u_t) f_t(j) \right]. \quad \text{(A.1)}
$$

But for all $t > T_1$, we know that $s_t \in I$ and that $p_{s_t j}(u_t) = 0$ for all $j \in S - I$ because $u_t \in A(s_t)$. Thus, for $t > T_1$ the right-most summation in Eq. (A.1) is zero. This means that the costs of the states in $S - I$ have no influence on the operation of RTDP after T_1. Thus, after T_1, RTDP performs asynchronous DP on a Markovian decision problem with state set I.

If no goal states are contained in I, then all the immediate costs in this Markovian decision problem are positive. Because there is no discounting, it can be shown that asynchronous DP must cause the costs of the states in I to grow without bound. But this contradicts the fact that the cost of a state can never overestimate its optimal cost, which must be finite due to the existence of a proper policy. Thus I contains a goal state with probability one.

After T_1, therefore, Trial-Based RTDP performs asynchronous DP on a stochastic shortest path problem with state set I that satisfies the conditions of the convergence theorem for asynchronous DP applied to undiscounted stochastic shortest path problems (Bertsekas and Tsitsiklis [12, Proposition 3.3, p. 318]). Consequently, Trial-Based RTDP converges to the optimal evaluation function of this stochastic shortest path problem. We also know that the optimal evaluation function for this problem is identical to the optimal evaluation function for the original problem restricted to the states in I because the costs of the states in $S - I$ have no influence on the costs of states in I after time T_1.

Furthermore, with probability one I contains the set of all states reachable from any start state via any optimal policy. Clearly, I contains all the start states because each start state begins an infinite number of trails. Trial-Based RTDP always executes a greedy action with respect to the current evaluation function and breaks ties in such a way that it continues to execute all the greedy actions. Because we know that the number of policies is finite and that Trial-Based RTDP converges to the optimal evaluation function restricted to I, there is a time after which it continues to select all the actions that are greedy with respect to the optimal evaluation function, i.e., all the optimal actions. Thus with probability one, I contains all the states reachable from any start state via any optimal policy, and there is a time after which a controller using RTDP will only execute optimal actions.

Finally, with trivial revision the above argument holds if RTDP backs up the costs of states other than the current state at each time step, i.e., if each B_t is an arbitrary subset of S. □

Appendix B. Simulation details

Except for the discount factor γ, which we set to one throughout the simulations, and the sets B_t, which we set to $\{s_t\}$ for all t, RTDP does not involve any parameters. Gauss–Seidel DP only requires specifying a state ordering for its sweeps. We selected an ordering without concern for any influence it might have on convergence rate. Both Adaptive RTDP and Real-Time Q-Learning require exploration during the training trials, which we implemented using Eq. (11). To generate the data described in Section 4.1, we decreased the parameter T with successive moves as follows:

$$T(0) = T_{\text{Max}}, \tag{B.1}$$

$$T(k+1) = T_{\text{Min}} + \beta(T(k) - T_{\text{Min}}), \tag{B.2}$$

where k is the move number (cumulative over trials), $\beta = 0.992$, $T_{\text{Max}} = 75$, and $T_{\text{Min}} = 0.5$.

Real-time Q-Learning additionally requires sequences of learning rate parameters $\alpha_t(i, u)$ (Eq. (14)) that satisfy the hypotheses of the Q-Learning convergence theorem [81,82]. We defined these sequences as follows. Let $\alpha_t(i, u)$ denote the learning rate parameter used when the Q-value of the state–action pair (i, u) is backed up at time step t. Let $n_t(i, u)$ be the number of backups performed on the Q-value of (i, u) up to time step t. The learning rate $\alpha_t(i, u)$ is defined as follows:

$$\alpha_t(i, u) = \frac{\alpha_0 \tau}{\tau + n_t(i, u)},$$

where α_0 is the initial learning rate. We set $\alpha_0 = 0.5$ and $\tau = 300$. This equation implements a *search-then-converge* schedule for each $\alpha_t(i, u)$ as suggested by Darken and Moody [19]. They argue that such schedules can achieve good performance in stochastic optimization tasks. It can be shown that this schedule satisfies the hypotheses of the Q-Learning convergence theorem.

References

[1] C.W. Anderson, Strategy learning with multilayer connectionist representations, Tech. Report TR87-509.3, GTE Laboratories, Incorporated, Waltham, MA (1987); (this is a corrected version of the report published in: *Proceedings Fourth International Conference on Machine Learning*, Irvine, CA (1987) 103–114).

[2] A. Barto, Reinforcement learning and adaptive critic methods, in: D.A. White and D.A. Sofge, eds., *Handbook of Intelligent Control: Neural, Fuzzy, and Adaptive Approaches* (Van Nostrand Reinhold, New York, 1992) 469–491.

[3] A. Barto and S. Singh, On the computational economics of reinforcement learning, in: D.S. Touretzky, J.L. Elman, T.J. Sejnowski and G.E. Hinton, eds., *Connectionist Models: Proceedings of the 1990 Summer School* (Morgan Kaufmann, San Mateo, CA, 1991) 35–44.

[4] A.G. Barto, R.S. Sutton and C.W. Anderson, Neuronlike elements that can solve difficult learning control problems, *IEEE Trans. Syst. Man Cybern.* **13** (1983) 835–846; reprinted in: J. A. Anderson and E. Rosenfeld, *Neurocomputing: Foundations of Research* (MIT Press, Cambridge, MA, 1988).

[5] A.G. Barto, R.S. Sutton and C. Watkins, Sequential decision problems and neural networks, in: D.S. Touretzky, ed., *Advances in Neural Information Processing Systems 2* (Morgan Kaufmann, San Mateo, CA, 1990) 686–693.

[6] A.G. Barto, R.S. Sutton and C.J.C.H. Watkins, Learning and sequential decision making, in: M. Gabriel and J. Moore, eds., *Learning and Computational Neuroscience: Foundations of Adaptive Networks* (MIT Press, Cambridge, MA, 1990) 539–602.

[7] R. Bellman and S.E. Dreyfus, Functional approximations and dynamic programming, *Math Tables and Other Aides to Computation* **13** (1959) 247–251.

[8] R. Bellman, R. Kalaba and B. Kotkin, Polynomial approximation—a new computational technique in dynamic programming: allocation processes, *Math. Comp.* **17** (1973) 155–161.

[9] R.E. Bellman, *Dynamic Programming* (Princeton University Press, Princeton, NJ, 1957).

[10] D.P. Bertsekas, Distributed dynamic programming, *IEEE Trans. Autom. Control* **27** (1982) 610–616.

[11] D.P. Bertsekas, *Dynamic Programming: Deterministic and Stochastic Models* (Prentice-Hall, Englewood Cliffs, NJ, 1987).

[12] D.P. Bertsekas and J.N. Tsitsiklis, *Parallel and Distributed Computation: Numerical Methods* (Prentice-Hall, Englewood Cliffs, NJ, 1989).

[13] S.J. Bradtke, Reinforcement learning applied to linear quadratic regulation, in: C.L. Giles, S.J. Hanson and J.D. Cowan, eds., *Advances in Neural Information Processing 5* (Morgan Kaufmann, San Mateo, CA, 1993) 295–302.

[14] D. Chapman, Penguins can make cake, *AI Mag.* **10** (1989) 45–50.

[15] D. Chapman and L.P. Kaelbling, Input generalization in delayed reinforcement learning: an algorithm and performance comparisons, in: *Proceedings IJCAI-91*, Sydney, NSW (1991).

[16] J. Christensen and R.E. Korf, A unified theory of heuristic evaluation functions and its application to learning, in: *Proceedings AAAI-86*, Philadelphia, PA (1986) 148–152.

[17] J.H. Curtiss, A theoretical comparison of the efficiencies of two classical methods and a Monte Carlo method for computing one component of the solution of a set of linear algebraic equations, in: H.A. Meyer, ed., *Symposium on Monte Carlo Methods* (Wiley, New York, 1954) 191-233.

[18] J.W. Daniel, Splines and efficiency in dynamic programming, *J. Math. Anal. Appl.* **54** (1976) 402-407.

[19] C. Darken and J. Moody, Note on learning rate schedule for stochastic optimization, in: R.P. Lippmann, J.E. Moody and D.S. Touretzky, eds., *Advances in Neural Information Processing Systems* 3 (Morgan Kaufmann, San Mateo, CA, 1991) 832-838.

[20] P. Dayan, Navigating through temporal difference, in: R.P. Lippmann, J.E. Moody and D.S. Touretzky, eds., *Advances in Neural Information Processing Systems* 3 (Morgan Kaufmann, San Mateo, CA, 1991) 464-470.

[21] P. Dayan, Reinforcing connectionism: learning the statistical way, Ph.D. Thesis, University of Edinburgh, Edinburgh, Scotland (1991).

[22] P. Dayan, The convergence of TD(λ) for general λ, *Mach. Learn.* **8** (1992) 341-362.

[23] T.L. Dean and M.P. Wellman, *Planning and Control* (Morgan Kaufmann, San Mateo, CA, 1991).

[24] E.V. Denardo, Contraction mappings in the theory underlying dynamic programming, *SIAM Rev.* **9** (1967) 165-177.

[25] M. Gardner, Mathematical games, *Sci. Amer.* **228** (1973) 108.

[26] D. Gelperin, On the optimality of A*, *Artif. Intell.* **8** (1977) 69-76.

[27] M.L. Ginsberg, Universal planning: an (almost) universally bad idea, *AI Mag.* **10** (1989) 40-44.

[28] S.E. Hampson, *Connectionist Problem Solving: Computational Aspects of Biological Learning* (Birkhauser, Boston, MA, 1989).

[29] P.E. Hart, N.J. Nilsson and B. Raphael, A formal basis for the heuristic determination of minimum cost paths, *IEEE Trans. Syst. Sci. Cybern.* **4** (1968) 100-107.

[30] J.H. Holland, Escaping brittleness: the possibility of general-purpose learning algorithms applied to rule-based systems, in: R.S. Michalski, J.G. Carbonell and T.M. Mitchell, eds., *Machine Learning: An Artificial Intelligence Approach, Volume II* (Morgan Kaufmann, San Mateo, CA, 1986) 593-623.

[31] D.H. Jacobson and D.Q. Mayne, *Differential Dynamic Programming* (Elsevier, New York, 1970).

[32] A. Jalali and M. Ferguson, Computationally efficient adaptive control algorithms for Markov chains, in: *Proceedings 28th Conference on Decision and Control*, Tampa, FL (1989) 1283-1288.

[33] M.I. Jordan and R.A. Jacobs, Learning to control an unstable system with forward modeling, in: D.S. Touretzky, ed., *Advances in Neural Information Processing Systems* 2 (Morgan Kaufmann, San Mateo, CA, 1990).

[34] L.P. Kaelbling, *Learning in Embedded Systems* (MIT Press, Cambridge, MA, 1991); revised version of: Teleos Research TR-90-04 (1990).

[35] S. Kirkpatrick, C.D. Gelatt and M.P. Vecchi, Optimization by simulated annealing, *Sci.* **220** (1983) 671-680.

[36] A.H. Klopf, Brain function and adaptive systems—a heterostatic theory, Tech. Report AFCRL-72-0164, Air Force Cambridge Research Laboratories, Bedford, MA (1972); a summary appears in: *Proceedings International Conference on Systems, Man, and Cybernetics* (1974).

[37] A.H. Klopf, *The Hedonistic Neuron: A Theory of Memory, Learning, and Intelligence* (Hemishere, Washington, DC, 1982).

[38] R.E. Korf, Real-time heuristic search, *Artif. Intell.* **42** (1990) 189-211.

[39] P.R. Kumar, A survey of some results in stochastic adaptive control, *SIAM J. Control Optimization* **23** (1985) 329-380.

[40] V. Kumar and L.N. Kanal, The CDP: a unifying formulation for heuristic search, dynamic programming, and branch-and-bound, in: L.N. Kanal and V. Kumar, eds., *Search in Artificial Intelligence* (Springer-Verlag, Berlin, 1988) 1-37.

[41] H.J. Kushner and P. Dupuis, *Numerical Methods for Stochastic Control Problems in Continuous Time* (Springer-Verlag, New York, 1992).

[42] W.H. Kwon and A.E. Pearson, A modified quadratic cost problem and feedback stabilization of a linear system, *IEEE Trans. Autom. Control* **22** (1977) 838-842.

[43] Y. le Cun, A theoretical framework for back-propagation, in: D. Touretzky, G. Hinton and T. Sejnowski, eds., *Proceedings 1988 Connectionist Models Summer School* (Morgan Kaufmann, San Mateo, CA, 1988) 21-28.

[44] M. Lemmon, Real-time optimal path planning using a distributed computing paradigm, in: *Proceedings American Control Conference*, Boston, MA (1991).

[45] L.J. Lin, Programming robots using reinforcement learning and teaching, in: *Proceedings AAAI-91*, Anaheim, CA (1991) 781–786.

[46] L.J. Lin, Self-improvement based on reinforcement learning, planning and teaching, in: L.A. Birnbaum and G.C. Collins, eds., *Maching Learning: Proceedings Eighth International Workshop* (Morgan Kaufmann, San Mateo, CA, 1991) 323–327.

[47] L.J. Lin, Self-improving reactive agents: case studies of reinforcement learning frameworks, in: *From Animals to Animats: Proceedings First International Conference on Simulation of Adaptive Behavior*, Cambridge, MA (1991) 297–305.

[48] L.J. Lin, Self-improving reactive agents based on reinforcement learning, planning and teaching, *Mach. Learn.* **8** (1992) 293–321.

[49] S. Mahadevan and J. Connell, Automatic programming of behavior-based robots using reinforcement learning, *Artif. Intell.* **55** (1992) 311–365.

[50] D.Q. Mayne and H. Michalska, Receding horizon control of nonlinear systems, *IEEE Trans. Autom. Control* **35** (1990) 814–824.

[51] L. Mérő, A heuristic search algorithm with modifiable estimate, *Artif. Intell.* **23** (1984) 13–27.

[52] D. Michie and R.A. Chambers, BOXES: an experiment in adaptive control, in: E. Dale and D. Michie, eds., *Machine Intelligence* **2** (Oliver and Boyd, Edinburgh, 1968) 137–152.

[53] M.L. Minsky, Theory of neural-analog reinforcement systems and its application to the brain-model problem, Ph.D. Thesis, Princeton University, Princeton, NJ (1954).

[54] M.L. Minsky, Steps toward artificial intelligence, *Proceedings Institute of Radio Engineers* **49** (1961) 8–30; reprinted in: E. A. Feigenbaum and J. Feldman, eds., *Computers and Thought* (McGraw-Hill, New York, 1963) 406–450.

[55] A.W. Moore, Efficient memory-based learning for robot control, Ph.D. Thesis, University of Cambridge, Cambridge, England (1990).

[56] A.W. Moore, Variable resolution dynamic programming: efficiently learning action maps in multivariate real-valued state-spaces, in: L.A. Birnbaum and G.C. Collins, eds., *Maching Learning: Proceedings Eighth International Workshop* (Morgan Kaufmann, San Mateo, CA, 1991) 333–337.

[57] A.W. Moore and C.G. Atkeson, Memory-based reinforcement learning: efficient computation with prioritized sweeping, in: S.J. Hanson, J.D. Cowan and C.L. Giles, eds., *Advances in Neural Information Processing* **5** (Morgan Kaufmann, San Mateo, CA, 1993).

[58] J. Peng and R.J. Williams, Efficient learning and planning within the dyna framework, *Adaptive Behavior* **2** (1993) 437–454.

[59] M.L. Puterman and M.C. Shin, Modified policy iteration algorithms for discounted Markov decision problems, *Manage. Sci.* **24** (1978) 1127–1137.

[60] S. Ross, *Introduction to Stochastic Dynamic Programming* (Academic Press, New York, 1983).

[61] A.L. Samuel, Some studies in machine learning using the game of checkers, *IBM J. Res. Develop.* (1959) 210–229; reprinted in: E.A. Feigenbaum and J. Feldman, eds., *Computers and Thought* (McGraw-Hill, New York, 1963).

[62] A.L. Samuel, Some studies in machine learning using the game of checkers. II—Recent progress, *IBM J. Res. Develop.* (1967) 601–617.

[63] J. Schmidhuber, Adaptive confidence and adaptive curiosity, Tech. Report FKI-149-91 Institut für Informatik, Technische Universität München, 800 München 2, Germany (1991).

[64] M.J. Schoppers, Universal plans for reactive robots in unpredictable environments, in: *Proceedings IJCAI-87*, Milan, Italy (1987) 1039–1046.

[65] M.J. Schoppers, In defense of reaction plans as caches, *AI Mag.* **10** (1989) 51–60.

[66] S.P. Singh and R.C. Yee, An upper bound on the loss from approximate optimal value functions. technical note, *Mach. Learn.* **16** (1994) 227–233.

[67] R.S. Sutton, Temporal credit assignment in reinforcement learning, Ph.D. Thesis, University of Massachusetts, Amherst, MA (1984).

[68] R.S. Sutton, Learning to predict by the method of temporal differences, *Mach. Learn.* **3** (1988) 9–44.

[69] R.S. Sutton, Integrated architectures for learning, planning, and reacting based on approximating dynamic programming, in: *Proceedings Seventh International Conference on Machine Learning* (Morgan Kaufmann, San Mateo, CA, 1990) 216–224.

[70] R.S. Sutton, Planning by incremental dynamic programming, in: L.A. Birnbaum and G.C. Collins, eds., *Maching Learning: Proceedings Eighth International Workshop* (Morgan Kaufmann, San Mateo, CA, 1991) 353–357.

[71] R.S. Sutton, ed., *A Special Issue of Machine Learning on Reinforcement Learning, Mach. Learn.* **8** (1992); also published as: *Reinforcement Learning* (Kluwer Academic Press, Boston, MA, 1992).

[72] R.S. Sutton and A.G. Barto, Toward a modern theory of adaptive networks: expectation and prediction, *Psychol. Rev.* **88** (1981) 135–170.

[73] R.S. Sutton and A.G. Barto, A temporal-difference model of classical conditioning, in: *Proceedings Ninth Annual Conference of the Cognitive Science Society*, Seattle, WA (1987).

[74] R.S. Sutton and A.G. Barto, Time-derivative models of pavlovian reinforcement, in: M. Gabriel and J. Moore, eds., *Learning and Computational Neuroscience: Foundations of Adaptive Networks* (MIT Press, Cambridge, MA, 1990) 497–537.

[75] R.S. Sutton, A.G. Barto and R.J. Williams, Reinforcement learning is direct adaptive optimal control, in: *Proceedings American Control Conference*, Boston, MA (1991) 2143–2146.

[76] M. Tan, Learning a cost-sensitive internal representation for reinforcement learning, in: L.A. Birnbaum and G.C. Collins, eds., *Maching Learning: Proceedings Eighth International Workshop* (Morgan Kaufmann, San Mateo, CA, 1991) 358–362.

[77] G.J. Tesauro, Practical issues in temporal difference learning, *Mach. Learn.* **8** (1992) 257–277.

[78] S. Thrun, The role of exploration in learning control, in: D.A. White and D.A. Sofge, eds., *Handbook of Intelligent Control: Neural, Fuzzy, and Adaptive Approaches* (Van Nostrand Reinhold, New York, 1992) 527–559.

[79] S.B. Thrun and K. Möller, Active exploration in dynamic environments, in: J.E. Moody, S.J. Hanson and R.P. Lippmann, eds., *Advances in Neural Information Processing Systems* **4** (Morgan Kaufmann, San Mateo, CA, 1992).

[80] P.E. Utgoff and J.A. Clouse, Two kinds of training information for evaluation function learning, in: *Proceedings AAAI-91*, Anaheim, CA (1991) 596–600.

[81] C.J.C.H. Watkins, Learning from delayed rewards, Ph.D. Thesis, Cambridge University, Cambridge, England (1989).

[82] C.J.C.H. Watkins and P. Dayan, Q-learning, *Mach. Learn.* **8** (1992) 279–292.

[83] P. Werbos, Approximate dynamic programming for real-time control and neural modeling, in: D.A. White and D.A. Sofge, eds., *Handbook of Intelligent Control: Neural, Fuzzy, and Adaptive Approaches* (Van Nostrand Reinhold, New York, 1992) 493–525.

[84] P.J. Werbos, Beyond regression: new tools for prediction and analysis in the behavioral sciences, Ph.D. Thesis, Harvard University, Cambridge, MA (1974).

[85] P.J. Werbos, Advanced forecasting methods for global crisis warning and models of intelligence, *General Systems Yearbook* **22** (1977) 25–38.

[86] P.J. Werbos, Applications of advances in nonlinear sensitivity analysis, in: R.F. Drenick and F. Kosin, eds., *System Modeling an Optimization* (Springer-Verlag, Berlin, 1982).

[87] P.J. Werbos, Building and understanding adaptive systems: a statistical/numerical approach to factory automation and brain research, *IEEE Trans. Syst. Man Cybern.* (1987).

[88] P.J. Werbos, Generalization of back propagation with applications to a recurrent gas market model, *Neural Networks* **1** (1988) 339–356.

[89] D. White and M. Jordan, Optimal control: a foundation for intelligent control, in: D.A. White and D.A. Sofge, eds., *Handbook of Intelligent Control: Neural, Fuzzy, and Adaptive Approaches* (Van Nostrand Reinhold, New York, 1992) 185–214.

[90] S.D. Whitehead, Complexity and cooperation in Q-learning, in: L.A. Birnbaum and G.C. Collins, eds., *Maching Learning: Proceedings Eighth International Workshop* (Morgan Kaufmann, San Mateo, CA, 1991) 363–367.

[91] R.J. Williams and L.C. Baird III, A mathematical analysis of actor-critic architectures for learning optimal controls through incremental dynamic programming, in: *Proceedings Sixth Yale Workshop on Adaptive and Learning Systems*, New Haven, CT (1990) 96–101.

[92] I.H. Witten, An adaptive optimal controller for discrete-time Markov environments, *Infor. Control* **34** (1977) 286–295.

[93] I.H. Witten, Exploring, modelling and controlling discrete sequential environments, *Int. J. Man–Mach. Stud.* **9** (1977) 715–735.

[94] R.C. Yee, Abstraction in control learning, Tech. Report 92-16, Department of Computer Science, University of Massachusetts, Amherst, MA (1992).

Artificial Intelligence 72 (1995) 139–171

Learning dynamics: system identification for perceptually challenged agents

Kenneth Basye [a,*], Thomas Dean [b,1], Leslie Pack Kaelbling [b,2]

[a] *Department of Mathematics and Computer Science, Clark University, 950 Main Street, Worcester, MA 01610, USA*

[b] *Department of Computer Science, Box 1910, Brown University, Providence, RI 02912-1910, USA*

Received September 1992; revised March 1993

Abstract

From the perspective of an agent, the input/output behavior of the environment in which it is embedded can be described as a dynamical system. Inputs correspond to the actions executable by the agent in making transitions between states of the environment. Outputs correspond to the perceptual information available to the agent in particular states of the environment. We view dynamical system identification as inference of deterministic finite-state automata from sequences of input/output pairs. The agent can influence the sequence of input/output pairs it is presented by pursuing a strategy for exploring the environment. We identify two sorts of perceptual errors: errors in perceiving the output of a state and errors in perceiving the inputs actually carried out in making a transition from one state to another. We present efficient, high-probability learning algorithms for a number of system identification problems involving such errors. We also present the results of empirical investigations applying these algorithms to learning spatial representations.

1. Introduction

System identification refers to inferring a model of the dynamics governing an agent's interaction with its environment. For instance, we might wish to infer a model of how

---

* Corresponding author. E-mail: kbasye@gamma.clarku.edu.

[1] This work was supported in part by a National Science Foundation Presidential Young Investigator Award IRI-8957601, by the Air Force and the Advanced Research Projects Agency of the Department of Defense under Contract No. F30602-91-C-0041, and by the National Science foundation in conjunction with the Advanced Research Projects Agency of the Department of Defense under Contract No. IRI-8905436.

[2] This work was supported in part by a National Science Foundation National Young Investigator Award.

fluctuations in the output of a parts supplier affect production for a factory or how an assembly robot interacts with the other devices in its work cell.

The inferred model might correspond to a system of differential equations, a set of production rules, or a set of states and transition probabilities for a stochastic process. The model is useful insofar as it enables the agent to predict consequences of performing actions in its environment. Such predictions might be used in planning, spatial inference, or diagnostic reasoning.

System identification has been studied in a variety of disciplines including control theory, neural networks, and automata theory. We focus on learning representations of environments that can be characterized as deterministic finite-state automata. There is a large literature even on this restricted problem, a portion of which is summarized in this paper. Our results address the effects of uncertainty on computational complexity. Our objective is to produce learning algorithms that infer accurate models with high probability in polynomial time when faced with noise in observing the inputs and outputs that determine the agent's interaction with its environment.

We are interested in how agents interact with their environments and, in particular, how uncertainty in observation complicates such interactions. We have chosen to focus on system identification as it appears to be critical in facilitating a wide range of interactions. It is clear that system identification is a means and not an end; however, we believe that studying system identification in isolation provides insight into many problems in which such identification plays a supporting role. Our basic findings are that uncertainty in observation is annoying and requires somewhat more bookkeeping but asymptotically it is not that hard to cope with. However, learning is hopeless in environments lacking any structure. Useful structure in the form of reasonably distributed landmarks or short sequences of distinctive features makes learning relatively easy.

It is certainly possible to function adequately even optimally without the use of a model. There are environments, however, in which having some sort of a model can help enormously. Perhaps, the clearest example of the utility of a model is in learning maps of large-scale space to support path planning. A dynamical model can also speed up learning plans [22] by allowing an agent to simulate its actions and the environment's reactions. Clearly there are tradeoffs involved in learning dynamical models; exactly what is worth learning will depend on the tasks of the agent. Again, we avoid addressing those tradeoffs in this paper (but see [9]) in order to focus on basic issues in how uncertainty in observation affects learning.

2. Modeling dynamical systems with automata

We model dynamical systems as deterministic finite-state automata (DFAs). Fig. 1 shows the state-transition graph for a DFA in which the inputs to the DFA are the agent's actions and the outputs from the DFA are the agent's perceptual inputs. We are interested in learning the *discernible* structure of real environments, where discernible is defined in terms of the agent's perceptual capabilities. Discernability does not require that, from the information available in a state, the agent can uniquely identify that state, but rather that there exists some sequence of actions and observations that can be used

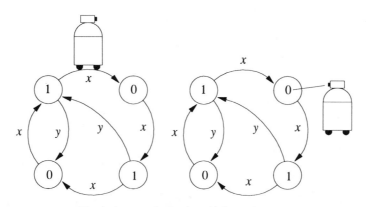

Fig. 1. An agent interacting with its environment.

by the agent to distinguish any two states.

For instance, the states of an automaton might correspond to the agent being in one of many locations in an office building, in which locations correspond to junctions where hallways meet. In this case, the observed outputs might correspond to the number of hallways incident on a junction, and the inputs to actions for traversing incident hallways. As another example, consider learning the structure of a voice-mail system. Here the states might correspond to various menus and services, actions to keys pressed by the user, and outputs to the announcements made at each state.

The DFA need not represent the whole of the agent's interaction with its environment; separate models could be used for different aspects of the interaction. We assume the state space has been reduced to a manageable size by careful choice of perception and action primitives. Actions are encapsulated abstract behaviors that serve to limit the agent's options for response in a given state. The set of possible observations is kept small through the use of perceptual apparatus that act as filters, thereby introducing equivalence relations on perceptual experiences.

Historically, AI researchers have kept the state space implicit, specifying only a set of state variables or fluents. In our view, the agent's observations need not correspond to observations of state variables and, even if this is desirable, the set of states of the automaton need not correspond to the cross product of the sets of values for all the state variables. We see the world as consisting of a relatively small number of perceptually distinguishable states. We admit that determining such state-space-reducing perception and action primitives requires a great deal of insight into the problem, and we offer no general advice on how to obtain such primitives. We claim, however, that without such primitives, learning will be very difficult.

Even in the deterministic case, uncertainty arises due to the fact that the observations available in a state do not uniquely determine that state. In this paper, we are particularly interested in stochastic sources of uncertainty. We allow there to be a noise process that occasionally results in the agent observing something other than the true output at a state or realizing one action while attempting to execute some other action. Fig. 2 illustrates both sorts of errors. Our polynomial-time performance results apply for quite extreme forms of uncertainty, but predict fairly poor performance in relatively

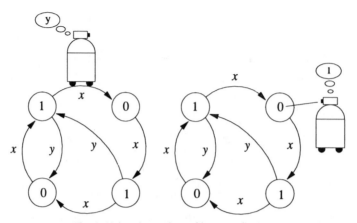

Fig. 2. Noisy observations of inputs and outputs.

benign environments. Our empirical investigations, however, indicate that our algorithms perform much better than our current theoretical bounds predict for benign environments of the sort we expect robots to encounter in the real world.

3. Formal model

In order to model system identification as inferring the structure of finite-state automata, we now introduce an extension of the familiar definition of finite-state automata. Recall that there are two varieties of finite-state automaton; in both versions, output follows some action, and the state reached by the action depends on the action taken and the previous state. In the Moore model, output depends only on the state reached by the action, whereas, in the Mealy model, output depends on both the previous state and the action taken. Alternatively, one may think of the Mealy model as having outputs that depend on the current state and the previous action. In terms of system identification, which model is appropriate depends on the nature of the agent's sensing systems and in particular on whether sensations depend in some way on the previous action. We use Moore automata for our model, which implies that our sensations for a given state are the same regardless of how we got to that state.

In this model, we explicitly distinguish between the actual states and actions of the automaton and the agent's possibly erroneous view of them. Thus, in any given true state of the environment, the agent observes a *label*, which may or may not be an accurate reflection of the state.[3] Similarly, an agent generates *commands* to the environment; these commands have a nominal correspondence to real actions, but the corresponding action is not always taken.

---

[3] It would be more technically correct to define an output alphabet for the automaton, give a function mapping states to outputs, then describe how the outputs generate observable labels that are sometimes not correct. For simplicity in the following treatment, we have chosen to collapse these processes into one, giving an account of how states give rise directly to possibly erroneous labels.

In order to make use of probabilistic functions as a means of modelling uncertainly, we introduce the following notation: for any finite set S, let

$$F_S = \left\{ f \mid f : S \to [0, 1], \sum_S f(s) = 1 \right\},$$

the set of probability density functions (PDFs) over S.

The structure of the agent's environment and its interaction with that environment is specified by the tuple $\mathcal{E} = (Q, B, L, C, \delta, \phi, \psi)$, where

- Q is a finite nonempty set of states,
- B is a finite nonempty set of basic actions,
- L is a finite nonempty set of observable labels,
- C is a finite nonempty set of executable commands,
- $\delta : Q \times B \to Q$, is the *state transition function*,
- ϕ is the probabilistic observation function, $\phi : Q \to F_L$, mapping each state into a distribution over possible observed labels, and
- ψ is the probabilistic action function, $\psi : C \to F_B$, mapping each executable command into a distribution over possible actions.

We write n for $|Q|$. We write $A = B^*$ for the set of all finite sequences of basic actions from B. We extend the state transition function δ to such sequences in the usual way by defining $\delta(q, \lambda) = q$, and $\delta(q, ab) = \delta(\delta(q, a), b)$ for all $q \in Q$, $a \in A$, and $b \in B$, where λ is the empty sequence. We write qa as shorthand for $\delta(q, a)$, the state resulting from execution of sequence a from state q.

We assume that every action may be executed in every state, so the function δ induces a set E of labelled edges (q_1, b, q_2) for every $q_1, q_2 \in Q$ and $b \in B$. An automaton is *strongly connected* if for any two states $q_1, q_2 \in Q$, there is some sequence $a \in A$ such that $q_1 a = q_2$.

We write $q\langle a \rangle$ to denote the sequence of outputs of length $|a| + 1$ resulting from executing the sequence a starting in state q, beginning with the output at state q. For example, if $a = b_0 b_1 b_2 \ldots b_n$, then $q\langle a \rangle = \langle \phi(q), \phi(qb_0), \phi(qb_0b_1), \ldots, \phi(qa) \rangle$.

Q, B, and δ specify the system itself apart from any agent. Note that the state transition function is deterministic; we are concerned with worlds or systems that have a fixed structure. The remaining elements represent the agent's ability to observe and act in its environment. When the agent reaches some state $q \in Q$, it observes a label drawn from the distribution $\phi(q)$. Similarly, when it is in state q and attempts to perform command c, it performs an action drawn from the distribution $\psi(c)$.

We assume that there is some "correct" observation at each state, and some "correct" action for each command. It is therefore useful to distinguish between a "correct" action or observation function and a "noisy" version of that function. We write ϕ^* (ψ^*) for a deterministic action (observation) function, which may be thought of as mapping each state (command) to a PDF in which some element has probability 1. Clearly, our inference procedures will have wider applicability if they require few assumptions about the stochastic functions governing observation and action. However, we certainly cannot expect to be able to learn in the presence of arbitrarily malicious noise. Instead, we exclude such situations by assuming that observation and action functions behave correctly with probability above some threshold value and that the distributions governing the errors made in the remaining cases are stationary (that is, they do not change during the lifetime of the agent). In some cases, it is also necessary to impose additional restrictions on the error distribution; these will be made explicit where they are required.

When each state has a different output under the correct observation function, we say that the observation function is *unique*. While not all environments present agents with unique observations, we shall see that unique observation functions provide additional structure that allows agents to infer automata in the presence of stochastic forms of uncertainty. Even in environments without unique observation functions, it may be the case that some states have unique outputs. We refer to such states as *landmarks*. In order to make use of landmarks the agent must not only be able to make a unique observation, it must also be capable of determining that the observation made *is* unique, that is, be capable of recognizing landmarks as landmarks.

When there are no landmarks, it becomes necessary to distinguish states by considering the outputs of sequences of states. In the following discussion, sequences of outputs are understood to arise from deterministic observations, that is, from the observation function ϕ^*. A sequence $a \in A$ is said to *distinguish* q_1 and q_2 if and only if $q_1\langle a \rangle \neq q_2\langle a \rangle$. The notion of distinguishability is extended to automata in the following way: M_1 and M_2 are distinguishable if there is a state q of M_1 (or M_2) and some action sequence a such that for all states q' of M_2 (or M_1), $q\langle a \rangle \neq q'\langle a \rangle$. An automaton is said to be *reduced* if, for all pairs of states $q_1 \neq q_2 \in Q$, there exists an action sequence that distinguishes them. The class of automata indistinguishable from a given strongly-connected automaton M has a unique (up to isomorphism) reduced member that is also strongly connected [16]; this automaton has the minimum number of states. We consistently assume that the environments we are attempting to learn are reduced, since there would be no experiment we could perform that would tell us otherwise. Note that this requirement does not mean there is one sequence that distinguishes all pairs of states. However, if there is a single sequence $a \in A$ that distinguishes all nonidentical pairs of states, then a is called a *distinguishing sequence* for M. More precisely, $a \in A$ is a distinguishing sequence if, for all $q_1, q_2 \in Q$, $q_1\langle a \rangle = q_2\langle a \rangle \Leftrightarrow q_1 = q_2$. The outputs resulting from the execution of a distinguishing sequence provide a unique signature for each state in an automaton, but note that the signature for a given state can only be determined by leaving the state, thus providing a way of knowing where you were when you began executing the sequence. A *homing* sequence is a sequence that provides a unique signature for the state reached at the end of its execution. More precisely, a sequence $a \in A$ is a homing sequence for M if and only if for all $q_1, q_2 \in Q$, $q_1\langle a \rangle = q_2\langle a \rangle \Rightarrow q_1 a = q_2 a$. Every distinguishing sequence is also a homing sequence, because knowing where you were when you started executing the distinguishing sequence (which is the result of having executed the sequence) implies that you also know where you are at the end of the sequence. Both distinguishing and homing sequences may be either *preset* or *adaptive* [11]. An adaptive sequence is one in which the next action in the sequence is determined by the previous outputs, thus it is really a tree of actions whose branches correspond to possible outputs. A preset sequence is fixed, and is executed "blindly," without regard for the outputs along the way.

The usual definition for finite-state automata includes a start state, where the machine is assumed to be prior to any actions. Some systems may have this feature, and if the agent has the ability to return to this state at will, we say that it has a *reset*. For many environments, however, the assumption of a reset is not realistic.

4. Theoretical results for the purely deterministic case

The main results of this paper are methods for learning automata in the presence of stochastic input and observation functions. In order to put those results in context, in this section we review some important previous results concerning the inference of automata in the purely deterministic case.

Some writers have made a distinction between inferring an automaton that behaves identically to the observed automaton and inferring an automaton that is isomorphic to the observed automaton. For any sequence of input/output data, there is a trivial automaton that agrees with the data that is constructed by building a chain of states as long as the data. If multiple sequences are allowed, this construction can build a tree with the start state as the root. For this reason, research has concentrated on finding the smallest automaton (in terms of $|Q|$) that agrees with a given set of data. Moore [16] showed that if the input/output pairs are assumed to have come from a reduced, strongly connected automaton, then inference of the smallest consistent automaton yields a result that is isomorphic to the original automaton. Thus, in this case, behaviorally correct inference and isomorphic inference are the same.

Gold [12] provides a method for inferring automata in the limit from their input/output behavior. The algorithm samples the automaton by generating inputs and recording the resulting outputs and periodically produces a description of the automaton. Inference in the limit means that the sequence of descriptions produced by the algorithm is guaranteed to converge on the description of the correct automaton eventually, but in this case there is no way to detect that this has happened. Gold's algorithm relies on the learner having the ability to reset the automaton to the initial state at any time.

The general problem of inferring the smallest automaton consistent with a given set of input/output pairs is NP-complete [1, 13]. Indeed, even finding an automaton polynomially close to the smallest is intractable assuming P $\neq$ NP [17].

Angluin [2], building on the work of Gold, provides a polynomial-time algorithm for inferring the smallest automaton given the ability to reset the automaton and a source of counterexamples. In this model, at any point, the algorithm can hypothesize an automaton and the source of counterexamples indicates whether it is correct and, if it is not, provides a sequence of inputs on which the hypothesized and actual automata generate different outputs.

Rivest and Schapire [19] show how to make use of a homing sequence as a substitute for a reset and how to dispense with both the reset and the source of counterexamples in the case in which a distinguishing sequence is either provided or can be learned in polynomial time [18, 20].

Several researchers have approached learning finite-state systems using neural networks. For example, Servan-Schreiber et al. [21] used a recurrent network to learn finite-state grammars, and Bachrach [3] used a neural net to implement one of the Rivest and Schapire algorithms mentioned above. This work has not stressed performance issues, nor has the issue of noise in inputs or outputs been considered.

5. Theoretical results for the stochastic case

In this section we provide polynomial-time algorithms for automata identification in three different stochastic settings. In the first, we assume that there is no error in the agent's actions, but allow error in its observations of outputs. In the second, we assume that observations of special landmark states are unique and perfect, but allow error in the action function. In the final case, we allow error in both the observations and actions of the agent, but impose the restriction that every state's nominal label be unique.

5.1. Deterministic actions and stochastic observations

In this section, we consider a situation in which there may be no uniquely labelled states. We show that by relying on a correct action function and knowledge of a distinguishing sequence, automata with non-unique observation functions can be learned even when the output function is noisy.[4]

5.1.1. Structural and interaction properties

Structurally, the requirements for this algorithm are quite weak: we require only that the automaton to be learned be strongly connected. We thus avoid the possibility that the agent becomes trapped in some part of the environment from which it cannot reach other parts. We also assume that the agent knows some upper bound on the number of states in the environment.

With regard to interactions, we assume that the agent moves deterministically, that is, that execution of actions is perfect. Observations, however, are assumed to be noisy, with the restrictions that the correct observation is made with probability greater than $\frac{1}{2}$ and that observations are independent events. Finally, we assume that the learner is provided with a preset distinguishing sequence for the environment. For many man-made and natural environments it is straightforward to determine a distinguishing sequence. For example, in most office environments, a short sequence of turns will serve to distinguish all junctions in the environment.

5.1.2. Algorithms

The algorithm we present here uses as a subroutine a procedure that moves the agent in the environment, collecting statistics on the labels it observes. The procedure provides as output a signature for the state reached at the end of the movement. Recall that a homing sequence is one for which the output uniquely determines the state reached at the end of the sequence and a distinguishing sequence is one for which the output

---

[4] The work described in this section was carried out jointly with Dana Angluin and Sean Engelson, and is described in more detail in [7].

uniquely determines the state from which the sequence was begun. In an environment with stochastic observations, homing sequences cannot be used because their signatures will not, in general, be observed correctly. This algorithm makes use of a procedure, called LOCALIZE, that, given a distinguishing sequence, achieves the effect of having a probably correct homing sequence. That is, it terminates with the automaton in a state and returns a signature for that state that is probably correct. The procedure is parameterized in such a way that it can be run longer in order to guarantee correctness with a higher probability.

We begin by explaining the LOCALIZE procedure, and then show how it can be used to learn environments with the properties discussed above.

The localization procedure works by exploiting the fact that movement is deterministic. The basic idea is to execute the given distinguishing sequence repeatedly until the agent is certain to be in a cycle, then execute it some number of times after that and collect the output. By finding the period of the cycle of locations, we can separate the observed outputs and use them as statistics on the outputs observed at each state. These statistics can then be used to determine (with high probability) the correct outputs at each state in the cycle, and hence to localize the agent by supplying the signature that would be returned by the distinguishing sequence in the deterministic case for the state the agent is in.

In order to determine the period of repetition of the walk with high probability, we keep statistics for alternative hypotheses for the period of the cycle. After the walk, these statistics are analyzed to determine with high probability the period of the cycle.

For an environment $\mathcal{E}$ with states $Q = \{q_1, q_2, \ldots, q_n\}$, let m be the given upper bound on $|Q|$. The set of outputs is $L = \{l_0, l_1, \ldots, l_k\}$. Let P_{ji} denote the probability of observing symbol l_j given that the agent is in state q_i. Let P denote a lower bound on all the P_{ji} for $i \neq j$.

Let $s = b_1 b_2 \cdots b_{|s|}$ be a preset distinguishing sequence for $\mathcal{E}$ consisting of one or more actions. For any integer $i > 0$, let s^i represent the sequence s repeated i times. Let $q\langle i \rangle$ be the state reached after executing the sequence s^{m+i}. The first m repetitions are sufficient to guarantee that the agent is in a cycle. Thus, the sequence of states $q\langle 0 \rangle, q\langle 1 \rangle, q\langle 2 \rangle, \ldots$ is periodic. Let p denote the least period of the cycle; this is the value we wish to find.

As we execute the second part of the walk (after the s^m prefix), we keep track of our position in the sequence, and keep statistics separately for each position. For each offset $\ell = 0, \ldots, |s| - 1$, let $q^\ell \langle i \rangle$ be the state reached from $q\langle i \rangle$ by executing the first ℓ actions of s, that is, $q\langle i \rangle b_1 b_2 \cdots b_\ell$. For each ℓ, the sequence $q_0^\ell, q_1^\ell, q_2^\ell, \ldots$ is also periodic of period p.

For each ℓ, consider the sequence of (correct) outputs from the states $q^\ell \langle i \rangle$:

$$\phi_i^\ell = \phi^*(q^\ell \langle i \rangle).$$

The output sequence

$$\phi_0^\ell, \phi_1^\ell, \phi_2^\ell, \ldots.$$

is also periodic, of some least period p_ℓ dividing p. Since outputs are not necessarily unique, we may have $p > p_\ell$. However, because s is a distinguishing sequence, p will

Table 1
Sequences of visited states for $\pi = 4$

Step #	States visited					
0	0	4	2	0	4	2 ...
1	1	5	3	1	5	3 ...
2	2	0	4	2	0	4 ...
3	3	1	5	3	1	5 ...

be the least common multiple (LCM) of all the p_ℓ's. Thus, it would suffice to find each of the values p_ℓ, and take their LCM. In fact, what we will do is to find (with high probability) values q_ℓ such that p_ℓ divides q_ℓ and q_ℓ divides p, so that the LCM of the q_ℓ is also p. We describe the procedure for the sequence $q_0, q_1, q_2, \ldots$; it is analogous for the others.

Consider any candidate period $\pi \leqslant m$, and let $g = \gcd(p, \pi)$. For each $0 \leqslant i \leqslant \pi - 1$, consider the sequence of states visited every π repetitions of s, starting with $m + i$ repetitions of s. This will be the sequence of states

$$q\langle i \rangle, q\langle i + \pi \rangle, q\langle i + 2\pi \rangle, q\langle i + 3\pi \rangle, \ldots.$$

Since $q\langle i \rangle$ is periodic of period p, this sequence visits each state of the set $\{q\langle i + kg \rangle : k = 0, 1, \ldots, p/g - 1\}$ in some order, and then continues to repeat this cycle of p/g states.

Table 1 shows an example with $p = 6$, $\pi = 4, g = 2$. In this case, row r gives the indices of the states visited by repeating s, starting from $q\langle r \rangle$, assuming that the cycle of states visited by repeating s is $q_0, q_1, \ldots, q_5$.

In the special case $\pi = p$, shown in Table 2, each row r will consist exclusively of visits to state q_r. It is this case that we wish to distinguish from the others.

We cannot observe the states themselves, but we can observe the labels at each state the agent visits. The algorithm will repeat the distinguishing sequence s a total of $\mathcal{N}$ times, with $\mathcal{N}$ chosen to ensure that, with high probability, our observed frequencies are close to the probabilities of the sampled distribution. For each candidate period $\pi \leqslant m$, we form a table with π rows, numbered 0 to $\pi - 1$, and k columns, one for each possible label l_j. During the second part of the walk, we increment the table in row r, column j each time we observe label l_j.

After the second part of the walk, we compute the frequency of each entry (label) relative to the other entries in the same row. Let $\rho = (P - \frac{1}{2})$, the *separation* between the lower bound on correct observation and $\frac{1}{2}$. We use the value $\frac{1}{2} + \frac{1}{2}\rho$ as a threshold. When every row in the table for some π has a value that is above the threshold, the table is said to be *plausible*. For each plausible table, we take the sequence of π outputs determined by the largest value in each of the π rows and find the minimum period π' of the sequence. We find the LCM of all π'; this is our candidate for p.

We now present the procedure in a precise manner.

Procedure Localize.

(1) For simplicity, we assume that all the possible outputs are known and correspond to the integers $1, \ldots, k$. Build a table $T(\pi, \ell, r, j)$ of size $m \times |s| \times m \times k$. Initialize

Table 2
Sequences of visited states for $\pi = 6$

Step #	States visited					
0	0	0	0	0	0	0 ...
1	1	1	1	1	1	1 ...
2	2	2	2	2	2	2 ...
3	3	3	3	3	3	3 ...
4	4	4	4	4	4	4 ...
5	5	5	5	5	5	5 ...

all the table entries to zero. [5]

(2) Execute the sequence s^m to ensure that the agent is in a closed walk that it will continually traverse for as long as it continues to execute s. [6]

(3) Initialize the sequence counter $R \leftarrow 0$ and the step counter $c \leftarrow 0$.

(4) Execute s at least $\mathcal{N}$ times, incrementing R after each time. After executing each individual step, do the following:

 (a) Let $\ell = c \bmod |s|$, and j be the label observed immediately following execution.

 (b) For each $\pi = 1, 2, \ldots, m-1$, increment the table entry $T(\pi, \ell, R \bmod \pi, j)$ by 1.

 (c) Increment the step counter: $c \leftarrow c + 1$.

(5) Let

$$F(\pi, \ell, r, j) = \frac{T(\pi, \ell, r, j)}{\sum_{j=0}^{k} T(\pi, \ell, r, j)}.$$

(6) Initialize the period list $\mathcal{L} \leftarrow \{_-\}$. For each π and each ℓ, consider the two-dimensional table $F(\pi, \ell, \cdot, \cdot)$. If, for each $r < \pi$, row r in this table contains an element larger than $\frac{1}{2} + \frac{1}{2}\mathbf{sep}$, build the sequence of outputs of length π by taking the outputs corresponding to the large elements, $\arg\max_j F(\pi, \ell, r, j)$ for $r = 0, 1, \ldots, \pi - 1$. Find the period of this sequence and add it to $\mathcal{L}$.

(7) Let Π be the LCM of all $\pi' \in \mathcal{L}$.

(8) Conclude that the agent is currently located at the last state before row $r = R \bmod \Pi$ in the three-dimensional table $F(\Pi, \cdot, \cdot, \cdot)$, and return, as the hypothesis for the correct outputs of the distinguishing sequence s from this state, the sequence of outputs $\arg\max_j F(\Pi, \ell, r, j)$ for $\ell = 0, 1, \ldots, |s| - 1$ concatenated after the single output $\arg\max_j F(\Pi, |s| - 1, (r - 1) \bmod \Pi, j)$.

Table 3 shows the tables that resulted from a run of LOCALIZE in the environment shown in Fig. 3. The distinguishing sequence given to the procedure was $\langle bb \rangle$. Recall that π is the conjectured period length (number of executions of s), l is an index into the sequence s, r is an index into the cycle of length π, and j is the observed label. We can see that the tables for $\pi = 2$ and $\pi = 4$ are all plausible. When $\pi = 2$ and $\ell = 0$,

---

[5] If the labels are not known, then the table can be constructed incrementally, adding new labels as they are observed.

[6] Following Step 2, the next action should be the first action in s.

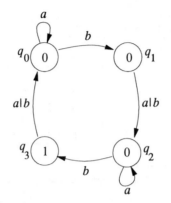

Fig. 3. A simple environment with a short distinguishing sequence.

Table 3
Tables built by LOCALIZE for the environment of Fig. 3

	$\pi = 1$		$\pi = 2$		$\pi = 3$		$\pi = 4$	
	$j = 0$	$j = 1$	$j = 0$	$j = 1$	$j = 0$	$j = 1$	$j = 0$	$j = 1$
$l = 0$	26(0.52)	24(0.48)	**21(0.84)**	4(0.16)	7(0.412)	10(0.588)	**11(0.846)**	2(0.154)
	0	0	5(0.2)	**20(0.8)**	10(0.588)	7(0.412)	2(0.514)	**11(0.846)**
	0	0	0	0	9(0.562)	7(0.438)	**10(0.833)**	2(0.167)
	0	0	0	0	0	0	3(0.25)	**9(0.75)**
$l = 1$	44(0.88)	6(0.12)	**21(0.84)**	4(0.16)	15(0.882)	2(0.118)	**13(1)**	0
	0	0	**23(0.92)**	2(0.08)	16(0.942)	1(0.0588)	**12(0.923)**	1(0.0769)
	0	0	0	0	13(0.812)	3(0.188)	**8(0.667)**	4(0.333)
	0	0	0	0	0	0	**11(0.917)**	1(0.0833)

we have the sequence 01, which has period 2; for $\pi = 2$ and $\ell = 1$, the period is 1; for $\pi = 4$ and $\ell = 0$ the period is 2; and for $\pi = 4$ and $\ell = 1$, the period is 1. The LCM of this set of periods is 2, so $\Pi = 2$. In the example, the agent starts in q_0, and so finishes either in q_0 (R is even) or in q_2 (R is odd). In the first case $r = 0$ and the signature returned by the algorithm is that of q_0: $\langle 000 \rangle$. In the other case $r = 1$ and the signature is $\langle 010 \rangle$.

5.1.3. Analysis

A formal proof of the correctness of the algorithm and a proof of the complexity in terms of the number of steps appears in a paper by Dean et al. [8]. We cite the final result concerning this complexity, and refer the reader to the paper for a complete proof.

Theorem 1. *In order to provide a correct signature with probability* $1 - \varepsilon$, LOCALIZE *must execute the distinguishing sequence s at least*

$$m + \frac{8m^2}{(2P - 1)^2} \ln \frac{2|s|km^3}{\varepsilon}$$

times. The number of steps taken is thus

$$O\left(\frac{|s|m^2}{(P - \frac{1}{2})^2} \ln \frac{|s|km^3}{\varepsilon}\right)$$

Recall that $|s|$ is the length of the distinguishing sequence, m is an upper bound on the number of states in the automaton, $P > \frac{1}{2}$ is a lower bound on the probability of the correct output from a state, k is the number of possible outputs, and ε is a bound on the probability that the procedure will fail.

The complete learning procedure which employs a distinguishing sequence s and LOCALIZE as subroutine is relatively straightforward and hence only sketched here. The detailed algorithm and proof of correctness is in [8]. Suppose for a moment that LOCALIZE always returns the agent to the same state and that the agent can always determine when it is in a state that it has visited before. In this case, the agent can learn the connectivity of the underlying automaton by performing what amounts to a depth-first search through the automaton's state transition graph. The agent does not actually traverse the state-transition graph in depth-first fashion; it cannot manage a depth-first search since, in general, it cannot backtrack. Instead, it executes sequences of actions corresponding to paths through the state transition graph starting from the root of the depth-first search tree by returning to the root each time using LOCALIZE. When, in the course of the search, a state is recognized as having been visited before, an appropriate arc is added to the inferred automaton and the search "backtracks" to the next path that has not been completely explored.

The actual inference algorithm is more complicated because our localization procedure does not necessarily always put the agent in the same final state and because we are not able to immediately identify the states we encounter during the depth-first search. The first problem is solved by performing many searches in parallel, one for each possible (root) state that LOCALIZE ends up in. Whenever LOCALIZE is executed the agent knows (with high probability) what state it has landed in and can take a step of the depth-first search that has that state as the root node. The second problem is solved by using a number of executions of the distinguishing sequence from a given starting state to identify that state with high probability.

It can easily be shown that it is possible to learn an automaton with high probability given a polynomial number of visits to a fixed starting state. LOCALIZE may not return the agent to the same starting state every time, but in a polynomial number of times executing LOCALIZE the agent will return to some state the required number of times. Of course, the agent is never absolutely sure that it has returned to the same state, but the agent can achieve any required probability of success in a number of steps polynomial in the reciprocal of the probability and the other measures of problem size.

The requirement that a distinguishing sequence be provided seems unlikely to be avoided in general. In particular, Dean et al. [8] show that learning such a sequence is not possible in polynomial time for environments as general as those we are considering here. Further, the results of Yannakakis and Lee [23] indicate that even computing preset distinguishing sequences for general environments is hard, although they provide an efficient way to compute adaptive distinguishing sequences. However, it is clear that an adaptive sequence will not work in place of a preset one in the LOCALIZE procedure.

The procedure relies on the ability to follow the sequence deterministically, so that it is certain to be in the right states, even if it perceives incorrect outputs along the way. With an adaptive sequence, correct movement would no longer be assured, since the action to perform at any point would depend on the previous, possibly incorrect, output.

5.2. Stochastic actions and deterministic observations

A *landmark environment* is one in which certain states have unique labels that can be detected as such. That is, not only are the labels unique, but one can think of the agent as having a detector that allows it to determine whether or not an observed label is unique. Although this seems to be a fairly strong condition, it is certainly something that people are quite good at. Indeed, people select landmarks precisely because they are sure that they present a unique aspect, and this surety comes without having examined all other locations. For example, almost anyone would identify the Transamerica pyramid in San Francisco as a good landmark, based on background knowledge of building styles that assures them that it is unique in appearance. This ability amounts to having learned what is unusual enough to count as a landmark; in this section we assume that agents have this ability. The problem of how this ability is learned or programmed is an interesting one, but is outside the scope of this work.[7]

5.2.1. Structural and interaction properties

In addition to the landmark property, we assume that the environment to be learned is reversible. This means that for every action that does not result in a self-transition, there is another action that reverses the effect of the first. While the agent's observation is perfect, no restriction is made on the structure of the labelling other than the landmark property. Thus, it is possible that all states that are not landmarks have the same label. With regard to movement, we assume that the agent takes the intended action with probability $\theta > \frac{1}{2}$, but allow any static distribution over actions that are in error. Finally, we assume that the agent has perfect knowledge of the action that would reverse its last action, that is, it knows perfectly from which way it arrived at its current location. We call the latter requirement *reverse movement certainty*. We assume that the agent has the ability to detect actions that will fail, that is, that will cause self-transitions. This obviously implies that the agent will also know which actions will succeed, and how many of these there are; we will sometimes refer to this as the degree of the state.

For convenience, we define D to be the subset of Q consisting of the landmark states and I to be the subset of Q consisting of the non-landmark states. We define the *landmark distribution parameter*, r, to be the maximum distance from any state in I to the nearest landmark (if $r = 0$, then I is empty and all states are landmarks). We say that a procedure learns the *local connectivity within radius r* of some $q \in D$ if it can provide the shortest path between q and any landmark within a radius r of q. We say that a procedure learns the *global connectivity of an environment $\mathcal{E}$ within a constant factor* if, for any two states q_1 and q_2 in D, it can provide a path between q_1 and q_2

---

[7] The work described in this section was carried out jointly with Jeff Vitter and is described in more detail in [4].

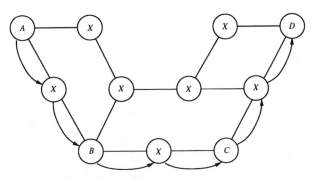

Fig. 4. A path found between landmarks A and D.

whose length is within a constant factor of the length of the shortest path between q_1 and q_2 in $\mathcal{E}$. The path will be constructed from paths found between locally connected landmarks (see Fig. 4).

Thus, we may summarize the agent's capabilities as follows. The agent's action function is not perfect, but serves to move the agent in the intended direction more than half the time. At each state, the agent knows what action to take to reverse the last action taken, even if it was not the intended action. In addition, the agent knows whether the state is a landmark, and if so, what its unique name is.

5.2.2. Algorithms

We begin by presenting a procedure that learns the local connectivity of an environment. We then show that the multiplicative error incurred in trying to answer global path queries can be kept low if the local error can be kept low and that the transition from a local uncertainty measure to a global uncertainty measure does not increase the complexity by more than a polynomial factor. We conclude that it is possible to build a procedure that directs exploration and map building so as to answer global path queries that are accurate and within a small constant factor of optimal with high probability.

The procedure for learning local connectivity begins with a search of the environment to locate all the landmarks. Once they have been found, the algorithm looks for short (less than cr, where $c > 2$ is an integer) paths between landmarks. This process has two phases: in the first, candidate paths are located, and in the second, these paths are verified. The need for this two-stage process arises from the possibility that some combination of movement errors could result in paths that appeared to connect two landmarks, but that, in fact, did not. We show that by exploiting reverse certainty we can statistically distinguish between the true paths and errors. By attempting enough traversals, the procedure can ensure with high probability that the most frequently occurring sets of directions corresponding to perceived traversals actually correspond to paths in $\mathcal{E}$.

The learning algorithm can be broken down into three steps: a landmark identification step in which the agent finds and identifies a set of landmarks, a candidate selection step in which the agent finds a set of candidate paths in $\mathcal{E}$ connecting landmarks, and a candidate filtering step in which the agent determines which of those candidate paths correspond to actual paths in $\mathcal{E}$.

We now present the procedure for learning local connectivity.

Procedure Connect.

(1) (Landmark location) A uniform random walk is made in the environment and landmarks encountered are added to a list.

(2) For each landmark A in the list from step (1):

    (a) For each sequence of directions of length cr, make multiple traversals of the path defined by the sequence, starting from A, recording the intended direction and reverse direction at each step. After each traversal, return to A with a random walk. Add any path which reaches some other landmark to the list of candidate paths.

(3) For each candidate path in the list from step (2), execute the path multiple times, beginning at the landmark at the head of the list and comparing reverse directions observed with those recorded for the path in step (2). Any failure in these comparisons is a failed traversal. If the landmark is reached without failure, the traversal is successful. If the landmark is not reached, return to the beginning landmark with a random walk. For each path, maintain a count of successful traversals.

(4) Return all paths from the list whose count from step (3) is above a threshold.

5.2.3. Analysis

We now state without proof (the detailed proof can be found in [6]) a series of lemmas leading up to the result that this algorithm is correct and has polynomial sample complexity.

Lemma 2. *For any $\varepsilon_l > 0$, the* CONNECT *procedure learns the local connectivity within cr of each state in any landmark environment with probability $1 - \varepsilon_l$ in time polynomial in $1/\varepsilon_l$, $1/(1 - 2\theta)$, and the size of $\mathcal{E}$, and exponential in cr.*

Lemma 3. *Let $\mathcal{E}$ be a landmark environment with distribution parameter r, and let c be any integer, $c > 2$. Given a procedure that, for any $\varepsilon_l > 0$, learns the local connectivity within cr of any landmark in $\mathcal{E}$ in time polynomial in $1/\varepsilon_l$ with probability $1 - \varepsilon_l$, it is possible to learn the global connectivity of $\mathcal{E}$ with probability $1 - \varepsilon_g$ for any $\varepsilon_g > 0$ in time polynomial in $1/\varepsilon_g$ and the size of the environment. Any global path returned as a result will be at most $c/(c - 2)$ times the length of the optimal path.*

Theorem 4. *It is possible to learn the global connectivity of any landmark environment with probability $1 - \varepsilon$ in time polynomial in $1/\varepsilon$, $1/(1 - 2\theta)$, and the size of $\mathcal{E}$, and exponential in r.*

Theorem 4 is a simple consequence of Lemmas 2 and 3. It has an immediate application to the problem of learning the global connectivity of an environment where all the states are landmarks. In this case, the parameter $r = 0$, and we need only explore paths of length 1 in order to establish the global connectivity of the environment. Because each candidate path has length one, this process works even if there is no reverse certainty.

Corollary 5. *It is possible to learn the connectivity of an environment $\mathcal{E}$ with only distinguishable locations with probability $1 - \varepsilon$ in time polynomial in $1/\varepsilon$, $1/1 - 2\theta$, and the size of G, even if there is reverse uncertainty.*

The notion of global connectivity defined above does not require that the environment be *completely learned* (i.e., to recover the structure of the entire environment). It is assumed that the indistinguishable states are of interest only in so far as they provide directions necessary to traverse a direct path between two landmarks. But it is easy to imagine situations where the indistinguishable states and the paths between them are of interest. For instance, the indistinguishable states might be partitioned further into equivalence classes so that one could uniquely designate a state by specifying its equivalence class and some radius from a particular global landmark (e.g., the bookstore just across the street from the Chrysler building). In [5], we show how to modify the above approach and try to completely learn the environment by first completely learning local neighborhoods of each landmark.

5.3. Stochastic actions and observations

In this section, we consider the case in which there is error in both the agent's actions and observations. In order to provide an algorithm with polynomial sample complexity, we are required to make restrictions on the environment. We present those restrictions, then give the algorithm and sketch a proof of its correctness and complexity.

5.3.1. Structural and interaction properties

Recall that an environment is reversible if, whenever there is an action a leading from q_1 to q_2 and $q_1 \neq q_2$, there is also a corresponding action from q_2 to q_1. Virtually all navigational environments have this property. Even one-way streets normally have corresponding parallel streets running in the opposite direction, providing an essentially undirected environment. Here, we assume the environment is reversible, but make no assumption that the agent knows the action that would reverse a given action.

The *conductance* of an environment is, informally, a measure of how many ways there are to get from one part of the environment to another. If there are a lot of bottlenecks, it is harder to learn the environment through random exploration. The algorithm presented here will work on environments of any conductance, but the lower the conductance (the more bottlenecks), the longer it will take.

We assume that the labelling of the environment is unique, so know that $|Q| \leqslant |L|$ (the number of states is less than or equal to the number of labels) and for simplicity of presentation we will assume that $|Q| = |L|$ and that for all i, label l_i is nominally correct for state q_i. Let $P_i = \phi(q_i)(l_i)$ be the probability that the agent correctly observes label l_i when it is in state q_i. For $i \neq j$, let $P_{ji} = \phi(q_i)(l_j)$ be the probability that the agent mistakenly observes label l_j when it is in state q_i. Finally, let P be a lower bound on all probabilities of correct observation, P_i. It is intuitively apparent that the higher the probability of correct observation is, the sooner the agent will be able to correctly identify its underlying environment.

The relationship between commands and actions is analogous to that between labels and states. We assume that $|A| = |C|$. Let $\theta_i = \psi(c_i)(a_i)$ be the probability that the agent correctly performs action a_i when it executes command c_i. Let θ be a lower bound on all the θ_i. In addition, we assume that the action function ψ is such that the agent can choose commands in such a way as to choose actions uniformly, allowing the agent to generate a random walk in the environment.

With regard to observation, we assume that the observation probabilities are *reflexive*; that is, for all i, j, $P_{ij} = P_{ji}$. The agent is just as likely to mistake state q_i for state q_j as it is to mistake state q_j for state q_i. As will be seen later, the point of this requirement is to limit the frequency with which a given label can be seen in those states where the observation is incorrect.

5.3.2. Algorithms

Given the restrictions from the previous section, the underlying structure of the environment can be learned by a very simple algorithm. The result of the algorithm will be, with high probability, an environment that is isomorphic to the original environment.

The algorithm uses a random strategy to explore the graph and records, for each pair of labels, (l_i, l_k), and each command, c_j, the number of times that an observation of l_i followed by performing c_j resulted in an observation of l_k. After enough exploration, a graph can be extracted from these statistics. If l_k is the most frequently observed label after doing command c_j when observing label l_i, then we assume that there is an edge for action a_j from state q_i to state q_k in the underlying graph.

More formally, the state-transition graph can be learned in the following way:

Algorithm CMFO (Choose Most Frequent Observation)
 (1) For each command $c \in C$, construct a two-dimensional table T_c indexed in each dimension by the labels in L.
 (2) Initialize all of the entries of all tables to 0.
 (3) Begin executing a uniform random walk in the environment. Whenever a transition is made from a state in which label l_i is observed to a state in which label l_j is observed by using command c, increment the value of $T_c(l_i, l_j)$.
 (4) After n action steps, stop and return edge set E' containing edge (q_i, a_h, q_j) only if $T_{c_h}(l_i, l_j) > T_{c_h}(l_i, l_k)$ for all k not equal to j.

Fig. 5 shows the results of a sample run of this algorithm on a very simple graph. The small tables specify the perception probabilities at each vertex; the large tables indicate, for each action, the frequency of sequential label pairs. The underlying graph is encoded by the largest element in each row of each table, which is in bold-face type.

5.3.3. Analysis

In this section we state specific conditions under which algorithm CMFO above succeeds and provide a bound on the number of observations the agent must make in order to have a given confidence of identifying the entire graph correctly.

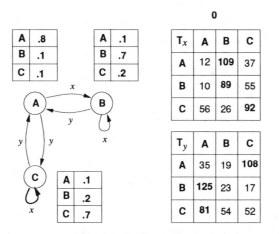

Fig. 5. Results of running the graph-identification algorithm in the simple environment shown for 1,000 steps. ($\theta = 0.8$).

In the following, we abuse notation slightly and let q_i stand for the event of visiting vertex q_i, l_i for the event of perceiving label l_i, and so on; in addition, we let $\circ q_i$ stand for the event of visiting q_i as a result of executing some action and $\circ l_i$ stand for the event of perceiving l_i as a result of executing some action. The algorithm can be seen as constructing estimates of the probabilities that a label l_j is seen after executing command c, given that the label l_i was seen just prior; this probability is notated as $\Pr(\circ l_j \mid l_i \wedge c)$. The observation probabilities depend on the details of the random walk being executed by the agent. This will be addressed later in the proof.

An important quantity for bounding the necessary number of trials is the *separation* of the probabilities $\Pr(\circ l_j \mid l_i)$ and $\Pr(\circ l_k \mid l_i)$, given that command c was executed. For a particular i, j, and k, the separation is defined as $s_i(j, k) = \Pr(\circ l_j \mid l_i) - \Pr(\circ l_k \mid l_i)$;[8] for a given label i, $s_i = s_i(j, k)$ where l_j is the "correct" successor label to label l_i (that is, that for action a corresponding to command c, $\delta(q_i, a) = q_j$) and l_k is the most likely incorrect successor label (that is, l_k is the label not equal to l_j that maximizes $\Pr(\circ l_k \mid l_i)$); a lower bound on all the s_i is written as s. If the value of s is high, then we are much more likely to see "correct" transitions than to see "incorrect" ones. For the CMFO algorithm to work correctly, we must guarantee that the separation is always positive, so that no incorrect transition is more likely to be observed than the corresponding correct one. The requirement that observation probabilities be reflexive derives from this need. Consider the sum of the probabilities of making a particular observation in error: $\sum_{i \neq k} P_{ki}$. Without any other restriction, it is possible to construct situations in which this is as high as $|Q|(1 - P)$, and in which positive separation is impossible for all but unrealistically high values of P. The reflexivity requirement is one of several possible requirements that eliminate such situations. In Section 6 we discuss one set of noise models that satisfy this requirement.

---

[8] Because the separation is always with respect to a particular command, we suppress the parameter throughout.

We can characterize the number of observations required by the algorithm as a function of the separation. The proof is omitted, but can be found elsewhere [6,14]. It uses Hoeffding's inequality to show that after a large enough number of samples, it is very likely that the observation with the largest sample frequency is also the observation with the largest true frequency.

Lemma 6. *If the separation s is greater than* 0, *then the output of algorithm* CMFO *is correct with probability at least* $1 - \varepsilon$ *after each vertex has been visited at least N times, where N is polynomial in* $1/s$, $1/\varepsilon$, $|Q|$, *and* $|A|$.

We will use a random walk to explore the environment, so we must turn our attention to the question of how long a walk is needed. Not only must we guarantee with high probability that the states are all visited enough times, we must also be able to characterize the distribution of state visitations, because it affects the transition probabilities, and, hence, the separation.

A *uniform* random walk in the environment is one in which actions are also chosen equiprobably; by our earlier assumption, the agent knows some distribution over commands that allows this. We can describe the walk by a Markov process with transition matrix R, defined by $r_{ij} = g/|A|$, where g is the number of edges in E from q_i to q_j. In a reversible environment, there are as many edges from q_i to q_j as there are from q_j to q_i, so R is symmetric; this implies that the columns, as well as the rows, sum to 1, making the matrix *doubly stochastic*. Any matrix that is doubly stochastic has a uniform stationary probability distribution [10]; that is, in the limit each state is visited with probability $1/|Q|$.

The next lemma concerns the rate at which the distribution of state visitations approaches the uniform stationary distribution. Let $\bar{x}_i(t)$ be the probability that the process is in state q_i at time t and let π_i be the stationary probability of state q_i. Define the discrepancy, ζ_t, to be the L_2 norm of the difference between π and $\bar{x}(t)$. This result is a direct consequence of Mihail's result [15] on the convergence of Markov chains.

Lemma 7. *Let t be the number of time steps needed to guarantee that the discrepancy between the state distribution at time t and its stationary distribution is less than ζ, when executing the process determined by the transition matrix R. Then t can be bounded above by*

$$t \leqslant \frac{2}{\Phi^2} \ln \frac{1}{\zeta},$$

where Φ is the merging conductance *of the process. It is defined by*

$$\Phi = \min_{S \subset Q: \sum_{q_i \in S} \pi_i \leqslant 1/2} \Phi(S),$$

where

$$\Phi(S) = \frac{\sum_{j_1 \in S} \sum_{j_2 \in Q-S} \sum_i r_{j_1 i} r_{j_2 i}}{|S|}.$$

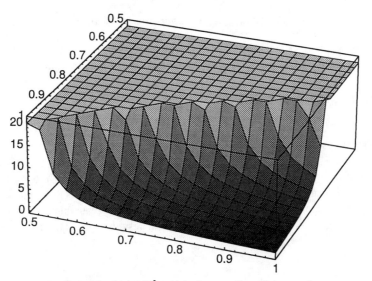

Fig. 6. A plot of $1/(2\theta P^2 - 1)$ in the area of positive separation.

Now, we give a bound on the separation, assuming a bound on the discrepancy.

Lemma 8. *Let ζ be an upper bound on the discrepancy after t steps, let $z = (1 + |Q|\sqrt{\zeta})/(1 - |Q|\sqrt{\zeta})$, let P be a lower bound on the probability of making a correct observation, P_i, and let θ be a lower bound on the probability of taking a correct action, θ_i. If the probabilities of making incorrect observations are reflexive, that is, if $\forall x, y, P_{xy} = P_{yx}$, then for all actions and all initial labels l_i, after a random walk of length t,*

(1) $s_i > 0$ if $P \geqslant (1 - z + \sqrt{z^2 + 8\theta z - 2z + 1})/4\theta$, and

(2) $s_i \geqslant P(2\theta P - 1)/z + P - 1$.

Note that for a long enough walk it is reasonable to approximate z by 1, which yields the simple requirement that $P > 1/\sqrt{2\theta}$; this has the intuitively pleasing consequence that θ, the lower bound on correct execution of commands, must be greater than $\frac{1}{2}$. In this case, the separation is bounded below by $2\theta P^2 - 1$, so the exploration complexity of algorithm CMFO contains a factor of $1/(2\theta P^2 - 1)$. Fig. 6 shows a plot of this factor for values of P and θ from $\frac{1}{2}$ to one in the area where the separation is positive. The "plateau" area in the figure represents the portions of (P, θ)-space for which the bound on the separation is negative.

Theorem 9. *The output of the CMFO algorithm is correct with probability at least $(1 - \varepsilon)(1 - \varepsilon_2)$ after a uniform random walk of length polynomial in*

$$P(2\theta P - 1)/z + P - 1,$$

$1/\varepsilon$, $1/\varepsilon_2$, $1/\Phi$, $|Q|$, and $|A|$, where P is the lowest probability of correct observation, θ is the lowest probability of correct action, Φ is the conductance, $z =$

$(1 + |Q|\sqrt{\zeta})/(1 - |Q|\sqrt{\zeta})$, and ζ is an upper bound on discrepancy of the state distribution, whenever

(1) $P > (1 - z + \sqrt{z^2 + 8\theta z - 2z + 1})/4\theta$,

(2) *a uniform distribution on C induces a uniform distribution on A,*

(3) $\forall x, y, P_{xy} = P_{yx}$, *and*

(4) *the environment is reversible.*

6. Empirical results

In the following sections we develop a particular class of noise model and present results of empirical simulations of our algorithms from Sections 5.1 and 5.3. In both cases, the results demonstrate that in automata representing plausible real-world environments, the actual number of samples needed is far less that predicted by the theoretical results.

6.1. Noise models

Two of the results of Section 5 require that the probability of correct action be above some threshold. Two others require that the probability of correct observation be above some threshold. In addition, algorithm CMFO requires that the probability of error be reflexive for observation. A large number of possible noise models satisfy these constraints, and the choice of noise model will certainly affect the actual performance of the algorithm. In our experiments, we have used one noise model for actions, and several different noise models for observations.

Our error model for actions is a simple *uniform* model. When an incorrect action is taken, it is chosen uniformly at random from all incorrect actions. For observations, we have developed a general class of noise models called *similarity partition* noise models. Such a model is constructed as follows. The set Q of states is partitioned into subsets $Q_1, Q_2, \ldots, Q_k$. Intuitively, the elements of the partition represent sets of states that look alike. Each state in a given partition, Q_i, has an observation function that gives the correct answer with probability P, and gives the label of some other state in the partition with probability $(1 - P)/|Q_i|$. The uniform error model is one special case of this scheme; it occurs when the partition has only one element that covers all of Q.

6.2. Deterministic actions and stochastic observations

The polynomial functions we have shown to bound the performance of the algorithms described in Section 5.1 are pessimistic. We now describe the results of experiments with LOCALIZE that indicate that this is so. There are similar results for the complete automaton inference algorithm provided in [8].

Our result requires environments with distinguishing sequences. We hypothesize that many natural environments, and hallway environments in particular, possess short distinguishing sequences. To test this hypothesis, we constructed a variety of hallway environments and determined the length of the shortest distinguishing sequence, assum-

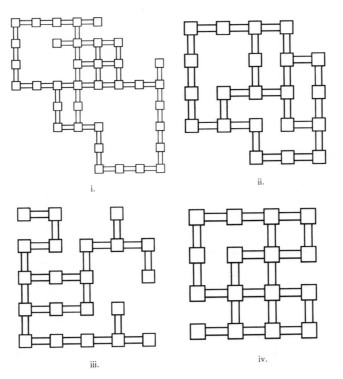

i.   ii.

iii.   iv.

Fig. 7. Graphs for hallway environments.

ing that such a sequence existed. Fig. 7(i) depicts the state-transition graph for the fifth floor of the Brown CS Department. Three other graphs typical of the ones that we used in our experiments are shown in Figs. 7(ii) through 7(iv). The length of the shortest distinguishing sequence for Fig. 7(i) is four. The lengths of the shortest distinguishing sequences for Figs. 7(ii), 7(iii), and 7(iv) are two, three, and two respectively.

We generated a large number of graphs by starting with a $d \times d$ grid of locations and constructing a graph of n edges by selecting n pairs of adjacent locations according to a uniform distribution without replacement. The actions available at a location consisted of movement in each of the four directions (i.e., N, E, W, S) along axes of the grid; if there was not an edge in a particular direction, the action corresponded to a self-transition. The labels for locations encoded the junction type (e.g., L-shaped or T-shaped) and orientation (e.g., facing N, E, W, or S) for a total of sixteen labels, including the degenerate label corresponding to a location with no adjacent corridors. A uniform error model was used, so the probability that the agent observed the correct label was P and the probability that it observed a label other than the correct one was $\frac{1}{15}(1 - P)$. For fixed d with n in the range of d to d^2, the length of the shortest distinguishing sequence was nearly constant. For the graphs that we have looked at, the length of the shortest distinguishing sequence seemed to increase roughly as the square root of the number of states. Fig. 8 shows the length of the shortest distinguishing sequence as a function of the number of states in the environment, averaging over sets of environments.

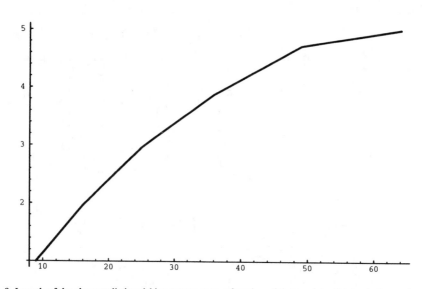

Fig. 8. Length of the shortest distinguishing sequence as a function of the number of states in the environment.

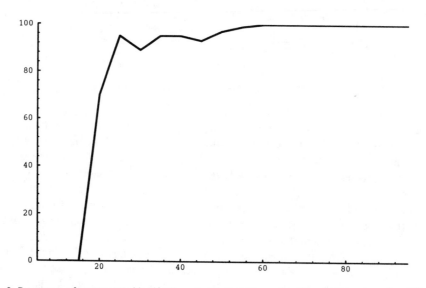

Fig. 9. Percentage of correct state identifications for LOCALIZE as a function of the number of repetitions of the distinguishing sequence.

The theoretical results indicate that for a DFA consisting of 21 states LOCALIZE needs as many as 76206 steps for $P = 0.8$. In our simulations, however, LOCALIZE is successful 100% of the time with no more than 50 steps using a distinguishing sequence of length three. We also observed that the performance of LOCALIZE is largely insensitive to P, continuing to perform with 100% accuracy having executed 50 steps with P as low as 0.5. We believe this is largely due to the fact that errors are distributed uniformly over the incorrect labels; it is straightforward to construct alternative error

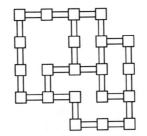

Fig. 10. An abstract environment used to test the CMFO algorithm.

distributions that require a lot more work on the part of LOCALIZE. Fig. 9 shows a graph of the percentage of correct state identifications for LOCALIZE running on the environment of Fig. 7(i) as a function of the number of repetitions of the distinguishing sequence. This graph typifies the performance of LOCALIZE running on the range of graphs that we considered in our experiments.

6.3. Stochastic actions and observations

In this section, we consider the performance of the CMFO algorithm in simulation. The environments used by the simulation are also constructed as abstract models of hallway environments. These environments have four actions, corresponding to moving North, South, East, and West. As before, actions that are not applicable for a given location result in self-transitions. Fig. 10 shows the environment, called *CIT 4*, used in our experiments; it models one floor of the Computer Science Department at Brown University and has 21 states. The experiments were performed using a range of values for the parameters P and θ.

With regard to the CMFO algorithm, the uniform error model is quite benign. This is because uniform distribution over a large number of states virtually guarantees that the most frequent observation will be correct. Indeed, under the uniform noise model, increasing the size of the problem actually helps in this regard, although the increased size also requires a longer walk to gather enough data. By using smaller partitions, more pernicious noise models may be created. For example, by partitioning Q into pairs, a significant competitor to the correct answer, in terms of frequency, is assured. It is easy to see that all similarity partition noise models satisfy the reflexivity requirement stated in the proof.

In these experiments, three different similarity partition error models were used. The first error model was the uniform model, the second and third were more complicated partitions based on the hallway structure of the environment. In these models, locations were partitioned according to the type of junction they represented in the world. For example, *CIT 4* has corner junctions, T-junctions and hall junctions. If the agent is able to detect the type of a junction reliably, then its sensors will conform to a noise model that partitions locations by junction type. Junction types may further be partitioned by considering the orientation of the junction. For example, a corner junction with South and West hallways might be distinguished from one with North and East hallways. In the *CIT 4* environment, the oriented junction-type partition results in a number of singleton elements, but also results in a number of pairs and triples.

6.3.1. Results

The experiments consisted of multiple runs of algorithm CMFO on the *CIT 4* environment. For each of the three error models, the algorithm was run in simulation with different values for the probability of correct action, θ, probability of correct observation, P, and number of steps. In these simulations, each time the algorithm issued a command, a random value from 0 to 1 was generated and compared against θ. If the value generated was greater than θ, an random incorrect action was chosen uniformly and executed, otherwise the correct action was executed. After each execution, a second number was generated and compared against P. If the number generated was greater than P, a random incorrect observation was returned from the similarity partition element of the current state. Otherwise, the correct label of the current state was returned. Values of θ and P from 0.5 to 1 in 0.1 increments were used; the walk length was varied from 1000 to 10,000. The walk length interval was chosen to give a range in which the algorithm's overall performance went from bad to nearly perfect. For each combination of walk length, θ, and P, the algorithm was given 20 tries to construct a map (50 tries per combination were used for the uniform error model).

Figs. 11–13 show the performance of algorithm CMFO on the *CIT 4* environment with the uniform, oriented junction-type and unoriented junction-type error models, respectively. Each figure shows that the algorithm's performance improves steadily as the uncertainty in action and in observation decrease and as the number of steps increases. The figures also provide a comparison of the different error models. Although the theorem guarantees the performance of the algorithm only when $P > 1/\sqrt{2\theta}$, data was collected with values of P and θ beginning at $\frac{1}{2}$. In the case of the uniform error model, complete success is obtained even for combinations of these parameters that are disallowed by the theorem. This is a result of the benign nature of the uniform noise model. In the oriented partition model, performance is very poor until the requirements are met (in particular until P reaches $1/\sqrt{2}$) because this model comes much closer to the pessimistic assumptions used in the theorem. The unoriented model performs much more closely to the uniform model, and this is attributable to the fact that the partitions are large in this model, none smaller than size 6. In addition, the walk lengths used in the simulation were much shorter than those suggested by the theorem, by roughly 2 orders of magnitude. The success of the algorithm on shorter walks is due both to the factors just mentioned and to the looseness of a result concerning random walks used in our proof. Fig. 14 shows the data gathered in a different form. Here, the number of steps (in thousands) needed by the algorithm to infer a correct map in each of twenty trials is shown for different values of P and θ. The "plateau" areas of these plots represent areas in which the algorithm failed to get twenty perfect answers with less than 10,000 steps. Comparison of these figures with Fig. 6, reproduced in the bottom right plot, shows that these failures are not unexpected; they occur in a region that may have very low or negative separation.

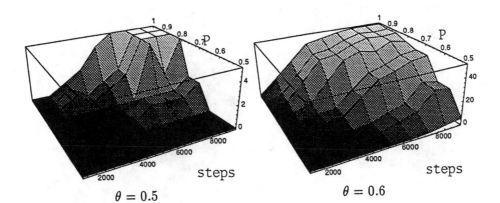

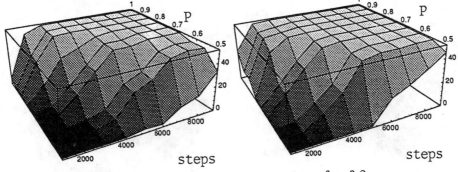

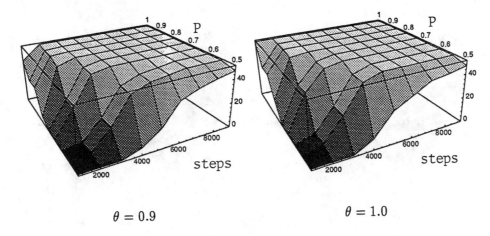

Fig. 11. Number of successes plotted as a function of p and the walk length for different values of θ for algorithm CMFO on the *CIT 4* environment with uniform error model.

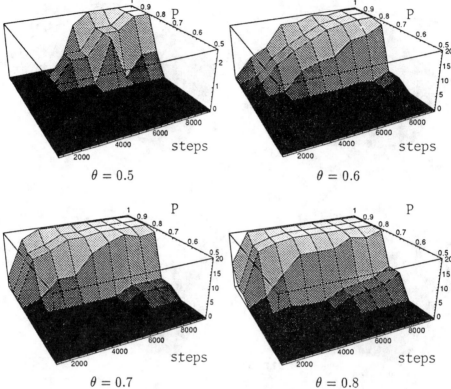

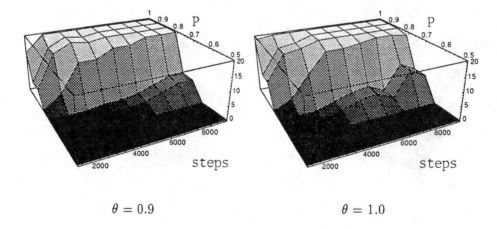

Fig. 12. Number of successes plotted as a function of p and the walk length for different values of θ for algorithm CMFO on the *CIT 4* environment with the oriented junction-type similarity partition error model.

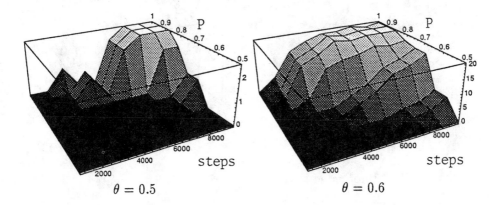

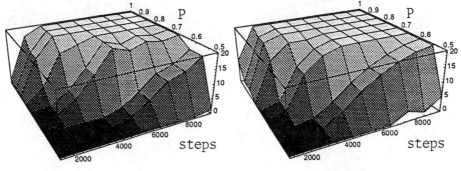

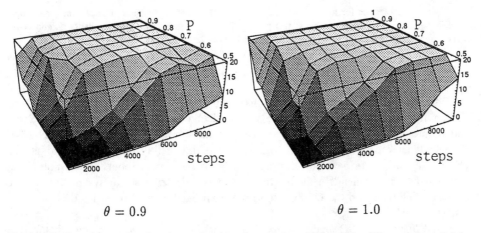

Fig. 13. Number of successes plotted as a function of p and the walk length for different values of θ for algorithm CMFO on the *CIT 4* environment with unoriented junction-type similarity partition error model.

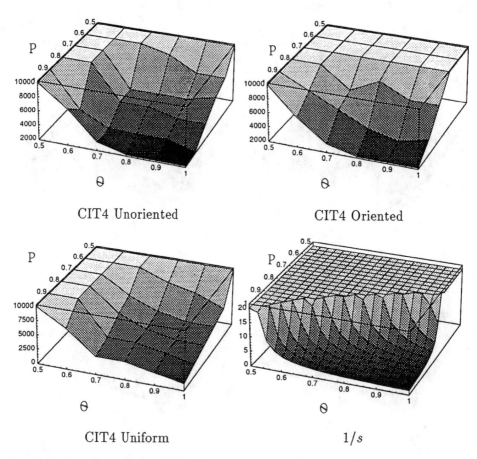

Fig. 14. Number of steps for first 100% success ($N = 20$) plotted as function of P and the walk length for different values of θ for algorithm CMFO on the *CIT 4* environment with three similarity partition error models; the bottom right plot is the $1/s$ factor from Theorem 2.

6.4. Application to a real mapping system

In the earlier analyses, simplifications were made for the sake of mathematical tractability. For example, we assume independent observation and movement errors and ignore sources of systematic error. Despite these simplifying assumptions, we believe that our models are relevant to a variety of interesting tasks and environments. Our simulations were based on the problem faced by mobile robots in learning about their spatial environment. In this section we briefly describe a real system for robotic map building based on the CMFO algorithm from Section 5.3; more detail is available elsewhere [6].

Recall that the CMFO algorithm required, in addition to several structural features, a nominally unique output at each state which whose observation probability was above some threshold. This requirement was satisfied by combining information about orientation, junction type and position at each location. The robot used was equipped with eight sonar transducers and an odometer which were used to generate this information. Robust high-level movement procedures were implemented as combinations of simpler traversal strategies; these procedures were used as the algorithm's actions. The robot's sensing and movement procedures were designed to operate in common hallway environment such as that corresponding to the *CIT 4* simulation environment. The CMFO algorithm was modified slightly from the version presented above; these modifications allowed more efficient exploration and avoided taking actions which could be predicted to fail.

The goal of the modifications and development of sensing and movement strategies was to allow correct identification of the environment using a number of steps well below the number required by the analysis of Section 5.3, on the order of a small constant times the number of states in the environment. This goal was achieved; The robot successfully built models using $3|Q|$ steps.

7. Discussion and open problems

The system identification problems discussed here can be thought of as points in a large space of such problems, each with its own set of structural and interaction properties. Our goal in this work has been to provide solutions to several representative problems from a portion of this space characterized by noisy inputs and/or outputs. Our interest in this part of the space derives directly from our interest in solving identification problems in the real world, where such noise is unavoidable.

These results provide indications about which problems might be realistically approached with current robotic systems. For example, although we have not provided direct comparisons of the complexity of the problems explored here, both our theoretical and empirical results suggest that having nominally unique labels is an enormous advantage. The robotic system described earlier was designed with this knowledge in mind. With regard to problems involving spatial exploration, there may be other assumptions that can be made which allow even better results.

The solutions to problems involving non-unique outputs generally involve sequences, in particular distinguishing sequences. Gill [11] provides a way to construct preset distinguishing sequences when they exist, but these may have length exponential in the number of states and the algorithm requires a complete description of the automaton. Yannakakis and Lee [23] show that the problem of determining whether an automaton has a preset distinguishing sequence is PSPACE-complete, but also give an efficient, constructive algorithm for determining whether an automaton has an adaptive distinguishing sequence. As regards uncertainty in perception, the following two important questions remain to be resolved.

- Suppose distinguishing sequences exist and observation and movement are uncertain? Are adaptive sequences still easy to find?
- Suppose the agent is given an adaptive distinguishing sequence. Is it easy to identify the underlying automaton with observation and movement uncertainty?

8. Conclusions

This paper investigates algorithms for agents to identify the input/output behavior of the dynamical system corresponding to their environment. In our model, the system is represented as a deterministic finite automaton with a relatively small number of states and actions. While we admit that the real world cannot be modeled by such automata to any high degree of predictive accuracy, expediency requires and nature has provided the means of simplifying the huge amounts of data available to our senses. Biological systems appear to be equipped with robust perceptual and motor routines that serve to abstract and considerably reduce the complexity of the real world. We believe that, lacking such routines, learning is impossibly hard. In addition, our approach does not require an agent to learn one automaton to represent the full range of its interaction with the environment; rather, different aspects of that interaction would be modeled with different automata. We claim then that, given appropriate perceptual and action routines, it makes sense to model system identification in terms of inferring automata.

In this paper, we address the problem of dealing with the inevitable errors that occur in perception and movement. Given our model, we show that errors in perception that do not affect movement are rather easy to contend with if the goal is polynomial-time, high-probability approximation. A general method of dealing with errors in both observation and movement without any means of establishing ground truth as a basis for filtering hypotheses has so far eluded us. We have, however, provided algorithms that work for the case in which there are landmarks distributed throughout the environment and the agent has some means of determining how it got somewhere without necessarily knowing where it came from. We have also provided algorithms for the case in which all states have unique signatures but both observation and movement are noisy.

In additional to our theoretical results, we have performed extensive experimental studies that indicate that, for a class of relatively benign but nevertheless realistic environments, our bounds are quite conservative. Ultimately, we are seeking algorithms that can learn a high-probability approximation to the correct, underlying environmental model in time some small constant factor of the size of the underlying model even in the presence of occasional errors. In our work on real mobile robots, we are approaching that goal.

Acknowledgments

Dana Angluin and Sean Engelson provided insights and corrections to the algorithm and proof of Section 5.1. Oded Maron and Evangelos Kokkevis also participated in discussions of these algorithms and provided helpful simulation results. Jeffrey Vitter participated in the development of the landmark algorithm. Philip Klein provided useful pointers to the literature of random walks in graphs. Several anonymous reviewers also provided helpful suggestions.

References

[1] D. Angluin, On the complexity of minimum inference of regular sets, *Inf. Control* **39** (1978) 337–350.

[2] D. Angluin, Learning regular sets from queries and counterexamples, *Inf. Comput.* **75** (1987) 87–106.

[3] J.R. Bachrach, Connectionist modeling and control of finite state environments, Tech. Report 92-6, Department of Computer and Information Science, University of Massachusetts at Amherst, Amherst, MA (1992).

[4] K. Basye, T. Dean and J.S. Vitter, Coping with uncertainty in map learning, in: *Proceedings IJCAI-89*, Detroit, MI (1989).

[5] K. Basye, T. Dean and J.S. Vitter, Coping with uncertainty in map learning, Tech. Report CS-89-27, Department of Computer Science, Brown University, Providence, RI (1989).

[6] K.J. Basye, *A framework for map construction*, Ph.D. Thesis, Department of Computer Science, Brown University, Providence, RI (1992).

[7] T. Dean, D. Angluin, K. Basye, S. Engelson, L. Kaelbling, E. Kokkevis and O. Maron, Inferring finite automata with stochastic output functions and an application to map learning, in: *Proceedings AAAI-92*, San Jose, CA (1992).

[8] T. Dean, D. Angluin, K. Basye, S. Engelson, L. Kaelbling, E. Kokkevis and O. Maron, Inferring finite automata with stochastic output functions and an application to map learning, Tech. Report CS-92-27, Department of Computer Science, Brown University, Providence, RI (1992).

[9] T. Dean, K. Basye, R. Chekaluk, S. Hyun, M. Lejter and M. Randazza, Coping with uncertainty in a control system for navigation and exploration, in: *Proceedings AAAI-90*, Boston, MA (1990).

[10] W. Feller, *An Introduction to Probability Theory and its Applications* (Wiley, New York, 3d ed., 1970), revised printing.

[11] A. Gill, State-identification experiments in finite automata, *Inf. Comput.* **4** (1961) 132–154.

[12] E.M. Gold, System identification via state characterization, *Automatica* **8** (1972) 621–636.

[13] E.M. Gold, Complexity of automaton identification from given sets, *Inf. Control* **37** (1978) 302–320.

[14] L. Kaelbling, K. Basye and T. Dean, Learning labelled graphs from noisy data, in: *Proceedings Seventh Yale Workshop on Adaptive and Learning Systems* (1992).

[15] M. Mihail, Conductance and convergence of Markov chains: a combinatorial treatment of expanders, in: *Proceedings 31st ACM Symposium on Foundations of Computer Science* (1989).

[16] E.F. Moore, Gedanken-experiments on sequential machines, in: *Automata Studies* (Princeton University Press, Princeton, NJ, 1956) 129–153.

[17] L. Pitt and M.K. Warmuth, The minimum consistent DFA problem cannot be approximated within any polynomial, in: *Proceedings 21st Annual ACM Symposium on Theoretical Computing* (1989).

[18] R.L. Rivest and R.E. Schapire, Diversity-based inference of finite automata, in: *Proceedings 29th ACM Symposium on Foundations of Computer Science* (1987).

[19] R.L. Rivest and R.E. Schapire, Inference of finite automata using homing sequences, in: *Proceedings 21st Annual ACM Symposium on Theoretical Computing* (1989).

[20] R.E. Schapire, The design and analysis of efficient learning algorithms, Tech. Report MIT/LCS/TR-493, MIT Laboratory for Computer Science (1991).

[21] D. Servan-Schreiber, A. Cleeremans and J.L. McClelland, Learning sequential structure in simple recurrent networks, in: D. Touretzky, ed., *Advances in Neural Information Processing* Vol. **1** (Morgan Kaufmann, San Mateo, CA, 1989).

[22] R.S. Sutton, Integrated architectures for learning, planning, and reacting based on approximating dynamic programming, in: *Proceedings Seventh International Conference on Machine Learning* (1990).

[23] M. Yannakakis and D. Lee, Testing finite state machines, in: *Proceedings 23rd ACM Symposium on Theoretical Computing* (1991).

Artificial Intelligence 72 (1995) 173–215

A dynamical systems perspective on agent-environment interaction

Randall D. Beer*

Dept. of Computer Engineering and Science and Dept. of Biology, Case Western Reserve University, Cleveland, OH 44106, USA

Received September 1992; revised March 1993

Abstract

Using the language of dynamical systems theory, a general theoretical framework for the synthesis and analysis of autonomous agents is sketched. In this framework, an agent and its environment are modeled as two coupled dynamical systems whose mutual interaction is in general jointly responsible for the agent's behavior. In addition, the adaptive fit between an agent and its environment is characterized in terms of the satisfaction of a given constraint on the trajectories of the coupled agent-environment system. The utility of this framework is demonstrated by using it to first synthesize and then analyze a walking behavior for a legged agent.

1. Introduction

This paper is concerned with properly characterizing the interaction between an autonomous agent and its environment. By *autonomous agent*, I mean any embodied system designed to satisfy internal or external goals by its own actions while in continuous long-term interaction with the environment in which it is situated. The class of autonomous agents is thus a fairly broad one, encompassing at the very least all animals and autonomous robots. An animal, for example, may simply be trying to survive, while a robot might be designed to carry out specific tasks, such as keeping some designated area clean or exploring the surface of another planet. The task is thus to abstract over particular details of implementation and embodiment (e.g., nerve cells vs. finite state machines or muscles vs. motors) in order to understand the essential character of this class of systems.

---

* E-mail: beer@alpha.ces.cwru.edu

However short of this ambitious goal the present paper may fall, the long-term aim is nothing less than a general theoretical framework for the explanation and design of autonomous agents.

The central problem for any autonomous agent, and thus the primary concern in this paper, is the generation of the appropriate behavior at the appropriate time as both its internal state and external situation continuously change. For an embodied agent, action must always take precedence over any other activity. Abstract reasoning, when it can be afforded at all, is profitable only insofar as it is ultimately reflected in improved behavior. This does not necessarily imply that an embodied agent must be purely reactive, reflexively responding only to its immediate situation. Rather, it means an autonomous agent must be able to flexibly combine its immediate circumstances with its long-term goals so as to continuously adjust its behavior in ways appropriate to both. An animal moving throughout its environment, for example, needs to adopt many different modes of behavior as it becomes hungry or tired and encounters potential food, predators and mates, all the while adjusting its posture and leg movements to the constantly changing terrain which it is traversing.

Traditionally, such "low level" concerns of embodiment have not played a major role in AI research. Instead, work in AI has tended to emphasize "high level" intellectual skills, such as language, problem solving and abstract reasoning. Embodied agents, when they have been considered at all, have been viewed as merely symbolic reasoning engines with sensors and effectors attached. Accordingly, the problems of embodied agents have usually been formulated as special cases of the problems of disembodied intelligent systems. Of course, it has long been realized that embodiment raises certain additional technical issues. Sensors, for example, introduce the problem of constructing, and maintaining the consistency of, internal representations of the environment from physical signals, while effectors introduce the problem of translating representations of action into actual motor commands. Furthermore, physical embodiment introduces real-time constraints on an agent's action that limit the amount of time that can be spent reasoning. However, these technical problems are usually seen as merely complicating, rather than invalidating, the classical picture.

In recent years, however, a growing number of AI researchers have begun to appreciate the fundamental importance of embodiment. There are a number of reasons for this change in perspective. Designing agents that can interact with the real world with the versatility and robustness of even simple animals has turned out to be considerably more subtle and difficult than originally realized, and approaches developed for disembodied agents have not in general translated well to the noisy, unpredictable, open-ended and dynamic nature of the real world. Furthermore, many problems that seemed intractable for disembodied systems have turned out to be considerably simplified by active participation in an environment. Work on animate vision, for example, has demonstrated that a number of visual problems are drastically simplified if the agent is given the ability to control its own gaze direction [8]. Likewise, work on situated agents has shown that the potentially brittle and combinatorially explosive nature of general planning can be significantly alleviated by using the immediate situation to guide behavior [3, 20]. Indeed, there is a growing realization that, far from being a mere complication for a disembodied intellect, embodiment may in fact be the more fundamental issue. Certainly, from an evolutionary perspective, the human capacity for language and abstract thought is a relatively recent elaboration of a much more basic capacity for situated action that is universal among animals.

This reassessment of the importance of embodiment has led to an explosion of recent work on autonomous agents. Brooks, working in the area of mobile robotics, was one of the first AI researchers to point out the limitations of classical AI techniques in the face of real-world complexity and the need for a renewed emphasis on embodiment and situated action [18, 20]. Agre and Chapman's work on routine activity grew out of a similar frustration with the limitations of classical planning in realistic environments and led to similar conclusions [2, 3, 22]. Building on Rosenschein's situated automata theory [56], Rosenschein and Kaelbling developed methods for deriving finite state machine controllers for an agent from a formal specification of its knowledge and goals [42]. My own work [11, 14] and that of Cliff [24] has demonstrated the significant potential for interaction between autonomous agent research and work on the neural basis of animal behavior. Biological design principles have also been stressed by Arbib and Liaw [5]. Surveys of recent work in autonomous agents can be found in the collections edited by Maes [45] and Meyer and Wilson [49].

This body of work is loosely characterized by a number of shared ideas. It emphasizes the primacy of actually taking action in the world over the abstract descriptions that we sometimes make of it. It focuses on the development of complete agents capable of carrying out open-ended tasks in unconstrained environments rather than isolated cognitive skills in restricted task domains. It emphasizes behavior and the fundamental importance that the immediate situation plays in guiding an agent's behavior, ideas historically associated with behaviorism, over reasoning and symbolic models of the world. Another common theme of this work has been that a significant fraction of behavior must be seen as emerging from the ongoing interaction between an agent and its environment, an idea often associated with cybernetics. This work has also begun to question the central role that internal representation has been assumed to play in intelligent behavior by most work in cognitive science.

In this paper, I will attempt to show that these and other ideas that are emerging from recent work on autonomous agents, as well as work on the neural basis of animal behavior, can be naturally cast into the language of dynamical systems theory. Furthermore, I will argue that this language can form the basis for a powerful theoretical framework for the explanation and design of autonomous agents in general. Section 2 reviews some of the basic concepts of dynamical systems theory that are required to present this framework. In Section 3, I sketch the theoretical framework itself and draw out some of its conceptual consequences. Section 4 demonstrates the utility of this framework by illustrating in some detail its application to the synthesis and analysis of a walking behavior for a simulated legged agent. Finally, Section 5 discusses the assumptions of the proposed framework, considers its broader implications, and suggests some directions for future work.

2. Dynamical systems

This section will briefly review the essential concepts and terminology of the qualitative theory of dynamical systems that will be required for the theoretical framework to be presented in Section 3. The presentation is necessarily informal and incomplete. The reader interested in a more thorough treatment should refer to one of the many available texts on dynamical systems including, in order of increasing mathematical sophistication, the books by Abraham and Shaw [1], Hale and Koçak [33] and Wiggins [66].

Consider the following three mathematical systems:

$$x_{n+1} = \mu x_n (1 - x_n) \tag{1}$$

$$ml \frac{d^2\theta}{dt^2} + \gamma \frac{d\theta}{dt} + mg \sin \theta = A \cos(\omega t) \tag{2}$$

$$\tag{3}$$

At first glance, these three systems may appear to have very little in common. The first equation is an example of an iterated map. The second system is a second-order differential equation describing the motion of a damped, sinusoidally-driven pendulum. The third system is a finite state machine with input. However, all of these systems are also instances of *dynamical systems* and the underlying similarity of many of the questions one might ask about each of these systems only becomes apparent in this formalism.

For our purposes here, a dynamical system is characterized by a set of *state variables* *x* and a *dynamical law* $\mathscr{F}$ that governs how the values of those state variables change with time. The set of all possible values of the state variables constitutes the system's *state space*. For simplicity, I will assume here that the state space is continuous (i.e., the state variables are real-valued), though most of the concepts that I will be introducing hold in some form for any metric space. Often the geometry of the state space is assumed to be simply Euclidean. Sometimes, however, other spaces arise. Perhaps the most common examples are cylindrical and toroidal state spaces, which occur naturally when some of the state variables are periodic (e.g., θ in Eq. (2)).

If the dynamical law depends only upon the values of the state variables and the values of some set of fixed *parameters* *u*, then the system is said to be *autonomous.*[1] In a continuous-time dynamical system, the dynamical law is given in terms of a set of differential equations: $\dot{x} = \mathscr{F}(x; u)$. In this case, the dynamical law defines a *vector field* on the state space. In a discrete-time dynamical system, the dynamical law is simply a map from current state to next state: $x_{n+1} = \mathscr{F}(x_n; u)$. A dynamical system is said to be *linear* or *nonlinear* according to the linearity or nonlinearity of $\mathscr{F}$ in the state variables.

As a concrete example, consider the following system of equations, which describe the behavior of a fully-interconnected network of two simple model neurons:

$$\dot{y}_1 = -y_1 + w_{11}\sigma(y_1 - \theta_1) + w_{21}\sigma(y_2 - \theta_2),$$
$$\dot{y}_2 = -y_2 + w_{12}\sigma(y_1 - \theta_1) + w_{22}\sigma(y_2 - \theta_2), \tag{4}$$

where y_i is the state of the ith neuron, $\sigma(\xi) = (1 + e^{-\xi})^{-1}$ is the standard sigmoidal (S-shaped) activation function, θ_i controls the offset or threshold of the activation function and w_{ij} is the weight of the connection from the ith to the jth neuron. This system is a simplification of a common neural network model that will be employed in Section 4. Note that this is a nonlinear system due to the nonlinearity of the activation function σ.

Starting from some *initial state* x_0, the sequence of states generated by the action of the dynamical law is called a *trajectory* of the system and is often denoted $\phi_t(x_0)$. A trajectory has the property that its tangent at each point is equal to the value of the vector field at that point. Some representative trajectories of the two-node network (4) are shown in Fig. 1. The set of all such trajectories through every point in the state space is called the *flow*, denoted ϕ_t. In the classical theory of differential equations, one is typically interested only in individual solutions, which correspond to individual trajectories of the dynamical system. In contrast, in the qualitative theory of dynamical systems, one is usually more interested in the geometrical or topological structure of the entire flow.

Of particular interest is the possible long-term behavior of a dynamical system. The state of some systems will simply diverge to infinity (e.g., the system $\dot{y} = y$), while others will eventually converge to *limit sets*. A limit set is a set of points that is invariant with respect to the dynamical law, so that if the state of a dynamical system ever falls on a limit set, the action of the dynamical law will keep it there indefinitely. The *stable* limit sets or *attractors* are especially important. An attractor has the property that the trajectories passing through all nearby states converge to the attractor. This means that if the state of the system is perturbed a sufficiently small distance away from an attractor, the action of the dynamical law will bring the state back to the attractor. The open set of initial states that converge to a given attractor is termed its *basin of attraction*. Those portions of the trajectories through such points which do not lie on the attractor itself are

---

[1] This is a technical term in dynamical systems theory whose meaning is unrelated to its use in the term "autonomous agents".

A

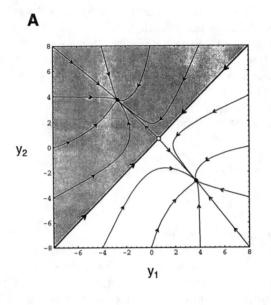

B   **C**

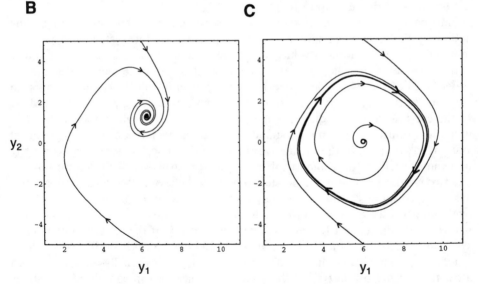

Fig. 1. Phase portraits for the two-neuron system (Eq. (4)) for several parameter settings. All of these systems are structurally stable, that is, the qualitative structures of their phase portraits persist for small variations in the parameters. (A) Here the system exhibits two stable equilibrium points near $(-3, 4)$ and $(4, -3)$ with basins of attraction shown in gray and white respectively. The open point near $(0, 0)$ is a repellor and the inset of this repellor (dark diagonal line) forms the separatrix between the two basins of attraction. The parameter values are $w_{11} = w_{22} = 4$, $w_{12} = w_{21} = -3$, $\theta_1 = \theta_2 = 0$. (B) Here the system exhibits a single equilibrium point attractor. The parameter values are $w_{11} = 2.75$, $w_{12} = -6$, $w_{22} = w_{21} = 6$, $\theta_1 = 6$, $\theta_2 = 0$. (C) Here the system exhibits a limit cycle (dark oval) and a repellor (open point near $(6, 0)$). This phase portrait was derived from the one shown in B by increasing the single parameter w_{11} from 2.75 to 6.

called *transients*. The solid point near $(-3, 4)$ in Fig. 1(A) is an example of an attractor, and its basin of attraction is shown in gray.

Repellors are limit sets that are *unstable*. Repellors have the property that at least some nearby trajectories diverge from them. Despite the fact that the repellor itself is invariant, if the state of the system is perturbed even an infinitesimal distance from the repellor, the action of the dynamical law will serve to carry it away. The open point near $(0, 0)$ in Fig. 1(A) is an example of a repellor. Attractors are important because they govern the long-term behavior of any physical system. Regardless of the initial state, a physically embodied dynamical system will always be found near an attractor after transients have passed. Due to their instability, repellors can only be observed by starting a dynamical system on a repellor and then never perturbing it. Since any physical system has some noise, it could never stay on a repellor indefinitely.

Four major classes of attractors are usually distinguished. *Equilibrium point* attractors are stable limit sets which consist of single points, such as the solid point near $(4, -3)$ in Fig. 1(A). An equilibrium point x^* represents a constant solution to the system: $\phi_t(x^*) = x^*$. *Periodic* attractors or *limit cycles* are stable limit sets which are closed trajectories in the state space. These correspond to periodic or oscillatory solutions, with the property that $\phi_t(x^*) = \phi_{t+T}(x^*)$ for some minimum period $T > 0$ and any point x^* lying on the attractor. An example of a limit cycle is shown in Fig. 1(C).

The remaining two classes of limit sets, *quasiperiodic* attractors and *chaotic* attractors, are much more complicated than either equilibrium points or limit cycles. Chaotic attractors, for example, possess a fractal structure and they exhibit a sensitive dependence on initial conditions. No matter how closely two unequal initial states are chosen, their resulting trajectories can diverge exponentially even while remaining bounded on the attractor until they become completely uncorrelated. For this reason, despite the underlying determinism of its dynamical law, the behavior of a chaotic attractor is in many ways indistinguishable from a random process. While I will not discuss quasiperiodic or chaotic attractors further in this paper, it is important to realize that such complicated behavior is quite common in higher dimensional nonlinear dynamical systems.

In general, the state space of a dynamical system will contain multiple attractors, each surrounded by its own basin of attraction. These basins are separated by unstable manifolds called *separatrices*. The dark diagonal line separating the white and gray basins of attraction of the two equilibrium point attractors in Fig. 1(A) is an example of a separatrix. Thus one can visualize these separatrices as dividing the flow of a dynamical system into a number of "cells" each containing an attractor of some type. A global characterization of this cellular structure is called the *phase portrait* of the system (Fig. 1).

We have been holding the parameters u of the dynamical law $\mathscr{F}$ constant and considering the global structure of the resulting flow. What happens when these parameters are changed? Since $\mathscr{F}$ is a function of u, the vector field that it determines, and hence the resulting flow ϕ_t that this vector field induces on the state space, will most certainly change as these parameters are varied. Thus a parameterized dynamical law actually defines a family of dynamical systems, with any particular flow corresponding to a single setting of the parameters.

Just as we were previously interested in the structure of any given flow in state space, we can now inquire into the structure of a family of flows in parameter space. Most dynamical systems are *structurally stable*, that is, for most parameter settings, small changes in the parameter values will produce small changes in the flow. Limit sets and basins of attraction may deform and move around a bit, but the new flow will be qualitatively similar (i.e., topologically equivalent, or *homeomorphic*) to the old one. However, at certain parameter values, dynamical systems can become *structurally unstable*, so that even infinitesimal changes in parameter values can cause drastic changes in the flow, producing phase portraits that are qualitatively different from the original. These qualitative changes in the types of limit sets are called *bifurcations*.

For example, as the parameter w_{11} in our example system (4) is increased from 2.75 to 6, the equilibrium point attractor shown in Fig. 1(B) loses its stability and bifurcates into the repelling point and limit cycle shown in Fig. 1(C) (the actual bifurcation, and therefore the structurally unstable flow that separates these two structurally stable flows, occurs around a w_{11} value of 3.25). Much more complicated bifurcations can occur. Thus, just as we can visualize separatrices as dividing the state space of any given dynamical system into basins of attraction of different attractors, we can think of the sets of bifurcation points corresponding to structurally unstable flows as dividing the parameter space of a family of dynamical systems into different structurally stable flows.

Up to this point, we have only considered autonomous dynamical systems, that is, systems in which the parameters have been held fixed for the duration of any particular trajectory. What happens when these parameters are allowed to vary in time as the trajectory evolves? A *nonautonomous* dynamical system is one in which one or more parameters are allowed to vary in time: $\dot{x} = \mathscr{F}(x; u(t))$. We can think of such parameters as *inputs* to the system. Because, as described above, the flow is a function of the parameters, in a nonautonomous dynamical system the system state is governed by a flow which is changing in time (perhaps drastically if the parameter values cross bifurcation points in parameter space). Nonautonomous systems are much more difficult to characterize than autonomous ones unless the input has a particularly simple (e.g., periodic) structure. In the nonautonomous case, most of the concepts that we have described above (e.g., attractors, basins of attraction, etc.) apply only on timescales small relative to the timescale of the parameter variations. However, one can sometimes piece together a qualitative understanding of the behavior of a nonautonomous system from an understanding of its autonomous dynamics at constant inputs and the way in which its input varies in time.

3. A theoretical framework

The qualitative theory of dynamical systems allows one to build up a global understanding of both the possible behaviors of a dynamical system and the dependence of those behaviors on external parameters even when the solutions have no closed-form expression in terms of elementary mathematical functions. In this section, I will use this formalism to sketch a theoretical framework for characterizing the interaction between autonomous agents and their environments. Only the basic framework will be described here. Some sample applications of the framework will be presented in Section 4, and Section 5 discusses the assumptions of the proposed framework and considers some of its broader implications and directions for future work. This framework owes a great debt to the perspective that the cybernetic tradition has long taken on many of these same questions. I have been particularly influenced by the work of Ashby [6] and Maturana and Varela [47, 48].

3.1. Agents and their environments

Following Ashby [6], I will model an agent and its environment as two dynamical systems $\mathscr{A}$ and $\mathscr{E}$, respectively. I will assume that $\mathscr{A}$ and $\mathscr{E}$ are continuous-time dynamical systems: $\dot{x}_{\mathscr{A}} = \mathscr{A}(x_{\mathscr{A}}; u_{\mathscr{A}})$ and $\dot{x}_{\mathscr{E}} = \mathscr{E}(x_{\mathscr{E}}; u_{\mathscr{E}})$. In addition, I will assume that both $\mathscr{A}$ and $\mathscr{E}$ have convergent dynamics, that is, the values of their state variables do not diverge to infinity, but instead eventually converge to some limit set. Note that the division between an agent and its environment is somewhat arbitrary (e.g., is an artificial limb or a tool part of the agent or part of the environment?) and therefore our theoretical framework should not depend overly much on the exact nature of this division. Our first act as scientific observers is to partition the world into individual components whose interactions we seek to understand, and there are many different ways to do this. For example, it will sometimes be convenient to view an agent's body as part of $\mathscr{A}$ and sometimes as part of $\mathscr{E}$.

An agent and its environment are in constant interaction. Formally, this means that $\mathscr{A}$ and $\mathscr{E}$ are coupled nonautonomous dynamical systems. In order to couple two dynamical systems, we can make some of the parameters of each system functions of some of the state variables of the other. I will represent this coupling with a sensory function S from environmental state variables to agent parameters and a motor function M from agent state variables to environmental parameters. $S(x_{\mathscr{E}})$ corresponds to an agent's sensory inputs, while $M(x_{\mathscr{A}})$ corresponds to its motor outputs. Thus, we have the following (Fig. 2):

$$
\begin{aligned}
\dot{x}_{\mathscr{A}} &= \mathscr{A}(x_{\mathscr{A}}; S(x_{\mathscr{E}}); u'_{\mathscr{A}}) \,, \\
\dot{x}_{\mathscr{E}} &= \mathscr{E}(x_{\mathscr{E}}; M(x_{\mathscr{A}}); u'_{\mathscr{E}}) \,,
\end{aligned}
\tag{5}
$$

where $u'_{\mathscr{A}}$ and $u'_{\mathscr{E}}$ represent any remaining parameters of $\mathscr{A}$ and $\mathscr{E}$ respectively that do not participate in the coupling. I will assume that this coupled agent-environment system also exhibits only convergent dynamics.

Note that I am using the terms "sensory input" and "motor output" in a fairly broad sense here. S, for example, is intended to represent *all* effects that $\mathscr{E}$ has on $\mathscr{A}$, whether or not this influence occurs through what is normally thought of as a sensor. This breadth of usage is justified by the observation that any such effect

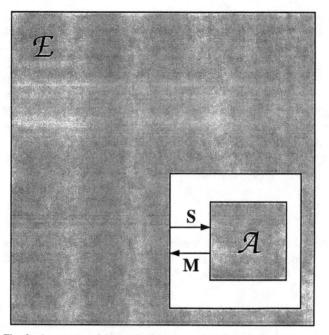

Fig. 2. An agent and its environment as coupled dynamical systems.

can influence the subsequent trajectory of $\mathcal{A}$. Likewise, M is intended to represent all effects that $\mathcal{A}$ has on $\mathcal{E}$, whether or not they occur through what is normally thought of as an effector.

I cannot overemphasize the fundamental role that feedback plays in this relationship. Any action that an agent takes affects its environment in some way through M, which in turn affects the agent itself through the feedback it receives from its environment via S. Likewise, the environment's effects on an agent through S are fed back through M to in turn affect the environment itself. Thus, each of these two dynamical systems is continuously deforming the flow of the other (perhaps drastically if any coupling parameters cross bifurcation points in the receiving system's parameter space), and therefore influencing its subsequent trajectory. Note that one dynamical system cannot in general completely specify the trajectory of another dynamical system to which it is coupled. Rather, a dynamical system follows a trajectory specified by its own current state and dynamical laws. By varying some of the parameters of these laws, a second dynamical system can certainly bias the intrinsic "tendencies" of the first (or even cause qualitative changes in behavior if bifurcations occur). However, one dynamical system cannot in general "steer" the trajectory of another dynamical system along any desired path. It is therefore perhaps most accurate to view an agent and its environment as mutual sources of perturbation, with each system continuously influencing the other's potential for subsequent interaction.

Given this tight coupling between an agent and its environment, we can equally well view the two coupled nonautonomous systems $\mathcal{A}$ and $\mathcal{E}$ as a single autonomous dynamical system $\mathcal{U}$ whose state variables are the union of the state variables of $\mathcal{A}$ and $\mathcal{E}$ and whose dynamical laws are given by all of the internal relations (including S and M) among this larger set of state variables and their derivatives. Neither of these perspectives is intrinsically better than the other, and one could switch between them as necessary. Given everything that has been said in Section 2, any trajectories observed in the interaction between the nonautonomous dynamical systems $\mathcal{A}$ and $\mathcal{E}$ must be trajectories of the larger autonomous dynamical system $\mathcal{U}$. Furthermore, after transients have died out, the observed patterns of interaction between $\mathcal{A}$ and $\mathcal{E}$ must represent an attractor of $\mathcal{U}$.

We thus have the basis for a dynamical understanding of one of the central themes of recent autonomous agent research, namely the idea that an agent's behavior arises not simply from within the agent itself, but rather through its interaction with its environment. Due to the higher dimensionality of its state space, a dynamical system formed by coupling two other systems can generate a richer range of dynamical behavior than either system could individually, and properties of the coupled system can therefore not generally be attributed to either subsystem alone. Therefore, an agent's behavior properly resides only in the dynamics of the coupled system $\mathcal{U}$ and not in the individual dynamics of either $\mathcal{A}$ or $\mathcal{E}$ alone. This suggests that we must learn to think of an agent as containing only a latent potential to engage in appropriate patterns of interaction. It is only when coupled with a suitable environment that this potential is actually realized through the agent's behavior in that environment.

3.2. Adaptive fit

What constitutes an "appropriate" pattern of interaction between an agent and its environment? It is often said that the behavior of animals is amazingly well adapted to the environments in which they must live. While, strictly speaking, evolution directly selects only for reproductive success, it is only animals whose behavior "fits" the dynamical and statistical structure of their environments that survive long enough to reproduce. We would like the behavior of the autonomous agents that we design to be similarly well-adapted to the environments in which they must function. Thus, the notion of adaptive fit is crucial to understanding the relationship between an agent and its environment. But what does it mean for an agent to be adapted to its environment?

Let us focus for the moment on animals, whose adaptive fitness is related to their survival. Then we can temporarily reformulate the question What does it mean for an agent to be adaptively fit to an environment? to the question What does it mean for an animal to survive? In order to answer this question, it will be useful to begin with a simple analogy to autonomous dynamical systems. As we have seen in Section 2, a dynamical law induces change on the state variables of a dynamical system. However, not all states are treated equally. While most states will be changed into other states through the action of the dynamical law, some states will persist indefinitely because they are invariant with respect to the changes caused by the dynamical law (i.e., an equilibrium point attractor of the system). Invariant states "survive" in the same way that rocks do, by resisting change.

Unlike rocks, animals actively engage their environments in order to stably maintain their existence. Similarly, we expect the agents that we design to accomplish particular tasks in their environments, not to sit immobile and ignore the world around them. In order to capture this more dynamic notion of survival, we can extend our analogy to periodic trajectories, which persist in a far more interesting way than do equilibrium points. In the case of a limit cycle, no single state is invariant with respect to the dynamical law. Rather, all of the states along a limit cycle have the property that the action of the dynamical law carries them to other states along the limit cycle, forming a closed curve which is itself invariant. Thus, the persistence of a limit cycle is achieved only by coordinating the effects of the dynamical law on all of the state variables of the system in such a way that a closed trajectory is formed.

Even such a dynamically maintained invariant as a limit cycle does not quite capture the notion of survival that we are after. It falls short in two ways. First, as explained in Section 3.1, an animal is not an autonomous dynamical system, but rather a nonautonomous one which is constantly perturbed by its environment. Second, an animal does not really have to maintain any *particular* trajectory in order to survive, as suggested by the limit cycle metaphor. Rather, in order to survive, any living organism must maintain the integrity of the network of biochemical processes that keep it alive. Maturana and Varela [47, 48] have termed this network of processes an *autopoietic* system.[2] If an animal's autopoiesis is sufficiently disrupted, either as a result of its own internal dynamics or as a result of environmental perturbations that it cannot properly compensate for, then the animal will cease to exist. Thus, an animal's autopoiesis serves as a crucial constraint on its behavioral dynamics. We can visualize this constraint as a (perhaps very complex and time-varying) volume in an animal's state space (Fig. 3; [6]). An animal is adaptively fit to an environment only so long as it maintains its trajectory within this constraint volume despite the perturbations that it receives from its environment.

In order to elaborate this basic account of adaptive fit, the nature of the constraint volume would need to be more completely characterized. For any real animal, this volume must obviously be very complicated, varying in time with its internal state. Indeed, the separation between the animal's behavioral dynamics and its constraint volume is fundamentally somewhat artificial, because any given animal's behavioral dynamics is clearly related to the particular way in which its autopoiesis is realized and this itself changes through evolution [47, 48]. However, for our purposes here, I take the existence of an agent (living or otherwise) for

---

[2] An autopoietic (lit. self-producing) system is a network of component-producing processes with the property that the interactions between the components produced generate the very same network of interactions that produced them.

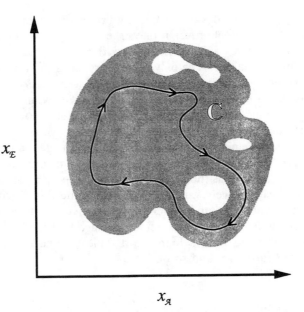

Fig. 3. An illustration of adaptive fit. This simple example assumes that both the agent and its environment are one-dimensional dynamical systems. As the state of the environment x_E moves up and down, the state of the agent x_A must move back and forth accordingly so that the trajectory of the coupled system always remains within the constraint volume $\mathbb{C}$. Here the two-dimensional coupled agent-environment system exhibits a limit cycle that satisfies the given constraint, but this is only one of an infinite number of possible agent-environment trajectories that satisfy $\mathbb{C}$.

granted and focus instead on the behavioral dynamics required to maintain that existence. This focus justifies the separation of behavioral dynamics from autopoietic constraints, and allows me to assume that the constraint volume is given *a priori*.

The adaptive fit of natural animals to their environments results from an evolutionary process involving reproduction with heritable variation and natural selection. When animals reproduce, mutations and sexual recombination of their genetic material lead to variations in their design. Because the genetic material of those animals which do not survive long enough to reproduce is not passed on to descendants, inappropriate designs are pruned away, while successful designs proliferate. In terms of our framework, we can think of evolution as trying out many different agent dynamics and retaining only those that, on average, are capable of satisfying their autopoietic constraints long enough to reproduce.

How might this notion of an autopoietic constraint apply to artificial agents? Homeostatic processes may be involved even for a robot. For example, an autonomous robot may need to regularly replenish its energy and avoid any potentially damaging situations. However, since the agents that we design are not living organisms, their existence does not strictly depend upon autopoiesis. Instead, the success of an artificial agent is typically measured in terms of its ability to accomplish some desired task in a given environment. For our purposes here, however, this external criterion plays the same role as autopoiesis in living animals, that is, it serves as a constraint on the admissible trajectories of the agent-environment dynamics. The only real difference is that, while autopoiesis is largely an intrinsic constraint on an animal's own state, it is usually an artificial agent's effects on its environment that are constrained by an external designer.

Thus, we can immediately generalize the above notion of adaptive fit to an arbitrary constraint $\mathbb{C}$ on the dynamics of a coupled agent-environment system (Fig. 3). I will say that an adaptive fit exists between an agent and its environment as long as the trajectory of the agent-environment dynamics satisfies this constraint, that is, as long as their interaction results in an adequate performance of the task for which the agent was designed. As a somewhat fanciful example, we might consider a robot vacuum cleaner to be adaptively fit to its environment as long as its interactions with its environment are such that the floor remains clean, despite the complicating factors found in a typical home (e.g., children, pets, rearrangement of furniture, and so on).

4. A concrete example

The basic theoretical framework sketched in the previous section is rather abstract in nature. In order to make the general framework that I have proposed more concrete, this section will show how it can be applied to examples of each of the two major problems in autonomous agents research, namely the *synthesis* problem and the *analysis* problem. Loosely speaking, the synthesis problem is the problem of constructing an agent that does what we want in a given environment, while the analysis problem is the problem of understanding how a given agent does what it does in a given environment. I will show how a walking behavior for a simulated legged agent can be synthesized and analyzed from the dynamical systems perspective of this framework. Along the way, I will point out some of the distinct advantages of this approach.

4.1. Synthesis of a walking agent

A major concern of much of the work on situated agents has been how to design agents that engage in some desired interaction with their environments. In terms of our framework, we can state this synthesis problem somewhat more formally as follows:

The Synthesis Problem. Given an environment dynamics $\mathscr{E}$, find an agent dynamics $\mathscr{A}$ and sensory and motor maps S and M such that a given constraint $\mathbb{C}$ on the coupled agent-environment dynamics is satisfied.

In order to illustrate the advantage of a dynamical systems perspective on the synthesis of autonomous agents, let us consider the problem of designing a dynamical neural network that will make a simulated insect-like agent walk (Fig. 4; [11]). In terms of our framework, the dynamics of the agent's body is $\mathscr{E}$ and the dynamics of the neural network that controls it is $\mathscr{A}$. $M(\boldsymbol{x}_{\mathscr{A}})$ gives the transformation from neural activity to body effectors, while the transformation from body sensors to neural inputs is given by $S(\boldsymbol{x}_{\mathscr{E}})$. Here $\mathbb{C}$ is a constraint on $\mathscr{E}$ only, namely that the average velocity of the body be greater than zero (where positive velocities correspond to forward motion and negative velocities correspond to backward motion). We will assume that S and M are given *a priori* in this example and the problem is to design a neural network controller whose dynamics are such that, when coupled to the agent's body, they cause it to walk. Note that the design of locomotion controllers for hexapod robots is currently a problem of some practical interest [15, 19, 26]. For a complete description of this work, as well as additional examples, see [13].

The body operates as follows. There are six legs, each with a foot that may be either up or down. When its foot is down, a leg provides support to the body and any forces that it generates contribute to the body's translation under Newtonian dynamics (the stance phase). When its foot is up, any forces generated by the leg cause it to swing (the swing phase). Each leg is controlled by three effectors: one governs the state of the foot and the other two determine the clockwise and counterclockwise torques about the leg's single joint. Each leg also possesses a single sensor that measures its angle relative to the body. The body can only move when it is stably supported, that is, when the polygon formed by the supporting feet contains the body's center of mass.

The agent is controlled by a continuous-time recurrent neural network. Such networks were briefly introduced in Section 2. In their most general form, an interconnected network of N such neurons is described by the following system of equations:

$$\tau_i \dot{y}_i = -y_i + \sum_{j=1}^{N} w_{ji}\sigma(y_j - \theta_j) + I_i(t) \quad i = 1, 2, \ldots, N \tag{6}$$

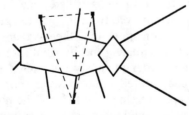

Fig. 4. The body model of the simulated insect. The legs can swing about their single joint with the body. A supporting foot is denoted by a black square. The body can only move when it is statically stable, i.e., when the polygon formed by the supporting feet (dashed line) contains the center of mass (cross) of the body.

where y is sometimes interpreted as the mean membrane potential of the neuron, $\sigma(\xi) = (1 + e^{-\xi})^{-1}$ is a sigmoidal (S-shaped) function which can be interpreted as its short-term average firing frequency, θ_j is a bias term associated with the cell's firing threshold, τ is a time constant related to the passive properties of the cell membrane, w_{ji} represents the strength of the connection from the jth to the ith neuron, and $I(t)$ represents a time-varying external input to the network (such as from a sensor). By restricting the matrix of connection weights to be zero-diagonal symmetric, Hopfield [38] demonstrated that such networks could be used as associative memories, with each pattern stored as a different equilibrium point attractor of the network dynamics. When no such restriction is placed on the connection weights, these networks are capable of exhibiting a much wider range of dynamical behavior. This is the form in which they will be used here. Note that no claim is being made about the general applicability of this particular neural model. It was merely selected to illustrate the framework due to its simplicity and widespread use.

Each leg of the agent was controlled by a 5-neuron fully-interconnected network (Fig. 5(A)). Three of these neurons are motor neurons whose outputs drive the three effectors of the leg, while the other two neurons are interneurons whose role is unspecified. All five neurons received a weighted input from the leg's angle sensor. Six copies of the single leg controller were combined in an architecture loosely based upon the organization of the neural circuitry underlying insect locomotion [11] to form a full locomotion controller with 30 neurons (Fig. 5(B)). Symmetry considerations were used to reduce the number of free parameters in this circuit to 50 (5 thresholds, 5 time constants, 25 leg controller weights, 5 sensor weights, 5 crossbody connection weights and 5 intersegmental connection weights). We wish to find settings of these 50 parameters such that the dynamics of the network causes the agent to walk when coupled to the body shown in Fig. 4.

Regardless of the particular control mechanism used, the majority of current work on situated agents relies on a human designer to manually construct a controller that will cause the agent to engage in some desired interaction with its environment. However, a number of researchers have begun to realize that manual design may not be the best approach. What is difficult about the synthesis problem is that the constraint to be satisfied may be very complex and its specification may be very far removed from the actual agent dynamics required to satisfy it. For example, the constraint that the average velocity of the body be greater than zero does not immediately specify what signals need to be sent to the body's eighteen effectors in order to satisfy this constraint. In addition, natural environments are rather complicated and somewhat unpredictable. Manual design often fails because designers, in trying to anticipate the possible opportunities and contingencies that might arise, build too many unwarranted assumptions into their designs. For these reasons, a number of researchers have begun to explore automated techniques for autonomous agent design, such as reinforcement and other forms of learning (e.g., [9, 10, 23, 41, 46]) or genetic algorithms (e.g., [17,

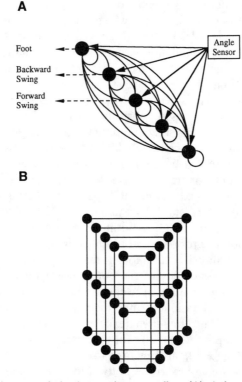

Fig. 5. Network architecture of the locomotion controller. (A) A leg controller. (B) Coupling between adjacent leg controllers.

40, 65, 67]). We used a genetic algorithm to search the space of network parameters for networks whose dynamics make the body shown in Fig. 4 walk.[3]

A genetic algorithm (GA) is a search technique whose operation is loosely based on natural evolution [31, 37]. The basic cycle of a genetic algorithm operates as follows. The space to be searched (in our case, the 50 network parameters) is usually encoded as a binary string. An initially random population of such strings is maintained. At each iteration, the performance of each individual is evaluated. A new generation of individuals is then produced by applying a set of genetic operators to selected individuals from the previous generation. Individuals are selected for reproduction with a probability propor-

---

[3] We employed a public GA simulator known as GAucsd (version 1.1). At the time of this writing, the latest version of GAucsd is available by anonymous ftp from cs.ucsd.edu in the pub/GAucsd directory. All network parameters were encoded in four bits, with time constants in the range [0.5, 10] and both thresholds and connection weights in the range [−16, 16]. The crossover rate was set to 0.6 and the mutation rate was set to 0.0001. Population sizes of 500 were used and good locomotion controllers typically took on the order of 100 generations to evolve. Full details of these experiments can be found in [13].

tional to their fitness. The standard genetic operators are mutation (in which bits are randomly flipped) and crossover (in which portions of the genetic strings of two individuals are exchanged). By iterating the processes of selection, recombination and mutation, the population accumulates information about the distribution of fitness in the search space. This information focuses subsequent search into fruitful subspaces.

In order to guide its search, a genetic algorithm requires a real-valued measure of performance rather than a rigid constraint to be satisfied. In this case, the constraint $\mathbb{C}$ can be thought of as some minimum acceptable level of performance. We used the total forward distance traveled by the agent in a fixed amount of time as the performance measure to be optimized.[4] Note that, by optimizing distance traveled in a fixed amount of time, we are not only demanding that the insect walk, but that it walk as quickly as possible. Because the insect can only make forward progress when it is statically stable, the GA must find a network dynamics that not only appropriately generates the three control signals required to operate each leg, but also properly coordinates the independent movements of the six legs so that stability is continuously maintained in order to satisfy the constraint that the average velocity of the body be greater than 0.

There are two different ways that we can think about these experiments. Abstractly, we can think of continuous-time recurrent neural networks as simply a basis dynamics out of which to build whatever agent dynamics is required and we can think of GAs as simply a technique for searching the family of flows defined by the parameterized network architecture for one whose dynamics cause the agent to walk when it is coupled to the body. More concretely, we can think of our neural network as a simple model of a nervous system and the genetic algorithm as a simple model of evolution. This second perspective can actually be quite useful because it allows comparisons to be made between the model and biology.

However, we must be careful not to lose sight of the many simplifications involved in this latter perspective. Both nervous systems and evolution are considerably more complicated than these simple models would suggest. To take just one example, while we have externally imposed a notion of fitness on the GA, no such external fitness measure exists in natural evolution. Indeed, because an animal's environment includes many other animals that are simultaneously evolving, the relationship of a given behavior to reproductive success may change significantly over time. Fitness is something intrinsic to natural environments rather than being externally specified. The significance of this difference between extrinsic and intrinsic fitness is that, by favoring particular behaviors over others in a fixed, *a priori* fashion, extrinsic fitness functions limit the range of behaviors that can possibly evolve in a way that intrinsic fitness does not.

We evolved eleven different locomotion controllers in all. Though the specific

---

[4] Because GAucsd is formulated to minimize an error measure rather than maximize a fitness measure, the actual measure used was the square of the difference between the maximum attainable distance and the actual distance covered in a given length of time.

parameter values found by the GA were quite different in these eleven networks, the dynamics of all of them have the property that, when coupled to the insect-like body shown in Fig. 4, they cause it to walk in such a way that stability is continuously maintained. The behavior of a typical controller is shown in Fig. 6(A). All of these controllers generate a pattern of leg movements known as the *tripod gait*, in which the front and back legs on each side of the body swing in unison with the middle leg on the opposite side. The tripod gait is ubiquitous among fast-walking insects [32].

As the networks evolved, they passed through several more or less distinct stages. Very early on, agents appeared that put down all six feet and pushed until they fell. These agents thus exhibit roughly the proper phasing of the three signals controlling each leg, but lack the ability to recover a leg after a stance phase as well as the ability to coordinate the motions of the different legs. In the next stage, agents evolved the ability to rhythmically swing their legs in an uncoordinated fashion. Such agents made forward progress, but they fell quite often. Finally, agents utilizing statically stable gaits began to appear, but their coordination was still suboptimal. Subsequently, the efficiency of locomotion slowly improved.

During these experiments, we discovered that the nature of the environment in

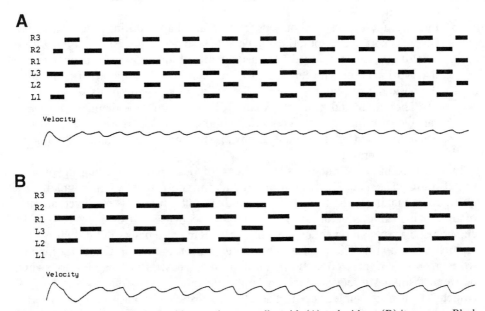

Fig. 6. Behavior of a typical mixed locomotion controller with (A) and without (B) its sensors. Black bars represent the swing phase of a leg and the space between bars represents a stance phase. The legs are labeled L for the left and R for right and numbered from 1 to 3 starting at the front of the agent. Note that the stepping frequency is higher, the swings of the three legs in each tripod are more tightly coordinated and the velocity varies less when the sensors are intact (A). However, this controller can generate a reasonably good tripod gait even in the complete absence of any sensory feedback from the body (B).

which the locomotion controllers were evolved had a major impact on their functional organization. In particular, the relative contributions of $\mathcal{A}$ and $\mathcal{E}$ to the generation of a walking pattern varied according to the dependability of sensory feedback during evolution. Three different classes of locomotion controllers were found:

(1) If sensors were enabled during the GA search, then *reflexive patterns generators* always evolved (5 trials). A reflexive controller is one which depends upon sensory feedback for its operation. If the sensors are later removed, reflexive controllers exhibit inappropriate phasing of motor outputs, and some cannot even oscillate in isolation. A reflexive controller is therefore not robust to sensor loss. Reflexive controllers take advantage of the fact that there is no point putting into the agent any dynamics that already appear to be in the environment. All that matters is that the coupled agent-environment system satisfy the given constraint.

(2) If the sensors were disabled during the GA search, then no access is provided to $\mathcal{E}$. In this case, so-called *central pattern generators* (CPGs; [25]) always evolved (4 trials). Even though the individual neurons are not oscillatory, a CPG is capable of generating the rhythmic control signals required for walking. The drawback of a CPG is that its output is stereotyped. It can make no use of sensory feedback to fine-tune its operation.

(3) Finally, if the presence of sensors was unreliable during the GA search (i.e., sensors were sometimes available and sometimes not), then *mixed pattern generators* evolved (2 trials). A mixed locomotion controller is one that works better with its sensors intact, but is quite capable of generating the basic motor pattern required for walking even without its sensors (Fig. 6). Though mixed controllers are robust to sensory damage, they are capable of using sensory feedback to improve their performance when it is available. Such mixed organizations are the most typical among biological pattern generators.

In this section, I formulated the problem of designing a walking agent as a search through a space of dynamical systems for those that, when coupled to a given body, maximize the forward distance that the body travels in a fixed amount of time. This same general approach has also been used to evolve a variety of chemotactic agents that were capable of using chemical signals to find their way to a patch of food [13]. The most notable result from these chemotaxis experiments were agents that utilized a bifurcation in their network dynamics to switch between distinct strategies depending upon the intensity of the chemical signal (which in turn depended upon the agent's distance from the food patch). Furthermore, I have demonstrated how manipulating characteristics of the environment (i.e., sensor dependability) puts selective pressure on the development of controllers with very different functional organizations. This ability to automatically tailor agent dynamics to fit the dynamical and statistical structure of a given environment is a significant advantage of automated agent design techniques.

4.2. Analysis of a walking agent

Given that some agent already exists, we might like to explain its behavior in a given environment. This is in fact the major problem faced by Neuroethologists, who seek to explain an animal's observed behavior in terms of its nervous system, its body and its environment. In terms of our framework, we can state this analysis problem somewhat more formally as follows:

The Analysis Problem. Given an environment dynamics $\mathcal{E}$, an agent dynamics $\mathcal{A}$, and sensory and motor maps S and M, explain how the observed behavior $M(x_{\mathcal{A}})$ of the agent is generated.

In order to illustrate the utility of a dynamical systems perspective on the analysis of autonomous agents, we would like to understand the operation of the evolved locomotion controllers described in the previous section. Unfortunately, a dynamical analysis of these 30 neuron networks would be far too complicated for our illustrative purposes here. However, in a set of closely related experiments, we also evolved five-neuron controllers for single-legged insects [13]. Note that, for the purposes of evolving single leg controllers, we had to modify the stability criteria so that a single-legged insect could move whenever its single foot was down. Except for the lack of an interleg coordination problem to be solved, these experiments were in every way analogous to those described in the previous section. These leg controllers passed through similar evolutionary stages and we also found reflexive, central and mixed pattern generators depending upon the conditions under which they were evolved. Fig. 7 shows the activity of a mixed leg controller with and without its sensors. Because these five-neuron networks are much more amenable to a dynamical analysis, we will focus on them here. For additional information on this analysis, see [12, 29].

4.2.1. Analysis of a central pattern generator
Because they have no sensory input, central pattern generators are autonomous dynamical systems. For this reason, CPGs are in some sense the simplest leg controllers to understand. In the case of a CPG, the dynamics of the neural network simply exhibits a limit cycle whose motor space projection $M(x_{\mathcal{A}})$ causes the insect's single leg to rhythmically stance and swing in a fashion appropriate to walking. The three-dimensional motor space projection of the five-dimensional limit cycle exhibited by one CPG is shown in Fig. 8. This limit cycle repeatedly takes the state of the system through the regions in motor space associated with stance phase (upper left-hand corner) and swing phase (lower right-hand corner). Since a limit cycle is a primitive concept in dynamical systems theory, there is really nothing more to be said at this level of discussion about the operation of a CPG (though there is of course much more that might be said about the way in which this limit cycle is realized in this particular circuit).

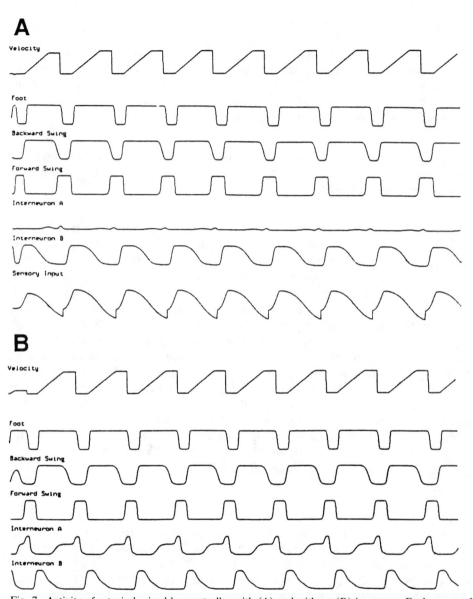

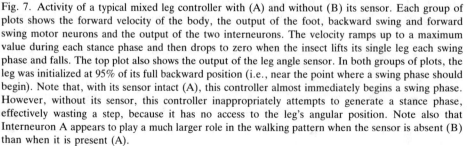

Fig. 7. Activity of a typical mixed leg controller with (A) and without (B) its sensor. Each group of plots shows the forward velocity of the body, the output of the foot, backward swing and forward swing motor neurons and the output of the two interneurons. The velocity ramps up to a maximum value during each stance phase and then drops to zero when the insect lifts its single leg each swing phase and falls. The top plot also shows the output of the leg angle sensor. In both groups of plots, the leg was initialized at 95% of its full backward position (i.e., near the point where a swing phase should begin). Note that, with its sensor intact (A), this controller almost immediately begins a swing phase. However, without its sensor, this controller inappropriately attempts to generate a stance phase, effectively wasting a step, because it has no access to the leg's angular position. Note also that Interneuron A appears to play a much larger role in the walking pattern when the sensor is absent (B) than when it is present (A).

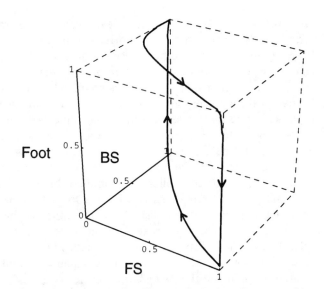

Fig. 8. A motor space projection of the five-dimensional limit cycle generated by a typical central pattern generator. The output of the foot, backward swing (BS) and forward swing (FS) motor neurons are plotted. Note that the foot is considered to be down when the output of the foot motor neuron is above 0.5 and up otherwise. A stance phase (foot and backward swing motor neurons active, forward swing motor neuron inactive) corresponds to a region near the back, upper left-hand corner of the state space, while a swing phase (forward swing motor neuron active, foot and backward swing motor neurons inactive) corresponds to a region near the front, lower right-hand corner of the state space.

4.2.2. Analysis of a reflexive pattern generator

Due to the presence of a sensory feedback signal, reflexive leg controllers are nonautonomous dynamical systems. When coupled to the body, the motor space projection of the dynamics of a reflexive controller also exhibits a suitable limit cycle (Fig. 9). However, we already know that reflexive controllers do not produce appropriate rhythmic output when their sensory input is removed. Unlike a CPG, the limit cycle of a reflexive leg controller arises only when it is coupled to the body. Technically, this limit cycle is a three-dimensional projection of a higher dimensional trajectory of the coupled agent-environment system $\mathcal{U}$. How does the interaction between a reflexive controller's autonomous dynamics and the sensory feedback that it receives from the body produce the observed limit cycle?

One way to approach this question is to think of a reflexive controller as an autonomous dynamical system whose flow is parameterized by the sensory input that it receives from the leg's angle sensor. At any given point in time, the network's state is flowing toward the attractor in whose basin it finds itself. However, because the angle of the leg is constantly changing, the structure of the network's flow is changing also, perhaps even undergoing bifurcations. We can visualize the instantaneous phase portrait of the autonomous network dynamics corresponding to any given leg angle. We can also visualize the network's state and the trajectory that it is instantaneously following at any point in the limit cycle. Of course, the system state generally never completely traverses these instantaneous trajectories because the phase portrait continuously changes as the leg moves. However, by piecing together these instantaneous pictures at many different points in time, we can build up a picture of the dynamics underlying the limit cycle observed when a reflexive controller is coupled to the body. Note that the leg actually passes through any given angle twice; once in swing phase and once in stance phase. While the phase portrait is the same in each case (since it depends only on the leg angle), the system's state, and hence the trajectory that it is following, will in general be different.

Such an analysis of one reflexive controller is presented in Fig. 9. The visualization of this particular controller is simplified by the fact that once transients have passed, the outputs of its two interneurons become constant. In other words, once the limit cycle is established, the dynamics of this network are essentially three-dimensional. The limit cycle that this reflexive controller exhibits when it is coupled to the body is shown at the center of Fig. 9. Surrounding this central plot are smaller plots showing the instantaneous autonomous dynamics of the network at different points in the swing/stance cycle. At (1), the foot has just been put down and a stance phase begun. At this point, the network's state is flowing toward the equilibrium point attractor in the upper left-hand corner of the state space. The position of this attractor corresponds to a situation in which the foot and backward swing motor neurons are active and the forward swing motor neuron is inactive (i.e., a stance phase). Due to the dynamics of the body, this pattern of motor neuron activity means that the foot is down and the leg is applying a force to the body that causes it to move forward, changing the leg angle and thus the output of the leg angle sensor. As the leg continues to stance at (2), the system state has essentially reached the equilibrium point. As the leg passes from (2) to (3), however, this equilibrium point suddenly disappears and is replaced by another equilibrium point near the lower right-hand corner of the state space that now begins to attract the system state. The position of this attractor corresponds to a state in which the foot and backward swing motor neurons are inactive and the forward swing motor neuron is active (i.e., a swing phase).

The system state now begins to flow toward this new attractor (3). Between (3) and (4), the output of the foot motor neuron falls below the activation threshold of the foot (0.5) and the foot is lifted, actually beginning a swing phase. As the leg passes from (4) to (5), the equilibrium point attractor in the lower right-hand corner of the state space disappears and the earlier equilibrium point attractor in the upper left-hand corner reappears. The network state now moves toward this attractor through (6) until the output of the foot motor neuron goes above the activation threshold for the foot at (1) and the foot is once again put down, beginning a new stance phase. Thus we can see how the limit cycle observed in the coupled network/body system arises as the network's state is alternately attracted by the two equilibrium points.

We can now explain the reason that this controller is a reflexive pattern generator by observing that, when its sensor is removed, the autonomous

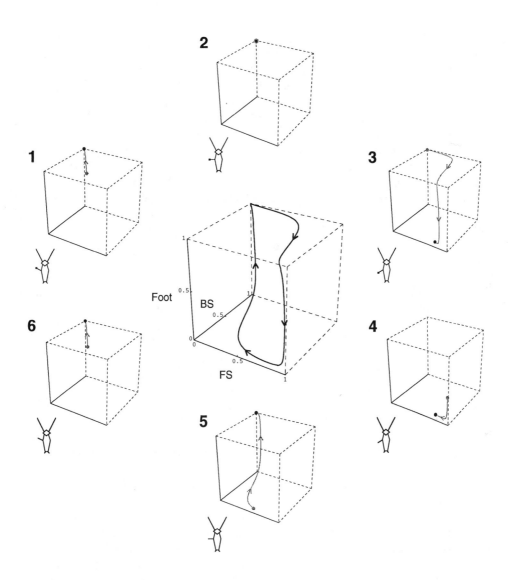

Fig. 9. Operation of a typical reflexive pattern generator. The output of the foot, backward swing (BS) and forward swing (FS) motor neurons are plotted. The limit cycle generated when this controller is coupled to the body is shown at the center. Surrounding this central plot are plots of the instantaneous autonomous dynamics of the network at different points in the step cycle. In each case, the solid point denotes an equilibrium point attractor, the gray point denotes the instantaneous system state, and the gray line shows the trajectory that the system would follow if the leg angle were to remain at its present angle. The top three plots roughly correspond to the beginning (1), middle (2) and end (3) of a stance phase, while the bottom three plots roughly correspond to the beginning (4), middle (5) and end (6) of a swing phase. Vertical columns of plots (i.e., (1) and (6), (2) and (5), and (3) and (4)) correspond to approximately the same leg angle and therefore the same phase portrait, though the system state and therefore the trajectory it is following differs between the upper and lower plots of each column.

dynamics of this controller is governed by an equilibrium point. By convention, a leg that is perpendicular to the long axis of the body is assigned a leg angle of 0. Since we modeled the removal of a sensor by setting its output to 0, the autonomous dynamics exhibited when the sensor is removed is identical to that exhibited when the leg is fixed in a horizontal position (i.e., plots (2) and (5) in Fig. 9). Thus, if the sensor is removed, the system state will flow toward the equilibrium point attractor in the upper left-hand corner of the state space and remain there, causing the leg to go into a permanent stance phase.

The switch between equilibrium points that occurs between (2) and (3) in Fig. 9, and again between (4) and (5), appears to be essential for the operation of this reflexive controller. How is this switch actually accomplished? This question is answered in Fig. 10, which shows a sequence of bifurcations that occur in the autonomous dynamics of this network as the leg moves from an angle of about 23 degrees past horizontal to 16 degrees past horizontal during swing phase (between plots (4) and (5) in Fig. 9). The sequence begins with a single equilibrium point attractor at the bottom of the state space (1). At (2), a second equilibrium point attractor appears at the top. Note that, during swing phase, the system state is still in the basin of attraction of the lower attractor at this point. At (3), the lower equilibrium point bifurcates into a limit cycle, which then begins to expand (4). Eventually, this limit cycle disappears, leaving behind only a single equilibrium point at (5). Now the system state is attracted by this upper equilibrium point. This sequence of bifurcations is reversed during stance phase. A complete bifurcation diagram for this network can be found in [12].

Because these bifurcations take place in such a narrow range of leg angles (approximately 7 degrees), the system state never really "sees" the intermediate attractors. For example, the limit cycle that briefly appears plays no functional role whatsoever in the network's dynamics because the system state never has a chance to get near it, let alone go around it. During the normal operation of this controller, this bifurcation sequence occurs in about 10 integration steps, during which the system state moves only an average Euclidean distance of 0.025 in the state space. However, the net effect of this sequence of bifurcations is to alternately switch the network's phase portrait between the two equilibrium points that are crucial to its operation. This particular sequence of bifurcations is unique to this controller, and was not observed in any of the other controllers that were analyzed.

From this dynamical analysis we can summarize the nature of the interaction between $\mathscr{A}$ and $\mathscr{E}$ that underlies the operation of this reflexive controller. The autonomous dynamics of $\mathscr{A}$, and its parameterization by S, is such that $\mathscr{E}$ can deform it, via a series of intermediate bifurcations, into essentially two kinds of flows. In one of these flows, there is a single fixed-point attractor near the upper left-hand corner of the state space, while in the other there is a single fixed-point attractor near the lower right-hand corner. The nature of $\mathscr{E}$, and its parameterization by M, is such that, when the network state is in the neighborhood of the upper left-hand attractor, the state of the body is changing in such a way that S will cause the lower right-hand attractor to appear in $\mathscr{A}$. Likewise, when the

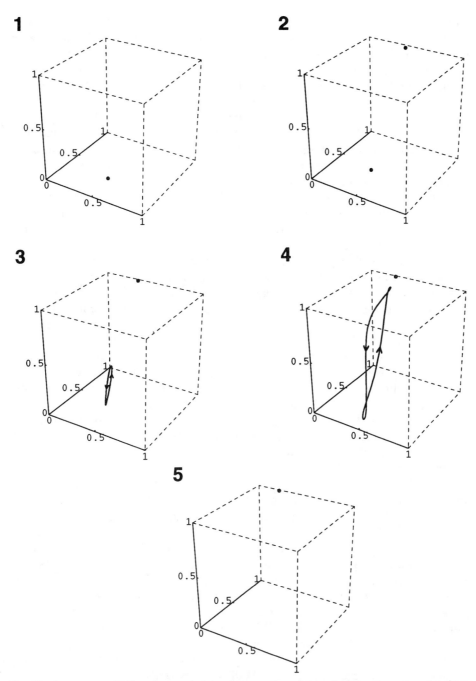

Fig. 10. A sequence of bifurcations underlying the operation of the reflexive pattern generator shown in Fig. 9. Only attractors are shown. During swing phase (between plots (4) and (5) in Fig. 9), the autonomous dynamics of the network undergoes the sequence of bifurcations shown here. During stance phase (between plots (2) and (3) in Fig. 9), this sequence of bifurcations is reversed.

network state is in the neighborhood of the lower right-hand attractor, the state of the body is changing in such a way that S will cause the upper left-hand attractor to appear in $\mathcal{A}$. This reciprocal relationship between $\mathcal{A}$ and $\mathcal{E}$ is what gives rise to the observed rhythmic walking pattern. Therefore, both $\mathcal{A}$ and $\mathcal{E}$ play absolutely essential and deeply intertwined roles in the operation of this reflexive controller.

4.2.3. Analysis of a mixed pattern generator

As shown in Fig. 11, we can approach the analysis of a mixed leg controller in a fashion similar to our analysis of the reflexive controller. However, because the dynamics of this circuit is fundamentally five-dimensional, we only plot the three-dimensional motor space projection of this system's trajectories. The limit cycle that this controller exhibits when it is coupled to the body is shown in the center. While the shape of this limit cycle is somewhat different from the one generated by the reflexive controller discussed above, they both exhibit the proper phasing of motor outputs necessary to make the leg walk. Surrounding this central plot are smaller plots that show the instantaneous autonomous dynamics at various points along this limit cycle. As for the reflexive controller, we can understand the dynamics of the coupled network/body system by piecing together these instantaneous snapshots. However, unlike the reflexive controller, the autonomous dynamics of this mixed controller exhibits limit cycles rather than equilibrium points through most of the cycle. When the mixed controller is coupled to the body, this limit cycle is continuously deformed as shown in Fig. 11 as the leg angle changes, and the system state is constantly attracted by this deforming limit cycle. The reason that this mixed controller can tolerate the loss of its sensor is because the autonomous limit cycle that it generates when the sensory input is set to 0 (see plots (2) and (5) in Fig. 11) is appropriate to make the leg walk. In the absence of any sensory input, the system state would follow this limit cycle rather than the limit cycle shown in the center of Fig. 11.

Since a mixed controller is capable of autonomously generating an appropriate limit cycle, what role if any is the sensory feedback it receives from the body actually playing in its operation? In order to explore this question, we examined how the controller responds when it is artificially driven with sinusoidal sensory input whose frequency is higher or lower than normal. Under these conditions, we found that the motor output pattern that the controller generates speeds up or slows down accordingly (Fig. 12). The sensory signal is thus capable of entraining the intrinsic oscillation produced by the controller itself. Despite the fact that the activity pattern of the interneurons changes considerably throughout this range of operating frequencies, the amplitude, shape and phasing of the motor outputs remains appropriate for walking. Within a significant range about its normal operating frequency, the motor pattern remains 1:1 phase-locked with the sensory signal. We have observed other ratios of phase-locking at higher or lower driving frequencies. Entrainment by sensory feedback is a common feature of biological pattern generators. For example, the pattern generator underlying locust flight can be entrained by rhythmic stimulation of wing stretch receptors [64].

This entrainment has an interesting functional consequence. Suppose that the

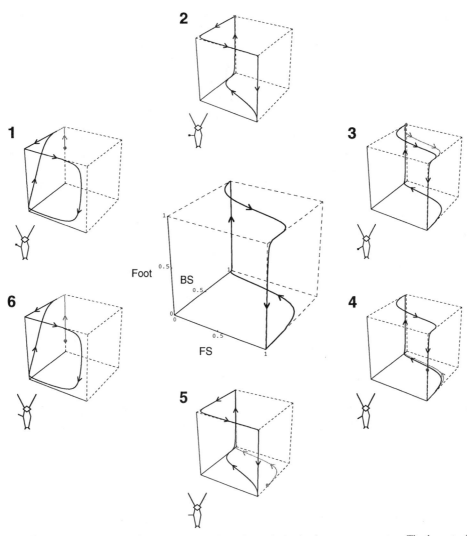

Fig. 11. Motor space projection of the operation of a typical mixed pattern generator. The layout of this figure is the same as for Fig. 9.

legs of the agent were to grow during its "life". For a given amount of applied torque, longer stancing legs will take more time to swing through a given angle than shorter legs. Thus, the sensory feedback signal from a longer leg will be spread out in time relative to that of a normal length leg. Since the mixed controller is entrained by the sensory feedback that it receives from the body, the sensory feedback from a longer leg will cause the leg controller to slow down its motor output pattern accordingly. Adapting their output to a changing periphery is a general problem that pattern generators have to deal with, for example in development or following peripheral damage. Note, however, that this adaptation

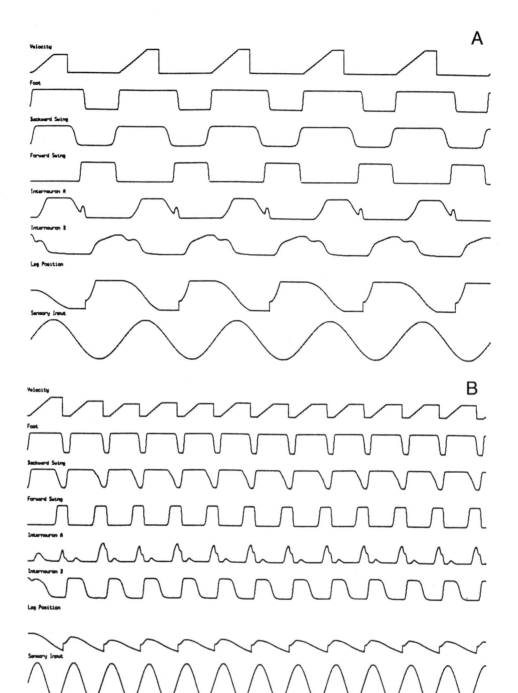

Fig. 12. Entrainment of the mixed pattern generator shown in Fig. 11 by sinusoidal sensory input. When the driving frequency is lower (A) or higher (B) than normal, the motor pattern slows down or speeds up accordingly.

does not come about through any structural change to the neural network itself, nor does it require a separate learning algorithm to modify the network parameters. Rather, it arises as a natural consequence of the dynamics of the mixed controller and its coupling with the body. This is a kind of functional plasticity which is quite different from what is normally thought of as learning. However, there are many examples of such plasticity in biology (for instance, the ability of an insect to immediately adjust its gait following the loss of a leg [32]).

The dynamical sophistication of this mixed leg controller is truly remarkable. With only *five neurons* (three of which are motor neurons), this controller can (1) generate the basic swing/stance leg movements necessary for walking; (2) take advantage of sensory feedback if it is available but can tolerate its absence with only a slight degradation in performance; and (3) adapt its operation to morphological changes in the body without requiring a separate learning mechanism. The likelihood of anyone designing such a flexible and compact leg controller by hand is probably rather low.

4.2.4. Conclusion

This section has illustrated how some of the tools of dynamical systems theory can be applied to the analysis of an agent interacting with its environment. For example, we have been able to explain why some locomotion controllers are robust to loss of sensory feedback and others are not in terms of the appropriateness or inappropriateness of their autonomous dynamics to the walking task. Furthermore, we have been able to gain significant insight into the specific nature of the interaction between the network dynamics and the body that gave rise to a walking pattern in each of the three controllers analyzed. For example, while the reflexive controllers make use of the body dynamics in a fundamental way in the generation of the limit cycle necessary for walking, the CPGs are capable of generating appropriate limit cycles completely autonomously and the mixed controllers use rhythmic sensory feedback to fine-tune autonomous limit cycles. Along the way, we discovered that, because it is entrained by sensory feedback, the mixed controller can adapt its motor output to a changing periphery.

What general conclusions can we draw from this analysis? One is struck by the variety of agent dynamics which evolved. Not only are the actual network parameters of each controller different, but the underlying dynamics vary widely. Yet they all lead to virtually indistinguishable walking behavior when coupled to the body under normal conditions. Furthermore, lesion studies of these controllers (not described here) have demonstrated that their operation is dynamically distributed, usually making it impossible to assign specific functional roles to individual interneurons. About the only thing that can be said about all of these controllers is that the coupled agent-environment systems in which they are embedded do what we asked them to do under the conditions in which they evolved. Indeed, as in natural evolution, this is all that they were selected for in the first place. We are thus led to conclude that it is simply inappropriate in general to attempt to impose our functional preconceptions on the organization of evolved systems.

5. Discussion

In this paper, I have attempted to use the language of dynamical systems theory to sketch a general theoretical framework for the design and analysis of autonomous agents. The framework focuses on the problem of generating the appropriate behavior at the appropriate time as both an agent's internal state and its external environment continuously change. The two key ideas of this framework are (1) that an agent and its environment must be understood as two coupled dynamical systems whose mutual interaction is jointly responsible for the agent's behavior and (2) that the adaptive fit between an agent and its environment can be characterized in terms of the satisfaction of a given constraint on the trajectories of the coupled agent-environment system. I have particularly emphasized that an agent's behavior is, strictly speaking, a property of the coupled agent-environment system only and cannot in general be attributed to either the agent or environment individually.

A concrete application of these ideas to the synthesis and analysis of a walking behavior for a six-legged agent was used to illustrate the framework. While I feel no particular commitment to either continuous-time recurrent neural networks or genetic algorithms, they represent at least one way in which agent dynamics satisfying a given constraint on the coupled agent-environment system can be designed. Such an "evolutionary" approach to agent design allows the agent's organization to be tailored to the particular dynamical and statistical structure of its environment and leads to remarkably adaptive, robust and compact controllers. I have also demonstrated that, despite the fact that they often exhibit no clean functional organization, the operation of these evolved systems can be understood from the perspective of interacting dynamical systems. Furthermore, this perspective can provide significant insight into the specific nature of the interaction between the agent and its environment that gives rise to the observed walking behavior in the various controllers.

5.1. Related work

There is currently a growing interest in dynamical explanations in the behavioral and brain sciences. The central idea dates back at least to cybernetics [6, 63]. More recently, concepts from dynamical systems theory have been making a substantial impact in such fields as neuroscience, cognitive science and mobile robotics. Within neuroscience, dynamical analyses have been applied to single neurons (e.g., [55]), small circuits (e.g., [62]) and complete brain systems (e.g., the model of olfactory cortex formulated by Skarda and Freeman [58], in which a chaotic attractor plays a central role). The concepts of dynamical systems are also beginning to play a major role in understanding the biological control of movement (e.g., [57]). Connectionism has made dynamics one of its founding principles [60] (though it is not clear that the full implications of this principle have yet been appreciated in connectionist research [36]) and has, for example, begun to propose theories of language in its terms [27, 53]. Both van Gelder [61] and Giunti [30] have begun to formulate a dynamical conception of cognition in cognitive science more generally. Finally, Smithers [59] has recently argued for a role for dynamical ideas in mobile robot research.

Within the autonomous agents literature, the theoretical framework that I have proposed is perhaps most closely related to Rosenschein's work on situated automata [56]. He models an agent and its environment as two interacting automata and he has emphasized that knowledge need not be explicitly encoded within an agent in order for it to engage in sophisticated interactions with its environment. He has used concepts from automata and formal language theory to characterize the behavior of such systems. In a sense, I have generalized this perspective to arbitrary dynamical systems and demonstrated how concepts from dynamical systems theory can be used to characterize the behavior of such systems, especially emphasizing continuous systems. On the other hand, while Rosenschein's major concern has been how propositional content can be assigned to correlations between an agent's internal states and the states of its environment, my interest is in how an agent can generate the appropriate behavior at the appropriate time.

5.2. Assumptions and extensions

This paper has focused on continuous, deterministic, convergent and low-dimensional dynamical systems as models for agents and their environments. In this section, I briefly consider the motivation behind these assumptions, their impact on the framework, and a number of ways in which they might be relaxed.

5.2.1. Continuity

The emphasis on continuous dynamics (i.e., continuous state spaces and continuous time) in this paper is motivated by the fact that the dynamics of both nervous systems and the macroscopic physical world are continuous in nature. For example, though many nerve cells fire action potentials (a seemingly discrete event), the current flows that underlie action potentials are continuous quantities. Furthermore, it has long been known that many nerve cells do not produce action potentials but instead communicate using graded potentials [52]. Likewise, the more discrete behavioral phenomena that we observe (e.g., decision making) must eventually be explained in continuous terms. In addition, it is my belief that the versatility and robustness of animal behavior resides in the rich dynamical possibilities of continuous state spaces.

However, it should be noted that any system with finite state which evolves deterministically can be described using the concepts of dynamical systems. Most of the concepts we have used hold in discrete-time systems as well, and many also hold in systems defined on discrete state spaces. For example, the transition table of a finite state machine defines a flow on a discrete state space. The lack of a metric on this state space limits the dynamical behavior that a finite state machine can exhibit, but such concepts as initial state, trajectory, flow, attractor, equilibrium point, limit cycle, basin of attraction, autonomous and nonautonomous still apply. Thus the present framework may still be useful even if the continuity assumption should turn out to be inappropriate.

5.2.2. Determinism

The theoretical framework sketched in this paper is purely deterministic in nature. This determinism derives from the common assumption in science that the macroscopic physical world is in principle completely determined by a knowledge of its state and the dynamical laws that govern its evolution. However, we often say that real environments, real sensors, etc. are somewhat unpredictable. What this usually means is that, because we have only incomplete knowledge of a system's state and laws, we are forced to use stochastic models to describe its behavior. In other words, regardless of whether or not the macroscopic physical world is deterministic in principle, we must sometimes treat it as stochastic in practice.

It should be noted that continuous-time recurrent neural networks show every sign of being robust in the face of unpredictable environmental contingencies. The locomotion controllers can often tolerate the loss of an interneuron or the loss of sensory feedback, and preliminary studies indicate that they are extremely robust to noise on the sensory feedback signal as well. However, regardless of the robustness of these controllers, the question naturally arises as to how the theoretical framework itself might be applied to unpredictable systems.

As I see it, there are two possibilities, depending upon whether a deterministic or stochastic model of unpredictability is adopted. Recall that nonlinear dynamical systems can exhibit dynamics that is completely deterministic in principle but unpredictable in practice (so-called chaotic dynamics). Significant progress has been made on extending the qualitative theory of dynamical systems to the analysis of chaotic dynamics [66]. If the unpredictability of a given system can be modeled with chaotic dynamics, then such techniques can be applied.

Otherwise, we must deal with a fundamentally stochastic model of unpredictability. In this case, we must consider stochastic dynamical systems (see, for example, [7]). Typical concerns in stochastic dynamical systems are understanding how some probability density function over the states of the system evolves with time and determining the asymptotic form of this distribution. The application of such techniques to autonomous agent problems is clearly an important research direction for the future development of the framework.

5.2.3. Convergence

In this paper, I have assumed that both the agent and environment dynamics are convergent, that is, the values of their state variables eventually converge to limit sets rather than diverging to infinity. In fact, even a flow that contains divergent regions is acceptable as long as the dynamics of interaction between the agent and environment never enters such a region. Divergent dynamical systems are a mathematical abstraction anyway. Due to resource limitations and saturation effects, no real physical system is truly divergent. Thus, the assumption of convergent dynamics is, I think, a fairly reasonable one.

However, it is important not to confuse this convergence assumption with the claim that the dynamics of agents and environments must settle onto limit sets before the framework applies. Indeed, the dynamics of the reflexive and mixed pattern generators never settle on an autonomous attractor, but instead are always in a transient because their flow is constantly perturbed by the sensory feedback that they receive. Of course, the dynamics of the coupled agent-environment system in these examples does eventually settle into a limit cycle, but even this need not be the case in general. If either the environment or the agent contains dynamics on time scales that are long relative to the lifetime of the agent, then the entire trajectory of interaction between them will take place on an extended transient.

Even in the case of an extended transient, however, the framework described in this paper still applies. The dynamics of interaction between the agent and its environment is still determined by the global structure of the flow of the coupled system and this structure is itself largely determined by the types and locations of its limit sets. Furthermore, in a system with multiple time scales, there may be a great deal of recurrence to the system's behavior over sufficiently short time scales. Under such conditions, it is often possible to treat the slower state variables as being approximately constant parameters of the faster dynamics and to study the dynamics of this reduced system. Though the attractors of this reduced system are not true attractors of the full system (because the slower state variables are in fact changing), they represent patterns of interaction that may show up repeatedly over sufficiently short time scales (cf. Agre and Chapman's notion of *routines* [3]).

5.2.4. Low dimensionality

Our ability to visualize the dynamics of the leg controllers described in Section 4 depended strongly on their relatively low dimensionality. Clearly, we will often need to analyze systems whose dimensionality makes direct visualization of the complete flow impossible. In this case, we must find ways to simplify the dynamics or rely upon nonvisual techniques. One obvious approach (utilized in Section 4) is to visualize higher dimensional dynamics with a set of carefully selected lower dimensional projections. More generally, one can sometimes find a series of coordinate transformations that map the dynamics of a higher dimensional system to a lower dimensional system while preserving most of its global structure. For example, such a technique has been used to reduce the four-dimensional Hodgkin-Huxley model of action potential generation to a two-dimensional system that preserves not only the qualitative behavior of the original system, but most of its quantitative behavior as well [43].

A number of other techniques are available for simplifying dynamical systems by reducing either their dimensionality or complexity in some spatial or temporal region of interest (e.g., Poincaré maps, center manifolds, normal forms, symbolic dynamics and the use of symmetries [66]). In addition, many of the analytical techniques of dynamical systems theory (e.g., computing limit sets, stability analysis, computation of Lyapunov exponents, etc.) do not require a global visualization of the flow. Finally, it should be pointed out that some progress has even been made on extending the qualitative theory of dynamical systems to infinite-dimensional systems (e.g., those arising from sets of partial differential, delay-differential and integro-differential equations; [34]). These and other techniques will undoubtedly need to be explored as larger systems are studied.

5.3. Modularity and design

Because the only requirement on an agent's dynamics is that the coupled agent-environment system satisfy a given constraint, there is a great deal of freedom both in how a desired dynamics of interaction is divided between the agent and its environment and in the internal organization of the agent's dynamics. We saw examples of this freedom in our analysis of the evolved leg controllers where, despite the fact that both their individual dynamics and the nature of their interaction with the body vary widely, all of these leg controllers produce virtually indistinguishable walking behavior when coupled to the body under normal conditions. Likewise, there is a growing realization within neuroscience that the neural circuits mediating nontrivial behaviors in even simpler animals are highly distributed and nonhierarchical and that traditional engineering principles may not apply to their design [4].

Because evolution only directly selects *against* agent dynamics that do not satisfy their constraint (rather than selecting *for* some optimal design), evolution tends to produce designs that take full advantage of the available freedom. This can lead to designs whose organization is very different from engineered systems. When an engineer designs a complex system, he or she typically performs a hierarchical decomposition of the problem to be solved, resulting in simpler subsystems with clean, well-defined functions and interfaces. Such a modular decomposition is necessary to ensure a correct, reliable and maintainable implementation, and it also appeals to a certain aesthetic sense of parsimony on the part of the designer. Evolution, however, operates under no such constraints. Natural selection preserves those animals that, as a package, work and discards those that do not. Of course, this is not to say that evolved systems are completely unstructured. Certainly, evolved systems exhibit modularity and it is likely that evolution would be unable to produce systems with the complexity of animals without it. However, because the internal organization of an evolved system does not reflect the conceptualization of any designer, whatever modules do exist are under no requirement to exhibit the sort of clean functional organization that we expect from an engineered system.

One might argue that this "messiness" is really just an implementation detail reflecting the blindness of evolution and not a fundamental part of the design. For example, we might be tempted to describe the leg controller dynamics as "really" just implementing a simple finite state machine that switches between two states labeled "swing phase" and "stance phase". However, it is important to realize that this is not a predictive explanation of these networks, but merely a descriptive summary of their normal operation. The predictive (and therefore explanatory) power of this summary is severely limited by the fact that it fails to capture the underlying dynamical laws that actually govern the system's operation. For example, the temporal patterns of motor neuron activations required to actually make the leg walk are not deducible from such a description. It also fails to capture how sensory feedback is capable of fine-tuning a walking pattern, or why some networks are robust to sensor loss while others are not. Yet these and other features are completely and succinctly explained by the qualitative dynamical analysis summarized in Figs. 8, 9, 10 and 11.

The fact that evolution can produce such messy designs is typically viewed as a shortcoming. However, it is also a source of freedom to cobble together counterintuitive but highly effective, versatile, robust and compact designs. Furthermore, this negative assessment overlooks a crucial difference between the task of an engineer and that of evolution. Engineers solve well-defined problems, and it is the detailed *a priori* specifications of those problems that allow modular solutions to be designed and their parsimony or optimality to be evaluated. In contrast, evolution has no clear specification of the "problem" that any given animal should solve. Even if such a specification existed, it would do little good since the "problem" itself is constantly evolving as the physical environment changes and the coevolution of conspecifics and other species modifies the relationship between behavior and reproductive success. Designing an artificial agent capable of autonomously accomplishing open-ended tasks in an unconstrained real-world environment is much closer to the sort of "problem" solved by evolution than it is to the problems for which traditional engineering methods have been successful.

While evolutionary design shows great promise as a practical method for designing autonomous agents, it is well known that the performance of the standard genetic algorithm does not scale well with the size of the parameter space using the direct encoding of neural network parameters employed here. These scaling problems will need to be addressed before such techniques can be applied to the design of more complicated agents. Toward that end, many different parameter encodings and many different variations of the basic genetic algorithm have been proposed (e.g., [16]) and their application to autonomous agent design needs to be explored. Where appropriate, other search techniques, such as simulated annealing and gradient techniques, should also be explored. When possible, biological data and symmetry considerations can be used to reduce the number of parameters to be searched, as in the adjacent coupling of the leg controllers in the full locomotion controller described in Section 4.1. Another strategy is to search not the parameter space of the agent's dynamics directly, but rather the parameter space of a developmental process that constructs the agent's dynamics (e.g., [35, 50]).

Yet another approach to the scaling problem is to evolve a complex agent dynamics incrementally. One possibility is to decompose a complex task into a set of simpler subtasks and to independently evolve solutions to these. A complete solution can then be obtained by evolving the coupling between these subnetworks on the original task. Another possibility is to evolve solutions to a simpler version of a difficult problem, successively increase the problem complexity, and then re-evolve the controllers to solve the harder versions of the problem. Finally, attempts to evolve controllers for physical robots instead of simulated agents introduce additional problems, since evolutionary search can only be carried out in simulation at present and there are nontrivial issues involved in transferring controllers from simulated to physical environments [21, 40].

5.4. Internal state and representation

Due to its emphasis on the unpredictable nature and real-time requirements of the real world, a great deal of recent work on autonomous agents has focused on the development of reactive agents whose actions are completely determined by their immediate situation. A purely reactive agent is a degenerate case of the present framework because it maintains no internal state. Rather, it is simply a function from sensory inputs to motor outputs. A reactive agent has no true autonomy because it is constantly pushed around by its environment.

In contrast, a dynamical systems perspective on autonomous agents emphasizes the importance of internal state to an agent's operation. Unlike a reactive agent, an agent with internal state can initiate behavior independently from its immediate circumstances and organize its behavior in anticipation of future configurations of its environment. This ability relies upon the fact that, while it is true that the real world is complicated and somewhat unpredictable, natural environments also exhibit a great deal of structure that a properly designed agent can depend upon and even actively exploit [39]. As a simple example, consider the way in which the reflexive controllers exploit the structure of the body dynamics to achieve walking.

The importance of internal state in the present framework raises an interesting question: Does the framework imply a commitment to internal representation? Much of the debate between proponents and critics of situated agent research has tacitly assumed the equation of internal state with representation, with proponents using criticisms of representation to argue the need for reactivity and critics using the limitations of state-free systems to argue the need for representation (e.g., [20, 44]). But are internal state and representation the same thing? Though this question clearly deserves a more detailed treatment than I can give it here, let me briefly explain why I believe that the answer must be no.

The problem with equating internal state and representation is that computationalism, the theoretical claim that a system's behavior derives from its instantiation of appropriate representations and computational processes [28, 51, 54], then becomes a tautological theoretical position. A scientific hypothesis must be falsifiable, that is, it must be formulated sufficiently clearly to be empirically tested and it must be possible that the test will come out negative. But all physical systems possess internal state on a variety of timescales. We would presumably hesitate in accepting, say, the temperature of the fuel-air mixture in a cylinder of an automobile engine as a representation of anything, or a thunderstorm as performing any computation. If, on the other hand, we did admit such a broad definition of representation and computation, then computationalism would become true by definition rather than by demonstration and would therefore be making no interesting theoretical claim about the nature of the processes underlying behavior. Similar problems exist with other commonsense notions of representation (e.g., correlation) and computation (e.g., systematicity of the relationship between input and output). For a more detailed discussion of these issues, see [12].

For this reason, representation must require additional conditions above and beyond the mere possession of internal state (or correlation, etc.) and computational systems must therefore be special cases of dynamical systems more generally [30, 61]. There is a great deal of controversy about the particular form of these extra conditions, but the details fortunately need not concern us here. What matters is that the framework's emphasis on internal state, while allowing it to transcend the limitations of purely reactive systems, does not necessarily imply a commitment to internal representation. Rather, the question of whether or not the notion of representation is appropriate for understanding the operation of any particular agent must be settled by an empirical investigation of the internal organization of that particular agent's dynamics. The framework is thus, strictly speaking, agnostic about the theoretical roles of representation and computation in the design and analysis of autonomous agents.

5.5. Conclusion

This paper has largely been presenting an argument about language, namely the language that we use to talk about autonomous agents and their environments. In particular, my primary goal has been to demonstrate that many of the ideas emerging from recent work on autonomous agents (as well as work on the neural basis of animal behavior, though I have not emphasized this aspect here) can be naturally cast into the language of dynamical systems theory.

One must never underestimate the power of language in shaping the way we think about the world. Our theoretical languages provide the metaphors we use to conceptualize the very phenomena we seek to understand. A computational language invites us to think about representations and their manipulation. Using this language, we become concerned with the structure of representations, where they are stored, how they are retrieved, what they mean, etc. From a computational perspective, observed regularities in an agent's behavior become windows into its program. If, for example, an agent persistently acts toward some end, then, computationalism tells us, it must be by virtue of possessing an internal representation of that goal. From a computational perspective, perception becomes a problem of reconstructing an accurate internal representation of the external environment. Taking action becomes a problem of constructing and executing representations of the actions to be performed. Learning becomes a problem of modifying existing representations and accumulating new ones. And so on.

This paper has only just begun the difficult task of developing a dynamical language for these and other phenomena exhibited by autonomous agents. A great deal of work remains to be done in developing this framework into a full-fledged theory. If this framework is to succeed in providing a foundation for our understanding of autonomous agents, then specific dynamical accounts of perception, action, goal-oriented behavior, decision-making, sequential behavior, learning, etc. will need to be developed and these accounts will need to be applied to specific agents, both natural and artificial. I strongly suspect that a dynamical perspective on these phenomena will significantly change the way we think about them.

Ultimately, like all work on embodied agents, the framework must face the fact that people can deliberately form and reason with conceptual representations. While I have taken the position that such intellectual capabilities are relatively recent elaborations of a far more fundamental capacity for situated action (and are therefore not nearly so crucial as is usually assumed for even highly complex but nondeliberative behavior), they must nevertheless eventually be explained. Will attempts to extend a dynamical perspective to such cognitive behavior as language and abstract reasoning turn out to require the implementation of computational processes on top of the dynamical substrate responsible for situated action? Or will the very way we think about such cognitive behavior, and the notions of representation and computation that currently seek to underwrite it, also have to change in the process?

Acknowledgments

I would like to thank Phil Agre, Hillel Chiel, John Gallagher, Ken Loparo, Leslie Picardo, and Beth Preston for many useful discussions and for their comments on earlier drafts of this paper. I would also like to thank the reviewers, as well as the attendees of the Workshop on Computational Theories of Interaction and Agency, for their many helpful suggestions. The simulation experiments reviewed in Section 4 were carried out in collaboration with John Gallagher. This work was supported by grant N00014-90-J-1545 from the Office of Naval Research. Additional support was provided by the Howard Hughes Medical Institute and the Cleveland Advanced Manufacturing Program through the Center for Automation and Intelligent Systems Research.

References

[1] R.H. Abraham and C.D. Shaw, *Dynamics—The Geometry of Behavior* (Addison-Wesley, Redwood City, CA, 2nd ed., 1992).

[2] P. Agre, The dynamic structure of everyday life, Technical Report 1085, MIT AI Lab., Cambridge, MA (1988).

[3] P.E. Agre and D. Chapman, Pengi: an implementation of a theory of activity, in: *Proceedings AAAI-87*, Seattle, WA (1987) 268–272.

[4] J.S. Altman and J. Kien, Highlighting *Aplysia*'s networks, *Trends Neurosci.* **13** (3) (1990) 81–82.

[5] M.A. Arbib and J.-S. Liaw, Sensorimotor transformations in the worlds of frogs and robots, *Artif. Intell.* **72** (1995) 53–79.

[6] W.R. Ashby, *Design for a Brain* (Wiley, New York, 2nd ed., 1960).

[7] K.J. Åström, *Introduction to Stochastic Control Theory* (Academic Press, New York, 1970).

[8] D.H. Ballard, Animate vision, *Artif. Intell.* **48** (1991) 57–86.

[9] A.G. Barto, S.J. Bradtke and S.P. Singh, Learning to act using real-time dynamic programming, *Artif. Intell.* **72** (1995) 81–138.

[10] K. Basye, T. Dean and L.P. Kaelbling, Learning dynamics: system identification for perceptually challenged agents, *Artif. Intell.* **72** (1995) 139–171.

[11] R.D. Beer, *Intelligence as Adaptive Behavior: An Experiment in Computational Neuroethology* (Academic Press, San Diego, CA, 1990).

[12] R.D. Beer, Computational and dynamical languages for autonomous agents, in: T. van Gelder and R. Port, eds., *Mind as Motion* (MIT Press, Cambridge, MA, to appear).

[13] R.D. Beer and J.C. Gallagher, Evolving dynamical neural networks for Adaptive behavior, *Adaptive Behav.* **1** (1992) 91–122.

[14] R.D. Beer, R.E. Ritzmann and T. McKenna, eds., *Biological Neural Networks in Invertebrate Neuroethology and Robotics* (Academic Press, San Diego, CA, 1993).

[15] R.D. Beer, H.J. Chiel, R.D. Quinn, K.S. Espenschied and P. Larsson, A distributed neural network architecture for hexapod robot locomotion, *Neural Comput.* **4** (3) (1992) 356–365.

[16] R.K. Belew and L.B. Booker, eds., *Proceedings of the Fourth International Conference on Genetic Algorithms* (Morgan Kaufmann, San Mateo, CA, 1991).

[17] L.B. Booker, Classifier systems that learn internal world models, *Mach. Learn.* **3** (1988) 161–192.

[18] R.A. Brooks, A robust layered control system for a mobile robot, *IEEE Trans. Rob. Autom.* **2** (1986) 14–23.

[19] R.A. Brooks, A robot that walks: emergent behaviors from a carefully evolved network, *Neural Comput.* **1** (2) (1989) 253–262.

[20] R.A. Brooks, Intelligence without representation, *Artif. Intell.* **47** (1991) 139–159.

[21] R.A. Brooks, Artificial life and real robots, in: *Toward a Practice of Autonomous Agents: Proceedings of the First European Conference of Artificial Life*, Paris, France (1992) 3–10.

[22] D. Chapman, *Vision, Instruction and Action* (MIT Press, Cambridge, MA, 1991).

[23] D. Chapman and L.P. Kaelbling, Input generalization in delayed reinforcement learning: an algorithm and performance comparisons, in: *Proceedings IJCAI-91*, Sydney, Australia (1991) 726–731.

[24] D. Cliff, Computational neuroethology: a provisional manifesto, in: *From Animals to Animats: Proceedings of the First International Conference on Simulation of Adaptive Behavior*, Paris, France (1991) 29–39.

[25] F. Delcomyn, Neural basis of rhythmic behavior in animals, *Science* **210** (1980) 492–498.

[26] M. Donner, *Real-Time Control of Walking* (Birkhauser, Boston, MA, 1987).

[27] J.L. Elman, Distributed representations, simple recurrent networks and grammatical structure, *Mach. Learn.* **7** (1991) 195–225.

[28] J.A. Fodor, *The Language of Thought* (Harvard University Press, Cambridge, MA, 1975).

[29] J.C. Gallagher and R.D. Beer, A qualitative dynamical analysis of evolved locomotion controllers, in: J.-A. Meyer, H. Roitblat and S. Wilson, eds., *From Animals to Animats 2: Proceedings of the Second International Conference on the Simulation of Adaptive Behavior* (MIT Press, Cambridge, MA, 1993) 71–80.

[30] M. Giunti, Computers, dynamical systems, phenomena and the mind, Ph.D. Thesis, Indiana University, Bloomington, IN (1992).

[31] D.E. Goldberg, *Genetic Algorithms in Search, Optimization and Machine Learning* (Addison-Wesley, Reading, MA, 1989).

[32] D. Graham, Pattern and control of walking in insects, *Adv. Insect Physiol.* **18** (1985) 31–140.

[33] J.K. Hale and H. Koçak, *Dynamics and Bifurcations* (Springer-Verlag, New York, 1991).

[34] J.K. Hale, L.T. Magalhaes and W.M. Oliva, *An Introduction to Infinite Dimensional Dynamical Systems—Geometric Theory* (Springer-Verlag, New York, 1984).

[35] S.A. Harp, T. Samad and A. Guha, Towards the genetic synthesis of neural networks, in: *Proceedings Third International Conference on Genetic Algorithms*, Fairfax, VA (1989) 360–369.

[36] I. Harvey, Untimed and misrepresented: connectionism and the computer metaphor, Technical Report CSRP 245, School of Cognitive and Computing Sciences, University of Sussex (1992).

[37] J.H. Holland, *Adaptation in Natural and Artificial Systems* (University of Michigan Press, Ann Arbor, MI, 1975).

[38] J.J. Hopfield, Neurons with graded response properties have collective computational properties like those of two-state neurons, *Proc. Nat. Acad. Sci.* **81** (1984) 3088–3092.

[39] I. Horswill, analysis of adaptation and environment, *Artif. Intell.* **73** (1995), to appear.

[40] P. Husbands and I. Harvey, Evolution vs. design: controlling autonomous robots, in: *Proceedings Third Annual Conference on AI, Simulation and Planning*, Perth, Australia (1992) 139–146.

[41] L.P. Kaelbling, *Learning in Embedded Systems* (MIT Press, Cambridge, MA, 1993).

[42] L.P. Kaelbling and S.J. Rosenschein, Action and planning in embedded agents, *Robotics and Autonomous Systems* **6** (1–2) (1990) 35–48.

[43] T.B. Kepler, L.F. Abbott and E. Marder, Reduction of conductance-based neuron models, *Biol. Cybern.* **66** (1992) 381–387.

[44] D. Kirsch, Today the earwig, tomorrow man?, *Artif. Intell.* **47** (1991) 161–184.

[45] P. Maes, ed., *Designing Autonomous Agents* (MIT Press, Cambridge, MA, 1990).

[46] S. Mahadevan and J. Connell, Automatic programming of behavior-based robots using reinforcement learning, in: *Proceedings AAAI-91*, Anaheim, CA (1991) 768–773.

[47] H.R. Maturana and F.J. Varela, *Autopoiesis and Cognition* (Reidel, Boston, MA, 1980).

[48] H.R. Maturana and F.J. Varela, *The Tree of Knowledge* (Shambhala, Boston, MA, 1987).

[49] J.-A. Meyer and S.W. Wilson, eds., *From Animals to Animats: Proceedings of the First International Conference on Simulation of Adaptive Behavior* (MIT Press, Cambridge, MA, 1991).

[50] G.F. Miller, P.M. Todd and S.U. Hegde, Designing neural networks using genetic algorithms, in: *Proceedings Third International Conference on Genetic Algorithms*, Fairfax, VA (1989) 379–384.

[51] A. Newell and H.A. Simon, Computer science as empirical inquiry: symbols and search, *Commun. ACM* **19** (1976) 113–126.

[52] K.G. Pearson, Nerve cells without action potentials, in: J.C. Fentress, ed., *Simpler Networks and Behavior* (Sinauer, Sunderland, MA, 1976).

[53] J.B. Pollack, The induction of dynamical recognizers, *Mach. Learn.* **7** (1991) 227–252.

[54] Z.W. Pylyshyn, *Computation and Cognition* (MIT Press, Cambridge, MA, 1984).

[55] J. Rinzel and G.B. Ermentrout, Analysis of neural excitability and oscillations, in: C. Koch and I. Segev, eds., *Methods in Neuronal Modeling* (MIT Press, Cambridge, MA, 1989).

[56] S.J. Rosenschein, Formal theories of knowledge in AI and robotics, *New Gen. Comput.* **3** (4) (1985) 345–357.

[57] G. Schöner and J.A.S. Kelso, Dynamic pattern generation in behavioral and neural systems, *Science* **239** (1988) 1513–1520.

[58] C.A. Skarda and W.J. Freeman, How brains make chaos in order to make sense of the world, *Behav. Brain Sci.* **10** (1987) 161–195.

[59] T. Smithers, Taking eliminative materialism seriously: a methodology for autonomous systems research, in: *Toward a Practice of Autonomous Systems: Proceedings of the First European Conference on Artificial Life*, Paris, France (1992) 31–40.

[60] P. Smolensky, On the proper treatment of connectionism, *Behav. Brain Sci.* **11** (1988) 1–74.

[61] T. van Gelder, What might cognition be if not computation?, Technical Report 75, Indiana University Cognitive Science, Bloomington, IN (1992).

[62] X.-J. Wang and J. Rinzel, Alternating and synchronous rhythms in reciprocally inhibitory model neurons, *Neural Comput.* **4** (1992) 84–97.

[63] N. Wiener, *Cybernetics* (MIT Press, Cambridge, MA, 2nd ed., 1961).

[64] G. Wendler, The influence of proprioceptive feedback on locust flight coordination, *J. Comput. Physiol.* **88** (1974) 173–200.

[65] G.M. Werner and M.G. Dyer, Evolution of communication in artificial organisms, in: C.G. Langton, C. Taylor, J.D. Farmer and S. Rasmussen, eds., *Artificial Life II* (Addison-Wesley, Reading, MA, 1991).

[66] S. Wiggins, *Introduction to Applied Nonlinear Dynamical Systems and Chaos* (Springer-Verlag, New York, 1990).

[67] S.W. Wilson, Knowledge growth in an artificial animal, in: K.S. Narendra, ed., *Adaptive and Learning Systems* (Plenum Press, New York, 1986).

Artificial Intelligence 72 (1995) 217–304

On information invariants in robotics [*]

Bruce Randall Donald [*]

Computer Science Department, Cornell University, 4130 Upson Hall, Ithaca, NY 14853-7501, USA

Received September 1992; revised April 1994

Abstract

We consider the problem of determining the information requirements to perform robot tasks, using the concept of *information invariants*. This paper represents our attempt to characterize a family of complicated and subtle issues concerned with measuring robot task complexity. We also provide a first approximation to a purely operational theory that addresses a narrow but interesting special case.

We discuss several measures for the information complexity of a task: (a) How much internal state should the robot retain? (b) How many cooperating agents are required, and how much communication between them is necessary? (c) How can the robot change (side-effect) the environment in order to record state or sensory information to perform a task? (d) How much information is provided by sensors? and (e) How much computation is required by the robot? We consider how one might develop a kind of "calculus" on (a)–(e) in order to compare the power of sensor systems analytically. To this end, we attempt to develop a notion of information invariants. We develop a theory whereby one sensor can be "reduced" to another (much in the spirit of computation-theoretic reductions), by adding, deleting, and reallocating (a)–(e) among collaborating autonomous agents.

[*] This paper describes research done in the Robotics and Vision Laboratory at Cornell University. Support for our robotics research is provided in part by the National Science Foundation under grants No. IRI-8802390, IRI-9000532, IRI-9201699, and by a Presidential Young Investigator award to Bruce Donald, and in part by the Air Force Office of Sponsored Research, the Mathematical Sciences Institute, Intel Corporation, and AT&T Bell laboratories.

[*] E-mail: brd@cs.cornell.edu.

SSDI 0004-3702(94)00024-U

Part I—State, communication, and side-effects

1. Introduction

In this paper we investigate the information requirements for robot tasks. Our work takes as its inspiration the *information invariants* that Erdmann[1] introduced to the robotics community in 1989 [24], although rigorous examples of information invariants can be found in the theoretical literature from as far back as 1978 (see, for example, [1, 35]).

Part I of this paper develops the basic concepts and tools behind information invariants in plain language. Therein, we develop a number of motivating examples. In Part II, we provide a fairly detailed analysis. In particular, we admit more sophisticated models of sensors and computation. This analysis will call for some machinery whose complexity is best deferred until that time.

A central theme to previous work (see the survey article [11] for a detailed review) has been to determine what information is required to solve a task, and to direct a robot's actions to acquire that information to solve it. Key questions concern:

(1) What information is needed by a particular robot to accomplish a particular task?
(2) How may the robot acquire such information?
(3) What properties of the world have a great effect on the fragility of a robot plan/program?
(4) What are the capabilities of a given robot (in a given environment or class of environments)?

These questions can be difficult. Structured environments, such as those found around industrial robots, contribute towards simplifying the robot's task because a great amount of information is encoded, often *implicitly*, into both the environment and the robot's control program. These encodings (and their effects) are difficult to measure. We wish to quantify the information encoded in the assumption that (say) the mechanics are quasistatic, or that the environment is not dynamic. In addition to determining how much information is encoded in the assumptions, we may ask the converse: how much information must the control system or planner compute? Successful manipulation strategies often exploit properties of the (external) physical world (e.g., compliance) to reduce uncertainty and hence gain information. Often, such strategies exploit mechanical computation, in which the mechanics of the task circumscribes the possible outcomes of an action by dint of physical laws. Executing such strategies may require little or no computation; in contrast, planning or simulating these strategies may be computationally expensive. Since during execution we may witness very little "computation" in the sense of "algorithm", traditional techniques from computer science have been difficult to apply in obtaining meaningful upper and lower bounds on the true task complexity. We hope that a theory of information invariants can be used to measure the sensitivity of plans

---

[1] Erdmann introduced the notion of measuring task complexity in *bit-seconds*; the example is important but somewhat complicated; the interested reader is referred to [24].

to particular assumptions about the world, and to minimize those assumptions where possible.

We would like to develop a notion of information invariants for characterizing sensors, tasks, and the complexity of robotics operations. We may view information invariants as a mapping from tasks or sensors to some measure of information. The idea is that this measure characterizes the intrinsic information required to perform the task—if you will, a measure of complexity. For example, in computational geometry, a successful measure has been developed for characterizing input sizes and upper and lower bounds for geometric algorithms. Unfortunately, this measure seems less relevant in robotics, although it remains a useful tool. Its apparent diminished relevance in embedded systems reflects a change in the scientific culture. This change represents a paradigm shift from *offline* to *online* algorithms. Increasingly, robotics researchers doubt that we may reasonably assume a strictly offline paradigm. For example, in the offline model, we might assume that the robot, on booting, reads a geometric model of the world from a disk and proceeds to plan. As an alternative, we would also like to consider *online* paradigms where the robot investigates the world and incrementally builds data structures that in some sense represent the external environment. Typically, online agents are not assumed to have an *a priori* world model when the task begins. Instead, as time evolves, the task effectively forces the agent to move, sense, and (perhaps) build data structures to represent the world. From the online viewpoint, offline questions such as "what is the complexity of plan construction for a known environment, given an *a priori* world model?" often appear secondary, if not artificial. In Part I of this paper, we describe two working robots, TOMMY and LILY, which may be viewed as online robots. We discuss their capabilities, and how they are programmed. We also consider formal models of online robots, foregrounding the *situated automata* of [1]. The examples in Part I link our work to the recent but intense interest in online paradigms for situated autonomous agents. In particular, we discuss what kind of data structures robots can build to represent the environment. We also discuss the *externalization* of state, and the *distribution* of state through a system of spatially separated agents.

We believe it is profitable to explore online paradigms for autonomous agents and sensorimotor systems. However, the framework remains to be extended in certain crucial directions. In particular, sensing has never been carefully considered or modeled in the online paradigm. The chief *lacuna* in the armamentarium of devices for analyzing online strategies is a principled theory of sensori-computational systems. We attempt to fill this gap in Part II, where we provide a theory of *situated sensor systems*. We argue that this framework is natural for answering certain kinds of important questions about sensors. Our theory is intended to reveal a system's information invariants. When a measure of intrinsic information invariants can be found, then it leads naturally to a measure of hardness or difficulty. If these notions are truly intrinsic, then these invariants could serve as "lower bounds" in robotics, in the same way that lower bounds have been developed in computer science.

In our quest for a measure of the intrinsic information requirements of a task, we are inspired by Erdmann's monograph on sensor design [25]. Also, we note that many interesting lower bounds (in the complexity-theoretic sense) have been obtained for motion planning questions (see, e.g., [9, 30, 43, 45]; for upper bounds see, e.g., [4,

6, 12]). Rosenschein has developed a theory of synthetic automata which explore the world and build data structures that are "faithful" to it [46]. His theory is set in a logical framework where sensors are logical predicates. Perhaps our theory could be viewed as a geometric attack on a similar problem. This work was inspired by the theoretical attack on perceptual equivalence begun by Donald and Jennings [14] and by the experimental studies of Jennings and Rus [33]. Horswill [32] has developed a semantics for sensory systems that models and quantifies the kinds of assumptions a sensori-computational program makes about its environment. He also gives source-to-source transformations on sensori-computational "circuits". In addition to the work discussed here in Section 1, for a detailed bibliographic essay on previous research on the geometric theory of planning under uncertainty, see, e.g., [11] or [13].

The goals outlined here are ambitious and we have only taken a small step towards them. The questions above provide the setting for our inquiry, but we are far from answering them. This paper is intended to raise issues concerning information invariants, survey some relevant literature and tools, and take a first stab at a theory. Part I of this paper (Sections 1–3) provides some practical and theoretical motivations for our approach. In part II (Sections 4–9) we describe one particular and very operational theory. This theory contains a notion of *sensor equivalence*, together with a notion of *reductions* that may be performed between sensors. Part II contains an example which is intended to illustrate the potential of a such a theory. We make an analogy between our "reductions" and the reductions used in complexity theory. Readers interested especially in the four questions above will find a discussion of "installation complexity" and the role of calibration in comparing sensors in Section 5 below. Section 8 discusses the semantics of sensor systems precisely; as such this section is mathematically formal, and contains a number of claims and lemmata. This formalism is used to explore some properties of what we call *situated sensor systems*. We also examine the semantics of our "reductions". The results of Section 8 are then used in Section 9 to derive algebraic algorithms for reducing one sensor to another.

1.1. Research contributions and applications

Robot builders make claims about robot performance and resource consumption. In general, it is hard to verify these claims and compare the systems. I really think that the key issue is that two robot programs (or sensor systems) for similar (or even identical) tasks may look very different. Part I of this paper attempts to demonstrate how very different systems can accomplish similar tasks. We also discuss why it is hard to compare the "power" of such systems. The examples in Part I are distinguished in that they permit relatively crisp analytical comparisons. We present these examples so as to demonstrate the standard of crispness to which we aspire: these are the kinds of theorems about information tradeoffs that we believe can be proved for sensorimotor systems. The analyses in Part I are illuminating but ad hoc. In Part II, we present our theory, which represents a systematic attempt to make such comparisons based on geometric and physical reasoning. Finally, we try to operationalize our analysis by making it computational; we give effective (albeit theoretical) procedures for computing our comparisons. Our algorithms are exact and combinatorially precise.

We wish to rigorously compare embedded sensori-computational systems. To do so, we define a "reduction" $\leq_1$ that attempts to quantify when we can "efficiently" build one sensor system out of another (that is, build one sensor using the components of another). Hence, we write $A \leq_1 B$ when we can build system A out of system B without "adding too much stuff". The last phrase is analogous to "without adding much information complexity". Our measure of information complexity is *relativized* both to the information complexity of the sensori-computational components of B, and to the bandwidth of A. This relativization circumvents some tricky problems in measuring sensor complexity. In this sense, our "components" are analogous to *oracles* in the theory of computation. Hence, we write $A \leq_1 B$ if we can build a sensorimotor system that simulates A, using the components of B, plus "a little rewiring". A and B are modeled as *circuits*, with wires (data-paths) connecting their internal components. However, our sensori-computational systems differ from computation-theoretic (CT) "circuits", in that their spatial configuration—i.e., the spatial location of each component—is as important as their connectivity.

We develop some formal concepts to facilitate the analysis. *Permutation* models the permissible ways to reallocate and reuse resources in building another sensor. Intuitively, it captures the notion of repositioning resources such as the active and passive components of sensor systems (e.g., infra-red emitters and detectors). *Geometric codesignation constraints* further restrict the range of admissible permutations. I.e., we do not allow arbitrary relocation; instead, we can constrain resources to be "installed at the same location", such as on a robot, or at a goal. *Output communication* formalizes our notion of "a little bit of rewiring". When resources are permuted, they must be reconnected using "wires", or data-paths. If we separate previously colocated resources, we will usually need to add a communication mechanism to connect the now spatially separate components. Like CT reductions, $A \leq_1 B$ defines an "efficient" transformation on sensors that takes B to A. However, we can give a generic algorithm for synthesizing our reductions (whereas no such algorithm can exist for CT.) [2] Whether such reductions are widely useful or whether there exist better reductions is open; however we try to demonstrate the potential usefulness both through examples and through general claims on algorithmic tractability. We also give a "hierarchy" of reductions, ordered on power, so that the strength of our transformations can be quantified.

We foresee the following potential for application of these ideas:

(1) (*Comparison*). Given two sensori-computational systems A and B, we can ask "which is more powerful?" (in the sense of $A \leq_1 B$, above).

(2) (*Transformation*). We can also ask: "Can B be transformed into A?"

(3) (*Design*). Suppose we are given a specification for A, and a "bag of parts" for B. The bag of parts consists of boxes and wires. Each box is a sensori-computational component ("black box") that computes a function of (i) its spatial location or pose and (ii) its inputs. The "wires" have different bandwidths, and they can hook the boxes together. Then, our algorithms decide, can we "embed" the components of B so as to satisfy the specification of A? The algorithms also

---

[2] For example: no algorithm exists to decide the existence of a linear-space (or log-space, polynomial time, Turing-computable, etc.) reduction between two CT problems.

give the "embedding" (that is, how the boxes should be placed in the world, and how they should be wired together). Hence, we can ask: "Can the specification of A be implemented using the bag of parts B?"

(4) (*Universal reduction*). Consider application 3, above. Suppose that in addition to the specification for A, we are given an encoding of A as a bag of parts, and an "embedding" to implement that specification. Suppose further that $A \leqslant_1 B$. Since this reduction is relativized both to A and to B, it measures the "power" of the components of A relative to the components in B. By universally quantifying over the configuration of A, we can ask, "can the components of B always do the job of the components of A?"

Our paper represents a first stab at these problems, and there are a number of issues that our formalism does not currently consider. We discuss and acknowledge these issues in Section 12.1.

2. Examples

2.1. A following task

2.1.1. A method of inquiry

To introduce our ideas we consider a task involving two autonomous mobile robots. One robot must follow the other. Now, many issues related to information invariants can be investigated in the setting of a single agent. We wish, however, to relate our discussion to the results of Blum and Kozen (in Section 2.2 below), who consider multiple agents. Second, one of our ideas is that, by spatially distributing resources among collaborating agents, the information characteristics of a task are made explicit. That is, by asking, "How can this task be performed by a team of robots?" one may highlight the information structure. In robotics, the evidence for this is, so far, largely anecdotal. In computer science, often one learns a lot about the structure of an algorithmic problem by parallelizing it; we would eventually like to argue that a similar methodology is useful in robotics.

Here is a simple preview of how we will proceed. We first note that it is possible to write a servo loop by which a mobile robot can track (follow) a nearby moving object, using sonar sensing for range calculations, and servoing so as to maintain a constant nominal following distance. A robot running this program will follow a nearby object. In particular, it will not "prefer" any particular kind of object to track. If we wish to program a task where one robot follows another, we may consider adding local infrared communication between the robots, enabling them to transmit and receive messages. This kind of communication allows one robot to lead and the other to follow. It provides an experimental setting in which to investigate the concept of information invariants.

2.1.2. Details of the following task

We now discuss the task of following in some more detail. Consider two autonomous mobile robots, such as those described in [44]. The robots we have in mind are the Cornell mobile robots [44], but the details of their construction are not important.

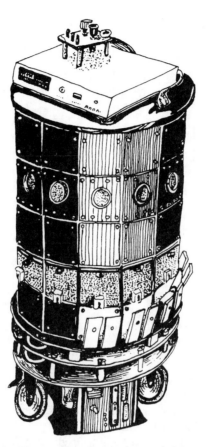

Fig. 1. The Cornell mobile robot TOMMY. Note (mounted top to bottom on the cylindrical enclosure) the ring of sonars, the IR Modems, and the bump sensors. LILY is very similar.

The robots can move about by controlling motors attached to wheels. The robots are autonomous and equipped with a ring of 12 simple Polaroid ultrasonic sonar sensors. Each robot has an onboard processor for control and programming.

We wish to consider a task in which one robot called LILY must follow another robot called TOMMY. It is possible to write such a control loop using only sonar readings and position/force control alone.

We now augment the robots described in [44] as follows. (This description characterizes the robots in our lab.) We equip each robot with 12 infra-red modems/sensors, arrayed in a ring about the robot body (see Fig. 1). Each modem consists of an emitter-detector pair. When transmitting or receiving, each modem essentially functions like the remote control for home appliances (e.g., TVs).[3] Experiments with our initial design [5] seemed to indicate that the communication bandwidth we could expect was roughly 2400 baud-feet. That is, at a distance of 1 foot between LILY and TOMMY, we

---

[3] The IR modems can time-slice between collision detection and communication; moreover, nearby modems (on the same robot) can "stagger" their broadcasts so as not to interfere with each other.

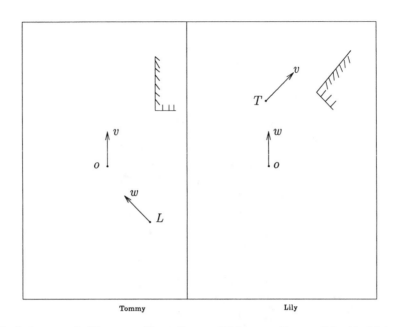

Fig. 2. The "radar screens" of TOMMY and LILY. TOMMY (T) is approaching a wall (on his right) at speed v, while LILY (L) follows at speed w.

could expect to communicate at 2400 baud; at 2 feet, the reliable communication rate drops to 1200 baud, and so forth.

We pause for a moment to note that this simple, experimentally-determined quantity is our first example of an information invariant.

Now, modem i is mounted so as to be at a fixed angle from the front of the robot base, and hence it is at a fixed angle θ_i from the direction of forward motion, which is defined to be 0.

Now, suppose that TOMMY is traveling at a commanded speed of v (note v need not be positive). For the task of following, each modem panel i on TOMMY transmits a unique identifier (e.g., 'Tommy), the angle θ_i, and the speed v. That is, he transmits the following triple:[4] $\langle id, \theta_i, v \rangle$.

In this task, LILY transmits the same information, with a different id of course. This means that when the robots are in communication each can "detect" the position (using sonars and IRs), the heading, and the name of the other robot.[5] In effect each robot can construct a virtual "radar screen" like those used by air traffic controllers, on which it notes other robots, their position and heading, as well as obstacles and features of

---

[4] The identifier is necessary for applications involving more than two robots. Also, using the id a robot can disambiguate other robots' broadcasts from its own IR broadcast (e.g., reflections off white walls).

[5] This data is noisy, but since an adequate servo loop for following can be constructed using sonars alone [44], the IRs only add information to the task. The IR information does not measurably slow down the robot, since the IR processing is distributed and is not done by the Scheme controller.

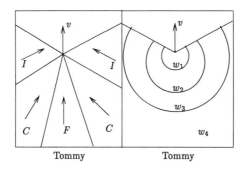

Fig. 3. The statespace "radar screen" of TOMMY is partitioned to indicate the control for LILY. (For the task of following, we could partition LILY's screen instead, but this is clearer for exposition). On the left is LILY's direction control; and the regions are F (follow), C (correct), and I (intercept). The commanded motion direction is shown as an arrow. On the right is LILY's speed control, with w_1 being very slow, w_4 fast, and $w_1 < w_2 < w_3 < w_4$. This control partition is conditioned on TOMMY's speed v.

the environment. The screen (see Fig. 2) is in local coordinates for each robot.[6] It is important to realize that although Fig. 2 "looks" like a pair of maps, in fact, each is simply a local reconstruction of sensor data. Moreover, these "local maps" are updated at each iteration through the servo loop, and so little retained state is necessary.

Now, robotics employs the notion of *configuration space*[7] [37] to describe control and planning algorithms. The *configuration* of one of our robots is its position and heading. *Configuration space* is the set of all configurations. In our case, the configuration space of one robot is the space $\mathbb{R}^2 \times S^1$. A related notion is *state space*, which is the space of configurations and velocities of the robot. After some reflection, it may be seen that Fig. 2 is a geometric depiction of a state space for the robot task of following (it is actually a representation of the mutual configuration spaces of the robots). Depending on where the robots are in Fig. 2, each must take a different control (servo) action. The points where one robot takes the same (parameterized) action may be grouped together to form an equivalence class. Essentially, we partition the state space in Fig. 2 into regions where the same action is required. This is a common way of synthesizing a feedback control loop. See Fig. 3.

The point is that in this analysis, we may ask, "What state must the robot LILY retain?". After some thought, the answer is, *very little*, since the "radar screens" in Fig. 2 may be drawn again from new sensor readings at each iteration. That is, no state must be retained between servo loop iterations, because in an iteration we only need some local state to process the sensor information and draw the information in Fig. 2. (We do not address whatever state TOMMY would need to figure out "where to lead", only how he should modify his control so as not to lose LILY.) One consequence of this kind of "stateless" following is that if communication is broken, or one robot

---

[6] In the language of [14], the sonar sensors, plus the IR communication, represent *concrete* sensors, out of which the *virtual* sensors shown in Fig. 2 can be constructed. The construction essentially involves adding the IR information above to the servo loop for following using sonar given in [44]. The details are not particularly important to this discussion.

[7] See [36] for a good introduction.

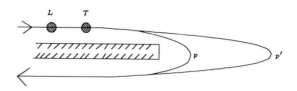

Fig. 4. Following around a wall. The shorter path p is quicker by Δt than p', but it cannot be executed without more communication or state.

is obscured from the other, then the robots have no provision (no *information*) from the past on which to base a strategy to reacquire contact. They can certainly go into a search mode, but this mode is stateless in the sense that it is not based on retained state (data) built up from before, before the break in contact. In short, at one time-step, LILY and TOMMY wake up and look at their radar screens. Based on what they see, they act. If one cannot see the other, perhaps it can begin a search or broadcast a cry for help. This is an essential feature of statelessness, or reactivity. Let us call a situation in which the robots maintain communication *preserving the control loop*. If they break communication it *breaks* the control loop.

Now, suppose that TOMMY has to go around a wall, as in Fig. 4. Suppose TOMMY has a geometric model of the wall (from a map or through reconstruction). Then it is not hard for TOMMY to calculate that if he takes a quick turn around the wall (as shown in trajectory p), that the line of sight between the robots may be broken. Since LILY is "stateless" as described above, when communication is broken the following task will fail, unless LILY can reacquire TOMMY. It is difficult to write a general such "search and reacquire" procedure, and it would certainly delay the task.

For this reason, we may prefer TOMMY to predict when line-of-sight communication would be broken, and to prefer a trajectory like p' (Fig. 4). When executed slowly enough, such trajectories as p' will allow the robots to maintain communication, and hence allow the following task to proceed. However, there is a cost: for example, we may reasonably assume that taking p' will take Δt longer than p. Now, let p^* denote the trajectory that follows the same path as p, but slowed-down so it takes the same time as p' [8]. It might also be reasonable to assume that if TOMMY slowed down enough to follow p^*, the robots could also maintain communication.

Hence, in this example, the quantity Δt is a measure of the "cost" of maintaining communication. It is a kind of invariant. But we can be more precise.

In particular, TOMMY has more choices to preserve the control loop. The distance at which LILY servos to TOMMY is controlled by a constant, which we will call the *following distance* [9] d. Hence, TOMMY, could transmit an additional message to LILY, containing the a new following distance d'. The meaning of this message would be "tighten up"—that is, to tell LILY to servo at a closer distance. Note that the message $\langle \texttt{heel}, d' \rangle$ essentially encodes a *plan D*—a new servo loop—for LILY. In this case, LILY will servo to follow TOMMY at the closer distance d', which will successfully permit the robots to navigate p while maintaining contact.

---

[8] So, p^* is the time-rescaled trajectory from p [19].

[9] For an explicit use of this constant in an actual servo loop, see, for example, [44].

Another possibility is that we could allow LILY to retain some state, and allow TOMMY to broadcast an *encoding* of the trajectory p. This encoding could be via points on the path, or a control program—essentially, by transmitting the message $\langle p \rangle$, TOMMY transmits a plan—a motion plan—for LILY. In this case, after losing contact with TOMMY, LILY will follow the path (or plan) p open loop, until TOMMY is reacquired.

In both these cases, we must allow LILY to retain enough state to store d or p. Since LILY already stores some value for d (see [44]), we need merely replace that. However, the storage for the plan (or path) p could be significant, depending on the detail.

Finally, we could imagine a scenario where LILY retains some amount of state over time to "track" TOMMY. For example, by observing TOMMY's trajectory before the break in communication, it may be possible to extrapolate future positions (one could, for example, use forward projections [23] or a kalman filter). Based on these extrapolations, LILY could seek TOMMY in the region of highest expectation. I will not detail this method here, but, it is not too difficult to see that it requires some amount of state for LILY to do this computation; let us call this amount s.

There is a tradeoff between execution time (Δt), communication (transmitting $\langle d' \rangle$ or $\langle p \rangle$), and internal state (storage for p or s). What is this relationship? Here is a conjecture one would like to prove about this relationship. For a path or a control program p or D, we denote its information complexity by $|p|$. For example, $|p|$ could measure the number of via points on p times their *bit-complexity* (the number of bits required to encode a single point).

Idea 2.1. There is an *information invariant* c for the task of following, whose units are bit-seconds. In particular,

$$c = |p| \, t_p = |D| \, t_D = s t_s, \qquad (1)$$

where t_p, t_D, and t_s are the execution times for the three strategies above.

Eq. (1) should be interpreted as a lower bound—like the Heisenberg principle. It is no coincidence that Erdmann's information invariants are also in bit-seconds. An information invariant such as (1) quantifies the tradeoff between speed, communication, and storage. Currently, to prove such crisp results we must first make a number of assumptions about dynamics and geometry (see Appendix F.1). Moreover, the methods we describe below typically yield results using "order" notation ($O(\cdot)$ or big-theta $\Theta(\cdot)$) instead of strict equality.

One example of provable information invariants is given in the *kinodynamic* literature [8, 19, 20]. This work is concerned with provable planning algorithms for robots with dynamics. We give some details in Appendix F.1. Here we note that Xavier, in [21, 49], developed "trade-offs" similar in flavor to Eq. (1). Both Erdmann and Xavier obtain "trade-offs" between information and execution speed. Their methods appear to require a performance measure (e.g., the "cost" of a control strategy). One might view our work (and also [1], below) as investigating information invariants in the absence of a performance measure. In this case, we cannot directly measure absolute information complexity in bit-seconds. Instead, we develop a way to relativize (or reduce) one sensori-computational system to another, in order to quantify their (relative) power. See Appendix F.1 for more details on information invariants with performance measures.

To summarize: the ambition of this work is to define the notions in Idea 2.1 so that they can be measured directly. Previous work [21,25,49] has required a performance measure in order to obtain a common currency for information invariance. In order not to use this crutch, we first define a set of transformations on sensori-computational systems. Second, we propose understanding the information invariants in terms of what these transformations preserve.

2.2. The power of the compass

In 1978, Blum and Kozen wrote a ground-breaking paper on maze-searching automata [1,35]. This section is devoted to a discussion of their paper, *On the power of the compass* [1], and we interpret their results in the context of autonomous mobile robots and information invariants.

In 1990, we posed the following question together with Jim Jennings:

Question 2.2 ([15]). "Let us consider a rational reconstruction of mobile robot programming. There is a task we wish the mobile robot to perform, and the task is specified in terms of external (e.g., human-specified) perceptual categories. For example, these terms might be "concepts" like *wall*, *door*, *hallway*, or *Professor Hopcroft*. The task may be specified in these terms by imagining the robot has *virtual* sensors which can recognize these objects (e.g., a wall sensor) and their "parameters" (e.g., length, orientation, etc.). Now, of course the physical robot is not equipped with such sensors, but instead is armed with certain *concrete* physical sensors, plus the power to retain history and to compute. The task-level programming problem lies in implementing the virtual sensors in terms of the concrete robot capabilities. We imagine this implementation as a tree of computation, in which the vertices are control and sensing actions, computation, and state retention. A particular kind of state consists of geometric constructions; in short, we imagine the mobile robot as an automaton, connected to physical sensors and actuators, which can move and interrogate the world through its sensors while taking notes by making geometric constructions on "scratch paper". But what should these constructions be? What program runs on the robot? How may these computation trees be synthesized?"

Let us consider this question of state, namely, what should the robot record on its scratch paper? In robotics, the answer is frequently either "nothing" (i.e., the robot is reactive, and should not build any representations), or "a map" (namely, the robot should build a geometric model of the entire environment). In particular, even schemes such as [39] require a worst-case linear amount of storage (in the geometric complexity n of the environment). Can one do better? Is there a sufficient representation that is between 0 and $O(n)$?

Blum and Kozen provide precise answers to these questions in the setting of theoretical, situated automata. This section didactically adopts the rhetorical "we" to compactly interpret their results. While these results are theoretical, we believe they provide insight into Question 2.2 above.

We define a *maze* to be a finite, two-dimensional obstructed checkerboard. A finite automaton (DFA) in the maze may, in addition to its automaton transitions, transit on each move to an adjacent unobstructed square in the N, S, E, or W direction. We say an automaton can *search* a maze if eventually it will visit each square. It need not halt, and it may revisit squares. Hence, this kind of "searching" is the theoretical analog of the "exploration" task that many modern mobile robots are programmed to perform. However, note that in this entire section there is no control or sensing uncertainty.

We can consider augmenting an automaton with a single *counter*; using this counter it can record state. (Two counters would not be an interesting enhancement, because then we obtain the power of a Turing machine). [10]

We say two (or more) automata *search a maze together* as follows. The automata move synchronously, in lock-step. This synchronization could be effected using global control, or with synchronized clocks. When two automata land on the same square, each transmits its internal state to the other.

Finally, we may *externalize* and *distribute* the state. Instead of a counter, we may consider equipping an automaton with *pebbles*, which it can drop and pick up. Each pebble is uniquely identifiable to any automaton in the maze. On moving to a square, an automaton senses what pebbles are on the square, plus what pebbles it is carrying. It may then drop or pick up any pebbles.

Hence, a pure automaton is a theoretical model of a "reactive", robot-like creature. (Many simple physical robot controllers are based on DFAs). The exchange of state between two automata models local communication between autonomous agents. The pebbles model the "beacons" often used by mobile robots, or, more generally, the ability to side-effect the environment (as opposed to the robot's internal state) in order to perform tasks. Finally, the single counter models a limited form of state (storage). It is much more restrictive than the tape of a Turing machine. We believe that quantifying communication between collaborating mobile robots is a fundamental information-theoretic question. In manipulation, the ability to structure the environment through the actions of the robot (see, e.g., [13]) or the mechanics of the task (see, e.g., [40]) seems a fundamental paradigm. How do these techniques compare in power?

We call automata with these extra features *enhanced*, and we will assume that automata are not enhanced unless noted. Given these assumptions, Blum and Kozen demonstrate the following results. First, they note a result of Budach that a single automaton cannot search all mazes. [11] Next they prove the following:

---

[10] A *counter* is like a register. A DFA with a *counter* can keep a count in the register, increment or decrement it, and test for zero. A single counter DFA (introduced by Fischer [28] in 1966) can be viewed as a special kind of push-down (stack) automaton (PDA) that has only one stack symbol (except for a top of the stack marker). This means we should not expect a single-counter machine to be more powerful than a PDA, which, in turn, is considerably weaker than a Turing machine (see, e.g., [31, Chapter 5]). The proof that a two-counter DFA can simulate a Turing machine was first given by Papert and McNaughton in 1961 [41] but shorter proofs are now given in many textbooks, for example, see [31, Theorem 7.9].

[11] See [1] for references.

(1) There are two (unenhanced) automata that together can search all mazes.

(2) There is a two-pebble automaton that can search all mazes.

(3) There is a one-counter automaton that can search all mazes.

These results are crisp information invariants. It is clear that a Turing machine could build (a perfect) map of the maze, that would be linear in the size of the maze. This they term the naïve linear-space algorithm. This is the theoretical analog of most map-building mobile robots—even those that build "topological" maps still build a linear-space geometric data structure on their "scratch paper". But (3) implies that there is a *log-space* algorithm to search mazes—that is, using only an amount of storage that is logarithmic in the complexity of the world, the maze can be searched. [12] This is a precise answer to part of our Question 2.2.

However, points (1–3) also demonstrate interesting information invariants. (1) = (2) demonstrates the equivalence (in the sense of information) of beacons and communication. Hence side-effecting the environment is equivalent to collaborating with an autonomous co-agent. The equivalence of (1) and (2) to (3) suggests an equivalence (in this case) and a tradeoff (in general) between communication, state, and side-effecting the environment. Hence we may credit [1] with a excellent example of information invariance.

2.2.1. *The power of randomization*

Erdmann's Ph.D. Thesis is an investigation of the power of randomization in robotic strategies [24]. The idea is similar to that of randomized algorithms—by permitting the robot to randomly perturb initial conditions (the environment), its own internal state, or to randomly choose among actions, one may enhance the performance and capabilities of robots, and derive probabilistic bounds on expected performance. [13] This lesson should not be lost in the context of the information invariants above. For example, as Erdmann points out, one finite automaton can search any maze if we permit it to randomly select among the unobstructed directions. The probability that such an automaton will eventually visit any particular maze square is one. Randomization also helps in finite 3D mazes (see Section 2.2.2 for more on the problems that deterministic (as opposed to randomized) finite automata have in searching 3D mazes), although the expected time for the search increases somewhat.

These observations about randomizing automata can be even extended to *unbounded* mazes (the mazes we have considered are finite). However, in a 2D unbounded maze, although the automaton will eventually visit any particular maze square with probability

---

[12] Here is the idea. First, [1] show how to write a program whereby an unenhanced DFA can traverse the boundary of any single connected component of obstacle squares. Now, suppose the DFA could "remember" the southwesternmost corner (in a lexicographic order) of the obstacle. Next, [1] show how all the free space can then be systematically searched. It suffices for a DFA with a single counter to record the y-coordinate y_{min} of this corner. We now imagine simulating this algorithm (as efficiently as possible) using a Turing machine, and we measure the bit-complexity. If there are n free squares in the environment then $y_{min} \leq n$, and the algorithm consumes $O(\log n)$ bits of storage. For details, see [1].

[13] While the power of randomization has long been known in the context of algorithms for maze exploration, Erdmann was able to lift these results to the robotics domain. In particular, one challenge was to consider continuous state spaces (as opposed to graphs).

one, the expected time to visit it is infinite. In 3D, however, things are worse: in 3D unbounded mazes, the probability that any given "cube" will be visited drops from one to about 0.37.

2.2.2. What does a compass give you?

Thus we have given precise examples of information invariants for *tasks* (or for one task, namely, searching, or "exploration"). However, it may be less clear what the information invariants for a *sensor* would be. Again, Blum and Kozen provide a fundamental insight. We motivate their result with the following

Question 2.3. Suppose we have two mobile robots, TOMMY and LILY, configured as described in Section 2.1. Suppose we put a flux-gate magnetic compass on LILY (but not on TOMMY). How much more "powerful" has LILY become? What tasks can LILY now perform that TOMMY cannot?

Now, any robot engineer knows compasses are useful. But what we want in answer to Question 2.3 is a precise, provable answer. Happily, in the case where the compass is relatively accurate, [14] [1] provide some insight:

Consider an automaton (of any kind) in a maze. Such an automaton effectively has a compass, since it can tell N,S,E,W apart. That is, on landing on a square, it can interrogate the neighboring N,S,E,W squares to find out which are unobstructed, and it can then accurately move one square in any unobstructed compass direction.

By contrast, consider an automaton in a graph (that need not be a maze). Such an automaton has no compass; on landing on a vertex, there are some number $g \geqslant 0$ of edges leading to "free" other vertices, and the automaton must choose one.

Hence, as Blum and Kozen point out, "*Mazes and regular planar graphs appear similar on the surface, but in fact differ substantially. The primary difference is that an automaton in a maze has a* compass: *it can distinguish N,S,E,W. A compass can provide the automaton with valuable information, as shown by the second of our results*" [1]. Recall point (1) in Section 2.2. Blum and Kozen show, that in contrast, to (1), no two automata together can search all finite planar cubic graphs (in a *cubic* graph, all vertices have degree $g = 3$). They then prove that no three automata suffice. Later, Kozen showed that four automata do not suffice [35]. Moreover, if we relax the planarity assumption but restrict our cubic graphs to be 3D mazes, it is known that no finite set of finite automata can search all such finite 3D mazes [3].

Hence, [1,35] provide a lower bound to the question, "What information does a compass provide?" We close by mentioning that in the flavor of Section 2.2.1, there is a large literature on randomized search algorithms for graphs. As in Section 2.2.1, randomization can improve the capability and performance of the search automata.

---

[14] In considering how a very accurate sensor can aid a robot in accomplishing a task, this methodology is closely allied with Erdmann's work on developing "minimal" sensors [25].

3. Discussion: measuring information

We have described the basic tools and concepts behind information invariants. We illustrated by example how such invariants can be analyzed and derived. We made a conceptual connection between information invariants and tradeoffs. In previous work, tradeoffs arose naturally in kinodynamic situations, in which performance measures, planning complexity, and robustness (in the sense of resistance to control uncertainty) are traded-off. We noted that Erdmann's invariants are of this ilk [24].

However, without a performance (cost) measure, it is more difficult to develop information invariants. We believe measures of *information complexity* are fundamentally different from *performance measures*. Our interest here is in the former; we will not discuss performance measures again until Appendix F.1. Here are some measures of the information complexity of a robotic task: (a) *How much internal state should the robot retain?* (b) *How many cooperating agents are required, and how much communication between them is necessary?* and (c) *How can the robot change (side-effect) the environment in order to record state or sensory information to perform a task?* Examples of these categories include: (a) space considerations for computer memory, (b) local IR communication between collaborating autonomous mobile robots, and (c) dropable beacons. With regard to (a), we note that, of course, memory chips are cheap, but in the mobile robot design space, most investigations seem to fall at the ends of the design spectrum. For example, (near) reactive systems use (almost) no state, while "map builders" and model-based approaches use a very large (linear) amount. Natarajan [43] has considered an invariant complexity measure analogous to (b), namely the number of robot "hands" required to perform an assembly task. This quantifies the interference kinematics of the assembly task, and assumes global synchronous control. With regard to (c), the most easily imagined physical realization consists of coded IR beacons; however, "external" side-effects could be as exotic as chalking notes on the environment (as parking police do on tires), or assembling a collection of objects into a configuration of lower "entropy" (and hence, greater information). *Calibration* is an important form of external state, which we explore in Part II.

In Part I, we exploited automata-theoretic results to explore invariants that trade-off internal state, communication, and external state. While Part I concentrates on information invariants for *tasks*, we did touch on how information invariants for *sensors* can be integrated into the discussion. In particular, we reviewed a precise way to measure the information that a compass gives an autonomous mobile robot. Somewhat surprisingly, trading-off the measures (a)–(c) proves sufficient to quantify the information a compass supplies.

The compass invariant illustrates the kind of result that we would like to prove for more general sensors. That is, we could add a fourth measure, (d) *How much information is provided by sensors?* While the examples we presented are perhaps didactically satisfying, we must introduce some more machinery in order to extend our discussion to include two additional important measures of the information complexity of a robotic task: (d), and (e) *How much computation is required of the robot?* In Part II we explore these issues in some detail. In particular, we describe how one might develop a kind of "calculus" on measures (a)–(e) in order to compare the power of sensor systems analytically. To this end, we develop a theory whereby one sensori-computational system can be "reduced" to another (much in the spirit of computation-theoretic reductions), by adding, deleting, and reallocating (a)–(e) among collaborating autonomous agents.

Part II—Sensors and computation

4. Sensors

Intuitively, we can imagine a *sensor system* being implemented as a tree of sensori-computational elements, in which the vertices are controllers and sensors, computing devices, and state elements. Such a system is called a *virtual sensor* by [14]. In a virtual sensor, outputs are computed from the outputs of other sensors in the same device. Given two sensor systems E and H, we would like to be able to quantify the information the sensors provide. In particular, suppose E and H are different "implementations" (in a sense we shall soon make precise) of superficially similar sensor systems. We would like to be able to determine whether the two systems are "equivalent" in the sense that they deliver "equivalent" information, that is, whether $E \cong H$. More generally, we would like to be able to write an "equation" like

$$E \cong H + \boxdot \tag{2}$$

where we can rigorously specify what box $\boxdot$ we need to "add" to H to make sensor E. For example, the box could represent some new sensing, or some computation on existing sensory and stored data. In Part II we discuss some methods for achieving these goals. To illustrate our techniques, we describe two sensors, the *radial* sensor [25], and the *beacon*, or *lighthouse* sensor. We then develop methods to compare the sensors and their information invariants. These sensors bear some relation to the *compass* discussed in Part I; it is our goal here to quantify this relationship precisely. In the beginning, we will allow informal definitions, which suffice for building intuition. The following concepts will be defined precisely in Section 8: the term *simulate*, the *output* of a sensor, a sensori-computational *resource*, the relation $\cong$, and the operator $+$. We begin as follows:

Definition 4.1 (*Informal*). [15] For two sensor systems S and Q we say Q *simulates S* if the output of Q is the same as the output of S. In this case we write $S \cong Q$.

The operator $+$ in Eq. (2) represents "adding" something to H. Informally, this "something" is what we would like to call a *resource* (later, in Section 4.2.1). We will later see that $\cong$ is an equivalence relation.

Here is a preview of the formalism we will develop. We view sensor systems as "circuits". We model these circuits as graphs. Vertices correspond to different sensori-computational components of the system (what we will call "resources" below). Edges

---

[15] This definition is formalized in Section 8.1.

correspond to "data-paths" through which information passes. Different embeddings of these graphs correspond to different spatial allocation of the "resources". We also permit resources to be *colocated*. This requires that we consider graph *immersions* as well as graph embeddings. *Immersions* are like embeddings, but they need not be injective. Under this model, the concepts above are easily formalized. For example, the operation + turns out to be like taking the union of two graphs.

One key idea involves asking: "What information is added (or lost) in a sensor system when we change its immersion?" and "What information is preserved under all immersions?". Our goal will be to determine what classes of immersions preserve information. Sections 4.1–7 explore this idea through an example.

4.1. The radial sensor

We begin with a didactic example. In [25] Erdmann demonstrates a method for synthesizing sensors from task specifications. The sensors have the property of being "optimal" or "minimal" in the sense that they convey exactly the information required for the control system to perform the task. For our purposes, it is sufficient to examine a particular sensor, called the *radial sensor*, which is the output of one of his examples. The radial sensor arises by considering manipulation strategies in which the robot must achieve a goal despite uncertainty.

The radial sensor works as follows. Consider a small robot in the plane. Suppose there is a goal region G which is a small disc in the plane. See Fig. 5. The robot is at some configuration $x \in \mathbb{R}^2$, and at some heading $h \in S^1$. Both these state variables are unknown to the robot. The robot can only command *relative* motions (relative to the local coordinate system specified by (x, h)). Thus, it would command a velocity $v_{\Delta\theta}$, and the robot would move in *relative* direction $\Delta\theta$, which is *global* direction $h + \Delta\theta$. The radial sensor returns the angle θ_r which is the angle between h and the ray between x and the goal. The robot need only command v_{θ_r} to reduce its distance to the goal.[16] This example easily generalizes to the case where there is uncertainty in the robot's control system (that is, the "aim" of $v_{\Delta\theta}$) see [25, 38]. It is plausible (and indeed, Erdmann proves) that this sensor is necessary and sufficient to write a feedback loop that provably attains the goal.

To summarize: the radial sensor returns information that encodes the relative heading θ_r of the goal G—relative to the robot's current heading h. See Fig. 5. We emphasize that the radial sensor does not reveal the configuration (x, h) of the robot beyond this. We will not describe possible physical implementations of the radial sensor, but see [25] for a discussion.[17]

---

[16] In the language of [14], the perceptual equivalence classes for this sensor are the rays emanating at x.

[17] Erdmann emphasizes the special cases where the robot always knows its heading, or, where the robot's heading is always fixed (say, due North, so that h is always identically zero). In these cases, the radial sensor returns the *global* heading to the goal. This special case arises in the domain of manipulation with a robot arm, which, of course, is why it is natural for Erdmann's theory. The radial sensor we present is just slightly generalized for the mobile robot domain.

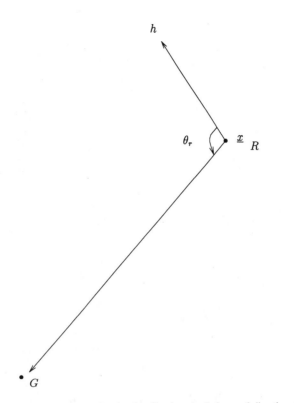

Fig. 5. The radial sensor E, showing heading h and relative goal direction θ_r.

4.2. Lighthouses, beacons, ships, and airplanes

We now describe another sensor. Our goal is to compare this sensor to the radial sensor using information invariants. See Fig. 6. We call this a *lighthouse* sensor system. We call this a sensor *system* since as described, it involves two physically separated "agents". We motivate this sensor as follows. Consider two mobile robots, which we denote L and R (see Fig. 6). L will be the "lighthouse" (beacon) and R will be the "ship". The robots live in the plane. In introducing the lighthouse system, we will informally introduce machinery to describe sensori-computational *resources*.

4.2.1. Resources

Now, to analyze the information invariants, we must be careful about the implementation of the sensor system, and, in particular, we must be careful to *count* how resources (a)–(e) (Section 3) are consumed and allocated—much the same way that one must be careful in performing a complexity analysis for an algorithm. Let us catalog the following kinds of *resources*:

- *Emitters*. On L, there are two lights which we call *physical emitters*. There is a unidirectional green light $\boxed{\text{g}}$ that rotates at a constant angular velocity. That is, the green light shines along a ray that is anchored (at its origin) at L. The ray sweeps

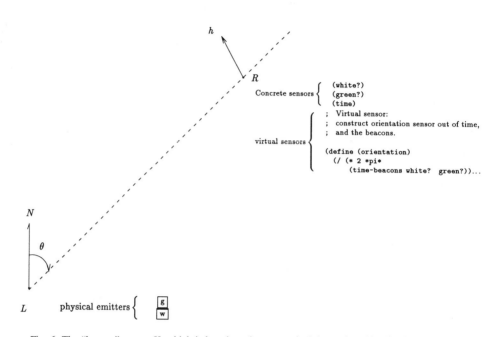

Fig. 6. The "beacon" sensor *H*, which is based on the same principle employed by lighthouses.

(rotates) about *L*. The green light can only be seen by points on that ray. Second, there is an omnidirectional white light $\boxed{\text{w}}$ that flashes whenever the green light is pointing due North. That is, the white light can be seen from all directions.

- *Concrete sensors.* On *R*, there is a photo-electric sensor that detects when a white light illuminates *R*. Another sensor detects green light. There is also a clock on *R*.
- *Computation.* There is a computer on *R* that we can program in Scheme, following [44]. The concrete sensors above are interfaced to Scheme via library functions (as in [44]). The functions (white?) and (green?) are of type UNIT → BOOL, and return #t when light is sensed and #f otherwise. The clock is available as the function (time), which returns the time measured in small units. We can measure the time and space requirements of a computation using standard techniques. Furthermore, we may quantify the amount of sensor information consumed by counting the number of calls to (white?), (green?), and (time) and the number of bits returned.

    Now, here is how lighthouses work. See Fig. 6. The "ship" *R* times the period t_w between white flashes. Then it measures the time *t* between a white flash and the next green flash. Clearly the "angle" θ of the robot—the angle between North and the ray from *L* to *R*—can be computed as $\theta = 2\pi t / t_w$. (Assuming the ship is moving slowly, relative to t_w).

- *Virtual sensors.* We can implement this as a *virtual sensor* [14] called (orientation) shown immediately below. The orientation sensor is specified as a computation that (i) calls concrete sensors, (ii) retains some local state (T0), and (iii) does some computation (*, /, etc.). It is easy to measure the time and space requirements of the "circuit" that computes θ. Hence, we can implement certain *virtual sensors* to compute orientation. We detail this implementation below:

Given the resources above, we can implement the following virtual sensors "on" R:[18]

```
;   Virtual sensor:
;     construct orientation sensor out of time,
;     and the beacons.

(define (orientation)
  (/ (* 2 *pi*
        (time-beacons white? green?))
     (time-beacons white? white?)))

;   time between beacons
;     event1  and event2  are type UNIT → BOOL.%
```
[19]
```
(define (time-beacons event1 event2)
  (sleep-until event1)
  (let ((T0 (time)))
    (sleep-until event2)
    (- (time) T0)))

:   utility in scheme48 [44].
;   sleep-until  waits until thunk  returns #t,
;     and then returns.
(define (sleep-until thunk) ....)
```

- *Resources R does not have.* Let us contrast our exemplar robot ship R with an *enhanced* version R' that corresponds to a real ship navigating at sea using lighthouse sensors. We should not confuse R with a real ship. A real ship R' has a map, on which are located *a priori* features, including a point which R' will assume corresponds to the location of L. True North is indicated on the map. R' computes θ as above (see Fig. 6), and draws a ray on the map, anchored at L, that is θ degrees from North. R' now knows that it is on that ray. In addition to possessing a map, and knowing the map coordinates of L, a real ship often has a compass. In the robotics domain, orientation odometry could approximate an accurate compass. Real ships also have communication devices like radios. We observe *communication* resources compare roughly to (b) in Section 3. Our *unenhanced* robot R, however, is not a real ship, and it has none of these resources.

Modern aircraft navigate using two sensors similar to the radial and lighthouse sensors. An *Automatic Direction Finder* (*ADF*) is a radial sensor. An ADF is simply a needle

---

[18] We must make some assumptions to prove this real-time program is correct. For example, we must assume the clock and the processor are very fast relative to the green light (and the ship).

[19] Objects of type UNIT → BOOL are called *boolean thunks*.

that points to a ground radio transmitter, in relative airplane coordinates. You do not need to know where you are or which way you are headed. You simply make the needle point straight ahead, by turning the airplane. So it is a radial sensor, and you track into the goal. A *VOR* (*VHF Omnirange*) is a lighthouse sensor. The VOR ground transmitter has the equivalent of a green and white light arrangement. The radio receiver in the plane decodes it, and then tells you the radial direction from the transmitter, in global coordinates. Then, if you actually want to fly to the VOR you have to have a compass, look at it, and turn the plane to fly in the same direction as your radio indicates. The VOR uses a clock, just like in the lighthouse. The "green emitter" in the VOR rotates at 30 Hz, and the white "North" light flashes 30 times a second. The receiver in the plane decodes the difference, just like in the lighthouse example, to give a direction. VORs do not use light, but they broadcast in the Megahertz range instead of the visual range.

To follow a radial sensor you only need to make the source be straight ahead of you; to follow a lighthouse sensor you need a compass. The radial sensor is in local coordinates and the lighthouse sensor is in global coordinates.

The ADF requires fewer instruments, but pilots tend to use the VOR. Why? Because that way you can look up your position on a chart, which is often what you care about (one VOR gives you a line; two give you your location). But if you just want to get somewhere, all you need is the ADF. [20]

5. Reduction of sensors

5.1. Comparing the power of sensors

Let us call the radial sensor E and the (unenhanced) lighthouse system H. The sensors are, of course, superficially similar: both have components at two spatially separated locations. Both sensors measure angles. Of course, they measure *different* angles. We cannot transform the information delivered by H into the information specification of E, without consuming more resources. These sensors deliver *incomparable* information, in that neither delivers strictly more information than the other.

We wish to be able to compare two sensors even when they deliver incomparable information. To do this, we introduce a mechanism called *reduction*, which allows us to compare the power of two sensor systems such as E and H. Hence, even though neither E nor H delivers strictly more information, they are comparable under a partial order induced by our reduction.

5.2. Sensor reduction

The analytic goal of sensor reduction is to be able to write "equations" like Eq. (2). The operational goal is to build one sensor out of another, and to measure the "power"

---

[20] There are some other reasons for using VORs, such as the fact that VORs are VHF while ADFs are LF/MF, so ADF reception gets blocked by thunderstorms while VOR reception does fine. On the other hand, VORs require line-of sight, whereas ADFs will work over the horizon.

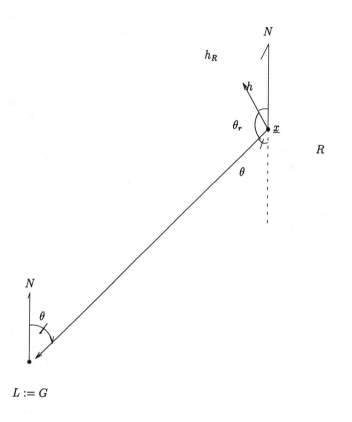

Fig. 7. Reduction using a compass h_R.

of the construction by a careful accounting for the resources we add. To illustrate the concept, we give two ways of constructing sensor E from sensor H. First, following Section 4.1, we assume that R is located at $x \in \mathbb{R}^2$ and has heading $h \in S^1$. However, R cannot sense these state variables and it does not know its configuration (x, h). Before we begin we stress the following: our goal is to change sensor H (by adding resources) so as to simulate sensor E. We have accomplished this task when R knows the angle θ_r, which is shown in Figs. 5, 7, and 8.

5.2.1. A reduction by adding a compass

We sketch a way to construct sensor E from H. This way is easy since it involves adding a powerful resource, namely a *compass*, to H. We will model this reduction as a function $\underline{s}$ from sensors to sensors. The reduction contains the following steps , which we denote s_1, s_2, and s_3 (see Fig. 7):

(s_1) We place the beacon L at the goal G.

(S_2) We add a concrete sensor called a *compass*[21] to R. The compass senses the heading h.

(S_3) The devices on R compute θ using the function (orientation) above, and then compute $\theta_r = \pi - h - \theta$. (See Fig. 7).

The reduction also adds a small amount of computation (but only a constant amount—two subtractions). We handle this by defining the compass to include this computation. Specifically, we define a sensor h_R to be a device that (i) computes the heading h, (ii) takes the output value of θ from (orientation) as an input, and (iii) outputs θ_r as specified in Step S_3. h_R could be implemented by a compass plus a small "circuit" to compute the value θ_r given h and θ. The subscript R of h_R denotes that it is installed on R. We will continue to refer call h_R a "compass" even though it is really a compass plus a small amount of computation.

In this reduction all the changes are made to R; L remains the same. Now, recall Eq. (2). Intuitively, we can substitute h_R for the box $\boxdot$ in this equation, and define the $+$ operator to encode how h_R is added to H, as specified in Steps $S_1, \ldots, S_3$ above.

5.2.2. Reduction using permutation and communication

The reduction in Section 5.2.1 requires adding new resources (the compass h_R). The next reduction we consider involves two new concepts. The first is *permutation*, and it involves redistributing resources in a sensor system, without consuming new resources. Surprisingly, a redistribution of resources can add information to the system. In order for permutation to add information, it is necessary for the sensor system to be spatially distributed (as, for example, H is; see Fig. 6). When permutation gains information, it may be viewed as a way of arranging resources in a configuration of lower entropy.

The second concept is *communication*. It measures resource (b) in Section 3. We consider adding communication primitives of the form COMM($L \rightarrow R$, *info*), which indicates that L sends message *info* to R. Like permutation, communication only makes sense in a spatially distributed sensor system. That is, because spatially colocated components can communicate "for free" in our model, only "external" data-paths add information complexity to the system. *Internal* data-paths have the same (spatial) source and destination. *External* data-paths have a different (spatial) source and destination. Hence, permutation (alone) can change the information complexity of a system by "externalizing" internal data-paths. To analyze a system like H, we view it as a system composed of autonomous collaborating agents L and R, each of which has certain resources. The COMM($\cdot$) primitive above we view as shared between L and R. We measure communication by counting the number of agents and the bits required to transmit *info*. This is the only kind of communication we will consider here (i.e., $L \rightarrow R$), and so we will henceforth abbreviate it by COMM(*info*).

---

[21] In using the term "compass" we make no commitment to a particular technology for implementation (such as sensing magnetic fields). In particular, the "compass" is an *orientation sensor* that could in principle be implemented using odometry or dead-reckoning, plus some initial calibration. Moreover, "North" N can be any fixed direction for our purposes, and need not be "true North". In the language of [38], the compass senses the projection of a perfect position sensor $p^* \in \mathbb{R}^2 \times S^1$ onto S^1.

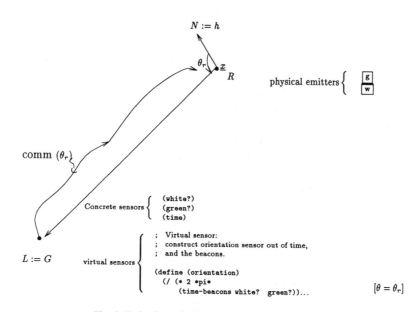

Fig. 8. Reduction using permutation and communication.

Given these concepts, we can sketch another reduction $\underline{Y}$. See Fig. 8. The reduction contains the following steps, which we denote Y_1, Y_2, and so forth.

(Y_1) As before, we place L at the goal G.

(Y_2) We move the physical emitters $\begin{array}{c}\boxed{g}\\\boxed{w}\end{array}$ from L to R (i.e., we mount them on the robot). "North" for the emitters should be installed in the direction of R's heading. That is, the white light flashes when the green light passes the local (to R) North, which is defined to be the robot's heading, h.

(Y_3) We move the concrete sensors (green?), (white?), and (time) from R to L.

(Y_4) We move the virtual sensor (orientation) coded above to L. That is, now this program will run on L.

See Fig. 8. Given ($Y_1, \ldots, Y_4$), by calling the procedure (orientation), L can now compute the value of the angle θ_r shown in the figure. However, although L now knows θ_r, R does not. We solve this problem by allowing L to communicate the value θ_r to R using the COMM($\cdot$) primitive described above:

(Y_5) L communicates the value of θ_r to R using the primitive COMM(θ_r).

Note that the permutation steps ($Y_2, \ldots, Y_4$) require no new resources. They merely require permuting the sensors and emitters. We do not view the relocation of the virtual sensor as "moving the computer to L". Instead, we view the virtual sensor (orientation) as a computational circuit; we move that circuit to L.

5.3. Installation notes

Crucial to installing a sensor is describing how the various physical resources should be lined up. We call these alignments *calibrations*. Since these calibrations constrain the spatial relationships among the various resources, as opposed to leaving them arbitrary, they effectively add information to the system. A calibration is some spatial relationship that is locked into place at the outset. This relationship may (or may not) change over time. Even when it does change, the initial calibration may still add information to the system, since the system can measure relative distances to the initial setting. Hence, calibration introduces an invariant that persists (at best) for the lifetime of the system. For example, by eliminating uncertainty at installation, we perform a kind of calibration, thereby eradicating that uncertainty for the duration of the calibration. Hence, calibration can displace the task of dealing with sensor uncertainty from the execution phase to the installation or layout phase. The purpose of this section is to introduce formal means for describing these calibrations, which we call *installation notes*. To make this more concrete, let us consider the calibrations necessary to permute and install sensor system H in the two reductions $\underline{s}$ (Section 5.2.1) and $\underline{y}$ (Section 5.2.2). [22]

The installation notes are numbered I_1, I_2, and so forth.

Note I_1 (Step s_1) and Note I_2 (Step y_1). The installation notes for Steps s_1 and y_1 are identical. When installing L at G, we must make sure that L and G line up perfectly; otherwise, the angle measured will not be exactly θ_r.

Note I_3. When installing the physical emitters on L, we must make sure that "North" for the emitters line up perfectly with true North. Compare Note I_5, below.

Note I_4 (Step s_2). When installing the compass, we must make sure that it lines up perfectly with the heading of the robot.

Note I_5 (Step y_2). We want the white light to flash when the green light passes through R's heading h. Hence, when installing the physical emitters on R, we must make sure that "relative North" for the emitters line up perfectly with the robot's heading h.

5.3.1. Calibration complexity

It is difficult to precisely measure the information gained in calibration. However, we note the following. First, the calibrations in I_3, I_4, and I_5 each add an equivalent amount of information to the system: each installation requires calibration of two 1 degree of freedom (1DOF) systems, each of which has configuration space S^1. Hence we say that I_3, I_4, and I_5 are *equivalent installation calibrations*.

Now let us consider calibrations I_1 and I_2 above. This installation requires a careful calibration of two 2DOF systems. To calibrate H so that at L is located at the point G clearly adds information. More precisely, note that we have so far considered the radial sensor E at a fixed goal G in the plane. Let us denote this particular installation by E_G. More generally, for a point y in the plane, we make the dependence explicit by writing E_y; thus we obtain a family of sensors $\{E_y\}$ parameterized by $y \in \mathbb{R}^2$.

---

[22] This section devolves to a suggestion of Mike Erdmann [22], for which we are very grateful.

Similarly, let us denote by H_y the sensor system H installed so that L is located at the point y. Now, our goal is to approximate one *particular* E_G using some H_y. Clearly, we could consider the case $G \neq y$; however in specifying E_G we specify G, and so this information is given. That is, it is no more work to locate H at G than to locate E at G, and the latter is unavoidable; it is the only way to implement E_G. Hence, we should be allowed to do at least this much work in installing H. In other words, merely in order to specify the sensor task, it is necessary to calibrate a 2DOF system to G—there is a sense in which the problem of approximating E cannot be specified without calibrating to some $y \in \mathbb{R}^2$. This argument is similar to saying that certain algorithms must at least read all their input. In this case, we say that the calibrations I_1 and I_2 are *necessary to specify the sensor E*. That is, the calibration required to install H_G is *necessary to specify E_G*. When the calibration parameter (the subscript G in this case) is understood, we will drop it.

Definition 5.1 (*Informal*). Consider two sensor systems S and Q. When S and Q require equivalent installation calibrations, and when the calibrations required to install Q are necessary to specify S, we say that S *dominates Q in calibration complexity*.

In Section 5.2.1 we described a reduction using a compass that yields a new sensor system from H. In Section 5.2.2 we described a reduction using permutation and communication, obtaining a different new sensor system from H. From the preceding discussion (Section 5.3), we conclude that E dominates both of these new sensor systems in calibration complexity.

Now it is clear that calibration is a source of information. We view calibration as a measure of the *external state* (see resource (c), Section 3) required for the task. Quantifying external state is tricky, since the time at which the resource is allocated (e.g., the time of calibration) may be much earlier than the time of the task execution. We developed the relatively sophisticated perspective of calibration complexity in this section, precisely to deal with this problem. Finally, it is worth noting the special role of *time* in this analysis (in that calibration and execution may be distant in time). We found it surprising that time would appear so crucial not only here, but also in the virtual sensor (orientation).

5.4. Comments on power

The reduction in Section 5.2.1 requires adding an orientation sensor (which may be implemented using a compass or odometry). The reduction in Section 5.2.2 requires permuting resources (sensors and emitters). It also requires adding communication, since L must now communicate θ_r to R.

Let H^* denote the permutation of H described in Steps $(Y_2, \dots, Y_4)$ in Section 5.2.2. Thus, in H^*, L has not been assigned any particular location, and while L knows θ_r, R does not. By installing H^* so that L is assigned the location G, we obtain a sensor called H_G^*. Now, recall the orientation sensor h_R for R, described in Section 5.2.1. Thus, in the language of Eq. (2), we have sketched how

$$E_G \cong H_G + h_R,$$
$$E_G \cong H_G^* + \text{COMM}(\theta_r). \tag{3}$$

Eq. (3) holds for all G. The operator $+$ denotes "combining" the two sensor subsystems. If this sounds somewhat operational, we will give a more analytic discussion below in Section 6 and a formal definition in Section 8, where we describe the semantics of our sensor model in detail.

5.4.1. Output communication

The term $\text{COMM}(\theta_r)$ in Eq. (3) says that we permit the permuted system H_G^* to route the information θ_r from one subsystem of H_G^* to another, spatially removed subsystem (these subsystems happen to be L and R in our case). First, note that θ_r is exactly the desired output of the sensor E_G. Hence the term $\text{COMM}(\theta_r)$ denotes an internal rerouting ($L \to R$) of this information within the permuted sensor system H_G^*. Let us generalize this construction.

Definition 5.2. Let b be a variable that ranges over all possible values that a sensor system can compute. We call b the *output* of the system. Let $\mathbb{K}(b)$ be the number of values b can take on, and define $\log \mathbb{K}(b)$ to be both the *size of b* and the *output size* of the sensor. The output size is an upper bound on the bit-complexity of b. For example, if b takes on integer values in the range $[1, q]$, then $\mathbb{K}(b) = q$, and $\log \mathbb{K}(b) = \log q$. In our example, θ_r is the output of E_G; the quantity $\log \mathbb{K}(\theta_r)$ is the output size of E_G. Now, suppose the information b is communicated over a data-path e. We will assume that the information is communicated repeatedly; without loss of generality, we take the unit of time to be the interval of the occasion to communicate the information. Thus we can take the size of the output b to be the *bandwidth* of e.

To return to our example, it is clear that we can make the permuted sensor system H_G^* satisfy the information specification of E_G if we merely add one internal re-routing operation of bandwidth $\log \mathbb{K}(\theta_r)$. In this case, we say we have added *output communication* to the permuted sensor system. [23]

More precisely, let S be a sensor system with output b. Let Q be another sensor system. We imagine Q as a "circuit" embedded in (say) the plane. Let $\text{COMM}(b)$ be a "sensor system" with one data-path e, that has bandwidth $\log \mathbb{K}(b)$. Then, adding output communication to Q can be viewed as the following transformation on sensor systems: $Q \mapsto Q + \text{COMM}(b)$. The transformation is parameterized by (the bandwidth of) S. The bounded-bandwidth data-path e can be spliced into Q anywhere. We note that this transformation can be composed with permutation (in either order):

$$
\begin{array}{ccccc}
Q & \mapsto & Q^* & \mapsto & Q^* + \text{COMM}(b) \\
\| & & & & \| \\
Q & \mapsto & Q + \text{COMM}(b) & \mapsto & (Q + \text{COMM}(b))^*.
\end{array}
$$

---

[23] To borrow a UNIX metaphor, this transformation allows the system to do an internal `rcp`, but not RPC—that is, it can copy information between subsystems, but it cannot request arbitrary remote evaluations.

We give a fully formal, graph-theoretic model of this transformation in Section 8.7.2.

6. A hierarchy of sensors

The examples above illustrate a general principle. This principle is analogous to the notion of *reduction* in the theory of computation. We would like our notion of reduction to do work analogous to the work done by computation-theoretic reductions. Consider two sensor systems S and Q. Recall the definitions of *simulation* (Definition 4.1) and *calibration complexity* from Section 5.3.1.

Definition 6.1. We define the *internal* (resp. *external*) *bandwidth* of a sensor system S to be the greatest bandwidth of any internal (resp. external) edge in S. The *output size* of S is given by Definition 5.2. We define the *maximum bandwidth* mb(S) to be the greater of the internal bandwidth, external bandwidth, and the output size of S. We call a sensor system *monotonic* if its internal and external bandwidths are bounded above by its output size.

Definition 6.2. We write $S \leqslant Q$ when
  (1) Q simulates S ($S \cong Q$),
  (2) S dominates Q in calibration complexity, and
  (3) mb(Q) is bounded above by mb(S).

Calibration exploits external state. Definition 6.2 allows us to order systems on how much information this external state (from calibration) yields. We will complete the formalization and analysis of calibration complexity later, in Sections 8.7.4 and A.1. Here is the basic idea. Calibration complexity measures how much information we add to a sensor system when we install and calibrate it. Installing a sensor system may require physically establishing some spatial relation between two components of the system. In this case we say the two components *codesignate* by the spatial relation. More generally, we may have to establish a relation between a component and a reference frame in the world. Most generally, when we compare two sensor systems S and Q, we typically must install and calibrate them in some appropriate relative configuration—again, in a spatial relation. When all these relations are (in)equalities of configuration, we say the system is *simple*. When all the relations are semi-algebraic (s.a.), we say the system is *algebraically codesignated*.

Now, let Q^* denote a permutation of sensor system Q, as described in Section 5.2.2. (For a formal definition, see Definition 8.6.)

Definition 6.3. We write $S \leqslant^* Q$ if there exists some permutation Q^* of sensor system Q such that $S \leqslant Q^*$.

Recall the meaning of COMM(*info*) from Sections 5.2.2 and 5.4.1. Finally,

Definition 6.4. Given two sensor systems S and Q, choose b such that $\log \mathbb{K}(b) = mb(S)$. We say S is *efficiently reducible* to Q if

$$S \leqslant^* Q + \text{COMM}(b). \tag{4}$$

In this case we write $S \leqslant_1 Q$.

For monotonic sensor systems, it suffices to take b to be the output of S (see Appendix B). This special case motivates the construction on the right-hand side of (4), where we add "output communication" to the sensor system Q (Section 5.4.1).

We now recap a couple of crisp results using reductions:

Claim 6.5.
   (a) $E_G \leqslant H_G + h_R$, *and*
   (b) $E_G \leqslant H_G^* + \text{COMM}(\theta_r)$.

Proof. Recall the discussion from Section 5.3.1 on calibration complexity. To obtain (a), we use the reduction that employs a compass (Section 5.2.1). The proof of (b) is obtained by the reduction using permutation and communication (Section 5.2.2).   □

Now, recall Eq. (3). The relation $E_G \cong H_G + h_R$, which derives from the compass reduction in Section 5.2.1, does *not* imply efficient reducibility, since adding a new concrete sensor h_R is too powerful to imply efficient reducibility. However, by the reduction in Section 5.2.2:

Proposition 6.6. *Erdmann's radial sensor E is efficiently reducible to the lighthouse sensor system H, that is $E \leqslant_1 H$.*

Proof. Recall from Eq. (3) that $E_G \cong H_G^* + \text{COMM}(\theta_r)$, and that θ_r is the output of E_G. From this, and Claim 6.5(b), we conclude that $E \leqslant_1 H$.   □

7. Information invariants

The relation $\leqslant_1$ defines a hierarchy of sensors. Compare the perceptual lattice of [14], who propose a geometric program for the analysis and synthesis of sensors based on their perceptual equivalence classes. The relation $\leqslant_1$ orders sensor systems on the complexity of their information invariants.[24]

---

[24] It is possible to develop a geometric account of information invariance by pursuing the direction of [14]. For more on this connection, see Appendix D. The account we give in Section 8 is also geometric but with a different flavor. Appendix D deals with the geometry of lattices, where an element of the lattice represents (essentially) a knowledge state. In Section 8 we examine different immersions of sensor systems. "Permutations" or "automorphisms" of the function space of immersions that preserve the sensor functionality are viewed as a kind of information-preserving transformation, and, hence, a model of information invariance.

At this point it would be useful to review the particular information invariants in our example. Here is the basic idea. The invariants may be analyzed by first examining Eq. (3). Since $\cong$ is an equivalence relation, we obtain the peculiar equation

$$H_G + h_R \cong H_G^* + \text{COMM}(\theta_r). \tag{5}$$

Now, what exactly does Eq. (5) mean? We understand that at present, this equation is not yet formal. Our goal is to understand this intriguing result. To do so, we must give a formal account of the colocation of resources. Here is a general idea of how we will proceed:

Recall the transformation described in Section 5.4.1 and Definition 6.4, where we added output communication to a sensor system. Recalling that h_R denotes the compass, at first glance, we would appear to obtain the following information invariant: *a compass is equivalent to permutation plus output communication*. This idea is tantalizing because it seems to define an information equivalence between normally unapposed categories: it yields an information invariant relating sensors, communication, and resource permutation. The invariant (5) is valid. However, it appears that this invariant is critically conditioned on the *type* of information being rerouted by the output communication. Output communication permits us to transform between local and global coordinates; however, if some form of orientation sensing (at L) is not present before the output communication step, then no amount of permutation and communication can simulate a global compass. [25] In Section 8.8, we address the generality of Eq. (5). There we model the colocation of resources as geometric *codesignation constraints*. This colocation can be modeled as a quotient map, and in Section 8.8 we discuss its relationship to information invariance.

8. On the semantics of situated sensor systems

In this section, we formalize our model of sensor systems. We give formal definitions of the reductions using permutation, and by "combining" sensor systems and "adding" resources. Below, we use the term "*sensor system*" to mean "*sensori-computational system*" where it is mellifluous.

8.1. Situated sensor systems

We formalize our model of sensor systems using a concept similar to the *communication graph* from distributed systems [27].

Definition 8.1. A *labelled graph* $\mathcal{G}$ is a directed graph (V, E) with vertices V and edges E, together with a labelling function that assigns a label to each vertex and edge. Where there is no ambiguity, we denote the labelling function by ℓ.

---

[25] In the language of [14], communication and permutation permit us to map between the perceptual equivalence classes (PECs) of E (the rays described in Section 4.1) and the PECs of H.

Definition 8.2. A *sensor system* S is represented by a labelled graph (V, E). Each vertex is labelled with a *component*. Each edge is labelled with a *connection*.

In Section 4.2.1 we defined components and connections operationally. We now give a formal definition. Components and connections are defined by their *simulation functions*. Simulation functions describe the behavior of both components and connections.

Consider a component $\ell(v)$ associated with vertex v. To simulate a component, we need to know (i) its inputs and (ii) its configuration. Suppose a component has r inputs and s outputs, each of which lies in some space R. Let C be the configuration space of the component. A *simulation function* for a component $\ell(v)$ is a map[26] $\Omega_v : R^r \times C \to R^s$.

Now we connect the components together. Assume for a moment that all the components have the same input–output structure as Ω_v above (i.e., that r and s are fixed throughout the system, but that the components themselves may perform different functions). We model an edge e between vertices v and u by its label, $\ell(e) = b$, and by a pair of integers, (i, j). $\log \mathbb{K}(b)$ is the *bandwidth* of the edge (Section 5.4.1) and the index i (resp. j) specifies to which of the r outputs of $\ell(v)$ (resp., s inputs of $\ell(u)$) we attach e $(1 \leqslant i \leqslant r$ and $1 \leqslant j \leqslant s)$.

Now, a simulation function for this edge e is taken to be a function $\Omega_e : R \to R$. We will usually restrict the edge functions to be the identify function (but they also check for bandwidth, i.e., that the transmitted data has size no greater than $\log \mathbb{K}(b)$).

We also define a resource called the "output device". Each sensor system must have exactly one vertex with this label, called the *output vertex*. The output vertex of the sensor system is where the output of the sensor is measured. The simulation function for the output device is the identity function, but the output value of this device defines the output value of the sensor system. In the examples introduced in Section 4 (the radial sensor E, lighthouse sensor system H, and the permuted lighthouse sensor H^*), we locate the output vertex on the "ship" at R.

A simulation function $\Omega_{\mathcal{U}}$ for an entire sensor system $\mathcal{U}$, then, is a collection of component simulation functions such as Ω_v and edge simulation functions such as Ω_e. The function $\Omega_{\mathcal{U}}$ simulates all the component simulation functions in the correct configuration, and simulates routing the data between them using the edge simulation functions. We adopt the convention that two components can communicate without an (explicit) connection when they are spatially colocated. When all these component and edge functions are semi-algebraic, then the sensor simulation function $\Omega_{\mathcal{U}}$ is also semi-algebraic (see Section 9). These concepts will be used to implement our notions of a "specification" for a sensor system (Section 1.1, application 3) and "universal reductions" (Appendix A.4).

Definition 8.3. Consider a sensor system $\mathcal{U}$ with simulation function $\Omega_{\mathcal{U}}$. The *output value* of $\mathcal{U}$ at a particular configuration is the value $\Omega_{\mathcal{U}}$ computes for that configuration.

---

[26] Components that retain state can be modeled by a function $\Omega_v : R^r \times C \times S \to R^s \times S$, where S is a *store* that records the state. For example, a state element with k bits of state would be modeled with $S = \{0, 1\}^k$. Alternatively, S can be absorbed as a factor subspace in the configuration space of the component.

Hence the output value of $\mathcal{U}$ is a function of $\mathcal{U}$'s configuration.

The notions *output value* and *output* (Definition 5.2) are related as follows. The *output* of $\mathcal{U}$ is a variable that ranges over all possible output values of $\mathcal{U}$. Given another sensor system $\mathcal{V}$, we say the *output of $\mathcal{U}$ is the same as the output of $\mathcal{V}$* when $\Omega_{\mathcal{U}}$ and $\Omega_{\mathcal{V}}$ are identical.

Under this model, we can simulate trees of embedded sensorimotor computation. It is also possible (in principle) to simulate more general graphs and systems with state, but in this case the value at the output vertex may vary over time (even for a fixed configuration). In this case we need some explicit notion of time and blocking to model the (a)synchronous arrival of data at a component. Such extensions are considered in [34]; for now we restrict our attention to trees, which suffice to model our examples. [27] In general our discussion is restricted to consider one clock-tick; however, generalizations are possible to consider the time-varying behavior of the system [34].

Let us relate these new definitions to the examples from Part I. Examples of components are given by the resources described in Section 4.2.1. *Connections* are like data-paths in that they carry information; a connection's label represents the information that will be sent along that path. Connections carry data between components. One common connection is specified using the COMM(*info*) primitive defined in Section 5.4.1. For example, recall the permuted sensor system H^* introduced in Section 5.4. Next, recall Eq. (3):

$$E_G \cong H_G + h_R,$$
$$E_G \cong H_G^* + \text{COMM}(\theta_r). \tag{3}$$

Consider the sensor system specified by the bottom right-hand side of Eq. (3):

$$H_G^* + \text{COMM}(\theta_r). \tag{$*$}$$

In the graph representation of $(*)$, the edge from the virtual (`orientation`) sensor at G to the output device at R, is labelled "θ_r".

Now, for each vertex v in V, we assume there is a configuration space C_v. A point in this space C_v represents a possible configuration of the component. Some components have configurations that change during the operation of the system (for example, in the lighthouse sensor system, all components mounted on the ship change configuration as the ship moves). Others are installed at fixed configurations. For example, the *emitters* $\boxed{g}$ $\boxed{w}$ in the lighthouse example, are installed at a specific position (L) and orientation (the white light flashes when the green light points North). So, the configuration space C for these emitters is $\mathbb{R}^2 \times S^1$. For convenience, let us assume that all components have the same configuration space C, and so $C = C_v$ (for all $v \in V$).

To summarize: a *component* is a primitive device that computes a function of (i) its inputs and (ii) its configuration $z \in C$. Each component is installed at a vertex

---

[27] Note the sensor system $H_G^* + \text{COMM}(\theta_r)$ in Eq. (3) is effectively a tree, and not a graph, even though there is data flow both from R to L and L to R. This is because the output vertex u_o on R does not feed back into the system.

of communication graph with d vertices, whose edges are the *connections* described above. The graph is immersed in a configuration space C^d, and the configuration z of a component is the configuration of its vertex. More generally, components can be *actuators*. An actuator is a component whose output forces the configuration of the graph to change or evolve through a *dynamics equation*. If the configuration of the entire graph is $z = (z_1, \ldots, z, \ldots, z_d) \in C^d$, then the dynamics equation models a mapping from the actuator component $\ell(v)$'s output at z to the tangent space $T_z C^d$ to the configuration space. See [17, 34] for more discussion of actuators.

Now, we give

Definition 8.4. A *situated* (or *immersed*) *sensor system* S is a sensor system $S = (V, E)$, together with an immersion $\phi : V \to C$ of the vertices. If $v \in V$, then we call $\phi(v)$ the *configuration of the vertex* v. When there is no ambiguity, we also call $\phi(v)$ the *configuration of the component* $\ell(v)$.

A situated sensor system is modeled by an immersed graph. If the map ϕ in Definition 8.4 is injective, then we call ϕ an *embedding*. Immersions need not be injective. In particular, in order to colocate vertices, it is necessary for immersions to be non-injective.

In Definition 8.4, the immersion ϕ may be a partial (as opposed to total) function, indicating that we do not specify the spatial configuration of those components whose vertices are outside the domain of the immersion. We denote the *domain* of a (partial) immersion $\phi : V \to C$ by $\phi^{-1}C$. We denote its *image* by $\operatorname{im} \phi$.

Example 8.5. H_G is a situated sensor system (H, ψ). H_G^* is a different immersion ψ^* of the same sensor system H, and so $H_G^* = (H, \psi^*)$.

This example illustrates a general concept: *permutation* of a situated sensor system corresponds to the choice of a different immersion with the same domain. Formally:

Definition 8.6. Let $\mathbb{S} = (S, \phi)$ be a situated sensor system. A *permutation* $\mathbb{S}^*$ of $\mathbb{S}$ is a situated sensor system (S, ϕ^*) such that the domain $\phi^{-1}C$ of ϕ and the domain $\phi^{*-1}C$ of ϕ^* are the same. [28]

Furthermore, for technical reasons, we also permit a permutation to change which vertex has the "output device" label. See Section C.2.

We can now formalize Definition 4.1 to say precisely what it means for two partially situated sensor systems to be equivalent:

Definition 4.1 (*Formalized*). Given two sensor systems S and Q, we say Q *simulates* S if the output of Q is the same as the output of S. In this case we write $S \cong Q$. More generally, suppose we write

---

[28] Technically, there are two kinds of permutation. Definition 8.6 is called *vertex permutation*; in Appendix A.2.1 we discuss a more general model called *graph permutation*. Vertex permutation suffices for all examples in this paper, but our results go through for graph permutation as well.

$$(\mathcal{S}, \phi) \cong (\mathcal{U}, \psi) \tag{6}$$

for two situated sensor systems. Eq. (6) is clearly well-defined when ϕ and ψ are total. Now, suppose that ϕ and ψ are partial, leaving unspecified the configurations of components $\ell(v)$ of $\mathcal{S}$ and $\ell(u)$ of $\mathcal{U}$. Then Eq. (6) is taken to mean that $(\mathcal{U}, \psi)$ simulates $(\mathcal{S}, \phi)$ for *any* configuration of v and u.

For Definition 4.1, in the case where (say) ϕ is partial, we operationalize Eq. (6) by rewriting it as a statement about all *extensions* $\overline{\phi}$ of ϕ. That is, we define ex ϕ to be the set of all extensions of ϕ. Then, we write: "$\forall \overline{\phi} \in$ ex ϕ, Eq. (6) holds" (with bars placed over the immersions). We treat ψ similarly, with an inner universal quantifier, although codesignation constraints (Sections 8.3 and 8.5.1) allow us to make the choice of extension $\overline{\psi}$ of ψ depend on the extension $\overline{\phi}$ that is bound by the outer quantifier. For example, Definition 4.1 becomes, "for all configurations $x \in C$ of v, for all configurations $y \in D_{\mathcal{S}}(x)$ of u, Eq. (6) holds". Here $D_{\mathcal{S}}(x)$ is a set in C that varies with x; the function $D_{\mathcal{S}}(\cdot)$ models the codesignation constraints. Definition 4.1 can be generalized to any number of "unbound" vertices; see Eq. (34) in Section 9.

Definition 4.1 uses a strong notion of simulation (in which the outputs of the sensor systems must be identical). A weaker notion, which merely requires the same equilibrium behavior, is introduced in Section 12.

8.2. Pointed sensor systems

Suppose we wish to consider a sensor system $\mathcal{S} = (V, E)$, where one component $\ell(v)$ for $v \in V$ is in a particular configuration $G_0 \in C$. This corresponds to immersion via the partial function ϕ with domain $\{v\}$ and range $\{G_0\}$. We may abbreviate the situated system $(\mathcal{S}, \phi)$ by writing $\mathcal{S}_{G_0}$, to distinguish it from the unsituated system $\mathcal{S}$. This is the notation we use in Section 5.3.1 and after. Of course, for this notation to capture all the information above about v, we must specify the preimage [29] of G_0 under ϕ, but we did that in Section 5.3.1 when we wrote down

"... let us denote by H_G the sensor system H installed with $L = G$".

We now explain the notation used in Example 8.5. First, we formalize our discussion of $\mathcal{S}_{G_0}$, above:

Definition 8.7. A *pointed immersion* of a sensor system $\mathcal{S} = (V, E)$ is a pair (ϕ, G) where $\phi : V \to C$ is an immersion of the vertices of $\mathcal{S}$, and $G \in$ im ϕ. G is called the *base point*. An *extension* of a partial pointed immersion (ϕ, G) is any total pointed immersion $(\overline{\phi}, G)$ where $\overline{\phi}$ is an extension of ϕ. [30]

Definition 8.8. A *pointed sensor system* is a triple $(\mathcal{S}, \phi, G)$ where $(\mathcal{S}, \phi)$ is a situated sensor system and (ϕ, G) is a pointed immersion (Definition 8.7) of $\mathcal{S}$. We abbreviate $(\mathcal{S}, \phi, G)$ by $\mathcal{S}_G$.

---

[29] More precisely: we must write down that the preimage of G_0 under the immersion ϕ contains v.

[30] (ϕ, G) is called *weakly pointed* if ϕ is partial and G is not necessarily contained in im ϕ.

Hence, H_G in Example 8.5 is a pointed sensor system. Next,

Definition 8.9. A *pointed permutation* of a sensor system $(\mathcal{S}, \phi)$ is a pointed sensor system $(\mathcal{S}, \phi^*, G)$, where ϕ^* is a permutation of ϕ.

Hence, H_G^* in Example 8.5 is a pointed permutation of the pointed sensor system H_G. In general, if $\mathcal{S}_G^*$ is a pointed permutation of $\mathcal{S}_G$, then $\mathcal{S}_G$ is a pointed permutation of $\mathcal{S}_G^*$.

8.3. Codesignation: basic concepts

If we view the configurations of components in a sensory system as "variables", then Convention 4.1 gives a "default" for determining which variables are "free" and which are "bound". Here is another view:

The partial immersion specifies which variables are specialized to be *constants*. These are the vertices in the domain of the immersion. Their configurations correspond to bound variables (constants). The configuration variables for vertices outside the domain of the immersion are not yet specialized, and hence are free.

We now have two concepts to define and investigate. First, we show how to specify systems which contain some constant configuration variables. After that, we must find a way to make two free variables *codesignate* (see [7]). Two vertices r and u codesignate under an immersion ϕ when $\phi(r) = \phi(u)$. More generally, r and u codesignate under *different* immersions ϕ and ψ when $\phi(v) = \psi(u)$. We now proceed with these two tasks.

Recall our example of a pointed sensor system $\mathcal{S}_{G_0}$ from Section 8.2 above. Recall $\mathcal{S}_{G_0} = (\mathcal{S}, \phi, G_0)$, and $\mathcal{S} = (V, E)$. The domain of ϕ is the single vertex $v \in V$. Now, to continue, suppose that $r \in V$ is the vertex of component $\ell(r)$, and that $r \neq v$ so that ϕ does not specify how to immerse r. Consider a different sensor system $\mathcal{U}$, with at least one vertex u. We wish to consider "combining" $\mathcal{U}$ and $\mathcal{S}$ by saying something like this:

> Immerse $\mathcal{S}$ with vertex v at G_0. Now, vertex r of $\mathcal{S}$ will be somewhere, say, R; but we want to immerse $\mathcal{U}$ so that u is at R also.

Hence, we don't care where R is, save that we wish to colocate r and u. To do this, we make r and u codesignate under the immersions of $\mathcal{S}$ and $\mathcal{U}$. We call this a *codesignation constraint* after [7]. Here is how we may say this more precisely:

> Let $\mathcal{S}_{G_0}$ denote sensor system $\mathcal{S}$ immersed with vertex v at G_0 (as above). Immerse the rest of $\mathcal{S}$ in any consistent manner, and denote this immersion by $\overline{\phi}$. Thus $\overline{\phi}$ is the *extension* of ϕ so that the restriction $\overline{\phi}|_{\{v\}}$ of $\overline{\phi}$ to $\{v\}$ is identical to ϕ. Now, let $R \in C$ be the configuration of r under $\overline{\phi}$, i.e., $R = \overline{\phi}(r)$. Denote by ψ the (partial) immersion of $\mathcal{U}$ defined as follows. ψ sends vertex u of $\mathcal{U}$ to R. Note that G_0 is a "constant" and R is a "free variable", in the sense that R depends on which extension $\overline{\phi}$ of ϕ we choose, whereas G_0 does not.

In Eqs. (2)–(5), we abbreviated this construction as follows:

$$\mathcal{S}_{G_0} + \mathcal{U}_R \tag{7}$$

which is short for $(\mathcal{S}, \phi) + (\mathcal{U}, \psi)$ with ϕ and ψ defined as above. Note that (7) is not sufficient to specify the desired (partial) immersion unless we also note that the preimage (under the immersion ϕ) of G_0 contains vertex v of $\mathcal{S}$, and that

$$\overline{\phi}(r) = R = \psi(u). \tag{$*$}$$

$(*)$ represents a codesignation constraint; we will define such constraints formally below in Section 8.5.1. We must also specify that G_0 is a constant and R is a free variable. The notation explained in (7) is used in the body of the paper, for example, in Eq. (3).

It remains for us to define precisely the $+$ operator we just used, and we do so in Definitions 8.10–8.12 below.

8.4. Combining sensor systems

The $+$ operator is defined on two graphs as a way of taking their union. Specifically:

Definition 8.10. Consider two graphs $\mathcal{G} = (V, E)$ and $\mathcal{G}' = (V', E')$. We define the *combination* $\mathcal{G} + \mathcal{G}'$ of $\mathcal{G}$ and $\mathcal{G}'$ as follows:

$$\mathcal{G} + \mathcal{G}' = (V \cup V', E \cup E').$$

We may define $+$ on sensor systems (Definition 8.2) by lifting the definition for graphs. We may define $+$ on two immersed graphs whenever the immersions are *compatible*. An immersion ϕ of $\mathcal{G}$ and an immersion ψ of $\mathcal{G}'$ are said to be *compatible* when the two immersions agree on the intersection $V \cap V'$ (for total immersions) or more generally, on $\phi^{-1}C \cap \psi^{-1}C$ (for partial functions). Given Definition 8.10, we have:

Claim 8.11. *The operator $+$ defined in Definition 8.10 is associative and commutative.*

Proof. Definitional. $\square$

8.5. The general case

Let $(\mathcal{S}, \phi)$ and $(\mathcal{U}, \psi)$ be two situated sensor systems. Let V denote the vertices of $\mathcal{S}$ and U the vertices of $\mathcal{U}$. Our notation above ($\mathcal{S}_G$, $\mathcal{U}_R$, H_G, h_R, etc.) is effective when the image of each partial immersion is a singleton, e.g., $\phi(V) = \{G\}$ and $\psi(U) = \{R\}$. In these cases it suffices to abbreviate

$$\mathcal{S}_G = (\mathcal{S}, \phi) \quad \text{and} \quad \mathcal{U}_R = (\mathcal{U}, \psi),$$

and to specify which (if any) of the configurations G and R is constant and which (if any) is free. We now generalize this notation for more complicated partial immersions.

Suppose $(\mathcal{S}, \phi)$ and $(\mathcal{U}, \psi)$ have compatible partial immersions. Now, $\phi(V)$ and $\psi(U)$ (which need not be singletons, in general) represent the "constant" configuration bindings of vertices (analogous to the singleton G above). We now consider codesignation constraints. All the codesignation constraints we have seen so far in Section 8 have this form: each was a pair $(v,u) \in V \times U$. A codesignation constraint is *compatible* with the immersions ϕ and ψ if one of the following is true:

(1) v is not in the domain $\phi^{-1}C$ of ϕ;

(2) u is not in the domain $\psi^{-1}C$ of ψ;

(3) $\phi(v) = \psi(u)$.

This definition is not quite general enough; we must also be able to specify (a) that two vertices of U (resp. V) codesignate—this means two components of S must be colocated. (b) we must also be able to specify that that two vertices *not* codesignate, for example, that $\phi(v) \neq \psi(u)$. The general definition is complicated and is given in Definition 8.14 below.

However, putting off the formal definitions for a moment, we can see what a combined sensor system really is. In summary: the immersions ψ and ϕ specify which component configurations are to be held constant. The codesignation constraints specify which components are to be co-located.

Definition 8.12. Let (S,ϕ) and (U,ψ) be two situated sensor systems with compatible partial immersions. The *combined sensor system*

$$(S,\phi) + (U,\psi) \tag{8}$$

is specified by (8), together with a set of codesignation constraints compatible with ϕ and ψ. We say the combination (8) is *defined* when the partial immersions ϕ and ψ are compatible.

Now, consider two sensor systems S and U. Both have output vertices, say, v_0 and u_0 resp. If $v_0 = u_0$ then this vertex remains the output vertex of $S + U$. In the case where $v_0 \neq u_0$, we must naturally specify which is the unique output vertex of the new, combined sensor system. By convention we will declare it to be either v_0 or u_0 (we must say which).[31] We adopt one default convention for this choice in Section 8.7.3. For more on output vertices, see Appendices C.1–C.2.

Definition 8.12 specializes to the particular cases such as Eq. (3) we have considered, by appropriate choice of partial immersions and codesignation constraints. To illustrate these choices, we give an example below, in Section 8.6. The operator $+$ is associative and commutative (see Claim 8.11 and Appendix C).

8.5.1. Codesignation constraints

Throughout this section, we let (S,ϕ) and (U,ψ) be two situated sensor systems with compatible partial immersions $\phi: V \to C$ and $\psi: U \to C$.

Definition 8.13. Define the partial immersion $\phi + \psi$ as follows:

---

[31] This is not a severe restriction when we are considering permutations like $(S + U)^*$ of $S + U$. See Appendix C.2.

$$\phi + \psi : \to C,$$
$$x \mapsto \begin{cases} \phi(x), & \text{if } x \in V, \\ \psi(x), & \text{if } x \in U. \end{cases}$$

We say the map $\phi + \psi$ is *defined* when the partial immersions ϕ and ψ are compatible.

Definition 8.14. A *codesignation constraint* is a pair $(x, y) \in (V \cup U)^2$.

Definition 8.15. We say a codesignation constraint (x, y) is *compatible with the partial immersions ϕ and ψ* if one of the following is true:
(1) x is not in the domain $(\phi + \psi)^{-1}C$ of $(\phi + \psi)$;
(2) y is not in the domain $(\phi + \psi)^{-1}C$ of $(\phi + \psi)$;
(3) $(\phi + \psi)(x) = (\phi + \psi)(y)$.

Noncodesignation constraints are modeled symmetrically to codesignation constraints. A codesignation constraint (x, y) indicates that we require that for any total immersion $\overline{\phi + \psi}$ that extends $\phi + \psi$,

$$(\overline{\phi + \psi})(x) = (\overline{\phi + \psi})(y) \tag{$*$}$$

holds. A *noncodesignation* constraint requires *inequality* (instead of equality) in $(*)$. Definitions 8.14–8.15 handle a single constraint. For sets of constraints, you have to employ the machinery of Appendix A, which generalizes these definitions.

8.6. Example: the basic idea

As an example, let us interpret Eq. (3). We give it again:

$$\begin{aligned} E_G &\cong H_G + h_R, \\ E_G &\cong H_G^* + \text{COMM}(\theta_r). \end{aligned} \tag{3}$$

Recall E_G and H_G are situated sensor systems. E_G is the radial sensor located at $G \in \mathbb{R}^2$. H_G is the lighthouse sensor with the emitters $\boxed{\substack{\text{g} \\ \text{w}}}$ located at G and oriented Northward.

When H is situated at G as above to obtain H_G, the immersion is partial, leaving the position R of the ship, unspecified in H_G. h_R denotes the compass installed at R, calibrated towards North. Eq. (3) (top) holds for any ship's position R so long as the sensor system h_R is co-located at R. Compare the right-hand side of Eq. (3) to (7). As in (7), in Eq. (3), once the preimages (under the immersion) of G and R are specified, the immersion of the combined sensor system becomes clear.

Now, H_G^* defines a new immersion of H (by "new" we mean different from H_G). The immersion depends on R but Eq. (3) holds for any R. $\text{COMM}(\theta_r)$ defines a graph with exactly one edge e. e is an edge with label $\ell(e) = \theta_r$, from the virtual sensor (orientation) to the ship (the output vertex) at R. Thus, e is an edge between two vertices of H^* (or H_G^*) but note that e is not part of the graph H^* (nor H_G^*); e is only present in the combination $H_G^* + \text{COMM}(\theta_r)$.

Finally, by convention, Eq. (3) (by itself) only holds for G. But, we specify in the sentence below Eq. (3) that it holds for any G. This is equivalent to placing the symbols "$\forall G$" before Eq. (3). This effectively "frees" G. The appearance of G as a subscript both on the left- and right-hand side of Eq. (3) indicates a codesignation constraint.

8.7. Example (continued) : a formal treatment

8.7.1. The top of Eq. (3)

We now rewrite Eq. (3) using the general notation of Section 8.5. In this example we do not explicitly consider orientation of components. However, the discussion can be generalized by taking the configurations G and R to lie in the configuration space $\mathbb{R}^2 \times S^1$.

Let ϕ be a partial immersion of E. Let ϕ_G be a partial immersion of E that installs it at G, so that $E_G = (E, \phi_G)$.

Let ψ be a partial immersion of H. Let ψ_G be a partial immersion of H that installs the emitters $\boxed{\dfrac{\text{g}}{\text{w}}}$ at G, so that $H_G = (H, \psi_G)$. We will define codesignation constraints so that all the concrete and virtual sensors are installed on the ship (i.e., at R).

Let v_1 and v_2 be the vertices of H such that $\ell(v_1) = \boxed{\text{g}}$, and $\ell(v_2) = \boxed{\text{w}}$.

Let $u_1, \ldots, u_k$ be the vertices of H corresponding to the concrete and virtual sensors described in Section 4.2.1. In particular, u_1 is the vertex of the virtual sensor (orientation).

Let u_0 be the output vertex of H.

Let ρ be a partial immersion of the compass h. Let w be the vertex of the compass in h. Then we can rewrite the top of Eq. (3) as:

$$(E, \phi_G) \cong (H, \psi_G) + (h, \rho) \tag{3--top}$$

together with the codesignation constraints [32]

$$\{(u_1, u_i)\}_{1 < i \leqslant k} \cup \{(v_1, v_2), (u_0, u_1), (u_1, w)\}. \tag{9}$$

8.7.2. The bottom of Eq. (3): the sensor system COMM($\cdot$)

Now, H^* denotes a different immersion of H. Call this immersion ψ^*. Let ψ_G^* denote the partial immersion that installs the concrete and virtual sensors at G. We will define codesignation constraints so that the emitters are installed on the ship. We must now precisely define what COMM($\cdot$) means.

We can be sure of getting the semantics of COMM($\cdot$) correct by treating it as a sensor system in its own right (albeit, a small one). Now, COMM(θ_r) defines the graph with

---

[32] A careful analysis will show that, while it is necessary that the rotating emitter $\boxed{\text{g}}$ be located at G, the omnidirectional $\boxed{\text{w}}$ can be anywhere. Hence the codesignation constraint (v_1, v_2) is unnecessary. However, by removing it, we are left with the problem of synchronizing $\boxed{\text{g}}$ and $\boxed{\text{w}}$. Either we must add communication, or else calibrate the emitters and give $\boxed{\text{w}}$ a clock. These issues complicate the example and so we will not deal with them further.

vertices [33] $\{u_1, u_o\}$ and a single edge $e = (u_1, u_o)$ with $\ell(e) = \theta_r$. We observe that the transformation on sensor systems whereby we add output communication (Section 5.4.1 and Definition 6.4) implies the following:

> The "head" vertex u_o of the edge $e = (u_1, u_o)$, is defined to be the output vertex of the sensor system COMM(θ_r).

Our model of communication is fairly abstract. External communication is probably not possible without some form of buffering by either the sender or the receiver. COMM($\cdot$) should include this buffer to be more realistic about modeling internal state.

Hence the bottom half of Eq. (3) may be written:

$$(E, \phi_G) \cong (H, \psi_G^*) + \text{COMM}(\theta_r) \tag{3-bot}$$

together with the codesignation constraints

$$\{(u_1, u_i)\}_{1 < i \leqslant k} \cup \{(v_1, v_2)\}. \tag{10}$$

Hence the bottom codesignation constraints (10) for (3-bot) are different from the top codesignation constraints (9) for (3-top), in that in the bottom constraints, w does not appear (since it is associated with the compass). Second, in the bottom equation, the output vertex is not constrained to be colocated with the virtual sensor (orientation). Thus the codesignation constraint (u_1, u_o) disappears.

8.7.3. Bandwidth and output vertices

We have defined COMM($\cdot$) as a graph with a single edge e. The argument (parameter) b to COMM(b) determines the *bandwidth* of e. Thus, for example, COMM(b) specifies a graph with one edge e whose label is b. This specifies that the edge is a data-path that can carry information b; if b requires $k = \log \mathbb{K}(b)$ bits to encode then k is the *bandwidth* of e.

Now recall the discussion on how to choose output vertices in combined sensor systems (Section 8.5). Here, (Section 8.7.2, Eq. (3-bot)) we have u_o as the output vertex of both H^* and COMM(θ_r), and so it unambiguously remains the output vertex of the combined system $H^* + \text{COMM}(\theta_r)$. More generally, we adopt the following

Convention 8.16. Let S be a sensor system. Unless otherwise stated, we take the output vertex of the combined sensor system $S + \text{COMM}(\cdot)$ to be the output vertex u_o of COMM($\cdot$).

For more on bandwidth, see Appendix B; for more on output vertices under permutation, see Appendices C.1–C.2.

8.7.4. Calibration complexity and codesignation

The size of the set (9) or (10) (number of codesignation constraints) is one measure of *calibration complexity* (see Section 5.3.1). However, this should be only part of the

---

[33] In this example, the vertices of COMM($\cdot$) are also vertices of H^*; but more generally the vertex sets can be disjoint.

measure. One reason that the number of codesignation constraints, alone, is not a good measure, is that one sensor system (say H, for argument) could have a single component that functions in the place of several colocated components in another sensor system (say, $\mathcal{V}$). For example, we could build a sensor $\mathcal{V}$ as follows: consider the emitter $\boxed{\text{g}}$ in H. Break up the emitter $\boxed{\text{g}}$ into all its tiny wires, power supply, filaments, rotating actuator, etc. All these components must then be colocated. This would result in more codesignation constraints for $\mathcal{V}$ than for H and thus, a spuriously high measure of calibration or installation complexity.

Instead, in order to measure calibration complexity we should compare "size" using something like order (Big-Oh $O(\cdot)$) notation. This is the basic idea we use, but there are some additional subtleties that we defer to Appendix A.1. There we propose a measure of calibration complexity that is more reasonable. This measure retains, however, one useful property: it is easy to compute it (in fact, like "size" above, it can be computed in the same time it takes to read the input).

8.7.5. Noncodesignation constraints and parametric codesignation constraints

To complete our model for this example, we must also introduce noncodesignation constraints so that $G \neq R$; this is necessary for our sensors to work. Suppose the radial sensor E has two vertices, t_0 and t_1, where t_0 is the output vertex, and t_1 is the "central vertex" of E (this is the vertex located at G in Fig. 5). The *non*codesignation constraints for both (3-top) and (3-bot) are

$$\{(u_1, v_1), (t_0, t_1)\}. \tag{11}$$

The former is a constraint on H (and H^*). The latter is a constraint on E. Finally, we require the *co*designation constraint

$$(t_0, u_0). \tag{12}$$

Eq. (12) is called a *parametric* codesignation constraint; it ensures that for all extensions $\overline{\phi_G}$, $\overline{\psi_G}$, and $\overline{\psi_G^*}$ of ϕ_G, ψ_G, and ψ_G^* resp., we have $\overline{\psi_G}(u_0) = \overline{\phi_G}(t_0) = \overline{\psi_G^*}(u_0)$. Parametric codesignation constraints are discussed further in Appendix A.3.

This completes our detailed discussion of the sensor systems in Eq. (3). The example is designed to explain most facets of our theory in a simple setting. Let us sketch how to make this analysis computationally effective. We choose two arbitrary points G and R in C. We begin with the two pointed immersions ϕ_G and ψ_G, with domains $\{t_1, t_0\}$ and $\{v_1, u_1\}$ resp. (So, ϕ_G is total and ψ_G is partial.) These functions and the desired permutation ψ_G^* are:

	t_1	t_0	u_1	v_1
ϕ_G	G	R		
ψ_G			R	G
ψ_G^*			G	R

We want our analysis to be true for any R and G (with $R \neq G$) and not just the ones we chose. To do this, we in effect wish to universally quantify over R and G and treat these configurations as variables. To do this carefully and computationally requires the quantification machinery from Section 9. Here, we give the basic idea. Now, after our first use of Eq. (3), we wrote

"Eq. (3) holds for all G."

This sentence effectively adds "$\forall G$" to the front of Eq. (3), and hence to Eqs. (3-top) and (3-bot). We call this *freeing G*. To obtain this effect, we rewrite Eqs. (3-top) and (3-bot) as follows: remove the G subscripts: that is, replace ϕ_G by any immersion ϕ of E. Similarly, replace ψ_G by ψ and ψ_G^* by ψ^*. (See Section 10 for more details). We have chosen this notation because our constructions are parameterized by the task, and the task is specified by G. The notation leaves this parameterization explicit. As we shall see below, perhaps the cleanest way to model this example is to treat all the sensor systems as initially unsituated, yet respecting all the (non)codesignation constraints above. This may be done using the tools developed in the sequel (Sections 8.8–10).

8.8. Generality and codesignation

Consider a sensor system S with d vertices V, immersed via a map $\phi: V \to C$. The configuration space of this sensor system can be viewed as C^d, since any immersion ϕ can be represented as a point in[34] C^d. Consider a codesignation constraint (u, v) for $u, v \in V$. This specifies a new immersion of S in a quotient $C^d/(u \sim v)$ of C^d in which the images of u and v are identified. This quotient construction can be used to analyze information equivalence in certain cases. We give an example below.

In Section 7, we discussed how general Eqs. (3) and (5) are. We can now address this question more precisely by noting that the top and bottom of Eq. (3) have different codesignation constraints. This means that equivalence only holds under the appropriate spatial identifications. (Recall that each codesignation constraint specifies such an iden-tification.) Hence, Eq. (5) is a relation that holds only on a quotient of configuration space. It is analogous to a "projective invariant" in geometry: an invariant relation that holds for projective space but not for affine space. To see this analogy, recall that, for example, real projective space $\mathbb{RP}^2$ is obtained as a quotient of real Euclidean space $\mathbb{R}^3$ by identifying all nonzero points on a line through the origin to a single point. There exist projective relationships in $\mathbb{RP}^2$ (for example, invariants in projective geometry) that do not hold in $\mathbb{R}^3$. In our case, it seems that by investigating the structure of these quotient relations one may measure the generality of information invariants, and, more generally, information-preserving transformations (e.g., reductions and immersions) on sensor systems.

It is interesting to note that the geometric structure of noncodesignation constraints is different from the quotient construction given above. The quotient construction can be viewed as follows. Let $\pi: C^d \to C^{d-1}$ be the projection of C^d onto C^{d-1}. This map models the quotient construction since C^{d-1} is isomorphic to $C^d/(u \sim v)$. Hence π models the identification of u and v. π then induces a new immersion $\tilde{\phi} = \pi(\phi)$:

---

[34] This just says that the function space C^V is isomorphic to C^d.

$$\phi \quad \in \quad C^a$$
$$\downarrow \pi \tag{13}$$
$$\widetilde{\phi} = \pi(\phi) \quad \in \quad C/(u \sim v).$$

One the other hand, noncodesignation constraints are essentially a kind of genericity requirement. To see this, let us assume that u and v are the first and second of the d vertices of V. We then consider an immersion to be "generic" when it sends u and v to different values. Define the diagonal $\Delta = \{(z, z) \in C^2 \mid z \in C\}$. Then the noncodesignation constraint insists that we avoid the embedded diagonal, that is, we must have an immersion

$$\phi' \in (C^2 - \Delta) \times C^{d-2}. \tag{14}$$

Combining (13) and (14) gives the general form for the configuration space of the sensor.

8.9. More general codesignation relations

8.9.1. The semantics of codesignation constraints

The codesignation constraints we have encountered so far model the necessary equality of images of vertices under immersions. For example,

$$\phi(u) = \psi(v) \tag{15}$$

for (some particular) $u \in U$ and $v \in V$:

$$\begin{array}{c} U \\ \quad \searrow^{\phi} \\ \qquad\qquad C. \\ \quad \nearrow^{\psi} \\ V \end{array} \tag{16}$$

Let us call this simple kind of codesignation constraints in (15), *equality* codesignation constraints.

More generally, we could consider relations of the form "The three points z, $\phi(u)$, and $\psi(v)$ are colinear" or "$\phi(u)$ is within distance d of $\psi(v)$", etc. This other kind of codesignation constraints could be called *general codesignation relations*. We could model such a relation as follows: consider a triple (u, v, Φ) where Φ is a semi-algebraic predicate on $C \times C$. So far, in considering equality codesignation constraints, all the predicates we have used have been diagonals: [35]

$$\Phi(x, y) \quad \text{iff} \quad x = y. \tag{17}$$

This choice (Eq. (17)) explicitly encodes the assumption that all working sensor configurations can be specified using colocation (or noncolocation). For example, for the lighthouse sensor H it is necessary for the green and white lights $\boxed{\mathrm{g}} \above{\boxed{\mathrm{w}}}$ to be colocated.

---

[35] For a noncodesignation constraint, we complement the diagonal.

Similarly, the sensor only works when the ship R is not at G. These statements give geometric constraints on the sensor semantics: the (non)codesignation constraints specify what (non)colocations must occur for the sensor to function properly. Hence, equality codesignation constraints such as Eq. (17) encode the assumption that the only geometric characteristic that affects sensor semantics is the colocation of components. Obviously this is not true for all sensors, but it is true for the sensors we have considered in this paper. We call such sensors *simple*, and they are worth a definition (Definition 8.17) below.

More generally, we could, in principle, require general codesignation relations to hold between component configurations—or, more generally, it may be true that there exist relationships other than (in)equality that must hold for the sensors to function properly. In this paper, we primarily discuss simple sensor systems, and only in Sections 8–9 do we consider the ramifications of such extensions. However, we feel our framework could (and should) be extended to handle at least restricted algebraic codesignation. To see how this would go, assume for a moment semi-algebraic predicates for general codesignation relations. The effect of general codesignation relations would be (geometrically) as follows. First, for a noncodesignation constraints, the "forbidden diagonal" would generalize to an arbitrary variety Y in C^d; Y would be characterized by some polynomial inequalities, and immersions $\phi \in Y$ would be forbidden. For general codesignation relations, we would construct a quotient whereby points in C^d would be identified via an algebraic map (a polynomial equation). The geometry of such spaces can be complicated; however, from a theoretical point of view, a line of attack can be seen.

We can summarize this discussion with a definition that captures the kind of sensor systems this paper addresses:

Definition 8.17. A sensor system that can be specified using only a finite number of equality codesignation (and noncodesignation) constraints is called *simple*. A sensor system that can be specified using only a finite number of semi-algebraic predicates in its general codesignation (and noncodesignation) constraints is called *algebraically codesignated*.

Since (17) is algebraically codesignated, all simple systems are algebraic codesignated. We consider only simple sensor systems in Sections 1–7. However, the algorithms in Section 9 apply to all algebraically codesignated systems.

8.9.2. The semantics of permutation

The semantics of permutations is intimately bound up in the semantics of codesignation. We now discuss the connection. The results of this section not only clarify our semantics, but also lead to a computational result, which we describe later in Section 9.

The meaning of a permutation (see Definition 8.6) is clear for a totally situated sensor system (i.e., a sensor system with a total immersion). Recall from Section 8.8 that we can view an immersion ϕ and its permutation ϕ^* as elements of the configuration space[36] C^d. Now, suppose, for a moment, that for every immersion $\phi \in C^d$ it is possible to choose[37] a permutation ϕ^* satisfying Definition 8.6. Imagine that for each $\phi_0 \in C^d$, we build a sequence of such choices, $\{\phi_0, \phi_1, \phi_2, \phi_3, \ldots\} \subset C^d$, where $\phi_{i+1} = \phi_i^*$. This defines a map

$$\begin{array}{ccccccc} C^d & \rightarrow & C^d & \rightarrow & C^d & \rightarrow & \cdots \\ \phi_0 & \mapsto & \phi_1 & \mapsto & \phi_2 & \mapsto & \cdots. \end{array} \tag{18}$$

Hence, a permutation can be viewed as a way of "permuting" the components of a sensori-computational system, or, it may be viewed as a kind of automorphism of sensor configuration space.

Now, suppose we now allow ϕ to be a *partial* immersion. Then by a permutation ϕ^* of ϕ we mean a different partial immersion with the same domain (Definition 8.6 still applies).

Permutations of a partial immersion have a structure that is related to codesignation constraints, in that each can be characterized geometrically via regions in C^d. Consider a partial immersion ϕ. Given ϕ we can define the set of *extensions* of ϕ:

$$\mathrm{ex}\,\phi = \{\overline{\phi} \in C^d \mid \overline{\phi}|_{\phi^{-1}C} = \phi\},$$

which is a region in C^d. A permutation ϕ^* of ϕ corresponds to selecting a new region $\mathrm{ex}\,\phi^*$ of C^d, with this property:

$$\phi^{-1}C = \phi^{*-1}C. \tag{19}$$

Now, it would be convenient if we could treat the regions $\mathrm{ex}\,\phi$ and $\mathrm{ex}\,\phi^*$ like "equivalence classes" in C^d. That way we could view ϕ and ϕ^* as the "generators" of different classes of immersions. A partial function then corresponds to a region in C^d, and permutation corresponds to choice of a different region in C^d. To take this view, we need the following:

Proposition 8.18. *Let ϕ^* be a permutation of ϕ. Then* $\mathrm{ex}\,\phi$ *and* $\mathrm{ex}\,\phi^*$ *are disjoint, unless* $\phi = \phi^*$.

Proof. Let $\overline{\phi} \in \mathrm{ex}\,\phi \cap \mathrm{ex}\,\phi^*$. Since $\overline{\phi}$ is an extension of both ϕ and ϕ^*, we have

$$\overline{\phi}|_{\phi^{-1}C} = \phi, \qquad \overline{\phi}|_{\phi^{*-1}C} = \phi^*.$$

But ϕ^* is a permutation of ϕ, which implies that ϕ and ϕ^* have the same domain (Definition 8.6). Since $\phi^{*-1}C = \phi^{-1}C$, therefore $\phi = \phi^*$. □

Let $\Sigma(\phi)$ denote all permutations of ϕ. Essentially, Proposition 8.18 tells us that the map $\mathrm{ex}: \Sigma(\phi) \rightarrow \{\text{Regions in } C^d\}$ has an injection-like property: the images of distinct permutations under ex do not intersect. The map ex also has a surjection-like property which we characterize as follows:

---

[36] We defer the necessity of quotienting C^d and removing diagonals, until Section 10.

[37] The choice will not, in general, be unique.

Claim 8.19. *Let $\phi, \psi : V \to C$ where ϕ is partial and ψ is total. Then there exists a permutation ϕ^* of ϕ such that ψ is an extension of ϕ^*.*

Proof. Take $\phi^* = \psi|_{\phi^{-1}C}$. $\quad\square$

Proposition 8.20. *Fix a partial immersion ϕ. The images of* ex : $\Sigma(\phi) \to$ {*Regions in C^d*} *cover C^d, that is,*

$$\bigcup_{\phi^* \in \Sigma(\phi)} \text{ex } \phi^* = C^d.$$

Proof. Immediate from Claim 8.19. $\quad\square$

We can summarize this as follows: we have viewed permutation as a bijective self-map of $\Sigma(\phi)$. It is equivalent to view permutation as a bijective self-map of the disjoint "equivalence" classes

$$\{\text{ex } \phi^*\}$$

(for all permutations ϕ^* of ϕ) in C^d. This viewpoint is justified by the following two claims:

Proposition 8.21. *The map*

$$
\begin{array}{rcl}
p_\phi : C^d & \to & \Sigma(\phi) \\
\psi & \mapsto & \phi^* \quad \text{s.t. } \psi \in \text{ex } \phi^*
\end{array}
\tag{20}
$$

is well-defined.

Proof. Observe that $p_\phi(\psi) = \psi|_{\phi^{-1}C}$ (see Claim 8.19). The map p_ϕ is defined for every $\psi \in C^d$, by Propositions 8.19 and 8.20. That $p_\phi(\psi)$ is uniquely defined by (20), we see from Proposition 8.18. $\quad\square$

Now, suppose the domain $\phi^{-1}C$ of ϕ contains k vertices, $1 \leqslant k \leqslant d$. We can represent any permutation ϕ^* of ϕ by the k images $(z_1, \ldots, z_k)$ of the vertices of $\phi^{-1}C$ under ϕ. That is, we can represent any such permutation ϕ^* by a point in C^k. Conversely, any point in C^k defines a permutation ϕ^*.

Lemma 8.22. *The following properties hold:* [38]
 (1) $\Sigma(\phi) \simeq C^k$.
 (2) *The map p_ϕ is a projection and we can give it in C-coordinates as:*

$$
\begin{array}{rcl}
p_\phi : \quad\quad C^d & \to & C^k \\
(z_1, \ldots, z_k, \ldots, z_d) & \mapsto & (z_1, \ldots, z_k).
\end{array}
\tag{21}
$$

---

[38] We use $\simeq$ to denote isomorphism.

(3) *Let ϕ^* be a permutation of ϕ. Then $\mathrm{ex}\,\phi^* \subset C^d$ is a cylinder over $\phi^* \in C^k$, and $\mathrm{ex}\,\phi^* = p_\phi{}^{-1}\phi^*$.*

(4) *The map p_ϕ is a quotient map.*

(5) $C^d/p_\phi \simeq C^k$.

Proof. Definitional. □

Finally, we note that our discussion of permutation for partially immersed sensor systems can be specialized to pointed sensor systems and pointed permutation (with the same base point). If ϕ^* is a pointed permutation of ϕ with point G, then the classes $\mathrm{ex}\,\phi$ and $\mathrm{ex}\,\phi^*$ have these additional properties (see Definition 8.7): [39]

$$G \in \mathrm{im}\,\phi = \bigcap_{\overline{\phi} \in \mathrm{ex}\,\phi} \mathrm{im}\,\overline{\phi}, \qquad G \in \mathrm{im}\,\phi^* = \bigcap_{\overline{\phi}^* \in \mathrm{ex}\,\phi^*} \mathrm{im}\,\overline{\phi}^*. \tag{22}$$

Thus for (partially) immersed systems, we have a handle on permutation, and now we know more precisely what the difference between (e.g.) H_G and H_G^* is, (see Section 5.3.1) in terms of permutation. Permutation corresponds to choosing a different equivalence class of C^d. For most of this paper we examine a special case, where the sensor systems are partially situated (that is, the domains of the immersions are nonempty). A powerful generalization is given in Section 10, where the sensor systems can be *unsituated*. This will allow us to understand the unsituated sensor system H^* precisely as a permutation of the (unsituated) system H.

8.10. The semantics of reductions

Recall the definition of *efficiently reducible* (Definition 6.4). To explore this notion, we first turn to the question of whether or not the relation $\leqslant^*$ in Definition 6.3 is transitive.

Consider three sensor systems, $\mathcal{U}$, $\mathcal{V}$, and $\mathcal{W}$, and their permutations: [40]

Sensor system	Vertices	Immersion	Permutation 1	Permutation 2	
$\mathcal{U}$	$U = \{u_0, u_1, \ldots\}$	$\mathcal{U} = (U, \alpha)$			(23)
$\mathcal{V}$	$V = \{v_0, v_1, \ldots\}$	$\mathcal{V} = (V, \beta)$	$\mathcal{V}^* = (V, \beta^*)$		
$\mathcal{W}$	$W = \{w_0, w_1, \ldots\}$	$\mathcal{W} = (W, \gamma)$	$\mathcal{W}^* = (W, \gamma^*)$	$\mathcal{W}^+ = (W, \gamma^+)$.	

If $\leqslant^*$ is transitive, then if $\mathcal{U} \leqslant^* \mathcal{V}$ and $\mathcal{V} \leqslant^* \mathcal{W}$, then $\mathcal{U} \leqslant^* \mathcal{W}$. We explore when this property holds. From Definitions 6.3 and 6.4 we can see that dominance in calibration complexity (Definition 5.1) is transitive, and so we will concentrate here on the less obvious aspects of transitivity. [41] To simplify the discussion we only deal with codesignation constraints, but the argument generalizes *mutatis mutandis* for noncodesignation constraints.

---

[39] For pointed sensor systems, the surjection-like properties (Propositions 8.19 and 8.20) only hold for the class of pointed immersions (with the same base point).

[40] Other permutations are possible, only a couple are shown.

[41] See Sections 8.7.4, and A.1 for more on computational calibration complexity.

8.10.1. Weak transitivity

First, let us observe that $\leqslant^*$ always obeys a property that is like transitivity, but "weaker". We now elaborate. Suppose $\mathcal{U} \leqslant^* \mathcal{V}$. Then (Definition 6.3), there exists some permutation $\mathcal{V}^* = (\mathcal{V}, \beta^*)$ of $\mathcal{V}$ such that $\mathcal{U} \leqslant \mathcal{V}^*$ (see Definition 6.2 for the definition of $\leqslant$). So, we have

$$(\mathcal{U}, \alpha) \leqslant (\mathcal{V}, \beta^*). \tag{24}$$

Now, suppose $(\mathcal{V}, \beta^*) \leqslant^* \mathcal{W}$. Then there exists a permutation $\mathcal{W}^* = (\mathcal{W}, \gamma^*)$ such that

$$(\mathcal{V}, \beta^*) \leqslant (\mathcal{W}, \gamma^*). \tag{25}$$

From Eqs. (24) and (25), and the definition of $\leqslant$ (Definitions 5.1, 6.3) we have

$$(\mathcal{U}, \alpha) \leqslant (\mathcal{W}, \gamma^*), \tag{26}$$

and therefore $\mathcal{U} \leqslant^* \mathcal{W}$. This property we call *weak transitivity*.

8.10.2. Strong transitivity for simple sensor systems

Simple sensor systems (Definition 8.17) obey *strong* transitivity, so long as all permutations are chosen to obey their codesignation constraints. Suppose $\mathcal{U}$, $\mathcal{V}$, and $\mathcal{W}$ are all simple. If $\leqslant^*$ is transitive: then, if $\mathcal{U} \leqslant^* \mathcal{V}$ and $\mathcal{V} \leqslant^* \mathcal{W}$, then $\mathcal{U} \leqslant^* \mathcal{W}$. In other words:

Suppose $\mathcal{U} \leqslant^* \mathcal{V}$ and $\mathcal{V} \leqslant^* \mathcal{W}$. Then there exist permutations $\mathcal{V}^* = (\mathcal{V}, \beta^*)$ of $\mathcal{V}$ and $\mathcal{W}^* = (\mathcal{W}, \gamma^*)$ of $\mathcal{W}$ such that

$$(\mathcal{U}, \alpha) \leqslant (\mathcal{V}, \beta^*) \tag{24}$$

and

$$(\mathcal{V}, \beta) \leqslant (\mathcal{W}, \gamma^*). \tag{27}$$

(Compare (27) with (25)). Then if $\leqslant^*$ is transitive, then there exists another permutation $\mathcal{W}^+ = (\mathcal{W}, \gamma^+)$ of $\mathcal{W}$, such that

$$(\mathcal{U}, \alpha) \leqslant (\mathcal{W}, \gamma^+). \tag{28}$$

Strong transitivity is a much stricter condition than weak transitivity. It requires that we be able to "compose" the immersions β^*, β, and γ^* to somehow construct the immersion γ^+. This may not, in general, be possible. However, it is possible for simple sensor systems, in which only equality codesignation constraints are employed to specify the system (Definition 8.17).

In order for strong transitivity to hold, we must make sure that both the permutations β and β^* for $\mathcal{V}$ and $\mathcal{V}^*$ respect the codesignation constraints for $\mathcal{V}$'s semantics. This is because we cannot expect *any* permutation of $\mathcal{W}$ to simulate $\mathcal{U}$ if either β or β^* are faulty configurations of $\mathcal{V}$. We call an immersion β^* of $\mathcal{V}$ *valid* if β^* respects the codesignation constraints for $\mathcal{V}$. This corresponds to restricting β^* to the valid regions of sensor configuration space C^d, as in Sections 8.9.2 and 10. We call a permutation

$\mathcal{V}^* = (\mathcal{V}, \beta^*)$ of $\mathcal{V}$ *valid* if its immersion β^* is valid. In this case we also say that the sensor system $\mathcal{V}^*$ is *valid*.

Lemma 8.23. *The relation $\leqslant^*$ (Definition 6.3) is transitive for valid simple sensor systems (Definition 8.17).*

Proof. Assume there exist valid permutations α, β, β^*, and γ^* so that (24) and (27) hold as above. We construct an immersion γ^+ so that (28) holds.

The picture we have is as follows:

$$
\begin{array}{ccc}
 & V & \\
 & \beta \Big\downarrow \Big\downarrow \beta^* & \\
U \xrightarrow{\ \alpha\ } & C & \qquad\qquad (29) \\
 & \gamma^* \Big\uparrow \Big\uparrow \gamma^+ & \\
 & W. &
\end{array}
$$

Consider Fig. 9. Certain vertices (for example v_0 and u_1) are colocated. Codesignation implies colocation, but the converse is not necessarily true. In constructing a new immersion we must simulate all colocations, because that way we will be sure to reproduce all codesignation constraints accurately in the new immersion. Because (only) colocation affects sensor semantics for simple sensor systems (Definition 8.17), this suffices to ensure that the new immersion preserves the sensor semantics. In short, colocation is evidence for codesignation.

We want to construct γ^+ as follows (see Fig. 9):

$$
\gamma^+ : W \to C
$$
$$
w_i \mapsto \beta^*(v_j) \quad \text{if } \beta(v_j) = \gamma^*(w_i).
$$

The general form of the set of colocations that γ^+ must simulate, is $\gamma^*(W) \cap \beta(V)$. This construction is general, and can be expressed as follows. Let

$$
f : \gamma^{*-1}(\gamma^*(W) \cap \beta(V)) \to C
$$
$$
w_i \qquad\qquad \mapsto \beta^*(\beta^{-1}(\gamma^*(w_i))).
$$

The map f is almost the map we want. When the image of f is a one-point set $\{z\}$, we define $\gamma^+(w_i) = z$. If $\beta^{-1}(\gamma^*(w_i)) \subset V$ is not a singleton (see Fig. 10), then we have a choice in the construction of γ^+. In this case we know that $\gamma^+(w_i) \in f(w_i)$. Since $f(w_i)$ is finite, we can enumerate all possible candidates for γ^+; one of them will be the correct one. $\square$

We note that our proof is not constructive: we only prove there exists a permutation $\mathcal{W}^+$. However, we can give a procedure for enumerating the finite number of candidates for the permutation γ^+. It is possible to check which is the correct one, by applying the results of the next section (Section 9).

We do not believe that the relation $\leqslant^*$ holds for arbitrary algebraically codesignated sensors. This is because the algebraic constraints may be incompatible. It would be of

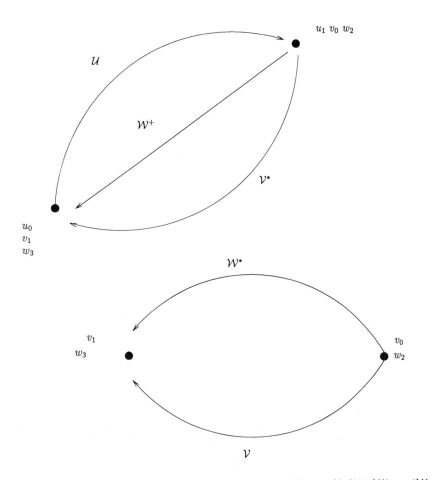

Fig. 9. The situated sensor systems $\mathcal{U} = (U, \alpha)$, $\mathcal{V} = (V, \beta)$, $\mathcal{V}^* = (\mathcal{V}, \beta^*)$, $\mathcal{W}^* = (\mathcal{W}, \gamma^*)$, and $\mathcal{W}^+ = (\mathcal{W}, \gamma^+)$ for Lemma 8.23. The vertices of $\mathcal{U}$, $\mathcal{V}$, and $\mathcal{W}$ are $U = \{u_0, u_1, \ldots\}$, $V = \{v_0, v_1, \ldots\}$ and $W = \{w_0, w_1, \ldots\}$, resp. Not all vertices are shown. $\gamma^+(w_2) = \beta^*(v_0) = \alpha(u_1)$ and $\gamma^+(w_3) = \beta^*(v_1) = \alpha(u_0)$. $\beta(v_1) = \gamma^*(w_3)$ and $\beta(v_0) = \gamma^*(w_2)$.

interest to find a restricted class that is larger than equality codesignation, for which transitivity holds.

8.10.3. A hierarchy of reductions

We now use our study of $\leqslant^*$'s transitivity to understand the reduction $\leqslant_1$ (Definition 6.4).[42] Now, even when $\leqslant^*$ is transitive, it appears that $\leqslant_1$ is not. To see this, suppose that $A \leqslant_1 B$ and $B \leqslant_1 C$. Then it appears that to reduce A to B we require one "extra wire" (namely, COMM(A)), and that to reduce B to C we could require (another) extra wire COMM(B), and therefore, in the worst case, to reduce A to C we could require *two* extra wires. That is, it could be that A cannot reduce to C with fewer

---

[42] I would like to thank Ronitt Rubinfeld for contributing key insights to this discussion of k-wire reductions.

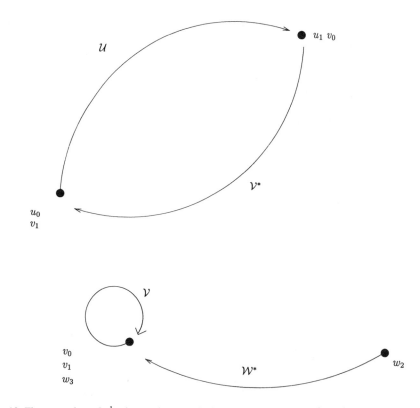

Fig. 10. The case where $\beta^{-1}(\gamma^*(w_i))$ is not a singleton (in this case, it is $\{v_0, v_1\} \subset V$). In this example, $\beta(v_0) = \beta(v_1) = \gamma^*(w_3)$. Now, we note that v_0 and v_1 colocate under β but not under β^*. However, this difference cannot be semantic (i.e., it cannot affect the sensor function), since we assume that both permutations are chosen to be valid with respect to the codesignation constraints for $\mathcal{V}$. In other words, (v_0, v_1) is not a codesignation constraint for $\mathcal{V}$ in this example.

than two extra wires. We have yet to find a non-artificial example of this lower bound but it appears to indicate that $\leqslant_1$ is not transitive (even for simple sensor systems).

Let us summarize. The reduction $\leqslant_1$ (Definition 6.4) is a "1-wire" reduction. It does not appear to be transitive. The reduction $\leqslant^*$ (Definition 6.3) is a "0-*wire*" reduction. It is transitive for simple sensor systems (Lemma 8.23). We could analogously define a 2-wire, or more generally, any *k-wire reduction* $\leqslant_k$ by modifying Eq. (4) in Definition 6.4 to

$$S \leqslant^* Q + k \cdot \text{COMM}(b), \tag{4'}$$

where $k \cdot \text{COMM}(b)$ denotes $\overbrace{\text{COMM}(b) + \cdots + \text{COMM}(b)}^{k \text{ times}}$.

Since $(\leqslant^*) = (\leqslant_0)$, this suggests a hierarchy of reductions, indexed by k. In general, we have the following:

Definition 8.24. We say a relation $\succ$ is *transitive* when $x \succ y$ and $y \succ z$ always implies

$x \succ z$. To distinguish this from *graded transitivity* (below), we call this *elementary transitivity* when necessary.[43]

We say a map $\mathcal{F} : \mathbb{N} \to 2^{X \times X}$, with $\mathcal{F}(i) = (\succ_i)$, is a *graded relation on $X \times X$*, when each $\succ_i$ is a relation on $X \times X$. We also write $\mathcal{F}$ as $\{\succ_i\}_{i \in \mathbb{N}}$.

We say that $\mathcal{F}$ has *graded transitivity* (or *is graded transitive*) if the following property holds: for every $x, y, z \in X$, if $x \succ_i y$ and $y \succ_j z$, then $x \succ_{i+j} z$.

Clearly, the k-wire reductions $\{\leqslant_i\}_{i \in \mathbb{N}}$ form a graded relation.

Corollary 8.25.
   (a) *The 0-wire reduction $\leqslant_0$ (called $\leqslant^*$ in Definition 6.3) is elementary transitive for simple sensor systems.*
   (b) *The k-wire reductions $\{\leqslant_i\}_{i \in \mathbb{N}}$ are graded transitive (Definition 8.24) for simple sensor systems.*

Proof. (a) is definitional from Lemma 8.23. To see (b), we use Lemma 8.23, and recall Definition 6.4, and that the $+$ operator is associative and commutative (Claim 8.11). To complete the argument, we also need a technical lemma, given by the "distributive" property[44] of Proposition C.3.   □

We call the k-wire reductions $\{\leqslant_i\}_{i \in \mathbb{N}}$ a *hierarchy* of reductions. We say such a hierarchy (i.e., any graded relation on X^2) *collapses* if it is isomorphic to an elementary relation (i.e., to a single subset of X^2).

Corollary 8.26. *The hierarchy of k-wire reductions ($k > 0$) on simple sensor systems collapses if $\leqslant_1$ is elementary transitive (on simple sensor systems).*

Proof. Suppose $X \leqslant_k Z$ ($k > 1$). To collapse the hierarchy, it suffices to show that $X \leqslant_1 Z$. (This follows from Lemma 8.23, by observing that the $+$ operator is commutative and associative, and by the "distributive" property of Proposition C.3).

Now, construct k sensor systems, $Y_i = Z^* + i \cdot \text{COMM}(b_X)$, where $\log \mathbb{K}(b_X) = \text{mb}(X)$ (for $1 = i, \ldots, k$). Hence each of the i "extra wires" in Y_i has bandwidth $\log \mathbb{K}(b_X)$ (see Sections 5.4.1, 8.7.3 and Definition 6.1; to see that this yields sufficient bandwidth, see Definition 6.2(3)). So, there exist k simple sensor systems $Y_1, Y_2, \ldots, Y_k$ with $1, 2, \ldots, k$ more wires than Z resp., such that $X \leqslant_0 Y_k \leqslant_1 Y_{k-1} \leqslant_1 \cdots \leqslant_1 Y_1 \leqslant_1 Z$. Recall that $(\leqslant^*) = (\leqslant_0)$, and observe that $(\leqslant_0) \subset (\leqslant_1)$. If $\leqslant_1$ and $\leqslant^*$ are transitive, then $X \leqslant_1 Z$.   □

For monotonic sensor systems, we can simply take b_X to be the output of X (see Section 6). Corollary 8.26 is stated for simple sensor systems, but it holds for the more general algebraic systems (in which case each Y_i is algebraic but not necessarily simple).

---

[43] Elementary transitivity is the sense used in Lemma 8.23.
[44] See Appendix C.

8.10.4. A partial order on simple sensor systems

In this section, all sensor systems are assumed to be simple.

Definition 8.27. We write $\mathcal{U} \leqslant_\infty \mathcal{V}$ if there exists some integer k such that $\mathcal{U} \leqslant_k \mathcal{V}$.

As a reduction, $\leqslant_\infty$ corresponds to adding an arbitrary amount of global, point-to-point communication. It is easy to see that $\leqslant_\infty$ is elementary transitive for simple sensor systems.

In a multi-agent sensor system, it makes sense to allow the "size" (i.e., number of components) of the system to grow, and to consider reductions parameterized by that size. For example, given a sensor system $\mathcal{U}$, we can use the notation $i \cdot \mathcal{U}$ to denote "i copies" of $\mathcal{U}$. Now, even if for another sensor system $\mathcal{V}$ we have $\mathcal{U} \leqslant_1 \mathcal{V}$, it is unlikely that we will have $i \cdot \mathcal{U} \leqslant_1 i \cdot \mathcal{V}$, for all $i \in \mathbb{N}$. However, it is easy to see the following

Claim 8.28. *If $\mathcal{U} \leqslant_k \mathcal{V}$, then for any $i, j \in \mathbb{N}$, $i \cdot \mathcal{U} \leqslant_\infty j \cdot \mathcal{V}$.*

The family $\{i \cdot \mathcal{U}\}_{i \in \mathbb{N}}$ is just one example of such a system; we could imagine other examples where the number of components, number of agents, or number of sensors varies with i. Our emphasis has changed slightly from the preceding. Before, we asked, what $k \in \mathbb{N}$ suffices such that $\mathcal{U} \leqslant_k \mathcal{V}$? Now, we ask to find that k *as a function of the size of $\mathcal{U}$ and $\mathcal{V}$.*

Now, we might deem it unfair to add arbitrary communication to the system. Let us instead consider adding only a polynomial amount of communication. In Definition 8.29, $\mathcal{U}$ and $\mathcal{V}$ are data and q is a fixed polynomial. n is the size of $\mathcal{U}$ and $\mathcal{V}$ (e.g., take n to be the total number of components). $q(n)$ (a function of n), is the amount of communication sufficient to reduce $\mathcal{U}$ to $\mathcal{V}$.

Definition 8.29. Let $\mathcal{U}$ and $\mathcal{V}$ be sensor systems. We write $\mathcal{U} \leqslant_\mathcal{P} \mathcal{V}$ if there exists some fixed polynomial function $q(n)$ of the size n of $\mathcal{U}$ and $\mathcal{V}$, such that $\mathcal{U} \leqslant_{q(n)} \mathcal{V}$ for all sizes n.

So, the assertion "$\mathcal{U} \leqslant_\mathcal{P} \mathcal{V}$" is a statement about a family of sensor systems. It says that $\mathcal{U}$ reduces to $\mathcal{V}$ by permuting $\mathcal{V}$ and adding an amount of communication that is polynomial in the size of $\mathcal{U}$ and $\mathcal{V}$. In particular, note that if $\mathcal{U} \leqslant_\mathcal{P} \mathcal{V}$, then for any $i, j \in \mathbb{N}$, $i \cdot \mathcal{U} \leqslant_\mathcal{P} j \cdot \mathcal{V}$. However, we can say something stronger:

Lemma 8.30 (Completeness of polynomial communication). $\mathcal{U} \leqslant_\mathcal{P} \mathcal{V}$ *if, and only if, $\mathcal{U} \leqslant_\infty \mathcal{V}$.*

Proof. "If" is trivial; we show the "only if" direction. If $\mathcal{U}$ and $\mathcal{V}$ have at most n vertices, then global point-to-point communication can be implemented by adding $O(n^2)$ new data-paths. Hence it is always true that $\mathcal{U} \leqslant_{O(n^2)} \mathcal{V}$. Any additional communication would be superfluous and would not add power to the system. $\square$

It follows that $\leqslant_{\mathcal{P}}$ is elementary transitive on simple sensor systems. Therefore it is a partial order on simple sensor systems.

9. Computational properties

In this section, we give a computational model of simulation (Definition 4.1), and discuss an algorithm for deciding the relations $\leqslant^*$ and $\leqslant_1$. This section relies heavily on the results of Section 8. Readers unfamiliar with algebraic decision procedures may wish to consult the review in Appendix A, where we review some basic facts about semi-algebraic sets. This section also yields benefits in terms of clarity. For example, pointed immersions are a somewhat awkward way to specify codesignation constraints; the machinery of this section enables us to dispense with them in an elegant matter.

9.1. Algebraic sensor systems

The algorithms in this section are algebraic and use the theory of real closed fields. In the first-order theory of real closed fields, we can quantify over real variables, but not over functions. This might seem to imply that we cannot quantify over immersions of sensor systems, since these immersions are functions. However, since our immersions have a finite domain, each immersion function can be represented as a point in a configuration space C^d. Therefore we can quantify over them in our algebraic theory. We now proceed to use this fact.

Definition 9.1. We say a function is semi-algebraic when its graph is semi-algebraic.

Consider a situated sensor system $(\mathcal{U}, \phi)$, and for the moment assume that ϕ is a valid immersion that is semi-algebraic and total. Let us define the *size* d of $\mathcal{U}$ to be the number of vertices in $\mathcal{U}$. Now,

Definition 9.2. A *simulation function* $\Omega_{\mathcal{U}}$ *for* $\mathcal{U}$ is a map $\Omega_{\mathcal{U}}: C^d \to R$, where R is a ring. We call the value $\Omega_{\mathcal{U}}(\phi) \in R$ of $\Omega_{\mathcal{U}}$ on a sensor configuration ϕ to be the *sensor value* or *output value* at ϕ.

Simulation functions compute the value of the sensor given a configuration of the sensor. The idea is that we can apply a simulation function to determine what value the sensor will return—what the sensor will compute in configuration ϕ. Definition 9.2 also formalizes our notion of a "specification" for a sensor system, alluded to in the context of design (Section 1.1, application 3). See Sections 8.1 and A.2 for more on simulation functions.

Example 9.3. Recall the "lighthouse" sensor system H (Fig. 6). A simulation function Ω_H for H computes the value of θ. We imagine Ω_H works by simulating the (orientation) sensor (see Section 4.2.1). Other, equivalent, simulations are also possible ("equivalent" means they compute the same value for θ). For example: let

$(x, h) \in \mathbb{R}^2 \times S^1$ be the configuration of the ship R. Let $(L, \theta_0) \in \mathbb{R}^2 \times S^1$ be the configuration of the "lighthouse". Then $\theta = \theta_0 + \tan^{-1}(x - L)$. We note that this simulation function is not algebraic (because arctangent is not algebraic). See Example 9.7, below.

Now, if the configuration space C is algebraic, then so is the function space C^d. Hence, every immersion ϕ of $\mathcal{U}$ with algebraic coordinates can be represented as an algebraic point in C^d. So ϕ is algebraic exactly when it can be represented as such an algebraic point.

Now, let $\mathbb{T}$ be a predicate on C^d in the theory of real closed fields. Then $\mathbb{T}(\phi)$ is either true or false, and we can decide it by applying $\mathbb{T}$ to ϕ.

Next, suppose we now permit ϕ to be partial. We call a partial function ϕ *semi-algebraic* when its restriction $\phi|_{\phi^{-1}C}$ to its domain $\phi^{-1}C$ is semi-algebraic. If ϕ is semi-algebraic, then the set of its extensions $\mathrm{ex}\,\phi \subset C^d$ is also semi-algebraic. We then observe that the expression denoting "for all extensions (resp., there exists an extension) $\overline{\phi}$ of ϕ, $\mathbb{T}(\overline{\phi})$ holds" namely

$$\Diamond \overline{\phi} \in \mathrm{ex}\,\phi : \mathbb{T}(\overline{\phi})$$

is also semi-algebraic ($\Diamond \in \{\forall, \exists\}$). To quantify over all extensions $\overline{\phi}$ of ϕ, we simply quantify over the configurations of the vertices *outside* the domain of ϕ. By Section 8.9.2 we can also "guess" permutations of ϕ—that is, it is possible to existentially quantify over permutations and hence to decide sentences of the form[45]

$$\exists \phi^* \in \Sigma(\phi) : \mathbb{T}(\phi^*)$$

which means, "there exists a permutation ϕ^* of ϕ, such that for any extension $\overline{\phi^*}$ of ϕ^*, $\mathbb{T}(\overline{\phi^*})$ holds". That is,

$$\exists \phi^* \in \Sigma(\phi), \ \forall \overline{\phi^*} \in \mathrm{ex}\,\phi^* : \mathbb{T}(\overline{\phi^*}). \tag{30}$$

To guess a permutation of ϕ we existentially quantify over the configurations of vertices *inside* the domain of ϕ.

Example 9.4. Let C be an algebraic configuration space. Let V be a set of three vertices, $V = \{v_1, v_2, v_3\}$. Now, we can encode any algebraic function $\psi : V \to C$ semi-algebraically, e.g., by a set of three ordered pairs $\{(v_1, z_1), (v_2, z_2), (v_3, z_3)\}$, where $\psi(v_i) = z_i$, $(i = 1, 2, 3)$. Let us call such an s.a. representation of ψ by the name $\sigma(z_1, z_2, z_3)$:

$$\sigma(z_1, z_2, z_3) = \{\psi : V \to C \mid \psi(v_i) = z_i, \ (i = 1, 2, 3)\}.$$

Now, consider a partial immersion $\phi : V \to C$ with domain $\{v_1\}$, such that $\phi(v_1) = G$, where G is algebraic. We can encode ϕ as

$$\exists z_2 \exists z_3 : \sigma(G, z_2, z_3).$$

---

[45] We call the existential quantification "guessing", since deciding a predicate in the existential theory of the reals is like guessing a witness to make the predicate true.

We can also encode the extensions and permutations of ϕ semi-algebraically. Specifically, we can encode any permutation ϕ^* of ϕ by a single point z_1 (the image of v_1); we can encode any extension $\overline{\phi^*}$ of ϕ^* by a pair (z_2, z_3) (the images of v_2 and v_3, respectively).

Thus, we can rewrite (30) as

$$\exists z_1 \; \forall z_2 \; \forall z_3 : \mathbb{T}(\sigma(z_1, z_2, z_3)). \tag{31}$$

If C has dimension r_c, then the formula (31) is a Tarski sentence in $3r_c$ variables.

We summarize:

Proposition 9.5. *If $\phi : V \to C$ is a semi-algebraic partial function, then the set $\mathrm{ex}\,\phi$ (ϕ's extensions) and the set $\Sigma(\phi)$ (ϕ's permutations) are also semi-algebraic.*

To guess a *valid* permutation, (Definition 8.10.2) we restrict the configurations to lie within the (algebraic) codesignation constraints, as described in Sections 8.9.2 and 10. (We are simply using algebraic decision procedures to make these choices effective.) Any s.a. codesignation constraints for an algebraically codesignated sensor system can be represented by an s.a. set $D \subset \mathbb{R}^r$. The structure of the region D, especially in relation to the region $\mathrm{ex}\,\phi^*$, is discussed in Sections 8.9.2 and 10. We must restrict our choice of permutation to D. To guess a valid permutation, we modify (30) to be:

$$\exists \phi^* \in \Sigma(\phi), \; \forall \overline{\phi^*} \in D \cap \mathrm{ex}\,\phi^* : \mathbb{T}(\overline{\phi^*}). \tag{32}$$

Definition 9.6. We call a sensor system $\mathcal{U}$ *algebraic* if it is algebraically codesignated (Definition 8.17), has an algebraic configuration space C, and a semi-algebraic algebraic simulation function $\Omega_{\mathcal{U}}$ (Definition 9.2).

Example 9.7. Recall Example 9.3, above. The simulation function Ω_H in Example 9.3 is not algebraic. However, we can define a (semi-)algebraic simulation function that encodes the same information, and is adequate, in the sense that we can use it to compare the sensor H's function to another orientation sensor. The algebraic simulation function we give now is adequate to decide the relation $\leqslant^*$.

To construct an algebraic version of Ω_H, we use a simple trick from calculus (also used in kinematics; see, for example [18]). Let ϕ be a configuration of sensor system H (Fig. 6). Define $\Omega'_H(\phi) = (\tan(\theta/2), q)$, where $\theta = \Omega_H(\phi)$ (see Example 9.3), and $q \in 4$ denotes which quadrant R is in relative to L. Ω'_H encodes the same information as Ω_H, but it is semi-algebraic.

We will not prove Ω'_H is algebraic but here is a brief argument. Substitute $u = \tan(\theta/2)$. Then we have $\sin\theta = (1 - u^2)/(1 + u^2)$ and $\cos\theta = 2u/(1 + u^2)$, and our simulation function is a rational function. By clearing denominators we obtain an algebraic function. See [18] for details. Essentially the graph of Ω'_H is an s.a. set in correspondence with the graph of the non-algebraic map Ω_H. The correspondence is given by $\theta \mapsto u$.

9.2. Computing the reductions $\leqslant^*$ and $\leqslant_1$

Now, suppose we have two algebraic sensor systems $\mathcal{U}$ and $\mathcal{V}$. We wish to decide whether $\mathcal{U} \leqslant^* \mathcal{V}$. If $\mathcal{U} = (\mathcal{U}, \alpha)$ and $\mathcal{V} = (\mathcal{V}, \beta)$, then we wish to decide whether there exists a permutation β^* such that

$$(\mathcal{U}, \alpha) \leqslant (\mathcal{V}, \beta^*).$$

(Here in Section 9.2 the relation $\leqslant$ is used as in Definition 6.2). That is, we wish to decide the following (assume that α and β are partial):

$$\left(\exists \beta^* \in \Sigma(\beta), \forall \overline{\alpha} \in \text{ex}\,\alpha, \forall \overline{\beta^*} \in \text{ex}\,\beta^* \right) : \quad \Omega_{\mathcal{U}}(\overline{\alpha}) = \Omega_{\mathcal{V}}(\overline{\beta^*}). \tag{33}$$

Eq. (33) does not incorporate the codesignation constraints. Since $\mathcal{U}$ and $\mathcal{V}$ are algebraically codesignated, their codesignation constraints may be represented as semi-algebraic sets $D_{\mathcal{U}}$, $D_{\mathcal{V}}$, and $D_{\mathcal{V}\mathcal{U}}(\overline{\alpha})$ in C^d. So (33) becomes:

$$\left(\exists \beta^* \in (\Sigma(\beta) \cap D_{\mathcal{V}}), \forall \overline{\alpha} \in (\text{ex}\,\alpha \cap D_{\mathcal{U}}), \forall \overline{\beta^*} \in (\text{ex}\,\beta^* \cap D_{\mathcal{V}\mathcal{U}}(\overline{\alpha})) \right) :$$
$$\Omega_{\mathcal{U}}(\overline{\alpha}) = \Omega_{\mathcal{V}}(\overline{\beta^*}). \tag{34}$$

Note that $\mathcal{V}$'s codesignation constraints depend on $\overline{\alpha}$: that is, the s.a. set $D_{\mathcal{V}\mathcal{U}}(\overline{\alpha})$ is an s.a. function of $\overline{\alpha}$. This technicality is necessary to allow for sufficient generality in specifying codesignation, and is explained further in Section A.3.

Using Grigoryev's algorithm (Theorem A.1) we can decide (34) in the following time. (We use (A.5) below to compute the time bound). Let n_Ω be the size of the simulation functions $\Omega_{\mathcal{U}}$ and $\Omega_{\mathcal{V}}$. Let r_c be the dimension of C. Let n_D be the size of the s.a. predicates for the codesignation constraints $D_{\mathcal{U}}$, $D_{\mathcal{V}}$, and $D_{\mathcal{V}\mathcal{U}}$. In (34), the outer existential quantifier binds some number $k \leqslant d$ vertices of $\mathcal{V}$ that are in the domain of ϕ. The inner universal quantifier binds the remaining $d - k$ vertices of $\mathcal{V}$. The middle universal quantifier binds up to d vertices of $\mathcal{U}$. Hence, we see there are at most $r = 2r_c d$ variables, and there are $a = 2$ alternations. Let us treat the maximum degree δ as a constant. The predicate has size $m = 2(n_\Omega + n_D)$. Therefore we can decide (34) in time

$$(m\delta)^{O(r)^{4a-2}} = (n_\Omega + n_D)^{O(r_c d)^6}. \tag{35}$$

Definition 9.8. Consider an algebraic sensor system $\mathcal{U}$, with d vertices. Recall we call d the *size* of $\mathcal{U}$. We call the size n_Ω of a sensor simulation function $\Omega_{\mathcal{U}}$ the *simulation complexity*. We call the size n_D of the codesignation constraints for $\mathcal{U}$ the *codesignation complexity*. We call $\mathcal{U}$ *small* if n_Ω and n_D are only polynomially large in d, i.e., $(n_\Omega + n_D) = d^{O(1)}$.

Now, let us assume that it is possible to compute dominance in calibration complexity (see Definition 6.2) in a time that much faster than (35) (see Section A.1 for how). Then we see the following

Lemma 9.9. *There is an algorithm for deciding the relation $\leqslant^*$ (Definition 6.3) for algebraic sensor systems. It runs in time polynomial in the simulation and codesignation*

complexity $(n_\Omega + n_D)$, *and sub-doubly exponential in the size of the sensor systems. That is, if the system has size d the time complexity is:*

$$(n_\Omega + n_D)^{(r_c d)^{O(1)}}, \tag{36}$$

where r_c is the dimension of the configuration space for a single component.

Corollary 9.10. *For small[46] sensor systems (Definition 9.8) of size d, there is an algorithm to decide the relation $\leqslant^*$ in time*

$$d^{(r_c d)^{O(1)}}. \tag{37}$$

Corollary 9.11. *For algebraic sensor systems, the relation $\leqslant_1$ (Definition 6.4) can be decided in the same time bounds as in Lemma 9.9 and Corollary 9.10.*

Proof. Consider deciding $S \leqslant^* Q + \text{COMM}(b)$, as in Definition 6.4. Recall the definition of *compatibility* for partial immersions (Section 8.4). We first observe that permutation (the * operation) and combination (the + operation) "commute" for compatible partial immersions. This is formalized as the "distributive" property[47] shown in Proposition C.3. We have already shown how to guess a permutation Q^* of Q. Our arguments above for guessing extensions and permutations can be generalized *mutatis mutandis* to compute the combination (Definition 8.10) of two algebraic sensor systems. Since $\text{COMM}(b)$ is a constant-sized sensor system (two vertices, one edge) with only a constant number of codesignation constraints (at most 2), we may guess how to combine it with a permutation Q^* of Q within the same time bounds given in Lemma 9.9 and Corollary 9.10. To complete the proof we require a technical argument (given in Appendix A.2) on how to simulate a permuted sensor system. □

10. Unsituated permutation

In Section 9 we examined a special case, where $\mathcal{U}$ and $\mathcal{V}$ are partially situated (that is, the domains of ϕ and ψ are non-empty). We now give a powerful generalization in which the sensor systems can be *unsituated*. Using the ideas in Sections 8.9.2 and 9, we can give an "abstract" version of permutation that is applicable to partially immersed sensor systems with codesignation constraints. Each set of codesignation constraints defines a different arrangement in the space of all immersions. Each cell in the arrangement, in turn, corresponds to a region in C^d.

Permutation corresponds to selecting a different family of immersions, while respecting the codesignation constraints. Since this corresponds to choosing a different region of C^d, the picture of abstract permutation is really not that different from the computational model of situated permutations discussed in Section 9. Suppose a simple sensor system $\mathcal{U}$ has d vertices, two of which are u and v. When there is a codesignation constraint

---

[46] Recall all small systems are algebraic.
[47] See Appendix C.

for u and v, we write that the relation $u \sim v$ must hold. This relation induces a quotient structure on C^d, and the corresponding quotient map $\pi: C^d \to C^d/(u \sim v)$ "identifies" the two vertices u and v. Similarly, we can model a non-codesignation constraint as a "diagonal" $\Delta \subset C^d$ that must be avoided. Abstract permutation of $\mathcal{U}$ can be viewed as follows. Let $D_{\mathcal{U}} = (C^d - \Delta)/(u \sim v)$. $D_{\mathcal{U}}$ is the quotient of $(C^d - \Delta)$ under π. For a partial immersion ψ^* to be chosen compatibly with the codesignation constraints, we view permutation as a bijective self-map of the disjoint equivalence classes

$$\{\pi(\operatorname{ex}\psi^* - \Delta)\}_{\psi^* \in \Sigma(\psi)}. \tag{38}$$

Thus, in general, the group structure for the permutation must respect the quotient structure for codesignation; correspondingly, we call such permutations *valid*. Below, we define the "diagonal" Δ, precisely.

Now, an unsituated sensor system $\mathcal{U}$ could be modeled using a partial immersion ψ_0 with an empty domain. In this case $\operatorname{ex}\psi_0 = C^d$ and Eq. (38) specializes to the single equivalence class $\{D_{\mathcal{U}}\}$. In this "singular" case, we can take several different approaches to defining unsituated permutation.

(i) We may define that $\psi_0^* = \psi_0$. Although consistent with situated permutation, (i) is not very useful. We choose a different definition. For unsituated permutation, we redefine $\Sigma(\psi_0)$ and $\operatorname{ex}\psi_0$ in the special case where ψ_0 has an empty domain.

(ii) When $\mathcal{U}$ is simple, we may define $\Sigma(\psi_0)$ to be the set of colocations of vertices of $\mathcal{U}$. That is, let $(x_1, \ldots, x_d)$ be a point in C^d, and define the ijth diagonal $\Delta_{ij} = \{(x_1, \ldots, x_d) \mid x_i = x_j\}$. Define permutation as a bijective self-map of the cells in the arrangement generated by all $\binom{d}{2}$ such diagonals $\{\Delta_{ij}\}_{i,j=1,\ldots,d}$. So, $\Sigma(\psi_0)$ is an arrangement in C^d of complexity $O(d^{2dr_c})$, $\operatorname{ex}\psi_0^* \in \Sigma(\psi_0)$ is a cell in the arrangement, and $\psi_0^* \in \operatorname{ex}\psi_0^*$ is a witness point in that cell. Hence ψ_0^* is a representative of the equivalence class $\operatorname{ex}\psi_0^*$. As in situated permutation, unsituated permutation can be viewed as a self-map of the cells $\{\operatorname{ex}\psi_0^*\}$ or (equivalently) as a self-map of the witnesses $\{\psi_0^*\}$. Perhaps the cleanest way to model our main examples is to treat all the sensor systems as initially unsituated, yet respecting all the (non)codesignation constraints. This may be done by (1) "algebraically" specifying all the codesignation constraints, (2) letting the domain of each immersion be empty, (3) using (ii) above, choose unsituated permutations that respect the codesignation constraints. The methods of Section 9 can be extended to guess unsituated permutations. In our examples, each guess (i.e., each unsituated permutation) corresponds to a choice of which vertices to colocate.[48] All our computational results (including our bounds) in Section 9 can be shown to hold for unsituated permutation by a simple extension of the arguments above.

10.1. Example of unsituated permutation

Unsituated permutation is quite powerful. Consider deciding Eq. (34) (in this example, we only consider vertex permutation of simple sensor systems). In particular, we

---

[48] The codesignation relation $u \sim v$, the quotient map π, the non-codesignation relation Δ, and definition (ii) of unsituated permutation, can all be extended to algebraic sensor systems using the methods of Section 9.

want to see that (33) makes sense for unsituated permutation, when we replace β by β_0, α by α_0, etc., to obtain:

$$
\begin{aligned}
&\left(\exists \beta_0^* \in (\Sigma(\beta_0) \cap D_\mathcal{V}),\right. \\
&\forall \overline{\alpha_0} \in (\text{ex } \alpha_0 \cap D_\mathcal{U}), \\
&\left.\forall \overline{\beta_0^*} \in (\text{ex } \beta_0^* \cap D_{\mathcal{V}\mathcal{U}}(\overline{\alpha_0}))\right): \\
&\quad \Omega_\mathcal{U}(\overline{\alpha_0}) = \Omega_\mathcal{V}(\overline{\beta_0^*}).
\end{aligned}
\tag{34$'$}
$$

With situated permutation (34), we are restricted to first choosing the partial immersion α. and thereby fixing a number of vertices of $\mathcal{S}$. Next, we can permute $\mathcal{U}$ to be "near" these vertices (this corresponds to the choice of β^*). This process gets the colocations right, but at the cost of generality; we would know that for any "topologically equivalent" choice of α, we can choose a permutation β^* such that (34) holds. For simple sensor systems, "topologically equivalent" means, "with the same vertex colocations".

Unsituated permutation (34$'$) allows us to do precisely what we want. In place of a partial immersion α for $\mathcal{S}$, we begin with a witness point $\alpha_0 \in C^d$. α_0 represents an equivalence class ex α_0 of immersions, all of which colocate the same vertices as α_0. So, α_0 says *which* vertices should be colocated, but not *where*. Now, given α_0, the outer existential quantifier in (34$'$) chooses an unsituated permutation β_0^* of $\mathcal{U}$. β_0^* represents an equivalence class ex β_0^* of immersions of $\mathcal{U}$, all of which colocate the same vertices of $\mathcal{U}$ as β_0^* does. The other, disjoint equivalence classes, are also subsets of C^d; each equivalence class colocates different vertices of $\mathcal{U}$, and the set of all such classes is $\Sigma(\beta_0)$ ($= \Sigma(\beta_0^*)$). Choice of β_0^* selects which vertices of $\mathcal{U}$ to colocate. The codesignation constraint $D_\mathcal{S}(\cdot)$ then enforces that, when measuring the outputs of $\mathcal{S}$ and $\mathcal{U}$, we install them in the same "place". More specifically: α_0 (given as data) determines which vertices of $\mathcal{S}$ to colocate; the choice of β_0^* determines which vertices of $\mathcal{U}$ are colocated; construction of $D_\mathcal{S}(\cdot)$ determines which vertices of $\mathcal{U}$ and $\mathcal{S}$ are colocated. Most specifically, given the configuration $\overline{\alpha_0}$ of $\mathcal{S}$, $D_\mathcal{S}$ in turn defines a region $D_\mathcal{S}(\overline{\alpha_0})$ in the configuration space C^d of $\mathcal{U}$. This region constraints the necessary coplacements $\overline{\beta_0^*}$ of $\mathcal{U}$ relative to $(\mathcal{S}, \overline{\alpha_0})$.

11. Application and experiments

We now describe an application of the theory in this paper, presented in [17]. This work is still preliminary, but we describe it here to give some feeling for the potential of our theory. The paper [17] relies heavily on the results and methods introduced here. Donald et al. [17] quantify a new resource: (f) *How much information is encoded or provided by the task mechanics?* The theme of exploiting task mechanics is important in previous work.[49] One could define "exploiting task mechanics" for robot manipulation as: *taking advantage of the mechanical and physical laws that govern how objects move and change.* Currently, in our framework the mechanics are embedded in the geometry

---

[49] For example, see the discussion of [25, 26, 40] in Part I.

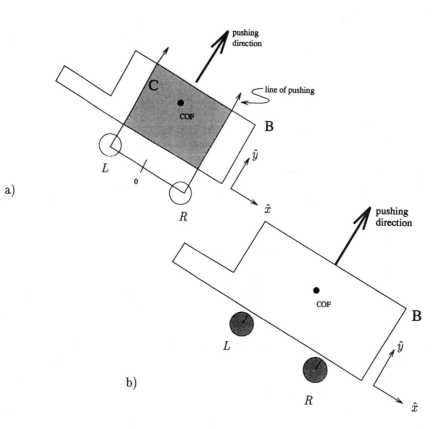

Fig. 11. (a) the "two-finger" pushing task versus (b) the two robot pushing task. The goal is to push the block B in a straight line.

of the system. In [17], we developed information invariants that explicitly trade-off (f) with resources (a)–(e) from the abstract, in the style of the preceding. Developing such invariants is quite challenging. We close with an example. This example opens up a host of new issues; see [17] for details.

Fig. 11(a) depicts a two-finger planar pushing task. The goal is to push the box B in a straight line (pure translation). The two fingers f_1 and f_2 are rigidly connected; for example, they could be the fingers of a parallel-jaw gripper. One complication involves the micro-mechanical variations in the slip of the box on the table. This phenomenon is very hard to model, and hence it is difficult to predict the results of a one-fingered push; we will only obtain a straight line trajectory when the center of friction (COF) lies on the line of pushing. However, with a two-fingered push, the box will translate in a straight line so long as the COF lies between the fingers. The nice thing about this strategy is that the COF can move somewhat and the fingers can keep pushing, since we only need ensure the COF lies in some region C (see Fig. 11(a)), instead of on a line. Second, if the COF moves outside C, then the fingers can move sideways to capture it again. For example, in [17] we implement the following control loop on our PUMA: *Sense the reaction torque τ about the point 0 in Fig. 11(a). If $\tau = 0$, push forward in*

```
(do-forever
  (let ((τ (measure-torque)))
    (cond ((zero? τ) (push ŷ))
          ((negative? τ) (move +x̂))
          ((positive? τ) (move -x̂))))))
```

Fig. 12. Protocol P1 (for a two-fingered gripper).

direction ŷ. If τ < 0 move the fingers in x̂; else move the fingers in -x̂. See Fig. 12.

From the mechanics perspective it might appear we are done. However, it is difficult to overstate how critically the control loop (Fig. 12) relies on global communication and control. Now, consider the analogous pushing task in Fig. 11(b). Each finger is replaced by an autonomous mobile robot with only local communication, configured as described in Section 2.1 of Part I. Each robot has a ring of one-bit contact ("bump") sensors. In addition, by examining the servo-loop in [44], it is clear that we can compute a measure of applied force by observing the applied power, the position and velocity of the robot, and the contact sensors.

Now, we ask, how can the system in Fig. 11(b) approximate the pushing strategy (Fig. 12), above? We observe the following. Each robot can compute its applied force and contact mode, and communicate these data to the other. The robots together must perform a control strategy (move in ŷ, move in ±x̂, etc.). Since the robots are not rigidly linked, there are five qualitative choices on how to implement a move in ±x̂. Our experiments suggest these strategies are aided by the ability to sense the box's surface normal, and to compliantly align to it. The IR-Modem mechanism described in Part I allows the communication of the following information: each robot's identity, orientation, and speed. In addition here are several kinds of information a robot might transmit for the pushing task: whether it is in contact with the box, the contact "bearing" (where the contact is on the bumper ring), the power being applied to the motors, and the local surface normal of the box. Next, a robot could communicate the message "Do this strategy: ..." or else "I am about to do this strategy: ..." Finally, the robots may have to transmit communication primitives like "Wait" and "Acknowledged".

While it is possible to specify and indeed implement sufficient communication to perform this task robustly, it is difficult to convince oneself that some particular communication scheme is optimal, or indeed, even necessary.

In [17], we analyze information invariants for manipulation tasks using the formalism presented here. For example, it is clear that the surface normal computation requires some internal state, and the compliant align can be viewed as consuming external state or as temporary calibration. Communication appears fundamental to performing the task in Fig. 11(b). So we ask: what communication is necessary between the robots to accomplish the (2-robot) pushing task? How many messages and what information is required? In [17] we use the methods introduced here to compare and contrast pushing protocols, and to answer these questions. First, we precisely describe two manipulation tasks for cooperating mobile robots that can push large, heavy objects. One task is shown

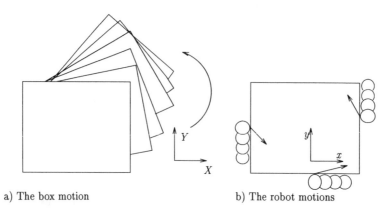

a) The box motion   b) The robot motions

Fig. 13. The task is to rotate the box by a specified angular amount. Here we illustrate the box being rotated by three cooperating autonomous agents. (a) The motion of the box viewed in world coordinates. (b) The relative motion of the pushing robots, viewed in a system of coordinates fixed on the box. The arrows illustrate the direction of the applied forces. From [17].

in Fig. 11(b), the other in Fig. 13. More specifically, we ask: *Can all explicit local and global communication between the agents be removed from a family of pushing protocols for these tasks?* [50] Donald et al. [17] answer in the affirmative—a surprising result—by using the general methods introduced here for analyzing information invariants.

11.1. Using circuits and reductions to analyze information invariants

In [17], we develop and analyze synchronous and asynchronous manipulation protocols for a small team of cooperating mobile robots than can push large boxes. The boxes are typically several robot diameters wide, and one to two times the mass of a single robot, although the robots have also pushed couches that are heavier (perhaps two to four times the mass, and 8 × 3 robot diameters in size). We build on the ground-breaking work of Mason and Erdmann [26,40] and others on planar sensorless manipulation. Our work differs from previous work on pushing in several ways. First, the robots and boxes are on a similar dynamic and spatial scale. Second, a single robot is not always strong enough to move the box by itself (specifically, its "strength" depends on the effective lever arm). Third, we do not assume the robots are globally coordinated and controlled. (More precisely, we first develop protocols based on the assumption that local communication is possible, and then we subsequently remove that communication via a series of source-to-source transformations on the protocols). Fourth, our protocols assume neither that the robot has a geometric model of the box, nor that the first moment of the friction distribution (the COF) is known. Instead, the robot combines sensori-motor experiments and manipulation strategies to infer the necessary information (the experiments have the flavor of [33]). Finally, the pushing literature generally regards the "pushers" as moving kinematic constraints. In our case, because (i) there are at least two robot pushers and (ii) the robots are less massive than the box, the robots are really "force-appliers" in a system with significant friction.

---

[50] This question was first posed as an open problem in a 1992 draft of this paper.

Of course, our protocols rely on a number of assumptions in order to work. We use the theory of information invariants developed here, to reveal these assumptions and expose the information structure of the task. We believe our theory has implications for the parallelization of manipulation tasks on spatially distributed teams of cooperating robots. To develop a parallel manipulation strategy, first we start with a perfectly synchronous protocol with global coordination and control. Next, in distributing it among cooperating, spatially separated agents, we relax it to an MPMD[51] protocol with local communication and partial synchrony. Finally, we remove all explicit communication. The final protocols are asynchronous, and essentially "uniform", or SPMD[51] —the same program runs on each robot. Ultimately, the robots must be viewed as communicating implicitly through the task dynamics, and this implicit communication confers a certain degree of synchrony on our protocols. Because it is both difficult and important to analyze the information content of this implicit communication and synchronization, we believe that using our theory of information invariants is justified.

The manipulation protocols in [17] are first modeled as circuits, using the formalism developed in Section 8. Source-to-source transformations on these protocols are then represented as circuit transformations. The circuit transformations are modeled using the reductions described in this paper. For the task in Fig. 11b, [17] consider three pushing protocols P1, P2, and P3, and their interreducibility under $\leqslant_1$. In particular, we transform an MPMD pushing protocol P2 with explicit IR communication to an asynchronous SPMD protocol P3 with no explicit communication. This transformation is then analyzed as an instance of reducing the latter to the former, using $\leqslant_1$. There are several things we have learned. We can determine a lot about the information structure of a task by (i) parallelizing it and (ii) attempting to replace explicit communication with communication "through the world" (through the task dynamics). Communication "through the world" takes place when a robot changes the environment and that change can be sensed by another robot. For example, protocol P2 uses explicit communication and protocol P3 makes use of an encoding in the task mechanics of the same information. Our approach of quantifying the information complexity in the task mechanics involves viewing the world dynamics as a set of mechanically implemented "registers" and "data-paths". This permits certain kinds of *de facto* communication between spatially separated robots.

In [17], we also consider three protocols R1, R2, and R3, for a reorientation task (see Fig. 13). A transformational approach to developing these protocols is viewed as a series of reductions. The final protocol R3 has several advantages over the initial protocols R1 and R2. Using protocol R3, two robots (instead of three) suffice to rotate the box. The protocol is "uniform" (SPMD) in that the same program (including the same termination predicate) runs on both robots. More interesting, in R3 it is no longer necessary for the robots to have an *a priori* geometric model of the box—whereas such a model is required for R1 and R2.

In terms of program development, synchrony, and communication, we have a correspondence between these protocols, shown in Fig. 14. We believe that a methodology for developing coordinated manipulation protocols is emerging, based on the tools described

---

[51] SPMD (MPMD) = Single (Multiple) Program, Multiple Data.

Pushing task	Reorientation task	
P1	R1	global coordination and control
P2	R2	local IR communication, partial synchrony, MPMD
P3	R3	uniform (SPMD), asynchronous, no explicit communication

Fig. 14. Summary of parallel manipulation protocols from [17].

here. This methodology helps transform an offline, synchronous manipulation strategy (e.g., P1 or R1) with global coordination and control, into an online, asynchronous, distributed strategy (P3 or R3) for the same task:

Developing parallel manipulation protocols [17]
  (1) Start with a sensorless [26] or near-sensorless [33, 47] manipulation protocol requiring global coordination of several "agents" (e.g., parallel-jaw fingers, or fingers of a dexterous hand).
  (2) Distribute the protocol over spatially separated agents. Synchronize and coordinate control using explicit local communication.
  (3) Define *virtual sensors* [52] for the quantities Step (2) measures.
  (4) Implement each virtual sensor using concrete sensors on mechanical observables.
  (5) Transform the communication between two agents L and R into shared data structures.
  (6) Implement the shared data structures as "mechanical registers".

Our circuits model the protocols in the steps above. Our reductions model the transformations between steps. By the results of Section 9, these reductions can be effectively computed. Therefore, in principle, the transformations in [17] could be synthesized automatically. We believe that our methods are useful for developing parallel manipulation protocols. We have implemented and tested our asynchronous, distributed, SPMD manipulation protocols using TOMMY and LILY, and found them robust and efficient. See [17] for a full discussion.

12. Conclusions

In this paper we suggested a theory of information invariance that includes sensors and computation. Our results generalize the work of [1]; first, we consider fairly detailed yet abstract models of physical autonomous mobile robots; second, we consider generalizations and variations on compasses and orientation sensors; third, we develop a generalized and stratified theory of the "power" of such sensori-computational devices. As such, perhaps our work could be called *On the generalized power of generalized compasses*.

---

[52] We use the term in the sense of [14]; others, particularly Henderson have used similar concepts. See Section 4.2.1 for examples of virtual and concrete sensors.

We think that information invariants can serve as a framework in which to measure the capabilities of robot systems, to quantify their power, and to reduce their fragility with respect to assumptions that are engineered into the control system or the environment. We believe that the equivalencies that can be derived between communication, internal state, external state, computation, and sensors, can prove valuable in determining what information is required to solve a task, and how to direct a robot's actions to acquire that information to solve it. Our paper proposes a beachhead on information invariance from which, we hope, such goals may be obtained. There are several things we have learned. First, we were surprised by how important *time* and *communication* become in invariant analysis. Much insight can be gained by asking *How can this sensor be simulated by a simpler system with a clock (resp. communication)?* Time-based sensors are ubiquitous in modern aircraft navigation systems (compare Section 4.2.1). In "DMEs" (*distance measuring equipment*) a ground station and the plane talk to each other, and measure differences in timing pulses to estimate their distance apart. GPS, which was approved in July, 1993 for use in airplanes, also operates on timing principles.

Robot builders make claims about robot performance and resource consumption. In general, it is hard to verify these claims and compare the systems. One reason is calibration: pre-calibration can add a great deal of information to the system. In order to quantify the "use" of external state, we suggested a theory of calibration complexity. Our theory represents a systematic attempt to make such comparisons based on geometric and physical reasoning. Finally, we try to operationalize our analysis by making it computational; we give effective (albeit theoretical) procedures for computing our comparisons. Our algorithms are exact and combinatorially precise.

Our reduction $\leqslant_1$ (Definition 6.4) attempts to quantify when we can "efficiently" build one sensor out of another (that is, build one sensor using the components of another). Hence, we write $A \leqslant_1 B$ when we can build A out of B without "adding too much stuff". The last is analogous to "without adding much information complexity". Our measure of information complexity is *relativized* both to the information complexity of the sensori-computational components of B, and to the bandwidth of A. This relativization circumvents some tricky problems in measuring sensor complexity (see Appendix B). In this sense, our "components" are analogous to *oracles* in the theory of computation. Hence, we write $A \leqslant_1 B$ if we can build a sensor that simulates A, using the components of B, plus "a little rewiring". A and B are modeled as *circuits*, with wires (data-paths) connecting their internal components. However, our sensori-computational systems differ from computation-theoretic (CT) "circuits", in that their spatial configuration—i.e., the spatial location of each component—is as important as their connectivity.

Permutation models the permissible ways to reallocate and reuse resources in building another sensor. *Codesignation constraints* further restrict the range of admissible permutations. *Output communication* formalizes our notion of "a little bit of rewiring". Like CT reductions, $A \leqslant_1 B$ defines an "efficient" transformation on sensors that takes B to A. However, we give a generic algorithm for synthesizing our reductions (whereas no such algorithm can exist for CT [53]). Whether such reductions are widely useful or whether there exist better reductions (e.g., our *"k-wire"* reductions in Section 8.10.3) is open; however in our laboratory we are using $\leqslant_1$ to design manipulation protocols [17] for multiple mobile robots. We also give a "hierarchy" of reductions, ordered on power, so that the strength of our transformations can be quantified. See Appendix A.4 for a discussion of "universal reduction" as per Section 1.1. See Appendices B and C.3 for more on relativized information complexity.

Our work raises a number of questions. For example, can robots "externalize", or record state in the world? The answer depends not only on the environment, but also upon the dynamics. A juggling robot probably cannot. On a conveyor belt, it may be possible (suppose "bad" parts are reoriented so that they may be removed later). However, it is certainly possible during quasi-static manipulation by a single agent. In moving towards multi-agent tasks and at least partially dynamic tasks, we are attempting to investigate this question in both an experimental and theoretical setting. We discuss these issues further in [17].

By analogy with CT reductions, we may define an equivalence relation $=_k$, such that $A =_k B$ when $A \leqslant_k B$ and $B \leqslant_k A$. We may also ask, does a given class of sensori-computational systems contain "complete" circuits, to which any member of the class may be reduced? Note that the relation $=_k$ holds between any two complete circuits.

Weaker forms of sensori-computational equivalence are possible. If we define the *state* of a sensor system $\mathcal{U}$ to be a pair (z, b) where z is the configuration of the system and b is the output value at z, we can examine the equilibrium behavior of $\mathcal{U}$ as it evolves in state space. Recall Definition 4.1; let us call this *strong simulation*. By analogy, let us say that a system $\mathcal{U}$ *weakly simulates* another system $\mathcal{V}$ when $\mathcal{U}$ and $\mathcal{V}$ have identical, forward-attracting compact limit sets in state space. [54] If we replace strong simulation ($\cong$ in Definition 4.1) with weak simulation, all of our structural results go through *mutatis mutandis*. The computational results also go through, if we can compute limit sets and their properties (a difficult problem in general). Failing this, if we can derive the properties of limit sets "by hand" then in principle, reductions using weak simulation instead of strong simulation ($\cong$) can also be calculated by hand.

Finally, can we record "programs" in the world in the same way we may externalize state? Is there a "universal" manipulation circuit which can read these programs and perform the correct strategy to accomplish a task? Such a mechanism might lead to a robot which could infer the correct manipulation action by performing sensorimotor experiments.

12.1. Future research

This paper represents a first stab at several difficult problems, and there are a number of issues that our formalism does not currently consider. We now acknowledge some of these issues here.

---

[53] For example: no algorithm exists to decide the existence of a linear-space (or log-space, polynomial time, Turing-computable, etc.) reduction between two CT problems.

[54] I am grateful to Dan Koditschek, who has suggested this formalism in his papers.

Our theory allows us to compare members of a certain class of sensor systems, and, moreover, to transform one system into another. However, it does not permit one to judge which system is "simpler" or "better" or "cheaper". In particular, for a given measurement problem, it does not permit a "simplest" sensor system to be identified. There are several reasons for this. The first is that there are inherent limitations on comparing absolute sensor complexity—and these problems represent structural barriers to obtaining good notions of "better" or "simpler". The theory is designed, in part, to get around some of these limitations. We discuss these problems—which are quite deep—in Appendix B at some length. Second, such comparisons would require an explicit performance measure. We discussed such measures as speed (or execution time) in Section 2.1.2. In Section F.1, we argue that such performance measures allow us to apply *kinodynamic* analysis tools [21,49]. There is no doubt that external performance measures such as "simpler" and "better" and "cheaper" could be used with our framework—but we don't know what exactly these measures are. It appears that efficient algorithms for exploiting these measures will have to take advantage of their structure.

Instead of investigating performance measures, we have argued that it is very hard to even measure or compare the "power" of sensorimotor systems. To address this problem, we developed our reductions. To make our stance clear, consider as an analogy the theory of computation (CT). CT does not tell us which algorithms are more "simple", but it does tell us which are more powerful (i.e., which can compute more). In our theory, as in CT, we can define transformations or reductions that we consider "fair", and then discuss equivalence of systems up to these transformations. Now, in CT, given performance measures (e.g., asymptotic complexity) we can also compare the performance of algorithms—although there are many different measures to choose from. But in CT, "faster" does not necessarily mean "simpler" in any sense. Our reductions are analogous to CT reductions. Execution time or speed is analogous to computational complexity. Finally, as in CT, notions of "simplicity" are orthogonal to notions of either reduction or performance.

However, the notion of performance measures opens up a host of practical issues.[55] Certainly some simple scheme of looking up the "cost" of components in a table could be used in conjunction with our system. An instrumentation engineer, confronted by a problem where one measurement strategy is ineffective, may choose to measure some other property to solve the problem rather than reconfigure the sensori-computational components of the system (for example, measuring the temperature rather than the pressure of a fixed volume of gas). This approach is not envisaged by our theorems, although the power of two given strategies could be compared. Furthermore, distinct measurement strategies have costs other than those considered here—for example, the cost of transducers, the effect on the measurement noise of measuring one observable and inferring another from its value, noise properties of transducers and common mode effects (for example, in positioning strain gauges). These issues should be considered in future work.

There is much to be done. Our model of reduction is very operational and others should be attempted. In addition to measuring the information complexity of commu-

---

[55] I would like to thank the anonymous referees for suggesting these issues and the wording to describe them.

nication, it may be valuable to quantify the *distance* messages must be sent. Similarly, it may make sense to measure the "size" of a resource permutation, or how far resources are moved. All these ideas remain to be explored. Finally, we have approached this problem by investigating information *invariance*, that is, the kind of information-preserving equivalencies that can be derived among systems containing the resources (a)–(e) (Section 3). An alternative would be to look at information *variance*, that is, it would be valuable to have a truly uniform measure of information that would apply across heterogeneous resource categories.

In the appendices we present a number of important extensions, and attempt to address some of the issues raised in this section.

Acknowledgments

This paper could never have been written without discussions and help from Jim Jennings, Mike Erdmann, Dexter Kozen, Jeff Koechling, Tomás Lozano-Pérez, Daniela Rus, Pat Xavier, and Jonathan Rees. I am very grateful to all of them for their generosity with their time and ideas. The robots and experimental devices described herein were built in our lab by Jim Jennings, Russell Brown, Jonathan Rees, Craig Becker, Mark Battisti, Kevin Newman, Dave Manzanares, and Greg Whelan; these ideas could never have come to light without their help and experiments. I would furthermore like to thank Mike Erdmann, Jim Jennings, Jonathan Rees, John Canny, Ronitt Rubinfeld, Seth Hutchinson, Sundar Narasimhan, and Amy Briggs for providing invaluable comments and suggestions on drafts of this paper. Thanks to Loretta Pompilio for drawing the illustration in Fig. 1. Debbie Lee Smith and Amy Briggs drew the rest of the figures for this paper and I am very grateful to them for their help. I am grateful to Jeff Koechling, Mike Erdmann, and Randy Brost for explaining to me how lighthouses, ADFs, and VORs work. This paper was improved by incorporating suggestions made at the *Workshop on Computational Theories of Interaction and Agency*, organized at the University of Chicago by Phil Agre and Tim Converse. I would like to thank Phil Agre, Stan Rosenschein, Yves Lesperance, Brian Smith, Ian Horswill, and all members of the workshop, for their comments and suggestions. I would also like to thank the anonymous referees for their comments and suggestions. I am grateful to Phil Agre who carefully edited this paper and made many invaluable suggestions on presentation.

Appendix A. Algebraic decision procedures

The algorithms in Section 9 are algebraic and use the theory of real closed fields;[56] for an introduction to algebraic decision procedures see, for example the classic paper of [2], or discussions in books such as [18, Chapters 1–4] and [10]. In Section 9, we reduce our computational problem to deciding the truth of a Tarski formula [48];

---

[56] Also called "Tarski's Language" or the "first-order language of algebra and geometry". One common mathematical term is "the first-order theory of real closed fields".

the algebraic algorithms can then decide such a sentence. Tarski's language is also called the *language of semi-algebraic sets*. Such sets are real semi-algebraic varieties defined by polynomial equalities and inequalities, where the polynomial coefficients are algebraic numbers. A Tarski formula is a logical sentence that quantifies existentially or universally over each of the real variables. A typical Tarski formula might be:

$$(\forall x \exists y \exists z \forall w) : \quad xy^2 - 16w^4 \leqslant 0$$
$$\vee \tfrac{3}{4}xw^2 + x^7 + 78w < 0 \tag{A.1}$$
$$\wedge z^4 + 5w^3 + 4x^2y^2 - y + 7x = 0.$$

More generally, we can think of a Tarski sentence as

$$(\Diamond_1 x_1 \, \Diamond_2 x_2 \, \cdots \, \Diamond_r x_r) : \quad s_1(x_1, \ldots, x_r) \ R_1 \ 0$$
$$C_1 \, s_2(x_1, \ldots, x_r) \ R_2 \ 0$$
$$\vdots \tag{A.2}$$
$$C_{m-1} \, s_m(x_1, \ldots, x_r) \ R_m \ 0,$$

where each $\Diamond_i$ is a *quantifier*, each R_j is a *real relation*, and $C_1, \ldots, C_m$ are *logical connectives*. A *quantifier* $\Diamond_i$ is either $\forall$ or $\exists$, and it quantifies over a real variable x_i. A *real relation* is a relation among real values, and is one of $<$, $>$, or $=$. A logical connective is one of $\vee$ or $\wedge$.[57] Each $s_1, \ldots, s_m$ is a polynomial in $\mathbb{R}[x_1, \ldots, x_r]$, and so (A.2) is a sentence in r variables. We call the set $Y \subset \mathbb{R}^r$ defined by (A.1) or (A.2) a *semi-algebraic set*, and, conversely, a set $Y \subset R^r$ is called *semi-algebraic* if it can be written in a form like (A.2). The set Y is called *algebraic* if the only real relation we require is equality ($=$). The boolean characteristic function $\mathbb{T}(\cdot)$ of a semi-algebraic set such as Y is defined as

$$\mathbb{T}(x_1, \ldots, x_r) \Longleftrightarrow s_1(x_1, \ldots, x_r) \ R_1 \ 0$$
$$C_1 \, s_2(x_1, \ldots, x_r) \ R_2 \ 0$$
$$\vdots \tag{A.3}$$
$$C_{m-1} \, s_m(x_1, \ldots, x_r) \ R_m \ 0.$$

$\mathbb{T}(\cdot)$ is called a *semi-algebraic predicate*. Hence, (A.2) can be written

$$(\Diamond_1 x_1 \, \Diamond_2 x_2 \, \cdots \, \Diamond_r x_r) : \quad \mathbb{T}(x_1, \ldots, x_r).$$

Let Φ be an s.a. predicate. Let x denote $(x_1, \ldots, x_r)$, and for a quantifier $\Diamond$, let $\Diamond x$ denote $(\Diamond x_1, \ldots, \Diamond x_r)$. If $\mathbb{T}_Y$ is an s.a. predicate for the s.a. set Y, we will abbreviate the sentence $\exists x : (\mathbb{T}_Y(x) \wedge \Phi(x))$ as follows:

$$\exists x \in Y : \Phi(x). \tag{A.4}$$

Given this convention (A.4), a little manipulation shows that as a consequence, the formula $\forall x : (\mathbb{T}_Y(x) \Rightarrow \Phi(x))$ is therefore equivalent to

$$\forall x \in Y : \Phi(x).$$

---

[57] So $\leqslant$ and $\geqslant$ can be built out of these.

Let δ be the total degree bound for the polynomials $s_1, \ldots, s_m$ in (A.2). We call the number of polynomials m the *size* of the Tarski sentence (A.2) and of the s.a. predicate $\mathbb{T}(\cdot)$ in (A.3). Observe however, that to calculate a bound $O(\delta rm)$ on the number of terms in (A.2), we would employ the degree bound δ and the number of variables r as well.

Now, it is remarkable that one can decide such sentences in complete generality: although Tarski's original algorithm [48] was non-elementary, [58] this bound has been improved by a chain of researchers since then. For example, Ben-Or et al. [2] showed how to decide the first-order theory of real closed fields with a purely algebraic algorithm in time $2^{2^{O(m)}}$ and space $2^{O(m)}$. In Section 9, we use this result:

Theorem A.1 (Grigoryev [29]). *Sentences in the theory of real closed fields can be decided in time doubly-exponential only in the number of quantifier alternations. More specifically, the truth of a Tarski sentence for m polynomials of degree $< \delta$ in r variables, where $a \leqslant r$ is the number of quantifier alternations in the prenex form of the formula, can be decided in time*

$$(m\delta)^{O(r)^{4a-2}}. \tag{A.5}$$

Proof. See [29]. □

A.1. Application: computational calibration complexity

Recall the discussion in Section 8.7.4. We wish to develop an algorithm for deciding the relation $\leqslant^*$ between sensor systems. Comparing the calibration complexity (Definitions 5.1, 6.2) of two sensor systems seems easier than the issues of immersion and simulation, because the calibration complexity does not change with the immersion, so long as the immersion respects the codesignation constraints. The essential idea behind computing calibration complexity is to measure the complexity of the codesignation constraints that specify a sensor system. One measure, of course, is the *number* of codesignation constraints, but other measures, such as the degree and the quantification, are also important. Using the algebraic methods from Section A, we can develop tools to measure the complexity of algebraic relations such as those encountered in algebraically codesignated sensor systems (Definition 8.17).

Now, to decide the relation $\leqslant^*$, we must be able to decide dominance in calibration complexity (see Definition 5.1). We propose to measure calibration and installation complexity by the complexity of the codesignation constraints. In general, one may measure the complexity of the codesignation constraints by comparing the complexity of the semi-algebraic varieties that the algebraic codesignations specify. One way to do this is to count the number, degree, quantification, and dimension of the semi-algebraic codesignation constraints. This gives numbers for m, δ, a, and r for an algebraic complexity measure such as (A.5), for example. Eq. (A.5) can then be used as a measure of the sensor's calibration complexity. These bounds can then be compared

---

[58] Tarski developed this algorithm around 1920, but it was not published until later.

(using big-Oh ($O(\cdot)$) notation) to determine which sensor dominates in terms of calibration complexity. The comparison can be done in essentially the same time it takes to read the input, and the time required is very small compared to (35), the time for the algebraic simulation.

Some of the complexity in our theory results from a decision to proceed through an abstract definition of a sensor system, independent of the underlying configuration space, and then to map that system into a particular space. One may ask whether this approach, though it mirrors much of modern geometry, is essential to the results obtained. We believe that it would be possible to start with an *a priori* configuration space (see Eq. (38)), instead of constructing it as a quotient of set differences. This would eliminate some of the technical baggage required (codesignation, non-codesignation and so forth). However, it appears that this approach would leave unanswered the question of measuring the complexity of the underlying configuration space—and hence it would not yield a computational theory of calibration complexity.

A.2. Application: simulation functions

Recall the discussion of simulation functions for components, edges, and sensor systems in Section 8. We now discuss simulation functions and their encodings. It is important that simulation functions work on permuted sensor systems. Here is how this might be accomplished.

A.2.1. Vertex versus graph permutations

We now consider two orthogonal kinds of permutation. In both models, the vertex and edge labels $\ell(v)$ and $\ell(e)$ never change. The first model is called *vertex permutation*, and is given in Definition 8.6. In this model, the vertices can move, and they drag the components and wires with them. That is, the vertices move (under permutation), and as they move, the edges follow. Vertex permutation suffices for all reductions in this paper, and the machinery in Sections 8.1 and 9 suffices to compute the reductions $\leqslant^*$ and $\leqslant_1$.

We can also consider an alternate model, called *edge permutation*, where the edge connectivity changes. An edge permutation can be modeled as follows. Consider a graph with vertices V and edges E. Start with any bijection $\sigma: V^2 \to V^2$. We call σ an *edge permutation*, since it induces the restriction map $\sigma|_E: E \to \sigma(E)$ on the edge set E. An edge permutation says nothing about the immersion of a graph.

We can also compose the models. We define a *graph permutation* to be a vertex permutation followed by an edge permutation. In a graph permutation, the vertices and the edges move independently. That is, vertices may move, but in addition, the edge connectivity may change. To illustrate the different models, consider a sensor system $\mathcal{U}$ with three vertices $\{v_1, v_2, v_3\}$ with labels $\ell(v_i) = B_i$ ($i = 1, 2, 3$). $\mathcal{U}$ has one edge $e = (v_1, v_2)$ of bandwidth k that connects B_1 to B_2. So, the B_i are the components of the system, and e is a data-path. A *vertex* permutation $\mathcal{U}^*$ of $\mathcal{U}$ would move the vertices (and therefore the components) spatially, but in $\mathcal{U}^*$, e would still connect v_1 and v_2, (and therefore, B_1 and B_2). An *edge* permutation σ of $\mathcal{U}$ would change the edge connectivity. So, for example, an edge permutation $\sigma(\mathcal{U})$ could be a graph with one edge $\sigma(e) = (v_2, v_3)$, connecting v_2 to v_3 (and hence B_2 to B_3). But in $\sigma(\mathcal{U})$ no edge would connect v_1 and v_2. Finally, consider a *graph* permutation $\mathcal{U}^\star$ of $\mathcal{U}$. Suppose $\mathcal{U}^\star = \sigma(U^*)$, that is, $\mathcal{U}^\star$ is the vertex permutation $\mathcal{U}^*$ followed by the edge permutation σ above. $\mathcal{U}^\star$ has the same edge connectivity as $\sigma(\mathcal{U})$. However, in $\mathcal{U}^\star$, the vertices are immersed as in $\mathcal{U}^*$.

To summarize: let $(\mathcal{U}, \phi)$ be a situated sensor system. A graph permutation of $\mathcal{U}$ is given by $\mathcal{U}^\star = (\mathcal{U}, \phi^\star)$ where $\phi^\star = (\phi^*, \sigma)$, ϕ^* is a vertex permutation, and σ is an edge permutation.

So, vertex permutation preserves the graph topology whereas edge permutation can move the edges around. Edge permutation permits arbitrary rewiring (using existing edges). It cannot add new edges, nor can it change their bandwidth. Although vertex permutation suffices for all the examples in this paper, graph permutation is useful (and required) in [17]. Graph permutation is also required for some of the applications discussed in Section 1.1 (particularly (3) *design* and (4) *universal reduction*—see Section A.4). Here, we will content ourselves with answering two questions: (i) if we permit graph permutation, does it change our complexity bounds? and (ii) does graph permutation give us a more powerful reduction?

We first turn to question (i). Fortunately, we can extend our computational results to graph permutation without difficulty. To do this, we model a graph permutation of a sensor system $\mathcal{U}$ as a vertex permutation of $\mathcal{U}$, followed by an edge permutation of $\mathcal{U}$. Using this scheme, we can compute all our reductions ($\leqslant^*$, $\leqslant_1$, etc.) within the same time bounds given in Lemma 9.9 and Corollary 9.10, permitting graph permutation in place of vertex permutation throughout. Our other lemmas also go through *mutatis mutandis*.

We now elaborate. An *adjacency matrix* for a sensor system with d vertices is a $d \times d$ binary matrix. An *adjacency matrix with bandwidth* has non-negative integer entries. An entry of b in row v, column u specifies a (directed) edge of bandwidth $\log \mathbb{K}(b)$ between[59] vertices v and u. Given an edge permutation σ, we can construct a new adjacency matrix, and the edge simulation functions (such as Ω_e in Section 8.1) can be constructed from the adjacency matrix. Now, we may view the edges (data-paths) in our sensor system as part of its configuration. Hence, in different configurations, the system may have different "wiring diagrams" (different edges). We now consider this such "configurations" and the resulting "configuration space". In particular, we wish to demonstrate their algebraicity.

Consider a sensor system $\mathcal{U}$ with d vertices V, and $\mathrm{O}(d^2)$ edges E. When we permit graph permutation, a configuration of this system can be specified by a pair (ϕ, σ), where $\phi: V \to C$ is an immersion (Definition 8.4) of $\mathcal{U}$, and σ is an edge permutation. As we have discussed, ϕ lives in the configuration space C^d. What about σ? σ is a member of the permutation group on d^2 elements. σ can be modeled as a $d^2 \times d^2$ binary matrix called a *permutation matrix*. Every permutation matrix has a single 1 in each row and column, the other entries being zero. Let $\mathbb{Z}_2$ denote the field $\mathbb{Z}/2$. Then, the space

---

[59] This representation is not hard to extend to components with multiple inputs and outputs, using an $rd \times sd$ matrix.

of permutation matrices is $\mathbb{O}(\mathbb{Z}_2, d^2)$, the *orthogonal* group of $d^2 \times d^2$ binary matrices. Each element is an orthogonal matrix, with determinant ± 1.

Every "rewiring" of $\mathcal{U}$ using only existing edges is encoded by a permutation $\sigma \in \mathbb{O}(\mathbb{Z}_2, d^2)$. So, to model vertex permutation plus rewiring, we extend our usual sensor configuration space from C^d to $C^d \times \mathbb{O}(\mathbb{Z}_2, d^2)$. It is not hard to extend this model to add one extra wire (output communication), or several extra wires (for k-wire reductions (Section 8.10.3)). The space $\mathbb{O}(\mathbb{Z}_2, d^2)$ is algebraic, and the computation of edge simulation functions from adjacency matrices is s.a.

Now, how expensive it is to compute the reductions $\leqslant^*$ and $\leqslant_1$ using graph permutation? Perhaps surprisingly, even with this extended configuration space (which has dimension $d^4 + r_c d$ instead of $r_c d$), we still obtain the same complexity bounds given in Lemma 9.9 and Corollary 9.10 (so long as r and s are constants). This is because [60] (see Eqs. (35–37)) $n^{(d^4 + r_c d)^{O(1)}}$ is still $n^{(r_c d)^{O(1)}}$.

We now address question (ii): does graph permutation give us a more powerful reduction? In answer we show the following:

Lemma A.2 (The clone lemma). *Graph permutation can be simulated using vertex permutation, preceded by a linear time and linear space transformation of the sensor system.*

Proof. Given a sensor system $\mathcal{U}$ we "clone" all its vertices, and attach the edges to the clones. The cloned system simulates the original when each vertex is colocated with its clone. Components remain associated with original vertices. We can move an edge independently of the components it originally connected, by moving its vertices (which are clones). Any graph permutation of $\mathcal{U}$ can be simulated by a vertex permutation of the cloned system.

More specifically: given a graph $G = (V, E)$ with labelling function ℓ, we construct a new graph $G' = (V', E')$ with labelling function ℓ'. Let the cloning function $\mathrm{cl}: V \hookrightarrow \mathbb{V}$ be an injective map from V into a universe of vertices [61] $\mathbb{V}$, such that $\mathrm{cl}(V) \cap V = \emptyset$. We lift cl to V^2 and then restrict it to E to obtain $\mathrm{cl}: E \to \mathrm{cl}(V)^2$ as follows: If $e = (u, v)$, then $\mathrm{cl}(e) = (\mathrm{cl}(u), \mathrm{cl}(v))$. Edge labels are defined as follows: $\ell'(cl(e)) = \ell(e)$.

Finally we define $V' = V \cup \mathrm{cl}(V)$ and $E' = \mathrm{cl}(E)$. We define the labelling function ℓ' on V' as follows. $\ell'(v) = \ell(v)$ when $v \in V$. Otherwise, $\ell'(v)$ returns the "identity" component, which can be simulated as the identity function. [62]

Suppose $\mathcal{U}$ has $d = |V|$ vertices and $|E|$ edges. This transformation adds only d vertices and can be computed in time and space $\mathrm{O}(d + |E|)$. $\quad\square$

---

[60] Another way to see this is as follows: even if we try each of the $(d^2)!$ edge permutations, this additional $(d^2)!$ factor is absorbed by the $\mathrm{O}(1)$ in the second exponent.

[61] See Section C.1.

[62] The proof can be strengthened as follows. Recall that two components can communicate without an (explicit) connection when they are spatially colocated. Therefore the proof goes through even if cloned vertices have no associated components, that is, $\ell'(v) = \emptyset$ for $v \notin V$. This version has the appeal of changing the encoding without adding additional physical resources.

Let us denote by $cl(\mathcal{U})$ the linear-space clone transformation of $\mathcal{U}$ described in Lemma A.2. Now consider any k-wire reduction $\leqslant_k$ (Section 8.10.3). We see that:

Corollary A.3. *Let* $k \in \mathbb{N}$. *Suppose that for two sensor systems* $\mathcal{U}$ *and* $\mathcal{V}$, *we have* $\mathcal{V} \leqslant_k \mathcal{U}$ *(using graph permutation). Then* $\mathcal{V} \leqslant_k cl(\mathcal{U})$ *(using only vertex permutation).*

Class edge permutation

In practice, we wish to impose some restrictions on edge and graph permutation. For example, suppose we have a sensor system $\mathcal{U}$ containing two cooperating and communicating mobile robots L and R. The sensori-computational systems for L and R are modeled as circuits. The data-paths in the system, in addition to bandwidth, have a *type*, of the form SOURCE $\rightarrow$ DESTINATION, where both SOURCE and DESTINATION $\in \{L, R\}$. When permuting the edges of $\mathcal{U}$ to obtain $\mathcal{U}^\star$, it makes sense to permute only edges of the same type. More generally, we may segregate the edge types into two *classes*, *internal* edges $L \rightarrow L$ and $R \rightarrow R$, and *external* edges $L \rightarrow R$ and $L \leftarrow R$. In constructing $\mathcal{U}^\star$, we may use an internal edge (of sufficient bandwidth) to connect any two components where SOURCE = DESTINATION. External edges (of sufficient bandwidth) can be used when SOURCE $\neq$ DESTINATION. Hence, in *class* edge permutation, we permute edges within a class. Class edge permutation leaves unchanged the complexity bounds and the lemmas of Section A.2.1.

In this example, maintaining exactly two physical locations can be done using simple codesignation constraints. More generally, we take SOURCE, DESTINATION $\in C$.

A.3. Application: parametric codesignation constraints

Recall Eq. (34), in which we formulated the sensor reduction problem as an s.a. decision procedure. We now discuss some technical details of this equation, using the notation and hypotheses of Section 9.2.

In order to allow for sufficient generality, we must permit $\mathcal{V}$'s codesignation constraints to depend on $\mathcal{U}$'s configuration $\overline{\alpha}$. That is, the s.a. set $D_{\mathcal{V}\mathcal{U}}(\overline{\alpha})$ is an s.a. function of $\overline{\alpha}$. Recall that $(\mathcal{U}, \overline{\alpha})$ denotes the sensor system $\mathcal{U}$ installed at configuration $\overline{\alpha}$. Now, given that sensor system $\mathcal{U}$ is at configuration $\overline{\alpha}$, we are interested in whether or not sensor system $\mathcal{V}$ can simulate $(\mathcal{U}, \overline{\alpha})$, but *only when* $\mathcal{V}$'s configuration $\overline{\beta^*}$ satisfies some constraint $D_{\mathcal{V}\mathcal{U}}(\overline{\alpha})$ that *depends* on $\overline{\alpha}$. That is we are interested in the question:

"Does $(\mathcal{V}, \overline{\beta^*})$ simulate $(\mathcal{U}, \overline{\alpha})$, given that $\overline{\beta^*}$ lies in $D_{\mathcal{V}\mathcal{U}}(\overline{\alpha})$?" [63]

For example, consider the reduction in Proposition 6.6. Here $\overline{\alpha}$ specifies (among other things) the ship's configuration (x, h) in the radial sensor E. We think of (x, h) as one "coordinate" of $\overline{\alpha}$. The parametric codesignation constraint $D_H(\overline{\alpha})$ is used to ensure that the corresponding ship in the lighthouse sensor H is also placed at (x, h). The question "Can H simulate E?" only makes sense given that (i) H and E are both installed at G and (ii) the ships in H and E are in the same configuration. Static codesignation constraints (that are invariant with $\overline{\alpha}$) ensure (i), whereas parametric codesignation

---

[63] In particular, we do not care what happens when $\overline{\beta^*} \notin D_{\mathcal{V}\mathcal{U}}(\overline{\alpha})$.

constraints (that vary with $\overline{\alpha}$) ensure (ii). This could be implemented as follows: let $\pi_{E,x}$ (resp. $\pi_{H,x}$) be the projection of E's (resp. H's) configuration that returns the ship's configuration. So, in particular, $\pi_{E,x}(\overline{\alpha}) = (x, h)$. These projections are clearly semi-algebraic functions. Then (this aspect of) the parametric codesignation constraint D_H could be implemented as

$$\beta \in D_H(\overline{\alpha}) \iff \left(\pi_{H,x}(\beta) = \pi_{E,x}(\overline{\alpha})\right). \tag{A.6}$$

The fact that we have an equality constraint ($=$) in Eq. (A.6) reflects the fact that E and H are *simple* sensor systems (Definition 8.17). In general (for arbitrary algebraic sensors systems), D_H could specify a more complicated s.a. relation between $\overline{\alpha}$ and β.

Formally, parametric codesignation constraints as D_H (A.6) and $D_{\mathcal{VU}}$ (see Eq. (34)) can be modeled as *parametric s.a. sets* (see [6]):

Definition A.4 (*Canny*). A *parametrically-defined semi-algebraic set* $D(\alpha)$ is defined as follows. $D(\alpha)$ is an s.a. set which is a function of some argument α. Hence there is an implicitly defined s.a. predicate $\mathbb{T}_D(z, \alpha)$ which is true iff $z \in D(\alpha)$. Now, let Y be an s.a. set with predicate $\mathbb{T}_Y$. So, when we write $D(\alpha) \subset Y$ we mean $\forall z \; \mathbb{T}_D(z, \alpha) \Rightarrow \mathbb{T}_Y(z)$, which gives us an s.a. predicate $\Phi_D(\alpha)$ which is true of those values of α such that $D(\alpha) \subset Y$.

A.4. Application: universal reductions

We can now use the tools from Sections A.2–A.3 to develop an algorithm for "universal reduction" (application 4 of Section 1.1). Universal reduction requires graph permutation (see Appendix A.2.1).

Let $\mathcal{U}$ and $\mathcal{V}$ be sensor systems. Suppose we are given a specification for $\mathcal{U}$, and a "bag of parts" for $\mathcal{V}$. The specification, as usual, is encoded as a simulation function $\Omega_{\mathcal{U}}$ as described in Section 8.1. We are also given a simulation function $\Omega_{\mathcal{V}}$ for $\mathcal{V}$. The bag of parts consists of boxes and wires. Each box is a sensori-computational component ("block box") that computes a function of (a) its spatial location or pose and (b) its inputs. The "wires" have different bandwidths, and they can hook the boxes together. Recall we are given a simulation function Ω_v for each component $\ell(v)$ and a simulation function Ω_e for each edge e (indeed, this is how the global simulation functions $\Omega_{\mathcal{U}}$ and $\Omega_{\mathcal{V}}$ are encoded; see Section 8.1). Then, our algorithms (above) decide, can we immerse the components of $\mathcal{V}$ so as to satisfy the specification of $\mathcal{U}$? The algorithms also give the immersion (that is, how the boxes should be placed in the world, and how they should be wired together). Hence, we can ask, can the specification of $\mathcal{U}$ be implemented using the bag of parts $\mathcal{V}$?

Now, suppose that in addition to the specification for $\mathcal{U}$, we are given an encoding of $\mathcal{U}$ as a bag of parts, and an immersion to implement that specification. Suppose further that $\mathcal{U} \leqslant_1 \mathcal{V}$. Since this reduction is relativized both to $\mathcal{U}$ and to $\mathcal{V}$, it measures the "power" of the components of $\mathcal{U}$ relative to the components in $\mathcal{V}$. By universally quantifying over the configuration of $\mathcal{U}$, we can ask, "can the components of $\mathcal{V}$ always do the job of the components of $\mathcal{U}$?"

More specifically: let α be a configuration of the sensori-computational system $\mathcal{U}$. Let $\mathcal{U}^\star = (\mathcal{U}, \alpha^\star)$ be a graph permutation of $(\mathcal{U}, \alpha)$ (Section A.2.1). Let $\Sigma^\star(\alpha)$ denote the set of all graph permutations of α, so, if $\mathcal{U}$ has d vertices, then $\Sigma^\star(\alpha) = \Sigma(\alpha) \times \mathbb{O}(\mathbb{Z}_2, d^2)$. Thus $\alpha^\star \in \Sigma^\star(\alpha)$, and $\alpha^\star$ encodes the spatial immersion of $\mathcal{U}$ as well as its wiring connectivity. By Sections 8.9.2 and A.2.1, $\Sigma^\star(\alpha)$ is s.a.

Similarly, let β be a configuration of $\mathcal{V}$. Hence, we can decide the Tarski sentence

$$\big(\forall \alpha^\star \in \Sigma^\star(\alpha), \; \exists \beta^\star \in D_{\mathcal{V}\mathcal{U}}(\alpha^\star) \cap \Sigma^\star(\beta)\big) : \; (\mathcal{U}, \alpha^\star) \leqslant_1 (\mathcal{V}, \beta^\star), \tag{A.7}$$

where $D_{\mathcal{V}\mathcal{U}}(\cdot)$ is a parametric s.a. codesignation constraint (Section A.3). When Eq. (A.7) holds, we say that $\mathcal{U}$ *universally reduces to* $\mathcal{V}$, (or that there is a *universal reduction* from $\mathcal{U}$ to $\mathcal{V}$). Hence, is possible to compute universal reductions algebraically. With the notation and hypotheses as above throughout Appendix A, the time complexity of deciding (A.7) is given by Eq. (A.5), which becomes

$$(m\delta)^{O(r)^{4a-2}} = (n_\Omega + n_D)^{O(r_c d + d^4)^{14}}. \tag{A.8}$$

Eq. (A.8) is still $(n_\Omega + n_D)^{(r_c d)^{O(1)}}$. Hence we have that

Corollary A.5. *Universal reductions (Eq. (A.7)) can be computed in the same time bounds given in Eqs. (35)–(37).*

Appendix B. Relativized information complexity

Let us specialize Definition 6.4 to monotonic sensor systems:

Definition 6.4 (*Monotonic*). Consider two monotonic sensor systems S and Q, and let b be the output of sensor S. We say S is *efficiently reducible* to Q if

$$S \leqslant^* Q + \mathrm{COMM}(b). \tag{4}$$

In this case we write $S \leqslant_1 Q$.

For the sensors we have considered, their complexity could essentially be characterized using the size $\log \mathbb{K}(b)$ of the *output* b. We now generalize this definition slightly. Our motivation is as follows. There are sensor systems whose complexity cannot be well-characterized by the number of bits of output. [64] For example: consider a "grandmother" sensor. Such a sensor looks at a visual field and outputs one bit, returning #t if the visual field contains a grandmother and #f if it doesn't. Now, one view of the sensor interpretation problem is that of information reduction and identification (compare [14], which discusses hierarchies of sensor information). However, consider a somewhat different perspective, that views sensors as *model matchers*. So, imagine a computational process that calculates the probability $P(G \mid V)$ of G (grandmother) given V (the visual field)—i.e., the probability that G is in the data (the visual field itself). The sensor in

---

[64] This discussion devolves to a suggestion of Sundar Narasimhan [42], for which we are very grateful.

the former case is something specific only to detecting grandmothers, while the latter prefers to see a grandmother as the model that best explains the current data. The latter is a process that computes over model classes. For example, this sensor might output TIGER (when given a fuzzy picture that is best explained as a tiger).[65]

In short, one may view a sensor system as storing prior distributions. These distributions bias it toward a fixed set of model classes. In principle, the stored distributions may be viewed either as calibration or internal state. To quantify the absolute information complexity of a sensor system, we need to measure the information complexity of model classes stored in the prior distribution of the sensor. This could be very difficult.

Instead, we propose to measure a quantity called the *maximum bandwidth* of a sensor system. Intuitively, this quantity is the maximum over all internal and external edge bandwidths (data-paths). That is:

Definition 6.1 (*First part*). We define the *internal* (resp. *external*) *bandwidth* of a sensor system S to be the greatest bandwidth of any internal (resp. external) edge in S. The *output size* of S is given by Definition 5.2. We define the *maximum bandwidth* $mb(S)$ to be the greater of the internal bandwidth, external bandwidth, and the output size of S.

The maximum bandwidth is an upper bound on the relative intrinsic output complexity (relativized to the information complexity of the components (Sections 8 and 12)). We explore this notion briefly below.

Maximum bandwidth is a measure of internal information complexity. The bandwidth is a measure of information complexity only *relative* to the sensori-computational components of the system. For example, imagine that we had a sensor system with a single component that outputs one bit when it recognizes a complicated model (say, a grandmother). The only data-path in the system has bandwidth one bit, because the single component in the system is very powerful. So, even though the maximum bandwidth is small, the absolute information complexity may be large.

So, some sensors are black boxes. We call a sensor system a *black box* if it is encoded as a single component. The only measure of bandwidth we have for a black box is its output size. For example, Erdmann's radial sensor E (Section 4.1) is essentially a black box plus output communication.

More generally, we call a sensor system *monotonic* if its internal and external bandwidths are bounded above by its output size. So, black box sensors are trivially monotonic. All the sensor systems in this paper are monotonic. But some of the systems in our forthcoming work [17] are not.

In light of this discussion, we now give a generalized definition of the reduction $\leqslant_1$, using relativized information complexity.

First, let S be a monotonic sensor system with output b as in Definition 6.4. In this case, we define COMM(S) to be COMM(b).

---

[65] Now one may ask why prefer one model over another and there can be many answers. [42] advocates *Minimum Description Length*, or *MDL*. This theory attempts to minimize $L(M) + L(D \mid M)$ where $L(M)$ is the length of model and $L(D \mid M)$ is the length of the data given that the model is minimal.

More generally, for (possibly) nonmonotonic sensors, we will let COMM(S) be COMM(2^k) where k is the *relative intrinsic output complexity* of S. Measuring this (k) in general is difficult, but we will treat the *maximum bandwidth* (Definition 6.1) of S as an upper bound on k. Finally, we generalize Definition 6.4 to nonmonotonic sensor systems as follows:

Definition 6.4 (*Generalized*). Consider two sensor systems S and Q. We say S is *efficiently reducible* to Q if

$$S \leqslant^* Q + \text{COMM}(S). \tag{B.1}$$

In this case we write $S \leqslant_1 Q$.

Appendix C. Distributive properties

In this appendix, we prove some technical properties about the permutation of partial immersions. These properties are algebraic, and we call them the "*distributive* properties". First, we consider "pure" permutation and combination (i.e., without output vertices, as in Definition 8.12). Then, in Sections C.1–C.2 we generalize to include permutation and combination of output vertices. Recall the definition of *compatibility* for partial immersions (Section 8.4).

Definition C.1. Let ϕ and ψ be compatible partial immersions. We say the permutations ϕ^* and ψ^* are *compatible permutations of ϕ and ψ*, if ϕ^* and ψ^* are also compatible.

We would like to show that for immersions, combination and permutation commute. That is: for two compatible partial immersions ϕ and ψ, if ϕ^* and ψ^* are compatible permutations, then

$$\phi^* + \psi^* = (\phi + \psi)^*?$$

In answer, we can now show the following:

Claim C.2. *Consider two compatible partial immersions ϕ and ψ, together with two compatible permutations ϕ^* and ψ^*. Then*
  (1) $\phi^* + \psi^* \in \Sigma(\phi + \psi)$.
  (2) *Let $\gamma^* \in \Sigma(\phi + \psi)$. Then there exists $\phi^* \in \Sigma(\phi)$, $\psi^* \in \Sigma(\psi)$, such that $\gamma^* = \phi^* + \psi^*$.*

Proof. (2) First, let γ^* be a permutation of $\phi + \psi$. Let $\phi^* = \gamma^*|_{\phi^{-1}C}$ and $\psi^* = \gamma^*|_{\psi^{-1}C}$. Then ϕ^* is a permutation of ϕ and ψ^* is a permutation of ψ, and $\phi^* + \psi^* = \gamma^*$.

  (1) Conversely, suppose ϕ^* and ψ^* are compatible permutations of ϕ and ψ. Then we observe that since the domains of ϕ and ϕ^* (resp., ψ and ψ^*) are identical, therefore the domains of $\phi^* + \psi^*$ and $\phi + \psi$ are identical. Hence, $\phi^* + \psi^*$ is a permutation of $\phi + \psi$. $\square$

Next, we ask, for sensor systems, do combination and permutation commute? That is: for two sensor systems S and U, is it true that

$$S^* + U^* = (S + U)^*$$

whenever $+$ is defined (see Definition 8.12)?

In answer, we show the following:

Proposition C.3. *Consider two sensor systems S and U as above. Assume their immersions are compatible, so that $S + U$ is defined. Then,*
  (1) *Let S^* and U^* be compatible permutations of S and U. Then $S^* + U^*$ is a permutation of $S + U$.*
  (2) *Let $(S+U)^*$ be a permutation of $S+U$. Then there exist compatible permutations S^* and U^* of S and U resp. such that $S^* + U^* = (S + U)^*$.*

Proof. Let $S = (S, \phi)$, $U = (U, \psi)$, $S^* = (S, \phi^*)$ and $U^* = (U, \psi^*)$, and apply Claim C.2. □

C.1. Combination of output vertices

Recall the definition of *combination* in Section 8.5. There, we considered two sensor systems S and U. Both have output vertices, say, v_o and u_o resp. When we combine the two sensor systems S and U to form $S + U$, we must specify the unique output vertex of the new, combined sensor system. We now show how to choose output vertices in a consistent manner so that the combination operation $+$ remains associative and commutative.

First, we view each sensor system as a *pointed graph*—a graph with one distinguished vertex called the *output vertex*.[66] We define $+$ on two pointed graphs in such a manner as to produce a new pointed graph. For example let (G_1, u_1) be a pointed graph with output vertex u_1. Let (G_2, u_2) be another pointed graph. Then

$$(G_1, u_1) + (G_2, u_2) = (G_1 + G_2, u_1 + u_2),$$

where $G_1 + G_2$ denotes combination (Definition 8.12). The output vertex $u_1 + u_2$ is defined as follows: let $\mathbb{V}$ be the universe of all possible vertices. So, for any graph G_i with vertices and edges (V_i, E_i), we have $V_i \subset \mathbb{V}$. We insist that $\mathbb{V}$ have a total-order $\succ$. Define $u_1 + u_2 = \min_\succ (u_1, u_2)$.

It is easy to see that under this definition, the operation $+$ on pointed graphs is both associative and commutative.

C.2. Output permutation

Recall Definition 8.6. There, we also permitted a permutation to change which vertex has the "output device" label. This kind of permutation is not required for the *monotonic*

---

[66] We must be careful not to confuse a *pointed graph* with a *pointed sensor system* (Definition 8.8).

sensor systems (Appendix B) considered in this paper, but it is needed for the general theory, and it is used explicitly in [17]. We formalize this notion here.

We define an operation called *output permutation* on pointed graphs (Section C.1). The effect of this operation is to choose a new distinguished vertex. For example, for a graph G with distinguished point u_0, we could choose a new distinguished vertex u_1. We represent this operation by

$$(G, u_0) \mapsto (G, u_1).$$

We call (G, u_1) an *output permutation* of (G, u_0).

Now, following Appendix A.2.1, let us call our existing notion of permutation (Definition 8.6) by the name *vertex* permutation (to distinguish it from *output* permutation). It is possible to compose output permutations and vertex permutations. We adopt

Convention C.4. We use the term *permutation* to include both output permutations and vertex permutations. Similarly, we will use the operator * for any permutation.

This convention is necessary to make combination and permutation commute in general.

C.3. Discussion

In Appendices B and C, we have made sure that combination (the + operation) and permutation (the * operation) commute. So, for example, for any sensor system $\mathcal{S}$, have ensured that $\mathcal{S}^* + \text{COMM}(\cdot) = (\mathcal{S} + \text{COMM}(\cdot))^*$, i.e., we can do the permutation and combination in any order. Second we have ensured that the combination operation + is commutative and associative. Third, in Definition 6.2, for the reduction $\leqslant_1$ (see generalized Definition 6.4) we have given the single edge e in $\text{COMM}(\cdot)$ enough bandwidth so that it still works when we switch it (e) around using permutation. Hence, the sensor system $(Q + \text{COMM}(S))^*$ in Eq. (B.1) may be implemented as the sensor system Q permuted in an arbitrary way, plus one extra data-path whose bandwidth is that of the largest flow in S.

Appendix D. On alternate geometric models of information invariants

We have presented a geometric model of information invariants. I am grateful to John Canny and Jim Jennings for suggesting that I provide an "abstract" example of information invariants, using the language and concepts developed in [14]. The resulting model is somewhat different in flavor from that of Section 8.

Here is a alternate geometric model for an example of information invariance. Let $\mathcal{U}$ be an arrangement of perceptual equivalence classes, as in [14, 5.1]. A simple control strategy may be modeled as a subgraph of the RR-graph [16] on $\mathcal{U}$. Now consider the lattice of perceptual equivalence classes formed by fixing the task environment and varying the sensing map, as in [14, 5.2]. Let $\mathcal{U}$ and $\mathcal{V}$ be two arrangements of perceptual equivalence classes in the lattice. Then there is an information invariant for $\mathcal{U}$ and $\mathcal{V}$

when they have a common coarsening [67] $\mathcal{W}$, together with a control strategy on $\mathcal{W}$. Note that by construction, this control strategy agrees on the overlap of $\mathcal{U}$ and $\mathcal{V}$.

This example is simple; it remains to develop and exploit this geometric model for other kinds of information invariants.

Appendix E. A non-geometric formulation of information invariants

There are several places where we have exploited the geometric structure of robotics problems in constructing our framework. First, our sensors are geometrical (in that they measure geometric quantities). Second, the configuration of a sensor is geometrical, in that each component is physically placed and oriented in physical space.

It is of some interest to derive an "abstract" version of our framework in which geometry plays no role. [68] Such a framework would be something like a "logical" framework.

It is not hard to formulate our approach in a geometry-free manner. First one would say that the "value" or the "output" of a sensor is simply a value in some set. Next, one would replace the configuration space C of a component by any set of the form

$$C = \{z \mid z \text{ is a location}\}. \tag{E.1}$$

C can be taken to have no structure whatsoever. All the definitions, constructions, and proofs of Section 8 then go through *mutatis mutandis*: there is no geometry anywhere. In particular, our (formerly geometric) codesignation constraints now reduce to Chapman's (propositional) codesignation constraints [7].

It is now worth asking, *what are the implications for Section 9*? It is easy to extend the definition of a simulation function $\Omega_{\mathcal{U}}$ for a sensor system $\mathcal{U}$: one obtains a set map $\Omega_{\mathcal{U}} : C^d \to R$ where C is as in (E.1), and R is an arbitrary set. At this point we lose the algebraic properties we exploited to derive the algorithms of Section 9. Hence our algorithms do not obtain when we remove the geometric structure. In particular, we lose our main computational result, Lemma 9.10. It seems plausible, however, that other deductive mechanisms might be used, instead, to obtain similar results in the abstract (non-geometric) case.

Appendix F. Provable information invariants with performance measures

F.1. Kinodynamics and tradeoffs

It is possible to develop provable information invariants in the special case where we have performance measures. Consider once again the information invariants discussed above in Section 2.1. That these invariants (Eq. (1)) are related to kinodynamics [8, 19, 20] should come as no surprise, since the execution time for a control strategy is taken

---

[67] A *coarsening* of $\mathcal{U}$ and $\mathcal{V}$ is a partition $\mathcal{W}$ such that both $\mathcal{U}$ and $\mathcal{V}$ are finer than $\mathcal{W}$.

[68] I am grateful to Stan Rosenschein for encouraging me to develop this generalization.

as "cost". In [49], Pat Xavier introduced a new algorithmic mechanism for measuring kinodynamic tradeoffs (see [21] for a brief description). These techniques were used to quantify the tradeoffs between planning complexity, executor complexity, and "safety" (clearance). Essentially, Xavier considers how closely (ε_T) one can approximate an optimal-time trajectory and how much "safety" ε_S—in the sense of headway—is required to execute the approximate solution with an uncertain control system. Xavier obtained "equicomplexity" curves in the ε_T-ε_S plane. These curves may be interpreted as follows. For a fixed "complexity" r (which may be equivalently viewed as (i) the running time of the planner, (ii) the space requirements of the planner, or (iii) the discretization density of the phase space for the dynamical system representing the robot), Xavier's planner obtains a kinodynamic solution which satisfies a one-parameter family of approximations of the form

$$\varepsilon_T = f_r(\varepsilon_S),\tag{F.1}$$

where f_r is a function conditioned on complexity r. Hence (F.1) represents an information invariant as well, and, if we view the "following distance" d as being similar to the clearance parameter ε_S, such kinodynamic methods appear attractive. We believe that these methods could be used to prove information invariants like (1); while they require specific assumptions about the dynamics and geometry, they are quite general in principle. Pursuing such theorems is a fruitful line of future research.

Kinodynamic tradeoffs are one source of information invariants, and one may even find provable, rigorous characterizations for information questions therein (e.g., [21, 49]). However, there is something a bit dissatisfying about this line of attack. First, it makes controls, not sensing, the senior partner, much in the same way that in the theory of Lozano-Pérez et al. [38] (see [11]), recognizability is a second-class citizen compared with reachability. In [38], this is a consequence of a bias towards sensorless manipulation [26]; in kinodynamics, it is a consequence of model-based control. Second, kinodynamics relies on a measure of cost (in this case, time), and hence the results emphasize performance, not competence.

Glossary of symbols [69]

		Section/ Appendix	Page	Definition	Figure (equation)
$\mathbb{R}$	real numbers	2.1.2	222		
S^1	unit circle	2.1.2	222		
p, p'	trajectories	2.1.2	222		
$S \cong Q$	Q simulates S	4.1	233,244,251	4.1	(3),(6)
$+$	combination of sensor systems	8.10	253,244	8.10	(3)
E	the radial sensor	4.1	234		5
G	the goal configuration	4.1	234		5

---

[69] For some symbols, the first page reference points to the beginning of the (sub)section explaining or containing that symbol.

		Section/Appendix	Page	Definition	Figure (equation)
R	ship	4.1	234		5
x, $\underline{x}$	ship's position	4.1	234		5
h	ship's heading	4.1	234		5
θ_r	angle between h and the goal direction	4.1	234		5
N	direction of North	4.2.1	235,236		6
H	the lighthouse (beacon) sensor	4.2.1	235,236		6
L	lighthouse	4.2.1	235,236		6
θ	R's bearing from L	4.2.1	235,236		6
$\boxed{g}$	rotating green light	4.2.1	235,236		6
$\boxed{w}$	flashing white light	4.2.1	235,236		6
(white?)	1-bit white light sensor	4.2.1	235,236		6
(green?)	1-bit green light sensor	4.2.1	235,236		6
(time)	clock	4.2.1	235,236		6
(orientation)	orientation sensor	4.2.1	235,236		6
h_R	generalized compass (installed on R)	5.2.1	239		7
p^*	sensed position	5.2.1	239		
COMM($\cdot$)	communication primitive	5.2.1	239		
COMM($L \rightarrow R$, info)	communicate info from L to R	5.2.1	239		
COMM(θ_r)	datapath labeled θ_r	5.2.1, 8.7.2	239, 256,244		(3)
$S, Q, \ldots$	sensor systems	5.2.1	239		
b	output of a sensor S	5.4.1, 8.1	244, 247,245	5.2, 8.3, 6.4	(4)
$\mathbb{K}(b)$	number of values b can take on	5.4.1, 6	244, 245	5.2	
mb(S)	maximum bandwidth of S	6, B	245, 294ff	6.1	
COMM(b)	datapath with bandwidth $\log \mathbb{K}(b)$	8.7.2	256,245,268	6.4	(4),(4$'$)
COMM(S)	datapath with bandwidth mb(S)	B	294,296		(B.1)
E_G	radial sensor installed at G	5.3.1	242,251,244	8.8	(3)
H_G	lighthouse sensor installed at G	5.3.1	242,244,251	8.8	(3)
*	(vertex) permutation	5.3.1	242,250,244	8.6	(3)
H^*	permutation of H	3	244		(3)
H_G^*	permutation of H_G	3	244		(3)
$\leqslant$	simulation and domination	6.2	245,265	6.2	(24)–(28)
$\leqslant^*, \leqslant_0$	0-wire reduction	6.3	245,264,268	6.3	(4), (4$'$)
$\leqslant_1$	1-wire ("efficient") reduction	6.4	245	6.4	
$\leqslant_k$	k-wire reduction	8.10.3	267		
$\leqslant_\infty$	reduction using global communication	8.10.4	270ff	8.27	
$\leqslant_{\mathcal{P}}$	reduction using polynomial communication	8.10.4	270ff	8.29	
$\mathcal{G} = (V, E)$	a graph with vertices V and edges E	8.1	247	8.1	
d	number of vertices in V	9.2	274,274		(35)
$\mathcal{S}, \mathcal{U}, \mathcal{V}, \mathcal{W}, \ldots$	sensor systems	8.2	247,267,268	8.2	9, 10
$\phi, \psi, \ldots$	immersions	8.1	247,250	8.4	
ℓ	labelling function	8.1	247,250	8.4	
C	configuration space	8.1	247		
$(\mathcal{S}, \phi)$	situated sensor system	8.1	247,250	8.6	
ϕ^*	permutation of an immersion	8.1	247,250	8.6	
$\mathcal{S}^*, (\mathcal{S}, \phi^*)$	permutation of a sensor system	8.1	247,250	8.6	
(ϕ, G)	pointed immersion	8.7	251	8.7	
$\mathcal{S}_G$	pointed sensor system	8.7	251	8.7	
$\mathcal{S}_G^*$	pointed permutation	8.7	251	8.7	

		Section/ Appendix	Page	Definition	Figure (equation)
$\overline{\phi}$	extension of a partial immersion	8.3	252		
$\overline{\phi^*}$	extension of a permutation	9.1	271		
u_o, v_o	output vertex	8.5	253		
Δ, Δ_{ij}	diagonal	8.8, 10	259, 275		(14),(38)
$\Phi, \mathbb{T} \ldots$	s.a. predicate	9.1, A	271, 286,287		(A.3)
$\mathrm{ex}\,\phi$	extensions of ϕ	8.9.2	261,263		(20)
$\Sigma(\phi)$	(vertex) permutations of ϕ	8.9.2	261,263		(20)
$\Sigma^\star(\phi)$	graph permutations of ϕ	A.4	293		(A.7)
$\mathrm{im}\,\phi$	image of ϕ	8.9.2	261,264		(22)
$\Omega_{\mathcal{U}}$	simulation function	9.1	271,247,274	9.2	(34)
$\diamondsuit$	quantifier	9.1	271,287		(A.3)
$D_{\mathcal{U}}, D_{\mathcal{V}}, D_{\mathcal{VU}}, \ldots$	s.a. codesignation constraints	9.2	274,274		(34)
r_c	dimension of C	9.2	274,274		(35)
δ	degree bound	9.2	274,274		(35)
n_Ω	simulation complexity	9.2	274,274	9.8	(35)
n_D	s.a. codesignation complexity	9.2	274,274	9.8	(35)
σ	edge permutation	A.2.1	289		
$\mathcal{U}^\star, (\mathcal{U}, \phi^\star)$	graph permutation of $\mathcal{U}, (\mathcal{U}, \phi)$	A.2.1	289		
$\mathbb{O}(A, d)$	group of orthogonal matrices	A.2.1	289		
cl	clone function	A.2.1	289,291	A.2	

References

[1] M. Blum and D. Kozen On the power of the compass (or, why mazes are easier to search than graphs), in: *Proceedings 19th Symposium on Foundations of Computer Science*, Ann Arbor, MI (1978) 132–142.

[2] M. Ben-Or, D. Kozen and J. Reif, The complexity of elementary algebra and geometry, *J. Comp. Syst. Sci.* **32** (1986) 251–264.

[3] M. Blum and W. Sakoda On the capability of finite automata in 2 and 3 dimensional space, in: *Proceedings 17th Symposium on Foundations of Computer Science* (1977) 147–161.

[4] A. Briggs, An efficient algorithm for one-step compliant motion planning with uncertainty, *Algorithmica* **8** (2) (1992) 195–208.

[5] R.G. Brown, Forthcoming Ph.D. Thesis, Computer Science Department, Cornell University, Ithaca, NY, USA.

[6] J. Canny, On computability of fine motion plans, in: *IEEE International Conference on Robotics and Automation*, Scottsdale, AZ (1989).

[7] D. Chapman, Planning for conjunctive goals, *Artif. Intell.* **32** (3) (1987) 333–378.

[8] J. Canny, B. Donald, J. Reif and P. Xavier, On the complexity of kinodynamic planning, in: *29th Symposium on the Foundations of Computer Science*, White Plains, NY (1988) 306–316.

[9] J. Canny and J. Reif, New lower bound techniques for robot motion planning problems, *28th Annual IEEE Symposium on Foundations in Computer Science*, Los Angeles, CA (1987).

[10] D. Cox, J. Little and D. O'Shea, *Ideals, Varieties, and Algorithms*, Undergraduate Texts in Mathematics (Springer-Verlag, New York, 1991).

[11] B.R. Donald, Robot motion planning, *IEEE Trans. Rob. Autom.* **8** (2) (1992).

[12] B.R. Donald, The complexity of planar compliant motion planning with uncertainty, *Algorithmica* **5** (3) (1990) 353–382.

[13] B.R. Donald, *Error detection and recovery in robotics*, Lecture Notes in Computer Science **336** (Springer-Verlag, New York, 1989).

[14] B.R. Donald and J. Jennings, Constructive recognizability for task-directed robot programming, *J. Rob. Autonom. Syst.* **(9)** (1) (1992) 41–74.

[15] B.R. Donald and J. Jennings, Constructive recognizability for task-directed robot programming, in: *Proceedings IEEE International Conference on Robotics and Automation*, Nice, France (1992).

[16] B.R. Donald and J. Jennings, Sensor interpretation and task-directed planning using perceptual equivalence classes, in: *Proceedings IEEE International Conference on Robotics and Automation*, Sacramento, CA (1991).

[17] B.R. Donald, J. Jennings and D. Rus, Information invariants for distributed manipulation, in: R. Wilson and J.-C. Latombe, eds., *The First Workshop on the Algorithmic Foundations of Robotics* (A.K. Peters, Boston, MA, 1994). A revised version of: B.R. Donald, J. Jennings and D. Rus, Towards a theory of information invariants for cooperating autonomous mobile robots, in: *International Symposium on Robotics Research (ISSR)*, Hidden Valley, PA (1993).

[18] B.R. Donald, D. Kapur and J. Mundy, *Symbolic and Numerical Computation for Artificial Intelligence* (Academic Press, London, 1992).

[19] B.R. Donald and P. Xavier, A provably good approximation algorithm for optimal-time trajectory planning, in: *Proceedings IEEE International Conference on Robotics and Automation*, Scottsdale, AZ (1989).

[20] B.R. Donald and P. Xavier, Provably good approximation algorithms for optimal kinodynamic planning for cartesian robots and open chain manipulators, in: *Proceedings 6th ACM Symposium on Computational Geometry*, (Berkeley, CA 1990).

[21] B.R. Donald and P. Xavier, Time-safety trade-offs and a bang-bang algorithm for kinodynamic planning in: *Proceedings IEEE International Conference on Robotics and Automation*, Sacramento, CA (1991).

[22] M. Erdmann, Personal Communication (1992).

[23] M. Erdmann, Using backprojections for fine motion planning with uncertainty, *Int. J. Rob. Res.* **5** (1) (1986).

[24] M. Erdmann, On probabilistic strategies for robot tasks, Ph.D. Thesis, MIT-AI-TR 1155, Department of EECS, MIT AI Lab, Cambridge, MA (1989).

[25] M. Erdmann, Towards task-level planning: action-based sensor design, Tech. Report, CMU-CS-92-116, Carnegie-Mellon School of Computer Science, Pittsburgh, PA (1991).

[26] M. Erdmann and M. Mason, An exploration of sensorless manipulation, in: *IEEE International Conference on Robotics and Automation*, San Francisco, CA (1986).

[27] M. Fischer, N. Lynch and M. Merritt, Easy impossibility proofs for distributed concensus problems, *Distrib. Comput.* **1** (1986) 26–39.

[28] P.C. Fischer, Turing machines with restricted memory access, *Inf. Control* **9** (4) (1966) 364–379.

[29] D.Y. Grigoryev, Complexity of deciding Tarski algebra, *J. Symb. Comput.* **5** (1) (1988) 65–108.

[30] J.E. Hopcroft, J.T. Schwartz and M. Sharir, On the complexity of motion planning for multiple independent objects; *PSPACE*-hardness of the "Warehouseman's Problem", *Int. J. Rob. Res.* **3** (4) (1984) 76–88.

[31] J.E. Hopcroft and J. Ullman *Introduction to Automata Theory, Languages, and Computation* (Addison-Wesley, Reading, MA, 1979).

[32] I. Horswill, Analysis of adaptation and environment, *Artif. Intell.* **73** (1995) (to appear).

[33] J. Jennings and D. Rus, Active model acquisition for near-sensorless manipulation with mobile robots, in: *International Association of Science and Technology for Development (IASTED) International Conference on Robotics and Manufacturing*, Oxford, England (1993).

[34] J. Jennings, Sensor interpretation and task-directed planning for autonomous agents, Ph.D. Thesis, Computer Science Department, Cornell University, Ithaca, NY (1994)

[35] D. Kozen, Automata and planar graphs, fundamentals of computing theory, in: L. Budach, ed., *Proceedings Conference on Algebraic, Arithmetic, and Categorical Methods in Computation Theory* (Akademie Verlag, Berlin, 1979).

[36] J.-C. Latombe, *Robot Motion Planning* (Kluwer, New York, 1991).

[37] T. Lozano–Pérez, Spatial planning: a configuration space approach, *IEEE Trans. Comput.* **32** (1983) 108–120.

[38] T. Lozano-Pérez, M.T. Mason and R.H. Taylor, Automatic synthesis of fine-motion strategies for robots, *Int. J. Rob. Res.* **3** (1) (1984).

[39] V.J. Lumelsky and A.A. Stepanov, Path-planning strategies for a point mobile automaton moving amidst unknown obstacles of arbitrary shape, *Algorithmica* **2** (1987) 403–430.

[40] M.T. Mason, Mechanics and planning of manipulator pushing operations, *Int. J. Rob. Res.* **5** (3) (1986).

[41] M. Minsky, Recursive unsolvability of Post's problem of 'Tag' and other topics in the theory of Turing machines, *Ann. of Math.* **74** (3) (1961) 437–455.

[42] S. Narasimhan, Personal Communication (1993).

[43] B.K. Natarajan, On planning assemblies, in: *Proceedings Fourth Annual Symposium on Computational Geometry*, Urbana, IL (1988) 299–308.

[44] J. Rees and B.R. Donald, Program mobile robots in scheme, in: *Proceedings IEEE International Conference on Robotics and Automation*, Nice, France (1992).

[45] J. Reif, Complexity of the mover's problem and generalizations, in: *Proceedings 20th Annual IEEE Symposium on Foundations of Computer Science* (1979); also in: J. Schwartz, J. Hopcroft and M. Sharir, eds., *Planning, Geometry and Complexity of Robot Motion* (Ablex, Norwood, NJ, 1987) Ch. 11, 267–281.

[46] S.J. Rosenschein, Synthesizing information-tracking automata from environment descriptions, Teleos Research, Tech. Report No. 2 (1989).

[47] D. Rus, Fine motion planning for dexterous manipulation, Ph.D. Thesis, Tech. Report CU-CS-TR 92-1323, Computer Science Department, Cornell University, Ithaca, NY (1992).

[48] A. Tarski, *A Decision Method for Elementary Algebra and Geometry* (University of California Press, Berkeley, CA, 2nd ed., 1951).

[49] P.G. Xavier, Provably-good approximation algorithms for optimal kinodynamic robot plans, Ph.D. Thesis, Tech. Report CU-CS-TR 92-1279, Computer Science Department, Cornell University, Ithaca, NY (1992)

Artificial Intelligence 72 (1995) 305–327

The stabilization of environments

Kristian J. Hammond[1], Timothy M. Converse*, Joshua W. Grass[2]

Department of Computer Science, University of Chicago, 1100 E. 58th Street, Chicago, IL 60637, USA

Received June 1992; revised October 1993

Abstract

In planning and activity research there are two common approaches to matching agents with environments. Either the agent is designed with a specific environment in mind, or it is provided with learning capabilities so that it can adapt to the environment it is placed in. In this paper we look at a third and underexploited alternative: designing agents which adapt their environments to suit themselves. We call this *stabilization*, and we present a taxonomy of types of stability that human beings typically both rely on and enforce. We also taxonomize the ways in which stabilization behaviors can be cued and learned. We illustrate these ideas with a program called FixPoint, which improves its performance over time by stabilizing its environment.

1. Introduction

The notion of "general purpose intelligence" is somewhat out of fashion these days. Early optimism in artificial intelligence has been tempered by the realization that the other face of generality is intractability. It is easy to find algorithms that solve general problems; the difficulty is to make problems specific enough that their solution is feasible. In AI models of activity, this injunction turns into a task of analysis; the question becomes "How is it possible to do the right thing in this domain?", and any answer that does not depend on the characteristics of that specific domain may well turn out be too general to work [3]. There is reason for skepticism even about assumptions of "domain-independent" intelligence in human beings; we may not be as general as we think we are (see [9]).

---

* Corresponding author. E-mail: converse@cs.uchicago.edu.

[1] This work was supported in part by DARPA contract number F49620-88-C-0058. E-mail: hammond@cs.uchicago.edu.

[2] E-mail: grass@cs.uchicago.edu.

This special volume of the journal *Artificial Intelligence* calls, among other things, for analyses that take into account how agents are fitted to their environments, and for theories that use such accounts to explain the success of agents, or that help in agent design. Our contribution here is to make an argument for a simple idea: that one way to ensure a good fit between agent and environment is to have the agent change the environment to suit itself. We call this kind of activity *stabilization*.[3]

1.1. Stabilization

We argue that, for an agent to interact successfully with a complex environment, one or more of the following things must be true:

- Either the agent or the environment, or both, must be designed with the other in mind (the "design" of the agent can be either evolutionary or intentional). In this case, agent and environment are well-matched from the start.
- The agent is able to learn to adapt to the particulars of its environment. In this case, through interaction, the agent comes to be better fitted to its environment over time.
- The agent is able to stabilize its environment to make it more hospitable. In this case, due to the action of the agent, the environment comes to be better fitted to the agent as time goes on.

Of course, *all* of the above may be true, and play a role in determining the success of the agent. Take the case of someone moving into a newly rented apartment, and the subsequent changes that occur in both the person and the apartment. The person (wonderfully designed, of course) occupies a new space, which (due to conventions about how buildings are constructed, as well as the particular skill of architects) is designed to make life easy in many ways for such a person. What follows is a process of mutual fitting. The person does quite a bit of learning about the particular space (becomes familiar with the floor plan, location of cabinets, electrical outlets, quirks of the plumbing, and so on). The new tenant also effects considerable change in the apartment (moving and arranging furniture, stocking the refrigerator, deciding where particular objects should be stored, and so on). As a result of *both* of these processes, the person develops a set of routines for interacting with the apartment, and is more effective and more comfortable than on the day of the move.

We use the term "stabilization" for this kind of organizing of the environment, and here is a more specific example of what we mean by it: Most people keep clean drinking glasses in some particular cabinet of their home, and when they want to drink something, they simply use one of them. This means that, at the time of deciding to have a drink of water, they need to do neither a lot of inference about whether they possess a suitable glass, nor a lot of physical search for a glass that meets their needs. The location of clean glasses is *stabilized*. Of course, this only happens due to the good efforts of someone in ensuring that glasses that are used are (at some point or other) cleaned and replaced in the cabinet.

---

[3] We use the term *stabilization* and *enforcement* (found in earlier papers) interchangeably here; the latter term more precisely captures the idea, but the former sounds less hostile.

In this paper we focus on this sort of stabilization, first of all because it has been neglected (in comparison with learning and more straightforward considerations in agent design), secondly because we believe that the notion can play a central role in understanding the successes of habitual human behavior, and, finally, because it seems like an unexploited research area in the analysis and design of agents that have a long-term interaction with their environments.

For the rest of the paper, we explore the idea of stabilization, and its use in the design of agents and in the analysis of agent–environment interaction. Finally we describe FIXPOINT, a program that implements some of these ideas, and some performance improvement results due to the stabilization of FIXPOINT's environment.

1.2. Models of long-term activity in AI

This paper is an entry in a long-standing debate in AI on appropriate methods for the construction of intelligent agents. Our central concern in this paper is with agents that have a long-term interaction with their environment. In the next two subsections we look very briefly at both classical and situated models, and explain why some concerns we have are addressed in neither tradition.[4] Then we will quickly present our "theory of agency", and explain how questions of stabilization fit into it. The rest of the paper will address stabilization itself.

1.2.1. Classical planning

Research on plan construction in AI can be viewed either as having produced a particular set of techniques for a well-defined computational problem, or as an *approach* that (in addition to the techniques) proposes a theory of action in which intelligent activity is seen as the result of plan construction and execution [2]. Either way, a consensus has arisen in AI that classical techniques for plan construction do not provide a complete and satisfying story about the generation of intelligent action.

There are a number of sources of this discontent: planning's formal intractability, the reliance on complete world descriptions, reliance on complete action models, and the questionable utility of plans produced when the restrictive assumptions are violated.

To this list, we would like to add one more: planning's view of activity is essentially *one-shot*. That is, classical planning techniques produce a plan to satisfy a given goal set, given a particular situation. There is no place for time-extended interaction [1] with an environment: presumably either a planner plans for the whole of time in advance, or is invoked at appropriate times to deal with particular goal sets. The former alternative multiplies the intractability of planning, while the latter requires, at the minimum, a theory of when to invoke the planner. Research on execution monitoring and interleaving of planning and execution can be seen as an attempt to develop such a theory; still, the original technology of this sort of planning was developed for one-shot goal achievement,

---

[4] These overviews will be so brief as to be caricatures; we apologize, but feel that these two extreme views have framed the debate on these issues to such an extent that we have to identify to the reader where we fit in the landscape defined by them.

and it remains to be seen whether it is appropriate for embedding in a longer-term context.

There is one line of planning research that is not "one-shot" in this sense: work on planning and learning (cf. the various learning attachments to the PRODIGY planning system [11]) This research concerns itself with planners that improve over time; nonetheless, the sense of performance improvement that is relevant is defined in terms of single tasks, rather than in interaction with an environment over time.

1.2.2. Situated action models

Discontents with planning models have led to an enormous variety of research in recent years—in this section we will focus on "situated action" models [1,4], and leave connections with closely related work to the reader.

This line of work stresses the *interaction* of agents and their environments, and their mutual dependence. It argues that design of an all-purpose agent is not feasible, and that it is incumbent on the designer of an agent to characterize the *dynamics* of an interaction (i.e. patterns of interaction that depend on both agent and environment, without being fully represented in either), and make use of that characterization in design. Chapman and Agre, along with championing this sort of analysis of agent–environment interactions, argue for a methodology of "machinery parsimony" (that is, a preference for the least complicated mechanisms in the agent that will explain an interaction). As illustrations of their theories of activity (and demonstration of sufficiency of simple mechanisms), they wrote programs that play videogames. In these programs, the minimal mapping between perception and action leads to the minimal proposal for a central system: a combinational logic circuit. As the central system diminishes, the peripheral systems grow in complexity. In his work on *Sonja*, for example, Chapman presents a sophisticated implementation of task-directed intermediate vision.

Our central difficulty with the models implied by the programs is that they are *steady-state*. That is, while they do provide an account of long-term interaction with an environment, they do not provide an account of how the interaction can arise (other than by careful characterization and resultant design work). It is difficult (for us, anyway), to see a place for learning in a combinational logic central system. (The only sort of learning that we are aware of that has actually been used with one of these systems is reinforcement learning; we believe that the same combinatoric problems that have dogged classical planning are likely to surface here.)

Of course, these programs were in part just sufficiency demonstrations to begin with— much of Agre's thesis has to do with analyses of how particular agent–environment interactions might arise [1], and our style of analysis here draws heavily from his. Whether our paper should be considered "situated action" research should probably depend on whether the reader will identify that term with programs or theories.

1.2.3. Our view of agency

We would like to have a theory of agency that is neither "one-shot" nor "steady-state", in that the account should explain the agent's extended interaction with an environment, while also telling a story about how that interaction can change and improve over time.

We come at this from a background in case-based planning [5], where the cost of synthetic planning is amortized by attempting to reuse prior plans as much as possible. In more recent work [6,7], we have come to see case-based planning as one part of a framework for the study of long-term agents.

In this framework, extended interaction with the environment consists of the use of a small set of plans[5] that cover the goals that typically arise, where the plans retrieved in response to environmental cues are incrementally debugged in response to failure, and are made as reliable as possible by stabilization of the environment.

Our main concern in this paper is the interaction of plan reuse and stabilization—how stabilization behaviors, external to episodes of using a particular plan, can impact the success of using the plan. To make this more concrete: imagine the "plan" to be knowledge of how to cook a particular dish, and the stabilization to be the set of behaviors that keeps the kitchen organized, cleaned, and stocked with the appropriate food and spices. Our interest is in how the plan use and the stabilization could be coordinated, particularly if the behaviors might be external to any particular episode of using the plan.

The most obvious thing to say about this is that there is clearly a tradeoff between the comprehensiveness of stabilization and the difficulties of plan reuse. For example, if a given plan achieves a given goal in a situation, the plan could obviously be reused later if the situation were *exactly* the same. If the later situation were the same in all respects relevant to the success of the plan, then (by definition) the plan could be reused as well. This will be true regardless of whether the similarity across the episodes is due to the natural stability of the world or due to the agent's efforts in stabilization. The more the "preconditions" of standard plans are stabilized, the less flexible and inventive the use of those plans will have to be.

2. Analysis versus design versus representation

There are several ways in which the concept of stabilization *might* be useful. First of all, it might be useful merely to help in understanding the dynamics that permit a particular agent to succeed in its environment. Secondly, such analysis might help in the *design* of an agent for a particular environment. Finally, such a designed agent might stabilize its environment because it happens to participate in the right dynamics, or (alternatively) because it explicitly represents and reasons about the types of stability it enforces.

As an example, consider an external view (say, by videotape) of a human in extended interaction with a kitchen. Take it as a fact about the kitchen that there is some limited number of drinking glasses, and that they cannot be used again without washing them. The behavior we observe is this: every so often the person goes to a

---

[5] We are torn between the desire not to use an ambiguous word like "plan", and the desire not to invent a new term when we don't mean anything really new by it. By "plan" we mean: the collection of knowledge used in pursuit of a particular (set of) goals, and that is used *only* in pursuit of those goals. This may or may not consist of a partially ordered set of "primitive actions"; we intend it usually to mean a sketchier representation used by a more flexible executive.

particular cabinet, takes out a glass, drinks from it, and puts it in the sink. At longer intervals, the person washes a number of glasses, dries them, and puts them back in the cabinet.

As a matter of analysis, we can notice that the washing-and-drying behavior supports the drinking behavior by replenishing the glasses (and that, in an odder sense, the reverse is true as well). Of course, we can only speculate on the *design* considerations that led to the behavior. Finally, does the person behave this way because of an explicit awareness that glass-washing supports glass use? Probably, but it is a subtle question, and one that might have a different answer if we wanted to design a robot to do the same task.

2.1. Analysis

We argue that the notion of stabilization is a powerful one, even just in explaining agent–environment interactions. In analyzing the role of stabilization in an interaction, several questions must be answered:
(1) What sorts of stability does the agent depend on?
(2) What sorts of stability are enforced by the agent?
(3) What does the agent *do* to perform the stabilization?
(4) How are the stabilizing behaviors organized and cued?
(5) How is the need for new kinds of stabilization recognized (if at all)?
For instance, in trying to account for what makes it possible to use clean drinking glasses at arbitrary times, the answers might be something like this:
(1) The agent depends on a wide array of types of stability including: the physics of the world, the fact that most household objects don't move unless someone moves them, and so on.
(2) Among other things, the agent enforces the fact that there is always at least one clean drinking glass in the cabinet.
(3) To ensure this, the agent periodically collects used glasses, washes them, dries them, and replaces them in the cabinet.
(4) The question of how the glass-washing behavior is organized and cued is by far the most interesting one here, and, in the case of a human being, is a question for psychologists and anthropologists rather than for us. We can, however, talk about some ways in which the behavior *might* be effectively cued:
   • Glasses could be washed immediately after use.
   • Glasses could be washed whenever a certain number of them collect in the sink.
   • All glasses could be washed every so often, say, once a day.
      These are only a few of the possibilities, and we will have more to say about this in a later section.
(5) Finally, there is the question of how the need for stabilization is recognized in the first place. This is somewhat beyond the scope of our example (which had to do with a successful "steady-state" pairing of behaviors), so we will postpone discussion of this until later in this section.

2.2. Design

Let us continue with the same example, but change our project from psychology to engineering; rather than speculating about how it is that people manage to get their dishes done, let's imagine that we have the task of designing a robot butler who must serve drinks in clean glasses at a moment's notice. How should our robot ensure that glasses are available when necessary?

Let's assume that the robot has the ability both to fill glasses and wash glasses—our concern will be with how those behaviors are linked. Of course, if the robot must always respond immediately to a request for a drink, then it is easy to see that there is the possibility of failure: all it would take would be simultaneous requests for more drinks than there were glasses in the household. As designers, we would want to ensure that, when possible, the robot did not rely on the assumption of clean glasses when none were clean, and also that the robot ensured that there were clean glasses when it was possible for it to do so.

The main source of possible failure here is that glass use will outstrip replenishment of glasses. In designing an agent to avoid that failure, there are a number of strategies to employ:

(1) Have the robot maintain an internal count of glasses used. When this count exceeds some threshold, insist that the robot collect and wash the glasses.

(2) Have the robot put used glasses into the sink, and scan the sink periodically. Whenever the number of glasses in the sink exceeds some threshold, insist that the robot wash the glasses.

(3) Assume some upper limit on the rate at which glasses are used, and insist that the robot wash glasses periodically (say, by using an internal timer).

(4) Have the robot wash glasses whenever it *notices* a dirty glass (whatever that would mean).

(5) Have the robot use glasses until they have all been used. Upon encountering a failure situation, where no clean glasses are available, have it wash all the glasses.

These suggestions vary along a number of dimensions: where information is carried (internally versus in the world), assumptions about future demands, assumptions about perceptual abilities, and the cost of occasional failure. The main point that we would like to make here is that there can be multiple ways to design an agent to enforce a single type of stability.

2.3. Representation

As we have seen, it is at least conceivable that an agent could be designed that
(1) enforced a certain kind of stability in the world,
(2) relied on that stability, and
(3) had no internal representation of either the stability or of its reliance on it.

For example, one might be able to design a robot that did three things: served drinks in glasses when asked, deposited used glasses in the sink, and washed glasses when enough glasses accumulated in the sink. Cleaning would be linked to use *only* via the external representation of glasses standing for themselves. Assuming that the robot were able to notice the accumulation of glasses, and that glass use did not vary unpredictably (as it might, say, during a party), then it is possible that this design strategy would be effective in the absence of any internal connection between use and cleaning.

Having said that, we have to say that we don't believe in that sort of strategy for the design of stabilizing agents, primarily because it requires too much precision from the designer. The *steady-state* behavior of our robot is plausible—relying on environmental cues to tell it when to wash glasses and when to use them. But it is a lot to ask of a designer to anticipate all of the dynamics that the designed agent might participate in, particularly if the design task includes ruling out unlikely sources of failure. If our robotic butler has no representation of the connection between washing glasses and their use, then what is it to do in the case when it runs out of glasses?

3. Types of stability and stabilizing behaviors

In our discussion of so far we have focused on a single example of stabilization. In this section we give a broader categorization of a number of types of stability and stabilizing behaviors that occur in daily life, and offer some intuitive arguments for their adaptiveness. At the end of the section, we discuss the problem of recognizing the need for a novel type of stabilization.

3.1. Types of stability

Here are some types of stability that people typically enforce. In addition to the common-sense examples, we offer reasons why it might be functional to perform this sort of stabilization.

3.1.1. Stability of location

The most common type of stability that arises in everyday activity relates to the location of commonly used objects. Our drinking glasses end up in the same place every time we do dishes. Our socks are always together in a single drawer. Everything has a place and we enforce everything ending up in its place.

Enforcing STABILITY OF LOCATION, then, serves to optimize a wide range of processing goals. First of all, the fact that an often used object or tool is in a set location reduces the need for any inference or projection concerning the effects of standard plans on the objects or the current locations of objects.[6] Second, it allows plans that rely on the object's locations to be run without explicit checks (e.g., no need to explicitly determine that the glasses are in the cupboard before opening it). Third, it removes the need at execution time for a literal search for the object.

---

[6] This strategy happens to be spatial, and provides stability for activity in the long term. See [8] (in the companion volume) for a more general treatment of use of the spatial world to support activity. Our concerns are similar, and to some extent the taxonomies are orthogonal.

3.1.2. Stability of schedule

Another common form of stability involves the construction of standard schedules that persist over time. Eating dinner at the same time every day or having preset meetings that remain stable over time are two examples of this sort of stability. The main advantage of this sort of stability is that it allows for very effective projection in that it provides fixed points that do not have to be reasoned about. In effect, the fixed nature of certain parts of an overall schedule reduces that size of the problem space that has to be searched.

A second advantage is that fixed schedules actually allow greater optimization of the plans that are run within the confines of the stable parts of the schedule. Features of a plan that are linked to time can be removed from consideration if the plan is itself fixed in time. For example, by going into work each day at 8:30, an agent might be able to make use of the traffic report that is on the radio at the half-hour. Because the schedule is stable, however, he doesn't actually have to reason about the times that the report is on the air to be assured of hearing it.

Finally, if the schedule is stabilized with regard to a pre-existing norm, (e.g., always have lunch at noon) coordination between agents is also facilitated.

Here we see an instance of a tradeoff between enforcement and planning flexibility. While an enforced schedule allows for optimization of search and execution for recurring goals, it often reduces the flexibility required to incorporate new goals into the preset agenda. As with any heuristic that reduces the combinatorics of a search space, there will be times when an optimal plan is not considered.

It is important to realize that the schedule enforced is optimized over the goals that actually do tend to recur. Thus, an agent who is enforcing this sort of stability is able to deal with regularly occurring events with far greater ease than when it is forced to deal with goals and plans outside of its normal agenda. This sort of tradeoff in which commonly occurring problems are easier to solve than less common ones seems to be an essential by-product of stabilizing an environment.

3.1.3. Stability of resource availability

Many standard plans have a consumable resource as a precondition. If the plans are intended to be used frequently, then availability of the resource cannot be assumed unless it is enforced. A good result of this sort of enforcement is when attempts to use a plan that depends on it will usually succeed. The ideal result is when enforcement is effective enough that the question of availability need not even be raised in connection with running the plan.

3.1.4. Stability of satisfaction

Another type of stability that an agent can enforce is that of the goals that he tends to satisfy in conjunction with each other. For example, people living in apartment buildings tend to check their mail on the way into their apartments. Likewise, many people will stop at a grocery store on the way home from work. In general, people develop habits that cluster goals together into compact plans, even if the goals are themselves unrelated. The reason that the plans are together is more a product of the conditions associated with running the plans than the goals themselves.

An important feature of this sort of stability is that the goals are recurring and that the plan associated with the conjunct is optimized with respect to them. Further, the goals themselves must be on loose cycles and robust with regard to over-satisfaction.

The advantage of this sort of STABILITY OF SATISFACTION is that an optimal plan can be used that is already tuned for the interactions between individual plan steps. Second, it can be run habitually, without regard to the actual presence of the goals themselves. As in the case of STABILITY OF LOCATION in which a plan can be run without explicit checks on the locations of objects, STABILITY OF SATISFACTION allows for the execution of plans aimed at satisfying particular goals, even when the goals are not explicitly checked.

A way to enforce this sort of stability is to associate the plan with a single cue—either a goal or a feature in the world—and begin execution of that plan whenever the cue arises. In this way, the habitual activity can be started even when all of the goals that it satisfies are not present.

3.1.5. Stability of plan use

We often find ourselves using familiar plans to satisfy goals even in the face of wide-ranging possibilities. For example, when one of us travels to conferences, he tends to schedule his flight in to a place as late as he can and plans to leave as late as he can on the last day. This optimizes his time at home and at the conference. It also allows him to plan without knowing anything about the details of the conference schedule. As a result, he has a standard plan that he can run in a wide range of situations without actually planning for them in any detail. It works, because it already deals with the major problems (missing classes at home and important talks at the conference) as part of its structure.

The major advantage here in enforcing the STABILITY OF PLAN USE is that the plan that is used is tuned to avoid the typical interactions that tend to come up. This means, of course, that the plans used in this way must either be the result of deep projection over the possible problems that can come up in a domain or be constructed incrementally. A further advantage is that little search through the space of possible plans for a set of goals needs to be done in that one plan is always selected.

3.1.6. Stability of cues

One effective technique for improving plan performance is to improve the proper activation of a plan rather than improve the plan itself. For example, placing an important paper that needs to be reviewed on his desk before going home improves the likelihood that an agent will see and read it the next day. Marking calendars and leaving notes serves the same sort of purpose.

One important area of enforcement is related to this use of visible cue in the environment to activate goals that have been suspended in memory. The idea driving this type of enforcement is that an agent can decide on a particular cue that will be established and maintained so as to force the recall of commonly recurring goals. One example of this kind of enforcement of STABILITY OF CUES is leaving a briefcase by the door every night in order to remember to bring it into work. The cue itself remains constant over time. This means that the agent never has to make an effort to recall the goal at execution time and, because the cue is stabilized, it also never has to reason about what cue to use when the goal is initially suspended.

The advantage of this sort of enforcement is that an agent can depend on the external world to provide a stable cue to remind it of goals that still have to be achieved. This sort of stability is suggested when an agent is faced with repeated failures to recall a goal and the plan associated with the goal is tied to particular objects or tools in the world.

3.2. Types of enforcement

To some extent the question of which sorts of stability an agent can profit from is separate from the question of how to ensure that stability. We now categorize some methods of ensuring stability, which differ from each other partly in what actions are taken and partly in how and when those actions are cued.

3.2.1. One-time change

It is often possible to make a single change to the environment which will persist without further effort on the agent's part. If this is a desirable state that facilitates normal activity, it may be worthwhile to perform.

A good example of this is rearrangement of furniture, say, to remove a couch from a frequently-traveled path. Once the change has been made, it can be forgotten about, and taken as a normal fixed part of the environment. But at the same time, the world has been made more hospitable to the normal activity of the agent.

3.2.2. Policy

Another type of enforcement is what McDermott calls "policy" [10]. For example, everyone always carries money. This is because we always need it for a wide variety of specific plans.

Enforcement of POLICY requires the generation of specific goals to satisfy the policy state whenever it is violated. In terms of policies such as always having money on hand, this means that the lack of cash on hand will force the generation of a goal to have cash, even when no specific plan that will use that cash is present.

Many policies have to do with ensuring resource availability. Here again, the advantage is that plans can be run without explicit reference to many of the conditions that must obtain for them to be successful. An agent can actually assume conditions hold, because he has a POLICY that makes them hold.

3.2.3. Plan modification

Enforcement of POLICY requires detecting when the desired state is being infringed upon. Another strategy for enforcing similar types of stability is to modify all the plans that normally disturb the stable state to include its re-establishment. This strategy is only possible when the state can only be disturbed by the agent, and there is a small set of plans that are implicated.

For example, one of us typically carries a transit pass in his wallet. There is only a single plan that requires taking it out of the wallet. If that plan includes the step of putting it back, then stability of location is effectively enforced, and the assumption that it is "always true" can be made.

Whether policy or plan modification is preferable depends also on the costs and utilities of establishing the state. For example, one method for ensuring having cash might be to add a trip to an automatic teller to every plan that uses cash, thereby ensuring that it is always replenished. It so happens that the trip is costly and the violation is easy to detect, so a policy makes more sense in this case.

3.2.4. Clean-up plans

One difference between PLAN MODIFICATION and POLICY is how the actions that re-establish a desirable state are cued. The first associates the actions with detecting the violation, while the second associates them with use of the plans that disturb the state. Another alternative is to have explicit plans that look for a certain category of states that need to be re-established, and then to use the plans in response to reliable cues.

For example, most people keep their kitchens stocked with food by some mixture of noticing depletion (policy) and periodically doing more exhaustive checking for what needs to be replenished (a clean-up plan). Similarly, people often maintain stability of location in their living spaces by a mixture of "putting things back" when done with them, and "cleaning up". The fact that clean-up plans are often dissociated from the plans that violate desired states as well as from recognition of the violation means that there must be other cues that indicate when it is time to employ them. For example, it is common to have a standard routine for leaving a home or office, cued by the activity of leaving, that involves looking for various standard states that need to be re-established.

3.3. Detecting the need for stabilization

In this section we are concerned with the question of how novel stabilizing behavior might be evolved. This can be slightly difficult to distinguish from the question of how enforcement behaviors are *cued*, which occupied us in the last section. Our suggestions here are also more tentative than the previous two taxonomies; the problem of learning when to change stabilization behaviors is difficult, and probably requires exactly the sort of deep reasoning that stabilization itself is designed to avoid.

3.3.1. Plan failure

Probably the central way to recognize the need for a particular kind of stabilization is to encounter the failure of a particular plan. If this plan is to be reused frequently, there are a number of alternative responses to the failure:
- Repair the plan.
- Substitute an alternate plan for the same goal that is not subject to the failure.
- Determine the circumstances in the world that are responsible for the failure and only use the plan when those conditions do not hold.
- Determine the circumstances responsible for the failure, and arrange to stabilize them so that the plan can always be used.

This categorization is quite abstract, so as an example: imagine that you have made coffee intending to drink it with milk, but find out that in fact there is no milk in your refrigerator. What should you do differently in the future?

- Repair—you could resolve to run out to the store to get milk whenever you encountered this problem in the future.
- Substitution—decide to have tea in the future instead.
- Selective use—decide that you should check for availability of milk before having coffee, and only have coffee when milk is available.
- Stabilization—decide that the problem is in the world, rather than in your specific plan for making coffee. Resolve that there will always be milk in the refrigerator in the future. (This, of course, leaves open the question of how the stabilization is to be accomplished and cued, which we discussed in the previous section.)

Of course, this example was constructed in such a way as to make stabilization the most attractive alternative. Also, the explanatory stance is a bit disingenuous, since it is unlikely that the notion of having to buy milk would be entirely novel to someone sophisticated enough to successfully make coffee. Still, we believe that plan failure is a good indication of the need for more subtle kinds of stabilization, and that it can also indicate the need for better tuning of stabilization behaviors that already exist. Encountering the failure in the above story might well indicate the need to buy milk more frequently or consistently, even for someone who had a well-tuned set of habits.

3.3.2. Critic application

Outright failure is not the only reason to be discontented with plans or patterns of activity—substandard results, inefficiency, or wasteful use of resources can indicate the need for learning, and possibly the need to learn stabilizing behaviors.

The problem is that inefficiency, for example, is difficult to recognize, and even more difficult to assign blame for. Depending on the action model and the expressiveness of a plan representation, it may (or may not) be possible to trace outright failure to the failure of a particular step or assumed precondition. But it is difficult to detect when a plan is taking "more time than it should", and even harder to diagnose what is wrong and what should be done.

One way that classical planners increased the efficiency of plans was by looking for certain patterns of steps and precondition relationships in the current versions of plans; for example, if two different steps relied on the establishment of identical preconditions, it indicated that the plan might be transformed by establishing the precondition once for both steps, eliminating one of the establishing steps.

This sort of critic application might be useful for pointing out the need for stabilization—rather than indicating a possible transformation to the plan, the critic would point out a change in the world that would make an improved version of the plan workable. For example, if a particular plan repeatedly established a particular condition, the corresponding stabilization might be an action external to the plan that ensured that the condition was always true. As we will see, FixPoint operates in part by means of something quite like this kind of plan criticism.

Of course, critic application depends on having a symbolic representation, either of a proposed plan or of a sequence of actions that had been performed in the past.

3.3.3. Profiling

A standard technique in software optimization is to *profile* the program—to study the amount of time the program spends in different function calls, in hopes of finding out where the bulk of execution time is being spent. This can be done either exhaustively or statistically (by periodically sampling the stack). Once the profiling has been done, efforts in optimization can be directed to the parts of the program that are actually responsible for most of the execution time. This may turn out to be fruitless, since it may well be that those parts of the program are already as fast as they can be made. But as a development strategy it makes sense to try to speed up the functions that account for most of the time.

One problem with critic application as an optimization strategy, or as an indicator of the need for stabilization, is that it relies on a representation of a sequence of actions (whether in the future or in the past). This is fine for a linear plan execution system, which must possess such a representation anyway, but may be restrictive for more flexible action systems. As the most speculative part of this paper, we would like to suggest that something like profiling might serve as an initial focusing mechanism to indicate where stabilization could be useful. Where plan critics might require, for example, a representation of a sequence of back-and-forth travel steps before suggesting a transformation to eliminate them, a profiling approach might detect (say, by sampling) that a large portion of the time spent in pursuit of a certain goal was spent in traveling. While there would be no associated transformation to suggest, stabilizations that reduced the need for travel could then be actively sought.

We now abandon these speculations, and turn to the FIXPOINT program, and what we have learned from it.

4. The FIXPOINT program

FIXPOINT is a computer program (written by Grass) which demonstrates some of the benefits of stabilization in a simple simulated domain. We make no great claims for it, either in the completeness with which it embodies what we have talked about or in the generality of its approach to stabilization. In particular, (as we will see) the stabilization it performs occupies just one point in the space defined by our earlier taxonomies.

4.1. The domain

The agent in the FIXPOINT program works in a simulated woodshop,[7] and its task is to construct little wooden boats. This involves several pieces of wood, and a number of operations using tools such as lathes, band-saws, and so on.

---

[7] The simulation was built on top of Firby and Hanks' Truckworld simulator.

The agent inhabits a world made up of six rooms, which contain woodworking machines, storage bins, and pieces of wood of various shapes and sizes. At any time, a given piece of wood may be in a machine, in a bin, or just in a room (as though it were lying on the floor).

The agent has nine basic actions available to it: The agent can move in a particular direction, to get from one room to another. The agent can grab the first available object of a given type in a room with one of its hands (i.e. it can pick up a random piece of wood in a room). With a more specific version of this action, it can also find and pick up a piece of wood of given dimensions (if any such are in the room). The agent can drop anything in a given hand, can transfer the contents of a hand to the internals of a particular machine, and can take an object from a machine (transferring it to a hand). Similarly, the agent can put objects into specific bins and take them out again. Finally, the agent can *operate* the various machines, which transforms or combines the objects inside the machine in a manner dependent on the type of machine.

These actions take varying amounts of time to execute, and in some cases expand into multiple actions in execution. For example, execution of the size-specific version of "grab" involves picking up and examining pieces of wood in a room until one of the right size is found, and so can take time proportional to the number of objects in a room.

FixPoint's agent's job is to use these actions to make as many toy boats as it can.

4.2. Planning and execution in FixPoint

FixPoint's agent has a single goal (to make toy boats), which it must repeatedly pursue over the course of a long-term interaction with its environment. The environment is different each time the goal is satisfied, largely due to the agent's own actions: the agent moves objects around, depletes resources, replenishes resources, and so on.

The agent uses a single (handcrafted) plan to satisfy its goal (see appendix). This plan is in the form of a sequence of STRIPS operators, augmented with descriptions of preconditions that are necessary for the subsequent chunk of the plan to execute successfully. In addition, the agent has the background tasks of ordering more wood when necessary, and "cleaning up".

4.2.1. What FixPoint does

The execution cycle for FixPoint is as follows:

(1) If the amount of available wood is insufficient to make a certain minimum number of boats, then more wood is "ordered". This means that the ordered wood will appear after a substantial delay.

(2) If there is sufficient wood to make a boat, then the agent attempts to use its standard plan to do so. Execution consists of stepping through the plan (which is a mix of actions and precondition statements). Preconditions are checked, and when they are false, a STRIPS planner is invoked to create a plan that will make them true. This "patch plan" is executed first, and then execution returns to the main plan.

(3) After creation of the patch plan, FixPoint examines it for evidence that the patch would have been unnecessary if prior stabilization had been done. In the current implementation, this can happen in two ways:
- If the patch plan involves moving wood from one room into another where it is needed, FixPoint makes an annotation that wood of that type "should" be in the room where it was used.
- If the patch plan involves moving wood to a room, then FixPoint also makes an annotation that, in the future, that type of wood should be put in a bin, since this reduces the physical search necessary to find it and use it.

(4) Finally, whenever ordered wood arrives, FixPoint's agent delivers it to the appropriate rooms and bins, according to the annotations derived from trying to use its standard plan.

4.2.2. World models in FixPoint

In some sense there is no interesting difference between planning and execution in FixPoint. FixPoint maintains an accurate internal model of the current state of the world, and plans that FixPoint constructs based on that model always succeed.

FixPoint spends its time in one of a small number of modes. Either it is executing a part of its main plan, or it is trying (by means of invoking Strips and using the resulting patch plan) to establish a precondition statement of the main plan, or it is cleaning up, or it is ordering more wood. In addition FixPoint may be analyzing patch plans to see where wood should be stored.

We are not advocating the assumption of complete world models, nor the use of Strips planners to establish preconditions in plan reuse. If FixPoint were operating exclusively by constructing and then executing plans, then there would be no need for a simulation (since the execution of plans would give no information that could not be gleaned from their construction). As it is, though, FixPoint combines construction and execution of very short plans with flexible reuse of a very long standard plan (in addition to extracurricular activities like ordering wood). Although the effect of any given action is predictable, the effect of use of the main plan, or the effect of ordering and restocking, is not projected by FixPoint. We intend the use of short constructed plans to establish preconditions as a stand-in for improvisation to establish them. The difference-reduction approach of Strips is not a bad stand-in, if the plans produced are very short.

4.3. An annotated trace

What follows is a set of excerpts from a long trace of the FixPoint program at work, with some explanatory comments.

At the beginning of the trace, FixPoint's agent begins to try to execute its standard plan for making boats. To negotiate the first part of the plan, the agent must start out in a particular room with a piece of wood of a particular size in its hand. As it turns out, the agent is in a different room with nothing in its hand.

```
Checking precondition ---
(AND (LEFT-SIZE 2 6 ?Z) (LOC ROBOT ROOM2))
Precondition failed. Attempting to replan and patch...
```

At this point, a conventional STRIPS planner is invoked to create a "patch plan" that can be run to make the desired initial conditions hold:

```
Working on: (AND (LEFT-SIZE 2 6 ?Z) (LOC ROBOT ROOM2))
  Trying to reduce differences.
    Differences =
      ((LOC ROBOT ROOM2) (LEFT-SIZE 2 6 ?Z))
[..]
The Plan is:

(LEFT-GRAB WOOD 2 6 24 (:RECT))
(MOVE ROOM1 ROOM2)
Executing patch ---
(LEFT-GRAB WOOD 2 6 24 (:RECT))
(MOVE ROOM1 ROOM2)
```

As it happens, there is wood of the right type in the current room, but no such wood in the room that contains the needed machine. So the result of invoking STRIPS is simply to grab the requisite wood and carry it to the room where it will be used.

After the patch plan is executed successfully, it is examined for optimizations in the world that could make the preconditions of the main plan easier to establish.

```
Patch successful, returning to main plan.
**************************************************
Looking at what was needed in patch and planning to
change the environment so the precondition is met
**************************************************
Looking for...
  Optimization of location...
    Location optimizations are:
      (ROOM2 WOOD 2 6 24 (:RECT))

  Optimization of bins...
    Bin optimizations are:
      (ROOM2 (1 2 6 24 (:RECT) WOOD 1))
```

Essentially, the program examines the patch plan to see whether it involves transporting wood from one room to another. If so, it makes an annotation to itself that wood of that type "should" be in that room. In addition, an annotation is made that wood of that type should be placed in a distinguished bin, since it is less time-consuming to get wood from a known bin than it is to physically search a room for it.

Execution of the main plan proceeds in this way, with precondition statements being established by creating and executing very short plans. Sometimes the patch plans involve nothing but moving the agent to an appropriate room, and (since the program has no knowledge of stabilizations that can ensure that the agent is always in a particular location) no annotations are made. Eventually, after about seventeen minutes of simulated time, with the help of five machines in different rooms, FixPoint's agent has constructed its first boat. In addition, it has made annotations about which rooms and bins should contain different types of wood:

```
Wood-room allocation:
  (ROOM2 WOOD 2 6 24 (:RECT))
  (ROOM2 WOOD 2 4 24 (:RECT))
  (ROOM2 WOOD 0.5 0.5 36 (:DOWEL))
  (ROOM2 WOOD 0.4 0.4 36 (:DOWEL))
  (ROOM1 WOOD 0.5 0.5 4 (:DOWEL))
  (ROOM1 WOOD 1 4 6 (:RECT (:HOLE :MEDIUM 0.5)
                            (:HOLE :LARGE 0.5)))
  (ROOM1 WOOD 0.4 0.4 3 (:DOWEL))
  (ROOM1 WOOD 2 6 10 (:SLANTED :POINTED :RECT))

Wood-bin allocation:
  (ROOM1 (1 1 WOOD 0.5 0.5 4 (:DOWEL))
         (2 1 WOOD 1 4 6 (:RECT (:HOLE :MEDIUM 0.5)
                                (:HOLE :LARGE 0.5)))
         (3 1 WOOD 0.4 0.4 3 (:DOWEL))
         (4 1 WOOD 2 6 10 (:SLANTED :POINTED :RECT)))
  (ROOM2 (1 1 WOOD 2 6 24 (:RECT))
         (2 1 WOOD 2 4 24 (:RECT))
         (3 1 WOOD 0.5 0.5 36 (:DOWEL))
         (4 1 WOOD 0.4 0.4 36 (:DOWEL)))
```

After completing its first boat, FixPoint's agent has depleted its stock of wood enough that it needs to order more. After ordering, FixPoint enters a period of "cleanup" (removing scrap wood, and putting useful pieces of wood into appropriate bins according to the annotations it has made). Then, when wood has arrived, the agent distributes the wood to appropriate rooms and bins.

```
+++ Alarms have fired:
  ((2 9 19 49)
   (ORDER-ARRIVED
     (3 (1 (:RECT) 2 4 24)
        (1 (:RECT) 2 6 24)
        (3 (:DOWEL) 0.5 0.5 36)
        (3 (:DOWEL) 0.4 0.4 36))))

  (1 (:RECT) 2 4 24)...is arriving. [..]
```

After the wood has been distributed, FixPoint begins to use its main plan again to build a second boat. Although the main plan is the same as it was when the first boat was made, it is being used in slightly different circumstances: the agent happens to be in a different location, and wood has been stored according to the annotations made on the first use of the plan.

```
Checking precondition ---
(AND (LEFT-SIZE 2 6 ?Z) (LOC ROBOT ROOM2))
Precondition failed. Attempting to replan and patch...

Working on: (AND (LEFT-SIZE 2 6 ?Z) (LOC ROBOT ROOM2))
   Trying to reduce differences.
     Differences =
        ((LEFT-SIZE 2 6 ?Z))
```

The agent is in the right room, but is not holding wood of the right type. Because the restocking of wood was done using the annotations made during the first use of the plan, there is now wood of the correct dimensions stored in a bin in the room it will be used in. The "patch plan" created in this case is simply to take a piece of wood from the bin.

```
The Plan is:

(LEFT-GET-FROM-BIN BIN5 1)
Executing patch ---
(LEFT-GET-FROM-BIN BIN5 1)
[..]
Patch successful, returning to main plan.
****************************************************
Looking at what was needed in patch and planning to
change the environment so the precondition is
*************************   ********************
Looking for...
  Optimization of location...
    No location optimizations.

  Optimization of bins...
    No bin storage optimizations.
```

In this way, FixPoint's agent constructs the second boat using the same plan as the first time around, but needs to perform fewer actions to make the various parts of the plan executable. Most of these actions that are omitted the second time involve either travel between rooms or search within a room for an object.

As a result, while it takes nearly eighteen minutes to construct the first boat (17:44), the second boat takes less than seventeen minutes (16:50). This is a small improvement, but is directly attributable to the stabilization performed. It is also larger than it seems, since more time is spent physically searching for wood in the second execution, simply because there is more wood in the rooms after the restocking.

4.4. Discussion

Now that we have discussed FIXPOINT, and have presented our taxonomy of stabilities and stabilizing behaviors, we are finally in a position to treat the first in terms of the second.

4.4.1. Types of stabilization in FIXPOINT

FIXPOINT has an inflexible commitment to stability of plan use; i.e. it has no choice but to construct boats using its standard plan. In the service of plan reuse, FIXPOINT enforces stability of location—by critiquing its patch plans, it makes annotations that enable it to ensure that the preconditions of its standard plans are either true or easily achieved. FIXPOINT tracks the use of resources internally, and periodically ensures their availability and distribution by use of a standard clean-up plan (ordering and distribution). FIXPOINT also enforces stability of schedule by tuning the minimum quantities of wood in stock that it will tolerate before ordering more (this capability was not covered in the trace). Finally, FIXPOINT displays some learning of stabilization of the location of objects: the annotations made during execution of the main plan persist, and are used during ordering. As a result, FIXPOINT decreases the total time necessary for execution of its standard plan.

4.4.2. What changes in FIXPOINT?

One possible objection the reader might have at this point is that FIXPOINT does not really change its environment—instead it changes its plans (i.e. learns), and any performance improvement should be viewed as the result of learning rather than stabilization, with change in the world a mere side-effect.

This is true in a sense, but the distinction is a subtle one. Any type of stability that needs to be actively maintained by an agent (i.e., that is not "one-time change" in our taxonomy) can be viewed as the direct product of the agent's plans and intentions. Improvement at stabilization, then, is a type of learning, and (in the long run) the changes in the world are simply the result of that learning.

The distinction (if one can be made) between improvement through stabilization and improvement through more straightforward learning depends in part on the way in which we segment the behavior we are trying to analyze. As an example of this, imagine that a person who cooks frequently learns grocery-shopping practices that ensure that the cupboard is always fully stocked with the spices typically used in that cooking. As a result, there may be fewer cooking failures, and in some sense we would want to say that the person had learned to be a better cook. To the extent that shopping is viewed as a separate activity from cooking, though, we might prefer to say that the same person now cooks in a better kitchen. The latter view may be preferable if the main connections between the activities are via this relatively stable environment that they both impact, rather than through internal representations.

4.4.3. Shortcomings and future work

The program trace we presented illustrates a particular type of stability, maintained in a particular way. In some sense, the program falls into a particular subcategory of each of the taxonomies presented in Section 3, rather than demonstrating them all at once.

The program is mainly intended to be illustrative of the idea of stabilization; we make no particular other claims for it, and don't want to be held to its representational commitments. Two shortcomings, however, are interesting to address, if only because they suggest directions for future work.

First of all, although the particular stabilization instances that FIXPOINT learns to enforce are not built into the program, the methods for detecting the need for them and the methods for enforcing those particular stabilizations are hand-coded. One direction for future research is to try to generalize these methods so that more of the work of making stabilization decisions can be made by the program. This work is underway in the RUNNER project [7].

Secondly, as we have said, there are no interesting differences between the (symbolic) internal model that FIXPOINT has of its world, and the (symbolic) simulation that is that world. In addition to the acknowledged implausibility of such perfect world models, the fact that FIXPOINT has such a model decreases the utility of stabilizing the location of objects. An extension of this implementation would be to have the program more thoroughly substitute learned stabilization policies for its models; in other words, have the program's knowledge of the world depend less on tracking it with a world model, and more on the program's knowledge of what the world should be like (due to its own efforts).

5. Conclusions

Agents involved in long-term interactions with their environments shape those environments, in addition to being shaped by them. In this paper we've presented the idea of *stabilization*, discussed its use in the analysis and design of agents, and categorized some of the different forms it can take. Finally, we presented FIXPOINT, a program that implements many of the ideas presented here, and showed how it achieves performance improvements by actively stabilizing its environment.

Acknowledgments

We thank Mark Roller for his work with Josh Grass on the implementation of FIX-POINT. We also thank Jim Firby for asking us questions that led us to thinking about the issues in Section 2, and an anonymous reviewer for detailed and helpful comments. Finally, we thank Phil Agre for not letting us get away with not writing this.

Appendix A. Plan representation

Both to give a sense of what FIXPOINT's plan representation is like, and as an aid in understanding the trace, we reproduce the first few statements of the standard plan used by FIXPOINT.

```
'( (precondition (and (left-size 2 6 ?z)
                      (loc robot room2)))
(put-in-machine 'left)
(operate-machine '(:z 10))
(get-from-machine 'left 'used)
(get-from-machine 'right 'scrap)
(drop 'right)
  (precondition (and (left-size 2 6 10)
                     (loc robot room5)))
(put-in-machine 'left)
(operate-machine '(:pointed))
(get-from-machine 'left 'used)
  (precondition (and (left-shape (:pointed :rect))
                     (left-size 2 6 10)
                     (loc robot room3)))
(put-in-machine 'left)
(operate-machine '(:slanted))
(get-from-machine 'left 'used)
  (precondition (loc robot room1))
(drop 'left)
  (precondition (and (left-size 2 4 ?z) (loc robot room2)))
(put-in-machine 'left)
(operate-machine '(:x 1))
(get-from-machine 'left 'scrap)
(drop 'left)
(operate-machine '(:z 6))
(get-from-machine 'left 'used)
(get-from-machine 'right 'scrap)
(drop 'right)
...)
```

References

[1] P.E. Agre. The dynamic structure of everyday life, Ph.D. Thesis, Technical Report 1085, MIT Artificial Intelligence Laboratory, Cambridge, MA (1988).

[2] P.E. Agre and D. Chapman, What are plans for? in: *Designing Autonomous Agents: From Biology to Engineering and Back* (MIT Press, Cambridge, MA, 1991).

[3] D. Chapman, On choosing domains for agents, Position paper prepared for the Workshop on Benchmarks and Metrics, NASA Ames (1990).

[4] D. Chapman, *Vision, Instruction, and Action* (MIT Press, Cambridge, MA, 1991).

[5] K.J. Hammond, *Case-Based Planning: Viewing Planning as a Memory Task*, Perspectives in Artificial Intelligence 1 (Academic Press, San Diego, CA, 1989).

[6] K.J. Hammond, T.M. Converse and C. Martin, Integrating planning and acting in a case-based framework, in: *Proceedings AAAI-90*, Boston, MA (1990).

[7] K.J. Hammond, M. Marks and T.M. Converse, Planning in an open world: a pluralistic approach, in: *Proceedings 11th Annual Meeting of the Cognitive Science Society*, Ann Arbor, MI (1989).

[8] D. Kirsh, The intelligent use of space, *Artif. Intell.* 73 (1995), to appear.

[9] J. Lave, *Cognition in Practice* (Cambridge University Press, New York, 1988).
[10] D. McDermott, Planning and acting, *Cogn. Sci.* **2** (1978) 71–109.
[11] S. Minton, Learning effective search-control knowledge: an explanation-based approach, Technical Report 133, Carnegie-Mellon University, Department of Computer Science, Pittsburgh, PA (1988).

Artificial Intelligence 72 (1995) 329–365

An architecture for adaptive intelligent systems

Barbara Hayes-Roth

Knowledge Systems Laboratory, Stanford University, 701 Welch Road, Building C, Palo Alto, CA 94304, USA

Received September 1992; revised May 1993

Abstract

Our goal is to understand and build comprehensive agents that function effectively in challenging niches. In particular, we identify a class of niches to be occupied by "adaptive intelligent systems (AISs)". In contrast with niches occupied by typical AI agents, AIS niches present situations that vary dynamically along several key dimensions: different combinations of required tasks, different configurations of available resources, contextual conditions ranging from benign to stressful, and different performance criteria. We present a small class hierarchy of AIS niches that exhibit these dimensions of variability and describe a particular AIS niche, ICU (intensive care unit) patient monitoring, which we use for illustration throughout the paper. To function effectively throughout the range of situations presented by an AIS niche, an agent must be highly adaptive. In contrast with the rather stereotypic behavior of typical AI agents, an AIS must adapt several key aspects of its behavior to its dynamic situation: its perceptual strategy, its control mode, its choices of reasoning tasks to perform, its choices of reasoning methods for performing chosen tasks; and its meta-control strategy for global coordination of all its behavior. We have designed and implemented an agent architecture that supports all of these different kinds of adaptation by exploiting a single underlying theoretical concept: *An agent dynamically constructs explicit control plans to guide its choices among situation-triggered behaviors*. The architecture has been used to build experimental agents for several AIS niches. We illustrate the architecture and its support for adaptation with examples from Guardian, an experimental agent for ICU monitoring.

1. Toward more comprehensive AI agents

"Intelligent agents" continuously perform three functions: perception of dynamic conditions in the environment; action to affect conditions in the environment; and reasoning to interpret perceptions, solve problems, draw inferences, and determine actions. Conceptually, perception informs reasoning and reasoning guides action, although in some cases perception may drive action directly. This abstract definition allows for a great variety of biological and artificial agents whose capabilities range from extremely limited and stereotyped behavior to extremely sophisticated and versatile behavior. Why should different agents exhibit different behavioral capabilities and what underlies these differences?

Differences in their behavioral capabilities allow different classes of agents to function effectively in different niches. A "niche" is a class of operating environments: the tasks an agent must perform, the resources it has for performing tasks, the contextual conditions that may influence its performance, and the evaluation criteria it must satisfy. Human beings are the most sophisticated existing agents. Given their broad range of potential behavior, individual human beings can function effectively in many challenging niches. By contrast, typical AI agents are extremely limited. Given their narrow range of potential behavior, individual agents can function effectively only in a small number (usually one) of severely restricted (usually highly engineered) niches.

We hypothesize that, to a large degree, an agent's architecture determines its potential behavior and, therefore, the niches in which it potentially can function:

Agent Architecture ⇒ Potential Behavior ⇒ Suitable Niches.

By "architecture" we mean the abstract design of a class of agents: the set of structural components in which perception, reasoning, and action occur, the specific functionality and interface of each component, and the interconnection topology among components. Under this hypothesis, human beings function effectively in many niches that no other animal or existing AI agent could fill—certainly because only human beings have acquired the necessary knowledge and skills, but more fundamentally because only the complex and powerful architecture embodied in the human nervous system [3] supports such a broad range of knowledge and skills.

Conversely, to function effectively in a particular niche, an agent must exhibit the range of behavior required in that niche and, therefore, must have an architecture that supports the required behavior:

Intended Niche ⇒ Required Behavior ⇒ Sufficient Architectures.

Typical AI agents have simple architectures for good reason: simple architectures are sufficient to support the behavior required in their intended niches. In fact, for restricted niches, architecture often plays a relatively small role in an agent's effectiveness, many alternative architectures may suffice, and architectural design is a relatively insignificant part of the agent-building enterprise. As the intended niche increases in complexity, however, architecture plays a larger role in the agent's effectiveness, fewer alternative architectures will suffice, and architectural design becomes a more critical and expensive part of the agent-building enterprise.

Thus, we argue that present AI agents are "niche-bound" both because they are "knowledge-bound" [33] and because they are "architecture-bound". Increasing only agents' knowledge can expand the very narrow niches in which they currently function. However, it will have diminishing returns as the intended niches increase in complexity and agents' ability to exploit the necessary knowledge and skills runs up against architectural limitations.

Our goal is to provide an architecture for more comprehensive AI agents that function effectively in more challenging niches. Thus, we are working very much in the spirit of Newell's call for "unified theories of cognition" [37]; see also [2,32]. We focus on a class of "adaptive intelligent systems (AISs)", which operate in a class of niches that is intermediate between the severely restricted niches of typical AI systems and the effectively unrestricted niches of human beings. As discussed below, AIS niches present dynamic variability in their required tasks, available resources, contextual conditions, and performance criteria. As a result, to function effectively in AIS niches, agents must possess a pervasive property of human behavior: *adaptation*. We have designed an agent architecture to support the several dimensions of adaptation required in AIS niches and used it to build experimental agents for several of the domain-specific niches in Fig. 1. To ground the discussion, we take examples throughout the paper from a particular niche, patient monitoring in an intensive care unit (ICU), and an experimental agent called Guardian [25,26], which was built with our agent architecture.

Let us begin by using the ICU monitoring niche to illustrate important shared properties of AIS niches. Intensive care patients are critically ill and depend on life-support devices (e.g., a ventilator) to perform vital functions until their own impaired organs heal and resume normal function, usually a period of several days. The high-level goals of ICU monitoring are to wean the patient from the devices as soon as possible (to minimize cost, discomfort, and undesirable side effects), while detecting and treating any additional problems that arise along the way. Effective patient-management involves: interpretation of many continuous-

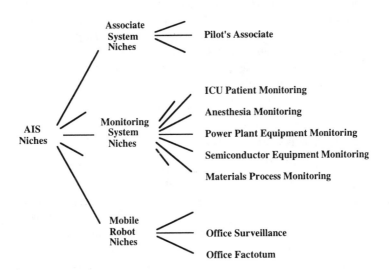

Fig. 1. Excerpt from the class hierarchy of AIS niches.

ly, periodically, or occasionally sensed physiological and device variables; planning and comparative evaluation of many interacting therapy alternatives; detection, diagnosis, and correction of unanticipated problems; control of many patient-management and device-control parameters; and reporting and consulting on patient progress with other members of the ICU team. The complexity of ICU monitoring can overwhelm even skilled clinicians.

As illustrated by ICU monitoring and summarized in Table 1, AIS niches are considerably more demanding than the niches occupied by typical AI agents. First, *AIS niches require performance of several diverse tasks, sometimes concurrently and often interacting*. For example, ICU monitoring requires tasks such as condition monitoring, fault detection, diagnosis, and planning. Second, *AIS niches provide variable resources for performing tasks*. For example, Guardian has both associative and causal modeling methods for performing diagnosis tasks. It may or may not have the particular class hierarchies or causal relations needed to apply these methods to a given diagnosis problem. Third, *AIS niches entail complex and variable contextual conditions*. For example, in ICU monitoring there may be 100 variables sensed automatically several times per second (e.g., blood pressure, pulse), as well as other variables that are sensed irregularly (e.g., laboratory results, X-ray analyses). Data representing these variables differ in criticality and criticality is context-dependent. A patient may manifest several problems simultaneously and therapies for simultaneous problems may interact. Finally, *AIS niches impose more qualitative performance criteria*, *replacing the usual correctness, efficiency, and completeness criteria with effectiveness, timeliness, and robustness*. For example, if an ICU patient manifests several problems simultaneously, any critical problems must be treated well enough and soon enough to save the patient's life, even if such treatment is sub-optimal and regardless of how many other problems go untreated.

To function effectively in AIS niches, an agent must be highly *adaptive* (Table 2): it must modify its behavior on each of several dimensions, depending on the situation in which it finds itself. First, *an agent must adapt its perceptual strategy to dynamic information requirements and resource limitations*. For example, when Guardian is monitoring a stable patient, it may divide its perceptual activities among all available patient data in order to maintain a good overview of the

Table 1
Shared properties of AIS niches versus typical AI niches

	AIS niches	Typical AI niches
Required tasks	Diverse, concurrent, interacting	Single isolated task
Available resources	Variable methods, data, models, facts available	Single correct method, relevant data, and appropriate model
Typical context	Competing: Percepts, tasks, actions	No competition
Evaluation criteria	Effective, timely, robust	Correct, efficient, complete

Table 2
Behavioral adaptations required of an AIS versus the static behavior of a typical AI agent

	Required AIS adaptations	Typical AI agent behaviors
Perception strategy	Adapt to information requirements and resource limitations	Fixed
Control mode	Adapt to goal-based constraints and environmental uncertainty	Fixed
Reasoning tasks	Adapt to perceived and inferred conditions	Single task
Reasoning methods	Adapt to available information and current performance criteria	Single reasoning method
Meta-control strategy	Adapt to dynamic configurations of demands and opportunities	Unnecessary

patient's condition and remain vigilant to possible problems. However, when it detects a serious problem, Guardian must perceive more selectively, focusing on patient data that help it diagnose the problem and identify an appropriate therapeutic action in a timely manner. Second, *an agent must adapt its control mode to dynamic goal-based constraints on its actions and uncertainty about its environment*. For example, when the patient has a critical, but slowly evolving problem, Guardian can plan and execute an optimal course of therapeutic actions. However, when urgent conditions arise, Guardian must be prepared to react immediately. Third, *an agent must adapt its choices among potential reasoning tasks to dynamic local and global objectives*. For example, when Guardian is monitoring a stable patient, it need only track patient data. When it detects a problem, it must perform a diagnosis task, along with its ongoing monitoring task. After completing its diagnosis, it must perform a therapy planning task, along with its ongoing monitoring task. Fourth, *an agent must adapt its reasoning methods to the currently available information and performance criteria*. For example, Guardian can use clinical experience to recognize commonly occurring problems and select standard therapeutic responses. However, when faced with unfamiliar problems, it must fall back on models of the patient's underlying pathophysiology to perform a more systematic diagnosis and design an appropriate therapy. Finally, *an agent must adapt its meta-control strategy to its dynamic configuration of demands, opportunities, and resources for behavior*. For example, Guardian ordinarily interleaves several unrelated or loosely-coupled activities, but may decide to suspend competing activities if a critical problem arises. An effective meta-control strategy may emerge from Guardian's independent decisions regarding co-occurring problems; in other cases it may decide to impose a particular meta-control strategy on a challenging configuration of competing demands and opportunities for behavior.

We have designed and implemented an agent architecture to support the several forms of adaptation required of an AIS. It enables an agent to modify its perceptual strategy, its control mode, its reasoning tasks, its reasoning methods, and its meta-control strategy, depending on relevant features of its dynamic situation. Moreover, our architecture has an important theoretical strength, a kind of architectural parsimony. Its support for all five dimensions of adaptation derives from a fundamental theoretical concept and its architectural embodiment [20,22,23]: *An agent dynamically constructs explicit control plans to guide its choices among situation-triggered behaviors.*

The remainder of the paper is organized as follows. Section 2 presents our agent architecture. Sections 3–7 examine the requirements for each of the five dimensions of adaptation in more detail and show how our architecture supports them. Section 8 discusses evaluation of the architecture, summarizes the status of experimental agents built with the architecture, and contrasts the architecture with others in the literature. Section 9 presents conclusions.

2. The agent architecture

Our agent architecture (Fig. 2) hierarchically organizes component systems for perception, action, and cognition processes. Perception processes acquire, abstract, and filter sensed data before sending it to other components. Action systems control the execution of external actions on effectors. Perception can

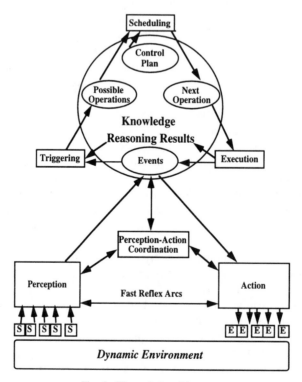

Fig. 2. The agent architecture.

influence action directly through reflex arcs or through perception-action coordination processes. The cognition systems interprets perceptions, solves problems, makes plans, and guides both perceptual strategies and external action. These processes operate concurrently and asynchronously. They communicate by message passing. Perception-action operations occur at least an order of magnitude faster than cognitive operations.

The cognition system, which is the architecture's most substantial component, is realized as a "blackboard architecture" [13], extended to support dynamic control planning [20,21,23]. For present purposes, we emphasize these features: (a) Perceptual inputs and internal reasoning operations produce changes to a global memory; (b) Each such event triggers some number of possible reasoning operations; (c) Possible operations are scheduled for execution based on active control plans; (d) Control plans are themselves constructed and modified by reasoning operations; (e) Possible actions and control plans are represented in an English-like machine-interpretable language that supports semantic partial matching of actions to plans.

For example, here is one of Guardian's reasoning operations for model-based diagnosis:

Name: Find-Generic-Causes

Trigger: Observe condition, C; where C exemplifies generic-fault, F

Action: Find generic-faults that can-cause F

Find-Generic-Causes is triggered and its parameters are instantiated whenever a prior reasoning operation indicates that a newly observed patient condition, C, "exemplifies" some generic-fault, F. For example, if C were a decrease in the patient's urine output or inspired air, it would exemplify the generic-fault: decrease in the flow of a flow process. When executed, the action of this reasoning operation consults the factual knowledge base and identifies all generic-faults that "can-cause" F (e.g., blockage or leakage of an upstream flow structure can cause a decrease in the flow of a flow process). By recording each such possible cause in the global memory, this operation creates internal events that trigger other reasoning operations. For example, some triggered operations might instantiate possible generic causes with respect to the observed condition, C (e.g., blockage or leakage of various structures in the urinary or respiratory system). Others might continue the backward chaining to identify other generic-faults that "can-cause" those currently hypothesized. Others might attempt to discriminate among alternative hypotheses by examining relevant patient data. To perform a reasoning task such as diagnosis, Guardian triggers and executes a sequence of such reasoning operations, under the control of an appropriate control strategy, incrementally building a solution to the diagnosis problem.

Here is an example of Guardian's control reasoning operations:

Name: Respond-to-Urgent-Problem

Trigger: Observe critical condition, C

Action: Record control decision with

Prescription: Quickly respond to C

Criticality: Criticality of C

Goal: Diagnosed problems related to C are corrected

Respond-to-Urgent-Problem is triggered and its parameter, C, is instantiated whenever the perception system delivers an observed condition with a high criticality. When executed, it creates a control decision to quickly respond to the condition and gives this decision a priority that is proportional to the criticality of C. While active, this control decision focuses (some of) Guardian's perception, reasoning (e.g., diagnosis and therapy planning), and action resources on activities related to quickly responding to C. For example, Respond-to-Urgent-Problem could produce a control decision to: Respond quickly to the observed decrease in the patient's inspired air. To identify possible operations that semantically match its control plans, an agent uses explicit knowledge of its own competence as well as its domain: (a) type hierarchies of actions and domain concepts; (b) other relations among actions and concepts; and (c) attached procedures for evaluating modifiers of actions and concepts. Thus, continuing the present example, Guardian would favor execution of possible operations that "quickly" (fast, relative to other operations) "respond to" (monitor, diagnose, correct) the observed decrease in inspired air. A control decision is deactivated when its goal is achieved, in this case, when all diagnosed problems related to C have been corrected. Using a small set of general control reasoning operations to generate a variety of specific control decisions, an agent such as Guardian can construct control plans (including plans that have sequential or hierarchical structure) that are appropriate to its situation and it can change those plans as the situation changes [30].

Fig. 3 illustrates the characteristic behavior of agents implemented in this architecture with a simplified episode from Guardian's monitoring of a simulated ICU patient.

At the start of the episode, Guardian has two active control plans: plan A, to update the control plan whenever possible with priority 5; and plan B, to monitor patient data whenever possible with priority 3. Because patient data are always available, the perception system filters continuously sensed patient data and sends selected values to the cognition system at a manageable global data rate. These perceived patient data repeatedly trigger monitoring operations for several variables, including blood pressure and heart rate, all of which match plan B. No events trigger any operations that match plan A. Therefore, for a time, Guardian executes various monitoring operations.

Soon, however, an executed monitoring operation reveals that the patient has abnormally low blood pressure. This observation triggers three new operations, one operation to update the control plan and two alternative operations to begin diagnosing the low blood pressure, all of which compete with recently triggered monitoring operations. Guardian chooses to update the control plan because that operation matches plan A, its highest priority active control plan. This operation produces control plan C, to respond quickly to the low blood pressure, with

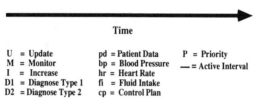

Control Plan

A. Update control plans -- P=5

B. Monitor all patient data
    P=3   P=1   P=3

              C. Quickly respond to low BP -- P=3

Possible Actions - Top Row Chosen for Execution

M:hr M:bp U:cp D1:bp I:fi   M:bp U:cp M: hr M:bp

M:bp M:hr M: hr M:hr M: hr M:hr M:hr M: bp M:hr

      M:bp M:bp M:bp   M:bp

      D1:bp D2:bp

      D2:bp

Time

U = Update	pd = Patient Data	P = Priority
M = Monitor	bp = Blood Pressure	— = Active Interval
I = Increase	hr = Heart Rate	
D1 = Diagnose Type 1	fi = Fluid Intake	
D2 = Diagnose Type 2	cp = Control Plan	

Fig. 3. Illustrative Guardian reasoning behavior.

priority 3, and lowers the priority of plan B to 1. As a result of the latter change, which is designed to focus resources on the more urgent blood pressure problem, the perception system filters sensed patient data more severely and sends values to the cognition system at a lower global data rate.

Now Guardian executes a series of actions that match plan C, temporarily ignoring repeatedly triggered monitoring actions because of plan B's lower priority. First, Guardian executes one of its pending diagnostic operations—types 1 and 2—for diagnosing the observed low blood pressure. Although both diagnostic operations "respond to low blood pressure" and, therefore, match plan C, diagnosis type 1 matches better because it embodies a "quicker" diagnostic method. Although Fig. 3 abstracts Guardian's diagnostic reasoning as a single executed action, in fact diagnosis involves execution of a sequence of reasoning operations. The result of each operation triggers the next, until the last operation identifies the cause of the high blood pressure, in this case low fluid intake. Identification of this underlying fault triggers an operation to take corrective action (via the action subsystem) by increasing the patient's fluid intake. Guardian executes this operation and, in so doing, triggers an operation to monitor blood pressure, which it expects to rise. This is the last operation Guardian executes under plan C. (Although this simple example involves only a single corrective action, Guardian is capable of performing several corrective actions in parallel—

coordinated actions to address a single problem or separate actions to address different problems.)

Confirmation of normal blood pressure indicates that the goal of plan C has been achieved, which triggers a new operation to update the control plan. Guardian executes this operation because it matches plan A, the highest priority active plan. It deactivates Plan C and returns the priority of Plan B to 3. As a result, the perception system filters sensed patient data less severely and sends values to the cognition system at its original higher global data rate. Guardian returns to executing monitoring operations repeatedly triggered by perceived patient data and chosen for execution under plan B.

This example illustrates the architectural mechanism underlying our fundamental theoretical concept: that an agent dynamically constructs explicit control plans to constrain and guide its choices among situation-triggered possible behaviors. Guardian always has some number of active control plans, varying in priority. Some control plans are quite general and favor the execution of a large class of potential operations. Others are more specific and distinguish operations that will help Guardian achieve well-defined objectives. Although the example of Fig. 3 shows only simple one-sentence control plans, the architecture allows (and Guardian typically employs) more complex control plans having sequential and hierarchical structure. Similarly, Guardian always has some number of possible behaviors. Some are triggered by inputs from its perception system, while others are triggered by the results of prior reasoning operations. Different operations, if executed, could change Guardian's knowledge of the environment, initiate or extend its performance of particular reasoning tasks, initiate performance of external actions by its action system, or modify its active control plans. At each opportunity, Guardian performs behaviors that best match its highest priority active control plans.

In the following sections, we show how this key architectural mechanism enables an agent to adapt its perceptual strategy, control mode, reasoning tasks, reasoning methods, and meta-control strategy to its dynamic situation.

3. Adaptation of perceptual strategy

In order to perform effectively in AIS niches, *an agent must adapt its perceptual strategy to changing cognitive requirements.*

In theory, we might like an agent to perceive all events in its environment and to reason about them in all promising ways, so that it can determine and carry out optimal courses of action. However, AIS niches present high, variable data rates for many environmental conditions; a resource-bounded agent cannot realize unbounded perception. In addition, AIS niches permit many different reasoning tasks and sometimes different methods for performing particular tasks. Each perceived event initiates a potential cascade of reasoning activities; the event itself triggers a number of possible reasoning operations, each of which produces new events, each of which triggers new operations, and so forth. Even if unbounded perception were feasible, the high and cascading demand for reasoning would swamp the cognitive resources of an agent such as Guardian (or a human being, for that matter).

In general, a resource-bounded agent ordinarily cannot—and, equally important, need not—perceive, reason, or act on every condition in its environment. Instead, the agent must be highly selective in its perception of the environment and it must adapt its perceptual strategy to balance two objectives. First, from a purely quantitative perspective, the agent must maximize its vigilance, perceiving as much information as possible about as many environmental conditions as possible, while avoiding perceptual overload. Second, from a qualitative perspective, the agent must maximize goal-directed effectiveness, readily acquiring data that are relevant to its currently important reasoning tasks, while avoiding distraction by irrelevant or insignificant data.

In our architecture, the perception system's basic functions (Fig. 4) are to abstract, prioritize, and filter sensed data before sending it to the cognition system. Five parameters determine how the perception system performs these functions. Two static compile-time parameters identify the domain variables to be sensed and ranges of critical values for those variables. Three dynamic run-time parameters (sent asynchronously by the cognition system) specify requested data abstractions, relevance values for different variables, and the desired global data rate. The perception system processes and sends to the cognition system all requested data abstractions at appropriately high rates and sends unrequested data at appropriately low (but usually non-zero) rates. It dynamically determines the "appropriate" rates at which to send each requested and unrequested observation by distributing the current desired global data rate among them in

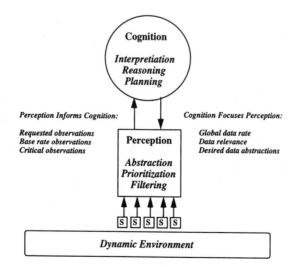

Fig. 4. Coordination of cognition and perception.

proportion to their current relevance values. There is one exception to this rule: The perception system sends critical values for all sensed variables, regardless of their current relevance values. Note that, since many variables are not sensed continuously, this provision does not guarantee perception of every critical value that occurs, but only every critical value that is sensed.

An agent dynamically adapts its perceptual strategy by modifying its three run-time parameters based on both feedback control and predictive control from the cognitive system.

The agent adapts its global data rate based on feedback control from activities in its cognitive system's limited-capacity event buffer. The event buffer is designed to insure that the cognitive system always retrieves the most important, up-to-date perceptions available. Events are ordered in the buffer by priority and recency, with best-first retrieval and worst-first overflow. (In theory, the buffer mechanism also uses a decay factor to remove unretrieved, out-of-data events, but we have not yet implemented a decay factor.)

The specific function used to integrate priority and recency factors to order events in the buffer should be tailored to characteristics of the agent's niche. For example, Guardian's niche presents events that vary widely in priority, with very high priority events occurring infrequently. Important features of its environment change relatively slowly and its deadlines are relatively long compared to the speed of its perception. Therefore, Guardian orders perceptual events by priority and then by recency. It always retrieves the most recent of the most important events and, in case of overflow, loses the least recent of the least important events. In practice, when critical events occur, Guardian retrieves and reasons about them immediately. When multiple critical events co-occur during a brief time interval, Guardian handles them promptly in priority order. Most of the time, however, no critical events occur and Guardian processes all of the incoming events within a few retrieval cycles of their arrival in the buffer—the exact order has no effect on the overall utility of its performance.

Regardless of the specific event-ordering function used, the buffer mechanism is designed for steady-state operation in which: (a) perceptual events enter and leave the buffer at roughly equal rates; and (b) all of the entering events ultimately are retrieved for reasoning. However, steady-state operation assumes that the perception system has been parameterized with a global data rate that is appropriate for the agent's reasoning rate. If there is a decrease in the pace of the agent's reasoning or an increase in the rate of critical sensed events, the event buffer will overflow—this is the architecture's "last line of defense" against perceptual overload. When the event buffer overflows, it means that the agent's reasoning cannot keep pace with perceptual events and, although it is still reasoning about up-to-date events, the agent is losing potentially important information. Conversely, when the buffer underflows (i.e., is empty), it means that the agent is waiting for perceptual events to reason about and, in the meantime, wasting cognitive resources. In either case, the agent corrects the imbalance between perception and reasoning rates by modifying the desired global data rate used by the perception system. An earlier version of this feedback mechanism implemented a "bang-bang" control response to actual over(under)flow. The current version implements an adaptive control response by monitoring trends in the number of items in the buffer and adjusting the global data rate in anticipation of over(under)flow occurring. As in conventional control applications, the adaptive control gives a smoother correlation between desired and actual global data rates.

The agent also adapts its global data rate predictively. It analyzes newly created or modified control plans to estimate its own future demand for cognitive resources and, complementarily, its future capacity to process perceptual events. Based on this estimate, it may increase or decrease its global data rate. For example, when Guardian adopts plan C in Fig. 3, to respond quickly to the patient's low blood pressure, it knows: (a) that the associated reasoning tasks will consume computational resources previously consumed by monitoring a variety of patient data; and (b) that the new tasks are more important than the monitoring task (priority 3 versus 2). It lowers its global data rate. Conversely, it raises its global data rate after achieving the goal of plan C. With a little knowledge about the computational properties of different reasoning methods, an agent can predictively modulate its global data rate more precisely.

The agent also analyzes control decisions to identify useful data abstractions and to determine the context-specific relevance of different variables. For example, in plan B of Fig. 3, Guardian's decision to monitor all patient "data" implies that the perception system should send the raw numeric data available from its sensors for all patient variables. Alternatively, given appropriate definitions for various data abstractions, Guardian might decide to monitor "criterial changes in value", "hourly high and low values", "running averages", etc. Plan B's initial priority of 3 translates into a mid-range relevance value for all patient variables. Guardian's subsequent reduction of plan B's priority translates into a reduction in relevance. However, Guardian's simultaneous introduction of plan C, to respond to the patient's low blood pressure with priority 3, preserves the medium relevance value for blood pressure. Although we do not illustrate it in Fig. 3, Guardian also could identify other variables that are relevant to its reasoning under plan C, either based on explicit domain knowledge or in the course of the reasoning itself.

In summary, our architecture enables an agent to adapt its perceptual strategy to its cognitive requirements in two ways. First, the agent maximizes its vigilance, while avoiding perceptual overload, by using feedback control and predictive control (based on control plans) to manage the global data rate underlying its perceptual strategy. Second, the agent acquires useful data, while avoiding distraction, by using dynamic control plans to adapt the relevance and abstraction parameters underlying its perceptual strategy. In an early experiment [50], Guardian's adaptation of its perceptual strategy reduced its input data rates to less than 10% of the original sensed data rates, with no degradation in the quality of its performance.

4. Adaptation of control mode

In order to function effectively in AIS niches, *an agent must adapt its control mode to changing features of its control situation.*

We can characterize control situations on several dimensions, including the uncertainty of events in the task environment, the degree of constraint on which sequences of actions will be effective in achieving goals, and the availability and cost of off-line and on-line computational resources. In simple niches, a characteristic control situation—representing a particular configuration of values on these several dimensions—may predominate. In that case, an agent should adopt the control mode that is most effective in its predominant situation. For example, the most effective control mode for some niches may be to plan and then execute carefully coordinated sequences of actions [16,44,50], while in other niches the most effective control mode may be to prepare and then execute more localized reactions to a range of possible run-time events [1,38,42,45].

However, AIS niches do not present characteristic control situations; they present control situations that vary over time on several dimensions. Two salient dimensions of variability, which we analyze here, are environmental uncertainty and constraint on effective actions. Environmental uncertainty determines how much monitoring an agent must do to determine run-time conditions. For example, a cold post-operative ICU patient presents low uncertainty; the patient is probably cold as a natural consequence of the surgery and quite likely to warm up gradually to normal body temperature, with no lingering after-effects. By contrast, a patient whose blood pressure is falling presents high uncertainty; it is unknown how long or how far the blood pressure will fall, what is causing the change, and what related effects may occur. Constraint on effective actions determines how many alternative courses of action the agent can pursue to achieve its goals. For example, there are many ways to help a cold post-operative patient regain normal body temperature, but there is only one way to enable a patient with a severe pneumothorax (a hole in the lung) to breathe: surgically insert a chest tube to allow accumulated air in the chest cavity to escape and thereby enable the lungs to inflate. As illustrated in Fig. 5, these two dimensions define a space of control situations.

To function effectively in AIS niches, therefore, an agent must possess and exploit a corresponding variety of control modes.

Like control situations, we can characterize control modes along several dimensions. Two salient dimensions, which we analyze here, are: the agent's sensitivity to run-time events and its advance commitment to specific actions. Sensitivity to run-time events measures how much the agent monitors its run-time environment. Commitment to specific actions measures how much the agent restricts in advance the actions it will execute at run time. (Control modes also vary, for example, on their demands for off-line and on-line computational and real-time resources; however these variables are not included in our analysis.) As illustrated in Fig. 5, these two dimensions, sensitivity and commitment, define a space of control modes.

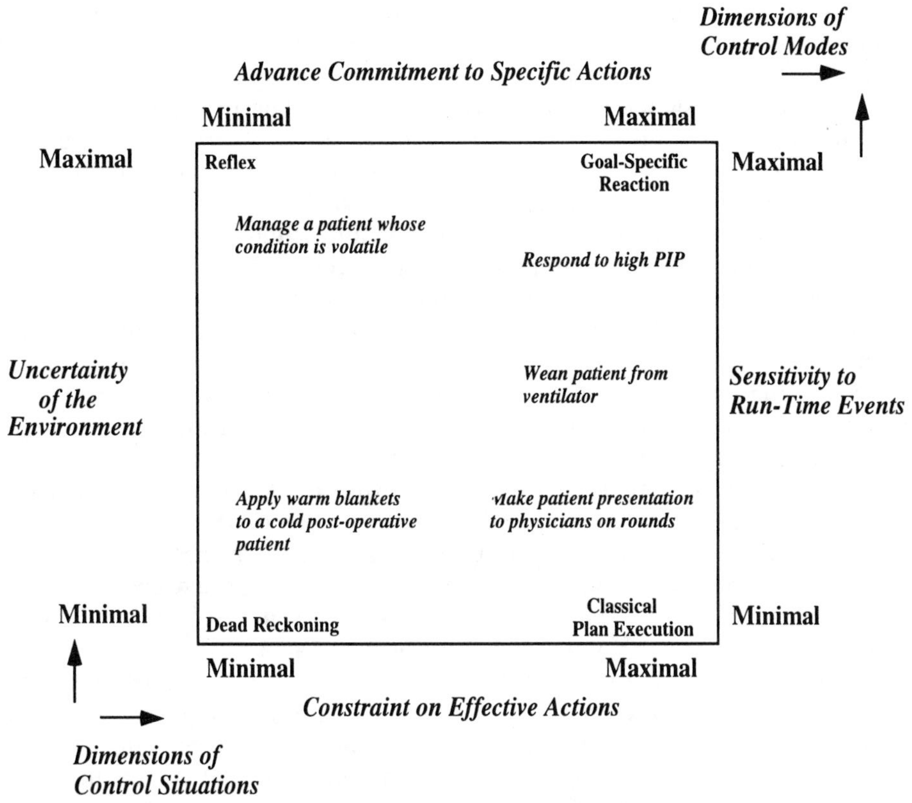

Fig. 5. Different control modes for different control situations.

By superimposing the spaces of control modes and control situations in Fig. 5, we suggest that particular control modes are appropriate for particular control situations—and, more importantly, that an agent could use a similar dimensional analysis to identify its dynamic control situation and adapt its control mode as appropriate. Let us consider the four corners of the space of control modes.

In a pure planning mode, an agent commits in advance to a sequence of actions, perhaps with limited conditionality, and then executes it at run time with minimal monitoring of run-time events. Planning mode is appropriate for control situations with low environmental uncertainty and high constraints on the selection and sequencing of effective actions. At the cost of preparation time, the agent exploits predictability in its environment to construct and execute an effective, efficient plan. For example, when requested to make patient presentations for physicians on rounds, Guardian should follow a standard protocol for presenting the relevant information in the correct order.

In a pure reactive mode, the agent commits in advance to a set of specific actions and conditions for their execution, but monitors run-time events to control invocation of particular actions from the set. Reactive mode is appropriate for control situations with high uncertainty and high constraints on effective actions. At the cost of preparation time and run-time resources, the agent can exploit its monitoring capabilities to respond flexibly to an uncertain environment. For example, Guardian should operate in reactive mode when responding to critical problems under time pressure, such as reacting to an observed increase in a patient's peak inspiratory pressure (a potentially life-threatening condition) by monitoring relevant data closely and using them to choose among a small set of predetermined diagnoses and associated therapeutic actions.

In both planning and reaction modes, an agent commits in advance to specific executable actions in order to meet strong constraints imposed by its goals. Planning mode exploits predictability of environmental events to minimize monitoring while following a single globally coordinated action sequence; thus it streamlines run-time performance. Reaction mode copes with greater uncertainty of environmental events by preparing a larger number of actions for a larger number of contingencies; run-time performance is less streamlined, but more robust. In intermediate modes between these two extremes, the agent modulates the amount of run-time monitoring and the conditionality of actions. In all regions along this border, however, the agent pays a high cost in advance preparation to choose the specific conditions it will monitor and the specific actions it will perform. The agent is maximally committed and cannot respond to a truly unanticipated event or perform a truly unanticipated action.

In what we might call a pure "dead reckoning" mode, an agent commits to a rough sequence of a few classes of actions and executes any sequence of specific actions within each successive class at run time. Dead reckoning mode is appropriate for control situations with minimal uncertainty of the environment and minimal constraints on actions. The agent can produce satisfactory behavior with a low cost of advance preparation. For example, Guardian should operate in dead reckoning mode when it has weak goals for non-critical conditions and plenty of time, such as improving the comfort and condition of cold post-operative patients by taking any of several different actions to help them warm up during their first couple of hours in the ICU.

In what we might call a pure "reflex" mode, the agent commits to a large class of actions, without specifying any of them individually, and monitors a similarly large set of run-time conditions to control its selection of actions for execution. Reflex mode is appropriate for control situations with high uncertainty and low constraint on effective actions. The agent can maximize its flexibility with a low cost of advance preparation. For example, Guardian should operate in reflex mode when a patient is very volatile, monitoring a broad class of patient data and letting observed irregularities elicit corrective actions.

In both dead reckoning and reflex modes, an agent is positioned implicitly to perform a larger number of specific actions and action sequences, compared to planning and reactive modes, respectively. Dead reckoning mode exploits predictability in environmental events to predetermine only the general shape of behavior, which the agent can instantiate as any of many alternative appropriate courses of action at run time. Reflex mode copes with greater environmental uncertainty by relying on run-time monitoring to invoke appropriate actions. In the intermediate modes between these two extremes, the agent modulates the amount of run-time monitoring and the balance of top-down versus bottom-up control of actions. In all modes of this border, however, the agent pays a minimal cost of advance preparation by identifying arbitrarily large classes of events to monitor and arbitrarily large classes of actions to perform. It does not commit to monitor any specific events or to perform any specific actions at all. Thus, unlike planning and reaction modes, the agent is always responding to "unanticipated" events and performing "unanticipated" actions.

Our analysis assumes that an agent has adequate monitoring and preparation resources for any control mode, but that, other things equal: (a) it prefers to spend resources on preparation rather than on monitoring in order to maximize the efficiency and global structure of run-time performance; and (b) it prefers to spend less resources when that will not compromise its goals. Alternatively, if we assume variations in availability or cost of these resources, the superimposed spaces show how run-time performance may be degraded in order to conserve particular resources. A more comprehensive analysis would introduce availability and demand for monitoring and preparation resources as higher-order dimensions of the superimposed spaces. The purpose of our analysis in the present context is to partially characterize the variability of control situations and differences in the situation-specific efficacy of alternative control modes.

To function effectively in AIS niches, an agent must continually identify its control situation, choose an appropriate control mode, and implement the chosen mode. We use examples from Guardian's niche to illustrate how our architecture supports this kind of adaptation.

First, an agent must identify its control situation. The agent can assess the uncertainty of its environment by recognizing that it is in states with known uncertainty. For example, Guardian might know that certain surgical procedures are more likely than others to be followed by recovery problems (higher uncertainty) in the ICU. The agent also can assess uncertainty empirically at run time, tracking the variance in its observations over time, noticing that planned actions are not having their expected effects, etc. The agent can assess the constraint on effective actions based on domain knowledge or on measurements of the search space associated with a particular goal. For example, Guardian might know that physicians want all patient presentations to follow the standard protocol (high constraint). As mentioned above, control situations also vary along other dimensions, such as the availability of computational and real-time resources during and prior to run time. As discussed in Section 3, an agent can estimate current and future demand for computational resources by analyzing its current and future control plans. It can estimate the availability of real-time resources on the basis of domain knowledge. For example, Guardian might know that some ICU problems evolve slowly, while others quickly become life-threatening.

Next, the agent must choose an appropriate control mode. The superimposed spaces in Fig. 5 provide one framework for making this choice. As mentioned above, control modes also vary along other dimensions, such as their demand for computational and real-time resources during and prior to run time. An agent can have qualitative knowledge of the resource requirements associated with generic control modes, such as those in Fig. 5. In addition, it might be able to quantify the requirements for a particular control mode in a particular parameterized situation.

Having identified its control situation and chosen an appropriate control mode, the agent must effect the chosen mode. Fig. 6 summarizes how our architecture enables an agent to adapt its control mode, modulating its sensitivity to run-time events and its commitment to specific actions by manipulating two properties of its control plan: the specificity of action class indicated in each component control decision and the degree of sequential organization among control decisions. Again we illustrate this capability with the control modes in the four corners of the space.

The agent goes into a pure planning mode by constructing a control plan that

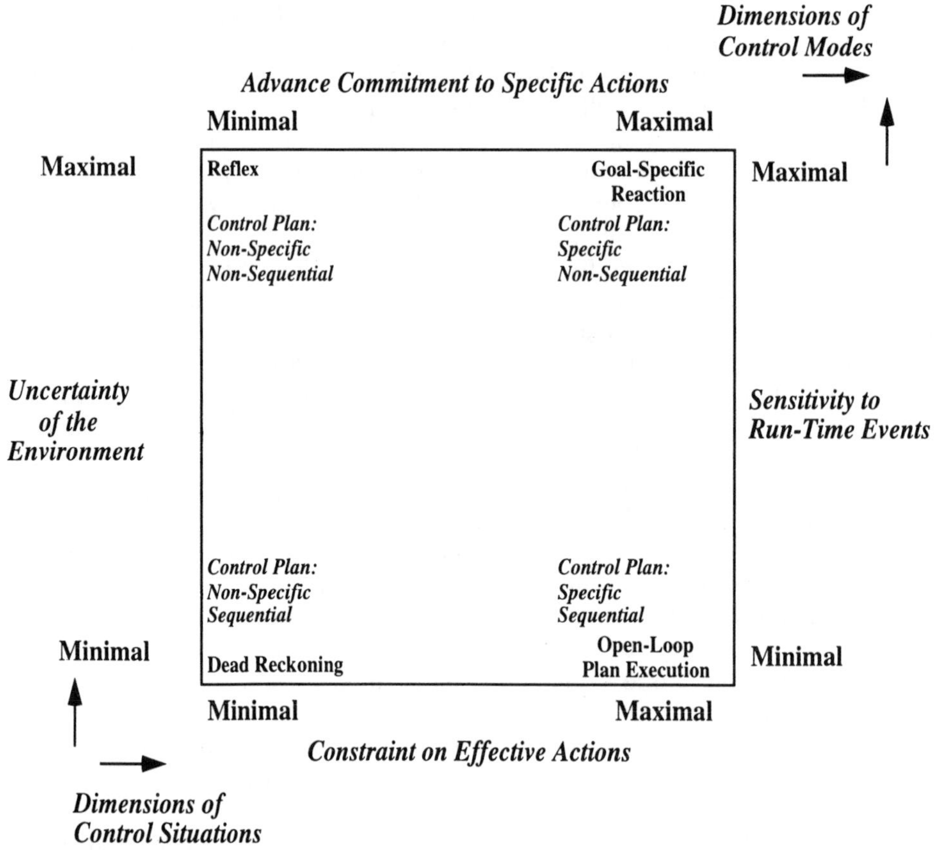

Fig. 6. Varying control plan properties to effect different control modes.

comprises a sequence of decisions, each identifying a specific executable action. It monitors only those events that are necessary to trigger the current next action in the plan. It tries to trigger only each successive next planned action. As a result, the agent triggers and executes the planned sequence of specific actions very quickly and reliably.

The agent goes into reactive mode by constructing a control plan that comprises an unordered set of decisions, each identifying a specific condition–action contingency. It monitors only those events necessary to evaluate the specified conditions. It attempts to trigger only the specified actions and executes whichever ones it triggers. As a result, the agent executes a less predictable sequence of a reliable set of planned actions. It is a little slower than in planning mode because it monitors all conditions all the time.

The agent goes into dead reckoning mode by constructing a control plan that comprises a sequence of a few general action classes. It monitors only those events that might trigger any member of the current planned action class. It attempts to trigger only actions that are members of the current planned action class and executes whichever ones it triggers until the local goal of the current planned action class is met. As a result, the agent executes a roughly predictable sequence of certain kinds of actions, with variability in the number and specific identities of executed actions within each successive class.

The agent goes into reflex mode by constructing a plan that comprises an unordered set of decisions, each identifying a class of condition–action contingencies. It monitors only those events that might trigger any member of any of the action classes and executes whichever ones it triggers. As a result, the agent's behavior is quite unpredictable in the number, identities, and sequence of specific actions it executes.

Our analysis can potentially be translated into the language of classical control theory. For example, the border between plans and reactive systems corresponds to the control-theoretic distinction between open-loop and closed-loop policies. Techniques for choosing optimal control modes also exploit our concept of uncertainty. Thus, it is known that in a deterministic environment, an optimal open-loop policy exists, while in a stochastic environment there exists a closed-loop policy that performs better than any open-loop policy. To our knowledge, adaptive control theory does not exploit our concept of constraint on actions (which corresponds to the control-theoretic concept of solution density) as a basis for prescribing control modes. In addition, although there exist control-theoretic approaches to run-time switching of control modes [43], these approaches typically switch among a much more homogeneous set of alternative controllers in the context of much simpler task environments. Finally, control-theoretic approaches do not provide a framework for smooth transitions in a continuous space of controllers.[1]

In summary, our architecture enables an agent to adapt its control mode among

---

[1] I am grateful to Satinder Pal Singh for calling my attention to the relationship between the present analysis and the classical control-theoretic analysis.

a diverse set of control modes, on the basis of its environmental uncertainty and internally determined constraints on its actions, by modifying two key parameters of its control plans: specificity and sequential organization of component control decisions.

5. Adaptation of reasoning tasks

In order to function effectively in AIS niches, *an agent must adapt its reasoning tasks to dynamic environmental conditions*.

In general, AIS niches demand performance of multiple component reasoning tasks. We define a task in terms of the types of domain entities it takes as inputs and produces as outputs and the relationships that must hold between particular instances of inputs and outputs. For example, in a diagnosis task, inputs are observed symptoms in a monitored system, outputs are conditions within the system, and the relationship is that the conditions cause the symptoms. For example, Guardian might diagnose the physiological condition that is causing a patient's observed low blood pressure. As a second example, in a prediction task, inputs are initial conditions in a monitored system, outputs are subsequent conditions in the system, and the relationship is that the subsequent conditions have a high conditional probability given the initial conditions. For example, Guardian might predict the consequences of leaving the patient's low blood pressure untreated. As a third example, in a planning task, inputs are initial conditions and desirable subsequent conditions, outputs are specifications for a pattern of actions, and the relationship is that performing the planned actions in the context of the initial conditions is expected to bring about the desirable subsequent conditions. For example, Guardian might plan therapeutic actions to raise the patient's low blood pressure back to normal range. An agent such as Guardian has many opportunities to perform different instances of each of these tasks and to perform sequences of related tasks, for example perceiving a problem, diagnosing it, then planning and executing a corrective response.

Our agent architecture provides a natural platform for realizing and integrating performance of diverse, potentially interacting tasks. As discussed in Section 2, each of an agent's reasoning methods is operationalized as a set of event-triggered reasoning operations, including some that construct control plans to organize the reasoning process appropriately in particular situations. Execution of each reasoning operation contributes to an incrementally growing solution in global memory and produces events that may trigger other reasoning operations. This "blackboard model" for reasoning is extremely general; it can support the inferential processes underlying many different reasoning tasks and potential interactions among tasks based on intermediate, as well as final results [12,29].

Within the architecture, any perceptual or cognitive event potentially can trigger operations involved in any known task. All triggered operations are placed on a global agenda, where they compete to be scheduled and executed. Depending on its control plan, the agent may execute all the operations in a given reasoning task prior to beginning a new one or it may interleave the operations of several tasks. In either case, the intermediate and final results of different tasks are recorded in the global memory, where they can influence one another. In Section 2 above, we illustrated how Guardian initiates, performs, and terminates a single task in response to a perceptual event: it reactively diagnosed and corrected a problem signaled by perceived low blood pressure. More generally, the event-based triggering of task-specific operations allows an agent to adapt its selection and sequencing of reasoning tasks to perceived conditions in the external environment and to internally generated conditions reflecting the intrinsic relations among reasoning tasks.

Table 3 illustrates Guardian's performance of a series of interacting perception, reasoning, and action tasks in which each task is triggered by preceding

Table 3
Illustrative chain of reasoning tasks initiated by cognitive and perceptual events

Triggering events	Tasks performed	Resulting events
1. Sense: Patient data	Perceive: Patient data	Observe: Many data values Intend: Normal patient state Expect: Normal patient data
2. Perceive: PIP value	Assess: PIP values	Observe: PIP high, rising $t1$–$t3$
3. Observe: PIP high, rising $t1$–$t3$	Diagnose: PIP rising	Hypothesize: Compliance Expect: Low arterial O_2
4. Expect: Low arterial O_2	Plan: Improve arterial O_2 now	Intend: Raise FIO_2 now Conditionally Expect: Raise arterial O_2 gradually
5. Intend: Raise FIO_2 now	Do: Raise FIO_2 Perceive: FIO_2 setting	Observe: Raise FIO_2 Expect: Raise arterial O_2 grad.
6. Hypothesize: Compliance	Diagnose: Compliance	Hypothesize: Pneumothorax $t1$ Expect: Falling arterial O_2 Expect: Possible death $> t8$

7. Expect: Falling arterial O_2
Expect: Possible death $> t8$
	Plan: Lower PIP now and
	Normalize arterial O_2
		(a) Step 1
		Intend: Insert chest tube now
		Conditionally Expect:
		    Lower PIP now
		Conditionally Expect:
		    Raise arterial O_2 promptly

8. Intend: Insert chest tube now	Do: Insert chest tube Perceive: Chest tube insertion Perceive: PIP data	Observe: Chest tube inserted Observe: Lower PIP now Expect: Raise arterial O_2
9. Observe: Lower PIP	Plan: Normalize arterial O_2	(b) Step 2 Intend: Lower FIO_2 now Conditionally Expect: Normal arterial O_2
10. Intend: Lower FIO_2 now	Do: Lower FIO_2 Perceive: FIO_2 setting	Observe: Lower FIO_2 Expect: Normal arterial O_2

perceptual or-cognitive events and produces cognitive events of its own that may trigger subsequent tasks. Table 3 does not show the triggering, execution, and results of each task's component reasoning operations. And it does not show the many triggered tasks that Guardian does not choose to execute.

In step 1, Guardian is observing a variety of patient data. It intends that the patient it is monitoring should be in a "normal" state (normal for a particular class of post-surgical patients) and, because it is not aware of any problems, expects that all patient data will be normal. As we shall see, much of Guardian's reasoning is driven by discrepancies between phenomena it *observes*, *expects* and *intends*. Our agent architecture makes these distinctions explicit and automatically detects mismatches to trigger reasoning activities.

In steps 2–3, Guardian detects an oxygen delivery problem and partially diagnoses it. In step 1, Guardian perceives patient data available from its sensors and produces a number of observations. In step 2, one of the new observations, the new value of PIP (peak inspiratory pressure), triggers a task to assess the dynamic state of the patient's PIP. The assessment task produces a new observation, that the patient's PIP is high and has been rising during the time interval $t1$–$t3$. This observation violates Guardian's expectation of normal patient data and so, in step 3, triggers a task to diagnose the cause of the discrepancy. The diagnosis task itself produces two results: a hypothesis that the patient is suffering from a compliance problem (inability to inhale sufficient air; as opposed to a sensor error in PIP measurement or a mechanical problem in the ventilator, for example); and an expectation that, as a result, the patient's arterial oxygen will be low.

At this point, the diagnosis is not complete: Guardian does not know what is causing the compliance problem. However, because the expected low arterial oxygen violates Guardian's intention that the patient should be in a normal state and because arterial oxygen is a life-critical physiological parameter, it does not immediately continue the diagnosis task. Instead, in step 4, the expectation of low arterial oxygen triggers a planning task to improve the patient's arterial oxygen now. The planning task produces an intention to raise the FIO_2 now (increasing the fraction of inhaled oxygen delivered by the ventilator), with the conditional expectation that doing so will raise the patient's arterial oxygen gradually. In step 5, the intention to raise FIO_2 now triggers the corresponding action and an associated perceptual task to confirm successful execution of the action. Guardian observes that it has indeed raised the patient's FIO_2 and, as a result, expects the arterial oxygen to rise. Note that, in the present scenario (without an oximeter in place), Guardian cannot observe the arterial oxygen directly and so must rely on the expected effects of its action of raising the FIO_2.

In step 6, Guardian continues its diagnosis of the oxygen delivery (compliance) problem. The previous hypothesis of a compliance problem (produced in step 3), which violates Guardian's intention of normal patient state, triggers a task to diagnose the underlying cause. This task produces three results: a more specific hypothesis, that the patient suffered a pneumothorax (a hole in the lung that allows inhaled air to rush out into the chest cavity, compressing the lungs and preventing subsequent inhalation) at time $t1$; an expectation that, as a result of the pneumothorax and despite Guardian's having raised the FIO_2, the patient's arterial oxygen will continue to fall; and a second expectation that, as a result of the falling arterial oxygen, the patient may die after time $t8$.

In step 7, these two expectations, which dramatically violate Guardian's intention of normal patient state, trigger a two-part planning task: (a) to lower the patient's PIP now so that any oxygen at all can be delivered; and (b) to normalize the patient's arterial oxygen. The first part of the planning task produces step 1: an intention to insert a chest tube immediately (to relieve pressure in the chest cavity and enable the lungs to inflate), with the conditional expectation that doing so will lower the patient's PIP immediately and, as a result, raise the arterial oxygen promptly.

At this point, the plan is not complete: Guardian has not determined how to normalize the patient's arterial oxygen. However, because the patient is in a life-threatening condition, it does not immediately continue its planning task. Instead, in step 8, the intention to insert a chest tube now triggers the corresponding action and associated perceptual tasks to confirm the insertion of the chest tube and the expected lowering of the patient's PIP. Again, Guardian cannot observe the expected rise in arterial oxygen directly and must rely on the expected effects of lowering the patient's PIP in the presence of a pneumothorax.

In step 9, Guardian's confirmation of the expected lower PIP triggers resumption of its interrupted planning task, producing step 2: an intention to lower the FIO_2 (back to its previous level), with the conditional expectation that arterial oxygen will gradually return to normal. In step 10, this intention triggers the corresponding action and an associated perceptual task to confirm the new FIO_2 setting. Again, Guardian expects, but cannot observe directly, that the patient's arterial oxygen gradually will return to normal. At this point in the scenario, with the crisis apparently resolved and the time pressure eased, Guardian may decide to place an oximeter so that it can monitor the patient's arterial oxygen directly or, alternatively, to send a blood sample to the laboratory for a gas analysis after twenty minutes or so.

As this scenario illustrates, our architecture allows an agent to perform a variety of reasoning tasks and, more importantly, to adapt its selection, ordering, and interleaving of reasoning tasks to dynamic perceived and inferred conditions in its environment. Triggering tasks with perceptual events enables the agent to adapt to exogenously produced changes in the world. Triggering tasks with cognitive events enables the agent to follow the intrinsic logical relations among tasks—where the intermediate or final results of one task provide the input to another. Explicit representation of the initial, intermediate, and final results of reasoning tasks allows the agent to interrupt and resume tasks deliberately.

6. Adaptation of reasoning methods

In order to function effectively in AIS niches, *an agent must adapt its reasoning methods to the available information.*

Given our input–output definition of tasks, there may be alternative methods for performing particular tasks. For example, an agent might perform a diagnosis task by means of a "model-based" method, in which it instantiates structure/ function models of phenomena observed in the monitored system and follows causal links to identify and instantiate hypothesized precursors. Alternatively, an agent might apply a "structured selection" method [10], in which it abstracts the observed data, performs a heuristic mapping into the hypothesis space, and refines the identified hypothesis back into the problem context. Alternatively, the agent might use a case-based method [49], in which it retrieves cases manifesting problems similar to the observed problem and hypothesizes that the diagnoses associated with those cases may explain the observed problem. Similarly, alternative methods may be applicable to other tasks, such as monitoring, prediction, and planning.

Following our analysis of situation-appropriate control modes (Section 4), we offer a similar analysis of situation-appropriate reasoning methods. Again, reasoning situations and methods vary along complementary dimensions: availability versus consumption of resources (e.g., domain knowledge, environmental data, real time, and computation); demand versus provision of performance properties (e.g., interruptability, potentially useful intermediate results); and requirement versus provision of response features (e.g., precision, certainty, quality, and justification).

Taking a subset of the dimensions defined by these variables for illustration, Fig. 7 superimposes two two-dimensional spaces, mapping methods that vary in their consumption of domain knowledge and run-time data onto situations that vary in the availability of these two resources. Methods in particular regions of the superimposed spaces are "appropriate" for situations in corresponding regions, based on two simplifying assumptions: (a) as more knowledge and data are brought to bear, the agent's response improves monotonically on all features; and (b) the agent prefers to expend whatever resources are available in order to produce the highest quality response. A more complete analysis would incorporate information about the actual cost of resources and the utility of particular performance and response features as higher-order dimensions of the superimposed spaces. But even with our simplifying assumptions, the present analysis illustrates the need and potential for agents operating in AIS niches to choose and use appropriate reasoning methods in different reasoning situations.

For illustration, we consider methods representing the four corners of the space in Fig. 7, applied to a prediction task.

Applying a quantitative simulation method [28] to a prediction task, an agent uses observed numeric data to instantiate parameters representing the initial conditions and other important variables in a set of differential equations and calculates the predicted values of the variables of interest after variable time t. Quantitative simulation produces precise, reliable, temporally specific quantitative results and explanatory justification in terms of the instantiated equations. Computation time may be high. Other things equal, quantitative simulation is appropriate when the reasoning context includes an appropriate set of differential equations and the run-time data necessary to instantiate the necessary parame-

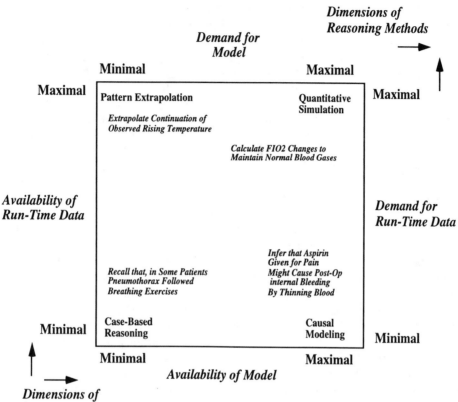

Fig. 7. Different methods for different contexts.

ters. For example, Guardian should use quantitative simulation to predict whether current values of FIO_2 (amount of oxygen provided by the ventilator on each breath) will maintain normal blood gases for the patient over some time period.

Applying a causal modeling method [40] to a prediction task, an agent uses qualitative observations to instantiate variables in a causal network with the initial conditions and follows causal links to identify predicted conditions. Causal modeling produces reliable, qualitative results, but no specific temporal information. It provides explanatory justification in terms of the instantiated conditions and causal links in the model. Run-time computation depends on the branching factor and depth of the model. Other things equal, causal modeling is appropriate when the reasoning context includes an appropriate causal model and when either: (a) the data, knowledge, or resources necessary to instantiate a more precise quantitative model are not available; or (b) the precision of quantitative simulation is not needed. For example, Guardian should use causal modeling to predict that aspirin given to a post-operative patient for pain will also thin the patient's blood (a side-effect) and, therefore, might also cause internal bleeding.

With both quantitative simulation and causal modeling, an agent exploits strong models to make predictions (or perform other tasks) and to explain its conclusions. Quantitative simulation also exploits larger amounts of run-time data to produce more specific, temporally constrained, quantitative predictions. Causal modeling compensates for a lack of relevant run-time data by producing more general, qualitative predictions with less specific temporal properties. Applying intermediate methods between quantitative simulation and causal modeling, the agent uses whatever data are available to quantify its model-based predictions as much as possible. With all methods along this border, however, the agent pays a high cost in run-time computation to reason out its predictions (or other conclusions). In addition, the agent's ability to perform its task with these methods is limited by the availability of appropriate models—which tend to be in short supply in some domains, such as ICU monitoring, but more available in other domains such as device monitoring.

Applying a pattern extrapolation method [46] to a prediction task, an agent incrementally instantiates time-varying patterns in observed data values and extraplates their completion to identify predicted conditions. Pattern extrapolation can produce predictions where no models are available, but with high uncertainty and no explanatory justification at all. Run-time computation depends on the number and complexity of known pattern definitions. Pattern extrapolation is appropriate when the reasoning context provides a lot of run-time data for developing and distinguishing among different potential patterns. For example, Guardian could use pattern extrapolation to predict that a monitored patient's rising temperature might continue to rise at its current rate, eventually reaching a dangerous region.

Applying a case-based method [19,31,41] to a prediction task, an agent retrieves a previous case in which conditions similar to those in the present case occurred and predicts that subsequent conditions in the present case will be similar to those in the previous case. Case-based reasoning can produce predictions in a broad range of situations, but with high uncertainty and no explanatory justification at all. Computation time depends on the agent's repertoire of cases and indexing mechanism. Case-based reasoning is appropriate when the task context includes a representative sample of cases and the run-time data necessary to index into the "right" prior case. For example, Guardian could use case-based reasoning about previous lung surgery patients to predict that a post-operative patient who is performing his breathing exercises very vigorously might develop a pneumothorax (a hole in the lung) in the area of a lung incision.

With both pattern extrapolation and case-based reasoning, an agent compensates for the absence of good models by using other kinds of knowledge (abstract pattern definitions or previous cases) to make predictions (or perform other reasoning tasks). Pattern extrapolation also exploits the availability of large amounts of run-time data to compensate for the absence of relevant cases. With all methods along this border, the agent pays a minimal cost in run-time computation. Its ability to perform its task is limited primarily by its repertoire of abstract pattern definitions and prior cases, which are readily available in medical domains such as ICU monitoring (often called "clinical experience"), as well as in engineering domains.

Our architecture provides a natural environment for representing, selecting, and applying situation-appropriate reasoning methods. Alternative methods for performing a given task can be represented as different collections of reasoning operations, all of which might be triggered by events signaling a need for that task to be performed. For example, Guardian's decision to give a patient aspirin to relieve pain might trigger a control decision to predict possible side effects, along with the initial reasoning operations underlying quantitative simulation, causal modeling, and case-based reasoning methods for performing prediction tasks. At that point, Guardian is free to apply any, all, or none of the triggered methods. Because reasoning skills are represented explicitly, an agent can determine what run-time data and models are required by a given method in a situation, and which of the required data and models are available in the situation. Continuing the example, Guardian could follow the analysis of Fig. 7 (or a similar analysis that incorporates other situational variables) to determine that, for the effects of aspirin, it has a very large number of potentially relevant cases varying on many dimensions, no quantitative models at all, and a simple causal model with a modest demand for run-time data. Under these circumstances, it would be appropriate to use the causal model. By modifying its initial control decision, so that it now intends to *causally* predict the side effects of giving aspirin, Guardian insures the selection of causal reasoning operations to perform its task.

In summary, our architecture allows an agent to adapt its reasoning methods to the availability of resources by representing a diverse collection of reasoning methods as sets of event-triggered reasoning operations, explicitly storing method-specific resource requirements, and allowing the agent to construct run-time control plans that reflect its assessment of situation-specific resource availability.

7. Adaptation of meta-control strategy

In order to function effectively in AIS niches, *an agent must adapt its meta-control strategy to dynamic configurations of demands and opportunities for activity*.

An agent's meta-control strategy places global constraints on its allocation of computational and physical (e.g., sensors, effectors) resources among competing activities. As a result, it determines which goals the agent achieves, to what degree, and with what side effects. As illustrated throughout this paper, our architecture permits an agent to adapt its perceptual strategy, control mode, reasoning task, and reasoning method to the requirements of a given activity. However, AIS niches characteristically present demands and opportunities for multiple activities during overlapping time intervals. For example, an ICU patient may manifest several simultaneous problems, varying in criticality. While Guardian is responding to one set of problems, it must continue to monitor other aspects of the patient's condition and, quite possibly, respond to newly occurring problems along the way. In addition, Guardian may perform other tasks not directly concerned with patient monitoring, such as describing a patient's progress during the preceding eight hours to a physician on rounds, explaining its diagnostic reasoning to a medical student, or advising a nurse of anticipated changes in the patient's condition. How should Guardian respond to each new demand or opportunity as it arises? How should its responses to new events impact on its prior commitments to ongoing activities—and vice versa? Thus, in AIS niches, the meta-control problem is: How should an agent allocate its limited computational resources among dynamic configurations of competing and complementary activities so as to achieve a high overall utility of its behavior?

Our architecture provides a natural framework for dynamic adaptation of explicit meta-control strategies for global coordination of behavior. Working within the basic architectural mechanism, an agent can trigger meta-control operations based on changes to its control plans. It can use some meta-control operations to monitor its activity-specific control decisions, their implications for resource consumption, and its actual progress toward associated objectives—all as they evolve over time. It can use other operations to revise activity-specific control decisions in light of global considerations. For example, Guardian might notice that it has made a series of control decisions to diagnose and treat a series of unanticipated problems. Although each of these decisions may be individually justifiable, together they may exhaust Guardian's computational and perceptual resources and, as a result, compromise its vigilance. Even worse, the division of available resources among the several problems may preclude treating any of them before its deadline. Having made this assessment, Guardian could make a meta-control decision to postpone its diagnosis and treatment of the least important of its pending problems to conserve resources for monitoring and to insure treatment of the most critical problems by deadline.

The architecture also allows an agent to use meta-control decisions prospectively to establish the desired global character of its intended behavior by constraining subsequent meta-level and activity-specific control reasoning. For example, in the episodes illustrated in Figs. 8 and 9, Guardian is monitoring a patient who develops two problems, first low blood pressure and then high PIP (peak inspiratory pressure). In both cases, Guardian diagnoses the low blood pressure as resulting from dehydration and treats it by increasing fluid intake. In both cases, it diagnoses the high PIP first as a hypoxia problem, which it treats by increasing the patient's oxygen, and then more specifically as the result of a pneumothorax, which it treats by inserting a chest tube. However, in the two figures these problems and treatments occur in different meta-level contexts, producing subtle, but significant differences in Guardian's behavior and, under some value models, in the overall utility of its behavior.

The two episodes differ in meta-control decision B versus B'. In Fig. 8, Guardian has made meta-control decision B, to give its highest priority to urgent problems, its next highest priority to monitoring, and its third highest priority to

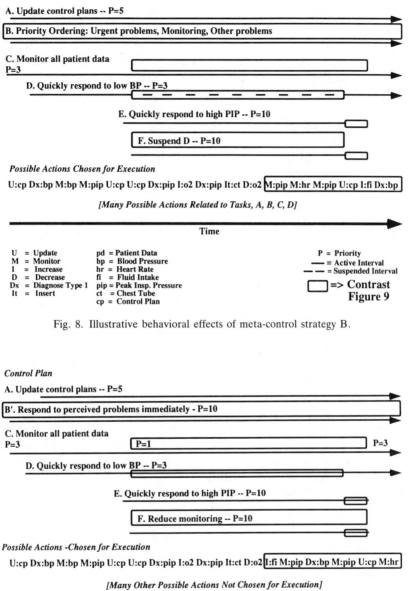

Control Plan

A. Update control plans -- P=5

B. Priority Ordering: Urgent problems, Monitoring, Other problems

C. Monitor all patient data
P=3

D. Quickly respond to low BP -- P=3

E. Quickly respond to high PIP -- P=10

F. Suspend D -- P=10

Possible Actions Chosen for Execution

U:cp Dx:bp M:bp M:pip U:cp U:cp Dx:pip I:o2 Dx:pip It:ct D:o2 | M:pip M:hr M:pip U:cp I:fi Dx:bp

[Many Possible Actions Related to Tasks, A, B, C, D]

Time

U = Update	pd = Patient Data	P = Priority
M = Monitor	bp = Blood Pressure	—— = Active Interval
I = Increase	hr = Heart Rate	— — = Suspended Interval
D = Decrease	fi = Fluid Intake	
Dx = Diagnose Type 1	pip = Peak Insp. Pressure	☐ => Contrast
It = Insert	ct = Chest Tube	**Figure 9**
	cp = Control Plan	

Fig. 8. Illustrative behavioral effects of meta-control strategy B.

Control Plan

A. Update control plans -- P=5

B'. Respond to perceived problems immediately - P=10

C. Monitor all patient data
P=3   P=1   P=3

D. Quickly respond to low BP -- P=3

E. Quickly respond to high PIP -- P=10

F. Reduce monitoring -- P=10

Possible Actions -Chosen for Execution

U:cp Dx:bp M:bp M:pip U:cp U:cp Dx:pip I:o2 Dx:pip It:ct D:o2 | I:fi M:pip Dx:bp M:pip U:cp M:hr

[Many Other Possible Actions Not Chosen for Execution]

Time

U = Update	pd = Patient Data	P = Priority
M = Monitor	bp = Blood Pressure	—— = Active Interval
I = Increase	hr = Heart Rate	— — = Suspended Interval
D = Decrease	fi = Fluid Intake	
Dx = Diagnose	pip = Peak Insp. Pressure	☐ => Contrast
It = Insert	ct = Chest Tube	**Figure 8**
	cp = Control Plan	

Fig. 9. Illustrative behavioral effects of meta-control strategy B'.

other problems. As a result, when it observes and decides to respond quickly to
the patient's high PIP, Guardian maintains its current monitoring activity, but
decides to suspend its activities related to the patient's low blood pressure, a less
important problem, until it has resolved the patient's high PIP. In Fig. 9,
Guardian has made a different meta-control decision B', to respond to perceived
problems immediately. As a result, when it observes and decides to respond
quickly to the patient's high PIP, Guardian continues its activities related to the
patient's low blood pressure, but reduces its monitoring activities until it has
resolved the patient's high PIP. A comparison of corresponding elements of Figs.
8 and 9 reveals other consequences of the difference in meta-level strategy. Under
strategy B in Fig. 8, Guardian completes its diagnosis and treatment of the high
PIP faster than under strategy B' in Fig. 9, but completes its diagnosis and
treatment of the low blood pressure problem later. Under strategy B in Fig. 8, it
remains sensitive to patient data not directly related to its current activities (e.g.,
heart rate), while under strategy B' in Fig. 9, its attention to patient data is
depressed by its attention to immediate problems. Depending on Guardian's
value model, each of these meta-control strategies could produce a higher overall
utility of behavior.

As these simple examples illustrate, our architecture uses the same underlying
mechanism to enable an agent to represent, reason about, and use both activity-
specific control plans and meta-control plans. An agent can adapt its meta-control
strategy to its dynamic configuration of potential activities by: (a) analyzing
control plans representing intended activities to estimate their resource requirements; (b) assessing the availability of required resources in the prospective
situation; and (c) making or modifying meta-control decisions that establish
appropriate constraints on the construction of activity-specific control plans. From
the agent's point of view, meta-control plans are no different from other control
plans, all of which simply establish local preferences for performing different
classes of reasoning operations—which may include different classes of task-level
reasoning operations, control operations, and meta-control operations. Similarly,
the agent need not treat meta-control planning any differently from its other
reasoning activities, all of which occur through the scheduling and execution of
event-triggered reasoning operations.

8. Evaluation

8.1. Evaluation paradigm

How can we evaluate the proposed architecture for adaptive intelligent
systems?

Given the complexity of the behavior we aim to support, we emphasize
empirical evaluation. Following Simon's observations on computer systems in
general, we believe that the problems we are trying to address more closely

resemble those of biology or psychology than physics and therefore so should our methods:

> We are never going to have three laws of motion in computer science. ... Now computing systems may or may not be as complicated as living organisms, but they are pretty complicated, and the principal way in which we are going to learn about them is to go into a laboratory and find facts. We do that by building systems and testing them. [47, p. 128]

Moreover, we believe that *challenging real-world domains* (rather than artificially structured games or toy problems) offer the richest experimental testbed for investigating adaptive intelligent systems, their architectures, and their behavior. In fact, it is difficult to define an artificial task domain that can simulate all of the dimensions of adaptation we observe in real-world AIS niches. Thus, for example, Feigenbaum explains how working on the DENDRAL project [15] played a critical role in the discovery that production rules could be used for knowledge representation:

> Buchanan succeeded where Waterman failed because Buchanan was immersed in the details of the chemistry, the knowledge representation problem, and the programming of the reasoning process. Waterman was only an onlooker. The immense importance of the experimental method in AI, and more broadly in CS, is that it provides the necessary mental data in sufficient detail to stimulate innovation and discovery. Perhaps it's easier to discover new ideas than to invent them! [14, p. 197]

Our goal is to develop an architecture that meets a *sufficiency criterion*, supporting adaptive intelligent systems throughout a large class of AIS niches. Thus, it is less important that any particular aspect of the architecture should embody the optimal approach to achieving any particular form of adaptation than that the architecture should gracefully integrate all of the required forms of adaptation—and that it should demonstrably be able to produce those behavioral adaptations as required by the operating environment. As Newell remarks on how best to evaluate unified theories of cognition:

> *Necessary* characteristics are well and good, but they are substantially less than half the story. *Sufficiency* is all important. [37, p. 158]

Finally, other things being equal—in particular, given that the sufficiency criterion has been met, we prefer *architectural parsimony*. A compelling architecture should minimize the number of component mechanisms with which it supports the several required forms of adaptation.

8.2. Current status of experimental agents

Our architecture has been implemented in an application-independent form and used to build experimental agents in several of the AIS niches in Fig. 1.

Guardian is the most substantial of our experimental agents. Guardian demonstration 4 [25] monitors on the order of twenty continuously sensed patient data variables and several occasionally sensed variables. Its tasks include monitoring, fault detection, diagnosis, prediction, explanation, and planning. It has relatively fast reasoning methods based on clinical knowledge of commonly occurring problems, their typical symptoms, and their standard treatments. It also has relatively slow, but more comprehensive reasoning methods based on symbolic knowledge of the underlying anatomy, physiology, and pathophysiology. Guardian demonstration 4 has been applied to a small number of simple, but realistic ICU scenarios. As illustrated in examples throughout the paper, this version of Guardian performs *rudimentary* versions of all of the different kinds of adaptation discussed above. Guardian demonstration 5, which is currently under development, will monitor on the order of 100 variables. It will perform the same set of tasks performed in demonstration 4, but with a more comprehensive set of methods. It will have a much larger medical knowledge base. Most important in the present context, Guardian demonstration 5 will provide a richer environment for evaluating the claimed architectural support for adaptation.

In addition to Guardian, several experimental monitoring agents have been developed in the architecture. In our laboratory, we have developed experimental agents to monitor power plant equipment [49] and semi-conductor manufacturing equipment [35]. Both of these agents possess symbolic representations of the structure, function, and behavior of the equipment being monitored. They perform model-based process tracking, diagnosis, prediction, and explanation. Each one has been demonstrated on two or three simple, but realistic scenarios. A similar agent has been developed to monitor materials processing [39]. These applications demonstrate the generality of our agent architecture across diverse domains within the AIS monitoring niche.

More recently, we have begun studying the application of our architecture to a class of niches for adaptive intelligent robots, which we call "AIbots". In a first demonstration [24], we developed a simulated robot that plans surveillance destinations and routes, gathers information from the environment, and responds to unanticipated alarms. Despite its simplicity, this agent exhibits several of the kinds of adaptation discussed in this paper. It uses reasoning to select and parameterize perceptual strategies and navigation strategies. It uses dynamic control plans to decide which high-level task to perform (e.g., situation assessment, planning, information gathering) and which method to use for a given task (e.g., a classical planner versus a case-based planner). In a second demonstration, we developed a simulated robot that acts as a general office factotum. It can deliver messages personally or electronically, fetch and deliver objects, and learn unanticipated features of its environment. It accepts asynchronous requests for instances of these message and object goals and generates learning goals for itself. It plans and executes behavior to achieve goals in various sequences and combinations, based on their priorities, deadlines, and interactions with one another. This agent continuously adapts whatever pending goals and plans it has in light of newly perceived information about its environment, new goals, or the unanticipated details of progress on current goals and plans. Finally, in a third demonstration, we have demonstrated the above-described behaviors on an actual Nomad 200 robot [52] operating in our offices.

The intelligent monitoring niches exemplified by Guardian and the intelligent robotics niches exemplified in our AIbots demand the array of behavioral adaptations characteristic of all adaptive intelligent systems, but they emphasize complementary subsets of these demands. The Guardian niche emphasizes broad and deep domain knowledge and reasoning, important requirements for adaptive selective perception (but no real signal processing), and minimal requirements for action control. The AIbots niche emphasizes signal interpretation as well as selective perception, important requirements for controlling physical action, and simpler cognitive behaviors. For this reason, we find them to be an interesting combination of niches in which to evaluate our architecture.

8.3. Comparison with other architectures

Although our architecture is not the only one that supports adaptation, it is one of a small set of candidate architectures currently in the literature. However, most of these other architectures focus on selected aspects of adaptation, as illustrated by the following examples. Soar [32,37] provides a very general search mechanism that can be applied to a variety of reasoning tasks and a learning mechanism that automatically moves the agent from search to a more reactive control mode based on experience. However, it does not provide a mechanism for perceptual adaptation or a mechanism for deliberately choosing reasoning tasks, reasoning methods, or control modes. The subsumption architecture [8] embodies a layered control model in which each layer adapts its behavior continuously to relevant perceptual information and imposes constraints on the responsiveness of the layer below itself. However, it has been applied primarily to the perceptual-motor behavior of mobile robots. It has not yet been extended to support reasoning and it does not provide a mechanism that allows an agent to dynamically choose among its own capabilities. CIRCA [36] and a similar architecture based on the Maruti real-time operating system [27] offer a two-layer architecture in which unpredictable AI methods are used to set goals and priorities for a real-time scheduler that guarantees to meet hard deadlines (assuming that is feasible) and to use slack resources effectively. This architecture adapts its real-time schedule to available resources and current priorities, but it does not provide other forms of adaptation, particularly within its use of the AI methods.

A caveat: We do not mean to suggest that these architectures are not capable of providing all of the required forms of adaptation, but only that their ability to do so has not yet been demonstrated and is not immediately obvious to us.

8.4. Other related work

Several researchers are working on particular forms of adaptation independent of architectural context. Notable examples are: anytime algorithms that trade reasoning time for solution quality [7], design-to-time scheduling algorithms for maximizing the use of available resources while meeting deadlines on critical tasks [17], reactive systems that provide bounded response times for specified events [42] or flexible adaptation to unanticipated event orderings [1,38], approximate processing techniques that provide acceptably degraded responses when resources are short [11]. We view these approaches as useful capabilities that we would strive to integrate within our architecture.

9. Conclusions

We have characterized a class of AIS niches. They require performance of diverse competing, and complementary tasks. They provide variable, possibly inadequate, resources for performing tasks. They present variably stressful contextual conditions. They impose conflicting performance criteria, which often cannot be satisfied completely. Therefore we have argued that, to function effectively in AIS niches, an agent must be highly adaptive. It must adapt its perceptual strategy to its dynamic cognitive requirements. It must adapt its control mode to uncertainty in its environment and constraints on its actions. It must adapt its reasoning tasks to demands and opportunities presented by its environment. It must adapt its reasoning methods to the available resources. It must adapt its meta-control strategy to its dynamic configuration of potential activities.

We find AIS niches motivating for three reasons. First, AIS niches represent a substantial increment in behavioral requirements compared to niches occupied by typical AI agents. They stress our science. They force us to deal with uncertainty and resource limitations. They force us to balance traditional efforts to design optimal solutions to isolated problems with efforts to design integrated solutions to complex problems. Second, AIS niches appear to represent an achievable objective. They do not overwhelm us with the complexity of all of human behavior, but focus our investigation on a powerful and pervasive property of human behavior: adaptation. Third, AIS niches represent significant real applications (e.g., intelligent monitoring systems, intelligent surveillance systems, intelligent associate systems). Agents that function effectively in these niches would have real practical and social utility.

In this paper, we argue on behalf of a particular agent architecture for AIS niches. However, as noted above, there are other sophisticated agent architectures that could be candidates for AIS niches. The success criteria for an AIS architecture are sufficiency, not necessity, followed by parsimony. It is quite possible that further evaluation of these candidates will identify several sufficient architectures. In the meantime, we have had a modest success in using our own architecture to build experimental agents in several AIS niches and in demonstrating the required kinds of adaptation. Moreover, we have been able to support the several required dimensions of adaptation parsimoniously, by means of a single architectural concept: *An agent dynamically constructs explicit control plans to guide its choices among situation-triggered possible actions.*

Acknowledgement

This research was supported by NASA contract NAG 2-581 under ARPA Order 6822, subcontract No. 71715-1 from Teknowledge Federal Systems under ARPA contract No. DAAA21-92-C-0028, and AFOSR grant AFOSR-91-0131. We thank Edward A. Feigenbaum for sponsoring the work in the Knowledge Systems Laboratory. We thank two anonymous reviewers for their many helpful criticisms and suggestions for improving earlier versions of the paper. Many individuals have contributed to different features of the AIS architecture and the Guardian system discussed in this paper: D. Ash, L.J. Barr, L. Boureau, L. Brownston, A. Collinot, V. Dabija, J. Drakopoulos, D. Gaba, G. Gold, M. Hewett, R. Hewett, A. Macalalad, A. Seiver, S. Uckun, A. Vina, R. Washington.

References

[1] P.E. Agre and D. Chapman, Pengi: an implementation of a theory of activity, in: *Proceedings AAAI-87*, Seattle, WA (1987).

[2] J.S. Albus, Outline for a theory of intelligence, *IEEE Trans. Syst. Man Cybern.* **21** (1991) 473–509.

[3] J.S. Albus, *Brains, Behavior, and Robotics* (BYTE Books, Peterborough, NH, 1981).

[4] J.S. Albus, System description and design architecture for multiple autonomous undersea vehicles, National Institute of Standards and Technology Report 1251, Gaithersburg, MD (1988).

[5] D. Ash, G. Gold, A. Seiver and B. Hayes-Roth, Guaranteeing real-time response with limited resources, *J. Artif. Intell. Med.* **5** (1) (1993) 49–66.

[6] D. Ash and B. Hayes-Roth, A comparison of action-based hierarchies and decision trees for real-time performance, in: *Proceedings AAAI-93*, Washington, DC (1993).

[7] M. Boddy and T. Dean, Solving time-dependent planning problems, in: *Proceedings IJCAI-89*, Detroit, MI (1989).

[8] R.A. Brooks, A robust layered control system for a mobile robot, *IEEE J. Rob. Autom.* **2** (1) (1986) 14–23.

[9] R.A. Brooks, Intelligence without reason, in: *Proceedings IJCAI-91*, Sydney, Australia (1991) 569–595.

[10] W.J. Clancey, Heuristic classification, *Artif. Intell.* **27** (1985) 289–350.

[11] K. Decker, V. Lesser and R. Whitehair, Extending a blackboard architecture for approximate processing, *J. Real-Time Syst.* **2** (1990) 47–70.

[12] R. Engelmore and T. Morgan, eds., *Blackboard Systems* (Addison-Wesley, Menlo Park, CA, 1988).

[13] L. Erman, F. Hayes-Roth, V. Lesser and R. Reddy, The Hearsay-II speech-understanding system: integrating knowledge to resolve uncertainty, *Comput. Surv.* **12** (1980) 213–253.

[14] E.A. Feigenbaum, A personal view of expert systems: looking back and looking ahead, *Expert Syst. Appl.* **5** (1992) 193–201.

[15] E.A. Feigenbaum, B.G. Buchanan and J. Lederberg. On generality and problem solving: a case study using the DENDRAL program, in: B. Meltzer and D. Michie, eds., *Machine Intelligence* **6** (Edinburgh University Press, Edinburgh, Scotland, 1971).

[16] R.E. Fikes and N.J. Nilsson, STRIPS: a new approach to the application of theorem proving to problem solving, *Artif. Intell.* **2** (1971) 198–208.

[17] A. Garvey and V. Lesser, Design-to-time real-time scheduling, *IEEE Trans. Syst. Man Cybern.* **23** (1993).

[18] A. Georgeff and A. Lansky, Reactive reasoning and planning, in: *Proceedings AAAI-87*, Seattle, WA (1987).

[19] K. Hammond, *Case-Based Planning: Viewing Planning as a Memory Task* (Academic Press, Boston, MA, 1989).

[20] B. Hayes-Roth, A blackboard architecture for control, *Artif. Intell.* **26** (1985) 251–321.

[21] B. Hayes-Roth, Architectural foundations for real-time performance in intelligent agents, *Real-Time Syst. Int. J. Time-Critical Comput. Syst.* **2** (1990) 99–125.

[22] B. Hayes-Roth, On building integrated cognitive agents: a review of Newell's *Unified Theories of Cognition*, *Artif. Intell.* **59** (1993) 213–220.

[23] B. Hayes-Roth, Opportunistic control of action, *IEEE Trans. Syst. Man Cybern.* (to appear).

[24] B. Hayes-Roth, P. Lalanda, P. Morignot, M. Balabanovic and K. Pfleger, Plans and behavior in intelligent agents, Stanford University Tech. Report, Stanford, CA (1994).

[25] B. Hayes-Roth, R. Washington, D. Ash, A. Collinot, A. Vina and A. Seiver. Guardian: a prototype intensive care monitoring agent, *J. Artif. Intell. Med.* (to appear).

[26] B. Hayes-Roth, R. Washington, R. Hewett, M. Hewett and A. Seiver, Intelligent real-time monitoring and control, in: *Proceedings IJCAI-89*, Detroit, MI (1989).

[27] J. Hendler and A. Agrawala, Mission critical planning: AI on the MARUTI real-time operating system, in: *Proceedings Workshop on Innovative Approaches to Planning, Scheduling, and Control* (1990) 77–84.

[28] T. Iwasaki and H.A. Simon, Causality in device behavior, *Artif. Intell.* **29** (1986) 3–32.

[29] V. Jagannathan, R. Dodhiawala and L. Baum, eds., *Blackboard Architectures and Applications* (Academic Press, Boston, MA, 1989).

[30] M.V. Johnson and B. Hayes-Roth, Integrating diverse reasoning methods in the BB1 blackboard control architecture, in: *Proceedings IJCAI-87*, Milan, Italy (1987).

[31] J.L. Kolodner, *Retrieval and Organizational Strategies in Conceptual Memory: A Computer Model* (Lawrence Erlbaum, Hillsdale, NJ, 1984).

[32] J.E. Laird, A. Newell and P.S. Rosenbloom, Soar: an architecture for general intelligence, *Artif. Intell.* **33** (1987) 1–64.

[33] D. Lenat and E.A. Feigenbaum, On the thresholds of knowledge, *Artif. Intell.* **47** (1991) 185–250.

[34] T.M. Mitchell, J.F. Allen, P. Chalasani, J. Cheng, O. Etzioni, M. Ringuette and J. Schlimmer, Theo: a framework for self-improving systems, in: K. VanLehn, ed., *Architectures for Intelligence* (Lawrence Erlbaum, Hillsdale, NJ, 1991).

[35] J.L. Murdock and B. Hayes-Roth, Intelligent monitoring and control of semiconductor manufacturing, *IEEE Expert* **6** (1991) 19–31.

[36] D.J. Musliner, E.H. Durfee and K.G. Shin, CIRCA: a cooperative intelligent real-time control architecture, *IEEE Trans. Syst. Man Cybern.* **23** (1993).

[37] A. Newell, *Unified Theories of Cognition* (Harvard University Press, Cambridge, MA, 1990).

[38] N.J. Nilsson, Action networks, Tech. Report, Stanford, CA (1989).

[39] W. Pardee, M. Shaff and B. Hayes-Roth, Intelligent control of complex materials processes, *J. Artif. Intell. Eng. Design Autom. Manufacturing* **4** (1990) 55–65.

[40] J. Pearl, Fusion, propagation, and structuring in belief networks, *Artif. Intell.* **29** (1986) 241–288.

[41] C.K. Riesbeck and R.C. Schank, *Inside Case-Based Reasoning* (Lawrence Erlbaum, Hillsdale, NJ, 1989).

[42] S.J. Rosenschein and L.P. Kaelbling, The synthesis of digital machines with provable epistemic properties, in: *Proceedings Conference on Theoretical Aspects of Reasoning about Knowledge*, Monterey, CA (1986) 83–98.

[43] W.J. Rugh, Analytical framework for gain scheduling, in: *Proceedings American Control Conference* (1990).

[44] E.D. Sacerdoti, The non-linear nature of plans, in: *Proceedings IJCAI-75*, Tblisi, Georgia (1975).

[45] M. Schoppers, Universal plans for reactive robots in unpredictable environments, in: *Proceedings IJCAI-87*, Milan, Italy (1987).

[46] Y. Shahar, A temporal abstraction mechanism for patient monitoring, in: *Proceedings SCAMC* (1991) 121–127.

[47] H.A. Simon, Artificial Intelligence: where has it been and where is it going? *IEEE Trans. Knowl. Data Eng.* **3** (2) (1991) 128–136.

[48] E. Simoudis, Using case-based retrieval for customer technical support, *IEEE Expert* **3**(2) (1992) 7–13.

[49] H. Sipma and B. Hayes-Roth, *Model-based monitoring of dynamical systems*, Tech. Report, Stanford, CA (to appear).

[50] R. Washington and B. Hayes-Roth, Managing input data in real-time AI systems, in: *Proceedings IJCAI-89*, Detroit, MI (1989).

[51] D.E. Wilkins, Domain-independent planning: representation and plan generation, *Artif. Intell.* **22** (1984) 269–301.

[52] D. Zhu, Nomadic host software development environment (Unix Version 1.1) (Nomadic Technologies, Mountain View, CA, 1992).

Artificial Intelligence 73 (1995) 1–30

Analysis of adaptation and environment

Ian Horswill *

MIT Artificial Intelligence Laboratory

Received September 1992; revised September 1994

Abstract

Designers often improve the performance of artificial agents by specializing them. We can make a rough, but useful distinction between specialization to a task and specialization to an environment. Specialization to an environment can be difficult to understand: it may be unclear on what properties of the environment the agent depends, or in what manner it depends on each individual property. In this paper, I discuss a method for analyzing specialization into a series of *conditional optimizations*: formal transformations which, given some constraint on the environment, map mechanisms to more efficient mechanisms with equivalent behavior. I apply the technique to the analysis of the vision and control systems of a working robot system in day to day use in our laboratory.

The method is not intended as a general theory for automated synthesis of arbitrary specialized agents. Nonetheless, it can be used to perform *post-hoc* analysis of agents so as to make explicit the environment properties required by the agent and the computational value of each property. This *post-hoc* analysis helps explain performance in normal environments and predict performance in novel environments. In addition, the transformations brought out in the analysis of one system can be reused in the synthesis of future systems.

1. Introduction

Scientists and mathematicians seek general principles: individual principles that each explain a large class of phenomena. Engineers seek general mechanisms, but are often forced for one reason or another to use highly specialized ones. When one needs to solve a wide range of problems, it may be more desirable to design a set of specialized mechanisms than to pay the price needed to build a single mechanism that can solve all problems.

---

* E-mail: ian@ai.mit.edu.

SSDI 0004-3702(94)00057-3

Computer science, being a curious combination of engineering and mathematics, often pushes both extremes of specialization and generality at once. Theorists and programming language designers search for ever simpler more compact abstract computing machines that are still Turing-equivalent (e.g. the 2-counter Turing machine [33] or the lambda calculus [10,41]), while computer architects search for the best collections of specialized circuits with which to emulate the behavior of these general computing machines [17]. Finally, compiler designers search for better methods for automatically mapping the general machines into specialized machines [3].

Throughout this paper, I will adopt the somewhat artificial distinction between specialization to a task (e.g. navigation vs. car assembly) and to an environment (e.g. forests versus highways). Specialization of an agent to a task is no different than the specialization of a normal computer program to a task. The designer usually has an explicit definition of the task and consciously uses that definition in the design of the agent or program. Often the internal structure of the mechanism reflects the internal structure of the task, with modules of the mechanism corresponding to subproblems of the overall task. (This is not as clear in the case of biological agents, see [7].) However, it is rare for a designer to have a complete formal description of the behavior of her agent's environment (the exception being simple virtual worlds). In addition, the agent's assumptions about its environment are often not explicitly represented within the agent. Such tacit knowledge may be spread diffusely throughout the agent. These factors conspire to make specialized agents difficult to understand.

The fundamental claim of this paper is that environmental specialization can be usefully described in terms of transformations over possible agents that provably preserve behavior when the agent is situated in some specific type of environment. The issue of when specialized mechanisms should be used in the first place is outside the scope of the paper.

2. Example

Fig. 1 shows an image of an office taken with a camera mounted on a robot. Suppose we want the robot to avoid obstacles by turning left when there is more free space to the left and right when there is more free space to the right. To do this, the robot must determine which side of the image has more free space. This amounts to the problem of finding which regions of the floor are free and which have objects on top of them. The problem is difficult because the image projection process loses information, depth information in particular, and so we cannot uniquely determine the structure of the scene without additional information either in the form of additional images or of additional assumptions.

A common way of solving the problem is to build a complete depth map of the scene and then project the features in the depth map into the floor plane. Those parts of the floor onto which no features are projected will be free space. A common way of building depth maps is to use two cameras in a stereo configuration. Distinctive features (usually edges) can be found in the two images and matched to one another. Given the matching of the features, we can compute each feature's shift due to parallax, and from

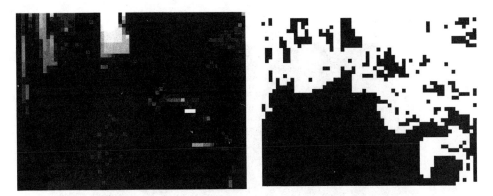

Fig. 1. (Left) Image of an office taken from the robot's camera. The dots in the lower middle of the image are artifacts due to the quantization in the rendering process. The structure in the lower right-hand portion of the image is a 5-legged office chair. The structures in the top-left are (left to right) a doorway viewed from an oblique angle, a small trash can, and a file cabinet. The homogeneous region in the lower and middle left is the carpet. (Right) The pixels with significant texture.

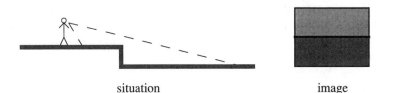

situation   image

Fig. 2. An observer views a cliff of a textureless surface (Left). Although variations in lighting of the two sides of the cliff may produce a local variation in image brightness at the point of discontinuity (Right), there is still no texture in the image above or below the discontinuity which would allow the observer to infer the depth, or even the presence, of the cliff from stereo data.

that, the 3D positions of the features (see [4]).

The stereo approach, while perfectly reasonable, does have undesirable properties. It is computationally expensive, particularly in the matching phase. It may also require very high resolution data. A more important problem is that the floor in this environment appears textureless from a distance, and so has no features to match. Fig. 1 shows a map of the image in which pixels with significant texture (actually, significant intensity gradients) are marked in white. The region corresponding to the floor is uniformly black. The stereo process cannot make any depth measurements in the most important region of the image because there are no features there to be matched. The problem can be remedied by interpolating a flat surface in the absence of texture from which to compute depth. In that case, the stereo system is working not because it is measuring the depth of the floor directly, but because it is making a smoothness assumption that happens to be true of floors in office environments. The assumption is not true in the general case (see Fig. 2).

This brings out two important points. First *truly general systems are extremely rare*, and so claims of generality should be considered carefully. Often the mechanisms we build have hidden assumptions. These can be particularly difficult to uncover in advance

Fig. 3. The carpet blob extracted from Fig. 1 using the coloring algorithm. Note that the blob is taller where there is more exposed carpet.

because we may unconsciously choose test data that fit them. This is not to say that implicit assumptions are bad. Quite the contrary: those assumptions can lead to great improvements in performance. However, we as engineers need to make *informed decisions* about our use of specialization. We need to understand more clearly what assumptions our agents make about their environments, and how often those assumptions are true of the particular environments in which they operate.

2.1. A more efficient algorithm

The stereo system worked on the scene in Fig. 1 because the floor was flat and the obstacles had texture. We can make a different system to solve the problem, one that is much more efficient, by using these facts directly and by treating the lack of texture on the floor as a useful feature of the environment rather than a problem to be overcome.

Notice that the floor forms a single, connected black blob at the bottom of Fig. 1. This blob is shown alone in Fig. 3. I will call this the carpet blob. The carpet blob is easily computed by region coloring: starting at the bottom of the screen, trace up each image column, marking pixels until a textured pixel is found in that column. The marked pixels will form the blob. The height of the blob varies with the amount of exposed floor in the corresponding direction, giving us a rough and ready measure of the amount of free space in that direction.

We can then solve our navigation problem simply by extracting the carpet blob and turning in the direction in which the carpet blob is tallest. This technique is the basis of the low level navigation capabilities the Polly system [18, 19], a mobile robot that gives simple tours of the AI lab at MIT. The navigation algorithm can easily be executed in real time on a low-end personal computer.

2.2. Preliminary analysis of coloring algorithm

Both the stereo algorithm and the coloring (blob-based) algorithm are specialized mechanisms that make assumptions about the structure of their environments. They perform properly when run in environments in which their assumptions hold, but may fail otherwise. Unfortunately, their assumptions are not explicitly represented. Neither algorithm would have any mention of the flatness of the floor in its source code listing, except, perhaps, as a comment.

We can understand the coloring algorithm by deriving it from the stereo algorithm by means of a series of transformations. The stereo system measures free space directly by computing a depth map and projecting it into the floor plane. Since we are only concerned with determining which side has more free space, however, we do not need to know the exact distances in any particular unit of measure. Any measure will do provided that we use it consistently. In fact, we can substitute for the stereo system *any system* that computes a strictly increasing function of the free space. It has been known at least since Euclid that image plane height is such a distance measure for points on a ground plane. This means, roughly, that we can replace stereo computations with the image plane heights of obstacles, provided that obstacles rest on the floor and we have some way of labeling each pixel as being either obstacle or carpet. A general obstacle detector might be more difficult to build than the original stereo system. However, the carpet in this environment has a very predictable appearance—it has no texture—and so we can substitute a texture detector for the obstacle detector.

We can summarize this analysis with the following general principles:

- We can substitute any monotonic measure of a quantity for a calibrated measure, provided that the measure will only be used for comparisons.
- We can substitute height in the image plane for some other distance calculation, provided that all objects rest on the floor and there is some way of classifying pixels as being floor or object.
- We can substitute a texture detector for a floor detector, provided that the floor is textureless, and the obstacles do have texture.

These principles concisely describe the specialization of the coloring algorithm. Each describes a general transformation from a possibly inefficient algorithm to a more efficient one, along with the conditions on the task and environment that make it valid. The transformations can be used to predict the performance of the coloring algorithm in novel environments, or reused in the design of new systems. For example, if we wanted to use the blob-based algorithm in an environment with a textured carpet, we would have to abandon the last transformation, but we would still be able to use the other two. If there was some property other than texture which allowed carpet pixels to be easily classified, then we could use that property as the basis of a new transformation.

3. Preview

The main point of this paper is that we can usefully analyze specialized systems by deriving them from general systems using a chain of conditional optimizations.

Implicit in these claims is the promise that such an analysis can be made formal and precise. However, the "analysis" in the previous section was handwavy, to say the least. Most of the rest of the paper is devoted to an extended example showing one way of making the analysis precise. This entails a great deal of formalism which is otherwise uninteresting. The reader may want to skim the most formal sections or skip them entirely.

The paper should not be interpreted as arguing for any particular choice of notation. The notations used here, while quite serviceable, were chosen largely because they were given to a more compact exposition than the alternatives in the literature. Nonetheless, alternatives do exist (see Section 4).

Section 4 surveys the literature on environmental analysis. The rest of the paper is devoted to a detailed analysis of the navigational systems of the Polly robot. The navigation system was not cooked up to suit the needs of the formalism. Polly is a real, working, vision-based robot in day-to-day use at the MIT AI lab. Section 5 fleshes out the notions of environment, transformation, and so on. Section 6 then fully formalizes these notions for the purpose of analyzing the blob coloring algorithm, the basis of Polly's low level navigation system. Section 7 extends the formalism to encompass state changes and actions. Section 8 uses this extended formalism to analyze Polly's high level navigation system. Section 9 then gives concluding remarks.

4. Related work

Relatively little attention has been devoted to environmental specialization in computer science, mostly likely because it is only recently that we have begun to construct computational systems that are closely coupled to natural environments.

In biology, a great deal of attention has been given to the specialization of complete agents to their environments. Cybernetics, the progenitor of artificial intelligence, also focused on agent/environment interactions, although not necessarily on the properties of specific, complex environments [45]. Ideas from these areas are now being applied to artificial intelligence and robotics (see [29, 30, 34]).

In perceptual psychology, Gibson proposed an "ecological" theory of perception that stressed the role of the environment in forming an agent's perceptions. Gibson argued that the structure of the environment determines a set of invariants in the energy flowing through the environment and that these invariants can be directly picked up by the perceptual apparatus of the organism via a process akin to resonance.

Marr [28] argued that in order to properly understand the operation of a perceptual system (or more generally, of any intelligent system), we must understand the problem it solves at the level of a *computational theory*.[1] The computational theory defines the desired input–output behavior of the perceptual system, along with a set of *constraints* on the possible interpretations of a given input. The constraints were necessary because a single stimulus can usually be generated by an infinite number of possible situations. The virtue of a computational theory is that it abstracts away from the details of an individual mechanism. A single computational theory can be used to explain and unify many different mechanisms that instantiate it. To Marr, the role of the constraints within computational theories was to show how the structure of the environment made interpretation possible at all, not how to make it more efficient. Marr believed that the human

---

[1] Marr's actual story is more complicated than this, and used three levels of explanation, not two. See [28].

visual system was a general mechanism for constructing three-dimensional descriptions of the environment and so was relatively unconcerned with understanding how a system could be specialized to take advantage of useful, but unnecessary, properties of the environment. This work extends Marr's ideas by using constraints to explain optimizations at the implementation level.

Most formal models of environments use state-space descriptions of the environment, usually finite-state machines. Rosenschein and Kaelbling used finite state machines to represent both agent and environment (see [36–38]). Their formalization allowed specialized mechanisms to be directly synthesized from descriptions of desired behavior and a formalization of the behavior of the environment. The formalization was powerful enough to form the basis of a programming language used to program a real robot. Later, Rosenschein developed a method for synthesizing automata whose internal states had provable correlations to the state of the environment given a set of temporal logic assertions about the dynamics of the environment. Donald and Jennings [12] use a geometric, but similar, approach for constructing virtual sensors.

Wilson [46] has specifically proposed the classification of simulated environments based on the types of mechanisms which can operate successfully within them. Wilson also used a finite state formalization of the environment. He divided environments into three classes based on properties such as determinacy. Todd and Wilson [43] used finite state machines to taxonomize grid worlds for a class of artificial agents created by a genetic algorithm. Littman [25] used FSM models to classify environments for reinforcement learning algorithms. Littman parameterized the complexity of RL agents in terms of the amount of local storage they use and how far into the future the RL algorithm looks. He then empirically classified environments by the minimal parameters that still allowed an optimal control policy to be learned.

There is also an extensive literature on discrete-event dynamic systems (see [23] for a readable introduction), which also model the environment as a finite state machine, but which assume that transition information (rather than state information) is visible to the agents.

Several researchers have discussed how time-extended patterns of interaction with the environment (called "dynamics" by Agre [1]) can be used to reduce the computational burden on an agent. Lyons and Hendriks have discussed how to derive and exploit useful dynamics from a formal specification of the environment [27]. They use a uniform formalization of both agent and environment based on process algebra. Using temporal logic, they are able to identify useful dynamics and design reactive behaviors to exploit them. Hammond, Converse, and Grass discuss how new dynamics can be designed into an agent to improve the stability of the agent/environment system [16].

5. Analyzing specialized agents

We will assume that we can reasonably separate the world into agent and environment. The world here need not mean the entire physical universe, only that portion of it which is relevant to our analysis. Let $\mathcal{A}$ denote some set of possible agents and $\mathcal{E}$ a set of environments. Each agent/environment pair will form a dynamic system with some behavior. We will also assume some task-specific notion of equivalence over possible behaviors. We will write $(a_1, e_1) \equiv (a_2, e_2)$ to mean that the behavior of a_1 operating in e_1 is equivalent to the behavior of a_2 in e_2. We can then say that two agents are equivalent if they are equivalent in all environments:

$$a_1 \equiv a_2 \quad \text{iff} \quad \forall e_1, e_2.(a_1, e_1) \equiv (a_2, e_2).$$

We will call them *conditionally equivalent* given some environmental constraint C if they are equivalent in all environments satisfying C. We will write this $a_1 \equiv_C a_2$. Thus

$$a_1 \equiv_C a_2 \quad \text{iff} \quad \forall e_1, e_2.C(e_1) \wedge C(e_2) \Rightarrow (a_1, e_1) \equiv (a_2, e_2).$$

Often, the designer has a particular behavior that they want the agent to achieve. Then the only useful behavioral distinction is whether the agent "works" or not, and so the $\equiv$ relation will divide the possible behaviors into only two classes, working and not working. Let the *habitat* H_A of agent A be set of environments in which it works. We will often refer to environment constraints as *habitat constraints*, since the habitat can be described as a constraint or conjunction of constraints.

5.1. Specialization as optimization

Suppose we want to understand an agent s that is somehow specialized to its environment. Although s might be more efficient than some more general system g, it may also have a smaller habitat, i.e. $H_s \subseteq H_g$. If we can find a sequence of mechanisms s_i and domain constraints C_i, such that

$$g \equiv_{C_1} s_1 \equiv_{C_2} s_2 \equiv_{C_3} \cdots \equiv_{C_n} s.$$

then we have that $g \equiv_{C_1 \cap \cdots \cap C_n} s$. We can phrase this latter statement in English as: *within the environments that satisfy* $C_1, \ldots, C_n$, g *and* s *are behaviorally equivalent— they will work in exactly the same cases*. This lets us express the habitat of s in terms of the habitat of g:

$$H_s \supseteq H_g \cap C_1 \cap \cdots \cap C_n.$$

Note that the left- and right-hand sides are not necessarily equal because there may be situations where S works but g does not. One of the constraints on the right-hand side might also be overly strong.

I will call such a sequence of equivalences, in which g is gradually transformed into s, a *derivation* of s from g, in analogy to the derivations of equations. We will restrict our attention to the case where each derivation step $s_{i-1} \equiv_{C_i} s_i$ can be seen as the result of applying some general optimizing transformation O_i that preserves equivalence given C_i (i.e. for which $s_i = O_i(s_{i-1})$ and for which $a \equiv_{C_i} O_i(a)$ whenever $O_i(a)$ is defined). Exhibiting such a derivation breaks s's specialization into smaller pieces that are easier to understand. It also places the constraints C_i in correspondence with their optimizations O_i, making the computational value of each constraint explicit. Teasing these constraints apart helps predict the performance of the agent in novel environments. If an environment satisfies all the constraints, the agent will work. If it does not, then we know which optimizations will fail, and consequently, which parts of the design to modify. In addition, if we can write a general lemma to the effect that $a \equiv_{C_i} O_i(a)$, then we can reuse O_i in the design of future systems. Such lemmas may be of greater interest than the actual agents that inspired them.

Note that we can equally well perform a derivation of one subsystem of an agent from another possible subsystem. For that reason, I will often use the term "mechanism" to mean either an agent or one of its subsystems.

6. Analysis of simple perceptual systems

In this section, we will perform a more detailed analysis of the coloring algorithm given in Section 2.1. To do this, we need to flesh out the notions of environment, behavior, and behavioral equivalence. Throughout the paper, we will use a state space formalization of the environment. In this section, we will only be concerned with the environment states themselves, not with the possible transitions between them. We will also ignore the internal state of the agent. In Section 7, we will add dynamics and internal state.

Let W be the set of possible world states. We will model environments as subsets of W (we will consider other state spaces in Section 7.1). Thus $\mathcal{E} = 2^W$. Habitats, which we have defined as sets of environments, will then effectively just be (larger) regions of the state-space themselves. Habitat constraints, constraints over possible habitats, are then also effectively just subsets of W.

Since we are ignoring dynamics and internal state, we will consider only those perceptual systems that give information about the instantaneous world state. Thus a perceptual system is a mechanism that has an identifiable output with an identifiable set of possible states S such that the state of the output is causally determined by the state of the world. Effectively, the perceptual system computes a function from W to S. We will call that function the *information type* that the perceptual system computes. We will say that two perceptual systems are behaviorally equivalent if they compute the same information type. An information type is finite if its range is finite. Note that information types should not be confused with the concept of information as inverse probability used in classical information theory (see [15]). While the two are certainly compatible, classical information theory is concerned with measuring quantities of information, whereas our concern here is with distinguishing among different kinds of information.

6.1. Derivability and equivalence

Often what is interesting about an information type is what other information types can be computed from it. We will say that one information type $I' : W \rightarrow S'$ is *derivable* from another, $I : W \rightarrow S$, if there exists a *derivation function* f for which $I' = f \circ I$. I_1 and I_2 are *equivalent* (written $I_1 \equiv I_2$) if they are interderivable.

The range of an information type is irrelevant to derivability; We can arbitrarily rename the elements of its range without changing what can be derived from it. Thus what really matters is the partition P_I it induces on the world states:

$$P_I = \{A \subseteq W \mid x, y \in A \Leftrightarrow I(x) = I(y)\}.$$

The elements of the partition are the maximal sets of world states that are indistinguishable given only I. One can easily show that[2]

Lemma 1. *The following statements are equivalent*:
  (1) *I_1 and I_2 are equivalent, that is, interderivable.*
  (2) *X is derivable from I_1 iff it is derivable from I_2, for all X.*
  (3) *The partitions P_{I_1} and P_{I_2} are identical.*
  (4) *I_1 and I_2 differ only by a bijection (a 1-1 onto mapping).*

We will say that I and I' are *conditionally identical given C* (written $I =_C I'$) if $I(w) = I'(w)$ for all $w \in C$. Note that $I =_W I$ and that $I_1 =_{C_1} I_2$ and $I_2 =_{C_2} I_3$ implies $I_1 =_{C_1 \cap C_2} I_3$. Finally, we will say that two perceptual systems are *behaviorally equivalent* if they compute the same information type and *conditionally equivalent given C* if their information types are conditionally identical given C.

6.2. Unconditional equivalence transformations

We will use a single box labeled with an information type I

$$\Rightarrow \boxed{I} \rightarrow$$

to represent a perceptual system that (somehow) computes the I. The double arrow is meant to represent a connection to the environment. When we want to expose the internal structure in the system, we will use single arrows to represent connections wholly within the system. Thus

$$\Rightarrow \boxed{I} \rightarrow \boxed{f} \rightarrow \boxed{g} \rightarrow \cdots$$

represents a system which first computes I and then applies the transformations f, g, … to it. Finally, we will denote predicates with a "?", thus

$$\Rightarrow \boxed{I} \rightarrow \boxed{> T?} \rightarrow$$

denotes a system which outputs true when $I(w) > T$, and false otherwise. These diagrams inherit the associativity of function composition:

$$\Rightarrow \boxed{f \circ I} \rightarrow \boxed{g} \rightarrow \quad \equiv \quad \Rightarrow \boxed{I} \rightarrow \boxed{f} \rightarrow \boxed{g} \rightarrow \quad \equiv \quad \Rightarrow \boxed{I} \rightarrow \boxed{g \circ f} \rightarrow$$

and so a simple optimization, which we might call "folding" (after constant-folding in compiler optimization), is the replacement of a series of computations with a single computation:

---

[2] See [19] for a proof.

$$\Rightarrow \boxed{I} \rightarrow \boxed{f} \rightarrow \quad \equiv \quad \Rightarrow \boxed{f \circ I} \rightarrow.$$

One example of an optimizing transformation is what might be called "decalibration". Estimating precise parameters such as depth can be difficult and can require precise sensor calibration. Often all that is done with this information is to compare it to some empirical threshold. For example, we might estimate the distance to an obstacle to decide whether we should swerve around it, or whether it is too late and we must brake to avoid collision. Generally, the designer arbitrarily chooses a threshold or determines it experimentally. In such situations, we can use *any* mechanism that computes distance in any units, provided that we correct the threshold.

Lemma 2 (Decalibration). *For any information type* $I : W \rightarrow \mathbb{R}$ ($\mathbb{R}$ *is the set of real numbers*) *and any strictly increasing function* $f : \mathbb{R} \rightarrow \mathbb{R}$,

$$\Rightarrow \boxed{I} \rightarrow \boxed{> T?} \rightarrow \quad \equiv \quad \Rightarrow \boxed{f \circ I} \rightarrow \boxed{> f(T)?} \rightarrow.$$

Proof. By associativity, the right-hand side is equivalent to

$$\Rightarrow \boxed{I} \rightarrow \boxed{(> f(T)?) \circ f} \rightarrow$$

and for all x, $f(x) > f(T)$ iff $x > T$, thus $(> f(T)?) \circ f = (> T?)$. $\square$

Decalibration allows a calibrated mechanism to be replaced with an uncalibrated mechanism, in certain cases.

6.3. Transformations over simple vision systems

The coloring algorithm used image plane height to discriminate depth and a texture detector to find obstacles. In this section, we will derive sufficient conditions for the validity of these techniques. We will show that image plane height is a strictly increasing function of object depth, provided the object rests on the floor and its projection into the floor is contained within its region of contact with the floor. We will also show that for floors whose surface markings have no spatial frequencies below ω and which are viewed from a distance of at least d, any low pass filter with a passband in the region $(0, d\omega)$ can be used to discriminate between objects and floor. The proof is not terribly interesting in itself. The reader may wish to skip to Section 6.4.

First, we need to define our coordinate systems, one camera-centered, in which the forward direction (z) is the axis of projection, and the other body-centered, in which the forward (Z) direction is the direction of motion (see Fig. 4). We will assume that the camera faces forward, but somewhat down, and so the camera- and body-centered frames share their left/right axis, which we will call X. We will call the up/down axes for the camera- and body-centered systems y and Y, respectively. We will assume that the ground plane lies at $Y = 0$. We will denote the image with range set X by $\mathcal{I}(X)$ so the b/w images are $\mathcal{I}(\mathbb{R})$ and the color images are $\mathcal{I}(\mathbb{R}^3)$.

The projection process can be specified in either of these coordinate frames. In camera-centered coordinates, the projection process maps a point (X, y, z) in the world

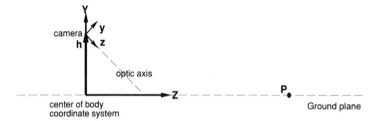

Fig. 4. A camera viewing a ground plane. The X axis (not shown) comes out of the page and is shared by the camera and body coordinate frames. The body coordinate frame is formed by X, Y and Z, the camera frame, by X, y and z. z is also the axis of projection, or optic axis, of the camera. h is the height of the camera and P is an arbitrary point on the ground plane.

to a point $(fX/z, fy/z)$ on the image plane, where f is the focal length of the lens. In the body-centered coordinate system, projection is best expressed with vector algebra. A point P in the world will be projected to the image plane point

$$p = \frac{f(P - h)}{z \cdot (P - h)}.$$

(These are 3D coordinates; the 2D coordinates are obtained by projecting it onto the image plane axes X and y, yielding the coordinates $(X \cdot p, y \cdot p)$).

6.3.1. Salience functions and figure/ground separation

Let O be a set of objects and $FG_O : W \to \mathcal{I}(\{T, F\})$ ("figure/ground") be the unique information type that, for all world states, returns an image in which pixels are marked "T" if they were imaged in that world state from one of the objects O, otherwise "F". A perceptual system that can compute FG_O within its habitat can distinguish O from the background. FG_O can be arbitrarily difficult (consider the case where O is the set of chameleons or snipers). Fortunately, there are often specific cues that allow objects to be recognized in specific contexts. We will call these cues *salience functions*. An information type is a salience function if it is conditionally equivalent to FG_O given some constraint (a "salience constraint"). The use of such simple, easily computed functions to find particular classes of objects is common both in AI (see [11,20,42,44,47]) and in the biological world (see [35] for a good introduction).

The coloring algorithm uses the texture detector as a salience function. We want to determine what salience constraint is required for a given texture detector. For simplicity, we will restrict ourselves to Fourier-based measures of texture. Effectively, a texture detector examines a small patch of the image. We can approximate the projection of a small patch with

$$(X, y, z) \mapsto (fX/z_0, fy/z_0)$$

where z_0 is the distance to the center of the surface patch. A sufficiently small patch can be treated as a plane with a some local coordinate system (x', y'). Suppose the patch's reflectance varies as a sinusoid with frequency vector $\vec{\omega}$. Then its reflectance R at a point (x', y') on the patch is given by:

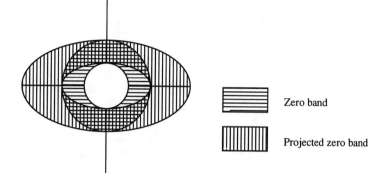

Zero band

Projected zero band

Fig. 5. The effect of perspective projection on local frequency distributions.

$$R(x', y') = \frac{1}{2}\left(\sin\frac{x'}{\omega_x} + \sin\frac{y'}{\omega_y}\right) + \frac{1}{2}.$$

If we view the patch:
- from a unit distance,
- through a lens of unit focal length,
- from a direction normal to the patch,
- with the X axis aligned with the x' axis, and
- with even illumination of unit intensity

then the image intensity will simply be

$$I(x, y) = R(x, y).$$

Now consider the effect of changing the viewing conditions. Doubling the distance or halving the focal length halves the size of the image.

$$I(x, y) = R(\frac{x}{2}, \frac{y}{2}) = \frac{1}{2}\left(\sin\frac{x}{2\omega_x} + \sin\frac{y}{2\omega_y}\right) + \frac{1}{2}.$$

The image is still a sine wave grating, but its projected frequency is doubled. Rotating the patch by and angle θ around the X axis shrinks the image along the Y axis by a factor of $\cos\theta$, producing a sine wave of frequency $(\omega_x, \omega_y/\cos\theta)$:

$$I(x, y) = R(x, y\cos\theta) = \frac{1}{2}\left(\sin\frac{x}{\omega_x} + \sin\frac{y\cos\theta}{\omega_y}\right) + \frac{1}{2}.$$

Rotating about the Y shrinks the X axis. Rotating about the optic axis simply rotates the frequency vector.

Thus a sine wave grating viewed from any position appears as a grating with identical amplitude but with a frequency vector modified by a scaling of its components and possibly a rotation. Since the projection process is linear, we can extend this to arbitrary power spectra: the power spectrum of the patch's projection will be the power spectrum of the patch, rotated and stretched along each axis (see Fig. 5). Frequency bands of the patch are transformed into elliptical regions of the frequency domain of its projection.

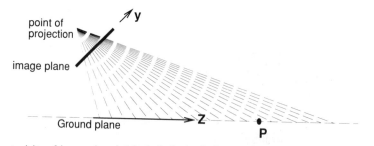

Fig. 6. Monotonicity of image plane height in body depth. Rays projected from the point of projection to points on the ground plane pass through successively higher points on the image plane as they move to more distant points on the ground plane.

Bounds on the possible viewing conditions yield bounds on how much the frequency bands can be deformed.

The *background texture constraint* (BTC) requires that all surface patches of the background have surface markings whose power spectra are bounded below by ω, that all objects have surface markings with energy below ω, and that no surface in view is closer than d focal lengths, and that the scene is uniformly lit. We have that

Lemma 3. *Any thresholded linear filtering of the image with a passband in the interval $(0, d\omega)$ is a salience function given the background texture constraint.*

Proof. By assumption, no patch of the background has energy in the band $(0, \omega)$, but all objects do. By the reasoning above, when any patch, either object or background, is viewed fronto-parallel from distance d, the band $(0, \omega)$ projects to the band $(0, d\omega)$. Thus a patch was imaged from an object iff its projection has energy in this band. But note that increasing the distance or changing the viewing orientation can only increase the size of the projected frequency ellipse. Thus for any distance greater than d and any viewing orientation, a patch will have energy in $(0, d\omega)$ iff it was imaged from an object. Thus a thresholded linear filter is a salience function given BTC. □

The corollary to this is that any thresholded linear filter with passband in $(0, d\omega)$ is conditionally equivalent to a figure/ground system given the background texture constraint.

6.3.2. Depth recovery

Depth can be measured in either a camera-centered or a body-centered coordinate system. We will call these "camera depth" and "body depth", respectively. The camera depth of a point P is its distance to the image plane, $z \cdot (P - h)$. Body depth, on the other hand, is how far forward the robot can drive before it collides with the point, $Z \cdot P$. We will concern ourselves with body depth.

Consider a world of flat objects lying on a ground plane. Then both object points and ground plane points have zero Y coordinates. The points must be linear combinations of X and Z. Since both z and Z are perpendicular to X, the X component of the point will make no contribution either to camera depth or to body depth and we can restrict our attention to the one-dimensional case, shown in Fig. 4, of a point $P = nZ$. Its body depth is simply n, while its camera depth $z \cdot (nZ - h)$ depends on camera placement. We can see by inspection, however, that the camera depth is linear in n and so camera depth and body depth are related by a linear mapping. More surprisingly, image plane height is a strictly increasing function of body depth. This can be seen from Fig. 6. It can also be shown analytically. The image plane height of P is

$$y \cdot \left(\frac{f(nZ - h)}{z \cdot (nZ - h)} \right) = \frac{y \cdot (fnZ - fh)}{nz \cdot Z - z \cdot h} = \frac{n\alpha - \delta}{n\beta - \gamma}$$

for $\alpha = fZ \cdot y$, $\beta = z \cdot Z$, $\gamma = z \cdot h$, and $\delta = fh \cdot y$. Differentiating with respect to n, we obtain

$$\frac{\alpha(n\beta - \gamma) - \beta(n\alpha - \delta)}{(n\beta - \gamma)^2} = \frac{\beta\delta - \alpha\gamma}{(n\beta - \gamma)^2}.$$

When the camera looks forward and P is in front of the agent, we have that $n, \beta, \delta > 0$, and $\gamma\alpha < 0$, so the derivative is strictly positive.

The *ground plane constraint* (GPC) requires that the camera view a set of the objects O resting on a ground plane G, and that for each $o \in O$, o is completely in view and o's projection in G is its set of points of contact with G.[3] Thus pyramids resting on their bases would satisfy the restriction, but not pyramids resting on their points. Given GPC, we can use least y coordinate as a measure of the depth of the closest object. Let Body-Depth$_O$ be the information type which gives the correct body depth for pixels generated by one of the objects O, or ∞ for pixels generated by the background.

Lemma 4. *Let R be a region of the image. Then $\min_R \circ$ Body-Depth$_O$ is conditionally equivalent to $\min\{y : FG_O(x, y) \text{ for some } (x, y) \in R\}$ given GPC, modulo a strictly increasing function.*

Proof. Note that there can only be one minimal depth, but there can be many minimal-depth object points. However, it must be the case that some contact point (an object point touching the floor) has minimal depth, otherwise there would be an object point whose ground plane projection was not a contact point, a contradiction. Let p be a minimal-depth contact point. We want to show that no object point can have a smaller projected y coordinate than p. Since the y coordinate is invariant with respect to changes in the X coordinate, a point which projects to a lesser y coordinate than p must have either a smaller Z coordinate or a smaller Y coordinate. The first would contradict p's being a minimal-depth point while the latter would place the point below the ground plane. Thus p must have a minimal y projection. We have already shown that for contact points the y projection is strictly increasing in body depth. $\square$

A trivial corollary to this lemma is that the height of the lowest figure pixel in an image column gives the distance to the nearest object in the direction corresponding to the column.

---

[3] Formalizing the notion of "touches" can be difficult (see for example [13, Chapter 8]), but we will treat the notion as primitive, since the particular formalization is unimportant for our purposes.

6.4. Derivation of the coloring algorithm

We can now derive the coloring algorithm from the stereo algorithm. Recall the stereo system:

$$\Rightarrow \boxed{\text{stereo}} \rightarrow \boxed{\text{project}} \rightarrow.$$

By Lemma 4, the stereo system is conditionally equivalent given GPC (modulo a monotonic function) to any system of the form

$$\Rightarrow \boxed{\text{FG}} \rightarrow \boxed{\text{column heights}} \rightarrow$$

where "FG" is some computation that performs figure/ground separation. By Lemma 3, this is conditionally equivalent given *BTC* to

$$\Rightarrow \boxed{\text{filter}} \rightarrow \boxed{\text{threshold}} \rightarrow \boxed{\text{column heights}} \rightarrow$$

where "filter" is any linear filter restricted to the frequency band $(0, d\omega)$, such as an edge detector operating at a scale larger than the floor texture:

$$\Rightarrow \boxed{\text{edges}} \rightarrow \boxed{\text{column heights}} \rightarrow.$$

Since the coloring system and the stereo system yield outputs which differ by monotonic functions, it remains to be shown that substituting one for the other leads to the same motor behavior. It can be shown that for a steering system based on balancing left and right distances the attractor and repeller basins in the robot's configuration space are invariant with respect to this substitution, provided that we can model the steering motor as a first order system. Doing so, however, requires the introduction of still more math, so the interested reader is directed to [19].

Even this is a restricted derivation, since it assumes fully textured objects. The derivation can be extended to untextured objects with different reflectances than the background. While space precludes a full derivation, the argument goes as follows. Untextured objects still trigger the texture detector at their boundaries. We can then compute the correct figure/ground map by filling the interiors of closed contours in the texture image. However, the column heights are invariant with respect to the interior filling operation, provided that the full object is in view (if part of it runs off the bottom of the screen, the coloring of the filled and unfilled versions will differ). Thus the raw coloring algorithm will still work on untextured objects, provided they have different reflectances than the background and they are in full view.

The derivation shows that the background texture constraint is used to simplify figure/ground separation. More importantly, it shows that it is not used for anything else. If we wish to run the system in an environment that does not satisfy the background texture constraint, but which does satisfy the ground plane constraint, then we can substitute any salience constraint that holds in the new environment. For example, if the background has a distinctive color or set of colors, then we might use a color system such as that of Turk et al. [44], or Crisman [11], to find the floor:

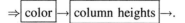

If we wanted to build a system that worked in both environments, then we could implement both systems and switch between them opportunistically, provided there was sufficient information to determine which one to use. We could even implement the original stereo system in parallel with these systems and add another switch.

7. Analysis of action selection

In this section we will apply transformational techniques to action-selection tasks with the goal of demonstrating a number of formal conditions under which we can reduce deliberative planning systems to reactive systems. We will continue to model the environment as a dynamic system with a known set of possible states. First, we will add actions (state transitions) to the environment, making it a full state-machine. We will then model both deliberative planning systems and reactive systems as variants of the control policies of classical control theory (see [26] or [7]). This gives us a uniform vocabulary for expressing both types of systems. We can then examine various formal conditions on the environment that allow simplifications of the control policy (e.g. substitution of a reactive policy for a deliberative one)

Again, the focus of this paper is the use of transformational analysis, not the specifics of the notation used below. The notation is needed to establish a framework within which to apply the transformations. The notation used here is largely equivalent to those used by Rosenschein and Kaelbling [38], and by Donald and Jennings [12]. It was chosen for largely for compactness of presentation. The formal trick of externalizing the agent's internal state also turns out to be useful.

7.1. Environments

We will now allow different environments to have different state spaces and will treat actions as mappings from states to states. An environment will then be a state machine $E = (S, A)$ formed of a state space S and a set of actions A which are mappings from S to S.

For example, consider a robot moving along a corridor with n equally spaced offices labeled 1, 2, and so on. We can formalize this as the environment $\mathbb{Z}_n = (\{0, 1, \ldots, n - 1\}, \{inc_n, dec, i\})$, where i is the identity function, and where inc_n and dec map an integer i to $i+1$ and $i-1$, respectively, with the proviso that $dec(0) = 0$ and $inc_n(n-1) = n-1$ (see Fig. 7). Note that the effect of performing the identity action is to stay in the same state.

7.1.1. Discrete control problems

We will say that a *discrete control problem*, or DCP, is a pair $D = (E, G)$ where E is an environment and G, the goal, is a region of E's state space. The problem of getting to the beginning of the corridor for our robot would be the DCP $(\mathbb{Z}_n, \{0\})$. By abuse of notation, we will also write a DCP as a triple (S, A, G). A finite sequence of

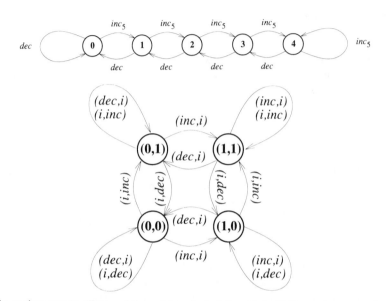

Fig. 7. The environment Z_5 (Top) and the serial product of $\mathbb{Z}_2$ with itself (Bottom), expressed as graphs. Function products have been written as pairs, i.e. $inc \times i$ is written as (inc, i). Identity actions (i and $i \times i$) have been omitted to reduce clutter.

actions $a = (a_1, a_2, \ldots, a_n)$ *solves D from initial state s* if $a_n(a_{n-1}(\cdots a_1(s))) \in G$. *D is solvable from s* if such a sequence exists. *D is solvable* (in general) if it is solvable from all $s \in S$.

7.1.2. Cartesian products

Often, the state space of the environment is structured into distinct components that can be acted upon independently. The position of the king on a chess board has row and column components, for example. Thus we would like to think of the king-on-a-chess-board environment as being the "product" of the environment $\mathbb{Z}_8$ with itself (since there are eight rows and eight columns), just as $\mathbb{R}^2$ is the Cartesian product of the reals with themselves. However, consider an environment in which a car drives through an 8×8 grid of city blocks. We would also like to think of this environment as being the product of $\mathbb{Z}_8$ with itself. Both the car and the king have 8×8 grids as their state spaces, but the car can only change one of its state components at a time, whereas the king can change both by moving diagonally.

We will therefore distinguish two different Cartesian products of environments, the *parallel product*, which corresponds to the king case, and the *serial product*, which corresponds to the car case. Let the Cartesian product of two functions f and g be $f \times g : (a, b) \mapsto (f(a), g(b))$, and let i be the identity function. For two environments $E_1 = (S_1, A_1)$ and $E_2 = (S_2, A_2)$, we will define the parallel product to be

$$E_1 \parallel E_2 = (S_1 \times S_2, \{a_1 \times a_2 : a_1 \in A_1, a_2 \in A_2\})$$

and the serial product to be

$$E_1 \rightleftharpoons E_2 = (S_1 \times S_2, \{a_1 \times i : a_1 \in A_1\} \cup \{i \times a_2 : a_2 \in A_2\}).$$

The products of DCPs are defined in the obvious way:

$$(E_1, G_1) \parallel (E_2, G_2) = (E_1 \parallel E_2, G_1 \times G_2).$$

$$(E_1, G_1) \rightleftharpoons (E_2, G_2) = (E_1 \rightleftharpoons E_2, G_1 \times G_2).$$

The state diagram for $\mathbb{Z}_2 \rightleftharpoons \mathbb{Z}_2$ is shown in Fig. 7.

We will say that a an environment or DCP is parallel (or serial) *separable* if it is isomorphic to a product of environments or DCPs.

7.1.3. Solvability of separable DCPs

The important property of separable DCPs is that their solutions can be constructed from solutions to their components:

Claim 5. *Let D_1 and D_2 be DCPs. Then $D_1 \rightleftharpoons D_2$ is solvable from state (s_1, s_2) iff D_1 is solvable from s_1 and D_2 is solvable from s_2.*

Proof. Consider a sequence S that solves the product from (s_1, s_2). Let S_1 and S_2 be the sequences of actions from D_1 and D_2, respectively, that together form S, so that if S were the sequence

$$(a \times i, i \times x, i \times y, b \times i, i \times z, c \times i)$$

then S_1 would be (a, b, c) and S_2 would be (x, y, z). S must leave the product in some goal state (g_1, g_2). By definition, g_1 and g_2 must be goal states of D_1 and D_2 and so S_1 and S_2 must be solution sequences to D_1 and D_2, respectively. Conversely, we can construct a solution sequence to the product from solution sequences for the components. $\square$

The parallel product case is more complicated because the agent must always change both state components. This leaves the agent no way of preserving one solved sub-problem while solving another. Consider a "flip-flop" environment $F = (\{0, 1\}, \{flip\})$ where $flip(x) = 1 - x$. F has the property that every state is accessible from every other state. $F \rightleftharpoons F$ also has this property. $F \parallel F$ does not however. $F \parallel F$ has only one action, which flips both state components at once. Thus only two states are accessible from any given state in $F \parallel F$, the state and its flip. As with the king, the problem is fixed if we add the identity action to F. Then it is possible to leave one component of the product intact, while changing the other. The identity action, while sufficient, is not necessary. A weaker, but still unnecessary, condition is that F have some action that always maps goal states to goal states.

Claim 6. *Let D_1 and D_2 be DCPs. If $D_1 \parallel D_2$ is solvable from state (s_1, s_2) then D_1 is solvable from s_1 and D_2 is solvable from s_2. The converse is also true if for every goal state of D_1 and D_2, there is an action that maps to another goal state.*

Proof. Again, let S be a solution sequence from (s_1, s_2). Now let S_1 and S_2 be the sequences of obtained by taking the first and second components, respectively, of each element of S. Thus, if S is

$$(a \times x, b \times y, c \times z)$$

then we again have that S_1 is (a, b, c) and S_2 is (x, y, z). Again, S_1 and S_2 are solution sequences for their respective component problems. Similarly, we can form a solution to the product from solutions to the components by combining them element-wise. To do this, the solutions to the components must be of the same length. Without loss of generality, let S_1 be the shorter solution. Since there is always an action to map a goal state to a goal state, we can pad S_1 with actions that will keep D_1 within its goal region. The combination of S_2 and the padded S_1 must then be a solution to the product. $\square$

7.2. Agents

We will assume an agent uses some *policy* to choose actions. A policy p is a mapping from states to actions. We will say that p:
- *generates a state sequence* s_i when $s_{i+1} = (p(s_i))(s_i)$ for all i.
- *generates an action sequence* a_i when it generates s_i and $a_i = p(s_i)$ for all i.
- *solves D from state s* when p generates a solution sequence from s.
- *solves D* when it solves D from all states.
- *solves D and halts* when it solves D and for all $s \in G$, $(p(s))(s) \in G$.

For example, the constant function $p(s) = dec$ is a policy that solves the DCP $(\mathbb{Z}_n, \{0\})$, and halts.

7.2.1. Hidden state and sensors

A policy uses perfect information about the world to choose an action. In real life, agents only have access to sensory information. Let $T : S \to X$ be the information type (see Section 6) provided by the agent's sensors. The crucial question about T is what information can be derived from it. We will say that an information type is *observable* if it is derivable from T.

To choose actions, we need a mapping not from world states S to A, but from sensor states X to A. We will call such a mapping a *T-policy*. A function p is a *T-policy* for a DCP D if $p \circ T$ is a policy for D. We will say that p *T-solves D* from a given state if $p \circ T$ solves it, and that p *T-solves D* (in general) if it *T*-solves it from any initial state.

7.2.2. Externalization of internal state

We have also assumed that the agent itself has no internal state—that its actions are determined completely by the state of its sensors. In real life, agents generally have internal state. We will model internal state as a form of external (environmental) state with perfect sensors and effectors. Let the *register environment* R_A over an alphabet A be the environment whose state space is A and whose actions are the constant functions over A. We will write the constant function whose value is always a as C_a. The action C_a "writes" a into the register. We will call $E \parallel R_A$ the *augmentation* of E with the alphabet A. An agent operating in the augmentation can, at each point in time, read the states of E and the register, perform an action in E, and write a new value into the register.

Using external state for internal state is not simply mathematical artifice. Agents can and do use the world as external memory. An agent need only isolate some portion of the world's state (such as the appearance of a sheet of paper) which can be accurately sensed and controlled. Humans do this routinely. Appointment books allow people to keep their plans for the day in the world, rather than in their scarce memory. Bartenders use the position of a glass on the bar to encode what type of drink they intend to mix and how far they are into the mixing (see [6]). For an example of a program that uses external state, see [2].

7.3. Progress functions

A *progress function* is a measure of distance to a goal. In particular, a progress function Φ for a DCP $D = (S, A, G)$ is a non-negative function from S to the reals for which

(1) Φ is nonnegative, i.e. $\Phi(s) \geqslant 0$ for all s.
(2) $\Phi(s) = 0$ iff $s \in G$.
(3) For any initial state i from which D is solvable, there exists a solution sequence $S = (a_1, \ldots, a_n)$ along which Φ is strictly decreasing (i.e. $\Phi(a_j(\cdots(a_1(i)))) > \Phi(a_{j+1}(a_j(\cdots a_1(i))))$ for all j).

The term "progress function" is taken from the program verification literature, where it refers to functions over the internal state of the program that are used to prove termination of loops. Progress functions are also similar to Liapunov functions (see [26]), admissible heuristics (see [5, Volume 1, Chapter II]), and artificial potential fields (see [21] or [24]).

We will say that a policy p *honors* a non-negative function Φ, if Φ steadily decreases it until it reaches zero, i.e. for all states s and some $\varepsilon > 0$, either $\Phi((p(s))(s)) < \Phi(s) - \varepsilon$ or else $\Phi(s) = \Phi((p(s))(s)) = 0$. A policy that honors Φ can be thought of as doing hill-climbing on Φ and so will run until it reaches a local minimum of Φ. When Φ also happens to be a progress function for the DCP, that local minimum will be a global minimum corresponding to the goal:

Lemma 7. *Let $\Phi: S \to \mathbb{R}$ be non-negative and let p be a policy for a DCP D that honors Φ. Then p solves D and halts exactly when Φ is a progress function on D.*

Proof. Consider the execution of p from an arbitrary initial state i. On each step, the value of Φ decreases by at least ε until it reaches 0, after which it must remain zero. Thus Φ must converge to zero within $\Phi(i)/\varepsilon$ steps after which the state of the system is confined to the set $\Phi^{-1}(0)$. We need only show that $\Phi^{-1}(0) \subseteq G$ iff Φ is a progress function for D. If Φ is a progress function $\Phi^{-1}(0) \subseteq G$ holds by definition. To see the converse, suppose $\Phi^{-1}(0) \subseteq G$. We want to show that from every state from which D is solvable, there is a solution sequence that monotonically decreases Φ. The sequence generated by p is a such a sequence. $\square$

Progress functions can be generated directly from policies. The *standard progress function* $\Phi_{p,D}$ on a policy p that solves D is the number of steps in which p solves D from a given state. An important property of product DCPs is that we can construct progress functions for products from progress functions for their components:

Lemma 8. *If Φ_1 is a progress function for D_1 and Φ_2 is a progress function for D_2, then $\Phi: (x, y) \mapsto \Phi_1(x) + \Phi_2(y)$ is a progress function for the serial product of the DCPs.*

Proof. Since $\Phi_1 \geqslant 0$ and $\Phi_2 \geqslant 0$, we have that $\Phi \geqslant 0$. Similarly, Φ must be zero for exactly the goal states of the product. Now suppose the product is solvable from (s_1, s_2). Then there must exist solution sequences for the components that monotonically decrease Φ_1 and Φ_2, respectively. Any combination of these sequences to form a solution to the product must then monotonically decrease Φ, and so Φ must be a progress function for the product. $\square$

Again, the parallel case is more complicated:

Lemma 9. *If Φ_1 is a progress function for D_1 and Φ_2 is a progress function for D_2, and for every goal state of D_1 and D_2 there is an action that maps that state to a goal state, then $\Phi: (x, y) \mapsto \Phi_1(x) + \Phi_2(y)$ is a progress function for the parallel product of the two DCPs.*

Proof. Again, we have that $\Phi \geqslant 0$ and that Φ is zero for exactly the goal states of the product. Now consider a state (s_1, s_2) from which the product is solvable. There must be solution sequences S_1 and S_2 to the component problems along which Φ_1 and Φ_2, respectively, are strictly decreasing. Without loss of generality, assume that S_1 is the shorter. Of the two solutions. We can pad S_1 and combine the solutions to produce a solution to the product. The padding cannot change the value of Φ_1, and so the value of Φ must be strictly decreasing along the combined solution. $\square$

7.4. Construction of DCP solutions by decomposition

7.4.1. Product DCPs

We now have the tools to construct solutions to product DCPs from the solutions to their components:

Lemma 10. *Let p_1 be a policy which solves D_1 and halts from all states in some set of initial states I_1, and let p_2 be a policy which solves D_2 and halts from all states in I_2. Then the policy*

$$p(x, y) = p_1(x) \times p_2(y)$$

solves $D_1 \parallel D_2$ and halts from all states in $I_1 \times I_2$. (Note that here we are using the convention of treating p, a function over pairs, as a function over two scalars.)

Lemma 11. *Let p_1 be a policy which solves D_1 from all states in some set of initial states I_1, and let p_2 be a policy which solves D_2 from all states in I_2. Then any policy for which*

$$p(x, y) = p_1(x) \times i \quad \text{or} \quad i \times p_2(y)$$

and

$$y \in G_2, x \notin G_1 \Rightarrow p(x, y) = p_1(x) \times i,$$
$$x \in G_1, y \notin G_2 \Rightarrow p(x, y) = i \times p_2(y)$$

will solve $D_1 \rightleftharpoons D_2$ and halt from all states in $I_1 \times I_2$.

Proof. We can prove both lemmas using progress functions. Let Φ_{p_1, D_1} and Φ_{p_2, D_2} be the standard progress for p_1 and p_2 on D_1 and D_2, respectively. Their sum must be a progress function for the product. This follows directly for the serial case, and from the fact that p_1 and p_2 halt for the parallel case. Since the policies for both products clearly honor the sum, they must solve their respective products. Note that the constraint given in the second lemma is sufficient, but not necessary. $\square$

7.4.2. Reduction

We can often treat one environment as an abstraction of another; The abstract environment retains some of the fundamental structure of the concrete environment but removes unimportant distinctions between states. An abstract state corresponds to a set of concrete states and abstract actions correspond to complicated sequences of concrete actions.

Let a projection of an environment $E = (S, A)$ into an abstract environment $E' = (S', A')$ be a mapping $\pi: S \rightarrow S' \cup \{\bot\}$. π gives the abstract state for a given concrete state or else $\bot$ if it has no corresponding abstract state. π^{-1} gives the concrete states corresponding to a given abstract state. For sets of states, we will let $\pi^{-1}(S) = \bigcup_{s \in S} \pi^{-1}(s)$.

We define a π-implementation of an abstract action a' to be a policy that reliably moves from states corresponding to an abstract state s' to states corresponding the abstract state $a'(s')$ *without visiting states corresponding to other abstract states*. Thus for any s' for which $a'(s')$ is defined, the implementation solves the DCP

$$(\pi^{-1}(\{s', \bot, a'(s')\}), A, \pi^{-1}(a'(s'))).$$

Note that we do not require p to stay in $\pi^{-1}(a'(s'))$ upon reaching it.

Given π-implementations $p_{a'}$ of each abstract action a', we can use an abstract policy p' to solve problems in the concrete environment by emulating the abstract actions. We need only look up the abstract state corresponding to our current concrete state, look up the abstract action for the abstract state, and run its implementation. This suggests the policy

$$p(s) = p_{p'(\pi(s))}(s).$$

This concrete policy works by taking the state s, looking up its abstract state $\pi(s)$, computing the proper abstract action $p'(\pi(s))$, and then computing and running the next concrete action in its implementation $p_{p'(\pi(s))}$. Note that since this policy has no internal state, it effectively recomputes the abstract action each time it chooses a concrete action. This is no problem when the concrete environment is in a state that corresponds to an abstract state, but the π-implementations are allowed to visit states that have no abstract state. To handle this problem, it is necessary to add a state register to the environment to remember what abstract action is presently being performed. The policy for the augmented environment computes a new abstract action whenever the environment is in a concrete state with a corresponding abstract state. It stores the name of the new abstract action in the register for later use, while also executing it its implementation. When the environment is in a concrete state with no abstract state, it uses the abstract action stored in the register and preserves the value in the register:

Lemma 12. *Let $D = (S, A, G)$, $D' = (S', A', G')$ be DCPs, π be a projection of D into D', and for each action $a' \in A'$, let $p_{a'}$ be a π-implementation of a' in D. If p' is a policy which solves D', then the policy*

$$p(s, a) = \begin{cases} p_a(s) \times C_a, & \text{if } \pi(s) = \bot, \\ p_{p'(\pi(s))}(s) \times C_{p'(\pi(s))}, & \text{otherwise,} \end{cases}$$

solves the augmentation of D with the alphabet A', from any state in $\pi^{-1}(S')$.

Proof. Let $\Phi_{p',D'}$ be the standard progress function for p' on D' and let $s \in P^{-1}(S')$. Then $\Phi_{p',D'}(\pi(s))$ is the number of abstract actions need to solve the problem from the concrete state s. If $\Phi_{p',D'}(\pi(s)) = 0$, then the problem is already solved, so suppose that p solves the problem from states s for which $\Phi_{p',D'}(\pi(s)) = n$ and consider an s for which $\Phi_{p',D'}(\pi(s)) = n + 1$. The policy p will immediately compute $p'(\pi(s))$, store it into the register. Call this action a'. The policy p will also immediately begin executing $p_{a'}$. Since this policy is a p-implementation of a', the system must reach a state in $\pi^{-1}(a'(\pi(s)))$ in finite time, which is to say that it will reach the next state in D'. By assumption, p' can solve D' from this high level state in n steps, and so p must be able to solve D from s, and so, by induction p solves D for all $s \in P^{-1}(S')$. $\square$

We will say that D is *reducible* to D' if there exists a projection π of D into D' and π-implementations of all of actions in D'. If D is reducible to D' then we can easily convert any solution to D' into a solution to D.

8. Analysis of a robot navigation system

Consider the problem of piloting a robot about the office environment shown in Fig. 8. At any given moment, the robot must decide given its destination how fast to turn and how fast to move forward or backward. Polly uses the policy of following corridors except when it reaches intersections. At intersections it compares the coordinates of the intersection to the coordinates of its goal (presumed to be another intersection) and turns north when the goal is to the north, south when the goal is to the south, and so on:

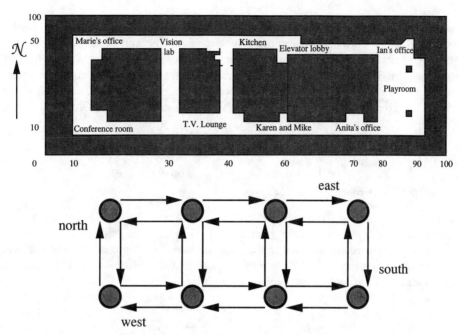

Fig. 8. Approximate layout of the seventh floor of the AI lab at MIT (Top) and its topological structure (Bottom).

$$p_{polly}(sensors) = \begin{cases} stop, & \text{if at goal,} \\ turn\text{-}north, & \text{if south of goal and at turn to north,} \\ turn\text{-}south, & \text{if north of goal and at turn to south,} \\ \dots \\ turn\text{-}north, & \text{if south of goal and pointed south,} \\ turn\text{-}south, & \text{if north of goal and pointed north,} \\ \dots \\ follow\text{-}corridor, & \text{otherwise.} \end{cases}$$

The details of the perception and control systems are given in [19].

8.1. Derivation from a geometric path planner

Geometric path planning is a common technique for solving this type of problem. Given a detailed description of the environment, a start position, and a goal position, a path planner computes a safe path through the environment from start to goal (see [24]). Once the path has been planned, a separate system follows the path. Geometric planning is versatile and can produce very efficient paths, but is not computationally efficient. It also requires detailed knowledge of the environment which the perceptual system may be unable to deliver.

We can clarify the relationship between a path planning system and Polly's reactive algorithm by deriving Polly's algorithm from the planing system. Let $\mathcal{N}$ be the DCP whose states are (position, orientation) pairs and whose actions are small (translation, rotation) pairs such as the robot might move in one clock tick. Clearly, Polly can be modeled as an $\mathcal{N}$ policy. However, the planner can equally well be modeled as an $\mathcal{N}$ policy. A planner/executive is simply a policy that uses internal state to compute and execute a plan. The planning portion uses scratch memory to gradually compute a plan and store it in a plan register, while the executive reads the finished plan out of the register and executes each segment in turn. Thus a planner/executive architecture has the form:

$$p_0(s, plan, scratch) = \begin{cases} i \times \mathrm{plan}_{\mathcal{N}}(s, scratch), & \text{if } plan \text{ incomplete,} \\ \mathrm{execute}(plan) \times i, & \text{otherwise;} \end{cases}$$

$$\mathrm{execute}(plan) = \mathrm{head}(plan) \times \mathcal{C}_{\mathrm{tail}(plan)}.$$

An agent in $\mathcal{N}$ will spend nearly all its time in corridors. The only real choice points in this environment are the corridor intersections. Thus only the graph of corridors and intersections $\mathcal{N}'$, need be searched, rather than the full state space of $\mathcal{N}$ (see Fig. 8). By Lemma 12, we can augment the environment with a register to hold the current north/south/east/west action and replace p_0 with the policy

$$p_1(s, action) = \begin{cases} p_{p_1'(I(s))}(s) \times \mathcal{C}_{p_1'(I(s))}, & \text{if at intersection,} \\ p_{action}(s) \times \mathcal{C}_{action}, & \text{otherwise,} \end{cases}$$

where:

- $I(s)$ is the intersection at state s,
- the different p_{action} policies implement following north, south, east, and west corridors, respectively, and,
- p_1' is an arbitrary $\mathcal{N}'$ policy.

The lemma requires that the goal always be a corridor intersection and that the robot always be started from a corridor intersection. We could now solve $\mathcal{N}'$ by adding plan and scratch registers and using a plan/execute policy:

$$p_1'(intersec, plan, scratch) = \begin{cases} i \times \mathrm{plan}_{\mathcal{N}'}(intersec, scratch), & \text{if } plan \text{ incomplete,} \\ \mathrm{execute}(plan) \times i, & \text{otherwise.} \end{cases}$$

We can simplify further by noting that $\mathcal{N}'$ is isomorphic to $\mathbb{Z}_4 \rightleftharpoons \mathbb{Z}_2$, that is, the corridor network is a 4×2 grid. By Lemma 11, we can replace p_1' with any policy that interleaves actions to reduce grid coordinate differences between the current location and the goal. We can then remove the plan and scratch registers from p_1 and reduce it to

$$p_2(s, action) = \begin{cases} p_{p_2'(I(s))}(s) \times \mathcal{C}_{p_2'(I(s))}, & \text{if at intersection,} \\ p_{action}(s) \times \mathcal{C}_{action}, & \text{otherwise,} \end{cases}$$

where p_2' is any $\mathcal{N}'$ policy satisfying the constraints that (1) it only stops at the goal, and (2) it only moves north/south/east/west if the goal is north/south/east/west of $I(s)$.

There are still two important differences between p_2 and p_{polly}: Polly uses a different set of actions ("turn north" instead of "go north") and it has no internal state to keep

Table 1
Summary of constraints and optimizations used in Polly's navigation system.

Constraint	Optimization
ground plane constraint	use height for depth estimation
background-texture constraint	use texture for obstacle detection
corridor network	replace planning in $\mathcal{N}$ with planning in $\mathcal{N}'$
grid structure	replace planning with difference reduction
orientation correlation	store state in orientation

track of its abstract action. While it appears to use a qualitatively different policy than we have derived, it does not. Within a short period of beginning a *north* action, an agent will always be pointed north. Similarly for *east*, *south*, and *west* actions. The orientation of the robot effectively is the *action* register and turn commands effectively write the register. There's no need for internal memory. Polly stores its state in its motor.

We can summarize the transformations used in the derivation as follows (see Table 1). The constraint that the environment consist of a network of corridors and that the goal be a corridor intersection allows us to replace geometric planning with planning in the corridor graph. The isomorphism of the corridor graph to a grid allows us to replace planning with difference reduction. Finally, the correlation of the robot's orientation with its internal state allows us to store the current action in the orientation.

It is important to note that either, both, or neither of the subproblems (the abstracted environment and corridor following) could be solved using deliberative planning; the two decisions are orthogonal. If both are implemented using planners, then the resulting system is effectively a hierarchical planner (see [39] or [22]). Polly's environment happens to allow the use of simple reactive policies for both, so it is a layered reactive system [9]. In an environment with a more complicated graph topology, one could reverse the second optimization and use a deliberative planner, leaving the first optimization intact. The result would then be a hybrid system with planning on top and reacting on the bottom (see [8, 14, 27, 40] for other examples). On the other hand, one could imagine an environment where the individual corridors were cluttered but were connected in a grid. In such an environment, the abstract problem could be solved reactively, but corridor following might actually require deliberative planning.

9. Conclusions

Fundamentally, this paper is about explanation. For one reason or another, we are often faced with agents or other mechanisms that operate properly in one type of environment but not in another. In such cases, we want to explain the agent's performance in different environments. Transformational analysis is a way of reverse-engineering ones own programs. It reduces an agent's environmental specialization to a series of lemmas giving the conditions under which different optimizations are possible. The lemmas are often more enlightening than the agents themselves. No one cares what edge detector Polly uses. The constraint (given in Lemma 3) which background surface markings place on the choice of edge detector is far more interesting. Once the lemmas have been obtained, they can be used to predict the performance of old agents in new environments or to suggest designs for new agents in old environments. Given a sufficient stock of optimization lemmas, one can imagine developing cookbook methods for designing particular kinds of situated agents, much as cookbook methods are currently used in electrical and mechanical engineering.

A discussion of when specialization is appropriate is outside the scope of this paper. The issue is not so much whether to build specialized systems or general systems as how we can be intelligent consumers of specialization. The literature is full of specialized systems, although they are often not billed as such. We must think carefully about whether an agent works because of the generality of its design or because of serendipitous properties of test data.

We must study the environment not only formally but experimentally. The knowledge we use of the external world to design our agents is necessarily incomplete. I have used the transformational techniques discussed here primarily for *post-hoc* analysis. It is rare that I understand the structure of my sensors and environment well enough for my first guess at an algorithm be robust. Performing a derivation based on plausible constraints that turn out to be empirically false is wasted effort. The environmental constraints we encode within our agents are partial theories of the environment. Theories must be tested. If we take this notion seriously, then we must view artificial intelligence as a form of natural science. To understand intelligence, we must study not only ourselves but our world.

Acknowledgements

Phil Agre, Rod Brooks, Bruce Donald, Eric Grimson, Maja Mataric, David Michael, Ray Paton, Stan Rosenschein, and Lynn Stein all provided much needed feedback during the development of these ideas. The reviewers provided many useful suggestions for improving the presentation. Support for this research was provided in part by the University Research Initiative under Office of Naval Research contract N00014–86–K–0685, and in part by the Advanced Research Projects Agency under Office of Naval Research contract N00014–85–K–0124.

References

[1] P.E. Agre, The dynamic structure of everyday life, Tech. Report 1085, MIT Artificial Intelligence Laboratory, Cambridge, MA (1988).

[2] P.E. Agre and I. Horswill, Cultural support for improvisation, in: *Proceedings AAAI-92*, San Jose, CA (1992).

[3] A.V. Aho, R. Sethi and J.D. Ullman, *Compilers: Principles, Techniques, and Tools* (Addison Wesley, Reading, MA, 1986).

[4] S.T. Barnard and M.A. Fischler, Computational and biological models of stereo vision, in: *Proceedings DARPA Image Understanding Workshop* (1990).

[5] A. Barr and E.A. Feigenbaum, *The Handbook of Artificial Intelligence* (William Kaufmann, Los Altos, 1981).

[6] K. Beach, Becoming a bartender: the role of external memory cues in a work-directed educational activity, *J. Appl. Cogn. Psychol.* (1992).

[7] R. Beer, A dynamical systems perspective on autonomous agent–environment interaction, *Artif. Intell.* **72** (1995) 173–215. CES 92-11, Case Western Reserve University, Cleveland, OH (1992).

[8] J. Bresina and M. Drummond, Integrating planning and reaction, in: J. Hendler, ed., *AAAI Spring Symposium on Planning in Uncertain, Unpredictable or Changing Environments* (AAAI Press, Asilomar, CA, 1990).

[9] R.A. Brooks, A robust layered control system for a mobile robot, *IEEE J. Rob. Autom.* **2** (1) (1986) 14–23.

[10] A. Church, *The Calculi of Lambda Conversion* (Princeton University Press, Princeton, NJ, 1951).

[11] J.D. Crisman, Color region tracking for vehicle guidance, in: A. Blake and A. Yuille, eds., *Active Vision* (MIT Press, Cambridge, MA, 1992), Chapter 7.

[12] B.R. Donald and J. Jennings, Constructive recognizability for task-directed robot programming, *J. Rob. Auton. Syst.* **9** (1992) 41–74.

[13] M.M. Fleck, Boundaries and topological algorithms, Tech. Report 1065, MIT Artificial Intelligence Laboratory, Cambridge, MA (1988).

[14] E. Gat, Integrating planning and reacting in a heterogeneous asynchronous architecture for controlling real-world mobile robots, in: *Proceedings AAAI-92*, San Jose, CA (1992).

[15] R.W. Hamming, *Coding and Information Theory* (Prentice-Hall, Englewood Cliffs, NJ, 1980).

[16] K.J. Hammond and T.M. Converse, Stabilizing environments to facilitate planning and activity: an engineering argument, in: *Proceedings AAAI-91*, Anaheim, CA (1991) 787–793.

[17] J.L. Hennessy and D.A. Patterson, *Computer Architecture: a Quantitative Approach* (Morgan Kaufmann, San Mateo, CA, 1990).

[18] I. Horswill, Polly: a vision-based artificial agent, in: *Proceedings AAAI-93*, Washington, DC (1993) 824–829.

[19] I. Horswill, Specialization of perceptual processes, Ph.D. Thesis, Massachusetts Institute of Technology, Cambridge, MA (1993).

[20] I. Horswill and R. Brooks, Situated vision in a dynamic environment: chasing objects, in: *Proceedings AAAI-88*, St. Paul, MN (1988).

[21] O. Khatib, Real-time obstacle avoidance for manipulators and mobile robots, *Int. J. Rob. Res.* **5** (1) (1986) 90–98.

[22] C.A. Knoblock, J.D. Tenenberg and Q. Yang, A spectrum of abstraction hierarchies for planning, in: *Proceedings AAAI-90*, Boston, MA (1990).

[23] J. Košecká, Control of discrete event systems, GRASP LAB Report 313, Department of Computer and Information Science, University of Pennsylvania, Philadelphia, PA (1992).

[24] J.-C. Latombe, *Robot Motion Planning* (Kluwer Academic Publishers, Boston, MA, 1991).

[25] M.L. Littman, An optimization-based categorization of reinforcement learning environments, in: J.-A. Meyer and S.W. Wilson, eds., *From Animals to Animats: The Second International Conference on Simulation of Adaptive Behavior* (MIT Press, Cambridge, MA, 1993) 262–270.

[26] D.G. Luenberger, *Introduction to Dynamic Systems: Theory, Models, and Applications* (Wiley, New York, 1979).

[27] D.M. Lyons and A.J. Hendriks, Exploiting patterns of interaction to achieve reactive behavior, *Artif. Intell.* **73** (1995) 117–148 (this volume).

[28] D. Marr, *Vision* (Freeman, New York, 1982).

[29] D. McFarland, What it means for robot behavior to be adaptive, in: J.-A. Meyer and S.W. Wilson, eds., *From Animals to Animats: Proceedings of the First International Conference on Simulation of Adaptive Behavior* (MIT Press, Cambridge, MA, 1991) 22–28.

[30] J.-A. Meyer and A. Guillot, Simulation of adaptive behavior in animats: review and prospect, in: J.-A. Meyer and S.W. Wilson, eds., *From Animals to Animats: Proceedings of the First International Conference on Simulation of Adaptive Behavior* (MIT Press, Cambridge, MA, 1991) 2–14.

[31] J.-A. Meyer and S.W. Wilson, eds., *From Animals to Animats: Proceedings of the First International Conference on Simulation of Adaptive Behavior* (MIT Press, Cambridge, MA, 1991).

[32] J.-A. Meyer and S.W. Wilson, eds., *From Animals to Animats: The Second International Conference on Simulation of Adaptive Behavior* (MIT Press, Cambridge, MA, 1993).

[33] M. Minsky, *Computation: Finite and Infinite Machines* (Prentice-Hall, Englewood Cliffs, NJ, 1967).

[34] R.C. Patton, H.S. Nwana, M.J.R. Shave and T.J.M. Bench-Capon, *Computing at the tissue/organ level (with particular reference to the liver)* (MIT Press, Cambridge, MA, 1992) 411–420.

[35] H.L. Roitblat, *Introduction to Comparitive Cognition* (Freeman, New York, 1987).

[36] S.J. Rosenschein, Formal theories of knowledge in AI and robotics, Research Report CSLI-87-84, Center for the Study of Language and Information, Stanford, CA (1987).

[37] S.J. Rosenschein, Synthesizing information-tracking automata from environment descriptions, in: R.J. Brachman, H.J. Levesque and R. Reiter, eds., *Proceedings First International Conference on Principles of Knowledge Representation and Reasoning*, Toronto, Ont. (1989) 386–393.

[38] S.J. Rosenschein and L.P. Kaelbling, The synthesis of machines with provable epistemic properties, in: J. Halpern, ed., *Proceedings Conference on Theoretical Aspects of Reasoning about Knowledge*, Monterey, CA (1986) 83–98.

[39] E.D. Sacerdoti, Planning in a hierarchy of abstraction spaces, *Artif. Intell.* **5** (2) (1974).

[40] L. Spector and J. Hendler, The supervenience architecture, in: A. Kak, ed., *Working notes of the AAAI Fall Symposium on Sensory Aspects of Robotic Intelligence* (AAAI Press, Asilomar, CA, 1991) 93–100.

[41] G.L. Steele and G.J. Sussman, The revised report on Scheme: an interpreter for the extended lambda calculus, AI Memo 452, MIT Artificial Intelligence Laboratory, Cambridge MA (1978).

[42] M.J. Swain, Color indexing, Tech. Report 390, Department of Computer Science, University of Rochester (1990).

[43] P.M. Todd and S.W. Wilson, Environment structure and adaptive behavior from the ground up, in: J.-A. Meyer and S.W. Wilson, eds., *From Animals to Animats*: *The Second International Conference on Simulation of Adaptive Behavior* (MIT Press, Cambridge, MA, 1993) 11–20.

[44] M.A. Turk, D.G. Morgenthaler, K. Gremban and M. Marra, Video road following for the autonomous land vehicle, in: *Proceedings IEEE International Conference on Robotics and Automation* (1987) 273–280.

[45] N. Wiener, *Cybernetics* (MIT Press, Cambridge, MA, 1961).

[46] S.W. Wilson, The animat path to AI, in: J.-A. Meyer and S.W. Wilson, eds., *From Animals to Animats*: *Proceedings of the First International Conference on Simulation of Adaptive Behavior* (MIT Press, Cambridge, MA, 1991) 15–21.

[47] J. Woodfill and R. Zabih, Using motion vision for a simple robotic task, in: *Proceedings AAAI Fall Symposium on Sensory Aspects of Robotic Intelligence* (1991).

Artificial Intelligence 73 (1995) 31–68

The intelligent use of space

David Kirsh*

Department of Cognitive Science, UCSD, La Jolla, CA 92093-0505, USA

Received September 1992; revised June 1993

Abstract

The objective of this essay is to provide the beginning of a principled classification of some of the ways space is intelligently used. Studies of planning have typically focused on the temporal ordering of action, leaving as unaddressed, questions of where to lay down instruments, ingredients, work-in-progress, and the like. But, in having a body, we are spatially located creatures: we must always be facing some direction, have only certain objects in view, be within reach of certain others. How we *manage* the spatial arrangement of items around us, is not an afterthought; it is an integral part of the way we think, plan and behave. The proposed classification has three main categories: spatial arrangements that simplify choice; spatial arrangements that simplify perception; and spatial dynamics that simplify internal computation. The data for such a classification is drawn from videos of cooking, assembly and packing, everyday observations in supermarkets, workshops and playrooms, and experimental studies of subjects playing Tetris, the computer game. This study, therefore, focusses on interactive processes in the medium and short term: on how agents set up their *workplace* for particular tasks, and how they continuously manage that workplace.

1. Introduction

How do we use the space around us? Studies of planning have typically focused on the temporal ordering of action, leaving questions of where to lay down instruments, ingredients, work-in-progress, and the like, as concerns that can be dealt with later. In having a body, we are spatially located creatures: we must always be facing some direction, have only certain objects in view, be within reach of certain others. How we manage the space around us, then, is not an afterthought; it is an integral part of the way we think, plan and behave, a central

---

* E-mail: kirsh@cogsci.ucsd.edu.

element in the way we shape the very world that constrains and guides our behavior.

The view I shall present is that whether we are aware of it or not, we are constantly organizing and re-organizing our workplace to enhance performance. Space is a resource that must be managed, much like time, memory, and energy. When we use space well we can often bring the time and memory demands of our tasks down to workable levels. We can increase the reliability of execution, and the number of jobs we can handle at once. The techniques we use are not always obvious, or universal. Some were taught to us, some naturally evolved as we improved our performance through practice, some are inevitable consequences of having the type of bodies, manipulators and sensors we have. In every case, though, the reason space can be used to simplify our cognitive and physical tasks is because of the way we are embedded in the world.

Here is a typical example of using space consciously to improve execution. When preparing an elaborate salad, one subject we videotaped, cut each vegetable into thin slices and laid them out in tidy rows. There was a row of tomatoes, of mushrooms, and of red peppers, each of different length. Our cook then brought over a large elliptical platter—one she had never used before—placed it beside the rows and began arranging the items along the circumference. The objective, as was evident from observation and later questioning, was to lay out on the platter all the cut items in a uniform and aesthetic manner. She did not want to run out of tomatoes early, leaving a tomatoless region, or to close the ring of vegetables before all ingredients, peppers, mushrooms, and tomatoes, were used up.

The placement problem our cook faced was to apportion ingredients in a uniform manner. This required either elaborate planning beforehand; recall of similar case experience, or online tracking of the relative number of remaining slices. Having never worked with an elliptical platter this size, our cook had no ready case knowledge to call on. Nor was she eager to count items and measure the circumference of the platter, a step she would perform if planning. Instead she relied on tracking the remaining slices and her moment by moment adaptive skills. To understand why lining up the ingredients in well ordered neatly separated rows is clever, requires understanding a fact about human psychophysics: estimation of length is easier and more reliable than estimation of area or volume. By using length to encode number she created a cue or signal in the world which she could accurately track. Laying out slices in lines allows more precise judgement of the property *relative number remaining* than clustering the slices into groups, or piling them up into heaps. Hence, because of the way the human perceptual system works, lining up the slices creates an observable property that facilitates execution.

The function of arrangement in this example is to encode, as *explicitly* as possible (see [22]), a key piece of information about the problem state. It is easy to analyze how it works. But, in general, how effectively information is encoded in environmental arrangements, depends on the memory, categories, and skills of an agent. There is substantial literature on memory of chess positions that shows that a single glimpse is enough to allow an expert chess player to remember far more of a game than is acquired by a novice player after many such glimpses [10]. This suggests that how an expert might store information in arrangements may not be evident to novices. It also suggests that even though we often do not realize that we are structuring our workplace to help us keep track of processes and a host of other useful functions I shall talk about, we should not assume that such cognitive or informational structuring is not taking place all the time. Informational structuring is commonplace.

I doubt that this idea will encounter deep opposition. Yet it has been rarely explored by psychologists. For instance, in a typical psychological experiment about memory, experimentalists set out to test a conjecture by systematically altering properties of the stimulus and observing the effect on certain dimensions of performance, such as how much, how reliably, how fast the stimulus material is remembered in free recall tests, in cued recall tests, or in recognition tests. Such tests are supposed to tell us something about how the agent organizes the stimulus material internally. Thus, the reason the string KXTNJQXTARWOYE is less memorable than the string IBMCIANBCDARPA is that it cannot be broken into known strings. After a while, many subjects (depending on background) will chunk IBMCIANBCDARPA into four more easily remembered strings IBM CIA NBC DARPA. Agents project structure onto the world. But curiously, experimentalists rarely allow the subject to play with the stimulus itself to highlight the chunks, as we note in scrabble. They do not set up experiments to determine how agents choose to structure the stimulus.

The tendency to delay study of the cognitive/computational virtues of spatial arrangement is not confined to psychology. Consider the following blocks world problem so fondly studied in planning. A child is asked to build two towers out of lettered blocks so that the first tower reads SPACE and the second reads MATTERS, as shown in Fig. 1. The blocks are currently scattered around the room. If we assume that standard AI blocks restrictions apply then only one block can be moved at a time, and only if there is no block on top of it. How shall the robot proceed? One method never discussed in the AI literature is to preprocess

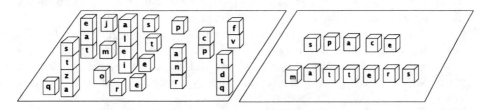

Fig. 1. In (a), a region of the floor is covered with blocks, some in small stacks, others just strewn about. In (b), the blocks that spell out the goal towers SPACE MATTERS have been ordered. Children often arrange blocks on the ground before stacking them, not simply because it is less demanding physically than stacking blocks stably, but because it is easier to solve the problem when one can readily see all the letters, and when one can order and re-order blocks without concern for balancing them.

the blocks so that they spell out the goal stacks SPACE MATTERS horizontally on the ground.

Why might this be a good idea? Because it serves as a proof that there exists a goal linearization that will work. If we can build SPACE MATTERS horizontally we know we can build it vertically. We can guarantee construction. At first this may not seem to be an advance over simply building the towers directly. The benefits of informationally structuring the world do not appear to be worth the effort. But if we factor in that the constraints on horizontal movement are weaker than those on vertical stacking, we can see that to solve the problem on the ground is to solve the problem in a more abstract space. On the ground, we can pick up and move a block regardless of whether it is sandwiched between blocks. And if we leave space between blocks we can insert a block without first shifting the others around. Hence, we can save many steps by solving the problem on the ground first, since if there is going to be external trial and error search in finding the goal ordering, there are far fewer moves to make on the ground. It is easier to solve the problem on the ground.

Such exploitation of the world to improve execution, or to simplify problem solving, is typical of situated reasoning. In a host of studies [17, 32, 43], it has been repeatedly shown how human agents make use of *resources* in the situation to help draw conclusions and solve problems rather than use abstract, symbolic computations. People make mental tools of things in the environment. Lave [31] emphasized the ubiquity of specialized "environmental calculating devices". For instance, in a famous example (de la Rocha [13], cited by Greeno [17]), an interviewer asked a subject who had recently enrolled in the Weight Watchers diet program, "How much cottage cheese would you have if you served three-fourths of the day's allotment, which is two-thirds of a cup?" After the man muttered that he had studied calculus in college, he measured two thirds of a cup of cottage cheese, put it on the counter, shaped it into a circle, put a horizontal and a vertical line through it, set aside one of the quadrants, and served the rest. Instead of multiplying $3/4 \times 2/3 = 1/2$, he used objects available in the situation to solve his problem.

Now space is always present, and the need to place objects somewhere is a constant fact of life. This makes space an invaluable resource to exploit in order to facilitate everyday problem solving and planning.

My goal in what follows is to provide the beginning of a principled classification of some of the ways space is intelligently used. The data for such a classification is drawn from videos of cooking,[1] assembly and packing, everyday observations in supermarkets, workshops and playrooms, and experimental studies of subjects playing Tetris, the computer game.

The remainder of the paper is divided into five parts. In the first, I introduce

---

[1] Among the videotapes of cooking I shall refer to is a valuable corpus gathered by Bernard Conein of University of Paris. These tapes record the activities of Parisian cooks preparing apple tarts in their home kitchens. This material has yet to be fully reported on and I thank Bernard for his permission to mention it here.

the general framework within which to think of intelligence and space. Our use of space is not a special case of intelligent activity which somehow deviates from our normal methods of interaction; the way to understand how we exploit spatial resources is part of a more general approach to the study of intelligent activity. In the next three parts, I present my classification organized into:

- spatial arrangements that simplify choice;
- spatial arrangements that simplify perception;
- spatial dynamics that simplify internal computation.

In the final part I draw some conclusions.

2. How to think about everyday activity

The approach I shall be endorsing falls squarely in the interactionist camp: to understand human behavior, and to design robots that scale up to complex dynamic environments, we must explore the interaction between agent and environment. Humans, to a significant degree, shape and even create the environment, which in turn, influences their behavior and development. We can study this interactive process along different time scales. As Hammond et al. [18] have done, we can study the way agents restore the environment to states which they (the agents) have methods to deal with, thereby diminishing uncertainty, reducing the number of contingencies that have to be built into programs, and allowing streamlining of plans because agents can rely on things being as they ought to be, more or less. The stabilizing processes Hammond discusses, are long term stabilizations.

But, equally, we can study interactive processes in the medium and short term—as I shall be doing here. For instance, we can study how agents set up their workplace for *particular* tasks, and how they continuously *manage* that workplace. To take an example, an agent who knows he will be acting as a short order cook may equip and maintain his kitchen with implements and standard resources that are regularly required—i.e. long term structuring. But, on being given a particular order, say a mushroom omelet, hash browns and whole wheat toast, the cook must still prepare the workplace specifically for that task—laying out the eggs, the cut mushrooms, and the requested number of pieces of bread. In setting up the workplace for a particular task the cook arranges items so that the work that has to be done in the high tempo phases of cooking is both simplified and reduced. This readying of the workplace is a *medium term* structuring of the environment.

Short term structurings arise when ingredients and implements are deployed adaptively in the cognitively demanding phase. Once the task has entered the main phase, we find that agents, particularly expert agents, constantly re-arrange items to make it easy to:

(1) track the state of the task;
(2) figure out, remember, or notice the properties signaling what to do next;
(3) predict the effects of actions.

To return to the diner, if several orders are being prepared, we have observed short order cooks, clustering the materials for orders together, and leaving knives, forks or other utensils near the ingredient to be used next, as if to mark their place in their plan.

Throughout this paper, I shall be operating with several assumptions it is best to make explicit. These have been instrumental in shaping the interpretations of behavior I shall be offering.

(1) The agents we observe are *experts*, or near experts, at their tasks, despite these tasks often being everyday tasks.

(2) Experts regularly find that enough information is available *locally* to make choices without having to plan on-line, using conscious analytical processes.

(3) Experts help to ensure that they have enough information locally by partially *jigging* or *informationally structuring* the environment as they go along.

(4) The human environments of action we shall be examining, the equipment and surfaces that comprise each workspace, are pre-structured in important ways to help compensate for limitations in processing power and memory.

Of these four tenets, number (3)—ways of informational structuring—will be my primary focus. It is worth elaborating numbers (2) and (4), as well, however, to get a proper perspective on this approach to embodied everyday activity. Readers who are impatient to see the classification of ways of using space intelligently may skip to Section 3.

2.1. *Experts don't plan much*

The hallmark of expertise, from a behavioral standpoint, is effectiveness and robustness. The hallmark of expertise, from a theoretical standpoint, is sufficient compiled knowledge to cope with normal contingencies without *much* on-line planning. A major factor in this compilation is expert perception: having the right perceptual categories, and knowing how to keep an eye on salient properties [10]. It is widely accepted that, for experts, there is tremendous local constraint on what should be done next [9]. Practice has tuned the perceptual systems of experts both to the microfeatures and cues that correlate with effective action [3, 6, 22, 23], and to the conditions when it is most helpful to attend to those cues.

Rasmussen [36, 37] and Reason [38] have elaborated this viewpoint in some detail. On their account, once an expert has decided what his goals are—what to cook for dinner, for example—the majority of activity that follows will be under what they call, *skill-based* and *rule-based* control (see also [34, 38, 41]; cf. [1]). These control structures, it is thought, are extremely responsive to current environmental conditions.

In the case of skills, this responsiveness is automatic and unreflective. When we make ourselves a cup of tea in our home kitchen, for example, we "automatically" comply with the orientation of faucet, kettle, cups, the water pressure, automatically retrieve the tea bag, milk, teapot, and so on. These actions are unreflective in the way habits are unreflective. That is, the actions are intentional, but not the product of deliberation.

In the case of rules, this responsiveness is also largely unreflective and automatic, triggered by perceived state information, but a rule has been invoked because the agent is aware that something unanticipated has occurred, that skill-based behaviors are beginning to drive things off course, and that corrective measures need to be taken. Thus, the need for a rule-based response will be triggered by one of the attentional checks on behavior that are part of skill-based activity. Once a disruption is noticed, the corrective action to be performed is determined by a rule in one of the "problem-solving packets" an expert has. For example, in the course of serving tea if we discover a dirty spoon, in normal circumstances, we will unreflectively wipe it clean, or reach into the drawer for another, or do whatever is obvious to put the process back on track. Even routine activities in familiar environments constantly give rise to such simple problems.[2] For most of these problems, it is suggested [36, 37] experts find sufficient cues in the situation to trigger a known rule without halting the activity in order to consciously and analytically take stock of the situation and reason or deliberate about a solution.

Conscious analytical processing—deliberation, as I have been calling it—is required when things begin to get too far out of control to rely on existing packets of problem-solving rules to manage the process. Only then must the agent consider non-local facts and goals, in order to formulate a plan to bring things back on track, or to find a new path to the goal. Accordingly, most expert activity is non-deliberate and locally driven.

2.2. Experts jig their environment

There are two obvious techniques which experts can use to increase the percentage of time they spend operating in skill and rule-based modes. The first is to broaden the range of cases their skills and rules cover, thereby coping with more diverse and uncertain environments. The second is to build into those skills and rules an environmental *dampening* factor that tends to decrease the variability of the environment. This is the force of tenet (3)—experts partially *jig* the environment as they go along. It is here that space becomes of paramount importance. Let me elaborate.

A jig is a device for stabilizing a process: it is a mechanism for reducing the degrees of freedom of a target object. A vice is a jig, a table top can serve as a jig, but so can a "pick" in basketball, or the slides on a cabinet drawer which determine the direction of free movement, or compliance. Jigging is one way of *preparing* or *structuring* the environment. The more completely prepared an environment is, the easier it is to accomplish one's task.

We can draw a logical distinction between physically jigging an environment

---

[2] Compare Agre's notion of hassles in his AI lab working paper of the same name [2].

and informationally jigging it; although in practice the two often go together. The distinction is between planting information in the environment to reduce the *perceived* degrees of freedom, and planting physical impediments or constraints in the environment to reduce the *physical* degrees of freedom an agent actually has. At the simplest level, the difference is between cues and constraints. In informationally jigging an environment an agent will usually arrange items (consciously or sometimes unconsciously) to draw attention, to cue cognitive events or processes in himself or herself, or another agent. For instance, in supermarkets, store managers succeed in biasing consumer choice by having large displays of 'specials' at the head of isles, by putting up flashy signs, by expanding the length of store shelf devoted to certain brands, and the like. These tricks alter a shopper's perceived choices, but do not actually restrict the range of physically possible actions. In physically jigging an environment, however, an agent arranges items (consciously or sometimes unconsciously) to physically constrain action. Thus, sticking a door jam under a door serves to constrain the physical freedom of an agent. If the agent can be counted on to notice the jam, then it can be relied on to serve as a cue, an informational jig, but there are many cases where the physical constraint goes unnoticed, and so acts as a physical jig alone.

I shall be concerned primarily with ways of arranging items to informationally jig the environment. As suggested, these include a variety of cueing techniques, but are not confined to those. For instance, the set of actions perceived possible may be reduced by hiding or partially occluding objects. Pull-down menus that display only some of the options available in a situation, is one such example. Another is found in the practice of dieters who keep certain foods in the pantry and out of the fridge, to prevent snacking. Out of sight is out of mind. Here, arrangements serve to *constrain* rather than cue perception.

Nonetheless, cueing is the key method of informationally structuring an environment. Agents "seed" the environment with attention-getting objects or structures. These can be harnessed to not only reduce perceived choice but to bias the *order* in which actions are undertaken. When I put a roll of film by the doorway, for example, I am using space to create a *reminder*[3] to prevent me from just marching out the door without remembering my earlier intention to get the film developed today. Reminders usually rely on attention-getting elements to draw our notice.[4] For instance, contextually unusual features, such as a surprising color, or an unexpected sound or smell, will often prompt reflection; as will being in just the right place at the time to be useful in a task. Such features work because we have sufficient knowledge of our tasks and plans that when, in the

---

[3] Reminders are one of the strategies agents have for improving prospective memory. "Prospective memory includes remembering a plan of action (i.e. what to do) and also remembering to do it. In most cases, the planned action has to be performed at a specified time, or within some time limits, so prospective memory also involves remembering when to perform the act" [12, p. 24].

[4] A different strategy for building reminders relies on "mentally linking the prospective task to another routine event or activity, like scheduling prospective phone calls for coffee-break time, or linking picking up the dry cleaning with going to work, so that one action cues another" [12, p. 28].

course of activity, we notice these felicitous events, or surprises, we are reminded of aspects of our tasks that must be performed. If successful, they capture our attention at the right time and alert us to opportunities we might have missed, or they reduce the likelihood of performing a so-called "double-capture slip".[5] These are slips arising from failure to notice a relevant choice, or a change in circumstances, with the effect that a "frequently done activity suddenly takes charge instead of (captures) the intended one" [35, p. 107].

Much of what I shall present in the following sections concerns ways of using spatial arrangements to informationally jig or structure the environment, and much of that focuses on ways of keeping attention properly directed. It is worth noting how environments that are dedicated to certain tasks already incorporate some of these ideas. This is the point of stressing tenet (4): that most task environments are pre-structured.

2.3. Pre-structured environments

Let us say that an environment E, is well designed for a particular task T, and a particular agent A endowed with skill S, and rules R, if, at every choice point, the environment provides sufficient physical and informational resources to locally determine A's choices. On the one hand, this will require E to be rich in task useful physical structures, for instance, E ought to have tools and surfaces which make it simple to satisfy regularly recurring preconditions in T. Thus, for cooking, where many tasks involve chopping, cutting, or slicing, we find kitchens equipped with knives in convenient reach, and hard flat surfaces—two obvious preconditions for most cutting-like actions. On the other hand, a well designed environment will also have to be rich in useful informational structures—cues and the like—to make it simple to cope with the cognitive demands of the task.

For example, in most kitchens [4], there are also timers, thermometers, oven lights and, of course, temperature settings to help us to see where in the process we are, and what must be done next. These devices populate the world with readily available task-relevant properties. Lids rattle when pressure builds up, kettles whistle or turn off automatically.

---

[5] A double capture error occurs when attention is drawn to something other than the choice at hand, and consequently behavior is then captured by a strong habit. Some examples cited by Reason and Mycielska [39] and Reason [38] are:

    (a) "I intended to stop on the way to work to buy some shoes, but 'woke up' to find that I had driven right past."

    (b) "I went into my room to change into something comfortable for the evening, and the next thing I knew I was getting into my pyjama trousers, as if to go to bed."

    (c) "I decided to make pancakes for tea. Then I remembered we didn't have any lemons, so I decided not to bother. Five minutes later, I started getting together the ingredients for pancakes having completely forgotten my change of mind."

In (a) inattention caused the agent to miss a choice point permitting the habit currently active to continue—*strong-habit exclusion*. In (b) inattention led to a missed choice point marking the branch point of two habits (i.e. the 'what to wear' choice point). In (c) forgetfulness, or inattention to the changed circumstances led the agent to revert to an earlier plan that had already been scrapped.

The distinction we introduced before between a purely informational jig or structure, and a purely physical structure, can be made more rigorous as follows. An action that structures the environment in a purely informational way achieves nothing that could not equally well be achieved by *asking an oracle*. This contrasts with actions that structure the environment *physically*, which reduce the physical complexity of a task by satisfying either preconditions or background conditions of actions.

This is worth explaining. An oracle is a device that can answer in unit time any instance of a particular decision problem. We might ask an oracle "what should I do next, given my current situation and goals?" Or "What are the likely effects of performing this action in this context?" Or even "What is the current state of the environment?" If the question asked is well-posed, i.e. decidable, the oracle will "instantly" return the correct answer. Oracles save computation. But they cannot save physical execution. Oracles can't slice or fry an egg; they never bring an agent physically closer to its goals.

For instance, to return to our blocks world example earlier, imagine we are dealing with blocks in which each block is lettered on one face only. As before, the goal assigned to the planner is to build a stack in which the letters form two sequences SPACE MATTERS, but, this time, the letters can be in any orientation. If not all the letters are visible, some of the blocks will have to be turned over before the stack can be built so that we know we are building the towers with the right ordering. These external epistemic actions[6] would not be necessary if we had an oracle or a partner in a better position to tell us a block's letter. The interesting thing is that the action of re-orienting a block does not satisfy any physical precondition of the goal.[7] The goal, as specified, allows the agent to place blocks without concern for direction. Accordingly, such actions are pragmatically superfluous. They are broadly equivalent[8] to placing an oracle in the environment which is able to remind us where each block is as soon as we ask (look).

Self-adjusting data structures provide a more formal model of the benefits of informational structuring. A data structure is self adjusting if each time an element is inserted or deleted, the structure executes an adjustment routine which performs simple changes to maintain certain "nice" properties. For example, in many sorting problems where binary trees are used to store the elements, it is possible that, due to some sequence of insertions and deletions the tree will become thin and long. Although traversing such a tree in left hand traversal is a linear time procedure, the process of deciding where to place the next element—that is, constructing the tree—is quadratic. If, however, certain small local

---

[6] For an in-depth analysis of the notion of external epistemic actions see [25].

[7] Unless, of course, the letter is printed on the top or bottom of a block, and the only way to expose the letter is by unstacking all the blocks above it.

[8] One important difference between an oracle and an environment that is appropriately informationally structured is that oracles provide answers in unit time whereas agents who must recover relevant information from an informationally structured environment may take considerably longer. This suggests that it is desirable to structure environments in ways that make relevant information most explicit. See [22].

changes are made to the tree whenever an operation is performed on it, we can guarantee keeping the tree wide and short. By incorporating such a scheme into the construction phase of our tree sorting algorithm we can improve performance, yielding an $O(N \log N)$ algorithm.[9]

Now the idea of making local changes in a data structure as we go along in order to improve performance is very much like making small rearrangements to the position of objects in our workspace to help us to find objects, to highlight change, or to allow us to use more efficient or familiar techniques. Both cases, self-adjusting data structures and reorganizing of the workspace, would be otiose if we had an oracle to advise us on what we must do next, or on where a particular element is to be found.

The implication is that rearrangements may be done just as much to make objects convenient mentally as to make them convenient physically. Restructuring often serves a cognitive function: to reduce the cost of visual search, to make it easier to notice, identify and remember items, and, of course, to simplify one's representation of the task.

2.4. A word about complexity analysis

Although I have been arguing that the point of informationally structuring space is to reduce the time and memory requirements of cognition, the actual reduction in computation achieved by the various methods I shall discuss does not, in general, lend itself to meaningful quantitative estimation.

For instance, from a classical information processing point of view, choice is the outcome of a heuristic search of options représented in a problem space. The problem space lays out decision points, feasible actions, and some fraction of the consequences of taking choices, and the agent relies on various heuristic methods to discover a goal path. The main ways to reduce the complexity of choice, then, are to revise the problem space so as to:

(1) reduce the fan-out of actions represented as available (feasible) at decision points—i.e. reduce the average branching factor;

(2) eliminate certain decision points—i.e. create a more abstract space with fewer nodes;

(3) represent the task in a way that exposes previously unnoticed constraints— i.e. add descriptions of state that lend themselves to better heuristic search, or, as in the mutilated checkerboard, to analytic solution.

Other ways of reducing the complexity of choice are to:

(4) improve search knowledge through chunking, caching, and so on;

(5) speed up the creation of a problem space representation;

---

[9] Tarjan has made an effort to quantify the value of self adjusting data structures under the rubric of amortized computation. His analysis relies on a cost–benefit evaluation: if the average expected benefit of having a data structure with nice properties exceeds the average cost of putting it into that form the self-adjusting algorithm is worth the effort. See especially [46].

(6) speed up the actual low level computation of search and heuristic evaluation.

Working within such a framework, it ought to be possible to determine, for any
given problem, what is the expected computational savings of an improvement in
one of these ways. Because there are external counterparts to most of these ways
we would expect it possible to generate similar complexity analyses. It should not
matter whether the change in the agent's computational task comes from
modifying the world to simplify choice, or modifying the internal representation
of the world to simplify choice. Yet, in practice, complexity analyses have limited
significance.

For instance, in Fig. 2(a) we see a graphical representation of the value of
having heuristics. Theoretically, an agent who modifies the description of state to
allow application of a heuristic powerful enough to single out a unique action at
each choice point, can reduce the complexity of search exponentially, from b^n to
n, where n is the average depth to the goal node and b is the average branching
factor. The agent can just choose the best action at each choice point without
checking for downstream consequences. Yet how many agents actually search
through all the steps in a plan before choosing the first step?

The external counterpart to method 3—modifying the description of problem
state—is to add new "heuristic cues" to the workplace. For example, in the
salad-making case mentioned in the introduction, we might argue that lining up
the vegetables not only helped determine the value of the cue "relative number
remaining", it altered the environment so that the heuristic based on it was now
usable. To realistically calculate the savings of such a cue, however, we would like
a cost–benefit analysis comparing the time lost by physically lining up the items,
versus the savings in improved layout performance. Empirical experiments can be

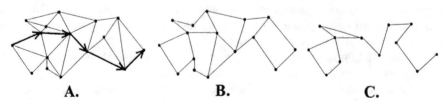

A.   **B.**   **C.**

Fig. 2. In these three graphs we see different ways a problem space can be modified to reduce search.
In (a), the information available at each node (which is not visible in this picture), has been
supplemented so that there is enough explicit information available locally to choose, on heuristic
grounds, a unique preferred action at each decision point. With the right heuristic cue a hard problem
can be made easy. In (b), the problem space has been set up so that the agent does not even represent
some of the feasible actions. In (c), we see the effects of revising the problem space to completely
eliminate the need for certain decisions. (c) is an abstraction from (a), in this case it is a sub-graph of
(a). External counterparts to each of these methods exist. To cause (a) by external means we modify
the environment so that there are heuristic cues available (e.g. lining up the vegetables). To cause (b),
we alter the environment so that actions are no longer locally afforded by the situation. Hiding food in
the pantry is a trivial example. To cause (c), we change the setting so that it is impossible to reach
certain decision points. For instance, locking the door to the kitchen to completely eliminate the
choice of a midnight snack. In actual cases, we often find varying degrees of each of these effects
present at once.

done. But these hardly count as formal results. They certainly will not tell us much about the internal computation saved, since different agents who use different methods will have tricks and shortcuts too, thereby frustrating appealing to empirical findings for worst case results. What is interesting about the examples, then, is not how much they reduce computation—for that we cannot meaningfully estimate—but *how easily* they reduce it.

3. Using space to simplify choice

3.1. Cues and constraints

Prima facie, choice is the product of search—visual search for the actions that are currently available, and mental search of the desirability of those available actions. Arrangements which reduce either type of search, simplify the computational burden of agents. In Fig. 2 there is a graph-theoretic portrait of three ways search can be so reduced. Information via cues and constraints can be added to a problem in order to:

(1) reduce the average fan-out of actions *perceived* as available at decision points;
(2) eliminate the need for previously necessary decisions;
(3) add new heuristic properties to simplify ranking the desirability of actions.

We will discuss each in turn.

3.2. Reducing perceived actions

To see an action as *available* for choice is to notice that it is *afforded* by the current situation. An affordance of a situation, crudely stated, is a way that a situation lends itself to being used [15]. An empty container affords filling, an active television affords viewing, and a hammer affords striking. Because of the relational nature of affordances, we need to tie them to the action repertoire of an agent. A television does not afford viewing to a blind person; a hammer does not afford hitting to a creature without manipulators. A situation has an affordance for a particular agent. Moreover, we can change the affordances of an object merely by altering its context. A television does not afford viewing when enclosed in a box; a cup does not afford filling in a liquidless environment. An affordance, as we shall use the term then, is a dispositional property of a situation defined by a set of objects organized in a set arrangement, relativized to the action repertoire of a given agent. Agents perceive an affordance, when they register that one of their possible actions is feasible in a situation.

Because an agent need not register all the actions feasible in a situation, the action set which is perceived as feasible (the perceived action set) is sensitive to properties of the situation, particularly arrangement. Two general ways of biasing the perceived action set are by:

(1) hiding affordances—*constraining* what is seen as feasible;

(2) highlighting affordances—*cueing* attention to what is feasible.
Clever placements do both, often at once.

Case 1: Production lines hide affordances

Production lines have been around since long before Henry Ford. Every time we serially decompose a complex task by dividing the space in which it is performed into functional *stations* where specific subtasks are performed, we create a production line. Of course, Ford added the notion of pipe-lining. But the principle is the same: by regionalizing subtasks we restrict the kind of actions an agent will consider undertaking. Only certain inputs find their way into each region, only certain tools are present, and so only certain actions are afforded. We may think of each spatial region as creating a task context, or task frame in which only certain skills and rules are appropriate. This has the effect of decreasing the fan-out of perceived options and eliminates the need to memorize anything more than the most abstract steps in a plan.

For example, in my kitchen at home, a task as simple as preparing a plain garden salad, reveals a latent production line because I wash vegetables by the sink and cut them on a chopping board. More precisely,

> I gather all the vegetables I intend to use, and place them beside the sink. As each vegetable is washed I place it aside, separating it from the unwashed vegetables. When all are washed I transfer them to beside the cutting board, where I keep my knives, and begin chopping each in the way I will need it.

When we examine this task we note two uses of space:
(1) by dividing the space by the sink into two, I segregate the vegetables by their cleanliness—a limiting case (binary) of using space to simplify classification. More on this in Section 4.
(2) by dividing the room into stations, where only certain subtasks are performed, I restrict the range of possible actions I consider at each station to a small subset of the possible actions that can in principle be performed on each ingredient.

The equipment and surfaces of a station effectively trigger an action frame or task context in which only a fraction of all actions are considered. Once a context of action has been triggered, the local affordances make clear what can and must be done. If a tomato were viewed in isolation, a cook in search of a salad might consider chopping it, washing it, placing it directly in a salad bowl or plate, or even eating it on the spot. To perform most of these tasks the cook would have to first find the relevant equipment—knives, sink, bowl, etc. Exactly which task the cook would do would depend on where in the plan he was. The virtue of spatially decomposing the task is that one need not consult a plan, except at the very highest level, to know what to do. Each task context affords only certain possibilities for action. You don't think of washing vegetables when they are sitting beside a knife and a cutting board, unless their unwashed state stands out and alerts you to a problem. Similarly, if an item is unwet and beside the sink, for all intents and purposes, it carries a "wash me" label. A cook entering the room can read off what is to be done, for there is enough information available in the set-up. The reason production line layouts are examples of hiding affordances rather than highlighting affordances is that the context of action delimits the range of immediately available actions to the ones that are "ready to go". When a knife and board are present, cutting actions are ready to go, and washing is not. (See Fig. 3).

Case 2: Cueing blocked actions

Manufacturing production lines often prevent workers from moving around to where tools are kept, create a set of dedicated workers. Actions are therefore not merely out of mind, they are out of bounds. In household kitchens, though, the same person does many tasks; stations are not fixed and tools move around. This means that although we have action frames, or task contexts, which have the effect of dropping from our sight certain actions that are still available in principle, we aren't physically or socially unable to perform those out of context actions. Such actions become impossible only when something in the environment restricts the physical freedom of the agent. For instance, by putting a door jam under a swing door one of the directions of opening can be blocked. One is free to open the door, but not to open it in the blocked direction. That action is physically unavailable. This practice of changing the task environment to eliminate degrees of freedom we call *blocking*.

Blocking usually restricts affordances by changing the action context so that certain preconditions are clobbered. This is seldom a permanent change—the door jam can be removed. But often the change is meant to be noticed; it signals the fact that a precondition has been intentionally clobbered. Some spatial arrangements say "Don't do X". They cue a prohibition. Here is an example.

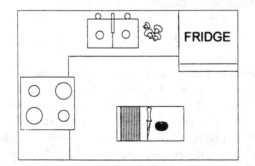

Fig. 3. In this figure we see a typical kitchen with its stations for chopping, using the burners, baking, and cleaning up. In professional kitchens separate staff may operate these stations, but in household kitchens, the same agent moves from station to station, often carrying tools along as he or she moves. The equipment and surfaces of a station effectively trigger an action frame or task context in which only a fraction of all actions are "live" options. This reduces the complexity of choice by creating a production line. A production line works successfully when a global task can be spatially decomposed into subtasks where the output of each subtask is a suitable input to the next subtask. This has the effect of decreasing the fan-out of perceived options, and eliminates the need to memorize a plan.

In physical plants, engineers regularly leave rags on hot handles or pipes to prevent burns. By placing a functionally significant item in a functionally significant place, the engineer creates a reminder or warning for himself and others.

Here is a second example:

One hassle notorious to owners of garbage disposal units is that it is easy for an implement, a knife or spoon, to slip into the machine's belly without one's knowledge. The next time the device is turned on the piece is mangled. To prevent this, a standard ploy is to cover the mouth with a plug, or failing that, to throw refuse into the mouth of the unit before placing cutlery in the same sink. The mouth is thereby blocked before implements can be swallowed up.

As is obvious from the examples, the physical context has not been irreversibly changed. An agent could undo a blocked precondition, in the same way that an agent could take a knife out of the drawer to cut a tomato. But, the distinction present is that a rag on a pipe, or a plug in a sink, are not just physical impediments to action; in most cases, they are intentional, meaningful cues. A visible wedge, a clamp, a boot on a car, a club on the steering wheel, a blockade, are further cases where knowledge of how a device functions can be counted on to make these physical impediments salient. In principle, any easy to notice clobbered precondition can be harnessed to signify that a particular path is obstructed, irregular, contaminated, or otherwise blocked. But the most reliable will rely on "natural mappings" [35] and will themselves satisfy the psychological conditions of being good cues. Thus, the absence of a knife is a less good cue than the presence of a pair of oven mits. That being said, a convention can be set up whereby almost any arrangement can be called into service to signal prohibition. For instance, a completely set table marks its being prepared for something special: other activities that are regularly performed on tables, such as writing, drinking tea, etc., are outlawed.

Case 3: *Arrangements that draw attention to affordances*

We have seen two ways of reducing an agent's perceived option set by structuring the workplace. The first eliminates actions from the perceived set by reducing affordances so that certain actions are not perceived as locally available, the second eliminates certain actions from consideration by prohibiting them—by creating cues that carry the message *don't do that*. Examples of arrangements created to steal attention—to *highlight affordances*—are not as straightforward. But they are prevalent.

We can distinguish two sorts:

(1) arrangements that highlight the obvious thing to do;
(2) arrangements that highlight opportunistic things to do.

The difference between the two turns on how habitual the action is that is cued. For instance, at the check-out counter of supermarkets the person bagging groceries operates in a strongly skill-driven manner. Owing to their accumulated knowledge about the items that must be packed, and the space available for buffering, baggers build up regular ways of solving their bin-packing problems. Among their other tricks, they rely on arrangements in the buffer zone to help call attention to obvious properties of the inventory.

> In bagging groceries the simple rules of practice are to put large heavy items at the bottom, more fragile items on the top, intermediate items go wherever they will fit. The flow of goods being cashed through, however, seldom matches the moment-by-moment requirements of packing. So the bagger is forced to buffer goods. Better baggers begin to create side pockets of goods in the buffer zone: thin fragile items, such as eggs or fresh pasta; items that must remain upright, such as raspberries, or a slice of cake, or firm cushioning items, such as magazines. Neither the choice of categories for clustering nor the location of these pockets is arbitrary. From informal observation it is evident that certain classifications are standard and that items in closer pockets are more likely to be used sooner.

Grocery packing is a complex interactive process in which control oscillates between being internally goal directed—"I need an intermediate object now"—and being feedback or data controlled—"can't I put this item in one of the bags I've started already?" By partitioning the space into identifiable clusters—"I need a heavy object—there's a bunch by the register"—the agent reduces the complexity of choice. This works in several ways. First, by creating equivalence classes of items, heavy, intermediate, fragile, small, the bagger makes it easier to spot a sought after type of item, and also easier to grab an item of that kind in a hurry. Three small items clustered together make it easier both to remember and to see where a small item is. Second, the urgency with which an item of a certain kind need be packed correlates nicely with the size of its build-up in the buffer zone. Because size is an attention-getting feature, the largest pile cries out for early use. This has the salutary effect that the agent is less likely to forget items in larger piles, and so, other things being equal, is more likely to use an item from that pile next. Third, items nearer to the center of the workplace are more likely to get noticed as vision sweeps over them in the normal course of packing. Hence, other things equal, they too have a greater likelihood of being used. It is not surprising that on questioning, baggers admit to often reserving that space for items they intend to use immediately after the next item. In each case, then, placement of items serves to highlight particular features that are useful. Clustering highlights the functional category of items; size highlights urgency; and centrality highlights what is next to be used. Each highlighted feature helps to bias choice.

The second class of attention-related biases relies on setting up the environment to increase the chance of noticing regularly unnoticed possibilities—of *seeding opportunities* (see Fig. 4). It is remarkably prevalent. Almost every activity produces by-products and side effects, some of which can be re-used. For instance, in repairing an old car the nuts and bolts removed when replacing a

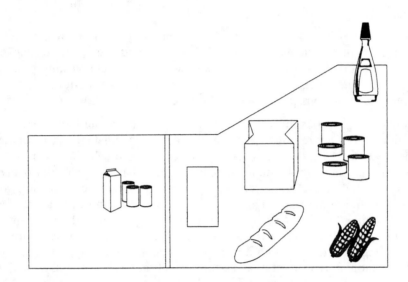

Fig. 4. A typical check-out scene in a supermarket reveals seeding the space around one with attention-getting clusters of goods. Skilled baggers build buffer zones that collect as yet unpacked items in functional groups such as fragile, heavy, keep upright. The groups of items that are nearby are likely to be used sooner than items more distant. The purpose of the groupings appears to be that of enhancing the affordances of the items. Thus heavy items afford support, hard items afford protection and so on. As baggers learn how to buffer and manage the space around the register better they begin to pack faster and more effectively. Not only do they have what they need more at hand, they can see what they have and so simplify choice.

worn out part are rarely thrown out immediately because they may prove useful later in bolting the new part in place, or in other repairs. "Don't throw out what might be useful" is a conservative but rational policy. Yet there is a trade-off. The more that is retained the more cluttered the space, with the result that the very opportunities that might be found go unnoticed. *How do agents manage task detritus?*

The principle behind clever by-product management is to leave around whatever has a good chance of promoting opportunism. Opportunism is the practice of taking advantage of opportunities the environment provides in order to fulfill a goal one did not originally set out to attain—the opportunistic goal lies outside one's current sub-goal context. Moreover, it is important that the cost to attain the opportunistic goal is lower than normal—the context provides the agent with a golden opportunity.[10]

A simple example of *cultivated opportunism* is found in the practice of carpenters:

---

[10] For example, I set out to go to the supermarket to buy dinner and note that the cleaners is nearby. In stopping to pick up the cleaning, I am satisfying a goal that I did not originally intend. But the environment provides me with an opportunity, which if noticed, can be exploited at less cost than satisfying the goal from scratch. I can piggyback the opportunistic goal and save the cost of a second trip.

In the course of making a piece of furniture one periodically tidies up. But not completely. Small pieces of wood are pushed into a corner or left about; tools, screwdrivers and mallets are kept nearby. The reason most often reported is that "they come in handy". Scraps of wood can serve to protect surfaces from marring when clamped, hammered or put under pressure. They can elevate a piece when being lacquered to prevent sticking. The list goes on.

By wisely leaving around a certain clutter, an agent multiplies the chances of getting something for nothing. But not just anywhere will do. The most successful ways of seeding the environment seem to require placing objects in positions which have the greatest chance of displaying their *affordances*. This is not always easy, for given the number of affordances an object has, it seems to require knowing which affordances are going to be useful, when they are going to be useful, and how to lay them about to call attention to just those affordances. Thus, the problem of facilitating opportunism is to find a way of leaving equipment, intermediate products, and task detritus around the workplace to highlight particular affordances.

If the agent has a system for placing objects—"I always keep the useful scraps over there"—their affordance will be known. But equally, if clusters of objects, organized by affordance, are built on the fly the agent also has a better chance of noticing opportunities. A clear example shows up in flower arranging:

In flower arranging it is customary to leave around discarded by-products, such as twigs and ferns, on the off-chance that they will prove useful in striking on a felicitous design. Pieces that seem most likely to be helpful are kept closer. Spatial layout partitions by-products into categories of possible use.

In general, cueing attention to bias choice is a hit or miss affair. But, given a clear understanding of what cues stand out, and how agents can encode meaningful pointers out of them, we might hope to build systems for exploiting cues to reduce task complexity.

3.3. Eliminating decisions

Let us say that a decision has been eliminated altogether if an agent has no choices to make when at that state. A state may be at the meeting place of several actions fanning in, or there may be only one previous state leading to it. In either case, if a state has no fanout, we shall say that it no longer marks a decision point. (See Fig. 5).

Good designers are forever looking for ways of contracting the number of decisions users must make: not just in the number of actions they must consider at any point but in the number of times they must make a decision at all. The fewer degrees of freedom an agent has the simpler its task, providing of course that the outcome is what the agent wants. Ultimate simplicity comes when there is only

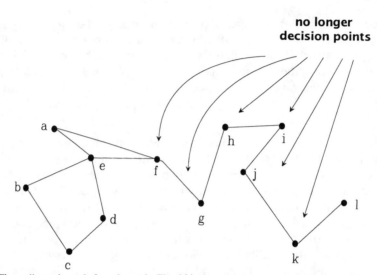

Fig. 5. The collapsed graph first shown in Fig. 2(c) shows us two types of eliminated decision points. In the first, at *f*, two paths that once were available have been eliminated so that the agent now has no alternative to moving along the one path available. In the second type, at *g*, *h*, *i*, *j* ,*k*, the agent again has no alternative, so in effect, behavior is determined from *f* onward.

one degree of freedom, or, more realistically, many degrees at the outset of a task, but then after that none: the outcome is ballistically determined. It is forced.

Most examples of informationally forced choices are limiting cases of blocking, narrowed action contexts, or attention stealing. Here is a different case that shows how properties of our three-dimensional topology can be exploited to simplify a problem, and so, in effect, do away with earlier choice points.

> A familiar problem faced by tailors is to reliably measure and record on cloth the given pattern they are to cut. The standard method is to first make a paper mock-up then trace the image right through the paper onto the material. In most cases the left pattern can be created simply by turning over the right pattern.

The key technique in eliminating decisions shown here is to substitute compliance for choice. Once the tailor has laid out the tracing paper, the rest is ballistic. There is no need to make moment-by-moment decisions about where to position the scissors: they are to follow the chalked line. Nor, for that matter, is it necessary to explicitly calculate the mirror image paper mock-up. The simple flip transform achieves that. By exploiting topological properties of the action space, certain otherwise key decision steps in trouser construction have been designed out of the process. The layout and cutout process are now so streamlined, and constrained, that there is no real choice.

3.4. Offloading heuristic properties

The third, and final way of using space to simplify choice is by creating arrangements that serve as heuristic cues that indicate the desirability of actions.

Let us understand a heuristic property to be an easily computed property of a local situation which allows us to rank the desirability of available actions. In rational decision theory, heuristics (or case knowledge) are supposed to serve as a plausibility filter, to be activated *after* a filter for availability has been applied [14]. Heuristic information is supposed to explain how live options can be ranked on the basis of local information. The distinction between this type of local information and the type of local information available in cues that prohibit, draw attention, or remind, is not hard and fast, but can be made by examining the scope of the information. A heuristic cue, unlike a plug left in a drain, normally applies to many choice points. For instance, in lining vegetables up into rows, our salad maker created a heuristic cue that was meant to apply repeatedly to decisions over the course of the task. It was a way of setting up the world to key into the skills of the agent over the long haul. Accordingly, the set-up costs could be amortized over the whole task. By contrast, in leaving a plug in the sink, or in placing the next item to be bagged close by, the cost of set-up must be paid off by the savings in the next few actions.

Case 4: Encoding the temporal order of actions

One of the most obvious and compelling ways of using space—and judging by conversation, the one most likely to leap to mind—is to lay down items for assembly, in the order in which they are to be put together, touched, handed off, or otherwise used. Space naturally encodes linear orders, and higher orders if the agent has an encoding system in mind. The obvious virtue of encoding orderings in the world is to *offload memory*. If I can arrange items to display the sequence they are are to be used in, then I don't have to remember that order, or figure it out, or consult the manual, as long as I know how to read the information off the local properties of the world.

Let us view an assembly problem as having two components: the *selection problem*—which piece is the one to attach next; and the *placement problem*— where and in what orientation should it be attached.

Here is an example of arranging pieces to simplify the selection problem:

> Imagine repairing an alternator. One takes the device apart, checks each piece, replaces the defective ones, cleans the old but usable pieces, and re-assembles the lot. In an untrafficked workplace, it is easy to create a geometrically simple spatial ordering that allows the property **next position in the arrangement** to be read off trivially. For instance, if the items are laid out in a straight line, interpretation of next is effortless. It is then trivial to decide that the next piece in the line is the next piece to use. But in busier workplaces and for harder assemblies, the orderings will often be more

baroque: sub-assemblies may be segregated into groups but left unordered within that, nuts and bolts may be put in small containers, larger pieces kept nearby, and so on. Determining the next piece to use, in such cases, may not be so simple.

Computationally, the advantage of having an ordering is obvious. In the extreme case, we reduce a doubly exponential problem of deciding which piece to select and where to place it, into an exponential problem. To see this, suppose the placement problem is regular: that at any moment there are two possible places a piece can fit, front or back of the assembly. If the agent knows the right ordering, and hence has a solution to the selection problem, then since there are two possible placements for each piece in an arrangement, there are, in the worst case, 2^n possibilites to search through. If the agent must solve both the selection and placement problems simultaneously, then all n factorial permutations of placements must be considered, generating $O(2^{2^n})$ possibilities to test. In the felicitous case, where the assembly forces a unique placement, and there is only one place a piece can fit at any moment, then given the right ordering the assembly problem is constant time. By contrast, if the agent must find an ordering, the problem is $O(n^2)$ even when the assembly forces a unique placement, because at each step the agent must try out the remaining pieces.

The trick in using space to encode placement order is obviously to have an ordering that is easy to read off an arrangement. Intuitively, linear orderings are just such an arrangement; they have a natural meaning for next. Moreover, arranging parts linearly, has the added virtue that it is hard to misplace items. If all parts are in a line, you know where to look. No surprise, then, that straight line orders are commonplace. But there is a danger, too, in using linear orders: the longer the line of pieces, the more likely the pieces are to be kicked out of order. Consequently, for the sake of robustness, assemblies involving many parts are better placed in a compact group. And indeed anecdotal reports suggest that small groups are popular: bolts and nuts clustered together, sub-assemblies off to a side. Furthermore, a simple linear order is not an expressive enough structure to carry information of the form: build sub-assemblies one and two first, then assemble those sub-assemblies, then assemble sub-assemblies three and four. (See Fig. 6.)

As arrangements become more complex, however, they lose much of their naturalness of interpretation, and depend more on an agent's ability to remember how things were laid out at set-up time. Memory for location is a current topic of psychological inquiry. In an early discussion of this topic, Malone [33] provided anecdotal evidence that subjects are surprisingly apt at locating documents in their office space. This was thought to reveal hidden virtues in messy desks, for the messier the desk, the more categories and cross-references one can achieve— at least, in principle. In a more recent study of locational recall, though, Lansdale [27, p. 1172] suggests that a subject's ability to recall the location of an object—a computer icon in an array—is disappointing in comparison to Malone's anecdotal

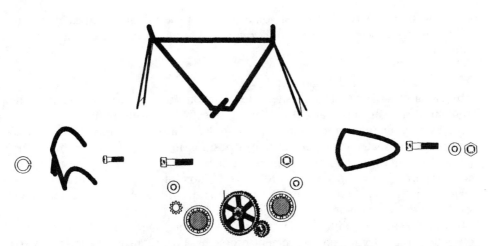

Fig. 6. In many assembly tasks it is necessary to complete sub-assemblies before all parts can be put together. A simple trick some repair people use is to cluster sub-assemblies in groups, themselves possibly strictly ordered, and to arrange the groups in ways that reflect the global order of assembly. Here we see a sub-assembly represented by a depression in a simple linear ordering.

evidence.[11] The reason the subjects themselves most often offered for their poor performance—as revealed by their most frequent complaint during the experiment—was that "different locations were arbitrary: there was no meaning to them, and hence the encoding of locational information was an abstract process" [27, p. 1174]. Further experiments which allowed subjects to exploit an encoding strategy—a method of location assignment that made sense with respect to the objects they were storing—showed that having a preexisting system was tremendously helpful.

Now, if linear orders are insufficiently expressive, agents must rely on known systems of arrangement, or on some design that makes sense relative to the subject matter. For instance, in organizing icons in a MacIntosh style environment, it would not be surprising if users arranged their icons for "peripheral" equipment, such as hard and soft disks, printer, waste basket, fax machine, remote terminal, around the physical periphery of the screen, and in a way that would make sense if the screen were their office and the equipment distributed around the walls. The semantics is clear here. Hence it is relatively easy to remember where a given icon is to be found. But it is less easy to find a system that conveys what piece to take next that does not rely on some perceptual cue, such as next biggest, next in line. It is possible to make the system more complex by incorporating a procedure of choice, such as, if one needs a hex bolt, then use the one at the end of the hex bolt line, whereas if one needs a washer use the

---

[11] Whether this low success rate is due to subjects not having themselves determined the shape or size of the matrix, or to the fact that subjects do not pick up locational information just by handling objects is still unknown.

biggest washer that is left. But at some point, as the visual search involved in finding the next piece becomes more complex, the virtue of structuring items is reduced.

Case 5: Encoding where to place it

In assembly tasks we distinguished the selection problem from the placement problem. Arrangements that help solve the selection problem reduce the search space by encoding the property **next piece to use** in an easy to read off manner. Position in the spatial arrangement marks position in assembly sequence, so the simple heuristic: use the next piece, is a reliable guide to action. The fact that more expert agents can encode orderings in non-linear and not immediately obvious arrangements proves only that they operate with sophisticated categories, not that they cannot determine **next** in a trivial way.

It would be attractive if a simple, or tractable, arrangement could be found that solves both the selection and placement problems. For instance, one might try to place the pieces on the floor in a manner that reveals **where** they go in the growing assemblage, but in a way that also encodes **next.** Unfortunately there is more information than can be encoded naturally[12] in two dimensions.

Consider the case of assembling a desk:

> In assembling a desk, standard practice is to arrange the key parts—the top, the right and left sides, the important struts—beside each other on the floor in a manner that reflects the way they will be put together. But temporal and topological structure pull apart, because it is hard to see how one can read which part to use next from the layout. For instance, if there is drilling to be done, it may be done on each piece before any two are joined. If there are intermediate steps which need be done before assembling the large pieces— such as attaching physical connectors, sanding edges, and so forth—the spatial display neither prohibits nor promotes that temporal ordering.

What should be apparent from this example is that as assemblages become more complicated it becomes harder to read next off the arrangement. This is not the same problem we discussed under non-linear orderings, above. The problem, now, is that if we lay out pieces in a way which encodes information about topological structure, we severely constrain the ways that remain for encoding sequence. As mentioned, it helps to have a systematic method of arranging items in mind beforehand. But, even so, the combinatorics are unbeatable. There is no escaping the fact that complex topologies will evade description in 2D layouts,

---

[12] By natural, in this case, I mean that there is a non ad hoc arrangement that an agent can call on to deal with the multi-dimensional problem of specifying when and where. Much of the problem lies in specifying where. Given a device with a multi-dimensional topology, it is extremely difficult to specify where an arbitrary part ought to be placed without using a general language with referential capacity to identify the pieces it touches. Consider the limitations in identifying the connectivity of a large cube made of smaller cubes. If the center cube touches cubes on all of its six sides there is no way of analogically representing that connectivity in 2D except in terms of a graph structure with labeled nodes.

and no escaping that even with simple topologies there will be occasions when the next piece to assemble lies on the other side of the floor, with no obvious spatial reason for assuming it to be the next piece.

There are a few ways of viewing topological encodings. The most interesting, in my opinion, sees them as the data set for a simple assemblage *program*. Observe Fig. 7(a). Suppose an agent is told "fold each piece 90° and connect it with screws to the pieces it touches". The layout on the floor is the data to this program. If the layout is properly set up, the three-dimensional connectivity will follow as a consequence of applying the program. The agent needn't review mentally the results of applying the program, any more than he would in using a set of compasses to draw a circle. If certain background conditions are correct—in the case of the compasses, that the paper is flat, in the case of the desk, that the layout folds correctly, then the algorithm will deliver the right answer given the data.

Now analytically a data set constitutes constraints on the output of a program. If the program is simple and the data set complex, the intelligence—the constraint—lies primarily in the data. This is the key idea behind logic programming. If, on the other hand, the data are simple and the program complex, the intelligence lies primarily in the program. This is the key idea behind standard procedural programming.

One technique expert assemblers learn is how to "logic program" with the environment. They learn to put into the spatial arrangement enough information

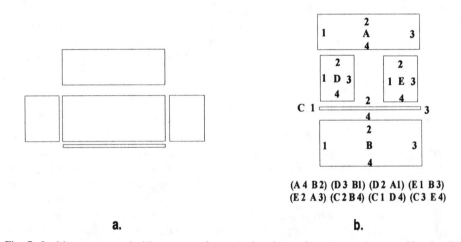

(A 4 B 2) (D 3 B1) (D 2 A1) (E 1 B 3)
(E 2 A 3) (C 2 B 4) (C 1 D 4) (C 3 E 4)

a.   **b.**

Fig. 7. In (a) we see a typical layout map for preparing the workspace to make assembly of a desk easy. The agent is advised to lay the parts down on the floor before assembly begins. The physical layout serves as input to a simple assembly program. By contrast, in (b) we see an alternative map that labels edges explicitly and explicitly states connectivity. Figuring out how to lay the assembly on the floor is itself a problem. So pieces tend to be labeled and stored in a pile. This leads to more visual search during assembly and more computation to ensure the right edges are connected. Not surprisingly, informal reports indicate that instructions that rely on matching numbers and edges prove to be harder in practice to follow.

to use a simple procedure to complete the task. There is no reason this arrangement may not be planned out beforehand. Indeed it often is. But the point is that expert assemblers can multiply the speed of on-line assembly if they lay out the parts well, as well as reduce the probability of error. (See Fig. 7.)

4. Spatial arrangements that simplify perception

In each of the examples just discussed the agent's decision problem was made *combinatorially* less complex by information that could be read off from the environment. One way or another, the amount of internal search required for choosing an action was reduced. A second fundamental way the problem of choosing an action can be simplified is by re-organizing arrangements to *facilitate* perception: to make it possible to notice properties or categories that were not noticed before, to make it easier to find relevant items, to make it easier for the visual system to track items.

Typically, in accounts of decision making, the cost of perception does not figure significantly in the combinatorics of choice. The cost of determining whether a perceptual operator applies to a world state or not, is assumed to have no effect on the size of the subgraph that must be searched, because search size is a function of the depth and breadth of a search, not how long it takes to identify a state, or test an operator. Hence, perceptual costs are treated as, at worst, contributing a constant increase in the complexity of a problem, they may increase the cost of a search from b^d to $a(b^d)$.

In absolute time, as opposed to asymptotic time, however, if there is a way to more readily determine the action affordances at a choice point, or the applicability of a heuristic, the agent will have more time to make a choice. Any change which makes recognition faster certainly simplifies the psychological hardness of a problem.

4.1. Clustering to categorize

Perhaps the most obvious way of simplifying perception is to arrange objects in space so that they form equivalence classes, or partitions, that reflect relevant preconditions, or properties that are useful to track, notice, or exploit. For instance, a standard precondition for washing a salad ingredient—a tomato—is that it has not already been washed. Clean and dirty tomatoes can be hard to tell apart. So one common ploy is to place washed tomatoes in one place, unwashed tomatoes in another. By segregating the two groups we highlight their differences. Examples of other objects already mentioned as being useful to classify include the side groups in the buffer region of checkout counters, scraps of wood in workshops, and playing cards which are usually ordered by suit and number in bridge, and by scoring category in gin rummy.

The primary value of such external partitioning is that it makes it easier:
- to keep track of where things are;

• to notice their relevant affordances.

Both factors are involved in recognizing the availability of actions and in monitoring the current state. If I can't find the garlic, I am not likely to think of rubbing it on the salad bowl—I miss some available actions. And, if I can't tell whether the dishes are clean or dirty—i.e. I fail to monitor correctly—then I can't decide whether I should wash them.

Clustering helps solve these problems because it is harder to lose big things than little ones, and harder to miss seeing what a whole group is good for. For instance, memory for location, as was mentioned before, is regularly overestimated. It is harder to remember where a pen is, than its color. But if the pen is in the group of like colored objects, the sheer size of the colored group will simplify the visual search problem. Color can be used as both a memory aid and a visual cue.

A similar story holds for affordances. The fact that a group of heavy glass bottles is building up by the cash register highlights the fact that heavy items are available. As merchandisers well know, one way to increase the chance of being noticed is to occupy more space—make bigger displays. The same method is used every day to simplify noticing affordances.

4.2. Other techniques for creating categories

Clustering is only one of the ways agents have of creating equivalence classes on the fly. According to Gestalt theory other factors besides proximity which determine whether we perceive a set of items as a group are such things as how similar the items are (similarity), whether the items move together (common fate), whether they fit into a smooth, continuous line (good continuation), whether they can be seen as a closed form, and whether they stand out together against a background (surroundedness). We have already seen examples of several of these. Good continuation, for instance, is relied on by assemblers to distinguish parts in their assembly plan from random parts in the workshop. Similarity is used by baggers working in tight spaces where large heavy items, though clustered, are directly beside small items.[13] An example of surroundedness was supplied by one reviewer of this paper. He mentioned that his father taught him to place the various pieces of his dismantled bicycle, many of which were small, on a sheet of newspaper. The newspaper served to mark out a region that was to be treated as special; it demarcated a boundary within which items of a particular sort were to be placed. Hence, it was easy to locate them, and they were less likely to be kicked about.

The idea of creating a special region applies not only to cases where there is a visible frame, a newspaper for instance, but to notional regions that an agent sets aside. By creating such regions it is sometimes possible to achieve tasks which

---

[13] Because common fate is a dynamic property we leave it for another time.

might otherwise be impossible. An interesting example can be found, once again, in the blocks world.

David Chapman [8] argued that it is possible to use a Pengi-like system to build a nine-block tower—spelling FRUITCAKE—from an environment of 45 blocks strewn about, provided that nine of those blocks already spell fruitcake and so can serve as an example tower to copy. The technique his system uses requires having snapshots of the entire environment, and moving markers around these snapshots to make it possible to keep track of where the next useful block is, which blocks must be removed to free that useful block, and so on. Using these markers as a way of recording state information it is possible to rely on a simple compiled rule system to copy the goal stack.

To scale this system up to cope with constructing arbitrary goal towers, however, requires adding additional markers: one set to mark towers that have been successfully built; and a second set to mark the goal towers already built. If we did not have these extra markers, then there would be nothing to stop the system from cannibalizing target towers for their parts, and nothing to stop the system from repeatedly copying goal towers. See Fig. 8(a). Since there is considerable cost in maintaining large numbers of markers this is an unattractive solution. But, it is not the only solution. If we allow *regionalizing* the environment, and building knowledge of where those regions are into the system, we can build arbitrary numbers of towers using just the original markers.

The trick is to divide the workplace into regions for storing the goal stacks, for foraging for blocks, and for building the target stacks, and to create a known ordering within those. Thus, region 1 will contain the original goal stacks organized in the order they are to be built; region 2 will contain the blocks currently available for building towers, possibly organized alphabetically, but that is not necessary; and region 3 will contain the new stacks currently being built. A pengi-like system will now work successfully as long as we add three more rules. As soon as the current goal stack is completed, move to the next stack on the right in the goal stack region; if there is no goal stack to the right, announce

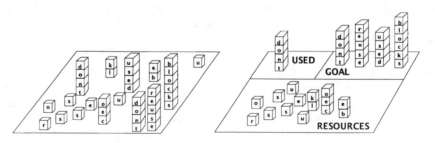

Fig. 8. In (a), we see a typical blocks world situation facing Blockhead, a Pengi-like tower copier. In order to reliably copy the goal stack, shown on the right, Blockhead must rely on five visual markers to keep track of the stack to copy, the block to copy, the current spot in the stack being cleared, the target block to be freed by clearing, as well as the stack being built. To copy more goal stacks would require more visual markers. In (b), we see the space regionalized into a goal stack region, a block foraging region, and a target stack region. Stacks in the goal and target regions are ordered from left to right. If Blockhead knows about these regions it can copy an arbitrary number of stacks without relying on more visual markers.

success. Build target stacks in the target stack region, starting from the left and moving right. Search for blocks only in the resource region. As can be seen in Fig. 8(b), this is a simple way of preventing cannibalism, duplication, and failure to halt. The point, to repeat, is that by creating external regions it is possible to keep memory demands within psychologically realistic limits.

4.3. Symbolic marking

Yet another technique for categorizing, or identifying an object is to *mark* the object with a cue that draws attention, or prods recall. For instance, when there is a pair of hard to distinguish items we wish to differentiate, such as two wooden spoons—one used for stirring a dark curry (currently cooking on the left front burner), the other for stirring a brown sauce (currently on the right front burner)—we may *mark* their difference by associating them with a known distinguisher. For instance, we might keep them on the lids of their respective saucepans (particularly if those are different in size), or we may place them beside one of the key ingredients (e.g. the curry tin). These are examples of symbolic positioning, or *marking*.

We have found marking to be an important resource for helping agents monitor task state. Here is another example.

> In the videotapes Bernard Conein made of French householders preparing apple tarts, we noticed that one cook, upon carefully measuring and cutting a butter stick nearly in two, promptly lays her knife on the measured piece as if to mark it as the piece to use. Both chunks of butter are similar in appearance, so it would be easy to confuse the one with the other. But by marking one piece with the knife, the cook has added extra information to the environment that can help make clear what to do next. Admittedly, the knife's position on the butter can serve many functions: it keeps the freshly used knife from dirtying the countertop, it keeps the knife itself from becoming unsanitary, and it places the knife in an orientation that facilitates grasping. But as well, it serves an informational function: it marks one half stick of butter as being the measured half, and also marks the fact that the measuring process itself has taken place.

Markers are a form of reminder. But with a twist. Whereas perfect reminders both signal that something is to be remembered and encode what that something is, markers really only serve the first function: they signal that there is something here to notice or remember, but not what that is. For a marker to be effective it must serve as an easy to use cue for recall. The knife's thoughtful positioning, particularly if regularly so used, can provide the context for recall.

4.4. Clustering to sharpen perceptual acuity

So far we have considered how clustering and thoughtful placement can highlight the category, or identity, of an item. By making more explicit the category of an item, agents can more readily perceptually track the functionally important elements in their environment. Few tasks make this more evident than solving jigsaw puzzles.

> Veteran jigsaw puzzlers are often found grouping pieces of similar shape or color into distinct piles. Pieces with straight edges are regularly grouped together, as are corner pieces, blues, greens, and pieces with similar male and female sockets. By sorting pieces that might otherwise be strewn about, players drastically reduce the expected time needed to perceptually locate appropriate pieces.

At first this may seem just another case of clustering to produce equivalence classes. But more is going on here. In solving a jigsaw puzzle the recurrent problem is to identify, from among a large set of pieces, the single one which correctly fits the target space. One of the properties of the game that makes it hard is that both coarse and fine discriminations are necessary. Coarse discriminations help with planning. "Cluster corner pieces! Look for parts of the sky!" But fine discriminations are necessary to determine exactly which individual piece will fit. Surprisingly, coarse grouping helps with noticing fine discriminations too.

The general strategy at work here is again a form of informational structuring. It is easier for an agent to narrow the search to the correct piece within a coarse group than to look for the piece from scratch. If the agent can create a hierarchical classification, visual search can be reduced from $O(N)$ to $O(\log N)$. Hence coarse grouping is a useful preprocessing technique.

Even more interestingly, a clever grouping can actually increase the fineness of distinctions the agent is capable of noticing. I call this the *vernier effect*. Vernier discrimination in visual perception refers to the eye's ability to distinguish very small displacements in the alignment of two objects or lines. This capacity to tell whether two lines are lined up or displaced is harnessed in vernier scales (see Fig. 9). In classification, a similar effect occurs. When a jigsaw piece is buried among a variety of rather differently shaped pieces, subjects pick it out on the basis of coarse differences. If it is buried among similar shaped pieces, subjects must pick it out on the basis of fine differences. These fine differences are noticeable precisely because we can lock in visually on subtle differences. Two objects that are otherwise indistinguishable can often be distinguished if their images can be superimposed. Proximity helps. So does quantity, for we thereby create a reference class for comparison which highlights the kind of differences to note. We change the resolution of our classification. (See Fig. 9.)

5. Saving internal computation

We have considered how spatial arrangements can reduce the amount of mental search involved in choice, and also reduce the amount of visual computation necessary to monitor current state, notice hints, and search for wanted items. A third way an embodied agent can enlist the world is to pass off computation. Familiar examples of such offloading show up in analog computations. When the

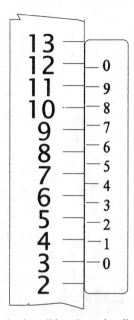

Fig. 9. A vernier is an auxiliary scale that slides along the divisions of a graduated instrument to indicate fractions of the divisions of the larger scale. It allows a user to make finer distinctions than possible with one scale alone. The perceptual principle verniers rely on is called vernier discrimination, which is the capacity of the eye to note when two lines are not perfectly aligned.

tallest spaghetti noodle is singled out from its neighbors by striking the bundle on a table, a **sort** computation is performed by using the material and spatial properties of the world. An agent who encodes size or rank in noodle length, can compute a fast sort by means of this physical process, as long as the result can be decoded quickly. The method does not involve symbolic computation, or an item-by-item comparison. It works by creating a visual cue that serves to make the property in question explicit.

Such computational exploitations of the world are more common than usually realized. When a tailor flips over a paper cutout, he is effectively computing a description of the mirror image of the original shape. It is not evident that such exploitation of the world qualifies as "using space" intelligently. But I shall include a discussion of some of the issues because the line between using the world, and using the spatial properties of the world, is not an easy one to draw.

Let us turn now to an example that shows that the mental use of the world can occur even at high speed.

5.1. High speed offloading

We have found in our laboratory studies of a fast-paced computer game, Tetris (see Fig. 10), that players will physically manipulate forms to save themselves

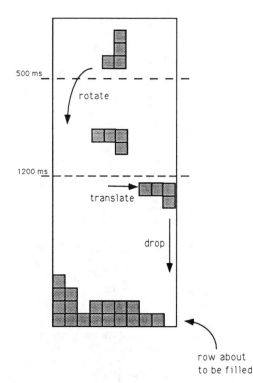

Fig. 10. In Tetris, pieces enter the board from the top and the player has to decide whether to move them right, left or to rotate them. We have found that there is a burst of rotational activity in a region about 800 ms to 1800 ms when the player is working out where to place the piece. External rotation can be as fast as 150 ms, whereas internal rotation takes five to ten times as long. By externally rotating pieces, players can save time in deciding where to place pieces.

mental effort [25]. They modify the environment to cue recall, to speed up identification, and to generate mental images faster than they could if unaided. In short, they make changes to the world to save themselves costly and potentially error-prone computations in the head.

The trick, in every case, is to modify visual input at exactly the right time to supply information needed by other computations. This is a version of just in time inventory control, only here, the inventory is informational. The effect is a highly interactional computation, where the information for a step in the computation is sometimes provided internally, and sometimes the information is provided externally. What binds the two together into a tightly coupled system is their timing. See Fig. 11 for a sketch of the kind of process model this suggests.

To take one example from Tetris, we found that about 800 to 1800 ms after a zoid enters the screen, players display a burst of rotations. See Fig. 10 for an explanation of Tetris. One hypothesis is that they rotate the piece rapidly to generate the mental icons they need to try out candidate placements. To rotate a zoid in the world takes far less time than to rotate its mental image. From our own studies we have determined that mental rotation of tetrazoids takes between

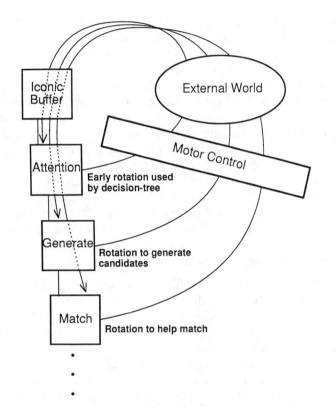

Fig. 11. In this figure internal processing components are nudged forward in their own computations by inputs caused by the agent's actions. The difference between this and standard cascade models of processing is that internal modules here can request motor output without much mediation, causing changes in the external environment that are specifically targeted at improving their own performance. From [25].

700 and 1500 ms; physical rotation can take place in 150 ms [25]. By shifting the burden of imagery formation away from the mental rotation component, and giving it, instead, to the faster working motor and perceptual systems, an agent can save hundreds of milliseconds. This is what is meant by saying the agent uses the world to save internal computation. External rotation solves the problem "what would this zoid look like if rotated 90 degrees?" Thus if there is a generate and test process occurring in players when they are trying to decide where to place a piece, a call to the motor system to physically rotate a piece can supply the generator with exactly what it needs. Computational steps are not actually eliminated; they are offloaded from the agent to the world.

5.2. Externalizing representations and perspective flipping

In high speed interactions, the agent and environment can be so tightly coupled that it may be plausible to view the two as forming a single computational system. In that case, some elements of the computation are outside the agent, some are inside, and the computation itself consists in the dynamic interaction between the two. The general idea that the dynamic relations holding between an embodied agent and its environment form a computational system has been advanced by Ed Hutchins [19, 20] and Sylvia Scribner [43].

One fact about human cognition that lends itself to such interpretation is that there are important psychological differences between external and internal representations, suggesting that sometimes it is more desirable to operate with external representations than internal ones, and vice versa. In [7] subjects were asked to form mental images of classically ambiguous figures, such as the Necker cube, the duck/rabbit. They had been shown several different ambiguous images, and understood the relevant notion of ambiguity, although importantly, they were naive to the test figures. Chambers and Reisberg found that none of the subjects could discover any ambiguity in their images. Evidently, internal representations, unlike their external counterparts, seem to come with their interpretation fixed. An agent conjuring an image cannot separate the interpretation of the image from the image itself. Reisberg [40] had this to say:

> "After subjects had tried (and failed) to reconstrue their image, they were asked to draw a picture from the image, and then attempt reconstrual of their own drawing. In sharp contrast to the imagery data, 100% of the subjects were able to reinterpret their own drawings. (These drawings were in fact ambiguous, as a new group of subjects was able to find both construals in them.) Once there was a stimulus on the scene (even a self-created one), subjects could set aside the understanding they had in mind in creating the stimulus, and interpret it anew. In imagery, the understanding is inherent in the representation, so that there simply is no representation separate from the understanding. With no freestanding icon to interpret, no reinterpretation is possible. . . . As long as ideas are internally represented, they exist only via a certain context of understanding, so that there can be neither doubt nor ambiguity about what is intended." [40, p. 8]

The implication is that if we want to discover important new elements in a structure, particularly if this requires looking for novel interpretations, we are better off depicting it externally, or consulting some pre-existing external representation of it. The skills we have developed for dealing with the external world go beyond those we have for dealing with the internal world. Hence, the reason creative activity tends to make such extensive use of external representations may be because, in the discovery phase, one wants to note as many possible extensions and variations to one's ideas as possible. This is easier if the representations are externalized.

Now, because computation regularly involves generate and test phases it is possible that the most intelligent use of space is to try out conjectures. For example, in the game of Scrabble, when we are searching for words, it is customary to shuffle tiles around in the hope of triggering an association. We may call activity of this sort, *self cueing*.

The principle of self cueing is a type of externalization that depends for its success on two factors: an internal module whose operations are, more or less, encapsulated from interference by other modules, and a tight coupling between internal and external processes. There would be no point fiddling with the outside world to jog our memories if we could do the same internally just as fast. The extra value flows from the way we associate items. We can get a fresh way of looking at our Scrabble tiles, if we shuffle them. This approach crops up in a range of self-help techniques. To solve an algebra problem we make explicit many of the obvious transformations. To solve a geometry problem we often draw a figure, or introduce constructions that alter the appearance of the structure. A theory of how externalization improves cognition would certainly go beyond ways of using spatial arrangements. But, we can be certain that in any such theory, more than lip service will be paid to the role of spatial arrangement.

6. Conclusion

Throughout this paper, I have presented ways agents have of managing the spatial arrangements of items in their workplace. To make it easier to stay in control of activity, we rely on techniques which reduce the memory load of tasks, the amount of internal computation necessary, or which simplify the visual search and categorization that is inevitably involved in performance. Some of these techniques we consciously apply, some we apply unwittingly. But all reflect our tight coupling to the world. A coupling becomes tight, when timing becomes important. In Tetris, for instance, zoids are rotated in the world to save mental rotation. Timing is crucial. A few hundred milliseconds later, and a given rotation will fail to carry useful information for a player. In bagging groceries, or in cooking, we place items around us at particular moments. If well-timed, such placements serve to remind us, to cue attention, to prevent us from considering irrelevant alternatives. The virtue of such cues and constraints is that they structure the information we take in as input. In fast-paced environments, this informational structuring supplies hints and clues that advance computations that are in progress. In slower-paced environments, such as Scrabble, jigsaw puzzle playing, and shelving books, informational structuring also helps supply ideas, hints and distinctions that facilitate problem solving. Even though slower-paced tasks involve choices that span tens of seconds, it is still important to have the right information at the right time. It is amazing how prevalent such phenomena are in our everyday activities.

One theme which has been recurring, but which I have left largely unexamined, is that many of our structuring actions serve to reduce the descriptive complexity of our environments. This makes it easier to track the state of the environment. The idea first surfaced in our discussion of the advantage of organizing lettered blocks alphabetically, or into known chunks, such as morphemes. A planner who first arranges blocks alphabetically reduces the need for visual search because he or she is able to describe the state of the environment more compactly. The position of a block in an alphabetical list is known by heart, so it can be generated without further knowledge of the particulars of the environment. The same applies if we organize blocks into well-known units. Given an environment in which the letters TEOEPPAPTTASSCERLAEP appear, we put a much smaller strain on Working Memory if we manage the environment so that the stimulus we see is chunked as in PET TAPE APPLE SOCRATES. Preprocessing the world saves processing the representation of the world. Put another way, the greater our understanding of the organization we maintain outside, the less we have to memorize.

It is in this spirit of reducing the descriptive complexity of the environment, that we can understand the virtue of creating critical cues, such as the relative length cue created by the cook who lined up the vegetables, described in the introduction. When a cue is both easy to monitor, and it carries all the information the agent need to know about the state of the ongoing process, it reduces the processing required to track the current state of the environment. It reduces the descriptive complexity of that state to a few bits.

Table 1 summarizes some of the examples discussed in the text. These cases span only a fraction of the range of intelligent uses of space in everyday life, but I believe they are representative.

Theorists in AI have dwelled on the intelligent use of time, hardly considering space. Yet vision, our primary spatial sense, is one of humanity's most powerful capacities. It is little wonder that diagrams facilitate problem solving. Should we not expect that much of our everyday competence might come from information-ally structuring our workspace? I have tried to show what, in certain cases, this might mean, and why it is a reasonable idea to develop.

Table 1

Capacity improved	What has been reduced	Mechanism
Recall	Probability of an error in prospective memory	Reminders
Visual search	Time complexity of search Descriptive complexity of environment Probability of an error	Use known orderings such as chunks or alphabets
Perceptual acuity	Granularity of perception Micro-categorization	Vernier effect
Reasoning	Time complexity of planning	Cue next action through a known ordering
Execution	Probability of capture error	Maximize cue separation

References

[1] P.E. Agre, *The Dynamics of Everyday Life* (Cambridge University Press, Cambridge, England, to appear).

[2] P.E. Agre, Hassles, MIT AI Lab Working Paper, Cambridge, MA.

[3] P.E. Agre and D. Chapman, Pengi: an implementation of a theory of activity, in: *Proceedings AAAI-87*, Seattle, WA (1987).

[4] P.E. Agre and I. Horswill, Cultural support for improvisation, in: *Proceedings AAAI-92*, San Jose, CA (1992).

[5] K. Beach, Learning to become a bartender: the role of external memory cues at work, Presented at Eastern Psychological Association, Boston, MA (1985).

[6] R.A. Brooks, Intelligence without representation, *Artif. Intell.* **47** (1991) 141–159.

[7] D. Chambers and D. Reisberg, Can mental images be ambiguous? *J. Experimental Psychol. Human Perception Performance* **11** (1985) 317–328.

[8] D. Chapman, Penguins can make cake, *AI Mag.* **10** (4) (1989) 45–50.

[9] N. Charness, Search in chess: age and skill differences, *J. Experimental Psychol. Human Perception Performance* **7** (1981) 467–476.

[10] W.G. Chase and H.A. Simon, Perception in chess, *Cogn. Psychol.* **4** (1973) 55–81.

[11] W.S. Cleveland and R. McGill, Graphical perception and graphical methods for analyzing scientific data, *Science* **229** (1985) 828–833.

[12] G. Cohen, *Memory in the Real World* (Lawrence Erlbaum, Hillsdale, NJ, 1989).

[13] O. de la Rocha, The reorganization of arithmetic practice in the kitchen, *Anthropology Education Q.* **16** (1985) 193–198.

[14] J. Elster, *Ulysses and the Sirens, Studies in Rationality and Irrationality* (Cambridge University Press, Cambridge, England, 1982).

[15] J.J. Gibson, The theory of affordances, in: R.E. Shaw and J. Bransford, eds., *Perceiving, Acting, and Knowing* (Lawrence Erlbaum, Hillsdale NJ, 1977).

[16] J.J. Goodnow, Some lifelong everyday forms of intelligent behavior: organizing and reorganizing, in: R.J. Sternberg and R.K. Wagner, eds., *Practical Intelligence: Nature and Origins of Competence in the Everyday World* (Cambridge University Press, Cambridge, England, 1986) 143–162.

[17] J.G. Greeno, Situations, mental models, and generative knowledge, in: D. Klahr and K. Kotovsky, eds., *Complex Information Processing* (Lawrence Erlbaum, Hillsdale NJ, 1989) 285–318.

[18] K.J. Hammond, T.M. Converse and J.W. Grass, The stabilization of environments, *Artif. Intell.* (1995).

[19] E. Hutchins, How a cockpit remembers its speeds, *Cogn. Sci.* (to appear).

[20] E. Hutchins, *Cognition in the Wild* (MIT Press, Cambridge, MA, to appear).

[21] M. Kamman, *The making of a Chef* (Atheneum, New York, 1982).

[22] D. Kirsh, When is information explicitly represented? in: P. Hanson, ed., *Information, Language and Cognition* (Oxford University Press, Oxford, England, 1991) 340–365.

[23] D. Kirsh, Today the earwig, tomorrow man? *Artif. Intell.* **47** (1991) 161–184.

[24] D. Kirsh and D. Maglio, Some epistemic benefits of action: Tetris, a case study, in: *Proceedings 14th Annual Conference of the Cognitive Science Society* (Morgan Kaufmann, San Mateo, CA, 1992).

[25] D. Kirsh and P. Maglio, On distinguishing epistemic from pragmatic actions, *Cogn. Sci.* (to appear).

[26] K. Kotovsky and D. Fallside, Representation and transfer in problem solving, in: D. Klahr and K. Kotovsky, eds., *Complex Information Processing* (Lawrence Erlbaum, Hillsdale, NJ, 1989) 69–108.

[27] M. Lansdale, Remembering about documents: memory for appearance, format, and location, *Ergonomics* **34** (8) (1991) 1161–1178.

[28] M. Lansdale and E. Edmonds, Using memory for events in the design of personal filing systems, *Int. J. Man-Mach. Stud.* (1992) 97–126.

[29] J.H. Larkin, Display-based problem solving, in: D. Klahr and K. Kotovsky, eds., *Complex Information Processing* (Lawrence Erlbaum, Hillsdale, NJ, 1989) 319–342.

[30] J.H. Larkin and H.A. Simon, Why a diagram is (sometimes) worth ten thousand words, *Cogn. Sci.* **11** (1987) 65–99.

[31] J. Lave, Cognitive consequences of traditional apprenticeship training in West Africa, *Anthropology Education Quart.* **8** (3) (1977) 177–180.

[32] J. Lave, *Cognition in Practice* (Cambridge University Press, Cambridge, England, 1988).

[33] T.W. Malone, How do people organize their desks? Implications for the design of office automation systems, *ACM Trans. Office Syst.* **11** (1983) 99–112.

[34] D.A. Norman, Categorization of action slips, *Psychol. Rev.* **88** (1981) 1–15.

[35] D.A. Norman, *The Psychology of Everyday Things* (Basic Books, New York, 1988).

[36] J. Rasmussen, What can be learned from human error reports?, in: K. Duncan, M. Gruneberg and D. Wallis, eds., *Changes in Working Life* (Wiley, London, 1980).

[37] J. Rasmussen, *Information Processing and Human-Machine Interaction* (North-Holland, Amsterdam, 1986).

[38] J.T. Reason, *Human Error* (Cambridge University Press, Cambridge, England, 1990).

[39] J.T. Reason and K. Mycielska, *Absent-Minded? The Psychology of Mental Lapses in Everyday Errors* (Prentice-Hall, Englewood Cliffs, NJ, 1982).

[40] D. Reisberg, External representations and the advantages of externalizing one's thoughts, in: *Proceedings Ninth Annual Conference of the Cognitive Science Society*, Seattle, WA (1987).

[41] W.B. Rouse, Models of human problem solving: detection, diagnosis and compensation for system failures, in: *Proceedings IFAC Conference on Analysis, Design and Evaluation of Man-Machine Systems* (1981).

[42] J.E. Savage, *The Complexity of Computing* (Wiley, New York, 1976).

[43] S. Scribner, Thinking in action: some characteristics of practical thought, in: R.J. Sternberg and R.K. Wagner, eds., *Practical Intelligence: Nature and Origins of Competence in the Everyday World* (Cambridge University Press, Cambridge, MA, 1986) 13–30.

[44] H.A. Simon and J. Hayes, The understanding process: problem isomorphs, *Cogn. Psychol.* **8** (1976) 165–190.

[45] J. Stevens, An observational study of skilled memory in waitresses, Presented at Eastern Psychological Association, Boston, MA (1985).

[46] R.E. Tarjan, Amortized computational complexity, *SIAM J. Comput.* 14 (1985) 306–318.

Artificial Intelligence 73 (1995) 69–115

Indexical knowledge and robot action—a logical account

Yves Lespérance [*], Hector J. Levesque [1]

Department of Computer Science, University of Toronto, Toronto, Ont., Canada M5S 1A4

Received October 1992; revised May 1993

Abstract

The knowledge required for action is generally indexical rather than objective. For example, a robot that knows the relative position of an object is generally able to go and pick it up; he need not know its absolute position. Agents may have very incomplete knowledge of their situation in terms of what objective facts hold and still be able to achieve their goals. This paper presents a formal theory of knowledge and action, embodied in a modal logic, that handles the distinction between indexical and objective knowledge and allows a proper specification of the knowledge prerequisites and effects of action. Several kinds of robotics situations involving indexical knowledge are formalized within the framework; these examples show how actions can be specified so as to avoid making excessive requirements upon the knowledge of agents.

1. Introduction

1.1. Motivation

Designing autonomous robots or other kinds of agents that interact in sophisticated ways with their environment is hard; you need good tools to do it. Designs should be based on well-developed theories of the interactions that agents have with their environment. There has been a widespread perception that *logic-based formalisms* are unsuitable for this task because classical logic can only represent objective knowledge, it cannot capture the context-relativity, the "situatedness" of action and of the knowledge required for action. In this paper, we will show that this view is inaccurate. We will present a logical theory of knowledge and action that does accommodate indexicality

---

* Corresponding author. E-mail: lesperan@ai.toronto.edu.
[1] Fellow of the Canadian Institute for Advanced Research.

SSDI 0004-3702(94)00010-X

and show that it provides a suitable framework for modeling many kinds of interactions that typically occur between a robot and its environment. Logic-based theories such as ours can help clarify many notions that are used in informal analyses of interaction. No doubt such theories do not capture all aspects of situatedness and much work remains to be done to show that they can be successfully applied to robot design. But we think that after having examined this work, one will agree that it makes an important contribution to the theoretical foundations of the field and has significant potential for applicability, no matter what kind of architecture turns out to be best for achieving reactive yet sophisticated behavior.

A key feature of agent-environment interaction is *incomplete knowledge*: agents typically know very little about their environment. Many theories of action and most existing planners have completely ignored the need to deal with what agents know and need to know by unrealistically assuming that agents always have perfect knowledge of the domain under consideration. But in the past decade, Moore [40,41], Morgenstern [42,43], and other researchers have proposed theories of knowledge and action that do address this need.

For example, it is *physically possible* for someone to withdraw funds at a teller machine by inserting a bank card and pressing a sequence of keys (assuming the machine is working, the card is not defective, there is money available, and so on). But this a very weak notion; by the same token, it is physically possible for a monkey to write a sonnet at a typewriter. To say that an agent is truly *able* to withdraw funds, we would want to insist that the agent *know* among many other things, his bank identification code. The reason this stronger notion of ability is so useful is that it allows us to make sense of actions that otherwise seem to have no relevant effect. For example, how else to explain an agent who always takes a small piece of paper out his wallet and looks at it carefully before pushing the keys on the teller machine?

To understand actions such as these, we need to consider agents that have knowledge about

- the *effects* various actions would have upon their knowledge;
- the *knowledge prerequisites* of the actions they might do—the conditions under which they are *able* to achieve goals by doing actions.

Theories such as Moore's and Morgenstern's do provide reasonable answers to the question of what the relationship between knowledge and action is and have considerably advanced our understanding of the issues involved. But many problems remain. This work deals with one aspect of the relationship between knowledge and action that has been neglected and is inadequately handled by these theories: the fact that the knowledge required for action is often relative to the agent's perspective—that it is often *indexical* (or relative) knowledge rather than objective knowledge. For example,

- if a robot knows the relative position of an object he can go and pick it up— knowing the absolute position of the object is neither necessary nor sufficient (he might not know where he is);
- one can soft-boil an egg if one has a timer—knowing at what time it will be done is neither necessary nor sufficient (one may not know what time it is).

In these cases, the agent has very incomplete knowledge of his situation, at least as far as objective facts are concerned, but this does not interfere with his ability to achieve his goals by doing actions. More generally, an agent may have sufficient knowledge to be able to achieve his goals even if he does not know

- where he is;
- what time it is;
- which objects are around him;
- where these objects are located (in absolute terms);
- who he is.

This is the case because the knowledge required for physical interactions with the environment is indexical knowledge, knowledge about how one is related to things in the environment or to events in one's history. This should not come as a surprise, since agents act upon their environment from a particular perspective, a particular place and moment in time. The same action done at different places and times has different effects. So it makes sense that the prerequisites of an action should involve knowledge that is relative to this perspective. Similarly and fortunately, the knowledge supplied by perception is indexical knowledge. For example, by using his sonar, a robot comes to know how far from him an object is (at the current time); he does not learn anything about the object's absolute position. Indexicality has of course been a central theme of the "situated action" paradigm [5, 51, 53]. Several researchers have argued that indexical knowledge plays a major role in the operation of reactive agents [2, 52].

Existing theories of the relationship between knowledge and action cannot handle these cases properly, as they do not accommodate the distinction between indexical knowledge and objective knowledge. They impose unnecessarily strong knowledge requirements upon agents before sanctioning their ability; they tend to require objective knowledge when indexical knowledge would be sufficient. They also cannot represent accurately the effects of action upon knowledge. We need an account of ability that squares with the fact that an agent may be missing very basic facts about his objective situation and that of the things around him and still be capable of achieving his goals. The reason we care about this is that this form of incomplete knowledge is the norm rather than the exception for agents in the world.

This is not to say that objective knowledge is never necessary for action. Because it is independent of the context, it can be stored or communicated without the need for adjustments to compensate for changes in the context. It is clear that human agents have all sorts of objective knowledge about the world and draw upon a variety of external sources of objective knowledge such as textbooks, databases, maps, timetables, etc. In hierarchical planning, it is likely that top-levels plans involve actions that are specified in a relatively objective way (e.g., in planning a car trip across the province, one first decides on what roads to follow and only later on whether to turn right or left). What this means is that a theory of knowledge and action must accommodate both the indexical knowledge involved in interaction with the physical environment and the objective knowledge involved in high-level planning and social interactions. As well, it must allow each kind of knowledge to be mapped into the other provided that knowledge of the context is available, so that objective knowledge can be exploited in physical interactions and indexical knowledge is available for communication, long-term storage, etc.

1.2. The approach

We want a theory of knowledge and action that handles the distinction between indexical and objective knowledge and accounts for indexical knowledge prerequisites and
effects of action. The approach taken is to develop a quantified modal logic that embodies the theory. The logic includes primitives that formalize notions of knowledge, time,
action, and historical necessity—the latter notion is used to capture the physical possibility of a course of action for an agent. The notion of ability is formalized as a derived
operator (i.e., defined in terms of the notions mentioned above). The epistemic and temporal parts of the logic adequately support the representation of indexical knowledge,
keeping it distinct from objective knowledge. We provide a formal semantics for the
knowledge operator that handles indexicality; it is a simple and natural extension of the
standard possible-world semantic scheme for the logic of knowledge [18,20]. The complete system permits an adequate characterization of indexical knowledge prerequisites
and effects of actions in a wide range of circumstances.

The specification of the theory as a logical system has several advantages. The properties that the theory attributes to agents correspond to provably valid sentences of the
logic; this ensures that the theory is precisely specified. Moreover, since attributions
of properties to agents emerge as sentences, they can themselves be objects of be-
lief/knowledge by agents; so for example, not only can you state that if an agent does
δ he will know whether φ, but also that the agent *knows* that if he does δ he will know
whether φ. In fact, our theory models not only interactions but also agents' knowledge
about interactions. In it, whenever an agent is able to achieve a goal by doing an action,
he knows that this is the case. Whenever a statement like "if agent a knows φ then a
can achieve ψ by doing δ" is valid in the logic, then this must be known by all agents.
The provision of a formal semantics clarifies the theory's claims and the ontological
commitments involved. Finally, the logic can be used to reason formally about knowledge, action, and ability—the kind of reasoning a designer might do in ensuring that the
agent being designed is able to achieve a goal. Our methodology differs little from that
used by Moore [40,41], Morgenstern [42,43], and others who have previously worked
on theories of knowledge and action.

Note that our theory is at the "knowledge level" [45], and as such, does not say much
about agent architecture. While it uses logic, it does not take any representational stance
(i.e., assume that knowledge is represented by sentence-like entities inside agents); this
is similar to the position taken by Rosenschein and Kaelbling in their situated automata
work [24,48]. But there is an emerging consensus that satisfactory architectural designs
for agents will need to be based on an adequate theory of agent-environment interaction.
Our work attempts to provide this kind of foundation.

A substantial part of our efforts has been devoted to the formalization of various
application domains within the logical system proposed. This is essential to ensure that
the theory is truly useful and that it handles adequately the kind of situations that it is
designed for. Moreover, the formalization of actions involves many decisions that have a
crucial effect upon what knowledge is required from an agent, but are not settled by the
theory; for example, decisions concerning the kind of parameters an action should take.
The applications developed show how actions can be specified so as to avoid making

excessive requirements upon the knowledge of agents, and how such specifications can be used to prove that an agent is able to achieve a goal by doing an action if he knows certain facts.

Much of our formalization efforts have been directed at a robotics domain, since this kind of application provides the most intuitive examples of situations where indexical knowledge is sufficient for ability. We will describe in detail our formalization of this domain, where a simple robot is involved in various types of interaction with its environment. In our formalization, perception does yield indexical knowledge and ability to act upon an object does not require knowing which object is involved or what its absolute position is. We also show how indexical knowledge and objective knowledge can be and must be related in our framework to deal with the use of maps for navigation. We discuss the representational issues that arise, which have general relevance to the formalization of actions with indexical knowledge prerequisites or effects.

In the next section, we briefly discuss related work. Then in Section 3, we give an overview of the logical system that forms the basis of our framework. The core of the paper is Section 4, where we describe our formalization of various types of interactions a simple robot has with its environment. Following that, Section 5 briefly describes other application domains that have been formalized, in particular cases where temporal knowledge is required for ability. Then in Section 6, we argue that the applications examined, in particular the ones involving temporal knowledge, provide convincing evidence that the distinction between indexical and objective knowledge supported by our framework has substantial practical value and that it cannot be done justice within existing accounts of ability. We conclude in Section 7 by discussing the contributions and limitations of this work, and suggesting various directions for further research; we discuss how this work might be applied to the design of autonomous robots and other types of agents.

2. Related work

This survey is selective and often sketchy; for a more complete discussion, see [29].

2.1. Theories of knowledge and action

As argued in the introduction, a theory that explains how agents manage to achieve their goals by doing actions, and in particular why they perform knowledge acquisition actions, must account for the effects of action upon knowledge and for the knowledge prerequisites of action; it must include an account of ability as opposed to mere "physical possibility". The most influential work in this area is Moore's theory of knowledge and action [40, 41]. His framework can be described as a combination of first-order dynamic logic (a modal logic of action) [13] with an S4 modal logic of knowledge [18, 19]. [2]

---

[2] Strictly speaking, the framework is not the modal logic just described, but the encoding in first-order logic of the semantics of this modal logic; thus the part of the logic dealing with action is closely related to the situation calculus [38].

On the matter of knowledge prerequisites of action, notice that one may know that an action would achieve a goal without knowing how to execute that action; for example, one may know that cooking beef bourguignon would impress the party's guests without knowing how to cook beef bourguignon. For Moore, knowing how to do an action amounts to knowing what primitive actions that action (description) stands for; knowing how to do an action requires having *de re* as opposed to *de dicto* knowledge of the action.

Let us review the philosophical lore on this distinction. *De re* knowledge attributions are said to assert the existence of some kind of epistemic relation between the knower and some entity. The intuition behind such attributions is that they apply to cases where the agent's knowledge is sufficiently precise to pick up a particular entity, as opposed to being about whatever satisfies a description. The latter cases are said to involve mere *de dicto* knowledge. For example, if John is told that someone among his co-workers has been selected to be the new manager, but is not told whom, he may then come to believe that the new manager (whoever he is) must be happy—a *de dicto* rather than *de re* belief. If he is later told that the new manager is Paul, he will then come to have a *de re* belief of Paul that he must be happy. Following Hintikka [19], knowing who/what θ is usually taken to amount to knowing of some x that it is θ (*de re*). The question of what precisely is required for an agent to have *de re* knowledge has been the subject of much philosophical debate (see [28] for a discussion). In AI, the common answer has been that having *de re* knowledge of some entity requires knowing a *standard name* for that entity [26,35], a view shared by Moore as well as the present work. Since what standard names refer to must be common knowledge; this means that they must be objective, and thus, that *de re* knowledge must in some sense always be objective knowledge. But this can be a bit misleading, as knowing what the relative position of an object is or knowing what primitive actions an action stands for hardly qualify as having objective knowledge. The domain over which one quantifies matters. In such cases, one can at best say that one has "objective" knowledge of a relational property.

So Moore uses this distinction in his formalization of ability. For atomic actions, his account goes as follows: an agent is able to achieve a goal by doing an action if and only if he knows what the given action is, and knows of himself that it is physically possible for him to do the action next and that his doing the action next necessarily results in the goal being achieved. Note that the agent is required to have *de re* knowledge of himself—to know who he is. Complex actions are handled recursively; for instance, an agent is said to be able to achieve a goal by doing a sequence of two actions if and only if by doing the first action, he is able to achieve the goal of being able to achieve the main goal by doing the second action. The agent need not initially know what all the actions that make up his plan are; he needs only know that he will know what to do next at each step of the plan. Note that in most cases, the specification of an action need not say anything explicit about its knowledge prerequisites; these fall out of the theory's general principles and the specification of the conditions under which one knows what the action is.

The requirement that the agent know what the action is has interesting results when the action is an instance of a parametrized procedure (e.g. DIAL(COMBINATION(SAFE1))); in many such cases, agents know what the procedure is and one wants to say that an agent knows what the action is if he knows what the arguments are; it is easy to state this in Moore's formalism (technically, one states that the procedure is an epistemically rigid function). But note that assuming that an instance of a procedure is known whenever one knows what the parameters are is often wrong. For example, whether one knows how to PICKUP(BLOCK1) has nothing to do with whether one knows a standard name for BLOCK1; it has more to do with whether one knows the relative position of BLOCK1, or more generally where BLOCK1 is relative to oneself. One has to be very careful as to how one parametrizes the actions, and in many cases, the parameters must be indexical descriptions.

But Moore's framework does not really accommodate the distinction between indexical and objective knowledge. His logic does not handle knowledge that is indexical with respect to the agent; it does not capture an agent's concept of himself, and knowledge that involves this concept (e.g., an agent's knowing that he himself is holding a block). So the account requires the agent to know who he is (know a standard name for himself, something clearly objective) in order to be judged able to achieve a goal by doing an action. This is clearly unnecessary. What need would a very simple agent, say a robot insect, have for knowing who he is? Because of this, the formalism cannot really model what knowing something under an indexical description amounts to. Yet this seems to be an important feature of how reactive agents deal with their environment (see Section 6 for more discussion of this). Moore's logic also does not handle knowledge about absolute times. So for instance, it is not possible to say that after looking at a clock, an agent knows what time it is.[3] These expressive limitations together with the way the account treats parametrized procedures mean that formalizations of various domains in Moore's framework tend to require too much objective knowledge and not enough indexical knowledge.

Let us point out a few other limitations of Moore's account of ability. Firstly, the notion formalized is a highly idealized version of the commonsense notion: one is taken as able to achieve a goal only if one knows that doing the action absolutely guarantees that the goal will be achieved; just knowing that it is highly likely to achieve the goal is not enough. It would be great to have a version of the account that deals with uncertainty, but this is not something we attempt in the present work. Secondly, it may be argued that ability is not just a matter of knowing what actions to take. For example, does knowing how to play a sonata only require knowing which notes to play and does knowing how to ride a bicycle only require knowing which movements to make? On the other hand, it is not clear that these examples point to some essential flaw in the account; perhaps it is just a matter of making explicit the temporal and memory constraints associated with the action (e.g., one needs to recover quickly from playing a note, as well as keep track of what note to play next). Finally, there are cases in commonsense discourse where we individuate actions in terms of their effects rather than in terms of what body

---

[3] Technically speaking, Moore models knowledge with an accessibility relation that ranges over (instantaneous) world states. He cannot represent knowledge that is indexical with respect to the agent because there is nothing to characterize who the agent thinks he might be in these states. He also cannot represent knowledge about absolute times because his states have no absolute time is associated with them. This should become clearer after our accounts of knowledge and ability have been introduced.

movements or effector commands get executed (e.g., one may say that at the end of every working day, a sales representative does the same action no matter where he might be, he goes home). But this is a different sense of "doing an action" from the one we are concerned with; we are not trying to produce a semantic account of natural language discourse about action.

Let us briefly discuss other theories of knowledge and action. One of the unattractive features of the logic of knowledge included in Moore's framework is that knowledge is assumed to be closed under logical consequence. Konolige [25] has developed a theory of knowledge and action, based on an account of knowledge as a predicate on sentences, that avoids this defect. [4] His account of ability is essentially a recasting of Moore's into his framework; only the same restricted class of actions is handled.

A theory that significantly extends this coverage has been developed by Morgenstern [42,43]. It handles both concurrent actions and plans involving multiple agents. Simpler cases are treated as in Moore's. Her account of knowledge is also syntactic, but differs significantly from Konolige's (she does not use the Tarskian approach to the paradoxes and there is a single truth predicate for all the languages in the hierarchy). Note that knowledge is, in fact, closed under logical consequence in her account. Her argumentation against classical logics of knowledge is not based on the consequential closure problem, but on the claim that they cannot express the weak knowledge prerequisites involved in multi-agent planning. For example, if Paul does not know how to fix a leaky faucet, but knows that his friend John is somehow able to do it, then he is able to fix the faucet by asking John to do it for him. However, our recent work [34] undermines this argument; we show that the notion of "somehow being able to achieve a goal" can in fact be modeled in a possible-world framework.

Neither Konolige nor Morgenstern recognize the role of indexical knowledge in action; their formalisms have the same limitations as Moore's in this respect. One researcher who did recognize it is Haas. In [16], he sketches how indexical knowledge might be handled in a specification of ability; but he does not formalize his proposals.

2.2. Theories of indexical knowledge

There has been a lot of work on indexical knowledge in philosophy, but we can only mention a few references here (see [29]). Our account of indexical knowledge is inspired from Lewis's view that having a belief involves ascribing a property to oneself and the current time [37]. In [46], Perry argues convincingly that indexicality is an essential feature of propositional attitudes.

Let us say a bit more about some recent work by Grove [14] and Grove and Halpern [15], where they propose a logic of knowledge that does handle indexicality. Their account of knowledge is quite similar to ours; in fact, their semantics is essentially the same as ours. However, their work is more narrowly focussed than ours; they do not account for action and its relationship to knowledge, and only handle time in a

---

[4] Note however that such "syntactic" accounts have been claimed to have the opposite defect, that is, to individuate knowledge states *too finely* [36]; for instance, it is far from clear that a belief that φ and φ' is any different from a belief that φ' and φ.

limited way. On the other hand, their work is technically very thorough; they discuss several logical systems with varying degrees of expressiveness, both propositional and first-order, and they provide complete axiomatizations and complexity results.[5] They also develop an appealing approach to quantification into epistemic contexts that permits a resolution of the ambiguity of *de re* reports with respect to the way the knower is referring to the object.

2.3. Reactive behavior and situated action

It has been argued that indexicality plays an important role in how agents manage to react in a timely manner to changing environmental conditions (e.g., avoid collisions with moving objects). Let us look at some recent work on *reactive agents* where this comes out. This is a promising application area for our work.

The classical AI paradigm with respect to the production of intelligent behavior involves a smart planner that searches for a plan that achieves the agent's goal and a dumb executor that carries out the plan in a mechanical way. In recent years, there has been a definite movement towards exploring alternatives to this paradigm. It is felt that because of the emphasis it places on search for complete plans, classical deliberative planning is too slow for producing reactive behavior. Moreover, it is not sufficiently grounded in perception; much of the effort expended on constructing a plan may be wasted if environmental conditions change in the meantime. The alternative architectures proposed achieve reactivity by emphasizing environment monitoring and the selection of actions appropriate to conditions; the focus is on developing a sophisticated executor.

Agre and Chapman [2, 3] have been among the most radical in their reevaluation of the classical paradigm. Their views have been influenced by anthropological theories of action [1, 53]. They emphasize the complexity of the real situations in which action occurs, the uncertainty of the information the agent may have about them, and the need for reactivity. This leads them to argue that the production of most activity does not involve the construction and manipulation of explicit representations of the world; the associated computational costs are just too prohibitive. They say that:

> Rather than relying on reasoning to intervene between perception and action, we believe activity mostly derives from very simple sorts of machinery interacting with the immediate situation. This machinery exploits regularities in its interaction with the world to engage in complex, apparently planful activity without requiring explicit models of the world. [2, p. 268]

The architecture they propose involves peripheral modules for perception and effector control and a central system that mediates between the two. They argue that combinational networks, that is, circuits computing logic functions, can form an adequate central system for most activities; thus in such cases, the central system has no state. They

---

[5] Interestingly, their results seem to show that the complexity of deciding whether a sentence is valid is no worse in systems that accommodate the distinction between objective and indexical knowledge than in comparable systems that do not.

have built various application systems to provide support for their analysis. One of these systems, called Pengi, plays a videogame where one controls a penguin that navigates in a maze, pushes away ice blocks, and confronts malicious "killer bees" [2].

From our point of view, the most interesting elements of Agre and Chapman's scheme are their notions of indexical-functional entities and aspects.[6] They claim that traditional domain representations involving objective facts such as "(AT BLOCK-213 427 991)" are inappropriate because they do not make reference to the agent's situation or goals. They see the machinery in their networks as registering indexical-functional entities such as "the block I'm pushing" and indexical-functional aspects such as "the bee I intend to clobber is closer to the projectile than I am". These entities and aspects are indexical because they depend on the agent's situation; they are also functional because they depend on his purposes. Clearly, Agre and Chapman find the notion of indexical information useful in designing their robots and explaining how they behave. However, they do not propose any formal version of this modeling scheme.

Subramanian and Woodfill [52] have recently proposed an interesting account of reactive agent architectures and the role indexical representations play in them; their work includes a computational complexity analysis that attempts to trace the source of the efficiency gains associated with the use of indexical representations. To model the world as viewed by reactive agents, they use a version of the situation calculus [38] with a vocabulary that includes indexical terms. The logical constant Now is used to refer the current situation. Constraints are introduced to ensure that every situation has at most one predecessor and the function Before is used to refer to a situation's predecessor (e.g., Before(Now) refers to the situation prior to the most recent action). Domain-dependent indexical terms, such as This-Block, are also used. Subramanian and Woodfill show how the kind of indexical control rules that determine what a reactive agent will do next (one-step planning) can be specified in this framework. This is also done for plan-monitoring rules, which are used to deduce what should be the case after an action has been performed. Their complexity analysis of this kind of setting traces the efficiency gains associated with the use of indexical representations to the fact that indexical theories can be propositionalized without the usual combinatorial explosion because they do not quantify over all entities of the relevant type; instead, they refer to the entities involved indexically. In their words: "the power of using these indexical terms is that it gives us implicit quantification."

Independently of whether this analysis is correct, it must be noted that Subramanian and Woodfill's framework inherits most of the limitations of the ordinary situation calculus, in particular, its inability to handle knowledge acquisition actions. Moreover, the semantics fails to distinguish between the context dependence of indexical terms and the simple world-dependence of non-rigid constants. Finally, the theory does not account for the distinctive logical behavior of indexical terms, for example, the fact that the past is determined while the future is not.

---

[6] This is Agre and Chapman's terminology. There are of course no such things as indexical (or agent-relative) *entities*; but there are indexical (or agent-relative) concepts or notions of things.

Another conception of how reactive behavior can be produced has been proposed by Rosenschein and Kaelbling [24,48]. Their approach is of particular interest to us because a logic is used to specify reactive agents and the environments in which they operate. Design tools based on the logic are also developed; these tools facilitate the specification of complex agents and allow high-level specifications to be "compiled" into circuit-level ones.

The architecture they propose for reactive agents [23] also avoids formal manipulation of explicit representations. It involves a perceptual component and an action selection component, both of which may have state (registers). They also argue that the lack of explicit representations does not mean that one loses the ability to ascribe semantic content to machine states. They propose an alternative way of doing this—the situated automata view. It involves viewing the agent and its environment as coupled automata. A machine state contains the information that φ (i.e., in that state, the machine knows that φ) if given the state transition functions of the machine and world, the fact·that the machine is in that state implies that φ must be the case. For example, the fact that a certain wire in a robot carries a "1" would mean that there is an object within a certain radius of his position, if given the state transition functions, the wire can only be carrying a "1" if there is an object within that radius. Thus the information content of a machine state is defined in terms of how it is correlated to environmental conditions.

Rosenschein and Kaelbling do not discuss the role of indexical knowledge in the production of reactive behavior. Their logic suffers from the same kind of expressive limitations as Moore's with respect to indexicality; it does not handle knowledge that is indexical with respect to the agent, and while it accommodates temporally indexical knowledge, it does not handle temporally objective knowledge. This may come as a surprise because their formalization of examples such as the one involving a robot that keeps track of whether a moving object is within shouting distance in [48] uses many indexical-sounding propositions. But their logic does not really model all of that indexicality. When indexical-sounding domain-dependent symbols are used, it's easy to lose track of what the formalism really handles. However, their work strongly suggests that a theory of knowledge and action that handles the distinction between indexical and objective knowledge would be very useful for producing better accounts of reactive behavior and better tools for the design of reactive agents.

3. A logic of indexical knowledge, action, and ability

In this section, we briefly review a formal theory of indexical knowledge, action and ability, and some of its properties. A much more detailed examination of the theory, including a discussion of the general issues involved can be found in [29, 33]. Here, we simply present the theory in sufficient detail to underwrite the applications of the next two sections.

Our theory is formulated in a many-sorted first-order modal logic with equality. We assume familiarity with conventional first-order logic as in [39], and at least some acquaintance with the standard apparatus of modal logics, as described in [21] or [8].

3.1. Syntax

We want to be able to express attributions of indexical knowledge in our logic, for example, that Rob knows that he himself was holding a cup five minutes ago. In such cases, what is known is a "proposition" that is relative. It may be relative to the knower, or to the time of the knowing, or perhaps to other aspects of the context. To handle this, our language includes two special terms: **self**, which denotes the current agent, and **now**, which denotes the current time; these terms are called *primitive indexicals*. Non-logical (domain-dependent) symbols may also depend on the current agent and time for their interpretation, for example, $\exists x \text{HOLDING}(x)$ may express the fact that the current agent is currently holding something—we say that such symbols are non-primitive indexicals. Our semantics handles this by interpreting terms and formulas with respect to *indices*, which consist of a possible-world, modeling the objective circumstances, and an agent and time, modeling the context. Note that **self** and **now** are *not* intended to be formal counterparts of similar sounding English words and behave differently from any such words (more about this shortly).

The language we use is called *LIKA* and as any first-order logical language, it divides syntactically into terms and formulas.[7] The terms here, however, are of four different sorts: terms for ordinary individuals (as usual), temporal terms, agent terms, and action terms. For each of these four sorts, there are both variables and function symbols (that is, functions whose values will be of the proper sort) and as usual, constants are taken to be 0-ary function symbols. We will use the metavariables v, F, and θ to range over variables, function symbols, and terms respectively, with superscripts i, t, a, and d used to indicate the sort: individual, temporal, agent, and action respectively. So, for example, v^t stands for a temporal variable, and θ^d stands for an action term. Syntactically, terms are formed in the obvious way, with the following restrictions: firstly, only temporal function symbols may take temporal terms as arguments, and secondly, action terms cannot appear as arguments to function symbols of any sort.

The atomic formulas include predications using predicate symbols and terms, written $R(\theta_1, \ldots, \theta_n)$, which are used to assert that $\theta_1, \ldots, \theta_n$ stand in static relation R at the current time and for the current agent. We also have equality expressions $(\theta_1 = \theta_2)$, between terms of the same sort, as well as expressions of temporal precedence $(\theta_1^t < \theta_2^t)$. Finally, $\textbf{Does}(\theta^d, \theta^t)$ is used to assert that the current agent does action θ^d starting from the current time and ending at time θ^t.

For non-atomic formulas, we have negations, implications, and universal quantifications, and all the standard abbreviations (such as disjunctions; see below). Finally, if φ is a formula, then so are $\textbf{At}(\theta^t, \varphi)$, $\textbf{By}(\theta^a, \varphi)$, $\textbf{Know}(\varphi)$, and $\Box \varphi$. $\textbf{At}(\theta^t, \varphi)$ means that φ holds at time θ^t, that is, when θ^t is taken to be the current time. $\textbf{By}(\theta^a, \varphi)$ means that φ holds when θ^a is taken to be the current agent. $\textbf{Know}(\varphi)$ is used to say that the current agent knows at the current time that φ. If φ contains indexicals, $\textbf{Know}(\varphi)$ should be taken as attributing indexical knowledge—knowledge the agent has about himself and the current time. For example, $\textbf{Know}(\exists x \text{HOLDING}(x))$ could mean that

---

[7] *LIKA* stands for "Language of Indexical Knowledge and Action". In [29], we used the name $\mathcal{L}_{index}$ instead of *LIKA*.

the agent knows that he himself is currently holding something. Finally, $\Box\varphi$ is used to say that φ is historically necessary, that is, that it must hold, given everything that has happened up to now. This completes the syntactic specification of the language.

The notions of free variable, bound variable, and term that is free for a variable in a formula are assumed to have their usual definition. We use $\varphi\{v \mapsto \theta\}$ to stand for the result of substituting θ for all free occurrences of v in φ, provided that v and θ belong to the same sort.

All symbols of the language other than the function symbols and the predicate symbols are considered to be *logical* symbols, and will have a fixed interpretation. In the examples of the next section, we will introduce domain-dependent function or predicate symbols (with names like POS or HOLDING) as well as axioms governing their interpretation.

3.2. Semantic structures

The terms and formulas of *LIKA* are understood in terms of the following semantic components: $\mathcal{A}, \mathcal{I}, \mathcal{T}, \mathcal{D}, \mathcal{W}, \Phi, \prec, \approx, \Delta$, and K. Instead of a single domain of discourse, we have non-empty domains for each sort: a set $\mathcal{A}$ of agents, a set $\mathcal{I} \supseteq \mathcal{A}$ of individuals, a set $\mathcal{T}$ of time points, and a set $\mathcal{D}$ of primitive actions. The terms of *LIKA* are taken to refer to elements of these domains, and quantification is handled in the usual way.

$\mathcal{W}$ is a set of temporally extended possible worlds. As explained earlier, we handle indexicals by interpreting terms and formulas with respect to *indices*, which are triples consisting of a world, an agent, and a time; so $\mathcal{E} = \mathcal{W} \times \mathcal{A} \times \mathcal{T}$ is the set of indices. We take a, i, t, d, w, and e (possibly subscripted, primed, etc.), as ranging over arbitrary elements of $\mathcal{A}, \mathcal{I}, \mathcal{T}, \mathcal{D}, \mathcal{W}$, and $\mathcal{E}$ respectively. The **By** and **At** operators are used to change the agent and time component of the index respectively. The denotations of terms and the truth of predications are handled in the obvious way using a function Φ which, at each index, maps function symbols to functions over the appropriate domains and predicate symbols to relations over the appropriate domains.

Turning now to the temporal aspects, formulas containing $<$ are understood in terms of $\prec$, which is a relation over $\mathcal{T}$ whose intended interpretation is "is earlier than". $\approx$ is a family of accessibility relations—one for each time point—that is used to interpret the historical necessity operator $\Box$. Intuitively, $w \approx_t w^*$ if and only if w and w^* differ only in what happens after time t. Formulas containing **Does** are interpreted in terms of $\Delta \subseteq \mathcal{D} \times \mathcal{E} \times \mathcal{T}$, which determines which actions are done by which agents in which worlds over which time intervals: $\langle d, \langle w, a, t_s \rangle, t_e \rangle \in \Delta$ if and only if action d is done by agent a from time t_s to time t_e in world w.

Finally, our semantics for knowledge is a simple generalization of the standard possible-world scheme [20, 27]. The knowledge accessibility relation K is taken to hold over *indices* rather than plain possible worlds: $K \subseteq \mathcal{E}^2$. Informally, $\langle\langle w, a, t\rangle, \langle w', a', t'\rangle\rangle \in K$ if and only if as far as agent a at time t in world w knows, it may be the case that w' is the way the world actually is *and* he is a' *and* the current time is t'. Thus, we model the knowledge state of an agent at a time in a world by a set of indices, which characterizes not only which worlds are compatible with what the agent knows, but also which points of view upon these worlds are compatible with what he knows. In other words, we allow an agent to be uncertain not only about what world he is in, but also about who he is and what time it is.

3.3. Denotation and satisfaction

More formally, we have the following: a semantic structure M is a tuple

$$\langle \mathcal{A}, \mathcal{I}, \mathcal{T}, \mathcal{D}, \mathcal{W}, \prec, \mathsf{K}, \approx, \varPhi, \varDelta \rangle.$$

An assignment is a function that maps variables into elements of the domain appropriate to them. $g\{v \mapsto x\}$ is the assignment that is identical to g except that it maps variable v into the entity x.

The *denotation* of a term θ in a structure M at an index e = $\langle w, a, t \rangle$ under an assignment g, written $\llbracket \theta \rrbracket_{e,g}^{M}$ is defined as follows (from now on, we omit the structure under consideration when it is clear from context):

- $\llbracket v \rrbracket_{e,g} = g(v)$,
- $\llbracket \mathbf{self} \rrbracket_{e,g} = a$,
- $\llbracket \mathbf{now} \rrbracket_{e,g} = t$,
- $\llbracket F(\theta_1, \ldots, \theta_n) \rrbracket_{e,g} = \varPhi(F, e)(\llbracket \theta_1 \rrbracket_{e,g}, \ldots, \llbracket \theta_n \rrbracket_{e,g})$.

We can now define what it means for a formula φ to be *satisfied* by a structure M, an index e = $\langle w, a, t \rangle$, and an assignment g, which we write $M, e, g \models \varphi$:

- $e, g \models R(\theta_1^i, \ldots, \theta_n^i)$ iff $\langle \llbracket \theta_1^i \rrbracket_{e,g}, \ldots, \llbracket \theta_n^i \rrbracket_{e,g} \rangle \in \varPhi(R, e)$,
- $e, g \models \mathbf{Does}(\theta^d, \theta^t)$ iff $\varDelta(\llbracket \theta^d \rrbracket_{e,g}, e, \llbracket \theta^t \rrbracket_{e,g})$,
- $e, g \models \theta_1 = \theta_2$ iff $\llbracket \theta_1 \rrbracket_{e,g} = \llbracket \theta_2 \rrbracket_{e,g}$,
- $e, g \models \theta_1^t < \theta_2^t$ iff $\llbracket \theta_1^t \rrbracket_{e,g} \prec \llbracket \theta_2^t \rrbracket_{e,g}$,
- $e, g \models \neg\varphi$ iff it is not the case that $e, g \models \varphi$,
- $e, g \models (\varphi_1 \supset \varphi_2)$ iff either it is not the case that $e, g \models \varphi_1$, or $e, g \models \varphi_2$,
- $e, g \models \forall v \varphi$ iff for every entity x in the domain appropriate to v, $e, g\{v \mapsto x\} \models \varphi$,
- $e, g \models \mathbf{At}(\theta^t, \varphi)$ iff $\langle w, a, \llbracket \theta^t \rrbracket_{e,g} \rangle, g \models \varphi$,
- $e, g \models \mathbf{By}(\theta^a, \varphi)$ iff $\langle w, \llbracket \theta^a \rrbracket_{e,g}, t \rangle, g \models \varphi$,
- $e, g \models \mathbf{Know}(\varphi)$ iff for all e', such that $\langle e, e' \rangle \in \mathsf{K}$, $e', g \models \varphi$,
- $e, g \models \Box\varphi$ iff for all w^* such that $w \approx_t w^*$, $\langle w^*, a, t \rangle, g \models \varphi$.

A formula φ is *satisfiable* if there exists a structure M, index e, and assignment g, such that $M, e, g \models \varphi$. A formula φ is *valid* (written $\models \varphi$) if it is satisfied by all structures, indices, and assignments.

As mentioned earlier, our logic is not intended to be a formalization of the behavior of English indexicals; we see it as a specification language, a tool for modeling how agents interact with their environment. In English, there are true indexicals (I, you, now, here, etc.), which refer to aspects of the utterance context no matter where they appear, and there are quasi-indexicals/quasi-indicators [7] (I myself, you yourself, he himself, etc.), which are used to report that an agent has an indexical mental state. The behavior of our *primitive indexicals* **self** and **now** displays characteristics of both categories. When **self** occurs outside the scope of **Know** or **By**, it behaves like the English indexical "I" and when **now** occurs outside the scope of **Know** or **At**, it behaves like the English indexical "now". In the scope of **Know** on the other hand, **self** and **now** behave like quasi-indexicals—there are no temporal quasi-indexicals in English, but one can imagine how a temporal analog of "he himself" would work. Finally, when **self** occurs in the scope of **By** and when **now** occurs in the scope of **At**, they behave like pronouns that are bound by the operator; this is similar to the way in which an expression like "the day before" depends on surrounding temporal operators as in "tomorrow, it will be the case that the day before, I wrote this line". We wanted to keep the logic simple and allow typical assertions about knowledge and action to be expressed concisely. This led to the chosen design. These features come at the cost of a simple relationship to English. But we feel that the logical behavior of our primitive indexicals is easily understood once one realizes it is different from that of any English analogs. This is not to say that formalizing the behavior of English indexicals is uninteresting. In fact, we think that our framework can be used as a foundation to build a model that relates the context sensitivity of language to that of mental states and action. We return to this topic in Section 7.2.

3.4. Constraints

To ensure that the semantics adequately models the notions that we are trying to capture (knowledge, historical necessity, etc.), we impose various constraints on semantic structures. When we speak of a valid or satisfiable formula we always mean relative to semantic structures that satisfy these constraints. Here we will simply list the constraints without justification (and minimal explanation):

(1) S4 *epistemic logic*. K must be reflexive and transitive.

(2) *Linear time logic.* $\prec$ must be a strict total order, that is, transitive, connected, and irreflexive. [8]

(3) *Start time is before end time.* If $\langle d, \langle w, a, t_s \rangle, t_e \rangle \in \Delta$, then $t_s \preceq t_e$.

(4) *Historical necessity is an S5 operator.* For all $t \in T, \approx_t$ must be an equivalence relation.

(5) *Possibilities do not increase over time.* If $w \approx_{t_2} w^*$ and $t_1 \preceq t_2$, then $w \approx_{t_1} w^*$.

(6) *Equivalent worlds support the same basic facts and knowledge.* If $w \approx_t w^*$, then, letting $e = \langle w, a, t \rangle$ and $e^* = \langle w^*, a, t \rangle$, it must be the case that
   (a) for any predicate R, $\Phi(R, e^*) = \Phi(R, e)$,
   (b) for any function symbol F, $\Phi(F, e^*) = \Phi(F, e)$,
   (c) for any e', $\langle e^*, e' \rangle \in K$ iff $\langle e, e' \rangle \in K$.

(7) *Equivalent worlds support the same actions.*
   (a) If $w \approx_{t_e} w^*$, then $\Delta(d, \langle w^*, a, t_s \rangle, t_e)$ iff $\Delta(d, \langle w, a, t_s \rangle, t_e)$,
   (b) if $w \approx_t w^*$ and $t_s \prec t$, then

   there exists t_e such that $t \prec t_e$ and $\Delta(d, \langle w, a, t_s \rangle, t_e)$

   if and only if

   there exists t'_e such that $t \prec t'_e$ and $\Delta(d, \langle w^*, a, t_s \rangle, t'_e)$.

---

[8] A relation R is connected if and only if for any x_1 and x_2, either $x_1 R x_2$ or $x_1 = x_2$ or $x_2 R x_1$; a relation R is irreflexive if and only if for no x is it the case that $x R x$.

(8) *Persistent memory and awareness of actions.* If $\langle\langle w, a, t\rangle, \langle w', a', t'\rangle\rangle \in K$ and $t_p \preceq t$, then there exists a time t'_p, where $t'_p \preceq t'$, such that $\langle\langle w, a, t_p\rangle, \langle w', a', t'_p\rangle\rangle \in K$ and if $\Delta(d, \langle w, a, t_p\rangle, t)$ then $\Delta(d, \langle w', a', t'_p\rangle, t')$.

See [33] for discussion of these constraints.

3.5. Abbreviations

To simplify writing formulas in *LIKA*, it is convenient to use certain abbreviations or notational conventions. Firstly, we assume the usual definitions for $\vee, \wedge, \equiv, \exists, \neq, >, \leqslant$, and $\geqslant$. We also introduce a dual to $\Box$: $\Diamond\varphi \overset{\text{def}}{=} \neg\Box\neg\varphi$. Next, using the operator **By**, we define a more common version of **Know** that specifies which agent knows the given proposition; similar definitions are assumed for **Does** and other operators that have yet to be introduced (**Res**, **Can**, etc.):

$$\mathbf{Know}(\theta^a, \varphi) \overset{\text{def}}{=} \mathbf{By}(\theta^a, \mathbf{Know}(\varphi)),$$

and similarly for **Does, Res, Can**, etc.

We have also developed a set of definitions that make it easy to state the occurrence of a large class of complex actions. We first define a new syntactic category, that of *action expressions*. We use the syntactic variable δ to represent members of this category. The category is defined by the following BNF rule:

$$\delta ::= \theta^d \mid \mathbf{noOp} \mid (\delta_1; \delta_2) \mid \mathbf{if}(\varphi, \delta_1, \delta_2).$$

It includes action terms, which represent simple actions, the **noOp** action which takes no time and changes nothing, $(\delta_1; \delta_2)$, which represents the sequential composition of the actions δ_1 and δ_2, and $\mathbf{if}(\varphi, \delta_1, \delta_2)$, which represents the action that consists in doing action δ_1 if the condition φ holds, and in doing action δ_2 otherwise.

We inductively extend **Does** to take action expression arguments as follows:

- $\mathbf{Does}(\mathbf{noOp}, \theta^t) \overset{\text{def}}{=} (\theta^t = \mathbf{now})$;
- $\mathbf{Does}((\delta_1; \delta_2), \theta^t) \overset{\text{def}}{=} \exists v_i^t(\mathbf{Does}(\delta_1, v_i^t) \wedge \exists v_e^t(v_e^t = \theta^t \wedge \mathbf{At}(v_i^t, \mathbf{Does}(\delta_2, v_e^t))))$, provided that v_i^t and v_e^t are distinct and do not occur anywhere in θ^t, δ_1, or δ_2;
- $\mathbf{Does}(\mathbf{if}(\varphi, \delta_1, \delta_2), \theta^t) \overset{\text{def}}{=} (\varphi \wedge \mathbf{Does}(\delta_1, \theta^t)) \vee (\neg\varphi \wedge \mathbf{Does}(\delta_2, \theta^t))$.

We also introduce the following abbreviations for action expressions:

- $\delta^k \overset{\text{def}}{=} \begin{cases} \mathbf{noOp}, & \text{if } k = 0, \\ (\delta; \delta^{k-1}), & \text{if } k > 0; \end{cases}$
- $\mathbf{ifThen}(\varphi, \delta) \overset{\text{def}}{=} \mathbf{if}(\varphi, \delta, \mathbf{noOp})$;
- $\mathbf{while}_k(\varphi, \delta) \overset{\text{def}}{=} \begin{cases} \mathbf{noOp}, & \text{if } k = 0, \\ \mathbf{ifThen}(\varphi, (\delta; \mathbf{while}_{k-1}(\varphi, \delta))), & \text{if } k > 0. \end{cases}$

Note that the numbers k ($\in \mathbb{N}$) in the above are not part of the language, and so cannot be quantified over. Also the last abbreviation above is a bounded form of "while loop"; properly capturing an unbounded form is problematic in the language as it stands.

Let us also define some dynamic-logic-style operators that will be used in our formalization of ability.[9] **AfterNec**(δ, φ), which is intended to mean "φ must hold after δ", is defined inductively as follows:

- **AfterNec**$(\theta^d, \varphi) \overset{\text{def}}{=} \Box \forall v^t (\mathbf{Does}(\theta^d, v^t) \supset \mathbf{At}(v^t, \varphi))$, where v^t is a temporal variable that does not occur free in φ;

- **AfterNec**$(\mathbf{noOp}, \varphi) \overset{\text{def}}{=} \varphi$;

- **AfterNec**$((\delta_1; \delta_2), \varphi) \overset{\text{def}}{=} \mathbf{AfterNec}(\delta_1, \mathbf{AfterNec}(\delta_2, \varphi))$;

- **AfterNec**$(\mathbf{if}(\varphi_c, \delta_1, \delta_2), \varphi) \overset{\text{def}}{=}$
  $(\varphi_c \supset \mathbf{AfterNec}(\delta_1, \varphi)) \wedge (\neg \varphi_c \supset \mathbf{AfterNec}(\delta_2, \varphi))$.

In terms of this, we define **PhyPoss**(δ), which is intended to mean that it is "physically possible" for **self** to do action δ next (even though he may not be able to it because he does not know what primitive actions δ stands for), and **Res**(δ, φ), read as "δ results in φ", which means that δ is physically possible and φ must hold after δ:

- **PhyPoss**$(\delta) \overset{\text{def}}{=} \neg\mathbf{AfterNec}(\delta, \mathbf{False})$;

- **Res**$(\delta, \varphi) \overset{\text{def}}{=} \mathbf{PhyPoss}(\delta) \wedge \mathbf{AfterNec}(\delta, \varphi)$;

True (**False**) stands for some tautology (contradiction).

Let us also define a few additional operators:

- **Kwhether**$(\varphi) \overset{\text{def}}{=} \mathbf{Know}(\varphi) \vee \mathbf{Know}(\neg\varphi)$;

- **DoneWhen**$(\delta, \varphi) \overset{\text{def}}{=} \exists v_s^t \exists v_e^t (v_e^t = \mathbf{now} \wedge \mathbf{At}(v_s^t, \mathbf{Does}(\delta, v_e^t) \wedge \varphi))$, provided that v_s^t and v_e^t are distinct and do not occur anywhere in φ or δ;

- **SomePast**$(\varphi) \overset{\text{def}}{=} \exists v^t (v^t < \mathbf{now} \wedge \mathbf{At}(v^t, \varphi))$, where v^t does not occur free in φ;

Kwhether(φ) means that **self** knows whether φ holds; **DoneWhen**(δ, φ) means that **self** has just done δ and that φ was true when he started; and **SomePast**(φ) means that φ held at some point in the past.

3.6. Ability

We base our formalization of ability on that of Moore [40], which in spite of its relative simplicity, does get at the essential connection between the ability of agents to achieve goals and the knowledge they have about relevant actions. It is simpler than his because we do not attempt to handle indefinite iteration (while-loop actions). Moore's formalization of this case is actually defective because it does not require the agent to know that the action will eventually terminate. We leave this case for future research.

Since we are not treating indefinite iteration, we can simply define ability in terms of the other constructs of the logic as follows:

- **Can**$(\delta, \varphi) \overset{\text{def}}{=} \mathbf{CanDo}(\delta) \wedge \mathbf{Know}(\mathbf{AfterNec}(\delta, \varphi))$;

- **CanDo**$(\theta^d) \overset{\text{def}}{=} \exists v^d \mathbf{Know}(v^d = \theta^d) \wedge \mathbf{Know}(\mathbf{PhyPoss}(\theta^d))$, where action variable v^d does not occur free in θ^d;

---

[9] These definitions are a bit different from the ones given in [29,31]. The ones given here make the operators behave exactly as their dynamic logic [13] analogs. The differences are discussed in [33].

- **CanDo(noOp)** $\stackrel{\text{def}}{=}$ **True**;
- **CanDo($\delta_1; \delta_2$)** $\stackrel{\text{def}}{=}$ **CanDo(δ_1)** $\wedge$ **Know(AfterNec(δ_1, CanDo(δ_2)))**;
- **CanDo(if($\varphi, \delta_1, \delta_2$))** $\stackrel{\text{def}}{=}$ (**Know(φ)** $\wedge$ **CanDo(δ_1)**) $\vee$ (**Know($\neg\varphi$)** $\wedge$ **CanDo(δ_2)**).

The definition says that the agent is able to achieve the goal φ by doing action δ, formally **Can(δ, φ)**, if and only if he can do action δ and knows that after doing δ, the goal φ must hold. **CanDo(δ)** is defined inductively. The first case takes care of simple actions—actions that are represented by action terms. It says that **self** can do a simple action θ^d if and only if he knows what that action is and knows that it is physically possible for him to do it. Note that the definition involves quantifying-in over the class of primitive actions (e.g. "send grasping signal to hand"), as opposed to arbitrary action descriptions. The second case handles the **noOp** action, which trivially holds. The third case handles sequentially composed actions: **self** can do $(\delta_1; \delta_2)$ if and only if he can do δ_1 and knows that after doing it he will be able to do δ_2. The final case takes care of conditional actions: **self** can do **if**($\varphi_c, \delta_1, \delta_2$) if and only if he either knows that the condition φ_c holds and can do δ_1, or knows that it does not hold and can do δ_2.[10]

Note that we eliminate Moore's requirement that the agent know who he is; instead, we require indexical knowledge. Thus, in the simple action case we require that the agent know what the action is, that he know that it is physically possible for *himself* to do it, and that he know that if *he himself* does it, the goal will necessarily hold afterwards. Mere *de re* knowledge is neither necessary nor sufficient for being able to achieve a goal; we discuss this further and give a concrete example in Section 4.2. Also, as discussed in Section 5, the fact that our account of ability is based on a more expressive temporal logic has important advantages when dealing with actions whose prerequisites or effects involve knowledge of absolute times and knowing what time it is.

3.7. Properties of the logic

In this subsection, we list some properties of the logic of *LIKA* that are used in the proofs of the robotics applications of the next section. We show that the logic indeed satisfies these properties in [29, 33], where we also discuss their significance.

The basis of our logic, that is, the part concerned with first-order logic with equality, is standard (the axiomatization in [39] can be used) with one exception: the "axiom" of specialization is restricted to prevent non-rigid terms from being substituted into modal contexts. This yields the following proposition:

Proposition 3.1 (Specialization). $\models \forall v \varphi \supset \varphi\{v \mapsto \theta\}$, *provided that θ is free for v in φ, no occurrence of a function symbol gets substituted into the scope of a **Know**, **At**, or **By** operator, no occurrence of **self** gets substituted into the scope of **Know** or **By**, and no occurrence of **now** gets substituted into the scope of **Know** or **At**.*

---

[10] This way of defining **Can** is preferable to the one in [29, 31] as it separates the knowledge prerequisites involving the goal from the rest; this makes it easier to prove results involving complex actions; see [33] for further discussion.

Knowledge obeys the following principles in our logic:

Proposition 3.2. $\models \mathbf{Know}(\varphi_1 \supset \varphi_2) \supset (\mathbf{Know}(\varphi_1) \supset \mathbf{Know}(\varphi_2))$.

Proposition 3.3. *If* $\models \varphi$, *then* $\models \mathbf{Know}(\varphi)$.

Proposition 3.4. $\models \mathbf{Know}(\varphi) \supset \varphi$.

Proposition 3.5. $\models \mathbf{Know}(\varphi) \supset \mathbf{Know}(\mathbf{Know}(\varphi))$.

Proposition 3.6. $\models \forall v\, \mathbf{Know}(\varphi) \supset \mathbf{Know}(\forall v \varphi)$.

Note that our handling of indexical knowledge affects how the above statements should be read. For instance, Proposition 3.5 says that if the agent knows that φ, then he knows that *he himself currently* knows that φ; $\forall a(\mathbf{Know}(a,\varphi) \supset \mathbf{Know}(a,\mathbf{Know}(a,\varphi)))$ is not valid.

We say that a formula φ is *future-blind* if and only if φ contains no occurrences of the **At** operator or the **Does** predicate outside the scope of a **Know** operator except in forms that can be represented as **SomePast** and **DoneWhen**. The following proposition says that a future-blind formula (i.e., one that does not talk about the future) is historically necessary if and only if it is true:

Proposition 3.7. $\models \Box \varphi \equiv \varphi$, *provided that* φ *is future-blind.*

Finally, we will need the following properties of **Can**:

Proposition 3.8. *If* $\models \varphi_i \supset \mathbf{Can}(\delta_2, \varphi_e)$, *then* $\models \mathbf{Can}(\delta_1, \varphi_i) \supset \mathbf{Can}((\delta_1; \delta_2), \varphi_e)$.

Proposition 3.9. $\models \mathbf{Can}(\delta, \varphi) \supset \mathbf{Can}(\delta, \mathbf{Know}(\varphi))$.

Proposition 3.10.

$$\models \mathbf{Can}(\mathbf{if}(\varphi_c, \delta_1, \delta_2), \varphi_g)$$
$$\equiv (\mathbf{Know}(\varphi_c) \wedge \mathbf{Can}(\delta_1, \varphi_g)) \vee (\mathbf{Know}(\neg\varphi_c) \wedge \mathbf{Can}(\delta_2, \varphi_g)).$$

4. Formalizing a simple robotics domain

In the previous section, we briefly reviewed a theory of indexical knowledge, action, and ability (described in detail in [33]). We claim that this theory forms an adequate framework for the formalization of actions involving indexical knowledge prerequisites or effects. Let us now substantiate this claim. We will formalize a robotics domain within the theory and prove that a robot is able to achieve certain goals by doing certain actions provided that he knows various facts. We will argue that our framework allows a much more accurate modeling of these cases than frameworks that ignore indexicality.

As will become clear, the framework we provide does not turn the formalization of actions that may have indexical knowledge prerequisites or effects into a trivial task. Many decisions must still be made in developing a formalization that have a crucial bearing on its adequacy from the point of view of how much and what kind of knowledge it requires from an agent; for example, decisions as to which parameters a procedure should take. What we provide on this front is some general advice on what to watch for, as well as the exemplary value of the situations that we formalize. Our central admonition in this respect is that *one should be careful not to impose excessive knowledge requirements upon agents in formalizing actions*; *in particular, one should merely require indexical knowledge, as opposed to objective knowledge, when that is sufficient.* Together with our formalization of the examples, we provide a discussion of how this guideline has been put into practice.

4.1. The domain

Our domain involves a robot, call him ROB, that moves about on a two-dimensional grid. Since our purpose is not to model situations where multiple agents interact, but to present and justify our account of indexical knowledge and action, our formalization will be based on the assumption that the robot is the only source of activity in the domain. We take our robot to have the following repertory of basic actions (primitives of his architecture): he may move forward by one square, he may turn right or left 90°, he may sense whether an object is on the square where he is currently positioned and if there is one, what shape it has, and he may pick up an object from the current square or put down the object he is holding on the current square. It should be clear that in spite of the simplicity of this domain, it contains analogs to a large number of problems faced by real robotic agents. For instance, one can view objects of particular shapes as landmarks and the robot can then navigate by recognizing such landmarks. We assume that there are no physical obstacles to the robot's movements; in particular, an object being on a square does not prevent the robot from being on it too (one can imagine the robot as standing over the object). Finally, note that the formalization does not model the uncertainty involved in predicting the effects of actions and acquiring knowledge by sensing; this limitation would have to be addressed for the framework to be applicable to real robotics problems.

4.2. Ability to manipulate an object

The indexicality of action manifests itself in many ways in this domain. One key way is that a robot can act upon (manipulate) an object if he knows where that object is *relative to himself*; he need not know either the object's absolute position or his own. First consider a simple instance of this where the robot wants to pick up an object and is actually positioned where that object is. Relevant aspects of the domain are formalized by making various assumptions,[11] most of which have to do with the types of action

---

[11] Assumptions are essentially non-logical axioms in a theory of a particular domain (they are not part of the logic proper). In reasoning within a theory, we only deal with semantic structures where the assumptions come out true. Note that due to this, assumptions not only hold at time **now**, but at all times, and it is common knowledge [18] that this is the case (i.e., everyone knows it, everyone knows that everyone knows it, and so on).

involved. The following assumption specifies the effects of the action PICKUP:

Assumption 4.1 (Effects of PICKUP).

$$\models \forall x(\text{OBJECT}(x) \land \text{POS}(x) = \textbf{here} \land \neg \exists y \, \text{HOLDING}(y)$$
$$\supset \textbf{Res}(\text{PICKUP}, \text{HOLDING}(x))).$$

Definition 4.2. $\textbf{here} \stackrel{\text{def}}{=} \text{POS}(\textbf{self})$

It says that if some object x is positioned where the agent currently is and he is not currently holding anything, then his doing the action PICKUP next will result in his holding x.[12]

This means that under these conditions, it is both physically possible for him to do PICKUP, and his doing so necessarily results in his holding the object. In fact, we assume that all basic actions are always possible. The view adopted is that such actions characterize essentially internal events which may have various external effects depending on the circumstances.[13] We also assume that agents always know how to do basic actions, that is, know what primitive actions they denote. This is formalized as follows:

Assumption 4.3 (Basic actions are known).

$$\models \exists d \, \textbf{Know}(d = \theta^{\text{d}}),$$

where $\theta^{\text{d}} \in \{\text{PICKUP}, \text{PUTDOWN}, \text{FORWARD}, \text{RIGHT}, \text{LEFT}, \text{SENSE}\}.$

We also make various frame assumptions for PICKUP (i.e., assumptions about what does not change as a result of the action). The following says that when the agent does PICKUP, the positions of all things must remain unchanged:

Assumption 4.4 (PICKUP does not affect POS).

$$\models \forall x \forall p (\text{POS}(x) = p \supset \textbf{AfterNec}(\text{PICKUP}, \text{POS}(x) = p)).$$

We also assume that PICKUP does not affect the orientation of anything and that unheld objects that are not where the agent is remain unheld after the action; these assumptions are specified analogously to the one above and we omit them here.

Now clearly, just having *de re* knowledge of some object is insufficient for being able to pick it up; something must be known about the object's position. Perhaps there are domains where as soon as an agent knows which object is involved, he would know

---

[12] Even though we are specifically talking about the agent and time of the context in the above, the attribution in fact applies to all agents and times, since it is assumed that the assertion is valid (i.e., satisfied at all indices), and it is a property of our logic that if $\models \varphi$, then $\models \forall a \forall t \textbf{By}(a, \textbf{At}(t, \varphi)))$. If several agents were involved, we might have to formalize the domain differently.

[13] For instance, Assumption 4.1 only specifies what happens when PICKUP is done under the conditions stated; what its effects are in other circumstances is not addressed.

how to get to it (or how to find out); in such a case, one might want to suppress all aspects of the process by which the agent determines the object's relative position and navigates to it, and thus one might develop a formalization where the formula in Proposition 4.5 turns out to be valid. However, this is clearly not the usual case; agents often fail to know where objects are. Our formalization reflects this; it models the situation at a level of detail sufficient to account for what agents need to know about the position of objects they want to manipulate. So the following proposition holds:

Proposition 4.5. $\not\models \exists x \mathbf{Know}(\text{OBJECT}(x)) \supset \mathbf{Can}(\text{PICKUP}, \exists x \text{ HOLDING}(x))$.

Proof. Consider a structure where $e, g \models \mathbf{Know}(\text{OBJECT}(x))$ but $e, g \not\models \mathbf{Know}(\exists x(\text{OBJECT}(x) \land \text{POS}(x) = \mathbf{here}))$, i.e., the agent the agent knows of some object, but does not know that this object is **here**, in fact, does not know that any object is **here**. Let there be an index e' be such that $\langle e, e' \rangle \in K$ and $e', g \models \mathbf{Does}(\text{PICKUP}, t) \land \neg\mathbf{At}(t, \exists x \text{ HOLDING}(x))$. This is consistent with Assumptions 4.1 and 4.3. It is easy to see that the above implies that $e, g \not\models \mathbf{Know}(\mathbf{AfterNec}(\text{PICKUP}, \exists x \text{ HOLDING}(x)))$ (using the fact that $\approx_t$ must be reflexive), i.e., the agent does not know that after he does PICKUP, he must be holding something. So the agent is not able to achieve the goal by doing PICKUP and the structure falsifies the formula. $\square$

In a discussion of the robot action of "putting a block on another block", Moore [41] recognizes that knowing what blocks are involved may not be enough and suggests that the action be defined in terms of lower-level actions involving arm motions to the objects' positions, grasping, and ungrasping. Now, knowledge of an object's absolute position is not sufficient for being able to act upon it (and nor is it necessary). One may not know what one's absolute position and orientation is and therefore may not be able to deduce where the object is relative to oneself. Our formalization reflects this fact. For instance, one can prove the following proposition with respect to the simple situation discussed earlier. It says that even if the agent is currently at some position p and knows that the absolute position of some object is p and that he is not holding anything, he still might not be able to achieve the goal of holding some object by doing the action PICKUP. The reason for this is simply that he may not know that he is at p.

Proposition 4.6.

$$\not\models \exists p(\mathbf{here} = p \land \mathbf{Know}(\exists x(\text{OBJECT}(x) \land \text{POS}(x) = p) \land \neg\exists y \text{ HOLDING}(y)))$$
$$\supset \mathbf{Can}(\text{PICKUP}, \exists x \text{ HOLDING}(x)).$$

The proof is similar to that of the previous proposition; it appears in [29].

On the other hand, we can also prove that if the agent knows that some object is *where he currently is* and that he is not holding anything, then he must be able to achieve the goal of holding some object by doing PICKUP:

Proposition 4.7.

$$\models \mathbf{Know}(\exists x (\text{OBJECT}(x) \wedge \text{POS}(x) = \mathbf{here}) \wedge \neg \exists y \, \text{HOLDING}(y))$$
$$\supset \mathbf{Can}(\text{PICKUP}, \exists x \, \text{HOLDING}(x)).$$

Proof. Suppose that the antecedent holds at e and g. By Assumption 4.3, we have that $e, g \models \exists d \, \mathbf{Know}(d = \text{PICKUP})$, i.e., the agent knows what the action is. By quantifier reasoning, Assumption 4.1 implies that

$$\models \exists x (\text{OBJECT}(x) \wedge \text{POS}(x) = \mathbf{here}) \wedge \neg \exists y \, \text{HOLDING}(y)$$
$$\supset \mathbf{PhyPoss}(\text{PICKUP}) \wedge \exists x \, \mathbf{AfterNec}(\text{PICKUP}, \text{HOLDING}(x)).$$

So by Propositions 3.3 and 3.2 and the supposition, it must be the case that $e, g \models \mathbf{Know}(\mathbf{PhyPoss}(\text{PICKUP}))$, i.e., the agent knows that the action is physically possible, as well as that $e, g \models \mathbf{Know}(\exists x \mathbf{AfterNec}(\text{PICKUP}, \text{HOLDING}(x)))$. It is straightforward to produce a semantic proof that $\models \exists v \mathbf{AfterNec}(\theta^d, \varphi) \supset \mathbf{AfterNec}(\theta^d, \exists v \varphi)$ (provided that v does not occur in θ^d). Thus by Propositions 3.3 and 3.2, it must be the case that $e, g \models \mathbf{Know}(\mathbf{AfterNec}(\text{PICKUP}, \exists x \text{HOLDING}(x)))$, i.e., the agent knows after doing the action, the goal must hold. Thus by the definition, $e, g \models \mathbf{Can}(\text{PICKUP}, \exists x \text{HOLDING}(x))$. $\square$

The agent can be totally ignorant of what his (and the object's) absolute position is and still be able to achieve the goal.

Note that Proposition 4.7 makes no requirement that the object that the agent ends up holding be the same as the one that was at his position before the action. This may appear too weak and an easy fix would involve assuming that the agent knows *which* object is involved. But it is possible to strengthen the above proposition without requiring such *de re* knowledge. For example, the following proposition captures the fact that the agent knows that after the action, he would be holding some object that was where he was before doing the action. Specifically, it says that if the agent knows that some object is currently at his position and that he is not currently holding anything, then he can by doing action PICKUP achieve the goal of holding some object that was at his own position before the PICKUP he has just done.

Proposition 4.8.

$$\models \mathbf{Know}(\exists x (\text{OBJECT}(x) \wedge \text{POS}(x) = \mathbf{here}) \wedge \neg \exists y \, \text{HOLDING}(y))$$
$$\supset \mathbf{Can}(\text{PICKUP}, \exists x (\text{HOLDING}(x) \wedge$$
$$\mathbf{DoneWhen}(\text{PICKUP}, \text{OBJECT}(x) \wedge \text{POS}(x) = \mathbf{here}))).$$

The proof is similar to that of Proposition 4.7; it appears in [29]. This result can be strengthened further to require uniqueness. But it should be clear that identifying the objects involved in the initial and goal situations, without requiring that it be known what objects they are, is not a trivial matter.

Before moving on, let's examine another variant of this situation. By the necessitation rule for **By** and universal generalization, an immediate consequence of Proposition 4.7 is that any agent who knows that there is an object where he himself is and that he is not holding anything must be able to achieve the goal of holding something by doing PICKUP, that is, $\models \forall a \mathbf{By}(a, \varphi_p)$, where φ_p is the formula of Proposition 4.7. However, if instead of this, an agent a merely knows that there is an object where a is, it no longer follows that he is able to achieve the goal.

Proposition 4.9.

$$\not\models \forall a \mathbf{By}(a, \mathbf{Know}(\exists x (\text{OBJECT}(x) \land \text{POS}(x) = \text{POS}(a)) \land \neg \exists y \, \text{HOLDING}(y))$$
$$\supset \mathbf{Can}(\text{PICKUP}, \exists x \, \text{HOLDING}(x))).$$

The reason why this is not valid is simply that a may not know that he is a. This shows that knowing of oneself (*de re*) that if one does the action, the goal will necessarily hold afterwards, as Moore's formalization of ability requires, is not sufficient for ability. One can similarly show that such *de re* knowledge is not necessary either (in some models of Proposition 4.7, the agent does not have such knowledge).

4.3. Going to a relative position

Let us now look at navigation. Since there are no obstacles in our robot's world, it seems that given any relative position, the robot should be able to go there. Let us show formally that this is the case. The effects of action FORWARD are specified as follows:

Assumption 4.10 (Effects of FORWARD).

$$\models \forall p \, \forall o (\mathbf{here} = p \land \mathbf{selfori} = o$$
$$\supset \mathbf{Res}(\text{FORWARD}, \mathbf{here} = p + \langle 1, 0 \rangle \times \text{ROT}(o))).$$

Definition 4.11. $\mathbf{selfori} \overset{\text{def}}{=} \text{ORI}(\mathbf{self})$.

Definition 4.12.

$$\text{ROT}(\theta_o^i) \overset{\text{def}}{=} \left\langle \begin{array}{cc} \cos \theta_o^i & \sin \theta_o^i \\ -\sin \theta_o^i & \cos \theta_o^i \end{array} \right\rangle.$$

Assumption 4.13. $\models \forall a (0 \leqslant \text{ORI}(a) < 2\pi)$.

Assumption 4.14. $\models \forall x (\text{HOLDING}(x) \supset \text{POS}(x) = \mathbf{here})$.

Assumption 4.10 says that as a result of doing FORWARD, the agent moves one square further along the direction he is facing; **selfori** represents the orientation of the agent with respect to the absolute frame of reference and $\text{ROT}(\theta_o^i)$ is the rotation matrix associated with angle θ_o^i. Assumption 4.14 says that objects held by the agent are where he is. We also need the following frame assumptions: that the agent's doing FORWARD, must leave his orientation unchanged (a formal version of this appears in Appendix A.1), that it must leave the position of objects that are not held by him unchanged; and that it has no effect on whether or not an object is being held.

Notice that we use expressions from the language of arithmetic and analytic geometry in formalizing this domain. We make the following assumptions regarding these forms:

Assumption 4.15. *All the constants and function symbols from arithmetic and analytic geometry used are rigid (i.e., have the same denotation at every index).*

Assumption 4.16. *All facts from arithmetic and analytic geometry are valid.*[14]

A consequence of Assumption 4.15 is that the restrictions on specialization do not apply for arithmetic or analytic geometry expressions:

Proposition 4.17. $\models \forall v \varphi \supset \varphi\{v \mapsto \theta\}$, *provided that θ is free for v in φ and all constants and function symbols θ contains are arithmetic or from analytic geometry.*

Finally, let us add a few more definitions:

Definition 4.18. $\text{RPOSToAPOS}(\theta_p^i) \overset{\text{def}}{=} (\mathbf{here} + \theta_p^i \times \text{ROT}(\mathbf{selfori}))$.

Definition 4.19. $\text{RORITOAORI}(\theta_o^i) \overset{\text{def}}{=} \text{MOD}_{2\pi}(\mathbf{selfori} + \theta_o^i)$.

Definition 4.20.

$$\text{MOVEDTOBY}(\theta_p^i, \theta_o^i, \delta)$$
$$\overset{\text{def}}{=} \exists v_p^i \exists v_o^i (\mathbf{DoneWhen}(\delta, v_p^i = \text{RPOSToAPOS}(\theta_p^i) \wedge v_o^i = \text{RORITOAORI}(\theta_o^i))$$
$$\wedge \mathbf{here} = v_p^i \wedge \mathbf{selfori} = v_o^i),$$

where v_p^i and v_o^i do not occur in θ_p^i, θ_o^i, or δ.

RPOSTOAPOS is a function that converts a relative position into an absolute one; similarly, RORITOAORI converts a relative orientation to an absolute one. MOVEDTOBY$(\theta_p^i, \theta_o^i, \delta)$ means that the agent has just done action δ and that by doing so, he has moved to the square that was at relative position θ_p^i (before the action) and has turned towards the direction that was relative orientation θ_o^i (before the action).

Now, let us discuss what these assumptions imply with respect to the ability of the robot to get to a given relative position. We start with a simple case: that the robot is able to go to the square directly in front of him (i.e., to relative position $\langle 1, 0 \rangle$) by doing FORWARD. In fact, the following proposition says something slightly stronger: that by doing FORWARD, one is able to achieve the goal of being on the square that was at relative position $\langle 1, 0 \rangle$ before the action and of having one's orientation remain unchanged.

---

[14] This is essentially a placeholder for an axiomatization of arithmetic and analytic geometry; there should be no problem coming up with one that gives us all the facts we need even though it would necessarily be incomplete.

Proposition 4.21. $\models \mathbf{Can}(\text{FORWARD}, \text{MOVEDTOBY}(\langle 1, 0 \rangle, 0, \text{FORWARD}))$.

A proof of this proposition is in Appendix A.1.

This result can then be extended to deal with squares arbitrarily far away along the row that the agent is facing (i.e., relative positions $\langle n, 0 \rangle$, where $n \in \mathbb{N}$). We can show that by doing FORWARD n times in sequence, one is able to achieve the goal of being on the square that was at relative position $\langle n, 0 \rangle$ before the action and of having one's orientation remain unchanged:

Proposition 4.22. *For all* $n \in \mathbb{N}$,

$$\models \mathbf{Can}(\text{FORWARD}^n, \text{MOVEDTOBY}(\langle n, 0 \rangle, 0, \text{FORWARD}^n)).$$

The proof is in Appendix A.2.

Now, let us look at the general case. The action of going to a relative position is defined below. The definition goes as follows: to go to relative position $\langle n, 0 \rangle$, where $n \in \mathbb{N}$, one simply goes forward n times; to go to relative position $\langle m, 0 \rangle$, where m is a negative integer, that is, to a position behind oneself, one turns left twice (i.e., 180°), then goes to relative position $\langle -m, 0 \rangle$, and then one turns left twice again, so as to return to one's original orientation; finally, to go to an arbitrary relative position $\langle n, m \rangle$, one first goes to $\langle n, 0 \rangle$, that is, to the right position on the x axis, then one turns left 90°, then one goes to $\langle m, 0 \rangle$, and then finally, one turns left three times (i.e., 270°) to return to the original orientation.

Definition 4.23.

$$\text{GORPOS}(\langle n, 0 \rangle) \stackrel{\text{def}}{=} \text{FORWARD}^n,$$

where $n \in \mathbb{N}$;

$$\text{GORPOS}(\langle m, 0 \rangle) \stackrel{\text{def}}{=} \text{LEFT}^2; \text{GORPOS}(\langle -m, 0 \rangle); \text{LEFT}^2,$$

where $m \in \mathbb{Z}$, $m < 0$;

$$\text{GORPOS}(\langle n, m \rangle) \stackrel{\text{def}}{=} \text{GORPOS}(\langle n, 0 \rangle); \text{LEFT}; \text{GORPOS}(\langle m, 0 \rangle); \text{LEFT}^3,$$

where $n, m \in \mathbb{Z}$, $m \neq 0$.

We also need provide a specification for the action of turning left. Its effects are formalized as follows:

Assumption 4.24 (Effects of LEFT).

$$\models \forall o(\mathbf{selfori} = o \supset \mathbf{Res}(\text{LEFT}, \mathbf{selfori} = \text{MOD}_{2\pi}(o + \tfrac{1}{2}\pi))).$$

This says that as a result of doing LEFT, the agent's orientation is rotated by 90°. We also make the frame assumptions that doing LEFT does not affect the position of anything nor whether any object is being held. Given this, it is straightforward to prove ability results for LEFT similar to the ones previously obtained for FORWARD. Let us only state our main result:

Proposition 4.25. *For all* $n \in \mathbb{N}$,

$$\models \mathbf{Can}(\mathrm{LEFT}^n, \mathrm{MOVEDToBY}(\langle 0,0 \rangle, \mathrm{MOD}_{2\pi}(\tfrac{1}{2}n\pi), \mathrm{LEFT}^n)).$$

This says that by doing LEFT n times in sequence, the agent is able to achieve the goal of having his orientation rotated by n times 90° to the left of what it was before the action and of having his position remain unchanged.

Then more generally, one can prove the following proposition about GORPOS; it says that one can, by doing $\mathrm{GORPOS}(\langle n, m \rangle)$, achieve the goal of being on the square that was at relative position $\langle n, m \rangle$ before the action and of having one's orientation remain unchanged:

Proposition 4.26. *For all* $n, m \in \mathbb{Z}$,

$$\models \mathbf{Can}(\mathrm{GORPOS}(\langle n, m \rangle), \mathrm{MOVEDToBY}(\langle n, m \rangle, 0, \mathrm{GORPOS}(\langle n, m \rangle))).$$

A proof of this proposition is in Appendix A.3.

Let us also point out that our formalization captures the fact that an agent need not be able to go to a given absolute position, for example, in a situation where he does not know where he is. The following proposition formalizes a simple instance of this; it states that the agent need not be able to go to absolute position p by doing FORWARD, even if p happens to be the position of the square directly in front of him.

Proposition 4.27. $\not\models \forall p(p = \mathrm{RPOSToAPOS}(\langle 1, 0 \rangle) \supset \mathbf{Can}(\mathrm{FORWARD}, \mathbf{here} = p)).$

A common reason for going somewhere is that one wants to get hold of or manipulate something that is there. It is straightforward to extend the results obtained so far and show that knowing the relative position of an object is sufficient for being able to go and manipulate it. Let $\mathrm{RPOS}(\theta^i)$ stand for the position of θ^i relative to **self**:

Definition 4.28. $\mathrm{RPOS}(\theta^i) \overset{\text{def}}{=} ((\mathrm{POS}(\theta^i) - \mathbf{here}) \times \mathrm{ROT}(-\mathbf{selfori})).$

In [29], we prove the following result:

Proposition 4.29. *For all* $n \in \mathbb{N}$,

$$\models \mathbf{Know}(\exists x(\mathrm{OBJECT}(x) \land \mathrm{RPOS}(x) = \langle n, 0 \rangle) \land \neg \exists y\, \mathrm{HOLDING}(y))$$
$$\supset \mathbf{Can}((\mathrm{FORWARD}^n; \mathrm{PICKUP}), \exists x\, \mathrm{HOLDING}(x)).$$

This says that if the robot knows that there is an object at position $\langle n, 0 \rangle$ relative to himself, that is, on the nth square directly in front of him, and knows that he is not holding anything, then he is able to achieve the goal of holding some object by doing

FORWARD n times followed by PICKUP. Note that this result requires the additional frame assumption that whether an entity is an object is not affected by any action. We omit details as no new techniques are required. It should be easy to generalize this result and show that by doing GORPOS($\langle n, m \rangle$) followed by PICKUP, the agent can come to hold something, provided that he knows that there is an object at relative position $\langle n, m \rangle$ and that he is not holding anything.

4.4. Perception

We will come back to this issue of what one *must* know in order to be able to go and manipulate an object, but now let's have a look at perception. As observed earlier, it too yields indexical knowledge.[15] In our domain, the action SENSE constitutes a limited form of perception. We formalize the effects of SENSE as follows:

Assumption 4.30.

$$\models \forall s \mathbf{Res}(\text{SENSE}, \mathbf{Kwhether}(\exists x(\text{OBJECT}(x) \land \text{POS}(x) = \mathbf{here} \land \\ \neg\text{HOLDING}(x) \land \text{OFSHAPE}(x, s))))).$$

This assumption says that doing SENSE results in the agent knowing whether an unheld object of a given shape is present at his current position (we are assuming that there can only be a single object resting on a square and that the robot's sensors are focussed on this object and not on any object that he might be holding). From this assumption and the fact that basic actions are assumed to be known, it follows trivially that by doing SENSE, the agent can find out whether there is an unheld object where he is and, if there is one, what its shape is.

We also make the following frame assumptions: that the agent's doing SENSE leaves his orientation and the positions of everything unchanged; that it does not change whether an object is held or not; and finally that no action affects the shape of objects.

4.5. Ability to go where an object is

Let's now go back to the issue of what one must know in order to be able to go and act upon an object. We said that knowing the relative position of the object was sufficient for this. But in real life, agents rarely know exactly what the relative positions of objects are. More typically, they know roughly where objects are and scan the general area until they find the object. The following proposition formalizes an instance of this; it says that by sensing and then scanning forward, up to k squares, until he senses that an unheld object is present, the robot can achieve the goal of either knowing that there is an unheld object where he is, or knowing that there are no unheld objects on the k squares behind him (including the one he is currently on). The SCAN$_k(\varphi)$ action involves repetitively moving forward and sensing (up to k times) until φ becomes true.

---

[15] Davis [10–12] has done interesting work on the topic of reasoning about knowledge and perception; however, he does not address the fact that the knowledge obtained from perception is indexical knowledge.

Definition 4.31. $\text{SCAN}_k(\varphi) \stackrel{\text{def}}{=} \textbf{while}_k(\neg\varphi, \text{FORWARD}; \text{SENSE})$.

Proposition 4.32. *For all $k \in \mathbb{N}$,*

$$\models \textbf{Can}((\text{SENSE}; \text{SCAN}_k(\exists x(\text{OBJECT}(x) \wedge \text{POS}(x) = \textbf{here} \wedge \neg\text{HOLDING}(x)))),$$
$$\textbf{Know}(\exists x(\text{OBJECT}(x) \wedge \text{POS}(x) = \textbf{here} \wedge \neg\text{HOLDING}(x))) \vee$$
$$\textbf{Know}(\neg\exists n(-k \leqslant n \leqslant 0 \wedge \exists x(\text{OBJECT}(x) \wedge \text{RPOS}(x) = \langle n, 0 \rangle \wedge \neg\text{HOLDING}(x))))).$$

Appendix A.4 contains a proof of this proposition.

So it is quite clear that ability to act upon an object does not require knowing its relative position. But then what is required? It seems that the best we can say is that the agent must *know of some procedure* that will take him to where the object is.

This creates problems in formalizing the knowledge prerequisites of certain high-level parametrized actions, for example, the action of "going to the position of an object θ" GOWHERE(θ). It would be inappropriate to treat this action as a primitive because we want to model how knowledge enables action at a more detailed level. The other way of dealing with such an action within our (and Moore's) framework involves defining it in terms of lower-level actions that are parametrized with the information that must actually be known in order to be able to do the high-level action. This allows knowledge prerequisites to be enforced by the requirement that one know which primitive action to do next. But for actions like GOWHERE(θ), it is not clear how this can be put into practice.

However, notice that GOWHERE(θ) is a strange kind of action, in that it appears to refer to anything that would achieve the goal that the agent be where θ is; it behaves as much as a *goal* as like an action. Perhaps we should rule out the introduction of such actions, but instead provide an action-less version of the **Can** operator: **CanAch**(φ) would mean that **self** is somehow able to achieve φ. Then, we may use **CanAch**(POS(θ) = **here** $\wedge \varphi$) instead of something like **Can**(GOWHERE(θ), φ).[16] A coarse "syntactic" way of formalizing **CanAch** goes as follows: e, g $\models$ **CanAch**(φ) iff there exists an action expression δ such that e, g $\models$ **Can**(δ, φ). A more general and robust approach is proposed in [34].

4.6. Map navigation

A general account of ability must be based on a formalism that handles both indexical knowledge and objective knowledge, as well as knowledge that relates the agent's perspective to the objective frame of reference, what we might call *orienting knowledge*. To see why this is the case, let us look at one last area of robotics, that of navigation with the help of a map. Maps (of the usual kind) contain objective information. To use this information, say to figure out how to get to a destination, an agent must first orient himself—find out where he is on the map, that is, what his absolute position is, and find out what his absolute orientation is. If he does not already have this information,

---

[16] This assumes that it is known that θ refers to the same entity before and after the action; the assumption can be dispensed with by referring to the denotation of θ prior to the action as illustrated in Section 4.2.

he might try to obtain it by searching his environment for landmarks represented on the map.

Our simple domain provides instances of this if we treat objects of various shapes as landmarks. Consider a variant of the scanning example of the previous section, where the robot knows what the absolute position of the unique object of shape s is (from having examined the map); then by scanning forward, the robot should be able to get into a state where he either knows where he is, or knows that the object is not in the region scanned. The following proposition shows that this is essentially correct. It says that if the robot knows that the unique object with shape s is at absolute position p and that it is not held, then by sensing and then scanning forward, up to k squares, until he senses that an unheld object with shape s is present, he can achieve the goal of either knowing that he is at absolute position p (i.e., knowing where he is), or knowing that the unheld object of shape s is on none of the k squares behind him (including the one he is currently on).

Proposition 4.33. *For all $k \in \mathbb{N}$,*

$$
\begin{aligned}
\models \forall p \forall s (\mathbf{Know}(\exists x (\text{OBJECT}(x) \land \text{POS}(x) = p \land \neg \text{HOLDING}(x) \land \\
\forall y (\text{OFSHAPE}(y, s) \equiv y = x))) \supset \\
\mathbf{Can}((\text{SENSE}; \text{SCAN}_k(\exists x (\text{OBJECT}(x) \land \text{POS}(x) = \text{here} \land \neg \text{HOLDING}(x) \land \text{OFSHAPE}(x, s)))), \\
\mathbf{Know}(\text{here} = p) \lor \\
\mathbf{Know}(\neg \exists n (-k \leqslant n \leqslant 0 \land \exists x (\text{OBJECT}(x) \land \text{RPOS}(x) = \langle n, 0 \rangle \land \neg \text{HOLDING}(x) \\
\land \text{OFSHAPE}(x, s)))))).
\end{aligned}
$$

The proof is omitted as it is similar to that of Proposition 4.32; a compete proof of a closely related result appears in [29].

Similarly, an agent might find out what its absolute orientation is by searching for a pair of landmarks whose orientation relative to one another is indicated on the map, or perhaps by searching for a single landmark whose faces have distinctive shapes that are represented on the map. Once the agent has found out where he is and what his orientation is, he will know which relative position corresponds to any absolute position; he can then use the information in the map to figure out how to go where he wants. [17] Orienting knowledge, that is, knowledge about how indexical notions are related to objective notions, allows objective knowledge to be mapped into indexical knowledge and vice versa. It is a key feature of our formalism that it allows all these kinds of knowledge to be represented.

5. Other applications

The notion of indexical knowledge and the important role it plays in action are most easily understood by looking at robotics examples as we did in the previous section. These involve actions taking place in physical space; the agent has knowledge that is relative to his point of view in physical space. This might suggest that the notion is bound to that of physical space. But this is not the case; the notion is really rather

---

[17] Many of these characteristics of the map navigation problem were pointed out by Israel [22].

abstract. It is useful as long as the domain involves agents that operate in some kind of space, from some kind of point of view into that space.

In [29], two non-robotics domains that involve very abstract notions of space are examined. The first involves an agent making a phone call. The phone system is naturally viewed as a kind of space structured into various kinds of regions and sub-regions. An agent can be quite ignorant of what characterizes his absolute position in that space, things like area code, country code, etc. This domain was formalized and it was proven that an agent is able to establish a connection to some phone if he knows what its number is and either knows that it is in his own area, or knows that it is not and knows what the phone's area code is (international and same-area long distance calls were ignored).

The other domain examined is that of data structure search and manipulation. At first, it might seem strange to look at this in terms of an agent located in some kind of space and having knowledge that is relative to his point of view into that space, yet this seems very much the outlook taken by many algorithms; one talks about following pointers and searching graphs. An example involving the heapsort algorithm [4] was partly formalized. We sketched a proof of the fact that an agent is able to heapify a tree consisting of a new node installed as root of two existing heaps by sifting the new node down the tree until its key is at least as large as that if its sons. [18] Note that the "space" involved in this example has a very different topology from that of physical space.

There is as much of a need for keeping track of one's place in time as of one's place in space. In the spatial examples of Section 4, we described cases where the agent is required to know his absolute position, other cases where he need only know where something is relative to himself, that is, know its relative position, and still other cases where neither kind of knowledge is needed—the agent needs only know a navigation procedure that gets him where he wants. The same kind of distinctions apply to situations where temporal knowledge is required for ability. Depending on the case, the agent might need to:

(1) *know what time it is*, e.g., an agent that needs to lock up a room at a specific time, say 5 p.m., and does so by checking a clock until the time comes,

(2) *know how much time some process needs to go on*, e.g., an agent who soft-boils an egg (i.e., cooks it without having the yolk solidify) using a timer,

(3) *monitor the environment for a condition indicating that a process has gone on long enough*, e.g., an agent who wants to fry a fish filet without overcooking it and who achieves this by frying it until its flesh is no longer translucent.

In [29], a formalization of the first two examples is sketched. The third example does not require time to be explicitly represented; it can be formalized much like the scanning example of Section 4.5. In [32], we also formalize an example of a common temporal reasoning/planning problem that can only be handled in a formalism that includes both indexical and non-indexical concepts and supports reasoning using both. The example involves an agent that does not initially know what time it is; he must keep track of time in relative terms (using a timer), but later convert this indexical knowledge into absolute

---

[18] A heap is a binary tree that satisfies the "heap property", that is, where the key stored at any node is greater or equal to the ones stored at its left and right sons (if they exist).

knowledge (by finding out what time it is) for communication to another agent. [19] It was found that the framework proposed provides the necessary tools for producing a satisfactory formalization in every one of these cases.

6. The need for distinguishing between indexical and objective knowledge

To someone accustomed to the objective point of view of science or mathematics, indexicality (context-sensitivity) may appear as little more than an artifact of natural language. One may thus claim that while using indexical descriptions is often convenient, in practice, indexical knowledge can always be understood objectively. One reason for wishing that this claim were true has to do with the fact that the semantic content of indexical representations depends on the context, so if the context changes you may have to adjust the representations to keep the semantic content unchanged. For instance, if an agent's knowledge base describes some facts as holding "now", then at the next time step, it should describe these facts as holding "one time step before now". [20] Haas [17] points out that the cost of adjusting a knowledge base that contains indexical time references for the passage of time would be high, if implemented in the obvious way. He proposes that a robot use its internal clock to eliminate all occurrences of "now" in its representations.

Let us discuss the claim that indexical knowledge can be reduced to objective knowledge. In our semantics for knowledge, indexical terms and formulas are treated as relative to an agent and a time; for example, knowing that something is **here** amounts to knowing that something is at one's position at the current time. Given this, it is clear that if one knows who one is and knows what time it is (remember that we are taking *de re* knowledge to require knowing a standard name), then anything that one knows in an indexical way is also known in an objective way. [21] But is it reasonable to assume that an agent always knows who he is and what time it is?

Let's consider the temporal part of this question (see [32] for a more detailed discussion). First, humans do not have internal clocks that they can use in the way a robot can, and they do not always know what time it is. A system that is interacting with humans will need to model this (e.g. to remind a user that his meeting is just starting). Even if we limit ourselves to simple robotics contexts, it seems unlikely that the internal clocks of robots could be guaranteed to be accurate. In such cases, Haas's

---

[19] Specifically, the agent has to set a turkey to roast in the oven and leave a message saying when the turkey started roasting, so that someone else can take it out when it is ready. But the agent (who sets the turkey to roast) does not initially know what time it is and only has access to the one-hour timer on the stove and a radio station that announces the time at least every 30 minutes. The plan we consider involves putting the turkey in the oven, setting the timer to one hour, then listening to the radio until the time is announced while keeping track of the roasting time with the timer, and finally calculating the time the turkey started roasting, and leaving a message to that effect.

[20] Subramanian and Woodfill [52] prove that such a transformation is truth-preserving within their indexical situation calculus framework.

[21] E.g., if at 10 a.m. Dec. 8, 1991, Rob the robot knows that there is currently a pop can one meter in front of him, and also knows who he is and what time it is, then he must know of Rob and of 10 a.m. Dec. 8, 1991 that there is a pop can one meter in front of that person at that time (*de re*).

scheme leads to indexical information being misrepresented. Moreover, Haas's robot cannot even represent the fact that his internal clock is incorrect; it could not monitor for this and plan to get its clock reset when appropriate. Also, for very simple (e.g. insect-like) robots, the cost of fitting them with internal clocks and setting them may be too high. Finally, as Haas recognizes, it is not at all clear that the cost of updating a temporal knowledge base that contains indexicals need be prohibitive; for example, if all occurrences of "now" are replaced by a new constant and the fact that this new constant is equal to "now" is added, then only this single assertion need be updated as time passes.

Work on reactive agent architectures supplies other reasons for wanting a formalism that can represent indexical knowledge. As pointed out by Agre and Chapman [2], the world can change in unexpected ways and reasoning about change can be very costly; in some cases it is better to rely on perception to get fresh information at every time step rather than try to update a representation of the world; in such cases, the problem of updating indexical representations does not arise. And as Rosenschein and Kaelbling [48] have shown, it is legitimate to ascribe knowledge to agents even when they have no explicit representation of this knowledge. In such cases, one needs a formalism that distinguishes between indexical and objective knowledge just to accurately model the agent's thinking. The output of the agent's perception module says nothing about time, and even if the agent has a correct internal clock, he may have no need to time-stamp his knowledge. We want a formalism that makes the distinctions required to model this.

Let us briefly discuss the other half of the above question, that is, whether agents need always know who they are (know a standard name for themselves). It is tempting to dismiss the usual amnesia examples as mere philosophical curiosities. But if we think of very simple agents, say insects; it would not seem all that unusual to have them not know who they are; in fact, one is hard pressed to come up with good reasons for them to need to know who they are. One can also imagine mass produced computers or robots that do not have their name etched in memory at the factory or even entered at boot-time. One might also look at processes running in a computer as agents. Grove [14] and Grove and Halpern [15] describe cases in the area of distributed systems and communication protocols where one does not want to assume that agents know who they are. One of their examples involves a set of processes that are running a leader-election protocol (to select one of them to play some special role later on); the processes are anonymous, they do not have any unique identifier as part of their state and they are all running the same program; they do not know who they are.

7. Conclusion

Agents act upon and perceive the world from a particular perspective. It is important to recognize this relativity to perspective if one is not to be overly demanding in specifying what they need to know in order to be able to achieve goals through action. In many cases (especially simple interactions with their physical environment) they need not know much about their objective situation; what they need is *indexical knowledge*, knowledge about how they are related to things in their environment or to events in their history. And perception yields just the kind of indexical knowledge that is needed.

Previous formal accounts of the ability of agents to achieve goals by doing actions, such as that of Moore [40,41] and Morgenstern [42,43], have ignored this, and thus end up imposing knowledge requirements that are neither necessary nor sufficient for ability; they fail to properly specify the knowledge prerequisites and effects of actions. In this work, we have developed a formal solution to the problem of how one should model the indexical knowledge prerequisites and effects of action. We have also shown how the theory can be used to formalize several common types of interaction between a robot and its environment.

7.1. Contributions

Let us review the ways in which our theory improves over previous accounts of the relationship between knowledge and action. Our account of knowledge formally captures the distinction between indexical and objective knowledge: it allows an agent to know something in an indexical way without knowing it in any kind of objective way and vice-versa. Knowledge about how objective notions are related to indexical notions can be expressed, thus allowing objective knowledge to be mapped into indexical knowledge and vice-versa. Also, the account fully handles time, in particular, temporally indexical knowledge. Its simple modal syntax provides succinct ways of expressing most matters of interest, in particular, attributions of indexical knowledge. Its model-theoretic semantics is a simple and natural extension of standard possible-world semantic schemes for the logic of knowledge. It retains what is perhaps the most attractive feature of possible-world semantics: the correspondence between constraints on the accessibility relation and important properties of the notion formalized. On the other hand, it also inherits some limitations of the possible-world approach, in particular, the "logical omniscience" problem (i.e., agents are taken to know all the logical consequences of their knowledge, as well as all validities). Finally, our account includes a formalization of the requirement that knowledge be persistent that works well with both temporally indexical and temporally absolute knowledge.

The temporal subset of our logic is simple and very expressive. Both objective and indexical temporal assertions can be made. Relations between indexically specified and objectively specified times can also be expressed. The fact that terms denoting times are included allows quantification over times into epistemic contexts, so one can make very weak ascriptions of temporal knowledge; for example, one can express the claim that John knows that Paul knows what time it is without John himself knowing it with the formula $\mathbf{Know}(\text{JOHN}, \exists t \mathbf{Know}(\text{PAUL}, \mathbf{now} = t))$. The occurrence of concurrent actions, continuous processes, and actions involving several agents can be expressed (even though our account of ability does not deal with these cases). There is one significant limitation: one cannot express the occurrence of actions involving indefinite iteration (unbounded while-loops). More generally, our account of the logic is limited by the fact that we have not identified a full axiomatization (even though the set of properties identified in [29,33] is an important step in that direction); in fact, we do not know whether the set of valid formulas is recursively enumerable.

Our formalization of ability improves over previous accounts in several ways. Firstly, it does not require an agent to know who he is in order to be able to achieve a goal by doing an action; all references to the agent within the knowledge required are indexical references. For instance, in the simple action case we require the agent to know that it is physically possible for *himself* to do the action and that if *he himself* does the action, the goal will necessarily hold afterwards (as well as knowing what the action is). *De re* knowledge of oneself is neither necessary nor sufficient for the agent to be able to achieve the goal (a concrete example was given in Section 4.2). Situations where an agent does not know who he is (in the sense of not knowing an objective standard name for himself) are perhaps unusual, but our theory could not claim to reflect a real understanding of indexicality if it did not deal with such cases.

Secondly, our account of ability is based on a very expressive temporal logic. We can thus handle prerequisites or effects of actions that involve knowledge of absolute times and knowing what time it is, as well as many cases of actions that refer to times (e.g., the action of "locking up at 5 p.m.", discussed in Section 5). This would also make it easier to extend the account to handle more complex actions than are currently treated, for instance concurrent actions, actions involving several agents, and actions that refer to time in very general ways.

Finally, the logic on which the account of ability is based includes an adequate treatment of indexical knowledge in general; as the applications in Sections 4 and 5 show, this allows a more accurate specification of the knowledge prerequisites and effects of actions.

On the other hand, our account of ability suffers from various limitations. The class of actions handled is quite restricted. Moreover, the notion modeled is extremely idealized: it requires that the action absolutely guarantee that the goal will be achieved—a high probability of success is not enough.

We have shown how the framework can be used to model various common types of interaction between a robot and its environment. These examples show how actions can be formalized so as to avoid making excessive requirements upon the knowledge of agents—so that only indexical knowledge, as opposed to objective knowledge, is required when that is sufficient. Our formalization accounts for the facts that perception yields indexical knowledge, and that ability to act upon an object does not require knowing which object is involved or what its absolute position is. It was also shown how indexical knowledge and objective knowledge can be related in the framework, to deal with the use of maps for navigation. Many representational issues that have general relevance to the formalization of actions with indexical knowledge prerequisites or effects were discussed. Applications of the theory in other domains, in particular, ones that involve temporal knowledge, were also briefly discussed. These applications provide evidence to that effect that the distinction between indexical and objective knowledge supported by our framework has substantial practical value and that it cannot be done justice within existing accounts of ability.

7.2. Directions for future research

A major difficulty in producing a usable framework for reasoning about action is the frame problem, that is, providing a way of specifying actions that does not require enumerating all properties that are not affected by them. Recently, Reiter [47] has proposed a solution to the frame problem within the situation calculus and Scherl and Levesque [49] have extended this solution to deal with knowledge and knowledge-producing actions. The approach allows a form of regression to be used to reduce reasoning about what facts hold in a situation to reasoning about what facts held in an initial situation. We are currently reformulating our framework into an extended version of the situation calculus so as to incorporate this approach to the frame problem [50].

As mentioned earlier, our formalization of ability has many limitations. It should be extended to handle more complex types of actions, such as those involving indefinite iteration, nondeterminism, and concurrency, as well as plans involving multiple agents. Morgenstern [42, 43] as well as our recent work [34] handle some of these cases, but these accounts do not deal with indexicality. Situations involving interacting agents are especially interesting from the indexicality point of view, since the difference in perspective between agents must be accounted for if they are to have indexical knowledge of the same facts. For example, imagine that we are cooperating in the dismantling of a motor, and are facing each other; suppose we need to jointly use a certain wrench in the next step; I might have to come to know that the wrench we are to use is the one on my left while you need to realize that it is the one on your right. However, multiple agents settings give rise to new difficulties for reasoning about change. One issue is whether agents know about all event occurrences that could affect their situation and if not, what assumptions they make about such events. Morgenstern [44] has proposed an approach to deal with this. Another issue connected to indexicality is the question of how agents refer to each other. In many cases, agents know of each other only under some indexical description (e.g., "the person in front of me now"); it would be inappropriate to assume that agents always know who all the agents involved are. The formalization proposed in [30] deals with this.

It would also be desirable to untangle various aspects of the notion of ability—distinguish between "being able to achieve a goal" and "knowing how to execute an action", between cases where the agent is aware of his ability and cases where he is not, between cases where the agent acts as a dumb interpreter of a program and cases where he does some optimization, etc. We are currently working on a formalization that deals with these distinctions, handles indefinite iteration and non-determinism, and is compatible with the approach to the frame problem mentioned earlier [34]. As well, the formalization of Section 3.6 requires that it be known that performing the action absolutely guarantees that the goal will be achieved. Yet, in most real situations, agents cannot hope to attain such a degree of certainty. It would be desirable to come up with an account that can cope with this. Both default and probabilistic approaches should looked at.

It would also be desirable to have a mathematically satisfactory axiomatization of the logic—one that is complete, if this is achievable. This might require a re-examination of some aspects of the logic.

Another issue that should be investigated is the interaction between indexicality and hierarchical plans. It seems that the top level actions in such a plan would usually be specified in a relatively objective way (e.g., go to City Hall), while the lower level actions would be indexically specified (e.g., turn right at the next light). How do the different levels in such a plan relate to each other? Route planning should be a good test domain.

Indexicality is but one aspect of situatedness. One should look at how other aspects can be modeled. For instance, Barwise [5] talks about how "situated inference" is often relative to background conditions; as an example, he describes how one might infer that an object will fall from the fact that it has been released in mid-air, an inference that is relative to the presence of gravity. In many cases, such background conditions play a role in ensuring that an agent's doing some action will achieve his goal, but the agent is totally unaware of it, or he simply ignores it because these conditions normally hold in his usual environment. It should be possible to extend our account to model this notion of "ability relative to background conditions". More challenging would be developing a propositional attitude model of the kind of opportunistic acting/planning that Agre and Chapman describe in [3], but not obviously beyond current techniques.

The theory holds great potential for applications in the modeling of communication (both natural-language and that involving artificial agents exchanging messages in designed languages), especially in conjunction with the extensions mentioned earlier. We have seen that the knowledge required for many types of action is indexical. Thus while many uses of indexical expressions in language are only communicative shortcuts, ways of succinctly referring to the relevant entities, it should not be surprising that there are also cases where the information that needs to be communicated is intrinsically indexical. For example, I can help you get to my place by telling you where it is *relative to your current position*. To model this, one needs a formal account of communication that relates the context sensitivity of language to that of mental states and action.[22] In [30], a preliminary version of such an account is developed, using our theory of indexical knowledge and action as a foundation. Some recent work [54] has focussed on providing agents that interact with the world with the ability to understand natural language instructions; this would be an ideal setting for exploring concrete applications of such an account.

Last but not least, the theory would appear to hold much promise for applications in the design of reactive agents. Rosenschein and Kaelbling [24, 48] use a logical formalism as a design notation and as a specification language in their robot design framework. Since indexical knowledge appears to be centrally involved in the production of reactive behavior [2, 52], it seems that elements of our logic could prove useful in these roles. It might even be useful as a representation language for a planner or

---

[22] No existing model of natural language use does this. Some, like Cohen and Levesque's [9], include sophisticated accounts of how the knowledge and intentions of agents are involved in speech acts, but ignore indexicality, in both utterances and mental attitudes. Others, such as Barwise and Perry's [6], include elaborate treatments of indexicality, but do not provide any kind of computational account of how an agent can draw inferences from his prior knowledge and the indexical representations that result from interpreting an utterance.

sophisticated executor. This kind of application might also yield back some insights into indexicality and suggest refinements to our theory.

Appendix A. Additional proofs

A.1. Proof of Proposition 4.21

First, let us formally state one of the frame assumptions for FORWARD mentioned in Section 4.3:

Assumption A.1 (FORWARD does not affect **selfori**).

$$\models \forall o(\textbf{selfori} = o \supset \textbf{AfterNec}(\text{FORWARD}, \textbf{selfori} = o)).$$

We prove Proposition 4.21 by first showing a more general result, Lemma A.3 below. The following lemma is used in its proof.

Lemma A.2.

$$\models \forall p \forall o(\text{MOVEDTOBY}(p, o, \delta) \supset$$
$$\textbf{AfterNec}(\text{FORWARD}, \text{MOVEDTOBY}(p + \langle 1, 0 \rangle \times \text{ROT}(o),$$
$$o, (\delta; \text{FORWARD})))).$$

Proof.

(1) Take arbitrary $e = \langle w, a, t \rangle$ and g. Assume that $e, g \models \text{MOVEDTOBY}(p, o, \delta)$.

(2) Take arbitrary w^* and t_e such that $w \approx_t w^*$ and $t \preceq t_e$. Let $e^* = \langle w^*, a, t \rangle$ and $e_e^* = \langle w^*, a, t_e \rangle$. Assume that $\Delta(\llbracket \text{FORWARD} \rrbracket_{e^*, g}, e^*, t_e)$.

(3) By Proposition 3.7, (1) implies that $e^*, g \models \text{MOVEDTOBY}(p, o, \delta)$.

(4) By this and (2), it follows that there exists t_s such that

$$\langle w^*, a, t_s \rangle, g\{t_e \to t_e\} \models \textbf{Does}((\delta; \text{FORWARD}), t_e).$$

Let $e_s^* = \langle w^*, a, t_s \rangle$. We must now show that $\llbracket \textbf{selfori} \rrbracket_{e_e^*, g} = \llbracket \text{RORITOAORI}(o) \rrbracket_{e_s^*, g}$ and

$$\llbracket \textbf{here} \rrbracket_{e_e^*, g} = \llbracket \text{RPOSTOAPOS}(p + \langle 1, 0 \rangle \times \text{ROT}(o)) \rrbracket_{e_s^*, g}.$$

(5) By Assumption A.1 and the reflexivity of $\approx_t$ (constraint (4) in Section 3.4), we must have that $\llbracket \textbf{selfori} \rrbracket_{e_e^*, g} = \llbracket \textbf{selfori} \rrbracket_{e^*, g}$. By (3), we have that $\llbracket \textbf{selfori} \rrbracket_{e^*, g} = \llbracket \text{RORITOAORI}(o) \rrbracket_{e_s^*, g}$. So it must be the case that $\llbracket \textbf{selfori} \rrbracket_{e_e^*, g} = \llbracket \text{RORITOAORI}(o) \rrbracket_{e_s^*, g}$.

(6) By Assumption 4.10 and the reflexivity of $\approx_t$, we have that

$$\llbracket \textbf{here} \rrbracket_{e_e^*, g} = \llbracket \textbf{here} \rrbracket_{e^*, g} + \langle 1, 0 \rangle \times \text{ROT}(\llbracket \textbf{selfori} \rrbracket_{e^*, g}).$$

By (3), we have that $\llbracket \textbf{here} \rrbracket_{e^*, g} = \llbracket \text{RPOSTOAPOS}(p) \rrbracket_{e_s^*, g}$, which implies that

$$\llbracket \textbf{here} \rrbracket_{e_e^*, g} = \llbracket \text{RPOSTOAPOS}(p) \rrbracket_{e_s^*, g} + (\langle 1, 0 \rangle \times \text{ROT}(\llbracket \textbf{selfori} \rrbracket_{e^*, g})).$$

By (5) we then get that

$$[\![\mathbf{here}]\!]_{e^*_e,g} = [\![\mathrm{RPOSTOAPOS}(p)]\!]_{e^*_s,g} + (\langle 1,0\rangle \times \mathrm{ROT}([\![\mathrm{RORITOAORI}(o)]\!]_{e^*_s,g})).$$

By the definitions of RPOSTOAPOS and RORITOAORI, this means that

$$[\![\mathbf{here}]\!]_{e^*_e,g} = [\![(\mathbf{here} + p \times \mathrm{ROT}(\mathbf{selfori}))$$
$$+ \langle 1,0\rangle \times \mathrm{ROT}(\mathrm{MOD}_{2\pi}(\mathbf{selfori} + o))]\!]_{e^*_s,g}.$$

Thus

$$[\![\mathbf{here}]\!]_{e^*_e,g} = [\![\mathbf{here} + (p + \langle 1,0\rangle \times \mathrm{ROT}(o)) \times \mathrm{ROT}(\mathbf{selfori})]\!]_{e^*_s,g}$$
$$= [\![\mathrm{RPOSTOAPOS}(p + \langle 1,0\rangle \times \mathrm{ROT}(o))]\!]_{e^*_s,g}.$$

(7) From (4), (5) and (6), it follows that

$$e^*_e,g \models \mathrm{MOVEDTOBY}(p + \langle 1,0\rangle \times \mathrm{ROT}(o), o, (\delta; \mathrm{FORWARD})).$$

Since w^* and t_e are arbitrary, this together with (2) implies that

$$e,g \models \mathbf{AfterNec}(\mathrm{FORWARD},$$
$$\mathrm{MOVEDTOBY}(p + \langle 1,0\rangle \times \mathrm{ROT}(o), o, (\delta; \mathrm{FORWARD}))). \qquad \square$$

Lemma A.3.

$$\models \forall p \forall o (\mathbf{Know}(\mathrm{MOVEDTOBY}(p, o, \delta))$$
$$\supset \mathbf{Can}(\mathrm{FORWARD}, \mathrm{MOVEDTOBY}(p + \langle 1,0\rangle \times \mathrm{ROT}(o),$$
$$o, (\delta; \mathrm{FORWARD})))).$$

Proof. Let $\varphi \stackrel{\mathrm{def}}{=} \mathrm{MOVEDTOBY}(p, o, \delta)$ and

$$\varphi' \stackrel{\mathrm{def}}{=} \mathrm{MOVEDTOBY}(p + \langle 1,0\rangle \times \mathrm{ROT}(o), o, (\delta; \mathrm{FORWARD})).$$

Take arbitrary e and g. Suppose that $e,g \models \mathbf{Know}(\varphi)$. We must show that $e,g \models \mathbf{Can}(\mathrm{FORWARD}, \varphi')$. By Assumption 4.3, we must have that $e,g \models \exists d\,\mathbf{Know}(d = \mathrm{FORWARD})$. It is easy to show that Assumption 4.10 implies that $\models \mathbf{PhyPoss}(\mathrm{FORWARD})$. Thus by Proposition 3.3, $\models \mathbf{Know}(\mathbf{PhyPoss}(\mathrm{FORWARD}))$. By Propositions 3.3 and 3.2, Lemma A.2 implies that $\models \mathbf{Know}(\varphi) \supset \mathbf{Know}(\mathbf{AfterNec}(\mathrm{FORWARD}, \varphi'))$. By the above supposition, this implies that $e,g \models \mathbf{Know}(\mathbf{AfterNec}(\mathrm{FORWARD}, \varphi'))$. $\square$

Let us now proceed with the proof of Proposition 4.21 proper. It is easy to show that $\models \mathrm{MOVEDTOBY}(\langle 0,0\rangle, 0, \mathbf{noOp})$. By Proposition 3.3, we must then also have that $\models \mathbf{Know}(\mathrm{MOVEDTOBY}(\langle 0,0\rangle, 0, \mathbf{noOp}))$. Thus, by Lemma A.3, we have that

$$\models \mathbf{Can}(\mathrm{FORWARD},$$
$$\mathrm{MOVEDTOBY}(\langle 0,0\rangle + \langle 1,0\rangle \times \mathrm{ROT}(0), 0, (\mathbf{noOp}; \mathrm{FORWARD}))).$$

Since $\models \mathbf{Does}((\mathbf{noOp}; \delta), \theta^t) \equiv \mathbf{Does}(\delta, \theta^t)$, the desired result follows by Proposition 4.17 and Assumption 4.16. $\square$

A.2. Proof of Proposition 4.22

As for Proposition 4.21, we proceed by first showing a more general result:

Lemma A.4. *For all* $n \in \mathbb{N}$,

$$\models \forall p \forall o (\textbf{Know}(\text{MOVEDTOBY}(p, o, \delta))$$
$$\supset \textbf{Can}(\text{FORWARD}^n, \text{MOVEDTOBY}(p + \langle n, 0 \rangle \times \text{ROT}(o),$$
$$o, (\delta; \text{FORWARD}^n)))).$$

Proof. By induction over n.

Base case: $n = 0$. In this case we only need to show that

$$\models \forall p \forall o (\textbf{Know}(\text{MOVEDTOBY}(p, o, \delta))$$
$$\supset \textbf{Know}(\text{MOVEDTOBY}(p + \langle 0, 0 \rangle \times \text{ROT}(o), o, (\delta; \textbf{noOp})))).$$

It is easy to show that $\models \textbf{Does}((\delta; \textbf{noOp}), \theta^t) \equiv \textbf{Does}(\delta, \theta^t)$. This together with Proposition 4.17 and Assumption 4.16 implies that

$$\models \text{MOVEDTOBY}(p + \langle 0, 0 \rangle \times \text{ROT}(o), o, (\delta; \textbf{noOp})) \equiv \text{MOVEDTOBY}(p, o, \delta).$$

From this, the desired result follows easily by Propositions 3.3 and 3.2.

Induction step: Assume that the formula is valid for n and show that it must then be valid for $n + 1$. By the induction hypothesis and Proposition 4.17, we have that

$$\models \textbf{Know}(\text{MOVEDTOBY}(p + \langle 1, 0 \rangle \times \text{ROT}(o), o, (\delta; \text{FORWARD})))$$
$$\supset \textbf{Can}(\text{FORWARD}^n, \text{MOVEDTOBY}(p + \langle 1, 0 \rangle \times \text{ROT}(o) + \langle n, 0 \rangle \times \text{ROT}(o),$$
$$o, ((\delta; \text{FORWARD}); \text{FORWARD}^n))).$$

It is easy to show that $\models \textbf{Does}((\delta_1; \delta_2); \delta_3) \equiv \textbf{Does}(\delta_1; (\delta_2; \delta_3))$. By this, Proposition 4.17, and Assumption 4.16, the above simplifies to

$$\models \textbf{Know}(\text{MOVEDTOBY}(p + \langle 1, 0 \rangle \times \text{ROT}(o), o, (\delta; \text{FORWARD})))$$
$$\supset \textbf{Can}(\text{FORWARD}^n, \text{MOVEDTOBY}(p + \langle n + 1, 0 \rangle \times \text{ROT}(o),$$
$$o, (\delta; \text{FORWARD}^{n+1}))).$$

By Propositions 3.8 and 3.9, it follows from this and Lemma A.3 that the formula is valid for $n + 1$. $\square$

Given this lemma, we can prove Proposition 4.22 in the same way that Proposition 4.21 was proved in the previous subsection (Lemma A.4 is used instead of Lemma A.3). $\square$

A.3. Proof of Proposition 4.26

In this case too, we proceed by first showing a more general result, Lemma A.6 below. The proof uses the following strengthened version of Proposition 4.25:

Lemma A.5. *For all* $n \in \mathbb{N}$,

$$\models \forall p \forall o (\mathbf{Know}(\text{MOVEDTOBY}(p, o, \delta))$$
$$\supset \mathbf{Can}(\text{LEFT}^n, \text{MOVEDTOBY}(p, \text{MOD}_{2\pi}(o + n\pi/2), (\delta; \text{LEFT}^n)))).$$

We omit its proof, which goes along the same lines as that of Lemma A.4.

Lemma A.6. *For all* $n, m \in \mathbb{Z}$,

$$\models \forall p \forall o (\mathbf{Know}(\text{MOVEDTOBY}(p, o, \delta))$$
$$\supset \mathbf{Can}(\text{GORPOS}(\langle n, m \rangle), \text{MOVEDTOBY}(p + \langle n, m \rangle \times \text{ROT}(o),$$
$$o, (\delta; \text{GORPOS}(\langle n, m \rangle)))))).$$

Proof. *Case* 1. $m = 0$ *and* $n \in \mathbb{N}$: Then

$$\text{GORPOS}(\langle n, m \rangle) = \text{FORWARD}^n$$

and the desired result follows immediately from Lemma A.4.

Case 2. $m = 0$ *and* $n < 0$: Then

$$\text{GORPOS}(\langle n, m \rangle) = \text{LEFT}^2; \text{GORPOS}(\langle -n, 0 \rangle); \text{LEFT}^2.$$

By Lemma A.5, Proposition 4.17, and Assumption 4.16, we have that

$$\models \mathbf{Know}(\text{MOVEDTOBY}(p, o, \delta))$$
$$\supset \mathbf{Can}(\text{LEFT}^2, \text{MOVEDTOBY}(p, \text{MOD}_{2\pi}(o + \pi), (\delta; \text{LEFT}^2))).$$

By Case 1 and Proposition 4.17, we have that

$$\models \mathbf{Know}(\text{MOVEDTOBY}(p, \text{MOD}_{2\pi}(o + \pi), (\delta; \text{LEFT}^2)))$$
$$\supset \mathbf{Can}(\text{GORPOS}(\langle -n, 0 \rangle),$$
$$\text{MOVEDTOBY}(p + \langle -n, 0 \rangle \times \text{ROT}(\text{MOD}_{2\pi}(o + \pi)),$$
$$\text{MOD}_{2\pi}(o + \pi), (\delta; \text{LEFT}^2; \text{GORPOS}(\langle -n, 0 \rangle))))).$$

By Propositions 3.8 and 3.9, one can chain these results to obtain:

$$\models \mathbf{Know}(\text{MOVEDTOBY}(p, o, \delta))$$
$$\supset \mathbf{Can}((\text{LEFT}^2; \text{GORPOS}(\langle -n, 0 \rangle)),$$
$$\text{MOVEDTOBY}(p + \langle -n, 0 \rangle \times \text{ROT}(\text{MOD}_{2\pi}(o + \pi)),$$
$$\text{MOD}_{2\pi}(o + \pi), (\delta; \text{LEFT}^2; \text{GORPOS}(\langle -n, 0 \rangle))))).$$

By chaining this again with an appropriate instance of Lemma A.5, one obtains that

$$\models \mathbf{Know}(\text{MOVEDTOBY}(p, o, \delta))$$
$$\supset \mathbf{Can}(\text{GORPOS}(\langle n, 0 \rangle),$$
$$\text{MOVEDTOBY}(p + \langle -n, 0 \rangle \times \text{ROT}(\text{MOD}_{2\pi}(o + \pi)),$$
$$\text{MOD}_{2\pi}(\text{MOD}_{2\pi}(o + \pi) + \pi), (\delta; \text{GORPOS}(\langle n, 0 \rangle))))).$$

Now it is easy to check that

$$\langle -n, 0 \rangle \times \text{ROT}(\text{MOD}_{2\pi}(o + \pi)) = \langle -n \cos(o + \pi), -n \sin(o + \pi) \rangle$$
$$= \langle n \cos(o), n \sin(o) \rangle$$
$$= \langle n, 0 \rangle \times \text{ROT}(o).$$

It is also the case that

$$\text{RORITOAORI}(\text{MOD}_{2\pi}(\text{MOD}_{2\pi}(o+\pi)+\pi))$$
$$= \text{MOD}_{2\pi}(\textbf{selfori} + \text{MOD}_{2\pi}(\text{MOD}_{2\pi}(o+\pi)+\pi))$$
$$= \text{MOD}_{2\pi}(\textbf{selfori} + o)$$
$$= \text{RORITOAORI}(o).$$

So by the definition of MOVEDTOBY and Proposition 4.16, we must have that

$$\models \text{MOVEDTOBY}(p + \langle -n, 0 \rangle \times \text{ROT}(\text{MOD}_{2\pi}(o+\pi)),$$
$$\text{MOD}_{2\pi}(\text{MOD}_{2\pi}(o+\pi)+\pi),$$
$$(\delta; \text{GORPOS}(\langle n,0 \rangle)))$$
$$\equiv \text{MOVEDTOBY}(p + \langle n, 0 \rangle \times \text{ROT}(o), o, (\delta; \text{GORPOS}(\langle n,0 \rangle))).$$

The desired result follows.

Case 3. $m \neq 0$: Then

$$\text{GORPOS}(\langle n, m \rangle) = \text{GORPOS}(\langle n,0 \rangle); \text{LEFT}; \text{GORPOS}(\langle m,0 \rangle); \text{LEFT}^3.$$

The proof is similar to Case 2. By chaining (Propositions 3.8 and 3.9) appropriate instances of Case 2 with instances of Lemma A.5, we show that

$$\models \textbf{Know}(\text{MOVEDTOBY}(p, o, \delta))$$
$$\supset \textbf{Can}(\text{GORPOS}(\langle n, m \rangle),$$
$$\text{MOVEDTOBY}(p + \langle n, 0 \rangle \times \text{ROT}(o) + \langle m, 0 \rangle \times \text{ROT}(\text{MOD}_{2\pi}(o+\pi/2)),$$
$$\text{MOD}_{2\pi}(\text{MOD}_{2\pi}(o+\pi/2)+3\pi/2),$$
$$(\delta; \text{GORPOS}(\langle n, m \rangle))))).$$

One then shows that

$$\models \text{MOVEDTOBY}(p + \langle n, 0 \rangle \times \text{ROT}(o) + \langle m, 0 \rangle \times \text{ROT}(\text{MOD}_{2\pi}(o+\pi/2)),$$
$$\text{MOD}_{2\pi}(\text{MOD}_{2\pi}(o+\pi/2)+3\pi/2), (\delta; \text{GORPOS}(\langle n, m \rangle)))$$
$$\equiv \text{MOVEDTOBY}(p + \langle n, m \rangle \times \text{ROT}(o), o, (\delta; \text{GORPOS}(\langle n, m \rangle)))$$

to obtain the desired result. □

Given this lemma, we can then prove Proposition 4.26 in the same way that Proposition 4.21 was proved in Section A.1 (Lemma A.6 is used instead of Lemma A.3). □

A.4. *Proof of Proposition 4.32*

Let us first introduce some shorthands:

- $\text{UOAT}(\theta_r^i) \overset{\text{def}}{=} \exists v^i(\text{OBJECT}(v^i) \wedge \text{RPOS}(v^i) = \langle \theta_r^i, 0 \rangle \wedge \neg\text{HOLDING}(v^i))$, provided v^i does not occur free in θ_r^i;
- $\text{UOH} \overset{\text{def}}{=} \text{UOAT}(0)$;
- $\text{UOBTW}(\theta_l^i, \theta_u^i) \overset{\text{def}}{=} \exists v^i(\theta_l^i \leqslant v^i \leqslant \theta_u^i \wedge \text{UOAT}(v^i))$, provided v^i does not occur free in θ_l^i and θ_u^i;

UOAT(θ_r^i) says that there is an unheld object θ_r^i squares directly in front of the agent (behind the agent if θ_r^i is negative); UOH says that there is an unheld object **here**; and finally, UOBTW(θ_l^i, θ_u^i) says that there is an unheld object between θ_l^i and θ_u^i squares directly in front of or behind the agent.

We prove Proposition 4.32 by first establishing a result concerning its scanning component, Lemma A.9 below. This result depends on two sublemmas. The first concerns the FORWARD action:

Lemma A.7. *For all $n \in \mathbb{N}$,*

$$\models \mathbf{Know}(\neg \text{UOBTW}(-n, 0))$$
$$\supset \mathbf{Can}(\text{FORWARD}, \neg \text{UOBTW}(-n-1, -1)).$$

This lemma can be proven from Assumptions 4.3 and 4.10, as well as the frame assumptions for FORWARD mentioned in Section 4.3; a detailed proof of a closely related result appears in [29]. The second preliminary lemma concerns the SENSE action:

Lemma A.8. *For all $n \in \mathbb{N}$,*

$$\models \mathbf{Know}(\neg \text{UOBTW}(-n, -1))$$
$$\supset \mathbf{Can}(\text{SENSE}, \mathbf{Know}(\text{UOH}) \vee \mathbf{Know}(\neg \text{UOBTW}(-n, 0))).$$

It can be proven from Assumptions 4.3 and 4.30, and the frame assumptions for SENSE mentioned in Sections 4.4 and 4.3.

Let us now proceed with the main lemma concerned with scanning:

Lemma A.9. *For all $k, n \in \mathbb{N}$,*

$$\models \mathbf{Know}(\text{UOH}) \vee \mathbf{Know}(\neg \text{UOBTW}(-n, 0))$$
$$\supset \mathbf{Can}(\text{SCAN}_k(\text{UOH}), \mathbf{Know}(\text{UOH}) \vee \mathbf{Know}(\neg \text{UOBTW}(-n-k, 0))).$$

Proof. By induction over k.

Base case: $\text{SCAN}_0(\text{UOH}) \stackrel{\text{def}}{=} \mathbf{noOp}$ and $\models \mathbf{Can}(\mathbf{noOp}, \varphi) \equiv \mathbf{Know}(\varphi)$, so all we need to show is that for all $n \in \mathbb{N}$,

$$\models \mathbf{Know}(\text{UOH}) \vee \mathbf{Know}(\neg \text{UOBTW}(-n, 0))$$
$$\supset \mathbf{Know}(\mathbf{Know}(\text{UOH}) \vee \mathbf{Know}(\neg \text{UOBTW}(-n, 0))).$$
This is easily done using Propositions 3.5, 3.3, and 3.2.

Induction step: Assume that the formula is valid for k and show that it must then be valid for $k+1$.

$$\text{SCAN}_{k+1}(\text{UOH}) \stackrel{\text{def}}{=} \mathbf{if}(\neg \text{UOH}, \text{FORWARD}; \text{SENSE}; \text{SCAN}_k(\text{UOH}), \mathbf{noOp}),$$

and so by Proposition 3.10, we have that

$$\models \mathbf{Can}(\text{SCAN}_{k+1}(\text{UOH}), \mathbf{Know}(\text{UOH}) \vee \mathbf{Know}(\neg \text{UOBTW}(-n-(k+1), 0)))$$
$$\equiv (\mathbf{Know}(\text{UOH}) \wedge \mathbf{Can}(\mathbf{noOp}, \mathbf{Know}(\text{UOH}) \vee \mathbf{Know}(\neg \text{UOBTW}(-n-(k+1), 0))))$$

$$\vee \, (\mathbf{Know}(\neg \text{UOH}) \wedge \mathbf{Can}(\text{FORWARD; SENSE; SCAN}_k(\text{UOH}),$$
$$\mathbf{Know}(\text{UOH}) \vee \mathbf{Know}(\neg \text{UOBTW}(-n-(k+1),0)))).$$

By Propositions 3.5, 3.3, and 3.2, it is easy to show that for all $n \in \mathbb{N}$,

$$\models \mathbf{Know}(\text{UOH}) \supset$$
$$\mathbf{Know}(\text{UOH}) \wedge \mathbf{Can}(\mathbf{noOp}, \mathbf{Know}(\text{UOH}) \vee \mathbf{Know}(\neg \text{UOBTW}(-n-(k+1),0))).$$

What remains to be proved is that for all $n \in \mathbb{N}$,

$$\models \mathbf{Know}(\neg \text{UOBTW}(-n,0))$$
$$\supset (\mathbf{Know}(\neg \text{UOH}) \wedge \mathbf{Can}(\text{FORWARD; SENSE; SCAN}_k(\text{UOH}),$$
$$\mathbf{Know}(\text{UOH}) \vee \mathbf{Know}(\neg \text{UOBTW}(-n-(k+1),0)))).$$

Clearly $\models \neg \text{UOBTW}(-n,0) \supset \neg \text{UOH}$ for $n \in \mathbb{N}$; so by Propositions 3.3 and 3.2, we have that for all $n \in \mathbb{N}$, $\models \mathbf{Know}(\neg \text{UOBTW}(-n,0)) \supset \mathbf{Know}(\neg \text{UOH})$. From Lemma A.8 and the induction hypothesis, it follows by Proposition 3.8 that for all $n \in \mathbb{N}$,

$$\models \mathbf{Know}(\neg \text{UOBTW}(-(n+1),-1)) \supset$$
$$\mathbf{Can}(\text{SENSE; SCAN}_k(\text{UOH}),$$
$$\mathbf{Know}(\text{UOH}) \vee \mathbf{Know}(\neg \text{UOBTW}(-(n+1)-k,0))).$$

By Propositions 3.8 and 3.9, this and Lemma A.7 imply that for all $n \in \mathbb{N}$,

$$\models \mathbf{Know}(\neg \text{UOBTW}(-n,0))$$
$$\supset \mathbf{Can}(\text{FORWARD; SENSE; SCAN}_k(\text{UOH}),$$
$$\mathbf{Know}(\text{UOH}) \vee \mathbf{Know}(\neg \text{UOBTW}(-n-(k+1),0))). \quad \square$$

We can now complete the proof of Proposition 4.32. By Lemmas A.9 and A.8 and Proposition 3.8, we must have that for all $n \in \mathbb{N}$,

$$\models \mathbf{Know}(\neg \text{UOBTW}(-n,-1)) \supset$$
$$\mathbf{Can}((\text{SENSE; SCAN}_k(\text{UOH})),$$
$$\mathbf{Know}(\text{UOH}) \vee \mathbf{Know}(\neg \text{UOBTW}(-n-k,0))).$$

Clearly $\models \neg \text{UOBTW}(0,-1)$, and thus by Proposition 3.3

$$\models \mathbf{Know}(\neg \text{UOBTW}(0,-1));$$

the desired result follows. $\quad \square$

Acknowledgements

This paper describes a revised version of work that was part of the first author's Ph.D. Thesis at the Department of Computer Science, University of Toronto, which was supervised by the second author (jointly with Graeme Hirst). Revisions were done while the first author was at NTT Basic Research Laboratories in Musashino, Japan and the School of Computing Science, Simon Fraser University, Burnaby, Canada. This work was funded by the Institute for Robotics and Intelligent Systems and the Natural Science and Engineering Research Council of Canada, and the Information Technology

Research Centre of Ontario. David Israel, Graeme Hirst, and the referees have provided many valuable suggestions. Discussions with Phil Agre, Adam Grove, Joe Halpern, and Joe Nunes have also been helpful.

References

[1] P.E. Agre, Review of L.A. Suchman, *Plans and Situated Action: The Problem of Human–Machine Communication* (Cambridge University Press, Cambridge, UK, 1987), *Artif. Intell.* **43** (3) (1990) 369–384.

[2] P.E. Agre and D. Chapman, Pengi: an implementation of a theory of activity, in: *Proceedings AAAI-87*, Seattle, WA (1987) 268–272.

[3] P.E. Agre and D. Chapman, What are plans for?, *Rob. Autonom. Syst.* **6** (1990) 17–34.

[4] A.V. Aho, J.E. Hopcroft and J.D. Ullman, *The Design and Analysis of Computer Algorithms* (Addison-Wesley, Reading, MA, 1974).

[5] J. Barwise, Information and circumstance, *Notre Dame J. Formal Logic* **27** (3) (1986) 324–338.

[6] J. Barwise and J. Perry, *Situations and Attitudes* (MIT Press/Bradford Books, Cambridge, MA, 1983).

[7] H.-N. Castañeda, On the logic of attributions of self-knowledge to others, *J. Philos.* **65** (15) (1968) 439–456.

[8] B.F. Chellas, *Modal Logic: an Introduction* (Cambridge University Press, Cambridge, UK, 1980).

[9] P.R. Cohen and H.J. Levesque, Rational interaction as the basis for communication, in: P.R. Cohen, J. Morgan and M.E. Pollack, eds., *Intentions in Communication* (MIT Press, Cambridge, MA, 1990) 221–255.

[10] E. Davis, Inferring ignorance from the locality of visual perception, in: *Proceedings AAAI-88*, St. Paul, MN (1988) 786–791.

[11] E. Davis, Reasoning about hand-eye coordination, in: *Working Notes, IJCAI Workshop on Knowledge, Perception, and Planning*, Detroit, MI (1989) 1–6.

[12] E. Davis, Solutions to a paradox of perception with limited acuity, in: *Proceedings First International Conference on Principles of Knowledge Representation and Reasoning*, Toronto, Ont. (1989) 79–82.

[13] R. Goldblatt, *Logics of Time and Computation*, CSLI Lecture Notes **7** (Center for the Study of Language and Information, Stanford University, Stanford, CA, 1987).

[14] A.J. Grove, Topics in multi-agent epistemic logic, Ph.D. Thesis, Department of Computer Science, Stanford University, Stanford, CA (1992).

[15] A.J. Grove and J.Y. Halpern, Naming and identity in a multi-agent epistemic logic, in: J. Allen, R. Fikes and E. Sandewall, eds., *Principles of Knowledge Representation and Reasoning: Proceedings of the Second International Conference*, Cambridge, MA (1991) 301–312.

[16] A.R. Haas, A syntactic theory of belief and action, *Artif. Intell.* **28** (1986) 245–292.

[17] A.R. Haas, Indexical expressions and planning, unpublished manuscript, Department of Computer Science, State University of New York, Albany, NY (1991).

[18] J.Y. Halpern and Y. Moses, A guide to the modal logics of knowledge and belief: preliminary draft, in: *Proceedings IJCAI-85*, Los Angeles, CA (1985) 480–490.

[19] J. Hintikka, *Knowledge and Belief* (Cornell University Press, Ithaca, NY, 1962).

[20] J. Hintikka, Semantics for the propositional attitudes, in: J.W. Davis, D.J. Hockney and K.W. Wilson, eds., *Philosophical Logic* (Reidel, Dordrecht, Netherlands, 1969) 21–45.

[21] G.E. Hughes and M.J. Cresswell, *An Introduction to Modal Logic* (Methuen, London, UK, 1968).

[22] D.J. Israel, The role of propositional objects of belief in action, Tech. Report CSLI-87-72 CSLI, Stanford University, Stanford, CA (1987).

[23] L.P. Kaelbling, An architecture for intelligent systems, in: *Reasoning about Actions and Plans: Proceedings of the 1986 Workshop*, Timberline, OR (1987) 395–410.

[24] L.P. Kaelbling and S.J. Rosenschein, Action and planning in embedded agents, *Rob. Autonom. Syst.* **6** (1990) 35–48.

[25] K. Konolige, A first order formalization of knowledge and action for a multi-agent planning system, in: J. Hays and D. Michie, eds., *Machine Intelligence* **10** (Ellis Horwood, Chichester, UK, 1982).

[26] K. Konolige, *A Deduction Model of Belief* (Pitman, London, 1986).

[27] S.A. Kripke, Semantical considerations on modal logic, *Acta Philos. Fennica* **16** (1963) 83–94.

[28] A. Kronfeld, *Reference and Computation: An Essay in Applied Philosophy of Language* (Cambridge University Press, New York, 1990).

[29] Y. Lespérance, A formal theory of indexical knowledge and action, Ph.D. Thesis, Department of Computer Science, University of Toronto, Toronto, Ont. (1991); also published as Tech. Report CSRI-248.

[30] Y. Lespérance, An approach to modeling indexicality in action and communication, in: J. Horty and Y. Shoham, eds., *Reasoning about Mental States: Formal Theories and Applications, Papers from the 1993 AAAI Spring Symposium*, Stanford, CA (1993) 79–85; also Tech. Report SS-93-05, AAAI Press; also in: *Proceedings IJCAI-93 Workshop on "Using Knowledge in its Context"*, Chambery, France (1993).

[31] Y. Lespérance and H.J. Levesque, Indexical knowledge in robot plans, in: *Proceedings AAAI-90*, Boston, MA (1990) 868–874.

[32] Y. Lespérance and H.J. Levesque, An argument for indexical representations in temporal reasoning, in: R. Elio, ed., *Proceedings Tenth Biennial Conference of the Canadian Society for Computational Studies of Intelligence*, Banff, Alta. (1994) 271–277.

[33] Y. Lespérance and H.J. Levesque, On the logic of indexical knowledge and action, Tech. Report, Department of Computer Science, University of Toronto, Toronto, Ont. (1995), to appear.

[34] Y. Lespérance, H.J. Levesque and F. Lin, A formalization of ability and knowing how that avoids the frame problem, in: *Proceedings Fourth International Conference on Principles of Knowledge Representation and Reasoning (KR'94)*, Bonn, Germany (1994), submitted.

[35] H.J. Levesque, Foundations of a functional approach to knowledge representation, *Artif. Intell.* **23** (1984) 155–212.

[36] H.J. Levesque, A logic of implicit and explicit belief, in: *Proceedings AAAI-84*, Austin, TX (1984) 198–202.

[37] D. Lewis, Attitudes *de dicto* and *de se*, *Philos. Rev.* **88** (4) (1979) 513–543.

[38] J. McCarthy and P. Hayes, Some philosophical problems from the standpoint of artificial intelligence, in: B. Meltzer and D. Michie, eds., *Machine Intelligence* **4** (Edinburgh University Press, Edinburgh, UK, 1979) 463–502.

[39] E. Mendelson, *Introduction to Mathematical Logic* (Van Nostrand, New York, 2nd ed., 1979).

[40] R.C. Moore, Reasoning about knowledge and action, Tech. Report 191, AI Center, SRI International, Menlo Park, CA (1980).

[41] R.C. Moore, A formal theory of knowledge and action, in: J.R. Hobbs and R.C. Moore, eds., *Formal Theories of the Common Sense World* (Ablex, Norwood, NJ, 1985) 319–358.

[42] L. Morgenstern, Knowledge preconditions for actions and plans, in: *Proceedings IJCAI-87*, Milan, Italy (1987) 867–874.

[43] L. Morgenstern, Foundations of a logic of knowledge, action, and communication, Ph.D. Thesis, Department of Computer Science, New York University, New York (1988).

[44] L. Morgenstern, Knowledge and the frame problem, in: K. Ford and P. Hayes, eds., *Reasoning Agents in a Dynamic World: The Frame Problem* (JAI Press, Greenwich, 1991).

[45] A. Newell, The knowledge level, *Artif. Intell.* **18** (1) (1982) 87–127.

[46] J. Perry, The problem of the essential indexical, *Noûs* **13** (1979) 3–21.

[47] R. Reiter, The frame problem in the situation calculus: a simple solution (sometimes) and a completeness result for goal regression, in: V. Lifschitz, ed., *Artificial Intelligence and Mathematical Theory of Computation: Papers in Honor of John McCarthy* (Academic Press, San Diego, CA, 1991) 359–380.

[48] S.J. Rosenschein and L.P. Kaelbling, The synthesis of digital machines with provable epistemic properties, in: J.Y. Halpern, ed., *Theoretical Aspects of Reasoning about Knowledge: Proceedings of the 1986 Conference*, Monterey, CA (1986) 83–98.

[49] R.B. Scherl and H.J. Levesque, The frame problem and knowledge-producing actions, in: *Proceedings AAAI-93*, Washington, DC (1993) 689–695.

[50] R.B. Scherl, H.J. Levesque and Y. Lespérance, Indexicals in the situation calculus, in preparation.

[51] B.C. Smith, The owl and the electric encyclopedia, *Artif. Intell.* **47** (1991) 251–288.

[52] D. Subramanian and J. Woodfill, Making the situation calculus indexical, in: *Proceedings First International Conference on Principles of Knowledge Representation and Reasoning*, Toronto, Ont. (1989) 467–474.

[53] L.A. Suchman, *Plans and Situated Action: The Problem of Human–Machine Communication* (Cambridge University Press, Cambridge, UK, 1987).

[54] B. Webber, N. Badler, B. di Eugenio, C. Geib, L. Levison and M. Moore, Instructions, intentions and expectations, *Artif. Intell.* **73** (1995) 253–269.

Artificial Intelligence 73 (1995) 117–148

Exploiting patterns of interaction to achieve reactive behavior

D.M. Lyons*, A.J. Hendriks

Philips Laboratories, Philips Electronics North America Corporation, Briarcliff Manor, NY 10510, USA

Received September 1992

Abstract

This paper introduces an approach that allows an agent to *exploit* inherent patterns of interaction in its environment, so-called dynamics, to achieve its objectives. The approach extends the standard treatment of planning and (re)action in which part of the input to the plan generation algorithm is a set of basic actions and perhaps some domain axioms. Real world actions are typically difficult to categorize consistently and are highly context dependent. The approach presented here takes as input a procedural model of the agent's environment and produces as output a set of action descriptions that capture how the agent can exploit the dynamics in the environment. An agent constructed with this approach can utilize context sensitive actions, "servo" style actions, and other intuitively efficient ways to manipulate its environment.

A process-algebra based representation, $\mathcal{RS}$, is introduced to model the environment and the agent's reactions. The paper demonstrates how to analyze an $\mathcal{RS}$ environment model so as to automatically generate a set of potentially useful dynamics and convert these to action descriptions. The output action descriptions are designed to be input to an Interval Temporal Logic based planner. A series of examples of reaction construction drawn from the *kitting robot* domain is worked through, and the prototype implementation of the approach described.

1. Introduction

In this paper we address the problem of constructing an agent capable of producing intelligent action in an uncertain and changing environment. The challenge the agent faces is to carry out tasks given new opportunities or difficulties that arise in the environment. The approach we propose is to construct agents that *exploit* inherent patterns of interaction in the environment to achieve their objectives. Chapman [6] calls

---

* Corresponding author. E-mail: dml@philabs.philips.com.

such a pattern a *dynamic*, and that usage is adopted here also. A dynamic may not be entirely controllable nor predictable by the agent; nonetheless, the agent can work with it to achieve its objectives in an intuitively efficient manner.

In previous work, we have developed the planner–reactor architecture as an approach to building such agents [19]. The reactor component of the planner–reactor handles uncertainty in the environment using reactions—hard-wired combinations of sensing and action—to "servo" out uncertainty. The planner component provides the deliberative capabilities to update the reactor component to best suit the current environment. It accomplishes this by adding new, or removing old reactions. The planner is implemented using an Interval Temporal Logic (ITL) language [24]; the reactor, using the $\mathcal{RS}$ language [17]. This paper presents an approach to the planner problem of constructing novel reactions that allow the agent to exploit the dynamics in its environment. The specific focus of the paper is on the problem of identifying dynamics that can be useful for building reactions. This extends the standard treatment of planning and (re)action where part of the input to the plan generation algorithm is a set of basic actions and (perhaps) some domain axioms. The set of actions, however, is normally invariant over the encountered instantiations of the problem domain.

The proposed approach, in contrast, derives additional, context-sensitive actions from an analysis of dynamics in the environment and how they interact with the basic sensory and motor actions available to the agent. A *procedural model of the environment*, representing the interactions between parts of the environment and the agent, is required for this analysis. The result of the analysis is a set of high-level action descriptions suitable for the ITL-based planner. Although the planner constructs reactions from these action schemas in a straightforward manner, the action schemas themselves ensure that the generated reactions can exploit context-sensitive actions, "servo" style actions, and other intuitively efficient ways to manipulate the environment.

Like Horswill [13], our objective is to allow the agent to take advantage of special features of the environment. His *habitat constraints* allow a designer to simplify the design of an agent so as to exploit its "niche" in the environment. Our approach is an attempt to automate the identification and use of a class of such constraints, namely constraints that express how an agent can exploit processes at work in the environment.

The proposed method for generating action schemas has a number of advantages. The construction of a good reactive system depends on the designer understanding the kinds of activities in which the environment engages. This information is not captured well by the classical planning concept of a set of basic action descriptions. Real actions for dealing with dynamic events are typically highly context dependent and difficult to categorize into a discrete set in a consistent and useful way. The proposed approach can handle such unseparable and context sensitive actions, since the dynamic provides the separation and the context of the action.

The remainder of this paper is laid out as follows. In the next two sections our previous work on the planner–reactor framework is introduced, and the motivation for investigating the problem of identifying and exploiting dynamics discussed. Section 3 introduces the concept of dynamics and of exploiting dynamics to achieve objectives. It includes a motivating example from our application domain, the kitting robot. Section 4 introduces the two formal representations used in the paper: the $\mathcal{RS}$ language and Interval Temporal Logic. This section explains the mechanisms for identifying dynamics and selecting reactions. Section 5 uses this formal framework to investigate exploiting dynamics in three kitting domain problems: visual tracking, guarded motion, and interaction with a conveyor belt. Section 6 describes the implementation of the approach.

2. The planner reactor framework

Reactive systems, e.g. [1,5], were introduced to address the fragility of classical approaches to plan generation and execution in an uncertain and changing environment. Previous work in constructing reactions has occurred in two fields: Learning better reactions based on feedback from the environment, e.g., DYNA [31], MD [7]; and the generation of reactive plans based on a model of the environment, e.g., the Universal Plan generator [25], ERE [4]. We are concerned with this latter area: constructing reactions or reactive plans. One solution to this problem has been to construct "off-line" systems, such as Kaelbling's GAPPS [14] and Schoppers' Universal Plan generator [25], that automatically generate reactive machines to suit a goal specification. Another response was to build systems, such as Hendler's APE [29], Arkin's AURA [3] and Bresina and Drummond's ERE [4], that integrated reactive and deliberative capabilities.

Our application domain is robotic kitting [27]. A kitting robot is a robot system that puts together assembly kits—trays containing all the necessary parts from which to build a specific product. Simpler and cheaper automation can construct the assemblies once they have been placed in the kits and routed appropriately. The key characteristic of the kitting robot is not so much its ability to reason about assembly, but rather its ability to choose timely and effective actions to suit an uncertain and changing environment. To deal with events as they happen, the kitting robot needs to be capable of *real-time, reactive response*. On the other hand, to deal with changes in the environment (e.g., bursts of errors in parts, or failures of resources) or new goals issued by factory management, the kitting robot needs to be able *to plan ahead "on the fly"*.

The definition of planning that we espouse is somewhat similar to that of Bresina and Drummond [4] and McDermott [23]: a planner is a module that continually modifies a concurrent and separate reactive system so that its behavior becomes more goal directed. The reactive component of the system will be referred to as the *reactor* after the terminology established by Bresina and Drummond. Fig. 1 illustrates our *planner-reactor* architecture. A reactor, a network of sensory-motor reactions, interacts directly with an uncertain and changing environment. The planner is a concurrent and separate module that monitors the reactor and its environment by issuing perception requests to the reactor. (These are distinct from the reactor's sensory actions.) When, in the planner's view, the reactor structure will not produce behavior that conforms to the planner's goals, the planner issues adaptations, structural changes to the reactor, to bring reactor behavior back into line with the goals. The planner can generate novel reactions and "add" them into the reactor, as well as remove existing reactions from the reactor, in a safe manner. Planner and reactor communicate asynchronously.

The specific focus of this paper will be on the planner problem of generating novel reactions for the reactor that exploit the dynamics in the environment. However, to

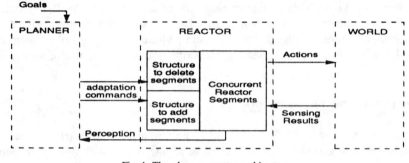

Fig. 1. The planner–reactor architecture.

explain the motivation for addressing this problem, a little additional detail on the planner–reactor work is necessary. The "full story" can be found in [19–21].

2.1. Reactor

The reactor contains a network of reactions. A reaction is a sensory process (or network) composed with an effector process (or network) in such a fashion that should the sensory process detect its triggering condition, then it will in turn trigger the effector process. The key property of the reactor is that it can produce action at *any* time. Unlike a plan executor, a reactor can act independently of the planner; it is always actively inspecting the world, and will act should one of its reactions be triggered. A reactor should produce timely, useful behavior even without a planner.

2.2. Planner

The planner is completely separate from, and concurrent with, the reactor. Rather than seeing the planner as a higher-level module that loads plans into a lower-level executor, we see the planner as an equal-level module that continually tunes the reactor to produce appropriate behavior (Fig. 1). The interaction between the planner and reactor is entirely asynchronous.

The input to the planner includes: a model of the environment in which the planner is operating; a description of the reactor's structure; and information from the user about objectives the reactor should achieve (e.g., in the kitting problem domain, geometric goals such as kit layouts) and constraints the reactor should obey in its behavior (e.g., batch mix or resource usage constraints). The planner continually determines if the reactor's responses to the current environment would indeed conform to the objectives. If not, then the planner makes an incremental change to the reactor configuration—adding in novel reactions, or deleting old reactions—to bring the reactor's behavior more into line with the objectives. The planner module has been implemented in a conventional manner using an ITL interval reasoner [19]. However, we found that approach to be somewhat limiting, as Section 2.4 will report, and this motivated the study of the approach proposed in this paper.

2.3. Planner–reactor interactions

As indicated in Fig. 1, there are two routes of interaction between planner and reactor. An adaptation is essentially an instruction to delete part of the reactor structure or to add in some extra structure. Each individual adaptation should be small in effect and scope; large changes in reactor behavior only come about as the result of iterated adaptation. Large adaptations would be equivalent to downloading "plans" to the reactor; something we need to avoid.

Perceptions are sensory data collected by the reactor to be sent to the planner. The knowledge needs of the planner and reactor are almost always different. The reactor uses sensory data to determine whether to fire its reactions. The planner needs sensory data to allow it to predict the future progress of the environment and the status of the reactor.

In [22] we demonstrate how it is possible to construct a reactor that can be adapted in a simple and concise manner. In [20] we describe how to make these adaptations in a safe manner despite the fact that the planner does know when or which reactions might be firing. In [19] we formalize the iterative improvement of a reactor by a planner to explore convergence. This latter paper gives the architecture of the ITL-based planner.

2.4. Generating reactions

The planner employed in the planner–reactor work [19] has some special features: it needs to consider repeated improvement of a reactor, and it reasons about building reactions as process networks. Nonetheless, it is conventional in that it expects a set of action schema, describing the basic domain actions, as part of its input.

Our experience was that this input severely restricted the reactions that could be devised by the planner. Many of the potentially useful modes of interaction with the environment were hidden by the choice of domain actions. One approach to solve this problem is to develop a very general set of basic actions. This is far from trivial, since real actions for dealing with dynamic events are typically highly context dependent and difficult to categorize into a discrete set in a consistent and useful way.

An alternate approach is to give the system a model of the environment and ask it to identify useful modes of interaction with its environment to achieve a given goal. This environment model needs to capture the interaction topology between parts of the environment as well as between the environment and the agent. This approach has the additional advantage that the designer's focus then becomes the building of an accurate environment model, rather than the devising of the correct view or interpretation of the environment for the agent, as seen through a set of action descriptions. It also has the advantage that the devised actions do not need to be consistent across different tasks, since they are extracted from the environment model on a per task basis, or even in the same task over time, since the processes at work in the environment may change over time.

The remainder of this paper is based on this second approach. A method will be introduced for automatically identifying dynamics, and for generating action descriptions based on the identified dynamics, which can be given as input to our ITL-based planner.

3. Planning to reactively exploit the environment

3.1. Modeling the environment as a set of processes

We will represent the environment model as a set of concurrent, communicating *processes* (in the computer science sense of the word). The key information that this procedural model captures is the interaction topology: what parts of the environment "are connected to" other parts and how "messages" are passed along those communication links. This kind of world model does *not* contain information about the current state of the world[1] such as e.g., (at-position object26 0.25 0.34 0.29); rather it contains information about how objects interact with each other, or how an object interacts with the agent's visual input sensors. In other words, the model describes the structural and temporal regularities, the patterns of interaction in the environment and how they evolve over time. The environment model may be partial and/or may contain uncertain information.

Modeling a dynamic environment as a set of processes is analogous to the approach taken by Hendrix [11] and in Qualitative Process Theory [9]. The sole mechanism assumption of QP-theory (but equally valid for Hendrix's work) states that all changes in (physical) systems are caused directly or indirectly by processes. Our modeling of the environment also subscribes to this assumption. This modeling only restricts the amount of interaction. It does not necessarily prescribe it, since the processes may contain uncertainty, e.g., random motion of objects, or the unpredictable occurrence of events such as a new object being introduced.

3.2. Exploiting dynamics

Constructing agents that *reactively exploit* their environment to achieve their objectives differs in some important aspects from the standard approach of building agents that plan and act to achieve their goals. In the latter approach, actions are considered similar to building blocks, which must be composed together in some ordering so that the agent can force the environment to a desired state. The first consequence of this viewpoint is that, because it demands well-defined "blocks", it guides a designer to choose actions that have a one-to-one mapping with effects on the environment.

Unfortunately, the actions typically available to an agent are not so well behaved—their effects are usually context dependent and they may indeed produce uncertain effects. Proper modeling of the effects and applicability conditions of such actions is very difficult for a designer; it may require elaborate descriptions encompassing extensive qualification axioms (e.g. Ginsburg [10]) or Causal Theories (Shoham [28]). More importantly, in this approach to action modeling the range of environments in which the agent operates must be known a priori, and an encountered environment which is slightly different can render such a model incorrect.

The second consequence is that it leads a designer to naturally considering the space of all compositions of the building blocks as the space in which to look for plans, i.e., tasks

---

[1] At least, not primarily.

which require a servoing behavior, achieving an objective through repetitive actions, are rarely considered. Schoppers [26] has begun to address this type of behavior. However, he chose to make the dynamics of the environment explicit in his action descriptions in terms of temporal *soon* and *sust* operators, modeling the servoing aspect of an action only as an uncertain completion time.

The approach proposed in this paper, exploiting environment dynamics, extends the traditional planning viewpoint principally in that it enriches an agent's action repertoire by inspecting the (procedural) model of the environment and looking for useful inherent patterns that an agent can capitalize on. Chapman [6] calls these patterns *dynamics*, and that usage is also adopted here. Dynamics are structural or temporal regularities of the environment. They exist independent of the agent and are essentially acausal. A simple example from the kitting robot domain is of a conveyor belt carrying parts past the robot. A part on the belt will start by being drawn inexorably towards the robot; after a certain time, it will be within the robots workspace; and, if it remains on the belt, a certain time after that it will be irrecoverably gone.

Some dynamics admit participation by the agent. That is, the actions available to the agent can be affected by and/or can affect the course of the dynamic. This is a much weaker concept that the notion of an event being within or partially within an agent's control [24]. For example, the motion of the belt may indeed be beyond the control of an agent. Nonetheless, an agent can participate in this dynamic to acquire an object. To participate in a dynamic, an agent must be capable of knowing about, or sensing components of, the dynamic and of producing actions that affect, or are affected by, the dynamic. For example to exploit the belt dynamic to acquire an object, the kitting robot needs to be able to tell when the part is in its workspace and it needs to be able to take a part from the belt. We say that an agent *participates* in a dynamic to achieve an objective when it uses a reaction triggered off the dynamic to carry out some action that in conjunction with the dynamic achieves the objective. Note that this allows us to utilize actions whose effects are context dependent, since the dynamic resolves the context. As will be shown later on, the generated reactions capture "closed loop" control law behavior, as opposed to plans generated in traditional planning approaches, which are essentially "open loop" strategies.

3.3. Example: the tracking reaction

To explain the concept of exploiting dynamics, consider the simple tracking environment shown in Fig. 2. This environment contains a number of objects. The objects may be moving, and that motion is beyond the control of the agent. The environment also contains a camera, the orientation of which can be controlled. If an object is in view, the camera will report the position of that object. We will assume that the agent has an object of type T in view initially, and that its objective is to know the position of this (possibly moving) object at all times.

The procedural model of this tracking environment TEM and the agent's reactor are shown in Fig. 3. (The formal representation for these will be described in a later section.) The central line denotes the sensory-motor interface of the agent. Above the line are the agents reactions. Below the line is the model of the environment. Reactions

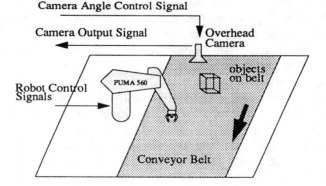

Fig. 2. The tracking environment.

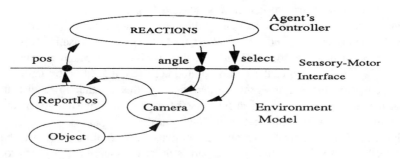

Fig. 3. Modeling the tracking environment.

and environment model interact only through the sensory-motor interface. In the reactor, of course, these reactions will affect, and be affected by, the actual environment the agent is in. The entire contents of Fig. 3 would be contained "inside" the planner and constitute its model of the environment and of the reactor.

The agent has access to the environment through its sensory-motor interface. This interface is a set of communication channels, ports, through which the agent can either affect the environment by transmitting a control value, e.g., a setpoint for a robot, or obtain information by receiving a value, e.g., the position of an object, given that the camera process is prodded to look for objects. For the agent to receive sensory information, it has to explicitly perform a sensing action, which is modeled as "hooking" into one or more of its sensory interface ports. This contrasts with systems such as ERE [4] and RAPS [8], where a hidden sensory subsystem continually updates a database with knowledge about the world, which the agent can access for free. This latter solution is only viable if the knowledge needs of an agent can be satisfied by sensing that is performed independent of the agent's course of action. At best this is inefficient. In the realistic case of limited sensing resources, it can lead to an agent waiting for crucial information, and possibly missing deadlines, while the sensing system is updating other pieces of knowledge (knowledge perhaps irrelevant to the agent's current needs).

The tracking environment model consists of a process representing the agent's visual sensor Camera, and some number of object processes, Object. The Camera process accepts communication on a port, *angle*, which selects the pose of the camera and *select*, which tells the camera the type of object the agent is interested in. If an object of the selected type is in view at the angle the camera is currently set to, then the position of that object is returned on the port *pos*. Camera determines what objects are in view as follows. It has communication port connections to all existing Object processes (only one such process is shown in Fig. 3). These processes represent objects in the environment. Each Object process continually reports its position and type to Camera, which applies a function InView based on the *select* and *angle* values to determine if a selected object is in view. The position of any object in view is echoed back on *pos*.

The agent can acquire position information via its sensory interface port *pos*. To find out what kind of information this port contains, it's necessary to trace back the connections from this port through the processes in the environment, and possibly back to the motor interface ports (in this case *angle* and *select*). As we trace back, we can annotate the connections with the conditions under which they actually transmit information. (The formalization of this analysis in our process model will be explained presently). For now, say that the connection from the Camera to the *pos* port is only transmitting whenever an object of type T is in the field of view of the camera, as determined by the condition $InView_{angle,pos}$.

Thus, in order to keep receiving information on port *pos* the agent has to keep this condition true. In other words, we have extracted a condition that should be the loop invariant for the tracking reaction. An example of a tracking reaction that maintains this invariant is as follows: The agent continually reads in the position of an object on port *pos*, transforms this position to a camera angle and transmits that angle to the motor interface port *angle*.

4. Representing and analyzing environments

To put the approach on a more formal footing, the following problems need to be addressed:

(1) A concise language for specifying environment models needs to be developed (the "input").
(2) A concise language for specifying action schemas needs to be developed (the "output").
(3) A method for identifying dynamics, based on the environment model language, needs to be designed.
(4) A method for translating identified dynamics into action schemas needs to be designed.

4.1. A concise language for representing environment models

$\mathcal{RS}$ is a formal model of computation targeted at sensory-based robotics [16, 18]. Plans, actions and world models are all represented in $\mathcal{RS}$ as hierarchical networks of concurrent processes. Techniques for analyzing $\mathcal{RS}$ process networks to capture the interaction between plans and environments have been developed [15, 17, 19]. Process networks allow us to more easily capture the recursion or interaction that is central to dynamics. However, $\mathcal{RS}$ doesn't help us to mechanize the automatic generation of reactions. For that we make use of an Interval Temporal Logic (ITL) based on Pelavin's model [24]. ITL on its own has difficulty capturing recursion. We will show that the mix of these two formalisms allows us to identify useful dynamics and then select reactions that achieve the objectives.

4.1.1. Processes in $\mathcal{RS}$

A description of a process, or network of processes, is called a *schema*. For example, $\text{Joint}_v\langle x \rangle$ denotes a process that is an instance of the schema Joint with one ingoing parameter v and one outcoming result x. A process can terminate either successfully (stop) or unsuccessfully (aborts). Networks are built by composing processes together using several kinds of *process composition operators*. These allow processes to be ordered in various ways, including concurrent, conditional and iterative orderings. At the bottom of this hierarchy, every network must be composed from a set of atomic, pre-defined processes. The set of *basic schemas* defines what processes are atomic.

$\mathcal{RS}$ notation has a *process algebra* [12] style: processes are specified as algebraic compositions of other processes. The relationship between this and state-machine models of computation is well understood. A process is essentially a state-machine; for $\mathcal{RS}$ a process is a special kind of automaton called a *port automaton*. A process composition operation is an instruction on how to combine automata: more specifically, how to combine state-transition graphs. Thus, $\mathcal{RS}$ provides a way to build processes without ever explicitly mentioning states. This allows us to avoid some of the problems of state-based approaches to representing and reasoning about actions [24].

4.1.2. Composing processes

We will make use of four atomic composition operations, namely, sequential, concurrent, conditional and disabling, and two non-atomic composition operations, namely, synchronous recurrent and asynchronous recurrent.

Sequential composition is used to enforce a strict ordering on operations. For example, ensuring that *part2* is always placed after *part1*, $\text{T} = \text{Place}_{part1}; \text{Place}_{part2}$.

Concurrent composition indicates that two or more processes should be carried out concurrently. This allows us to represent a lack of ordering between activities, e.g., $\text{T} = \text{Place}_{part1} \mid \text{Place}_{part2}$, or actions which need to be done simultaneously, e.g., squeezing an object *obj* with two fingers $f1$ and $f2$, $\text{T} = \text{ApplyForce}_{f1,obj} \mid \text{ApplyForce}_{f2,obj}$. The process T terminates once all its arguments have terminated.

Concurrent processes can communicate with each other via *communication ports*. Two special basic processes are defined for this purpose: $\text{IN}_p\langle v \rangle$ reads a value from port p and can pass it on through its result v; $\text{OUT}_{p,v}$ writes the value v out on port p. All port communication is synchronous [2] and there can be fan-in and fan-out on ports. For

---

[2] Asynchronous communication can be built from dynamic process creation plus synchronous communication.

example, if $X_p = IN_p$ and $Y_q = OUT_{q,n}$ then $N = X_a \mid Y_a$ is a network of an input process in parallel with, and connected to, an output process [3].

Conditional composition allows the construction of networks whose behavior is conditional. The network of $T = P:Q$ behaves like $P;Q$ iff P terminates successfully. If P aborts, then Q is not carried out, and T aborts. For example, in $LidOpen_{box} : Place_{x,box}$ whether $Place$ is carried out or not depends on whether $LidOpen$ terminates successfully or not. Conditional composition can be used to pass results between processes in a "pipelined" fashion. If $X_p = IN_p \langle v \rangle : A_v$ the value read in on the port p is used as a parameter to the process A.

Disabling composition allows one process to terminate another. The network $T = A\#B$ behaves like $A \mid B$ except that it terminates whenever *any* of its arguments terminates.

Finally, two useful non-atomic composition operations are defined in terms of these four: *synchronous recurrent* $A:;B = A : (B;(A:;B))$, and *asynchronous recurrent* $A::B = A : (B \mid (A::B))$. Synchronous recurrent composition is similar to *while-loop* iteration. Asynchronous recurrent composition does not iterate, but rather "spawns" off a set of concurrent processes every time its "condition" is satisfied. These special forms of guarded recursion are useful (and can be implemented efficiently).

One technique for analyzing process networks is based on the algebraic properties of these compositions operators. These properties can be used to develop a set of "process identities" that can be used to rewrite networks into alternate forms (e.g., simplify networks). One such technique that we will make reference to in the next section is to rewrite a network so that all "local" processing is hidden and treated simply as a time delay. For example, in the network $T = IN_p \langle u \rangle : A_u \langle v \rangle : OUT_{q,v}$ if the process A does not use the ports p and q, then from the perspective of communication on these ports, A is local. The network can be written as $T = IN_p \langle u \rangle : Delay_t : OUT_{p,f(u)}$, for some time t and mapping f.

The network $STREAM_{y,v} = OUT_{y,v} ::STOP$ will reappear often in our examples. This network offers to transmit the value v on the port y infinitely often.

4.2. A concise language for representing action schemas

We have already developed a planner based on an interval temporal logic (ITL) similar to that described by Pelavin [24]. Thus, the output of our proposed dynamics identification system should be compatible with the action schema input language for this planner.

Formulae in our ITL language are first order logic predicates augmented with a modal operator @, e.g., *InView(P)@i1* specifies that the predicate *InView(P)* should be evaluated over interval $i1$. In addition the special predicate *ITL(interval1, itlrelation, interval2)* is used to specify constraints between intervals, e.g., *ITL(i1, [e], i2)* specifies that the interval $i1$ should denote the same interval of time as $i2$, with e denoting equal. Other relevant time relation are s for starts, d for during and f for finishes. The i

---

[3] The concept of a *port variable*, a variable referring to a port, is being used here in place of the port connection relation used in previous $\mathcal{RS}$ work, e.g., [18].

postfix denotes the inverse and including more than one relation denotes disjunction of the relations (see [2] for more details).

Processes are described by action schemas which specify executability conditions and effects (executability conditions are generalized "pre"-conditions which may specify constraints that must hold *while* the process is executing). For instance, below, the specifications are given for the processes *LOOK(outport)* and *MOVECAMERA(inport)*. The process *LOOK* has one output port *outport*, which will hold the position information of the object, if it is in view.

```
atp_actionschema LOOK
output: outport
intervals i1,i2
executability: InView(obj) @ i2 and
                  ITL(i2, [si e di fi],LOOK)
effects:       ObjectPosition(outport) @ LOOK
endactionschema
```

(We will assume that every action schema has an associated interval of the same name that refers to the interval of execution of the process). The process *MOVECAMERA* is similarly defined but has an input port *inport*, which needs position information about the object, and will keep that object in view as long as that port has the up-to-date position of the object.

```
atp_actionschema MOVECAMERA
input: inport
intervals i1,i2
executability: ObjectPosition(inport) @ i1 and
                  ITL(i1, [si e di fi], MOVECAMERA)
effects:       InView(obj) @ MOVECAMERA
endactionschema
```

Note that the ports *inport* and *output* "carry" the (possibly changing) position information of the object. In addition to predicates denoting static information and process models, the planner can accept rules specifying consistency conditions, e.g., that only one process is allowed to transmit information to a port.

Reactions are straightforward to construct when the component actions are represented as producing or consuming port values over an interval in this continuous way. Consider constructing a *TRACKING* reaction that moves the camera to maintain an object in view. The output port of *LOOK* always has the current position of the object if that object is in view of the camera. If we place the position of an object on the input port of *MOVECAMERA* then the camera will be moved so as to place that object in view. Carrying out these actions concurrently, with the ports connected, allows us to ensure that the current position of the camera is always set to the current position of the object and thus ensure that the object is always kept in view.

4.3. A method to identify dynamics

4.3.1. Process evolution

To analyze how process networks (world models and/or plans) execute over time, it is important to be able to derive how networks evolve as component processes dynamically terminate. To this end, we introduce the *evolves* operator. We say that process P evolves into process Q under condition Ω if P possibly becomes equal to Q when condition Ω occurs; we write this as $P \xrightarrow{\Omega} Q$. If there is a set of processes that P can possibly become equal to on condition c, then P necessarily becomes equal to exactly one of these when c occurs.

To define the evolves operator, we need two pieces of information: First, we need to know for each basic process under what conditions it terminates. Second, we need to know for each composition operator, how the composition is affected by the termination conditions of each argument process.

The conditions under which the basic process P terminates successfully will be written ΩP. In some cases, we will also need to use the conditions under which P terminates unsuccessfully, i.e., *aborts* itself; these necessary (but not sufficient[4]) conditions we write as $\mho P$.

We start by defining *single-step* evolution; this captures the concept of the very next single process creation/termination change that a network can undergo. Consider a sequential composition of processes $T = P1;P2$, where P1 and P2 are basic. This network can only change as follows

$$P1;P2 \xrightarrow{\Omega P1 \vee \mho P1} P2.$$

I.e., P1;P2 always evolves into P2 whether P1 terminates successfully or aborts. In this fashion, we can define the way in which evolves interacts with all the composition operators. Appendix B contains the full description of this interaction.

A specific network P might be capable of more than one possible next evolution. We define the set of next possible evolutions as

$$poss(P) = \{(c, Q) \text{ such that } P \xrightarrow{c} Q\}. \tag{1}$$

In general we will be interested in the ultimate effect of a single chain of successive one-step evolutions. Thus, we define the evolves operator as the transitive closure of a chain of one-step evolutions:

$$P \xrightarrow{c1} P1 \xrightarrow{c2} P2 \xrightarrow{c3} \ldots \xrightarrow{cn} Q \iff P \xrightarrow{c} Q \quad \text{where } c = c1.c2.c3.\ldots.cn. \tag{2}$$

We write temporal ordering of conditions using a period, e.g., $A.B$ is read A then B.

The set of all possible evolutions is the transitive closure of $poss(P)$ over the one-step evolves operator (analogous to the concept of "reachability" and the "reachable set" in linear systems theory). We can define this recursively in terms of one-step evolution as

---

[4] A process can also be forced to abort in disabling composition "#".

"every network that can be reached in one evolution plus everything that can be reached from there", or, equivalently, in terms of the transitive evolves operator as:

$$poss^*(\mathrm{P}) = \{(c, \mathrm{Q}) \text{ such that } \mathrm{P} \xrightarrow{c} \mathrm{Q}\}. \tag{3}$$

4.3.2. Process limits

To pull out dynamics from an environment model, we need to understand how that environment behaves in the following sense. We need to understand how sensory input reflects change in the model, and ultimately how that change is related to motor output (if it is). That is, we need to construct something equivalent to the usual transfer function of linear systems theory: the result of transitively closing all the internal evolution steps between the motor and sensory interfaces. For a set of reactions, this gives us a sensory input to motor output mapping; for an environment model, it gives us a motor output to sensory input mapping. The concept of process limits and bound processes is introduced below as an approach to pulling out dynamics from an environment model expressed in $\mathcal{RS}$.

A *process limit* is a process that has evolved from the initial process, but cannot evolve any further. The significance of the limit is that it prevents any further change of behavior by the process. Any process may have zero or more limits; we call the set of limits of a process P, *limitset*(P); this is a subset of $poss^*(\mathrm{P})$:

$$(c, \mathrm{Q}) \in limitset(\mathrm{P}) \quad \begin{array}{l} \text{(i) } \mathrm{P} \xrightarrow{c} \mathrm{Q}, \text{ and} \\ \text{(ii) there exists no } (cr, \mathrm{R}) \text{ s.t. } \mathrm{Q} \xrightarrow{cr} \mathrm{R}. \end{array} \tag{4}$$

The evolves operator provides us a way to determine process limits. In the case that a process does have limits, then we can use evolves to "simulate" the execution of the network until we reach a limit. To get *all* the limits of a network we need to produce $poss^*$ for the network. Therein lies a problem: If the process is in an endless loop, however, then the "simulated" execution will also be in a loop! This can be addressed by stopping the production of $poss^*$ whenever a process recursion is detected. In the remainder of the paper, *limitset*(P) will refer to this augmented concept: all the process limits *plus* any recursive process invocation by P.

A process, such as Q in the above definition, that does not evolve to anything, we call a *bound*, since it may bound the evolution of any process it occurs in. Any basic process that never terminates is a bound. The basic processes STOP and ABORT are also bounds. Strictly speaking, whether or not a process is a bound is just a question of its definition. However, we will find it convenient to also designate specific processes as bounds for the purpose and duration of some analysis. Such processes will be referred to as pseudo-bounds.

Let EM be an $\mathcal{RS}$ model of the environment, i.e., a process network. First, we treat any sensory processes in EM as pseudo-bounds. That is, whenever one of those processes is produced in the evolution of EM, then the evolution will go no further, and this bound and the conditions under which it was evolved, will become part of the limitset. This will tell us the ultimate sensory process(es) produced due to any motor input or any environment changes. This will also tell us about internal cycles in the environment,

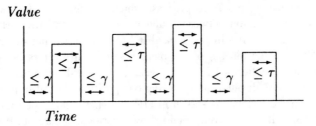

Fig. 4. Timing characteristics.

e.g., the motion of an autonomous object, since recursive process invocations are now also contained in the limitset.

We will look at a number of examples of limitset generation in Section 5 and our implementation of limitset generation is discussed in Section 6.

4.4. Translating dynamics into action schemas

In Section 4.2 we discussed the actions *LOOK* and *MOVECAMERA* and noted how easily they could be reasoned given the assumption that their associated ports continuously carried data values. Recall that our objective is to build action schemas such as these two by combining the basic sensory and motor capabilities of the agent with dynamics in the environment. The tool introduced to extract dynamics is the $\mathcal{RS}$ limitset. The limitset is a discrete concept and will tell us about the sequence processes and/or of values on a port. Before we can reason in the aforementioned fashion with ITL formalizations like *LOOK MOVECAMERA* we need to be able to say when discrete port communication can approximate a continuous signal.

The intuition here is that if a value is produced sufficiently often, then it is a reasonable approximation to continuous. So, the first criterion is that the network producing the value must be in a "loop", continually producing new values. The second criterion is that new values must be produced "often enough". We will begin by introducing some canonical network forms that produce outputs in a continual sequence with some associated time delays. These definitions will formalize the first criterion. We will then place a constraint on the timing delays to formalize the second criterion.

4.4.1. Characterizing denseness

Definition 1. For any network that can be reduced to the form

$$T_v = \text{Term}_\gamma \; ; \; (\text{STREAM}_{x,v}\#\text{Term}_\tau) \; ; \; T_v$$

for small τ and γ, we say that x is (γ, τ)-dense.

This definition establishes when a signal source (there is no input in this network) is considered (γ, τ)-dense. By "dense" we mean that the network continually produces signal values. The γ and τ are the timing characteristics for the network. It is realistic to expect that the transit from input to output will incur some small, bounded delay.

This delay is modeled by the `Term` process, which we define as follows: `Term` waits for an arbitrary time duration between 0 and its argument, and then terminates. Once a new value is calculated, it will be "locked in" for a time so that other networks can read it. `STREAM` never terminates on its own; it continually offers output on its port (see its definition in Section 4.1.2). The Term_τ process will terminate, however, after at most a time τ. Thus, through the disabling composition, "#", it terminates `STREAM`. This produces a discrete signal as shown in Fig. 4. (This is *not* a periodic signal in the standard sense [30]. It is, however, bounded by a periodic square pulse train of period $\gamma + \tau$ and duty ratio $\tau/(\tau + \gamma)$.)

We also need to consider the case when a value is transformed by a network. So given a $(\gamma i, \tau i)$-dense value on an input port x, for what kinds of network that transform that value onto a value on the output port y do we consider the value on y to be dense? This leads to our next two definitions:

Definition 2. For any network that can be reduced to the form

$$T = \text{IN}_x\langle v \rangle : (\text{Term}_{\gamma o}; (\text{STREAM}_{y,f(v)}\#\text{Term}_{\tau o})) ; T$$

for small values of τo and γo and a continuous function f then y is locally $(\gamma o, \tau o)$-dense with x.

A process being locally dense on a port means that the internal transfer of information from input to output conforms to our intuition of denseness.

Definition 3. If an input port x is $(\gamma i, \tau i)$-dense and an output port y is locally $(\gamma o, \tau o)$-dense with x then y is $(\gamma i + \gamma o, MAX(\tau i, \tau o))$-dense.

This says that in composing dense signals, the signal delays add in the resultant signal, and the resolution factor of the result is the same as larger of the two resolutions.

These (γ, τ)-denseness definitions can now be applied to a model of the environment to find the characteristics associated with environment dynamics. They are applied as indicated at the end of Section 4.1.2: rewriting networks so that all "local" processing, processing that doesn't refer to the output and/or input ports in question, is hidden and treated simply as a time delay (modeled for example by `Term`). We can use the denseness definitions in two ways. Firstly, we can use them to filter out processes that cannot be utilized in our ITL reaction generation approach. This is essentially a qualitative approach, since we don't need to know the values of τ and γ, just that the process is of the right form. But we can also use these definitions in a quantitative way, to ensure a stable mating between the timing characteristics of reactions and the environment in which they operate.

4.4.2. Denseness constraints for reactions

We say a reaction is *sufficiently dense* with respect to a port in the model of the environment if that reaction generates or consumes data more quickly than the environment does.

Let us assume that the environment model provides data, for example the position of an object, on a $(\gamma e, \tau e)$-dense port, p. Let us assume that values on p are consumed by a reaction that is $(\gamma r, \tau r)$-dense. For the reaction to be sufficiently dense with respect to this environment, we demand that the bounding period of the reaction be less than that of the environment, i.e., that $\tau r + \gamma r < \tau e + \gamma e$.

In the case that the reaction is writing to p, rather than reading from it, then we additionally constrain the reaction to enforce $\gamma r < \gamma e$. This ensures that from the point of view of the environment, the reaction is always ready to produce new data.

Under what time constraints can this combination of environment and reaction be considered stable? We will consider the system stable if the reaction is sufficiently dense, i.e., able to generate responses at a faster rate than the environment can change. Thus, if it can follow the amplitude of the changes in the environment, the reaction will indeed provide a stable behavior, by undoing the (assumed small) deviation in a single correction step each cycle.

If, on the other hand, the controls become saturated or the amplitude of the changes is large enough to lose sensor coverage in a single environment change, the interaction pattern gets broken. Saturation is a difficult subject in control theory in general, and, in our work, the implicit assumption is made that this doesn't occur.

If these denseness constraints are met, we can abstract from the interactive generation or consumption of data. Thus, the ITL description just needs to mention that the port "carries" the information. For the examples in this paper, we will employ denseness to filter out dynamics that cannot be used in our ITL reasoner. We will assume, however, that the timing characteristics of the reactions do ensure that they are sufficiently dense.

5. Detailed examples of exploiting dynamics

Sufficient structure has now been established to apply the proposed approach to some detailed examples. The following examples are from the kitting robot domain. The first is the tracking example introduced back in Section 3.3. Subsequent examples build on this one. The guarded motion example introduces motions of the robot to acquire an object. The belt example introduces environmental motions that can be exploited to acquire an object. In each case, the environment will be specified as a set of $\mathcal{RS}$ network definitions, the limitset concept used to find useful dynamics in this environment, and action schemas generated by combining these dynamics with the sensory-motor capabilities of the agent.

5.1. The tracking example

The $\mathcal{RS}$ network to implement the environment model for the tracking example discussed previously is presented below. The model is comprised of a set of mutually recursive process equations. The topmost process is the TEM (for tracking environment model) network. Its parameters are the initial position of the object to be tracked p, and the camera angle a. For simplicity, the *select* port has been omitted from the camera model; this allows us to focus more directly on the reactive portion of the problem. We will assume for now that the camera only recognizes objects of the desired type.

$$\text{TEM}_{p,a} = (\text{Object}_p \mid \text{Camera}_a),$$

$$\text{Object}_p = (\text{STREAM}_{op,p}\#\text{Delay}_{t0}) \ ; \ \text{Ran}_{-\varepsilon,\varepsilon}\langle\gamma\rangle \ : \ \text{Object}_{p+\gamma},$$

$$\text{Camera}_a = (\text{Monitor}_a\#\text{IN}_{angle}\langle na\rangle) \ : \ \text{Camera}_{na}, \tag{5}$$

$$\text{Monitor}_a = (\text{Delay}_{ts0}; \text{IN}_{op}\langle p\rangle; \text{Delay}_{ts1}) \ :: \ (\text{InView}_{p,a} : \text{ReportPos}_p),$$

$$\text{ReportPos}_p = \text{STREAM}_{posn,p}\#\text{Delay}_{ts0}.$$

The basic process $\text{Ran}_{l,h}$ is defined as producing an arbitrary result value between l and h. Ran is being used here to model the uncertainty in object motion. Thus, Object_p continually repeats the following behavior: it offers its current position p for a time $t0$ on the port op, and then "moves" (updates its position) some arbitrary amount between $+\varepsilon$ and $-\varepsilon$ relative to p. Camera_a is continually checking (via Monitor) for any object in view at the current position, while concurrently being ready to accept a new position and repeat the behavior for that position. Monitor polls the position data from Object processes and spawns off a subnetwork to determine if the object is in view and passes on the position data if it is. The process InView carries out the calculations to determine if the object is in view. If it is, then the ReportPos process continually offers the position of the object on port pos. If the object is not in view, the subnetwork just aborts. The values of $t0, ts0$ and $ts1$ are constant and are timing characteristics of the model. (The use of $ts0$ and $ts1$ in Monitor and ReportPos is necessary for denseness reasons explained later.)

The TEM model describes the environment itself. However, the agent interacts with this environment through its sensors and actuators. These sensors and actuators may impose limitations on this interaction, so we need to model them also. We will assume the sensory-motor interface is defined by the two processes sense1 and motor1 defined as follows:

$$\text{sense1} = (\text{IN}_{pos}\langle v\rangle; \text{Delay}_{gl}) \ :; (\text{STREAM}_{s1,v}\#\text{Delay}_{tl}),$$

$$\text{motor1} = (\text{IN}_{m1}\langle v\rangle; \text{Delay}_{gm}) \ :; (\text{STREAM}_{angle,v}\#\text{Delay}_{tm}). \tag{6}$$

These primitive "actions" affect or are affected by parts of the environment model, i.e., sense1 is affected by pos and motor1 affects $angle$. There is an important issue of style here that needs to be emphasized: the agent does not invoke whatever effect motor1 has on the environment by creating an instance of motor1. The action is invoked by writing a message on motor1's input port $m1$. A single instance of each of sense1 and motor1 is always present and these constitute the sensory-motor interface. Each is in a loop, continually reading a value and passing that value to/from the environment.

The timing delays in these actions, gl, tl, gm, and tm, model the timing delays in real sensor and effector hardware. These actions have been given neutral names, rather than names such as "movecamera" and so on, to reinforce the fact that they do not constitute actions usable by the ITL planner. Rather the *combination* of one of these actions plus some dynamic extracted from the environment is what is presented to the ITL planner as an action.

The environment model and sensory-motor interface have now been described. Any *specific* environment and agent will be characterized by an instance of TEM with its initial parameters and instances of `sense1` and `motor1`, e.g.,

$$\text{ThisWorld} = \text{TEM}_{pinit,ainit} \mid \text{sense1} \mid \text{motor1} \tag{7}$$

where *pinit* and *ainit* are constants.

Notice that all these networks produce values on ports in a *discrete* fashion. For example, the port *pos* does not present a continuously changing value, rather it holds a value that changes in discrete time increments of $ts0$. The value $ts0$ models the rate at which object position information changes in the environment. In contrast, the timing delays in `sense1` and `motor1` model the rate at which *the agent's* sensors and actuators interact with the environment.

The next step is to proceed with extracting dynamics from the environment model. As discussed in Section 4.3.1, this is done by looking at the limitset of the environment model network assuming that the sensory input processes (and any recursive calls) are pseudo-bounds. This produces the following set (the mechanization of this operation is described in Section 6):

$$\begin{aligned} limitset(\text{TEM}_{p,a}) = \{ \quad &(\gamma \in [-\varepsilon, \varepsilon] \quad ,\text{TEM}_{p+\gamma,a}), \\ &(\Omega \text{IN}_{angle}\langle na \rangle \quad ,\text{TEM}_{p,na}), \\ &(inview(p) \quad ,\text{TEM}_{p,a} \mid \text{ReportPos}_p) \\ &\}. \end{aligned} \tag{8}$$

The first element of the limitset tells us that left on its own (no conditions) the object process may "move" (i.e., the location value that it transmits may change). The second element tells us that changing the value on the *angle* port changes the camera position. Let the termination condition of the process `InView` be written as $inview(p)$. The final element tells us that if the predicate $inview(p)$ holds then the port *pos* holds the value of the object position. We are now in a position to combine the information on the dynamics in the environment with the basic sensory and motor definitions, based on what will provide dense information, and generate a set of high-level abstractions for ITL.

Based on Definitions 2 and 3 and the assumption that tm and gm are small enough, we can say that if the value on *angle* in `motor1` is dense, then so is the position of the camera. Therefore we can add an ITL actionschema $MOVECAMERA(a)$ with the formalization as given earlier in Section 4.2. When $MOVECAMERA(a)$ is applied on an interval I then the position of the camera in that interval is always the same as the value set in a.

Now considering *pos*, we can say that if $inview(p)$ holds, then *pos* reflects the position of the object. But is it (γ, τ)-dense? TEM employs an asynchronous recurrent composition (the "::") to spawn off a `ReportPos` process to report on the position of the object. Our denseness definitions were based on a simpler recursive form. (We have to use the asynchronous composition for `ReportPos` to appear as part of the limitset.) As it happens, the denseness of the asynchronous form can be related to Definition 2 *as*

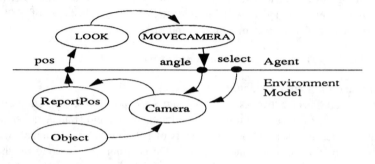

Fig. 5. The tracking reaction.

long as the signal is periodic and we "sandwich" the input process between two delay processes as shown in Monitor. This result is demonstrated in Appendix A. A more general result can be obtained at the expense of a slightly more complex environment model.

Thus, by Appendix A, *pos* is dense if the position reported by the object is dense and if the object is in view. Definition 1 establishes that the position reported by the object is dense. Thus, the abstract ITL action $LOOK(p)$, defined as in Section 4.2, can be constructed: If $LOOK(p)$ holds on an interval I then if the object is in view, then the value of p is the value of the position of the object.

From these candidate actions, it is straightforward for the ITL planner to construct the TRACK reflex to maintain an object in view. This consists of running the LOOK and MOVECAMERA actions concurrently with their ports connected. Translating this ITL specification back into $\mathcal{RS}$ produces the network:

$$\text{TRACK} = (\text{LOOK}_p \mid \text{MOVECAMERA}_p). \tag{9}$$

The mechanization of this example is reported in Section 6.

5.2. *The guarded motion environment*

The guarded move environment model GEM is shown in Fig. 6. This is similar to the tracking environment except that we now additionally represent the robot itself and a tactile sensor mounted on the robot's gripper. There is an additional control port that allows us to *incrementally* move the robot, and an additional sensor port that reports back when an object has been contacted.

The objective in this example is for the robot to acquire the object. To do this, it needs to reach out by incrementally updating its position in the direction of the object, and when the tactile sensor indicates that contact has occurred, to grasp the object.

The $\mathcal{RS}$ network to implement the environment for the guarded move environment is the set of process equations for the tracking environment *plus* the equations given below:

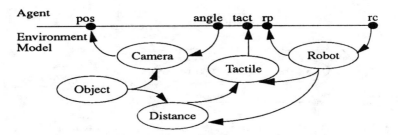

Fig. 6. The guarded motion environment GEM.

$$\text{GEM}_{p,a,rp} = (\text{TEM}_{p,a} \mid \text{Robot}_{rp} \mid \text{Tactile} \mid \text{Dist}),$$

$$\text{Robot}_p = (\text{IN}_{rc}\langle\delta\rangle \# \text{STREAM}_{rp,p}) \; ; \; \text{Robot}_{p+\delta},$$

$$\text{Dist} = (\text{IN}_{op}\langle p1\rangle \mid \text{IN}_{rp}\langle p2\rangle) \; :; \; \text{OUT}_{d,p1-p2}, \tag{10}$$

$$\text{Tactile} = (\text{Delay}_{tt0}; \text{IN}_d\langle v\rangle; \text{Delay}_{tt1}) \; :: \; (\text{Equal}_{v,0} : \text{ReportTact}_1),$$

$$\text{ReportTact}_v = \text{STREAM}_{tact,v} \# \text{Delay}_{tt0}.$$

The highest-level process is GEM and its arguments are the initial object and camera positions and the initial position of the robot arm. $tt0$ and $tt1$ are constant values, timing characteristics of the model.

The additional basic sensory-motor interface processes we need are now:

$$\text{touch} = (\text{IN}_{tact}\langle v\rangle; \text{Delay}_{gto}) \; :; \; (\text{STREAM}_{t,v} \# \text{Delay}_{tto}),$$

$$\text{move} = (\text{IN}_r\langle d\rangle; \text{Delay}_{gmv}) \; :; \; (\text{STREAM}_{rp,d} \# \text{Delay}_{tmv}). \tag{11}$$

We can build on the tracking reaction established in the previous section. The tracking reaction ensures that the object always remains in view. This in turns establish that $LOOK(p)$ always returns the object's position. To determine what other high-level actions we can construct, we need to again identify dynamics in the environment model.

This gives us the following set (duplicating partially the results from TEM):

$$limitset(\text{GEM}_{p,a,pr}) = \{ \; (\gamma \in [-\varepsilon, \varepsilon] \quad , \; \text{GEM}_{p+\gamma,a,pr}),$$

$$(\Omega\text{IN}_{angle}\langle na\rangle \quad , \; \text{GEM}_{p,na,pr}),$$

$$(inview(p) \quad , \; \text{GEM}_{p,a,pr} \mid \text{ReportPos}_p),$$

$$(\Omega\text{IN}_{rc}\langle\delta\rangle \quad , \; \text{GEM}_{p,a,pr+\delta}), \tag{12}$$

$$(dist(p,pr) = 0 \; , \; \text{GEM}_{p,a,pr} \mid \text{ReportTact}_1)$$

$$\}.$$

The first three entries parallel those of TEM. The fourth entry reports that sending a value of δ to the rc port will cause the robot to move δ from its current position. The final entry claims that when the distance between the robot and the object is zero, then the tactile sensor will signal a 1. This is sufficient to allow us to construct a high-level process *CONTACT* whose behavior is to terminate whenever the tactile sensor signals a

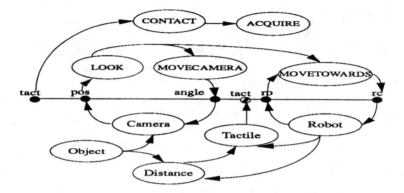

Fig. 7. The guarded motion reaction.

contact. However, our definitions of denseness are not sufficient to allow us to build a $MOVETOWARDS(r)$ action that we can connect with a concurrent $LOOK(p)$ to push us towards the object. We are missing the notion of approximating continuous increasing or decreasing values. This motivates the following definition:

Definition 4. For any network that can be reduced to the form

$$T_v = \text{Term}_\gamma \; ; \; (\text{STREAM}_{x,v} \# \text{Term}_\tau) \; ; \; T_{v+\delta}$$

for small values of τ and γ then x is
   (1) (γ, τ)-densely increasing if $\delta > 0$,
   (2) (γ, τ)-dense if $\delta = 0$,
   (3) (γ, τ)-densely decreasing if $\delta < 0$.

Definitions 2 and 3 now need to be extended so that they "transfer" the densely increasing/decreasing properties also. If Definition 4 is used along with the others in our generator of high-level actions then we can suggest some interesting new actions. The third entry in the limitset combined with move tells us that for a positive value, r will be densely increasing on robot position, suggesting a high-level action $MOVEUP(r)$. For a negative value, r will be densely decreasing, suggesting a high-level action $MOVEDOWN(r)$. More interestingly, if r is $p - pr$, then it is densely decreasing with respect to $dist(p, pr)$, suggesting an action $MOVETOWARDS(r)$ and, if r is $pr - p$, then it is densely increasing with respect to $dist(p, pr)$, suggesting an action $MOVEAWAY(r)$.

We can now construct a useful reaction from these actions as follows. We make a concurrent combination of $LOOK(p)$ and $MOVETOWARDS(r)$ with p connected to r. We can tell from the descriptions of these actions that this will eventually produce $dist(p, pr) = 0$. We can recognize this fact with $CONTACT$ and begin the acquisition at that point. Let us assume an action $ACQUIRE$ to complete the acquisition. Translating this ITL specification back into $\mathcal{RS}$ we produce the reaction network:

$$\text{GuardedMove} = (\text{CONTACT} \# (\text{LOOK}_p \mid \text{MOVETOWARDS}_p)); \text{ACQUIRE}. \tag{13}$$

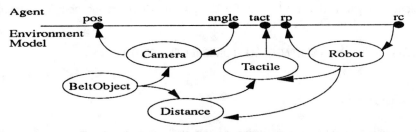

Fig. 8. The belt environment BEM.

5.3. The belt environment

The belt environment model BEM is shown in Fig. 8. This is very similar to the guarded move environment except that we replace the `Object` process with a `BeltObject` process. This process represents an object on the belt.

The objective in this example is the same as in the previous example: to acquire the object. The interesting variation here is that the belt motion will carry the object to the robot if it's "smart enough" to take advantage of it.

The $\mathcal{RS}$ network to implement the environment for the belt environment is the guarded move environment with `Object` replaced by `BeltObject` defined below:

$$\text{BeltObject}_p = (\text{STREAM}_{op,p} \# \text{Delay}_{tm0}) \; ; \; \text{LST}_{p,\nu} \; : \; \text{Object}_{p+\mu}. \tag{14}$$

`BeltObject` is a version of `Object` in which the position of the object only increments in a fixed direction and amount μ in time $tm0$. Once the position of the object hits the end of the belt, ν, the process recursion terminates, indicating that the object is now off the end of the belt and no more position signals are generated. The process $\text{BEM}_{p,a,pr}$ is the same as GEM but with `Object` replaced by `BeltObject`.

Applying the limitset approach to identifying dynamics, we get the following set (duplicating partially the results from GEM):

$$
\begin{aligned}
limitset(\text{BEM}_{p,a,pr}) \; = \{ \; &(p < \nu &&, \text{BEM}_{p+\mu,a,pr}), \\
&(\Omega\text{IN}_{angle}\langle na \rangle &&, \text{BEM}_{p,na,pr}), \\
&(inview(p) &&, \text{BEM}_{p,a,pr} \mid \text{ReportPos}_p), \\
&(\Omega\text{IN}_{rc}\langle \delta \rangle &&, \text{BEM}_{p,a,pr+\delta}), \\
&(dist(p,pr) = 0 \;, &&\text{BEM}_{p,a,pr} \mid \text{ReportTact}_1) \\
&\}.
\end{aligned}
\tag{15}
$$

The first entry tells us that as long as the position of the object is less than ν, then the object will move incrementally in the direction μ. If we look at this entry with respect to Definition 3, then in addition to the actions we pulled out of GEM, we can suggest a high-level action that is densely decreasing with respect to $dist(p,pr)$ as long as $p < \nu$. This high-level action is *WAITFOROBJECT*. The reaction generated for the guarded move is equally valid in this environment. However, we can now also generate a reaction in which the robot waits for the part to arrive on the belt. This translates to

GuardedWait = (CONTACT#WAITFOROBJECT); ACQUIRE.

6. Mechanization

This section contains a description of our prototype implementation. The purpose of this implementation is to demonstrate that the mechanization of our approach to identifying dynamics and constructing action descriptions based on them is indeed possible. The implementation is an action generation module designed to fit into our current planner–reactor framework. Its input is a world model described in $\mathcal{RS}$, and its output is a set of ITL action descriptions that the ITL planner can use to construct reactions or reactors. This prototype implementation is in PROLOG.

The generation of actions from world models is completed in three steps: First, the limitset of the world model is generated, to identify candidate dynamics in the environment. Secondly, those dynamics that can be sensed or affected by the agents sensors or actuators respectively, are identified and selected. This set is further reduced by considering only those dynamics that convey port information in a manner compatible with our definitions of denseness. Finally, ITL action schemas are generated from this reduced set of dynamics.

6.1. Limitset generation

Recall from Section 4.3.1 that a limit of a process P is a process that P has evolved into and which will not evolve into anything further; it "caps" the evolution of P. The limitset of P is a set of couples, one for each limit of P, containing the limit and the conditions under which P will evolve to that limit.

The concept of process evolution is central to the definition of the limitset of a process. The easiest approach to implementing the limitset function is to implement evolution as *simulated execution*. Evolution is defined in [17] in terms of the simulated execution of each composition operator and the conditions under which basic processes terminate. This definition is easily implemented in PROLOG. To do this, of course, we need to construct a PROLOG notation for process names, parameters, and results and for composition operations. To simplify this exposition, however, we will continue to use $\mathcal{RS}$ notation for the PROLOG examples below.

The termination conditions of basic processes need to be supplied as an input to the implementation. We do this with the predicate stopcondition(T,I,O,C) defined for each basic process T, where I and O are the parameter and result lists of the process, and C is the termination condition (which may contain references to the parameters or results). These condition statements will eventually be used as part of the executability conditions and effects of candidate actions.

Here are the PROLOG definitions of the stopcondition predicate for some of the basic processes we have used in this paper:

```
stopcondition( Delay ,[T]      , _ , duration(T)          ).
stopcondition( Ran    ,[L,H]  ,[N] , (N=random(L,H))  ).
stopcondition( In     ,[PN]    ,[N] , (N=commin(PN))   ).
stopcondition( Out    ,[PN,V] , _ , (commout(PN)=V) ).
```

The first statement establishes that the termination condition of Delay_T is the condition *duration*(T). In this case, we interpret *duration*(T) as that a time T has passed. The termination condition of $\text{Ran}_{L,H}\langle N \rangle$ is that the result N is set to an arbitrary value between the values L and H. The termination condition for $\text{In}_{PN}\langle N \rangle$ is that the result N is set to whatever communication arrives on the port *PN*. The termination condition for Out is interpreted similarly. These termination conditions need to be predicates that can be understood or translated by the ITL planner.

The evolves predicate ev() can now be written as follows, based on the stopcondition predicate and the definition of evolution in the Appendix.

```
ev( N_P⟨R⟩ ,STOP ,C) :- stopcondition(N,P,R,C).
ev( X;Y    ,Z    ,C) :- ev(X,STOP,A),  ev(Y,Z,B), C=A.B.
ev( X:Y    ,Z    ,C) :- ev(X,STOP,A),  ev(Y,Z,B), C=A.B.
ev( X:Y    ,Z    ,C) :- ev(X,ABORT,C), Z=ABORT.
```

and so on for $X \mid Y$, $X\#Y$, $X:;Y$ and $X::Y$. The notation $A.B$ indicates the temporal ordering between conditions A and B.

A process may evolve to more than one other process, so sometimes we will need to return a list of processes and conditions. For example, in the network P#Q either process could terminate first, so we need to return both possibilities. Applying the ev() function to the TEM world model (suitably transcribed into PROLOG, of course) we get:

```
?- ev(TEM_{p,a},P,C).
P = [ Object_{np} Camera_{na} ReportPos_{pos,p,ts} ].

C = [ (streamout(op,t0)=p) . (np=random(p+e,p-e))
         na=commin(ang)
         duration(ts) . (p=commin(op)) . objectinview(p)
      ].
```

P and C above contain the same data as the *limitset*(TEM) shown in the previous section, but in a different format. Each list element of P is a limit process, and the corresponding list element of C is the condition under which that limit occurs. Notice also that ev() only lists the element of the network TEM that has become a limit, this is more convenient for generating action schemas than the limitset definition.

6.2. *Selection of candidate dynamics*

Having obtained the candidate dynamics, the next step is to determine which of these can be influenced by, or can influence the agent. We accomplish this by looking at the port connections between the sensory-motor interface of the agent and each of the dynamics. We define a PROLOG predicate sensible() (the dynamic can be sensed by the agent)

> sensible(D,P,N) :- basicsense(P), usesport(N,P), usesport(N,D).

That is, dynamic D is sensible by the agent using sensory process P and port N if P is a basic sensory process and if P and D communicate via some port N. The predicate effectable() can be defined similarly for basic motor processes. Note that applying these predicates to the three candidate actions from the limitset analysis results in the first dynamic, that of Object, being rejected, and the sensory and motor connections for the second and third dynamics being identified.

> ?- effectable(Camera,P1,N1), sensible(ReportPos,P2,N2).

> P1 = motor1,   P2 = sense1,
> N1 = *ang*,   N2 = *pos*.

To validly translate port communications into ITL, it is necessary to ensure that the communications are dense in the manner we have already discussed. Definition 1 defines dense "output-only" processes. Definition 2 defines local, i.e., input-to-output, denseness. Definition 3 gives the rule for determining under what conditions a locally dense process is dense. Definitions 1 and 2 require implementing a syntactic scan of the world model to determine for each process if it obeys the dense and/or local dense definitions. This only need be done once and off-line. For now, we assume that this scan has been done and we concentrate on implementing Definition 3: A process is dense if it obeys Definition 1, or if it is locally dense on a port and that port receives data from (if it's an input) or transmits data to (if it's an output) a dense process:

> dense(IP,P) :- locallydense(IP,OP,P),usesport(OP,DP),not(DP=P), dense(OP,DP).
> dense(OP,P) :- locallydense(IP,OP,P),usesport(IP,DP),not(DP=P), dense(IP,DP).

To finish the selection of candidate dynamics, we use dense() to ensure that the candidate dynamic is dense on the port returned by sensible() or effectable(). In this case, both are. In our current system, this is the only use that is made of the *duration* information. After this step, the duration information is dropped from all conditions.

6.3. *Generation of action schemas*

The final step is to generate the ITL action schemas from the candidate dynamics. An ITL action schema has the following fields:

> Name
> Input Port and Basic Sensory Process
> Output Port and Basic Motor Process
> Temporal intervals used
> Executability
> Effects

Most of these are straightforward to fill in from the description of the dynamic and its associated sensory-motor connection. The executability condition is derived from the condition element of the dynamic. For example, the condition on the `ReportPos` dynamic is $duration(ts).(p = commin(op)).objectinview(p)$. After some cleaning up (described in the following paragraph), this roughly translates into saying that there should be an object in view. The effect comes from the limit process element of the dynamic, `ReportPos` in this example. However, this latter is a process. It is necessary to have a predicate effects() that translates a process into a language that the ITL planner can use, namely, a form similar to the condition generated by ev(). The mapping from process to effects, like the stopcondition predicate, needs to be supplied as input for our mechanization. For example, the effect of the process $Camera_{na}$ is that the camera position is set to na, and any object that is at position na is now in view. The effect of $ReportPos_{p,v,t}$ is that the object position is reported on port p.

There is also some minor housekeeping to be done. ITL actions refer to ports, not to values on the ports. Thus whenever we have a $v = commin(p)$ or $commout(p) = v$ statement in a condition or effect, we need to replace all occurrences of the variable v with p throughout the rest of that condition. We can then remove the $commin$ or $commout$ from the condition. The condition for the `ReportPos` dynamic then becomes $objectinview(op)$ (duration has been dropped after the denseness step, op has been substituted for p, and the $commin$ dropped). Finally in all conditions and effects, we replace references to all ports which are connected to sensory or motor ports, with the name of the sensory or motor ports to which they are connected.

The following are the action schema generated by the two dynamics:

```
atp_actionschema camera-55 Input: [ m1 ]
Output: [ ]
Intervals: [int-camera-55, int-54]
Executability:
    objectposition(m1) @ int-54 and
        ITL(int-54, [si,e,di,fi], int-camera-55)
Effects:
    cameraposition(m1) @ int-camera-55 and
        objectinview(m1) @ int-camera-55
endactionschema camera-55

atp_actionschema reportpos-57
Input: [ ]
Output: [ s1 ]
Intervals: [int-reportpos-57, int-56]
Executability:
    objectinview(op) @ int-56 and
        ITL( int-56, [si,e,di,fi], int-reportpos-57)
Effects:
    objectposition(s1) @ int-reportpos-57
endactionschema reportpos-57
```

6.4. Extensions

The purpose of this implementation has been to demonstrate that mechanization of the approach is feasible. The primary work was in mechanizing the limitset product, and this was based on simulated execution using the evolves operator. The limitset implementation is surprisingly robust, given its simplicity and the brute force approach taken. It doesn't explicitly know about variable or result scope, or about recursion, yet in general it handles both of these in a satisfactory manner. This is not altogether surprising for two reasons: Firstly, simulated execution is a technique already used in many branches of computer science and is not that challenging to implement correctly. Secondly, much of the work of interpreting the limitset results is actually done by the ITL planner—the limitset implementation doesn't worry about variable scope, for example, because the ITL planner handles this in processing the executability condition and effects derived from the limitset.

Nonetheless, the limitset implementation used here is simplified in that it doesn't reason about port communication between concurrent processes, and certain kinds of recursion will trigger an endless loop. In [17], a set of limit theorems are developed that directly relate the structure of the limitset and the structure of the process network. Employing that approach to synthesizing the limitset promises a more efficient implementation, and one which handles recursion in a more elegant way.

The connectivity analysis, to determine which dynamic is connected to which sensory or motor port, is straightforward. Indeed, the entire processing could be done off-line and accessed when necessary. The denseness definitions (Definitions 1 and 2) can also be performed off-line. However, Definition 3 needs to be carried out for each dynamic. It can only be done off-line at the expense of analyzing all possible connections. The implementations of densely increasing/decreasing were not shown here, but can be addressed in a manner similar to the implementations of Definitions 1 and 2; that is, carried out off-line and accessed on-line.

The implementation of the denseness definitions is in progress. The approach is that all processes in a process network that do not concern input or output on a port are reduced to time delays. In the case that a process uses only one port, or a single input and output port, the implementation is not difficult. In the case that more ports are involved, the problem may be complicate, and we have not developed any general solutions yet.

7. Conclusions

We have presented an approach to identifying and exploiting dynamics—patterns of interaction—in the environment. The work has been done in the context of, but not yet integrated with, the planner–reactor architecture. The approach divides the problem into two related sub-problems: Firstly, the environment model is analyzed to identify dynamics. This analysis is carried out using the limitset concept from the $\mathcal{RS}$ model. Secondly, the dynamics are used to construct high-level ITL actions, each representing a process with inputs and outputs, that can be used to construct reactions. The concept of the "denseness" of the information on a communication port is important for addressing the timing and continuity issues. ITL reasoning can then be used to select high-level actions and connect them together appropriately. Although we did not pursue the derivation of the timing characteristics in reactions, we did lay the groundwork for it. That information becomes important in real-time scheduling of the processes that implement reactions.

There are a number of architectures in the literature similar to our planner–reactor architecture: Bresina and Drummond's ERE [4], McDermott's Transformational Planner [23] and Sutton's DYNA [31] among others. The principle novelty of the planner–reactor architecture is in the loose and well-defined interaction between planner and reactor, and in the characterization of the reactor as a concurrent network of processes using the $\mathcal{RS}$ language. These two features enable the formalization of the on-going, iterative process of adaptation to explore the issue of the convergence of the reactive system [19].

Our definition of the planner as incrementally generating reactions to exploit the environment has few comparisons in the planning literature. Chapman [6] introduces the definition of dynamics as acausal patterns of interaction. However, he does not investigate the problem of analyzing an environment to derive dynamics. Schoppers [26] addresses a problem very similar to ours. However, he chooses to make the dynamics of the environment explicit in his action descriptions in terms of temporal *soon* and *sust* operators. In our case, these dynamics are implicit in the process model description of the environment, and are only identified by the limitset calculation.

Our approach means that it's not necessary to be aware of the agent's objectives when constructing the environment model; no action repertoire needs to be modeled, justified and qualified a priori. Rather, the on-line construction of reactions based on the *current* environment enables an agent to achieve its objectives using environment dynamics which may only partly be in its control. The generated reactions capture "closed loop" control law behavior, derived from "open loop" actions. This context-sensitive abstraction of repetitive behavior is a major contribution of this approach.

We earlier made the comparison with Horswill's *habitat constraints* and his language of equivalence transformations to simplify agents so as to exploit their environment. Our limitset analysis allows us to derive dynamics that do work the agent may want to do and offer these as candidate portions of reactions. It does not address equivalence in the sense Horswill does, and it may be possible to enrich our system by developing analogs of his transforms in our limitset analysis.

There are two drawbacks to the approach. It presumes that a (possibly partial) model of the environment can be put together beforehand, and its usefulness hinges on the environment having dynamics to exploit that are relevant to the agents objectives. The latter, we argue, is a reasonable "richness" assumption to make about "real-life" environments. The former can only be addressed by learning.

Future work needs to address the following points:

(1) Focusing in on a set of environment processes given the planner's objectives and constructing a subnet of the environment from these. (The *Snet* algorithm discussed in [17] may be of use in this problem.)

(2) The planner–reactor policy of assumption relaxation needs to be incorporated. Assumptions are a second way to limit the size of the subnet of the environment

model under consideration. However, the reactions chosen will need to obey the convergence constraints for the planner–reactor developed in [19].

Appendix A. Denseness for asynchronous composition

The following lemma and theorem establish a denseness result for asynchronous recurrent composition. We will show this result only for the periodic case (where delays of exactly γ and τ are incurred). The same results can be proven for the non-periodic case (where γ and τ are upper bounds) at the expense of a slightly more complex network.

Lemma 5. *For the network*

$$\text{ST} = (\text{IN}_x\langle v \rangle; \text{Delay}_{\gamma o}) \; ::; \; (\text{STREAM}_{y, f(v)} \# \text{Delay}_{\tau o})$$

for small values of γo and τo and a continuous function f then if y is $(\gamma i, \tau i)$-dense then x is $(\gamma i + \gamma o, MAX(\tau i, \tau o))$-dense.

This is straightforward to show, since the ::; operator is defined recursively. Applying its definition to the network of Lemma 5 yields the exact form of the network in Definition 2. More difficult to show, and more useful in our case, is the next theorem:

Theorem 6. *For the network*

$$\text{AT} = (\text{Delay}_{\tau o}; \text{IN}_x\langle v \rangle; \text{Delay}_{\gamma o}) \; :: \; (\text{STREAM}_{y, f(v)} \# \text{Delay}_{\tau o})$$

for small values of γo and τo and a continuous function f then if y is $(\gamma i, \tau i)$-dense then x is $(\gamma i + \gamma o, MAX(\tau i, \tau o))$-dense.

The two τo delay processes end up being activated in parallel. Output then ceases, input happens, and γo passes before the next output. Thus, the delays sequence the IN process to begin only once the previous STREAM network has been terminated. This allows the reduction of AT to the form ST which Lemma 5 establishes is dense.

Appendix B. Definition of one-step process evolution

The following definitions capture one-step evolution. All process terminations below are of basic processes.

- $P \xrightarrow{\Omega P} \text{STOP}$ (definition of termination condition).
- $P \xrightarrow{\upsilon P} \text{ABORT}$ (definition of abort condition).
- Sequential: $P \; ; \; Q \xrightarrow{\Omega P \vee \upsilon P} Q$.
- Concurrent:
    - $(P \mid Q) \xrightarrow{\pi(cp, cq)} (P' \mid Q')$ iff $P \xrightarrow{cp} P'$ and $Q \xrightarrow{cq} Q'$ (where $\pi(c1, c2, \ldots)$ maps a set of conditions onto the disjunction of all their orderings).

- $\quad\Big|_{i\in I} \mathrm{P}i \xrightarrow{c} \mathtt{ABORT}$ iff all the processes abort, $c = \bigwedge\limits_{i\in I} \mho\mathrm{P}i$.

- $\quad\Big|_{i\in I} \mathrm{P}i \xrightarrow{c} \mathtt{STOP}$ iff at least one process terminates successfully,

$$c = (\bigwedge\limits_{i\in A} \mho\mathrm{P}i) \wedge (\bigwedge\limits_{j\in S} \Omega\mathrm{P}j),$$

where $A \cup S = I$, $A \cap S = \emptyset$ and $S \neq \emptyset$.

- Conditional:
  - $\mathrm{P}\langle i\rangle : \mathrm{Q}_i \xrightarrow{\Omega\mathrm{P}} \mathrm{Q}_i$, and
  - $\mathrm{P}\langle i\rangle : \mathrm{Q}_i \xrightarrow{\mho\mathrm{P}} \mathtt{ABORT}$.

  Different behavior on termination versus abortion is what makes this operator "conditional".

- Disabling:
  - $(\mathrm{P\#Q}) \xrightarrow{\pi(cp,cq)} (\mathrm{P'\#Q'})$ iff $\mathrm{P} \xrightarrow{cp} \mathrm{P'}$ and $\mathrm{Q} \xrightarrow{cq} \mathrm{Q'}$.
  - $\#_{i\in I}\mathrm{P}i \xrightarrow{c} \mathtt{ABORT}$ iff all processes abort.
  - $\#_{i\in I}\mathrm{P}i \xrightarrow{c} \mathtt{STOP}$ iff at least one process terminates.

Note that disabling composition can force a component process to abort. Thus, components of disabling composition need to have their abort conditions extended to include the cases under which the network forces them to abort. It is important to distinguish these (necessary and sufficient) extended conditions $\overline{\mho\mathrm{A}}$ from the (necessary) spontaneous conditions $\mho\mathrm{A}$. The relationship between these conditions is, for A in a disabling network with P1, P2, ...,

$$\overline{\mho\mathrm{A}} = \mho\mathrm{A} \vee (\bigvee\limits_{\mathrm{P}i\neq\mathrm{A}} (\mho\mathrm{P} \vee \Omega\mathrm{P})). \tag{B.1}$$

References

[1] P. Agre and D. Chapman, Pengi: an implementation of a theory of action, in: *Proceedings AAAI-87*, Seattle, WA (1987) 268–272.

[2] J.F. Allen, Towards a general theory of action and time, *Artif. Intell.* **23** (2) (1984) 123–154.

[3] R.C. Arkin, Motor schema-based mobile robot navigation, *Int. J. Rob. Res.* **8** (4) (1989) 92–112.

[4] J. Bresina and M. Drummond, Integrating planning and reaction, in: J. Hendler, ed., *AAAI Spring Workshop on Planning in Uncertain, Unpredictable or Changing Environments*, Stanford, CA (1990).

[5] R. Brooks, A robust layered control system for a mobile robot, *IEEE J. Rob. Autom.* **2** (1) (1986) 14–22.

[6] D. Chapman, *Vision, Instruction, and Action* (MIT Press, Cambridge, MA, 1992).

[7] S. Chien, M. Gervasion, and G. DeJong, On becoming decreasingly reactive: learning to deliberate minimally, in: *Ninth Machine Learning Workshop* (1991) 288–292.

[8] R.J. Firby, Adaptive execution in complex dynamic worlds, Ph.D. Dissertation and Research Report YALEU/CSD/RR#672, Yale University, New Haven, CT (1989).

[9] K.D. Forbus, Qualitative process theory, *Artif. Intell.* **24** (1984) 85–168.

[10] M. Ginsberg, Reasoning about action II: the qualification problem, *Artif. Intell.* **25** (1988) 311–342.

[11] G. Hendrix, Modeling simultaneous actions and continuous processes, *Artif. Intell.* **4** (1973) 145–180.

[12] C.A.R. Hoare, *Communicating Sequential Processes* (Prentice-Hall, Englewood Cliffs, CA, 1985).

[13] I. Horswill, Analysis of adaptation and environment, *Artif. Intell.* **73** (1995) 1–30 (this volume).

[14] L.P. Kaelbling, Goals as parallel program specifications, in: *Proceedings AAAI-88*, St. Paul, MN (1988) 60–65.

[15] D. Lyons and A. Hendriks, A practical approach to integrating reaction and deliberation, in: *First International AI Conference on Planning Systems*, College Park, MD (1992).

[16] D.M. Lyons, A formal model for reactive robot plans, in: *Second International Conference on Computer Integrated Manufacturing*, Troy, NY (1990).

[17] D.M. Lyons, Representing and analysing action plans as networks of concurrent processes, *IEEE Trans. Rob. Autom.* **9** (3) (1993).

[18] D.M. Lyons and M.A. Arbib, A formal model of computation for sensory-based robotics, *IEEE Trans. Rob. Autom.* **5** (3) (1989) 280–293.

[19] D.M. Lyons and A.J. Hendriks, Planning for reactive robot behavior, in: *IEEE Int. Conf. Rob. Autom.* (1992); (see also video proceedings).

[20] D.M. Lyons and A.J. Hendriks, Safely adapting a hierarchical reactive system, in: *SPIE Intelligent Robots and Computer Vision XII* (1993).

[21] D.M. Lyons and A.J. Hendriks, Planning by adaptation: experimental results, in: *IEEE Int. Conf. Rob. Autom.*, San Diego CA (1994).

[22] D.M. Lyons, A.J. Hendriks, and S. Mehta, Achieving robustness by casting planning as adaptation of a reactive system, in: *IEEE Int. Conf. Rob. Autom.* (1991).

[23] D. McDermott, Robot planning, Tech. Report YALEU/CSD/RR#861, Yale University, New Haven, CT (1991).

[24] R. Pelavin, A formal approach to planning with concurrent actions and external events, Ph.D. Thesis, Department of Computer Science, University of Rochester, Rochester, NY (1988).

[25] M. Schoppers, Representation and automatic synthesis of reaction plans, Tech. Report UIUCDCS-R-89-1546 (also Ph.D. Thesis), Department of Computer Science, University of Illinois at Urbana-Champaign, (1989).

[26] M. Schoppers, Building plans to monitor and exploit open loop and closed loop dynamics, in: J. Hendler, ed., *AI Planning Systems* (1992) 204–213.

[27] C.J. Sellers and S.Y. Nof, Performance analysis of robotic kitting systems, *Rob. Comp. Integ. Manuf.* **6** (1) (1989) 15–24.

[28] Y. Shoham, *Reasoning about change*, MIT Press Series in Artificial Intelligence (MIT Press, Cambridge, MA, 1988).

[29] L. Spector and J. Hendler, Knowledge strata: reactive planning with a multi-level architecture, Tech. Report UMIACS-TR-90-140, Institute of Advanced Computer Studies, University of Maryland, MD (1990).

[30] H. Stark and F. Tuteur, *Modern Electrical Communications: Theory and Systems* (Prentice Hall, Englewood Cliffs, NJ, 1979).

[31] R. Sutton, First results with Dyna, in: J. Hendler, ed., *AAAI Spring Symposium on Planning in uncertain and changing environments*, Stanford CA (1990).

Artificial Intelligence 73 (1995) 149–173

A situated view of representation and control

Stanley J. Rosenschein [1], Leslie Pack Kaelbling [*,2]

Computer Science Department, Box 1910, Brown University, Providence, RI 02912-1910, USA

Received December 1993; revised September 1994

Abstract

Intelligent agents are systems that have a complex, ongoing interaction with an environment that is dynamic and imperfectly predictable. Agents are typically difficult to program because the correctness of a program depends on the details of how the agent is situated in its environment. In this paper, we present a methodology for the design of situated agents that is based on *situated-automata theory*. This approach allows designers to describe the informational content of an agent's computational states in a semantically rigorous way without requiring a commitment to conventional run-time symbolic processing. We start by outlining this situated view of representation, then show how it contributes to design methodologies for building systems that track perceptual conditions and take purposeful actions in their environments.

1. Introduction

Humans, delivery robots, and automated factories are all systems that have an intelligent, ongoing interaction with environments that are dynamic and imperfectly predictable. Such systems are often called *situated agents*. They constitute an important class of systems that are very difficult to program because of their close interaction with the environment in which they are situated. Specifications of correctness for situated agents amount to specifications of their interactions with the environment: what action should the agent take when the environment is in a particular configuration? Programs

---

[*] Corresponding author. E-mail: lpk@cs.brown.edu.
[1] Work on this paper was supported in part by the National Aeronautics and Space Administration under contract NAS2-13326 and by the Defense Advanced Research Projects Agency under NASA contract NAS2-13229 and under TEC contract DATA76-93-C-0017.
[2] Work on this paper was supported in part by National Science Foundation National Young Investigator Award IRI-9257592 and in part by ONR Contract N00014-91-4052, ARPA Order 8225.

SSDI 0004-3702(94)00056-5

for situated agents must allow them to respond appropriately to diverse, rapidly changing situations.

The emphasis on an agent's connection to its environment is an important change from that of traditional theories of representation and control. In this paper, we present an informal overview of a particular methodology for the design of situated agents. This methodology, based on *situated-automata theory* [14, 16], allows system designers to use high-level symbolic languages to describe the informational content of agents without requiring the symbolic structures to be implemented in the agent. It has become folk wisdom that "situated agents" and "representation" are incompatible concepts. In our view, this is not at all the case, and we feel there is much to gain from analyzing the semantics of representations from a situated perspective. In this spirit, we start by outlining this situated view of representation, then show how it contributes to design methodologies for building systems that track perceptual conditions and take purposeful actions in their environments.

2. Situated representation

Our ultimate aim, in designing and building situated agents, is to have them perform a rich set of tasks correctly; that is, at each moment to carry out actions that are appropriate to their situations and goals. In order to specify correct behavior, and then to show that a particular program will satisfy that specification, we need to make precise the relationship between internal states of an agent and conditions in its environment. Once this relationship is made precise, we can give clear specifications of desired behavior for an agent in an environment and then generate a program for manipulating the internal states of the agent that satisfies those specifications.

For example, suppose we are designing an agent whose task it is to water a plant if and only if it is dry. From the outset, we must take into account the interaction between the agent and the environment: the specification of our problem contains a statement about the agent, *water the plant*, and a statement about the environment, *when it is dry*. In order to design such a controller, we must have a systematic way of talking about the relationship between the agent and its environment.

2.1. Existing approaches

There has been a variety of approaches to describing the relationship between agents and their environments.

Many simple embedded systems are designed according to the principles of control theory. These systems usually have very little internal state, which typically consists of estimates of a set of real-valued variables that describe the state of the environment directly in parametric form. The designer of the control system chooses the real-world quantities upon which correct control responses depend, then designs machinery to estimate those quantities inside the agent based on incoming sensory signals. The control actions taken by the agent depend on the estimates of the quantities. This approach works well when the agent's interaction with the environment can be described by simple continuous functions and when the quantities that must be estimated can be sensed fairly directly. As agents and their environments become more complex, more abstract information will have to be represented, and this approach will no longer suffice.

In the artificial intelligence community, an agent's information about the state of its environment is typically represented symbolically. A formal language is developed by the system's designer, including an intended semantics that relates sentences stored in the agent's memory to the propositions about the world that they denote. This approach is applicable to arbitrarily complex relationships between states of the agent and the world, but it can be computationally intractable to maintain such a representation.

Many researchers have found it useful to provide ascriptional accounts of the relationship between states of an agent and states of the environment. McCarthy [10], for example, speaks of attributing knowledge of the temperature to a thermostat, and Newell [12] gives a definition of knowledge of an agent in terms of what would have to be true in the world in order for that agent's actions to be rational (in service of some goal). More formal notions of an agent's having knowledge about its environment are found in the work on *epistemic logic*: Moore [11] uses epistemic logic to model the knowledge of one agent about another's knowledge for the purpose of asking questions, for example. Halpern and Moses [2] provide a concrete computational model of knowledge in their applications of epistemic logic to the formalization of communication protocols in distributed systems. We use an approach similar to that of Halpern and Moses for specifying embedded agents, finding the concept of knowledge to be an effective way of describing the relationship between agent and environment.

2.2. The situated-automata model

Traditional theories of computation are based on the notion of computation as *computation of a function*. The inputs are presented to the computational process, it works for some amount of time, then generates the answer and terminates. There is only one question and only one answer; of course, the question can be arbitrarily complex, potentially including many simple questions, but once the computation has started, it cannot be changed.

2.2.1. Interaction model

It is more appropriate to think of an agent embedded in an environment as performing a *transduction*. It has a stream of inputs from the environment and generates a stream of outputs or actions to the environment. For the purposes of this work, we model the coupling between the agent and the environment as that of a pair of automata that are operating synchronously with one another; that is, their interaction can be seen as taking alternating turns, with the world generating an input (or "perception") to the agent, then the agent generating an output (or "action") to the world. In order to make this synchronous interaction a plausible model of interacting with a dynamic environment, we require the agent to generate actions, without fail, at strictly timed intervals.

In the transduction model, then, an agent is viewed as an automaton that generates a mapping from inputs to outputs, mediated by its internal state. Fig. 1 shows the coupling of the agent and its environment. We note in passing that although there is only one agent

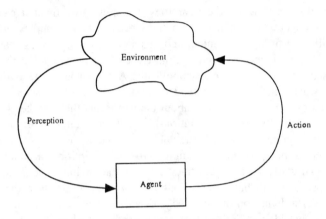

Fig. 1. Interaction between agent and environment.

in this model, most interesting environments have large numbers of agents. From the perspective of this model, however, all of the other agents, whether robotic or biological, are taken to be part of the environment. This gives us a way to discuss the properties of a single agent from *its* perspective.

2.2.2. *Correlational definition of information*

Agent tasks are often specified in the form: *when P is true of the state of the* environment, *then the agent should take action A*. This specification could only be implemented immediately if the agent had direct access to arbitrary properties of the world. In general, that is not the case. Because an agent's actions in reality can only depend on its inputs and internal state, agent programs must ultimately be expressed in the form: *when P′ is true of the state of the* agent, *then the agent should take action A*. Our problem, then, is to give a systematic account of the relationship between P and $P′$; if we can find some $P′$ that implies P, then taking action A when $P′$ holds of the agent's state is sufficient to satisfy the specification.

One way to view this relationship is in terms of a correlation between states of the agent and states of the external world. We will say that when an agent x is in state v, it *carries the information that φ* if and only if whenever it is in state v, φ is true in the world. This definition was originally articulated [14] in terms of equivalence classes of strings that would leave an automaton in the same state.

Given this definition, we can specify the simple robot plant-watering task more precisely: whenever the agent carries the information that the plant is dry, it should water the plant. Of course, as it stands, this is a fairly weak specification. For example, it could be satisfied trivially by any agent whose internal state is simply uncorrelated with the state of the plant. To rule out such a consequence, we might require further that the agent *track* whether the plant is dry: that is, if the plant is dry, the agent should carry the information that it is dry, and if it is not dry, the agent should carry the information that it is not dry. These two informational requirements taken together specify an agent that will water the plant if and only if it is dry.

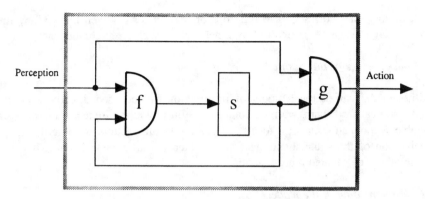

Fig. 2. Circuit model of a finite-state machine.

2.2.3. Circuit model of computation

We motivated the concept of information as a way to describe the relation between internal states of an agent and the external state of the world. In this section, we will introduce a way of describing the structure of agents and their internal states.

Considering an agent as an automaton does not, in itself, give us much help in its design or analysis. We take a finer-grained view here, considering an agent to be made up of parts, called *locations*, each of which is capable of assuming a set of local states (or "values") over time. The set of possible global states of the agent, then, will be the cross-product of the local state sets of the atomic locations.

A machine is a set of locations whose values depend on one another over time. We can construct arbitrarily complex machines from machines of two primitive types: pure functions and delays. Pure function machines consist of two (possibly complex) locations and specify the values of one location (the output) as a function of the values of the other (the input). Delay machines also consist of two locations, but constrain the values of the output location to be the values that the input location had on the previous tick. [3]

Given a network of delay and function elements, complete with feedback connections, it is possible to organize it into a circuit of the form shown in Fig. 2, in which there is a state-update function, f, that maps the input and the old value of the internal state into a new value of the internal state, and an output function, g, that maps the input and the old value of the internal state into the output. It is often useful to think of the internal state as being a "state vector" containing the state of all the individual delay elements in the machine.

Although these definitions can be satisfied by machines made up of infinitely many locations, each of which can take on infinitely many values, we will focus our attention on machines with finite sets of atomic locations, each of which can take on only a finite set of values.

One obvious model for this abstract notion of machine exists in the form of digital hardware: locations correspond to wires, function machines correspond to logic gates,

---

[3] We use "tick" to mean one discrete time unit.

and delay machines correspond to flip-flops or registers. As is well known, any finite-state transduction can be carried out by a network of such basic components.

2.3. Consequences of the situated-automata model

Although the correlational model of information can be used directly without the need for logical formalism, we have found it useful to adopt a logical framework, with a suitable syntax and semantics, for its application. In this section, we describe a logical formalization of the situated-automata model, then consider some insights it gives us into the nature of situated representation.

2.3.1. Formalization of the model

We have adopted logic as a means of describing the structure of machines, characterizing their interactions with the environment, and stating criteria for their correctness. This use of logic as a specification language is independent of its use as an implementation strategy. This is crucial because machines with complex logical descriptions often have very simple implementations and *vice versa*. Because a location x, in a certain state, carries information about any proposition that is true whenever x is in that state, there can be an infinity of propositions φ such that x carries the information that φ. Those propositions could not all be written down and manipulated symbolically. A simple example will illustrate this point. Consider a machine that consists of a single and gate. Behaviorally, the device is very simple: the output of the machine is 1 if and only if both its inputs are 1. Semantically, it may be more involved: if a 1 at the first input carries the information that φ and a 1 at the second input carries the conditional information that $\varphi \rightarrow \psi$, then whenever the output location has value 1, it carries the information that ψ. The inference rule *modus ponens* is not implemented in the machine, but it can be applied freely to reason about the information that locations of the machine have about the state of the world.

The correlational definition of information, introduced in Section 2.2.2, can be directly formalized in epistemic logic [16], using the form $K(x, \varphi)$ to indicate that agent x carries the information that φ. This definition of information induces an equivalence relation on possible worlds, thus giving rise to an accessibility relation satisfying the S5 axioms [3]:

$$K(x, \varphi) \rightarrow \varphi \qquad \text{(truth)},$$
$$K(x, \varphi \rightarrow \psi) \rightarrow (K(x, \varphi) \rightarrow K(x, \psi)) \qquad \text{(consequential closure)},$$
$$K(x, \varphi) \rightarrow K(x, K(x, \varphi)) \qquad \text{(positive introspection)},$$
$$\neg K(x, \varphi) \rightarrow K(x, \neg K(x, \varphi)) \qquad \text{(negative introspection)}.$$

We view an agent as the union of all of its locations, so states of agents are comprised of states of component locations. We find it useful to apply the K operator not only to the agent as a whole, but also to its constituent locations. Information can be carried in simple locations or in compound locations, and aggregating locations leads us to an important corollary of the axioms, the principle of *spatial monotonicity*: an aggregate location carries the conjunction of the information carried by its constituent locations:

$$K(x,\varphi) \wedge K(y,\psi) \rightarrow K([x,y],\varphi \wedge \psi).$$

The formal model can be used to prove correctness properties of agents: given a description of the circuit that makes up the agent and a description of the informational properties of the inputs to the agent, it can, for example, be shown that the outputs have certain informational properties [16]. This constitutes a correctness proof for an embedded agent.

2.3.2. Properties of representations

In both standard programming methods and AI inference systems, the semantics of machine states is typically *stipulated*: the designer of the machine has a particular meaning in mind for values in designated locations and strives to construct the machine so that those stipulated semantics will hold. The situated-automata view allows us to attribute semantics to values in locations more "objectively" based on the correlational definition of knowledge. In the following sections, we examine aspects of the relationship between these two kinds of semantics.

Time is meaning

The correlational definition of knowledge assigns information content to locations *at a point in time* as a function of the value they contain at that time and the world states with which that value can co-occur. One immediate consequence of this definition is that a location containing a value at time t and continuing to hold that value until time $t + k$ will be assigned as its information content the disjunction of world conditions satisfied at any time instant in the interval $[t, t + k]$. Unless the designer has taken special care to design mechanisms for updating values in time to track external change, the objective information at a location may not be what he intended at all. For example, consider a robot that senses an object, stores the sensor reading, which the designer takes to be a representation of the distance to that object, and only updates the state every 10 seconds. The actual information content of the stored representation *all along* will in all likelihood not be what was intended but some weaker (though not necessarily vacuous) proposition that bounds the distance to the object, depending on the possible maximum relative velocity between the robot and the object.

Given the situated view of knowledge, this is not very surprising; but standard AI systems often operate in a way that does not take seriously the degradation of information over time. They get certain sensory inputs that are written down symbolically in the memory of the machine and manipulated over time. Even if the stipulated semantics of the formulae were true when the process began, it is entirely possible that the world will change enough during the course of the inference process that the data on which the conclusions were based are no longer valid.

Machines that manipulate symbols

The situated-automata framework can also be applied to computations that perform symbol manipulation. The requirement that intended semantics match real ones is emphasized in symbolic systems. It is possible, in theory, to design a system that manipulates symbolic representations of propositional information about the world in such a way that a proposition is only symbolically written in memory when it is justified by the correlational theory; that is, when those locations carry that same propositional information. This can be achieved through careful use of time stamps and axioms that describe the dynamics of the world, but it has proven very difficult in practice and is rarely done.

It is interesting to consider, in more detail, an example illustrating two different ways of encoding information. In the first case, we dedicate a particular bit in a machine to the representation of whether there is an obstacle within two meters of the agent; if it is on, then there is an obstacle and if it is off, it is not known whether there is an obstacle. In the second approach, the symbols `distance(robot,obstacle) < 2` (or symbols in some other language with compositional semantics) can be written anywhere in memory and, if the system is designed properly, those locations will carry the same information as the single bit of the first example being on. In the first case, we say that the information is encoded "by location"; that particular bit is devoted to the representation of a single condition, so the location of the encoding of the bit is crucial. In the second case, the information is encoded "by value"; the values of the locations involved in representing the information are crucial, but that same combination of values occurring at any location would carry the same information.

To see how a correctly functioning symbolic representation system yields the correct correlational semantics, consider a very simple language with symbols of two types: unary predicates (e.g., `fully-charged`, `red`, `tired`, `distant`) and individual constants (e.g., `robot1`, `ball37`, `john`, `wall2`). Sentences in this language could be represented by simple juxtaposition of symbols as in this sequence:

> `[fully-charged robot1 red ball37 tired john distant wall2]`.

While the correlational account of information assigns time-varying propositions as the meanings of a value at a location, under a more standard Tarskian account, these symbols might be interpreted differently: the unary predicates might denote mappings from individuals to temporally-indexical propositions (e.g., mappings from time to truth values), while individual constants might denote individuals (or perhaps temporally-indexical individuals). Note that if the representation is uniformly veridical, that is, if the sentence is in memory only when it is true, then at the level of propositions, the two semantics agree. Importantly, however, the situated-automata framework would have attached that meaning to the symbol sequence whether or not the designer had that Tarskian semantics in mind. In other words, the attribution of semantic content need not be externally stipulated.

There is clearly a trade-off between using these two kinds of representation (and a whole spectrum of intermediate cases). When information is represented largely by location, the number of bits or atomic locations used can be very small, making this form of representation quite efficient. Symbolic representations are notoriously space-inefficient, requiring many bits to encode syntactically the propositional content to be represented. However, these representations are also very flexible. When storing information by value, any proposition expressible in the language can be represented; when storing information by location, on the other hand, each individual proposition must be thought of in advance by the designer of the machine (or, as we will see, by a compilation system).

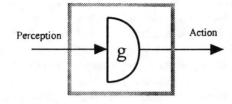

Fig. 3. Pure-action case.

As observed above, when a location carries the information that P, so does every super-location; there is a minimal location that carries the information that P. We will say that information is *localized* to a minimal location that carries it. An especially important consideration in the decision between encoding by value and by location is the amount of work that must be done to localize important information. In order to take a particular action when P is true, the locations that control the effector must eventually carry the information that P; it is insufficient for that information to be encoded in some collection of locations in a uniformly-interpreted memory. The amount of work that has to be done to take the information that P and localize it into the effector bits, or any other location where it might be further combined with other information, can crucially depend on how it was initially represented. When information is encoded by value, it can often take many complex operations of indexing and pattern matching to localize; information that is encoded by location can often be used directly. Such considerations should guide the representational choices that are made in designing and building agents.

3. Designing agents

Given the situated view of agents and environments as interacting automata and the circuit model of computation, we can build a design methodology for agents situated in dynamic environments. We first consider the case in which the agent has no internal state, then the case in which the agent monitors, but does not affect, the environment. We conclude by combining our design methodologies for an entire agent.

3.1. Pure action

We begin by considering control in a very simple setting, namely stimulus–response systems that map current inputs to outputs without any dependence on prior inputs. At each instant, the inputs carry information about the immediate state of the environment, but the agent has no internal memory by which to distinguish otherwise similar states through residues of past experiences. In the automaton model, the state set of a stimulus–response automaton contains only one state, and inputs are simply passed on to the output relation. This is illustrated schematically in Fig. 3. Although stimulus–response agents are extremely limited, they are complete agents, nonetheless, and constitute a relatively easy-to-analyze starting point.

By what criteria can a stimulus–response system, or any action-selection system, be judged successful? A natural way to answer this question is to relativize success to some stated goal specification that is taken to be part of the problem statement. Different families of control problems arise, depending on what is meant by the term "goal".

One dimension of variability in defining goals is whether the goals are fixed or dynamic. With fixed goals (or design-time goals), action-selection mappings are evaluated relative to the entire trajectory of states they engender. To model an agent as pursuing dynamic goals, on the other hand, assumes some method for defining moment-to-moment variations in what the agent seeks. Even with dynamic goals, the agent is seen as having at least the fixed goal of acting rationally, that is, at each moment selecting actions consistent with its current goals and information. (Interesting subtleties arise in pathological situations where agents might preserve rationality by choosing not to want or not to know.)

Another dimension of variability in goal definition arises from the complexity of the goal and the form in which it is expressed. Goals can vary in complexity from that of maintaining simple environmental invariants, to satisfying arbitrary temporal predicates, to optimizing complex numerical evaluation criteria (e.g., maximize throughput while minimizing energy, with complex trade-offs). Regarding the form of presentation, complexity can vary from a simple enumeration of states, for goals of maintenance, to complex formulas in expressive logical languages, closed under Boolean operations, quantification, and rich temporal operators.

Because, in extreme cases, agent synthesis can be intractable, it is not a reasonable objective to try to develop universal solution methods. Rather, it is preferable to develop a methodology for specifying particular action strategies, and to develop an inventory of solved special cases that can expedite agent construction in practical situations. As with goal specification, the specification of action-selection mappings can take many forms, direct and indirect. One family of direct methods includes notations for defining functions of one or more input variables in a suitable language, such as look-up tables (only in very simple cases), functional expressions, circuit descriptions, or data-flow graphs. A related family of methods uses the calculus of relations rather than functional expressions, in some cases with a determinization operator applied as the last step, after the output relation has been composed by applying operations like union, intersection, and restriction to primitive relations. The base-level relations can be represented either enumeratively or in more compact form.

Rex [4, 8] is a language for specifying action mappings (as well as machines with internal state) as abstract circuit descriptions. Rex served as a substrate for Gapps [5, 7], which takes a symbolic specification of an action mapping and compiles it into fixed run-time circuitry. A Gapps program consists of a set of goal reduction rules, which specify how a high-level goal is transformed to a more specific and simpler low-level goal. When given a fixed goal to satisfy, the Gapps compiler generates a provably correct (though possibly partial) reactive program (input-to-output map) for that goal. A Gapps program is guaranteed to be correct, but not necessarily complete; if it outputs an action, it is appropriate to the situation, but it will not necessarily output an action in every situation. One of the main strengths of Gapps is its least-commitment approach: if many low-level actions satisfy a particular goal, they are all returned as part of the result, which allows nondeterministic choice of action; this greatly simplifies the compositional construction of programs that satisfy multiple goals.

Although Gapps programs are specified using symbolic rules, they still require the programmer to do a great deal of the work, especially in determining what chains of actions will result in desired outcomes. Gapps does not support the reduction of goals into sequences of action, so the programmer has to maintain any such commitments himself based on perceived conditions. In many cases, we would like programs to be derived from much more abstract specifications.

3.1.1. Maintaining invariants through goal regression

Indirect methods define the action-selection mapping by deriving it from some description of the environment and the goal, whether in the form of an explicit combinatorial object like a graph, or in the form of declarative assertions, such as operator descriptions found in classical AI planning systems. To illustrate how a stimulus–response agent can be constructed algorithmically from an explicit description of an environment and goal, we consider the special case of agents that maintain invariants. Although the method illustrated does not scale well with large state sets, it does introduce important concepts and build up intuitions about properties of action strategies.

A stimulus–response agent that maintains invariants can be synthesized as follows. Let the environment be represented as a nondeterministic automaton $\langle S, P, A, init, \nu, out \rangle$, where

- S is a finite set of states of the environment;
- P is a finite set of outputs (these are usefully viewed as *percepts* from the agent's perspective);
- A is a finite set of actions that the agent can generate as input to the environment;
- *init* is a set of states containing the one that the environment is known to be in initially;
- ν is a relation on $S \times A \times S$ where $\nu(s_1, a, s_2)$ holds if it is possible for the world to make a transition from state s_1 to state s_2 when action a is generated by the agent; and
- *out* is a function mapping S to P

For the simple pure-action case, we assume that the environment automaton outputs its full state as output. In other words, the percept set P is identical to the state set S and *out* is the identity function on states. Let the goal be represented by G, a subset of S, that the agent is to maintain as an invariant condition.

A solution to this problem is G^*, a subset of G within which the environment can be made to stay indefinitely, and a mapping from G^* to A, specifying the actions the agent should take in order to stay within G^*. The set G^* can be computed iteratively, as follows:

Let $G_0 := G$
For $n = 0$ to $\ldots$
   Let $G_{n+1} = \emptyset$
   For all $g \in G_n$
     If $\exists a. \forall g'. \nu(g, a, g') \rightarrow g' \in G_n$ then
       add g to G_{n+1}
   When $G_n = G_{n+1}$, terminate and return G_n.

Each intermediate set G_n is the set of states from which G can be maintained for at least n steps. For any state $g \in G$, if there exists an action such that from every possible successor state g', G can be maintained for n steps, then in state g, G can be maintained for $n + 1$ steps. This step is called "goal regression", because G_{n+1} is the weakest precondition under which G_n can be made true on the next step (see Rosenschein [13] or Waldinger [17] for a more complete description of regression-based planning). When this process reaches a fixed point, then we have determined the set, G^* of states from which G can be maintained indefinitely. In order to maintain G^* from some state g, the agent can do any action a such that $\forall g'. \nu(g, a, g') \rightarrow g' \in G^*$.

3.1.2. Goal regression example

Consider a simple domain in which a robot must keep plants alive by watering them. The action set of the robot contains actions to water each plant and *no-op*, the action that does nothing. The state of the world can be expressed as a vector describing the moisture level of each plant, where 4 is wet (just watered) and 0 is dead. For example, the vector (4 3 0) describes a situation in which the first plant is wet, the second slightly drier, and the third is dead. Moisture decreases by one every time step on which the plant is not watered. Plants that die (reach moisture level 0) stay dead forever.

We consider a situation in which there are three plants and the goal is to maintain the condition "no plants are dead"; G is enumerated below (with equivalent states under different orderings of plants deleted, because the identity of the individuals is irrelevant to the maintenance of this goal):

(4 4 4) (4 4 3) (4 4 2) (4 4 1) (4 3 3) (4 3 2) (4 3 1) (4 2 2)
(4 2 1) (4 1 1) (3 3 3) (3 3 2) (3 3 1) (3 2 2) (3 2 1) (3 1 1)
(2 2 2) (2 2 1) (2 1 1) (1 1 1)

The G^* resulting from the goal regression algorithm is:

(4 4 4) (4 4 3) (4 4 2) (4 4 1) (4 3 3) (4 3 2) (4 3 1) (4 2 2)
(4 2 1) (3 3 3) (3 3 2) (3 3 1) (3 2 2) (3 2 1)

The most constrained state in G^* is (3 2 1). By watering the plant at moisture level 1, it is changed to (4 2 1), and then to (4 3 1), and then to (4 3 2). At this point, the *no-op* action is allowed, and the robot can rest, leading to the original starting state of (3 2 1). Note that there are no states in G^* with two plants at level 1 or three at level 2; although these states are in G (no plants are currently dead), they are not in G^*, because it is not possible to keep all the plants from dying in the future.

3.1.3. Discussion

As mentioned above, this construction does not scale well as the number of environment states increases, and this motivates the use of other representations. Although ordinarily used to handle run-time goals of achievement, the declarative operator descriptions used in AI planning systems encode the same information as state-transition graphs, and can be used to drive the construction above. Operator descriptions provide a more intuitively interpretable form of expression and can often be manipulated more

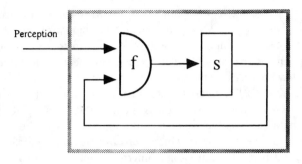

Fig. 4. The pure-perception case.

efficiently because they refer to large subspaces of the state space with terse symbolic labels. Rather than calculating G^* through enumeration, operator descriptions allow it to be calculated through symbolic regression. This may be more or less efficient that the alternative, depending on specifics of the problem domain. This technique has been implemented and explored as an extension to the Gapps programming system [6].

3.2. Pure perception

Until now we have assumed that inputs from the environment are sufficiently informative, in that they encode all the world-state information needed to drive action. In cases where less information is available, the inputs to action selection must be derived by accumulating partial information over time, and for this purpose additional machinery is necessary. We refer to this additional machinery as the "perception system" and explore its properties in this section.

As in the case of action selection, it will be useful to approach perception by beginning with a study of the *pure* phenomenon. By pure perception we mean agent–environment systems in which the outputs of the agent have no influence on the environment at all, and the agent is simply a tracking system, or monitor: a passive observer, seeing, but not seen by, the environment. This special type of agent, again, will be of limited practical use but does illustrates the essential features of information extraction. The set-up for pure perception is illustrated in Fig. 4. The lack of influence of the agent on the environment cannot be depicted graphically; the environment's next state function is independent of the output of the agent.

The focus in analyzing the perception system is on the kind of correspondence maintained between its internal states and states of the environment. This correspondence, in fact, is a form of invariant of exactly the type investigated in the previous section, but over the states of the agent–environment pair rather than just the environment. Even when the environment is indifferent to the actions of the agent, it makes sense to ask how the perception component might be designed to maximize the degree of correlation between its states and those of environment, hence maximizing its information.

To see this most clearly, consider an environment, modeled once again as a nondeterministic automaton $\langle S, P, A, init, \nu, \mathrm{out} \rangle$. What is the maximum amount of information encoded in an instantaneous percept? In general, the best we can do is to associate with each percept p the set of environment states with which it is compatible (i.e., those s such that $out(s) = p$). What is the maximum amount of information about the environment that could be accumulated by the agent automaton over time? Given a rich enough inventory of internal states, a pure-perception agent could optimally track the environment by having states isomorphic to the powerset of environment's states. Let $\Sigma = \text{powerset}(S)$ be the set of internal states of the agent, with the agent in state σ_i if and only if every world state $s \in \sigma_i$ is consistent with the agent's perceptual history so far. The agent's initial state is the set of possible initial states of the environment, *init*, and its transition function $N(\sigma, a, p)$ which maps the previous internal state σ, the last action a, and the last percept p, into a new internal state, is given by

$$N(\sigma, p, a) = \{s' \mid \exists s \in \sigma . \nu(s, a, s') \wedge \text{out}(s) = p\}.$$

This *powerset automaton* might be cumbersome, indeed, but its tracking behavior would be optimal.

Although as the number of environment states rises, the powerset construction quickly becomes infeasible, it is useful as a thought experiment because much of its value can be preserved through efficient but information-rich approximations. Mathematically, these approximations are homomorphic images of the ideal powerset automaton, and thus are consistent with, but not as complete as, that ideal, or optimal, tracker. Nevertheless, these homomorphic images allow useful information to be monitored, while carefully trading off computational space and time, under the designer's control. One simple approach to constructing homomorphic projections of the powerset automaton is to choose a set of *interesting* or *significant* states in the powerset automaton, and close these under union and intersection. The result is a lattice, which will be a sub-lattice of the powerset Boolean algebra. The construction of the initial state and transition function of the perception system then proceeds as in the case of the powerset automaton above, but with the true powerset elements approximated by least upper bounds in the sub-lattice. For example, if in the original powerset automaton the transition function maps a state to a successor state that is not an element of the homomorphic-image lattice, the element of that lattice which best approximates the successor state will be returned instead. Thus the lattice transition function *approximates* the optimal transition function and degrades gracefully with the precision of the representation. The lattices themselves would typically be cartesian products of simpler lattices, with elements that could be represented compactly as parameter vectors.

This technique forms the basis of the RULER system [15]. RULER takes an approach analogous in many ways to AI planning systems. In RULER, the environment is described by a set of assertions, including temporal assertions that describe conditions that are either true initially or that will be true in the next state, depending on current conditions. The RULER compiler synthesizes perceptual machinery (an initial state and next state function) by chaining together these individual assertions, not with a view toward constructing action sequences, but rather with a view toward computing descriptive parameters in the next state's world model. The use of lattices as the semantic domain of interpretation of the model parameters, along with effectively closing the parameter space under intersection, allows incremental information to be folded in nicely and leads to a compositional methodology for constructing perceptual update mechanisms.

3.2.1. Ruler compilation

RULER's compilation method works as follows. The compiler takes as input a description of information carried by the run-time inputs to the program and the internal state variables, as well as a background theory containing temporal facts about the world. The compiler operates by deriving theorems about what is true initially and about what will be true at any time, given what was true at the previous time. In the course of the derivation, free variables are instantiated in the manner of logic programming systems. From the instantiated formulas, the compiler extracts a program for initializing and updating a state vector with the desired informational properties.

More precisely, the compiler's inputs consist of the following:

- a list $[a_1, ..., a_n]$ of input locations,
- a list $[b_1, ..., b_m]$ of internal state locations,
- for each input location a, a formula $P_a(U)$ with free variable U,
- for each internal location b, a formula $P_b(U)$ with free variable U and a function $rconj_b$,
- a finite set Γ of facts.

The formulas $P_x(U)$ express propositions parameterized by U, where U ranges over run-time values of location x; for example, $P_{b4}(6)$ might denote "current soil mosture level ≥ 6". These values are drawn from a lattice so that degrees of partial information can be represented. The *rconj* operations are binary functions that take a pair of lattice values and combine them into a single lattice value summarizing their conjunctive content as precisely as possible. (The *rconj** operation extends *rconj* to sets of lattice values in the natural way.) Using formulas in this way, the propositions that were merely implicit in the information of the machine can be made explicit and manipulated by the compiler.

For each internal location b, the compiler computes two sets of runtime value terms I_b and N_b defined as follows (the $\Box$ symbol is the temporal logic operator representing "necessarily always"):

$$I_b = \{e \mid \Gamma \vdash \Box init\ P_b(e)\},$$
$$N_b = \{e' \mid \Gamma \vdash \Box(P_{a_1}(a_1) \wedge \cdots \wedge P_{b_n}(b_n) \rightarrow next\ P_b(e'))\},$$

where $e' = f([a_1, \ldots, a_n], [b_1, \ldots, b_m])$. If we are initially ignorant of soil moisture, we might have only $\Box P_{b4}(0)$, so $I_{b4} = \{0\}$. If our lower bound on moisture decreases 1 per time step, then we might have $\Box(P_{b4}(n) \rightarrow next\ P_{b4}(n-1))$. Each set I_b contains terms representing properties that can be proved from the background theory Γ to hold initially in the world. Each set N_b contains terms for properties that can be proved to hold "next", given the properties that hold now as represented by the values of the input and state locations. If these sets are infinite, they can be generated and used incrementally. This is discussed more fully below.

From these collections of sets the compiler computes the initial value of the state vector, v_0, and its update function, f. The initial value is computed as follows:

$$v_0 = [rconj^*_{b_1}(I_{b_1}), \ldots, rconj^*_{b_m}(I_{b_m})].$$

In other words, the initial value of the state vector is the vector of values derived by *rconj*-ing values representing the strongest propositions that can be inferred by the compiler about the initial state of the environment in the "language" of each of the state components. Similarly, for the next state function:

$$f([a_1, \ldots, a_n], [b_1, \ldots, b_m]) = [rconj^*_{b_1}(N_{b_1}), \ldots, rconj^*_{b_m}(N_{b_m})].$$

Here the compiler constructs a vector of expressions that denote the strongest propositions about what will be true next, again in the language of the state components.

In the case of the initial value, the *rconj* values can be computed at compile time because the values of all the arguments are available. In the case of the next state function, however, the *rconj* terms will not denote values known at compile time. Rather, they will generally be nested expressions containing operators that will be used to compute values at run time. Assuming the execution time of these operators is bounded, the depth of the expressions will provide a bound on the update time of the state vector.

Without restricting the background theory, we cannot guarantee that the sets I_b and N_b will be finite. However, even in the unrestricted case the finiteness of terms in the language guarantees that whichever elements we *can* derive at compile time can be computed in bounded time at run time. Furthermore, the synthesis procedure exhibits strongly monotonic behavior: the more elements of I_b and N_b we compute, the more information we can ascribe to run-time locations regarding the environment. This allows incremental improvements to be achieved simply by running the compiler longer; stopping the procedure at any stage will still yield a correct program, although not necessarily the program attuned to the most specific information available. Since, in general, additional *rconj* operations consume run-time resources, one reasonable approach would be to have the compiler keep track of run-time resources consumed and halt when some resource limit is reached.

As we have observed, without placing restrictions on the symbolic language used to specify the background theory Γ, the synthesis method described above would hardly be practical; it is obvious that environment-description languages exist that make the synthesis problem not only intractable but undecidable. However, as with Gapps and other formalisms in the logic programming style, by restricting ourselves to certain stylized languages, practical synthesis techniques can be developed.

We have experimented with a restriction of the logical language that seems to offer a good compromise between expressiveness and tractability. This restriction is to a weak temporal Horn-clause language resembling Prolog but with the addition of *init* and *next* operators. The derivation process proceeds as described above using backward-chaining deduction techniques as the specific form of inference. A prototype system has been built implementing the Horn-clause version of the synthesis algorithm. One of the ways the language differs from Prolog is in the strong distinction between compile-time and run-time expressions. Compile-time expressions undergo unification in the ordinary manner; run-time expressions, by contrast, are simply accumulated and used to generate the final program. The RULER system was run on several small examples involving object tracking and aggregation, and the synthesis procedure has proved tractable in our test implementation.

Using off-line synthesis techniques, conditions that are semantically complex can still be recognized with limited machinery, and for this reason it is entirely consistent with the "reactive" bias to admit sophisticated semantic information and models. With some care, the designer can have the best of both worlds: declarative forms can be used to clarify the semantics of the domain representation, and finite parametric representations can be generated by the compiler to guarantee bounded-time updates and real-time response.

3.2.2. Ruler example

This section sketches out a simple example of a pure-perception system synthesized by the RULER system. Imagine that we again have a plant-watering robot, but we are now concerned with constructing its perceptual system so that it maintains, at all times, as much information as it can about the moisture level of a collection of plants. The representation used by the system must be able to accommodate uncertainty, so we use an interval, representing known lower and upper bounds on the true moisture level of the plant. This gives us our first rule,

```
moisture(p,[0, max]).
```

which states that the moisture of plant p is always between 0 and some maximum level. Additionally, if the robot is at the plant, it can get an approximate reading of the moisture level from its sensor:

```
moisture(p,[v-1,v+1]) :-
    at_plant(p,1),
    moisture_sensor(v).
```

The at_plant(p,1) term requires that the robot know that it is at plant p at the time the moisture is being sensed. In this case, there is an input bit, a, such that at_plant(n,a). The robot has been constructed in such a way that if a has value 1, then the robot is known to be at plant n; if it has value 0, the robot is not known to be at that plant. We will treat other propositions similarly.

The dynamics of the world are specified in terms of next rules. If we know that the robot's last action was not to water the plant (either because we know it didn't water or because we know it wasn't at the plant), then the moisture may either increase (perhaps due to rain) or decrease by 1:

```
next moisture(p,[l-1,h+1]) :-
    not_watering(1),
    moisture(p,[l,h]).

next moisture(p,[l-1,h+1]) :-
    not_at_plant(p,1),
    moisture(p,[l,h]).
```

If we know that the robot did just water the plant, then the moisture will increase to its maximum level:

```
next moisture(p,[max,max]) :-
    at_plant(p,1),
    watering(1).
```

If we don't know whether the robot watered the plant (either because we don't know whether it watered or because we don't know whether it was at the plant), the bounds spread quickly:

```
next moisture(p,[l-1,max]) :-
    moisture(p,[l,h]).
```

Note that the last rule does not conflict with other rules that provide tighter bounds on the moisture. We combine the results of these rules by specifying an *rconj* rule for moisture. In this case, it is simply to intersect the intervals. Running RULER on this set of rules results in a circuit that retains as much information as possible about the moisture of the plant, given its inputs and the specified representation.

3.2.3. Objects, properties, and relations

While conceptually adequate for generating provably correct perceptual subsystems, at least for nonprobabilistic domain models, RULER is limited in that it makes no special provision for modeling worlds in which objects and their properties and relations are of special importance. This is the case, for example, in visual perception where objects move in and out of view, and a prime form of information to be extracted from the scene concerns the identity of objects and their spatial relations to one another and to the observer. To begin to address domains of this type, we developed an information-update schema we named Percm.

The Percm schema can be thought of as a specialized form of RULER in which a finite, but shifting, set of objects is being tracked and described. The descriptions are represented as labeled graphs, with node labels representing unary properties of objects, and edge labels representing binary relations between objects. One of the objects is the agent, and the rest of the objects can vary, moving in and out of attentional focus. This scheme bears some relationship to the indexical-functional representations developed by Chapman and Agre for Pengi, but with rigorous correlation-based semantics. The node and edge labels are drawn from a space of data values representing lattice elements, just as in the RULER case, only now the propositional matrix is fixed (i.e., a fixed conjunction of properties and relations) and the lattice elements are constrained to be of semantic type *property* or *relation*, or to be coercible to such values.

Fig. 5 shows the basic runtime data structures that underlie a Percm with n elements. There is a vector of length n, each of whose elements contains the unary properties of the ith element being tracked. Often, index 1 is reserved for the agent. In addition, there is an $n \times n$ matrix in which cell $\langle i, j \rangle$ contains the strongest representable information available about the relation between objects i and j. In many cases, the relations will be symmetric (or canonicalizable) so that only the upper triangle of the matrix needs to be explicitly represented.

The update cycle for this data structure is similar to RULER's, but in the Percm context, fixed background descriptions of the environment are provided not in the form

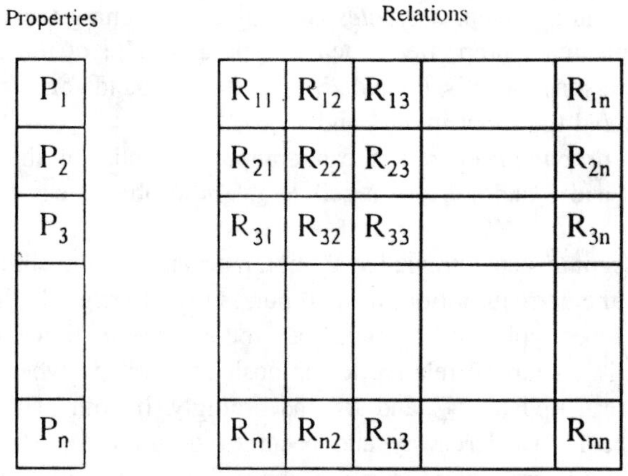

Fig. 5. Data structures supporting an instance of the Percm schema with n objects.

of propositional assertions about world-state transitions, but rather as rules, both temporal and atemporal, for computing object properties and relations. This information is built into a set of operations used to update the data structures. These operations are:

- *create*: maps an input value to initial object properties and relations inferable from that input;
- *propagate*: strengthens properties and relations among objects x and y by deriving what can be inferred from existing properties and relations between each of x and y and some third object, z;
- *merge*: combines descriptions of objects x and y if their properties and relations imply that they are identical;
- *aggregate*: creates a new object y whose existence can be inferred from the existence of constituent objects $x_1, ..., x_n$ with appropriate properties and relations, and initializes y's description based on descriptions of constituents;
- *degrade*: maps properties and relations at time t to new values inferable for time $t + 1$.

The perceptual system is synthesized by composing and iterating these operations to update the object descriptions, with values again drawn from lattices to obtain gracefully degrading approximations. Because Percm is a finite schema of bounded size, to complete the specification of an instance of the Percm schema, the designer must also define how, in the case of object overflow, objects are to be discarded or withdrawn from active attention. Circuitry to keep the data structures updated can be large, but is of bounded size. Operations like finding an empty cell for a new object can be done in a very shallow circuit with size $O(n)$.

3.2.4. Percm example

In order to illustrate the ideas behind the Percm schema, we present a simple example of its operation. A mobile robot, traveling through a new environment, needs to construct a representation of the salient objects and their spatial relations.

The robot might begin by perceiving, instantaneously, that there are two objects in front of it: a chair and a person. It *creates* two objects, assigning them indices 2 and 3, stores some of their unary properties (such as type and color of the chair, gender and hair-color of the person) in cells P_2 and P_3, and stores bounds on the spatial relations between each one and the robot in $R_{1,2}$ and $R_{1,3}$.

Immediately, a *propagate* operation can compute bounds on the spatial relations between objects 2 and 3 and store it in cell $R_{2,3}$. These objects can be neither *merged* nor *aggregated.*

Finally, in the *degrade* step, knowledge about the generic motion abilities of chairs and people, as well as the current motion of the robot, is used to degrade the spatial relation information. The robot typically has good local odometry (motion information), so it knows how much it has moved relative to the position it was in when it first perceived these objects and can update $R_{1,2}$ and $R_{1,3}$ accordingly. If both of these objects were static, the robot could wander away and become confused about its relation to the objects, but still retain precise information about the relation of the objects to each other. However, in this case, people are far from static, so the degrade step will increase the bounds on all spatial relations between the person and other objects, because the person could potentially move in any direction.

On the next cycle, the robot again sees the person, but because of its changed perspective, is able to measure the person's height. This person gets *created* as object 4 in the Percm data structures. This time, on the *merge* step, the robot is able to infer that, because of their close spatial positions (and perhaps because two people were not seen simultaneously), that objects 3 and 4 must really be the same. They are merged by conjoining their properties and their relations to other objects and storing them in a single index. The other index is marked as free. Now, the height and hair color are both known about a single person.

The *aggregate* operation is useful when entire complex objects cannot be perceived instantaneously. Thus, a robot attempting to identify a large truck might individually identify wheels, a cab, and a flat bed, then aggregate them into a truck object.

As the data structures begin to get full, it will be important to purge items in a useful way. Objects may be purged because their information is weak, or they are superseded by a complex object, or for a variety of attentional reasons based on the robot's current goals.

3.3. Combined perception and action

The techniques illustrated in the two previous sections can be combined directly to synthesize control systems containing both perception and action components. For instance, using the Gapps approach, one could develop mappings from information states to actions, where the information states are the output of a perceptual subsystem synthesized using the RULER or Percm methodologies. If there were no interactions among design decisions needed for the two subsystems, the definition of the *information state* of the agent would act as a clean interface, and the combined system would exhibit the intended behavior. In general, however, there are interactions, and in this section we explore the nature of those interactions and potential methods of dealing with them.

The first problem is the specification of the information-state interface between the two modules. This problem exists even when the perceptual mechanism is degenerate. It is possible that the perceptual inputs from the environment do not provide enough information for the goal to be satisfied. Another difficulty arises if the information is available, but is encoded in such a way that the localization machinery is of intractable complexity.

The design of the system becomes much more complex when the actions taken by the agent in the environment affect the information that will be available to it. When choosing action strategies, attention must be given to how actions chosen now will maintain the flow of information necessary for distinguishing among future states to be acted on. In AI, this problem often goes under the label of the *knowledge precondition* problem [11]: it is not enough to *be* in an environmental state when a certain action is appropriate; the agent must *know* that it is in an environmental state in which that action is appropriate.

The problem grows more complex when perceptual machinery distills information contained in the sensory input stream, and still more complex when the goal itself pertains to affecting the agent's own information state. In these cases, the internal structure of the perception module is, from the point of view of the action-selection module, part of some external environment whose dynamic properties are critical to the success or failure of its strategy. Unfortunately, without elaborating the internal structure of the perception module first, statements of fact about this environment cannot be made, and hence no valid action strategy can be chosen. In general, action strategies intended to satisfy information goals can only coherently be developed in the context of fixed perceptual machinery, or, at least, in the context of articulated assumptions about the perceptual machinery.

A natural development methodology, then, would be to design the perception module first, choosing conditions to be tracked and defining update circuitry that tracks these conditions in the passive sense introduced in the previous section, but does not guarantee the input streams that will force it to the right state. After defining this fixed machinery, an action strategy can be defined, relying on the definition of the perception component as if it were part of the environment. This strategy is designed to cause input streams flowing into the perception component to drive it into the appropriate states and actively makes use of constraints imposed by the previously chosen structure of the perception module. In principle, when perception and action modules are generated from declarative domain descriptions, a single set of facts about the environment should suffice to generate both modules. In other words, RULER-like state-transition rules, combined with operator-description-like action descriptions, contain enough constraints to generate systems that seek information. The RULER rules generate a perceptual system that maintains, as an invariant, correlations with conditions that the action system needs to test. This approach can involve a search, albeit at design time, for suitable conditions that can be effectively tracked.

In all of these approaches, the result is an automaton with an objective informational relation to its environments. This is unlike the usual case in AI, in which knowledge pre- and post-conditions have been analyzed using theories that link internal states of agents to their environment only through stipulated semantic-denotation relations attributed by designers somewhat arbitrarily to symbolic data. This distinction is substantial, and it is encouraging that many of the same semantic desiderata that have been pursued in traditional AI planning and representation systems can be achieved in a more mechanistic, and potentially far more efficient, control-theoretic setting.

A final area of complexity is the pervasive uncertainty found in natural environments. Throughout this work, we have modeled uncertainty using simple nondeterminism. While this allows designers and machines to avoid committing to information they do not possess, these models are extremely conservative in that they regard all alternative states that are not ruled out by hard constraints to be of equal importance. In real task domains, however, some of those alternatives are far more likely than others, and this fact is essential to the proper exploitation of the information. A model that is midway between deterministic and nondeterministic models is the probabilistic model in which state transitions, under a given input, are described by probability distributions. A natural mathematical model for such systems is the Markov process, which has been studied extensively by applied mathematicians.

The difficulty in using probabilistic models together with the symbolic techniques described above is the nonmonotonicity of probabilities, which leads to noncompositionality of the design technique. By conditioning on further evidence, the probability of a proposition can either be reduced or increased. This means that a designer cannot, in general, define a module of the perceptual component, prove a strong statement about the semantics of its outputs, and then proceed to use that module together with other modules; conditioning on the joint states of the modules may completely undermine the intended semantics of the first module. Furthermore, the action strategy embodied in the action-selection component is integral to the definition of the probabilistic state-transition matrix of the entire system. Just as before when we could not, in principle, define an action strategy before providing a fixed definition of the perception component, here we cannot define the perception component without constraining action first. The apparent circularity only points to the fundamental need to consider the agent as an integrated whole; the behavior of the entire system, agent plus environment, is determined only when all the boundary conditions have been specified. Interim constraints and incremental refinement may be useful, but must be used cautiously, especially when modeling domains probabilistically. The theory of partially observable Markov decision processes [1, 9] provides a theoretically well-founded methodology for deriving controllers in stochastic domains, but it seems to be computationally very intractable.

4. Conclusions

The aim of situated-automata theory is to provide a new semantic perspective on intelligent agents. Traditional AI has been dominated by "reasoning" metaphors drawn from folk psychology in which programs are seen as actors manipulating linguistic elements, drawing conclusions from premises, and constructing representations of action. The semantics of these systems have been made rigorous, but are almost always imposed by their designers. Moreover, traditional models have often failed to explain how so much "reasoning" can get done so fast with so little hardware. Reactive-agent architectures have been proposed as an alternative to traditional AI, but to date theoretical foundations for this work have been less developed.

Situated-automata theory provides a semantic analysis of information processing that is intended to apply to all embedded control systems without requiring designer-conceived interpretations of machine state or computational models based on run-time inference. It is based on a direct mathematical model of how the states of natural processes, in the ways they unfold over time, reflect one another through intricate cross-dependencies and correlations that give rise to semantically meaningful states. The theory brings the semantic precision associated with traditional logic-based AI to the analysis of systems that are not structured as conventional reasoning systems at all. Nor are systems that *do* seem to "reason" excluded from this style of analysis; they are simply a special case.

Note that none of this analysis is inconsistent with the construction of agents as symbolic systems; it simply makes explicit the constraints that must hold for their intended interpretation to be valid and provides methods for using symbolic characterizations as program specifications rather than as an implementation strategy.

The shift from the traditional AI view to the situated view brings us to an outlook reminiscent of early cybernetic feedback models, but with more semantic subtlety and sophistication (derived from traditional symbolic AI) in describing conditions being tracked and controlled by an agent. In this view, the fundamental phenomenon to be explained is not "reasoning" but the mutual constraint exhibited between parts of a physical system over time. The key lies in understanding how a process can naturally mirror in its states subtle conditions in its environment and how these mirroring states ripple out to overt actions that eventually achieve goals. The fundamental questions include how the enormous set of discernible conditions can be modeled and grasped, how computational elements can be arranged to preserve distinctions that matter for controlling the environment while perhaps blurring others, and how can this be done in real time with high reliability using relatively modest computational resources.

While the analytical approach presented here is very general in scope, its application to synthesis problems and to the design of particular systems remains quite challenging. In this paper we have attempted to sketch directions we regard as promising, primarily involving the use of stylized off-line symbolic reasoning to generate tractable run-time machinery with desired properties of information and control. Work remains to be done on the integration of automated learning techniques as well as the modeling and exploitation of statistical covariance in ways analogous to the discrete logic-based techniques presented here.

Acknowledgments

We derived a great deal of help and inspiration from our colleagues over the years of this project. Stanley Reifel built Flakey, an experimental mobile robot platform, and constantly challenged us to match in working software what we derived in elegant formulas. Sandy Wells brought a knowledge of computer vision, hardware, and hacking that was invaluable. Nathan Wilson implemented endless versions of and variations on Rex and wrote some crucial navigational code for Flakey. Stuart Shieber was a valuable adjunct to the group and implemented natural language modules for the robot programs. Fernando Pereira was an important influence on the early development of situated-automata theory. David Chapman spent some summers with us and helped make Rex a much better language, through both ideas and implementation. He also worked on Ruler and some of its precursors. We are generally indebted to and appreciative of our colleagues at the Artificial Intelligence Center of SRI International, at Stanford University's Center for the Study of Language and Information, and at Teleos Research. We gratefully acknowledge financial support from these institutions as well as from sponsors at the Defense Advance Research Projects Agency, the National Aeronautics and Space Administration, the Air Force Office of Scientific Research, General Motors Research, and FMC.

References

[1] A.R. Cassandra, L.P. Kaelbling and M.L. Littman, Acting optimally in partially observable stochastic domains, in: *Proceedings AAAI-94*, Seattle, WA (1994).

[2] J.Y. Halpern and Y. Moses, Knowledge and common knowledge in an distributed environment, in: *Proceedings Third ACM Conference on Principles of Distributed Computing* (1984) 50–61; revised version: IBM RJ 4421.

[3] G.E. Hughes and M.J. Cresswell, *An Introduction to Modal Logic* (Methuen and Company, London, 1968).

[4] L.P. Kaelbling, Rex: a symbolic language for the design and parallel implementation of embedded systems, in: *Proceedings AIAA Conference on Computers in Aerospace*, Wakefield, MA (1987).

[5] L.P. Kaelbling, Goals as parallel program specifications, in: *Proceedings AAAI-88*, Minneapolis–St. Paul, MN (1988).

[6] L.P. Kaelbling, Compiling operator descriptions into reactive strategies using goal regression, Technical Report, Teleos Research, Palo Alto, CA (1991).

[7] L.P. Kaelbling and S.J. Rosenschein, Action and planning in embedded agents, *Rob. Autonomous Syst.* **6** (1) (1990) 35–48; also in: P. Maes, ed., *Designing Autonomous Agents: Theory and Practice from Biology to Engineering and Back* (MIT Press, Cambridge, MA, 1991).

[8] L.P. Kaelbling and N.J. Wilson, Rex programmer's manual, Technical Report 381R, Artificial Intelligence Center, SRI International, Menlo Park, CA (1988).

[9] W.S. Lovejoy, A survey of algorithmic methods for partially observed Markov decision processes, *Ann. Oper. Res.* **28** (1) (1991) 47–65.

[10] J. McCarthy and P.J. Hayes, Some philosophical problems from the standpoint of artificial intelligence, in: B. Meltzer and D. Michie, eds., *Machine Intelligence* **4** (Edinburgh University Press, Edinburgh, 1969).

[11] R.C. Moore, A formal theory of knowledge and action, in: J.R. Hobbs and R.C. Moore, eds., *Formal Theories of the Commonsense World* (Ablex, Norwood, NJ, 1985).

[12] A. Newell, The knowledge level, *Artif. Intell.* **18** (1982) 87–127.

[13] S.J. Rosenschein, Plan synthesis: a logical perspective, in: *Proceedings IJCAI-81*, Vancouver, BC (1981); reprinted in: J.F. Allen, J. Hendler and A. Tate, eds., *Readings in Planning* (Morgan Kaufmann, San Mateo, CA, 1990).

[14] S.J. Rosenschein, Formal theories of knowledge in AI and robotics, *New Gen. Comput.* **3** (4) (1985) 345–357.

[15] S.J. Rosenschein, Synthesizing information-tracking automata from environment descriptions, in: *Proceedings International Conference on Principles of Knowledge Representation and Reasoning*, Toronto, Ont. (1989).

[16] S.J. Rosenschein and L.P. Kaelbling, The synthesis of digital machines with provable epistemic properties, in: J.Y. Halpern, ed., *Proceedings of the Conference on Theoretical Aspects of Reasoning*

About Knowledge (Morgan Kaufmann, San Mateo, CA, 1986) 83–98; updated version: Technical Note 412, Artificial Intelligence Center, SRI International, Menlo Park, CA.

[17] R.J. Waldinger, Achieving several goals simultaneously, in: E.W. Elcock and D. Michie, eds., *Machine Intelligence* **8** (Ellis Horwood, Chichester, 1977); reprinted in: J.F. Allen, J. Hendler and A. Tate, eds., *Readings in Planning* (Morgan Kaufmann, San Mateo, CA, 1990).

Artificial Intelligence 73 (1995) 175–230

The use of dynamics in an intelligent controller for a space faring rescue robot

Marcel Schoppers *

Robotics Research Harvesting, P.O. Box 2111, Redwood City, CA 94062, USA

Received November 1992; revised November 1993

Abstract

The NASA Extra Vehicular Activity Retriever (EVAR) robot is being designed to retrieve astronauts or objects that become detached from the orbiting Space Station. This task requires that the robot's intelligent controller must rely heavily on orbital dynamics predictions, without becoming blind to the wide variety of anomalies that may occur.

This article describes the controller's Universal Plan (U.P.) and some technical lessons learned from it. The U.P. reacts not to actual current states but to estimated states, which are obtained using goal-directed active perception. A modal logic formalization of discrete-event dynamics allows us to finely analyze and specify the interactions of knowledge, belief, sensing, acting, and time within the U.P. The U.P. now acts like a hands-off manager: it makes regular observations, grants some leeway for unobservable or ill-modelled processes, has faith in subsystem dynamics, and takes action only to manipulate subsystems into delivering desired progress. Most of the time, the appropriate action is to do nothing.

Finally we examine properties of the application that allowed the U.P. to deliver robust goal achievement despite misleading state estimates, weak models of relevant processes, and unpredictable disturbances.

---

* E-mail: mjs@hpp.stanford.edu.

1. Project overview

The control system to be discussed herein was implemented for the NASA Extra-Vehicular Activity Retriever [1] (EVAR), a robot that will be deployed in space later this decade to locate and retrieve astronauts or other objects that become untethered from Space Station or Shuttle. Each retrieval mission will involve sensor acquisition of the target object, rendezvous with the object, stand-off, grappling, sensor acquisition of home base, return with the object, stand-off, and delivery.

The project of implementing the control system had two purposes. One was the production of the control system itself. The other, imposed on us by forward-thinking NASA staff, was to provide a demonstration of the value of putting intelligent hardware in space. NASA is very cautious about the workings of anything that goes into space, and for good reason: a malfunction can cost billions of dollars. A natural consequence is that NASA mistrusts the AI enterprise because it is deliberately building programs that do things even the systems' own programmers can't predict in detail. Our control system was to be an example of such a program, and we were to demonstrate that, despite the unpredictability of our intelligent software's behavior—or rather, because of it—the control system could be reliable and safe.

At the heart of the control system was a Universal Plan (U.P.) [53]—a representation for robotic discrete-event control laws that is amenable to automatic synthesis, and which is highly conditional and very fast by virtue of its ready translation into equivalent decision trees. As required for the project's higher purpose, the plan's sequence of decisions was largely unpredictable, depending heavily on what was happening in the environment outside the control system.

To demonstrate the safety of our control system in a convincing way, NASA decided that they would themselves build the simulator for testing our controller. (Testing our controller on a real robot in space was impossible for obvious reasons.) NASA programmers were then free to make the physical dynamics as realistic as they wished, and to smuggle into the simulation whatever strange events they wished (including some unintended malfunctions). The simulator included not only the usual physical environment such as orbital motion, a space station, astronauts, and the robot's own hardware and physics, but also the robot's laser-based perception subsystem, so that from our point of view there was no difference between a perceptual misinterpretation and a strange physical event. The simulator also provided a menu of accidents that could be introduced at the user's will.

The project's final demonstration for NASA successfully rescued a free-floating astronaut despite such events as space station windows that looked like astronauts until the robot got close enough; an astronaut being instantly moved further way or closer in; an astronaut rescuing herself by grabbing the robot instead of waiting to be grabbed; successfully grabbed astronauts who then escaped; failed attempts to grab an astronaut; collisions with meteorites large enough to impart arbitrary rotations and translations; effector commands and data requests that were either deliberately ignored or inexplicably

---
[1] Extra-vehicular activity is anything happening in open space. The name might be taken to mean either that the robot is extra-vehicular, or that it retrieves other things engaged in extra-vehicular activity.

lost in transmission; and so forth. The success of our approach may be judged from the fact that our clients decided at one point not to bother fixing certain bugs in their simulator, because our control system works in spite of them. Our control system is now routinely demonstrated to senior NASA officials by allowing them to interfere with the robot's activities as they choose.

Universal Plans (U.P.s) were initially designed to display robust recovery from unpredictable events, and this feature was central to our success, but the robotic application demanded several technical innovations to enlarge the range of realizable behaviors. Our plan had to monitor its own activities by performing sensor control actions and requesting world state estimates from the perception subsystem, and also needed to act to forestall events that had not happened yet. These problems required, and were solved by, adding new dimensions to the state space/domain model, in the form of new kinds of conditions the plan could test and react to. The required additional subtlety was achieved with modal logic operators for knowledge, belief, and branching time, which were introduced into the representation in such a way that all aspects of the domain description—predicates, actions, domain constraints, and states—could be infiltrated with the necessary modal operators. Although these innovations have been described in earlier papers [56, 57], they will be presented here in greater detail and from a more control-theoretic viewpoint.

The focus of this paper will be our last representational extension, providing the ability to monitor dynamics, hold beliefs about the future, and react to the presence of particular expectations. Thus we added, to the U.P. representation's prior ability to recover robustly from disturbances, a new ability to distinguish disturbances from dynamics and use the latter to advantage.

We begin by describing prior constraints on how the project was carried out; these constraints motivated some design decisions and also limited our progress. Next we present our modal logic formalization of dynamics, and then the implementation of our U.P. as an experiment on the validity and utility of our formalization. Finally we report on what we learned from our experiment, listing the capabilities accrued from our representational extensions, and the principles and issues we discovered.

Included among our "lessons learned" (Section 6) are the following:

- where to put the boundary between the control system and the controlled system (hint: beliefs about the state of the operating environment comprise yet another independent dynamic subsystem);
- why the architecture became neither a synchronous sense–act cycle, nor two asynchronous acting and monitoring subsystems, but a hybrid in which several asynchronous sensori-motor loops were managed by a synchronous belief-monitoring cycle;
- how to rely on dynamics without becoming defenceless against abnormal or unpredictable events, and why plan execution came to mean doing nothing most of the time;
- why we believe that knowledge restricting possible courses of events belongs in the state estimation subsystem, not in action selection;
- what it was about the astronaut retrieval domain that enabled our controller to be effective, and why similar effectiveness is likely to be achievable in general;

- why standard control systems notions split the qualification problem into two sub-problems addressable with appropriate solution techniques;
- the need for action decisions to directly affect beliefs, even before the decisions have any physical consequences.

2. Prior constraints

In this section we present the constraints on our work. We explain the general Universal Plan (U.P.) concept and how the U.P. for this project relates to it; we review some control theory; and we describe the simulated robot we controlled.

2.1. Robust reactive behavior

U.P.s were designed to display an extreme robustness against unexpected events [52]. This was accomplished by making U.P.s equivalent to decision trees, which apply a sequence of tests to map every possible situation to one of the tree's leaf nodes, where the response appropriate to that type of situation is stored. Iterated execution of such a decision tree will then map each new situation to a response, no matter what the previous situation was. Thus, U.P.s may be summarized as conveying highly conditional advice of the form

If a situation satisfying condition P should ever arise while you are trying to achieve goal G, then the appropriate response is action A.

Consequently U.P.s are capable of responding to all sequences of events—even physically impossible ones—and the behavior of an agent executing a fixed U.P. depends critically on which situations arise at plan execution time.

In this respect U.P.s can be compared to the differential equations of control theory, which create attractor and repulsor states in the state space without "representing" any actual behavior over any period of time. To explicitly predict behavior in advance of its occurrence, the equations must be integrated from a given starting point. Similarly, planning was traditionally approached as a problem of finding suitable sequences or trajectories through the state space, assuming a given initial state and some constraints on state transitions. The U.P. philosophy, akin to that of control theorists, is: why bother to guess a starting point, integrate the equations, and search for trajectories, when the devices being controlled will invariably depart from any behavior predicted in detail. It is possible to achieve good control by analyzing the equations themselves. In the case of U.P.s, it is similarly possible to obtain robust goal-directed control by analyzing the plans themselves, without analyzing any state or action sequences. (What is analyzed instead is the ability to reach one state space region from another, where a region is the set of all states satisfying some test.)

The extreme robustness of U.P.s, even to the point of allowing physically impossible courses of events, was found to be indispensible to our work with EVAR. While it may be obvious that reality is not accessible except via error-prone perception software, so that the plan is reacting not to its physical environment but to its estimations and guesses thereon, this has the less obvious consequence that physically impossible courses of events do occur—not in nature, of course, but certainly in the robot's perceptions. We shall come back to this topic in Section 6.4.

2.2. Automatic synthesis

U.P.s were the first form of "reactive plan" for which automated synthesis was demonstrated [53] (in [38] no mention is made of automated goal conflict resolution during the compilation of situated automata). Nevertheless, for the present work, automated U.P. synthesis was deliberately avoided: had we so much as modified a U.P. planner during this project, our employer could legally have prevented us from pursuing related research anywhere else. Therefore, the U.P. to be described below was built by hand in C, but with great vigilance for a future return to automated synthesis—we consciously viewed the C code as the *compiled* U.P. that might have been produced by suitable reasoning algorithms. To ensure that our C code remained faithful to the output of our imaginary U.P. compiler and hence to the U.P. formalism itself, we:

- reduced the U.P. as much as possible to a small number of macros that encoded our understanding of how an automatically synthesized U.P. would have worked;
- complied with such macros even if it meant defining C functions to do nothing but return **true**, and even if it meant defining the same subplan under several different names (e.g. when a subplan achieved several goals);
- formalized (e.g. with modal logic) any new capabilities needed by the plan;
- operationalized the achievement of modally qualified goals by modifying the relevant macros;
- marked all deviations from an automatically synthesized U.P. with "HACK!" comments.

This discipline continued throughout the project. As a result the C code was rife with function names like `ach_b_soon_sust_kw_clamp_open()`, which was the name of the subplan for requesting an update on the status of the robot's gripper—our formalizations were very evident in our C code.

Since the completion of the U.P. written in C we have modified our U.P. interpreter and planning algorithms, and have checked that the newly introduced modal logic operators generate the proper deductions and goal conflicts. Consequently we can confidently assert that our modal logic extensions to the U.P. formalism have both preserved the ability to synthesize U.P.s automatically, and solved the control problems we intended them to solve. However, because of a few deliberate "HACKs" in the C version of the U.P. (see Section 7.2) it is not yet possible to synthesize a functionally equivalent U.P. automatically.

Our concern with automated synthesis is also a large factor in understanding some of the limitations of our final U.P. Most obvious in this respect is our choice of modal logic to distinguish knowledge goals. We made this choice even though we were well aware at the time that sensors deliver uncertain data, while the modal formula "$k\ P$" is either true or false, with nothing in between. And indeed, our formalism's inability to reflect uncertainty at the symbol level has left us currently unable to encode multi-sensor fusion within the existing U.P. formalism. However, modal logic has very clear formal semantics and, beginning with [42], has made several appearances in planning systems, in contrast to more quantitative formalisms such as Bayes nets and utility models, which could not be usefully assembled from simple context-independent components when our work began [32,62]. We chose to protect automatic synthesis of U.P.s at the expense of leaving a few other problems temporarily unsolved.

2.3. Avoiding instability in the control hierarchy

At the beginning of our work, NASA decided that they would themselves build the simulation to be used for testing our U.P.-based controller. In the simulation they would use the actual perception and control algorithms that were being used by the hardware robot, to deprive us of direct access to simulated world state. In this way NASA retained complete control of simulation realism, and relieved us of the need to write fast servo loops for the robot's effectors, but gave us instead the control issues attending hierarchical control systems: the software would have at least two levels, one for the servo loops and one for our U.P.

In "hierarchical multi-rate" control systems slow loops control fast loops, as in our case, by changing set-points or other parameters in the servo loops. Even if it is known that the fast loops are stable for fixed parameter values, the combined system in which the parameters are variable may be unstable. One way to see this is to think of the textbook example of stability: a spring that is fixed at one end, has a movable weight at the other, and experiences some friction. If we pull the weight from its rest position and then release it, it will be pulled back and will eventually stop. Now consider the position of the fixed end to be a parameter, and suppose that we start moving the previously fixed end back and forth by a fixed distance. If we do that at just the right frequency, the weight at the other end will make larger and larger oscillations. This is the phenomenon of instability, caused in this case by our constant meddling with a parameter of an otherwise stable system.

A similar phenomenon arises when a controller tries to control a nonlinear plant by treating it as several operating regions in which it is linear. The controller then dynamically switches between the control laws for the operating regions, in a procedure commonly known as "gain scheduling" [59]. Here too it is possible that, even when the control law for each operating region is stable, the switching could happen in just the right way to make the complete system unstable.

The control engineer's rule of thumb for avoiding instability in these cases is to ensure that parameter adjustment (the slow loop) runs at much lower frequency than the system being controlled (i.e. the fast loop). This is one of the reasons that the number 10 comes up frequently in descriptions of hierarchical architectures such as NASREM [3]—in such contexts the number 10 is an implicit reference to a serious outstanding problem. The control theory required to solve this problem properly has only recently been developing [49,59].

Obeying the applicable rule of thumb, our U.P. executes approximately twice per second. This is much less than 1/10 the natural frequencies of the subsystems being controlled, so the danger of instability is minimal.

2.4. The Nyquist Sampling Theorem

When a control loop is not instantaneous, the data being used to compute a reaction may change in mid-loop, leading to inappropriate reactions. The usual solution is to "sample and hold": take a snapshot of world state at the beginning of a loop, and hold that data constant until the reaction has been computed. If the variables being monitored are oscillating, it is possible that this technique will take its snapshots at just the right frequency so that the variables appear to be stationary. Similarly, it is also possible that transient behavior is missed completely, or that the perceived frequency of oscillation is some fraction of the actual one.

The Nyquist Sampling Theorem (see e.g. [4]) states that to determine the actual frequency of an oscillating input signal, that signal must be sampled at more than twice the frequency of the signal.

It follows that, executing twice per second, the U.P. cannot respond properly to any process with a frequency of $\geqslant 1$ hertz. The U.P. could have been executed at much higher frequency—at some risk to total system stability, see Section 2.3—but since high-frequency oscillations relating to the control of individual effectors had been delegated to servo loops, < 1 hertz was thought to be fast enough for the U.P.

2.5. The robot's construction

To understand the plan fragments presented in this paper it is necessary to know something of EVAR's capabilities and construction. EVAR is designed for free flight on orbit. It can accelerate in any direction at any time, and can rotate about all three of its body axes at the same time, if required. It has two arms, one of which is equipped with a clamp. The clamp is instrumented with a sensor to indicate whether the clamp is open; at present there is no contact or proximity sensor. EVAR has three chest cameras mounted side by side so that their fields of view overlap slightly, and so that their combined fields of view span 180 degrees horizontally. (This arrangement allows EVAR to perform a visual scan in all directions by doing a backwards somersault.) A directable scanning laser range finder is mounted on top of EVAR's "shoulders", and has a rectangular field of view 60 degrees wide and high. The laser can be pointed at anything above the plane of EVAR's shoulders, hence cannot look at anything that is more than 30 degrees below that plane unless the whole robot is rotated.

3. On the modal formalization

Our work began with a conception of U.P.s wherein plans simply stated what should be done in various circumstances, much like a production system. But because we wished to build embedded systems, we were immediately forced to diverge from production systems by including some way to describe actions that brought information from the outside world into the executing plan. A modal logic of knowledge was introduced to play that role. Since some actions are valuable even if some of their preconditions have not been recently sensed, we also needed a way to represent information that had been derived from earlier knowledge using a dynamics model. A modal logic of belief was introduced to fill that gap. Finally, it was necessary to represent some of the dynamics of the application domain, so that approaching events could be anticipated and appropriate measures taken, whether those measures consisted of doing nothing, of initiating corrective action, or of continuing existing activities. This last gap was filled by a modal logic of branching time, adapted to model both open- and closed-loop dynamics. An intuitive feeling for the results may be had from the following interpretations of the modal operators:

- *Knowledge* of the state of the world is obtainable only by performing sensing actions at plan execution time. Such knowledge lasts only a few seconds, or until an action negates it, whichever comes first.
- *Beliefs* about current and future states of the world arise either as projections of earlier beliefs forward through time, or as expectations following on the heels of goals communicated to robot subsystems. Both sets of beliefs are licensed by the continuous and discrete domain models provided by the system designer.
- After initiating robotic action, the executing plan may believe the *eventual* attainment of desired effects, but may specifically *not* believe that the desired effects have been obtained, unless the action is described as being instantaneous.
- Sensing actions are described as enabling the belief that it will eventually be the case that

    P is known to be true *or* P is known to be false,

    so that at plan construction time the results of such actions are ambiguous, with disambiguation occurring only during plan execution. Sensing actions rarely have instantaneous results.
- All relevant processes (including environmental processes, robotic actions, and sensing) are monitored not only for their success but also for their progress, and are evaluated for their compatibility with desired futures.

The modal logic formulations of knowledge, belief, and branching time were adopted for U.P.s on the following pragmatic grounds.

(1) Modal logics were well understood formalisms with soundness and completeness theorems.
(2) If all conditions appearing in action preconditions, postconditions, domain constraints, and goals were systematically infiltrated with modal operators, this would safeguard the ability to automatically check the logical consistency of domain models and of plans.
(3) Modal conditions in plans could be operationalized for plan execution (by means of tests on perception-based data) without imposing any formalism-specific computational burden at plan execution time.

We now discuss the modal logics in greater detail.

3.1. Knowledge and belief

When a plan or procedure is being carried out by a system embedded in the real world (e.g. a robot), there must be some way to determine whether the plan is working.

Given that sensing is necessary and that the *flexible* use of a sensor will require effector activity (such as moving the sensor platform relative to the robot body, or moving the whole robot body), the sensory activities and their supporting effector activities had better become part of the plan, and both had better be represented in such a way that their effects and interactions can be reasoned about during plan construction.

The U.P.s formalization of sensing actions closed a gap between three bodies of planning work. First, there was work on automated reasoning about knowledge and action. This work had not represented sensing actions whose outcomes were unpredictably either true or false, and had not planned the use of sensing actions to check whether other executed actions had worked as desired. For example, when Moore [42, pp. 121f] had a safe-opening action produce the knowledge that the safe was open, this was done not by planning a sensing action to find out at plan execution time whether the safe was open or closed, but by showing that if the safe were *assumed* open (or closed) then, after simulating the safe-opening action, *the planner* would "know" that the safe was open (or closed). Of course, the planner could equally well assume that the safe was still closed, and actually had no reason to make either assumption. Similarly, none of the formalisms of Drummond [15, Section 5.12], Haas [31], Konolige [40] or Morgenstern [43] were used to represent actions whose execution would check the outcomes of other planned actions.

Second, there was work on automatically creating or modifying plans to include sensing actions that verified progress during plan execution, but none of that work had made use of logical formalisms for reasoning about knowledge, e.g. [9, 14, 19, 28, 60].

Third, there was a body of work on situated agency wherein relatively sophisticated execution-time sensing was common-place, but here again, the knowledge preconditions of actions were not formalized. The previous work closest to our needs was that of Rosenschein [48], which presented a formal account of the knowledge obtainable by embedded systems at execution time, but did not use that formalism for action representation.

This gap was closed by Schoppers [56] who infiltrated the first-order terms of an otherwise ordinary planning domain model with modal operators for knowledge and belief [33, 37]. Consequently, the pre- and post-conditions of actions, and the declarative domain constraints, could all make use of modal terms. This preserved the value of logical deduction for plan synthesis purposes. "Knowledge" was then interpreted as "perceptually verified information", and the achievement of knowledge goals was enabled by means of two axioms:

$$\mathbf{kw}\ P \equiv \mathbf{k}\ P \lor \mathbf{k}\neg P. \qquad\qquad (\text{Axiom 1})$$

$$\mathbf{k}\ P \equiv \mathbf{b}\ P \land \mathbf{kw}\ P. \qquad\qquad (\text{Axiom 2})$$

Axiom 1 defines "knowing-whether" as an undetermined outcome, and is used to describe sensing actions and pose sensing goals. Since ordinary physical effects do not automatically provide perceptual information, goals involving the **kw** modality can only be achieved by sensing. Axiom 2 is used to resolve, into two subgoals, goals requiring the achievement of definite knowledge **k** P of some condition P.[2] One subgoal can

---

[2] In earlier papers this axiom required P rather than **b** P because the distinction between actual and believed facts had not been completed.

initiate the use of effector actions; the other can initiate the use of sensing actions to perceive whether an effector action is necessary and/or successful.

To support the representation of information other than knowledge—for example, estimates of present world state or convictions about future events—a modal belief operator **b** was also introduced into the plan representation. The logic S5 was chosen for the knowledge modality, in part because the S5 system was the simplest suitable system, and in part because the formalization of [48] turned out to be S5 (cf. [17]). The logic weak-S5 was chosen for the belief modality. Both systems contain the following as axioms or theorems, in which **b** may be uniformly replaced by **k**:

$$\mathbf{b}(P \supset Q) \supset (\mathbf{b}\, P \supset \mathbf{b}\, Q).$$
$$\mathbf{b}\, P \supset \neg\mathbf{b}\neg P.$$
$$\mathbf{b}\, P \equiv \mathbf{b}\, \mathbf{b}\, P.$$
$$\neg\mathbf{b}\, P \equiv \mathbf{b}\neg\mathbf{b}\, P.$$

In addition, the stronger S5 system contains the axiom characterizing knowledge as true:

$$\mathbf{k}\, P \supset P.$$

Finally, the knowledge operator was related to the belief operator in the usual way:

$$\mathbf{k}\, P \supset \mathbf{b}\, P.$$
$$\mathbf{b}\, P \equiv \mathbf{k}\, \mathbf{b}\, P.$$

These modal operators for knowledge and belief, and especially Axiom 2 above, were central to the design of our C-language U.P., but were not used to support automated reasoning until long after that U.P. had been completed.

3.2. Dynamics, disturbances, and system boundaries

At the beginning of our work with EVAR, U.P.s suffered from several time-related problems, including:

- The plan insisted on acting as long as a desired condition was false, even if that condition would eventually become true without any further action on the plan's part. For example, an early EVAR U.P. repeatedly told the laser scanner to move to a given position, even though the scanner was already on its way there and couldn't move any faster.
- The plan refused to act as long as a desired condition was true, even if that condition was about to become false very predictably and could be kept true with appropriate action. For example, an early EVAR U.P. coolly waited for an astronaut to drift out of the laser scanner's field of view before bothering to move the scanner. Since the astronaut was gathering speed as she left the scanner's field of view, the time required to re-find her could be unbearable to onlookers, and as a result the robot seemed chronically inept.

Solving these problems demanded (among other things) an ability to encode and utilize, within an executing plan, beliefs about the near future. More specifically, since automatically constructed plans (including U.P.s) execute an action only if that action is achieving a goal, it was necessary to define, for each primary goal G_1 that needed to be kept true over some extended interval, a type of supporting goal G_2 having the following properties:

- G_2 could be constructed from G_1 by means of a simple device such as prefixing G_1 with a modal operator;
- if G_1 had not yet been achieved, then G_2 should be false if and only if action was required to make G_1 true;
- if G_1 had already been achieved, then G_2 should be false if and only if action was required to keep G_1 true;
- G_2 could sensibly be made the postcondition of an action, and as such could "clobber" other goals;
- the truth or falsity of G_2 could be determined by sensing the present state of the world.

Furthermore, it was necessary to specify a mechanism for attaching G_2 to G_1 in plans, and to find a formalism capable of representing G_1, G_2, and their logical relationship.

None of the existing formalisms for modelling actions and processes over time ([27, 41, 46, 50], along with temporal modal logics and dynamic logic) provided a clean answer. In all cases it was either difficult or impossible to derive a condition G_2 that was false at any time if and only if, no matter what actions were actually being taken at that time or later, *lack of action would have* resulted in G_1 becoming true or false.

Consideration of the differing consequences of action and inaction brings us directly to the distinction between closed-loop and open-loop control. Hence we now present some background information on controllers and dynamics.

Feedback controllers are characterized by a *closed loop* from the controller through effectors to the system being controlled, through sensors, and back to the controller. If that loop is broken anywhere, be it because sensors are broken or nonexistent, or because the controller is turned off, the system becomes *open-loop* and feedback compensation becomes impossible. However, in an open-loop system in which the controller can still influence the effectors, *feedforward* compensation remains possible. Feedforward compensation can observe a disturbance coming from somewhere outside the controlled system, can utilize a model of the controlled system to predict the effects of the disturbance on system behavior, and can counteract those predicted effects before any actual effect occurs (like bracing for an expected collision). For this to work the disturbance itself must be measurable and the model being used to predict its effects must be good, since a feedforward compensator will not be able to observe and correct any results differing from its intentions. Because of its complete dependence on a good system model, feedforward compensation is brittle and is usually combined with feedback compensation. Feedback compensation allows a disturbance to have effects on the controlled system and then counteracts the observed (actual) effects. This is a much more robust control method, provided that the effects of disturbances can be tolerated. Almost all control systems are closed-loop. A sizeable fraction utilize both feedforward and feedback compensation.

The terms "open-loop" and "closed-loop" are also loosely applied as qualifiers of dynamics. A *dynamic* is a rule about change over time. *Open-loop dynamics* are the principles governing the behavior of a system when it is running open-loop, which—given the brittleness of feedforward compensation—usually means that it is completely uncontrolled. *Closed-loop dynamics* are the principles governing the behavior of a closed-loop system, including the effects of a feedback controller. As a simple example, a door may or may not stay open by itself, depending on the presence of a spring for closing it, and/or a door-stop for keeping it open. A spring-loaded door's open-loop dynamics cause the door to close. When our robot continuously holds the door open, the door's response to the ongoing action of our robotic agent is a closed-loop dynamic.

Similarly, *open-loop stability* is a property of systems that possess a stable equilibrium without the continuous help of an automatic controller. All commercial passenger aircraft are open-loop stable for safety's sake. If an aircraft is not *closed-loop stable* it cannot be flown. Most military aircraft are closed-loop stable but open-loop unstable, i.e. they can only fly with the continuous help of an automatic controller. This allows greater maneuverability, at cost of some risk to the pilot's life.

Implicit in the open/closed-loop distinction is a *conceptual boundary* around the system being controlled. When we say that a spring-loaded door's closing behavior is open-loop, we are assuming a system containing both the door and the spring, with any controlling influence coming from somewhere else. If we were to consider the spring to be a trivial controller for a system consisting of the door only, then the door's closing behavior would be closed-loop under the influence of the spring, and its open-loop behavior would then be to stop moving.

Derived from this distinction are the two related concepts of unmodelled dynamics and disturbances. *Unmodelled dynamics* are dynamics we either know about and can safely ignore, or do not know about and may or may not be able to ignore. The behavior of any physical system can be analyzed and modelled only down to some level of abstraction determined by the modeller's energy and measuring equipment. Below that level of abstraction there will be behaviors the modeller is initially unaware of—it is a given that unmodelled dynamics will exist. After building a controller and testing it on a simulation of the system being controlled, the modeller has only verified that the controller works on the model. The controller may not (or may) work when applied to the real system, depending on the unmodelled dynamics being (or not being) excited by the controller's influence on the plant. In the worst case, unmodelled dynamics may be dependent on an infrequently occurring aspect of the controller's action, so may not be discovered even during flight testing, yet may be so serious that, when finally excited, they cause the controlled system to become unstable and crash.

The primary distinction between dynamics and *disturbances* is that dynamics arise somewhere in the control loop while disturbances do not. Disturbances may or may not be stochastic and may or may not be modelable, but they are not controllable. For example, a disk spinning inside a CD player will not be perfectly centered, so to follow a given track the laser head may have to oscillate at the same frequency as the disk. This oscillation is expected and very regular, yet is considered a disturbance because it cannot be controlled, it can only be compensated for.[3]

Only these few terms already allow useful characterizations of AI planning work. Most of the planners built to date have been open-loop because there was neither any

---

[3] For this excellent example we thank Kjell Gustafsson, of the Department of Automatic Control, Lund Institute of Technology, Sweden.

effect on a physical plant, nor any feedback from sensors. A famous exception was STRIPS [20], which was a closed-loop controller because it did control a real robot and replan when sensor data warranted it, but STRIPS was largely a feedforward controller because Shakey, the robot it controlled, moved by dead reckoning and visually examined its environment only between movements, and the plan itself did nothing and received no feedback except between movements.

The plans built by pre-1985 planners were brittle because the planners were operating as feedforward controllers, whether or not the plans were used to control a physical system. The dominant feature of the post-1985 "reactive planning" work was greater reliance on feedback.

In the reactive planning literature one finds frequent assertions that the technology is especially suited to "dynamic, unpredictable, uncertain" domains. This conflation of dynamics with unpredictability is mistaken. Dynamics are predictable by definition (down to some level of abstraction). The real driver of reactive planning work—and the reason why feedback is essential—is robustness against disturbances. This has so far been pursued without any concern for exploiting open-loop dynamics.

In summary, awareness of dynamics is necessary for efficient behavior:

(1) If a system's open-loop dynamics are such that the system will evolve toward certain desired conditions of its own accord, then it is not necessary to act on the system at all to achieve the desired ends.

(2) If a system's open-loop dynamics are such that the system will evolve away from certain desired conditions of its own accord, then it may be necessary to keep acting on the system even though the desired conditions are already true. That is, the plan must be able to react to the unwanted open-loop dynamic by replacing it with a suitable closed-loop dynamic.

The latter case is sometimes referred to as "maintenance" or "prevention". In U.P.s the distinction between open- and closed-loop dynamics serves to distinguish situations in which no action is necessary (because open-loop dynamics suffice) from situations in which action (a closed-loop dynamic) is required. Consequently the open- versus closed-loop distinction pervades our formalization of time.

3.3. Branching time

In this section we present our complete formalization of the distinction between open-loop and closed-loop dynamics, in terms of a modal logic of branching time (refer to Fig. 1).

We begin with a model of world state, and subdivide that state into two parts, the state of the system being controlled, also called the "plant", and the state of the controller, in this case the U.P. An *estimate* of plant state, encoded with real-valued variables, was obtained from sensor interpretation software and Kalman filtering software provided by NASA. This real-valued state estimate was intermittently requested by, and communicated to, our U.P., which applied various thresholding and comparison tests to the real-valued data. As described in Section 4.2, these tests evaluate the truth or falsity of modally qualified atomic formulae such as **b soon sust kw** in_laser_fov(X). The collection of such test outcomes translates the real-valued state estimate into a

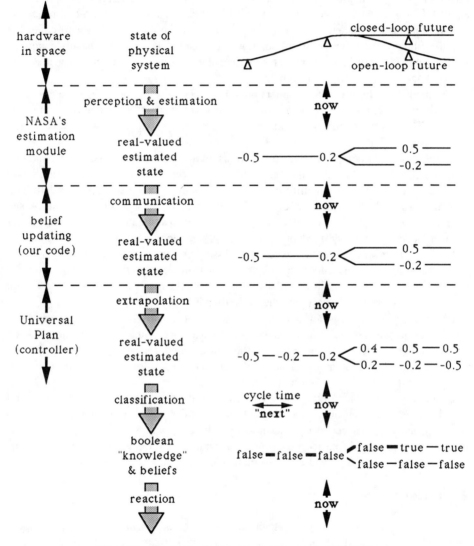

Fig. 1. Mapping perceived plant states into temporal model states.

(partial) Boolean state estimate. The Boolean state estimate is a partial "world state" in the planning sense, with the important difference that its contents are computed by abstracting from measurements of the actual plant, not by simulating action effects. This Boolean state estimate is used by the U.P. to decide what to do.

U.P. execution is assumed to manifest a kind of "sense–act cycle" of classifying the estimated state of the plant, acting accordingly, then repeating. The classification step computes the Boolean state estimate "on the fly" as the U.P. applies Boolean tests to the real-valued state estimate. The perceived state of the plant, in both its real-valued and Boolean forms, can change only between sense–act cycles, so that each sense–act cycle is working off a frozen snapshot of the plant state.

The U.P. needs to examine not only the Boolean abstraction of the currently perceived plan state, but also what might happen at various future times and under various scenarios. To provide a basis for answering such questions we construct a standard semantic model for the logic of branching time, as follows. We now imagine not only the current real-valued state estimate, but all possible real-valued state estimates, and we map each such estimate into the corresponding Boolean state estimate, thus obtaining the set of all possible Boolean state estimates. It is likely that many real-valued state estimates will map into a single Boolean state estimate. We can induce two relations on the set of Boolean state estimates, one relating each state to its successors under the open-loop behavior of the plant, and a similar relation for the plant's closed-loop behavior. From these two relations we can construct a third relation, their union, which relates Boolean state estimates to their successors under *either* open- or closed-loop dynamics. In each of the two base relations a state estimate may give rise to different future developments, in the open-loop case because physics may be nondeterministic, and in the closed-loop case because we may choose to control the plant in different ways. Hence both successor relations are 1:N and the temporal conception is one of branching futures. From here the development of the relevant modal logics is well studied, see e.g. [47]. Time is assumed to be infinite.

The amount of time τ that passes between the successive Boolean state estimates of the temporal model is determined by the plan execution machinery. We will assume $\tau > 0$.

Since the U.P. is perceiving the plant, and since the plant can only be in one state at a time, the U.P.'s Boolean state estimate will correspond to a particular one of the states in the temporal model, and the actual behavior of the plant over time will correspond to a particular one of the possible futures in the temporal model. However, the importance of the model is that it influences the U.P.'s choices of action, and those choices in turn influence which possible future becomes actual.

The following branching time modal logic operators were used in this work. To avoid confusion between actual plant states and the Boolean states of the temporal model, the latter will be called "model states".

- **next** P is true at a given model state if condition P is true in the immediately succeeding model states in all *open-loop* futures.
- **soon** P is true at a given model state if condition P becomes true eventually in all possible *open-loop* futures *not* including the present state.
- **sust** P is true at a given model state if condition P is true not only in that state, but remains true forever in *some* possible future, whether or not action is required to keep it true. Then we say that P is "sustainable" from that state.
- **cont** P is true at a given model state if condition P is true not only in that state, but remains true forever in *all open-loop* futures. Then P will "continue" to be true at least as long as the controller does nothing.

The primary use of **next** is to test, when P is true of the perceived plant state in the current sense–act cycle, whether P will remain true at least until the next sense–act cycle, even if no action is taken to make it so. If that is true, the plan execution machinery may do nothing now, and can reconsider later (next) whether P should go on being true even longer. If it is false, e.g. if P *should* remain true but inaction would cause it to become false, the appropriate response is to perform an action that achieves **next** P. Over a sequence of sense–act cycles, the plan's determination that **next** P should remain true turns out to be a moment-by-moment way of keeping P true continuously—a way that does not need to commit to whether P's truth will ever end. It may be the case that P can be kept true continuously by taking action on every other sense–act cycle, or even less often. The ability to represent continuously true conditions is provided by numerous temporal modelling approaches, but ours is the first one to allow that conditions may be kept continuously true by means of *intermittent* action, determining the frequency of the necessary action at plan execution time.

When the operators **soon** and **sust** are composed, we obtain the crucial modality **soon sust** P, which is true at a given moment if, without further action being required (open-loop dynamics), it will eventually (still or again) be the case that P is true and can be kept that way. Conversely, **soon sust** P is false at a given moment when

(1) the U.P. must perform some action to make P true in a sustainable way, regardless of whether P is temporarily true at any earlier time; or
(2) P is already true and sustainable, but will become false or unsustainable unless the plan does something immediately.

Nearly all of the goals occurring in the EVAR U.P. were of the form **sust** P and needed to be kept true for some period of time, either because several preconditions needed to be made true conjunctively (so that those achieved first had to stay true) or because actions were not instantaneous (and preconditions had to stay true throughout the action). For conditions of the form **sust** P our plan used

$$(\neg\mathbf{sust}\ P \wedge \mathbf{soon\ sust}\ P) \vee (\mathbf{sust}\ P \wedge \mathbf{next\ sust}\ P)$$

as a necessary and sufficient condition for inaction. This formula is almost equivalent to **soon sust** P except that it demands action even when

$$\mathbf{sust}\ P \wedge \mathbf{soon\ sust}\ P \wedge \neg\mathbf{next\ sust}\ P.$$

Consequently **soon sust** P was a necessary and sufficient condition for inaction when **sust** P was being *achieved*, while **next sust** P was a necessary and sufficient condition for inaction when **sust** P was being *maintained*. (A pendulum repeatedly swinging through the desired end point should not count as sustainment.)

This choice of formalization worked because our U.P. had no interest in the specific amount of time before a desired condition would become true. In a more quantitative formalization, action might be desirable to speed up the attainment of an outcome that was already assured.

We show in Section 4.5 how the achievement of modally qualified goals was operationalized in our C code.

3.4. Possible futures versus actual futures

At this point it will be useful to address a potential misinterpretation of our formalization. Some readers express concern that, in the case where a robot is continually acting, **soon** P implies the existence of futures in which the robot is initially not acting, whereas in fact such futures will not exist. This is a simple confusion between what is possible and what is actual. It is possible that through my inaction, the Little Nell who is lying on the train tracks will die in a few moments; it is also possible that I run and manage to save her. Indeed, the possibility of her dying is the *reason* for my running to save her, so that by acting, I remove from actuality exactly the possible future that motivated my acting [41]. Similarly, our U.P. is full of reaction to future possibilities that will be determinedly prevented.

On the other hand, it is conceivable that the plan could find the possible open-loop futures to be desirable in certain respects, and could then perform an action which side-stepped those very futures. If those futures were being counted on to become real, however, this scenario would be a destructive interaction wherein a subgoal was being "clobbered" by a badly timed action. It is part of the task of any planner to prevent just such interactions.

3.5. Encoding the EVAR domain

In parallel with developing the C-language U.P. we also used the modal logic extensions to encode the EVAR domain. That representation made clear which effects were primitive, or derivable by inference, or conditional. For example, opening EVAR's clamp has the primitive effect of the clamp's being open, and has the derived effect that nothing is being held, and has the conditional effect that the astronaut being held has been delivered to the Space Station. These relationships between actions and effects were apparent in our C code. For derived effects the relevant deductions were encoded (see Fig. 6, line 72), and several effects were commented as being conditional.

We are now developing a new U.P. interpreter and planner on top of a specially modified Prolog interpreter. The interpreter is now able to back-chain from modally qualified goals, testing exactly the same conditions and in the same order as our C-language U.P. (except for a few special cases commented as being "HACKs", see Section 7.2), including that it can execute several subplans pseudo-concurrently.

Figs. 2 and 3 show part of our modalized domain model.

- By virtue of the axiom ($\mathbf{k}$ P $\supset$ $\mathbf{b}$ P), the first set of rules in Fig. 2 can be used to derive either knowledge or belief.
- The domain constraint

    $\mathbf{k}$ located(X) -> $\mathbf{k}$ in-fov(X).

  holds because an object can only be *known* to be located, at a given time, if it is being perceived at that time, and it can only be perceived if it is in some sensor's field of view. The corresponding rule for belief does not hold because the plan is entitled to have beliefs about an object's location without that object being seen at the time.
- Action descriptions are written action-name first, followed by goal-reduction rules in Prolog style, with postconditions on the left, a state transition arrow "<+" in the middle, and preconditions on the right. A "?" appearing among the preconditions separates the "qualifiers" preceding it from the "subgoals" following it. Both must be true to use the effect but qualifiers are not to be achieved when false; they serve

```
% rules for both knowledge & belief, forever

clamp_open <-> ~ clamp_closed.

facing(X) -> in_camera_fov(X).
in_fov(X) <-> ( in_camera_fov(X) | in_laser_fov(X) ).
in_fov(X) -> laserable(X).
laserable(X) -> located(X).

% rules constraining knowledge, forever

k located(X) -> k in_fov(X).
k located(X) -> kw in_laser_fov(X).
k located(X) -> kw in_camera_fov(X).
k in-fov(X) -> kw facing(X).

k in_laser_fov(X) <-> kw clamp_near(X).
k in_laser_fov(X) <-> kw standing_off(X).
k in_camera_fov(X) <-> kw low_spin(X).

% some of the above hold for belief, forever

b located(X) -> bw in_laser_fov(X).
b located(X) -> bw in_camera_fov(X).
% hence b located(X) -> bw in_fov(X).
b in_fov(X) -> bw facing(X).

% eternal rules about persistence

% the clamp never moves by itself
b clamp_open -> b cont b clamp_open.
b clamp_closed -> b cont b clamp_closed.
% an inert object can't accelerate
b low_spin(X) -> b cont b low_spin(X).
b ~ low_spin(X) -> b cont b ~ low_spin(X).
% the arm stays where it was put
b arm_out -> b cont b arm_out.
b ~ arm_out -> b cont b ~ arm_out.
```

Fig. 2. Domain constraints for the EVA Retriever.

only as applicability filters. Where "&&" separates two effects the second effect is a conditional effect, occurring only if the preconditions of *both* effects are satisfied. Conditional effects can be nested to any depth. Disjunctive effects are also allowed but are rarely used.

```
% action descriptions

opening --            % open the clamp
   b next b clamp_open <+ true
&& b next b delivered(X,Y) <+
              b coupled(X), b clamp_near(Y).

closing --            % close the clamp
   b next b clamp_closed <+ true
&& b next b coupled(X) <+
              b clamp_open, b clamp_near(X).

extending --          % extend arm with clamp
   b soon sust b arm_out <+ true.

translating1(X) --    % move to standoff
   b soon sust b standing_off(X) <+ b sust k located(X).

translating2(X) --    % move to contact
   b soon sust b clamp_near(X) <+
                   b sust k low_spin(X) ?
                   b sust k facing(X),
                   b sust k standing_off(X),
                   b sust b arm_out.

rotating1(X) --       % turn to look at-X
   b soon sust b laserable(X) <+ b located(X).

rotating2(X) --       % turn to face X
   b soon sust b facing(X) <+ b located(X).

rotating3(X) --       % somersault
   b soon sust b in_camera_fov(X) <+ true.

tracking(X) --        % track w range finder
   b soon sust b in_laser_fov(X) <+ b sust b laserable(X).

get_status --         % read internal sensors
   b soon sust kw clamp_open,
   b soon sust kw arm_out    <+ true.

get_info(X) --        % get data from sensors
   b soon sust kw located(X) <+ true.
```

Fig. 3. Action descriptions for the EVA Retriever.

- For all actions but the last two, the postconditions are free of knowledge modalities; the last two actions are knowledge-generating.
- Preconditions of actions are qualified by a belief (or knowledge) modality, subject to the domain engineer's view that each action may (or may not) be performed on the strength of unverified projections derived from earlier states.
- The temporal modalities on action postconditions indicate both the expected delay until effects are achieved, and whether effects are achieved in a sustainable way. Almost all conditions in the EVAR domain had to be sustained.
- The temporal modalities on action preconditions indicate whether preconditions must be true only initially or throughout the action.
- Although GET-INFO(X) is described as achieving only **b soon sust kw** located(X), the deduction rules provided enable our interpreter to use the GET-INFO(X) action to achieve all of the following goals: **b soon sust kw** in-camera-fov(X), **b soon sust kw** in-laser-fov(X), **b soon sust kw** in-fov(X), **b soon sust kw** laserable(X), and **b soon sust kw** facing(X). This deduction ability was one of the main motivations for the modal formalization.

3.6. Using the formalism

Fig. 4 shows a list of modal conjunctions and whether/how they can be simultaneously true.

We now discuss several unusual aspects of our modal formalization.

Preconditions are usually of the form **sust** P. Since the effects of actions are usually delayed and of the form **soon sust**¬P, actions usually cannot "clobber" preconditions.

From Fig. 5 it is clear that **soon sust**¬P is consistent with **sust** P because the two sustainments can take place in different possible futures. This is not unreasonable, however. I recently mailed off a check that would have overdrawn my checking account, thus achieving **soon sust**¬sufficient-funds, and yet at the same time I intended **sust** sufficient-funds, as demonstrated by the fact that soon after mailing the check, I requested a 24-hour transfer from my savings to my checking account, thus preempting the open-loop future I had set up. Observe that my preemption worked because the transfer process was much faster than the mailing process and was initiated early enough to be complete before the check was cashed. Also observe that the actual sequence of events paid my creditors more speedily than if I had delayed the mailing until after the transfer.

Effects of the form **soon sust**¬P are only *possibly* in conflict with a sustained precondition P: whether a conflict exists depends upon timing information not currently encoded by the modal formalism. Until the necessary timing information is available, our planner will treat merely *possible* conflicts as conflicts. This was also the spirit of TWEAK's modal truth criterion [11].

The second consequence of our use of the **sust** operator is that **soon sust** effects do not imply **sust** preconditions. There is no obvious solution to this particular problem: at present we have preconditions that are not directly achievable by any action's effects, but if action effects were strengthened to imply sustained preconditions, we

condition 1	condition 2	resolution
soon sust P	soon sust¬P	sust¬P <> sust P
soon sust P	next sust¬P	sust¬P < sust P
soon sust P	sust¬P	sust¬P < sust P
soon sust P	sust¬P ∧ next sust¬P	sust¬P < sust P
next sust P	soon sust¬P	sust P < sust¬P
next sust P	next sust¬P	*conflict*
next sust P	sust¬P	sust¬P < sust P
next sust P	sust¬P ∧ next sust¬P	*conflict*
sust P	soon sust¬P	sust P < sust¬P
sust P	next sust¬P	sust P < sust¬P
sust P	sust¬P	*conflict*
sust P	sust¬P ∧ next sust¬P	*conflict*
sust P ∧ next sust P	soon sust¬P	sust P < sust¬P
sust P ∧ next sust P	next sust¬P	*conflict*
sust P ∧ next sust P	sust¬P	*conflict*
sust P ∧ next sust P	sust¬P ∧ next sust¬P	*conflict*
soon sust P	soon cont¬P	sust P < cont¬P
soon sust P	next cont¬P	*conflict*
soon sust P	cont¬P	*conflict*
next sust P	soon cont¬P	sust P < cont¬P
next sust P	next cont¬P	*conflict*
next sust P	cont¬P	*conflict*
sust P	soon cont¬P	sust P < cont¬P
sust P	next cont¬P	sust P < cont¬P
sust P	cont¬P	*conflict*
sust P ∧ next sust P	soon cont¬P	sust P < cont¬P
sust P ∧ next sust P	next cont¬P	*conflict*
sust P ∧ next sust P	cont¬P	*conflict*
soon cont P	soon cont¬P	*conflict*
soon cont P	next cont¬P	*conflict*
soon cont P	cont¬P	*conflict*
next cont P	soon cont¬P	*conflict*
next cont P	next cont¬P	*conflict*
next cont P	cont¬P	*conflict*
cont P	soon cont¬P	*conflict*
cont P	next cont¬P	*conflict*
cont P	cont¬P	*conflict*

Fig. 4. Analysis of potential conflicts.

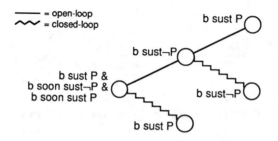

Fig. 5. Some interactions are not inconsistent.

would get side-effect conflicts even if the effects were actually temporary and non-overlapping.

Thirdly, the appropriateness of using **sust** in preconditions is debatable. The intent on the knowledge engineer's part is that **b sust** P appearing as a precondition should cause P to be not only sustainable but actually sustained. Our C plan and our U.P. interpreter act accordingly, by achieving and maintaining **b next sust** P, and performing the action that required **b sust** P only when **b sust** P is also true, so that the plan actually achieves and maintains

b sust P ∧ **b next sust** P

—which is the moment-by-moment way of keeping P true we discussed in Section 3.3. However, making preconditions reflect this strengthened condition of being actually sustained only increases the logical gap between effects and preconditions. Since for all other purposes it is good enough to represent preconditions as requiring mere sustainability, we have chosen to define only one modal operator **sust**, meaning sustainable, and our C code and U.P. interpreter simply do the right thing when actual sustainment is meant.

Lest the reader think these problems arise from a poor choice of formalism, we point out that there is no other formalism for representing processes over time which distinguishes open-loop futures, invokes intermittent action for maintaining desired conditions, and solves all the above problems.

4. The U.P. implementation in C

We now present both the operational and structural details of our U.P. for EVAR control. We begin by describing our implementation of indexical–functional reference, which determined what state estimate information was relevant at any time. Using that data, the U.P. determined which goals and reactions were appropriate from moment to moment. In particular we describe how the U.P. monitored the dynamics of EVAR's physical subsystems. Then we note that, since state estimates degrade over time, state estimate data are also a dynamic subsystem, and our U.P. treated them as such. Finally we present the C macros used to construct the U.P., and we exhibit a part of the plan.

4.1. Indexical–functional reference

Indexical–functional reference was introduced by Agre and Chapman [1,2] and was adapted by Schoppers and Shu [58] for use in logic-based systems such as U.P.s, as follows. Instead of building plans to manipulate representations of objects, we build plans to contain any number of indexical–functional variables which become associated with particular physical objects at plan execution time. In the EVAR U.P. implementation, each such variable is in fact a pointer to a data record/struct that contains information about where to find a physical object relative to EVAR. This information includes vectors for relative location, velocity, and acceleration estimates in EVAR's body-centered coordinate system; an object type; and a numeric tag for communication with the NASA-supplied world state estimation module. At plan execution start-up the tags are null and the location vectors are zeroed. The plan can request from the NASA world state estimation module a list of tags for known physical objects, and can then request more information about the object identified by each tag. When data is obtained for an object identified as an astronaut, the plan can store the astronaut's data into the appropriate variable's data record. By regularly using the NASA-provided object tag to request updates from the NASA world state estimation module, the plan can ensure that it keeps track of where the object is. New data arriving from the NASA state estimation module simply replaces the old data in the existing record (this is handled by an interrupt service routine).

The data record associated with a given variable is available to all predicates and actions which occur in the plan and take that variable as an argument.

This mechanism qualifies as indexical–functional reference because each variable appearing in the plan is associated with a time- and body-relative (indexical) pointer into physical space. At any given moment a variable picks out, via its data record, one object being interacted with, and over time a variable can pick out any sequence of objects that satisfy the tests on the variable's referent, such that the variable's referent is always "(the data about) the astronaut I am fetching" (functional), no matter how many other astronauts there are, nor how many are fetched over time. The U.P. does not remember anything about objects that aren't relevant to its current activities.

Unfortunately, the NASA state estimation module remembers all the objects ever seen, identifies each object with a numeric tag, and forces our U.P. to use those tags when requesting tracking updates. This means both that our plan's efficiency-conscious focus on particular physical objects is ignored by NASA's software, and also that the plan's indexical–functional variables range over NASA-provided object tracks rather than over physical objects (the U.P.'s operation is indexical and functional nevertheless). The resulting indirection is transparent to most of the U.P. code; it matters only to the primitive actions that must use the object tags to request track updates from the NASA software.

The collection of data records associated with the plan's indexical–functional variables, plus another record for robot-internal state, together comprise the "local real-valued state estimate" described in Section 3.3.

4.2. Monitoring dynamics

The information stored in the data records associated with the plan's variables is examined by C functions which evaluate such conditions as

```
b soon sust b standing_off(X).
```

Although the C code does not reason symbolically, it nevertheless depends crucially on our modal logic formalizations, as evidenced by such function names as

```
b_soon_sust_b_standing_off(X).
```

The soon P operator described in Section 3.3 evaluates whether P will become true by virtue of some open-loop dynamic. For example, if a door was standing open and there was a goal to have it be shut, b soon b door-shut would be false, inducing the U.P. to take an action like kicking the door. Thereafter, as long as the door continued to look like it would eventually be shut, b soon b door-shut would be true and no further action would be necessary.

To elaborate on the door example, swing-doors can behave in nontrivial ways, such as:
(a) slowly closing but never quite shutting;
(b) closing completely, flying past the shut position, swinging to and fro a few times, and finally stopping still slightly open; or
(c) swinging to and fro a few times before finally closing.

These cases would be discriminated as follows. The b soon b door-shut test will come out true at the beginning of all three cases, since the door looks like it will eventually be shut, even if only momentarily. From there the test would (case (a)) remain true until some time before the door stops moving, (case (b)) remain true until some time after the last door-closing, and (case (c)) remain true until, and as long as, the door remains closed. The exact moment at which the test becomes false in cases (a) and (b) depends on the precision of the model being used to predict the door's open-loop motion.

In the EVAR domain, our U.P. cares not just about the momentary truth of things, but about their ongoing truth. For such cases we defined the sust P ("sustainable") operator. How sust b door-shut is interpreted depends on the application. Suppose θ is the variable to be controlled, namely the angle between the door and its shut position, and so define b door-shut $\equiv (\theta = 0)$. If a U.P. is not allowed to cause a robot to intercept a moving door, then we must define

$$b \text{ sust } b \text{ door-shut} \equiv (\theta = 0 \wedge \dot{\theta} = 0),$$

i.e. the door must be both closed and at rest before the U.P. can conclude that the door can be kept shut. If however the robot is allowed to intercept moving doors, we can define

$$b \text{ sust } b \text{ door-shut} \equiv (\theta = 0),$$

for then the robot can stop the door at the exact moment when it is shut. In the EVAR domain, the kinetic energies involved were too large to allow interceptions, so sustainability generally required $\dot{\theta} \approx 0$, and here we proceed with that interpretation. Then it follows that b soon sust b door-shut is true just in case the U.P. observes that the door's state $\langle \theta, \dot{\theta}, \ddot{\theta} \rangle$ is consistent with the eventual truth of $(\theta = 0. \wedge \dot{\theta} = 0)$. To implement such a test we would model open-loop door motion with a second-order differential equation, solve the equation to obtain a closed-form expression for the door's trajectory, plug in the desired end state, solve for a criterion on the antecedent motion, and encode the resulting criterion as a C function. It was never necessary to make the U.P. explicitly model possible futures.

Reconsidering cases (a)–(c) above, we see that unlike the b soon b door-shut test, the b soon sust b door-shut test may come out false at the beginning of cases (a) and (b), because the door motion model may be precise enough to detect, even before the door has swung through the shut position once, that the door will finally remain slightly open. In case (c) the b soon sust b door-shut test will still be true from beginning to end, but now it is true at the beginning because the door will eventually remain shut, not because the door is about to swing through the shut position.

Our U.P. for controlling EVAR took action to achieve all goals b sust Q for which b soon sust Q was false. To push the swing-door example to its breaking point: b soon sust b door-shut being false would induce the U.P. to somehow apply a *small acceleration* $\ddot{\theta}$ to the door, thus modifying the door's motion just enough to make the door, several swings later, come to a halt ($\dot{\theta} = 0$) at the precise moment when the door was also closed ($\theta = 0$). After observing the door's new motion, the U.P. would find b soon sust b door-shut to be true and would, long before the door stopped swinging, deem further action against the door unnecessary.

4.3. State estimates as dynamic subsystems

The distinction between open-loop and closed-loop dynamics bears directly on the issue of how often to sense something. An agent's beliefs about current environmental state can be viewed as a dynamical system whose open-loop dynamics have to do with a decay of accuracy and/or certainty over time. If an agent's beliefs about environmental state are subject to decay, and if those same beliefs must be maintained for plan execution purposes, then the plan is faced with a situation that is exactly analogous to an opening door that should be forced shut. Then, one appropriate response is to resort to a closed-loop dynamic, e.g. by occasionally updating the decaying information.

In congruence with the encoding of effector goals, the U.P. encoded knowledge goals—conditions of the form b sust kw P—with correspondingly named C functions, i.e. b_sust_kw_P(), and monitored their dynamics with the expected supporting C functions, b_soon_sust_kw_P() and b_next_sust_kw_P(). However, since achieving a knowledge goal consisted only of sending an update request to the NASA state estimation module and receiving a reply containing the requested data, there was nothing to watch to evaluate satisfactory progress. In such cases the b_soon_sust_kw_P() function was purely a function of time, evaluating to true for 1 or 2 seconds after transmission of the update request, and remaining true only if the requested data was received.

Some time after reception of the requested data, b_soon_sust_kw_P() would become false again to force another update. The period over which knowledge could be sustained depended on the nature of the knowledge. Knowledge of the position of other objects lasted a few seconds; knowledge of the positions of the robot's effectors lasted until those effectors were moved.

4.4. A referential subtlety

All object positions were calculated in a body-centered coordinate system that translated and rotated with EVAR. This was done so that EVAR would not be dependent on an external coordinate system obtainable only via a breakable radio link. It was also convenient for controlling EVAR's effectors. However, it also generated some surprises.

The C function b_laserable(azim,elev) could compare the given azimuth and elevation with the current pan and tilt of the laser scanner, and so could determine whether the given direction was currently visible. Since the given direction was body-relative, this function was unaffected by any rotation of EVAR's body. The function b_sust_b_laserable(azim,elev), on the other hand, tested the sustained visibility of the "absolute" direction that was aligned with the given relative direction at the moment the function was called. If EVAR was rotating, that "absolute" direction might not remain visible for long. To be consistent we then mentally redefined b_laserable(azim,elev) to test the momentary visibility of the "absolute" direction picked out by the given relative direction. This produced a paradox: if EVAR was rotating, repeated calls to b_laserable(0,0) could return **true** forever, while yet b_sust_b_laserable(0,0) correctly returned **false**. The paradox is resolved by noting that each successive call to b_laserable(0,0) would be referring to a different "absolute" direction.

4.5. Operationalizing goal achievement

The EVAR U.P. was constructed by means of a small number of macros. These macros were defined specifically to ensure that our hand-coding of goal achievement and monitoring would comply with our modal logic formalization. This section provides a complete list of the macros used by the EVAR U.P.

We distinguish macros according to the type of precondition they achieve and monitor. Preconditions can be either *momentary* or *sustained*, with the obvious meaning; and they can be *knowledge* preconditions, *effector* preconditions, or *combined* preconditions. Knowledge preconditions achieve **kw** P and change the U.P.'s knowledge, effector preconditions achieve **b** P and change the external world, combined preconditions achieve **k** P and change both.

In these macros, the pseudo-action NO-OP does exactly nothing, while the pseudo-action busy=1 sets a flag to indicate that the plan has not yet achieved the desired preconditions/subgoals. When set, this flag can be used to inhibit the achievement of later preconditions, and will certainly inhibit execution of the action having the unsatisfied preconditions. Actions are finally executed when *none* of the macros around their preconditions set the busy flag.

(1) Instead of directly achieving a *momentary knowledge* precondition **kw** P of action A, the plan actually achieves **b soon kw** P, thus inherently exploiting any relevant open-loop dynamics. Nevertheless, the action A of which **kw** P is a precondition can only be performed when the original precondition **kw** P is true-at-the-time. The appropriate macro is:

```
kw P ?
T: NO-OP
F: b soon kw P ?
    T: busy=1  % wait for kw P
    F: busy=1, ACHIEVE b soon kw P
```

(2) The macro for achieving a *momentary effector* precondition **b** P is similar to macro #1, but with **kw** P replaced by **b** P throughout.

(3) To achieve a *momentary combined* precondition **k** P of action A, the plan utilized the equivalence

$$\mathbf{k}\ P \equiv \mathbf{kw}\ P \wedge \mathbf{b}\ P$$

which makes clear that achievement of knowledge of P may require several inter-dependent actions, namely
- perceiving whether P is perhaps already true before anything has been done,
- acting to make P true, and
- perceiving whether P has successfully been made true.

Exploiting any relevant open-loop dynamics, the complete macro became a straightforward nesting of macros #1 and #2:

```
kw P ?
T: { b P ?            % b P subtree
     T: NO-OP         % = k P
     F: b soon b P ?
         T: busy=1  % wait for b P
         F: busy=1, ACHIEVE b soon b P
   }
F: b soon kw P ?
    T: busy=1         % wait for kw P
    F: busy=1, ACHIEVE b soon kw P
```

This nesting allows for action to achieve P only when P is known to need achieving (**kw** P $\wedge$ ¬**b** P $\equiv$ **k**¬P).

(4) Instead of directly achieving a *sustained knowledge* precondition **b sust kw** P of action A, the plan actually achieves **b soon sust kw** P, thus inherently exploiting any relevant open-loop dynamics. Nevertheless, the action A of which **b sust kw** P is a precondition can only be performed when the original precondition **b sust kw** P is true-at-the-time (assuming disturbance-free controllability). Furthermore, in order to perform the action A that requires the truth of **b sust kw** P and simultaneously act to sustain **kw** P, the plan may have to do several things in parallel. Consequently, we defined the following macro:

```
{ b sust kw P ?
  T: b next sust kw P ?
     T: NO-OP
     F: ACHIEVE b soon sust kw P
  F: { busy=1 % delay A until b sust kw P
       ||
          b soon sust kw P ?
          T: NO-OP
          F: ACHIEVE b soon sust kw P
}     }
```

The "||" denotes parallel performance of busy=1 with the lower decision fragment. Since the busy flag is not set when **b sust kw** P is true, the action requiring **b sust kw** P and the action sustaining it can be running simultaneously.

(5) The macro for achieving a *sustained effector* precondition **b sust b** P is similar to macro #4, but with **kw** P replaced by **b** P throughout.

(6) To achieve a *sustained combined* precondition **b sust k** P of action A, the plan again utilized the equivalence

$$\mathbf{k}\ P \equiv \mathbf{kw}\ P \wedge \mathbf{b}\ P.$$

The complete macro became a straightforward composition of macros #4 and #5:

```
b sust kw P ?
T: { b next sust kw P ?
     T: NO-OP
     F: ACHIEVE b soon sust kw P
   ||
     { b sust b P ?
       T: b next sust b P ?
          T: NO-OP
          F: ACHIEVE b soon sust b P
       F: { busy=1
            % wait for b sust b P
            ||
            b soon sust b P ?
            T: NO-OP
            F: ACHIEVE b soon sust b P
   } }     }
F: { busy=1
     % wait for b sust kw P
     ||
     b soon sust kw P ?
     T: NO-OP
     F: ACHIEVE b soon sust kw P
   }
```

This macro has twice the parallelism of macro #4. In particular, when

b sust kw P $\wedge$ $\neg$**b soon sust kw** P $\wedge$
b sust b P $\wedge$ $\neg$**b soon sust b** P

this macro allows the plan to do all of the following in parallel:
- checking beliefs about sensory information about P (**b sust kw** P),
- acting to sense the current truth value of P (achieving **b soon sust kw** P),
- checking beliefs about P itself (**b sust b** P),
- acting to sustain the truth of P (achieving **b soon sust b** P),
- performing the action having **b sust** P as precondition,

and furthermore, these things may be happening simultaneously for all the other preconditions conjoined with P, and for all the supergoals of P, and even for preconditions in unrelated parts of the plan. While this much parallelism is not necessary, it is efficient and is permitted in the absence of destructive interactions between activities.

(7) There are also a couple of macros for testing what we have called the qualifiers of actions—the preconditions that act as applicability filters but whose falsehood should not cause attempts to make them true. The macro for testing a *momentary* qualifier **k** P is:

```
kw P ?
T: b P ?
    T: NO-OP      % = k P
    F: REJECT     % don't allow A
F: b soon kw P ?
    T: busy=1     % wait for kw P
    F: busy=1, ACHIEVE b soon kw P
```

This can be seen to be similar to the macro for achieving momentary knowledge, except that achieving **b soon** P has been replaced by a rejection of the action A whose qualifier is being evaluated. In the C version of the U.P. there was only one way to achieve each goal, and REJECT could be implemented as busy=1. In the more general U.P. interpreter, a rejection of one candidate action results in backtracking to find another.

(8) The macros for testing other qualifiers are similarly related to their counterparts for achieving preconditions, namely, actions to achieve physical effects are replaced by REJECT. We are still debating whether this approach is correct. Qualifiers may currently initiate sensing actions whose preconditions may in turn initiate physical motions to enable the sensing. Stricter interpretations of qualifiers might prohibit all physical actions, or might prohibit all action. We have not yet encountered a situation that clearly forces one of the stricter interpretations, in part because there were few qualifiers in the EVAR domain.

For pedagogical purposes it is convenient to derive the macros for combined preconditions (#3 and #6) from those for knowledge and effector preconditions (#1, #2, #4, #5) as above. By virtue of some theorems of the modal logics of knowledge and belief, the reverse derivations are also possible. If we set P $\equiv$ **kw** Q and use the reductions

kw P ≡ **kw kw** Q ≡ **true**

and

b P ≡ **b kw** Q ≡ **kw** Q

in macro #3, we recover macro #1; using them in macro #6 we recover macro #4. Similarly, if we set P ≡ **b** Q and use the reductions

kw P ≡ **kw b** Q ≡ **true**

and

b P ≡ **b b** Q ≡ **b** Q

in macro #3, we recover macro #2; using them in macro #6 we recover macro #5. Thus, of macros #1–#6, only macros #3 and #6 are strictly necessary.

4.6. Example of a subplan

Here we present a piece of the final C-language U.P. for EVAR control. The complete U.P. differs in being larger; in having less transparent names for some of its subplans; in the fact that the `marker-bound` subplan was not primitive; and in including functions for testing goal-related modal conditions as described in Section 4.2. The SUST_K_MACRO refers to macro #6 exhibited above.

The code in Fig. 6 implements a subplan for grappling with an astronaut. The topmost goal of the subplan is to become coupled to the astronaut. This goal is invoked by an endless loop (line 3). On each iteration, the U.P. tests a number of conditions, determines what response is appropriate (if any), and exits. For example, if the top-level call to SUST_K_MACRO(coupled(X)) finds that **b sust b** coupled(X) and **b next sust b** coupled(X) are true, then the function `ach_next_sust_b_coupled(X)` is not even entered. On the next iteration, of course, the astronaut may have escaped, and then `ach_next_sust_b_coupled(X)` *would* be entered.

The `ach_next_sust_b_coupled(X)` function (line 4) is an encoding of a conditional effect: if the world is set up so that the robot's clamp is in the right place relative to the astronaut, then closing the clamp will catch the astronaut. "Setting up the world" in this case means—in any order, or in parallel—bringing the clamp near the astronaut, facing the astronaut, and having the clamp open. The call to SUST_K_MACRO(clamp_near(X)) on line 7 may invoke none, one, or both of the functions `ach_soon_sust_kw_clamp_near(X)` and `ach_soon_sust_b_clamp_near(X)`, depending on how the various tests come out in the course of executing SUST_K_MACRO(clamp_near(X)); and similarly for the calls on lines 8 and 9. If any of the six conditions **b sust b** clamp_near(X), **b sust kw** clamp_near(X), **b sust b** approx_facing(X), **b sust kw** approx_facing(X), **b sust b** clamp_open, or **b sust kw** clamp_open evaluates to **false** the SUST_K_MACRO will set busy=1 and the SERIALIZE macro at line 10 will cause an exit. Only when all six preconditions have been achieved will the SERIALIZE macro allow performance of a clamp closing action. In sum, when `ach_next_sust_b_coupled(X)` exits it may or may not have invoked any of

```
1   #define SUBGOALS      int busy = 0
2   #define SERIALIZE     if (busy) return

3   while (1) SUST_K_MACRO(coupled(X));

4   ach_next_sust_b_coupled(marker X)
5   { SUBGOALS;
6     /* only clamp_near(X) is shown */
7     SUST_K_MACRO(clamp_near(X));
8     SUST_K_MACRO(approx_facing(X));
9     SUST_K_MACRO(clamp_open);
10    SERIALIZE;
11    close_clamp;
12  }

13  ach_soon_sust_kw_clamp_near(marker X)
14  { SUBGOALS;
15    SUST_K_MACRO(robot_status);
16    SUST_K_MACRO(percepts_of(X));
17    /* deduction: if we know arm pos and
18    /* and pos, kw_clamp_near follows, so
19    /* there's nothing else to achieve */
20  }

21  ach_soon_sust_b_clamp_near(marker X)
22  { SUBGOALS;
23    /* these two subplans not shown */
24    SUST_K_MACRO(facing(X));
25    SUST_K_MACRO(standing-off(X));
26    SERIALIZE;
27    translate2_to_contact(X);
28  }

29  ach_soon_sust_kw_percepts_of(marker X)
30  { /* either there are fresh percepts, or
31    /* not, so kw_percepts must be true, &
32    /* this subplan will never be used. */
33  }

34  ach_soon_sust_b_percepts_of(marker X)
35  { SUBGOALS;
36    SUST_K_MACRO(in_laser_fov(X));
37    /* deduction: if X is in FOV there are
38    /* fresh percepts, so there's nothing
39    /* else to achieve              */
40  }
```

Fig. 6. Simplified version of part of current grappling plan.

```
41   ach_soon_sust_kw_estimate_of(marker X)
42   { /* either there's an estimate, or not,
43     /* so kw_estimate_of must be true, so
44     /* this subplan will never be used. */
45   }

46   ach_soon_sust_b_estimate_of(marker X)
47   { SUBGOALS;
48     SUST_K_MACRO(marker_bound(X));
49     SERIALIZE;
50     /* we have a tag for the object, so.. */
51     get_info_on(X);
52   }

53   ach_soon_sust_kw_in_laser_fov(marker X)
54   { SUBGOALS;
55     SUST_K_MACRO(robot_status);
56     SUST_K_MACRO(estimate_of(X));
57     /* deduction: if there's a new estimate
58     /* we can tell if the laser is looking
59     /* there; if there's an old one we know
60     /* X is not in view; so after the two
61     /* subgoals there's nothing to achieve */
62   }

63   ach_soon_sust_b_in_laser_fov(marker X)
64   { SUBGOALS;
65     SUST_B_MACRO(laserable(azim(X),elev(X)));
66     SERIALIZE;
67     start_tracking(X);
68   }

69   ach_soon_sust_kw_laserable(float Azim,Elev)
70   { SUBGOALS;
71     SUST_K_MACRO(robot_status);
72     /* deduction: since <Azim,Elev> is a
73     /* direction relative to the robot
74     /* right now, the robot's current mo-
75     /* tion determines whether the laser
76     /* can keep that dir'n in sight.  */
77   }
```

Fig. 6. Simplified version of part of current grappling plan (*continued*).

```
78   ach_soon_sust_b_laserable(float Azim,Elev)
79   { SUBGOALS;
80     SUST_K_MACRO(robot_status);
81     SERIALIZE;
82     rotate1_toward(Azim,Elev);
83   }

84   ach_soon_sust_kw_marker_bound(marker X)
85   { /* kw_marker_bound(X) tests whether X
86     /* is now associated with a tag. it is
87     /* or it isn't, so kw_marker_bound(X)
88     /* is true and this subplan will never
89     /* be used.                          */
90   }

91   ach_soon_sust_b_marker_bound(marker X)
92   { SUBGOALS;
93     SUST_K_MACRO(robot_status);
94     SERIALIZE;
95     rotate3_to_bind(X);
96   }
```

Fig. 6. Simplified version of part of current grappling plan (*continued*).

the six relevant subplans, and may or may not have performed a clamp closing action. If any of the six relevant subplans *were* invoked, then they, in turn, might or might not have invoked other subplans to achieve *their* preconditions. All the same options arise again in the next iteration of the U.P.

In the U.P. fragment shown here, all preconditions happen to be achievable in parallel. The SERIALIZE macro may also appear between preconditions, in which case false preconditions preceding it can prevent even the testing of preconditions appearing after it.

5. Capabilities of the formalism

5.1. Active vision

The **kw** modal operator allows us to give effector actions preconditions that require sensing, and also allows us to represent sensing actions, which can then be given effector preconditions. Thus we have enabled arbitrary inter-dependence of sensing and acting. A prime example from the EVAR U.P. is (refer to Fig. 6):

- Grabbing an astronaut (acting, line 11), requires (line 7):
- Knowing how far away she is (deduction, line 17), which requires (line 16):
- Knowing where she is (deduction, line 37), which requires (line 36):

- Knowing whether the laser range finder is seeing her (deduction, line 57), which requires (line 56):
- Having a location estimate (sensing, line 51), which requires (line 48):
- Having seen the astronaut in the first place, if necessary performing a physical search by tumbling the whole robot body (action, line 95), which requires (line 93):
- Proprioception (sensing, not shown).

Our plan enables *eye-to-hand* coordination in the sense that the perceived positions of particular objects are continuously used to control body motion. Among other examples, our U.P. supports and uses visual tracking, which is built into the NASA-provided software as a closed loop from laser scanner input to laser gimbal control. Our U.P. initiates and monitors the execution of the relevant software.

Our U.P. also enables *hand-to-eye* coordination in the sense that the body can be controlled to make desired percepts available. Our existing U.P. does not provide for active perception in the sense of acting to simplify the perception process itself, unless the required motion can be induced via a precondition on a sensing action.

Active perception researchers' interest in attentional mechanisms is addressed by Section 5.2.

5.2. Task-directed attention

It is sometimes thought that "classical" planners require "complete" information about the initial state; that execution monitoring of action-ordered plans is similarly afflicted; and that U.P.s have the same problem. The first assertion is correct, the last two are mistaken.

For action-ordering planners the entire initial state must be known (as represented), to allow the planner to simulate the effects of *arbitrary* action sequences on that state. For plan *execution*, even of action-ordered plans, it is necessary to know only the bare minimum that will allow performance of the next action, namely the truth of that action's preconditions. That much is usually a very small subset of a "complete" world state. Some plan execution systems additionally want to know, before performing some actions, that those actions are still needed, so may examine a small number of extra conditions, as in triangle tables [21].

U.P. execution similarly involves checking the preconditions of the actions being performed next (in parallel), plus some verification that all those actions are still needed. This too is usually a small subset of a world state. U.P.s differ most significantly from earlier technology in two respects: all the potentially relevant sensing actions are automatically incorporated as an integral part of the plan, and U.P.s can be synthesized automatically without requiring the planner to assume any initial state at all [53].

The fact that sensing actions are incorporated only when they are demanded by knowledge preconditions means that the set of conditions being sensed changes as the current activity changes. Hence U.P.s embody a dynamic perceptual focus. This focus has been present since the earliest exposition of U.P.s [52], awaiting only the formalization of sensing actions [56] to enact it. An analysis of the sensory bandwidth of U.P. execution was given in [54], along with implications for the engineering of reactive and/or intelligent software.

5.3. Efficient perceptual experiments

When the EVAR state estimation subsystem projects the motion of a previously seen object forward to the present under orbital dynamics, the resulting prediction of object location is considered a belief by our U.P., and the U.P. is defined so that a believed position is sufficient basis for pointing the laser scanner at that position (rotating the robot's body as necessary). If the object is seen near where it was expected, its location then becomes "known". If it is not seen its location becomes unknown, the previous location-belief is cancelled, and the U.P. reacts to the absence of that belief by resorting to a visual search. (This search is from the robot's current location, we did not implement search procedures involving locomotion other than body rotation.)

The predicted location serves as heuristic guidance toward efficient behavior. If the prediction is accurate enough a relatively time-consuming visual search can be avoided, and otherwise the predicted location would be scanned anyway.

The plan's behavior amounts to a perceptual experiment to determine the veracity of the predicted location. From the plan representation viewpoint this particular experiment is very much like the perceptual verification of the expected effects of attempted actions.

5.4. Monitoring helpful dynamics

Predicates of the form **b soon** P (where P was usually **sust b** Q) were implemented as C functions that applied tests to the current estimate of the world state and its time-derivatives. It bears emphasizing that the truth of these conditions was monitored, not assumed, see Section 4.2. Since the **b soon** P tests usually came out true far in advance of P itself being true, the U.P. spent much of its time just watching, see Section 6.3.

5.5. Forestalling unhelpful dynamics

Progress monitoring continued after desired conditions had been achieved, when it verified continued success. Action could be initiated when the desired condition itself was true but was about to become false, e.g. when the astronaut being rescued was about to drift out of the laser scanner's field of view.

A special example of preventive action forestalled loss of access to a current world state estimate. State estimates ("knowledge") were considered valid for a limited amount of time. When that time was about to expire, the action to forestall the imminent loss of knowledge consisted of sending off a request for an update.

In all cases of preventive action, the setback was considered imminent if current inaction would not leave enough time for successful preventive action, although the setback itself might be quite some time away. This test of imminence was encapsulated in the C functions implementing the **next** P predicates.

Certain cases of preventive action were not solved in the most general way due to subsystem interactions, see Section 7.3.

5.6. Parallel activities

The large amount of potential parallelism in U.P.s was used to good effect. For example, before actually grappling an astronaut the robot was required to "stand off" the astronaut at a short distance and for some time. This served both as extra precaution against collisions, and as time available for obtaining a good estimate of the astronaut's rotational motion. During stand-off the robot was required to be directly facing the astronaut and to have its arms out in case the astronaut could take the initiative. Hence, along the way to achieving a stand-off, the plan simultaneously
- accelerated into the astronaut's orbit,
- rotated the robot body to face the astronaut,
- tracked the astronaut with the laser scanner,
- opened the grappling clamp, and
- refreshed its state estimate information.

In principle it would be possible for the goals of rotating the body and tracking the astronaut to conflict, since the laser scanner platform had a limited kinematic range and its use could require body rotations. This was dealt with by implementing all the astronaut-related body rotations so that they tumbled the robot about the same axes, differing only in the angle to be rotated. In this way, rotating to precisely face the astronaut prior to grappling would also satisfy the goal of rotating to approximately face the astronaut during approach, as well as the goal of rotating to track the astronaut with the laser scanner. The more "relaxed" orientation goals would be achieved first, leaving the more precise goals to demand additional rotation. (The body rotation for searching visible space was an exception.)

6. Underlying principles

As documented in the previous sections, our distinctions between estimated/believed and perceived/known information, together with the ability to hold beliefs about expected behavior under open- and closed-loop dynamics, allowed the construction of a U.P. in which sensing, estimating, acting and timing supported each other in sophisticated ways.

This section presents some lessons we learned and were able to test. Section 7 discusses issues we encountered and did not resolve satisfactorily.

6.1. The controlled system: robot hardware, software, and beliefs

In considerations of dynamics it is important to be clear about the location of the boundary between the controlling and controlled systems. We began our work under the influence of "embodied agent" discussions, assuming that the controlling system was the robot and the controlled system was the space environment. We ended—after having completed the U.P.—with the realization that we had built something else: as far as the U.P. was concerned, the robot body and its servo loops were just another part of the world.

The most surprising aspect of this realization was that the information being managed by the plan, namely the plan's local copy of the robot's world state estimate, was also part of the controlled system, and had an open-loop dynamic causing it to diffuse over time. The appropriate response was of course to replace that unwanted dynamic with a closed-loop dynamic, by intermittently requesting updates from NASA's world state estimation module. The plan was doing the right thing before we properly understood what it was doing.

From our point of view "the controller" ultimately consisted only of our U.P., a few implementation-specific flags, and some bits to encode past activity (e.g. the phase of the visual search, how long ago certain activities were initiated, whether certain processes had been monitored continuously since initiation, and in some cases the last command sent to a robot subsystem). The controller contained no bits for encoding the current state of anything outside the U.P.; all such information was part of the controlled system.

6.2. Synchronous belief checking, asynchronous subsystems

As noted in Section 6.1 the controlling system consists of little more than the executing U.P., while the controlled system consists of the robot hardware, its servo loops, aspects of the space environment, and even the plan's beliefs about present and future world state. It follows that our architecture does not fit very well into either of the well-known architectural categories for intelligent embedded agents—the synchronous sense–plan–act architecture [39] and the asynchronous-monitoring-and-acting architecture [35].

If we consider the controller to consist of the U.P. only, then it is best described as a sense–act cycle wherein sensing means examining state estimates, and acting means instantaneously re-parameterizing subsystems. If we consider *all* software as part of the controller, then the architecture is closest to those recently proposed by [7,25], wherein a reactor contains servo loops, subsumption-style behaviors, and small U.P.s; a sequencer coordinates and configures potentially concurrent reactions; and a deliberator selects tasks and constructs plans. A similar architecture was developed on information-theoretic grounds in [51,61], comprised of execution, coordination, and management/organization levels. Our U.P. for EVAR control belongs at the middle level. (Consequently U.P.s have now been successfully demonstrated in two of the three layers.)

Our architecture can also be compared to the NASREM architecture [3] as follows: in both, higher levels synchronously coordinate asynchronous subsystems, and subsystem capabilities are fixed at design time; but our architecture currently contains only two levels, and communicates subsystem parameters as well as subsystem goals.

6.3. Relying on dynamics without ignoring disturbances

A reasonably useful vision of our U.P. is to see it as a bedouin in an undulating desert criss-crossed with trails, being pulled along by a loosely coordinated camel train. The bedouin can see a short distance ahead, knows when there are choices to be made, can use the locally visible landscape to navigate, and from long experience knows which

choices lead to the next oasis. Occasionally, some camel will either try to wander off
on its own or try to lie down, and hence will need to be curbed, but most of the time
there is nothing for the bedouin to do besides glance around intermittently while the
temporal landscape glides by, effortlessly and inevitably.

Each camel in the train represents a subsystem operating under its own dynamics.
The U.P.'s job is to bend the pre-existing subsystem dynamics to a specific coordinated
purpose. To successfully manipulate a dynamic (viewed as a function from initial to
successor states) the U.P. must know the corresponding "inverse dynamic", namely, what
initial states/conditions induce the dynamic to produce the final conditions desired by the
U.P. A subsystem need not be aware that it is being manipulated: the mere existence of
an "invertible" dynamic is sufficient to allow effective manipulation. Manipulable initial
conditions include subsystem parameters such as target positions, maximum velocities,
and amounts of available resources, as well as external circumstances like getting the
robot's clamp near an astronaut body part before the clamp-closing dynamic is enabled.

Observe that the plan's actions are instantaneous, generally serving only to change
parameters of subsystem dynamics, while the subsystem controllers and the processes
they affect carry the plan along its chosen trails. From the plan's point of view, the
subsystems are largely open-loop: give them suitable initial conditions and they'll do
the desired thing by themselves in good time. (Leave some cheese in a mouse trap, and
the mouse will trap itself.)

All this can be done, and the end goal reached, purely reactively, i.e. the plan can
react to its current temporal vicinity and its knowledge of what comes next, without ever
explicitly visualizing (symbolically constructing) any part of the desired path. (Many
people born in Pittsburgh can drive infallibly all over town using landmarks, but can
neither reliably describe their routes nor reliably relate them to a street map.)

The key ingredients in the U.P.'s ability to exploit dynamics are predicates of the form
b next sust P and **b soon sust** P. By virtue of their veto power on corrective action,
these tests had better be right about the subsystems' expected behavior, for the price of
being too confident is that an effector will arrive in the wrong place or at the wrong
speed. In the worst case, when **b soon sust** P remains true and **b sust** P remains false,
the plan can be misled to wait forever.

Disturbances can be small, just large enough to move an effector off its ideal trajectory,
as when a thruster hiccups, or they can be so large that the plan needs to initiate an
entirely new set of activities, as when a previously caught astronaut escapes. U.P.s
recover easily from large disturbances, which were a driving factor in the invention of
U.P.s. A sufficiently large change of context will cause the plan's predicates to evaluate
the current state differently, and so will lead to very different choices of action. Small
disturbances, however, under poorly designed **b soon sust** P predicates, could induce
the endless waiting just mentioned. Hence these predicates are also key ingredients in
the ability to compensate for small disturbances.

Beyond the obvious solution of implementing the **b soon sust** P predicates to carefully
monitor and cautiously project the robot's motions (see Section 4.2), a very reliable
solution would be to build time limits into all **b soon sust** P predicates, causing them to
become false eventually whether or not the controlled subsystem was thought to be still
"on track" at the time. This would force the plan to re-initiate all overdue processes by

giving them new target positions. (We did not need to try this, choosing instead to get our **b soon sust** P predicates right.)

6.4. On impossible events, inertia, and reactivity

In control systems, a special class of disturbance is the injection of sensor noise and/or error in state estimation. In real-valued control systems, such disturbances are handled by means of frequent updating and action reselection. We have come to the same approach, which might be paraphrased paradoxically as: if your perception is unreliable, rely on it often. There is also more to be said about the roles of inertia and reactivity.

If the state of the world reported by a perception subsystem is not guaranteed to be an accurate portrayal of reality, then it follows that the perception subsystem may also report state sequences (i.e. events) that could not occur in reality. Our favorite example of this was an observed astronaut who was seen to turn into a space station window. Another example is of objects transferring from one orbit into a non-intersecting one with apparently massive expenditures of energy, although the objects were unpowered— this phenomenon occurred when a Kalman filter found objects on the edge of their positional uncertainty envelope.

An agent's "inertia" against believing perceived impossible events can be beneficial, or not, if the state estimate prior to the impossible event was (respectively) correct, or not. Observe that in the case of the astronaut turning into a window, believing the perceived impossible event was beneficial (the initial state estimate was incorrect). We came to the conclusion that it was better for the state estimator to accept what it thought it was seeing, thus to be right on average, than to stand on principle ("astronauts can't turn into windows") and thus risk being very wrong indefinitely.

If there is any way to judge the value of accepting an impossible event, such a judgment must be based on other information already available in the state estimation module (e.g. belief strengths before and after the event) and the state estimation module is the right module to make the judgment. Therefore, a reasonable way to design reactive agents is have the state estimation module determine the appropriate amount of "inertia", and allow the action selection module to react quickly to whatever interpretation the state estimation module selects, even if that means reacting to an impossible sequence of states. This is the approach taken by Universal Plans.

It follows that any agent designer who makes assumptions about what events will be perceived, and who makes a control system design or implementation dependent on such assumptions, may be responsible for a disaster. Unfortunately, being endowed with excellent perception systems, people very easily fall into this trap. Worse, people are not very good at imagining impossible events, nor are they naturally inclined toward the labor of constructing exhaustive lists of perceptually unlikely events.

In view of these understandable shortcomings of human designers, it is important to provide robotic controllers with automated support for dealing with the supposedly impossible. Under the U.P. approach the solution is to design the controller in such a way that assumptions of impossibility have nowhere to hide: by virtue of their reliance on dynamic classification of perceived world states, U.P.s begin with no restrictions on possible courses of events and demand effort to impose restrictions. This contrasts with many previous approaches to discrete-event control systems design, wherein state sequences or procedures are primitive, so that enlarging the set of possible futures adds to the workload, e.g. [18, 22, 24, 26, 34, 44].

6.5. The Rapid Feedback Principle

If sensors are noisy and foolable, and if algorithms for interpreting sensor data can be wrong even about perfect data, how can an embedded agent "know" anything through perception? A novel answer is proposed by Rosenschein [48], who considers belief states (or bit states) of an agent to be encoding knowledge of a fact if-and-only-if, whenever the agent is in the relevant states, the encoded fact is really true (this finds "knowledge" not within the agent but in a correlation between agent states and environment states). To engineer a "knowing" agent under this view, noisy sensors must be compensated for by very cautious sensor interpretation. The embedded agent is then likely to err by refusing to believe things that *are* true. In the astronaut rescue domain, where windows or other objects may be mistaken for astronauts, these considerations reveal a cruel dilemma: should perception be so cautious in its professions of knowledge that the robot could stare at an astronaut with disbelieving eyes even as she died for lack of oxygen, or should perception be less skeptical and perhaps cause the robot to chase a perceived astronaut while the real astronaut died somewhere else?

The notion of "knowledge" embedded in our actual work is: model-based predictions, perceptually corroborated. This notion applies very nicely to observations of object positions, which can be predicted under orbital motion; to effector motions, which are voluntary; and even to object recognition, which utilizes previous observations as predictions for later ones. Even so, EVAR's so-called "knowledge" may intermittently be wrong.

One of the surprises emerging from our work is that for EVAR, misinterpretation of sensor data seems not to matter very much. EVAR's state estimation software invariably corrects itself, and in the vast majority of cases perceptual mistakes last for only a fraction of a second. The U.P. representation recovers so rapidly, even from the apparent perception of physically impossible events, that momentary misperceptions have no humanly noticeable effect on the robot's behavior. Consequently, here too it was better to be right on average, and to act on possibly mistaken beliefs, than to wait for certainty.

Nevertheless, there clearly are situations in which a perceptual mistake could become extremely serious. What makes mistakes serious, and what makes domains unforgiving?

An obvious difficulty is the impossibility of recovering, or more generally, the cost of recovering, given that sometimes the cost is infinite. Since the control system is by hypothesis unable to know exactly what the world's state is, a state estimate is a probability distribution over possible states; then a small probability times an infinite cost is still a disaster. However, having the robot do nothing for fear of pursuing the wrong thing also leads to disaster, and even the time required to get a better state estimate may mean disaster. When all the available courses of action may lead to infinitely bad consequences, utility theory breaks down, but the robot can still act to minimize the probability of failure.

Considerations like these lead to the following insight, which we call the "Rapid Feedback Principle":

> *a domain containing infinitely bad disasters can yet be forgiving if the domain provides processes that generate disaster-related (or goal-related) feedback at the cost of only a small fraction of disaster avoidance (or goal achievement) resources.*

Such a domain gives a robot multiple opportunities to avoid disaster, and rewards attempts with helpful information. Moreover, this combination allows application of the Marginal Utility heuristic [16, pp. 137,148]: it is optimal to perform the action that delivers the highest goal-achieving likelihood per unit cost of goal-achieving resources. If it is not known which action is most likely to successfully avoid disaster, then the action of choice is the one that delivers the most valuable information as cheaply as possible. It is still possible that disasters will happen anyway, but only if the robot had little chance from the outset.

Fortuitously, the design of EVAR's hardware and software satisfies the Rapid Feedback Principle for the astronaut retrieval task. Long-range target recognition is early feedback, and motions can consume arbitrarily small amounts of rescue time and fuel. From there, the Marginal Utility heuristic says that EVAR should investigate the nearest and most astronaut-like objects first.

Notice that the rapid feedback principle is satisfied by vertebrates for the task of survival (by virtue of long-range sensors and high maneuverability); that humans achieve both survival and efficient behavior by modifying their physical environment to make the principle true (e.g. with early feedback consisting of signs, obstacles, or error messages); that robots of anthropomorphic design, and robots in human habitats, may well satisfy the principle accidentally, for many physical tasks; and that in general, a robot may be engineered to satisfy the principle for specific tasks through suitable choices of sensors and effectors.

6.6. Redefining the qualification problem

We now turn to consider some aspects of our modal logic formalization. In particular, our practice of describing actions as having effects in all post-action open-loop futures requires explanation, since the range of open-loop futures might include meteorites, earthquakes, and volcanic eruptions.

In early work, the practice of proving plans correct was insufficiently distinguished from the practice of proving disembodied programs correct, and the descriptions of actions were taken literally (promised effects were guaranteed to result from action performance, preconditions were supposed to be necessary and sufficient for action success, and plans could be proved to work). These assumptions lead to one form of the qualification problem in which preconditions should be not only necessary [4] for

---

[4] Necessary = the action will work *only if* P, so that preconditions may be missing, the set of satisfying situations may be a superset of the set in which the action works, and the action may be tried when in fact it could not work.

action success but also sufficient.[5] For example, the frequent observation that starting my car works *whenever* there is no potato in the tailpipe, and the battery is not flat, and... is motivated by the desire that preconditions should be sufficient to guarantee successful performance, hence necessary and sufficient.

Instead of this philosophy we came to the position that

> *preconditions should be necessary and sufficient to guarantee achievement of the postconditions under an assumption of disturbance-free controllable behavior, and sufficient to enable likely achievement of the postconditions across the range of situations that satisfy the preconditions.*

We now discuss this idea in some detail, starting at its end.

By saying that preconditions should be sufficient to enable likely success we are allowing both that the preconditions may not be "necessary", and that they may not be sufficient to guarantee every-time success. If an action's preconditions are "not necessary"[6] the action may occasionally not be tried when it could work, but that does not matter if there are alternative actions; and if there was some circumstance in which it did matter, that circumstance could be detected automatically as a conditionally unachievable goal, e.g. during plan synthesis or domain model checking. (The U.P.'s synthesis algorithms perform precisely the required analysis [53].) If an action's preconditions are not sufficient to guarantee every-time success, we can compensate by trying the action again, or by trying a different action [22]. Thus, it turns out that for many problems—including starting a car—there is no need for a guarantee that any particular attempt will be successful. Indeed, many actions, despite their frequent reliability, are better seen as experiments. Perhaps the car will start this time, perhaps it won't; perhaps the car will start eventually, perhaps not. Humans, and our robot control plan similarly, make up for the lack of absolute guarantees by simply making an attempt and perceiving the results.

[Aside: If p_0 is the probability that a desired result holds before the first attempt to achieve it, and if an action attempt succeeds with probability $p > 0$, then the probability that at least n ($n \geqslant 1$) attempts will be required is $(1 - p_0)(1 - p)^{n-1}$, and the expected number of attempts to achieve success is $(1 - p_0)/p$.]

If actions have sufficient preconditions for likely success, it is possible that, in some strange circumstance, *all* the actions described as being likely to achieve a desired condition are in fact useless. Then there remains the option of trying alternative solutions to supergoals: after a few failed attempts to start one car, both we and a robotic system can start a different car, or catch a bus, or work at home, or take a vacation day. This line of argument finally breaks down only when every goal in the entire chain of supergoals of our present activity—including the goal that is the final purpose of the whole plan, e.g. having enough to eat—is not achievable in the present circumstance. If enough energy is spent on providing the robotic system with alternative courses of action, that

---

[5] Sufficient = the action will work *whenever* P, so that superfluous preconditions may be present, the set of satisfying situations may be a subset of the set in which the action works, and the action may be ruled out when in fact it would work.

[6] Not necessary = the set of satisfying situations does not contain all situations in which the action works.

possibility can be made arbitrarily remote, and having sufficient preconditions on likely action success is good enough.

Thus, in our opinion the primary reason to desire sufficient preconditions on *guaranteed* action success is not to ensure plan robustness, which can be achieved by other means, but to achieve ideally efficient robotic behavior (avoiding futile attempts)—which in fact is rather inefficient because it requires checking a much longer list of preconditions that are very likely to be already true (no potato in tailpipe just now). It is debatable whether a given amount of domain engineering effort is better spent on increasing the likelihood of multi-try goal achievement or the likelihood of first-try action success.

Next we come to the modal formalism's assumption of disturbance-free controllability. Bearing in mind that a disturbance is technically defined as something that affects the behavior of a closed-loop system from outside the control loop, it is easy to see that to a first approximation the qualification problem is about disturbances. Earthquakes, meteorites, potatoes in tailpipes and flat batteries are not "in the driving loop", and they are not phenomena one can prevent. One can deal with them in two ways, by compensating for their occurrence, or by changing both the definition of the controlled system and the design of the controller so that the disturbances become controllable. Often, the latter is not feasible.

Controllability is a technical term as well. A system is controllable if it is possible to drive the system to a particular desired state no matter what the system's initial state is. The synthesis of U.P.s amounts to a constructive controllability analysis, in this narrow sense of the word. A wider use of the term is to imply that all the important process variables can be changed conveniently and that appropriate feedback can be obtained. In either sense, the assumption of controllability rules out most system malfunctions and breaks in the control loop.

Our control plan occasionally issued commands that seemed to vanish into hyperspace, perhaps due to bugs in the communications software. Such breakages make a system temporarily open-loop and eventually uncontrollable. By allowing action descriptions to assume the absence of such events we licensed stronger postconditions and weaker sufficient preconditions than would otherwise be valid. Thus, we represented most of our plan's actions as being guaranteed to work in all possible (disturbance-free controllable) futures, despite the fact that the system was intermittently uncontrollable.

It might be felt that our use of control-theoretic terms has merely legitimized ignoring the qualification problem, but in fact there are qualification problems that are not attributable to either disturbances or uncontrollability. The examples of blocks attached to each other with bars, and of pulley systems that cause blocks to move when the robot reaches for them, do not qualify as disturbances because their effects are due to the robot's own actions—they are in-the-loop. In the control systems community such effects are called "unmodelled dynamics". As that name implies, they arise from an incorrect or incomplete model of the system to be controlled. It is precisely this aspect of the qualification problem that has yielded to work on automated explication of previously implicit model structure, e.g. [30].

It follows that our definitions have split the qualification problem in a useful way.

Using the notions of disturbances and (lack of) controllability we have drawn a boundary around one set of things that cause problems. Our boundary is defined by the design of a complete closed-loop system, which inherently determines both what is controllable and what is a disturbance. It accepts as fact that some things are inherently uncontrollable. The qualification problem, however, is generally thought of as a problem of inadequate domain modelling, but defining it that way makes automated discovery the only solution and further makes the problem unsolvable. The qualification problem could usefully be redefined to include only unmodelled dynamics, leaving disturbances as a separate problem to be tackled with robust compensation at plan execution time.

The acknowledged invalidity of the assumptions underlying our modal formalization—adopted only for action representation purposes—results in an inability to give hard guarantees that an action will definitely have a represented effect, but that's why preconditions should also be sufficient to enable likely action success in general. The upshot is that when our action descriptions posit, using **next** and **soon** modalities, an outcome in "all possible" (post-action) open-loop futures as opposed to "some possible" open-loop futures, the assertion being made is that the action can confidently be expected—without absolute guarantees—to work after a single attempt. Two examples from opposite sides of this distinction are the action of moving the robot's arm to a desired position, which can be expected to work (under suitable assumptions), and the action of looking in a random place for a lost object, which cannot. This distinction was to be used by our plan execution machinery to limit the system's patience: actions that were expected to work were to be tried only a few times, actions that were not expected to work could be tried more often and as less desirable options; but we have not implemented this yet.

Said differently, our action descriptions (operator types) encoded the *heuristic* knowledge that, if any of an action's purported effects were desired, then (under suitable preconditions) the action was *a good one to try*. Rephrasing the position stated at the beginning of this section, we conjecture that preconditions should describe, not the conditions on action success, but the conditions under which an action can be attempted and frequently succeed. Having a tailpipe free of obstruction is not a precondition on *attempting* to start a car. (However, if the car subsequently fails to start, a blocked tailpipe may become relevant as an explanation.)

For similar reasons, planning does not prove that a plan will work. Planning is no more (and no less!) than the automatic synthesis of a proof to the effect that, given a goal and an assumption of controllability in the broad sense, the modelled system is in fact controllable in the narrow sense, and as a bonus the planner constructs an appropriate trajectory or control law (a plan). Action-ordering planners yield only the part of the control law that is required for a narrow range of expected trajectories through the state space. A U.P. is a complete control law.

6.7. Acting on beliefs

The title of this section is deliberately ambiguous, referring to three related facts:
(1) Our controller operates continuously on large amounts of faith in Newtonian dynamics, as mentioned in Section 6.3;

(2) The plan's beliefs about current world state are themselves a dynamical subsystem with degerative open-loop behavior, and that dynamic must be replaced with a closed-loop dynamic, as described in Section 5.5;

(3) There are three mechanisms by which beliefs might become false:

    (a) open-loop dynamics, which can be modelled and so allow the plan to predict when its current state-estimate beliefs will become false;

    (b) disturbances, which cannot all be predicted and so force the state estimation subsystem to weaken all its beliefs uniformly with the passage of time; and

    (c) newly initiated processes, which require the plan to act directly on the state estimation subsystem (even before the processes have any noticeable effects) so as to cancel that subsystem's faith that its predictions are still plausible. The exact cancellations required can be deduced from the descriptions of the actions taken.

As an example of point 3(c), performance of the clamp-opening action had to invalidate the belief that **b next/soon sust kw** clamp_closed. Since the clamp will not open by itself there is no reason, besides the effects of the plan's own actions, to request updates on the clamp's state. Making the plan invalidate the relevant state estimate caused the plan (in the next sense–act cycle) to immediately request a robot status update. In the absence of such an update the plan would have gone on "knowing" that the clamp was closed even after the plan had opened it.

Some of the effects of actions upon beliefs can be expressed and inferred under our modal logic formalization. The effect of clamp-opening is **b next b** clamp_open from which we can deduce **b next¬k** clamp_closed. Assuming that **k** clamp_closed was true before the action (so that there was indeed some "knowledge" to be undermined) we see that clamp-opening immediately undermines the knowledge we had. Moreover, we also have the domain axioms

    b clamp_open ⊃ **cont b** clamp_open

    b clamp_closed ⊃ **cont b** clamp_closed

—a pleasing variety of "frame" or "inertia" axioms not requiring mention of any actions—which allow us to deduce

    b next b clamp_open ⊃ **b next cont¬k** clamp_closed

    k clamp_closed ⊃ **b next cont¬k**¬clamp_closed.

Putting the consequents together we obtain **b next cont¬kw** clamp_closed, from which it follows that ¬**b soon sust kw** clamp_closed and ¬**b next sust kw** clamp_closed, thus demanding immediate sensing to *sustain* knowledge even though present knowledge may be valid.

If the effect of clamp_opening were **b soon b** clamp_open the deduction would not work. The domain axioms allow us to deduce

    b soon b clamp_open ⊃ **b soon cont¬k** clamp_closed

    k clamp_closed ⊃ **b soon cont¬k**¬clamp_closed.

Conjoining the consequents we get **b soon cont¬kw** clamp_closed, but from there to
¬b soon sust kw clamp_closed fails because **b soon cont¬kw** clamp_closed and **b soon
sust kw** clamp_closed are consistent: an eventual problem may allow prior corrective
action (cf. Section 3.5).

In sum, when an action has **next** effects, the representation of those effects can be used
to automatically disable the believed sustainability of the knowledge that the action's
effects are false, provided that suitable domain axioms are present.

6.8. Plan size

This section discusses the size of the complete U.P. for controlling EVAR. The C
code defined, and the U.P. made use of, 191 functions implementing true/false tests.
[29] proved that a domain of that size would on average require a Boolean circuit of
$2^{191}/(4 \times 191) \approx 10^{55}$ gates, and then interpreted that as a result about the expected
size of U.P.s. This result continues to be frequently cited as an argument against the
feasibility of U.P.s.

In our code, subplans were implemented as C functions which invoked other subplans
to achieve preconditions (if necessary), and which performed an action only if all
preconditions were true. Each subplan was defined only once in the C code, although
of course subplan functions could be invoked any number of times—just as a symbolic
goal reduction rule needs to be defined only once but can be used to achieve any number
of goal instances. Thus it was nontrivial to find out how big the U.P. would have been if
all invocations of subplan functions were replaced with textual subplan copies. This size
was determined as follows. We started with the primitive subplans (no preconditions),
assigning them a weight of 1, and then proceeded upwards from invoked subplan to
invoking subplan, adding the subplan weights. The number of leaf nodes produced by
the **sust k** P macro was calculated as

$$2 \times (\#sust\_kw\_P\_leaves + 1)$$
$$+ 2 \times (\#sust\_b\_P\_leaves + 1)$$
$$- 2.$$

In this way we found that a textually explicit plan would have had 291,028 leaf nodes
(condition–action rules). At its deepest the plan applied 26 Boolean tests to the world
state estimate.

This plan size measurement is nowhere near the predicted 10^{55} leaf nodes. The most
obvious reason for the difference is that our U.P. executes subplans in parallel, allowing
a "reaction" to be a combination of several actions taken independently by parallel
subplans—a possibility Ginsberg did not consider. How large would our plan have been
if all composite reactions had to be explicitly identified and selected? Equivalently, how
many types of world states does our plan actually distinguish and react to?

To calculate this size we again started with the primitive subplans, assigning them
a weight of 1 and proceeding upwards as before, but noting whether subplans were
invoked in parallel or in serial, and either multiplying or adding the subplan weights.
Plan size below each **sust k** P macro was calculated as

$$(\#sust\_kw\_P\_leaves + 1)$$
$$+ (\#sust\_kw\_P\_leaves + 1) \times$$
$$2 \times (\#sust\_b\_P\_leaves + 1)$$
$$- 2 \sum \#shared\_subplan\_leaves^2$$
$$+ 2 \sum \#shared\_subplan\_leaves.$$

This formula takes into account that two identical subplans being executed in parallel can be replaced with one such subplan. We also took into account that in U.P.s, a protected achieved goal can eliminate the need for whole subplans. Thus we found that, if made textually explicit without parallelism, our U.P. would have had 1.3×10^{10} leaf nodes (condition–action rules), associating each with an appropriate composite reaction.

We are still 45 orders of magnitude short of the predicted 10^{55} leaf nodes. To account for the difference we observe that Ginsberg's circuit size argument tacitly assumed that the Boolean inputs would be independent. If there are N independent Boolean inputs, there are $S = 2^N$ combinations of inputs and 2^S different Boolean functions, most of which need $S/(4 \log_2 S)$ gates to implement them. If the inputs are not independent, there will be $S' < S$ combinations of inputs and $2^{S'} \ll 2^S$ different Boolean functions requiring only $S'/(4 \log_2 S')$ gates. For example, if our 191 Boolean variables were constrained with 360 binary clauses, the number of possible value assignments on those variables would, on average, decrease to $S' = S \times (3/4)^{360} \approx S \times 10^{-45}$ (cf. [23]), and the expected size of a Boolean circuit on those variables would shrink by approximately the same factor.

In summary, in the astronaut retrieval domain defined by 191 true/false tests on world state, dependencies between tests (and perhaps some other unknown factors) reduce the expected size of our U.P. from 10^{55} to 1.3×10^{10} leaf nodes; parallel execution of subplans reduces that to 2.9×10^5 leaf nodes; and lastly, replacing a fully assembled decision tree with dynamically assemblable subtrees reduces the plan to 47 subtrees. (The complete C code for our U.P. consisted of 1,900 lines of code, not counting comments, instrumentation, and lines of 1 character or less.)

These dramatic plan size reductions are possible by virtue of specific features of the domain, namely:
(1) the utility of parallel execution of subplans indicates separately controllable sub-domains; and
(2) the effectiveness of factoring a U.P. into subplans indicates "domain symmetry", specifically the number of action types that share the same precondition type; and
(3) indexical–functional variables are useful in proportion to the number of domain objects that may assume a given role relative to the robot.

These points deserve some elaboration. First, in the EVAR domain there is lots of room for parallelism because goal achievement and goal monitoring *sustainment* never interfere.

Second, U.P.s are uniquely well suited to achieve the same precondition in different contexts. Since all subplans of a U.P. are themselves reactive and universal, Universal subplans are context-independent. Hence for each precondition or goal type, only one subplan needs to be defined, and that subplan can be reused without change to achieve that goal type in any context. This multi-context relevance is especially noticeable for subplans that control sensors, since such subplans are involved in the achievement of all knowledge goals, and knowledge goals number half of the goals occurring in the plan.

Third, our U.P. also exploits indexical–functional variables which are dynamically assigned to track physical objects. If only one astronaut is *the-astronaut-I'm-rescuing-now*, the existence of any number of other astronauts multiplies domain complexity without affecting plan size.

Thus our plan size experience bears out the arguments of [12] and [55].

Our U.P., in defining 1.3×10^{10} different classes of world states and specifying an appropriate reaction for each such class, may be the most discriminating Boolean classifier ever produced in software.

7. Loose ends

This section presents questions and problems we encountered but did not solve to our satisfaction.

7.1. Limits of U.P. capability

Now that we have augmented the original U.P. ability to compensate for disturbances with a new ability to exploit dynamics, what can the formalism not handle?

A general answer is that U.P.s are Turing-equivalent: U.P.s can include actions that directly modify beliefs, and other actions that react to those beliefs. It follows that there is little that U.P.s cannot compute. In particular, there is nothing to prevent a U.P. from including actions that keep count of their number of consecutive performances (both the C code and the U.P. interpreter provide an execution cycle counter), so that when a patience limit is reached, a different action may be used to achieve the same goal, cf. Section 6.6.

However, Turing-equivalent computing in isolation is a different problem than embedded control of dynamics, and the current U.P. synthesis algorithms leave some control problems unsolved. Observe that all the actions modelled in Section 3.5 require action on EVAR's part. Encoding *open-loop* dynamics at the symbolic level may also be useful. Some cases are trivial. For example, suppose that a robot wanted to close a door which happened to be spring-loaded, so that the only needed action was to release the door. This could be encoded with an "open-loop pseudo-action" such as:

```
open_loop --
  b soon sust b door_closed(X)
      <+ b cont b spring_loaded(X) ?
        b sust b unobstructed(X).
```

where the open_loop action is a no-op. (Our existing U.P. interpreter can store and manipulate any number of effects under the same action name.) For a more problematic example, suppose that a U.P. wanted a robot to pick up an object that happened to be covered with grease. Also suppose that the domain model had no concept of grease, but could encode that in some situations, successfully grasped and raised objects would invariably slip out of the robot's grasp under the influence of an open-loop dynamic (gravity). U.P. synthesis should then realize that it would be futile to perform any lifting that set up a situation enabling the grasp-defeating open-loop dynamic. The present U.P. synthesis machinery will not notice the futility of such actions because it ignores (open-loop) processes that are not accomplishing a task-related goal. We are currently working on a fusion of U.P.s with CIRCA [44], which considers both wanted and unwanted processes along with any timing constraints (see also Section 7.4).

7.2. Unterminated processes

Recall that our U.P. performs "actions" to initiate potentially lengthy processes in the robot or its environment. We found that some disturbances could shift the plan's focus of attention so radically that previously needed processes became irrelevant and were therefore ignored, while the process itself continued as previously requested and sometimes produced behavior that was strange but not wrong. As an example that did not actually occur but that makes the point very graphically, a disturbance occurring in the middle of a robotic arm motion, if it rendered the existing motion irrelevant without requiring the arm for a new purpose, could leave the arm in an out-stretched position while the robot went about its new business unawares.

This was one of the motivations for our explicitly marked "HACK" code. The problem could be fixed by inserting, at judicious points in the C code, a goal to terminate the stray process, e.g. by moving the arm to a more "natural" or "relaxed" position. However, such "stand-down" subgoals often could not be interpreted as preconditions on any action.

A solution to this problem must meet the constraint that in any control system, no subsystem may ever be left unsupervised. It is not a solution to design the coordination level so that all its "actions" on subsystems consist of small procedures. While this would ensure that subsystems eventually reached a stand-down posture, it would also interfere with proper reactive behavior and could still look silly, leaving a procedure to run to completion when the entire procedure was no longer relevant. A slightly better solution is to have "actions" consist of only two steps, one for the desired effect and one for a stand-down, with the stand-down to be performed only if the coordinator forgets to say otherwise. This approach would need to decide under what conditions the stand-down should be performed, i.e. at what point can a process consider itself to have become "stray". The same question arises if the stand-down behavior is built into a subsystem as a default or emergency response. The ideal solution would be for the coordination level to monitor its own focus of attention, issuing subsystem-specific stand-down commands as soon as a subsystem's services were no longer needed for any current goal.

7.3. Inadequate representation of quantitative information

Our current formalism has obvious limitations in that it does not support the explicit representation of quantitative information about either certainty or time. Thus it is not possible to automatically make use of two sensors simultaneously when that would deliver higher certainty than either sensor used alone. Similarly, there is a built-in assumption that perceived information is always more reliable than information obtained by model-based estimation. On the topic of quantitative time, it is not possible to symbolically represent the amount of time it usually takes to complete an action.

Fortunately, these limitations turned out to be nearly irrelevant to the EVAR domain. The inability to use two sensors never became an issue because no two sensors delivered readings of the same quantity; the assumption that perceived information is more reliable than projected information turned out to be true because projections were based on earlier readings whose certainty was no higher than that of new readings; and a lot of quantitative temporal information could be built into the C code that evaluated the plan's conditions. An example of the latter is that it was possible to evaluate the condition **b soon** P as true for 1 second after attempting to achieve P, and thereafter to evaluate it as true if observed movements were appropriate.

Indeed, the formalism exhibited only one serious problem deriving from the representational lack of quantitative timing. The plan sometimes wanted to carefully measure distance to the Space Station (to avoid a collision) while also watching the retrieved astronaut (to make sure we still had her), but could not watch them both at once. The resulting behavior was that the robot looked at the Space Station, got the knowledge it wanted, believed that knowledge to be good for some indefinite time and so turned to look at the astronaut, then lost confidence in the Space Station's position before the astronaut had actually been seen, and so looked back at the Space Station, losing track of the astronaut entirely. This problem was solved with a hand-coded hack because the formalism did not represent enough information to support automated detection of the problem. On the other hand it is also not clear that a more explicit formalism is the only answer: a dynamic resource scheduler/arbitrator such as that of [6] might do as well.

Another timing problem could have arisen when an object moved to exit the laser scanner's field of view at its bottom edge. Until the scanner's elevation (or tilt) became zero the object could be tracked by moving only the laser scanner. After that, keeping the object in view required rotation of the robot's entire body, and furthermore, the time at which this "downward" rotation should be initiated depended on the object's trajectory and on the robot's inertia (see Fig. 7). Our plan was able to rotate the body as necessary to catch up with the target object, but we did not try to get the timing right, largely because this problem either never arose or was accidentally solved, so we did not realize its possible existence until well after the project was over. This particular example might have been properly solvable with suitable re-working of the **b next sust b** laserable(X) condition, but we can imagine that some subsystem interactions might require even more foresight—what if something else had to be done before the body could be rotated—and at some point it becomes undesirable for the **b next sust b** laserable(X) predicate to have to consider the entire robot's kinematics and dynamics when deciding if it is time to begin rotating the body.

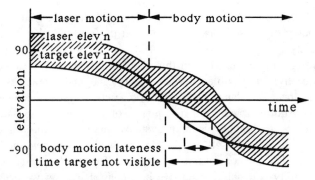

Fig. 7. Tracking can require well-timed body rotation.

7.4. Coincidental real-time performance

U.P. execution is currently only "coincidentally real-time": it can cycle at least an order of magnitude faster than the dynamics of the EVAR domain, but there are currently no hard real-time guarantees.

Nevertheless, it will be important in future work that the U.P. is not directly involved in controlling sensors or effectors, it only tells the robot's servo loops how the sensors and effectors should be controlled. The main reason for this division of labor is that the time constraints on servo loops are much more severe than those on changing loop parameters.

We are already working to provide hard real-time guarantees on U.P. execution. We expect to use an adaptation of the CIRCA approach [44].

8. Concluding remarks

We have presented extensions of the Univeral Plans representation that: provide for dependencies of sensing on action and vice versa; allow monitoring of the progress and outcomes of processes; enable exploitation and/or forestalling of the consequences of domain dynamics; and protect the original provisions for robust plan execution and automated plan synthesis. We have also discussed the control-theoretic underpinnings of U.P.s, including: the relation between the qualification problem and our assumptions about the nature of action primitives; our view that perception-based state estimates comprise a subsystem with a degenerative open-loop dynamic; the fact that actions must have effects on beliefs even before they have effects on the physical world; and the danger of ignoring any sequence of perceived states, no matter how unlikely. See especially Sections 6 and 7.

A complex and highly parallel U.P. for EVA Retriever control, built using the formalisms described herein, has been thoroughly tested by randomly chosen NASA officials against a NASA-built simulation of the EVA Retriever robot undergoing realistic dynamics and worst-case disturbance scenarios. The plan exploits known helpful dynamics for economy of effort; neutralizes known counter-productive dynamics (but see

Section 7.1); recovers robustly from disturbances, including intermittent bugs in the control system being supervised; also recovers robustly from mistaken perceptions; and runs very efficiently.

A summary insight to be gained from this paper is that there is no inherent conflict between highly reactive and flexible behavior on one hand, and guarantees about system behavior on the other. The "unpredictability" of reactive systems is worrisome only if "predictability" requires tracing out a sequence of (partial) world and/or machine states, as is done by traditional planning systems, finite state machines, instruction address registers, and so forth—all of which embody the computer science notion of predictability rather than the control theoretic notion. To see why the computer science notion of predictability is counter-productive in a controls setting we need only recall the limitations of feedforward controllers (cf. Section 3.2): they are brittle because they are at once unable to compensate for the inevitable disturbances, and extremely dependent on the correctness of their assumptions about the system being controlled. This weakness has long been known for continuous-variable control systems, and has now been reproduced in AI planning systems. In both cases the relevant fields have discovered and embraced feedback and after-the-fact compensation for disturbances. The U.P. representation takes the analogy between the fields a step further by taking dynamics seriously, and by enabling controllability analyses of control laws (a.k.a. plans) over entire state spaces rather than over a few trajectories (see Sections 2.1 and 2.2). There is yet more progress to be made in the direction of theoretical knowledge about what stability is and how to achieve it, how to trade off responsiveness against stability, and how to control with limited observability, see e.g. [10,36]. Inability to predict trajectories merely forces us into a more control-theoretic approach wherein feedback controllers are much more robust and no less amenable to guarantees.

The foundation of this paper is the nature of dynamics as patterns of events. Newtonian orbital dynamics represent an extreme of reliability but are by no means the only useful dynamics, nor is physical law the only useful kind of causality. Indeed, the ability of humans (and animals) to utilize dynamics far outstrips our ability to theorize about the dynamics being exploited, as the following examples show.

- Steam engines with flyball governors were in use long before there were theories for thermodynamics and control.
- Some people make provocative statements as a way of testing a hearer's beliefs, then assume that lack of argument implies agreement. Knowing about this dynamic is helpful both to avoid silly discussions and to prevent otherwise inexplicable rumors. Conversations are dominated by informal dynamics of this sort.
- The book *Games People Play* [5] is a long list of the vicious circles and self-destructive behaviors that routinely result from human emotional dynamics (for which there is no underlying theory). Many of the "games" can be terminated by refusing to behave habitually.
- Until human babies learn that parents continue to exist even when out of sight, a parent's departure is deeply frightening and causes the baby to scream, which in turn causes the parents to exist again.

These examples put inaccurate domain models into a broad perspective which makes approximations and heuristics the norm. As mentioned in Section 3.2, control systems engineers are inevitably stuck with a certain amount of abstraction and ignorance, such that even thoroughly flight-tested aircraft can crash due to previously undiscovered dynamics (air is not an ideal gas, aircraft surfaces may bend and even vibrate, etc). In particle physics—the technical field most renowned for penetrating many layers of abstraction—quark theory is now widely believed to be an approximation. In many areas of human activity, such as social interactions, there are currently no predictively useful theories at all. But dynamics do not need to be based on deep theories: conversational dynamics are important information nevertheless. Nor do dynamics models need to be precisely correct to be useful: misguided or not, a baby's screaming generally does bring the parents back.

The above examples also point to the implicit faith all people have in dynamics, since reliance on abstractions requires faith. Recall that even the Newtonian gravitation law is an abstraction: no-one knows what gravity is. Hence the orbital dynamics arising from Newton's theory can be exploited only with some measure of faith. From babies accepting the constant existence of their parents, to astronauts shooting for the moon, the human race is adrift on an ocean of faith, separated from brute reality through lack of time and the limitations of human intelligence. Philosophers know the magnitude of the faith, examine it even to questioning their own existence, and despair at the chasm between themselves and true knowledge. Seen in such philosophic light, all our knowledge becomes mere belief, and all our action becomes mere attempt (cf. Section 6.6). It becomes unsurprising that even our most sophisticated artifacts occasionally malfunction in unexpected ways. Nevertheless, on the whole, the human race has learned to manipulate many aspects of reality very effectively indeed. That this success finally rests on faith in dynamics is a clue to the importance of that faith.

Acknowledgements

Rebecca Schmitt provided large amounts of risk funding for the invention and prototyping of U.P.s, even before the author had obtained his Ph.D. degree. Additional concept development was financed by Advanced Decision Systems from IR&D funds. The work reported herein was funded by NASA contract NAS9-18162, under the far-sighted supervision of Jon Erickson. The C version of the plan was implemented during 1990-1991 while I was employed by Advanced Decision Systems. During that time Dan Shapiro and Dave Gaw contributed project management skills, helpful discussions, and code. (All three of us have subsequently taken other jobs.) The current paper, and rationalization of the formalism, were funded in part by NASA contract NAS9-18931, and in part by Robotics Research Harvesting.

The author's visit in February–May 1991 to the Department of Automatic Control, Lund Institute of Technology, Sweden, was both foundational to this paper and very enjoyable. My wife and I especially thank Karl-Erik Årzén and Karl-Johan Åström for making that trip possible, and Eva Schildt for streamlining it. Klas Nilsson, Kjell Gustafsson and Jan Eric Larsson answered many questions about basic control theory and also plied us with excellent company.

Dan Shapiro provided comments on a draft of this paper over some good cuppas (coffee) in the park opposite Peet's. Bruce D'Ambrosio's comments prodded me to clarify the rapid feedback principle. Phil Agre reminded me that I was an existentialist when Universal Plans were conceived, and seem to be one still.

The many constructive comments provided by the over-worked reviewers enabled large improvements in the presentation.

References

[1] P.E. Agre and D. Chapman, Pengi: an implementation of a theory of activity, in: *Proceedings AAAI-87*, Seattle, WA (AAAI/MIT Press, Cambridge, MA, 1987) 268–272.

[2] P.E. Agre, The dynamic structure of everyday life, Ph.D. Thesis, Tech. Report 1085, AI Lab, MIT, Cambridge, MA (1988).

[3] J. Albus, *Brains, Behavior and Robotics* (Byte Books, Chichester, England, 1981) Chapter 5.

[4] K. Åström and B. Wittenmark, *Computer Controlled Systems—Theory and Practice* (Prentice Hall, Englewood Cliffs, NJ, 2nd ed., 1990).

[5] E. Berne, *Games People Play* (Grove Press, New York, 1964).

[6] A. Bestavros, J. Clark and N. Ferrier, Management of sensori-motor activity in mobile robots, in: *Proceedings IEEE International Conference on Robotics and Automation* (1990) 592–597.

[7] R.P. Bonasso, Coordinating perception and action with an underwater robot in a shallow water environment, *Proceedings of the SPIE Conference on Sensor Fusion* IV, SPIE vol. **1611** (1991) 320–330.

[8] R.P. Bonasso and M. Slack, Ideas on a system design for end-user robots, *Proceedings of the SPIE Conference on Cooperative Intelligent Robotics in Space* III, SPIE vol. **1829** (1992) 352–358.

[9] R. Brooks, Symbolic error analysis and robot planning, AI Memo 685, MIT, Cambridge, MA (1982).

[10] C. Cassandras and P. Ramadge, eds., Toward a control theory for discrete event systems, *IEEE Control Syst. Mag.* **10** (4) (1990) 66–112.

[11] D. Chapman, Planning for conjunctive goals, *Artif. Intell.* **32** (1987) 333–377.

[12] D. Chapman, Penguins can make cake, *AI Mag.* **10** (4) (1989) 45–50.

[13] P.R. Cohen, M.L. Greenberg, D.M. Hart and A.E. Howe, Trial by fire: understanding the design requirements for agents in complex environments, *AI Mag.* **10** (3) (1989) 34–48.

[14] R. Doyle, D. Atkinson and R. Doshi, Generating perception requests and expectations to verify the execution of plans, in: *Proceedings AAAI-86*, Philadelphia, PA (AAAI/MIT Press, Cambridge, MA, 1986) 81–87.

[15] M. Drummond, Plan nets: a formal representation of action and belief for automatic planning systems, Ph.D. Thesis, Department of AI, University of Edinburgh, Scotland (1986).

[16] O. Etzione, Embedding decision-analytic control in a learning architecture, *Artif. Intell.* **49** (1991) 129–159.

[17] R. Fagin, J.Y. Halpern and M. Vardi, What can machines know? On the epistemic properties of machines, in: *Proceedings AAAI-86*, Philadelphia, PA (AAAI/MIT Press, Cambridge, MA, 1986) 428–434.

[18] L. Ferrarini, An incremental approach to logic controller design with Petri Nets, *IEEE Trans. Syst. Man Cybern.* **22** (3) (1992) 461–473.

[19] R.E. Fikes, Failure tests and goals in plans, AI Group Tech Note 53, SRI International, Menlo Park, CA (1971).

[20] R.E. Fikes and N.J. Nilsson, STRIPS: a new approach to the application of theorem proving to problem solving, *Artif. Intell.* **2** (1971) 189–208.

[21] R.E. Fikes, P.E. Hart and N.J. Nilsson, Learning and executing generalized robot plans, *Artif. Intell.* **3** (1972) 251–288.

[22] R.J. Firby, An investigation into reactive planning in complex domains, in: *Proceedings AAAI-87*, Seattle, WA (AAAI/MIT Press, Cambridge, MA, 1987) 202–207.

[23] J. Franco and M. Paull, Probabilistic analysis of the Davis-Putnam procedure for solving the satisfiability problem, *Discrete Appl. Math.* **5** (1983) 77–87.

[24] J. Freedman, Time, Petri Nets, and robotics, *IEEE Trans. Rob. Autom.* **7** (4) (1991) 417–433.

[25] E. Gat, Integrating planning and reacting in a heterogeneous asynchronous architecture for controlling real-world mobile robots, in: *Proceedings AAAI-92*, San Jose, CA (AAAI/MIT Press, Cambridge, MA, 1992) 810–815.

[26] M.P. Georgeff, A. Lansky and P. Bessiere, A procedural logic, in: *Proceedings IJCAI-85*, Los Angeles, CA (1985) 516–521.

[27] M.P. Georgeff, The representation of events in multiagent domains, in: *Proceedings AAAI-86*, Philadelphia, PA (AAAI/MIT Press, Cambridge, MA, 1986) 70–75.

[28] M. Gervasio, Learning general completable reactive plans, in: *Proceedings AAAI-90*, Boston, MA (AAAI/MIT Press, Cambridge, MA, 1990) 1016–1021.

[29] M.L. Ginsberg, Universal planning: an (almost) universally bad idea, *AI Mag.* **10** (4) 1989) 40–44.

[30] M.L. Ginsberg and D.E. Smith, Reasoning about action II: the qualification problem, *Artif. Intell.* **35** (1988) 311–342.

[31] A.R. Haas, A syntactic theory of belief and action, *Artif. Intell.* **28** (1986) 245–292.

[32] P. Haddawy and S. Hanks, Issues in decision-theoretic planning: symbolic goals and numeric utilities, in: *Proceedings DARPA Workshop on Innovative Approaches to Planning, Scheduling and Control*, San Diego, CA (1990) 48–58.

[33] J.Y. Halpern and Y. Moses, A guide to the modal logics of knowledge and belief, in: *Proceedings IJCAI-85*, Los Angeles, CA (1985) 480–486.

[34] D. Harel, Statecharts: a visual formalism for complex systems, *Sci. Comput. Program.* **8** (1987) 231–274.

[35] B. Hayes-Roth, Architectural foundations for real-time performance in intelligent agents, *J. Real-Time Syst.* **2** (1) (1990) 99–125.

[36] Y.-C. Ho, ed., Dynamics of discrete event systems, *Proc. IEEE* **77** (1) (1989) 3–208.

[37] J. Hughes and J. Cresswell, *An Introduction to Modal Logic* (Methuen, London, England, 1972, reprinted 1985).

[38] L.P. Kaelbling, Goals as parallel program specifications, in: *Proceedings AAAI-88*, St. Paul, MN (AAAI/MIT Press, Cambridge, MA, 1988) 60–65.

[39] L.P. Kaelbling and S.J. Rosenschein, Action and planning in embedded agents, in: P. Maes, ed., *Designing Autonomous Agents* (MIT Press, Cambridge, MA, 1990) 35–47.

[40] K. Konolige, A first-order formalization of knowledge and action for a multi-agent planning system, Tech Note 232, AI Center, SRI International, Menlo Park, CA (1980).

[41] D. McDermott, A temporal logic for reasoning about processes and plans, *Cogn. Sci.* **6** (1982) 101–155.

[42] R. Moore, *Reasoning about knowledge and action*, Tech Note 191, AI Center, SRI International, Menlo Park, CA (1980).

[43] L. Morgenstern, Foundations of a logic of knowledge, action and communication, Ph.D. Thesis, Department of Computer Science, New York University (1987).

[44] D. Musliner, E. Durfee and K. Shin, CIRCA: a cooperative intelligent realtime control architecture, *IEEE Trans. Syst. Man Cybern.* **23** (6) (1993) 1561–1574.

[45] K. Passino and P. Antsaklis, A system- and control-theoretic perspective on AI planning systems, *Appl. Artif. Intell.* **3** (1) (1989) 1–32.

[46] R. Pelavin and J. Allen, A formal logic of plans in temporally rich domains, in: *Proc. IEEE* **74** (10) (1976) 1364–1382.

[47] N. Rescher and A. Urquhart, *Temporal Logic* (Springer Verlag, New York, 1971).

[48] S.J. Rosenschein, Formal theories of knowledge in AI and robotics, *New Gen. Comput.* **3** (4) 1985) 345–357.

[49] W. Rugh, Analytical framework for gain scheduling, *IEEE Control Syst. Mag.* **11** (1) (1991) 79–84.

[50] E. Sandewall and R. Ronnquist, A representation of action structures, in: *Proceedings AAAI-86*, Philadelphia, PA (AAAI/MIT Press, Cambridge, MA, 1986) 89–97.

[51] G. Saridis, Knowledge implementation: structures of intelligent control systems, in: *Proceedings Second IEEE International Symposium on Intelligent Control* (1987) 9–17.

[52] M. Schoppers, Universal plans for reactive robots in unpredictable environments, in: *Proceedings IJCAI-87*, Milan, Italy (1987) 852–859.

[53] M. Schoppers, Representation and automatic synthesis of reaction plans, Report UIUCDCS-R-89-1546, Dept of Computer Science, University of Illinois at Urbana-Champaign (1989).

[54] M. Schoppers, Sensory bandwidth and the information content of goal structures, *Int. J. Expert Syst. Res. Appl.* **2** (3) (1989) 257–292.

[55] M. Schoppers, In defense of reaction plans as caches, *AI Mag.* **10** (4) (1989) 51–60.

[56] M. Schoppers, Automatic synthesis of perception driven discrete event control laws, in: *Proceedings Fifth IEEE International Symposium on Intelligent Control* (1990) 410–416.

[57] M. Schoppers, Building plans to monitor and exploit open- and closed-loop dynamics, in: *Proceedings First Conference on AI Planning Systems* (Morgan Kaufmann, San Mateo, CA, 1992) 204–213.

[58] M. Schoppers and R. Shu, An implementation of indexical-functional reference for the embedded execution of symbolic plans, in: *Proceedings DARPA Workshop on Innovative Approaches to Planning, Scheduling and Control*, San Diego, CA (1990) 490–496.

[59] J. Shamma and M. Athans, Gain scheduling: potential hazards and possible remedies, *IEEE Control Syst. Mag.* **12** (3) (1992) 101–107.

[60] A. Tate, Planning and condition monitoring in a FMS, Tech Report 2, AI Applications Institute, University of Edinburgh, Scotland (1984).

[61] K. Valavanis and G. Saridis, Probabilistic modelling of intelligent robotic systems, *IEEE Trans. Rob. Automation* **7** (1) (1987) 164–171.

[62] M.P. Wellman and J. Doyle, Preferential semantics for goals, in: *Proceedings AAAI-91*, Anaheim, CA (AAAI/MIT Press, Cambridge, MA, 1991) 698–703.

Artificial Intelligence 73 (1995) 231–252

On social laws for artificial agent societies: off-line design [*]

Yoav Shoham, Moshe Tennenholtz [*]

Robotics Laboratory, Department of Computer Science, Stanford University, Stanford, CA 94305, USA

Received January 1992; revised November 1993

Abstract

We are concerned with the utility of social laws in a computational environment, laws which guarantee the successful coexistence of multiple programs and programmers. In this paper we are interested in the off-line design of social laws, where we as designers must decide ahead of time on useful social laws. In the first part of this paper we suggest the use of social laws in the domain of mobile robots, and prove analytic results about the usefulness of this approach in that setting. In the second part of this paper we present a general model of social law in a computational system, and investigate some of its properties. This includes a definition of the basic computational problem involved with the design of multi-agent systems, and an investigation of the automatic synthesis of useful social laws in the framework of a model which refers explicitly to social laws.

1. Introduction

This paper is concerned with the utility of social laws in a computational environment, laws which guarantee the successful coexistence of multiple programs and programmers. We imagine an environment in which multiple planners/actors are active; we will call these "agents" here, without attaching precise technical meaning to the term (but see the formal development in the next sections). These agents' actions, and perhaps also goals, may be either facilitated or hindered by those of others. [1]

---

[*] This work was supported in part by a grant from the US-Israel Binational Science Foundation.

[*] Corresponding author. Current address: Industrial Engineering and Management, Technion – Israel Institute of Technology, Haifa 32000, Israel. E-mail: moshet@ie.technion.ac.il.

[1] As a special case, we are interested in extending the framework of Agent Oriented Programming (AOP) [15]. This framework, which attaches a precise meaning to the term "agent" (briefly, it defines agents to have mental state, consisting of components such as beliefs and commitments), currently accounts for the design of individual agents; we are interested in a theory for the design of successful societies of such agents. However, this paper will not be specific to the AOP framework.

To illustrate the issues that come up when designing a society, consider the domain of mobile robots. Although still relatively simple, state-of-the-art mobile robots are able to perform several sorts of tasks. They can move from place to place, identify and grasp simple objects, follow moving objects, and so on. Each of these tasks involves sophisticated techniques, but is, broadly speaking, achievable with existing planning and control technology. However, when we consider gathering several robots in a shared environment, a host of new problems arises. The activities of the robots might interfere with one another: The planned space–time paths of robots might intersect, an object needed by one robot might be removed by another, bottlenecks might occur, and so on. Similarly, robots may require the assistance of other robots to carry out their task: It may take two robots to lift a particular object, one robot may lack a capability possessed by another, and so on.

How is one to deal with these phenomena? There are two extreme answers, neither of which is in general acceptable. One is to assume a single programmer, whose job it is to program all the robots. As such, he will need to worry about all possible interactions among them, in exactly the same way as he worries about the interactions among the different actions of a single robot (this is the approach usually taken in robotics; see for example [1,5]). This answer is unsatisfactory for several reasons. First, it is unreasonable to expect that a single individual will control all agents. For example, in the Gofer project [2] the goal is to populate the planned Information Sciences building at Stanford with 100 or so mobile robots, each programmed individually by members of the department in much the same way as workstations are used. Second, the set of agents can be expected to change over time, and one would hardly want to have to reprogram all agents upon each addition or deletion of an agent. Finally, even if a single programmer was given the task of programming all the agents, we have given him no guidelines as to how to achieve the task. To the extent that he will proceed by programming each agent individually, he will be forced to deal with the interactions among the different programs.

An alternative extreme answer is to admit that agents will be programmed individually in an unconstrained fashion, to acknowledge that as a result interactions will occur, and to equip the agents with the means for handling these interactions during execution. These means may take various forms. For example, one approach is to merely detect the interactions as they occur, and appeal to a central supervisor for resolution. An alternative method for handling interactions is to equip the agents with communication capabilities, and program them to engage in series of communications to resolve interactions. Again, using the domain of mobile robots for illustration, when two robots note that they are on a collision course with one another, they may either appeal to some central traffic controller for coordination advice, or alternatively they might engage in a negotiation resulting (say) in each robot moving slightly to its right. The use of negotiation to resolve conflicts is common in the distributed AI literature (see for example [3,7,14]).

Nonetheless, there are limitations to this second approach as well. By placing no constraints in advance, the number of interactions may be prohibitive; either the central arbiter may be deluged by pleas, or else agents will have to enter into negotiations at every step. While we certainly do not argue against the utility of either a central coordinator or a negotiation mechanism, we do argue that it is essential to add a mechanism that will minimize the need for either. Again, we draw on the domain of mobile robots for intuition. Suppose robots navigate along marked paths, much like cars do along streets. Why not adopt a convention, or, as we'd like to think of it, a social law, according to which each robot keeps to the right of the path? If each robot obeys the convention, we will have avoided all head-on collisions without any need for either a central arbiter or negotiation.

This then is the image, which is not original to us; it is implicit in many places in AI, and was made explicit already by Moses and Tennenholtz [10, 11]. The society will adopt a set of laws; each programmer will obey these laws, and will be able to assume that all others will as well. These laws will on the one hand constrain the plans available to the programmer (in the above example, plans which call for driving on the left are ruled out), but on the other hand will guarantee certain behaviors on the part of other agents. The two approaches discussed above simply mark the endpoints of this tradeoff continuum. The first, "single programmer" approach stretches the notion of a social law so as to completely dictate the behavior of each agent, leaving no freedom to the individual programmer. The second approach adopts an opposite, degenerate form of social law, the vacuous law. The goal of the intended theory of social laws will be to relax the restriction to these extreme solutions, and instead to strike a good balance between allowing freedom to the individual programmers on the one hand and ensuring the cooperative behavior among them on the other.

How is one to decide on appropriate social laws? One approach is to hand-craft laws for each domain of application. This is the approach we take in the first part of this work, where we present a number of traffic laws for a restricted domain of mobile robots; in this part we show social laws which ensure that no collisions or deadlocks occur, and agents are still allowed enough freedom to plan close to optimal paths.

In the second part of the paper we tackle a different problem; we are interested in a general model of social law in a computational system, and in general properties that can be proved in that model. We argue that the notion of social law, or constraints, is not epiphenomenal, but rather should be built into the action representation; we then offer such a representation. Second, we define the basic computational problem involved in the design of multi-agent systems in the framework of this model. In addition, we investigate the complexity of *automatically* deriving useful social laws in this model, given descriptions of the agents' capabilities, and the goals they might encounter over time. We show that in general the problem is NP-complete, and identify precise conditions under which it becomes polynomial.

The remainder of the paper is structured as follows. Section 2 is devoted to the case study of mobile robots. Section 3 is devoted to the more general model and computational problem. In Section 2.1 we present the multi-robot grid system. In Section 2.2 we introduce two sets of traffic laws for that system. The first is trivial, restrictive, and produces inefficient behavior on the part of the robots. The second is more flexible, and allows very efficient behaviors while still avoiding collisions among the robots. Section 2.3 briefly discusses a number of extensions to the basic framework. In Section 3.1 we set up the formal (and, we believe, natural) model of multi-agent actions. In Section 3.2 we state the computational problem precisely, and show that in its full generality the problem is NP-complete. We also show a similar result for one natural restriction on the general model. In Section 3.3 we formulate additional natural restrictions on the general model; we show that these conditions are both necessary and sufficient for the problem to become polynomial. Finally, in Section 3.4 we look at a special case in which the (possibly many) states of agents happen to be encodable concisely, and show that there too the problem is polynomial. We conclude with a summary, discussion of related work, and planned future work. The proofs of the theorems concerning the traffic laws appearing in Section 2 follow from the details of these laws. Proof sketches of the theorems stated in Section 3 appear in an enclosed appendix.

2. A case study: mobile robots

Building efficient multi-robot systems is an attractive task for the relatively near future. Although it might be the case that building a sophisticated robot is a very complex task, gathering many simple state of the art robots in a shared environment can be attacked at this point and might be simpler than the task of building a single sophisticated robot. In this section we investigate the idea of social laws for artificial agent societies in the context of mobile robots. Our aim is to prove analytic results about the usefulness of our approach in that framework. The specific domain we look at is an idealized one. Hence, although the results presented in this section can be used for practical systems, the reader should treat them mainly as a nontrivial demonstration of the artificial social systems approach in a particular domain of application.

2.1. The multi-robot grid system

The domain we investigate will be called the *multi-robot grid system*. It consists of an $n \times n$ grid, and a set of m robots. It might be useful for the reader to keep in mind that the rows and columns of the grid can refer to lanes in a supermarket, or to paths in a warehouse, etc. When mobile robots have to move along these lanes and paths we get a multi-robot grid system structure. At each point in time each robot is located at some grid coordinate. The fact that several robots occupy the same coordinate denotes a collision among them; part of our goal as designers of the system will be to ensure that collisions are avoided. We assume that each robot has the capability at each stage to move to one of its neighbor coordinates or stay in place. Each such operation lasts a certain amount of time and consumes a certain amount of energy. We assume that the system is synchronous and that movement to a neighbor coordinate takes one time unit and consumes one energy unit, unless this motion follows a stop (that is, taken from a resting position). In the latter case we assume that movement to a neighbor coordinate takes c time units and consumes c energy units, where $c > 1$ (identical constants are used for time and energy only for ease of exposition). Remaining motionless wastes no energy, although of course it does waste time.

This is the bare-bones framework, on which we concentrate in this paper, but it can be extended in a number of ways. In order to reason about assembly tasks, we will extend the system to contain (in the spaces between coordinates) various items and substances that the robots might need for their tasks. Or, we may allow robots to travel at different velocities. Such extensions are discussed briefly in Section 2.3.

We have so far discussed *how* robots might travel, but not *why*. For the latter we assume that at random times robots are given target locations, and their goal is to reach those destinations, minimizing either time, or energy consumption, or both (they are not required to stay at the location for any period of time, just get there). In the simplest case, at any time each robot has at most one target destination; in the general case robots may accumulate several destinations. In addition, robots are required to avoid collisions.

The job of the programmer of an individual robot will be to implement an efficient path-planning program. In the absence of other robots, the task is conceptually simple: In the case in which at all times each robot has at most one destination it is trivial, and in the general case it is some variation on the familiar Traveling Salesman Problem. However, the existence of other robots may render useless an otherwise perfect plan. There has been some work in robotics on the coordinated operation (and, in particular, motion) of multiple robots (see for example [1,5]). However, much of this work has assumed a centralized controller which has full information about the system. As we have argued in the introduction, this assumption, while reasonable in some applications, is in general untenable, as would be a decentralized solution which relied only on on-line negotiations among robots. Although there exist local techniques for collision avoidance, such as artificial potential fields (see [6]), the reader should not confuse them with a global mechanism of coordination such as social laws.

Again, without detracting from the merit of the above mechanisms, we argue that it is necessary to design social (or, in this special case, traffic) laws to minimize the need for on-line conflict resolution. In fact, we will be interested in eliminating this need altogether. In other words, our job as designers of this small social system will be to impose on it traffic laws which will guarantee that no collisions will occur—provided that all programmers abide by the law. However, in our zeal to prevent collision we must be careful not to preclude the possibility of robots reaching their destinations (so, for example, forbidding all motion would be inappropriate). In fact, we will be interested in traffic laws that not only allow robots to reach their destinations without collision, but allow them to do so reasonably efficiently.

2.2. First two traffic systems

Any system of laws must assume certain capabilities on the part of agents. For example, a law against disposal of garbage in public places assumes the ability to identify garbage as well as public places. The situation regarding traffic laws is similar, and laws will differ depending on assumptions we can make about the robots. The assumptions that will be relevant here regard sensory capabilities: Can robots detect other robots? If so, at what distance? In this section we will consider two cases: In the first the robots lack all sensory capabilities, and in the second they can detect "close" robots.

From this point on we will assume that n is even. Rows and columns in the grid will be numbered from bottom to top, and from left to right, respectively. We assume that $m \leqslant n$, but that m is still large. In the rest of this paper with the exception of Section 2.3.4 we will assume that $m = O(\sqrt{n})$.[2]

We start by assuming that robots cannot sense each other's presence. The question is whether there exists a traffic law which will allow the robots to reach their destinations guaranteeing that no collisions occur. The answer is positive, although perhaps in a somewhat disappointing way. The first traffic law requires that all robots snake their way around the grid in a regular pattern, passing sequentially through all nodes. More explicitly, we have the following:

Traffic Law 1. Each robot is required to move constantly. The direction of motion is fixed as follows. On even rows each robot must move left, while in odd rows it must move right. It is required to move up when it is on the rightmost column. Finally, it is required to move down when it is on either the leftmost column of even rows or on the second rightmost column of odd rows. The movement is therefore in a "snake-like" structure, and defines an Hamiltonian cycle on the grid.

It is trivial to show that the following holds, even when robots are given new goals while still on the way to an existing one:

Theorem 2.1. *Traffic Law 1 guarantees that that no collisions will occur, and that each agent will reach each goal it is given in* $O(n^2)$ *steps from the time it is given that goal.*

Clearly, Traffic Law 1 is an example of the extreme case discussed in the introduction, in which the laws completely dictate the behavior of agents, leaving no room for individual planning. Intuitively, such rigid laws lead to suboptimal behavior, and indeed, while the Traffic Law 1 does guarantee a certain minimal performance, this performance is quite suboptimal: Robots might have to snake around the entire grid just to get to a nearby node. It is possible to do much better, but for that we must make further assumptions about the perceptual capabilities of the robots. In the following we assume that each robot in the multi-robot grid system is able to perceive robots that are at a distance of one coordinate away from it (including robots that are at a distance of one on both rows and columns).

One use of the perceptual capability could be to assign each robot a unique number, and rely on time-slicing to avoid collisions (each time slice would be devoted to one of the robots, which would be able to move to an unoccupied neighboring node). This class of solutions has a number of drawbacks. Chief among them are the facts that robots might be blocked and that in such solutions each robot ends up spending either $O(mn)$ or $O(mt)$ time units, where t is the complexity of the best solution in the absence of other robots (recall that m is the number of robots and $n \times n$ is the grid size); we would

---

[2] We recall the standard big-O and little-o notation. Given a pair of functions $f(n)$ and $g(n)$, $g(n) = O(f(n))$ means that $g(n)/f(n)$ converges to a constant when n converges to infinity. Similarly, $g(n) = o(f(n))$ means that $g(n)/f(n)$ converges to 0 when n converges to infinity.

like a solution that is truly linear in n or, yet better, in t. An additional drawback is that we envision an open system in which robots may be added and removed without having to reprogram the entire system.

We opt for a different use of the sensory capabilities. The capability to perceive the immediate environment is similar to our experience in everyday life, and our second traffic law too derives from that experience. The basic idea is to adopt familiar traffic laws such as giving way to a robot arriving from the right. However, naive laws of this kind quickly give rise to deadlocks and related problems, and so we will craft a somewhat more sophisticated law. The following law might seem strange at first. However, its importance follows from the results we are able to prove concerning it. In fact, all parts of this law excluding the sixth restriction of it are quite natural and can be related to our everyday experience. However, this sixth restriction is crucial for the particular results we got. Moreover, this restriction seems to be extremely useful when we consider modifications of the basic framework (see Section 2.3:4).

We now briefly discuss the idea of the following law, and then present its details. The basic idea is to superimpose on the original grid a coarser one. The key point is that when agents move on the coarse grid several simple traffic laws will prevent them from getting stuck, and will guarantee that each robot will have to wait only a small number of times for any other robot before entering an internal grid (leaving the coarse grid). In an internal grid we ensure that each robot is able to reach any possible coordinate of that grid. This requires a somewhat complex behavior presented by the sixth requirement of the following law.

Traffic Law 2.
  (1) Superimpose on the original grid a coarser one. The squares of the coarser grid will be subgrids of size $2m \times 2m$ of the original grid. A sketch of the "multi-grid" created appears in Fig. 1. [3]
  (2) In odd rows of the coarse grid robots will be required to move only right, while in even rows of it they will be required to move only left.
  (3) In odd columns of the coarse grid robots will be required to move only down while in even columns of it they will be required to move only up.
  (4) In junctions of the coarse grid, priority will be given on the basis of "first in first out". More specifically, when a robot is in a distance of 1 from entering one of the coarse grid's junctions, then it should not enter that junction if there is another robot which is in a distance of 1 from that coarse grid's junction and arrived there first. The default priority (in the case where robots arrive to the corresponding locations at the same time) will always be given to robots moving on columns.
  (5) While a robot is moving along the coarse grid, it is allowed to change its movement direction (from "along a row" to "along a column" and vice versa)

---

[3] Our results hold also for smaller coefficients of m, but although this would make our results even stronger, we will not discuss these cases here. Similarly, for ease of exposition we assume that the coarse grid "fits nicely" on top of the original fine grid. Our results don't depend on this assumption.

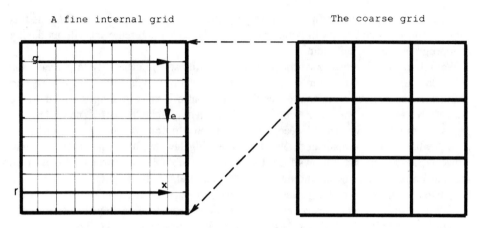

Fig. 1. A coarse grid imposed on the fine grid.

     only k times before leaving the coarse grid (and entering an internal grid), where k is a small constant.

(6) Inside each $2m \times 2m$ grid each robot will move in the following way (see Fig. 1): The entrance point to the grid will be from the leftmost coordinate of the row denoted by r (from the leftmost coordinate of that grid's "lowest internal row"). The robot will then be required to move along the row r to the coordinate denoted by x (the rightmost internal coordinate of row r). During the movement along r, if the robot perceives the existence of a robot in the coordinate in front it or finds that it reached x, then it has to stop and wait for $2n + cmk$ time units. Then, it has to continue (if still necessary) along r to x. After reaching that coordinate (x) and waiting there (if still necessary) for the above mentioned period, the robot has to reach the coordinate denoted by g (which is in distance $4m - 2$ from it) in exactly $4m - 2$ steps without entering any of the areas appearing in thick lines (both in the internal grid and on the coarse grid) in Fig. 1. Afterwards, the robot will be required to move from g to the coordinate denoted by e along the path appearing in thick lines in Fig. 1, and leave that grid from there.

(7) Robots are not allowed to stop moving unless the robot in front of them does not move or when they are required otherwise by the social law.

(8) The points of return from an $2m \times 2m$ grid to the coarse grid will be considered as additional junctions of the coarse grid (i.e. the traffic laws of the coarse grid will have to be obeyed there).

    The following two theorems show that Traffic Law 2 has attractive properties; they both assume that there are $m = O(\sqrt{n})$ robots in the $n \times n$ multi-robot grid system, and that the robots can perceive their neighbors (that is, those robots that are at distance of at most one coordinate away along rows and columns).

Theorem 2.2. *Traffic Law 2 guarantees that no collisions occur.*

Theorem 2.3. *Traffic Law 2 guarantees that, given a goal which can be achieved in isolation (that is, assuming no other robots are present) in t time and energy units,*[4] *there exists a plan that achieves it in $t + 2n + o(n)$ time units, and (for t satisfying $m = o(t)$), in $t + o(t)$ energy units.*

The proofs of these theorems follow from the details of Traffic Law 2. Here we only make the following remarks. The fact that we have a coarser grid enables the agents to not get stuck at junctions. By having complex movements only in the $2m \times 2m$ grids, the robots will move freely most of the time (while keeping distance from others). The law enables each robot to achieve its goal while waiting at most k times for each other robot. This is achieved by the traffic arrangements in the coarse grid, and by the fact that each robot waits for the other robots to reach their goals when it reaches an internal grid. The above need to wait for others might be sometimes relaxed, and then we are able to get even better results (see Section 2.3.1). The traffic law enables to reach an internal grid, in which the goal is, in a simple way. This is due to the rules of behavior regarding movement on the coarse grid. Inside an internal grid each coordinate is reachable (i.e., liveness is guaranteed). Whenever two different robots enter an internal grid and move towards the coordinate g, the one that enters the internal grid earlier is always closer to g than the other one (i.e., safety is guaranteed; it is easy to see that after a robot reaches g it cannot collide with others given the above traffic law).

Notice that although the robots are assumed to obey the traffic law, there is still much freedom (and local planning to be done) for the robots. In a typical problem an agent might need to visit several coordinates. Planning the shortest path will be part of the planning stage. This decision might depend on many possible criteria that are *not* known to the designer(s) and to other robots. However, when a robot decides that its next destination is a certain coordinate then it can reach it efficiently (in a reasonable amount of time and with close to optimal consumption of energy), *regardless of the goals and plans of other agents*—as long as all agents play by the rules of the social system.

Notice that the average time which is required for a robot working in isolation to reach a coordinate is linear in n. Therefore, we get a relatively good coordination. For a goal which can be achieved in isolation in n time units, our social laws will guarantee that we will lose only a factor of 3 (in many cases we can do even better and get close to optimal solutions; see Section 2.3.1). If we are interested in the units of energy that are spent, and we consider destinations that are reasonably far, then the existence of other agents causes us to lose almost no energy at all.

There are a number of ways in which to improve, refine and extend the system; some of these are explored in the next section. Notice for example that the above traffic laws might require a robot which is assigned no goal to move constantly. In order to treat this issue we will have to specify locations where robots can "rest". This can be easily handled if we assume that there is enough space for two robots in each coordinate of the grid. However, in this paper we concentrate mainly in extensions where the original format of the grid will be preserved.

---

[4] Notice that for a robot working in isolation, the optimal path will be without stops. As a result, the time consumption and the energy consumption of the robot moving along that path will be identical.

2.3. Various extensions

In this section we briefly discuss various extensions to the basic framework presented in the previous sections.

2.3.1. On a single robot ability and social law efficiency

Recall that c is the amount of time and energy spent on the first movement after a stop. Recall also the qualitative difference between the energy and time consumptions guaranteed by Traffic Law 2. However, if we assume that c is small (say $c = 1.5$), then we can achieve excellent results concerning time consumption also. In this case, we will drop the requirement of waiting for $2n + ckm$ time units in an $2m \times 2m$ grid (this requirement is part of the sixth requirement of Traffic Law 2). If we denote the traffic law generated by dropping the above requirement from Traffic Law 2 by Traffic Law 3, then we can show that Traffic Law 3 guarantees that instead of spending t time units (when working in isolation) each robot will need to spend only about ct time units in the multi-agent case.[5] This result sheds light on some interesting practical issues. For example, making robots that can accelerate without wasting much energy and in a relatively fast fashion might be (as is shown here) more important than building a sophisticated communication scheme for coordinating activity. On the other hand, Traffic Law 2 shows that if our main interest is to minimize the energy spent by the robots (while still requiring that their time consumption will be reasonable), then the appropriate way for achieving it might not necessarily be the option in which they will finish each task in the fastest way. In our traffic law, when a robot has to wait for $2n + ckm$ time units, it can shut its engine and batteries and spend no energy during that period (no perception or movement is needed). As a result, each robot will be able to achieve close to optimal energy consumption even for large c.

2.3.2. Allowing multiple velocities

Other interesting issues arise when we consider robots moving in different velocities (we capture the notion of velocity by enabling robots to move along several coordinates in one time unit). In this subsection, we assume that moving in a certain velocity is a matter of decision. Each robot might have a different optimal velocity, and we assume that the cost of deviating from this velocity is proportional to the size of that deviation.[6] Therefore, we would like to enable the robots to move most of the time in a velocity which is close to their optimal velocity. We treat the above "velocities problem" by devoting different lanes on the coarse grid for different velocities while still requiring moving in a particular constant velocity inside the $2m \times 2m$ grids. If the robots' optimal velocities can range between v_1 to v_j, we can decide on s velocities, $v_i = v_1 + i \cdot (v_j - v_1)/s$, and associate with column and row l of the coarse grid the velocity v_i iff $l = i(\mathrm{mod}(s))$ (robots moving there will be required to move in that velocity). The velocity of movement inside each $2m \times 2m$ grid will be v_1. Now, we

---

[5] In fact this holds also for a large c, but then Traffic Law 2 will be unsatisfactory for distant goals.

[6] The case when a certain robot cannot move in a certain velocity which is optimal to another is an extreme case that (although interesting) will not be discussed in this paper.

augment Traffic Law 2 by the above mentioned requirements, and refer to the augmented law as Traffic Law 4. It is easy to show that Traffic Law 4 guarantees that each robot will be able to reach any goal it receives while moving in a velocity that differs by at most $(v_j - v_1)/s$ from its optimal velocity, with the exception of o(n) coordinates along which it will have to move in a different velocity. However, before using this result, some cautions should be taken. Because of the fact that the o(n) obtained is proportional to the size of s, then when considering an n which is not large we will still have to optimize the size of s for getting satisfying behavior (whenever n is larger, s will be chosen to be larger).

2.3.3. A few words on workstations

The next problems to be discussed are concerned with assembly issues. When considering assembly issues, there might be a need to change some of the traffic rules, because robots might need to stop at certain workstations in order to carry out assembly tasks. For example, if a robot decides to assemble a certain unit with/from the elements it gathered, then it might need to stop in order to perform the task. This might of course disturb others. We can treat the above problem using a similar idea to the idea used in the "velocities problem". This will be achieved by designating "workstation" areas, in which the assembly activity will be performed. The frequency of such locations should be calculated carefully in order to minimize the length of paths the robots will have to follow in order to achieve their goals. Different assembly locations will be devoted to different robots and to different expected assembly times in order to decrease the amount of unnecessary stops. Notice that all of the above is still concerned with traffic laws. However, the general framework suggested does not restrict itself to these laws. When we consider assembly issues, we might look at totally different social laws: return public tools to their places, notify other robots about the place of a certain tool you used, etc.

2.3.4. The $m = O(n)$ case

In the previous sections we showed how close to optimal coordination can be achieved when we are interested in the total energy consumption, and how such results are obtained concerning time consumption when the constant c is small. However, the optimality of these results relies on the assumption that $m = o(n)$. Therefore, when we consider a system of many robots we have to assume that our grid is quite large. An interesting complementary problem is concerned with our ability to devise social laws that will be good for the case where $m \leqslant n$ but still $m = O(n)$. Of course we can use the O(n^2) result of Theorem 2.1, but the question is whether we can do better. The following traffic law relies on Traffic Law 2 and points to the fact that, when we are interested in reaching relatively distant goals, then we can achieve close to optimal coordination even in the $m = O(n)$ case.

Traffic Law 5. This traffic law will be similar to the sixth requirement of Traffic Law 2 when we replace the $2m \times 2m$ grid by the whole grid, and use the following modifications. Row r will be the bottom row of the whole grid, and x will be the second rightmost coordinate of that row. The coordinate g will be the leftmost coordinate of the top row of the grid, and the column of e will be the rightmost column of the grid. However, instead of stopping at e, each robot will have to move along the rightmost column until the bottom of the grid and then return back to x. When a robot is in x, it will have to reach g in one of the shortest paths possible without entering the top row. We assume that the robots start operating from the lowest row (but will have to return only to x and continue from there). In the first iteration (when first arriving at x) the robots must move from x to g without entering r.

We can show:

Theorem 2.4. *Given that there are* $m = O(n)$, $m \leqslant n$, *robots in the multi-robot grid system, Traffic Law 5 guarantees that each goal can be achieved in* $4n$ *time units.*

Notice that, if we are interested in reaching coordinates at a distance of about n, then this result can be considered as a very good performance. Notice also that no stops or perception are needed in order to achieve goals according to this law. In the case that robots might be working towards several goals, meaningful local planning will still be needed in order to try achieving several goals before reaching g. However, this traffic law is more restrictive than Traffic Law 2. This has a significant drawback: a robot might not be able to achieve all its goals before reaching g, and then it will have to achieve some of them in later iterations. This of course might badly affect the efficiency of the robots in cases where robots have several goals at the same point in time. The above situation points to the fact that although the social law must restrict the behavior of agents in order to enable individual achievement of goals, we have to be careful not to be too restrictive in order to enable the agents to devise efficient plans for achieving their goals.

3. The general framework

This section introduces a more general treatment of social laws in a computational setting. We see this part as complementary to the previous one. In fact, we believe that both of them have to be understood in order to have an initial theory of artificial social systems.

3.1. The model

The term "agent" is common in AI, and used in diverse ways. Here we will take an agent to have state, and to engage in actions which move it among states. Although this basic definition is consistent with most uses of the term in AI,[7] it is perhaps somewhat too impoverished to be worthy of the lofty name. However, our goal here is not to contribute to the theory of individual agents but to the theory of social law, and so it will be illuminating to initially adopt a model in which all the complexity arises from the existence of multiple agents, and not from the behavior of individual agents.

---

[7] For example, it is consistent with its definition in Agent Oriented Programming, mentioned earlier.

We adopt a synchronous model: Agents repeatedly and simultaneously take action, which leads them from their previous state to a new one. The actions of an agent are taken from a given repertoire. The problem in defining the transition functions of agents is due to the fact that the state in which the agent ends up after taking a particular action at a particular state depends also on actions and states of other agents. Thus, in principle, we could think of the transition function of the entire system, a mapping from the states and actions of all agents to the new states of all agents. In this view, for example, in order to determine the effect of one car turning left at an intersection, we would have to specify the states and actions of all other cars. An alternative view would be to define the transition function of each agent independently, and account for the effects of other agents by making the function nondeterministic. In this view, for example, the effect of turning left at an intersection would be either a new position and direction of the car, or a collision.

These are two extreme approaches to modelling concurrent actions. In the first approach, *all* information about other actions must be supplied, and the transition function produces the most specific prediction. In the second approach, *no* information about other agents is supplied, and the transition function produces the most general prediction. Instead of adopting either extreme view, we propose an intermediate approach. We propose adding the concept of *social law*, or constraints on the behavior of agents. The constraints specify which of the actions that are in general available are in fact allowed in a given state; they do so by a predicate over that state. The transition function now takes as an argument not only the initial state and the action taken by the agent, but also the constraints in force; it produces a prediction about the set of possible next states of the agent. For example, it might predict that as a result of turning left at the intersection, *given certain traffic rules*, the car will successfully complete the turn.

We claim that this is a natural representation of actions, and an advantageous one. Generally speaking, the prediction based on constraints will be more general than the prediction that is based on the precise states and actions of all other agents, and more specific than the prediction based on *no* information on the other agents.

A final comment, before we present the formal model. We make an assumption of *homogeneity*; specifically, we assume that the sets of states and the available actions are common to all agents. We do not assume that the agents will necessarily be in the same state at any time, nor that they will take the same action when in the same state; only that they "have the same hardware". Similarly, we assume an egalitarian society, in which the same constraints apply to all agents. None of these assumptions are crucial to our approach or results, but they simplify the discussion.

The formal model

Definition 3.1. Given a set of states S, a first-order language $\mathcal{L}$ (with an entailment relation $\models$), and a set of actions A, a *constraint* is a pair (a, φ) where $a \in A$ and $\varphi \in \mathcal{L}$ is a sentence. A *social law* is a set of constraints (a_i, φ_i), at most one for each $a_i \in A$.

The language $\mathcal{L}$ will be used to describe what is true and false in different states. Given a state $s \in S$ and a sentence $\varphi \in \mathcal{L}$, s might satisfy or not satisfy φ. We denote the fact that s satisfies φ by $s \models \varphi$. The intuitive meaning of (a_i, φ_i) will be that φ_i is the most general condition about states which *prohibits* taking action a_i.

In the sequel, we will use the following notation. Given a pair of social laws, sl_1 and sl_2, we denote by $sl_2 < sl_1$ the fact that for every $(a_i, \varphi_i) \in sl_2$ there exists $(a_i, \varphi_j) \in sl_1$ such that $\varphi_j \models \varphi_i$. Intuitively, it will mean that sl_1 is more restrictive than sl_2.

Definition 3.2. A *social agent* is a tuple $(S, \mathcal{L}, A, SL, T)$ where S, $\mathcal{L}$, A are as above, SL a set of social laws, and T is a total transition function $T : S \times A \times SL \rightarrow 2^S$ such that:

- For every $s \in S$, $a \in A$, $sl \in SL$, if $s \models \varphi$ holds and $(a, \varphi) \in sl$ then $T(s, a, sl) = \emptyset$, the empty set.
- For every $s \in S$, $a \in A$, $sl_1 \in SL$, $sl_2 \in SL$, if $sl_2 < sl_1$ then $T(s, a, sl_1) \subseteq T(s, a, sl_2)$.

In practice, the transition function T will be only partially specified. If $T(s, a, sl)$ is not explicitly defined for a particular sl, then $T(s, a, sl)$ is assumed to be the conjunction of all explicitly defined $T(s, a, sl_i)$ satisfying that $sl_i < sl$. If this conjunction is over an empty set, then $T(s, a, sl) = \emptyset$, the empty set.

Definition 3.3. A *social multi-agent system* is a collection of social agents which share the set of states, the language for describing states, the set of potential actions, the set of potential social laws, and the transition function.[8]

3.2. The computational problem

The multi-agent system defined in the previous section provides one degree of freedom in addition to those present in standard multi-agent models: the social law in effect. Once we fix the social law, the social multi-agent system reduces to a standard one, since all transitions which are incompatible with this law are now ignored. (Note, however, that the remaining transitions may still be nondeterministic.) Thus, a social multi-agent system and a particular social law together induce a standard multi-agent system, which makes no reference to social laws. Loosely speaking, the computational problem will be to select from among the candidate social laws one that, given the social multi-agent system, will induce a "good" standard system. But what makes for a "good" system?

For this purpose we identify a subset of the set of states, which we call *focal states*. We will be interested in a social law which will ensure that each agent, given two focal states, is able to construct a plan guaranteed to move him from one state to the other—*no matter what actions are taken by other agents*. Note the existence of a certain tradeoff: The more restrictive the law, the more can the planner rely on the effects of his actions, but, on the other hand, the more restrictive the law, the fewer actions are available to the planner in the first place. In selecting a social law we wish to strike a

---

[8] Recall again that this only means that the agents "have the same hardware", not that they will in fact be in the same state or take the same actions in a given state.

good balance, allowing each agent enough freedom to achieve its goals but not enough freedom to foil those of others.

Before proceeding with the formal development, we note two (probably obvious) points regarding the complexity of deriving useful social laws:

- Unlike planning, which occurs frequently over time, social laws need only be computed once (assuming that the characteristics of the system do not change; see discussion in last section). We might therefore not mind spending more time in this off-line stage of deriving the social laws. Still, if we show (say) an exponential lower bound on the problem of deriving these laws, it will limit the sizes of the problem for which we can expect a solution, even off-line.
- It might at first seem that deriving social laws is inherently harder than planning, since in the former "one must simulate the planning of agents anyway". This is clearly false; for example, the utility of the law requiring keeping to the right of the road can be demonstrated without simulating the route-planning agents might perform.

We now turn to the formal development. Intuitively, an agent's *legal plan* is a decision on how to act in each state, in a way which is consistent with the law in force:

Definition 3.4. Given a social agent $(S, \mathcal{L}, A, SL, T)$ and a social law $sl \in SL$, a *legal plan* is a total function $DO : S \to A$ such that if $(a, \varphi) \in sl$ and $s \models \varphi$ holds, then $DO(s) \neq a$. An *execution* of the plan from a state s_0 is a sequence of states $s_0, s_1, s_2, \ldots$ such that $s_{i+1} \in T(s_i, DO(s_i), sl)$.

Note that a plan forces the agent to take action at every step, but we certainly allow the user to include the null action, which might leave states unchanged. Also note that even if the null action is included, some social laws may prohibit it in certain states!

Definition 3.5. Given a social multi-agent system and a subset F of the set of states (the focal states), a *useful law* is a law for which, given any $s_1, s_2 \in F$, there exists a legal plan such that *every* execution of that plan in s_1 includes s_2.

Note that, strictly speaking, we cannot speak of a plan "leading" to the goal, since the plan is by definition infinite. Also note that this definition does *not* mean that there necessarily exists one *fixed* sequence of actions that will connect two focal states; an action of the agent may have nondeterministic effects, and the following action in the execution of the plan may depend on the state in which the agent landed.

We are now in a position to phrase a precise computational problem:

Definition 3.6 (*The Useful Social Law Problem* (*USLP*)). Given a social multi-agent system and a set of focal states, find a useful law if one exists, or, if no such law exists, announce that this is the case.

The technical results of this section concern the computational complexity of the USLP. In order to present quantitative results we have to be more precise about some of the details of our model. In the following we will assume that the number of states in the representation of an agent is finite and is denoted by n, and we will measure the computational complexity as a function of n. We assume that the total size of an agent's representation is polynomial in n. We also assume that each property of the form $s \models \varphi$, and of the form $sl_1 < sl_2$ can be efficiently verified.

The following theorem shows that the general USLP is intractable, although its complexity is lower than the complexity of many other problems discussed in multi-agent activity.

Theorem 3.7. *The USLP is NP-complete.*

We point again that, since the USLP is computed off-line, this result is not entirely negative. Still, it would be satisfying to be able to achieve lower complexity by imposing various restrictions on the structure of agents. This is what we do in the next two sections.

3.3. Several restrictions on the general model

We start by imposing the following restriction: For each state s, the number of transitions which might change s is bounded by $O(\log(n))$.[9] This is a straightforward generalization of the natural "bounded fan-out" restriction which is common for classical automata. Intuitively, this restriction says that the number of actions an agent might perform at a given state is small relative to the total number of states, while the quality of the information about constraints which might be relevant to the effects of a particular action in a particular state is relatively high. Our logarithmic bound enables us to treat the case in which the number of transitions which are applicable in any given state is small relative to the total number of states, while it is still a function of that number. Notice that the total number of actions and social laws appearing in the representation might still be much more than logarithmic.

The computational problem related to the above restriction is defined as follows:

Definition 3.8 (*The Bounded Useful Social Law Problem* (*BUSLP*)). Given a social multi-agent system where the number of transitions which might change a particular state is bounded by $O(\log(n))$, and a set of focal states, find a useful law if one exists, or, if no such law exists, announce that this is the case.

On its own, this natural restriction does not buy us a whole lot as far as the computational complexity goes:

Theorem 3.9. *The BUSLP is NP-complete.*

However, we have not presented this restriction as a mere curiosity; we now present precise conditions under which the BUSLP become tractable. Consider the following three restrictions:

---

[9] If $T(s, a, sl_1) = T(s, a, sl_2)$ for $sl_2 < sl_1$, then we do not count $T(s, a, sl_1)$ as one of the transitions.

(1) The number of focal states is bounded by a constant c.

(2) For any pair of focal states $s_1, s_2 \in F$, there exists a legal plan all of whose executions reach s_2 starting at s_1 *while visiting the same sequence of states.* Intuitively, this requirement states that it is not enough that there be a plan, as required in the definition of a useful law; the plan must be deterministic.

(3) For any pair of focal states $s_1, s_2 \in F$, there exists a legal plan all of whose executions reach s_2 starting at s_1 *in no more than* $O(\log(n)/\log(\log(n)))$ *steps.* Intuitively, this requirement states that it is not enough that there be a plan; the plan must be short. [10]

These three restrictions may or may not be acceptable; although we expect that they are reasonable in some interesting applications, we take no stance on this here. The significance of these restrictions is that they allow us to state precise conditions under which the BUSLP becomes polynomial:

Theorem 3.10. *The BUSLP is polynomial if restrictions* (1), (2), *and* (3) *hold; if we drop any of these restrictions* (*and do not add additional ones*), *then the BUSLP is NP-complete.*

3.4. Succinct representation of agents

In the previous section we provided necessary and sufficient conditions under which the BUSLP becomes polynomial; note that this result does not provide necessary conditions for the USLP to become polynomial (it provides only sufficient conditions for that). Indeed, in this section we mention a different restriction of the USLP which guarantees polynomial time complexity.

The general framework imposes no structure on the set of states, and places no restrictions on the number of laws which affect the results of any particular action. In practice, there is much more structure in the makeup of agents. For example, while the set of states might be very large, it is usually possible to identify components of the agent, such that the set of states of the agent consists of the Cartesian product of the sets of states of the individual components. If we consider for example the representation of a robot, then one component may relate to its location, another to its orientation, and another to its arm position.

This modularity of states is the first restriction we consider here; specifically, we assume that there exist $O(\log(n))$ components, each of which can be in one of a constant number of states. Thus the state of an agent consists of the Cartesian product of these states. The total number of an agent's states is still n; note that this is no contradiction.

The modularity of state gives rise to a modularity of action; usually, only a small number of social laws will be relevant to determining the change in the state of a particular component as a result of a particular action. In the robotic setting, for example,

---

[10] Notice that the $\log(\log(n))$ factor can be treated as a small constant for any social agent model of a manageable size, and thus, practically speaking, the restriction is to plans of a length that is logarithmic in the number of states. However, the theorem below requires the precise term given here.

a change in the particular location of the robot might depend on particular traffic laws, but not on laws requiring one to shut windows after opening them, on laws prohibiting one from taking the last cookie without announcing the fact, and perhaps not even on many of the possible traffic laws. We capture this intuition by requiring that the change of a particular state of a particular component can depend on only a constant number of social laws.

We will use the term *modular social agent* to denote an social agent whose structure has these two properties of modularity, and *modular social multi-agent system* to denote a collection of such agents. Notice that these restrictions are independent from those discussed in the previous section. Modular systems have the following property:

Theorem 3.11. *Given a modular social multi-agent system, the USLP is polynomial.*

4. Conclusions

A basic approach to coordinating multiple agents is to restrict their activities in a way which enables them to achieve their dynamically-acquired goals while not interfering with other agents. Although this is, we believe, a commonsensical approach, it has not received much attention so far within AI; exceptions include [10,11], where the authors investigate several basic principles and formal aspects of this approach.

The contribution of the case study presented in the first part of this paper is twofold: We have offered a new approach to designing multi-robot systems, and have demonstrated the general approach of artificial social system in a concrete domain. In the second part of this paper we treated the more general computational theory of social laws. We have presented model of multi-agent action whose novel feature is the explicit mention of social laws in the definition of agents. We then defined and investigated the fundamental computational problem involved with finding useful social laws. We showed that the general problem is intractable, and then identified restrictions which achieve tractability. We believe that the formal model, computational problem definition, and complexity results constitute an essential contribution to our understanding of the role of social law in artificial intelligence. Some work had been concerned with issues related to topics discussed in this paper. This includes work in the areas of organization theory (see [8]), team theory [9], and DAI (see for example [4]). The related work in these areas of research is especially concerned with the design of agents' roles and communication structures which enable a cooperative achievement of a common goal. The work on artificial social systems concentrates on a somewhat complementary issue: the off-line design and computation of laws which enable each agent to work individually and successfully towards its own goals during the on-line activity given that all the agents obey these laws. Additional related work includes the synthesis of multi-agent programs [12] and work on cooperative discrete event systems (DES) [13]. A main difference between these lines of research and the work in the framework of artificial social systems stems from the fact that the latter gives more structure for the design of multi-agent systems (first find a social law and then enable agents to tend to work individually) while concentrating on the fundamental problems of social design (we have to restrict the behavior of agents but not restrict them too much). A crucial difference between our setting and that of DES is that in our case the effects of actions taken locally by an agent depend on actions taken by other agents; the result of taking action A by one agent depends on whether another agent took action B. In DES the supervisor restricts the actions available to machines so that the sequence of actions in the systems ends up belonging to a given language; however the effect of each individual action is unaffected by the supervisor. This is also true of so-called "product automata"; there too the job of the coordinator is to ensure global properties such as mutual exclusion by restricting actions of agents, but the effect of any allowed action is not altered. [11] It can be shown that various extended notions, such as "shared events" in DESs still operate within the basic DES framework, and thus address quite separate issues that in our work.

Much remains to be done. For example, as was mentioned in Section 3.1, we have assumed a homogeneous society, both in term of the makeup of agents and in terms of the applicability of social laws. In future work we will relax this assumption, made here only for convenience. Harder assumptions to relax include the assumption of law-abiding citizenship; here we have assumed that all agents obey the social laws, but what happens if some don't? How vulnerable is the society to rogue agents? Similarly, we have assumed that the useful social law is computed off-line. Sometimes this is infeasible, however, either because the makeup of the agents is not known in advance, or because it changes over time. In such cases, can we devise methods by which, through trial and error, the agents will over time converge on a social law? These are some of the questions in which we are currently interested; experimental results on these matters appear in [16].

Appendix A. Proof sketches

Proof of Theorem 3.7 (*Sketch*). It is easy to check that the problem is in NP. We prove NP-hardness by a reduction from 3-SAT. Clause i in the 3-SAT instance will correspond to transitions which change from state i to state $i + 1$. For each literal appearing in the 3-SAT instance there will be a corresponding action. The transition which corresponds to performing l (i.e., the action which corresponds to the literal l) in state i (l should appear as a literal in clause i) will change from state i to state $i + 1$ if and only if the social law which says that $\neg l$ is disallowed will hold. For example, if clause i is $x \wedge y \wedge \neg z$, then we will have actions which correspond to x, y, $\neg z$ that will lead from state i to state $i + 1$ given that the actions which correspond to $\neg x$, $\neg y$, z will be disallowed respectively. We assume the existence of an auxiliary action that leads with no conditions from any state to state 1. We assume that the focal states include state 1 and the "final" state (whose number is determined according to the number of clauses). Our result can be easily verified now. □

---

[11] To quote from Ramadge and Wonham's survey article [13], "... we assumed that the components of the open loop product system were independent, and that any interaction between the components could be modeled as part of a control constraint".

Proof of Theorem 3.9 (*Sketch*). The proof follows from the fact that the reduction presented in the proof outline of Theorem 3.7 is useful for the BUSLP case as well (in fact, we get an instance of the BUSLP). ☐

Proof of Theorem 3.10 (*Sketch*). The polynomial result is achieved by applying a DFS (depth-first search algorithm) starting from each possible focal state where the actions which usually appear in classical DFS are replaced by transitions containing also social laws, and where the depth of the search is bounded by $O(\log(n)/\log(\log(n)))$. An additional difference is that along each such DFS we have to check whether we use an action which is already disallowed (by a previous transition in the appropriate path). The above algorithm is polynomial and finds all the possible paths of the appropriate length (where each path includes both actions and social laws) between a given pair of focal states. The number of such possible paths is polynomial. Because of the fact that there is only a constant number of focal states, we remain only with a polynomial number of alternatives that we have to check (there is a polynomial number of relevant paths for each pair of focal states, and there is a constant number of such pairs).

The NP-complete results are achieved again by a reduction from 3-SAT. The idea is to associate with each literal of each clause of the 3-SAT instance a distinguished action, and to build an agent that needs to be able to perform for each clause at least one action from among the actions that correspond to that clause. However, in order that an action which corresponds to a literal l will have desired effects, all the actions that correspond to $\neg l$ should be disallowed. Let us illustrate this idea in the case where we allow any number of focal states (where restriction (1) is dropped). In that case the structure of our agent (the reduction's outcome) will be of an "almost" acyclic graph (where the states are the nodes and the transitions are the edges of that graph). In fact, it will be "almost" a tree where we also allow several edges (with the same direction) between adjacent nodes. The depth of that tree will be $O(\log(n)/\log(\log(n)))$ where the degree of each internal node is $O(\log(n))$ (where n is the number of clauses in the 3-SAT instance). We associate the set of edges connecting a particular pair of adjacent nodes with a particular clause of the 3-SAT (there will be a 1–1 correspondence between clauses and pairs of adjacent nodes in that graph). We will associate several actions with the pair of states which corresponds to clause i: a unique action for each literal appearing in that clause. However, an agent which performs in a given state a particular action that corresponds to the literal l will reach the adjacent state if and only if the actions which correspond to $\neg l$ will be disallowed. We also assume that there is an auxiliary action that leads with no condition from any leaf state to the root state (and therefore the graph is only "almost" acyclic). If we assume that the focal states are the root state and the leaves states, we get the appropriate result.

A similar idea is used for proving the case where we drop the second restriction. In that case the reduction will be quite similar to the one mentioned before, but we will change a little bit the structure of the above tree. We will assume that the only focal state is the root state (and therefore there is only a constant number of focal states now), and will force the need to pass from each vertex in the previous graph to its son in that graph using the nondeterminism (in the previous case this was forced by the fact that we had to reach any focal state and therefore any leaf). In order to do so, we will replace the direct connection between each given non-leaf vertex x of the previous graph and its sons by a connection from x to $O(\log(n))$ new vertices each of which will be connected to a different and unique vertex which previously was a son of x. The connection from a new vertex n_y to the vertex y which was previously a son of x will be by edges mentioning the same actions that were mentioned by the connection from x to y. However, in x itself the agent will be able to perform now only one action: a new distinguished action which leads nondeterministically to all the previously mentioned new vertices. It is easy to verify that this construction will force us to select for each clause a particular appropriate action (in order to reach the focal state given all the possible nondeterministic effects). Given that an action which corresponds to a literal l will have the desired effects only if the actions which correspond to $\neg l$ are disallowed, we get the desired reduction.

The case where we drop restriction (3) follows immediately from the construction used in the proof of Theorem 3.7. $\quad\square$

Proof of Theorem 3.11 (*Sketch*). The proof of this theorem follows immediately from the fact that on that natural case the number of possible alternatives for useful social laws which we have to consider is polynomial. More precisely, there is a logarithmic number of components each of which might relate to a constant number of focal states, and therefore the total number of potential social laws is polynomial and can be enumerated in a polynomial time. For each such law we can verify in polynomial time whether each particular focal state is reachable from all the other focal states. This is based on the facts that the number of focal states as well as the problem of verifying reachability between a pair of focal states are polynomial. As a result, we get a full polynomial procedure for determining a useful social law. $\quad\square$

References

[1] S.J. Buckley, Fast motion planning for multiple moving robots, in: *Proceedings 1989 IEEE International Conference on Robotics and Automation*, Scottsdale, AZ (1989) 322–326.

[2] P. Caloud, W. Choi, J.C. Latombe, C.L. Pape and M. Yim, Indoor automation with many mobile robots, in: *Proceedings IEEE International Workshop on Intelligent Robots and Systems*, Tsuchiura, Japan (1990).

[3] R. Davis and R.G. Smith, Negotiation as a metaphor for distributed problem solving, *Artif. Intell.* **20** (1) (1983) 63–109.

[4] E.H. Durfee, V.R. Lesser and D.D. Corkill, Coherent cooperation among communicating problem solvers, *IEEE Trans. Comput.* **36** (1987) 1275–1291.

[5] M. Erdmann and T. Lozano-Perez, On multiple moving robots, *Algorithmica* **2** (4) (1987) 477–521.

[6] O. Khatib, Real-time obstacle avoidance for manipulators and mobile robots, *Int. J. Rob. Res.* **5** (1) (1986).

[7] S. Kraus and J. Wilkenfeld, The function of time in cooperative negotiations, in: *Proceedings AAAI-91*, Anaheim, CA (1991) 179–184.

[8] T.W. Malone, Modeling coordination in organizations and markets, in: A.H. Bond and L. Gasser, eds., *Readings in Distributed Artificial Intelligence* (Morgan Kaufmann, San Mateo, CA, 1988).

[9] J. Marschak and R. Radner, *Economic Theory of Teams* (Yale University Press, New Haven, CT, 1972).

[10] Y. Moses and M. Tennenholtz, Artificial social systems, Part I: basic principles, Tech. Rept. CS90-12, Weizmann Institute, Rehovot, Israel (1990).

[11] Y. Moses and M. Tennenholtz, On computational aspects of artificial social systems, in: *Proceedings DAI-92* (1992).

[12] A. Pnueli and R. Rosner, Distributed reactive systems are hard to synthesize, in: *Proceedings 31th IEEE Symposium on Foundations of Computer Science* (1990).

[13] P. Ramadge and W. Wonham, The control of discrete event systems, *Proc. IEEE* **77** (1) (1989) 81–98.

[14] J.S. Rosenschein and M.R. Genesereth, Deals among rational agents, in: *Proceedings IJCAI-85*, Los Angeles, CA (1985) 91–99.

[15] Y. Shoham, Agent oriented programming, Tech. Rept. STAN-CS-1335-90, Department of Computer Science, Stanford University, Stanford, CA (1990).

[16] Y. Shoham and M. Tennenholtz, Emergent conventions in multi-agent systems: initial experimental results and observations, in: *Proceedings KR-92*, Cambridge, MA (1992).

Artificial Intelligence 73 (1995) 253–269

Instructions, intentions and expectations

Bonnie Webber *, Norman Badler, Barbara Di Eugenio, Chris Geib,
Libby Levison, Michael Moore

*Department of Computer and Information Science, University of Pennsylvania, 200 South 33rd Street,
Philadelphia, PA 19104-6389, USA*

Received September 1992; revised June 1993

Abstract

Based on an ongoing attempt to integrate Natural Language instructions with human figure animation, we demonstrate that agents' understanding and use of instructions can complement what they can derive from the environment in which they act. We focus on two attitudes that contribute to agents' behavior—their intentions and their expectations—and shown how Natural Language instructions contribute to such attitudes in ways that complement the environment. We also show that instructions can require more than one context of interpretation and thus that agents' understanding of instructions can evolve as their activity progresses. A significant consequence is that Natural Language understanding in the context of behavior cannot simply be treated as "front end" processing, but rather must be integrated more deeply into the processes that guide an agent's behavior and respond to its perceptions.

1. Introduction

This is a short position paper on what we have learned about language, behavior and the environment from an ongoing attempt to use Natural Language instructions to guide the task-related behavior of animated human figures. While the project, AnimNL (for "Animation and Natural Language"), is not yet ready to deliver a prototype, we believe that what we have so far learned from this attempt to produce a complete vertical integration from language to animated behavior will be of interest and benefit to others as well.

AnimNL builds upon the *Jack*™ animation system developed at the University of Pennsylvania's Computer Graphics Research Laboratory. In *Jack*, animation follows

---

* Corresponding author. E-mail: bonnie@central.cis.upenn.edu.

Fig. 1. SodaJack placing a glass on the counter.

from model-based simulation of virtual agents acting in an environment. The agents of primary interest are *Jack*'s biomechanically reasonable and anthropometrically-scaled human models (see Fig. 1). The models have 138 joints, including an accurate torso, and a growing repertoire of naturalistic behaviors such as walking, stepping, looking, reaching, turning, grasping, strength-based lifting, and both obstacle and self-collision avoidance [5]. Each of these behaviors is environmentally reactive. That is, incremental computation is able to adjust an agent's performance to the situation, as the situation progresses, *without further involvement of the higher-level processes* [10] unless an exceptional failure condition is signaled. Different limits can be placed on an agent's vision, strength and comfort threshold, for more realistic environmental response, and different environments can easily be constructed, so as to vary the situations in which the figures are acting.[1]

With these features, we believe that *Jack* can provide a fairly realistic target for linking Natural Language with behavior. This is because *Jack* agents "naturally" face limits on their ability to understand Natural Language utterances, much as people do: their ability to understand language relies on their knowledge, their knowledge is mediated by what they can perceive, and their perception is limited. Moreover, since *Jack* agents can, like people, effect changes on their world, their understanding of language can evolve through intentional activity in the world (cf. Section 2).

From our work with *Jack*, what we have been led to believe about language, behavior and the environment is that:

---

[1] In discussing agents, we will use the pronoun "he", since we will be using a male figure in our illustrated example—i.e., a figure with male body proportions. The *Jack* animation system provides anthropometrically-sizable female figures as well.

- Just as an agent may be motivated by its environment to consider adopting particular goals as *intentions* that will guide its subsequent behavior, so an agent may also be motivated by Natural Language instructions. Moreover, goals recognized as being situationally relevant either through perceiving the environment or processing instructions, can clarify the meaning of other instructions. (Huffman and Laird [32] see a similar complementarity of roles between language and the environment in an agent's *acquisition* of procedural knowledge.)
- Just as an agent uses its perception of the current environment to augment its knowledge and guide its current behavior, so too can an agent use *expectations* derived from instructions about how a situation will evolve, to augment its beliefs and guide its current and future behavior.

Intentions and expectations can complement one another. Intentions can embody an agent's expectations that the agent can act in ways to satisfy those intentions, while expectations can lead an agent to form intentions to check that those expectations are satisfied and to take corrective actions if not.

Three caveats are necessary here: one involving the quality of everyday instructions, a second involving the sources of an agent's intentions, and a third involving the existence of a distinct "instructor".

First, the task of formulating instructions is clearly not without problems for human language users, as the prevalence of incomprehensible and/or useless instructions shows. Two of our own favorites are:

- "Replace items on vehicle with items contained in this kit." (ANCO Replacement Windshield-Washer Pump, Stock No. 61-14);
- "To access the next highest programmed station setting, or to switch to a lower programmed station, the SCAN buttons must be repeatedly pressed." (VCR, Mitsubishi Electronics).

There are many possible things to blame for the prevalence of poor instructions, including (1) the prevalence of poor writing, in general; (2) a writer's inability to be too specific, because they lack detailed knowledge of the exact situation in which the task will be carried out; and (3) the difficulty people have in converting narrative accounts of past behavior or experience into effective instructions for future behavior. (Recall, for example, the joke about the bus rider who asks a fellow passenger where he should get off for City Hall. The latter replies, "Just get off one stop before I do".)

While significant work is being done to improve the quality of instructions [3, 17, 25, 45, 46], in the end, one may have to accept that no fixed instruction set can serve all agents in all situations.

Secondly, real agents will always have additional intentions that come from sources other than instructions: intentions arise from personal goals and desires, as well as from the policies (social, governmental, etc.) an agent agrees to adhere to. However, we have simplified the situation to one of semi-autonomous agents who have no other intentions than those that follow from their given instructions. This does not mean, however, that nothing else influences their behavior. Since *Jack* agents are environmentally reactive, features in the changing environment affect their behavior as well. For example, an agent instructed to go to the door may also have to take action to avoid obstacles it finds blocking its way. In future work, we plan to address instructions that convey general policy, and to allow it to affect agent behavior as well. For animated agent behavior that follows from particular personality traits, the reader is referred to work by Bates et al. [9, 37] and by Morawetz [14].

Thirdly, in real life there is often no distinct instructor around. In the case of multi-person tasks, this means the conduct of a task is often a product of negotiation by the participants, each with their own knowledge and beliefs [29, 47]. The intentions and expectations of any one of them then may then reflect what has been negotiated by the group. We argue though that the situation with a distinct instructor can show more simply that instructions can allow an agent to form beliefs about the world that it can act on with relative confidence.

The paper is structured as follows: in the next section, we discuss plans and instructions in general, as well as some related work. We also give a brief overview of AnimNL, in support of the points we will be making about instructions, intentions and expectations. Intentions are then discussed in Section 3, and Expectations in Section 4.

2. Background

2.1. Plans and instructions

Early views of Natural Language *instructions* corresponded to the early views of *plans*: instructions were treated as specifying nodes of a plan that, when completely expanded into primitive action specifications, would control agent behavior. This view, for example, underlies SHRDLU's successful response to instructions such as "Pick up the green pyramid and put it in the box" [54].

That *plans* should not be viewed as control structures has already been well argued by Agre and Chapman [1], Pollack [42], Suchman [48], and others in the field. Agre and Chapman show that when people form plans in response to instructions, they appear to use those plans as *resources*. The actual task situation may then lead them to interpolate additional actions not mentioned in the instructions, to replace actions specified in the instructions with other ones that seem better suited to the situation, and to ground referring terms as a *consequence* of their actions rather than as a precondition for them. Other researchers, working in what has come to be called a *BDI* framework ("beliefs, desires and intentions") now view planning in terms of agents adopting (and dropping) intentions to act [13, 16, 29, 43].

A plan's relationship with a set of instructions is also not rigid. It depends, *inter alia*, on various features of the instructions, including:
- whether the instructions convey *doctrine* (general policy regarding behavior in some range of situations) or *procedure* (actions to be taken now or at some specified time in the future);
- in the case of procedural instructions, whether they are given *before*, *during*, or *after* action;
- whether the instructions are meant as *advice*, *suggestion*, *order*, *request*, *warning*, or *tutorial*.

These features are apparent in recent work involving instructed agents. For example, in Chapman's work [15], instructions are given as advice to agents already engaged in an activity. They are treated as additional evidence for an action alternative already identified by the agent as being relevant to the current situation. That alternative may not, however, be taken immediately (or ever) if other alternatives have more evidence in their favor. Chapman derives this view from observing how arcade game players follow instructions given to them by kibbitzers watching them play. (Chapman also notes that negative instructions can be similarly understood as evidence against actions.)

Vere and Bickmore treat most instructions to their "basic agent", Homer, as orders to carry out specific tasks [50]. However, they have also enabled Homer to interpret negative instructions as policy that can override orders that conflict with it. They give an example in which Homer (a small submarine) is told not to leave its island, and it subsequently refuses to comply with an instruction to take a picture of the Codfish (a ship) because to do so would require leaving the island.

Work by Alterman and his students [2] shows how instructions given after an incorrect action has been performed are treated as assistance, helping agents to accommodate their existing routines to the device currently at hand. In this approach, routines evolved over many different instances of engagement help focus an agent on the details of the situation that require attention and on the decisions that must be made. Instructions may interrupt activity to call attention to other relevant details or decisions, or to correct decisions already made. Neither plans nor instructions function as control structures that determine the agent's behavior.

Our own work has focussed on procedural instructions given to agents before undertaking a task. Such instructions can be found in user's manuals, owner's manuals, maintenance manuals, and "how to" books—for example,

- Depress door release button to open door and expose paper bag. (*Royal* CAN VAC™ Owner's Manual, p. 5.)
- Remove safety wire from access unit adjusting bolt and adjusting link and loosen bolt. (Air Force Manual T.O.IF-16C-2-94JG-50-2, Ammunition Drum, Removal and Installation.)
- If candle wax falls on a piece of furniture, wait until it solidifies, then pick it off with your fingernail or a plastic spatula. (McGowan and DuBern, *Home Repair*. London: Dorling Kindersley Ltd. 1991, p. 22.)

One application that could benefit from the ability to understand and animate agent behavior that would follow from such instructions is *task analysis* in connection with Computer-Aided Design. By enabling virtual human agents to carry out maintenance and repair tasks in the CAD environment itself, a designer could determine before the artifacts were built whether people would be able to carry out those tasks in anticipated environments.

There are at least three ways to make different virtual agents interact with objects in different virtual environments. One way is through direct manipulation, which would require a designer to directly control a range of different agents in a range of different environments, in order to observe and evaluate their behavior. A second way is through direct motion sensing (e.g. "Virtual Reality" kinesthetic input [4]). The third way is through Natural Language level instructions. This could be the most economical, since it would allow the designer to simply "rerun" the same instructions with different agent–environment pairs, in order to accomplish the same ends.

Other potential application areas for using instructions to direct the behavior of animated agents include group training activities and multi-agent simulations. Thus we feel that enabling virtual human agents to understand instructions is of practical as well as theoretical interest.

2.2. Overview of the AnimNL architecture

We begin with a brief overview of the AnimNL architecture, since it captures our beliefs that language understanding is a process that evolves, in part, through principled interaction with the world. Roughly speaking, AnimNL consists of three interacting modules:

- A module consisting of processes that work towards understanding an instruction step in terms of an initial structure of intentions, which we call a *plan graph*. These processes include parsing, interpretation and plan inference [18–21].
- A module consisting of a high-level incremental planner and two specialized processes able to adapt highly-parameterized plans for search and for object manipulation to the exact situation at hand [26–28, 35, 41].
- A simulator that coordinates motion directives and perceptual requests from the planning components with ones corresponding to environmental responses, and schedules their performance. An agenda allows multiple behaviors to be carried out in parallel, and other behaviors to be initiated and terminated asynchronously with respect to each other [10].

The result is that an agent's behavior at any time reflects both its low-level responses to the current environment and the current state of its high-level intentions. A more detailed description of the AnimNL architecture can be found in [53].

3. Intentions from instructions

Intentions have been identified as a factor in rational behavior by various researchers (e.g., [12, 13, 15, 42]), who see them as playing at least two roles: (1) they can constrain the courses of action an agent need consider to those consistent with what the agent already plans to do; and (2) they can be used to determine when an action can be said to be relevant, to have succeeded or to have failed.

We have found that goals specified in instructions—which, in the case of positive instructions, are goals that agents are being ordered or advised or requested to adopt as their intentions—can also affect (1) how an agent interprets action descriptions in those instructions and (2) how the agent behaves in carrying out actions. In the first case, instructions perform a role that Chapman's Ph.D. thesis [15] shows can also be performed by the environment. In Chapman's work, apparently underspecified instructions are interpreted simply as evidence for a response to the current environment that has already been deemed relevant on the basis of perception. Therefore, if a knife can be used either to kill a monster or to jimmy a door, and if a monster is threatening the agent and no door needs to be jimmied (e.g., to enable the agent to escape), an instruction such as "use the knife" will be understood only as advice to kill the monster.

In Section 3.1, we show how goals specified in Natural Language instructions can function in a similar way, and in Section 3.2, we comment on how intentions derived from instructions can affect low-level behavioral features. We conclude in Section 3.3 with a brief discussion on how the action representation used in AnimNL allows its high-level planner to use intentions effectively.

3.1. Behavioral import of purpose clauses

Comments are often made about the *efficiency* of Natural Language—how much of an utterance's meaning can be left unspecified, to be filled in by listeners able to draw on an appropriate context. In this light, we have come to understand that *purpose clauses*—infinitival clauses that convey the goal of an action—provide a helpful source of information for understanding underspecified action descriptions which convey information implicitly through context. While this information could of course be made explicit, people seem not to expect this: speakers commonly leave it for hearers to figure out for themselves. [2]

Consider the following example (from [18]):

Place a plank between two ladders to make a simple scaffold.

The action description in the main clause is "place a plank between two ladders". The goal conveyed in the purpose clause is "make a simple scaffold". Now, by itself, the main clause conveys no explicit constraints on the orientation of what have to be two *step-ladders* and only one constraint on the placement of the plank—that it be somewhere in the three-dimensional space "between" wherever the step-ladders are. However there are significant implicit constraints that follow from the purpose of making a simple scaffold: the ladders should be aligned with their treads facing outwards in opposite directions, at a distance spannable by the plank, which should be placed horizontally on treads of the two ladders that are the same height off the ground. (How high off the ground will depend on the purpose of the scaffold: it is not determinable from the given instruction alone.) An (incremental) plan can then be formulated to comply with both the explicit and implicit constraints on the procedure and its intended result.

Our second example is intended to show that an agent can use a goal expression and perceptual tests on when that goal is achieved to determine the referent of a noun phrase and hence what action he or she is meant to carry out. The instruction to be considered is:

Vacuum the rug or carpet against the direction of the pile to leave it raised.

---

[2] There are, of course, other linguistic means of conveying purpose—free adjuncts [52], means clauses [7,8], and even simple conjunction [24]. Moreover, clauses that convey purpose do serve other functions as well, such as making an action description easier to understand [22,23] or justifying why an action should be done [8]. Our point here is simply that any linguistic specification of goals (purpose clauses being a clear example) can serve, like the environment, as the context in which an *underspecified* action description can be elaborated and thereby correctly understood.

To follow this instruction, an agent must know the direction referred to as "against the direction of the pile". If the agent does not know the referent of this phrase before starting, the purpose clause ("to leave it raised") can be used to guide his or her search for it. That is, the agent can plan to vacuum a bit in various directions and observe which direction of sweep leaves the pile raised. At this point, the agent can begin to elaborate a plan for vacuuming the entire rug or carpet in that direction and thereby finish the job.

A further example is related to a matter we return to in Section 4, and concerns the termination conditions associated with perceptual tests. (The instructions are for removing wine stains from a rug or carpet.)

> Blot with clean tissues to remove any liquid still standing. Sprinkle liberally with salt to extract liquid that has soaked into the fabric. Vacuum up the salt.

In the first sentence, blotting with clean tissues specifies a *type* of activity but not the extent to which it should be pursued. (In the terminology of Moens and Steedman [40], it is simply a *process* like "running", not a *culminated process* like "running a mile": it has no intrinsic endpoint.) How long an agent should blot the stained area comes from the purpose clause "to remove any liquid still standing": the agent should plan to interleave blotting with perception, until no standing liquid is left visible.

The purpose clause in the second sentence conveys in a somewhat different way the condition under which the agent can start the final step, vacuuming up the salt. It is not the termination point of the sprinkling (which is terminated when the agent decides there is now a "liberal" amount of salt on the stain [34]), but that of the subsequent waiting. How long the agent should wait comes from the purpose clause "to extract liquid that has soaked into the fabric". The agent must plan to interleave waiting with perception, continuing until he perceives that the salt is damp (i.e., a change in visual texture). At this point, the salt has extracted as much liquid as it can, and the agent can commence vacuuming.

This example illustrates the complementary relation between intention and expectation: the intention to remove the standing liquid leads to an expectation that blotting it will eventually accomplish this removal, which in turn leads to an intention to observe the situation, monitoring for the expected point at which no liquid will be left standing.

To say the above is not to say that an agent's only intentions are those derived from instructions, but rather that goals specified in instructions, which the agent may adopt as intentions, can provide a context for fully understanding underspecified action description in instructions.

Di Eugenio has designed and implemented the machinery to be used in AnimNL for computing many of the inferences that follow from understanding that the action α described in the main clause of an utterance is being done for the purpose π described in a purpose clause. This relationship between α and π can be characterized more specifically as either *generation* or *enablement*. In *generation*, executing α under appropriate circumstances is all that is required to achieve π. In *enablement*, α brings about circumstances in which π can be generated by subsequent actions.

Di Eugenio's approach makes use of both linguistic knowledge and planning knowledge. A knowledge base of plan schemata (or *recipes*) complements a taxonomic structure of action descriptions. The latter is represented in Classic [11] and exploits *classification* to allow an inference algorithm to find related action descriptions. These descriptions index into the knowledge base of recipes which includes information about generation, enablement and sub-structure relationships between actions. The inference algorithms on these linked structures are described in detail in [18, 19].

An instruction may convey to the agent that a generation or enablement relationship holds between two actions, without the agent being able to determine which one, from the text alone. This may lead to confusion when the agent comes to act on the instruction. For example, recall the *Royal* CAN VAC instruction given in Section 2.1:

> Depress door release button to open door and expose paper bag.

(This is from a procedure for replacing the dust bag when it is full.) Whether a generation or enablement relation holds between "depressing the button" and "opening the door" will depend simply on the orientation of the canister. If the canister is horizontal when the button is depressed and the catch released, the door will fall open of its own accord because of gravity. In this case, depressing the button will generate opening the door, without the need for further action. If however, the agent has up-ended the canister to make the button more accessible, depressing the button will just release the catch: the agent must still grasp the door and pull it open. An agent who expected the former may think he didn't press the button hard enough and try again, rather than think an additional action was called for. Although this is a relatively trivial example, readers will probably recognize the problem. It could be solved by making the instruction more specific:

> Holding canister horizontally, depress door release button to open door and expose paper bag.

However, making the text longer seems to decrease the likelihood that it will be read. Trying to convey the information graphically [25] relies on the reader distinguishing between necessary features of the depicted scene and accidental ones. This suggests that producing instructions of guaranteed reliability may be an impossible task.

3.2. Intentions and behavioral features

In the previous section, we distinguished two relations, generation and enablement, holding between an action and its current purpose. Viewing purpose in terms of an agent's intention to achieve it, we now discuss the need we have discovered to take account of that intention when computing low-level features of the action to be performed and animated. Such features may include the place at which the agent locates itself to perform the action, and the manner in which it grasps an object involved in the action or moves it. While our current implementation of this capability is simply via table look-up, a more general and extensible solution is being pursued [35] for a wide class of object manipulation tasks. In the meanwhile, we believe it is still worthwhile to illustrate the phenomenon, if only by example, since such a difference can be made to human figure animation by a figure's carrying out a task-related action "naturally", even when particular behavioral choices are not necessary to simply the success of the specified action.

Our first example involves the region in which an object will be grasped. If a hammer is to be grasped simply to enable it to be moved from place to place, any region of the hammer is a viable grasp location, although somewhere near its center of mass may make it easier for the agent to lift and transport. If however, the hammer is to be grasped to enable its use in hammering a nail, a more appropriate grasp region would be towards the end of its shank. Even then, re-orientation may be required, once the hammer is lifted.

Our second example involves constraints on an agent's target in moving to a location. Consider the simple instruction

Go over to the mirror.

By itself, this tells an agent little about where he or she is supposed to end up being positioned with respect to the mirror. On the other hand, specifying a goal that will be enabled by reaching a target location can help an agent to better identify that location. For example,

Go over to the mirror and straighten it.
Go over to the mirror and straighten your bow tie. [3]

Straightening a mirror requires manipulating it, so an agent will target a comfortable arm's reach. Straightening one's bow tie requires seeing oneself clearly: this may target a location either closer to or further away from the mirror, depending on the agent's eyesight. Note that the instructor may not know enough about the agent to specify a target location in more detail: it is something that only the agent can determine. Thus no further explicit guidance can be provided.

The capabilities of our existing implementation are demonstrated in an animated simulation of "SodaJack", a soda fountain agent who can respond to requests for a soda or ice cream [28]. In this domain, the intention to perform a basic task action such as moving a glass so as to *generate* serving it to a "customer", posts a constraint on the agent's movements that the glass not be tipped to one side. On the other hand, moving a glass so as to *enable* wiping it off posts no such constraint. While a few simple things such as these can be done by table look-up, the problem of systematically characterizing those features of intended actions that affect low-level physical activity is of considerable difficulty. While the significance of this boundary between symbol and action has been recognized and formalized in [33], much more work is needed in order to actually cross it.

3.3. Intentions in means/end reasoning

Given that instructions only convey certain features of an agent's behavior, situated decision making is necessary to expand and amplify the agent's intentions, to fill in

---

[3] These are examples of purposive "and", mentioned earlier in footnote 2 and discussed in more detail in [24]. The "and" form sounds more natural here than the "to" form.

gaps. To enable decision making to use an agent's intentions effectively, we have found it worth replacing fixed set of preconditions, with reasoning about the effects of actions in the context in which they will be performed.

This reflects our analysis of preconditions [27] as encoding claims about the universal desirability or undesirability of certain effects of an action. For example, failing to clear off a block before picking it up, may mean that objects on top of it will slide off and break or disturb other objects. Sometimes an agent will be concerned about this possibility; other times, not. (We assume that agents may desire to avoid particular actions or actions that may lead to particular states.) The problem with fixed preconditions is that they prevent an agent from considering an action, even if the agent doesn't care about its possibly destructive side-effects.

Limited simulation, on the other hand, can enable an agent to reason roughly about the effects of performing an action in a given world state. The agent can then decide whether or not performing the action will satisfy his intentions without violating any behavioral constraints. In some cases, the consequences will be acceptable given the agent's current intentions, in other cases, they won't. This use of situated reasoning through limited simulation allows the system to use intentions to define, in a situation-specific way, when an action is applicable and can be successful rather than using an *a priori* definition. (Another use of limited simulation in planning is discussed in [38].)

The removal of preconditions from action operators has multiple effects. One benefit is to give the system more flexibility in choosing which actions to use to achieve its ends. However, the cost of this increased flexibility is that actions may fail to achieve these ends. In short, using intentions and limited simulation to perform action selection means the possibility of action failure must be allowed for.

The current version of AnimNL's planner, which eliminates preconditions in favor of situated reasoning about the effects of actions, is described in more detail in [26, 27].

4. Expectations from instructions

Here we address the role of instructions in raising *expectations* that complement an agent's current perceptions in influencing its behavior. Expectations can lead to further perceptual activity—not just observation but also activities that enable observation. As such, expectations from instructions complement the signals coming in from the outside world. Here we discuss three types of expectations generated by different elements in instruction, and the "active perception" [6] they can engender.

4.1. Expectations about processes

In some earlier work designed for creating animations from recipes, Karlin [34] analysed a range of temporal and frequency adverbs found in instructions. One particular construction she analysed is the following:

Do α for ⟨duration⟩ or until ⟨event⟩
e.g. Steam two minutes or until mussels open.

Karlin notes that this is not a case of logical disjunction, where the agent can choose which disjunct to follow: rather, the explicit duration suggests the usual amount of time that it will take to just cook the mussels. This can be detected when all the mussels that were closed when they were put into the pot (already open ones having been discarded as dead) are now open. If they are not open after two minutes, the agent should wait a bit longer. Those that have not opened after another short wait should then be discarded, since they are full of mud.

The usefulness of an expectation such as this comes from the cost of sensing. Steaming is usually done in a closed, opaque cooking pot, so the lid must be removed in order to check the state of the contents. Whenever this is done, steam escapes, setting the process back. The result of sensing too often then is that the mussels become tough through over-cooking. The expectation can therefore be used to gauge how long to wait before beginning to make costly sensing tests.

4.2. Expectations about consequences

Processes often have more than one possible outcome, depending on how long they proceed and how much resources they consume. Another type of expectation arising from instructions concerns the properties of objects that will result from such processes. (This is described in more detail in [51].)

Consider for example, mixing flour, butter and water.[4] Depending on the relative amounts of these three ingredients and the absorbency of the flour (different for different types of flour and for winter and summer wheat), the result may be anything from a flakey mass to a viscous batter. Instructions can indicate the intended result, so that the agent can modify and/or augment his actions so as to produce it. How instructions convey the intended result can vary: In example (1a)–(1c), the expected viscosity of the resulting mixture is conveyed through the verb:

> (1a) Mix the flour, butter and water, and *knead* until smooth and shiny.
> (1b) Mix the flour, butter and water, and *spread* over the blueberries.
> (1c) Mix the flour, butter and water, and *stir* until all lumps are gone.

while in example (2a)–(2b), it is conveyed through the noun phrase:

> (2a) Mix the flour, butter and water. Let *the dough* relax for 15 minutes.
> (2b) Mix the flour, butter and water. Let *the batter* sit for 15 minutes.

There are several ways in which expectations such as these can affect an agent's behavior. The simplest is to *monitor the result*: if it doesn't meet the agent's expectation (too liquid or too solid), the agent can compensate with additional amounts of flour in the former case or water in the latter. Alternatively, the agent can *monitor the process*: that is, he can add the specified amount of water to the specified amounts of butter and flour *gradually*, mixing it in. If it is becoming too viscous, he can stop before adding all the ingredients.

---

[4] This is not something we are capable of animating without simulating the properties of semi-viscous fluids, but it is the best example for making our point.

4.3. Expectations about locations

Actions can effect changes in the world that alter what an agent can perceive. Part of an agent's cognitive task in understanding instructions is therefore to determine for each referring expression, the perceptual context in which the agent is meant to find (or *ground*) its referent. Some referring expressions in an instruction may be intended to refer to objects in the currently perceivable situation, while others may be intended to refer to objects that only appear (i.e., come into existence or become perceivable) as a consequence of carrying out an action specified in the instruction.

The difference can be seen by comparing the following two instructions

(3a) Go into Fred's office and get me the red file folder.
(3b) Go into Fred's office and refile the red file folder.

At issue is the referent of the expression "the red file folder". In (3a), it is clearly the red file folder that the listener will find in Fred's office, a file folder whose existence the listener may previously have not been aware of. That is, (3a) leads a listener to develop the expectation that *after* they perform the initial action and go into Fred's office, they will be in a context in which it makes sense to determine the referent of "the red file folder". In contrast, given instruction (3b), it is reasonable for a listener to first try to ground "the red file folder" in the context in which the instruction is given. If successful, the listener can then go into Fred's office and refile it. If unsuccessful though, a listener will not just take the instruction to be infelicitous (as they would in the case of an instruction like "Pick up the file folder", if there were currently no file folder around). Rather they will adopt the same locational expectation as in the first example, that the red file folder is in Fred's office. What is especially interesting is the *strength* of this expectation: a cooperative agent will look around, if an object isn't where they expect it to be until they find it. This has led Moore to develop flexible procedures he calls *search plans* [41] following [39], that can be used to guide an agent in grounding both definite and indefinite referring expressions. Moore's search plans are able to incorporate expectations about the context in which a referring expression will receive its intended grounding, to limit search.

In AnimNL, Di Eugenio has attempted to derive some of these expectations through plan inference techniques described in more detail in [19,20]. In this case, the inferences are of the form: if one goes to place μ for the purpose of doing action α, then expect to do α at μ. If α has among its *applicability conditions*—conditions that must hold for α to make sense, in terms of its potential for success in the circumstances [36,44,49]—that one or more of its arguments be at its performance site μ, then a locational expectation develops as in (3a). If not, a weaker expectation arises, as in (3b). (Notice that this can even arise on the basis of a single clause: "Bring me the red file folder from downstairs" leads to a similar expectation as (3a), while "Give the man downstairs the red file folder" leads to a similar expectation as (3b). Haas [31], citing examples such as "Pick up the book behind you", points out a problem with indexical descriptions such as "the book behind you". A listener must decide whether such descriptions are to be grounded before they act—in this case, so that it makes sense to turn around to see the book in order to pick it up—or whether they must act on the description as given.)

In addition to expectations concerning the location of an object satisfying a particular description, an agent may also develop expectations concerning the particular description that needs to be satisfied. Here, an instruction like "Open the paint can" is more illustrative than "Get the book". An agent who simply seeks to ground the expression "the paint can" in its current situation may identify several objects of type "paint can". On the other hand, an agent who expects to be able to open the referent of "the paint can" will seek to ground a more specific expression such as "the closed paint can" or "the paint can that needs opening".[5]

5. Conclusion

The central theme of this special issue is "principled characterizations of agent–environment interactions". What we have tried to characterize in this short position paper are ways in which agents' understanding and use of instructions can complement what they can derive from the environment in which they act, lessons we have learned from attempting a complete vertical integration from Natural Language instructions to animated human figures. We have focussed on two attitudes that contribute to agents' behavior—their intentions and their expectations—and shown how Natural Language in the form of instructions provides a source of such attitudes in ways that complement the environment. We have also made the point that instructions can require more than one context of interpretation. Thus agents' understanding of instructions will evolve as their activity progresses. Understanding instructions is thus not a one-shot process that occurs entirely prior to activity. Language understanding is not just something that takes place "at the front end".

Acknowledgments

The authors would like to thank Brett Achorn, Breck Baldwin, Welton Becket, Moon Jung, Michael White, and Xinmin Zhao, all of whom have contributed greatly to the current version of AnimNL. We would also like to thank Phil Agre, Joseph Rosenzweig, Jeffrey Siskind, Mark Steedman, Michael White, and two anonymous reviewers for their comments on the many drafts this paper has gone through. The research has been partially supported by ARO Grant DAAL03-89-C-0031 including participation by the U.S. Army Research Laboratory (Aberdeen), Natick Laboratory, and the Institute for Simulation and Training; U.S. Air Force DEPTH contract through Hughes Missile Systems F33615-91-C-0001; DMSO through the University of Iowa; National Defense Science and Engineering Graduate Fellowship in Computer Science DAAL03-92-G-0342; NSF Grant IRI91-17110, CISE Grant CDA88-22719, and Instrumentation and

---

[5] This is similar, in some ways, to Haddock's "the rabbit in the hat" example [30] in which the phrase as a whole may refer uniquely in a context, even though neither of its component noun phrases ("the rabbit" and "the hat") do. Haddock's solution makes use of constraint satisfaction, the "in" relation constraining possible rabbit referents to ones that are in hats and possible hat referents to ones that contain rabbits.

Laboratory Improvement Program Grant USE-9152503, and DARPA grant N00014-90-J-186.

References

[1] P.E. Agre and D. Chapman, What are plans for? *Rob Autonomous Syst.* **6** (1) (1990) 17–34; also in: P. Maes, ed., *Designing Autonomous Agents* (MIT Press, Cambridge, MA, 1990); first published as: Technical Report, MIT AI Laboratory, Cambridge, MA (1989).

[2] R. Alterman, R. Zito-Wolf and T. Carpenter, Interaction, comprehension and instruction usage, *J. Learn. Sci.* **1** (4) (1991).

[3] E. André and T. Rist, The design of illustrated documents as a planning task, in: M. Maybury, ed. *Intelligent Multimedia Interfaces* (AAAI-Press, Cambridge, MA, 1993); also: DFKI RR-92-45 (1993).

[4] N. Badler, M. Hollick and G. Granieri, Real-time control of a virtual human using minimal sensors, *Presence* **2** (1) (1993) 82–86.

[5] N. Badler, C. Phillips and B. Webber, *Simulating Humans*: *Computer Graphics, Animation and Control* (Oxford University Press, New York, 1993).

[6] R. Bajcsy, Active perception, *Proc. IEEE* **76** (8) (1988) 996–1005.

[7] C.T. Balkanski, Actions, beliefs and intentions in rationale clauses and means clauses, in: *Proceedings AAAI-92*, San Jose, CA (1992).

[8] C.T. Balkanski, Actions, beliefs and intentions in multi-action utterances, Ph.D. Thesis, Harvard University, Cambridge, MA (1993).

[9] J. Bates, A.B. Loyall and W.S. Reilly, An architecture for action, emotion, and social behavior, *Proceedings 4th European Workshop on Modeling Autonomous Agents in a Multi-Agent World*, St. Martino al Cimino, Italy (1992).

[10] W. Becket and N.I. Badler, Integrated behavioral agent architecture, *Proceedings Workshop on Computer Generated Forces and Behavior Representation*, Orlando, FL (1993).

[11] R.J. Brachman, D. McGuinness, P. Patel-Schneider, L. Resnick and A. Borgida, Living with classic: when and how to use a KL-ONE-like language, in: J.F. Sowa, ed.. *Principles of Semantic Networks* (Morgan Kaufmann, San Mateo, CA, 1991) 401–457.

[12] M. Bratman, *Intentions, Plans and Practical Reason* (Harvard University Press, Cambridge, MA, 1987).

[13] M. Bratman, D. Israel and M. Pollack, Plans and resource-bounded practical reasoning, *Comput. Intell.* **4** (4) (1988) 349–355.

[14] T. Calvert, Composition of realistic animation sequences for multiple human figures, in: N. Badler, B. Barsky and D. Zeltzer, eds., *Making Them Move* (MIT Press, Cambridge, MA, 1991) 35–50.

[15] D. Chapman, *Vision, Instruction and Action* (MIT Press, Cambridge, MA, 1991).

[16] P.R. Cohen and H.J. Levesque, Persistence, intention, and commitment, in: M.P. Georgeff and A. Lansky, eds., *Reasoning about Actions and Plans, Proceedings of the 1986 Workshop* (Morgan Kaufmann, Los Altos, CA, 1986) 297–340.

[17] J. Delin, D.R. Scott and A. Hartley, Knowledge, intention, rhetoric: levels of variation in multilingual instructions, *Proceedings ACL-93 Workshop on Intentionality and Structure in Discourse Relations*, Columbus, OH (1993).

[18] B. Di Eugenio, Understanding Natural Language instructions: the case of purpose clauses, *Proceedings 30th Annual Conference of the Association for Computational Linguistics*, Newark, DE (1992).

[19] B. Di Eugenio, Understanding Natural Language instructions: a computational approach to purpose clauses, Ph.D. Thesis, University of Pennsylvania, Philadelphia, PA (1993).

[20] B. Di Eugenio and B. Webber, Plan recognition in understanding instructions, *Proceedings 1st International Conference on Artificial Intelligence Planning Systems*, College Park, MD (1992).

[21] B. Di Eugenio and M. White, On the interpretation of Natural Language instructions, *Proceedings COLING-92*, Nantes, France (1992).

[22] P. Dixon, The processing of organizational and component step information in written directions, *J. Memory Language* **26** (1) (1987) 24–35.

[23] P. Dixon, The structure of mental plans for following directions, *J. Experimental Psychol. Learn. Memory Cogn.* **13** (1) (1987) 18–26.

[24] C. Doran, Purposive "and" clauses in spoken discourse, Unpublished paper, University of Pennsylvania, Philadelphia, PA (1993).

[25] S. Feiner and K. McKeown, Automating the generation of coordinated multimedia explanations, *IEEE Comput.* **24** (10) (1991).

[26] C. Geib, Intentions in means/end planning, Technical Report MS-CIS-92-73, Department of Computer and Information Science, University of Pennsylvania, Philadelphia, PA (1992).

[27] C. Geib, A consequence on incorporating intentions in means-end planning, in: *AAAI Spring Symposium Series: Foundations of Automatic Planning: The Classical Approach and Beyond*, Working Notes, Stanford, CA (1993),

[28] C. Geib, L. Levison and M. Moore, SodaJack: an architecture for agents that search for and manipulate objects, Tech. Report MS-CIS-94-16, Department of Computer and Information Science, University of Pennsylvania, Philadelphia, PA (1994).

[29] B.J. Grosz and C. Sidner, Plans for discourse, in: P. Cohen, J. Morgan and M. Pollack, eds., *Intentions in Communication* (MIT Press, Cambridge, MA, 1990).

[30] N. Haddock, Computational models of incremental semantic interpretation, *Language Cogn. Process.* **4** (1989) 337–368.

[31] A.R. Haas, Natural language and robot planning, Technical Report, Department of Computer Science, SUNY Albany, NY (1993); also: *Comput. Intell.* (submitted).

[32] S. Huffman and J.E. Laird, Acquiring procedural knowledge through tutorial instruction, *Proceedings 1994 Workshop on Knowledge Acquisition for Knowledge-Based Systems*, Banff, Alta. (1994).

[33] D. Israel, J., Perry and S. Tutiya, Executions, motivations and accomplishments, *Philos. Rev.* (to appear).

[34] R. Karlin, Defining the semantics of verbal modifiers in the domain of cooking tasks, *Proceedings 26th Annual Meeting of the Association for Computational Linguistics*, Buffalo, NY (1988) 61–67.

[35] L. Levison and N. Badler, How animated agents perform tasks: connecting planning and motor control through object-specific reasoning, *AAAI Spring Symposium on Physical Interaction and Manipulation*, Stanford, CA (1994).

[36] D. Litman and J.F. Allen, Discourse processing and commonsense plans, in: P. Cohen, J. Morgan and M. Pollack, *Intentions in Communication* (MIT Press, Cambridge, MA, 1990) 365–388.

[37] A.B. Loyall and J. Bates, Real-time control of animated broad agents, *Proceedings 15th Annual Conference of the Cognitive Science Society*, Boulder, CO (1993) 664–669.

[38] D. McDermott, Transformational planning of reactive behavior, Research Report 941, Computer Science Department, Yale University, New Haven, CT (1992).

[39] G. Miller, E. Galanter and K. Pribram, *The Structure of Plans and Behavior* (Holt, Rinehart and Winston, New York, 1960).

[40] M. Moens and M. Steedman, Temporal ontology and temporal reference, *Comput. Linguistics* **14** (2) (1988) 15–28.

[41] M.B. Moore, Search plans, Ph.D. Dissertation Proposal, Technical Report MS-CIS-93-55, Department of Computer and Information Science, University of Pennsylvania, Philadelphia, PA (1993).

[42] M. Pollack, Inferring domain plans in question-answering, Ph.D. Thesis, Department of Computer and Information Science, Technical Report MS-CIS-86-40, University of Pennsylvania, Philadelphia, PA (1986).

[43] A. Rao and M.P. Georgeff, An abstract architecture for rational agents, *Proceedings KR-92*, Boston, MA (1992) 439–448.

[44] M. Schoppers, Universal plans of reactive robots in unpredictable environments, *Proceedings IJCAI-87*, Milan, Italy (1987).

[45] K. Schriver, Plain language through protocol-aided revision, in: E.R. Steinberg, ed., *Plain Language: Principles and Practice* (Wayne State University Press, Detroit, MI, 1991) 148–172.

[46] K. Schriver, Teaching writers to anticipate readers needs: a classroom-evaluated pedagogy, *Written Commun.* **9** (2) (1992) 179–208.

[47] C. Sidner, Using discourse to negotiate in collaborative activity: an artificial language, *Proceedings AAAI Workshop on Cooperation among Heterogeneous Agents*, San Jose, CA (1992).

[48] L.A. Suchman, *Plans and Situated Actions* (Cambridge University Press, New York, 1987).

[49] A. Tate, Generating project networks, *Proceedings IJCAI-87*, Milan, Italy (1987).

[50] S. Vere and T. Bickmore, A basic agent, *Comput. Intell.* **6** (1) (1990) 41–60.

[51] B. Webber and F. Baldwin, Accommodating context change, *Proceedings 30th Annual Conference of the Association for Computational Linguistics*, Newark, DE (1992).

[52] B. Webber and B. Di Eugenio, Free adjuncts in Natural Language instructions. *Proceedings COLING-90*, Helsinki, Finland (1990) 395–400.

[53] B. Webber, N. Badler, F. Baldwin, W. Becket, B. Di Eugenio, C. Geib, M. Jung, L. Levison, M. Moore and M. White, Doing what you're told: following task instructions in changing but hospitable environments, in: Y. Wilks and N. Okada, eds., *Language and Vision across the Pacific* (to appear); also: Technical Report MS-CIS-92-74, Department of Computer and Information Science, University of Pennsylvania, Philadelphia, PA (1992).

[54] T. Winograd, *Understanding Natural Language* (Academic Press, New York, 1972).

Artificial Intelligence 73 (1995) 271–306

Reinforcement learning of non-Markov decision processes

Steven D.Whitehead [a,*], Long-Ji Lin [b,1]

[a] *GTE Laboratories Incorporated, 40 Sylvan Road, Waltham, MA 02254, USA*
[b] *School of Computer Science, Carnegie Mellon University, Pittsburgh, PA 15213, USA*

Received September 1992; revised April 1993

Abstract

Techniques based on reinforcement learning (RL) have been used to build systems that learn to perform nontrivial sequential decision tasks. To date, most of this work has focused on learning tasks that can be described as Markov decision processes. While this formalism is useful for modeling a wide range of control problems, there are important tasks that are inherently non-Markov. We refer to these as *hidden state* tasks since they arise when information relevant to identifying the state of the environment is *hidden* (or missing) from the agent's immediate sensation. Two important types of control problems that resist Markov modeling are those in which (1) the system has a high degree of control over the information collected by its sensors (e.g., as in active vision), or (2) the system has a limited set of sensors that do not always provide adequate information about the current state of the environment. Existing RL algorithms perform unreliably on hidden state tasks.

This article examines two general approaches to extending reinforcement learning to hidden state tasks. The *Consistent Representation (CR) Method* unifies recent approaches such as the Lion algorithm, the G-algorithm, and CS-QL. The method is useful for learning tasks that require the agent to control its sensory inputs. However, it assumes that, by appropriate control of perception, the external states can be identified at each point in time from the immediate sensory inputs. A second, more general set of algorithms in which the agent maintains internal state over time is also considered. These *stored-state* algorithms, though quite different in detail, share the common feature that each derives its internal representation by combining immediate sensory inputs with internal state which is maintained over time. The relative merits of these methods are considered and conditions for their useful application are discussed.

---

* Correponding author. Fax: (617) 890-9320. E-mail: swhitehead@gte.com.

[1] Currently at Siemens Corporate Research Incorporated, 755 College Road East, Princeton, NJ 08540, USA. Fax: (609) 734-6565. E-mail: ljl@learning.scr.siemens.com.

1. Introduction

Computational theories of agent–environment interaction need to include an account of learning. Learning is necessary to develop and maintain intelligent agents. Sophisticated real-world robots cannot be achieved through meticulous programming alone. The real world is much too complex, idiosyncratic, and uncertain to know ahead of time, and programming languages are too rigid and inexpressive for programming alone to be feasible. Intelligent agents must bear at least some of the burden of skill acquisition themselves. Also, because the world does not stand still, to maintain a high level of performance, agents must learn new skills and adapt old ones to changes in the environment.

Though there are many kinds of learning, and many things that an agent might learn, in the end, all learning boils down to learning control. The value of anything learned can only be measured in terms of its effect on the agent's interaction with its environment, in terms of its ability to control the environment to a desired end.

This article focuses on reinforcement learning, a paradigm that is well suited to learning control in highly interactive environments [7, 46]. In reinforcement learning the agent–environment interaction is modeled as a controller coupled to a finite state machine (whose transition probabilities are unknown). At each time step, the controller performs an action which causes the environment to change state and generate a payoff. The agent's objective is to learn a state-dependent control policy that maximizes a measure of the total payoff received over time.

Some of the features that make reinforcement learning (RL) appealing are:

(1) RL is a weak method in that
   (a) learning occurs through trial-and-error experimentation with the environment;
   (b) the feedback used for learning takes the form of a scalar payoff—no explicit teacher, who offers the "correct answer" is required;
   (c) on sequential decision making tasks, payoffs may be sparse and considerably delayed; and
   (d) little or no prior knowledge is required.
(2) RL is incremental and can be used online.
(3) RL can be used to learn direct sensory–motor mappings, and is, thus, appropriate for highly reactive tasks in which the agent must respond quickly to unexpected events in the environment.
(4) RL is valid in nondeterministic environments.
(5) When used in conjunction with temporal difference (TD) methods [19, 44], RL has proven to be effective on difficult sequential decision making tasks (e.g., checkers [38], pole balancing [8, 30], and backgammon [49]).
(6) RL architectures are extensible. Recently, RL systems have been extended to incorporate aspects of planning [25, 45, 58], intelligent exploration [21, 23, 51], supervised learning [15, 24, 56] and hierarchical control [16, 26, 41, 62].

Traditionally, research in RL has focused on Markov decision processes (MDPs). Described formally in Section 2, a Markov decision process intuitively corresponds to a control task in which at each point in time (a) the agent directly observes the state of the environment and (b) the effects of actions depend only upon the action and the current state. In most applications, the agent does not observe the state of the environment directly, in the sense of being given a label which names the state. This assumption that the agent, at each point in time, encodes in its internal representation all the information relevant to predicting the effects of actions is known as the *Markov* assumption. It is important for two reasons. First, it has been important to the theoretical development of RL, because focusing on Markov decision processes has allowed researchers to apply the classical mathematicals of stochastic processes and dynamic programming [7,44,54,55]. Second, existing reinforcement learning methods, which use TD-methods [44], rely on the Markov property during credit assignment, and may perform badly when the assumption is violated [18,59]. Nevertheless, there are important learning control problems that are not naturally (or easily) formulated as Markov decision processes. These non-Markov tasks are commonly referred to as *hidden state tasks*, since they occur whenever it is possible for a relevant piece of information to be *hidden* (or missing) from the agent's representation of the current situation.

Hidden state tasks arise naturally in the context of autonomous learning robots. The simplest example of a hidden state task is one which occurs when the agent's sensors are inadequate for the task at hand. Suppose a robot is charged with the task of sorting blocks into bins according to their color, say Bin-1 for red, Bin-2 for blue. If the robot's sensors are unable to distinguish red from blue, then for any given block it can do no better than guess a classification. If there are an equal number of blocks of each color, then guessing can do no better than chance. On the other hand, if the robot can detect color, it can easily learn to achieve 100% performance. The former case corresponds to a non-Markov decision problem, since relevant information is missing from the agent's representation. The latter case is Markov since once a color sense is available the information needed to achieve optimal performance is always available. In general, if a robot's internal representation is defined only by its immediate sensor readings, and if there are circumstances in which the sensors do not provide all the information needed to uniquely identify the state of the environment with respect to the task, then the decision problem is non-Markov.

Hidden state tasks are also a natural consequence of integrating learning with active/selective perception [60]. In active perception, the agent has a degree of control over the allocation of its sensory resources (e.g., controlling visual attention or selecting visual processing modules) [3,5,6]. This control is used to sense the environment in an efficient, task-specific way. However, if control is not properly maintained then the data generated by the sensors may fail to code a relevant piece of information, and the resultant internal representation may be ambiguous with respect to the current state of the environment. It follows that if the agent must learn to control its sensors, there will be periods of time when the internal representation will be inadequate. Therefore the decision task will be non-Markov.

Techniques for applying reinforcement learning to non-Markov decision processes is the central focus of this article. We describe a generalized technique called the *Consistent Representation (CR) Method* that can be used to learn control in systems with active perception [57]. The principal idea underlying the CR-method is to split control into two phases, a perceptual phase and an overt phase. During the perceptual phase, the system performs sensing (or sensor configuration) actions in order to generate an adequate (i.e., Markov) representation of the current external environment. During the overt stage, this representation is used to select overt action; that is, an action that changes the state of the external environment. Systems using the consistent representation method learn not only the overt actions needed to perform a task, but also the perceptual actions needed to construct an adequate, task-specific representation of the environment. Although, the CR-method unifies such recent algorithms as the Lion algorithm [60], CS-QL [48], and the G-algorithm [13], it is restricted to tasks in which the agent can always identify the current state of the environment through proper control of its sensors. It is not appropriate for tasks in which the agent must store state information over time, or remember previous events in order to infer the current state.

To overcome this restriction, several, more general approaches are considered that retain state information over time. We refer to these as *stored-state methods*. The simplest of these approaches is one which augments immediate sensory inputs with a delay line to achieve a crude form of short term memory [25]. This approach has been successful in certain speech recognition tasks [53]. Another alternative is called the method of *predictive distinctions* [4, 14, 25, 39]. Following this approach, the system learns a predictive model of the sensory inputs (i.e., environmental observables) and then uses the internal state of this model to drive action selection. A third approach uses a recurrent neural network in combination with existing reinforcement learning methods to learn a recurrent state-dependent control policy directly [28]. Each of these methods is described in detail and conditions for their useful application are considered.

The remainder of the article is organized as follows. Section 2 provides a basic review of concepts from reinforcement learning. Section 3 discusses non-Markov decision processes and considers the difficulties they cause for learning control. Section 4 presents the Consistent Representation Method as a technique for learning to control perception and reviews examples of this technique. Section 5 describes and compares three stored-state methods and specifies preference conditions for each. Section 6 discusses all of these methods in the broader context of scalability and conclusions are drawn in Section 7.

2. Review of reinforcement learning

In this section the basic concepts from reinforcement learning are reviewed. We begin by describing a simple model of agent–environment interaction. Next, we review the principles of Markov decision processes and Q-learning [54], a popular reinforcement learning algorithm. A thorough review of Markov decision processes and reinforcement learning, however, is beyond the scope of this article. Throughout the article, we shall focus primarily on Q-learning and the difficulties caused for it by non-Markov decision processes. Other algorithms [8, 19, 44, 63] suffer a similar fate. For a more complete review of Markov decision processes and Q-learning, the reader may wish to consult [10] and [54]. For a review of reinforcement learning in general, see [7].

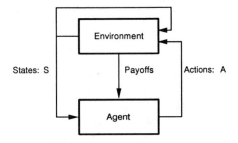

Fig. 1. A simple model of agent–environment interaction.

2.1. Modeling agent–environment interaction

Fig. 1 illustrates a model of agent–environment interaction that is widely used in reinforcement learning. In this model the agent and the environment are represented by two synchronized finite state automatons interacting in a discrete time cyclical process. At each time point, the following sequence of events occurs.
(1) The agent senses the state of the environment.
(2) Based on this current state, the agent chooses an action to perform.
(3) Based on the current state and the action selected by the agent, the environment makes a transition to a new state and generates a payoff.
(4) The payoff is passed back to the agent.

2.1.1. The environment

The environment is modeled as a Markov decision process. Formally, a Markov decision process is described by the tuple (S, A, T, R), where S is the set of possible states, A is the set of possible actions, T is the *state transition function*, and R is the *reward function*. At each time, the environment occupies exactly one state from S, and accepts one action from A. S and A are usually assumed to be discrete and finite. State transitions are modeled by the transition function, T, which maps state–action pairs into new states $(T : S \times A \rightarrow S)$. The transition function is in general probabilistic, and typically specified in terms of a set of *transition probabilities*, $P_{x,y}(a)$, where

$$P_{x,y}(a) = Prob(T(x, a) = y). \tag{1}$$

Payoffs generated by the environment are determined by a reward function, R, which maps state–action pairs into scalar-valued rewards $(R : S \times A \rightarrow \mathbb{R})$. The reward function may also be probabilistic.

Notice that in a Markov decision process (MDP), the effects of actions (i.e., the next state and the immediate reward generated) depend only upon the current state. Process models of this type are said to be memoryless and to satisfy the *Markov property*. The Markov property is fundamental to this model of the environment because it implies that knowledge of the current state is always sufficient for optimal control (i.e., to maximize the reward received over time) [10]. Thus, even though it may be possible to devise action-selection strategies whose decisions depend upon additional information (e.g., a history trace), these strategies cannot possibly outperform the best decision strategies that depend only upon knowledge of the current state.

2.1.2. The agent

The agent is responsible for generating control actions. At each time step it senses the current state, selects an action, and observes the new state and reward that result. Rewards are used as feedback for learning.

One way to specify an agent's behavior is in terms of a control *policy*, which prescribes, for each state, an action to perform. Formally, a policy f is a function from states to actions ($f : S \rightarrow A$), where $f(x)$ denotes the action to be performed in state x.

In reinforcement learning, the agent's objective is to learn a control policy that maximizes some measure of the total reward accumulated over time. In principle, any number of reward measures can be used, however, the most prevalent measure is one based on a discounted sum of the reward received over time. This sum is called the *return* and is defined for time t as

$$ return(t) = \sum_{n=0}^{\infty} \gamma^n r_{t+n}, \tag{2} $$

where γ, called the *temporal discount factor*, is a constant between 0 and 1, and r_{t+n} is the reward received at time $t + n$. Because the process may be stochastic, the agent's objective is to find a policy that maximizes the *expected return*.

For a fixed policy f, define $V_f(x)$, the *value function* for policy f, to be the expected return, given that the process begins in state x and follows policy f thereafter. The agent's objective is to find a policy, f^*, that is uniformly best for all possible states. That is, find f^*, such that

$$ V_{f^*}(x) = \max_f V_f(x) \quad \forall x \in S. \tag{3} $$

An important property of MDPs is that f^* is well defined and guaranteed to exist. In particular, the *Optimality Theorem* from dynamic programming [9] guarantees that for a discrete time, discrete state Markov decision process there always exists a deterministic policy that is optimal. Furthermore, a policy f is optimal if and only if it satisfies the following relationship:

$$ Q_f(x, f(x)) = \max_{a \in A}(Q_f(x, a)) \quad \forall x \in S \tag{4} $$

where $Q_f(x, a)$, the *action-value function*, is defined to be the expected return given that the agent starts in state x, applies action a once, and follows policy f thereafter [9, 10]. Intuitively, Eq. (4) states that a policy is optimal if and only if in each state, the policy specifies an action that maximizes the local "action-value". That is,

$$ f^*(x) = a \text{ such that } Q_{f^*}(x, a) = \max_{b \in A}[Q_{f^*}(x, b)] \quad \forall x \in S, \tag{5} $$

and

$$ V_{f^*}(x) = \max_{a \in A}[Q_{f^*}(x, a)] \quad \forall x \in S. \tag{6} $$

$Q \leftarrow$ a set of initial values for the action-value function (e.g., uniformly zero)
Repeat forever:
    1) $x \leftarrow$ the current state.
    2) Select an action a to execute that is usually consistent with $f(x)$
        but occasionally an alternate.
    3) Execute action a, and let y be the next state and r be the reward
        received.
    4) Update $Q(x,a)$:
$$Q(x,a) \leftarrow (1-\alpha)Q(x,a) + \alpha[r + \gamma U(y)]$$
        where $U(y) = Q(y, f(y))$.
Here for each $x \in S$: $f(x) \leftarrow a$ such that $Q(x,a) = \max_{b \in A} Q(x,b)$.

Fig. 2. A simple version of the one-step Q-learning algorithm.

For a given MDP, the set of action-values for which Eq. (4) holds is unique. These values are said to define the optimal action-value function Q^* for the MDP.

If an MDP is completely known (including the transition probabilities and reward distributions), then the optimal policy can be computed directly using techniques from dynamic programming [9, 10, 36]. However, in many cases, the structure and dynamics of the environment are *not* known. Under these circumstances the agent cannot compute the optimal policy directly, but must explore its environment and learn an effective control policy by trial-and-error.

2.2. Q-learning

Q-learning [54] is an incremental reinforcement learning method. It is a good representative for reinforcement learning because it is simple, mathematically well founded, and widely used. For our purposes Q-learning is useful for illustrating the difficulties caused by non-Markov decision problems. Also, because other reinforcement learning algorithms use similar credit assignment techniques (namely TD-methods [44]), an understanding of the difficulties for Q-learning is useful for understanding weaknesses of other algorithms.

In Q-learning the agent estimates the optimal action-value function (also called the Q-function) directly and uses it to derive a control policy using the greedy strategy mandated by Eq. (5). A simple Q-learning algorithm is shown in Fig. 2. The first step of the algorithm is to initialize the agent's action-value function, Q. Q is the agent's *estimate* of the optimal action-value function. If prior knowledge about the task is available, that information may be encoded in the initial values, otherwise the initial values can be arbitrary (e.g., uniformly zero). After initialization, the agent enters the main control/learning loop. The first step is to sense the current state, x. Next, the agent selects an action a to execute. Most of the time, this action will be the action specified by its policy $f(x)$ as defined by Eq. (5), but for the purposes of exploration the agent will occasionally choose an action that appears sub-optimal. For example, one might choose to follow f with probability p and choose a random action otherwise. [2] The agent executes the selected action and notes the reward r and state y that result. Finally, the action-value estimate for state–action pair (x, a) is updated. In particular, an estimate for $Q^*(x, a)$ is obtained by combining the immediate reward r with a utility estimate for the next state, $U(y) = \max_{b \in A} [Q(y, b)]$. The sum

$$r + \gamma U(y), \tag{7}$$

called a one-step corrected estimator, is an unbiased estimator for $Q^*(x, a)$ when $Q = Q^*$, since, by definition

$$Q^*(x, a) = E[R(x, a) + \gamma V^*(T(x, a))], \tag{8}$$

where $V^*(x) = \max_{a \in A} Q^*(x, a)$. The one-step estimate is combined with the old estimate for $Q(x, a)$ using a weighted sum:

$$Q(x, a) \leftarrow (1 - \alpha) Q(x, a) + \alpha[r + \gamma U(y)], \tag{9}$$

where α is the learning rate. Q-learning is guaranteed to converge to an optimal policy for any finite Markov decision process if, in the limit, every state–action pair is tried infinitely often and if the learning rate decreases according to a proper schedule [55].

3. Non-Markov tasks

To see how non-Markov decision tasks arise in agent–environment interactions, one need only make a distinction between an abstract (agent-independent) specification for a task and the actual decision problem faced by a learning agent. We shall refer to these as the *external* and the *internal* decision problems, respectively, since the former is agent-independent and exists outside the agent, while the latter is endogenous and agent-specific.

3.1. An example

To illustrate the distinction, consider the task of inspecting apples in a packaging plant. Suppose apples are to be sorted according to whether or not they are ripe. Ripe apples are shipped to the supermarket, green apples are crushed for their juice. If apples come down a conveyor one at a time, then a Markov decision process model of the task might be formulated as follows. We could define a state variable called ripeness to characterize the current apple as either "ripe" or "green"—this state variable would induce a state space of size 2. The model could have two actions, which would be to either "accept" or "reject" an apple. A reward function could be defined to give a unit of reward whenever a ripe apple was accepted and a green apple was rejected, and a unit of penalty otherwise. A transition function could be defined to model the dynamics

---

[2] Occasionally choosing an action at random is a particularly simple mechanism for exploring the environment. Exploration is necessary to guarantee that the agent will eventually learn an optimal policy. For examples of more sophisticated exploration strategies, see [21,45,51].

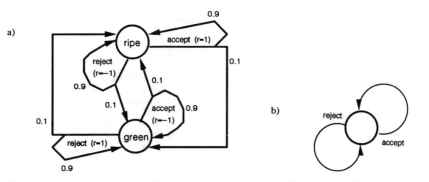

Fig. 3. The apple sorting example. (a) An abstract (external) model of the task. (b) The actual (internal) task facing a robot with no sensors.

of the apple sequence. If the types of apples coming down the conveyor are temporally dependent, as might be the case if apples were loaded into the hopper in crates from different orchards, then nonuniform transition probabilities could be used to model this dependence. For example, we might assume that the next apple down the conveyor will be the same type as the last one with probability 0.9, and different with probability 0.1.

This process model, illustrated in Fig. 3(a), corresponds to a specification of the task. It is a mathematical abstraction. The states, actions, rewards, and transitions exist in the mind of the modeler, and are intended to capture the essence of the environment and the task requirements. It makes no explicit reference to the physical agent that might perform the task. It defines the *external* decision problem.

Conversely, consider the decision problem facing a control system embedded inside a robot's head. For simplicity, consider a robot that has a single binary sensor $S1$ that it uses to represent its environment, and a single binary actuator $A1$ that it uses to affect action. In a totally situated agent, the sensors and affectors determine the basic structure of the internal decision problem: two states: $S1 = 0, S1 = 1$; and two actions: $A1 = 0, A1 = 1$. The transition and reward dynamics of this internal process are determined not only by the dynamics of the external environment, but also by the physics of the sensory–motor interface. For example, if the robot's sensor is able to detect the color of the apple on the conveyor (say, red or green), and if its affector is a lever that can be used to select apples then the internal decision process may closely match the external task (assuming red apples are "ripe" and green apples are "green"). On the other hand, if the agent's sensor or affector is not closely matched (e.g., say the sensor detects bruises), then the internal problem may bear little resemblance to the external one.

3.2. Accounting for perceptual–motor processes

The distinction between external and internal decision tasks can be incorporated into our model of agent–environment interaction by augmenting Fig. 1 to explicitly account for the mappings performed by the agent's perceptual–motor processes. The new model is shown in Fig. 4. On the sensory side the agent's perceptual processes map states in

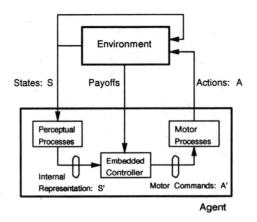

Fig. 4. A model of agent–environment interaction that explicitly accounts for the agent's perceptual–motor processes. Perceptual processes map states from the external world model onto internal representations. Motor processes map internal motor commands onto actions in the external world model.

the external world onto states in the agent's internal representation. On the motor side, the agent's motor processes map internal motor commands to actions in the external task model. [3] In general, these mappings could be of considerable complexity. A perceptual mapping might involve immediate precepts, attentional mechanisms, and stored history information; and a motor mapping might involve complex motor sequences or parallel actions. For the purposes of the present discussion we shall restrict consideration to simple mappings only. Indeed, for the remainder of the article, we will concentrate only on sensory mappings and assume that there is a one-to-one mapping between motor commands and external actions. We also assume reward is passed directly to the embedded controller. That is, whenever a situation arises in the world that would generate a reward in the external model, that reward is correctly passed to the embedded controller.

3.3. Non-Markov internal tasks

Formally, a decision task is non-Markov if information above and beyond knowledge of the current state can be used to better predict the dynamics of the process and improve control. [4]

In general, an agent's internal decision problem will be non-Markov if there are internal states that can represent multiple external states. We call this phenomenon *perceptual aliasing* since it occurs when two or more external states, through the perceptual

---

[3] Notice that these mappings are conceptual more than physical, in that they run through the world and then into the external (abstract) task model. For example, a state in the agent's internal representation may represent certain situations in the physical universe, which (via the modeling process) get mapped into states in the external task model.

[4] Strictly speaking, this definition is slightly overstated. Traditionally a process is said to be non-Markov if information about the *history* of the process (in addition to its current state) can be used to improve prediction and control. However, because we are dealing with systems that have the potential to collect additional information through sensing we have chosen to adopt a definition that is slightly more general.

mapping, get superimposed onto a single internal state. Intuitively, perceptual aliasing occurs when the agent is uncertain about the state of the external world. For example, in a situated agent, it occurs when the agent's sensors fail to code a relevant piece of information. Perceptual aliasing results in non-Markov decision tasks because, by definition, there are states in the internal representation that do not code all the information needed to characterize the future dynamics of the task.

Returning to our apple sorting robot, suppose the robot's color sensor is temporarily disconnected (i.e., always made to read zero). In this case, the robot is unable to distinguish apples by their color and the internal representation collapses to a single state, (see Fig. 3(b)). Clearly, this decision problem is non-Markov since (1) knowledge of the current apple's color could be used to improve the systems performance—without its sensor, the robot is reduced to guessing; and (2) knowledge of the recent history of the process could be used to improve performance. For example, knowledge that the last action resulted in a positive reward could be exploited to yield a control policy that performs better than chance. This follows since according to the external model, 90 percent of the time the current apple is the same type as the previous one.

3.3.1. The ubiquity of non-Markov tasks

Markov decision tasks are an ideal. Non-Markov tasks are the norm. They are as ubiquitous as uncertainty itself. An agent that can be uncertain about the state of the external task necessarily faces an internal decision problem that is non-Markov. And sources of uncertainty abound. Sensors have physical limitations. Rarely are they perfectly matched to the task. Sensor data are typically noisy, unreliable, and full of spurious information. Sensors have limited range, and relevant objects are often occluded. Also, information can be hidden in time. The spoken word is transient and lost unless it is actively processed and stored. Short term memory too is limited and subject to deterioration. Lin [28] provides a good example:

> Consider a packing task which involves 4 steps: open a box, put a gift into it, close it, and seal it. An agent driven only by its current visual precepts cannot accomplish this task, because when facing a closed box the agent does not know if the gift is already in the box and therefore cannot decide whether to seal or open the box.

In this case occlusion of the gift by the lid prevents immediate perception of a vital piece of information. Such hidden state tasks also arise when temporal features (such as velocity and acceleration) are important for optimal control, but not included in the system's primitive sensor set.

Even if perfect sensors were available, many control problems are too ambiguous or ill-posed to specify a state space in advance. Indeed, part of the agent's task may be to discover a useful state space for the problem. For example, integrating learning and active perception invariably leads to non-Markov decision tasks [57]. Active perception refers to the idea that an intelligent agent should actively control its sensors in order to sense and represent only information that is relevant to its immediate ongoing activity [1,3,5,6,12,52]. If an agent must, as part of the task, learn to control its sensors, its internal control problem will necessarily be non-Markov. This follows since during learning there will be periods of time when the agent will improperly control its sensors, fail to attend to a relevant piece of information, and fail to unambiguously identify the state of the external task.

3.4. Effects on control

The level of performance that can be obtained by an agent whose internal decision problem is non-Markov is generally inferior to that of its Markov counterpart. That is, a non-Markov decision problem usually leads to sub-optimal control if the agent mistakenly assumes the problem is Markov. This can be seen in the apple sorting task, where the robot with its color sensor intact can achieve perfect classification, but the robot without the sensor (and no memory) can perform no better than chance. Notice that the degree of performance degradation depends on the problem. For example, if 95% of the apples are ripe, then a blind policy that "accepted" every apple would fail only 5% of the time. On the other hand, perceptual aliasing can lead to non-Markov decision tasks whose best fixed policies are arbitrarily bad. [5]

3.5. Difficulties for reinforcement learning

The straightforward application of traditional reinforcement learning methods to non-Markov decision problems in many cases yields sub-optimal control and in some cases severely degraded performance. These difficulties stem from the agent's inability to obtain accurate estimates of the utility and action-values for the underlying decision process. In particular, because of perceptual aliasing, there are states in the agent's internal representation that represent two or more distinct states in the external world model. The utility and action-value estimates learned by the agent for these non-Markov internal states tend to reflect a mix (or average) of the values for the external states they represent. Because of this averaging, it is inevitable that the agent's internal utility and action-value estimates will be erroneous for some situations. These errors, in turn, may result in the selection of sub-optimal actions for the non-Markov states, as the agent may inaccurately perceive a sub-optimal action to be of higher value than the true optimal action, or the agent may incorrectly degrade the value of the optimal action.

Unfortunately these difficulties are compounded by use of temporal difference methods [44] which cause errors to propagate throughout the state space, thus infecting action selection even for non-aliased states. In particular, most reinforcement learning algorithms employ utility (action-value) estimators that combine values for recently observed rewards with utility estimates for subsequent states—in one-step Q-learning, action-value estimates are obtained by adding the immediate reward with a utility estimate for the next state (cf. Eq. (7)). Thus, for a given state if the agent constructs estimators that use utility estimates from non-Markov states, those estimators will likely

---

[5] This is significant because most reinforcement learning algorithms aim to learn fixed policies. Opening the door to probabilistic policies could improve performance under these circumstances.

be erroneous and the error will be propagated to that state. Once infected a state may propagate its error to other states in a similar manner.

4. Consistent representation methods

In the last few years several RL algorithms have been developed to deal with selective perception. The Lion algorithm [60] learns to control visual attention in a primitive deictic sensory–motor system; the CS-QL algorithm [48] learns efficient, task-specific sensing operations; and the G-algorithm [13] learns to extract task-relevant bits from a large input vector. [6] In this section, we review these algorithms in turn. We then present the *Consistent Representation Method*, a computational framework that unifies these different algorithms [62].

4.1. The Lion algorithm

The Lion algorithm was perhaps the first reinforcement learning algorithm specifically designed to address an adaptive perception task [59]. It was used to learn a simple manipulation task in a modified Blocks World. The distinguishing feature of this task is that the agent is equipped with a controllable sensory system that provides it with only partial access to the environment. To learn the task, the agent must learn to focus its visual attention on relevant objects and select appropriate motor commands. The details of the task are as follows.

4.1.1. The block-stacking task

The learning task is organized into a sequence of trails. On each trial, the agent is presented with a pile of blocks. A pile consists of a random number of blocks (ranging from 1 to 50) arranged in arbitrary stacks. Blocks are distinguishable only by color; they may be red, green, or blue. Each pile contains a single green block. The agent's goal is simply to pick up the green block as quickly as possible. If the robot achieves the goal before the trial's time limit expires, it receives a fixed positive reward, otherwise it receives no reward. The dynamics of the environment are such that a block can be grasped only when it is uncovered and the agent's hand is empty. Thus in some cases it is necessary to unstack blocks to reach the goal. In this task the effects of block manipulating actions are completely deterministic.

What differentiates this task from other Block World problems (and other reinforcement learning tasks) is the agent's sensory–motor system. Instead of assuming a sensory system that provides a complete and objective description of every object in the scene, the system is equipped with a deictic sensory–motor system which provides the controller with an ability to flexibly access a limited amount of information about the scene at a time [1]. In a deictic sensory–motor system, selective perception is implemented using

---

[6] Note that these methods differ from supervised feature selection methods [35] that rely on the presentation of preclassified samples. The algorithms presented here operate without explicit supervision in the context of an embedded reinforcement learning task.

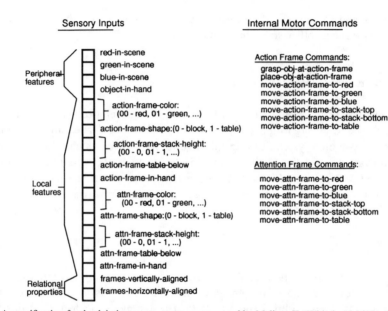

Fig. 5. A specification for the deictic sensory–motor system used by Meliora-II (Whitehead [60]). The system has two markers, an *action-frame* marker and an *attention-frame* marker. The system has a 20-bit input vector, 8 overt actions, and 6 perceptual actions. The values registered in the input vector and the effects of internal action commands depend upon the bindings between markers in the sensory–motor system and objects in the environment.

markers [1, 52]. Conceptually, a marker corresponds to a focus of attention. In practice, markers are used to establish frames of reference for both perception and action. On the sensory side, placing a marker on an object in the environment brings information about that object into view (i.e., into the internal representation). On the motor side, marker placement is used to select targets for overt manipulation. A specification for the sensory–motor system used by the agent is given in Fig. 5. This system employs two markers: the action-frame marker and the attention-frame marker, respectively. On the sensory side, the system generates a 20-bit input vector at each point in time. Most of these bits represent local, marker-specific information, such as the color and shape of a marker's bound object. Other bits detect relational properties such as vertical and horizontal alignment, while others detect spatially non-specific properties such as the presence or absence of red in the scene. By moving markers from object to object the agent can multiplex a wide range of information onto its relatively small input register.

Listed on the right-hand side of Fig. 5 are the internal motor commands supported by the sensory–motor system. These commands are partitioned into two groups: those related to the action-frame marker and those related to the attention-frame marker. Both groups contain commands for controlling marker placement. These actions index objects by their primitive features (e.g., color) or by spatial relationship (e.g., top-of-stack). The action-frame marker has additional commands that are used for manipulating blocks. The "grasp-object-at-action-frame" command causes the system to grasp (if possible) the object marked by the action-frame marker. Similarly, the "place-object-at-action-

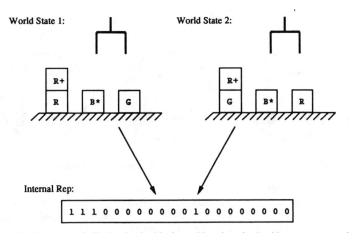

Fig. 6. An example of perceptual aliasing in the block-stacking domain. In this case, two world states with different utilities and optimal actions generate the same internal representation. The "*" indicates the location of the attention-frame marker; the "+" the location of the action-frame.

frame" command causes the system to place a held object at the location marked by the action-frame.

The decision problem facing the agent's embedded controller is non-Markov since improper placement of the system's markers fails to multiplex relevant information onto the agent's internal representation. This point is illustrated in Fig. 6 which shows two different external world states (each corresponding to a different state in a Markov model of the task) that, because of an improper placement of markers, generate the same internal representation.

4.1.2. Control

To tackle this non-Markov decision problem, the Lion algorithm adopts an approach which attempts to select overt (manipulative) actions based only on the action-values of internal states that are unaliased (Markov). To accomplish this, the Lion algorithm breaks control into two stages. At the beginning of each control cycle a perceptual stage is performed. During the perceptual stage, a sequence of commands for moving the attention-frame marker is executed. These so-called "perceptual actions" cause a sequence of input vectors to appear in the input register. These values are temporarily buffered in a short term memory. Since perceptual actions do not change the state of the external environment, each buffered input corresponds to a representation of the current external state. If the perceptual actions are selected with care one of these internal states will be Markov (i.e., will encode all information relevant to determining the optimal action). Once the perceptual stage is completed, the overt stage begins. During the overt stage an action for changing the state of the external environment is selected. These so-called "overt actions" correspond to commands for the action-frame marker.[7] To guide

---

[7] Notice that moving the action-frame marker from one object to another changes the state of the external environment since it changes the set of objects that can be effected by the grasp and place commands.

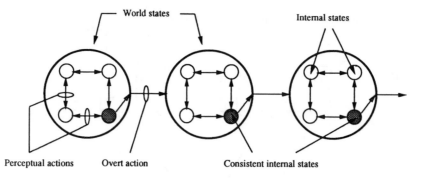

Fig. 7. A graphical depiction of the Lion algorithm. The large (super) graph depicts the overt control cycle, where large nodes correspond to world states and arcs correspond to overt actions. The subgraphs embedded within each large node depict perceptual cycles, with nodes corresponding to internal representations of the current world state and arcs corresponding to perceptual actions.

selection of an overt action, the Lion algorithm maintains a special action-value function which is defined over internal-state, overt-action pairs. This overt action-value function is special in that the action-values for perceptually aliased states are suppressed (i.e., ideally they are equal to zero), whereas the action-values for unaliased states are allowed to take on their nominal values. Given this action-value function, the Lion algorithm, during the overt stage, selects an overt action by simply examining the action-values of each buffered internal state and choosing the action with the maximum action-value. Since aliased states tend to have suppressed action-values, the selected action tends to correspond to the optimal action from a unaliased internal state. Fig. 7 illustrates this two-stage control cycle graphically.

4.1.3. Learning

A special learning rule is used to learn the overt action-value function. The learning procedure operates as follows. First, the internal state with the maximal action-value is identified as the *Lion*. The action-value for this state is updated according to the standard rule for one-step Q-learning (i.e., Eq. (9)). Next, the error term in the updating rule for the Lion state is used to update the action-values for the remaining buffered states. This is done so that once an accurate action-value is learned for an unaliased state, further changes in the action-values for aliased states cease. Finally, each buffered state is tested to see if it is aliased. If a state tests positive, its action-value is reset to zero.

A very simple procedure is used to identify potentially aliased states. The rule simply examines the sign of the error term in the one-step Q-learning rule (that is, the sign of the difference between a state's current action-value and the action-value estimate constructed after a one-step delay). If all action-values are initially set to zero, the task is deterministic, and rewards are nonnegative, then aliased states tend to regularly overestimate their action-values (i.e., show a negative error). Unaliased states, on the other hand, tend to monotonically approach the optimal action-value from below (i.e., positive error only). Therefore, aliased states can be detected by monitoring the sign in the estimation error.[8]

The learning rule for the perceptual stage is much simpler. For perceptual control a *perceptual action-value function* is estimated over internal-state, perceptual-action pairs. During the perceptual stage, actions are selected by choosing the perceptual action that maximizes the action-value for the current input bit vector (internal state). The perceptual action-value function is updated within the perceptual stage, using the standard one-step Q-learning rule except that the overt utility of the internal state is also accounted for. Since aliased states tend to have suppressed overt action-values, perceptual actions that lead to unaliased internal states tend to have higher action-values than those that do not. (See [57] for further details.)

4.1.4. Discussion

The Lion algorithm is able to learn the block manipulation task described above. It learns a perceptual control strategy that focuses the attention-frame marker on the green block, and learns an overt control policy that moves the action-frame marker as needed to unstack covering blocks. Detailed experimental results can be found in [57].

The Lion algorithm exploits several assumptions in order to deal with non-Markov decision problems. These limiting assumptions are:

(1) The effects of actions must be deterministic.
(2) Only nonnegative rewards are allowed.
(3) For each external state, there must exist at least one configuration of the sensory system that generates an internal state that is unaliased.

4.2. CS-QL

There is much work in machine learning that focuses upon the predictive power of information, but fails to account for its cost [2, 35]. Tan recognized that to be efficient it is necessary to explicitly account for the cost of sensing. In [48], he develops two cost-sensitive learning algorithms for classification tasks: CS-ID3 and CS-IBL, respectively. CS-QL, which stands for Cost-Sensitive Q-Learning, resulted when he combined ideas for cost-sensitive learning with reinforcement learning [47]. In CS-QL, the learning agent not only learns the overt actions needed to perform a task, but also learns an efficient procedure for identifying the current state of the environment.

CS-QL and the Lion algorithm share the same basic control cycle. That is, in CS-QL control is decomposed into a two-stage process of sensing (perceptual control) and action (overt control). However, the sensing model used in CS-QL is considerably different. Instead of using a deictic sensory–motor system, CS-QL adopts a sensing model in which the agent has a set of primitive sensing tests. Each test provides a specific piece of information about the external environment. Also, instead of learning a perceptual control policy, as in the Lion algorithm, CS-QL constructs a classification tree,

---

[8] Subtle interactions sometimes cause unaliased states to overestimate their action-values. This sometimes leads to suppression of unaliased states. However these states tend to bounce back from such suppressions and eventually stabilize. For a detailed discussion of this technique for detecting aliased states, see [57] and [48].

where each internal node corresponds to a sensing operation, each branch corresponds to a test result, and each leaf corresponds to a state in the agent's internal representation (for example, see Fig. 8). In CS-QL, the agent has learned an adequate classification tree when every leaf in the tree is unaliased; that is, when each leaf represents a unique state in a Markov model of the task.

The classification tree is learned incrementally. Initially, the tree consists of a single root node. In other words, the entire external state space is collapsed onto a single internal state. As aliased leaves are detected, they are expanded (converted to internal nodes) by attaching sensing operations to them. The new leaf nodes that result introduce new distinctions into the representations. The tree is expanded until a Markov representation is achieved.

When expanding a node, CS-QL simply selects the least expensive sensing operation, among those that remain, to attach to the target leaf. This heuristic favoring low-cost tests tends to explore inexpensive sensing procedures first, but may not always generate the most efficient trees. By incorporating a more sophisticated selection method that accounts for both cost and the discriminatory power of each sensing test (see the G-algorithm below), more efficient classification trees should result. To detect aliased leafs, CS-QL uses the same technique employed by the Lion algorithm. Thus, CS-QL shares the same limitations as the Lion algorithm.

CS-QL has been successfully demonstrated in a simulated robot navigation task in which the robot must learn to deduce its position from limited information gathered from its selective sensors. One very simple instance of this type of navigation task, along with a classification tree learned by CS-QL, is shown in Fig. 8. In this example, the robot's sensing operations allow it to detect properties (e.g., empty, barrier, cup) of nearby cells in the maze. The cost of sensing a cell is proportional to its distance from the robot. By accumulating features from nearby cells the robot can successfully (and efficiently) identify its position within the maze.

4.3. The G-algorithm

The G-algorithm is a third technique developed to address a kind of adaptive perception task. However, unlike the Lion algorithm and CS-QL, its development was not specifically motivated by the desire to minimize the cost of sensing or by the need to control an active sensory system. Instead, the G-algorithm was developed to mitigate problems caused by the availability of too much information. In particular, when Chapman and Kaelbling [13] tried to apply Q-learning to learn a simple align-and-shoot subtask in the context of a more general video-game domain (called Amazon), they found that their learning system was being overwhelmed by the sheer volume of information generated by the sensors. The subtask they were studying involved aligning the agent with a target, orienting to it, and firing a weapon. At each point in time, the agent's sensory system generated 100 bits of input. Using all this information resulted in an internal state space containing 2^{100} states. Most of these bits, however, were irrelevant to *the* specific subtask they were studying and just interfere with learning by introducing unnecessary distinctions in the internal representation. On the other hand, the bits that are specifically relevant are not necessarily known ahead of time and at

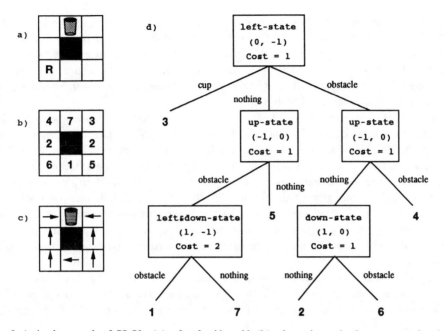

Fig. 8. A simple example of CS-QL: (a) a 3 × 3 grid world, (b) a learned mapping between state descriptions and states, (c) a learned optimal decision policy, and (d) a learned cost-sensitive classification tree. (Reproduced with permission.)

other stages of the game, the bits that were irrelevant "now" were vitally important "then". The G-algorithm was developed to learn a control policy which could generalize over irrelevant information in the input.

The G-algorithm works by identifying bits in the input vector that are important for control. It is very similar to CS-QL in that both grow classification trees incrementally. That is, both start with a single root node (i.e., assuming no information is relevant), then construct a tree-structured classification circuit by recursively splitting nodes based on the values of sensory inputs. In CS-QL, the information used to split nodes in the tree corresponds to the results of sensing acts (or tests), in the G-algorithm nodes are split based on the values of bits in the input. As in CS-QL, the leaves of the G-algorithm's tree define the agent's internal state space. Unlike CS-QL, the G-algorithm does not associate a cost with sensing/reading a bit.

What sets the G-algorithm apart from both CS-QL and the Lion algorithm, is the method it uses to detect non-Markov (aliased) internal states. CS-QL and the Lion algorithm both monitor the sign in estimation error to detect non-Markov states; a method that is limited to deterministic tasks only. The G-algorithm uses a much more general statistical test. In general, a leaf in the classification tree is non-Markov if it can be shown that there are bits in the input vector (that have not already been tested in traversing the tree from root-to-leaf) that are statistically relevant to predicting future rewards. To detect if a leaf is non-Markov, the G-algorithm uses the Student's T-test [42] to find statistically significant bits. That is, over time as the agent experiences a variety of external states, reward data is collected and stored for each leaf, target-bit pair. Data for a given leaf is separated into one of two bins. One bin corresponds to situations when the target bit is on; the other when the bit is off. Given these two sets of data, a Student's T-test is used to determine how probable it is that distinct distributions gave rise to them. If after sufficient sampling, this estimate is above a threshold, the bit is deemed relevant and the leaf is split.

The insight provided by the G-algorithm is to use statistical methods to test bit relevance (and consequently detect non-Markov states). The specific algorithm is limited in that the T-test assumes that the reward distributions being compared are Gaussian. This is clearly not the case in general, since reward distributions can be arbitrary. However, this problem can be mitigated by comparing distributions of *cumulative* rewards. Also, the G-algorithm is not guaranteed to detect bits that are relevant in higher order pairings. A bit's relevance must be apparent in isolation. Finally, additional memory and sensing is required to gather statistics for relevance testing. Nevertheless these difficulties and limitations seem to be a minor price to pay for a method that extends to stochastic domains.

The G-algorithm was successfully demonstrated on the orient-and-shoot task. It was found to significantly outperform an alternative approach that used error backpropagation in a neural network. See [13] for details and a discussion of some difficulties they did encounter.

4.4. The Consistent Representation Method

While the algorithms described above vary considerably in their detail, they share the same basic approach. We refer to this common framework as the *Consistent Representation (CR) Method*.[9] The key features of the CR-method are:

(1) At each time step, control is partitioned into two stages: a perceptual stage followed by an action (or overt) stage.

(2) The perceptual stage aims to generate an internal representation that is Markov.

(3) The action stage aims to generate optimal overt actions.

(4) Learning occurs in both control stages. For the action stage, traditional reinforcement learning techniques are used. These techniques impose a Markov constraint on the internal state space. This constraint, in turn, drives adaptation in the perceptual stage in that the perceptual stage constantly monitors the internal representation for non-Markov states. When one is found, the perceptual process is modified to eliminate it.

(5) It is assumed that the external state can always be identified from immediate sensory inputs.

---

[9] The term *Consistent Representation* is derived from the fact that it is not absolutely necessary for the internal state space to be Markov. In particular, it is sufficient for each state to be Markov with respect to predicting future rewards (but not necessarily future states). For instance, in Fig. 8, two different external states are classified into the same state, state 2. This "mis-classification", however, does not result in a sub-optimal policy. This slightly weaker concept of being "partially Markov" or "Markov with respect to reward" has been associated with the term "consistent". See [57] for a further discussion of this distinction.

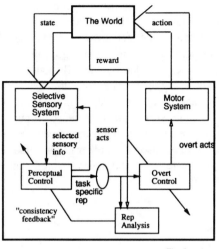

Fig. 9. The basic architecture of a system using the Consistent Representation Method. Control is accomplished in two stages: a perceptual stage, followed by an overt stage. The goal of the perceptual stage is to generate a Markov, task-dependent internal state space. The goal of overt control is to maximize future discounted reward. Both control stages are adaptive. Standard reinforcement learning algorithms can be used for overt learning, while perceptual learning is driven by feedback generated by a representation analysis module, which monitors the internal state space for non-Markov states.

Fig. 9 illustrates an architectural embodiment of the CR-method. The major components include: a selective sensory system, a motor system, a perceptual control, an overt control, and a representation monitor. The line from the perceptual control to the selective sensory system represents perceptual control (or selection) acts. The line from the overt control to the motor system represents overt acts. Both the perceptual and overt controllers are adaptive. Reward from the environment is received by both the overt controller and the representation monitor. The representation monitor detects non-Markov states and provides feedback to the perceptual control.

The correspondence between the components of this architecture and each of the previous algorithms is as follows. The Lion algorithm assumes a deictic sensory–motor system which includes commands for moving perceptual (or attentional) markers; CS-QL assumes a sensory–motor interface that consists of a set of discrete sensing acts; and the G-algorithm assumes a binary input vector from which individual bits are selected as relevant. The identification procedure implemented in the perceptual control takes the form of a "perceptual policy" in the Lion algorithm, and the form of a binary classification tree in CS-QL and the G-algorithm. The task-specific internal representation generated by the Lion algorithms corresponds to a subset of input bit vectors; while in CS-QL and the G-algorithm it is defined by the leaves of a classification tree. The Lion, CS-QL, and G-algorithm all use a form of Q-learning for overt control. For representation monitoring, both the Lion and CS-QL algorithm use an overestimation technique, while the G-algorithm relies on a more general statistical method. [10]

Relating the Lion, CS-QL and G-algorithm in the common framework of the CR-method is useful for two reasons. First, it promotes cross-fertilization of ideas between specific algorithms. For instance, the statistical methods used by the G-algorithm can be incorporated into Lion and CS-QL to yield algorithms that function in stochastic domains. Second, the structure provided by the CR-method highlights shared assumptions and limitations, and it suggests extensions to overcome them. In particular, a fundamental assumption made by all these algorithms is that all external states can be identified at each point in time from immediate sensor inputs. This assumption makes these techniques inappropriate for many interesting tasks that require memory to keep track of information that for one reason or another has become perceptually inaccessible. These more general hidden state tasks and several stored-state approaches to them are the subject of the next section.

5. Stored-state methods

One obvious approach to dealing with inadequate perception and non-Markov decision problems is to allow the agent to have a memory of its past. This memory can help the agent identify hidden states, since it can use differences in memory traces to distinguish situations that based on immediate perception appear identical. The problem is: given a huge volume of information available about the past, how should the agent decide what to remember, how to encode it, and how to use it. There are two approaches to this problem that have been discussed in the literature. In one approach the agent keeps a sliding window of its history, in the other approach the agent builds a state-dependent predictive model of environmental observables [4, 14, 28, 39, 50]. In addition to these two approaches, this section describes a third approach, which learns a history-sensitive control policy directly from reinforcement.

5.1. Three stored-state architectures

Fig. 10 depicts three stored-state architectures for reinforcement learning in non-Markov domains. In our experiments with all three, a neural network (Q-net) was trained using temporal difference methods to incrementally learn an action-value function (Q-function).

In the *window-Q architecture*, instead of relying only upon immediate sensory inputs (or sensations) to define its internal representation, the agent uses its immediate sensations, the sensations for the N most recent time steps, and the N most recent actions to represent its current state. In other words, the window-Q architecture allows direct access to the information in the past through a sliding window. N is called the *window size*. The window-Q architecture is simple and straightforward. However, to use this

---

[10] A version of the Lion algorithm has also been developed where feedback from an external supervisor is used to detect non-Markov states. This external supervision dramatically improves both perceptual and overt learning [57].

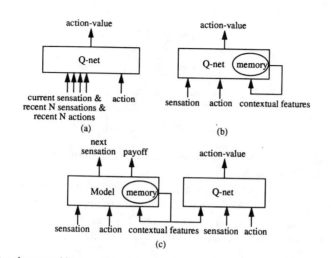

Fig. 10. Three stored-state architectures for reinforcement learning in non-Markov domains: (a) window-Q, (b) recurrent-Q, and (c) recurrent-model.

architecture one must choose a window size, which may be difficult to do in advance. On the one hand, if the selected window size is too small, the internal representation may not be sufficient to define a state space that is Markov. On the other hand, an *input generalization* problem may arise if the window size is chosen to be too large, or if the window must necessarily be large to capture relevant information that is sparsely distributed in time. Under these circumstances excessive amounts of training may be required before the neural network can accurately learn the action-value function and generalize over the irrelevant inputs. In spite of these problems, the window-Q architecture is worthy of study, since (1) this kind of *time-delay neural network* has been found to be useful in speech recognition tasks [53], and (2) the architecture can be used to establish a baseline for comparing other methods.

The window-Q architecture is sort of a brute-force approach to using memory. An alternative is to distill a (small) set of *contextual features* out of the large volume of information about the past. This historical context together with the agent's current sensory inputs can then be used to define its internal representation. If the contextual features are constructed correctly then the resultant internal state space will be Markov and standard RL methods may be used to learn an optimal control policy. The *recurrent-Q* and *recurrent-model* architectures illustrated in Fig. 10 are based on this basic idea. However, they differ in the way they construct their contextual features. Unlike the window-Q architecture, both of these architectures can in principle discover and utilize historical information that depends on sensations arbitrarily deep in the past, although in practice this has been difficult to achieve.

Recurrent neural networks, such as Elman networks [17], provide one approach to constructing relevant contextual features. As illustrated in Fig. 11, the input units of an Elman network are divided into two groups: the (immediate) sensory input units and the *context units*. The context units are used to encode a compressed representation of relevant information from the past. Since these units function as a kind of memory and

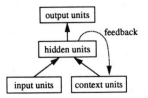

Fig. 11. An Elman network.

encode an aggregate of previous network states, the output of the network depends upon past as well as current inputs.

The recurrent-Q architecture uses a recurrent network to estimate the action-value function directly (Fig. 10(b)). To predict action-values correctly, the recurrent network (called recurrent Q-net) must learn contextual features which enable the network to distinguish between different external states that generate the same immediate sensory inputs.

The recurrent-model architecture (Fig. 10(c)) consists of two concurrent learning components: a *one-step prediction module* or action model, and a Q-learning module. The prediction module is responsible for learning to predict the immediate sensory inputs (and payoffs) that result from performing an action. Because the agent's immediate inputs do not completely code the state of the external environment, the model must learn and use contextual features to accurately predict the effects of an action on the the environment. If we assume that an accurate predictive model can be learned, and that the model's contextual features can be extracted, then a Markov state space can be generated for the Q-learning component by defining its inputs (internal state space) to be the conjunction of the agent's immediate sensory input and the contextual features. This follows since, at any given time, the next state of the environment can be completely determined by this new state representation and the action taken.

Both the recurrent-Q and recurrent-model architectures learn contextual features using a gradient descent, least-mean-square method (e.g., error back-propagation), but they differ in an important way. In learning the predictive model, the goal is to minimize errors between actual and predicted sensory inputs and immediate rewards. In this case, the environment provides all the needed training information, which is consistent over time as long as the environment does not change. For recurrent Q-learning, the goal is to minimize errors between temporally successive predictions of action-values (see Eq. (9)). In this case, the error signals are computed based partly on information from the environment and partly on the agent's current estimate of the optimal action-value function. Since this latter term changes over time and carries little or no useful information during the early stages of learning, these error signals may be in general weak, noisy, and even inconsistent over time. Because of this the practical viability of the recurrent-Q architecture is uncertain.

Having introduced these architectures, it is worthwhile to note that combinations of these approaches are also possible. For example, we can combine the first two architectures: the inputs to the recurrent Q-net could include not just the current sensory input but also recent inputs and recent actions. We can also combine the last two architectures. For instance, one approach would be to share the context units between

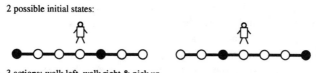

2 possible initial states:

3 actions: walk left, walk right & pick up
4 binary inputs: left cup, right cup, left collision & right collision
reward: 1 when the last cup is picked up
        0 otherwise

Fig. 12. Task 1: a two-cup collection task. The cup locations are denoted by filled circles.

the model network and the Q-network such that the contextual features learned would be based on prediction errors from both networks. Although there are many possibilities, this article is only concerned with the three basic architectures. Further investigation is needed to see if other combinations will result in better performance than the basic versions.

5.2. Network training

The (nonrecurrent) Q-nets of the window-Q and recurrent-model architectures can be trained using a straightforward combination of temporal difference methods [44] and the connectionist back-propagation algorithm [37]. This combination has been successfully applied to solve several nontrivial reinforcement learning problems [24, 25, 49].

Training the model of the recurrent-model architecture is slightly more complicated. Recurrent networks can be trained by a recurrent version of the back-propagation algorithm called *back-propagation through time* (BPTT) or *unfolding of time* [37]. BPTT is based on the observation that any recurrent network spanning T steps can be converted into an equivalent feed-forward network by duplicating the network T times. Once a recurrent network is unfolded, back-propagation can be directly applied. The Q-net of the recurrent-Q architecture can also be trained by BPTT together with temporal difference. For detailed network structures and implementation, see [28].

5.3. Simulation results

This subsection presents simulation results of a study in which the three history-based architectures were applied to a series of non-Markov decision tasks. Through this study, we have gained insight into the behavior of these architectures, and a better understanding of the relative merits of each and the conditions for their useful application. (Detailed descriptions of the simulation and results can be found in [28].)

5.3.1. Task 1: two-cup collection

We begin with a simple two-cup collection task (Fig. 12). This task requires the learning agent to pick up two cups located in a 1-D space. The agent has three actions: walking right one cell, walking left one cell, and pick-up. When the agent executes the pick-up action, it will pick up a cup if and only if the cup is located at the agent's current cell. The agent's sensory input includes four binary bits: two bits indicating if there is a cup in the immediate left or right cell, and two bits indicating if the previous action results in a collision from the left or the right. An action attempting to move the agent out of the space will cause a collision.

The cup collection problem is restricted so that there are only two possible initial states (Fig. 12). In each trial, the agent starts with one of the two initial states. Because the agent can see only one of the two cups at the beginning of each trial, the location of the other cup can only be learned from previous trials. To collect the cups optimally, the agent must use contextual information, such as which initial state it starts with, to decide which way to go after picking up the first cup. Note that the reason for restricting the possible initial states is to avoid perceptual aliasing at the onset of a trial when no contextual information is available.

This task is nontrivial for several reasons: (1) The agent cannot sense the cup in its current cell, (2) it gets no reward until both cups are picked up, and (3) it often operates with no cup in sight especially after picking up the first cup.

The three memory architectures were tested on this cup collection task. The experiment was repeated 5 times, and every time each architecture successfully learned an optimal control policy within 500 trials. (The window size N was 5.) One interesting observation, however, was the following: The recurrent-model architecture *never* learned a perfect model within 500 trials. For instance, if the agent has not seen a cup for 10 steps or more, the model normally is not able to predict the appearance of the cup. But this imperfect model did not prevent Q-learning from learning an optimal policy.

The two main results of this experiment were:

- To demonstrate that each of the architectures is capable of learning to perform this simple hidden state task, and in particular, to demonstrate that the two recurrent architectures are able to develop and use memory-based contextual features.
- To notice that for the recurrent-model architecture, even when the model is only partially correct it may provide sufficient contextual features for optimal control. This is good news, since a perfect model is often difficult to obtain.

5.3.2. Task 2: Task 1 with random features

Task 2 is simply Task 1 with two random bits in the agent's sensory input. The random bits simulate two difficult-to-predict and irrelevant features accessible to the learning agent. In the real world, there are often many features which are difficult to predict but fortunately not relevant to the task to be solved. For example, predicting whether it is going to rain outside might be difficult, but it does not matter if the task is to pick up cups inside. The ability to handle difficult-to-predict but irrelevant features is important for a learning system to be practical.

The simulation results are summarized as follows: The two random features had little impact on the performance of the window-Q architecture or the recurrent-Q architecture, but had a noticeable negative impact on the recurrent-model architecture.

The system using the recurrent-model architecture exhibited streaks of optimal performance during the course of 300 trials. However, it apparently could not stabilize on the optimal policy; it oscillated between the optimal policy and several sub-optimal policies. It was also observed that the model tried in vain to reduce the prediction errors on the two random bits. There are two possible explanations for the poorer performance compared with that obtained when there are no random sensation bits. First, the model might fail to learn the contextual features needed to solve the task, because much of the effort was wasted on trying to learn to predict the random bits. Second, because the activations of the context units were shared between the model network and the Q-net, a change to the representation of contextual features on the model part could simply destabilize a well-trained Q-net, if the change was significant. The first explanation is ruled out, since the optimal policy indeed was found many times. To test the second explanation, we fixed the model at some point of learning and allowed only changes to the Q-net. In such a setup, the agent found the optimal policy and indeed stuck to it.

This experiment revealed two lessons:

- The recurrent-Q architecture is more economic than the recurrent-model architecture in the sense that the former will not try to learn a contextual feature if it does not appear to be relevant to predicting action-values.
- A potential problem with the recurrent-model architecture is that changes to the representation of contextual features on the model part may cause instability on the Q-net part.

5.3.3. Task 3: Task 1 with control errors

Noise and uncertainty prevail in the real world. To study the capability of these architectures to handle noise, we added 15% control errors to the agent's actuators, so that 15% of the time the executed action would not have any effect on the environment. (The two random bits were removed.)

In three out of the five runs, the window-Q architecture successfully found the optimal policy, while in the other two runs, it only found sub-optimal policies. In contrast, the recurrent-Q architecture always learned the optimal policy (with little instability).

The recurrent-model architecture always found the optimal policy after 500 trials, but again its policy oscillated between the optimal one and some sub-optimal ones due to the changing representation of contextual features, much as happened in Task 2. If we can find some way to stablize the model (for example, by gradually decreasing the learning rate to 0 at the end), we should be able to obtain a stable and optimal policy.

Two lessons have been learned from this experiment:

- All of the three architectures can handle small control errors to some degree.
- Among the architectures, recurrent-Q seems to scale best in the presence of control errors.

5.3.4. Task 4: pole balancing

In the pole balancing problem, the system's objective is to apply forces to the base of a movable cart in order to balance a pole that is attached to the cart via a hinge (Fig. 13). This problem has been studied widely in the reinforcement learning literature. It is of practical interest because of its resemblance to problems in aerospace (e.g., missile guidance) and robotics (e.g., biped balance and locomotion). It is of theoretical interest because of the difficult credit assignment problem which arises due to sparse

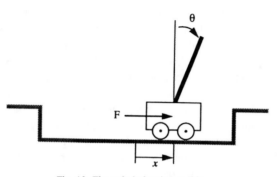

Fig. 13. The pole balancing problem.

reinforcement signals. In particular, in most formulations of the problem, the system only receives nonzero reinforcement when the pole falls over. For instance in our simulations the system receives a penalty of -1 when the pole tilt exceeds 12 degrees from vertical.

In the traditional pole balancing task, the system's sensory inputs include the position and velocity of the cart and the angular position and velocity of the pole [43]. This information completely characterizes the state of the system and yields control problem that is Markov. In our experiments, only the cart position and pole angle are given. This yields a non-Markov decision problem, and in order to learn an adequate control policy the system must construct contextual features resembling velocities for the cart and pole. In this experiment, a policy was considered satisfactory whenever the pole could be balanced for over 5000 steps in each of the seven test trials where the pole starts with an angle of 0, ±1, ±2, or ±3 degrees. In the training phase, pole angles and cart positions were generated randomly. The initial cart velocity and pole velocity were always set to 0. $N = 1$ was used here.

The input representation used here was straightforward: one real-valued input unit for each of the pole angles and cart positions. The following table shows the number of trials taken by each architecture before a satisfactory policy was learned. These numbers are the average of the results from the best five out of six runs. (A satisfactory policy was not always found within 1000 trials.).

method	window-Q	recurrent-Q	recurrent-model
# of trials	206	552	247

While the recurrent-Q architecture was the most suitable architecture for the cup collection tasks, it was outperformed by the other two architectures for the pole balancing task.

5.4. Comparisons

The above experiments provide some insight into the performance of the three memory architectures. This subsection considers problem characteristics that may be useful in determining when one architecture may be preferred over another.

5.4.1. Problem parameters

Some of the features (or parameters) of a task that affect the applicability of these architectures are:

- *Memory depth.* One important problem parameter is the length of time over which the agent must remember previous inputs in order to generate an internal representation that is Markov. For example, the memory depth for the pole balancing task is 1, as evidenced by the fact that the window-Q agent was able to obtain satisfactory control based only on a window of size 1. Note that learning an optimal policy may require a larger memory depth than that needed to represent the policy. For instance, for Task 1 (cup collection) the window-Q agent was able to represent (and occasionally learn) the optimal policy based on a window of size as small as 2, but it could only reliably learn the optimal control when using a window of size 5.

- *Payoff delay.* In cases where the payoff is zero except for the goal state, we define the payoff delay of a problem to be the length of the optimal action sequence leading to the goal. This parameter is important because it influences the overall difficulty of Q-learning. As the payoff delay increases, learning an accurate Q-function becomes increasingly difficult due to the increasing difficulty of credit assignment.

- *Number of contextual features to be learned.* In general, the more perceptual aliasing an agent faces, the more contextual features the agent has to discover, and the more difficult the task becomes. In general, predicting sensations (i.e., a model) requires more contextual features than predicting action-values (i.e., a Q-net), which in turn requires more contextual features than representing optimal policies. Consider Task 1 for example. Only two binary contextual features are required to determine the optimal actions: *"is there a cup in front?"* and *"is the second cup on the right-hand side or left-hand side?"*. But a perfect Q-function requires more features such as *"how many cups have been picked up so far?"* and *"how far is the second cup from here?"*. A perfect model for this task requires the same features as the perfect Q-function. But a perfect model for Task 2 requires even more features such as *"what is the current state of the random number generator?"*, while a perfect Q-function for Task 2 requires no extra features.

  It is important to note that we do not need a perfect Q-function nor a perfect model in order to obtain an optimal policy. A Q-function needs to only assign values to actions so that their relative values are in the correct order. Similarly, a model needs to only provide sufficient features for constructing a good Q-function.

5.4.2. Architecture characteristics

Given the above problem parameters, we would like to understand which of the three architectures is best suited to particular types of problems. Here we consider the key advantages and disadvantages of each architecture, along with the problem parameters which influence the importance of these characteristics.

- *Recurrent-model architecture.* The key difference between this architecture and the recurrent-Q architecture is that its learning of contextual features is driven by learning an action model rather than the Q-function. One strength of this approach is that the agent can obtain better training data for the action model than it can for the

Q-function, making this learning more reliable and effective. In particular, training examples of the action model (<sensation, action, next-sensation, payoff> quadru-ples) are directly observable with each step the agent takes in its environment. In contrast, training examples of the Q-function (<sensation, action, action-value> triples) are not directly observable since the agent must estimate the training action-values based on its own changing approximation to the true action-value function.

The second strength of this approach is that the learned features are dependent on the environment and independent of the reward function (even though the action model may be trained to predict rewards as well as sensations). As a result, these features can be reused if the agent has several different reward functions, or goals, to learn to achieve.

- *Recurrent-Q architecture.* While this architecture suffers the relative disadvantage that it must learn from indirectly observable training examples, it has the offsetting advantage that it need only learn those contextual features that are *relevant* to the control problem. The contextual features needed to represent the optimal action model are a superset of those needed to represent the optimal Q-function. This is easily seen by noticing that the optimal control action can in principle be computed from the action model (by using look ahead search). Thus, in cases where only a few features are necessary for predicting action-values but many are needed to predict completely the next state, the number of contextual features that must be learned by the recurrent-Q architecture can be much smaller than the number needed by the recurrent-model architecture.

- *Window-Q architecture.* The primary advantage of this architecture is that it does not have to learn the state representation recursively (as do the other two recurrent network architectures). Recurrent networks typically take much longer to train than nonrecurrent networks. This advantage is offset by the disadvantage that the history information it can use is limited to those features directly observable in its fixed window which captures only a bounded history. In contrast, the two recurrent network approaches can in principle represent contextual features that depend on sensations that are arbitrarily deep in the agent's history.

Given these competing advantages for the three architectures, one would imagine that each will be the preferred architecture for different types of problems:

- One would expect the advantage of the window-Q architecture to be greatest in tasks where the memory depths are the smallest (for example, the pole balancing task).

- One would expect the recurrent-model architecture's advantage of directly available training examples to be most important in tasks for which the payoff delay is the longest (for example, the pole balancing task). It is in these situations that the indirect estimation of training Q-values is most problematic for the recurrent-Q architecture.

- One would expect the advantage of the recurrent-Q architecture—that it need only learn those features relevant to control—to be most pronounced in tasks where the ratio between relevant and irrelevant contextual features is the lowest (for example, the cup collection task with two random features). Although the recurrent-model architecture can acquire the optimal policy as long as just the relevant features are learned, the drive to learning the irrelevant features may cause problems. First of all, representing the irrelevant features may use up many of the limited context units at the sacrifice of learning good relevant features. Secondly, as we have seen in the experiments, the recurrent-model architecture is also subject to instability due to changing representation of the contextual features—a change which improves the model is also likely to deteriorate the Q-function, which then needs to be re-learned.

The tapped-delay line scheme, which the window-Q architecture uses, has been widely applied to speech recognition [53] and turned out to be quite a useful technique. However, we do not expect it to work as well for control tasks as it does for speech recognition, because of an important difference between these tasks. A major task of speech recognition is to find the temporal patterns that already exist in a given sequence of speech phonemes. Whereas in reinforcement learning, the agent must look for the temporal patterns generated by its own actions. If the actions are generated randomly as it is often the case during early learning, it is unlikely to find sensible temporal patterns within the action sequence so as to improve its action selection policy.

On the other hand, we may improve the performance of the window-Q architecture by using more sophisticated time-delay neural networks (TDNN). The TDNN used here is quite primitive; it only has a fixed number of delays in the input layer. We can have delays in the hidden layer as well [20,53]. Bodenhausen and Waibel [11] describe a TDNN with adaptive time delays. Using their TDNN, window-Q may be able to determine a proper window size automatically.

6. Discussion

This paper has described learning techniques that were developed to handle tasks that involve either selective perception or state hidden in time. However, many tasks of interest in fact involve both selective perception and memory, and solutions to these tasks may require integration of both Consistent Representation Methods and stored-state methods.

One simple approach to extending the CR-method would be to extend the agent's selective sensory system to include remembered sensory–motor events. That is, instead of selecting bits of information from the current sensory input only, the system could also select bits from a memory trace of previous inputs and actions. This approach is similar to the window-Q architecture in that a memory trace is maintained, however it differs in that only a relatively small amount of information would be selected at each point in time. Moreover, under this scheme it might be possible to devise reference-based rules for updating the history-trace in a way that would preserve relevant memories while dropping irrelevant ones.

Other architectures that combine features from both the CR-method and history-based architectures may also be very useful. For example, one problem with the CR-method as it currently stands is that it uses no information about the previous state of the environment when trying to identify the current state. In a sense the system re-identifies the state of the environment starting from "scratch" after each action. Knowledge of the last state and the most recent action could considerably reduce the effort required to identify the current state, since in most environments transitions between states tend to be local and predictable. Thus instead of "rediscovering" the state after each action, the agent could merely verify the current state, or in the worst case, identify the outcome from a limited number of possibilities.

In addition to further exploring variations on the above architectures, future work must also assess the scalability to these algorithms. These algorithms were derived from a desire to extend reinforcement learning beyond Markov decision problems and to problems that involve selective perception and/or state hidden in time. To some extent we have been successful. However, the tasks we have explored remain painfully simple compared to the scale of problems required for truly autonomous, intelligent behavior. A few of the issues that must be addressed to achieve scalability include:

- *Learning bias*: Reinforcement learning can be viewed as a kind of search through the space of possible control policies. If that search can be biased in an appropriate direction, learning can proceed much more quickly than it might otherwise. One approach to introducing bias into a learning agent is to allow it to interact with other intelligent agents performing similar tasks. Other agents can serve as role models, advice givers, instructors, critics, and supervisors, and in general can strongly bias an agent's learning. Simple versions of these methods have been demonstrated in the context of reinforcement learning and have produced significant improvements in learning time [15, 25, 61]. Nevertheless, more work is needed.

- *Fast/efficient credit assignment*: Credit assignment is the fundamental problem in reinforcement learning: given reward from the environment, which actions were responsible for generating that payoff and how should the system be changed to improve performance. Most reinforcement learning algorithms solve this problem by making incremental changes to the system over a long period of time. If additional knowledge about the causal structure of the environment (for example, an action model) can be made available, more efficient credit assignment methods can be developed. For example, see [25, 31, 33, 34, 45, 64].

- *Generalization*: A reinforcement learning agent must generalize from its experiences. In particular, when the state space is so large that exhaustive search for optimal control is impractical, the agent must guess about new situations based on experience with similar situations. Instead of representing action-value functions (i.e., Q-function) with look-up tables, we must develop function approximators that promote useful generalization across states and actions. For example, see [13, 27, 29, 32, 47–49].

- *Hierarchical learning*: To date much of the work in reinforcement learning has focused on problems that are small compared to those facing real robotic systems. For example, a walking robot may require precise (continuous) information from dozens of sensors, and may need to control dozens of effectors. The combinatorics associated with such problems quickly overwhelm the simplest RL methods. Another source of complexity arises when agents pursue multiple goals. Hierarchical learning is approach to turning intractable problems into tractable ones: First, a complex task is decomposed into multiple elementary tasks that can be solved effectively. Then control policies that are learned for solving the elementary tasks can be integrated to solve the original complex task. Once the agent has learned to solve one complex task, solving a new one task may be easier if the two share the same elementary subtasks. For work in this direction, see [22, 26, 27, 40, 62].

Of course there are many other issues that stand between current technology and the development of intelligent autonomous agents, and reinforcement learning is no panacea. However, the autonomy afforded by reinforcement learning methods makes them likely to play an important role.

7. Conclusions

Intelligent control systems must deal with information limitations imposed by their sensors. When inadequate information is available from the agent's sensors or when the agent must actively control its sensors in order to select relevant features, the internal decision problem it faces is necessarily non-Markov. Learning these control tasks can be very difficult.

In this article we have presented several approaches to dealing with non-Markov decision problems. The Consistent Representation (CR) Method was proposed as an approach to dealing with tasks that involve control/selection in an active sensory system. In the CR-method, control is partitioned into two phases: a perceptual control phase, which aims to identify the current state of the environment; and an overt control phase, which aims to maximize reward. Three instances of this method, the Lion algorithm [60], the G-algorithm [13], and CS-QL [47], were described and examples of their uses presented. The major assumption made by the CR-method is that the state of the environment can be identified at each point in time by appropriately controlling the sensory system. This assumption prevents it from being applied to tasks in which relevant state information is temporarily hidden from view.

Stored-state methods are more appropriate for tasks in which information is hidden in time. Three stored-state architectures were described: window-Q, recurrent-model, and recurrent-Q. The window-Q architecture uses a tapped-delay line to maintain a fixed length history of recent sensory–motor events. The recurrent-model architecture constructs a predictive model of the external environment, whose own internal state is used, in conjunction with sensory inputs, to drive control. The recurrent-Q architecture uses a recurrent neural network to learn the action-value function for the non-Markov task directly. Because the recurrent network can encode state information across time steps, its own internal state is used to resolve ambiguities caused by inadequate sensory input. These three architectures were demonstrated on a series of hidden state tasks, and conditions for their useful application were discussed.

The methods described in this article are preliminary in that they have only been demonstrated on relatively simple tasks and they have not been extensively tested or compared in very complicated domains. Nevertheless, these algorithms represent a significant advance over traditional reinforcement learning algorithms, which do not address non-Markov tasks at all. Perhaps these rather modest algorithms will serve as stepping stones to more sophisticated and capable methods for dealing with the ubiquitous problems of hidden state.

Acknowledgements

We gratefully acknowledge the contributions made to this article by Dana Ballard, Tom Mitchell, Rich Sutton, Lonnie Chrisman, Ming Tan, Sebastian Thrun, and Rich Caruana. Thank you for sharing your thoughts and ideas, your comments and criticisms, and most of all your time and energy.

References

[1] P.E. Agre, The dynamic structure of everyday life, Ph.D. Thesis, Tech. Report No. 1085, MIT Artificial Intelligence Lab., Cambridge, MA (1988).

[2] D.W. Aha and D. Kibler, Noise-tolerant instance-based learning algorithms, in: *Proceedings IJCAI-89*, Detroit, MI (1989) 794–799.

[3] J. Aloimonons, I. Weiss and A. Bandyopadhyay, Active vision, *Int. J. Comput. Vision* **1** (4) (1988) 333–356.

[4] J.R. Bachrach, Connectionist modeling and control of finite state environments, Ph.D. Thesis, University of Massachusetts, Department of Computer and Information Sciences, Amherst, MA (1992).

[5] R. Bajcsy and P. Allen, Sensing strategies, in: *Proceedings U.S.–France Robotics Workshop*, Philadelphia, PA (1984).

[6] D.H. Ballard, Animate vision, Technical Report 329, Department of Computer Science, University of Rochester, Rochester, NY (1990).

[7] A.B. Barto, S.J. Bradtke and S.P. Singh, Real-time learning and control using asynchronous dynamic programming, Technical Report 91-57, University of Massachusetts, Amherst, MA (1991).

[8] A.G. Barto, R.S. Sutton and C.W. Anderson, Neuron-like elements that can solve difficult learning control problems, *IEEE Trans. Syst. Man Cybern.* **13** (5) (1983) 834–846.

[9] R.E. Bellman, *Dynamic Programming* (Princeton University Press, Princeton, NJ, 1957).

[10] D.P. Bertsekas, *Dynamic Programming: Deterministic and Stochastic Models* (Prentice-Hall, Englewood Cliffs, NJ, 1987).

[11] U. Bodenhausen and A. Waibel, The Tempo 2 algorithm: adjusting time-delays by supervised learning, in: D.S. Touretzky, ed., *Advances in Neural Information Processing Systems* **3** (Morgan Kaufmann, San Mateo, CA, 1991).

[12] D. Chapman, *Vision, Instruction, and Action* (MIT Press, Cambridge, MA, 1993).

[13] D. Chapman and L.P. Kaelbling, Learning from delayed reinforcement in a complex domain, in: *Proceedings IJCAI-91*, Sydney, Australia (1991); also: Teleos Technical Report TR-90-11 (1990).

[14] L. Chrisman, Reinforcement learning with perceptual aliasing: the predictive distinctions approach, in: *Proceedings AAAI-92*, San Jose, CA (1992) 183–188.

[15] J. Clouse and P.E. Utgoff, A teaching method for reinforcement learning, in: *Proceedings Ninth International Conference on Machine Learning*, Aberdeen, Scotland (1992).

[16] P. Dayan and G. Hinton, Feudal reinforcement learning, in: J.E. Moody, S.J. Hanson and R.P. Lippmann, eds., *Advances in Neural Information Processing Systems* **5** (Morgan Kaufmann, San Mateo, CA, 1993).

[17] J.L. Elman, Finding structure in time, *Cogn. Sci.* **14** (1990) 179–211.

[18] J.J. Grefenstette, Credit assignment in rule discovery systems based on genetic algorithms, *Mach. Learn.* **3** (1988) 225–245.

[19] J.H. Holland, Escaping brittleness: the possibilities of general-purpose learning algortihms applied to parallel rule-based systems, in: *Machine Learning: An Artificial Intelligence Approach* **II** (Morgan Kaufmann, San Mateo, CA, 1986).

[20] A.N. Jain, A connectionist learning architecture for parsing spoken language, Ph.D. Thesis, Technical Report CMU-CS-91-208, Carnegie Mellon University, School of Computer Science (1991).

[21] L.P. Kaelbling, Learning in embedded systems, Ph.D. Thesis, Stanford University, Stanford, CA (1990).

[22] L.P. Kaelbling, Hierarchical learning in stochastic domains: preliminary results, in: *Proceedings Tenth International Conference on Machine Learning* (1993).

[23] S. Koenig and R. Simmons, Complexity analysis of real-time reinforcement learning applied to finding shortest paths in deterministic domains, Technical Report CMU-CS-93-106, School of Computer Science, Carnegie Mellon University, Pittsburgh, PA (1992).

[24] Long-Ji Lin, Programming robots using reinforcement learning and teaching, in: *Proceedings AAAI-91*, Anaheim, CA (1991) 781–786.

[25] Long-Ji Lin, Self-improving reactive agents based on reinforcement learning, planning and teaching, *Mach. Learn.* **8** (1992) 293–321.

[26] Long-Ji Lin, Hierarchical learning of robot skills by reinforcement, in: *Proceedings 1993 IEEE International Conference on Neural Networks* (1993).

[27] Long-Ji Lin, Reinforcement learning for robots using neural networks, Ph.D. Thesis, Technical Report CMU-CS-93-103, Carnegie Mellon University, School of Computer Science, Pittsburgh, PA (1993).

[28] Long-Ji Lin and T.M. Mitchell, Reinforcement learning with hidden states. in: *Proceedings Second International Conference on Simulation of Adaptive Behavior: From Animals to Animats* (MIT Press, Cambridge, MA, 1993).

[29] S. Mahadevan and J.H. Connell, Scaling reinforcement learning to robotics by exploiting the subsumption architecture, in: *Proceedings Eighth International Workshop on Machine Learning*, Evanston, IL (1991).

[30] D. Michie and R.A. Chambers, 'Boxes' as a model of pattern-formation, in: C.H. Waddington, ed., *Toward a Theoretical Biology* **1**, *Prolegomena* (Edinburgh University Press, Edinburgh, 1968) 206–215.

[31] T.M. Mitchell and S.B. Thrun, Explanation-based neural network learning for robot control, in: J.E. Moody, S.J. Hanson and R.P. Lippmann, eds., *Advances in Neural Information Processing Systems* **5** (Morgan Kaufmann, San Mateo, CA, 1993).

[32] A. Moore, Variable resolution dynamic programming: efficiently learning action maps in multivariate real-values state spaces, in: *Proceedings Eighth International Conference on Machine Learning*, Evanston, IL (1991) 333–337.

[33] A.W. Moore and C.G. Atkeson, Prioritized sweeping: reinforcement learning with less data and less real time, *Mach. Learn.* **13** (1) (1993) 103–130.

[34] Jing Peng and R.J. Williams, Efficient learning and planning within the Dyna framework, in: *Proceedings Second International Conference on Simulation of Adaptive Behavior: From Animals to Animats* (MIT Press, Cambridge, MA, 1993).

[35] J.R. Quinlan, Induction of decision trees, *Mach. Learn.* **1** (1986) 81–106.

[36] S. Ross, *Introduction to Stochastic Dynamic Programming* (Academic Press, New York, 1983).

[37] D.E. Rumelhart, G.E. Hinton and R.J. Williams, Learning internal representations by error propagation, in: D.E. Rumelhart and J.L. McClelland and the PDP Research Group, eds., *Parallel Distributed Processing: Explorations in the Microstructure of Cognition* **1** (MIT Press, Cambridge, MA, 1986) Chapter 8.

[38] A.L. Samuel, Some studies in machine learning using the game of checkers, in: E.A. Feigenbaum and J. Feldman, eds., *Computers and Thought* (Krieger, Malabar, FL, 1963) 71–105.

[39] J. Schmidhuber, Reinforcement learning in Markovian and non-Markovian environments, in: D.S. Touretzky, ed., *Advances in Neural Information Processing Systems* **3** (Morgan Kaufmann, San Mateo, CA, 1991) 500–506.

[40] S.P. Singh, Transfer of learning across compositions of sequential tasks, in: *Proceedings Eighth International Workshop on Machine Learning*, Evanston, IL (1991) 348–352.

[41] S.P. Singh, Transfer of learning by composing solutions of elemental sequential tasks, *Mach. Learn.* **8** (1992) 323–339.

[42] G.W. Snedecor and W.G. Cochran, *Statistical Methods* (Iowa State University Press, Ames, Iowa, 1989).

[43] R.S. Sutton, Temporal credit assignment in reinforcement learning, Ph.D. Thesis, University of Massachusetts at Amherst (1984); also: COINS Tech. Report 84-02.

[44] R.S. Sutton, Learning to predict by the method of temporal differences, *Mach. Learn.* **3** (1) (1988) 9–44.

[45] R.S. Sutton, Integrating architectures for learning, planning, and reacting based on approximating dynamic programming, in: *Proceedings Seventh International Conference on Machine Learning*, Austin, TX (1990).

[46] R.S. Sutton, ed., *Reinforcement Learning* (Kluwer, Boston, MA, 1992).

[47] Ming Tan, Cost sensitive reinforcement learning for adaptive classification and control, in: *Proceedings IJCAI-91*, Sydney, Australia (1991).

[48] Ming Tan, Cost sensitive robot learning, Ph.D. Thesis, Carnegie Mellon University, Pittsburgh, PA (1991).

[49] G. Tesauro, Practical issues in temporal difference learning, *Mach. Learn.* **8** (1992) 257–277.

[50] S.Thrun and K. Moller, Planning with an adaptive world model, in: D.S. Touretzky, ed., *Advances in Neural Information Processing Systems* **3** (Morgan Kaufmann, San Mateo, CA, 1991).

[51] S. Thrun, Efficient exploration in reinforcement learning, Technical Report CMU-CS-92-102, School of Computer Science, Carnegie Mellon University, Pittsburgh, PA (1992).

[52] S. Ullman, Visual routines, *Cognition* **18** (1984) 97–159; also in: S. Pinker, ed., *Visual Cognition* (MIT Press, Cambridge, MA, 1985).

[53] A. Waibel, Modular construction of time-delay neural networks for speech recognition, *Neural Comput.* **1** (1989) 39–46.

[54] C.J.C.H. Watkins, Learning from delayed rewards, Ph.D. Thesis, University of Cambridge, England (1989).

[55] C.J.C.H. Watkins and P. Dayan, Technical note: Q-learning, *Mach. Learn.* **8**2, (1992) 39–46.

[56] S.D. Whitehead, Complexity and cooperation in reinforcement learning, in: *Proceedings AAAI-91*, Anaheim, CA (1991); a similar version also appears in: *Proceedings Eighth International Workshop on Machine Learning*, Evanston, IL (1991).

[57] S.D. Whitehead, Reinforcement learning for the adaptive control of perception and action, Ph.D. Thesis, Department of Computer Science, University of Rochester, Rochester, NY (1991).

[58] S.D. Whitehead and D.H. Ballard, A role for anticipation in reactive systems that learn, in: *Proceedings Sixth International Workshop on Machine Learning*, Ithaca, NY (1989).

[59] S.D. Whitehead and D.H. Ballard, Active perception and reinforcement learning, *Neural Comput.* **2** (4) (1990); also in: *Proceedings Seventh International Conference on Machine Learning*, Austin, TX (1990).

[60] S.D. Whitehead and D.H. Ballard, Learning to perceive and act by trial and error, *Mach. Learn.* **7** (1) (1991); also: Technical Report 331, Department of Computer Science, University of Rochester, Rochester, NY (1990).

[61] S.D. Whitehead and D.H. Ballard, A study of cooperative mechanisms for faster reinforcement learning, Technical Report 365, Computer Science Department, University of Rochester, Rochester, NY (1991).

[62] S.D. Whitehead, J. Karlsson and J. Tenenberg, Learning multiple goal behavior via task decomposition and dynamic policy merging, in: J.H. Connell and S. Mahadevan, eds., *Robot Learning* (MIT Press, Cambridge, MA, 1993).

[63] R.J. Williams, Reinforcement learning in connectionist networks, Technical Report ICS 8605, Institute for Cognitive Science, University of California at San Diego (1986).

[64] R.C. Yee, S. Saxena, P.E. Utgoff and A.G. Barto, Explaining temporal-differences to create useful concepts for evaluating states, in: *Proceedings AAAI-90*, Boston, MA (1990).

Artificial Intelligence 73 (1995) 307–322

Book Review

Jean-Arcady Meyer and Stewart W. Wilson, eds., *From Animals to Animats*: *Proceedings of the First International Conference on Simulation of Adaptive Behavior* ★

Matthew Brand [a,*], Peter Prokopowicz [b], Clark Elliott [c,d]

[a] *The Media Lab, MIT, Cambridge, MA 02139, USA*
[b] *Department of Computer Science, University of Chicago, Chicago, IL 660637, USA*
[c] *The Institute for the Learning Sciences, Northwestern University, Evanston, IL 60201, USA*
[d] *Institute for Applied Artificial Intelligence, DePaul University, Chicago, IL 60604, USA*

In the mid-eighties Valentino Braitenberg published *Vehicles* [8], a short but splendid book describing a canny progression of thought experiments, each in the form of a robotic go-cart driven by a simple circuit (reviewed in this column [24]). Subtly building upon neuroethological theories of how simple nervous systems relate sensation to action, Braitenberg designed successive vehicles to demonstrate behaviors that looked increasingly lifelike and intelligent. Braitenberg explained the exercise thus:

> We will talk only about machines with very simple internal structures, too simple in fact to be interesting from the point of view of mechanical or electrical engineering. Interest arises, rather, when we look at these machines or vehicles as if they were animals in a natural environment. We will be tempted, then, to use psychological language in describing their behavior. And yet we know very well that there is nothing in these vehicles that we have not put in ourselves. This will be a very interesting educational game.

One need only read about a few vehicles to see the appeal of the book's main theses: that simple automata can produce interesting behavior in appropriate environments, and that animal nervous systems might prove instructive examples for the designs of such automata. This "educational game" has a long history, rooted in the anatomical inquiries of Descartes [12], Bonnet [7], and Huxley [14]. Recently, it has attracted practitioners from fields as diverse as ethology, neurobiology, robotics, and artificial intelligence. *From*

★ (MIT Press/Bradford Books, Cambridge, MA, 1991); 551 pages, ISBN 0-262-63138-5.
* Corresponding author.

SSDI 0004-3702(93)E0078-Z

animals to animats is the most extensive publication to date to represent the work and ambitions of this group, whom we will call *animatists*: those who seek the rudiments of intelligence in the rudimentary intelligences of lower animals, or, alternatively, in simulations thereof. *Animats* is the proceedings of the First International Conference on Simulation of Adaptive Behavior (1990) and contains 62 papers out of roughly 90 submissions. It advertises itself as a field-heralding document, laying out the ambitions, methods, and subject matters of what several contributors call "the animat way".

Although animal behavior is the leitmotif of the conference, the dominant theme is situatedness—the production of competent behavior from minimal (often decentralized) control systems in tight sensory-motor loops with the environment. Animatists take the situated stance to explain why their virtually behaviorist models—generally stimulus–response architectures with highly impoverished representations—are adequate for a wide variety of animal-like behaviors. In a few variations, mainly reinforcement learning and evolution, and a proliferation of architectures, this theme dominates the proceedings. For the most part, these papers are *not* concerned with the contingencies of animal or even robot behavior, such as the actual distribution and detectability of food, the problems of sensing behaviorally significant states, or how real environments demand specific forms of locomotion and navigation. Rather, those concerns are addressed by a smattering of ethological and neuroethological papers, which, partly because of the light they shed on the animat programme, may be the most interesting part of the proceedings.

Animats is the work of many people and consequently records many points of view. To give a flavor of the proceedings, we will identify some of its unifying themes, then examine some of the divergences between its various constituencies, especially between the simulators and the ethologists. In examining the simulators' approach to animats, we will consider animat simulations and algorithms, and adaptivity and evolution in particular. We will then discuss the animatist's view of situatedness, and how this relates to the project of building actual robots with interesting, robust, and perhaps even useful behaviors. Because there are strong contrasts between the state of the art of animat science in 1990 and what the biological record seems to say about control strategies, perception, and neural organization of behavior in real organisms, we will devote the latter half of the review to these issues, drawing upon the germane and often remarkable ethological side of the proceedings. Rather than examine the papers in the proceedings one-by-one, we will sketch the framework of theoretical assumptions that motivate animat research and discuss the papers that best and worst serve these interests.

1. "The animat way"

Animat researchers aspire to capture and represent the causal structure of environments and tasks in a way that will produce robust and composable behaviors with minimal representational overhead. Their methods generally employ learning, evolution, or minimalist design. Some authors (e.g., [Meyer, Cliff, Wilson, Brooks, Arbib] [1]) de-

---

[1] Papers are referred to by last name of first author; see table of contents duplicated in Appendix A.

clare that successful animat designs will lead to parsimonious but potent representations upon which more complicated behaviors and intelligences may be built. Ultimately, by synthesizing behaviors and building robot animats, these researchers may well be able to tell artificial intelligence something about the kinds of representations the body and the senses can provide to cognition. There has been a long-running debate over whether this would be a rude awakening for AI [23]. Animatists have already demonstrated successful behaviors that use unusual representation schemes—for example, a robot that learns to robustly navigate cluttered offices using a network of landmark-specific behaviors [Mataric], and simulations that mimic the information processing and pathologies of salamander, frog, and cockroach nervous systems by topographical maps [Manteuffel], schema networks [Arbib], and neuromorphic circuits [Beer], respectively.

Many authors in *Animats* argue that minimal representations and distributed control systems are preferred for their robustness, reactivity, and adaptability (e.g., [Brooks, Wilson, Maes]). The work in this vein deserves a certain admiration: many papers describe successful control strategies for locomotion, navigation, exploration, and nest-tending that are ingeniously dumb. Many of these strategies, especially those reported in ethological studies, are splendid examples of how the task decompositions underlying natural behaviors often surpass the rational analyses of tasks that lie at the heart of artificial intelligence. Indeed, the consensus of the ethological evidence in the proceedings is that nature prefers such solutions, at least for small animals and insects, where "the small size of a bee's brain impresses upon us the need to keep Occam's razor sharp" [11]. As we will illustrate later, the ethological papers provide an excellent counterpoint to the studies of man-made systems, revealing animal behaviors that are striking in the simplicity of their control strategies, and in the sophistication of their sensorimotor support.

2. Are animats algorithms?

Much of *Animats* will be familiar to the AI reader. The proceedings contains a proliferation of reinforcement learning algorithms that have been situated in simulated environments and trained to forage, follow walls, evade predators, or run mazes. Like many animals, these adaptive algorithms must apprehend only a small part of the world's complexity. Unlike animals, their environments don't have any real complexity, as the typical animat simulation resembles a gridded board game (e.g., [Paredis, Riolo, Sutton, Lin, Collins, Tyrrell]) or video game (e.g. [Wood, Ceccioni, Pierce]). Robotic investigations, few in number, are evenly divided between impoverished environments such as nonbranching mazes [Nehmzow] and realistically cluttered environments such as student offices [Mataric].

As the proceedings indicate, the general practice adopted by these researchers is to show that unfit individuals can adapt well to a *particular* environment by trial-and-error learning, either by tuning individual control policies (e.g., [Sutton, Cecconi, Pierce]) or adapting a mix of control policies (e.g., [Koza, Kurtz, Luigi]). The environment is often little more than a specific fixed problem (e.g., play a short game [Koza], run a particular maze [Sutton], or maximize foraging in a static field [Collins]). This does little to support the contention that adaptive control architectures might perform robustly across many simple but highly varying or novel problems (i.e., environments). Ants incorporate an analysis of the world so successful that they can thrive in widely varying habitats, and even adapt to new environmental regimes brought on by changes in weather and season. By contrast, there are animats that would be stymied by navigational variations as simple as curved walls (e.g., [Nehmzow]).

It is not surprising that these models of behavior, being largely statistical (e.g. [Roitblat, Nehmzow, Schmidhuber, Booker, Sutton, Lin, Riolo, Pierce, Cecconi, Paredis, Vonk, Davidor]), may only capture components of world causality that are highly specific to a particular task; the problem of coaxing inductive systems toward more general causal properties of the world is a general concern throughout the proceedings (e.g., [Booker, Collins]), though often honored in the breach. In this regard, many animatists are hobbled by a conceit that frequently arises in AI: They attribute their success with a specific problem more to the synthetic aspects of their solution—the quality of their algorithm—than to the analytic aspects—their analysis of the task and the representations they've chosen.

Even with such simplified environments, researchers have found that many tasks and settings require strategies beyond stimulus–response control and trial-and-error learning. [Sutton] and [Riolo], for example, suggest that knowledge of the task domain should not just be implicitly embedded in the acquired control mechanism, but should be explicitly available for "mental" operations. [Riolo] augments a stimulus–response architecture with the ability to look several steps ahead before choosing a response, thus departing from the extreme animat position and moving closer toward traditional AI projective planning. [Sutton] makes a curious suggestion: His Dyna-Q architecture uses acquired world knowledge for mental trial-and-error learning, thereby acquiring an optimal control policy with fewer real-world trials. Here explicit world knowledge is used only for off-line practice, not for on-line decision-making. Similarly, in an echo of Minsky's [22] and Braitenberg's [8] "double brain" schemes, [Schmidhuber] proposes a world-modeling neural network to monitor a control network and direct the animat toward "interesting" parts of the environment. Thus the animat may prefer opportunities to learn over more extrinsic rewards.

Evidently, animatists are learning lessons that evoke the early history of experimental challenges to behaviorism. Particularly relevant in this regard are the Gestalt demonstration that animals can solve problems that require temporarily retreating from a goal (e.g., Kohler's experiments with apes, suspended bananas, and movable platforms [16], and Tolman's demonstration of "latent learning", or learning in the absence of reward and punishment [27]).

3. Flirting with evolution

Since many animatists model simple behaviors that can be implemented in small circuits, some are interested in combining blind search techniques with environmentally determined fitness measures to see if circuits encoding useful behaviors can be evolved. Animat evolution comes in two flavors: with and without phenotype. The latter, which we will discuss in the next paragraph, accretes, merges and mutates control mechanisms as if they were genes. The former generally uses genes to specify the connectivity and parameters of a neural network. The chief empirical result here appears to be that the search space for useful behaviors is, predictably, exploded by such an arrangement; one set of simulations which evolves behaviors for a simplified foraging task required six days on a Connection Machine [Collins]. The authors of this experiment were engaged in a question of interest to the artificial life community—which phenotype tends to evolve to fitness faster: feedforward neural networks (show), recurrent neural networks (place), or handcrafted modular neural networks (win). Given their highly particular nature, it is not clear what general claims these experiments could support. It is interesting to note, however, that their results are in line with the hypotheses that (1) causal insulation (i.e., modularity) is important for reducing complex interactions and (2) some internal state (i.e., recurrent networks) can aid even the simplest behaviors by integrating environmental cues over time. That the authors did not note these old AI chestnuts is a reminder that a substantial number of the animat papers come from outside the traditional AI community, which has a history of errors, dead ends, and general wisdom about information-processing architectures that would be of use to new communities of computational modelers.

Many animatists seem determined to discover these notions independently. For example, some papers describing phenotype-less evolution—where the direct causal properties of the genetic code are selected for—applied evolutionary processes directly to Lisp S-expressions and machine codes. [Koza] presents a game-player that uses the results from competition with other game-players to evolve small Lisp decision trees; these trees eventually comprise a 5-ply minimax strategy. [Harvey] outlines an approach for discovering interesting mathematical functions by subjecting random machine-code expressions to fitness criteria of interest and vacuity. Although these works are vaguely reminiscent of Eurisko [18] and highly reminiscent of AM [17], they seem to have been conducted without the benefit of Lenat's hindsight [19] and, curiously, reported without a citation.

4. Situatedness without situations

Some researchers suggest that the goal of animat research is to characterize tasks and environments in terms of their causal complexity, and identify appropriate robust control architectures (e.g., [Wilson, Brooks, Cliff, Meyer]). In contrast to much of AI, the spotlight is on the relationship between the individual and the environment, rather than the relationship between intelligence and a task. It is worth understanding this difference because it motivates the entire animat programme. Moreover, we think that it is the seed of what will ultimately be the animat contribution to AI.

The glue that makes the animat and its environment an analytic whole is the oft-invoked principle of situatedness [1]. This slightly mystical term means nothing more (or less) than taking seriously the problems and privileges of having a body: sensing, effecting, the significance of place, the use of space, the constraint of time. In the extreme situated view, animats are relieved of the crushing responsibilities of representing the world because all the necessary information is available in the immediate environment, and, presumably, freely available through the senses.

The situated analysis of task intelligence is liberating in that it emphasizes subjectively useful representations over objectively correct world models, and thus frees robot designers to attend only to information that has significance vis-à-vis the task [2]. However, situatedness implies—or should imply—a greater commitment to the root of subjective representations: sensing and perception. AI researchers who are fluent in *situatednese* often speak of "offloading representation overhead into the world"; many, though, are aware that they are really offloading to the senses, which have evolved to detect behaviorally significant patterns and anomalies in the environment [9,6]. *Nihil in intellectu nisi prius in sensu.* [2]

Oddly enough, the questions of how to sense and what to sense for have been side-stepped by nearly all animat researchers; many of the animat models presume information not usually available to animals, such as absolute position and reliably detectable gradients (e.g., [Sutton, Riolo, Collins, Cecconi, Paredis]). If not working in robotics or ethology, animatists also dispense with the problem of discovering what kinds of information the environment actually offers. This is unfortunate, as that is exactly where animatists could best advance their field. High-level situated systems are typically based on extensive analyses of the informational affordances that support behavior in man-made environments [25]. One would expect animatists to do similar analyses of natural environments, but one-up AI situatedness by showing that these analyses make sober assumptions about sensing and perception. If the animatists succeed in this regard, AI researchers will have much to learn from them.

As for the animat contribution to robotics, it may well prove to be that the main obstacle to achieving animal-like behavior is not the development of control mechanisms, but the engineering of useful sensors and perceptual systems. The ethological papers in the proceedings, which we will review in the next section, have much to say about this matter.

5. Sharp senses, simple minds

If there is a lesson to be learned from the ethological papers in the proceedings, it is that animals' highly specialized perceptual systems and rich proprioceptive representations are often the key to strikingly simple control mechanisms. Two papers from the proceedings—[Teitelbaum] and [Jamon]—illustrate this nicely.

One approach to teasing apart the basic components of behavior is selective lesioning and suppression of parts of the brain. [Teitelbaum] used transectioning and drugs to suppress central motor programs used for spontaneous (voluntary) behavior in rats. As they describe it, the impaired behaviors break down into sets of "allied reflexes". For example, injections of the dopamine receptor-blocker haloperidol will make a rat cataleptic. Despite the suppression of all voluntary motion, if pushed from behind, the rat will leap into the air. The authors explain, "As the cataleptic animal is pushed

---

[2] Nothing in the mind unless previously in the senses.

forward, it braces ... by shifting its weight backwards. When its hind legs begin to slip, a leap is triggered ... When it lands ... it immediately resumes immobility". All these reflexes are allied in a static postural module, which homeostatically maintains the rat's stability.

Nearly all the reflexes catalogued by the authors require fairly complex proprioceptive, tactile, and vestibular triggers. For example, a twisting reflex, which helps an upside-down rat get back onto its feet, requires a twisted supine posture and forepaw contact with the ground in order to trigger rotation of the shoulders. The entire righting behavior is a simple concatenation of such reflexes, each initiated by a complex set of proprioceptive and tactile cues.

Several animal studies in *Animats* found fairly sophisticated sensory triggers in behaviors that, from a control point of view, appear relatively simple. The sensory aspects of animal behavior contrast strongly with the sensation-poor animat simulations. Most of these simulations have environments and sensory attributes that are impoverished even by AI standards, let alone in comparison with robotics and vision domains. Outside of robotics (e.g., [Brooks, Mataric]), animatists are not grappling with animals' or robots' real information-processing needs. This certainly does not invalidate any animat paradigm; it merely indicates that in order to show that their adaptive control systems solve problems, animat builders will have to get into the robot business. Fortunately, for simple animats at least, researchers won't have to solve general computer vision problems. Ethologists point out that behavioral triggers are often quite specialized—a male stickleback fish will attack a red underbelly sported by just about any stickleback-sized object [26]. For these animals, evolution has found features that can be reliably detected and which correlate highly with appropriate conditions for a behavior. With few exceptions, animatists have done no such analysis of real-world environments, nor have they considered whether feature detectors could be built to meet the informational needs of their simulated animats.

In support of the animatists, it does appear to be the case that many animals do use remarkably simple control mechanisms. In fact, the simplicity and elegance of the control strategies proposed in the ethological studies easily exceeds that of the control algorithms of the animat architectures.

6. Long trips, little navigation

An important hypothesis in the animat literature is that environments are rich enough in local information to support nonlocal behaviors such as navigation without full-blown internal maps. Many animat navigation systems use one-dimensional representations to "tunnel through" the world using landmarks and gradients for guidance [Mataric, Pierce, Lin]. One-dimensional representations, such as landmark networks, are far easier to build and revise than two-dimensional representations such as maps. Animatists have found it profitable to ignore two-dimensional systematicities in the world, such as the fact that two paths may intersect or that curved paths have shortcuts.

Nature, evidently, has found it profitable to use even simpler mechanisms. [Jamon] surveys recent debates in the ethological literature about some of nature's more famous travellers: salmon returning to spawn, bees returning to waggle, and pigeons and rodents returning to home. As the examples we recount below suggest, the navigational talents of these animals may have been greatly overestimated.

Transported a relatively long distance from home, rodents have a better than chance ability to return. Although this suggests a special orientation mechanism or extensive topological maps, a model requiring only a random walk biased by gradual variations in vegetation suffices to explain experimental data. Supporting evidence comes from the observation that of the mice who were tested, those who were released in patches of vegetation with locally inverted gradients started off in the wrong direction and were lost for several days. A similar model accounts for the ability of salmon to return from the Pacific to their spawning streams. Assuming that salmon are scattered at sea, swim straight in a random direction until they reach a coast, and then wander up and down the coast until the home stream is found by chance, statistical simulations yield return rates that are only slightly below those reported in wildlife studies. This gap can be closed by various reasonable assumptions, such as uneven distribution of the salmon population in the ocean, and environmental irregularities such as ocean currents.

Stochastic process models are also consistent with the map-like abilities of homing pigeons. Homing pigeons are widely believed to use orientation mechanisms when they are far from their familiar home territory. Atmospheric gradients are not reliable over long distances, so gradient-based orientation is highly subject to noise. [Jamon] describes a computer simulation by Wallraff [28] in which model pigeons have learned the local intensities and directions of several gradients at home. Far from home, a model pigeon determines the probable home vector from each of these gradients with a polynomially declining probability of correctness. It then tosses a weighted coin for each vector, and averages the results with the current heading for a new heading. [Jamon] notes that "remarkably low" probabilities sufficed for simulated homing performances comparable with those of actual pigeons.

As these examples attest, stochastic algorithms may form the basis for some impressive map-like behaviors. However, some caveats are in order here. First, the simplicity of such a control algorithm is intimately related to powers of perception and locomotion; none of the random processes will work well if an animal cannot make a straight line, a daunting task for a day's worth of swimming. Secondly, the reader may object that some of these animals are known to have more sophisticated powers of navigation. This is correct, but generally pertains to home territory; homing pigeons, for example, are thought to have detailed mental maps of the area around their loft. Finally, these behavioral accounts are merely statistical simulations that have been parameterized to match the observed success rates of real populations. Animals may use different processes and informational affordances to produce the same behavior. In order to establish the biased random walk model, for example, ethologists will need to show that biological navigation algorithms fail in predictable ways, as did the few mice that got lost after an initial misorientation. However, even with all these objections, we find the stark modesty of the algorithms that might guide such remote travels quite noteworthy.

One of the most delightful examples of a simple algorithm yielding an apparently sophisticated behavior is reported in [Deneubourg]. Deneubourg and colleagues set out to model ants' facility for clustering and sorting larvae in the nest. Their model is a random walk combined with two simple rules for picking up and dropping larvae: the probability of picking up an object is high if there are no similar objects nearby; the probability of putting it down is high in the opposite situation. Using this algorithm, a simulated ant colony will order itself in a manner remarkably similar to that of real ants reordering a scattered nest.

One is tempted to speculate that nature uses stochastic control strategies because (1) they are often adequate, and (2) they presumably require less precise genetic coding of neural structures. Indeed, this may be one of a repertoire of strategies that nature has for encoding behavior in a nervous system.

7. The neural encoding of behavior

After reading so many animat algorithms, one must wonder: Are there natural neural organizing principles that we would ultimately recognize as behavior architectures? From an architectural point of view it makes sense to segregate function so as to prevent unwanted interaction, hence it would seem logical to envision behaviors as encoded by individual modules or layers. This design strategy appears to be at work in the brains of higher mammals: the human cortex, for example, is characterized by localities of specific interconnection patterns, selectively linked by large white-matter pathways [15].

However, in lower animals, arthropods, and probably the most ancient structures of the mammalian brain, the neural organization of behavior seems to be much less systematic—sometimes key functions are subsumed by individual cells. It is also rather hodgepodge. Looking at the nervous system schematic of, say, the mollusc Hermissenda [4], it is quite believable that the neural circuits developed through accretion and random rewiring. Instead of modular or laminal organization, we see a multiplicity of neural arbitration mechanisms.

The neuroethological papers in the proceedings describe a smorgasbord of neural devices for behavior arbitration. [Beer] describes an artificial cockroach controlled by a neuromorphic circuit. Like many of the animals from whose nervous systems its circuits were cribbed, the artificial cockroach incorporates several mechanisms for arbitrating between competing behaviors. In some cases, a "command cell" is inhibited; in others, rhythm-generating cells are perturbed. Connections between cells serving one behavior can be suppressed by another behavior, effecting a temporary rewiring of the behavior. [Manteuffel]'s simulation of how salamanders visually home in on prey demonstrates an organizing principle common in higher brains: the salamander brain has a number of topographical maps which project to each other, thereby converting retinotopic position to neck-muscle position, which in turn governs the salamander's direction of approach. [Arbib]'s artificial toad, simulated at the much higher level of schemas, often assimilates the output of two competing schemas simply by adding their outputs; this coarse-coding [3] is a familiar computer vision and neural network representational strategy. With all these different mechanisms for arbitration and representation, it seems somewhat less likely that any single algorithmic architecture will support the full range of behavior we see even in a single insect.

Indeed, it may be a long time before we see an animat as complicated as an insect. Behaviors such as hunting and courtship remain well beyond the state of the art (though we are ready to be surprised by their algorithmic simplicity). Conversely, it may also be a long time before we see an animat as simple as an insect. This is because of the physics of scale. Small animals may get by with simple control mechanisms simply because many errors have benign consequences at diminutive physical scales. Insects collide and crawl over each other, fall from heights, and stumble and roll without damage. Their behavioral repertoire assumes a very forgiving physical world. Where the world isn't forgiving enough, individuals are expendable. Larger size, however, may require more intelligence simply because coordination, efficient use of energy, and longevity are more important. Ironically, when animatists build robots, the larger scale regimen forced on them by modern engineering may require more complicated intelligences than they would like.

8. Related reading

Ethological and behavior-centered models have had a promising impact in the robotics community, where the constraints of body, sensation, and limited computation are real, not simulated. Some readers may prefer Maes' *Designing Autonomous Agents* [20] to the *Animats* proceedings. Although the two collections have several contributors in common, articles in *Designing Autonomous Agents* are technically more substantive and represent a more sober approach to building animal-like robots. Although the book does not provide as interesting a window into recent developments in ethology as *Animats* does, one article [5] does present a useful introduction to ethology for roboticists.

Those who are more interested in ethology itself may prefer to consult a book surveying the field (e.g., the *Oxford Companion to Animal Behavior* [21]), or classics which have influenced AI researchers (e.g., Tinbergen's *The Study of Instinct* [26]). Those more interested in neuroethology or computational models of perceptual pathways may wish to consult Ewert's *Neuroethology* [13], or a text of the same name by Camhi [10].

9. Summary

Animats explicitly represents itself as an effort to create a new scientific community drawing from the fields of artificial intelligence, ethology, and robotics. The primary goal is to discover the underpinnings of animal-like intelligence through the synthesis of behavior and analysis of tasks and environments. The quality of the contributions varies greatly. The most vivid reading comes from the researchers who have worked with real animals, real robots, and real environments. The ethology-meets-computer-modeling articles in particular are fascinating, both as a lesson as to how simple brains are viable in sophisticated sensorimotor platforms (e.g., [Jamon, Teitelbaum, Cruse,

Manteuffel]), and simply as an opportunity to marvel at natural designs (e.g. [Theraulaz, Deneubourg]). By contrast, the papers which do not contend with the real physical world only offer vague characterizations of the animat problem along with questionable algorithms for its solution. *Animats* contains a good number of manifestos, proposals, critiques of other fields, and algorithms that only superficially address the information processing needs of real animals and real robots. This is somewhat understandable, in that *Animats* is a conference proceedings, not a book, and in that the field itself is something of a novelty.

The papers in *Animats* raise many issues that are or should be of concern to artificial intelligence researchers: What are the informational affordances of tasks and real environments? What kinds of error will environments tolerate? What kinds of representations do competent behaviors really need? What aspects of behavior can be learned? What innate predispositions can or should be assumed? What kinds of representation are sustainable with real sensors and limited computation? And finally, what might we learn about these matters from studying evolution's answers? It is quite conceivable that when animatists gain experience with real robots, sensors, tasks, and environments, they will propose answers to these questions that artificial intelligence researchers will have to take seriously. Unfortunately, in much of the proceedings, these questions are used as a pretense to put reactive and machine learning algorithms through their paces in woefully impoverished simulated worlds. Of all these questions, only the last two—sustainable representations and the biological record—are well served in the proceedings, the former by an occasional robotics paper, and the latter by an intriguing sampling of ethological and neuroethological papers. Apparently, the ethologists have gained much more by adding computational modeling to their repertoire than computational modelers have gained by reading ethology.

Appendix A. Table of contents from the proceedings

A.1. The Animat Approach

Simulation of Adaptive Behavior in Animats: Review and Prospect
  Jean-Arcady Meyer and Agnes Guillot
The Animat Path to AI
  Stewart W. Wilson
What it Means for Robot Behavior to be Adaptive
  David McFarland
Computational Neuroethology: A Provisional Manifesto
  Dave Cliff
On the Feasibility of Computational Artificial Life—A Reply to Critics
  Harold C. Morris
The Animat and the Physician
  Alexandre Parodi and Pierre Bonelli
Extended Classifiers for Simulation of Adaptive Behavior
  Renaud Dumeur

A.2. Perception and Motor Control

Biomimetic Sonar Processing: From Dolphin Echolocation to Artificial Neural Networks
   H.L. Roitblat, P.W.B. Moore, P.E. Nachtigall and R.H. Penner
Hierarchical Dishabituation of Visual Discrimination in Toads
   DeLiang Wang and Michael A. Arbib
The Computational Hoverfly: A Study in Computational Neuroethology
   Dave Cliff
Can Allied Reflexes Promote the Integration of a Robot's Behavior?
   Philip Teitelbaum, Vivien C. Pellis, and Sergio M. Pellis
Coordination of Leg Movement in Walking Animals
   Holk Cruse
A Biological Visuo-Motor System: How Dissimilar Maps Interact to Produce Behavior
   Gerhard Manteuffel
Biological and Computational Stereo Vision
   Stephen T. Bernard
Modeling and Simulation of Animals' Movements
   Simon Benhamou and Pierre Bovet

A.3. Cognitive Maps and Internal World Models

Schemas for Prey-Catching in Frog and Toad
   Michael A. Arbib and Alberto Cobas
Mapbuilding Using Self-Organising Networks in "Really Useful Robots"
   Ulrich Nehmzow and Tim Smithers
The Contribution of Quantitative Models to Long Distance Orientation Problems
   Marc Jamon
Navigating with a Rat Brain: A Neurobiologically-Inspired Model for Robot Spatial Representation
   Maja J. Mataric
Four Important Issues in Cognitive Mapping
   W.K. Yeap and C.C. Handley
Attracting Similar Shapes towards Each Other
   Mitch R. Harris

A.4. Motivation and Emotion

Ethological and Psychological Models of Motivation—Towards a Synthesis
   Frederick Toates and Per Jensen
Pleasure: The Answer to Conflicting Motivations
   Michel Cabanac
Machine Motivation
   J.R.P. Halperin

A Possibility for Implementing Curiosity and Boredom in Model-Building Neural Controllers
  Jürgen Schmidhuber

A.5. Action Selection and Behavioral Sequences

Instinct as an Inductive Bias for Learning Behavioral Sequences
  Lashon B. Booker
A Bottom-Up Mechanism for Behavior Selection in a Artificial Creature
  Pattie Maes
The Neural Basis of Behavioral Choice in an Artificial Insect
  Randall D. Beer and Hillel J. Chiel
An Investigation of Two Mediation Strategies Suitable for Behavioural Control in Animals and Animats
  Martin Snaith and Owen Holland
Computer Simulation of an Animal Environment
  Toby Tyrrell and John E.W. Mayhew

A.6. Ontogeny and Learning

Ontogeny of Preferences in Guppies (Poecilia Reticulata) Exposed to Food and Conspecifics
  Patrick W. Colgan, T. Lynne Jamieson, Janice E. Frame and J. Terry Smith
Simulation Studies of Song Learning in Birds
  James M. Williams and P.J.B. Slater
Reinforcement Learning Architectures for Animats
  Richard S. Sutton
Self-Improving Reactive Agents: Case Studies of Reinforcement Learning Frameworks
  Long-Ji Lin
Exploring Adaptive Agency II: Simulating the Evolution of Associative Learning
  Peter M. Todd and Geoffrey F. Miller
Lookahead Planning and Latent Learning in a Classifier System
  Rick L. Riolo
Learning Hill-Climbing Functions as a Strategy for Generating Behaviors in a Mobile Robot
  David Pierce and Benjamin Kuipers
Some Parallels between Associative Learning and Object Classification
  David R. Shanks

A.7. Collective Behaviors

Task Differentiation in Polistes Wasp Colonies: A Model for Self-Organizing Groups of Robots
  Guy Theraulaz, Somon Goss, Jacques Gervet, and Jean-Louis Deneubourg

The Dynamics of Collective Sorting: Robot-Like Ants and Ant-Like Robots
  J.L. Deneubourg, S. Goss, N. Franks, A. Sendova-Franks, C. Detrain, and L. Chretien

A.8. *Evolution of Behavior*

Evolution and Co-Evolution of Computer Programs to Control Independently-Acting
  Agents
  John R. Koza
The Evolution of Information-Gathering: Operational Constraints
  Cynthia Kurtz
Representations for Artificial Organisms
  Robberts J. Collins and David R. Jefferson
Evolving Organisms that Can Reach for Objects
  Federico Cecconi and Domenico Parisi
The Artificial Evolution of Behavior
  Inman Harvey
The Rise of Interaction: Intrinsic Simulation Modelling of the Onset of Interacting
  Behaviour
  Fabio De Luigi and Vittorio Maniezzo
The Evolution of Behavior: Some Experiments
  Jan Paredis
A Von Neumann Approach to a Genotype Expression in a Neural Animat
  Dan Wood

A.9. *Architectures, Organizational Principles, and Functional Approaches*

Challenges for Complete Creature Architectures
  Rodney A. Brooks
Cognitive Action Theory as a Control Architecture
  H.L. Roitblat
Towards a Theory of Emergent Functionality
  Luc Steels
Eight Principles for Building an Intelligent Robot
  David L. Waltz
Robot Ethology: A Proposal for the Research into Intelligent Autonomous Systems
  Uwe Schnepf
A Model of the Mechanisms Underlying Exploratory Behavior
  Liane M. Babora and Patrick W. Colgan
The Causal Analysis of an Adaptive System: Sex-Ration Decisions as Observed in a
  Parasitic Wasp and Simulated by a Network Model
  Marijke Vonk, Felix Putters and Berend-Jan Velthuis
Evolution as Pattern Processing: TODO as a Substrate for Evolution
  P. Hogeweg and B. Hesper
Matching, Maximizing, and Melioration as Alternative Descriptions of Behaviour
  Alasdair I. Houston

An Adaptation Anomaly of a Genetic Algorithm
Yuval Davidor
Autonomous Agents, AI, and Chaos Theory
George Kiss
Incrementing Intelligent Systems by Design
Brendan McGonigle

A.10. Animats in Education

Animal Simulations with *Logo: Massive Parallelism for the Masses
Mitchel Resnick
Lego Vehicles: A Technology for Studying Intelligent Systems
Jim Donnett and Tim Smithers

References

[1] P. Agre, The dynamic structure of everyday life, Ph.D. Thesis, Department of Electrical Engineering and Computer Science, MIT, Cambridge, MA (1988).

[2] P. Agre and D. Chapman, Pengi: an implementation of a theory of activity, in: *Proceedings AAAI87*, Seattle, WA (1987).

[3] J. Albus, A new approach to manipulator control: the cerebellar model articulation control (CMAC), *J. Dyn. Syst. Measurement Control* **97** (1975) 220–227.

[4] D. Alkon, *Memory Traces in the Brain* (Cambridge University Press, Cambridge, England, 1987).

[5] T. Anderson and M. Donath, Animal behavior as a paradigm for developing robot autonomy, in: P. Maes, ed., *Designing Autonomous Agents* (Bradford Books/MIT Press, Cambridge, MA, 1990).

[6] D. Ballard, Reference frames for animate vision, in: *Proceedings AAAI-89*, Detroit, MI (1989) 1635–1641.

[7] C. Bonnet, Essai de psychologie, in: *Oeuvres d'Histoire Naturelle et de Philosophie* (Samuel Fauche, Neuchatel, 1779).

[8] V. Braitenberg, *Vehicles* (Bradford Books/MIT Press, Cambridge, MA, 1984).

[9] R.A. Brooks, Intelligence without reason, *Proceedings IJCAI-91*, Sydney, Australia (1991) 569–595.

[10] J. Camhi, *Neuroethology: Nerve Cells and the Natural Behavior of Animals* (Sinaur Associates, 1984).

[11] B. Cartwright and T. Collet, Landmark maps for honeybees, *Biol. Cybern.* **57** (1983) 85–93.

[12] R. Descartes, *Passions de L'Ame* (Amstelodami, 1685).

[13] J. Ewert, *Neuroethology* (Springer-Verlag, New York, 1980).

[14] T. Huxley, On the hypothesis that animals are automata, in: *Method and Results: Essays* (D. Appleton and Company, New York, 1874).

[15] J. Kelly, Principles of the functional and anatomical organization of the nervous system, in: E. Kandel and J. Schwartz, eds., *Principles of Neural Science* (Elsevier Science, New York, 1985) 209–221 (Chapter 19).

[16] W. Kohler, *Mentality of Apes* (Vintage Books, New York, 1956).

[17] D. Lenat, AM: an artificial intelligence approach to discovery in mathematics as heuristic search, Tech. Rept. AIM-286, STAN-CS-76-570, HPP-76-8 Department of Computer Science, Stanford University, Stanford, CA (1976).

[18] D. Lenat, EURISKO: a program that learns new heuristics and domain concepts, *Artif. Intell.* **21** (1983) 61–98.

[19] D. Lenat and J. Brown, Why AM and EURISKO appear to work, *Artif. Intell.* **23** (1984) 269–294.

[20] P. Maes, ed., *Designing autonomous agents: theory and practice from biology to engineering and back* (Bradford Books/MIT Press, Cambridge, MA, 1990); reprinted from: *Rob. Autonomous Syst.* **6** (1–2).

[21] D. McFarland, ed., *The Oxford Companion to Animal Behavior* (Oxford University Press, Oxford, England, 1987).

[22] M. Minsky, *The Society of Mind* (Simon and Schuster, New York, 1985).

[23] J. Searle, Minds, brains, and programs, *Behav. Brain Sci.* **3** (1980) 417–457.

[24] M. Stefik, Review of Braitenberg's Vehicles: Experiments in Synthetic Psychology, *Artif. Intell.* **27** (2) (1985) 246–248.

[25] L. Suchman, *Plans and Situated Action* (Cambridge University Press, Cambridge, England, 1987).

[26] N. Tinbergen, *The Study of Instinct* (Clarendon Press, Oxford, 1951).

[27] E. Tolman, Cognitive maps in rats and men, *Psychol. Rev.* **55** (1948) 189–208.

[28] H. Wallraff, Simulated navigation based on unreliable sources of information (models of pigeon homing, part 1), *J. Theor. Biol.* **137** (1989) 1–19.

Artificial Intelligence 73 (1995) 323–369

Book Review

Kenneth M. Ford and Patrick J. Hayes, eds., *Reasoning Agents in a Dynamic World: The Frame Problem* ⋆

Jozsef A. Toth *

Department of Information Science and Intelligent Systems Program, University of Pittsburgh, 600 Epsilon Drive, Pittsburgh, PA 15238, USA

This book, the first volume in a JAI Press series entitled *Advances in Human and Machine Cognition*, is a collection of fifteen papers edited by Kenneth M. Ford and Patrick J. Hayes. These papers were originally presented at The First International Workshop on Human & Machine Cognition, Pensacola, Florida, May 11–13, 1989. The workshop is a biannual affair which at each meeting addresses a core interdisciplinary topic in artificial intelligence (AI) and cognitive science. The special topic for the conference, and book, is the *frame problem*. The papers in the book incorporate an interdisciplinary approach drawing from AI, cognitive science, psychology and philosophy. The book is quite formal and some chapters require a background in logic, computer science and AI principles—although a few will appeal to the general reader. There is a six-page introduction by the editors that provides a brief synopsis of the frame problem and related problems as well as a brief organization and summaries of the papers presented in the book.

1. Introduction

The frame problem originally emerged from McCarthy's situation calculus and was first identified by McCarthy and Hayes in 1969. The conceptual framework of the situation calculus involved the basic idea that changes of *states* in the world are caused by *actions*. The frame problem came about as a formal representation problem stemming from the design and implementation of intelligent systems. The term *frame* itself arose

---

⋆ (JAI Press, Greenwich, CT, 1991); 290 + xiv pages.

* E-mail: jtoth@pitt.edu.

from McCarthy's conception of a system of frames or, "frames of reference". Each frame comprised properties, known as fluents, to which the consequences of an action would not affect the entire frame, only parts of it:

> ... if a person has a telephone he still has it after looking up a number in the telephone book. If we had a number of actions to be performed in sequence, we would have quite a number of conditions to write down that certain actions do not change the values of certain fluents. In fact with n actions and m fluents we might have to write down mn such conditions.
>
> We see two ways out of this difficulty. The first is to introduce the notion of frame, like the state vector in McCarthy (1962). A number of fluents are declared as attached to the frame and the effect of an action is described by telling which fluents are changed, all others being presumed unchanged. (Mc-Carthy & Hayes, 1969, p. 38)

The phrase, *all others being presumed unchanged*, is the crux of the original frame problem. It was quickly discovered that presuming any aspect of the world to be unchanged, and representing those presumptions, was a very deep problem. The frame problem also gave rise to a lineage of related problems which were grounded in the same conceptual framework regarding states and actions in the world. In addition to the many subtle variations of the original frame problem, which will be explicated later in the survey of the book, the most noteworthy of these descendants are the qualification, ramification and persistence problems. The *qualification* problem involves the inability to specify enough preconditions to merit the validity of an action in any given state. The *ramification* problem entails the inability to specify all the side effects of an action. The *persistence* problem is the problem of representing which facts endure and which cease to endure from one state to the next.

1.1. Goals of the review

In the introductory chapter of the book, "Framing the Problem", a brief history, as well as two basic kinds of frame problem are highlighted by the editors. The first type is the original McCarthy & Hayes (1969) *narrow* frame problem which is strictly defined as a *representation* problem of artificial intelligence (AI). The representational nature of the narrow frame problem entails the problem of finding an appropriate means of describing the absence of change between states. The typical representations associated with the narrow frame problem include data, or "knowledge", structures such as multi-attribute schemas and predicates in logic. The second type is the *broad* frame problem, which captures the idea that the frame problem might be solved by concentrating on computational resources and control structures rather than representations. The broad frame problem also appears, however, to take in topics of a more expansive nature including: the relationship between representation and computation, laws of motion, philosophy and potential bridges between human and machine cognition. Regarding the issue that tugs at representation and computation for instance: If an electromechanical reasoning agent were to be endowed with boundless computational resources, one argument against this kind of broad solution (Hayes, 1987) maintains that the agent would still lack the ability to make inferences about changes between states since such computations would be performed on what are presumed to be ineffective representations, such as frame axioms, vis-à-vis the narrow frame problem. Thus, exploration into new and different aspects of computability might or might not lead to a "solution" to the frame problem. By applying this narrow/broad distinction to the book, the editors classify the contributions of Haugh, Morgenstern, Tenenberg, Weber and Weld as closer to the narrow frame problem. The chapters by Nutter and Perlis assume the broader stance. The remaining eight chapters are left unclassified by the editors. In general, as witnessed by the myriad approaches and opinions discussed in the book, it is safe to say that a consensus built towards what the frame problem actually *is*, becomes sorely lacking:

> The frame problem poses a frustrating and tantalizing enigma. It has been defined very tightly, and so loosely that it seems to be the entire problem of cognition. It has been viewed as absolutely central and as artifactual. It has been characterized as essentially an issue of complexity and as an issue to which questions of complexity are irrelevant. It is hardly surprising that some people doubt that it is there at all. (Nutter, p. 171) [1]

For the purposes of this review, whenever I use the term "frame problem", I am referring to any known treatment of the frame problem. Otherwise, I will explicitly refer to a particular instance or descendent of the frame problem by name (e.g., "the qualification problem"). Given the breadth and discontinuity of opinions provided by the various contributors, what one will most likely *not* gain from the book is a sense of closure regarding the frame problem. What the reader will most likely acquire is an enhanced appreciation for the depth and complexity of this problem and perhaps a renewed insight into one's own particular realm of interest—even if only remotely related to the frame problem. The title of the book, *Reasoning Agents in a Dynamic World*, and the series to which it belongs, *Advances in Human and Machine Cognition*, imply to me a particular setting for the frame problem. In particular I interpret these to mean a coupling of the common qualities which human cognition (i.e., cognitive science) and machine cognition (i.e., artificial intelligence) share as both divergent and convergent disciplines. I kept this in mind as I read the book and have also adopted this conceptual union as the basic theme of this review. Therefore, my goals in this review are:

- in Section 2, to provide a general survey of some of the major contributions in the book;
- in Section 3, to discuss and to establish how the myriad ideas advanced by contributors in the book interact with specific scientific methodologies regarding human and machine cognition.

Clarifying my second goal: Upon reading the book, I have been able to surmise that the frame problem, rather than an end in itself, is actually a *symptom* of the method by which the researcher in AI or cognitive science chooses to characterize, through abstraction, the relationship between the reasoning agent and its environment. This

---

[1] All nondated name and page references refer to the book.

abstraction is typically realized in a representation either for the purposes of modeling in AI, or to explain a particular behavioral phenomenon in cognitive science. The frame problem is "the tip of the iceberg", as it were, of certain scientific and methodological approaches in AI and cognitive science. The germinal issue, then, does not appear to entail whether the frame problem is solvable or not. Rather, it seems to pertain to whether a particular representational approach in AI or cognitive science will lead to the intractability which has been identified as the frame problem. The contributions of Nutter, Perlis and Stein, in particular, provide important insights to an argument of this kind, suggesting that the frame problem is really an unsolvable obstacle—much like the mathematical impossibility of dividing any number by zero or infinity. For the past two decades, the frame problem appears to have served as an ontological and epistemological "litmus test" for those who have cared to notice its significance, such as Chapman (1987, 1991), Agre & Chapman (1987) or Pollack & Ringuette (1990) have demonstrated in the domain of planning. I maintain that the narrow/broad distinction introduced by the editors, which is also discussed by some of the contributors, does not effectively capture the essence of the frame problem. Therefore, in the discussion (Section 3), I will assume a more expansive posture and examine in greater detail the methodological issues pertaining to the relationship between the reasoning agent and its environment. For the remainder of this Section however, I will introduce some of the fundamental intractabilities associated with certain modes of abstraction and representation that lead to the frame problem, in an attempt to set the stage for the survey of the book in Section 2 and the ensuing discussion in Section 3.

1.2. Machine cognition and omniscience

Certain assumptions of *omniscience* underlie most approaches to abstraction and representation in AI and cognitive science. Omniscience means that in order for a particular representation to work, the reasoning agent endowed with that representation must have complete knowledge of all objects and events in the world and complete knowledge of itself. This general assumption was inherent in McCarthy's situation calculus, where describing the external world was accomplished by saying that a state S_{n+1} in the world results from an action A_n in state S_n.[2] Characterized by McCarthy & Hayes, "A situation S is the complete state of the universe at one time" (1969, p. 33). The terms *state* and *situation* are more or less synonymous. Frame axioms were the first, albeit defunct, attempt at providing a solution to, or way around, the original frame problem discovered in the situation calculus. Frame axioms are logic expressions that maintain information about what properties do not change in the transition from one state to the

---

[2] As a historical note, McCarthy's earlier thinking which eventually led to the situation calculus had involved the requirement for "a kind of means–ends analysis used in ordinary life" (1963, p. 410). Likewise, relating to what would later come to be identified as the frame problem, "Causality logic should be extended to allow inference that certain propositional fluents will always hold" (1963, p. 417). A *fluent* can be thought of as an attribute or property whose value can change or remain the same over time.

next as the result of an action. The following expression is an example of a frame axiom in a simple world involving blocks:

> If block x has a color c in situation S_n and situation S_{n+1} results from moving block x in S_n, then block x will have the same color c in S_{n+1}. (Morgenstern, p. 135)

Simply put, a block in this pedagogical world does not change color as the result of being moved. In order for this frame axiom to work however, one kind of omniscient assumption that must be made is that nothing else can occur *between* states other than what is described by this frame axiom regarding the block's color c. This omniscient assumption holds that, "all intervening events are known" (Haugh, p. 110). For example, if a five year old child, holding a full, quality-assured can of spray paint of a different color c' were to come along *between* the states S_n and S_{n+1}, and paint the block x to the new color c', the frame axiom described a moment ago would be rendered invalid. In turn, if other frame axioms were to depend on the validity of this frame axiom, the constancy of a particular color c, those would also become invalid. One can see how the reasoning agent could rapidly become confused if events in the world did not occur exactly as prescribed. A reasoning agent equipped with the situation calculus and frame axioms, or even with a more recent representation in AI or cognitive science, can only truly function with the assumption of omniscience. Other varieties of omniscience will be covered later in the survey of Haugh's chapter in Section 2.3.

In a sense omniscience is a fallacy since a biological or electromechanical reasoning agent cannot possibly be aware of everything that transpires around it. Nevertheless, omniscience mandates that the agent be aware of everything and that this awareness must be represented and maintained internally by the reasoning agent. Hence, in general, if *any* representation-related change in the world occurs, it must be acknowledged by the electromechanical agent; and, in turn, the corresponding internal representation that is maintained to describe the agent's model of the world must also be updated to reflect this change. The agent cannot be made aware on a "need to know" basis. In the case of the simple scenario presented above, whenever block x in S_n is moved in the world, either by the reasoning agent or as the result of some other external cause, information about the block's new state in S_{n+1} must be propagated to the corresponding internal representation in the reasoning system, from $\#S_n$ to $\#S_{n+1}$ (the '#' symbol denotes "in the mind of the agent"). The formalism of situation theory (Devlin, 1991; Barwise & Perry, 1983) effectively represents this principle of external–internal correspondence, as depicted in Fig. 1. Moreover, this new internal information must be exhaustively propagated, and verified, among all the other objects in the internal representation in order to curtail any potential conflicts and contradictions. For instance, two different blocks cannot occupy the same x, y, z location at the same time. This intricate practice of bookkeeping, in particular, has been one of the main thrusts of the nonmonotonic reasoning research community. In the review of Perlis' and Goodwin & Trudel's chapters, potential uses for the maintenance of co-existing, conflicting values of properties will be explicated.

Even if the world of the electromechanical reasoning agent involves thousands or millions of objects, because of omniscience, each relevant external object, $\{x_0, \ldots, x_m\}$,

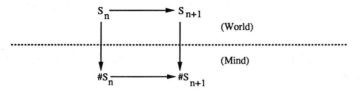

Fig. 1. Mapping external states S to internal mental states $\#S$ (adapted from Devlin, 1991).

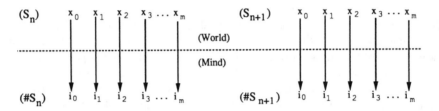

Fig. 2. Omniscient mapping of external objects $\{x_0,\ldots,x_m\}$ to internal representations $\{i_0,\ldots,i_m\}$ from one state n to the next $n+1$.

must be mapped to a unique corresponding internal representation, $\{i_0,\ldots,i_m\}$. Fig. 2 illustrates how this omniscient mapping is maintained from the transition of one pair of external–internal states $\{S_n, \#S_n\}$ to the next, $\{S_{n+1}, \#S_{n+1}\}$. Note in Fig. 2 how each external object x is mapped, via the vertical arrow, to its corresponding internal representation. The "mapping" referred to pertains not so much to individual objects, but more importantly, to the *properties* which make up an agent's conception of an object. Like the property of color mentioned before, other examples of properties might involve the physical location of one object, spatial orientations between two or more objects, ownership of a set of objects, absolute and relative velocity, and so forth. An external *event* is a perceivable change in one or more properties related to one or more objects. Actions such as those in the situation calculus, are only one of many phenomena that might give rise to events. As external events occur, which cause the transitions from one external state S_n to the next S_{n+1}, the internal representation must be expressive enough to represent the changes which occur within and between the actual properties used to describe external objects. Objects in and of themselves do not change, rather the unique properties that describe and individuate objects change. In the situation calculus and other representations of AI and cognitive science, the properties of objects that are subject to change, via events and actions, do so owing to the principle of *causality*. Thus, some force or entity is always responsible for effecting the change of a property from a value to a different value. The force, or cause, that results in a change might originate in the mind of the agent ($\#S$), such as in the generation of a new goal based on the current circumstances. Or, it can also exist external to the agent (S), manifested perhaps as another agent or as the result of a law of nature, such as wind or gravity.

As Chapman (1987) discovered in the domain of planning however, the omniscient method of representation described so far becomes combinatorially intractable in a fast-changing, complex world. Mandating that the agent must apprehend and internally maintain a complete, omniscient copy of the world, including causal relations among

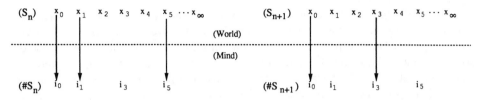

Fig. 3. Non-omniscient mapping of external objects to internal representations from one state to the next.

properties, presumably on a constant and real-time basis, is unrealistic and unsound. This entire discussion relating to omniscience, causality and the frame problem will be resumed in Section 3.

1.3. Human cognition without omniscience

In biological agents such as humans, the set of internal mental representations corresponding to the potentially infinite set of external objects and events is considerably smaller than the exhaustive, omniscient case presented a moment ago. The reason why this must be so is because true biological agents are not omniscient. The biological agent's perceptual and attentional faculties only permit a constrained apprehension of externally occurring information. Yet, biological agents intuitively "know" which properties of external objects to attend to and which ones to ignore. Biological reasoning agents do not have a frame problem. The attempt to capture this biological capability in a representation is a cyclic theme throughout many of the contributions in the book. Fig. 3 illustrates a non-omniscient scenario involving an infinite set of external objects $\{x_0, \ldots, x_\infty\}$ and a finite set of internal representations $\{i_0, \ldots, i_5\}$. In this case, the external–internal mapping is neither omniscient as described in the previous Section 1.2, nor are the mappings consistent from one state to the next. More precisely, in state n, there is no mapping between x_3 and i_3, but there are mappings between $\{x_0, i_0\}$, $\{x_1, i_1\}$ and $\{x_5, i_5\}$. Yet, in state $n + 1$, (a) the mapping between $\{x_0, i_0\}$ still exists, (b) the mappings between $\{x_1, i_1\}$ and $\{x_5, i_5\}$ are absent, unlike state n, where they were present, and (c) the mapping between x_3 and i_3 is present, whereas in state n it was not. Also, in the case of x_2, x_4 and $\{x_6, \ldots, x_\infty\}$, the internal representations i_2, i_4 and $\{i_6, \ldots, i_\infty\}$ that could potentially map to these corresponding external objects do not even exist for any state.

Therefore, in this non-omniscient scenario, although in certain cases a mapping does not exist (e.g., $\{i_3, x_3\}$ in state n), the *potential* for a mapping always exists (e.g., $\{i_3, x_3\}$ in state $n + 1$). This state of affairs is certainly more congruent with biological cognition. Consider the phenomenon of object recognition. In the presence of a pre-learned stimulus, the mapping can be established through the faculties of attention and perception. But in absence of the stimulus, the potential for a mapping still exists. In the case where external objects exist but for which an internal representational placeholder does not (e.g., x_2, x_4), it might be the case that the external object will eventually be perceived, then through learning, an internal representation is established to correspond to this external object and any events (changes of property) associated with it and other internal representations.

It must be noted that the omniscience/non-omniscience issue so far discussed ultimately bears on the intra-agent case as well, in which two or more sets of internal
states (e.g., #S, ##S) correspond to each other in a fashion identical to the "standard"
external S, internal #S case. The reason for this is because once a particular representation is internalized, through learning, the agent also utilizes internal representations, in
conjunction with or even in the absence of any external stimuli.

To summarize, standing in direct contrast with machine cognition and omniscience
is the relative ease by which biological organisms appear to solve frame-like problems
(e.g., Nutter). In the lives of biological organisms, there are many objects and events
that occur in the world which the organism either is aware of yet ignores, or simply
has no awareness of. In either case, even with incomplete and partial knowledge, the
organism's ongoing perceptions, deliberations and actions typically meet with relative
success. One of the main functions of evolution has been to ensure that, by attending to
the more necessary and relevant things in the world, such as the acquisition of food and
a mate, as well as the evasion of predators, there is a higher probability that ontogenetic,
phylogenetic and, in the case of humans, sociocultural success will follow. In order to
survive, a successful biological reasoning agent must know what to attend to and what to
ignore in a wide variety of situations. This phenomenon can be observed in the simplest
of insects to the most complex of mammals. Moreover, with humans, this capability
appears to have extended far beyond the basic survival requirements of evolution and
has resulted in reasoning processes which transcend a wide variety of domains including
language and problem solving. Some of these types of reasoning will be covered in more
detail in the survey of Nutter's and Perlis' chapters.

In the quest for artificial intelligence then, if biological organisms can appropriately
attend and ignore with such effortlessness, why has it been so difficult, if not impossible,
for the AI researcher to replicate the same phenomenon in a non-biological medium such
as a computer or a robot? In particular, biological entities are able to function without
omniscience, and appear to solve frame-like problems (Nutter). As the progenitors of
the frame problem have argued, being able to successfully *represent* this ability is the
challenge of the frame problem—appropriately attending to or ignoring the presence and
absence of change and non-change in a dynamic world:

> One feels that there should be some economical and principled way of succinctly
> saying what changes an action makes, without having to explicitly list all the
> things it doesn't change as well; yet there doesn't seem to be any other way to
> do it. *That* is the frame problem. (Hayes, 1987, p. 125) [original emphasis]

1.4. A dynamic world

Complementing the issue of omniscience, there is also the title of the book to be
considered, *Reasoning Agents in a Dynamic World*, and how it applies to the various
contributions in the book. I assume "dynamic" refers to a world which changes constantly, is unpredictable, and happens in a real-time fashion. To put it another way,
the granularity of the dynamic world should correspond to the least noticeable change
detectable by the reasoning agent. For a rapidly changing world, the metrics might

involve distances of centimeters or meters and time intervals of milliseconds. For a slowly changing world, perhaps millimeters and minutes. Finally, I interpret *reasoning agent* to mean either a biological organism, such as a human, or a non-biological entity resembling a computer or a robot. With basic ideas, terms and goals intact, I now turn to the book.

2. Survey of the book

The book is not organized into sections. The fifteen chapters are presented alphabetically according to the first author's last name. I have separated eleven of these contributions into five general topics which are organized in this section into the following subsections: 2.1, Object-based models (Nutter, Sandewall); 2.2, Philosophical approaches (Perlis); 2.3, Persistence (Goodwin & Trudel, Haugh, Weber); 2.4, The qualification problem and circumscription (Etherington et al., Tenenberg, Weld); and 2.5, Modal and temporal logics (Stein, Morgenstern). In each of these subsections for each chapter that I survey, I have used the actual title of the chapter in the book as the opening paragraph header. Using this format, the reader of this review has the option to read only those subsections that might be of interest. I would like to point out though that central to my discussion later in Section 3 will be the contributions of Nutter, Perlis and Stein and, to a lesser extent, Etherington et al., Goodwin & Trudel, Haugh and Weber.

2.1. Object-based models

Focus of Attention, Context and the Frame Problem

J. Terry Nutter (pp. 171–188) has three main points: (1) there is a class of *frame-like* problems across AI that share features with the frame problem, (2) there is a single, potentially sufficient mechanism to deal with these frame-like problems involving the *focus of attention*, and (3) the underpinnings of this mechanism are a rich notion of *context* and an understanding of *salience*. She supports McDermott's (1987) claim that the frame problem is unsolvable by people and that one should not worry about trying to get machines such as robots to solve problems that humans cannot. Rather, it is postulated that people do things that *look* like they are solving the frame problem. Hence, Nutter asserts that the solutions we do come up with should be generalizable, not specific to one domain such as the Yale shooting problem (introduced in Section 2.3 below). Unsolvable problems should be avoided, and we should try to find the most economic and interesting solutions.

Nutter emphasizes the fact that since the specification of the representational aspect of the original frame problem is narrow (i.e., the narrow/broad distinction) relating to the qualification, ramification and persistence problems, the solutions will be narrow as well. Instead of narrow solutions, she suggests that we look in suitable areas to find broader, generalizable solutions. Hence, Nutter's conception of the frame problem is the problem of too much knowledge. Her central conjecture is, "every time we *appear* to solve a general problem of change and relevance, what we have *actually* done is replaced it by a much simpler problem, and solved that" (p. 176).

In turn, it is claimed that people solve frame-like problems *iteratively*, by adopting a simplification of a problem, considering the solution, then using information about the failure of the solution (if it fails) to adjust the simplification and try again. She cites three exemplary frame-like problems: *natural language understanding,* which implications to attend to and which to ignore; *learning,* which features to try to project to the new model being learned and which ones to ignore; and *analogical reasoning,* which features to project between analogies and which ones to ignore. The practice of these three domains all share the process of *limitation*. According to Nutter, the key mechanism to realize context and salience is the *focus of attention*. She asserts that intuition is content-driven. Frame-like reasoning can be realized by using content to restrict content through impoverishment of a working model of the world, and by attending only to salient, relevant features through this focus of attention.

Nutter sketches a proposed implementation of her attention model as a propositional semantic network. The structure of the network entails an exhaustive *static* world model that, by default, is inactive. The nodes are activated (made salient) via a metaphorical "gas" that spreads through the network. The spreading activation of the "gas" in localized regions in the network corresponds to the focus of attention. The flow of the gas can be attenuated either by fixing the quantity of gas or by limiting the number of edges from the activated area through which the gas can spread.

Towards a logic of dynamic frames

Erik Sandewall's thesis (pp. 201–217) entails combining McCarthy & Hayes' (1969) and Minsky's (1975) concepts of "frame" along with Hayes' (1985) *histories*. It is argued that the McCarthy & Hayes frame and the Minsky frame differ only on the principle of methodology; the former being a predicate logic-based approach, the latter being presented as an alternative to predicate logic realized instead as an object-based formalism (e.g., Stefik & Bobrow, 1986). Likewise, a history is "a piece of spacetime with natural boundaries, both temporal and spatial" (Hayes, 1985). Sandewall sees a relationship between Minsky frames and histories because they both are an attempt to assign a structure to the modeling of the world.

Sandewall coins the term *dynamic frame* to describe his proposed structure. He describes the application of designing an electronic automobile co-driver as a suitable domain for dynamic frames. The co-driver is intended to be a control system for maneuvering a motor vehicle in real world traffic environments. The knowledge base for the co-driver is called the model of the current traffic situation (MCTS). A simple instance of the MCTS consists of frames which contain information about the cars in front and cars behind the vehicle being controlled. The dynamic aspect of the frame entails the quantitative change of parameters such as distances and velocities which are maintained as individual parameter values (i.e., fluents) in the frames. Sandewall introduces two dynamic frame management concepts: *intra-frame change*, the smooth change and discontinuities in parameter values, and *inter-frame change*, managing the structure of frames including creation, destruction and modification. He denotes two types of inter-frame change: *actuated* change caused by an agent (e.g., driver of the vehicle), and *mechanical* change caused by the physical world. His goal is to characterize, in logic, dynamic frames and the histories they describe. The requirements for this proposed logic are to (1) write differential control equations as axioms, and (2) characterize inter-frame change as well as decide which control axioms hold under which conditions. Although he says, "no such logic exists today" (p. 211), Sandewall turns to Forbus' (1985) Qualitative Process Theory (QPT) for some clues to a potential ontology of such a logic. He touches on three components from QPT: *processes* which create, terminate and influence objects—similar to his inter-frame change; *physical objects* which closely resemble his dynamic frames; and *influences*, those things that affect parameter values—synonymous with his intra-frame change. I provide a simple analogy which captures the essence of dynamic frames. The phase changes of water are discontinuous at 0 and 100 degrees Celsius. This motivates the requirement for the creation and management of three dynamic frames to represent the three unique states of water; solid, liquid and gas. With such a representation Sandewall's logic-frame hybrid would mediate the intra-frame aspects of each state such as volume and temperature, obtained from physical sensors. It would also control the inter-frame transition from one state, or frame, to another as the temperature of the medium rises or falls.

2.2. Philosophical approaches

Intentionality and Defaults

Donald Perlis (pp. 189–199) provides a philosophical and theoretical discussion describing his theory of intentionality. Intentionality is the notion of *aboutness*, e.g., the word "cat" is *about* a living organism with fur and four legs that makes a meowing sound. Perlis' account involves a cycle of postulating an error about a belief, detecting the error and correcting the erroneous belief. It is assumed that a reasoning agent must be able to distinguish between error and truth. This approach addresses an extended realm of default reasoning comprising a complex world in which a reasoning agent will always make mistakes and is compelled to correct these mistakes in order to survive.

Perlis' definition of the frame problem is that it is an aspect of the problem of default reasoning and there are two types: the numerical and conceptual. The numerical frame problem entails a precisely-defined world in which most entities possess the property of *inertia*, many axioms are required for description, nothing is uncertain and default reasoning is not required (i.e., blocks-world). The conceptual frame problem relates to a world of uncertainty. This is a world that is too complex to fully axiomatize in which only rules of thumb can be used and described with imprecise and vague concepts. Default reasoning was born out of uncertainty (Reiter, 1980; Lifschitz, 1987; Haugh, 1987). The problem, according to Perlis, is that standard approaches to default reasoning have focused on capturing defaults in the domain, but not on what to do with something that comes along and defeats a default—the solution has been to throw away the defeated default and retain the defeater.

Presented as the Appearance Reality Distinction (ARD), Perlis defines *appearance* to be those things that are maintained internally (machine or mind) as conceptual or mental entities. Likewise, *reality* corresponds to the "real" things occurring in the world external to the reasoning agent. Reasoners are forced by circumstances to distinguish between

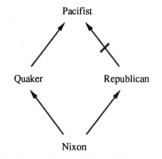

Fig. 4. The Nixon Diamond (from Thomason, 1992).

appearance and reality. In the case where appearance and reality are not congruent, error results. Standard default reasoning and frame problem notions of inertia do not find conclusions about error. Hence, what ARD does is to build error into its framework. Perlis enumerates several examples where the strength of this approach is applied to different modes of reasoning. These include: (a) in the absence of enough information, such as in the Nixon Diamond,[3] either leaving the problem unresolved or seeking more data to resolve it, (b) having to remember past thinking in order to accomplish a current task, (c) remembering a past false belief during a course of reasoning, (d) remembering a past course of reasoning, and (e) separating goals from the current state of progress.

The last two sections discuss topics of past philosophical approaches to linking internal mental states to external physical entities. These include the word–world connection in Mill's direct reference theory (1875), the idea that words relate to things out in the world. Perlis also discusses Frege's (1960) and Russell's (1964) notions of *reference meaning* (i.e., word–world) and *sense meaning*, using different words to relate to or describe the same entity; e.g., the phrases "Silver Fox's husband" and "Former President of the U.S." share the same reference meaning, George Bush, but different sense meaning. Kripke (1980) and Putnam (1988), in turn, derived a causal theory in order to describe another kind of sense meaning that describes the traditional notion of sense meaning. For example, what would be a consistent sense meaning for the phrase "top dog"? The argument surrounding the causal theory is that one does not necessarily have to know the detailed origins of "top dog", an aspect of hierarchical behavior in canine social life, in order to purposefully use such a phrase.

To provide an illustrative example of the merits of the ARD, Perlis finishes his discussion with a section describing Dennett's 2-bitser, a vending machine that accepts quarters. The gist of the 2-bitser is that the machine can only "mean" a quarter by virtue of an outside observer. Its intentionality is derived, not intrinsic. Perlis argues that the ARD is a step towards intrinsic or directed intentionality. By arguing that the 2-bitser machine can be fooled with bogus quarters, the error detection feature of the ARD comes to the rescue. With a quarter-verification feature built in, the 2-bitser could

---

[3] Richard Nixon is both a Republican and a Quaker. Republicans are not pacifists, yet Quakers are. Since Nixon inherits attributes from both, this results in a contradiction. The directed graph used to describe these four relationships assumes the shape of a diamond (Fig. 4).

then be able to detect the fallacious coins via a specialized camera and reject them. The principal question he asks is, how do humans develop the same capacity to recognize the fact that they are wrong? He cites Kripke (1980) and Devitt & Sterlny (1987) as providing the most recent and robust answers to this puzzling question. Their answer lies in the cultivation of causal features with respect to the growth and usage of *features* of prototypical things from the perspective of the language user (i.e., reasoning agent).

2.3. Persistence

Omniscience Isn't Needed to Solve the Frame Problem

Brian A. Haugh (pp. 105–131) challenges the presumptions of omniscience which surround extant technical solutions to the frame problem. He focuses on the omniscience relating to *temporal persistence*, the assumption that facts hold over time unless there is a specific reason to doubt the truth of those facts. Historically, this concept has been the principal alternative to frame axioms and has provided an elegant basis for certain solutions to the frame problem such as the *add* and *delete* lists in STRIPS (Fikes & Nilsson, 1971). In the STRIPS planning system, current, true facts about the world were maintained on the *add* list. Whenever a fact about the world was rendered invalid it was moved from the *add* list to the *delete* list. The popular term for this process of defeating or negating a persistent fact is known as "clipping".

Haugh enumerates six existing approaches to persistence and demonstrates how the omniscient assumptions within each detract from what appeals to common-sense reasoning:

- *All successful actions known.* This is associated with the concept of chronologically minimized clipping (Kautz, 1986; Lifschitz, 1986), where more distant events are preferred to be clipped over more recent ones. In other words, facts about the world fade, become false or irrelevant, over time. The omniscient assumption inherent in chronological minimization is that all successful action-attempts are known for both recent and distant events.
- *All fact changes known* (Kautz, 1986; Lifschitz, 1986). A reasoning agent has no means by which all changes in the world could be known. Therefore, this does not appeal to common sense since we ignore so many things that change during the course of reasoning.
- *All event occurrences known.* The motivated action theory of Morgenstern & Stein (1988) presumes that events are "motivated" by the situation or are provable in the situation. In the Yale shooting problem (Hanks & McDermott, 1986) [4] it is assumed by the omniscience of this theory that there are no other motivated events outside the scope of the axioms describing the problem that lead to an accidental unloading of the gun.

---

[4] The scenario involves *Fred* (who is alive), an unloaded gun, ammunition and a *Gunman*. (a) The gun is loaded with the ammunition by *Gunman*, (b) *Gunman* waits, (c) *Gunman* then points and fires the loaded gun at *Fred*. The compelling question: at the end of this sequence of events, is *Fred* alive or dead? Various treatments of the problem result in either *Fred*'s death, or *Fred* remaining alive due to the mysterious unloading of the gun during the waiting period.

- *All intervening events known.* In the McCarthy & Hayes situation calculus a state S_{n+1} results from an action A_n in state S_n. The omniscient assumption is that no other events can occur between S_n and S_{n+1}. However, there are many events that occur between states that we have no knowledge of.
- *All causal laws are known.* Other than action, the other principal means of change are physical laws or rules that describe what changes are the result of events in given circumstances (Hayes, 1971; Lifschitz, 1987; Morgenstern & Stein, 1988). In most formalisms, it is almost always the case that all laws must explicitly be known. This assumption is unrealistic in the face of what appeals to common sense.
- *Sole suspects are culprits.* Challenging Baker (1989), Baker & Ginsberg (1989), Lifschitz (1987) and Morgenstern & Stein (1988), "the actual cause of some change (culprit) is amongst the known potential causes of such a change (the suspects) whenever there are such suspects" (p. 113). Again, this assumption can only work in a context-free world in which all cause–effect relationships are known.

In the face of all this omniscience, Haugh presents his theory of unpresumptuous temporal persistence which entails four components: avoiding unjustified changes, distinguishing explicit knowledge, minimizing unexplained changes and minimizing unjustified changes. This is accomplished by providing a means to distinguish as well as describe *explicit* and *derived* facts. The derived facts in particular, Haugh states, will, in the long run, have to be of an autoepistemic nature. What this means is that knowledge derived from the environment and internalized by the reasoning agent must be integrated with existing knowledge in order to form new knowledge.

The Myth of Domain-Independent Persistence

Jay C. Weber (pp. 259–274) argues that, "solving the frame problem reduces to the problem of inferring the nonexistence of causes for change" (p. 259). He addresses action occurrence omniscience, i.e., knowledge of all actions, and argues the reason that certain solutions to the frame problem are not generalizable is because of their inherent *domain-independence*. Weber shows how the minimization of action occurrences may not necessarily lead to intuitively consistent solutions to problems. Domain knowledge is required to provide contextual information that is not possible in a domain-independent paradigm. He shows that this can be accomplished in three different causal theories involving the use of deductive, nonmonotonic[5] and statistical *domain details*.

Weber illustrates his idea of deductive domain details by introducing six additional domain-dependent axioms to the original Yale shooting problem. For example he suggests adding the axiom, "*Gunman* waits briefly, without unloading or shooting the gun" to the original problem. This axiom eliminates the need for earlier explanations such as motivated action theory (Morgenstern & Stein, 1988) where the continuous loaded state of the gun and subsequent death of *Fred* is explained by the absence of a third agent who could come along and unload the gun.

---

[5] Nonmonotonic logics satisfy the requirement that facts about the world cannot be derived *ad infinitum* (i.e., monotonically) since at least two separate facts will eventually contradict each other. Therefore, the general function of a nonmonotonic logic is to guarantee that contradictory facts will not co-occur, such as in the Nixon diamond where Nixon is both a pacifist and a non-pacifist.

With nonmonotonic domain details Weber extrapolates that the qualification problem is also applicable to the notion of requiring the preconditions for *lack of change*. For example, if an agent parks her car, then goes to work, she should expect her car to be there at the end of the day (Allen, 1984). There are certain things that *could* happen to the car, such as being stolen or impounded; but the assumption that the car will probably be there at the end of the day is a reasonable one. Hence, Weber suggests the introduction of domain-dependent assumptions written in the style of Reiter's (1980) default rules.[6] Thus, regarding the car scenario:

> ... it seems reasonable at first, to assume that my car is still where I left it this morning, unless I have information that is inconsistent with that assumption. However, this premise gets *less and less reasonable* [emphasis added] as hours turn into days, weeks, months, years and centuries—even if it is quite *consistent* to make such a premise. This puts the problem where it should be— namely in the area of making reasonable assumptions, not in the area of *defining* the effects of actions ..., the persistence of facts ..., or causal laws ....
> (Georgeff, 1987, pp. 118–119)

This passage sets the stage for Weber's final topic, the notion of statistical domain details, which is a hybrid of statistics and nonmonotonic logic. The principal goal is to "assign numerical beliefs to assertions about the persistence of properties" (p. 269). The heart of this approach is to find the means to express the idea of *less and less reasonable* in the quote above. Using the statistical inference of Kyburg (1974) the basic *statistical persistence inference* form is:

$$\%p \, (\text{true}(p, \, t') \mid \text{true}(p, \, t)) = x.$$

This has a Bayesian flavor and reads, "x is the belief that p is true immediately after t' given that p is true at t". In the car example, the persistent belief that "the car almost always stays in the parking lot" would be expressed as:

$$\%t(\text{true}(\text{inLot}, \, t') \mid \text{true}(\text{inLot}, \, t)) \approx 1.$$

Persistence in Continuous First Order Temporal Logics

Scott D. Goodwin and André Trudel (pp. 87–104) point out that much work has been done in both *discrete temporal logics* such as the situation calculus (Kautz, 1986; Shoham, 1986; Goebel & Goodwin, 1987; Haugh, 1987; Lifschitz, 1987; Loui, 1987; Goodwin & Goebel, 1989) and *continuous first-order temporal logics* (McDermott, 1982; Allen, 1984; Shoham, 1988); but the study of persistence in the latter case has received little attention. It is asserted that the requirements for a continuous temporal logic are (1) *point-based* information that is true or false at a point in time and (2) *interval-based* information that is true or false over an interval of time (i.e., between two points in time). Ontologically, intervals subsume points; but points do not subsume intervals. The gist of their work involves a *persistence rule* in which (1) point-based

---

[6] These rules are of the form $\left[\dfrac{p_s \, : \, p_{do(a,s)}}{p_{do(a,s)}} \right]$ which means that if p is true in situation s and p is still consistent after the action a then we can infer p after the action.

information persists by default until defeated and (2) the persistence of interval-based information is determined by the persistence of point-based information.

This is accomplished by combining a temporal logic, GCH, with a statistically motivated semantics for defaults called Extended Theorist (Goodwin & Goebel, 1989) derived from Poole's (1987) Theorist. This type of default differs from the standard notion of the default, i.e., "assume true in the absence of evidence to the contrary" (e.g., Reiter, 1980). Instead the authors "interpret defaults as asserting statistical knowledge which can be used to justify particular beliefs" (p. 94). Using the Yale shooting problem as a sample domain, the authors re-axiomatize the problem so that it is continuous rather than discrete. The continuous temporal domain knowledge is represented as facts and defaults. The Yale shooting problem from Hanks & McDermott (1986) results in two extensions.[7] The authors translate these two extensions from discrete form into their continuous representation. What follows is the syntax that describes these continuous versions, then text which explains the syntax and semantics:

$$\Gamma_a = \{\text{persists}([1,2],\text{loaded}), \text{persists}([0,3),\text{alive})\},$$
$$\varepsilon_a = \{\text{true}(3,\text{alive}) : \text{persists}([1,2],\text{loaded})\},$$
$$\Gamma_b = \{\text{persists}([1,2),\text{loaded}), \text{persists}([0,3],\text{alive})\},$$
$$\varepsilon_b = \{\text{true}(2,\text{loaded}) : \text{persists}([0,3],\text{alive})\}.$$

Γ_a, which reads "extension a", states that the gun is loaded from time 1 up to and including time 2, denoted by "]", and *Fred* is alive from time 0 up to but *not* including time 3, denoted by ")". Γ_b reads that the gun is loaded from time 1 up to but not including time 2 and that *Fred* is alive from time 0 up to and including time 3. These are illustrated in Fig. 5. In the scenario the gun is fired sometime during the interval [2,3] (including time 2 and time 3). The question is asked as to whether *Fred* is alive or dead at time 3. There are at least three ways to evaluate these two extensions. I enumerate these in detail here since they comprise a principal subset of several methods to evaluate problems such as the Yale shooting problem.

The first way is to evaluate them according to the standard facts and deductions strictly associated with the axiomatization of the problem. In Γ_a it is not explicitly known if *Fred* is alive or dead at time 3. But since the gun is loaded from time 1 to time 2 and the gun is fired somewhere between time 2 and time 3, we can infer at time 3 that *Fred* is dead through the domain axiom, "*IF* someone fires a loaded gun at a living person *THEN* the person will die". In Γ_b, since it is stated *Fred* is alive at time 3, it can be deduced that the gun was unloaded at time 2. This is the original interpretation of the problem; and it cannot be determined whether *Fred* is alive or dead at time 3, since both extensions possess reasonable, yet contradictory, interpretations. Γ_a suggests that *Fred* is dead and Γ_b says that *Fred* is alive.

The second way is to evaluate the extensions Γ_a and Γ_b according to the *exceptions* ε_a and ε_b respectively. Exceptions are meta-level inferences made by the researcher that

---

[7] An extension is one of several outcomes in a nonmonotonic logic in which a contradiction has occurred. In the Nixon Diamond for example, one extension maintains that Nixon is {Republican, Quaker, Pacifist}; and a second extension holds that Nixon is {Republican, Quaker, ¬Pacifist}. Note that {Republican, Quaker, Pacifist, ¬Pacifist} is not a legal extension since Nixon cannot be both a pacifist and a non-pacifist.

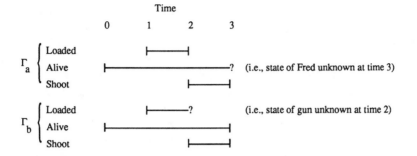

Fig. 5. Two continuous extensions from Yale shooting problem.

are not a result of the original axiomatization of the problem. Exceptions can either be *discountable* (refutable) and do not affect the validity of an extension or *nondiscountable* (irrefutable) and invalidate an extension. ε_a is an exception to Γ_a since it is not known if *Fred* is alive at time 3. If *Fred* is alive at time 3, this fact would invalidate the truth of the assumption, persists([1,2],loaded). ε_b is an exception to Γ_b since it is not known if the gun is unloaded at time 2. If the gun is loaded at time 2, this fact would invalidate the truth of the assumption, persists([0,3],alive). Both ε_a and ε_b are nondiscountable; and, as a result, both extensions Γ_a and Γ_b cannot be considered as reasonable outcomes to the scenario.

Finally, the third way involves the authors' notion of *temporal independence* (Goodwin & Goebel, 1989), which means that the state of affairs at any point in time depends only on the states of affairs at past points in time. Conversely, past states of affairs are fixed, independent and unaffected by the future. In this context ε_a, is now a discountable exception to Γ_a since the gun was loaded in the past and the truth of this assumption cannot be dependent on the fact that *Fred* is alive or dead in the future. Given temporal independence, since the gun was loaded, then fired, *Fred* is dead. However, ε_b is still a nondiscountable exception to Γ_b, since the truth of the gun being unloaded at time 2 depends on *Fred* being alive in the future, which he is not, thus violating temporal independence. Given this outcome, *Fred* dies.

2.4. The qualification problem and circumscription

Limited scope and circumscriptive reasoning

David Etherington, Sarit Kraus and Donald Perlis (pp. 43–54) claim "a proper foundation for the frame problem must rest on a theory of non-monotonic reasoning [(NMR)]" (p. 43). They argue, however, that extant forms of NMR tend to be overeager to jump to default assumptions. "The problem is that agents frequently know that there must be individuals who do not have the default properties, without knowing *who* those individuals are" (p. 46).

In particular, McCarthy's (1980, 1986) circumscription approach was a proposed solution to the qualification problem; i.e., how many preconditions must be satisfied before we know a particular action can happen? Circumscription implements an inference rule for deriving sets of assumptions on the basis of available information. For example, suppose we know only one red-haired person, Jane. If we see someone who has red hair, by circumscription we assume it is Jane. However, if we learn that Jane has an identical twin Joan, we can no longer assume by circumscription that it is Jane; the best we can do is to assume that it is either Jane *or* Joan (Cohen & Feigenbaum, 1989, pp. 118–119).

Hence, what is required is the additional capability of *scope* in the NMR system. The term "scope" in this context means *something of concern*, or *relevant to making a decision* (p. 47). It is suggested that there are two kinds of scope; *wide* (e.g., all red-haired people) and *narrow* (e.g., Jane). If the scope is narrow, it is safe to reason with a default conclusion. But if the scope is wide, default conclusions cannot be trusted. The authors provide another illustration. There is an engineer who routinely inspects hundreds of bridges a year. Although safe bridges tend to remain safe, every year she fully expects to find several that are unsafe. Thus, during the year she does not make the default assumption that any given bridge is safe—within the *wide scope* of her professional concern, there are exceptions to the safety default and it is her job to find them. Likewise, when she is away on vacation and happens upon an unfamiliar bridge that she would have not inspected, in her *narrow scope* of interest she would have no reason to believe that the bridge is unsafe and crosses it without reserve. A system of logic is advanced by the authors to capture this idea of scope in circumscriptive reasoning.

Abandoning the completeness assumptions

Josh D. Tenenberg (pp. 231–257) challenges extant approaches that require complete knowledge of the world (i.e., omniscience). He strikes theoretical ground somewhere between two prevailing views he refers to as the *permissive* and *conservative* approaches. The permissive approach comprises the frame axiom, procedural and nonmonotonic approaches that assume the agent precipitates change, knows of all action in the world and is aware of all causal relationships between an action and its effects. Historically, this has been described as:

> conditions P do not change when action A occurs

The conservative approach entails *explanation closure* (Schubert, 1989; Weber, 1989; Haas, 1987) and *multiple agency and concurrency* (Allen, 1984; Pollack, 1985; Mc-Dermott, 1982; Georgeff, 1987). Explanation closure is phrased as:

> condition P changes between time T and $T + 1$, only when one of actions $A_1, \ldots, A_n$ occurs at time T (p. 240).

Multiple agency and concurrency address the issue of outside actions overlooked by explanation closure but still assume that the agent is aware of all events in the world (i.e., omniscience).

Tenenberg suggests, as an alternative, that "actions achieve goals relative to a context with some likelihood of success" (p. 232). Like Weber, Tenenberg implements Kyburgian statistics and attacks the qualification problem by arguing that most qualifications defeat the success of certain actions only a fraction of the time. Exemplifying the Yale Shooting Problem, he argues that all treatments of the problem to date have predicted *Fred*'s death. Schubert (1989) and Weber (1989) have shown that the gun can only be unloaded by *unload* axioms, which do not exist in the original problem. Kautz (1986) and Shoham (1986) suggest that all propositions, unless defeated, must persist right up until *Fred*'s death. Lifschitz (1987), Haugh (1987) and Weber (1988) have also shown that, by minimizing causative acts, there is no way the gun can become unloaded. Tenenberg, suggests however, that these approaches, although sound, can become strained when the waiting period, for example, becomes increasingly longer. Tenenberg has developed inference statistics such as,

$$\%(\text{alive}' \mid \text{shoot} \wedge \text{alive} \wedge \text{loaded}) \in [0.1, 0.3]$$

which reads, "given a person is initially alive and has been shot at with a loaded gun, the probability that s/he is now alive is somewhere between the interval 0.1 and 0.3". Tenenberg strikes the middle ground as "an approach that associates statistically bounded probabilities with temporally scoped assertions" (p. 254).

System dynamics and the qualification problem

Daniel S. Weld (pp. 275–286) sees the qualification problem as part of a larger problem where "every model of reality is an approximation" and "the qualifications of an action are violated when the model's simplifying assumptions are inappropriate" (p. 275). He introduces a three-phase approach to managing the qualification problem by (1) choosing a model, (2) reasoning within the model, and (3) validating that the choice of model is appropriate—if the choice fails, compare models and switch to a different model. Weld points out that according to the Heisenberg uncertainty principle—as certain quantities are measured more precisely the ability to determine others is lost—it has been shown that perfect deterministic models are theoretically impossible. Even if a perfect model of the world were to exist, the only way to manage tractability within a system would be by the introduction of simplifying assumptions. Engaging McCarthy's potato-in-the-tailpipe scenario, [8] Weld discusses the advantages of *inter-model* over *intra-model* qualifications by asking the question; what happens if the key is turned with a potato in the tailpipe? These types of dynamics belong to models outside of the realm of just starting a car—unless one insists on including the behavior of potatoes in the ontology of a car.

Weld has developed a domain-independent algorithm for discrepancy-driven model switching that uses a method of generate and test. Implemented as a Lisp system, SAM, the algorithm is given a *Graph of Models* (GoM) which entails a directed graph where the nodes are models and the edges comprise sets of simplifying assumptions that distinguish between adjacent models. The current deficit of SAM is that it is dependent on continuous representations such as those involving physics mechanics problems. Also, unless explicitly specified, the algorithm does not know how to deal with unknown discrepancies; in these cases, Weld suggests that an approach involving theory formation would be an appropriate direction of research.

---

[8] This is the canonical example used to illustrate the qualification problem. In order to start a car, an infinite number of preconditions are necessary; electrical system intact, fuel in the tank, turning the key, ..., and there cannot be a potato in the tailpipe. The purpose of the potato is to illustrate the point that although the first three preconditions are probably in the knowledge base of most drivers, the potato is most likely not, yet is a necessary precondition for the action of starting a car.

2.5. Modal and temporal logics

An atemporal frame problem

Lynn Andrea Stein (pp. 219–230) argues that the frame problem is "generally assumed to be a problem of temporal reasoning" (p. 219) and usually entails the effects
of actions. Instead, she claims there is another problem *independent* of time called the
counterfactual validity problem that looks very much like the frame problem. One goal
of her chapter is to open a new doorway for research on the frame problem that does not
depend solely on the structure of time. Hence, instead of the causalities that arise from
the results of actions, Stein asserts that what really requires attention among reasoning
states is what is *relevant*. This more general idea of relevance subsumes the more specific *causal* relevance encountered in action-based temporal reasoning. Counterfactuals
have the form:

If *a* were true, then *b* would be,

but actually mean something more like:

In the world(s) most like this one
but where *a* holds, *b* holds as well.

Stein provides some examples of counterfactual statements, one of which is:

If I moved the dining room table to the living room,
it would still be white.

Stein remarks that the problem with solving counterfactuals involves the ability to
determine what facts about the world are *relevant* to the change being made in the world
or to the agent vis-á-vis the *antecedent* of the counterfactual. In the case of the dining
room table, the basic question is, what else is relevant to the movement of the table;
e.g., is the color of the table really relevant simply because it has been moved from one
room to another? Citing Ginsberg (1986), Ginsberg (1987a), Ginsberg & Smith (1988a,
1988b) and Lewis (1973), Stein maintains that any instance of the frame problem can
be restated in terms of a counterfactual validity problem. This is accomplished through
a *possible worlds* approach in which the reasoner must determine the closeness between
the current world (e.g., dining room) and other worlds (e.g., living room) including
any action and its results. This also involves the principle of truth maintenance such that
transitions between worlds result in consistent facts. For example, by moving the table
from the dining room to the living room, in a new world, the table can obviously not
be in two different places. In a new living room world, the fact about the table being in
the dining room must be retracted.

> The counterfactual validity problem is concerned with the differences between
> this world and [a world] in which I move the table, while the frame problem is
> concerned with the effects (and non-effects) of moving the table in *that* world.
> (p. 225) [original emphasis]

Stein also summarizes some basic differences between the frame problem and the
counterfactual validity problem. In the frame problem, change is over time and causes

are directly related to their effects. Also, in the context of the qualification and ramification problems, the frame problem is constrained whereas counterfactuals are *not*—any antecedent or side-effect of a counterfactual must be acceptable, no matter how far-fetched.

Knowledge and the frame problem

Leora Morgenstern (pp. 133–170) discusses the integration of a theory of action with a theory of knowledge that allows for multiple agents. She refers to these as the *third agent* and *vicarious planning* frame problems. The former happens when a planning agent, depending on another person, does not know if that person will know enough to participate in the plan when it comes time to perform his part in the plan. The latter occurs when a planning agent delegates a part of the plan to another person and is uncertain as to what the state of the world will be once the delegate is finished. An example of the third agent frame problem:

> Bill wants to open a safe at time *1*. To open the safe, he needs to know the combination of the safe. He does not know the combination, but knows that his friend Susan knows a friend of his (the third agent) who does. Assume that friendly agents cooperate and give information when requested to do so. To further simplify the problem, assume that in this particular problem situation, concurrent actions are not allowed. How can Bill plan to open the safe?

If the above example is modified so that the person who knows the combination is Susan's friend, rather than Bill's, we then have an instance of the vicarious planning frame problem. For the third agent problem, intuition says that Bill should plan to (a) ask Susan for the name of his friend (i.e., the third agent), (b) Susan tells Bill the name of his friend, (c) Bill asks his friend for the combination, and (d) Bill's friend tells him the combination. Unfortunately, Bill cannot *prove* that his plan will work because he cannot prove that his friend will know the combination at a later time such as time *3*. The reason why this is so is because neither Bill, his friend, nor Susan know of all the actions that transpire between times *1* and *3*—even if the activities of all three agents transpire in a synchronized fashion, without concurrency. The "frame" aspects of both of these problems entail knowing what stays the same about the world when portions of the plan are delegated to other agents.

Morgenstern asserts that standard frame problem solutions such as frame axioms and nonmonotonic temporal logics (McDermott, 1982; McCarthy, 1986) do not work for multi-agency because they were designed with single-agency in mind. Two omniscient properties of those approaches are highlighted; *dense*, the system knows of something that occurs at any point in time—there are no gaps in knowledge; and *complete*, all actions are known to the system. Concepts such as concurrent actions and incomplete knowledge about actions and the world are not expressible in extant paradigms. Thus, Morgenstern's chief requirements are (1) "to develop a non-monotonic temporal logic that allows an agent, if he does not know of a particular action, to conclude that the action has not taken place" (p. 148), (2) the reasoning system should prefer situations "... in which actions happen only if they are *motivated* ..." (p. 148), and (3) to support both forward and backward reasoning. The Motivated Action Theory (MAT) of Morgenstern & Stein (1988) accommodates these requirements. The gist of the theory is that an action is motivated if there is a *reason* for it to happen. In forward temporal projection, applied to the original Yale shooting problem, MAT will predict *Fred*'s death. In turn, if told that *Fred* is alive after the gun has been fired, MAT will reason via backward temporal projection and conclude that the gun must have been unloaded. In general, MAT prefers logical conclusions in which the *fewest* unmotivated actions take place, "... based on the principle that an agent typically knows all that he needs to know in order to make predictions about the world in which he lives" (p. 149).

Based on the above requirements, she introduces EMAT, which is the integration of MAT, a theory of action and planning, with an epistemic (i.e., related to knowledge) logic. EMAT essentially allows "reasoning agents to reason about how other agents perform temporal reasoning" (p. 157). Some of the basic features of EMAT include, (1) a "weak" epistemic operator *believe* that allows the nonmonotonic reasoning system to construct plans around knowledge that may or may not be true, (2) a theory of relativized instantiation i.e., all the propositions an agent *a* believes at time *t*, and (3) the capability of nesting multi-agent beliefs (e.g., Bill knows that Susan knows that a friend-of-Bill's knows the combination).

3. Discussion

Although various authors cannot seem to agree on what the fundamental problem or solution is, there certainly appears to be a *special* phenomenon or human capability that workers are trying to capture in these bodies of theories.[9] Humans and other biological organisms are very skilled at what appears to be the effortless discernment between change and the absence of change and the adeptness to suitably attend to either under a wide variety of circumstances. Along with the term *frame problem*, aspects of this phenomenon are also referred to in the book as *scope* (Etherington et al.), *salience*, *context*, *intuition* (Nutter), *common sense* (e.g., Haugh), *relevance* (Stein), *meaning*, *sense* and *reference* (Perlis), among others. No matter what it might be called, the issue from the perspective of human or machine cognition remains—precisely *how* does one go about representing these phenomena while avoiding the perplexing singularity known as the frame problem? In the absence of a consensus as to what the frame problem or solution is, when considering each approach in the book, and for the purposes of the ensuing discussion, I suggest that the reader default to the traditional McCarthy & Hayes (1969) *narrow* frame problem. For any representation, there exists a set of assumptions that are driven by a scientific perspective within which that representation is developed. In this section, my goal is to discuss the issue of

---

[9] There are three earlier volumes dedicated to the frame problem and related problems (Brown, 1987; Ginsberg, 1987b; Pylyshyn, 1987). The editors also mention another book under development edited by Kenneth Ford and Zenon Pylyshyn titled, *The Robot's Dilemma Revisited: The Frame Problem in Artificial Intelligence* (Ablex Press) which has arisen from the same body of Workshop papers that inspired this book.

representation in the context of scientific methodology. Most central to this issue is how the researcher in AI or cognitive science chooses to look at the phenomenon involving the intelligent agent and its environment. Depending on how the researcher chooses to view such phenomena invariably affects the mode of abstraction which then results in a representation. From certain methods stem the assumption of omniscience and the frame problem.

3.1. Abstraction and representation

I would like to revisit the assumption of omniscience explicated in Sections 1.2, 1.3 and Figs. 1–3. To summarize, omniscience is the unattainable ideal which propounds that the reasoning agent must be completely aware of all objects and events external and internal to it. The representations in most extant AI architectures and cognitive models depend on the assumption of omniscience as part of their ontology and epistemology. The same representations however, typically involving structures and processes, ultimately depend on a general method, or mode, of abstraction. In turn, the mode of abstraction depends on a particular scientific point of view through which the researcher has decided to study a phenomenon. The purpose of this discussion is to make apparent that the frame problem is a problem owing to particular scientific world views through which AI researchers or cognitive scientists (hereinafter, referred to as *researcher*) have attempted to abstract and represent the relationship between reasoning agents and the dynamic worlds in which they exist.

> Unlike McDermott, however, I don't think the frame problem is unreal or insignificant: It seems to point up a basic error in the way we try to describe the everyday world. We aren't carving nature up at the right ontological joints, if you ask me. But time will tell. (Hayes, 1987, p. 130)

This passage by Hayes occurred in a time during which the legitimacy of the frame problem had been brought into serious question. McDermott, in the same volume, argued that no known AI researcher was working on the frame problem. McDermott also maintained that the frame problem was, "of interest mainly to a fringe group, those who believe that logical analyses are relevant to building knowledge representations. I count myself in this group..." (1987, p. 116). Yet, in the passage above, it is clear that Hayes is calling into account matters regarding the philosophy of science and scientific methodology. He suggests that methodology plays a role in how the researcher chooses to approach a given problem in AI or cognitive science, which then results in a representation. In certain cases, the desired approach *leads* to an obstacle known as the frame problem. Following Hayes' cue then, I wish to further his line of reasoning and explore what other means might exist that would allow the researcher to "carve nature up" at a different set of "ontological joints".

Pepper (1942, 1967), Dewey and Bentley (1949), Altman & Rogoff (1987) and Wertsch (1991) are among a few who have brought into perspective particular scientific *world views* which reflect how the researcher defines relationships between (a) the reasoning agent, (b) the agent's environment, and (c) the observer of the agent and environment; whether the observer be the researcher, or, an observer that is an aspect of the phenomenon itself. The term "world view" is derived from the notion of *world hypothesis*. These terms collectively refer to the manner by which an observer of nature, usually a physical, natural or social scientist, chooses to characterize the phenomena that he or she witnesses. Although several different types of world views have been advanced, there are three in particular that I would like to highlight for the purposes of this discussion—the interactional, organismic, and transactional world views of Altman & Rogoff (1987). Each of these world views possess six distinguishing attributes which render them distinct: (i) the units of analysis; the characterization of (ii) time, (iii) change, (iv) causation and (v) context; and (vi) the role of the observer. Below, I will describe each of these three world views and show how they are representative of various approaches to human and machine cognition. In the case of the interactional and organismic world views, omniscience and the frame problem exist. Yet, in the transactional world view, as will be illustrated later in Section 3.4, omniscience and the frame problem are entirely absent.

In addition, since the traditional narrow frame problem is a scientific problem of representation, I maintain that it is prudent to discuss such matters in terms of testable hypotheses. One means of validating a representational hypothesis is by way of mathematical *proof*. Unfortunately, a proof does not provide much insight into how the representation will actually perform, particularly in a dynamic, unpredictable world. Another effective way to test a specific hypothesis concerning a representation is to see how the representation actually performs in the actual or simulated environment it was originally abstracted from. This is usually accomplished by implementing the representation as an aggregation of data structures and algorithms in a computational system. Two parameters that are typically analyzed in this setting are *space complexity,* the amount of memory and secondary storage consumed by the data structures and algorithms, and *time complexity,* the amount of computational (i.e., CPU) cycles consumed by the data structures and algorithms. From this perspective of space and time complexity, the contributions in the book have not yet been realized as intelligent computing systems that reason about dynamic worlds.[10] Therefore, I will usher in two implemented, computational architectures, *Tileworld* and *Pengi*, which serve as very reasonable intelligent systems that (a) address many of the requirements idealized by the contributors in the book, and (b) also serve as exemplars for many of the underlying traits of the interactional (Tileworld) and transactional (Pengi) world views.

3.2. The interactional world view

The *interactional* world view is the prevailing method of scientific abstraction in both human and machine cognition.

> Pepper's mechanistic perspective, Dewey and Bentley's interaction approach, and our interactional world view are similar in their common assumption that phenomena are composed of independent elements that *interact* according to

---

[10] In the book, Sandewall's dynamic frames are a candidate for a computational system which reasons about a dynamic world, but only appear to be in the phase of conceptual design.

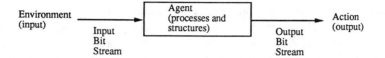

Fig. 6. Interactional world view of human and machine cognition.

certain laws or principles. Although context and time can be included in these approaches, they are usually treated as independent domains, not as intrinsic parts of psychological phenomena. Thus space and time are "locations" of phenomena and are external to their functioning. (Altman & Rogoff, 1987, p. 10) [emphasis added]

Analysis of the intelligent phenomenon in the interactional world view involves the structured, sometimes recursive, decomposition of the agent and the environment into separable "atoms". These atoms are encapsulated and share direct cause-and-effect relationships with each other. Instances of this world view can be traced back to the philosophy of Aristotle and the physical laws of Newton. Atoms can be aggregated functionally and structurally into larger systems. The interactional world view has found wide appeal in the development of intelligent systems and cognitive models. This particular interactional world view of human and machine cognition is grounded in the sender–receiver communication theory of Shannon & Weaver (1949) and the computational models of Von Neumann (1961) and Turing (1946), comingled with information processing theories of cognition beginning with Newell & Simon (1956) and Chomsky (1957, 1959), among others. Fig. 6 highlights the basic constituents of this world view. The units of analysis typically comprise five atoms: (a) environment, or the input domain, (b) a stream of input bits which is transmitted from the environment to the agent, (c) the agent, which processes the input bits with internal processes and bits, i.e., aggregated, multiple recursive instances of this top-level model (e.g., see Fig. 7), (d) an output stream of bits, and (e) action, which affects the environment. Causation is of an antecedent (input), consequent (output) nature. Likewise, change, context and time, which involve internal and external objects and events, are treated as independent, disjunct entities. A principal feature of the interactional world view of human and machine cognition (hereinafter referred to as the *cognitive world view*) entails the law-like *causal* relationships that are exhaustively sustained between all atoms.

Two comparable examples of the interactional world view are behaviorism and certain forms of connectionism, for which the units of analysis are very similar to those of the cognitive world view. In the interactional world view of stimulus–response behaviorism, research efforts are principally focused on the *environment* (stimulus) and *action* (response) atoms. Behaviorism is unlike the cognitive world view, for in the cognitive world view the locus of study is instead on theoretical structures and processes internal to the *agent* atom, and to a lesser extent, the *environment* and *action* atoms. Likewise, in certain varieties of connectionism, the points of study at present appear to be primarily centered around the *input* and *output* bit stream atoms and the internal structures and processes of the *agent* atom. The connectionism interactional world view is quite similar to the cognitive interactional world view appearing to differ in two important ways; (a) the *input* bit stream atoms are presumably at the feature or sub-symbolic level,[11] and (b) the structures and processes internal to the *agent* atom are continuous, rather than discrete and symbolic. Almost ironically, although these three exemplary disciplines are essentially of the same *genre*, the interactional world view, many contentious debates have transpired regarding which atoms should be the emphasis of study and what the ontology of those atoms should be (e.g., Chomsky, 1959; Fodor & Pylyshyn, 1988). In addition, recent disputes have broken out *between* world views regarding for instance, interpretations of a transactional world view, such as situated action (Agre, 1993), from the perspective of the interactional, cognitive world view (Vera & Simon, 1993).

The frame problem: is the interactional world view the culprit?

Omniscience and the frame problem emerge from the cognitive world view. During the 1950s the cognitive world view had arisen as a response to behaviorism and the strident emphasis on a stimulus–response account of intelligence. The then new cognitive researchers, as part of their anti-behaviorist insurrection, turned to the investigation of hypothetical structures and processes internal to the *agent* atom, by and large passing over the *environment* and *action* atoms. A fundamental problem has arisen from the cognitive world view, however, regarding how the internal structures and processes are typically represented. The problem stems from the immutable law intrinsic to the interactional world view which involves the causal or antecedent–consequent relationships sustained between atoms. In other words, any atom identified by the researcher, which is subsequently abstracted and realized in a representation, is affected by and affects all other atoms that have been abstracted into the same representation. By abstraction, I mean the process of mapping or translating the observable phenomenon into a form more suitable for analysis, representation or computation (see (Brooks, 1991), for an interesting account of abstraction in cognition). In the book, first-order logic is a preferred means of abstraction. Likewise, explicit causality is usually expressed either in terms of *Modus Ponens* ($P \rightarrow Q$), IF–THEN production rules, or inferential statistics (e.g., Tenenberg, Weber).

To provide a very simple, worst-case illustration of the effects of causation, omniscience and the corresponding intractability in an internal representation, consider a world consisting of 200 same-sized blocks which are situated on a two-dimensional plane (no stacking allowed). The reader might recall from Section 1.2 that the physical blocks correspond to S_n, S_{n+1} and $\{x_0, \ldots, x_m\}$ discussed in Figs. 1 and 2. For an action such as moving a block, the property of spatial orientation among the blocks will change as the result of this action. One such useful representational property for a reasoning agent might be *left-of*(m, n) and *not*(*left-of*(m, n)) used to describe the (x, y) locations of blocks relative to each other. These internal entities correspond to #S_n, #S_{n+1} and

---

[11] The issue of precisely *what* a symbol is has always been a somewhat murky issue, and appears to depend on how one chooses to abstract the world in the setting of a particular world view. In the cognitive world view, a symbol is "meaningful"—e.g., something like the letter "A", the word "CAT", or a mental image of a cat. Examples of "meaningless" sub-symbols in connectionism are the "/", "\" and "-" features which constitute the letter "A". What is "meaningful" in either case seems to be more of a function of what is meaningful to the researcher, rather than what is meaningful to the intelligent agent being studied.

$\{i_0, \ldots, i_m\}$ that were discussed in Figs. 1 and 2 from Section 2.1. If one block is moved from its current (x, y) location (i.e., S_n) to a new location (x', y') (i.e., S_{n+1}), the *left-of*(m, n) and *not*(*left-of*(m, n)) relationships between it and the remaining 199 blocks in the internal representation must be checked, so as to maintain consistency, and updated to reflect the side-effects of this action (i.e., from #S_n to #S_{n+1}). If this checking is not done, contradictory or inconsistent facts about the world could arise in the internal representation. Most importantly, the frame problem would be encountered, since any change or lack of change would remain unknown. In the worst case, n^2 causal relationships must be somehow reflected in the internal representation for each pair of (i.e., *left-of*, *not*(*left-of*)) properties used to describe this world. For a world of 200 blocks, this would amount to 40,000 separate, unique *left-of* and *not*(*left-of*) pieces of knowledge, known as axioms. If we introduce a second property such as *in-front-of*(m, n) and *not*(*in-front-of*(m, n)), 40,000 additional axioms must be added to the representation bringing the total to 80,000. To fully represent the property of spatial orientation for 200 blocks, by the addition of *right-of*(m, n), *not*(*right-of*(m, n)), *behind*(m, n) and *not*(*behind*(m, n)), 160,000 axioms would be required to fully represent the concept of spatial orientation in this world of 200 blocks. Space complexity is poor.

In a dynamic environment, the reasoning agent would have to attend to the plane of blocks on a relatively frequent basis since it, or some other external entity, could be responsible for the movement of one or more, even all of the blocks. For smooth detection assume that the internal representation must be updated twenty times per second. For 200 blocks this would mean that the update of each property in the representation could consume at most 0.0000003125 seconds, or 0.3125 microseconds, of machine processing time including the feature-based recognition of the blocks, attention, perception and the updating of the internal representation. Time complexity is poor. By present computing standards even this simple representation approaches the upper-limits of computational tractability. This is indicative of Hayes' (1987) argument against *broad* approaches to potential computational solutions (Section 1.1). Even allowing the circumvention of object recognition, attention and perception by abstracting the characterization of the external environment into very simple atoms (which is usually the case in this world view), one can see that by adding a few more properties, with stacking allowed, such as *on-top*(m, n) and *not*(*on-top*(m, n)), the representation inevitably becomes computationally intractable. This simple scenario has not even taken into account what the reasoning agent does with the representation once it has been internalized; whether it be planning, problem solving or search. In a representation such as this, it is clear that below certain thresholds of complexity, the frame problem and related problems relating to the property of spatial orientation are "solved", or at least curtailed. But, it should also be apparent that the space and time complexity eventually attains intractability as the size and complexity of the agent's world increases (Chapman, 1987).

Therefore, the preferred method to constrain this intractability has been for researchers to select domains of study in which most or all the characteristics of the *environment* atom are static. For intrinsically dynamic environments where static assumptions are prohibitive, the solution has been to constrain the complexity of the internal representation through abstraction, assumption and simplification of the entities in the external world. Most approaches first consider a *static world* hoping that the representation will

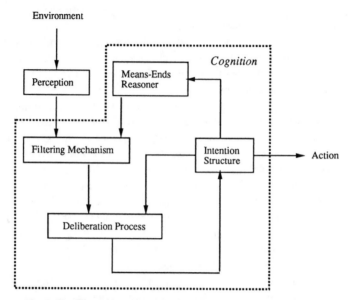

Fig. 7. The Tileworld architecture (from Pollack & Ringuette, 1990).

"scale up" to the demands of a dynamic world. This is the principal reason why I have pursued the title of the book, *Reasoning Agents in a Dynamic World*, to such an extent. As Brooks (1991) recounted, the general divide-and-conquer strategy in early AI and cognitive science had been to decompose the domain of human and general biological intelligence into separate subdisciplines such as vision, perception, natural language, planning, robotics, and so forth, while maintaining the aspiration that the individual sub-problems would and could be solved as separate efforts. Once each of the sub-problems was solved, it was hypothesized that the individual solutions could then be reconstructed through integration and aggregation into the Final Solution. It should be obvious to the reader that this scientific strategy is symptomatic of the atomism intrinsic to the interactional world view.

The *Tileworld* architecture (Pollack & Ringuette, 1990) provides a superior example of an *implemented* intelligent reasoning system that is grounded in the tradition of the cognitive world view and which reasons about an unpredictable dynamic world. At present, Tileworld reasons about a dynamic, simulated environment which consists of approximately 150 abstracted objects. The Perception module (Fig. 7) performs no function in this architecture, with the assumption that the earlier phases of object recognition (e.g., Marr, 1982), attention and perception have already occurred. Therefore, each object in the simulated environment is mapped to a corresponding internal representation (as was discussed in Fig. 2 from Section 1.2) which Tileworld's cognitive planning subsystem reasons about (Bratman, 1987). In particular, this involves both immediate reasoning about the present and deliberative reasoning about the future. Information about the complete state of all 150 abstracted objects in its environment is periodically scanned and internalized into 150 corresponding internal objects; i.e., "... the agent can access a global map of the world that indicates the locations of all objects ..." (Pollack & Ringuette, 1990, p. 4). This practice of updating the internal representation with a complete copy of the external world is symptomatic of the omniscience assumption. Instead of having to perform a worst-case update of twenty times per second however, as illustrated before with the 200 blocks, Tileworld curtails the frame problem by scanning the entire external world, then updating the internal representation with this information only on a demand-driven basis. Thus, any change, or non-change, in the environment is not reflected in the internal representation of the system until it is required by some aspect of the internal reasoning process. Once internalized, only the relevant entities are attended to. It is clear that Tileworld's approach to the frame problem is elegant, albeit with the assumption of omniscience intact (e.g., Haugh, Tenenberg). Both space and time complexity are very well constrained for a world of 150 abstracted objects. It is not clear however, how space and time complexity would scale up to the demands of a dynamic world comprising thousands or millions of objects.

There is also another point to be considered. Suppose for a moment, that a reasonable *interactional* divide-and-conquer solution to object recognition, the focusing of attention (e.g., Nutter) and perception were to arrive, thus providing Tileworld's Perception module with functionality. These questions, indeed, could be asked of *any* interactional approach to human or machine cognition. Would the integration of inputs, outputs, structures and processes within and between the Perception module and Tileworld's other modules be possible? For instance, since the characterization of the environment would be more concrete, perhaps comprising real physical entities as in Sandewall's traffic situation model, would the output of Tileworld's new Perception module be similar to its current output, an omniscient series of abstracted objects? With its new perceptual and attentional capabilities, the output of the Perception module would in all likelihood, comprise a non-omniscient subset of the external world, as described in Section 1.3 (Fig. 3). But, how would this affect the extant internal reasoning structures and processes in Tileworld, which are singularly equipped to function with an omniscient internal representation of the world? Given the causally-governed bookkeeping problem illustrated in the example with the 200 blocks, the omniscient internal representation in Tileworld coupled with a non-omniscient attentional and perceptual module would mean that portions of the internal representation would not be updated with changing, relevant information about the world. This would eventually result in inconsistencies relating to change and lack of change, which as we already know is the frame problem. In other words, this kind of atomistic integration does not appear to be plausible, when representing a dynamic, unpredictable world. Given that systems such as Tileworld serve to promote principles of resource-boundedness and resource-limited reasoning (Pollack, 1992; Simon, 1955), the assumption of omniscience, as it is realized in Tileworld's exhaustive internal representation of the world—which instead implies boundless resources via the frame problem—contradicts the very thesis it endeavors to help bring about.

The reason I have pursued this tangent at such great length is to accentuate the fact that in the interactional world view, no matter how the researcher attempts to abstract the world, causal laws and their related consequences invariably underlie, and are intrinsic to, the ensuing representation. From this originates the assumption of omniscience; in any representation which results from an abstraction in this world view, the researcher and the representation must be ready to account for all causal relationships between all atoms.

Recalling the discussion in Sections 1.2 and 1.3, the fallacy of omniscience is that a true biological reasoning agent is neither aware of all objects and events in its world, within itself, nor of all causal relationships between objects. The frame problem falls out of this assumption since it inevitably becomes prohibitive, if not paradoxical, to represent *all* change and non-change in a causally-governed world. But, as Hayes aptly put it, "there doesn't seem to be any other way to do it, *that* is the frame problem" (1987, p. 125) [original emphasis]. (However, I will illustrate, later in Section 3.4, there *are* "other ways to do it", such that the frame problem is altogether avoidable.) Therefore, after the initial publication of the frame problem in 1969, most if not all, potential solutions have concentrated on strategies of elimination, reduction or minimization in order to restrict the prohibitive combinatorics, such as those illustrated in this Section, to a more tractable magnitude. As I have illustrated, Tileworld performs quite well within the limitations of omniscience and the frame problem. With the presence of atomism and causal relationships however, it appears that any potential approach in this world view, including Tileworld, inevitably attains a combinatorial asymptote as the size and complexity of the world increases (Chapman, 1987), thus making the frame problem unavoidable.

The interactional world view in the book

With the exception of the chapters of Nutter, Perlis, Stein and Sandewall, for most of the contributions in the book, the interactional world view is pre-eminent in one form or another (see Table 1). Change, context and time are treated as separate dimensions. Even in the cases utilizing inferential statistics (e.g., Tenenberg, Weber), the approach is not immune from the standpoint of causal relationships. Rather than discrete, binary causes i.e., *True* or *False*, causes are instead assigned continuous probabilities ranging from 0 to 1. Regarding the representation of time, the approaches of Morgenstern and particularly Goodwin & Trudel also follow the tenets of the interactional world view. Time is treated as a dimension separate from other entities in the abstractions. Excluding the systems of Brown [12] and Weld, the remaining contributions exist only in the early phases of conceptual development or as theoretical analyses. Keeping in mind the capabilities of the Tileworld architecture and the intractabilities imminent in the cognitive world view; I encourage the reader to ask: how effectively each of the proposed approaches in the book would scale up in a dynamic, fast-changing, unpredictable world consisting of hundreds or thousands of objects and events. There is another fundamental question that I encourage the reader to ask, or at least consider: if the frame problem, in all likelihood, "point[s] up a basic error in the way we try to describe the everyday world" (Hayes, 1987), could one consider alternate ways to (a) look at and (b) describe intelligent phenomena? This is precisely the kind of question Stein asks in her chapter. Particularly for those researchers that are plagued with issues relating to unpredictable and dynamic worlds, other world views exist in which the frame problem may either be attenuated, or simply does not exist. These issues owe to the manner by which elements and relationships are characterized between and within the agent and environment. Two

---

[12] Brown's chapter proposes and describes an implementation of a software meta-language which combines features from a wide variety of logics.

such candidates are the organismic and transactional world views. These are not widely known and might be awkward to apprehend in the present setting of human and machine cognition. I will do my best however, to explicate them below in relation to the book and this discussion.

3.3. The organismic world view

The *organismic* world view involves a separation of agent and environment as in the interactional world view. However, regarding the agent, "organismic approaches require an appreciation of how elements fit together in terms of system-wide principles of organization" (Altman & Rogoff, 1987, p. 19). Any element therefore, must be analyzed in the context of the whole system. The whole of the agent is characterized as more than the sum of its parts (i.e., Gestalt). In turn, "organismic world views consider the whole and certain part–whole relationships to be the proper unit of analysis ..." (Altman & Rogoff, 1987, p. 19). Regarding causality, rather than an emphasis on uni-directional, cause–effect relationships between atoms which is reminiscent of the interactional world view (e.g., Fig. 6), causality can be reciprocal (e.g., bi-directional), can follow multiple paths, and can also assume complex patterns. Regarding time and change, the organismic world view stresses teleological mechanisms which "pull" the organism towards certain "ideal states", also known as homeostasis; whereupon time and change cease to be relevant. The organismic world view also permits a separation of the analysis of the agent and the environment. The intra-agent elements are context-dependent. Regarding the agent and the environment however, time, change and context are separate entities, much as in the interactional world view.

Certain connectionist models for instance, reflect most aspects of the organismic world view. The interactive activation model of McLelland & Rumelhart (1981) consists of an interconnected network of linguistic "units" at the feature (i.e., sub-symbolic), letter and word level which share either excitatory or inhibitory bi-directional relationships with each other. As the constituents of a printed word such as "CAT" for example, are presented to such a network, the feature units (e.g., "/", "\", "-") become activated, which in turn activate letter units (e.g., "C", "A", "T"). The activation spreads through the entire system until the word units (e.g., "CAT"), and presumably other concepts related to "CAT", such as "MORRIS", are activated as well. As the end-result of this spreading i.e., once homeostasis or the "final state" is attained, most units associated with a cat are fully excited and other similar, yet unrelated entities, such as "BAT" and "CAR" are inhibited. Nutter's contribution in the book is akin to the organismic world view and proposes a spreading activation model similar to McLelland & Rumelhart. Nutter's is designed to focus the attention of the agent only to those concepts that are relevant in a model of a static world. Sandewall's contribution also adheres to most aspects of the organismic world view. Rather than the spreading of activation though, he seeks a system of dynamic frames wherein the selection and activation of frames is contingent on higher-order parameters extracted from the environment via physical sensors.

In all three of these cases, however, omniscience is still a factor which contributes to the characterization of the relationship between the agent and the environment; and ultimately the internal representation. The reason why owes to the quality intrinsic to the organismic world view which treats the agent and environment as separate entities. Even though the elements within the agent are context-dependent, the agent is still context-independent with respect to the environment (see Table 1). The causal universals intrinsic to the interactional world view thus also affect the organismic world view in much the same fashion. To put this another way, even though causality in the organismic world view can be complex, multi-directional, reciprocal and even teleological, it still carries along with it the same pernicious assumption of omniscience. Nutter's internalized static "world model" for instance, must ultimately account for every object and event in the external world. Moreover, for each of these three approaches, when something changes in the environment, the change must be acknowledged by the reasoning agent in order for the internal representation to remain consistent. This, as we have already observed, gives birth to the frame problem.

3.4. The transactional world view

The *transactional* world view considers the agent and environment as being melded into indivisible, inseparable contexts.

> The transactional approach is ... the study of the changing relations among psychological and environmental aspects of holistic unities. [emphasis removed] The transactional whole is not composed of separate elements but is a *confluence* of inseparable factors that depend on one another for their very definition and meaning. Furthermore, transactional approaches focus on the *changing* relationships among aspects of the whole, both as a tool for understanding a phenomenon and because temporal processes are an integral feature of the person-environment whole.
>
> [Unlike the organismic and interactional world views] ... the transactional world view does not deal with the relationship *between elements*, in the sense that one independent element may cause changes in, affect, or influence another element. Instead, a transactional approach assumes that the *aspects* of a system, that is, person and context, coexist and jointly define one another and contribute to the meaning and nature of a holistic event. [original emphasis] (Altman & Rogoff, 1987, p. 24)

The unit of analysis is, in principle, purely contextual. Hence elements, also referred to as "aspects", of both the agent and the environment, including change and context, can only be described *in terms of each other*. In her chapter, Stein pursues ideals such as these regarding her attempt to describe the world in terms of acausal, atemporal counterfactuals rather than through temporal and causal logics. The transactional world view has also been realized in disciplines such as situated action (Suchman, 1987; Agre, 1993; Chapman, 1991; Agre & Chapman, 1987, 1991), situation theory (Devlin, 1991; Barwise & Perry, 1983), the theory of affordances (Gibson, 1979), subsumption architectures (Brooks, 1991), activity theory (Wertsch, 1991; Vygotsky, 1986), psychology (Greeno, 1989) and psycholinguistics (Van Orden et al., 1991). Fig. 8 illustrates, in a superficial way, a diagrammatic characterization of the relationship be-

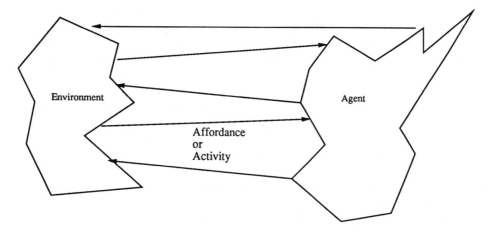

Fig. 8. Activity- or affordance-based transactional world view.

tween the agent and the environment in this world view. The diagram highlights the attributes of cognition intrinsic to the agent which correspond to distinctive features germane to the environment, typically realized as activity. Note that the linear conception of time—past, present, future—in the interactional sense, is absent from this world view. Causality also lacks any tangible interpretation in this world view in the sense of antecedent–consequent, cause–effect, or input–output relationships among "atoms" (e.g., Figs. 6 and 7), since they do not exist in this world view. Now it is necessary, to once again get at the biological and mechanical crux of the frame problem.

Interpretations of attention and perception in the cognitive world view

Backtracking a bit, the cognitive world view explicated earlier considers cognition as a centralized, information-theoretic management system for abstracted information. This abstracted information has presumably been extracted from the environment via the faculties of attention and perception. Hence, attention and perception have historically been idealized as processes that are *ancillary* rather than essential to cognition; i.e., their foremost roles have been to acknowledge incoming stimuli from the world (e.g., Fig. 6) and reconstruct such stimuli into internalized, abstracted collections of objects, or "symbols". These internalized symbols are then presumably manipulated by myriad internal "cognitive processes" (e.g., Fig. 7). In the cognitive world view there are two prevailing interpretations regarding the roles of attention and perception and how they relate to cognition; (1) a mechanistic, or machine, interpretation and (2) a biological, or human, interpretation.

In the mechanistic interpretation (Section 1.2), because of the assumption of omniscience, (a) the role of perception has been to extract *each and every* entity from the environment, and (b) the capabilities of attention, are instead, utilized internally as part of the cognitive reasoning process, such as they are in Tileworld, focusing on relevant and salient aspects of the internal representation, rather than the external representation. In the biological interpretation (Section 1.3), by contrast, the typical functions ascribed to the phenomena of perception and attention are: (a) object individuation and recognition capabilities (e.g., Marr, 1982), and (b) an attentional mechanism which allows the system to focus only on *relevant* and *salient* entities that are present in the external, perceptual (e.g., visual) flux (e.g., Treisman, 1985; Allport, 1989; Wolfe, 1992). The precise relationships between the functions of attention, perception and cognition in *either* interpretation have historically remained elusive, since these three functions have been treated as separate sub-disciplines in accord with the divide-and-conquer atomism intrinsic to the interactional world view. To put it another way, the nature of the "interfaces" between these three functionally disparate entities remain unclear. Thus, even within the same world view, there are major discrepancies between the interpretations of human and machine cognition and what the roles of attention and perception are in either.[13]

The presence of omniscience in machine cognition versus the ostensible absence of it in human cognition appears to be one of the primary sticking points in the cognitive world view. In the biological, or human interpretation (Section 1.3), attention is one of the *earlier* processes to occur. In the machine interpretation (Section 1.2), such as in Tileworld, attention is one of the *later* processes to occur. This inconsistency in the machine interpretation of the cognitive world view, when abstracted and realized in a representation, has been the basis for many of the nonmonotonic, and temporal persistence issues addressed in the book (e.g. Haugh, Weber, Goodwin & Trudel) and elsewhere. Lacking any other way around this, the methodological, tractable and representational constraints intrinsic to the cognitive world view typically result in the simplifying assumption that the "output" of attention and perception (e.g., Fig. 7) is simply an omniscient stream of abstracted objects—constituting many of the approaches to the frame problem and the family of nonmonotonic logics. For many of the contributions in the book, this assumption is realized in representations which ignore attention and perception outright, and which only reason about abstracted objects that have been presumably processed by attention and perception (see Table 1). By the same token, some of the very same contributions (e.g., Etherington et al.) argue that salience, relevance and the focus of attention, functions that are intrinsic to the biological interpretations of attention and perception, are vital to the "solution" to the frame problem. The theoretical gulf that separates these two conflicting interpretations of human and machine intelligence is thus, quite vast.

Interpretation of attention and perception in the transactional world view

In the transactional world view by contrast, the agent, environment and the relationship between the two are all considered as a single, unified unit of analysis. Thus, it is impossible to presume intelligence to be solely "internal" to the agent as it typically is in the interactional and the organismic world views. *Both* biological and mechanistic transactional interpretations of these three functions, such as discussed in Section 1.3, focus more directly on the "confluence" of agent and environment. From

---

[13] These incongruencies are typically rationalized by arguing that the goals of AI and certain forms of cognitive science are not necessarily to follow strict biological principles. But the willingness to embrace a biological phenomenon when it suits the purpose of a non-biological approach (e.g., "perception", "cognition", "attention", "memory") belies this posture.

the perspective of developing requirements for a computational architecture, particularly for a representation, such interpretations differ markedly from what have historically been considered the "standard", mainstream representations in AI and cognitive science. Since transactional *aspects*, rather than internalized abstractions of the environment are the primary unit of analysis, the biological functions that negotiate most directly with such agent-environment aspects are first perception and attention, *then* cognition. There currently exist a few intelligent architectures, in which the developers have focused their efforts on the functions of perception and attention and the relation of these externally to the environment, as well as internally to cognition in attempts to capture this "confluence". These approaches take on many of the characteristics of the transactional world view. Most noteworthy have been Brooks' insect-like robotic creatures (1991), Pengi (Agre & Chapman, 1991) and Sonja (Chapman, 1991). The mode of representation is known as a *deictic*. A prototypical verbalization of a deictic is:

> *the-cup-I-am-drinking-from.* (Agre, 1993)

This deictic neither uniquely denotes an internal structure or process, an external object, nor an action, such as would be described in the situation calculus. Referring to Fig. 8, a deictic such as *the-cup-I-am-drinking-from* entails aspects of (a) the environment, *from-the-cup*; (b) the agent, *I-am*; and (c) the activity, *I-am-drinking*. The reader should not be misled however, into believing that a deictic is somehow decomposable into three subordinate categories. The Gestalt property of the deictic is also akin to what Gibson (1979) had distinguished by name as the *affordance*. As a consequence, in deictic representations, the relationship between agent and environment possess most of the qualities that are intrinsic to the transactional world view.

As an example, the video game domain which Pengi reasons about, called Pengo, contains hundreds of moving objects, and change is fast, as well as unpredictable. The Pengi domain (Fig. 9) comprises (a) a single penguin which is manipulated by the Pengi system, (b) several predatory bees which can either kill the penguin or be killed by the penguin, and (c) about two hundred cubes of ice—some of which can be kicked by the penguin at a predatory bee in order to kill it. The design strategy chosen by the developers of Pengi was to avoid the intractabilities inherent in omniscient, interactional world view approaches. Instead of omnisciently internalizing the world, as Tileworld does, Pengi treats external objects and events in the world, and its transactions with them, as the principal representation. The objects in the Pengi domain are thus individuated into deictic elements such as *the-penguin*, *the-ice-cube*, *the-enemy-bee*, and so forth. In this non-omniscient fashion, *the-enemy-bee* might refer to a particular bee in one situation, but perhaps a different bee in another situation; contingent perhaps on the property of physical proximity between *the-penguin* and an infinite set of potentially threatening *enemy-bees*. Then, activities entailing many potential situations in which *the-penguin* might find itself, comprising objects and events (i.e., changes in property discussed in Sections 1.2 and 1.3), are also represented deictically.

The implementation of these transactions are grounded in Ullman's (1984) *visual routines*. These basic perceptual procedures are postulated to transpire at the stage of intermediate vision *after* object detection and individuation have taken place (Marr, 1982).

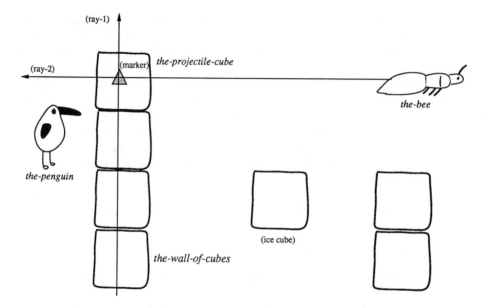

Fig. 9. Situated use of visual routines in Pengi (view is from above).

Visual routines are theorized to co-occur with other attentional and higher-order processes which help constrain, or make salient, only those entities in the visual field that are relevant in the current context; other irrelevant entities are simply ignored.[14] Fig. 9 illustrates two visual routines, known as *markers* and *rays*, which allow Pengi to "visualize" a way to maneuver *the-penguin* next to a cube of ice in order to kick it at a predatory bee and kill it. This particular scenario is best described by the following deictic: *Finding the-projectile-cube-to-kick-at-the-bee when lurking behind the-wall-of-cubes.* Based on the situation depicted in Fig. 9, the Pengi system wishes to kill *the-bee* using the cube-kicking capabilities of *the-penguin*. Two visual routines are utilized that work directly with the visual information "perceived" from the video screen. So in order to locate the cube that *the-penguin* should kick in order to kill *the-bee*, two rays are traced. The first ray (ray-1) is traced along *the-wall-of-cubes* in a vertical fashion where the candidate *projectile-cube*s are known to be. The second ray (ray-2), which reflects the flight path of *the-bee* is traced indefinitely in a horizontal direction until it intersects with another ray, in this case (ray-1). A marker is "dropped" where these two rays, (ray-1) and (ray-2), intersect, yielding *the-projectile-cube* that should be kicked. The very next situation (not illustrated) would then locate *the-penguin* adjacent to *the-projectile-cube* so that it can be kicked at the bee.

---

[14] As an example, consider that while you are reading this footnote, you have focused your attention to this text and are ignoring the text you had just been reading above. In reality, as you read, you are ignoring most things around you other than the eight or so character window in front of and behind the words that you are reading. As in most non-omniscient intelligence, you do not have to internalize the entire situation around you in order to read this text.

Regarding abstraction and representation, note that such visual activity, involving markers and rays, is not conveniently captured in an atomistic representation like predicate logic. But this is not to imply that Pengi is "representationless", contrary to Brooks' (1991) argument. It simply means that at present, Pengi escapes a convenient nomenclature, hence, the deictic verbalizations. [15] Also note that even though approximately two hundred blocks of ice and many moving, potentially predatory bees comprise the overall state in the Pengi game, only focused *situations* relevant to Pengi's purview, such as the one depicted in Fig. 9, are reasoned about. The other objects and events are simply ignored until they become relevant in another situation. This is characteristic of the non-omniscient scenario discussed in Section 1.3 where it was described how actual and potential mappings between external objects and internal representations can either be present or absent (Fig. 3). Since Pengi reasons about information *external* to it in terms of itself and the world, omniscience and internal bookkeeping problems do not exist the way they do in the interactional world view. Thus, both space and time complexity remain within very reasonable, biologically plausible limits. The Pengi system is not without its critics however. Although the planning-like reasoning that Pengi exhibits is emergent and mirrors certain aspects of standard temporal projection paradigms, it can only reason about its present context. Reasoning forward in time, such as is accomplished in Tileworld, is not possible. Since Pengi is an atemporal and acausal system, it is not equipped to reason about dimensions such as time and causality—partly owing to the transactional world view.

The transactional world view: no frame problem

The Pengi system focuses its "attention" to the current, relevant context that is defined both in terms of the environment and the agent. This is accomplished through the aggregation of simple attentional and perceptual operations known as visual routines. The functions of these routines are mediated by internal "combinational networks", the analog to cognitive processes, which essentially decide what set of routines are relevant within a given context. The objects in the environment remain external to the reasoning agent and are not internalized. Hence, Pengi does not have to worry about what has changed and what has not changed with respect to the entire set of two hundred or so objects which make up the game. In fact, if thousands or millions of the same objects were added to the game, neither space nor time complexity would be affected. Owing to the tenets of the transactional world view, Pengi and the situated environment are a unified whole, therefore agent, environment, change, causality, time and action are inseparable. The objects and events outside of Pengi's purview are simply ignored— change or lack of change relating to what is ignored does not matter; there is not an internal representation of the external world; hence, no need for an assumption of omniscience and more importantly, no potential for a frame problem. In fact, there *is no* frame problem in this incarnation of the transactional world view.

The principal feature offered by the transactional world view, and the example provided by Pengi, is that many of the requirements set forth by the contributors in the

---

[15] There have been recent developments in the realm of situation theory (Devlin, 1991) attempting to formalize such ideas.

Table 1
Three scientific world views (derived from Altman & Rogoff, 1987)

World view	Time and change	Causation	AI & Cognitive Science
Interactional: Qualities of agent and physical or social environment treated as separate underlying entities, with interaction between parts. Context is characterized as separable from the agent and environment.	Change results from interaction of separate agent and environment entities; change sometimes occurs in accord with underlying regulatory mechanisms; time and change not intrinsic to phenomena.	Emphasizes *efficient causes*, i.e., antecedent–consequent relations, notions of causation. Observers are separate, objective, and detached from phenomena; equivalent observations of same phenomenon by different observers.	Omniscience and frame problem exist. *Methods:* Logic, situation calculus, modus ponens, production and statistical inference rules, cognition, behaviorism and connectionism. *Book:* Brown, Etherington et al., Goodwin & Trudel, Haugh, Morgenstern, Perlis, Tenenberg, Weber, Weld. *Computational Models:* Tileworld.
Organismic: Holistic entities composed of separate agent and environment components, elements or parts whose relations and interactions yield qualities of a whole that are "more than the sum of the parts". Elements within agent are context-dependent and affected by system-wide principles.	Change results from interaction of agent and environment entities. Change usually occurs in accord with underlying regulatory mechanisms, is teleological and irrelevant once ideal state is reached; assumes system stability is goal.	Emphasizes *final causes*, i.e., teleology, "pull" toward ideal state. Observers are separate, objective and detached from phenomena; equivalent observations by different observers.	Omniscience and frame problem exist. *Methods:* Activity and situation theories, connectionism. *Book:* Nutter, Perlis, Sandewall *Computational Models:* McLelland & Rumelhart (1981).
Transactional: Holistic entities composed of "aspects", not separate parts or elements; aspects are mutually defining; temporal qualities are intrinsic features of wholes. Agent and environment comprise a unified, indivisible context.	Stability/change are intrinsic and defining features of phenomena; change occurs continuously; directions of change emergent and not preestablished.	Emphasizes *formal causes*, i.e., description and understanding of patterns, shapes and form of phenomena. No antecedent–consequent relationships between elements. Observers are aspects of phenomena; different observations by different observers in different contexts.	Omniscience and frame problem *do not* exist. *Methods:* Situation, activity and affordance theories, connectionism, counterfactuals. *Book:* Perlis, Stein. *Computational Models:* Pengi.

book appear to be satisfied to a certain extent: *scope* (Etherington et al.), *salience, context, intuition* (Nutter), *common sense* (Haugh), *relevance* (Stein), *domain-specificity* (Weber) and *abandoning completeness* (Tenenberg). It is very clear that many of the contributors in the book are completely aware of the requirements that would lead a given approach away from omniscience and the frame problem. Unfortunately, with the exception of Stein and Perlis, the proposed solutions are carried out from the vantage point of the interactional or organismic world views, which as I have already argued, are predisposed to assumptions of omniscience and the frame problem. These distinctions are summarized in Table 1.

3.5. World view "roundup"

In the last three sections, I have attempted to describe a continuum that points up various perspectives through which the researcher might choose to characterize the relationship between a reasoning agent and its environment. At one end of the continuum, known as the interactional world view, such phenomena are decomposable into arbitrarily complex "atoms" which exhaustively share cause–effect relationships with each other. It was discussed that within this world view, exist the assumption of omniscience and the frame problem. The Tileworld architecture was illustrated as an example of this world view in which the omniscience assumption regarding external–internal mappings are intact, yet the frame problem is curtailed through a selective sampling of a complete copy of the world on a need-to-know basis. This perspective places little or no emphasis on biological perception and attention, and instead, focuses on internal cognitive processes that reason about complete, internalized copies of the external world. Anchoring the opposite end of the continuum, is the transactional world view, in which the agent and environment comprise an inseparable, embeddedness in context. Likewise, the Pengi architecture was presented as an exemplar of this world view in which it was demonstrated that omniscience and the frame problem do not exist. Following the agent-environment-action qualities of the deictic representation, this perspective emphasizes attention and perception in which cognition serves only a mediatory role between the agent and the environment, in terms of deciding which action to select next, given the demands of the present situation. This view supports many of the requirements idealized in the book. By focusing only on relevant and salient aspects of the situation, all else can be ignored, and a frame problem does not exist. Finally, somewhere in the middle of this spectrum lies the organismic world view, in which the agent comprises a holistic entity, yet the separability between the agent and the environment still exists, much like the interactional world view.

Thus, the question remains, what does each world view have to offer to the realms of research in human and machine cognition? Also, are these world views mutually exclusive, or, as has been accomplished in other sciences such as physics and biology, might they be better utilized and integrated to produce more powerful and explanatory theoretical frameworks? For instance, in Perlis' discussion, he provides compelling examples which show that it is sometimes necessary to remember, as well as reason about, past experiences from which certain facts might either be congruent or contradictory with similar or identical facts relevant in the present situation. Since humans appear to exhibit the phenomenon of being able to reason about time; past, present and future, this is clearly a trait that is part and parcel of an interactional world view—where time is treated as a separate dimension. However, given what we *now* know about omniscience and the frame problem (by way of this review), reasoning about time in the interactional world view, particularly in an unpredictable and dynamic world, has severe limitations. We also know that the transactional world view does not inherently possess such limitations, however this world view is also atemporal and acausal. Thus, I pose the question, might it be possible to develop abstraction and representation methodologies which combine desirable aspects from some or all of these current, or to-be-discovered, world views? In the case of Tileworld and Pengi, for instance, could aggregations of

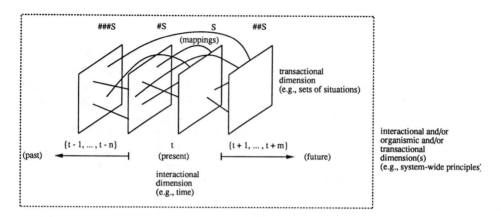

Fig. 10. Integration of interactional, organismic and transactional world views.

transactional Pengi-like situations be reasoned about along an interactional Tileworld-like dimension of time?

In order to provide a sketch of this, Fig. 10 depicts a visualization in which transactional dimensions, realized as four distinct sets of situations, S, $\#S$, $\#\#S$, and $\#\#\#S$, are organized along the interactional dimension of time from $t - n$ to $t + m$, i.e., past, present and future. The two sets of situations, S and $\#S$, reflect the "standard" non-omniscient external–internal mapping (i.e., Fig. 3 rotated 90 degrees) at a present time t. Recalling the discussion from Section 1.3, once transactions among situations are learned or remembered through experience, they are then internalized, and realized as the phenomenon of long-term memory. Thus, in Fig. 10, $\#\#\#S$ reflects a very large set of transactional situations, perhaps organized along, but certainly not constrained to, the interactional dimension of time, from $t - 1$ to $t - n$, that reflect learned, past transactional experiences. [16] Likewise, $\#\#S$ reflects a set of "working memory"-like (e.g., Baddeley, 1986) transactional situations, that comprise the present course of reasoning, as in Tileworld, which draws from past experiences, $\#\#\#S$, as well as from the environment, S and its immediate perceptions of the environment, $\#S$. Potential situations about the future, from $t + 1$ to $t + m$, are temporarily "deliberated" about as alternatives in $\#\#S$, before being committed to in $\#\#\#S$.

Thus, one can see that the phenomenon of attention and perception, through a transactional perspective, is not only utilized for the immediate negotiation between agent ($\#S$) and environment (S) as it is in Pengi, but is also generalized to involve the phenomena of working memory ($\#\#S$) and long-term memory ($\#\#\#S$) (e.g., Schneider & Detweiler, 1987). In this scenario, attention is not only an aspect of the canonical biological variety, such as the use of visual routines in Pengi, but is also "turned inward",

---

[16] Of course, as in Stein's discussion, time in a transactional sense takes on an altogether different meaning. Rather than viewing time as a separate, linear dimension as it is in the interactional and organismic world views, in this case time is embedded in the remembered transactional situation as some aspect of the situation. This characterization of transactional memory is similar to the "reentrant value mapping" discussed in Clancey (1993, pp. 95–96).

as is currently reflected in the omniscient internal reasoning structure of Tileworld. The phenomenon of mental imagery (Kosslyn, 1983) illustrates one way in which perception and attention might be directed inward in the presence and absence of external stimuli. An integrated architecture such as the one described in Fig. 10, I maintain, is congruent with many of the requirements advanced by the various contributors in the book in terms of (a) avoiding the frame problem altogether, (b) conforming to what is know to occur biologically (e.g., Olshausen et al., 1992), and (c) still accurately capturing certain phenomena of human intelligence, non-omnisciently, such as reasoning about time. Architecturally, these two dimensions might be subsumed by a larger system-wide dimension, or dimensions, in which system-wide principles in one, two or all three world views, negotiate interactions and/or transactions between the interactional ($t - n$ to $t + m$) and transactional dimensions (S, #S, ##S, ###S) so-far discussed. As in Perlis' example, or like in Tileworld, such information drawn from the past (###S) might bear on reasoning that takes place in the present (S, #S) and about the future (##S), even if the information that crosses temporal boundaries (via mappings, Fig. 10) is contradictory. This scenario is also loosely related, but certainly not isomorphic, to Stein's reasoning about counterfactual worlds.

4. Conclusion

In this review, I have attempted to accomplish several things. Foremost, I have tried to organize and highlight some of the major contributions in the book. I have also attempted to show how the presence or absence of the frame problem is dependent on the scientific perspective, or world view, through which the researcher in AI or cognitive science chooses to perform his or her research activities. I have endeavored to demonstrate that the frame problem is present in the interactional and organismic world views yet is absent in the transactional world view. The reason why pertains to the relationship between the agent and environment, as interpreted by the researcher, from the perspective of one of these scientific world views. The characterization of time, causality, change and context, ultimately bear on this relationship. A journey quite far afield has been required in order to sufficiently integrate, to my satisfaction, the contents of the book, and what it represents to AI and cognitive science as well as to the reader of this review and the reader of the book. Each contribution in the book, as I have discussed, is representative of one, two, or all three world views. Given the broader philosophical and methodological issues that have been explicated and pursued in this review, I believe that the frame problem has been cast into a stronger and more convincing exegetic role.

Science is human activity. When scientists encounter naturally-occurring phenomena, by working with existing tools and methods, as well as creating new ones—hypotheses, observations, experiments, theories, frameworks, paradigms, world views and social movements are constructed. Underneath all of this however, remains the simple fact that *any* observer of Nature is simply observing, but is never completely capable of explaining what he or she has observed. Owing to the cultural milieu in which any scientific observer is active, tendencies towards certain world views, tools, methods and so forth are fostered. Some of these tendencies originate by individual choice, others are constrained by sociocultural and historical factors, such as meeting the needs or expectations of the benefactor funding the research. Yet others are privileged or conform to a particular *genre* (Wertsch, 1991, pp. 124 and 135). Conventional scientific wisdom might suggest that scientists gain glimpses at ultimate, immutable truths about nature by way of scientific discovery. The truth however, I maintain, is in the eye of the beholder; thus, there are *at least* as many truths as there are people. Moreover, the semiotic devices, realized as accepted tools and nomenclatures, serve scientists well in order to mediate and collectivize their activities (Merrell, 1982; Wertsch, 1991).

I have few opinions about which world view is the "right" one to pursue in AI or cognitive science. I do have many opinions however, about what is *reasonable* within a given world view—and I encourage the reader of the book to entertain such opinions as well. Thus, attempting to establish a theory of context from an interactional perspective could prove to be a fruitless enterprise, since it appears to be better suited for development from a transactional outlook. On the other hand, there are many aspects of human and machine cognition that are fundamentally interactional, such as that of reasoning about time in the work of Pollack and Bratman. Or, consider the case where a researcher in human or machine cognition ascribes a term such as "internal structure" or "internal process" to an intelligent phenomenon. It should not be unrealistic to expect this researcher to: (a) explain how the structure or process deals with intractabilities such as the frame problem, (b) if simplifying assumptions are made, such as an abstracted static world, or an omniscient internal representation of the world, how the researcher intends to "scale up" the structure or process to the demands of a real-world situation and (c) what is the goodness of fit between human and machine cognition as it pertains to the structure or process.

In the Introduction, I had provided the analogy that the frame problem is similar to well-known mathematical intractabilities, such as the inability to divide any number by zero or infinity. Coincidental to this review, recent developments in cosmological physics, in attempts to describe the origins of the universe, have forced a re-interpretation of the linear concept of time (past, present, future) to a dimension of "imaginary time" in order to overcome certain mathematical intractabilities (Hawking, 1988). The crux of the problem involves the singularity at the moment, or "time zero", at which the Big Bang is postulated to have occurred. At this singular moment, all laws of physics are invalid since the descriptive equations, owing to the value of time being zero, call for denominators that involve the quantity of infinity (∞), which is mathematically impossible. A proposed solution to this problem has been achieved by a shift from a temporal, interactional perspective to an atemporal, quasi-transactional characterization of time. By reinterpreting time as a nonlinear, holistic aspect of the universe, this singularity is eliminated and imposes the alternate view of the universe as an atemporal phenomenon in which the universe simply "is", for lack of a better word, rather than "was", "is" and "will be" (past, present, future). In other words, in this alternate view, describing the evolution of the universe is not contingent on the dimension of time, thus altogether avoiding the "time zero" singularity. I only call on this example to emphasize the analogy between it and what we have seen to be true of the frame problem intrinsic to the interactional and organismic world views versus the absence of the frame problem in the transactional world view. This leads me to suggest that any strides toward "unification" (e.g., (Newell, 1990) which posits an ostensibly interactional unification, although some would disagree) could be better served in two, three or even other to-be-discovered world views (a sketch of which was illustrated in the last section; e.g., Fig. 10), as has been achieved in other scientific disciplines.

A topic not given much coverage in this review has been the role of the observer as it relates to a phenomenon. The discipline of physics has had much experience with this. For instance:

> Whereas transactional perspectives, exemplified by relativity and quantum theories in physics, consider the position and rate of movement of observers to be part of the phenomenon, interactional perspectives (including the Newtonian approach in physics) assume that observers are separate from the phenomenon and that observation can be done without the observer's influencing or altering the phenomenon. (Altman & Rogoff, 1987, p. 18)

It is no secret that scientific progress in human and machine cognition has been painfully slow, and this partly owes to the complexity of the problem—the mind often being characterized as the single, most intricate phenomenon in the observable universe. *Advances in Human and Machine Cognition* ultimately rest on scientific activity which as already mentioned, is carried out by people. Therefore, the most significant role that I see the scientific observer as having, is the awareness that she or he in point of fact, *does* play a role in all of this.

Acknowledgment

I extend many thanks to Phil Agre, William Clancey, Keith Devlin, Ellice Forman, Alan Lesgold, Mike Lewis, Mark Bickhard, Martha Pollack, Marc Ringuette, Walter Schneider, Stephen Smoliar, Mark Stefik, Richmond Thomason, Ann Ward and William Wilson, bearing on my many frames of reference.

References

Agre, P.E. (1993), The symbolic worldview: reply to Vera and Simon, *Cogn. Sci.* **17**, 61–69.

Agre, P.E. and Chapman, D. (1987), Pengi: an implementation of a theory of activity, in: *Proceedings AAAI-87*, Seattle, WA, 268–272.

Agre, P.E. and Chapman, D. (1990), What are plans for? *Rob. Autonomous Syst.* **6**, 17–34.

Allen, J.F. (1984), Towards a general theory of action and time, *Artif. Intell.* **23**, 123–154.

Allport, A. (1989), Visual attention, in: M.I. Posner, ed., *Foundations of Cognitive Science* (MIT Press, Cambridge, MA) 631–682.

Altman, I. and Rogoff, B. (1987), World views in psychology: trait, interactional, organismic, and transactional perspectives, in: D. Stokols and I. Altman, eds., *Handbook of Environmental Psychology* 1 (Wiley, New York) 7–40.

Baddeley, A.D. (1986), *Working Memory* (Clarendon, Oxford).

Baker, A.B. (1989), A simple solution to the Yale shooting problem, in: R.J. Brachman, H.J. Levesque and R. Reiter, eds., *Proceedings First International Conference on Principles of Knowledge Representation and Reasoning* (Morgan Kaufmann, San Mateo, CA) 11–20.

Baker, A.B. and Ginsberg, M.L. (1989), Temporal projection and explanation, in: N.S. Sridharan, ed., *Proceedings IJCAI-89*, Detroit, MI (Morgan Kaufmann, San Mateo, CA) 906–911.

Barwise, J. and Perry, J. (1983), *Situations and Attitudes* (Bradford Books/MIT Press, Cambridge, MA).

Bratman, M.E. (1987), *Intention, Plans and Practical Reason* (Harvard University Press, Cambridge, MA).

Brooks, R.A. (1991), Intelligence without representation, *Artif. Intell.* **47**, 139–159.

Brown, F.M. (1987), *The Frame Problem in Artificial Intelligence: Proceedings of the 1987 Workshop, April 12–15, 1987, Lawrence, Kansas* (Morgan Kaufmann, Los Altos, CA).

Chapman, D. (1987), Planning for conjunctive goals, *Artif. Intell.* **32**, 333–377.

Chapman, D. (1991), *Vision, Instruction and Action* (MIT Press, Cambridge, MA).

Chomsky, N. (1957), *Syntactic Structures* (Mouton, The Hague, 1978 printing).

Chomsky, N. (1959), A review of B.F. Skinner's *Verbal Behavior*, *Language* **35**, 26–58.

Clancey, W.J. (1993), Situated action: a neuropsychological interpretation (response to Vera and Simon), *Cogn. Sci.* **17**, 87–116.

Cohen, P.R. and Feigenbaum E.A. (1989), *The Handbook of Artificial Intelligence, Volume III* (Addison-Wesley, New York).

Devitt, D. and Sterlny, K. (1987), *Language and Reality* (MIT Press, Cambridge, MA).

Devlin, K. (1991), *Logic and Information* (Cambridge University Press, New York).

Dewey, J. and Bentley, A.F. (1949), *Knowing and the Known* (Beacon, Boston, MA).

Fikes, R.E. and Nilsson, N.J. (1971), STRIPS: a new approach to the application of theorem proving to problem solving, *Artif. Intell.* **2**, 198–208.

Fodor, J. and Pylyshyn, Z.W. (1988), Connectionism and cognitive architecture: a critical analysis, *Cognition* **28**, 3–71.

Forbus, K.D. (1985), Qualitative reasoning about physical processes, *Artif. Intell.* **24**; also in: D.G. Bobrow, ed., *Qualitative Reasoning about Physical Systems* (MIT Press, Cambridge, MA) 85–168.

Frege, G. (1960), On sense and reference, in: P. Geach and M. Black, eds., *Translations from the Philosophical Writings of Gottlob Frege* (Blackwell, Oxford, England).

Georgeff, M.P. (1987), Actions, processes and causality, in: *Proceedings 1986 Workshop on Reasoning about Actions and Plans* (Morgan Kaufmann, Los Altos, CA).

Gibson, J.J. (1979), *The Ecological Approach to Visual Perception* (Houghton Mifflin, Boston, MA).

Ginsberg, M.L. (1986), Counterfactuals, *Artif. Intell.* **30**, 35–79.

Ginsberg, M.L. (1987a), Possible worlds planning, in: *Proceedings 1986 Workshop on Reasoning about Actions and Plans* (Morgan Kaufmann, Los Altos, CA).

Ginsberg, M.L. (1987b), *Readings in Non-Monotonic Reasoning* (Morgan Kaufmann, Los Altos, CA).

Ginsberg, M.L. and Smith, D. (1988a), Reasoning about action I: a possible worlds approach, *Artif. Intell.* **35**, 165–195.

Ginsberg, M.L. and Smith, D. (1988b), Reasoning about action II: the qualification problem, *Artif. Intell.* **35**, 311–342.

Goebel, R.G. and Goodwin, S.D. (1987), Applying theory formation to the planning problem, in: F.M. Brown, ed., *The Frame Problem in Artificial Intelligence: Proceedings of the 1987 Workshop* (Morgan Kaufmann, Los Altos, CA) 207–232.

Goodwin, S.D. and Goebel, R.G. (1989), Non-monotonic reasoning in temporal domains: the knowledge independence problem, in: M. Reinfrank, J. de Kleer, M.L. Ginsberg and E. Sandewall, eds., *Non-Monotonic Reasoning: 2nd International Workshop* (Springer-Verlag, Berlin) 187–201.

Greeno, J.G. (1989), Situations, mental models, and generative knowledge, in: K. Kotovsky, ed., *Complex Information Processing: The Impact of Herbert A. Simon* (Lawrence Erlbaum, Hillsdale, NJ) 285–318.

Haas, A. (1987), The case for domain-specific frame axioms, in: F.M. Brown, ed., *The Frame Problem in Artificial Intelligence: Proceedings of the 1987 Workshop* (Morgan Kaufmann, Los Altos, CA) 343–349.

Hanks, S. and McDermott, D. (1986), Default reasoning, non-monotonic logic, and the frame problem, in: T. Kehler, S.J. Rosenschein, R. Filman and P. Patel-Schneider, eds., *Proceedings AAAI-86*, Philadelphia, PA (Morgan Kaufmann, Los Altos, CA) 328–333.

Haugh, B. (1987), Simple causal minimization for temporal persistence and projection, in: K.D. Forbus and H.E. Shrobe, eds., *Proceedings AAAI-87*, Seattle, WA (Morgan Kaufmann, Los Altos, CA) 218–223.

Hayes, P.J. (1971), A logic of actions, in: *Principles for Designing Intelligent Robots* (Metamathematics Unit, University of Edinburgh) 495–519.

Hayes, P.J. (1985), The second naive physics manifesto, in: J.R. Hobbs and R.C. Moore, eds., *Formal Theories of the Commonsense World* (Ablex, Norwood, NJ) 1–36.

Hayes, P.J. (1987), What the frame problem is and isn't, in: Z.W. Pylyshyn, ed., *The Robot's Dilemma: The Frame Problem in Artificial Intelligence* (Ablex, Norwood, NJ) 123–137.

Hawking, S.W. (1988), *A Brief History of Time: From the Big Bang to Black Holes* (Bantam Books, New York).

Kautz, H.A. (1986), The logic of persistence, in: T. Kehler, S.J. Rosenschein, R. Filman and P. Patel-Schneider, eds., *Proceedings AAAI-86*, Philadelphia, PA (Morgan Kaufmann, Los Altos, CA) 401–405.

Kosslyn, S.M. (1983), *Ghosts in the Mind's Machine: Creating and Using Images in the Brain* (Norton, New York).

Kripke, S.A. (1980), *Naming and Necessity* (Harvard University Press, Cambridge, MA).

Kyburg Jr, H.E., (1974), *The Logical Foundations of Statistical Inference* (Kluwer Academic, Dordrecht, Netherlands).

Lewis, D.K. (1973), *Counterfactuals* (Harvard University Press, Cambridge, MA).

Lifschitz, V. (1986), Pointwise circumscription: preliminary report, in: T. Kehler, S.J. Rosenschein, R. Filman and P. Patel-Schneider, eds., *Proceedings AAAI-86*, Philadelphia, PA (Morgan Kaufmann, Los Altos, CA) 406–410.

Lifschitz, V. (1987), Formal theories of action, in: F.M. Brown, ed., *The Frame Problem in Artificial Intelligence: Proceedings of the 1987 Workshop* (Morgan Kaufmann, Los Altos, CA) 35–57.

Loui, R.P. (1987), Response to Hanks and McDermott: temporal evolution of beliefs and beliefs about temporal evolution, *Cogn. Sci.* **11**, 283-297.

Marr, D. (1982), *Vision* (Freeman, San Francisco, CA).

McCarthy, J. (1962), Towards a mathematical science of computation, *Proceedings IFIP Congress* **62** (North-Holland, Amsterdam).

McCarthy, J. (1963), Programs with common sense, in: M. Minsky, ed., *Semantic Information Processing* (MIT Press, Cambridge, MA, 1968).

McCarthy, J. (1980), Circumscription—a form of non-monotonic reasoning, *Artif. Intell.* **13**, 27–39.

McCarthy, J. (1986), Applications of circumscription to formalizing common-sense reasoning, *Artif. Intell.* **28**, 89–116.

McCarthy, J. (1987), The frame problem today, in: F.M. Brown, ed., *The Frame Problem in Artificial Intelligence: Proceedings of the 1987 Workshop* (Morgan Kaufmann, Los Altos, CA) 3.

McCarthy, J. and Hayes, P.J. (1969), Some philosophical problems from the standpoint of artificial intelligence, in: B. Meltzer and D. Michie, eds., *Machine Intelligence* **4** (American Elsevier, New York)463–502; also in: B.L. Webber and N.J. Nilsson, eds., *Readings in Artificial Intelligence* (Morgan Kaufmann, Los Altos, CA) 431–450.

McDermott, D.V. (1982), A temporal logic of reasoning about processes and plans, *Cogn. Sci.* **6**, 101–155.

McDermott, D.V. (1987), We've been framed: Or, why AI is innocent of the frame problem, in: Z.W. Pylyshyn, ed., *The Robot's Dilemma: The Frame Problem in Artificial Intelligence* (Ablex, Norwood, NJ) 113–122.

McLelland, J.L. and Rumelhart, D.E. (1981), An interactive activation model of context effects in letter perception, Part 1: an account of basic findings, *Psychol. Rev.* **88**, 375–407.

Merrell, F. (1982), *Semiotic Foundations* (Indiana University Press, Bloomington, IN).

Mill, J.S. (1875), *A System of Logic* (Longmans, New York).

Minsky, M. (1975), A framework for representing knowledge, in: J. Haugeland, ed., *Mind Design* (MIT Press, Cambridge, MA, 1981).

Morgenstern, L. and Stein, L.A. (1988), Why things go wrong: a formal theory of causal reasoning, in: R. Smith and T.M. Mitchell, eds., *Proceedings AAAI-88*, St. Paul, MN (Morgan Kaufmann, San Mateo, CA) 518–523; longer version in: Stein, L.A. and Morgenstern, L. (1989), *Motivated Action Theory*, Tech. Report 89-12, Computer Science Department, Brown University, Providence, RI.

Newell, A. (1990), *Unified Theories of Cognition* (Harvard University Press, Cambridge, MA).

Newell, A. and Simon, H.A. (1956), The logic theory machine: a complex information processing system, *I.R.E. Trans. Inf. Theory* **2**, 61–79.

Newell, A. and Simon, H.A. (1972), *Human Problem Solving* (Prentice-Hall, Englewood Cliffs, NJ).

Olshausen, B., Anderson, C. and Van Essen, D. (1992), A neural model of visual attention and invariant pattern recognition, CNS Memo 18, Computation and Neural Systems Program, California Institute of Technology, Pasadena, CA.

Pepper, S.C. (1942), *World Hypotheses: A Study in Evidence* (University of California Press, Berkeley, CA).

Pepper, S.C. (1967), *Concept and Quality: A World Hypothesis* (Open Court, La Salle, IL).

Pollack, M. (1985), Generating expert answers through goal inference, Doctoral Dissertation, Computer Science Department, University of Pennsylvania, Philadelphia, PA.

Pollack, M. (1992), The uses of plans, *Artif. Intell.* **57**, 43–68.

Pollack, M. and Ringuette, M. (1990), Introducing the Tileworld: experimentally evaluating agent architectures, SRI Technical Note 489, Menlo Park, CA; also in: *Proceedings AAAI-90*, Boston, MA.

Poole, D., Goebel, R. and Aleliunas, R. (1987), Theorist: a logical reasoning system for defaults and diagnosis, in: N.J. Cercone and G. McCalla, eds., *The Knowledge Frontier: Essays in the Representation of Knowledge* (Springer-Verlag, New York) 331–352.

Putnam, H. (1988), *Representation and Reality* (MIT Press, Cambridge, MA).

Pylyshyn, Z., ed. (1987), *The Robot's Dilemma: The Frame Problem in Artificial Intelligence* (Ablex, Norwood, NJ).

Reiter, R. (1980), A logic for default reasoning, *Artif. Intell.* **13**, 81–132.

Russell, B. (1964), *The Problems of Philosophy* Oxford University Press, New York.

Schneider, W. and Detweiler, M. (1987), A connectionist/control architecture for working memory, in: G.H. Bower, ed., *The Psychology of Learning and Motivation* **21** (Academic Press, Orlando, FL) 53–119.

Schubert, L.K. (1989), Monotonic solution of the frame problem in the situation calculus, in: H.E. Kyburg and R. Loui, eds., *Selected Papers from the 1988 Society for Exact Philosophy Conference.*

Shannon, C.E. and Weaver, W. (1949), *The Mathematical Theory of Communication* (University of Illinois Press, Urbana, IL).

Shoham, Y. (1986), Chronological ignorance: time, non-monotonicity, and causal theories, in: T. Kehler, S.J. Rosenschein, R. Filman and P. Patel-Schneider, eds., *Proceedings AAAI-86*, Philadelphia, PA (Morgan Kaufmann, Los Altos, CA) 389–393.

Shoham, Y. (1988), *Reasoning about Change: Time and Causation from the Standpoint of Artificial Intelligence* (MIT Press, Cambridge, MA).

Simon, H.A. (1955), A behavioral model of rational choice, *Quarterly J. Economics* **69**, 99–118.

Stefik, M. and Bobrow, D.G. (1986), Object-oriented programming: themes and variations, *AI Mag.* **6** (4), 40–62.

Suchman, L.A. (1987), *Plans and Situated Actions: The Problem of Human-Machine Communication* (Cambridge University Press, New York).

Thomason, R. (1992), NETL and subsequent path-based inheritance theories, *Comput. Math. Appl.* **23** (2–5), 179–204.

Treisman, A.M. (1985), Preattentive processing in vision, *Comput. Vis. Graph. Image Process.* **31**, 156–177.

Turing, A.M. (1946), Proposal for the development in the mathematics division of an automatic computing engine (ACE), in: D.C. Ince, ed., *Mechanical Intelligence, Collected Works of A.M. Turing* (North-Holland, New York, 1992).

Ullman, S. (1984), Visual routines, *Cognition* **18**, 97–159.

Van Orden, G.C., Pennington, B.F. and Stone, G.O. (1990), Word identification in reading and the promise of subsymbolic psycholinguistics, *Psychol. Rev.* **97** (4), 488–522.

Vera, A.H. and Simon, H.A. (1993), Situated action: a symbolic interpretation, *Cogn. Sci.* **17**, 7–48.

Von Neumann, J. (1961), *Design of Computers, Theory of Automata and Numerical Analysis* **5**: *Collected Works* (Pergamon Press, New York).

Vygotsky, L.S. (1986), *Thought and Language* (MIT Press, Cambridge, MA).

Weber, J. (1988), A versatile approach to action reasoning, Tech. Report 287, University of Rochester, Rochester, NY.

Weber, J. (1989), Principles and algorithms for causal reasoning with uncertain knowledge, Doctoral Dissertation, Computer Science Department, University of Rochester, Rochester, NY.

Wertsch, J.V. (1991), *Voices of the Mind: A Sociocultural Approach to Mediated Action* (Harvard University Press, Cambridge, MA).

Wolfe, J.M. (1992), Guided Search 2.0, a revised model of visual search, Unpublished Manuscript, Harvard Medical School and Brigham and Women's Hospital, Boston, MA.

Artificial Intelligence 73 (1995) 371–377

Book Review

Christopher G. Langton, ed., *Artificial Life*[1]

Christopher G. Langton, Charles Taylor, J. Doyne Farmer, Steen Rasmussen, eds., *Artificial Life II* [2]

Christopher G. Langton, ed., *Artificial Life II*: *Video Proceedings*[3]

Stephen W. Smoliar *

Institute of Systems Science, National University of Singapore, Heng Mui Keng Terrace, Kent Ridge, Singapore 0511

1. The ill-defined vision of artificial life

A seductive name is often more confusing than informative to the imagination of the general public. Names like "catastrophe theory" and "chaos theory" (not to mention "artificial intelligence") never fail to attract popular attention but rarely direct that attention to the substance of their respective disciplines; and serious practitioners often wish those names had never been coined in the first place. Now we are confronted with "artificial life", whose origins can be traced back to the late Sixties when John Conway began work on his "Game of Life" [2]. This was simply an array of cellular automata whose two states were metaphorically dubbed by Conway "live" and "dead". Conway further pursued his metaphor by explaining the transition rules in terms of "birth", "death", and "survival". This metaphor was subsequently picked up by Christopher

---

* E-mail: smoliar@iss.nus.sg.

[1] (Addison-Wesley, Redwood City, CA, 1989); xxxi+655 pages.

[2] (Addison-Wesley, Redwood City, CA, 1992); xxi+854 pages.

[3] (Addison-Wesley, Redwood City, CA, 1992); 120 minutes.

Langton in the course of his doctoral research at the University of Michigan [5]:

> Cellular automata provide us with the logical universes within which we can embed artificial molecules in the form of propagating, virtual automata. We suggest that since virtual automata have the computational capacity to fill many of the functional roles played by the primary biomolecules, there is a strong possibility that the "molecular logic" of life can be embedded within cellular automata and that, therefore, artificial life is a distinct possibility within these highly parallel computer structures.

The paper from which the above quotation was taken, entitled "Studying Artificial Life with Cellular Automata", appeared in the 1986 volume of *Physica D*; and in September of 1987, Langton organized "an interdisciplinary workshop on the synthesis and simulation of living systems" at the Center for Nonlinear Studies of the Los Alamos National Laboratory. The proceedings of this workshop were published under the title *Artificial Life* by the Santa Fe Institute as the sixth volume of their "Studies in the Sciences of Complexity". A second workshop was held in the city of Santa Fe in February of 1990; and *its* proceedings were subsequently published under the same auspices as *Artificial Life II*, along with a two-hour videotape.

While these workshops have now led to over 1500 pages of published material and two hours of video, I think it is fair to say that the discipline has yet to converge upon any unifying principles or themes. The workshops have been highly eclectic events, bringing together participants from disciplines which were often almost entirely unaware of each other. Yet while the resulting diversity is impressive, even the most enthusiastic reader cannot help but come away from some of the papers without wondering whether or not he has gone beyond the lunatic fringe.

One source of confusion likely to face the reader is that there are actually quite a few things happening in the name of artificial life. Consequently, for the sake of the readers of this journal, it will be desirable to sort out those aspects of artificial life which are related to artificial intelligence from those which are not. The next section will provide a brief review of the latter, where the areas of greatest interest are biology and the philosophical study of emergence. This will be followed by a more thorough discussion of three aspects of artificial intelligence which have been impacted by artificial life research: robotics, implementing Marvin Minsky's "society of mind" [8], and an evolutionary approach to learning. This exposition will be followed by some concluding observations.

2. Aspirations of artificial life (not related to artificial intelligence)

2.1. Biology

If one of the objectives of artificial intelligence has been a better understanding of what we tend to call "thought", then one may say that artificial life wishes to take on the more general question of life itself. This can be approached from a variety of points of view. One is to ask whether or not the manifestations of life on earth are the *only* such manifestations: Can you have life without the building blocks of carbon, oxygen, and hydrogen which are common to all life-forms on this planet? Another is to recognize that there are still major lacunae in our understanding of terrestrial biology, many of which can not be resolved by conventional experimental practices. Artificial life may be viewed as a potential laboratory tool for addressing questions which are beyond the grasp of those experimental practices.

Unfortunately, it may also be viewed as wishful thinking by highly speculative theoretical biologists and camp-followers with limited background in the life sciences. As a result there is precious little which would count as "hard science"; and the reader with a pedestrian knowledge of biology will be ill-equipped to judge the potential value of the "softer" contributions. Fortunately, one of the most concrete presentations is also very well written: " 'Non-Optimality' via Pre-adaptation in Simple Neural Systems", by David Stork, Bernie Jackson, and Scott Walker in *Artificial Life II*. This paper confronts the question of apparently "useless" synapses in certain life forms (in this case the tailflip circuit in the crayfish). The analysis invokes the principle of co-evolution: The circuit is a product of a previous evolutionary stage for which there were different criteria for fitness. However, those fit organisms led to changes in the environment which, in turn, led to new fitness criteria to which the organisms were then obliged to adapt. Such adaptation was not a matter of "optimizing from scratch" but one of seeking a path from a previously optimal state to a new one. Stork and his colleagues lucidly demonstrate how such a path could carry along vestigial remains of the previous state.

Most of the other biology papers are far "softer" in content. In his own contribution to the second volume, "Life at the Edge of Chaos", Langton continues his study of cellular automata by addressing which sets of state-transition rules are likely to yield automata with "life-like" behavioral properties (such as reproduction). However, Langton is clearly more at home with thermodynamics than with biology; and he does little to convince the reader of the biological implications of his investigation. Similarly, there are several papers concerned with the modeling of "autocatalytic sets", chemical mixtures such as the "primordial soup" [7] which has been hypothesized to be the source of life on this planet; but none of those models can yet explain the presence of the molecules common to terrestrial life forms (such as RNA).

2.2. "Philosophy/emergence"

An aspect of the second volume of proceedings which was not present in the first was that of philosophical speculation. Two papers were products of a panel discussion on the "Ontology of Artificial Life": "Aspects of Information, Life, Reality, and Physics", by Steen Rasmussen, and "Emergence and Artificial Life", by Peter Cariani. Rasmussen's presentation was extremely sketchy; but it is important to note his observation that "physics also gives rise to chemistry and biology, and through them, an observer participation, namely the emergence of life and later the evolution of man" (p. 769). This reduction of biology to physics was contested in Robert Rosen's paper, "What Does It Take to Make an Organism?" It is unfortunate that this opposing position never appeared in print. Cariani's paper, on the other hand, is more valuable for its expository discussion of three approaches to emergence: computational emergence, thermodynamic emergence, and emergence relative to a model. This analysis is potentially valuable in that it raises the possibility that studies which are concerned with computational emergence (such as Langton's work with cellular automata) may not necessarily impact the physical phenomena of thermodynamic emergence, which include the origin of life. However, it would be a mistake to view Cariani as a defeatist. Rather, his philosophical analysis clearly illustrates a need for focus which is sorely lacking in the biological contributions to these two volumes.

3. Artificial life and artificial intelligence

3.1. Robotics

From the perspective of artificial intelligence, robots are the most viable examples of artificial life, particularly those which are androids or emulations of other animal life forms. The second workshop featured a presentation by Rod Brooks with the humble title, "Real Artificial Life". Much of the substance of this talk can be found in Brooks' paper, "Intelligence without Representation", which has been published in this journal [3]. Nevertheless, it is unfortunate that *some* statement of these results did not appear in *Artificial Life II*.

3.2. Implementing the Society of Mind

One of the more perplexing editorial decisions of the first proceedings volume was the allocation of an explicit section to reports on projects at the MIT Media Lab. While the association between artificial life and media studies seemed tenuous at best, this decision resulted in the publication of one of the most interesting papers in the entire two volumes of proceedings: "Animal Construction Kits", by Michael Travers. The name of the paper, itself, should justify its relevance to artificial life. What is important for purposes of this review, however, is its contribution to artificial intelligence: This paper constitutes an excellent account of an implementation of a system based on the principles outlined in Minsky's book, *The Society of Mind* [8]. One reason for Travers' success may be that he is building upon the same foundation that inspired Minsky, Nikolaas Tinbergen's pioneering study of animal instinct [10].

Travers' system is called Agar, and it was developed as part of the work on the Vivarium Project at the Media Lab. Its long-term goal is to model the three-spined stickleback which Tinbergen had studied extensively. However, one of the more important contributions of Agar is the recognition that an effective implementation of a creature like the stickleback cannot be achieved unless one also implements a realistic world which it can inhabit. Thus, Travers' success can be attributed, at least in part, to his ability to come up with a suitable implementation scale for both his artificial creatures and the world in which they exist.

Travers summarizes the implementation of his creatures as follows:

An Agar creature's behavioral control system is made up of entities called *agents*, loosely based on those described in Minsky's Society of Mind theory [8]. In Agar's implementation of the theory, agents are computational objects that can:

- Execute concurrently,
- Maintain local state,
- Access the state of other agents through connections, and
- Take actions automatically when environmental conditions are met.

An agent is to be thought of as semi-autonomous. This means that an agent is not necessarily doing the bidding of some other agent or outside entity such as the user, but is responding to conditions in its environment, which can include other agents as well as the world. In this sense, an agent is similar to a production rule.

An agent's *condition* can be stated as a boolean function of sensor predicates and other agents' activations. An agent's *action* can be an arbitrary behavior expressible in Lisp. . . .

Actions that an agent may want to perform include:

- Activate or suppress other agents,
- Activate a motor function,
- Activate a script,
- Remember the current activation state of other agents (K-line creation . . .), and
- Create a new agent or alter an existing one. (p. 429)

Agar was subsequently demonstrated during the second workshop. However, no paper was presented; and there was no follow-up document in the proceedings volume.

3.3. Learning and evolution

A major theme of the second workshop which was virtually ignored during the first workshop concerned the application of principles of evolution to learning. Five excellent papers were delivered during the workshop, all of which appeared in the proceedings volume along with some papers which had their origins as posters. Because these results are of particular interest to current work in artificial intelligence, I shall summarize several of the more interesting of these contributions.

"Interactions between Learning and Evolution", by David Ackley and Michael Littman, addresses a very fundamental question of survival:

> How can an organism learn in . . . circumstances, where the only unarguable sign of failure is the organism's own death, and the reproduction process preserves only the genetic information, which is unaffected by any learning performed during the organism's life? (p. 489)

To answer this question, Ackley and Littman propose a new approach to learning algorithms:

"Evolutionary Reinforcement Learning" [1] (ERL) provides one answer to this question. In ERL, we allow evolution to specify not only inherited *behaviors*, but also inherited *goals* that are used to guide learning. We do this by constructing a genetic code that specifies two major components. The first component is a set of initial values for the weights of an "action network" that maps from sensory input to behavior. These weights represent an innate set of behaviors that the individual inherits directly from its parents.

The second component is an "evaluation network" that maps from sensory input to a scalar value representing the "goodness" of the current situation. By learning to move from "bad" situations to "better" situations—modifying its action network weights in the process—an individual achieves the goals of learning passed down from its predecessors. Whether those inherited goals are actually sensible or not is, of course, a separate issue; insofar as learning is a factor, each organism stakes its life on the *assumption* that its inherited evaluation function is reliable. (p. 489)

The idea of a genetic code which governs not only an organism's "behavioral hardware" but also the goals it has which must be satisfied through behavior places this work very much in sympathy with Tinbergen's perception of instinct and Minsky's interpretation of Tinbergen's work. Indeed, the relationship between behavior and goals is one of the more neglected areas in the current "Neural Darwinism" work of Gerald Edelman and his colleagues [9]. Ackley and Littman have presented a bold piece of experimental work, supplemented by an excellent display of results incorporated in the video proceedings.

The artificial life team at UCLA is represented by several papers, the most interesting of which is "AntFarm: Towards Simulated Evolution", by Robert Collins and David Jefferson. The project is basically concerned with the study of a colony of artificial "ants". The issues are "simulated evolution of complex behavior in complex environments, the evolution of cooperation among closely related individuals, and the evolution of chemical communication" (p. 579). Of greatest interest is the extent to which this work has been guided by attempts to model the actual behaviors observed in ant colonies.

Communication receives more specific examination in another UCLA paper by Gregory Werner and Michael Dyer, "Evolution of Communication in Artificial Organisms". Werner and Dyer populate a world with artificial male and female organisms in order to investigate the evolution of mate-finding strategies. Not only do effective strategies emerge from their model; but also subspecies develop which communicate through different "dialects". While Collins and Jefferson began from the position of observing life and trying to explain the behavior they saw, Werner and Dyer have explored a particular objective of life which may ultimately provide new ways of looking at the "real thing".

4. Conclusions

The "bottom line", then, is that there *is* much of substance in these volumes which may interest members of the artificial intelligence community. There is also much to encourage wild speculation, and whether or not any of that speculation may ultimately benefit the study of artificial intelligence remains to be seen. Resources such as the published work of Edelman [4] seem to offer evidence that the time is ripe for a more fruitful interaction between artificial intelligence and biology. However, on the basis of these two volumes, it is unclear that "artificial life" will provide a foundation for that interaction. Furthermore, because these volumes have been relatively poorly edited, they do not provide a particularly good introduction to the literature for readers who might wish to learn more about potentially relevant biological issues. Perhaps this means that the time is not yet quite right for artificial intelligence to turn to biology for inspiration. For now, unless the next workshop brings a bit more focus to the discipline of artificial life, its impact on artificial intelligence is likely to be rather peripheral.

References

[1] D.H. Ackley and M.L. Littman, Learning from natural selection in an artificial environment, in: M. Caudhill, ed., *Proceedings of the International Joint Conference on Neural Networks, IJCNN-90-WASH-DC*, Washington, DC (Erlbaum, Hillsdale, NJ, 1990) 189–193.

[2] E.R. Berlekamp, J.H. Conway and R.K. Guy, *Winning Ways for Your Mathematical Plays* (Academic Press, London, England, 1982) two volumes.

[3] R.A. Brooks, Intelligence without representation, *Artif. Intell.* **47** (1–3) (1991) 139–159.

[4] G.M. Edelman, *Neural Darwinism: The Theory of Neuronal Group Selection* (Basic Books, New York, 1987).

[5] C.G. Langton, Studying artificial life with cellular automata, *Phys. D* **22** (1986) 120–149.

[6] D.B. Lenat and J.S. Brown, Why AM and Eurisko appear to work, in: *Proceedings AAAI-83*, Washington, DC (1983) 236–240; also: Artif. Intell. **23** (1984) 269–294.

[7] S.M. Miller and L.E. Orgel, *The Origins of Life on Earth* (Prentice-Hall, Englewood Cliffs, NJ, 1974).

[8] M. Minsky, *The Society of Mind* (Simon and Schuster, New York, 1986).

[9] G.N. Reeke Jr et al., Synthetic neural modeling: a multilevel approach to the analysis of brain complexity, in: G.M. Edelman, W.E. Gall and W.M. Cowan, eds, *Signal and Sense: Local and Global Order in Perceptual Maps*, The Neurosciences Institute Publications (Wiley, New York, 1990) Chapter 24, 607–707.

[10] N. Tinbergen, *The Study of Instinct* (Clarendon Press, Oxford, England, 1989).

Artificial Intelligence 73 (1995) 379–386

Book Review

Thomas Dean and Michael Wellman, *Planning and Control* ★

James Hendler *

Computer Science Department, A.V. Williams Building, University of Maryland College Park, MD 20742, USA

Received March 1993

It's a pretty frustrating thing these days to be a "Good Old Fashioned AI" researcher, as we've been branded by Searle and others. Neural network and genetic algorithms researchers are taking us to task over low-level data, our industrial partners are demanding increasingly complex real-time performance, and our funding agents are talking about high performance computing and intelligent control. Let's face it, it's a tough time for symbolic approaches—these guys demand numbers, and they want them soon! Many of us have faced this challenge using a time tested strategy—hunkering down in our research trenches and hoping that this firestorm will eventually pass. Let the engineers give them equations, logic will serve us in the future as it has in the past. Unfortunately, as AI people look to building more and more complex systems, hiding from numbers seems to be less and less successful—we must come forth and do battle, lest we are blown away by the winds of the research wars, losing the spoils to the eventual victors.

One of the places in AI where this conflict has become clear is in the area of planning and robotics. Over the past fifteen years or so, a schism has developed between the fields. AI research in planning has focused on the search-related problems of computing complete and correct solutions to conjoined-goal symbolic problems. Roboticists, on the other hand, have been focusing on problems such as the theories of kinematics and control. AI researchers have largely ignored sensors and effectors; roboticists use "planning" to mean finding paths through space, ignoring issues of long-term goals. The AI planning toolkits are filled with logics, situation calculus and the STRIPS assumption; the engineer worries about proving convergence, Kalman filtering, and adaptive control.

In the past few years, however, a small vanguard of researchers in both areas have been realizing that there is some merit to the work done by the others. A few roboticists

---

★ (Morgan Kaufmann, San Mateo, CA, 1991) 486 pages, $44.95.

* E-mail: hendler@mimsy.umd.edu.

have started worrying more about autonomous robots and intelligent controllers, while a small number of AI researchers have been starting to try to anchor our theories on more realistic simulators and actual robots. A number of workshops and AAAI symposia have recently been held, trying to bring together these researchers to discuss common problems. The robotics competitions at the AAAI Conference reflect the sorts of problems and challenges that emerge from this synthesis—recognition of obstacles, planning paths to map environments, determining what obstacles to move, etc.

Unfortunately, the long separation between AI and Engineering roboticists has led to a major problem: paraphrasing George Bernard Shaw, we are two communities separated by a common language. Terms such as "controller", "filter", "plan", "goal", and many others have been used by the two differing sets of researchers in very different ways. The AI researcher with a "planning system" is probably worried about the ordering of operations in a Blocks World; the roboticist is trying to generate an optimal trajectory through a space of fixed obstacles. Finding a way to bridge the terminological confusion is a major problem—the need for an "AI–Robotics, Robotics–AI" translator is manifest.

Luckily for this growing community, a first approximation to exactly such a translator has recently been published: Thomas Dean and Michael Wellman's *Planning and Control*. Essentially, Dean and Wellman have attempted to write a book that teaches AI people enough of the mathematics of control for them to understand, and profit from, the work done by roboticists and control engineers. At the same time, the book presents an overview of AI planning ideas, in a manner that lets an engineer understand what we have in mind. In short, this book fills a significant need in the growing "perception, planning, and robotics" area—one of the newer subfields in the AI arena.

What's in the book

In their preface, Dean and Wellman explain that this text is a "tentative first step towards an integrated view of planning and control ... a first approximation of the theory we were seeking" (p. ix), which covers ideas from "artificial intelligence, control theory, operations research and the decision sciences" (p. vii). The framework for tieing these areas together is presented in the first chapter, which discusses the issues involved in the control of dynamic, embedded systems. Such systems, for example a real robot interacting with a possibly changing world, are a real challenge both for traditional AI planning work and for control engineers. A number of examples of systems and situations which need such an integration of planning and control are presented. These examples are often presented in TEMPLOG, a Prolog-like language extended to include temporal reasoning, making them accessible to an AI audience. [1] The book also contains a large amount of mathematics and equations—it is not for the numerically shy reader.

To really understand what this book is all about requires a realization of what the book is *not* about: This is not a general book on AI planning systems. From the title, some

---

[1] I should note that a weakness of the book is that, as far as I can ascertain, TEMPLOG is only partially implemented and is not easily available even in the partial form. As such, one cannot actually experiment with the examples that are presented.

have assumed that the book presents an overview of the work in the planning community. However, in actuality the book is motivated by one specific (and important) aspect of AI planning systems—dynamic embedded systems (think of this as "robotic planning" for a more intuitive notion). An examination of the table of contents makes this quite clear. The chapters include: "Dynamics of Control", "Temporal Reasoning", "Designing Control Systems", "Knowledge-Based Planning", "Stochastic Control", "Planning under Uncertainty", "Controlling Inference", "Learning", and "Integrated Planning and Execution".

To get a feel for the sort of material in the book, consider what is covered in one of the chapters, Chapter 4, "Designing Control Systems". This chapter starts with a section on "Basic issues" in which the authors lay out a simple problem—that of moving a robot through a set of city streets laid out in a rectangular grid. The authors use this example to explain control issues, in particular to provide an intuition behind the concepts of feedforward and feedback control, which are the bases of most modern work in control. Having defined these concepts, the authors can then offer problems that arise in control and present the known solutions (in the form of equations) for dealing with a number of situations.

Sections 4.2–4.5 explain many of the basic ideas of "controllable" systems. Important concepts such as "observability", "stability", and "optimality" are introduced, and many of the basic theories of control are presented. These sections move very quickly into the math and theories and can be difficult going. The authors do not dwell on the sort of prosaic argumentation that one most often encounters in AI texts, rather they move quickly into the details. For example, one important property of controlled systems is "stability". Informally speaking, a dynamic system is "asymptotically stable" if small disturbances and perturbations will not cause large changes in the system's behavior. Dean and Wellman briefly present this intuition, and then move into a discussion of "stability in the sense of Lyapunov" and "asymptotic stability". These ideas are presented directly through equations and theorems such as

Theorem 5 The system described by the state equation,

$$\dot{x} = Ax(t) + Bu(t),$$

is asymptotically stable if and only if all of the eigenvalues of the matrix A have negative real parts. (p. 124)

quite different from the usual AI text, but critical if one is to talk with control engineers beyond a surface level. As should be clear from this theorem, however, your old college math is needed to really work through this stuff—time to review your multivariate calculus texts. Still, the main ideas can be gleaned without fully understanding the intricacies, and one can begin to appreciate the complexities inherent in proving that a controlled system is stable or that a control policy is optimal.

These definitions in hand, the authors then take the reader into sections on feedback control and the computational issues in control. These sections include a number of simple control examples and a discussion of how processes are controlled via feedback from sensors. The mathematics of the previous four sections is now put aside, and computational issues take precedence. This discussion is one of the strongest in the book and is absolutely crucial to the AI researcher who wants to communicate with his or her engineering colleagues. The issues presented, the examples shown, and the concepts covered are critical to an understanding of control.

The chapter continues with a section on navigation and control, describing the use of potential fields in navigating around obstacles.[2] This chapter not only helps to show how the ideas in the previous sections are brought together, but also shows the strength of Dean and Wellman within these non-traditional areas for AI researchers. They present a coherent discussion of potential field computation (a difficult area in its own right) and, more importantly, provide a uniform treatment of navigation and control. Although these topics are extremely related, they are usually discussed separately in engineering texts; and the relation gets muddled. At the University of Maryland, for example, our top control researchers are in Electrical Engineering, while our main researchers in kinematics (critical to navigation) are in a separate Aerospace Engineering Department. Mobile robotics, however, requires understanding of both sorts of problems, and the treatment in this book is one of the most accessible discussions I've found.

The final pages of the chapter provide a "further reading" section. While in many books these chapters simply mention a few texts or recent papers, in this book they provide crucial pointers. In this chapter, for example, the authors cite a number of useful (and well-known) papers that an AI researcher can read to get more of the engineering background; and they also cite a number of well-known AI papers that a control engineer might find useful. Not omitted, of course, are pointers into the literature that might not be as well known to *either* group—thus allowing the knowledgeable reader to further pursue the ideas presented in the chapter.

This chapter is possibly the strongest in the book, but it is not atypical of the others. In choosing to describe one of the more engineering-oriented chapters, however, I may have given the impression that the AI ideas are not covered. This is not the case, as would have been demonstrated if I'd chosen to discuss, for example, Chapter 5, "Knowledge-Based Planning". The subjects in this chapter include: plans and tasks, task reduction, planning for deadlines, conditional plans, planning and reaction, and goals and preferences. These are clearly more mainstream AI, and the presentation looks more like what one would find in an AI textbook. The ideas are not presented in full detail, just as the topics in Chapter 4 fill whole engineering textbooks; but enough is presented to give an engineer an idea of what AI people mean when they talk about planning.

What's right about this book

Clearly, this book provides a lot of technical material and has a broad coverage of a number of issues not typically presented to the AI researcher. I've talked with a number of other people who have read the book, and we've all been very impressed with the breadth of the material and with the coverage of control. In fact, I suspect the thing

---

[2] A discussion of potential-field-based navigation is well beyond this review, but the quick intuition is that you consider your robot to be like a charged particle moving through a field of attractive (goals) and repulsive (obstacle) forces.

that's most right about the book is not the details of its technical material, but rather exactly this breadth of coverage. It helps makes it clear to us AI folks what the control engineers worry about (particularly their evaluation criteria for control solutions) and vice versa.

An anecdote: for about three and a half years now, I've been trying to set up a joint research project with my colleague P.S. Krishnaprasad, a roboticist in the Electrical Engineering Department. We are both members of an interdisciplinary research institute, and have been under continuing pressure to forge joint research projects. Thus, the will was there. Unfortunately, for a long time we simply talked past each other. I could not understand why my roboticist friend was interested in the problems he kept presenting, or why he couldn't see that the work I described was clearly important. He, of course, felt the reverse.

The situation changed, however, during the past year. As I read *Planning and Control*, I asked my colleague to do the same. I learned that his concerns with potential field computations and imperfect sensors had a lot to do with the concerns of control engineers (as discussed previously in my description of Chapter 4) . He learned why I was concerned with reactive planning and long-term projection. We have reached the point where this term we jointly hired a graduate student, and our first journal paper is nearing completion. The Dean and Wellman book didn't provide the solutions to the problems of concern to us, but it provided the backbone of communication we needed to communicate enough to do serious joint research.

Another important aspect of the book, related to bridging the gulf between roboticist and AI researcher, is that it makes it much clearer to the AI researcher why the engineers insist on numbers and equations. The criteria for control systems are not only that "they work well", but also that they can be proven to be stable and/or converge (essentially, that the behavior can be proven not to cause the system to go into states which are counterproductive or dangerous). The control engineer building a controller that must function within a nuclear plant not only wants to know that it will function well in typical situations, but also that the controller is unlikely to throw the plant into a dangerous state. Ditto for the designer of an airplane wing, an industrial robot arm, a chemical process controller, a telephone network control system, etc., etc. Unfortunately, if symbolic AI systems have a weakness, it's that we typically cannot prove such things: how do you show your theorem prover could never conclude that valve-17 should be opened past half way (unless certain other conditions hold) or that your expert system will never cause chemical flow to go beyond a certain threshold? Proving (as opposed to claiming) such things often requires an appeal to numbers and mathematical proof techniques. The Dean and Wellman book helps one to understand the techniques to use and, perhaps more importantly, why to do these things in the first place.

To summarize, with AI researchers and robotic engineers focusing on different aspects of similar problems, using different evaluation criteria, and using similar language often to mean differing things, communication has often been difficult and embarrassingly full of errors. The Dean and Wellman book is an invaluable aid in helping to bridge translation barriers and to enable AI researchers to pursue robotics in a more serious way. In short, the book serves as a "Rosetta Stone" for translation between "robotic speak" and "AI talk".

What's wrong with this book

Let me be clear before I begin this section that I think this book is useful, important, and well worth your time. You should buy it, read it, and be excited by the new research directions that the book will enable you to pursue. That said, there are a number of problems with the volume, and I'd be remiss as a reviewer if I did not point them out.

Perhaps the greatest problem in the book is that, although it discusses a number of different, and important, control theoretical issues, and also presents a nice overview of AI planning approaches, it fails to present a compelling overall framework for helping to integrate the ideas. The discussion of embedded dynamic systems, presented in the first chapter and followed throughout the book, makes an important start at providing such a framework, but there is still a lot more to be done. In this book a number of different topics are presented, and not enough effort is made to tie it all together. The sections on uncertainty and learning, for example, while relevant to many control problems, seem poorly integrated into the rest of the book. It is not clear how much of the detail one needs to know, what of value is to be taken from these chapters, and what other work it bears the most relation to. A short section on uncertain reasoning in AI, with a pointer into the literature on uncertainty and to Wellman's thesis, would have sufficed, and would have kept the book more focused. Similarly, the learning section is somewhat uneven, and might have been forgone in favor of sections on (hierarchical) adaptive control, which might have fit into the overall framework better than some of the sections on AI learning techniques. The sections on path planning and other navigation issues are also presented more as separate problems than as part of an integrated whole. The book's reader comes away with a lot of new knowledge, but lacking a firm framework to fit it on.

Similarly, the lack of a framework makes it hard to know what topics that have been omitted might also be of importance—although the book uses robotic planning systems as an example in many cases, it contains a wealth of material on control and decision theory, but little, for example, on kinematics. When my colleagues discuss trying to use Kalman filters for handling nonlinear control of a chemical process, this book has helped me to understand what they meant. When they discuss developing models of smooth non-holonomic motion, the book is of little help. Yet, this is an issue that several of the people who work in AI and robotics have tackled (Brooks, Latombe, Arkin, etc.) so one might expect it to be there. While it would be unfair to expect a book to cover everything, the lack of structure makes it hard to guess which issues will be covered and which ones won't.

Another problem I had with the book results from the fact that Dean and Wellman are two of the better mathematicians in AI circles, while some of the rest of us (including me) are a bit rusty. The book presents complex equations unabashedly and right from the beginning. Perhaps it is my own failure that I can no longer solve complex partial differential equations this many years since my last math course, but at times I felt a more graceful touch would have been appreciated. More importantly, many of the control ideas presented in the book have relatively simple intuitions that would make it easier for one to understand the ideas without working through the math. After much work the reader can work backwards from the equations to understand what is happening, but the intuitions behind the math are often omitted. To be fair to the authors, however, I will point out that they do provide a number of examples in the book, and do give the reader enough material to figure out what is going on. Still, again and again in this book I had to work quite hard to understand what was going on, when a little more guidance and intuition from the authors would have made my life easier (and the book much simpler to read).

These two problems make the book hard going. These are definitely not reasons to avoid the book in one's research life, but they do limit the book's utility as a text. I've talked to several people who've attempted to use the book in classes, typically with mixed success. Where the professor had a broad background and could provide the intuitions and framework, the book was somewhat of a success (typically the best students in the class got a lot out of it, while the others were lost). In two cases where the professor had to work through the book with the students, it was felt that the class had lacked coherence and that even the best students felt lost. Those who approached the class as an advanced topics course focusing on mathematical AI and/or robotic control were satisfied. Those using the book in a "planning" seminar were uniformly disappointed.

Thus to summarize, I ended the previous section comparing this book to the Rosetta Stone. By analogy, my summary of the book's faults would have to be that at times it is more analogous to the Dead Sea Scrolls. That is, the book is missing some important sections, includes some parts that are well-nigh impossible to decipher, and assumes the reader shares certain knowledge and background with the authors. These things make this book extremely difficult going at times, and a number of sections beg for improvement. Still, the material contained in the book exposes the determined reader to important and interesting new areas—assuming he or she is willing to put the effort into understanding the details of the text.

Summary

As should be clear by now, this book stresses certain aspects of planning research, while relegating others to the sidelines. This makes the coverage of the book significantly different than that of other recent publications in the AI planning area. For example, very little is presented on the sort of systems and formalizations of the "classical AI planning paradigm" (as in the collection *Readings in Planning* [1] or Wilkins' *Practical Planning* [3]) or to reasoning about actions and plans (as in Allen et al's *Reasoning about Plans* [2]). Instead, this book really concentrates on *robotic planning* and control; and, as long as that is what the reader is looking for, he or she will not be disappointed. If, on the other hand, the reader is looking for an overview of traditional AI planning work, then these other references may be more appropriate.

However, that said, I think this book is an important one. It's hard for me to remember how I faked it with my engineering colleagues before reading this book; and while I still cannot claim to be "up" on my control and decision theory, I can now follow research papers, work cooperatively with engineering colleagues, and know where to look for reference pointers when dealing with those of my graduate students involved with my robotics and control efforts. Let me be clear, I'm still a hardcore AI type; but this book has been a tremendous help as I've been attempting to make a connection between my AI work and many of the real-world control and robotics problems that arise in the interdisciplinary aspects of many of the problems I'm now examining. The book is well worth reading, and I recommend it highly, especially to those prepared to put in the time and effort required to really understand the material.

References

[1] J. Allen, J. Hendler and A. Tate, *Readings in Planning* (Morgan Kaufmann, San Mateo, CA, 1990).
[2] J. Allen, H. Kautz, R. Pelavin, and J. Tenenberg, *Reasoning about Plans*, (Morgan Kaufmann, San Mateo, CA, 1991).
[3] D. Wilkins, *Practical Planning*: *Extending the Classical AI Planning Paradigm* (Morgan Kaufmann, San Mateo, CA, 1988).

Artificial Intelligence 73 (1995) 387–401

Book Review

David Chapman,
Vision, Instruction, and Action [*]

Damian M. Lyons [*]

Philips Laboratories, Philips Electronics North America Corporation, 345 Scarborough Rd, Briarcliff Manor, NY 10510, USA

Received June 1992; revised September 1992

1. Introduction

Chapman's aptly named book *Vision, Instruction, and Action* is a first-rate exposition of the *concrete-situated* approach that he and Phil Agre have been advocating for some time. The book describes the theory and implementation of Sonja: an *integrated* system that uses instruction in the course of visually guided activity to produce sensible behavior in a domain characterized by complexity, uncertainty and immediacy. The domain is a video game called Amazon—a game with most of the complexities of the Pengo video game (the domain for Sonja's forerunner, Pengi [2]) plus some. While Sonja is an integrated system, it's not by any means a complete system: Chapman emphasizes one kind of visual system, the use of advice in decision making, and the selection of action, in that order. Nonetheless it provides a good concrete illustration of the tenets of the concrete-situated approach. Researchers familiar with this approach as well as those new to the area will find this book useful.

This review is structured as follows. Section 2 contains a description of the approach and constraints that Chapman brings to the problem of building an integrated system. Section 3 describes the architecture and some of the mechanisms used to build Sonja. Section 4 is a description of the system in action. Section 5 is an overview of the appendix material: proposed extensions to handle collaboration and skill-acquisition.

---

[*] (MIT Press Cambridge, MA, 1991); 295 pages, $35.00, (paperback).

[*] E-mail: dml@philabs.Philips.Com.

SSDI 0004-3702(93)E0079-2

2. Approach

2.1. Concrete-situated approach

In previous work [8], Chapman has argued that the 'classical' approach to planning (e.g., STRIPS, NOAH) has problems with computational complexity, and has suggested that it might be appropriate to take an entirely different approach to the problem of producing sensible behavior in complex environments. That new approach, called the *concrete-situated approach,* has since been described in a series of research papers with Phil Agre [1, 2]. The book does a lucid job of explaining this approach in Chapter Two, and I found this section to be both compelling and rewarding to read.

There are seven key aspects of the approach espoused by Chapman:

(1) *Routineness.* The approach assumes that activity is mostly routine—regular, non-problematic, practised. In routine activity, no 'new thoughts' (a term which Chapman defines more precisely) are required. The approach doesn't deny the need for non-routine activity. However, it states that the mechanisms that support activity should *primarily* support routine activity.

(2) *Situatedness.* The key decision-making resource available to an agent is its concrete situation—the configuration of the environment in which the agent is situated, the here-and-now. Appropriate use of this resource, through perception, avoids the problems of approximate and out-of-date representations.

(3) *Interactivity.* One of the most interesting aspects of this approach is that it proposes that the organization of activity is not a sole property of the agent nor its environment. Rather the organization of activity is *shared* between them. Chapman describes this by saying "Causality rapidly loops in and out of the agent, rather than looping around inside the agent's head and occasionally emerging to affect the world." This aspect of the approach shifts the focus from building agents that attempt to completely control the environment to agents that exploit patterns of interaction with the environment.

(4) *Dynamics.* A dynamic is a pattern in this interaction of agent and environment. Such patterns may be noted by an external observer but are not explicitly represented in their entirety in either the agent or the environment. Dynamics are acausal; although an observer can attribute effects to a dynamic, the dynamic does not necessarily exist just for the purpose of producing those effects. This is not to say that dynamics cannot be exploited to accomplish work.

(5) *Routines.* A routine is "a regular, practiced pattern of activity"—a dynamic that has been exploited so that the agent gets work done. The routine is the unit of activity in the concrete-situated approach. Designing an agent requires considering what mechanisms will allow the agent to engage in appropriate routines with the environment.

(6) *Improvisation.* The concrete-situated approach claims that the best strategy for an agent to adopt in determining what to do next is for the agent to continually inspect its concrete situation and use it to redecide what to do. Chapman calls this improvising. It ensures that an agent's actions are always chosen based on the latest data about the environment; uncertainty about the state

of the environment is simply not allowed to build up. Improvisation strongly constrains what mechanisms can be used for computing what to do next—there is not sufficient time to engage in theorem proving or problem solving.

(7) *Deictic representation.* The concrete-situated approach espouses an unusual kind of representation referred to as 'deictic'. The environment is segmented and represented in units which are *relative* to the agent and its ongoing activities. There is no objective view of the environment. (Subramanian and Woodfill [18] describe some of the advantages and trade-offs implicit in this agent-centered view of representation.)

2.2. Choice of domain

Pengi [2] was constructed by Agre and Chapman as a first illustration of the concrete-situated approach. Pengi played a video game called Pengo. This video game modeled many of the characteristics of real-world domains that were problematic to classical planning systems: there was an enormous number of objects that had to be tracked, objects in the game exhibited unpredictable behavior, and the game required a response time of well under a second. Chapman has also designed a video game, Amazon, as the domain for Sonja. The game is similar to Pengo in demanding a timely response to a complex, uncertain and changing environment, but was also designed to test advice taking, handling longer-term interactions, and handling a more ontologically complex domain.

Amazon is a dungeon-and-dragons style video game. The objective of the game is to make the amazon wander the dungeon, which is partitioned into rooms, collecting goodies (amulets, scrolls, keys, etc.) and not get it killed by the hordes of monsters that inhabit the place (ghosts, demon bunnies, piles of bones, etc.). The amazon can fight by throwing shuriken (nasty three-pointed objects) or by using a knife. As you might guess, amulets and scrolls have special powers which if understood can be used to fight more effectively. Tools such as knives can be used for multiple purposes. Amazon health is a variable quantity which is decreased when monsters attack and increased when food is eaten. Amazon lacks the treasure 'reward' normally part of such video games. Chapman doesn't allude to this point; however, it's clear from his implementation that Sonja explores without recourse to reward motivation. It's important to note that Sonja plays Amazon from the same perspective a human would, an overhead view of a portion of the dungeon.

Chapman emphasizes that Sonja's domain is *not* a simulation. The point is that Sonja's domain is *not* exploring dungeons; rather it is playing the video game called Amazon. Sonja is not the amazon object in the game; it moves the amazon around the same way a human player does and with the same kind of visual input. Playing video games is a realistic and demanding human activity. Admittedly, the interface to the video game is quite simplified: rather than using a camera and mechanical hand hooked to a joystick, Chapman hooks Sonja's perceptual and motor structures up to the video game data structures. Human video game players seem to 'identify' themselves with the agent in the game. Even reading about video game playing seemingly invokes this effect, and it can be difficult at times to appreciate the separation between Sonja's perceptions and those of the amazon.

2.3. Essential connectionism

We find out in Chapter Three that Chapman has two objectives for his work; not just to build an integrated, intelligent system but to do so with *biologically plausible* hardware. To address this second objective, he sets forth the following set of well-established facts about the brain by which, he claims, an implementation must abide to be biologically plausible.

- The brain is composed of a great many components,
- each of which is connected to many others, and
- each of which carries out some relatively simple computation,
- slowly, and
- using information mainly from its connections.

Chapman calls these the *essential connectionist* constraints and argues that they prohibit the use of pointers, variables, inspectable data structures, interpreters and dynamic storage. Pointers are disallowed because they cannot be easily implemented in a connectionist framework (they would require a crossbar switch); and, while the jury is still out, the evidence is against the brain implementing them. If pointers are disallowed then variables and inspectable data structures cannot be implemented in a general fashion.

Disallowing pointers also makes the usual computing concept of dynamic storage more difficult to implement. However, in a connectionist framework the concept of dynamic storage maps to the concept of creating *new connections* between components. Chapman additionally claims that his routineness assumption (no 'new thoughts') rules out this analog of dynamic storage. Routine activity is therefore defined as activity that can be engaged in by an architecture with a fixed connection pattern.

Interpreters (virtual machines) are ruled out for speed reasons. Given the slowness assumption of essential connectionism, if connectionist hardware were to 'emulate' other hardware, then this emulated machine would run too slowly to handle activities such as video game playing. Connectionist computation "must stay 'close to the hardware'."

Chapman chooses depth-bounded digital circuits—a digital circuit with a bound on the length of the paths between inputs and outputs—as his implementation medium. While these are not a plausible model of detailed neural functioning, they do obey the list of essential connectionist constraints.

2.4. Criteria of success

Chapter Nine presents an interesting discussion of how Chapman would like to see his work evaluated. I think this discussion is worth reading early on since it motivates the style and content of the book.

Chapman argues that AI needs an evaluation criterion—a definition of what constitutes good work—of its own. He claims that an implicit criterion seems to have arisen, and cites as evidence the fact that several highly regarded and seminal AI papers (Minsky's

Frames [13], Hayes' Naive Physics [10], and McCarthy's Advice Taker [12]) would fail evaluation criteria from math, science, philosophy or engineering. Nonetheless they are widely regarded as examples of good AI work. These papers do not focus on results, on demonstrations of superior technology or on producing new theorems. Rather what these papers offer are *approaches*: "a way of doing research: a way of looking at phenomena, of choosing issues to explore, of stating and attacking problems". From this viewpoint, the role of implementation is not to test a theory or demonstrate superior technology, but to provide concrete illustrations of an approach. An implementation is successful when it persuades other researchers to adopt the approach. Chapman cites NOAH as a particularly successful implementation since it has engendered much imitation.

This argument is in part a response to the school of thought that considers AI to be an unscientific pursuit simply because it has as yet featured little rigorous experimentation and few widely known theoretical results. Chapman admits this lack. However, he maintains that this state of affairs is fine because, "AI is *largely about* approaches", as evidenced by the Minsky, Hayes and McCarthy papers. Thus he argues for an explicit, privileged role for work describing approaches. I think he's taking the point a little too far here. Approach papers do indeed play a strong and vital role in AI. I would not consider this due to the intrinsic nature of the field, however, just to its relative immaturity. A field matures by finding which approaches are good for which problems— by the evaluation of works (such as this book) which propound an approach and attempt to establish its usefulness. On the other hand, the point that implementations are exemplary of approaches is well made. The evaluation of approach papers can be difficult precisely because they lack concrete results. Describing the implementation of a suggested approach is one way to make the work more concrete and hence more open to evaluation and (potentially) imitation. It is important to value implementations for this reason *as well* as for reasons of performance testing.

It is worth bearing in mind when reading this book that Chapman does not set out to produce formal results or to exhaustively compare Sonja with other work. The main objective of the book is to describe his approach in a concrete fashion. The book is rewarding when read from this perspective: I found the implementation clarified issues raised in the descriptive early chapters and I found a number of ideas I plan to make use of myself. However, I would have liked also to see the results of some test runs, some performance figures and some more detailed comparisons with other technologies. I wanted to see these not necessarily because I believe scientific or engineering evaluation criteria should be applied, but because these kinds of results are also illustrative devices, aids to understanding the Chapman approach.

3. Architecture

Sonja's architecture follows precedent in being divided into a central system (concerned with choosing what to do) and a peripheral system (concerned with sensory and motor processing). The exact division between central and peripheral systems, however, lies along an unusual line. The central system is homogeneous and non-modular, and

Chapman does not argue for its generality. The design of the peripheral system is modular and follows neurophysiological evidence. The only peripheral system considered is vision. Sonja also takes and uses advice; however, advice input is not seriously modeled as a peripheral system. Sonja's motor system is a direct connection to the video game controls.

3.1. The central system

Sonja's central system has three kinds of components: registrars, which interpret sensory data in a deictic fashion; proposers, which signal the appropriateness for specific courses of action based on registrar input; and arbiters, which arbitrate between the proposed courses of action. Registrar, proposer and arbiter components are each small parallel and interconnected circuits that remain continuously active. Chapman cites Minsky's Society of Mind [14] for comparison; another example would be Selfridge's Pandemonium [17].

Note that the segmentation of sensory data along deictic lines is done in the central system. This gives an important advantage. In more conventional renditions, such as Albus' RCS [3], sensory data is segmented in a separate sensory hierarchy. The large amounts of raw sensory data that occupy the bottom levels of the hierarchy are compressed into more compact, "object"-related representations at higher levels. This hierarchy can usually communicate laterally with a parallel modeling or task hierarchy (the equivalent of Chapman's central system). However, such communication is restricted to occur only between nodes at the same level. Thus, not only is a task restricted to the sensory segmentation provided in the hierarchy, it is also restricted to just the sensory primitives available at its own level. Thinking of perception in this way, as a separate, general-purpose module, is both inaccurate from a neurophysiological perspective and is a barrier to generality.

It is reasonable to assume that perception and action developed in animals hand-in-hand [21]. Perception was used to solve quite specific and time-constrained problems, and the solutions so derived were not necessarily generally applicable. Arbib [4] cites the existence of multiple, distinct visual systems in the frog—one for prey acquisition, another for predator avoidance, another for barrier navigation, etc. This argues for considering perception–action units as the basic unit, rather than considering a perception action split. Sonja's central system captures this distinction nicely for (at least one kind of) vision.

Separating off perception also limits the generality of an implementation. In robotics the 'standard' approach is to build a sensory subsystem capable of recognizing the occurrence of any one of a set of geometric object models in a scene. This sensory subsystem then updates a central database [11]. The remaining components of the robot control system query this database when they need perceptual information. Although this approach sounds eminently reasonable, it is next to impossible to implement in a general fashion in a nontrivial environment. For a start, the notion of what constitutes 'objects' in a task—obvious to humans—often does not coincide with what geometric matching pulls out of the image. The system ends up doing either too much work, or too little. It ends up doing too much work if precise geometric information is not important for the task; it ends up doing too little if the correct recognition criteria were not geometric but were, say, functional ('cup-ness' for example). Even when the environment is controlled sufficiently to support geometric matching, a good set of models for one task is often not so convenient for another.

The problem is not with geometric modeling or returning precise descriptions. The problem is with the 'one size fits all' approach to breaking the environment down into the right perceptual units for the task at hand. Different tasks require different definitions of 'objectness'. Their requirements include functional and relational as well as geometric models and they require differing degrees of data precision. Sonja's architecture supports this flexibility by including registrars as part of the central system.

Chapman uses MACNET, a LISP-based digital circuit specification language to write the central system. MACNET translates a circuit specification program into a (somewhat optimized) circuit description that can then be executed on a circuit emulator. Use of MACNET enforces the digital circuit hardware constraint. The book presents a special macro language designed to support the easy specification of proposers and arbiters (registrars are written directly in MACNET). The macro language provides for defining proposers and associating activation conditions with them. It provides for defining default, override and hierarchical abstraction relationships between proposers. A 'competition and cooperation' style of computation [4] is provided for by allowing proposers to support or object to other proposers and proposals.

The book contains some useful comments on building and debugging this kind of circuitry. One interesting problem arises from the 'fixed-connection' assumption. Various proposers may want to use the same chunks of, or connections to, the peripheral system at the same time. This gives rise to a problem because rather than there being a subroutine that calculates, say, the distance between two points, there is a piece of circuitry that does this. If two proposers need to evaluate the distance between different sets of points, then this circuitry has to be shared out sequentially between them, and the results must then be routed to the right proposer. This complicated allocation approach was used in Pengi. In Sonja, the approach is to duplicate the circuitry as necessary. This makes sense for operations in which speed is essential. However, both allocation and duplication seem inadequate solutions in general and I suspect that a limited kind of instantiation framework is necessary.

3.2. Vision

Sonja's vision system is described in detail. It is inspired by, and meant to model, theories of human vision. Chapman argues strongly that vision needs to be task-specific in the sense that it must support the activities in which the system engages. Amazon requires relational data of low precision. Relational data is tough to make explicit in a 'standard' (geometric-model/common-database) vision system because of the sheer quantity of relations and the problems of updating them when the scene changes. One solution is have the vision system produce only the requisite data needed by actions; i.e., to wire actions up to get the very specific pieces of information they need from sensors. This approach, which Chapman calls 'insect vision' and attributes to Brooks [7] does not require distinguishing vision processing from task or action processing.

The insect approach is somewhat too task-specific: it requires that an entire new pathway between sensors and effectors be constructed for each new task or subtask. This is the one place where Chapman uses learning as a constraint in addition to the tenets of the concrete-situated approach and essential connectionism. He argues that learning implies the usefulness of a set of relatively high-level visual primitives to "act as a tinkertoy-like kit from which new visual machinery can be built". Ullman's *visual routines* model [20] provides this framework for Sonja.

The visual routines model says that visual processing is accomplished by applying the members of a small set of *visual operators* in various combinations and sequences, *visual routines,* to an image. Visual operators model what is called intermediate vision and visual routines model late vision. Early vision refers to the retinotopic phase of vision. Intermediate vision refers to the phase where retinotopic mappings are reduced to more compact encodings. Late vision refers to processes that use these compact encodings. In Sonja, the registrars of the central system implement late vision. Sonja does not engage in any pixel-level early processing, instead the visual system is connected to the game data structures. This sidesteps one of the key problems in early vision—noise. Chapman agrees that whether this structure will handle noisy input well is an open question. He notes that video game screens are designed to be easy to process visually anyway.

Early properties are made available to the central system via *visual attention.* The mechanisms of visual attention allow the differential application of visual processing to parts of the image. Chapman implements a 'spotlight' model of attention using an addressing pyramid. The pyramid is a tree structure in which each level is exponentially smaller than the one below it. Leaf nodes in the pyramid contain information on early properties of regions of the image. Interior nodes can either average the information at all their inferior nodes, or select information from one of their inferior nodes, and pass that upwards. Sonja has a 16×16 resolution pyramid. The pyramid turns out to be prohibitively slow on a serial machine, so Sonja can run with or without the pyramid (in which case the game data structures are accessed directly). Chapman points out that the concept of an addressing pyramid rescues pointers, at least in a very limited form, from the prohibition of the essential connectionism constraints.

Sonja employs two kinds of visual search described in the psychophysics literature: *parallel* and *serial-self-terminating* [19]. Parallel search involves computation of early properties at all points in an image. Not all properties can be computed in this fashion; some properties have to be computed on one candidate region of the image at a time. Chapman uses retinotopic maps to implement parallel search and uses the attention pyramid (routing all the early properties of an addressed candidate location to the root, candidate by candidate) to implement serial search. Chapman reports that Sonja's speed at serial search roughly matches human performance (about 17 locations per second). Although, it's not clear if this is with or without the full pyramid mechanism (and hence if it's a real or estimated performance measure).

Visual routines need to maintain state between calls to operators. For example, to find the nearest instance of an object, it's necessary to 'mark' the current position of the agent and then check the distance between this and each object instance. Chapman uses a set of globally accessible marker objects, *intermediate objects*, to store intermediate

state. There are four types:
- markers (which flag point locations),
- lines (which flag the line segment between two points),
- rays (which flag a direction), and
- activation planes (which flag regions).

There are a fixed number of each kind of object and they are uniquely named.

Each visual operator used in Sonja was chosen to be generally useful, abide by essential connectionism and have some biological evidence to support it. Chapman admits this last constraint was not always met. The set itself was chosen to span the domain and facilitate writing/learning new visual routines. Without a formal definition of the domain, it's very hard to show that the set of operators spans it. This gets back to the 'standard' robotics concept of a separate and self-sufficient perceptual system that can be used for any task. I'm still not convinced this sort of question is even well-defined; but given that it could be made so, then I would expect it to be easier to determine if a set of visual operators spans a domain than to determine if a 'standard' object recognition system spans the domain. Sonja's operators include tracking, determination of distances, directions and angles, and various region operations. Again, because of the fixed hardware assumption, it's necessary to have multiple copies of those operators which could potentially be needed simultaneously.

3.3. Advice

One of the major ways that Sonja differs from Pengi is in its use of advice. Agre and Chapman have maintained that the concept of plans-as-programs—plans composed of detailed instructions which are directly executed by the agent—is flawed. They argue instead for plans as resources that can be consulted by an agent in deciding what to do "on an equal basis with other resources such as the configuration of your equipment, external memory devices like a string tied around your finger or a scratch pad, or your feelings" [1]. Sonja's use of instructions illustrates this approach.

Sonja's vocabulary of instructions consists of a small set of imperative sentences and their negatives. Chapman chooses to ignore many linguistic issues in favor of concentrating on the issues of grounding the instructions in concrete activity and on the use of instructions as decision-making resources. So, for example, Sonja does not look at the syntax of the instructions, nor will it engage in a running dialog with an advice-giver.

To understand what is involved in video game advice-giving, Chapman videotaped a number of human players and their advice-giving friends during play. Human players rely on the fact that the advice-giver shares the same sense of the game that they do—sees things in the same way and has understood objectives. In this kind of framework, communication becomes part of maintaining a shared view of reality. Chapman advocates a passive approach to this issue—Sonja and its advisor share a common world view not so much because they actively establish it, but because Sonja's mechanisms embody this common view and because much of Sonja's design is modeled on human psychophysical studies. So, for example, 'visual attention' is a phenomenon common to Sonja and its advisor; this means instructions such as "on your left" (a warning to watch out for something on the left) can be understood and are actually of some use to the system. At a more general level, this suggests that the reasons for using biological models in AI are not limited to inspiration or Cognitive Science modeling, but also include the need to ensure that an adequate level of communication is possible between humans and the AI system.

The mechanism for issuing instructions to Sonja is a bit stiff: at a point in the game when advice is to be offered, the advisor hits suspend, types in the advice, and then resumes the system. Sonja stores instructions using a fixed set of instruction buffers. Instruction strings (e.g., "on your left") activate one or more of the instruction buffers (and buffers can be activated by one or more instructions). A buffer stays active until it has been consulted and explicitly cleared by the central system. Instruction buffers can be chained to achieve sequential ordering of instructions. For example, the instruction string "get the potion and set it off" activates the chain of instruction buffers `register-the-potion`, then `pick-up-the-goody`, and then `use-a-potion`. This sequence would motivate Sonja to determine if there is a magic potion nearby that it would make sense to get, and then possibly to acquire and use that potion.

Sonja understands instructions by relating them to the current Amazon situation. Instructions (and instruction buffers) are *not* high-level programs. So `use-a-potion` is not a program/subroutine that results in motor signals being sent to Sonja's effectors. Rather the instruction simply adds in an extra 'vote' for the proposed action. This vote competes and cooperates with all the other proposals active in Sonja's arbitration network. The instruction is consulted to arrive at a decision, not executed to produce motor commands.

An instruction may support or object to courses of action already under consideration, or it may permit or even require new registration. For example, "use a knife" or "no, the other one" (setting buffers `use-a-knife` and `no-the-other-one` respectively) may cause Sonja to look around for a sensible candidate object to use and discover new possibilities for using it. The instruction buffer `no-the-other-one` effects what Chapman calls a *repair*, a correction of a misunderstanding. It causes Sonja to reregister "*all* the entities referred to by pending instructions".

4. Sonja at play

About one sixth of the book is devoted to describing Sonja in action. I think Chapman missed a chance here to drive home the concepts of dynamics and routines—agent and environment sharing the responsibility for organizing complex behavior—that he describes so well in the early chapters. The description of Sonja in action is filled with detailed descriptions of mechanisms and how they give rise to specific kinds of behavior. It reads a bit too much like the sort of maintenance documentation that programmers are urged to provide for their latest creations. Having come from the 'high' of reading the early chapters, I expected this section to give a description of Sonja's behavior from an observer's viewpoint: what routines are engaged in, what part Sonja plays and what part the environment plays in each routine, how the resultant interaction exploits the dynamic to achieve work. Given that perspective, then it would be appropriate to describe in detail how Sonja's mechanisms cause it to play its 'part' in the routine (and thus illustrate why they are appropriate mechanisms). This section of the book does contain a description of the routines Sonja engages in, but these seem to take a back seat to the details of the mechanism.

I separated out four interesting routines in which Sonja engages and I list them in the next few subsections in the 'observational' (as opposed to mechanistic) style that I had expected. The first two, wandering and bypassing obstacles, rely on relatively static contributions from the environment. The second two, both combat related routines, incorporate dynamic contributions from the actions of entities such as ghosts and demons. In almost all cases I have simplified out the special cases from the routines, and I have omitted a detailed discussion of Sonja's mechanisms.

4.1. Wandering

In this relatively simple routine Sonja interacts with the environment to effect a random wandering behavior. The relevant parts of the environment are obstacles (which will cause the amazon to stop moving if it moves against them) and the amazon's direction of motion (which can be sensed). The relevant parts of Sonja's mechanism are the two local rules:

(1) if the amazon is not moving then it is kicked into motion in a random direction;
(2) if the amazon is moving then it is advanced in its current direction of motion.

Sonja and the environment interact as follows: The amazon is stopped if the game has just started, if Sonja has been engaged in some activity, or if the amazon has just hit a wall; in all these cases rule (1) produces a new random heading. As long as the amazon is moving, Sonja uses that current direction of motion to continue motion (rule (2)). The wandering routine may, of course, be interrupted or interleaved with other routines such as passing obstacles or fighting ghosts.

4.2. Passing obstacles

Sonja engages in this routine to get by obstacles. The relevant parts of the environment are obstacles (which can be sensed visually). The relevant parts of Sonja's mechanism are the two rules:

(1) if there is an obstacle between the amazon object and the goal location, then rotate the direction of motion until the obstacle is no longer in the way;
(2) if passing an obstacle, every so often rotate the heading back towards the goal until the heading intersects either the goal or the obstacle.

Sonja and the environment interact as follows. When an obstacle is sensed, rule (1) results in Sonja choosing and following a new unobstructed direction of motion close to one side of the obstacle. Rule (2) results in Sonja continually choosing a direction directly to the goal (if it is reachable) or encountering the obstacle again. Encountering the obstacle again triggers rule (1). Note that in this routine, two parts of Sonja's mechanism communicate via the obstacle.

4.3. Fighting ghosts

The two previous routines relied on some rather static contributions by the environment. Fighting routines must incorporate dynamic contributions from the actions of entities such as ghosts and demons. The 'fighting ghosts' routine is used by Sonja to kill off ghosts which otherwise might attack it. The relevant parts of the environment are any ghost instances. Ghosts travel at a constant speed, slower than the amazon object, and always move towards the amazon. They will sap the amazon's strength if they ram up against it, but can't fire at it from a distance. The relevant parts of Sonja operate as follows. Sonja selects the most dangerous ghost: the nearest ghost which has a net component of motion towards the amazon object. If such a ghost exists, then Sonja fires at it until it vanishes or ceases to be the most dangerous ghost.

Sonja and the environment interact as follows. Ghosts are always drawn towards the amazon, but since the amazon can travel faster, only those ghosts it is moving towards have a chance of catching it. Sonja always selects the nearest ghost moving towards it and targets that ghost. This routine (on its own) thus results in Sonja killing all ghosts which could kill it, *unless* the ghost appears extremely close to the amazon icon [1] or a ghost 'wall' of sufficient size and distance advances on the amazon object (a detailed analysis of the interaction should produce numeric values for size and distance). Interleaving this routine with other routines may result in weakening its ghost busting abilities.

4.4. Fighting demons

Sonja also has a routine for fighting demons. The relevant parts of the environment are instances of demons and the fireballs they generate. Demons, unlike ghosts, are monsters that can fire (fireballs) from a distance; thus demons are always dangerous. Apart from this, they behave the same as ghosts, being drawn towards the amazon at a constant speed. Fireballs are destroyed when hit. The relevant parts of Sonja operate as follows. If a demon is the nearest monster, then the mechanisms described under ghost fighting will be triggered for the demon. Detecting an instance of a fireball causes Sonja to fire back along the trajectory of the fireball.

Sonja and the environment interact as follows. If a demon registers as the nearest monster then a routine similar to the ghost fighting routine will result. If a fireball is detected, then Sonja fires back along the fireball. This will result in the destruction of the fireball and, since demons always move towards the amazon, also in the eventual destruction of the demon. Notice that shots fired at a single demon might be the result of interleavings of the fireball-based and nearest-monster-based routines. And of course, with multiple ghosts and demons, Sonja's behavior will be a complex interleaving of instances of these routines. The very fact that these routines are *not* perfectly guaranteed to kill off all threats means that advice is a useful commodity to Sonja.

---

[1] I don't know if this is allowed in Amazon.

5. Collaboration and learning

The book has two appendices. The first describes proposed extensions to Sonja to allow it to play in a collaborative fashion with another player. The second describes an experiment in skill acquisition and some conclusions and discussions.

The key extension needed to enable Sonja to play collaboratively is for it to be able to register the intentions of its collaborator. This activity is often called *plan recognition*. The general case of plan recognition is hard. However, Chapman claims plan recognition is relatively easy in a concrete domain such as Amazon. The concrete situation not only constrains what the agent can/should do, it also constrains what any other agent can/should do in the same situation. Thus, determining what a collaborator's intentions are boils down to determining what your intentions would be in the same situation.

The skill-acquisition experiment consisted of building a learning system called WOM-BAT. This work predated Sonja, and its application domain was a video game called Robots. Chapman's objective was to combine top-down and bottom-up learning methods in a synergistic fashion. WOMBAT used a temporal-difference method combined with backpropagation as the bottom-up component, and brute-force, breadth-first search with dependency analysis generalization as the top-down component. Chapman reports that the system wasn't very successful, for a host of reasons. Backpropagation temporal-difference methods were too slow and unreliable and required domain-specific tuning of various parameters. Dependency analysis offered little advantage in generalization for the Robots domain. The remainder of the section, taking off from the failure of WOMBAT, is a very interesting discussion of filling out the concrete-situated approach to address skill acquisition.

6. Conclusions

On the whole, I liked this book. Chapman has demonstrated that the concrete-situated approach can be used to build an agent capable of intelligent action in a complex and time-constrained domain, a domain which has real-world flavor and in which a classical planning approach would be a liability. The book gives us two very interesting concrete illustrations of the approach: the model of advice and the model of vision; and Appendix B contains a provoking discussion of the application of the concrete-situated approach to learning.

However, I would argue with the use of the phrase "biologically plausible" to describe hardware that obeys connectionist constraints. The neural network literature distinguishes work on artificial neural networks (connectionism) from work on biological neural networks (computational neuroscience). Connectionists have abstracted computational characteristics from neural models and used them to construct artificial systems. Chapman clearly falls in this class. Computational neuroscientists attempt to build computational models of biological systems and such models have to match the behavior of the actual neural systems, e.g., Arbib's *Rana Computatrix,* a model of the neural circuitry underlying visuomotor coordination in frog and toad [5]. Implementations guided by the essential connectionist constraints can be called, at most, biologically inspired. Chapman does claim that components of Sonja's visual system are sufficiently precise "that they could be taken as theories about the human brain and subjected to psychophysical experiment". However, he expresses no interest in following up on this avenue of investigation.

Chapman comments that navigation took an inordinate amount of effort: "Half the central system code and well over half the time I spent implementing Sonja went into navigation." Motion, like vision, is one of those things that animals do without much conscious effort; and hence it appears simple. There is much evidence that motion control has highly specific neural control circuitry (e.g, basal ganglia, cerebellum, superior colliculus) [4,9,16]. The experience in robotics has been that motion planning is well addressed with motion-domain specific techniques and algorithms, e.g., [6]. Sonja attempts to solve general motion problems completely within its central system. It is more likely that only 'late' motion (by analogy with late vision) should be addressed in Sonja's central system. [2] Other highly specialized and parallel systems should handle 'intermediate' (e.g., obstacle avoidance) and 'early' (e.g., actuator control) motion.

Looking back at his effort in building Sonja, Chapman writes that he initially thought the arbitration network would be the most complex component to build. Instead he found that the visual systems and the registrars were the problem. This (and other evidence) leads him to claim that for concrete domains action selection is in general easy and the harder problem is perception. Hence, future research should concentrate in that area. I think it's important to be careful here. Studying perception on its own is as bad as studying action selection on its own. Perception and action evolved together in animals [21] and the concrete-situated approach argues well from a problem-directed viewpoint that they need to be tightly coupled. Sonja's visual system is constructed so that its only connection with action selection is through the late vision registrars of the central system. It effectively studies just *one* perception–action system (and one which apparently won't handle navigation well). In a system with many perception–action modules, what we need to study is not just perception or action, since these components may differ remarkably between modules, but rather ways to *integrate* perception and action.

I have already mentioned that I would have preferred to have seen something more in the way of performance studies and comparisons with other technologies. I think Chapman ignores the illustrative powers of such studies as a matter of principle. He wants to be clear that, for example, the sort of tests Sacerdoti runs on NOAH [15] would not stand up as an engineering evaluation of the technology, so he doesn't provide any such tests for Sonja. To a certain extent I agree, but I'd still argue that these tests have illustrative value and would be of use in understanding and duplicating parts of Sonja.

In summary, this book presents us with a very concrete example of the approach that Chapman and Agre have been advocating for some time. Chapman does a first-rate job of presenting that approach, especially in the early chapters. My only real quibble is that he misses a dynamite chance to drive home the concrete-situated notions of dynamics and routines in the section describing Sonja in operation.

---

[2] Sonja's central system seems to have a functionality corresponding to what Ewert [9] calls *command neurons*—cells which are tightly involved in the decision making to carry out a specific behavior.

References

[1] P.E. Agre and D. Chapman, From reaction to participation, in: *DARPA Planning Workshop*, Santa Cruz, CA (1987) 123–154.

[2] P.E. Agre and D. Chapman, Pengi: an implementation of a theory of action, in: *Proceedings AAAI-87*, Seattle, WA (1987) 268–272.

[3] J. Albus, RCS: a reference model architecture for intelligent control, *IEEE Comput.* **25** (5) (1992) 56–59.

[4] M.A. Arbib, Perceptual structures and distributed motor control, in: V.B. Brooks, ed., *Handbook of Physiology—The Nervous System II. Motor Control* (American Physiological Society, Bethesda, MD, 1981) 1449–1480.

[5] M.A. Arbib, Levels of modelling of neural interactions underlying visuomotor coordination, Technical Report 85-36, University of Massachusetts, Computer and Information Science Department, Amherst, MA (1985).

[6] M. Brady et al., *Robot Motion* (MIT Press, Cambridge, MA, 1984).

[7] R.A. Brooks, A robust layered control system for a mobile robot, *IEEE J. Rob. Automation* **2** (1) (1986) 14–22.

[8] D. Chapman, Planning for conjunctive goals, *Artif. Intell.* **32** (1987) 333–377.

[9] J.-P. Ewert, *Neuroethology* (Springer-Verlag, Berlin, 1980).

[10] P.J. Hayes, The naive physics manifesto, in: D. Michie, ed., *Expert Systems in the Micro-Electronic Age* (Edinburg University Press, Edinburgh, Scotland, 1978).

[11] E. Kent, M. Shneier and T. Hong, Building representations from fusions of multiple views, in: *IEEE International Conference on Robotics & Automation*, San Francisco, CA (1986) 1634–1639.

[12] J. McCarthy, The advice taker, in: M. Minsky, ed., *Semantic Information Processing* (MIT Press, Cambridge, MA, 1968).

[13] M. Minsky, A framework for representing knowledge, in: P.H. Winston, ed., *The Psychology of Computer Vision* (McGraw-Hill, New York, 1975).

[14] M. Minsky, *The Society of Mind* (Simon and Schuster, New York, 1986).

[15] E.D. Sacerdoti, *A Structure for Plans and Behavior* (Elsevier, New York, 1977).

[16] R.F. Schmidt, ed., *Fundamentals of Neurophysiology* (Springer-Verlag, New York, 2nd ed., 1978).

[17] O.G. Selfridge, Pandemonium: a paradigm for learning, in: *Mechanisation of Thought Processes* (Her Majesty's Stationary Office, London, 1959) 511–531.

[18] D. Subramanian and J. Woodfill, Subjective ontologies, in: J. Hendler, ed., *AAAI Spring Workshop on Planning in Uncertain, Unpredictable or Changing Environments*, Stanford CA (1990).

[19] A. Treisman and S. Gormican, Feature analysis in early vision: evidence from search asymmetries, *Psych. Rev.* **95** (1) (1988) 15–48.

[20] S. Ullman, Visual routines, *Cognition* **18** (1984) 97–159.

[21] C. von Hofsten, Catching, in: *Perspectives on Perception and Action* (Lawrence Erlbaum, Hillsdale, NJ, 1987) 33–46.

Artificial Intelligence (selected titles)
Patrick Henry Winston, founding editor
J. Michael Brady, Daniel G. Bobrow, and Randall Davis, current editors

Artificial Intelligence: An MIT Perspective, Volumes I and II, edited by Patrick Henry Winston and Richard Henry Brown, 1979

NETL: A System for Representing and Using Real-World Knowledge, Scott Fahlman, 1979

The Interpretation of Visual Motion, Shimon Ullman, 1979

Turtle Geometry: The Computer as a Medium for Exploring Mathematics, Harold Abelson and Andrea di Sessa, 1981

Computational Models of Discourse, edited by Michael Brady and Robert C. Berwick, 1982

Robot Motion: Planning and Control, edited by Michael Brady, John M. Hollerbach, Timothy Johnson, Tomás Lozano-Pérez, and Matthew T. Mason, 1982

Robot Hands and the Mechanics of Manipulation, Matthew T. Mason and J. Kenneth Salisbury, Jr., 1985

The Acquisition of Syntactic Knowledge, Robert C. Berwick, 1985

The Connection Machine, W. Daniel Hillis, 1985

Legged Robots that Balance, Marc H. Raibert, 1986

ACTORS: A Model of Concurrent Computation in Distributed Systems, Gul A. Agha, 1986

Knowledge-Based Tutoring: The GUIDON Program, William Clancey, 1987

AI in the 1980s and Beyond: An MIT Survey, edited by W. Eric L. Grimson and Ramesh S. Patil, 1987

Visual Reconstruction, Andrew Blake and Andrew Zisserman, 1987

Reasoning about Change: Time and Causation from the Standpoint of Artificial Intelligence, Yoav Shoham, 1988

Model-Based Control of a Robot Manipulator, Chae H. An, Christopher G. Atkeson, and John M. Hollerbach, 1988

A Robot Ping-Pong Player: Experiment in Real-Time Intelligent Control, Russell L. Andersson, 1988

The Paralation Model: Architecture-Independent Parallel Programming, Gary Sabot, 1988

Automated Deduction in Nonclassical Logics: Efficient Matrix Proof Methods for Modal and Intuitionistic Logics, Lincoln Wallen, 1989

Shape from Shading, edited by Berthold K.P. Horn and Michael J. Brooks, 1989

Ontic: A Knowledge Representation System for Mathematics, David A. McAllester, 1989

Solid Shape, Jan J. Koenderink, 1990

Theories of Comparative Analysis, Daniel S. Weld, 1990

Artificial Intelligence at MIT: Expanding Frontiers, edited by Patrick Henry Winston and Sarah Alexandra Shellard, 1990

Vector Models for Data-Parallel Computing, Guy E. Blelloch, 1990

Experiments in the Machine Interpretation of Visual Motion, David W. Murray and Bernard F. Buxton, 1990

Object Recognition by Computer: The Role of Geometric Constraints, W. Eric L. Grimson, 1990

Representing and Reasoning with Probabilistic Knowledge: A Logical Approach to Probabilities, Fahiem Bacchus, 1990

3D Model Recognition from Stereoscopic Cues, edited by John E.W. Mayhew and John P. Frisby, 1991

Artificial Vision for Mobile Robots: Stereo Vision and Multisensory Perception, Nicholas Ayache, 1991

Truth and Modality for Knowledge Representation, Raymond Turner, 1991

Made-Up Minds: A Constructivist Approach to Artificial Intelligence, Gary L. Drescher, 1991

Vision, Instruction, and Action, David Chapman, 1991

Do the Right Thing: Studies in Limited Rationality, Stuart Russell and Eric Wefald, 1991

KAM: A System for Intelligently Guiding Numerical Experimentation by Computer, Kenneth Man-Kam Yip, 1991

Solving Geometric Constraint Systems: A Case Study in Kinematics, Glenn A. Kramer, 1992

Geometric Invariants in Computer Vision, edited by Joseph Mundy and Andrew Zisserman, 1992

HANDEY: A Robot Task Planner, Tomás Lozano-Pérez, Joseph L. Jones, Emmanuel Mazer, and Patrick A. O'Donnell, 1992

Active Vision, edited by Andrew Blake and Alan Yuille, 1992

Recent Advances in Qualitative Physics, edited by Boi Faltings and Peter Struss, 1992

Machine Translation: A View from the Lexicon, Bonnie Jean Dorr, 1993

The Language Complexity Game, Eric Sven Ristad, 1993

The Soar Papers: Research on Integrated Intelligence, edited by Paul S. Rosenbloom, John E. Laird, and Allen Newell, 1993

Three-Dimensional Computer Vision: A Geometric Viewpoint, Olivier Faugeras, 1993

Contemplating Minds: A Forum for Artificial Intelligence, edited by William J. Clancey, Stephen W. Smoliar, and Mark J. Stefik, 1994

Thinking between the Lines: Computers and the Comprehension of Causal Descriptions, Gary C. Borchardt, 1994

Rules of Encounter: Designing Conventions for Automated Negotiation among Computers, Jeffrey S. Rosenschein and Gilad Zlotkin, 1994

Qualitative Reasoning: Modeling and Simulation with Incomplete Knowledge, Benjamin Kuipers, 1994

Computational Theories of Interaction and Agency, edited by Philip E. Agre and Stanley J. Rosenschein, 1996